PUBLIC PAPERS OF THE PRESIDENTS

OF THE UNITED STATES

PUBLIC PAPERS OF THE PRESIDENTS

OF THE UNITED STATES

Richard Nixon

Containing the Public Messages, Speeches, and

Statements of the President

1969

UNITED STATES GOVERNMENT PRINTING OFFICE

WASHINGTON : 1971

PUBLISHED BY THE
OFFICE OF THE FEDERAL REGISTER
NATIONAL ARCHIVES AND RECORDS SERVICE
GENERAL SERVICES ADMINISTRATION

For sale by the Superintendent of Documents, U.S. Government Printing Office
Washington, D.C. 20402 - Price $14.50

FOREWORD

ON January 20, 1969, America was nearing the end of a decade that had been marked by tumult and tragedy, and in which many Americans had grown uncertain about the Nation's present and fearful of its future.

Against that backdrop, the new Administration took office dedicated to the reform of the American Government, to the restoration of America's spirit, and to the renewal of its promise.

The first priority was ending the war in Vietnam, and building toward a stable peace not only there but worldwide. No problem so occupied my own time and attention during 1969. I considered it vital that the war be ended, but also that it be ended in a way which would contribute to a larger and a lasting peace. This required standing firm against those who pressed for a precipitate withdrawal regardless of the consequences. But it also called for new initiatives that would reverse the trend of ever greater U.S. involvement, that would give the North Vietnamese incentives to negotiate, and that at the same time would strengthen the capacity of the South Vietnamese to manage their own defense.

By the end of 1969 we had laid a far-reaching set of peace proposals on the negotiating table at Paris, a carefully phased process of "Vietnamization" was well underway, American troops were coming home, and the South Vietnamese themselves were rapidly improving their position.

In enunciating the "Nixon Doctrine," in opening serious talks with the Soviet Union, in revitalizing America's alliances, in reviewing our defense posture, and in many other initiatives that are discussed in these pages, we sought systematically and comprehensively to lay the groundwork for what America has not had in this century: a full generation of peace.

At home, serious problems of crime, disorder, social progress, and inflation all stood high on the Nation's list of concerns as the new Administration took office. But beyond these and the many

v

other pressing issues that faced us, we were confronted by a more fundamental question: whether the Government itself was still sufficiently responsive and sufficiently effective to cope with the emerging needs of the 1970's and beyond.

We were convinced that the policies, the programs, and the organizational structures that had grown in such sometimes haphazard profusion during the middle third of the century, however appropriate for their own time, were not adequate for the final third. Reform therefore would have to be sweeping. It would have to be coordinated. It would have to reflect a fresh assessment not only of what could be learned from past mistakes, but also of the changed dynamics of the new age we now were entering. It would have to provide a far more sophisticated means of assessing second-order consequences: that is, the chain of effects in what might seem unrelated areas that would be set in motion by any given action. One of the central lessons of recent decades is that the most significant impacts of particular actions or policies (on the environment, for example, or on patterns of migration) have often been those that were unforeseen and therefore not considered when the decision was made. We were determined to do better.

"Reform" thus was more than the watchword of the Administration's first year. It was a need that we urgently perceived as the key to whether government could be made to work in the decades ahead. Taken in their entirety, the papers in this volume reflect a first-year record of reforms initiated or proposed—in welfare, in the postal service, in the draft, and in many other basic areas—a record that has few precedents in modern times.

The final test, of course, will be how well it all works—and precisely because our central focus has been on long-term needs, the verdict of history will not be in for many years. But if the soundness of our judgment has matched the vigor of our determination, then I believe that 1969 will be looked back upon as a year of profoundly significant beginnings, in which the foundations were securely laid for achieving peace in the world and for making real the promise of America at home.

Richard Nixon

PREFACE

IN THIS VOLUME are gathered most of the public messages
and statements of the 37th President of the United States that
were released by the White House during the period January 20,
1969–December 31, 1969. Similar volumes are available covering
the administrations of Presidents Truman, Eisenhower, Kennedy,
and Johnson.

The series was begun in 1957 in response to a recommendation
of the National Historical Publications Commission. Until then
there had been no systematic publication of Presidential papers.
An extensive compilation of the messages and papers of the
Presidents, covering the period 1789 to 1897, was assembled by
James D. Richardson and published under congressional authority
between 1896 and 1899. Since then various private compilations
have been issued but there was no uniform publication comparable to the *Congressional Record* or the *United States Supreme
Court Reports*. Many Presidential papers could be found only
in mimeographed White House releases or as reported in the
press. The National Historical Publications Commission therefore
recommended the establishment of an official series in which
Presidential writings and utterances of a public nature could be
made promptly available.

The Commission's recommendation was incorporated in regulations of the Administrative Committee of the Federal Register
issued under section 6 of the Federal Register Act (44 U.S.C.
1506). The Committee's regulations, establishing the series and
providing for the coverage of prior years, are reprinted at page
1099 as Appendix F.

CONTENT AND ARRANGEMENT

The text of this book is based on Presidential materials issued
during the period as White House releases and on transcripts of

news conferences. Original source materials, where available, have been used to protect against errors in transcription. The President's spoken words are checked for accuracy against tape recordings when these are available. An asterisk preceding an item in the List of Items indicates that no tape was available and therefore the item follows the text as released by the White House Press Office.

The dates shown at the end of item headings are White House release dates. In instances where the date of the document differs from the release date that fact is shown in the note immediately following the item. Textnotes, footnotes, and cross references have been supplied where needed for purposes of clarity.

Remarks or addresses were delivered in Washington, D.C., unless otherwise indicated. Similarly, statements, messages, and letters were issued from the White House in Washington unless otherwise indicated. All times shown are local time.

Items published in this volume are presented in chronological order, rather than being grouped in classes. Most needs for a classified arrangement are met by the subject index. For example, a reader interested in recipients of the Congressional Medal of Honor during 1969 will find them listed in the index under the heading "Awards and Citations."

Appendices A through E have been provided to deal with special categories of Presidential issuances and actions, as noted below.

White House releases not included as items in this volume and not appearing in later appendices are listed in Appendix A at page 1051.

Though not all proclamations, Executive orders, and similar documents required by law to be published in the *Federal Register* and *Code of Federal Regulations* were issued as White House releases during 1969, a complete listing of these documents by number and subject appears at page 1081 in Appendix B.

Directives to members of the Cabinet and Presidential assistants and task forces established by the President are listed in Appendix C at page 1087.

Presidential Unit Citations awarded during 1969 are listed in Appendix D at page 1095.

Preface

The President is required by statute to transmit numerous reports to the Congress. Those transmitted during the period covered by this volume are listed in Appendix E beginning at page 1097.

The planning and publication of the first 24 volumes of this series was under the direction of David C. Eberhart of the Office of the Federal Register. Beginning with the present volume, the series is under the direction of Fred J. Emery. The editors of the present volume were Dorothy G. Chance and Peter J. Haley, assisted by Faye Q. Rosser. Special Assistant to the President James Keogh, Executive Assistant to the President William J. Hopkins, and Cecilia Bellinger of Mr. Keogh's staff, provided aid and counsel in the selection and annotation of the materials. C. W. Shankland of the Government Printing Office developed the typography and design.

JAMES B. RHOADS
Archivist of the United States

ROBERT L. KUNZIG
Administrator of General Services
January 1971

CONTENTS

LIST OF ITEMS

[Asterisks preceding items containing the President's remarks indicate that there was no tape recording available to compare with the released text. These items, therefore, follow the text as released by the White House Press Office.]

List of Items

39–861—71——2

List of Items

List of Items

List of Items

39–861—71——3

39–861—71——4

List of Items

Richard Nixon

January 20–December 31, 1969

I Inaugural Address.

January 20, 1969

Senator Dirksen, Mr. Chief Justice, Mr. Vice President, President Johnson, Vice President Humphrey, my fellow Americans—and my fellow citizens of the world community:

I ask you to share with me today the majesty of this moment. In the orderly transfer of power, we celebrate the unity that keeps us free.

Each moment in history is a fleeting time, precious and unique. But some stand out as moments of beginning, in which courses are set that shape decades or centuries.

This can be such a moment.

Forces now are converging that make possible, for the first time, the hope that many of man's deepest aspirations can at last be realized. The spiraling pace of change allows us to contemplate, within our own lifetime, advances that once would have taken centuries.

In throwing wide the horizons of space, we have discovered new horizons on earth.

For the first time, because the people of the world want peace, and the leaders of the world are afraid of war, the times are on the side of peace.

Eight years from now America will celebrate its 200th anniversary as a nation. Within the lifetime of most people now living, mankind will celebrate that great new year which comes only once in a thousand years—the beginning of the third millennium.

What kind of a nation we will be, what kind of a world we will live in, whether we shape the future in the image of our hopes, is ours to determine by our actions and our choices.

The greatest honor history can bestow is the title of peacemaker. This honor now beckons America—the chance to help lead the world at last out of the valley of turmoil and onto that high ground of peace that man has dreamed of since the dawn of civilization.

If we succeed, generations to come will say of us now living that we mastered our moment, that we helped make the world safe for mankind.

This is our summons to greatness.

I believe the American people are ready to answer this call.

The second third of this century has been a time of proud achievement. We have made enormous strides in science and industry and agriculture. We have shared our wealth more broadly than ever. We have learned at last to manage a modern economy to assure its continued growth.

We have given freedom new reach. We have begun to make its promise real for black as well as for white.

We see the hope of tomorrow in the youth of today. I know America's youth. I believe in them. We can be proud that they are better educated, more committed, more passionately driven by conscience than any generation in our history.

No people has ever been so close to the achievement of a just and abundant society, or so possessed of the will to achieve it. And because our strengths are so great, we can afford to appraise our weaknesses with candor and to approach them with hope.

Standing in this same place a third of

a century ago, Franklin Delano Roosevelt addressed a nation ravaged by depression and gripped in fear. He could say in surveying the Nation's troubles: "They concern, thank God, only material things."

Our crisis today is in reverse.

We find ourselves rich in goods, but ragged in spirit; reaching with magnificent precision for the moon, but falling into raucous discord on earth.

We are caught in war, wanting peace. We are torn by division, wanting unity. We see around us empty lives, wanting fulfillment. We see tasks that need doing, waiting for hands to do them.

To a crisis of the spirit, we need an answer of the spirit.

And to find that answer, we need only look within ourselves.

When we listen to "the better angels of our nature," we find that they celebrate the simple things, the basic things—such as goodness, decency, love, kindness.

Greatness comes in simple trappings.

The simple things are the ones most needed today if we are to surmount what divides us, and cement what unites us.

To lower our voices would be a simple thing.

In these difficult years, America has suffered from a fever of words; from inflated rhetoric that promises more than it can deliver; from angry rhetoric that fans discontents into hatreds; from bombastic rhetoric that postures instead of persuading.

We cannot learn from one another until we stop shouting at one another—until we speak quietly enough so that our words can be heard as well as our voices.

For its part, government will listen. We will strive to listen in new ways—to the voices of quiet anguish, the voices that speak without words, the voices of the heart—to the injured voices, the anxious voices, the voices that have despaired of being heard.

Those who have been left out, we will try to bring in.

Those left behind, we will help to catch up.

For all of our people, we will set as our goal the decent order that makes progress possible and our lives secure.

As we reach toward our hopes, our task is to build on what has gone before—not turning away from the old, but turning toward the new.

In this past third of a century, government has passed more laws, spent more money, initiated more programs than in all our previous history.

In pursuing our goals of full employment, better housing, excellence in education; in rebuilding our cities and improving our rural areas; in protecting our environment and enhancing the quality of life—in all these and more, we will and must press urgently forward.

We shall plan now for the day when our wealth can be transferred from the destruction of war abroad to the urgent needs of our people at home.

The American dream does not come to those who fall asleep.

But we are approaching the limits of what government alone can do.

Our greatest need now is to reach beyond government, to enlist the legions of the concerned and the committed.

What has to be done, has to be done by government and people together or it will not be done at all. The lesson of past agony is that without the people we can do nothing—with the people we can do everything.

To match the magnitude of our tasks, we need the energies of our people—en-

2

listed not only in grand enterprises, but more importantly in those small, splendid efforts that make headlines in the neighborhood newspaper instead of the national journal.

With these, we can build a great cathedral of the spirit—each of us raising it one stone at a time, as he reaches out to his neighbor, helping, caring, doing.

I do not offer a life of uninspiring ease. I do not call for a life of grim sacrifice. I ask you to join in a high adventure—one as rich as humanity itself, and exciting as the times we live in.

The essence of freedom is that each of us shares in the shaping of his own destiny.

Until he has been part of a cause larger than himself, no man is truly whole.

The way to fulfillment is in the use of our talents. We achieve nobility in the spirit that inspires that use.

As we measure what can be done, we shall promise only what we know we can produce; but as we chart our goals, we shall be lifted by our dreams.

No man can be fully free while his neighbor is not. To go forward at all is to go forward together.

This means black and white together, as one nation, not two. The laws have caught up with our conscience. What remains is to give life to what is in the law: to insure at last that as all are born equal in dignity before God, all are born equal in dignity before man.

As we learn to go forward together at home, let us also seek to go forward together with all mankind.

Let us take as our goal: Where peace is unknown, make it welcome; where peace is fragile, make it strong; where peace is temporary, make it permanent.

After a period of confrontation, we are entering an era of negotiation.

Let all nations know that during this administration our lines of communication will be open.

We seek an open world—open to ideas, open to the exchange of goods and people—a world in which no people, great or small, will live in angry isolation.

We cannot expect to make everyone our friend, but we can try to make no one our enemy.

Those who would be our adversaries, we invite to a peaceful competition—not in conquering territory or extending dominion, but in enriching the life of man.

As we explore the reaches of space, let us go to the new worlds together—not as new worlds to be conquered, but as a new adventure to be shared.

With those who are willing to join, let us cooperate to reduce the burden of arms, to strengthen the structure of peace, to lift up the poor and the hungry.

But to all those who would be tempted by weakness, let us leave no doubt that we will be as strong as we need to be for as long as we need to be.

Over the past 20 years, since I first came to this Capital as a freshman Congressman, I have visited most of the nations of the world. I have come to know the leaders of the world and the great forces, the hatreds, the fears that divide the world.

I know that peace does not come through wishing for it—that there is no substitute for days and even years of patient and prolonged diplomacy.

I also know the people of the world.

I have seen the hunger of a homeless child, the pain of a man wounded in battle, the grief of a mother who has lost her son. I know these have no ideology, no race.

I know America. I know the heart of

America is good.

I speak from my own heart, and the heart of my country, the deep concern we have for those who suffer and those who sorrow.

I have taken an oath today in the presence of God and my countrymen to uphold and defend the Constitution of the United States. To that oath I now add this sacred commitment: I shall consecrate my Office, my energies, and all the wisdom I can summon to the cause of peace among nations.

Let this message be heard by strong and weak alike:

The peace we seek—the peace we seek to win—is not victory over any other people, but the peace that comes "with healing in its wings"; with compassion for those who have suffered; with understanding for those who have opposed us; with the opportunity for all the peoples of this earth to choose their own destiny.

Only a few short weeks ago we shared the glory of man's first sight of the world as God sees it, as a single sphere reflecting light in the darkness.

As the Apollo astronauts flew over the moon's gray surface on Christmas Eve, they spoke to us of the beauty of earth—and in that voice so clear across the lunar distance, we heard them invoke God's blessing on its goodness.

In that moment, their view from the moon moved poet Archibald MacLeish to write: "To see the earth as it truly is, small and blue and beautiful in that eternal silence where it floats, is to see ourselves as riders on the earth together, brothers on that bright loveliness in the eternal cold—brothers who know now they are truly brothers."

In that moment of surpassing technological triumph, men turned their thoughts toward home and humanity—seeing in that far perspective that man's destiny on earth is not divisible; telling us that however far we reach into the cosmos, our destiny lies not in the stars but on earth itself, in our own hands, in our own hearts.

We have endured a long night of the American spirit. But as our eyes catch the dimness of the first rays of dawn, let us not curse the remaining dark. Let us gather the light.

Our destiny offers not the cup of despair, but the chalice of opportunity. So let us seize it not in fear, but in gladness—and "riders on the earth together," let us go forward, firm in our faith, steadfast in our purpose, cautious of the dangers, but sustained by our confidence in the will of God and the promise of man.

NOTE: The President spoke at 12:16 p.m. from the inaugural platform erected at the East Front of the Capitol, immediately following administration of the oath of office by Chief Justice Earl Warren.

The address was broadcast on radio and television.

2   Remarks at a Reception for Campaign Workers. *January* 21, 1969

IN SPEAKING to all of you here this morning, I think you should know how this little gathering was set up.

What we had planned was to have a few friends in, particularly those who would be going back to faraway places—to California, Florida, and the rest—and also those who had worked in the campaign headquarters in New York and also in Washington.

Well, the party began to grow, as you can see. Everybody got together. We think it is wonderful. It is more than we expected, but we are so glad to have you here and to welcome you to your house. It is ours, too, but it is yours, and we are glad to be here.

We are also very glad to have the Vice President and his wife here. I feel that with him by my side, we are going to be able to provide some direction and leadership to the Nation that the Nation wants and that the Nation needs.

I am particularly happy to have him here because when I went over to my office—I was over there quite early this morning—I found that the desk that I have in my office is the Vice President's desk. I took it out of the office down there.

The reason that I took that desk, incidentally—and you will be reading this in the papers tomorrow—was that for about 50 years it has been the desk in the Vice President's office. It was there when I was there for 8 years. It was the desk that Woodrow Wilson had used when he was President.

I had always liked the Wilsonian background, and also liked the desk itself. The President has always been given a choice of the various desks that he can have. That is one of the prerogatives. So I took the Wilson desk, and I think he has the Jefferson desk.

We had hoped and expected this morning, too, that we would have a chance to give you some refreshment of some sort. I think there will be something down in the other end of the room.

We had hoped, too, that we could have a chance, at least, to talk with everybody here, to have one of those nice little chats. I see so many people here that I would just love to sit down with and really find out how to settle Vietnam and a few other things, but that will come.

I think perhaps more than anything else what I wanted you to know was this: that a President has to make a determination, a very important determination, as to who will be the first guests in the White House. Naturally, your first guests have to be and should be the members of your family, so I had members of my family yesterday, about 200 or 300, and we had a nice affair here just before the inaugural ball.

The second group, of course, that you want in are members of your family that are not related but who are members of what we call "the official family." That is this group. By "the official family" I mean not only people who worked in campaigns, as all of you did, people who helped out, as all of you did, but people I have known going back over the years. I see so many here, some of those who entertained during the course of the campaign. I know that some of you are here.

Wasn't that a great group that went to those inaugural balls and put on the programs for it? I really thought they did a wonderful job.

I think perhaps the best way I can describe it is by one of my favorite stories that I got out of studying the various inaugurals and the backgrounds which involved President Buchanan.

As you know, he did not go down in history as one of our most distinguished Presidents, probably because he was followed by Lincoln, and the comparison was difficult for anybody. But in any event, Buchanan became President at an older age—he thought it was older—at a later time than he had expected or wanted.

5

Consequently, he felt at that time that the office had come to him too late. He was disappointed that it had come so late.

It is reported that as he was driving down from the Capitol to the White House, he made a comment to this effect: that all of his friends that he wanted to reward had died, and all of his enemies that he hated and wanted to punish were now his friends. I just want you to know you are all our friends here.

There is a lot of business, of course, that has to be undertaken today. We are going to have the first meeting of the National Security Council. I have already been through quite a few state papers, signed some more appointments, and a few other things—no pardons yet, though.

As far as business is concerned, I can assure you that nothing on this first day, the first day of being officially in the White House, will mean more to us than to be here with our friends. We are grateful for your friendship. We are grateful for your support.

We want you back here in this house on other occasions when it won't be quite as crowded as it is, when we will have a chance to at least see that you do have some refreshment and a few other things.

I can only say that this is a great house. It has a great history. It has a magnificent presence, as we walked through it for the first time, with nobody in it at all.

But what really makes the house, what really gives the feel to this house, is the presence of people for whom you have affection and people you love. This house right now, I think, means more to us than it will ever mean in the future, because you are our friends and our people. We are thankful to you and we wish you the very best.

The Vice President has to go up to open the Senate. I used to have to do that for 8 years. I don't want to make him late, but I wanted him to see this house and have an opportunity for you to see him, because he was a great campaigner in this last campaign, believe me.

You never know what a man is until you put him in the fire, and he has been through the fire, believe me. He knows how to take the heat. Since he will be presiding over the Senate, the body in this Nation's Capital where there is a rule of unlimited debate, I think we ought to give him a chance to talk as long as he wants to talk right now.

THE VICE PRESIDENT. Thank you, Mr. President.

One thing that the President didn't mention was that that unlimited debate rule does not apply to the Vice President. He is a very silent, austere member of that honorable body.

I do want to say that it seems as if no one's desk is secure any more, Mr. President. We had one thing to warn the rest of the staff about: that their desks are not secure, either.

Whatever the President wants is what I want. I envisage that as the principal role of the Vice Presidency—to implement the policies of the Chief Executive.

Not many people have had the chance to come to the Office, to work for a man like Richard Nixon, and I deeply appreciate the opportunity. He has been a towering source of strength to me through that campaign he mentioned, which had its traumatic moments.

I think the measure of a man rests in his first actions and his thoughts, and his consideration. I believe that your presence here today gives you an accurate measure of Richard Nixon—the fact that you are here as invited guests to receive his appreciation, to which I certainly want to add mine. It is wonderful to have this chance to greet you.

As the President has indicated, I must make my way to the tender mercies of the Senate. Thank you.

THE PRESIDENT. I know that some of you were not at the balls yesterday and, consequently, I will share with you, if you weren't listening to the morning news report, what I thought was the best crack of the day—and there were many, I am sure, which I didn't hear.

This one was Art Linkletter.[1] As we walked in with Tricia, my older daughter, and David and Julie, and I made a little talk, then Art came on to respond. He said, "Well, you know, I would have liked to have had the opportunity to introduce the President because if I had introduced him, I would have done it in this way: I would have presented him as General Eisenhower's grandson's father-in-law."

Last night, you will be interested to know, we didn't have much time for dinner because we had the family reception and then we went on to the balls. We had to get into that white tie, and my neck is still hurting. Anyway, we went into the little family dining room upstairs and had something to eat.

The people who served there were the same ones who served the General, General Eisenhower, when he was President. Of course, David used to be here quite often in those days, and he is going to be here quite often these days, too.

We sat down and I wondered what they were going to serve. They brought out steak. They said from the time he was this high, whenever he came there he al-

ways wanted steak. So that is the way we are going to get Julie back. We are going to have steak all the time.

Maybe you would like to hear a word from Pat, David, and Julie. How about that?

I see so many others we could have words from. I see Jim Drury out here. We could have "The Virginian." [2]

Here is Pat.

MRS. NIXON. I just want to add my thanks to those expressed already, and that we hope to see you soon. You will be invited often. This time, instead of having the "big shots," so-called, we are going to have all our friends on a rotation basis. We hope to see you here again soon.

THE PRESIDENT. Just to keep the record clear, in my book all of our friends are "big shots."

JULIE NIXON EISENHOWER. I just think I will tell you about our first night in the White House.

David and I are carrying on a tradition. In 1953, when his grandfather spent the first night in the White House, David's father [John S. D. Eisenhower] was flown over from Korea as a surprise so he could be at the inauguration. President Truman had him flown over. He surprised the whole family.

David's family spent the night in the Queen's Room, so to carry on the tradition, last night we spent the night in the Queen's Room and it was a thrill.

THE PRESIDENT. I was just going to say, isn't it nice to have an Eisenhower in the White House again?

DAVID EISENHOWER. In line with what the President was saying, I remember thinking last night when John [Ficklin], the Chief Butler, came up to me and he

---

[1] Radio and television personality.

[2] A television series featuring James Drury.

said, "No, Mr. David, no steak tonight." Then he brought out the steak. I knew that happy days were here again.

THE PRESIDENT. We do want you to know, again, that you are always welcome in this house. We can never express in words our appreciation for your loyalty, friendship, support, and hard work far beyond the call of duty over the years.

Now we are going to have to—not "have to," but we are going to want to return it manyfold. We are going to get up early and work late and do everything we can so that this house will always be a happy house, and your home will always be a happy home.

Thank you.

NOTE: The President spoke at 11:05 a.m. in the East Room at the White House.

3 Remarks at the Swearing In of New Members of the White House Staff. *January 21, 1969*

Mr. Chief Justice, ladies and gentlemen:

This is the first official swearing in of this new administration. I do not think there will be any that will be more important.

The people who will be sworn in are members of the White House Staff. They are supposed to be faceless men and women.

For faceless men and women, I think they look very good, though, don't you, Mr. Chief Justice?

We mean by that that these are the men and women who will be working long hours in the White House and in the Executive Office Building; who will be working, many of them, as is the case with many people in Government, at less compensation than they have had in private life; who, in addition to that, will be away from their families a great deal.

That is one of the reasons we invited the families. We want you to take a good look at them now. You may not see too much of them later.

I should tell you that as far as my own work habits are concerned, some of you who have been with me in campaigns know what they are. We usually start fairly early in the morning and go reasonably late in the afternoon or evening, but I try not to call after midnight.

I have an interesting story on that that I just recalled as I was walking down the hall.

Ten years ago, when I was in the Soviet Union, I recall a conversation in which Mr. Khrushchev was talking to Mr. Mikoyan. Mr. Mikoyan, who had a very keen sense of humor, often was used by Mr. Khrushchev as a foil for some of his jokes, and sometimes Mr. Mikoyan would turn it on him.

In some way, after we had had lunch, and the conversation was in that easy stage when no very heavy subjects were up, the question of sleep came up and how much sleep each of us got.

Mikoyan pointed out that during the Stalin era, Stalin had very unusual sleep habits; that he would work during the day and then he would call members of his staff at 2, 3, or 4 o'clock in the morning. Then they would work the rest of the night. Then he smiled and said, "You know, we sleep much better now that Mr.

Khrushchev is the head of the Soviet Union." You can take that a number of ways, of course.[1]

I simply want you to know that while the hours will be long, and the work will be hard, I hope it will be rewarding. As far as any of the wives are concerned, of the husbands who are here, if they are away after midnight, don't blame me; blame them.

Now, for the purpose of this swearing-in ceremony, we have the honor of having the Chief Justice of the United States.

I pointed out at luncheon yesterday that it was to me a very great honor to be sworn in by the Chief Justice and I thought it had some significance historically, because I was the first President born west of the Rockies, in the State of California, to be elected President, and I was sworn in by the Chief Justice of the United States, who also came from California.

So that swearing in, and this one today, is an all-western swearing in, but we are glad to invite you easterners, midwesterners, and southerners to the club as well.

Mr. Chief Justice.

[At this point Chief Justice Earl Warren administered the oath of office. The President then resumed speaking.]

Thank you very much, Mr. Chief Justice.

I should tell the members of the White

House Staff, Mr. Chief Justice, how fortunate they are that you, with great experience, knew exactly how to administer the oath.

In 1953, when I was sworn in as Vice President, we used this same oath. As you may have noted yesterday, the oath for the Vice President is this one, whereas, the oath for the President is a much shorter one.

In 1953, Senator Knowland—who had been appointed to the Senate by the Chief Justice when he was Governor of California—at my request, swore me in. He proceeded, in swearing me in, to read the entire oath, and then I had to repeat it from memory. Even though I had been a Member of the Senate, I did forget a line. Some people were even wondering whether I was really the Vice President or not.

But the Chief Justice, both today—and I want to say I appreciated the fact that yesterday on the shorter oath—did it phrase by phrase. When you are standing there for that one moment, even though I sometimes can remember 30 minutes of speech, shorter or longer as the case may be, without dropping too many words, for that one moment you can imagine what you might forget.

We welcome you now officially to the White House Staff. We know that this is going to be a very dedicated Staff. I know it from the work that you have all done during the transition.

I do want your families to know that after all I have said about these long hours and the rest, you will see your fathers, your mothers, and others on occasion. I know, too, that despite what you have heard about Washington, that this is an exciting city in which to live. It is

---

[1] The President's reference to Mr. Mikoyan's statement had particular meaning to the audience because of a widely publicized 1965 speech made by Jack Valenti, Special Assistant to President Lyndon B. Johnson before the Advertising Federation of America in Boston, in which he said: "I sleep each night a little better because Lyndon Baines Johnson is my President."

the capital of the world. There are many interesting things to do. Enjoy it; savor it while you are here. You will look back on it later and remember what a wonderful experience it was.

Thank you very much. We wish you well.

NOTE: The President spoke at 1 : 13 p.m. in the East Room at the White House where 81 new members of the White House Staff, including

clerks and secretaries, were sworn in by Earl Warren, Chief Justice of the United States. During his remarks the President referred to Nikita S. Khrushchev, former Premier of the Soviet Union and Anastas I. Mikoyan, former Chairman of the Presidium of the Supreme Soviet.

Before administering the oath of office, Chief Justice Warren spoke. His remarks are printed in the Weekly Compilation of Presidential Documents (vol. 5, p. 157).

4   Remarks at the Swearing In of the Cabinet. *January 22, 1969*

Mr. Chief Justice, Mr. Vice President, ladies and gentlemen:

This is an historic occasion in any administration. It involves, of course, the swearing in of our Cabinet.

Before coming down this morning, I was reading a little background with regard to the appropriate term to apply to a Cabinet.

Andrew Jackson was the man who first used the term Kitchen Cabinet.

Theodore Roosevelt called his Cabinet a Tennis Cabinet, because he played tennis.

Herbert Hoover's Cabinet was a Medicine Ball Cabinet.

I have been asked what this Cabinet is. In view of the fact that we started at 8 o'clock in the morning for the swearing in, we will call it a Working Cabinet.

We are honored today to have the Chief Justice of the United States to swear in each member of the Cabinet.

As I call the name of the member of the Cabinet, if he would step forward with his wife—his wife will hold the Bible as the Chief Justice swears in each member of the Cabinet.

The Secretary of State, Mr. William P.

Rogers, and Mrs. Rogers.

The Secretary of the Treasury, Mr. David M. Kennedy, and Mrs. Kennedy.

The Secretary of Defense, Mr. Melvin R. Laird, and Mrs. Laird.

The Attorney General, Mr. John N. Mitchell, and Mrs. Mitchell.

The Postmaster General, Mr. Winton M. Blount, and Mrs. Blount.

The Secretary of Agriculture, Mr. Clifford M. Hardin, and Mrs. Hardin.

Since I missed the name of the next Cabinet officer on nationwide television a few weeks ago, I want to be sure that everybody on television knows that I remembered it on this occasion.

The Secretary of Commerce.

I congratulate you, *Mr. Stans.* [*Laughter*]

The Secretary of Labor, Mr. George P. Shultz, and Mrs. Shultz.

The Secretary of Health, Education, and Welfare, Mr. Robert H. Finch, and Mrs. Finch.

Mr. Chief Justice, just another historical note. This is the first time in the history of this Nation that the President of the United States, the Chief Justice of the United States, and the Cabinet officer being sworn in were all born in the State of California.

The Secretary of Housing and Urban Development, Mr. George W. Romney, and Mrs. Romney.

The Secretary of the Department of Transportation, Mr. John A. Volpe, and Mrs. Volpe.

Mr. Chief Justice, you will note that I almost automatically started to raise my hand, too, on that occasion.

[*To Secretary Volpe*] The other night, with all the traffic conditions in Washington, it was very difficult to get a cab. I got a ride with the Secret Service.

Another historical note: George Washington in his first Cabinet—there were four members of that Cabinet.

Since that time the Cabinet has begun to grow until now we have 12 official members of the Cabinet. There have been several recommendations from time to time that new members should be added.

President Harry Truman suggested there should be a Secretary for Columnists for one, and also a Secretary for Semantics.

We have no plans to add to the Cabinet as far as its official stature is concerned, but there are two who will be members of the Cabinet in everything except the official position.

One is the Director of the Budget, Mr. Robert P. Mayo.

Mr. Mayo and Mrs. Mayo.

When President Eisenhower set up his Cabinet procedure, he invited as a member of the Cabinet the Ambassador to the United Nations, because of the importance that that role plays in our foreign policy, and particularly in seeking roads to peace.

I am also following that practice.

The Ambassador to the United Nations, our designee, Ambassador Charles W. Yost, and Mrs. Yost.

Mr. Chief Justice, ladies and gentlemen, that completes the swearing in of the Cabinet this morning.

For the benefit not so much of the Cabinet members, but for the benefit of their families, and particularly their children who are here, one other historical note:

I found that during the course of our history, eight men who have served as members of the Cabinet went on to become President of the United States.

My grade school mathematics tells me that each member of this Cabinet then has one chance in 48 to be the tenant of this house in which I now live, the White House, and to become President of the United States.

Those odds are pretty good.

The only thing I would suggest now is that if any one of you is going to come through, we must get to work. It is time for the Cabinet meeting, 8:30.

Thank you very much.

NOTE: The President spoke at 8:03 a.m. in the East Room at the White House.

5   Statement on Signing Executive Order Establishing the Council for Urban Affairs. *January* 23, 1969

THE ESTABLISHMENT of the President's Urban Affairs Council is an historic occasion in American Government. Half a century ago the census of 1920 revealed that a majority of Americans had come to live in cities. But only decades later did the American National Government begin to respond to this changed reality. By

1960, 70 percent of the population was urban and today probably 73 percent is.

For all this, the American National Government has responded to urban concerns in a haphazard, fragmented, and often woefully shortsighted manner (as when the great agricultural migrations from the rural South were allowed to take place with no adjustment or relocation arrangements whatever). What we have never had is a policy: coherent, consistent positions as to what the National Government would hope to see happen; what it will encourage, what it will discourage.

Having a policy in urban affairs is no more a guarantor of success than having one in foreign affairs. But it is a precondition of success. With the creation of the Urban Affairs Council we begin to establish that precondition: the formulation and implementation of a national urban policy.

NOTE: The Council for Urban Affairs was established by Executive Order 11452 of January 23, 1969.

A White House announcement concerning the creation and membership of the Council is printed in the Weekly Compilation of Presidential Documents (vol. 5, p. 161).

At a White House news briefing following the Council's first meeting Dr. Daniel P. Moynihan, Assistant to the President for Urban Affairs and Executive Secretary of the Council, announced the formation of nine subcommittees of the Council, each to be chaired by a Cabinet officer. Dr. Moynihan also announced the formation of an interim staff committee under the chairmanship of Budget Director Robert P. Mayo to work out plans for transition to a peacetime economy at the end of the Vietnam conflict.

6 Statement Announcing the Appointment of Dr. Arthur F. Burns as Counsellor to the President. *January 23, 1969*

TODAY I am pleased to announce a major appointment. Dr. Arthur Burns, a longtime friend and trusted adviser, has agreed to join the White House Staff as the Counsellor to the President. Dr. Burns will have Cabinet rank.

He will head up a small group whose prime responsibility will be the coordination of the development of my domestic policies and programs. Dr. Martin Anderson, one of my Special Assistants, will serve as his deputy. Dr. Burns' role will be that of a generalist, dealing with a broad province of legislative and executive actions.

Besides being a brilliant scholar with a worldwide reputation in economics, Dr. Burns is an able administrator who has been in charge of the National Bureau of Economic Research for many years.

Dr. Burns will, of course, work closely with members of the Cabinet, Dr. McCracken, Mr. Harlow, and others on the White House Staff.

NOTE: Dr. Paul W. McCracken was Chairman-designate of the Council of Economic Advisers and Bryce N. Harlow was an Assistant to the President.

7   Remarks at the Swearing In of Walter J. Hickel as Secretary of the Interior.   *January 24, 1969*

Mr. Chief Justice, Mr. Vice President, all of our distinguished guests this morning:

This is an historic moment in the history not only of this administration, its early history, but also in the history of the country.

For the first time a member of the Cabinet comes from the largest State of the Union and one of the newest States, the State of Alaska.

It is also of historical note to mention that this is somewhat of a precedent, at least for two administrations, because he succeeds Secretary Udall who came from the 48th State to be admitted, the State of Arizona in 1912, and Alaska, of course, was the 49th.

In presenting the Secretary to the Chief Justice for his oath, I would also like to be permitted just another remark with regard to his presence here.

It will be noted that he is alone insofar as his taking the oath. But all of his colleagues are here with him and the distinguished Members of the Senate and House leadership and particularly the Members of the Senate and House Interior Committees are here.

I am sure that enough editorial note has been taken of the fact that his confirmation has taken a little longer than some of the other members of the Cabinet. If I may paraphrase him, however, that does not concern us. We are not interested in confirmation for confirmation's sake.

I should also point out that he takes an office which, throughout the history of this country, has been somewhat controversial. We all recall some of the great Secretaries of the Interior.

I recall particularly—and some of the older members of the press as well as some of the older people in political life will remember—Secretary Ickes.[1] He felt that he had a number of responsibilities, not only to handle his office, which he did with some controversy and considerable distinction, but also to keep the press in line. He once referred to columnists as Public Enemies No. 1. Secretary Hickel will never do that, I am sure.

He also considered it his responsibility to keep the President humble. Secretary Ickes was the one who once said that the President is not a descendant of a sun goddess. And I am sure that Secretary Hickel will assume that great responsibility to see that this President also remains humble.

But I should point out, too, that he already has rendered service far beyond the call of duty. In the first 4 days of this administration he, rather than I, has been the subject of the Herblock cartoons. I am grateful for that.

So if I may present him now with the Biblical scripture, "The last shall be first," as far as this administration is concerned. Secretary Hickel.

NOTE: The President spoke at 10 a.m. in the East Room at the White House.

----

[1] Harold L. Ickes, Secretary of the Interior 1933–1946.

8 Letter to the Chairman, Civil Aeronautics Board, Relating to the Transpacific Route Investigation. *January 24, 1969*

Dear Mr. Chairman:

Upon a review of the actions taken by your Board and President Johnson in connection with the Transpacific route investigation (your Docket 16242 et al.), I have come to the conclusion that it is both appropriate and necessary for me to rescind the prior Presidential action taken and recall the matter for my further review and decision.

Please do not take any further action in connection with the international aspects of this matter until I have had an opportunity to finally advise you of my decision upon the merits.

Very truly yours,

RICHARD NIXON

[The Honorable John H. Crooker, Jr., Chairman, Civil Aeronautics Board, Washington, D.C. 20428]

NOTE: The President's letter was made public as part of a White House release announcing the President's action concerning the investigation.

9 Statement Announcing Disaster Assistance for Mississippi. *January 25, 1969*

I HAVE BEEN deeply saddened by reports of the natural disaster which struck the State of Mississippi last Thursday. I note that the grief caused to that State by the tornado of 2 days ago has been compounded by a gas explosion near Laurel, Miss., early this morning. To the families of those who have lost their lives and to other victims of these disasters, I extend my deep personal sympathy and that of the Nation.

I have asked the Office of Emergency Preparedness and other agencies of the Federal Government to thoroughly investigate the situation in Mississippi and to take immediate actions which they deem appropriate. A representative of the Office of Emergency Preparedness was quickly at the scene of tornado damage on Thursday and met with citizens of the communities which had suffered damage. Another OEP representative accompanied Governor John Bell Williams in an aerial inspection of the explosion area today.

The Federal Government has already responded to the request for assistance in the following ways:

1. A Disaster Assistance Coordinator currently is in the State working with local, State, and Federal officials on disaster assistance efforts.

The OEP conducted a meeting last night in Hazlehurst for State and local officials and citizens of the affected area. The purpose of the meeting was to evaluate damages and possibilities for assistance. At the meeting, State and Federal agency officials discussed their assistance programs.

2. The Small Business Administration has designated Copiah, Simpson, and Smith Counties as disaster loan areas eligible for long-term, low-interest rate loan assistance. The SBA regional office in Jackson, Miss., will provide service for the disaster area.

3. The U.S. Department of Agriculture also is active in providing disaster assistance. The Consumer and Marketing Service has supplied food for Red Cross feeding operations in Hazlehurst.

10   The President's News Conference of *January 27, 1969*

THE PRESIDENT. Ladies and gentlemen, since this is my first press conference since the inauguration, I can imagine there are a number of questions. Consequently, I will make no opening statement, and we will go directly to your questions.

QUESTIONS

PRESENTATION OF LEGISLATIVE PROPOSALS

[1.] Mr. Cormier [Frank Cormier, Associated Press].

Q. Sir, do you plan to make your own State of the Union Message, and do you have a major legislative program to present to Congress this year?

THE PRESIDENT. I shall have a major legislative program to present to the Congress this year. Whether that would best be presented by a series of individual messages or a State of the Union Message, supplemented by some individual messages, is yet to be determined. I will make a determination within the next 2 weeks, after consultation with the legislative leaders.

PEACE PLAN FOR VIETNAM

[2.] Miss Thomas [Helen Thomas, United Press International].

Q. Mr. President, now that you are President, what is your peace plan for Vietnam?

THE PRESIDENT. I believe that as we look at what is happening in the negotiations in Paris, as far as the Amercian side is concerned we are off to a good start. What now, of course, is involved is what happens on the other side.

We find that in Paris, if you read Ambassador Lodge's [1] statement, we have been quite specific with regard to some steps that can be taken now on Vietnam. Rather than submitting a laundry list of various proposals, we have laid down those things which we believe the other side should agree to and can agree to: the restoration of the demilitarized zone as set forth in the Geneva Conference of 1954; mutual withdrawal, guaranteed withdrawal, of forces by both sides; the exchange of prisoners. All of these are matters that we think can be precisely considered and on which progress can be made.

Now, where we go from here depends upon what the other side offers in turn.

RELATIONS WITH COMMUNIST CHINA

[3.] Q. Mr. President, now that you are President, could you be specific with us about what your plans are for improving relations with Communist China, and whether you think they will be successful or not?

---

[1] Ambassador-at-Large Henry Cabot Lodge, head of the United States delegation at the Paris peace talks.

THE PRESIDENT. Well, I have noted, of course, some expressions of interest on the part of various Senators and others in this country with regard to the possibility of admitting Communist China to the United Nations.

I also have taken note of the fact that several countries—including primarily Italy among the major countries—have indicated an interest in changing their policy and possibly voting to admit Communist China to the United Nations.

The policy of this country and this administration at this time will be to continue to oppose Communist China's munist China to the United Nations.

There are several reasons for that. First, Communist China has not indicated any interest in becoming a member of the United Nations.

Second, it has not indicated any intent to abide by the principles of the U.N. Charter, and to meet the principles that new members admitted to the United Nations are supposed to meet.

Finally, Communist China continues to call for expelling the Republic of China from the United Nations; and the Republic of China has, as I think most know, been a member of the international community and has met its responsibilities without any question over these past few years.

Under these circumstances, I believe it would be a mistake for the United States to change its policy with regard to Communist China in admitting it to the United Nations.

Now, there is a second immediate point that I have noted. That is the fact that there will be another meeting in Warsaw. We look forward to that meeting. We will be interested to see what the Chinese

Communist representatives may have to say at that meeting, whether any changes of attitude on their part on major, substantive issues may have occurred.

Until some changes occur on their side, however, I see no immediate prospect of any change in our policy.

MAJOR PROBLEMS OF CONCERN TO THE PRESIDENT

[4.] Q. Mr. President, what problems that you have to cope with do you feel require your most urgent attention now?

THE PRESIDENT. Well, Mr. Kaplow [Herbert Kaplow, NBC News], the major problems with which I have been concerned in this first week have been in the field of foreign policy, because there only the President can make some of the decisions.

And consequently the Security Council, as you ladies and gentlemen are aware, has had two very long meetings, and, in addition, I spent many long hours at night reading the papers which involve the foreign policy of the United States.

This afternoon I will go to the Pentagon for my first major briefing by military officials on our military situation.

Going beyond that, however, I would say that the problems of our cities, which have been discussed at length at the Urban Affairs Council, and our economic problems, which were discussed at the meeting we had in the new Cabinet Committee on Economic Policy,[2] require urgent attention.

It is very difficult to single one out and

---

[2] The Cabinet Committee on Economic Policy was established by Executive Order 11453 of January 24, 1969.

put it above the other. There are a number of problems which this administration confronts; each requires urgent attention. The field of foreign policy will require more attention because it is in this field that only the President, in many instances, can make the decisions.

NONPROLIFERATION TREATY AND MISSILE
TALKS

[5.] Q. Mr. President, on foreign policy, nuclear policy, particularly, could you give us your position on the Nonproliferation Treaty and on the starting of missile talks with the Soviet Union?

THE PRESIDENT. I favor the Nonproliferation Treaty. The only question is the timing of the ratification of that Treaty. That matter will be considered by the National Security Council, by my direction, during a meeting this week. I will also have a discussion with the leaders of both sides in the Senate and in the House on the Treaty within this week and in the early part of next week. I will make a decision then as to whether this is the proper time to ask the Senate to move forward and ratify the Treaty. I expect ratification of the Treaty and will urge its ratification at an appropriate time, and, I would hope, an early time.

As far as the second part of your question, with regard to strategic arms talks, I favor strategic arms talks. Again, it is a question of not only when, but the context of those talks. The context of those talks is vitally important because we are here between two major, shall we say, guidelines.

On the one side, there is the proposition which is advanced by some that we should go forward with talks on the reduction of strategic forces on both sides—we should go forward with such talks, clearly apart from any progress on political settlement; and on the other side, the suggestion is made that until we make progress on political settlements, it would not be wise to go forward on any reduction of our strategic arms, even by agreement with the other side.

It is my belief that what we must do is to steer a course between those two extremes. It would be a mistake, for example, for us to fail to recognize that simply reducing arms through mutual agreement—failing to recognize that that reduction will not, in itself, assure peace. The war which occurred in the Mideast in 1967 was a clear indication of that.

What I want to do is to see to it that we have strategic arms talks in a way and at a time that will promote, if possible, progress on outstanding political problems at the same time—for example, on the problem of the Mideast and on other outstanding problems in which the United States and the Soviet Union, acting together, can serve the cause of peace.

THE MIDEAST PROBLEM

[6.] Q. Mr. President, do you or your administration have any plan, outside the United Nations proposal, for achieving peace in the Middle East?

THE PRESIDENT. As you ladies and gentlemen are aware, the suggestion has been made that we have four-power talks. The suggestion has also been made that we use the United Nations as the primary forum for such talks. And it has also been suggested that the United States and the Soviet Union bilaterally should have talks on the Mideast, and in addition to that, of course, that the problem finally should be settled by the parties in the area.

We are going to devote the whole day on Saturday to the Mideast problem, just as we devoted the whole day this last Saturday on the problem of Vietnam.

We will consider on the occasion of that meeting the entire range of options that we have. I shall simply say at this time that I believe we need new initiatives and new leadership on the part of the United States in order to cool off the situation in the Mideast. I consider it a powder keg, very explosive. It needs to be defused. I am open to any suggestions that may cool it off and reduce the possibility of another explosion, because the next explosion in the Mideast, I think, could involve very well a confrontation between the nuclear powers, which we want to avoid.

I think it is time to turn to the left now [*turning to reporters on his left*].

BUDGET PROSPECTS

[7.] Q. Mr. President, sir, could you tell us whether you have had a chance to examine the Johnson budget, and whether you see any hopes for a reduction in the Johnson budget?

THE PRESIDENT. Yes, I have examined it. As far as hopes for reduction are concerned, the Director of the Bureau of the Budget has just Friday issued instructions to all of the departments to examine the budgets in their departments very closely and to give us recommendations as to where budget cuts might be made.

This is for two purposes: One, because we would like to cut the overall budget; and two, because we want to have room for some of the new programs that this ad-

ministration and the new approaches that this administration would like to implement.

At this time I cannot say where and how the budget can be cut. I will say that we are taking a fresh look at all of the programs and we shall attempt to make cuts in order to carry out the objectives that I set forth during the campaign.

POSSIBILITY OF A CEASE-FIRE IN VIETNAM

[8.] Q. Mr. President, do you consider it possible to have a cease-fire in Vietnam so long as the Vietcong still occupy Vietnamese territory?

THE PRESIDENT. I think that it is not helpful in discussing Vietnam to use such terms as "cease-fire" because cease-fire is a term of art that really has no relevance, in my opinion, to a guerrilla war.

When you are talking about a conventional war, then a cease-fire agreed upon by two parties means that the shooting stops. When you have a guerrilla war, in which one side may not even be able to control many of those who are responsible for the violence in the area, the cease-fire may be meaningless.

I think at this point this administration believes that the better approach is the one that Ambassador Lodge, under our direction, set forth in Paris—mutual withdrawal of forces on a guaranteed basis by both sides from South Vietnam.

NUCLEAR WEAPONS AND THE SOVIET UNION

[9.] Q. Mr. President, back to nuclear weapons. Both you and Secretary Laird have stressed, quite hard, the need for superiority over the Soviet Union. But what is the real meaning of that in view of the fact that both sides have more than enough already to destroy each other, and how do you distinguish between the validity of that stance and the argument of Dr. Kissinger[3] for what he calls "sufficiency"?

THE PRESIDENT. Here, again, I think the semantics may offer an inappropriate approach to the problem. I would say, with regard to Dr. Kissinger's suggestion of sufficiency, that that would meet, certainly, my guideline and, I think, Secretary Laird's guideline, with regard to superiority.

Let me put it this way: When we talk about parity, I think we should recognize that wars occur, usually, when each side believes it has a chance to win. Therefore, parity does not necessarily assure that a war may not occur.

By the same token, when we talk about superiority, that may have a detrimental effect on the other side in putting it in an inferior position and, therefore, giving great impetus to its own arms race.

Our objective in this administration, and this is a matter that we are going to discuss at the Pentagon this afternoon, and that will be the subject of a major discussion in the National Security Council within the month—our objective is to be sure that the United States has sufficient military power to defend our interests and to maintain the commitments which this administration determines are in the interest of the United States around the world.

I think "sufficiency" is a better term, actually, than either "superiority" or "parity."

---

[3] Henry A. Kissinger, Assistant to the President for National Security Affairs.

CRIME IN THE DISTRICT OF COLUMBIA

[10.] Q. Mr. President, you talked quite a bit during the campaign about crime in the District of Columbia. We have had quite a bit of it since January 1st, and I wondered how you proposed to deal with it.

THE PRESIDENT. Mr. Healy [Paul F. Healy, New York Daily News], it is a major problem in the District of Columbia, as I found when I suggested to the Secret Service I would like to take a walk yesterday. I had read Mary McGrory's column and wanted to try her cheesecake.[4] But I find, of course, that taking a walk here in the District of Columbia, and particularly in the evening hours, is now a very serious problem, as it is in some other major cities.

One of the employees at the White House, just over the weekend, was the victim of a purse snatching, which brings it very close to home.

Incidentally, I might point out in that case that my advisers tell me that by seeing that the area is better lighted, that perhaps the possibility of purse snatching and other crimes in the vicinity of the White House might be reduced. Therefore, we have turned on the lights in all of that area, I can assure you.[5] [*Laughter*]

---

[4] Mary McGrory of the Washington Evening Star and United Features Syndicate. Her column of January 26, 1969, was in the form of a letter to the President and referred to the problem of crime in the District of Columbia. In the column Miss McGrory mentioned that the policemen of Precinct 8, after investigating four robberies at her residence, had sampled cheesecake which she had prepared in her kitchen.

[5] The President was referring to President Johnson's economy move that all unnecessary lights in the White House be turned off.

39–861—71——5

But to be quite specific with regard to the District of Columbia, it was not only a major commitment in the campaign; it is a major concern in the country. I noted an editorial in one of the major papers, the New York Times, for example, that Washington, D.C. was now a city of "fear and crime." That may go too far, but at least that was their judgment. All three of the Washington papers indicate great concern.

Consequently, I have on an urgent basis instructed the Attorney General to present to me a program to deal with crime in the District of Columbia, and an announcement of that program and also an announcement as to what we will ask the Congress to do, in addition to what we will do administratively, will be made at the end of this week.

WITHDRAWAL OF NOMINATIONS AND RE-EXAMINATION OF PACIFIC AIRLINE ACTION

[11.] Q. Mr. President, why did you decide to withdraw all the appointments [6] that had been sent to Capitol Hill by your predecessor, and can you tell us why you decided to cancel the decision, for the time, in the Pacific airline case?

THE PRESIDENT. Well, first, with regard to the appointments, I had two precedents to follow. And so consequently, I took my choice. In the one instance, President Kennedy, as you will recall, did not withdraw the appointments of judgeships which he inherited from President Eisenhower. On the other hand, President

_____
[6] For list of withdrawals, see Weekly Compilation of Presidential Documents (vol. 5, p. 166).

Eisenhower had withdrawn all appointments and then proceeded to make new appointments, including some from the list that had been withdrawn.

I felt that the Eisenhower approach was the more efficient way to handle it.

I should point out that among those names that have been withdrawn, I already know that some will be reappointed. But I felt that the new administration should examine the whole list and make its own decision with regard to whether the individuals that had been appointed would serve the interests of the Nation according to the guidelines that the new administration was to lay down.

With regard to the action that had been taken by the previous administration on the airlines, I received recommendations or, shall I say, requests on the part of both the Chairman of the House Foreign Affairs Committee and the Chairman of the Senate Foreign Relations Committee that this matter be returned to the White House for further examination.

As you know, the President has authority in this field only where it involves international matters. Under the circumstances, since both Chairmen were members of the other party, and since also I had received suggestions from a number of other Congressmen, both Democratic and Republican, as well as Senators, that this should be reexamined, I brought it back for reexamination.

One other point that should be made: There is no suggestion, in asking for a reexamination of that decision, of impropriety or illegality or improper influence. We will examine the whole situation, but particularly with regard to its impact on foreign relations.

DISCUSSIONS OF NOMINATIONS WITH THE
FORMER ATTORNEY GENERAL

[12.] Q. Mr. President, Ramsey Clark stated this morning that you gave President Johnson assurances through Attorney General Mitchell that you would not withdraw the judicial nominations of Mr. Poole and Mr. Byrne [7] and several others. Could you comment on that, sir?

THE PRESIDENT. Well, I remember exactly what did occur, and it may be that we did not have an exact meeting of the minds in the event that Ramsey Clark, former Attorney General Clark, had that understanding. What happened was that Ramsey Clark discussed this matter during the period between the election and the inauguration with Attorney General Mitchell. He asked Attorney General Mitchell to ask me whether I would object to action on the part of President Johnson in the event that he did submit these appointments to the Senate.

My reply was that I would not object to President Johnson's submitting such—submitting names to the Senate, just as I did not object to his action in the trans-Pacific case or in any other area. As you ladies and gentlemen are quite aware, I have scrupulously followed the line that we have one President at a time, and that he must continue to be President until he leaves office on January 20.

However, I did not have any understanding with the President directly, and

no one, including Attorney General Mitchell, as far as I was concerned had any discretion to agree to a deal that these nominations, having been made, would be approved by me. I have withdrawn them and now I am going to examine each one of them. As I have already indicated, I have decided that in at least some instances some of the names will be resubmitted.

THE TFX AND CONGRESSIONAL
COMMITTEES

[13.] Q. Mr. President, in the last administration, the McClellan Committee [8] ran into a considerable problem in obtaining information on costs, performance, and development on the TFX [Tactical Fighter Experimental aircraft], F–111 contract. I wondered if you will open the records on this, and what your general view is with regard to dealing with congressional committees?

THE PRESIDENT. I understand not only the McClellan Committee, but Mr. Mollenhoff [9] did some examination in this field, too.

With regard to the TFX, and also with regard to all of the matters that you have referred to, this administration will reexamine all past decisions where they are not foreclosed, where the reexamination is not foreclosed, by reason of what has gone before.

I will not, however, at this time, prejudge what that examination will in-

---

[7] Cecil F. Poole and William M. Byrne, Jr. Their nominations as United States District Judges for the Northern and Central Districts of California, respectively, were submitted to the Senate by President Johnson on January 9, 1969.

[8] The Senate Committee on Government Operations under the chairmanship of Senator John L. McClellan of Arkansas.
[9] Clark R. Mollenhoff, Des Moines Register and Tribune, who asked the question.

dicate. I believe that it is in the best interests of the Nation, when a new administration comes in, with a new team, that the President direct the new team, as I have directed it very strongly during this first week, to reexamine all decisions that may have been questioned, either by Senate committees or by responsible members of the press, or by other people in public or private life. This we are doing and this is one of the areas in which a reexamination is going forward.

PLANS FOR CURBING INFLATION

[14.] Q. Inflation and rising prices, Mr. President, are of great concern. What specific plans do you have to curb them?

THE PRESIDENT. In the meeting of the Cabinet Committee on Economic Policy, which I set up, one of the three new institutions I set up—I say three new institutions—if I might digress for a moment, I suppose the Nation wonders what a President does in his first week and where is all the action that we have talked about. We have done a great deal, particularly in getting the machinery of government set up which will allow us to move in an orderly way on major problems.

I do not believe, for example, that policy should be made, and particularly foreign policy should be made, by off-the-cuff responses in press conferences, or any other kind of conferences. I think it should be made in an orderly way. So it is with economic policy. That is why, in addition to the Urban Affairs Council and a revitalized National Security Council for foreign affairs, we now have a Cabinet Committee on Economic Policy. That Cabinet Committee has con-

sidered the problem of inflation, and the problem is, first, that we are concerned about the escalation of prices to a rate of 4.8 percent, and we do not see, if present policies continue, any substantial reduction in that.

And, second, we are considering what actions can be taken which will not cause an unacceptable rise in unemployment. By unacceptable rise in unemployment, I want to emphasize that we believe it is possible to control inflation without increasing unemployment in, certainly, any substantial way.

I should make one further point. Unless we do control inflation, we will be confronted, eventually, with massive unemployment, because the history of economic affairs in other countries indicates that if inflation is allowed to get out of hand, eventually there has to be a "bust" and then unemployment comes. So what we are trying to do, without, shall we say, too much managing of the economy, is, we are going to have some fine tuning of our fiscal and monetary affairs in order to control inflation.

One other point I should make in this respect: I do not go along with the suggestion that inflation can be effectively controlled by exhorting labor and management and industry to follow certain guidelines. I think that is a very laudable objective for labor and management to follow. But I think I am aware of the fact that the leaders of labor and the leaders of management, much as they might personally want to do what is in the best interests of the Nation, have to be guided by the interests of the organizations that they represent.

So the primary responsibility for controlling inflation rests with the national administration and its handling of fiscal and monetary affairs. That is why we will have some new approaches in this area. We assume that responsibility. We think we can meet it, that we can control inflation without an increase in unemployment.

THE OUTLOOK FOR PEACE IN VIETNAM

[15.] Q. Mr. President, during the transition period in New York, several persons who conferred with you came away with the impression that you felt the Vietnam war might be ended within a year. Were these impressions correct, sir?

THE PRESIDENT. I, of course, in my conversations with those individuals, and any individuals, have never used the term "6 months, a year, 2 years, or 3 years," because I do not think it is helpful in discussing this terribly difficult war, a war that President Johnson wanted to bring to an end as early as possible, that I want to bring to an end as early as possible.

I do not think it is helpful to make overly optimistic statements which, in effect, may impede and perhaps might make very difficult our negotiations in Paris. All that I have to say is this: that we have a new team in Paris, with some old faces, but a new team. We have new direction from the United States. We have a new

sense of urgency with regard to the negotiations.

There will be new tactics. We believe that those tactics may be more successful than the tactics of the past.

I should make one further point, however: We must recognize that all that has happened to date is the settlement of the procedural problems, the size of the table, and who will sit at those tables.

What we now get to is really that hard, tough ground that we have to plow: the substantive issues as to what both parties will agree to, whether we are going to have mutual withdrawal, whether we are going to have self-determination by the people of South Vietnam without outside interference, whether we can have an exchange of prisoners.

This is going to take time, but I can assure you that it will have my personal attention. It will have my personal direction. The Secretary of State, my Adviser for National Security Affairs, the Secretary of Defense—all of us—will give it every possible attention and we hope to come up with some new approaches.

Helen Thomas, United Press International: Thank you, Mr. President.

NOTE: President Nixon's first news conference was held in the East Room at the White House at 11 a.m. on Monday, January 27, 1969. It was broadcast on radio and television.

---

11 Memorandum on the Need for a Review of the Budget. *January 27, 1969*

Memorandum for Heads of Executive Departments and Agencies:

As we set the course of the new Administration, a careful and thorough review of the budget must be the first order

of business. The American people have a right to expect that their tax dollars will be properly and prudently used. They also have a right to expect that fiscal policy will help to restrain the present excessive rate of price inflation in our economy.

At my request, the Budget Director has asked you to begin promptly a review of the budget requests sent to the Congress by the outgoing administration. This task must receive your personal attention. As you evaluate the programs of your agency in that review, I want each of you particularly to:

- identify activities of low priority which can be reduced or phased down and perhaps, over time, eliminated completely;
- start now to redirect ongoing Federal programs toward this Administration's goals and objectives.

We must act promptly along these lines in order to make room for new programs that seem urgent.

For the fiscal year ending June 30, 1969, we must operate under the spending ceilings set in the Revenue and Expenditure Control Act of 1968. Fiscal year 1969

is more than half over, and our flexibility for making changes is limited.

However, we need to begin now to lay the foundation for our future actions. I want you, therefore, to examine in detail the spending plans of your agency through this June and to achieve all the savings that you can—not by deferrals or stretchouts which will have to be made up later, but by actions that will provide a sound base for future programs we will want to undertake. The Director of the Budget should be informed of your plans within the next 30 days. Our examination of the Government's programs and budget levels in the coming weeks is of central importance to the success of the new Administration in achieving a more efficient and responsive Government. I ask each of you to cooperate fully in this endeavor.

RICHARD NIXON

NOTE: The memorandum was dated January 25, 1969, and released January 27, 1969.

12 Remarks to Key Personnel at the Department of State. *January* 29, 1969

Mr. Secretary, ladies and gentlemen:

I am very honored and privileged to be here in this auditorium on my first official visit with the key personnel of one of the departments.

I recall, incidentally, that on Inauguration Day the first building I visited was this one. We had then a prayer breakfast, not a breakfast—we had prayer without breakfast.

Now that we have had the prayers, we are back here to get the advice so that I can go back to the Senate and get the con-

sent for everything that we have to do from now on.

I do want you to know, too, that in appearing here with the Secretary of State, I think his relationship with the President is of great interest to those in this Department.

I have been reading some dope stories lately about the rivalries that may develop between the various departments in Government and particularly the traditional struggles for power that sometimes take place when the State Department is concerned and the White House Staff is concerned when it delves into foreign policy. I have often answered those who had concern in this point by saying that what really counts is not the table of organization, but what really counts is the relationship between the two men—the President and his Secretary of State.

I am sure that all of you know that my relationship with Secretary Rogers goes back many, many years. We came into Government virtually together; as a matter of fact, we came into the service together—the Navy—when we were at Quonset Point in 1942. Since that time I have learned to respect his judgment, his courage, his basic intelligence, as I know and I am sure that you in this Department who have the opportunity to know him will learn to respect it.

I also am aware of the fact that in the presence of a Secretary of State I may be in the presence of someone who may turn out to be my successor in this office.

I did a little historical research before coming over here, just as I did historical research before I went to the House yesterday and to the Senate today at noon. So, in each place I pay proper tribute to the Members of the body concerned.[1]

In the House of Representatives, for example, I was able to point out that in a period between 1840 and 1880, 10 out of

the 12 Presidents of the United States in that period had served in the House of Representatives. Then for a considerable period of time, up until the time of the election in 1960, the Nation moved to other areas for their Presidents, except for the election of Harry Truman in 1948.

I pointed out when I was at the Senate today that Andrew Johnson, in the 19th century, was the last President before John F. Kennedy who had served in both the House and the Senate. Then John F. Kennedy, Lyndon Johnson, and now the present occupant of the Presidency, have served in both the House and the Senate.

Now, as far as the State Department was concerned, my history had to go back a little further.

I found, for example, that in days long gone—not gone, but long past—that in the past the Secretary of State was the office that was the logical one for anyone to seek in the event he wanted to be President.

You will all remember that Jefferson was Washington's Secretary of State. Madison was Jefferson's Secretary of State. Monroe was Madison's Secretary of State. John Quincy Adams was Monroe's Secretary of State. And Martin Van Buren was Jackson's first Secretary of State.

In fact, the tradition continued, and I found ended in the passing of the office from President Polk to President Buchanan. President Buchanan was the last who had been Secretary of State who became President of the United States. Now, whether that tells us something or not as to why it has not happened since, I do not know.

President Buchanan, as some of you

---

[1] On January 28, 1969, the President paid a visit to the House of Representatives and had luncheon with the leadership, members of the House Committee on Rules, and chairmen of various other committees. Earlier on January 29, he visited the Senate and lunched with the Senate leadership in the minority leader's office.

may recall—if you were following me on inaugural night [2]—was one who came to the Presidency at a time that he thought was much too late for that honor to be accorded him. As he was riding down from the White House to the Capitol he turned to a friend and said that he didn't feel particularly happy about becoming President at this late stage in his political career because he found that all of his friends that he wanted to reward had now died. And he said all of his enemies that he hated and wanted to punish were now his friends.

Now, of course, we have Secretary Rogers. I should point out that there is another way that he can go up if he would like. He has been the Attorney General of the United States and consequently could qualify for the Chief Justiceship. I am not suggesting that, incidentally, he will be Earl Warren's [3] successor—not right now.

But you will recall that the first Chief Justice of the United States, John Jay, started as Secretary to the Confederation before the United States became the Government that it was under the Constitution. And John Marshall had served as Secretary of State too, as did Charles Evans Hughes. That is a great tradition.

All that I am suggesting to you by these opening remarks is that those of you who may plan to be Secretary of State can look forward possibly to being either President of the United States or Chief Justice.

I will only add one further thought, however, that in each body, any House Member, naturally, who heard what I

said could see himself becoming President some day, any Member of the Senate could see that if things worked out he might become President, and, of course, any person in this audience with your foreign policy background and your futures could see yourself becoming President.

Which is the best way? I think perhaps the best answer I have for that is in a favorite anecdote. An Episcopal priest was asked by a young parishioner who was very troubled about all of the theology he had heard about, asked that question that I am sure all leaders in religious thought are often asked.

The young parishioner said, "Father, is the Episcopal Church the only true path to salvation?" The priest smiled and answered. He said, "No, son, there are other ways, but no gentleman would choose them."

I am sure the Secretary would say that there may be other ways to the Presidency than the Secretary of State, but no gentleman would choose them.

Now, may I speak to you quite directly about the work that you do and my association with it, and what I hope would be our association in the future?

As I look at this front row here, I see men whom I met 20 years ago when I first went to Europe with the Herter Committee.[4] I can see in rows way back there people who have briefed me on my trips abroad during the period I was a Congressman, a Senator, the 8 years I was Vice President, and then in the period

---

[2] During the evening of January 20, 1969, the President visited six Inaugural Balls.

[3] Chief Justice Earl Warren had informed President Johnson in 1968 that he wished to retire as soon as a successor had been qualified.

[4] In the summer of 1947 the President was serving as a member of the House Select Committee on Foreign Aid, named after its Chairman, Representative Christian A. Herter of Massachusetts. The Committee toured 18 European nations to survey war damage and make suggestions on need for aid.

of 7 or 8 years when I was out of Government.

During that time, I have visited over 60 countries. I always prided myself on trying to be well briefed before I made those visits, and consequently I became well acquainted with the career men and women in the State Department.

Not just because I stand before you today, but because I believe this—and I have often said it publicly and privately—I do think we have the best career service in the world. I think that was the case based on what I have seen, what I have heard, and on the advice that I have received.

I think it is vitally important to the future of this country that the morale of that career service be kept at its highest level possible and that those who make the foreign policy of this country have the best possible advice that we can get from those who serve in the career service.

That is one of the reasons, when Secretary Rogers assumed his position and when the Under Secretaries as well as the Assistant Secretaries talked to me, that I set forth a policy, a policy that I want followed throughout this administration, somewhat different from some of the policies of the past. Each President must work differently, of course, in developing his foreign policy decisions.

That policy is this: I consider the Secretary of State to be my chief foreign policy adviser and when we have a difficult decision and I ask him what should we do, I do not want him to come in and say, "Well, you could do this or you could do that." I want him to say, "You could do this or you could do that," but I want him to give me his advice on what we should do.

But I have also told him, and as I understand he has informed you, that where there is a strong minority view or where there may be two other viewpoints or more held by responsible people, that I want to see that view too. The reason that I want to see the minority views as well as the majority views, and as well as his advice which may be either one or the other because he may not agree with the majority view even in the Department, is that I have the conviction that a policy is improved by having the decision maker consider the options and consider the alternatives. Even if he decides to reject one point of view that is strongly urged, he may develop from considering that point of view a more effective and stronger position in the position which he eventually considers to be the preferable one.

I say this because as I have traveled throughout the world I've been sometimes concerned that people in the career service in various posts develop a sense of frustration that they have ideas with regard to the conduct of foreign policy that are quite relevant that ought to be considered, but that some way they will never get to the top in the bureaucracy.

Now, I recognize in the huge responsibilities we have around the world, in all the cables that come pouring in here, that every idea that anybody has in the world can't always come to the President of the United States or even to the Secretary of State or even to the Under Secretaries or the Assistant Secretaries. But I do want to urge everyone here who has responsibility for preparing any materials that come to my office, that I am interested in, and want to see, points of view that may differ from those that eventually may become the policy of this country.

I think the more that we have that kind

39–861—71——6

of dialogue, that kind sometimes, of debate, of consideration, which is not simply papering over differences, negotiating them out—and I know you are very skilled in that, too, you have to be—but I think when we have that kind of dialogue we can improve our policies. It will certainly be of very good assistance to me.

I say that, too, because I realize that in this Department are so many who have varied backgrounds, who have done a great deal of thinking, a great deal more than I will ever have the opportunity to do, on special problems and special areas.

I will, therefore, appreciate the best that you can present and I can assure you that to the extent my time permits, those viewpoints will be considered.

Finally, as you may have noted if you read or heard my first press conference on Monday—I was glad the Secretary had read it, incidentally—you will note that I pointed out—when one of the questioners said, "What is the most important decision that you have to make? What is the greatest problem that you have to confront?"—I pointed out what is the fact: And that is that it is difficult to try to select priorities among the many problems that confront this Nation at home and abroad, but I do know that there are certain decisions in foreign policy that only the President of the United States can make. It is here that he must devote that extra effort if there is any extra effort he can devote to it because if he makes a mistake in this area, it is a mistake that no one else is going to be able to correct.

For that reason, I asked that the Secretary arrange this meeting, that I come here to say to those who have worked in the field—many of you I have met around the world, many of you I hope to meet during the course of my service in the present office that I hold—to say to you that I appreciate what you have done. I respect the members of this Department, the career service, for the contribution you have made and are making to the foreign policy of this country.

I hope that when this administration completes its service in Washington we will have made real progress toward settling differences between nations, toward bringing the peace that we all want in the world.

I know that if that comes, it will come only because of the quality of our State Department personnel. I know that I have to count on you. I can only say that as I stand here today, as I see you, I believe that I, as the chief executive officer of this Nation, have the best advice of any chief executive officer of any nation in the world.

Thank you.

Before Mr. Rogers responds, I should say that in giving that little history I can also tell you about the last Attorney General who became Secretary of State. I am sure some of the veterans may remember, it was President Taft's Secretary of State, Philander Knox. He was famous for a reason that I hope Mr. Rogers does not become famous for. He was a man who loved the good life. He used to arrive in the office about 10 o'clock to look over the cables. At 11:30 he would leave and go to the best club in town for a leisurely two-martini lunch. Then in the afternoon, if it was a good day, he would go out to Chevy Chase and play golf and that evening attend a diplomatic reception.

I understand that things have changed, but that was one of your predecessors.

NOTE: The President spoke at 3:06 p.m. in the auditorium at the Department of State.

13   Statement About the Nomination of Gerard C. Smith as Director, United States Arms Control and Disarmament Agency.   *January 29, 1969*

GERARD SMITH has the experience, the knowledge, and the dedication for this job. He was engaged in developing proposals for a test ban as early as a decade ago. President Kennedy credited him with the original proposal for the Washington-Moscow "hot line."

The tasks of the Arms Control and Disarmament Agency belong to the most important of my administration. I know that Mr. Smith will address them with all the urgency and emphasis that they deserve.

To this end I am directing that the role and status of the ACDA within the United States Government be upgraded. Mr. Smith will have direct and ready access to the Secretary of State and to the President and will participate in all meetings of the National Security Council at which matters within the scope of his mission are considered.

NOTE: The statement was read by Press Secretary Ronald L. Ziegler at his news briefing at 5:42 p.m. on Wednesday, January 29, 1969.

14   Remarks at the 17th Annual Presidential Prayer Breakfast.   *January 30, 1969*

Mr. Vice President and Mrs. Agnew, Senator Carlson, all the distinguished Members of the Congress, representatives of the administration, and particularly to our distinguished guests from other countries and those listening on radio and those who may see bits and pieces on television:

I am honored to be here on one of the first public appearances since the inauguration; and particularly so because I have had the opportunity to share with you in these very eloquent moments in which we have heard from people in both parties, in which we have also heard from a representative of another nation. There is, however, a common theme that runs through it all. That theme is religious faith which, despite the differences we may have, brings us together—brings us together in this Nation and, we trust, may help bring us together in the world.

As I was preparing my Inaugural Address, I did what I am sure every President who has had that responsibility did—I read all the ones that had previously been made. They were very different. Some were much longer than others. One was an hour and 40 minutes. Another, the shortest, was 10 minutes. Some spoke of all the great issues, as the State of the Union Message does, and others were rather brief, speaking only of the principles which were to be held to by the next President of the United States.

But there was one theme that was common to every one of them. That was that each President, as he was being inaugurated, in his own way, recognized the spiritual heritage of this Nation and asked for the blessing of God on this country, in not only its affairs at home, but its affairs abroad.

In talking to Billy Graham, who has spoken to us so eloquently today, he told me he had made a study of the Presidents of the United States. He had reached an interesting conclusion. Some of them came to the Presidency with a much deeper and more basic religious faith than other, but however they may have come to that awesome responsibility, all had left the Presidency with a very deep religious faith.

Yesterday, Speaker McCormack gave me a striking example of this. One of the early great Presidents, Andrew Jackson, came to the Presidency from the battlefields. Perhaps those who had read history were not aware of the deep religious faith which he perhaps had then but had not expressed, but which in his later years— and particularly after he left the Presidency—he often attested to.

The Speaker referred to an occasion when President Jackson was asked to participate in a dedication ceremony marking the Battle of New Orleans. He refused because the ceremony was set for Sunday.

Those who were inviting him said, "But, Mr. President, you fought the Battle of New Orleans on Sunday." And President Jackson answered, "Well, that was a matter of necessity. I am speaking now from choice."

During these past few days, as is the case with any newly inaugurated President, I have found very little time to do what I would like to do; to meet people, to read the thousands of letters that come in from all over the country. But each evening at the end of the day I try to read a few, to get a feeling of the country, so as not to get out of touch—in that Oval Room—with all of the deep feelings that people around this country have about the Presidency and our Nation.

I found one common theme that ran through a majority of those letters. I was somewhat surprised that it did so. In these days in which religion is not supposed to be fashionable in many quarters, in these days when skepticism and even agnosticism seems to be on the upturn, over half of all the letters that have come into our office have indicated that people of all faiths and of all nations in a very simple way are saying: "We are praying for you, Mr. President. We are praying for this country. We are praying for the leadership that this Nation may be able to provide for this world."

As I read those letters I realized how great was my responsibility and how great was your responsibility, those who share with me these days in Government.

I realize that people whom we will never meet have this deep religious faith which has run through the destiny of this land from the beginning.

I realize that we carry on our shoulders their hopes, but more important, we are sustained by their prayers.

I say to all of you joining us here today in this Presidential Prayer Breakfast that in the many events that I will participate in, none will mean more to me, personally, none, I think, will mean more to the Members of the Cabinet and the Congress, than this occasion.

You have inspired us. You have given us a sense of the continuity of history which brings us together from the beginning to now. You have told us in a very simple and eloquent way that, great as the problems are which now confront us, with faith, faith in our God, faith in the ideals of our country, and also with a deep dedication to what our role is in this Nation and the world, we are going to be able to make these next years great years for this Nation and great years for the world.

I believe that and it is to that end that we dedicate ourselves today. That objective transcends all partisan considerations. I am proud to stand here today in the presence of those who, by your being here, indicate that you have not lost faith in this Nation. You have not lost faith in the religious background that has sustained us.

As a matter of fact, we are entering a period when, sustained by that faith, we will be able to meet the challenge which is ours—a challenge which comes to very few people in the history of man. It is America's now. Whether we succeed or we fail will determine whether peace and freedom survive in this world.

We will meet the challenge. We will meet it because we are going to devote every hour of the day to seeing that we meet it properly. But we will meet it also because we will be sustained and inspired by the prayers of millions of people across this world. Those prayers do mean something. Through the medium of these words I wanted to thank the people of this Nation, the people of this world who are praying for us. We trust that we can be worthy of your prayers and worthy of your faith.

Thank you.

NOTE: The President spoke at 10:15 a.m. at the Sheraton Park Hotel in Washington. The nondenominational prayer breakfast was attended by some 2,000 guests, including religious and political leaders and Federal officials. Former Senator Frank Carlson of Kansas was chairman of the Prayer Breakfast Committee.

The Rev. William F. (Billy) Graham, noted evangelist and personal friend of the President, gave the principal address.

15   Remarks Announcing a Goodwill Tour to Western Europe by Col. Frank Borman, USAF. *January* 30, 1969

Ladies and gentlemen:

These three men who stand with me need no introduction. [*The President referred to the Apollo 8 astronauts: Col. Frank Borman, USAF; Capt. James A. Lovell, Jr., USN; and Lt. Col. William A. Anders, USAF.*]

I think, if anything, they are probably better known than the President of the United States as a result of television and their recent very great exposure for the whole world to see.

It is my very great privilege today to welcome them not only here again to this house and this office, but to announce that Colonel Borman, his wife, and two sons are going to make a goodwill trip to Western Europe. The number of countries to be visited is, at present, eight. The number may be extended.

We think this is a very appropriate trip for him to make for several reasons.

First, a personal note with regard to the inaugural ceremonies to indicate the sense of continuity of the space program. Naturally, when the inauguration invitations went out I suggested that we invite the three astronauts who are with me today to come to the inauguration. The NASA director [1] very appropriately pointed out that the invitation should be extended to a larger group, because these three men, as Colonel Borman and his colleagues have taken every opportunity to point out, could not have done what they have done without building on what has gone on before them. So, consequently, a group of nine came as guests to the inauguration.

As Colonel Borman goes to Europe, he pointed out to me just a few minutes ago that his two colleagues have a misison here at home that they need to undertake and consequently will not be going with him. But Colonel Borman will be representing not only these three, but the men who have gone before.

I should also point out that as he goes to Europe he emphasizes a fact we often forget: that the knowledge which made possible these great discoveries is not limited to this Nation; that it comes from the whole history of scientific discovery, and there is certainly no national monopoly on that kind of knowledge.

It is significant to note that when we look at the national backgrounds of these men here we find represented the Canadians, the British, the Germans, and the

Czechoslovakians here in this group.

So I think it is very appropriate for Colonel Borman to go to Western Europe and to bring to them not only the greetings of the people of the United States, but to point out what is the fact: that we in America do not consider that this is a monopoly, these great new discoveries that we are making; that we recognize the great contributions that others have made and will make in the future; and that we do want to work together with all peoples on this earth in the high adventure of exploring the new areas of space.

So, consequently, Colonel, I think they would like to hear from you, as they have heard so often.

I told the Colonel and his colleagues before that they have been appearing so often and so well in various parts of the country that these exposures to the national press corps causes them much less concern than it does me when I come before you.

NOTE: The President spoke at 11 a.m. in the Fish Room at the White House before a group of reporters.

Colonel Borman's response and announcement of his itinerary are printed in the Weekly Compilation of Presidential Documents (vol. 5, pp. 190, 208).

---

[1] Thomas O. Paine, Acting Administrator.

16 Special Message to the Congress Requesting New Authority To Reorganize the Executive Branch. *January 30, 1969*

To the Congress of the United States:

New times call for new ideas and fresh approaches. To meet the needs of today and tomorrow, and to achieve a new level of efficiency, the Executive Branch requires flexibility in its organization.

Government organization is created to serve, not to exist; as functions change, the organization must be ready to adapt itself to those changes.

Ever since the Economy Act of 1932, the Congress has recognized the need of the President to modernize the Federal Government continually. During most of that time, the Congress has provided the President the authority to reorganize the Executive Branch.

The current reorganization statute—Chapter 9 of Title 5 of the United States Code—is derived from the Reorganization Act of 1949. That law places upon the President a permanent responsibility "from time to time to examine the organization of all agencies" and "to determine what changes therein are necessary" to accomplish the purposes of the statute. Those purposes include promoting the better execution of the laws, cutting expenditures, increasing efficiency in Government operations, abolishing unnecessary agencies and eliminating duplication of effort. The law also authorizes the President to transmit reorganization plans to the Congress to make the changes he considers necessary.

Unfortunately, the authority to transmit such plans expired on December 31, 1968. The President cannot, therefore, now fulfill his reorganization responsibilities. He is severely limited in his ability to organize and manage the Executive Branch in a manner responsive to new needs.

I, therefore, urge that the Congress promptly enact legislation to extend for at least two years the President's authority to transmit reorganization plans.

This time-tested reorganization procedure is not only a means for curtailing ineffective and uneconomical Government operations, but it also provides a climate that enables good managers to manage well.

Under the procedure, reorganization plans are sent to the Congress by the President and generally take effect after 60 days unless either House passes a resolution of disapproval during that time. In this way the President may initiate improvements, and the Congress retains the power of review.

This cooperative executive-legislative approach to reorganization has shown itself to be sensible and effective for more than three decades, regardless of party alignments. It is more efficient than the alternative of passing specific legislation to achieve each organizational change. The cooperative approach is tested; it is responsive; it works.

Reorganization authority is the tool a President needs to shape his Administration to meet the new needs of the times, and I urgently request its extension.

RICHARD NIXON

The White House
January 30, 1969

---

17   Remarks to Employees at the Department of Justice.
January 30, 1969

Mr. Attorney General, ladies and gentlemen:

I think of all the departments of Government that I have visited, and will be visiting in these next 2 to 3 weeks, I will feel more at home here.

I don't mean because the Bureau of Narcotics is here or the Bureau of Prisons or anything of that sort. But when I look over this room and I see the senior people in the Department of Justice, when I know your backgrounds, when I realize that we come basically from the same backgrounds, I realize that but for the accident of politics I might be here and you might be where I am.

I, too, want you to know that in saying that, I speak with very great appreciation of the activities of your new Attorney General. I was trying to check on his political credentials before I came over here today and I think you might be interested in some of his background.

I find that there is a story to the effect, which he has not denied, that he was one of the commanding officers for John F. Kennedy in the Pacific. Before he became my campaign manager or director during the campaign of 1968, he was Counsel to Governor Nelson Rockefeller of New York. I say Counsel to Governor Rockefeller. He was Counsel to the State of New York in its activities in the field of bonds.

I remember in that respect a conversation I had with the Governor, at which your new Attorney General was present, shortly after I had won the nomination of the Republican Party in Miami Beach and the Governor came in to congratulate me. Mr. Mitchell was there. I started to introduce the two and Governor Rockefeller very graciously said, "I know John Mitchell. You know, he is my lawyer. Or, I should say, he was my lawyer."

But in any event, with that common background, I do want you to know that I am aware of the tremendous responsibility the men and women in this room have. All of you know that for these past few years, and particularly over the past few months, there has been an increasing interest in the United States in the activities in which you have primary responsibility.

I want to make it very clear when we talk about the fields in which you are en-

gaged—the fields of law enforcement, antitrust, civil rights, all of these areas— that we are not talking in any partisan sense. The interest of all Americans is involved here.

There has never been a time in this Nation's history when more Americans were more concerned about the enforcement of law and reestablishing not only respect for laws but laws that deserve respect, and that means how the laws are enforced will bring that respect.

So a great deal rides on the competence of the men and women in this room—the leadership that you provide.

I simply want you to know that I have great confidence in you. I realize that only a few of you, those who sit in these front rows, are here because of the appointments that I have made, appointments that I have made after consultation with the Attorney General and with his, of course, strong approval.

I know that most of you in this room are people who have dedicated your adult lives to the service of government. I want all of you to know who are not political appointees, those of you who are in the career service, that I have great respect for those who have been in the career service. I know what a tremendous contribution you have made and what a tremendous contribution you are going to make.

No one can be a successful Attorney General, no one can be a successful Assistant Attorney General or Deputy Attorney General unless he has the backing and the enthusiastic support of those in his Department.

We need your support. We want it and we hope to be worthy of it.

I can simply say, as I look back over the years that I was in the Congress—

34

going back 22 years ago, 4 years in the House, 2 years in the Senate, and 8 years as Vice President—I have had many opportunities to know the men and women in the Department of Justice. I always had the very highest respect for their caliber. And I learned then that when you look over the entire Government, you would not be able to name any department where, in terms of dedication, in terms of sacrifice for the public interest, there was a higher standard than here. Let me be quite precise in that respect.

I am sure all of you are aware of the fact that there was considerable publicity at the time the Attorney General took this assignment that he had to come down in pay as a result.

I know, too, that there is a reverse side of that coin. I know that in this room are many people who, when they had the choice of whether to go into private practice—with all of the opportunities to go up financially—you chose Government service. You chose it not because the financial remuneration was low. But you chose it because the opportunity for service was high. I therefore respect you for what you have done.

I know that over the years you sometimes may have had doubts as to whether that decision was the right one, particularly when those years came when you were old enough, as some of you are, to have to meet the responsibilities of sending children to college and all the other activities in maintaining a balanced family budget.

But I can assure you that speaking as one who has been at the highest level—and I can say the highest level in the company of my former law partner [Attorney General Mitchell]—at the highest level of remuneration in the private practice of the law, and one who has also served in the Congress of the United States, in the Senate of the United States, as Vice President and, years ago, I should also point this out, started out as a P–3—I think that was the classification in the old Office of Price Administration before World War II—I can tell you that if I had the choice to make today, the choice between going into Government service, and doing what you are doing in this Department, and going into one of the great law firms with a much higher remuneration, I would do what you are doing here.

You are going to look back on your lives, I think, later on, and you can be proud that when you had that choice to make you chose to make this contribution to public service.

Now, understand, I am not running down those who are in the private sector. After all, without them we would not have the tax monies with which to make that pay increase which we all want. But what I am suggesting here is this: that we in this country sometimes are not too much aware, enough aware, of how much of a financial sacrifice people may make to go into Government service. We are not, therefore, appreciative enough of how much they have contributed.

It has become rather fashionable to run down the career servant; and sometimes, I must say, the career servant, like the political appointee, needs a little jacking up. And there will be some of that in this next administration, I can assure you. With all that, I simply want to conclude with this final thought.

As the new President of the United States, working with the new Attorney General, I want you to know that we both understand your problems. We both recognize that there will be virtually no index of the success of this administration that will be more closely watched than what happens in the conduct of the enforcement of the law by the Department of Justice.

In this room is the brain power. In this room is the dedication. In this room is the ability that will determine whether we succeed or fail in that great venture. We will provide the leadership. I am con-

fident as I stand here that you will provide, also, that strong support that we need so that we can look back on these years and be proud of what we have accomplished, not only for our profession of the law, but be proud of what we have accomplished for this Nation.

NOTE: The President spoke at 4:03 p.m. in the Great Hall at the Department of Justice.

18 Statement on the Death of Allen Dulles. *January* 30, 1969

AT ELEVEN O'CLOCK last night, America lost a most valued public servant and the world lost a dedicated and courageous defender of freedom.

The death of Allen Dulles came at a time when his qualities of deliberation, integrity, and intelligence are more than ever those on which free men must rely. He served his country in the great tradition of his family and with unstinting devotion to duty.

During the years he served as Director of the Central Intelligence Agency, I had the opportunity to meet with him on many occasions. My impression of him

then is my impression now: He was a man who brought civility, intelligence, and great dedication to everything he did. In the nature of his task, his achievements were known to only a few. But—because of him—the world is a safer place today.

I know that all Americans join with Director Helms, Mrs. Nixon, and with me in extending our deepest sympathy to his family.

NOTE: Allen W. Dulles, who served as Director of the Central Intelligence Agency 1953–1961, died at the age of 75 at Georgetown University Hospital in Washington, D.C.

19 Remarks at the Pentagon to Top Officials of the Department of Defense. *January* 31, 1969

Mr. Secretary and gentlemen:

It is a very great honor to be here in the Defense Department and to have received today the colors of the various forces of our Defense Establishment, to have had another briefing from the Defense Department a few moments ago, and now to address the key men who are responsible for the defense of the United States and who

also play the major role in the defense of peace and freedom in the world.

As I stand here today, I would perhaps have to admit that this is one department where I feel particularly humble. Like so many Americans, I, of course, have served in the Armed Forces and I always feel just a little bit embarrassed when an admiral comes up to me and says "sir." I think it should be the other way around. I am sure the Secretary has this same problem.

All I can say is that I hope that in these years ahead, as the President of this Nation, and as the Commander in Chief of the Armed Forces, I can be worthy of the men and women who serve in the Defense Department.

In speaking to that point, I was asking the Secretary, as we moved through the halls and saw all of the civilian personnel and some of the military personnel standing in the corridors to welcome us, about the numbers that were involved. We know that this Department is the biggest in our Government. Approximately 60 percent of our personnel and budget comes from this Department. We know, too, that as far as the numbers of people who are involved, I understand there are approximately 4 million in the Defense Department, both civilian and military personnel.

In reflecting on that number, I want to particularly emphasize to the men here how important it is to see that all of those 4 million, to the extent that it is possible, realize that they play, collectively and individually, a vital role in the defense of this country and in developing the strength that is essential if we are going to be able to provide peace with freedom in the world.

Last night we had a very fascinating briefing by the astronauts, with some of the slides they had taken, as well as some of the motion pictures they had taken on their trip around the moon.

Colonel Borman made a very significant point as the briefing was concluded. He said that he was speaking not just for himself, and not just for the three who had made this trip, but for 400,000 men and women in the Nation who at one time or another had played a part in making this great, spectacular feat possible.

Here in this room are the top people. I suppose we would refer to most of you as the "top brass." You are the people who will have direct contact with the Secretary and with the President. You will be briefing him and me and the other top officials of this Government.

But I think it is vitally important for all of us to recognize that all over this Nation, and all over the world, are men and women who will never have that opportunity, men and women who do jobs, sometimes very routine jobs, that can become very, very boring and that they constantly need reassurance that what they do matters.

I was glad to see Colonel Borman bring it home that way. Four hundred thousand made it possible for this magnificent achievement to occur. I trust that all of you can convey that kind of spirit to those who work in the Defense Department, in all their capacities that they may be filling here and around the world.

In that respect, too, I would like to pay a tribute which I think should be paid to those who are in the career forces. I am referring now to the Army, the Navy, the Air Force, the Marine Corps, the Coast Guard, to the American military man.

It is rather fashionable these days to speak of the military man as a class apart. He knows about the hardware. He knows about military strategy. He knows how to conduct a war. Sometimes it goes so far that well-intentioned individuals say, "Well, we have a Department of War, this one, and we need a Department of Peace."

I have never thought of it that way. This is the Defense Department. Without what this Department, through its efficiency and through the dedication of its personnel, creates we would not be able to have the negotiations which can bring peace. This is an integral part of our peace forces in the world.

The other point that I wish to make is that individually I have been privileged to know the top military commanders of this Nation, going back over 20 years. I know that the military man in the United States today is a broad-gauged man. His knowledge is not limited simply, and his interests are not limited simply, to the military responsibilities that are his.

He knows the world in which we live. He can give valuable advice on the great diplomatic and political considerations that have to be considered when great decisions are made. He is a specialist, true, and I can assure you of one thing: I do not presume to be a specialist in this field and I am going to rely, when it comes to purely military matters, on what my military advisers tell me should be done.

But I do know this: I do know that due to the magnificent education that is provided for those who finally achieve the top ranks in our military services, they are men who are not just specialists; they are generalists in the best sense of the word. They can make a contribution, a contribution to the overall policy of this Nation.

I want you to know that I want to hear what they have to say. I will take that into consideration in developing our policies, because I know that your interests are the same as ours.

I know often the tendency is to take the Department of Defense and the Department of State and constantly to assume that they will be at odds; they will be working against each other; and that it is the job of the President of the United States, or his national security advisers, to try to negotiate the differences and then

present some kind of, shall we say, negotiated peace treaty between the two before we can get a policy.

I don't consider it that way at all. We will have our differences. There are differences within the State Department as to what our policy should be. There are differences within the Defense Department, although it is very hard to get General Wheeler to tell me what they are.

But on the other hand, while those differences do exist, I believe that we are all working together toward the same end. I want to hear those differences expressed. I will then have to make the decision, a decision that only the President of the United States can make in determining what our policy will be.

But only if I hear from the Defense Department and from within the Department the differences that may be there, and from the State Department and any other interested departments of Government what their views are on the great problems that confront this Nation at home and abroad—only if I hear that can I make the kind of decision that is going to be the best decision.

So I want to say, Mr. Secretary, that I am going to depend upon you and General Wheeler to bring to me and the National Security Council the viewpoints of the Defense Department, and even those minority viewpoints that may exist here which may not agree with that which you have eventually considered should prevail.

By seeing that those viewpoints are brought to the attention of the National Security Council, and through that Council to the President of the United States, you will assure that our policy will be a better policy than it would otherwise be.

Finally today, I would like to say one

thing about a subject that is often mentioned in Government and which is the reason for the visit that I am making to this Department and all the 12 major departments of Government in the first 3 weeks that I am in office: It is that question of morale.

I know we hear all sorts of stories about morale in one department is low, and morale in another department is going down, and the rest. I know perhaps less than particularly our military commanders know what really brings morale.

What brings morale is not what happens down in the ranks, but the leadership and the example that is set at the top.

I have one favorite story that I would like to impose upon you, a story that I think indicates my philosophy with regard to morale, and one that I hope you will take to heart and try to apply in these days and months and years ahead.

In reading General Pershing's memoirs of World War I, he told of the very difficult time that he had immediately after assuming command of the American Expeditionary Force of having to remove some of his closest friends who were commanders of divisions; and when he had to make those very difficult decisions, of course, this tore him apart, but he did it.

Because he was decisive and did move effectively, that Force became a very powerful force before the end of World War I. He told of one particular case which illustrates the point that I wanted to make.

An attack had been ordered in a certain area and he, on a certain day, was visiting one of the divisions. The commander of that division, an old friend of the General's, said to him, "General, we cannot make this attack. My men are tired; my men are disheartened; their morale is low.

We simply aren't going to be able to launch another attack, go over the top tomorrow."

General Pershing answered him in this way: He said, "General, your men are not tired. Your men are not disheartened. Their morale is not low. You are tired. Your morale is low. I am going to relieve you."

So he relieved the general and he put another man in charge, another general. He said within a matter of 2 to 3 weeks, as a result of the change in command, and the new spirit that came to that division, it was one of the best fighting units on the whole Western Front, after a record previous to that time which had been one of the worst.

I want all of you to know that I trust that in my position I can provide the kind of leadership that will keep up your morale, but by the same token, we count on you to let every one of the 4 million people in the armed services of this country know that what each one of them does really counts. It really matters. Failing to do even the smallest job may affect the efficiency and the effectiveness of our overall defense policy.

This sounds like a little sermon to a group of very sophisticated and top leaders in our military and business community, but I say it to you today because I do know this: You can have the most efficient organization possible, you can have all the money that you need, and you can still not have that spirit, that high, extra quotient that can only come from leadership which brings the highest morale and which gets it right down through the ranks, through all the civilians who dedicate their lives to public service, through all the military men who do that.

I know most of you personally. I have

appointed some of you who are on the civilian side, and I understand, too, that I make some of the appointments on the military side. I sign lots of sheets which indicate what you are going to do.

I can only say in conclusion that we are counting on you. I will respect your advice and I know that you will see to it that this whole great Defense Establishment has a new sense of purpose, a new sense of that great dedication which has made us always proud of the defense forces of this country.

Thank you.

NOTE: The President spoke at 11:37 a.m. in the auditorium at the Pentagon. Col. Frank Borman was commander of the Apollo 8 space mission.

The remarks of Secretary of Defense Laird are printed in the Weekly Compilation of Presidential Documents (vol. 5, p. 196).

20   Statement Outlining Actions and Recommendations for the District of Columbia. *January* 31, 1969

RESPONSIBILITY begins at home.

The District of Columbia is the Federal City, and the Federal Government cannot evade its share of responsibility for the conditions of life in the District.

For many who live here, those conditions have become intolerable. Violent crimes in the District have increased by almost three times in the last 8 years; only 2 days ago, the local newspapers carried a report that armed robberies had more than doubled in the past year alone.

This violence—raw, vicious violence, hurting most of all those who are poor and work hard—is the surface manifestation of far deeper troubles.

These troubles have been long building. In part, Washington today is reaping a whirlwind sown long since by rural poverty in the South, by failures in education, by racial prejudice, and by the sometimes explosive strains of rapid social readjustments.

Because its roots are deep and closely woven, crime in the District cannot be brought under control overnight. Neither can poverty be ended nor hatred eliminated nor despair overcome in a year. But we can begin.

In the 11 days since the new administration took office, I have asked the departments and agencies concerned to make an intensive study—as a matter of first priority—of actions that could be taken now toward curbing crime and improving the conditions of life in the city of Washington.

I wish I could report that we had produced a magic formula that would end crime and sweep away despair overnight. We have not. I have determined on a number of actions and recommendations which will provide a start.

These include:

—a swift start on restoring those areas devastated nearly 10 months ago,

—a package of proposals that can at least help toward restoring the safety of life and property,

—a commitment to give the people of the District of Columbia the voice they legitimately should have in the public policies that affect their lives.

Before detailing these measures I would

like to make two points, both of which may help set the measures themselves in perspective.

I am pleased to report, first, that Mayor Washington and I, together with key members of our respective administrations, have established the basis for what I confidently expect will be the most effective cooperation yet achieved in the relations between the Federal and city governments.

The basic framework within which we both intend to operate is one of local initiative and responsibility, and the fullest possible Federal support—not only in terms of the necessary money, but also by involving the vast array of technical assistance available from within the Federal departments and agencies headquartered here.

Second, the great majority of these actions and recommendations are in the fields of crime control and the administration of justice. I recognize full well that crime and violence are only part of the complex interweave of problems the District faces, and that in the long run crime itself also requires much more far-reaching and subtle approaches. But the rapidly mounting urgency of the crime crisis in the District marks immediate, direct anti-crime measures as the first-priority task.

There is another reason for this early and urgent emphasis. Crime in America today is both a primary local responsibility and a primary national concern. Here in the District, the Federal Government bears a special responsibility and has a unique opportunity. By searching for new ways of applying the resources of the Federal Government in the war against crime here, we may discover new ways of advancing the war against crime elsewhere.

These measures are by no means a comprehensive list. They represent things that are clearly needed and can be done now. Other crime control measures will follow, and also additional measures to meet the vast array of the District's other needs.

RESTORING THE DEVASTATED AREAS

Scarcely any of the shops and homes destroyed during the riots of last April have been rebuilt, and very few of those damaged have been made habitable or usable again. These rotting, boarded-up structures are a rebuke to us all and an oppressive, demoralizing environment for those who live in their shadow. They remind us again of the basic fact that the principal victims of violence are those in whose neighborhoods it occurs.

It is not enough merely to patch up what now exists; we must truly rebuild.

The people of the District—especially, of course, the people who live in these areas, and those who own the land—must decide the purposes for which these blocks will be used. The Federal Government can, however, pledge its full support for those Federal programs which can enable such redevelopment to proceed, and can further pledge the utmost Executive energy in responding to formal applications from the District.

We have already begun. Specifically, Secretary Romney informed me today that the Department of Housing and Urban Development has approved a $29.7 million neighborhood development plan for the Shaw area, including the major portion of the 7th Street neighborhood damaged during last April's riots. This plan, the result of several years of preparation, is an accomplishment of which this city can be proud.

It took Secretary Romney's Department less than 24 hours to approve this plan for the Shaw area, once it was approved by the City Council last Tuesday and submitted for Federal approval Wednesday evening. This unprecedented process illustrates the commitment of this administration to the meeting of the urgent needs of the Capital City.

Mayor Washington has indicated that he intends to seek similar assistance under the Housing and Urban Development Act of 1968 for rehabilitation of the two major areas of riot damage not covered in the Shaw plan—the areas along 14th Street and H Street. I can assure him that this administration will respond with the same sense of urgency to his requests for help in these areas.

He has promised me a tight but serious timetable under which the first construction in these areas would begin next fall.

While the city prepares for this construction, and decides what to do with the 14th and H Street areas, the Department of Housing and Urban Development will make available $1 million in special interim assistance for improvements in some of the blighted areas. This morning, I watched the first cranes at work clearing rubble to make way for a temporary playground. The District has plans for swings, slides, and swimming pools where now there is charred rubble. Street lighting will be improved, roads and sidewalks repaired.

Under section 514 of the 1968 Housing and Urban Development Act, Mayor Washington has undertaken to provide one-third matching funds for this $1 million, and the District Government will take the initiative in deciding how this money will be spent. The limited assistance to be provided by the Federal Government under this interim program cannot by itself remake these areas. But it is a first step toward making them more livable, an earnest demonstration of our concern, and a first sign of hope.

In this connection, I can announce that the 1969 Inaugural Committee, through its chairman, Mr. J. Willard Marriott, has agreed to devote the net proceeds of the inaugural to the cost of providing playground equipment and other improvements for these parks and playground areas.

CRIME AND ADMINISTRATION OF JUSTICE

A meaningful assault on crime requires action on a broad array of fronts. But in the midst of a crime crisis, immediate steps are needed to increase the effectiveness of the police and to make justice swifter and more certain.

Toward these ends and as a beginning, I have taken or will propose action in 12 major areas.

1. THE COURTS OF THE DISTRICT OF COLUMBIA

I am asking Congress to provide 10 more judges for the courts of the District of Columbia. I will ask later for additional judges as they become necessary upon the reorganization of the District of Columbia court system.

As an interim measure, I would hope that the existing visiting judges program would be expanded in the District. The Chief Judge of the District of Columbia Circuit here has diligently sought the services of visiting judges. I will encourage and aid him in his effort to obtain the services of more judges.

To improve the administration of justice in the District, I have directed the Attorney General to consult with the bench, the bar, and the various interested groups, to assist in the drafting of appropriate legislation providing for a reorganization and restructuring of our present court system toward the eventual goal of creating one local court of general, civil, criminal, and juvenile jurisdiction for the District of Columbia. It is consistent with my support for home rule to urge the creation of a local court system similar to that of the States and other large municipalities.

To perform with full effectiveness, a modern court needs modern computer and management techniques. I have asked the Attorney General to offer his Department's assistance to the study groups in the District that are presently seeking to apply such techniques in the court system.

I have asked the Attorney General to submit specific recommendations for such additional courthouse personnel, including United States Marshals, court clerks, probation officers, law clerks, and bailiffs, as are necessary to support not only the present judges but the additional judges that will be requested.

2. UNITED STATES ATTORNEY'S OFFICE

The chronic understaffing of the prosecutor's office has long hampered the efficient administration of justice in the District. It is widely recognized that a ratio of at least two prosecutors for each judge is needed. To achieve that goal, 20 new assistant U.S. attorneys are required immediately. With the creation of 10 additional judgeships and the contemplated court reorganization, another

20 prosecutors will be required. Consequently I am recommending the authorization of 40 more assistant U.S. attorneys.

A comprehensive reorganization of the Office of the U.S. Attorney is imperative. This should include a restructuring of the Office to provide for two-man prosecutor teams in important cases; the development of specialized functions for technical cases, such as frauds and other economic crimes; and the creation of a special "violent crimes unit" to handle such crimes as armed bank robberies on a priority basis, as is presently being tried experimentally.

In addition, greater emphasis is needed on developing policy guidelines and training programs. On January 14, $120,-000 was awarded by the National Institute of Law Enforcement and Criminal Justice for a special study committee. Included in its study is an examination of the prosecutor's office, with a view toward recommending improvements in its operation. I strongly support this study and have instructed the Attorney General to make available the resources of the Department of Justice to assist the committee and to facilitate reorganization found desirable.

In addition, I will seek authorization for the hiring of law clerks and sufficient other personnel for the proper staffing of the U.S. Attorney's Office and for the hiring and use of trained investigators, who are necessary to the effective functioning of the prosecutor's office.

3. COURTHOUSE FACILITIES

The local courts already are overflowing the existing Court of General Sessions buildings. Judges are sitting in three different buildings, and some in temporary courtrooms. With the creation of additional judges and the eventual transfer of greatly expanded jurisdiction to the local courts, a new courthouse complex becomes a pressing necessity. One hundred thousand dollars has already been utilized for planning for a new courthouse and $3.5 million has been appropriated for site selection. But we must have these facilities now. Consequently, I am vigorously endorsing the requests presently pending before the Congress for $1,240,-000 to be used to complete acquisition and for additional planning. The administration will fully support the Mayor in such additional requests as are needed to speed the building program. Meanwhile, I have instructed the General Services Administration to assist in providing temporary facilities.

4. BAIL REFORM AND THE BAIL AGENCY

Problems arising out of the operation of the Bail Reform Act of 1966 are now being considered by the Congress. But substantial changes in this area are needed quickly. Increasing numbers of crimes are being committed by persons already indicted for earlier crimes, but free on pretrial release. Many are now being arrested two, three, even seven times for new offenses while awaiting trials. This requires that a new provision be made in the law, whereby dangerous hard-core recidivists could be held in temporary pretrial detention when they have been charged with crimes and when their continued pretrial release presents a clear danger to the community.

Additionally, crimes committed by persons on pretrial release should be made subject to increased penalties.

Insufficient staffing of the Bail Agency is one of the contributors to crime by those on pretrial release. I support immediate lifting of the ceiling that now constricts the Agency's funding. I will seek appropriations for an initial expansion of the Agency from 13 to 35 permanent positions. If the pretrial release system is to protect the rights of the community, the Agency must have the capacity for adequate investigation and supervision.

5. THE DISTRICT OF COLUMBIA DEPARTMENT OF CORRECTIONS

As the local government is painfully aware, the existing facilities and programs of the Department of Corrections are woefully inadequate. On January 16, 1969, the Director of the Bureau of Prisons submitted a comprehensive report to Mayor Washington identifying the deficiencies and making a number of recommendations. I join with the Mayor in urging immediate implementation of those recommendations, and I will offer whatever Federal assistance is possible in doing so.

All who have studied the problem agree that far-reaching changes are needed in the penal facilities and programs serving the District. I will press vigorously for accomplishment of the needed reforms.

6. OFFICE OF PUBLIC DEFENDER

The recent bail reform hearings before the Senate Judiciary Subcommittee on Constitutional Rights have emphasized the important contributions skilled defense counsel can make toward expediting criminal trials.

Too often, inexperienced lawyers who are appointed to represent indigent defendants complicate and delay the trial process by their unfamiliarity with the law and criminal practice. Experience has shown that professional public defenders, on the other hand, not only better safeguard the rights of defendants, but also speed the process of justice. The Legal Aid Agency in the District is a pilot project which has given every indication of great success if properly supported. I believe the time has come to convert this project into a full-fledged public defender program. To make this project possible, I will support the Legal Aid Agency's 1970 budget request for $700,000 to allow an increase in its staff from 22 to 34 attorneys and to assume responsibility for a successful project in offender rehabilitation. This would allow it to become a full-fledged public defender's office with the capacity to represent almost half of the indigent adult and juvenile defendants in the District.

7. THE METROPOLITAN POLICE DEPARTMENT

There is no deterrent to crime quite so effective as the public presence of policemen. Several immediate steps are needed to bolster and improve the local police force in the District of Columbia.

The first step is more effective recruitment. Despite diligent recruitment efforts, the police force has hundreds of unfilled vacancies. I have pledged to the Mayor the assistance and full support of this administration to improve the recruitment process. I will sponsor the establishment of a procedure by which the District can draw upon the experience of other cities. Imaginative and innovative approaches may be necessary.

But even bringing the Department up to its presently authorized strength will not secure adequate public protection in these troubled times. Consequently, I am recommending to the Mayor that he request authorization of an additional 1,000 police officers for the District, and I will support such a request.

I endorse the Mayor's efforts and those of the Police Department to reorganize the structure of the Department, so as to consolidate functions, reduce duplication, and free additional police officers for patrol and enforcement duties. I offer the assistance of the Federal Government in this effort.

I urge our local police officials to give a high priority to planning and development, making use of the increased Federal funds now available for the introduction of new law enforcement techniques.

The Police Department also needs the increased assistance of competent legal advisers in this era of ever more complicated criminal law and procedures. I laud the Mayor for his recent appointment to the Police Department of a legal adviser. However, with the increased burdens on the Department it seems advisable to increase the staff and capability of such an office. Not only do the police need to be properly advised as to the performance of their duties, but it is also necessary for the Police Department to be assured of the Government's support of an interest in the officer's performance of his individual duties.

8. DIRECTOR OF PUBLIC SAFETY

The potential of this office is great. It is presently vacant. The Mayor informs me that he is diligently searching for the right man to fill the job. I have offered the Mayor this administration's resources to assist him in selecting the best possible Director.

9. CITIZEN PARTICIPATION

Increased citizen involvement is essential to any program of crime control and prevention; it is also in keeping with the American tradition. I strongly support the Mayor in his plan to appoint a Criminal Justice Coordinating Committee patterned after similar successful programs in other large cities. It is important that the Council be properly staffed. This could be done with help from the recently created Criminal Justice Planning Office and funded under the Law Enforcement Assistance Act, which provides financial support of up to 90 percent for such planning activity involving citizen participation. Policy making and planning must have citizen participation and coordination if they are to produce programs that are widely acceptable to the community. I pledge the Mayor the support and assistance of the Federal Government in this area.

10. NARCOTICS

Although the narcotics traffic in the District of Columbia is apparently not dominated by organized crime, it has become an acute and growing problem. It is a direct cause of much of the District's crime, by driving the narcotic user to commit crime to support his "habit." Many armed robberies, assaults, and bank holdups are directly related to narcotics use.

Consequently, I have instructed the U.S. Bureau of Narcotics and Dangerous Drugs to increase significantly its role in the District of Columbia in enforcing the narcotic and dangerous drug laws. The

Bureau has assured me that they will also increase their cooperation with the Metropolitan Police Department in enforcement, training, and in making available additional laboratory facilities and expert and technical assistance.

I have also directed the Bureau and the Department of Justice to seek more effective application of the civil commitment provisions of the Narcotics Rehabilitation Act of 1966 which has not yet been widely used.

11. JUVENILE CRIME

In recent years the median age of those charged with crime has been ominously dropping. The National Commission on Violence warned this month: "The key to much of the violence in our society seems to lie with the young. Our youth account for an ever-increasing percentage of crime, greater than their increasing percentage of the population . . . . It may be here, with tomorrow's generation, that much of the emphasis of our studies and the national response should lie."

I strongly support the city government's efforts to draft a new Juvenile Code, and I am making available technical assistance by Federal authorities. The Department of Justice is already cooperating with the Corporation Counsel and other local officials on the project.

Under the proposed court reorganization, the now isolated and undernourished Juvenile Court would be brought into the new District of Columbia court of general jurisdiction. Thus juveniles would have the advantage of the comprehensive facilities of the new court, including family services and probation assistance.

The pilot Group Home Rehabilitation

Project, in which juveniles enjoy retention of community ties, close adult supervision, and peer-group controls, gives every appearance of success. Expansion of the project as a substitute for institutionalization and as a possible supplement to probation is desirable. I support the Mayor in his request for increased funding and authorization for such facilities.

The lack of sufficient psychiatric services for the youthful disturbed is a serious obstacle to crime prevention. Young minds gone astray must be helped while still malleable. I will assist the Mayor in his forthcoming request for a well-staffed psychiatric care residential facility for adolescent delinquents.

I also urge that the local government, together with local school officials, prepare a plan to provide for the education of those schoolchildren whose disciplinary and truant absence from schools for long periods now causes them to reach adulthood educationally stunted. A substitute educational program must be devised for them, lest they become a burden to themselves and the community.

12. NEW ATTENTION TO THE DISTRICT

The Attorney General has created a new post within the Justice Department, that of Associate Deputy Attorney General for the Administration of Criminal Justice, with one of the new official's special and continuing responsibilities, that of helping improve the administration of justice in the District of Columbia. He has named to the post Mr. Donald Santarelli, a widely experienced expert on the special problems of crime control in the District. One of Mr. Santarelli's functions will be to evaluate and help implement new ideas for more effective anticrime measures in the District.

HOME RULE AND DISTRICT REPRESENTATION

For more than 20 years I have supported home rule for the District of Columbia. I continue to support home rule, but I consider the timing of that effort the key, as is proven by its past history of failure. For the present, I will seek within the present system to strengthen the role of the local government in the solution of local problems.

Beyond this, I will press for congressional representation for the District. In accordance both with my own conviction and with the platform pledge of my party, I will support a constitutional amendment to give the 850,000 people of the District at last a voting representative in Congress.

Adding an amendment to our Constitution, however, is a long and difficult process. As an interim measure, I will press this year for legislation that would give the District a nonvoting delegate. The District is a Federal city, but it should not be a Federal colony. Nearly 200 years ago, the people of America confronted the question of taxation without representation. It was not acceptable then; it hardly is justifiable today.

I cannot overemphasize the fact that these reforms are not a panacea. They are a beginning. Some will show modest results quickly; others may show greater results over a longer period of time. More must be done. But as the city moves to modernize its own government, as improved Federal cooperation provides the support so desperately needed, as the citizens of Washington develop a greater awareness of ways in which citizen action can make their city safer and more livable, as progress is made in tackling the stubborn social problems that have sapped the spirit of so many of the District's people, I am confident that together we can make measurable progress toward reviving the spirit and restoring the safety of the Nation's Capital, and making it once again what it ought to be: a proud, glorious city, cherished by every American as part of his heritage and cherished by those who live here as a place of beauty, neighborliness, and decency.

NOTE: On Friday morning, January 31, 1969, the President joined Mayor Walter E. Washington and Secretary of Housing and Urban Development George Romney in a ceremony at 7th and T Streets, NW., in Washington. The ceremony marked the beginning of work to clear the site of rubble remaining from the civil disorders of April 1968 in order to build a playground area.

21 Remarks Following a Visit With General Eisenhower. *February 2, 1969*

THE PRESIDENT. Gentlemen, this is the longest conversation I have had with General Eisenhower since his heart attack.

I was very impressed by how well he looked. He was sitting up, as the photographs indicate. This was the first time he has been photographed since that time, at least when I have been present.

What we primarily discussed were the problems of NATO, the European alliance, and the problems of the Middle East. As usual—and I would say even more than usual—I was impressed by General Eisenhower's great understanding of this area of the world, of the personalities involved, and also of the great forces that are involved there.

As we now enter a period when we are reexamining our policies in Europe and also reexamining our policies in the Mideast, I am trying to talk to as many people who are experienced in these areas as I can.

General Eisenhower gave us some excellent advice—Dr. Kissinger was with me—

some excellent advice and also some comments on the policy decisions that we are to make in the very near future in both areas.

Q. How did he refer to you, Mr. President?

THE PRESIDENT. He said, "Mr. President," and I was a little embarrassed, frankly.

Finally, I was trying to think how the semantics went. He said, "Well, Mr. President, I am glad to see you." I was a little embarrassed. Then I started to refer to him as "General," but when the conversation became quite animated, as it did during a discussion of the European situation and its relationship to the Mideast, I slipped almost automatically into "Mr. President" again, and he smiled.

Reporter: Thank you, Mr. President.

THE PRESIDENT. Thank you.

NOTE: The President spoke with reporters at 6 p.m. at Walter Reed Army Medical Center following a 50-minute visit with General Eisenhower in his hospital suite.

22   Remarks to Top Officials at the Department of Housing and Urban Development. *February 3,* 1969

I first want to tell you how very delighted I am to be visiting this new building and this relatively new Department. I understand you have moved in quite recently.

As I saw the building, I could certainly understand why the working conditions could be perhaps much improved over what it was. My reports are that Secretary Romney jogs to work. And as I understand, previously he would have to jog to 18 different buildings. So at least he is setting an example for me, however, that is very hard to find. I do not know whether these reports are true, but they tell me that as he jogs along that some of the people who are working in the Department wave to him as they go in their limousines.

Of course, knowing the Secretary's background and having remembered some of those striking television commercials he used to do when he was the head of the American Motors—I was going to say General Motors—I know that it is just very hard for him to ride in one of those gas guzzlers.

As I had the opportunity to come through the halls and come up in the elevator, I saw many hundreds of employees. And as I stand before you, I realize that the 300 in this room are those who will determine the morale of those who work in this great Department, this tremendously important Department, that you will provide the leadership that will make the difference between success and failure, not only for your Department but for so many of the objectives of the American people in the new administration.

One of the reasons I am paying these visits—I guess they are somewhat unprecedented visits right at the beginning of an administration—to each of the major departments of Government is that I want you to know, first of my interest in work, and, second, of my interest in your leadership, and, third, I particularly want those who are career civil servants, those that were not appointed by the new administration, to know that I have an interest in what you are doing, that interest which is shared by all of the members of this Cabinet.

We bring in very few new people, as you know, those that can be appointed at the assistant secretary and at the certain exempt areas, exempt from civil service. But the success of a government, the success of any department, depends upon the competence, depends upon the dedication of the hundreds at the top and the thousands down in the ranks who are the career people.

We need their help—and to the extent that they are in this room, we need your help. And I thought the best way to make it clear that we did first support those who have given their careers to Government service was to come to the agencies, as I am presently doing.

Now in referring specifically to this agency, it has, of course, a very interesting name—Housing and Urban Development. And as I look at this building and recognize it is the only one of its kind in the United States, it shows innovation that the agency already has been responsible for. I understand, incidentally, there are two like this in France.

What, of course, interests me, and I understand also has made a great impression on the Director of the Budget, is that it cost $3 million less than the Congress appropriated. I don't know whether the Secretary can maintain that kind of a record in the future. But if he does, he will be the first one in history that has ever done that.

But more important than that, more important than the dollars, more important than what we think of as the housing, housing and urban development—in a sense that is a very impersonal phrase—is the human factor that is involved.

I was pointing out to the Secretary, as we were chatting upstairs before coming down here, that in my travels around the world, and particularly in some of the countries that do not have the freedom and the diversity that goes with freedom, that one thing that has been appalling to me is the great dullness of huge housing projects without character.

We need, of course, to rebuild America's cities. We are going to have to put billions of dollars into this rebuilding program in the years ahead, looking down to the end of the century when the cities of America will be rebuilt. The question is not whether we do it and not how many units we are going to build. That will be done. But the question is, can we do it and still maintain some character? Can we still maintain for the individuals that will live in this housing, a sense of identity, a sense of dignity which does not come when they are just numbers in a huge, big block that you are unable to find unless somebody guides you to it, particularly if it is very late in the evening?

Under the circumstances, then, I think you have an exciting challenge in that respect. And I am happy to inform the members of this group that I have had an opportunity to sit now with Secretary Romney in several meetings of the Cabinet Council on Urban Affairs. I have noticed what he brings to that Council. I was not surprised that he brings this particular viewpoint to it.

But he constantly emphasizes in the discussions of that Council that we are not just concerned about things, we are not just concerned about buildings, but we are concerned about people. It is this individual, human characteristic which is so important.

And I just want to emphasize to the group in this room, this group so essential to the future of America, so essential because you will provide the leadership that will determine the kind of housing in the broadest sense that we are going to have, that if at the same time you can have that sense of mission with regard to not only retaining character in American life insofar as the shelter that we have, but even, as I might suggest, making it more meaningful, because we can do better than we have done in the past.

And I think this is a charge, a challenge, which your Secretary has been giving to you and which I wish, too, to underline.

Another thought that I wish to leave with you is this: The other night—I say the other night, it seems like a long time ago—but one day last week we had a very great responsibility within the administration in developing a program for the District of Columbia.

Part of that responsibility, a major part of it, had to be met by this agency. Governor Romney reported to me that a very large group of people in this agency worked clear around the clock in order to meet the deadline that I had set for having a positive report about what we were going to do about the District of Columbia, rather than having that report limited simply to the tremendously important objective of controlling the growth of crime in this area. I just want to express my appreciation to the individuals in this room that worked on that project.

And I would appreciate it, too, if you would express my thanks, personal thanks, to all of those down the line—the secretaries, the others, people who never have a chance to meet a President, who perhaps even see him just on television, or perhaps see him coming through the hall— to let them know that we recognize, those of us at the top, you at the top, that we all recognize that up and down the line, everyone, every individual in this Department counts, every individual in this Government counts.

There are 4 million people at the present time who are in one way or another in the Government of the United States of America. And I think that sometimes, with our emphasis on the people at the top, we forget that down the line are people who, in many instances, are not making as much money as they might if they were in private enterprise, but who are here because of a sense of dedication and a sense of purpose. They want to be here. This is the contribution that they want to make.

And what they live for is not only what they create, but they also live for a recognition, from those who may be the senior officials, of the fact that they are appreciated, that they are making a contribution that is meaningful. I want you to know that I am aware of what they are doing. And I would appreciate it if you would convey that same sense of appreciation to those down the ranks.

Then, finally, another point that I would like to emphasize in talking to this group is that we are going to be doing some new things in the new administration. This is no reflection on the old. What we are doing at the present time is to examine all of the programs, a lot of exciting new programs, that have come along in the last few years. We are attempting to improve on some of them. Some of them we will discard.

But our main purpose is to move forward in an effective way to solve these immense problems that we have in our cities. And I know of no department in this Government which will make a greater contribution to those solutions than this Department.

I urge you to give us the benefit of your thinking. We won't always agree. I say "we" speaking only in terms at the Cabinet level. But only by having the excitement that comes from people who disagree as to the solutions to problems, only by having that competition of good ideas, do we get the superior ideas that America needs in this and in so many other fields.

So with that, Mr. Secretary—I have already kept this group longer than I should have, for I know of the many tasks that they have to undertake for the balance of this day and the weeks and months ahead—I again tell you how grateful I am for what you have done. I look forward to working with you, to supporting you and your colleagues in the work that you are undertaking.

I appreciate the fact that you in Government service have in many instances made a sacrifice, not only to be in it but to stay in it. And I just want you to know that the Nation is grateful, too.

And speaking of housing and urban

51

development, Mr. Secretary, I was only going to suggest, this is a brand new building, that certainly you ought to have room for a little larger auditorium up here for all of these people to begin with.

Thank you very much.

NOTE: The President spoke at 2:30 p.m. to some 200 top officials of the Department of Housing and Urban Development in the departmental conference room.

23 Remarks to Employees at the Department of Agriculture. *February 3, 1969*

Mr. Secretary, and ladies and gentlemen:

It is a very great privilege for me to return to this Department and to this auditorium. I well remember that visit in 1954. Some of you were here then, but most of you were not here then. I think some of you may have been in school then. Who knows?

But in any event, I did want to come to this Department, as well as some of the other departments of Government, for several reasons that I will enunciate, I trust, rather briefly, but with great feeling as far as this group is concerned.

In the first place, I wanted to say a word about your new Secretary. Now, I know in this group that is before me for the most part you are people who have been in this Department for most of your lives, your adult lives. I know that very few of you, as this is the case in Government, have been appointed by the new President and the new Secretary. So, consequently, a new Secretary, I suppose, is always being tested by the Department. They wonder: "Well, what kind of a man is he going to be? Is he going to be an effective advocate of the points of view of that Department in the Cabinet? Is he going to be a good leader of the people in this great Department?"

When I selected the Secretary, it was one of the more difficult of the Cabinet selections. They are all difficult, because

you are choosing among many very competent men and women. But I do want to say that since his selection and in watching him not only in his appointments that he has made and recommended to me, watching him also in the very effective and eloquent way that he has represented the Department of Agriculture and its points of view in the Cabinet, as well as in the meetings of the Council of Urban Affairs and the other groups on which he sits, I believe that in Secretary Hardin we have a man that you will be proud to work for. I think he is going to be one of the great Secretaries of Agriculture.

He has already indicated some of the substance that I wanted to emphasize in my remarks.

In the old days—I say the old days, looking back 25 years ago when I first came to Washington or knew it well, or 30 years ago—this Department was considered to be primarily the Department interested in providing better facilities and better incentives for production by America's farmers. That is still, of course, a major responsibility, a major mission for this Department.

I know that the Secretary in his opening statement made it quite clear that one of the first priority assignments of his administration of this Department would be to see to it that America's farmers received their fair share of the increasing growth and wealth and productivity of this Nation. That, however, while it is the primary function of this Department, and traditionally when it first began perhaps its only major function, there are others which the Secretary very properly has emphasized.

The fact that now the role of this Department in waging effectively the battle against poverty and particularly the battle against hunger as it relates to poverty, not only in the United States and the world, this is something which goes beyond simply producing more agricultural products, as all of you know better than I. It goes to other problems.

I noted the tremendous interest—and I think it is encouraging that such an interest finally is developing among the people at large—the interest in the problem of hunger in the United States. You will recall when the public conscience finally became aroused, really aroused, about the problem of hunger in the United States. It was a CBS television program a few months ago in which millions of Americans for the first time, living in what is really the best fed, the best housed, the best clothed Nation in the world, millions of Americans saw on television that in this rich land there is hunger—hunger not simply due to lack of food, but also hunger due to failure to have the right kind of food, the problem of nutrition to which the Secretary has referred.

And so as we look at this problem, it seems to me that there is no department in Government that has a more exciting opportunity, for a reason that you are more aware of than I am.

When we consider America's problems today, one at the top of the list is our agricultural surpluses. We are constantly worrying about that and the budget, and we are worrying about it in terms of our agricultural programs.

But I know that all of you are aware, as I am, that those surpluses are a great bounty for the United States of America. It means that we can effectively deal with the problems of hunger in this country and help with the problems of hunger in the world because we are able to produce so much.

And so that presents the challenge to the men and women in this room, the leaders of this Department, those upon whom the Secretary is going to rely to obtain the advice so that we can effectively use this tremendous productive capacity which this Department has helped to build through the years; so that we can effectively use it in a scientific way to attack the problems of hunger, of malnutrition and all of its facets in this Nation, and thereby also perhaps to set an example to other nations in the world.

It is an exciting problem. It is one in which I have asked the Secretary to assume a special responsibility in the meetings in the Cabinet and in the other various groups in which he sits and in which I am also present. We are going to work on this problem. Other administrations have, too. But we have had it brought to our attention, it seems to me, more directly than has been the case in other administrations for the reasons that I have already mentioned.

I want you to know that this is one of the missions that I trust this Department will undertake with all the success that it has been able to apply to its primary mission of increasing production of agricultural products in the United States.

Then, the third point that I wish to urge upon the group here again is one that I know will be like carrying coals to Newcastle or as the Japanese say, bringing sake to Nada.

What I wish to emphasize is that as we consider the problems, as we did this morning in our Urban Affairs Council, the new Cabinet committee, it was significant to note—and I am sure you noticed this as you checked the press reports—that the Secretary of Agriculture is a member of the Urban Affairs Council. That was at my insistence, at my insistence for two reasons, because we know that the problems of rural America today will be the problems of urban America tomorrow. We know that as life in rural America is less attractive, there is a tendency for people from the farms and from agricultural America to move into the cities.

Of course, we also know that when we look at the very thing that I mentioned a moment ago as being an asset, the productivity, the new methods whereby less farmers, less people on the farm can produce more, this means that all of these new developments result in unemployment for farm workers and eventually they gravitate from the farms to the cities.

So the Secretary of Agriculture is on that particular Council, the Urban Affairs Council, for that reason—but for another reason as well. And the reason is that as we look to America down the road to the end of this century, to the kind of a nation we are going to be, present projections are that our population will increase from 200 million to 300 million and that 80 percent, possibly even 90 percent of that increase will be in the cities of America.

It will happen that way unless there is a change with regard to life in rural America. I am glad that we have in the Secretary of Agriculture a man who understands this problem, understands it and

has done some very exciting thinking about it. He is also a man that understands the problems of hunger and nutrition, a man who understands the role that the United States has in the world.

As you know, he has had some publications in this field most recently. But referring particularly to the problems of rural America as they relate to urban America, I think that you would be interested to know that on the evening that I made the sale to the Secretary of Agriculture and was able to convince him that he should lose—he didn't lose it; he wasn't fired; most college presidents are these days—but in any event, that he should leave—he was a very successful chancellor of the University of Nebraska—that he should leave that post and come into Government.

He will remember, I am sure and I am telling you, that over half of the discussion was on this great, exciting mission which this Department and other departments in the Government in support of this Department must work on: That is to look at rural America—the 50 million people who live in what is called "rural America"—to deal with its problems in just an effective way and with the same sense of urgency that we deal with the problems of urban America.

I mention these things which are routine to you. I noted that the Secretary in his opening statement had covered them when he addressed the members of his Department after he was confirmed.

I mention them to you only to indicate to you that at the Presidential level, at the White House level, that I understand the importance of the work of this Department. I understand that your primary responsibility is to the farmers of America and to increasing farm production, more effective methods for production.

I understand, too, your responsibility to those who live on the farms in terms of income and the rest. But I also want you to know that I put a special emphasis, as does your new Secretary, on the other problems that are mentioned: the problems of hunger in this Nation as it affects not only the amount of food, but as it affects also nutrition and diet generally and, finally, that we put a special emphasis on this overall problem of the kind of nation we are going to build looking down the road to the end of this century.

There is no department in this Government that will play a bigger role in seeing what kind of a nation this is going to be than the members of this Department.

You are referred to, as you know, as an "old line department." But I would remind you that when this Department was set up by Abraham Lincoln or during his administration, he said that it was "the department of the people," because it was more concerned with people than any other department of Government.

That was undoubtedly true in the rural America of Lincoln's time. What I am saying to you today is this is still the department of the people because you are concerned with the problems of people. And while it is an old line department, you have a new, fresh challenge.

I am glad that you have here the new thinking, the new ideas, that this country needs in these fields.

And Mr. Secretary, if I could conclude with one final thought that I have tried to emphasize in my visits to the various departments. I do not think it is necessary to emphasize here but if you will permit me, I would like to spend just one moment on this point.

In this room are the leaders. In this room are those who are responsible for the conduct of the thousands of employees of the Department of Agriculture in Washington and across the Nation.

The kind of leadership that you provide in this room will determine the morale of the people in this great Department and it will also determine their effectiveness.

And I simply want you to know that, as I mentioned at the outset, I am completely aware of the fact that only a very few people, those in these front rows, were appointed by the new administration.

I recognize that no matter how effective those people that were appointed by this administration are, that they are going to fail unless they have the backing, unless they have the dedication of the thousands of career people who have been in the Department of Agriculture and who will make the difference between success and failure for whatever administration comes in.

I respect the career service in this Government. I respect the fact, as I came through the hall, that one man told me that he had been in the Department for 35 years. I appreciate the fact that that man had he gone perhaps into business or into some other kind of activity, he might have done better economically. But he was in government because he felt that this gave his life a sense of purpose that he could not get in some other kind of activity.

And I want you to know that in this new administration, we not only respect those who are the career servants. We realize that you have made and are making a tremendous contribution to this country. We realize that our successes in administration will depend upon what you do.

We want you to know that we are going to back you up because we are convinced that as we back you up, you are going to give us the support that we need to give America the kind of leadership it wants.

Thank you.

NOTE: The President spoke at 3:18 p.m. to approximately 450 employees of the Department of Agriculture in the Department's fifth wing auditorium.

24 Statement Announcing the Nomination of Dr. James E. Allen, Jr., as Assistant Secretary for Education and Commissioner of Education. *February 3, 1969*

GOVERNMENT, at whatever level, has no more important responsibility than education. At this time when our cities, towns, the States, and the Nation, are making and must make intensive efforts to improve the quality of education for all our people and give special attention to all those for whom adequate opportunity has been denied, I am pleased to announce the nomination of Dr. James E. Allen, Jr., as Assistant Secretary for Education and U.S. Commissioner of Education.

For the past 13 years, Dr. Allen has served with distinction in New York State as Commissioner of Education and President of the University of the State of New York, one of the most highly regarded and comprehensive educational posts in the Nation. In this position, he has had general responsibility for all levels of edu-

cation in that State from preschool to graduate school, public and private, involving more than 5 million students. As the highest educational official in the Government, Dr. Allen will play a leading role in shaping the policies and plans of this administration for the support and improvement of education in the Nation.

The Federal responsibility for education and training has been growing and must continue to grow. Dr. Allen will bring to his task experience and commitment commensurate with the importance which I, as President, attach to the role of education at the Federal level. Dr. Allen will assume his position as soon as he can fulfill his obligations in New York State, and will join the Department [of Health, Education, and Welfare] no later than May 1.

25 Remarks at the Swearing In of Members of the Executive Office of the President and the White House Staff. *February 4, 1969*

Ladies and gentlemen:

We are today swearing in five very important members of the Executive Office of the President and of the White House Staff.

We shall begin with that very important group, the Council of Economic Advisers.

If Dr. Paul McCracken, Dr. Houthakker, and Dr. Stein will step up here.

Before swearing these three gentlemen

in, of course, as all of you know, they have been working prior to this swearing in and I have been reminded over and over again that as economists they are known as part of the "Dismal Science."

I can say it may be a dismal science, but from the reports I have been receiving, it is not a dull science by any manner of means.

I hope during this administration it might be a happy science, that their predictions may turn out that way.

[Judge Warren Earl Burger of the U.S. Court of Appeals, District of Columbia, administered the oath of office.]

Now, Dr. Arthur Burns, if you will step up.

Dr. Burns is being sworn in as Counsellor to the President and we will have his wife, Mrs. Burns, to stand here with him.

[Judge Burger administered the oath of office.]

Now, the fifth man to be sworn in today is the only one who has a different title. As you will note, the first four have very properly been described as doctors, meaning of course they are scholars, and our fifth is a general.

So we have four doctors and a general. I should point out that General Lincoln, however, could have been introduced as a doctor,[1] I believe, and he has written a book. So he is in the proper company at the present time.

Mrs. Lincoln, would you step in here between us?

[Judge Burger administered the oath of office.]

That concludes our ceremony this morning. We appreciate you all being here. We are particularly glad to see the members of the families that are here.

Thank you very much.

NOTE: The President spoke at 12:17 p.m. in the Fish Room at the White House.

---

[1] General Lincoln received an honorary degree of doctor of laws from the University of Pittsburgh in 1968.

26   Remarks to Top Officials at the Department of Labor. *February 4, 1969*

Mr. Secretary, ladies and gentlemen:

I am very privileged and honored to meet with you today—the top officials of the Labor Department.

As I was saying to the Secretary when I came into the building, I think that during the years when I was Vice President, except for, of course, the White House, this Department of Government was one that I visited more often than any other.

I was involved at times in various matters involving labor disputes in which I worked with Secretary Jim Mitchell.

As some of you will remember, and particularly, George, you will remember—George Weaver[1] here—that I was Chairman of the President's Committee on Government Contracts, a duty that the Vice President had. The meetings were held right here. So I was quite familiar with this building and was privileged to know many of the fine career people who work in the Labor Department.

I have, incidentally, something in common with the Department. I did a little

---

[1] Assistant Secretary of Labor for International Affairs 1961–1969.

57

background beforehand as to the Labor Department—when it began and all of that.

I found that the Labor Department was founded in the year 1913. That was the year I was born. And I think I can probably say we both have our best years ahead of us.

I want to begin, as I have in the other departments, by saying a word about your Secretary. He is one of the men that I selected for the Cabinet, having in mind the responsibilities that he would have to meet and the background that I felt qualified him for those responsibilities.

I think, too, that in selecting him that we have brought to this Department a man who will be able to carry out the new responsibilities that are going to be given to this Department—and I will mention them briefly later—but also who will continue in the high tradition of the Secretaries over the years.

Of course, the man that I knew the best was Jim Mitchell, who brought such a high degree of professional competence in the manpower field to the Department. And I believe that your new Secretary has that same ability.

I think, too, I should mention the fact that he has shown that he is a man of very great talent in getting along with people. I checked his background a bit before coming over here. I found that he had worked in the Eisenhower administration; he was a consultant to the Kennedy administration; and he worked on a task force in the Johnson administration.

Now, anybody who can stay employed in those three administrations can keep down unemployment in the United States of America.

I know, too, there has been some con-

cern in the Department about the desire, naturally, to see that we have a broad regional representation as far as the people who are in the top echelons of Government.

I remember I attended, on one occasion, the swearing in of one of the Under Secretaries of Labor during the Mitchell regime. The Under Secretary was Jock O'Connell,[2] who came from New Jersey. He was sworn in by Justice Brennan, who came from New Jersey, and the Secretary of Labor was Mr. James Mitchell, who came from New Jersey. Now we thought that was simply keeping too many of the jobs in one place.

I am glad to see that the new Secretary of Labor has appointed one new Secretary from South Chicago, another from West Chicago, and another one from the Chicago suburbs. If I don't watch him, I will have Mayor Daley in here next.

Of course, we do want to say some words that have to do with the mission of this Department. On that score, I know that the new Secretary has talked to his top officials indicating to you the interest I have strongly emphasized to him in having a strengthened Labor Department, strengthened in terms of not only its capability of handling its current assignments but strengthened also in terms of some new assignments in the manpower area, which I think properly belong to this Department.

Now, just a word to indicate where we began. When you look back to the year 1913—I checked some of the statistics then and found that there were 21 million wage earners in the United States—employees.

---

[2] James T. O'Connell, Under Secretary 1957–1962.

Today there are 77 million. Then the average wage was 21 cents an hour; today it is $3.10 an hour.

Those are some indications of how things have changed. But beyond that, the mission of this Department has changed. The unsophisticated observer thinks of the Department of Labor as being one that is almost completely absorbed in the problems of labor-management relations and avoiding controversies. As a matter of fact, I am expecting the Secretary of Labor to tell us how the dock strike is to be settled before the day is over.

But you know and I know that the Department's mission goes far beyond that; that the Department's mission relates to the problems of the disabled, to the problems of employment for minority groups, also to the whole general area of manpower which is becoming increasingly a part of our concern in this Nation.

I refer to the fact that as we look over the next 30 years and look back over the last 55 years of the Department, so much more will happen in terms of the manpower force and the labor needs in this country than has happened over that period, much as did happen in those dramatic figures that I just quoted.

We know that the practices of automation—the new devices that are going to not bring unemployment, but change the character of needs for labor in this country—that that is something we must plan for.

It means forward thinking with regard to America's youth—what we train them for, what kind of education they will have. As the Secretary will tell you in a meeting that we had of our Urban Affairs Council this week, a couple of days ago, I emphasized the necessity for all of our departments to be thinking ahead as to how we can meet the new problems that are going to arise.

And I would say that there is perhaps no department in Government, more than the Department of Labor, that has this responsibility, because those who work in the great productive complexes of the United States, whether in factories or on the farm or wherever they may be, 10 years from now, 15 years from now, may not have that same kind of job opportunity.

We must train them for the new responsibilities, for the new skills that are going to be needed.

Consequently, I am particularly glad to note to this group that you have in your Secretary a man who thinks that way; a man who is not thinking simply in the limited terms of labor-management relations, as vitally important as that is, but who is thinking in terms of the vision that we all need to have of the future and the kind of America we want this to be, not only in terms of jobs for America, but the kind of jobs and the environment that we want people in our working force to have.

All of these are certainly concerns that every man and woman in this room—you who are the leaders of this Department—will have in your minds in the years ahead as you provide advice and counsel to the new administration.

In terms of the new responsibilities, as far as manpower is concerned, it seems to me that the primary responsibility for manpower, for manpower training, job training, really belongs here. That is why, in terms of some of the reorganization plans that we are considering—and we have already discussed this with the Secretary—we are going to give this Depart-

59

ment some more responsibility.

We are doing so for two reasons: One, because it belongs here; but, two, because I know that in this Department is the competence—the technical competence and the expertise—to handle the problem.

We are going to give you the challenge and we are sure that you will meet that challenge and meet it effectively.

There is nothing more important than this whole manpower area, more important as we, for example, defuse the crises that we have in our cities and the crises that also may exist in rural America as well.

With all of these things in mind, I simply want to leave you with the thought that this Department, old as it is—it is as old as I am, 55 or 56 years of age—that old as it is, it has problems that are new, it is going to have new responsibilities. It is a very exciting place to be, an exciting place to be in this Department, to be working in it.

One final thought I wish to leave with you, which I perhaps need to say less here than in any of the departments I have visited to date or will be visiting for the balance of the week, is with regard to those that I am not meeting today as I will meet you.

I know that there are thousands of people here in Washington assigned to this Department, working under the people in this room, and others throughout this Nation that I, as the President of the United States, will never have the opportunity to meet.

I would hope that you would convey to them that I recognize how very important their contribution is to the success of an administration.

Now, the only people that I personally will appoint to positions in this Department can probably be put in two or three rows in this room. I recognize that right in this room the great majority are people who have given their lives to the career service in Government. It is rather fashionable to knock that career service, wherever it may be.

But I have been in Government much of my adult life. And I know how many dedicated and very competent people there are; people who have come into Government not because of the remuneration that they could get, but they have come here because of a sense of purpose and a sense of vision that they had and they came here because they thought more important than how much compensation they received was that they could make a contribution to their Nation. We are grateful for that.

I also know that as far as the Secretary of Labor is concerned and the Assistant Secretaries and all of the top people that we may have appointed, that their leadership will make a great deal of difference insofar as seeing that this Department has the kind of a record that will be outstanding. But I know that without the support of the career public servants in this room and the thousands of others attached to the Department, no matter how good these men are and these women who are appointed to these top jobs, they will not be able to succeed without that support.

What I am really trying to say is this: We need you. We need all of the career people, particularly. We need your help. We need your dedication. We need your enthusiasm.

I only can assure you, we will try to be

worthy of it—worthy of the people who have given so much of their time, so much of their lives to public service. We hope to provide the leadership along with you that will make the American people look at the record of this Department at the conclusion of this administration and say, "This was the best period in the life of the Labor Department."

Thank you.

NOTE: The President spoke at 2:30 p.m. at the Department of Labor.

27 Message to the United Nations Economic Commission for Africa Meeting in Addis Ababa on the Occasion of Its 10th Anniversary. *February 4,* 1969

THE UNITED STATES sends warm congratulations on this tenth anniversary of the United Nations Economic Commission for Africa. We join in celebrating the solid achievements of the Commission. We wish it continued success.

Through a decade of hard work and dedication, the Commission has pioneered in promoting international efforts to developing Africa. It has inspired fruitful new cooperation both within the Continent and between Africa and other regions. It has helped African Governments approach the challenges of growth with confidence and careful planning. And it has encouraged the translation of plan to practice that builds the progress we all seek.

I have seen at first hand Africa's remarkable potential. The Commission, under the able leadership of its Executive Secretary, has certainly brought that potential nearer to reality. I know it will continue to point the way in African development.

As we look ahead to the next decade, all of us have high hopes for the future of the Continent. The United States is proud to be associated with the common quest for a better life. You have my very best wishes as you meet to chart the goals of the Commission for the years of promise ahead.

RICHARD NIXON

28 Statement on the Death of Ralph McGill. *February 4,* 1969

THERE IS a kind of courage which not only calls forth praise from friends but also elicits respect from adversaries. It was this kind of courage, intellectual and moral, which distinguished Ralph McGill.

Proud of the deepest traditions of his Southern heritage, loyal to the concepts of integrity and honor which are the pride of his region, he brought to journalism a sense of responsibility and a devotion to truth.

I was privileged to talk with him on many occasions when he accompanied me on my trip to Russia in 1959. His high intelligence and deep sense of compassion made an indelible impression on all who knew him.

Mrs. Nixon joins me in extending deepest sympathy to his wife and family.

NOTE: Mr. McGill died on February 4 in Atlanta, Ga., of a heart attack at the age of 70. Since 1942 he had been editor, and since 1962 publisher, of the Atlanta Constitution. In 1958 he won the Pulitzer Prize for editorial writing.

29 Message to the Senate Requesting Advice and Consent to Ratification of the Treaty on Non-Proliferation of Nuclear Weapons. *February 5, 1969*

To the Senate of the United States:

After receiving the advice of the National Security Council, I have decided that it will serve the national interest to proceed with the ratification of the Treaty on Non-Proliferation of Nuclear Weapons. Accordingly, I request that the Senate act promptly to consider the Treaty and give its advice and consent to ratification.

I have always supported the goal of halting the spread of nuclear weapons. I opposed ratification of the Treaty last fall in the immediate aftermath of the Soviet invasion of Czechoslovakia. My request at this time in no sense alters my condemnation of that Soviet action.

I believe that ratification of the Treaty at this time would advance this Administration's policy of negotiation rather than confrontation with the USSR.

I believe that the Treaty can be an important step in our endeavor to curb the spread of nuclear weapons and that it advances the purposes of our Atoms for Peace program which I have supported since its inception during President Eisenhower's Administration.

In submitting this request I wish to endorse the commitment made by the previous Administration that the United States will, when safeguards are applied under the Treaty, permit the International Atomic Energy Agency to apply its safeguards to all nuclear activities in the United States, exclusive of those activities with direct national security significance.

I also reiterate our willingness to join with all Treaty parties to take appropriate measures to insure that potential benefits from peaceful applications of nuclear explosions will be made available to non-nuclear-weapon parties to the Treaty.

Consonant with my purpose to "strengthen the structure of peace," therefore, I urge the Senate's prompt consideration and positive action on this Treaty.

RICHARD NIXON

The White House
February 5, 1969

30   Statement Announcing Continuation of Advance
     Payments to Participants in the Feed Grain Program
     for 1969.   *February 5, 1969*

I HAVE today instructed the Secretary of Agriculture to continue, for 1969 only, the practice followed in recent years making available a 50 percent advance payment to participants in the feed grain program. I have taken this action because I feel the Government has a moral obligation to honor this implied commitment.

Initial announcement of the 1969 feed grain program on December 26, 1968, did not indicate any change in the way advance payments were to be made to farmers. The budget submitted to the Congress on January 15, 1969, stated that the advance payment rate was being reduced from 50 percent to 25 percent in 1969, and that no advance payments would be made for the 1970 program.

A great many feed grain producers have been cooperating with this Federal Government program for crop diversion over the years. We feel farmers are entitled to proper and sufficient notice about any change in the ground rules on such payments. Many of them are already beginning to sign up for the program.

The major reason for the initiation of an advance payment system on feed grains some 8 years ago was to bolster a sagging agricultural economy by advancing the actual receipt of benefit payments by the farmer. Our appraisal as to whether or not that reason will be relevant later on this year will influence the decision on advance payments in 1970.

As a result of my decision, budget outlays for the current fiscal year will rise by $168 million in comparison with the expenditure figures presented by the outgoing administration. However, if there are no advance payments in 1970, the combined effect for the 2 fiscal years 1969 and 1970 will be approximately as contemplated in the budget document.

In view of the serious budget problem which we now face in the current fiscal year, I have directed the Secretary of Agriculture to recommend to the Director of the Budget specific areas in which savings might be obtained to offset as much as possible the additional outlays which my decision requires.

31   Remarks About a New Policy on Appointment
     of Postmasters.   *February 5, 1969*

Ladies and gentlemen:

The Postmaster General appeared today before the Republican leaders meeting at the White House. After that meeting, a decision has been made which is historic, one that he will announce to you.

I will summarize it briefly before asking him to elaborate on it and to answer any questions you may have with regard to the decision.

As most of you who have covered Washington know, from the beginning of this Republic, as a matter of fact, even before the Constitution was adopted, when Benjamin Franklin was the Postmaster General during the Articles of Confederation, postmasters have always been the subject of patronage.

The party in power had the right to appoint the postmasters and the party out of power, of course, was waiting for the time when it would get that right as a result of winning an election.

It has been generally agreed by experts who have examined the operations of the Post Office Department that this had a detrimental effect on morale in the career service and that it also might have had a very detrimental effect on the efficiency of the operations of the Department.

As you will recall, during the course of the last campaign, one pledge I made emphatically over and over again was that we were going to take politics out of the Post Office Department and that we were going to improve postal service.

As far as the second objective is concerned, by bringing the Postmaster General into this position, a man with immense success in the business community, and a team, I would say among all the Cabinet teams, one of the best that I have in the whole Government, we think that we have moved toward efficient operation of the Department.

The first responsibility of taking politics out of the appointment of postmasters is one that is not only mine, but it is one in which we have to have the support of the members of our party in Congress.

This is difficult for a fundamental reason: When the party in power has the right to name postmasters, they don't want to give it up. It is always the party out of power that passes the resolutions suggesting that postmasters should be appointed on a merit basis. This is the time, we believe, to bite that bullet.

Consequently, I have made the decision, which has been recommended by the Postmaster General, that beginning now postmasters will be appointed on a merit basis without the usual political clearance which has been the case for the 190 years or more that this Nation has been a nation, and even before that time.

The Postmaster General will explain the significance of this particular action, and I hope he will elaborate a bit on what he thinks it may do in terms of more efficient postal service.

NOTE: The President spoke at 2:14 p.m. in the Fish Room at the White House. The statement by Postmaster General Winton M. Blount which followed the President's remarks is printed in the Weekly Compilation of Presidential Documents (vol. 5, p. 224). Mr. Blount's responses to reporters' questions on the new policy were made public on the same day in the form of a White House press release.

32 Remarks About an Increase in the Expenditure Ceiling of the National Science Foundation. *February* 5, 1969

Ladies and gentlemen:

As you will recall, during the last campaign I expressed a great interest in basic research and particularly in the field of science.

As you know, there has been considerable concern expressed in scientific circles and in educational circles with regard to the ceiling on expenditures for the National Science Foundation.

After a very vigorous discussion of this item, having in mind the fact that we have a difficult expenditure situation in the present budget, I have finally decided to authorize the Director of the Bureau of the Budget to raise the ceiling by an amount of $10 million. This is covered in the statement which you have before you.

Dr. DuBridge will indicate what this will mean. Also, I think, Doctor, if you could indicate why the imposition of the ceiling had such a detrimental effect not just on the scientific community, but on higher education generally.

Thank you very much.

NOTE: The President spoke at 2:30 p.m. in the Fish Room at the White House. At the conclusion of the President's remarks Dr. Lee A. DuBridge, Director of the Office of Science and Technology, answered reporters' questions concerning the announcement. This news briefing was made public on the same day in the form of a White House press release.

33   Statement Announcing an Increase in the Expenditure Ceiling of the National Science Foundation.   *February* 5, 1969

THE COLLEGES and universities of this Nation provide a critical resource which needs to be fostered and strengthened. Our higher educational system provides the advanced training needed for tomorrow's leaders in science and technology, industry and government, and also conducts the basic research which uncovers the new knowledge so essential to the future welfare of the country. It is essential that these programs of education and research be sustained at a level of high excellence.

In recent years the Federal Government has become the mainstay in the support of university graduate study and research, to the great benefit of the Nation. However, in more recent years the support levels have stabilized or have even declined in spite of rising costs. But university activities cannot be turned on and off like a faucet, as I have previously stated, and hence substantial damage has been done to important programs and to many colleges and universities. In particular I believe that the previous administration made a serious error in limiting so severely the ex-penditure ceiling of the National Science Foundation, which plays a very important role in the support of educational and research activities. Because of the unique nature of the National Science Foundation's operations, the imposition of this ceiling by the Revenue and Expenditure Control Act of 1968 created undue hardship. While the Government as a whole must continue to operate within the severe restraints of this act, it seems evident that this unique situation in regard to the National Science Foundation requires special attention.

Therefore, I have instructed the Director of the Budget and the Director of the National Science Foundation to increase immediately the expenditure ceiling for the National Science Foundation by $10 million, in order to deal with the many serious disruptions which have occurred in academic programs of education and research. Furthermore, I have instructed the Director of the Budget, in consultation with my Science Adviser, to examine other research and development programs to ascertain where offsetting savings can

65

be obtained. I also call upon the university community to cooperate with the Government's program of fiscal restraint in view of our serious concern about current inflationary trends in our Nation.

This action is taken in recognition of what I believe to be unique circumstances of compelling urgency and in no way indicates a relaxation of this administration's intentions to reduce Government expenditures wherever possible.

34   The President's News Conference of *February 6, 1969*

THE PRESIDENT'S TRIP TO EUROPE

THE PRESIDENT. [1.]   Ladies and gentlemen, as you will note from a release from the Press Office, I will leave on the 23d of this month for a trip to Europe which will take me to Brussels, to London, to Berlin and Bonn, to Rome and to Paris.

I will be accompanied on the trip by the Secretary of State, Mr. Rogers, and by my Adviser for National Security Affairs, Dr. Kissinger.

The purpose of the trip I will describe as being a working trip rather than a protocol trip. I plan to see in each of the countries I visit the head of government, and in addition to that, I will have a visit with the members of our United States delegation in Paris, headed by Ambassador Lodge, and will have a meeting with Pope Paul in Rome.

While I am in Brussels, I will see leaders of the NATO community. As far as the agenda is concerned for these meetings, it is wide open. I have some ideas about the future of the European community which I will discuss, and I am sure that my colleagues in that community have some ideas that they will want to discuss.

I have requested that, in addition to the usual group meetings which will take place, I have an opportunity to have an individual, face-to-face meeting with each head of government, with no one present except a translator when needed.

As I look at this trip and what it may accomplish, I want to make very clear that this is only a first step in achieving a purpose that I have long felt is vital to the future of peace for the United States and for the world. That is the strengthening and the revitalizing of the American-European community.

This will be the first, I would hope, of several meetings of this type that will take place in the years ahead. I would trust that, as a result of this meeting and as a result of other meetings that will take place, this great Alliance which, in my view, has been the greatest force for peace, to keep the peace, over the last 20 years— this great Alliance which was brought together by a common fear 20 years ago— will be held together now and strengthened by a common sense of purpose.

I will go now to your questions.

QUESTIONS

THE PRESIDENT AND THE PEACE TALKS

[2.]   Q. Mr. President, in connection with your visit to Paris and your talks with Ambassador Lodge, do you see any possibility of your having any direct contact with the other side in these negotiations, specifically, the representatives of North Vietnam or the NLF [National Liberation Front]?

THE PRESIDENT. Mr. Smith [Merriman Smith, United Press International], I do not see any possibility of that kind of conversation at this time. I would not rule it out at some later time, if Ambassador Lodge and others who have responsibility for negotiation thought it were wise.

With Ambassador Lodge and his colleagues, I hope to get a complete report on the progress of the negotiations and also any recommendations that he or they may have with regard to new initiatives that we might take to make more progress than we have made.

I think we have made a good start in Paris, incidentally. I believe that we can now move forward to some substantive achievements.

FUTURE MEETINGS WITH SOVIET
LEADERS

[3.] Q. Mr. President, looking beyond this trip, could you give us a clue to your attitude toward the possibility of future meetings with Soviet leaders?

THE PRESIDENT. I believe that a meeting with Soviet leaders should take place at a future time. I should make clear that I think that where summitry is concerned I take a dim view of what some have called "instant summitry," particularly where there are very grave differences of opinion between those who are to meet.

I believe that a well-prepared summit meeting, where we have on the table the various differences that we have on which we can perhaps make progress, would be in our interest and in their interest, and it will be my intention after this trip is completed to conduct exploratory talks at various levels to see if such a meeting could take place.

I should point out, incidentally, that one of the reasons that this trip takes precedence is that I have long felt that before we have meetings of summitry with the Soviet leaders, it is vitally important that we have talks with our European allies, which we are doing.

AMERICAN TROOP WITHDRAWAL IN
VIETNAM

[4.] Q. Mr. President, this morning South Vietnamese President Thieu said that the South Vietnamese army is capable of relieving a sizable number of American troops in Vietnam. What is your understanding of "sizable," and do you think there will actually be a reduction of the number of American troops?

THE PRESIDENT. Well, speaking personally, and also as the Commander of the Armed Forces, I do not want an American boy to be in Vietnam for one day longer than is necessary for our national interest. As our commanders in the field determine that the South Vietnamese are able to assume a greater portion of the responsibility for the defense of their own territory, troops will come back. However, at this time, I have no announcements to make with regard to the return of troops.

I will only say that it is high on the agenda of priorities, and that just as soon as either the training program for South Vietnamese forces and their capabilities, the progress of the Paris peace talks, or other developments make it feasible to do so, troops will be brought back.

THE PARIS PEACE TALKS

[5.] Q. Mr. President, on your trip to Paris, do you plan to see the South Vietnamese negotiators there? In that connection, a general question on the talks themselves: Do you think you can continue to separate the military issues from the political issues and the political settlement of South Vietnam in the negotiations in Paris?

THE PRESIDENT. Well, Mr. Lisagor [Peter Lisagor, Chicago Daily News], that is one of the matters that I want to discuss with Ambassador Lodge, to get his judgment on that point. It is our view that at this time the separation of those two items is in our interest and in the interest of bringing progress in those talks.

Now, as far as meeting with the South Vietnamese leaders is concerned, we have no present plans to do so. If Ambassador Lodge advises that it would be wise to do so, such meetings will be scheduled. There will be enough time in the schedule for a meeting if he does suggest it.

AMBASSADOR CHARLES W. YOST

[6.] Q. Mr. President, your nominee and now your Ambassador to the United Nations, Mr. Yost, has been under attack from some conservative groups, such as the Liberty Lobby, for his past associations with certain individuals, particularly including Alger Hiss. In light of your more than passing familiarity with the

Hiss case,[1] would you comment on these attacks on Mr. Yost and whether they should be given any credence?

THE PRESIDENT. As far as Mr. Yost's background is concerned, I am completely aware of it because, of course, all of these matters are brought to my attention before appointments are made. But what I am looking to now is his capability to handle the problems of the future and not events that occurred over 20 years ago.

There is no question about his loyalty to this country. And I also think there is no question about his very good judgment on critical issues confronting the United States, particularly in the Mideast.

As I pointed out, he is one of our prime experts in the Mideast. He sat in on the National Security Council meetings when we discussed the Mideast and made some very valuable contributions.

U.S. POLICY ON THE MIDDLE EAST

[7.] Q. Mr. President, on the Middle East, now that you have completed your review with the NSC [National Security Council], you spoke of a need for new initiatives, can you tell us what your policy is going to be now and what initiatives you do expect to take?

THE PRESIDENT. Mr. Bailey [Charles W. Bailey 2d, Minneapolis Tribune, Minneapolis Star], our initiatives in the Mideast, I think, can well be summarized by

---

[1] As a member of the House Un-American Activities Committee, Congressman Nixon spearheaded the 1948–1949 investigation of Communist activity which subsequently led to the perjury conviction of former State Department official Alger Hiss.

that very word that you have used. What we see now is a new policy on the part of the United States in assuming the initiative. We are not going to stand back and rather wait for something else to happen.

We are going to assume it on what I would suggest five fronts:

We are going to continue to give our all-out support to the Jarring mission.[2] We are going to have bilateral talks at the United Nations, preparatory to the talks between the four powers. We shall have four-power talks at the United Nations. We shall also have talks with the countries in the area, with the Israelis and their neighbors, and, in addition, we want to go forward on some of the long range plans, the Eisenhower-Strauss plan for relieving some of the very grave economic problems in that area.[3]

We believe that the initiative here is one that cannot be simply unilateral. It must be multilateral. And it must not be in one direction. We are going to pursue every possible avenue to peace in the Mideast that we can.

TAX REFORM PROPOSALS

[8.] Q. Mr. President, how do you feel about the Johnson administration's tax

---

[2] United Nations mediation mission in Arab-Israeli dispute headed by Gunnar Jarring, Swedish Ambassador to the Soviet Union.

[3] A project to employ nuclear energy for water desalination and irrigation to further economic development of the Middle East. Proposed in the summer of 1967 by Lewis L. Strauss, former Atomic Energy Commissioner, and supported by former President Eisenhower, the plan was approved by Senate Resolution 155 of December 12, 1967, sponsored by Senator Howard H. Baker, Jr., of Tennessee.

reform proposal that would exempt many poor families from paying any taxes at all, but would guarantee that wealthy families at least pay some minimum income tax? We are told that you are sending up a tax reform proposal and would like to get your opinion.

THE PRESIDENT. Tax reform has been a matter of discussion within administration councils during the past week. In a discussion, which I understand has already been widely publicized, that I had with Chairman Mills of the Ways and Means Committee, and the ranking Republican, Mr. Byrnes, we went over the agenda and also the timetable as to when the proposals should come down.

The Secretary of the Treasury will have a preliminary announcement to make on tax reform tomorrow. He will make major tax reform recommendations to the Congress at a later time.

But at this time I do not want to indicate in advance the areas in which we are going to move. I will say that the two areas that you mentioned were considered and were discussed in the conference that we had here in the White House with the ranking members of the Ways and Means Committee.

LATIN AMERICA

[9.] Q. Sir, would you please tell us how you plan to move in solving some of the problems of Latin America? Have you decided on your Assistant Secretary of State in that field?

THE PRESIDENT. I believe we have decided on the Assistant Secretary of State, but I am not yet prepared to make the announcement because the necessary clearances have not taken place.[4]

May I make one thing very clear: I have noted news stories to the effect that the job was going begging and we were unable to find a qualified man. We have several qualified people but the Secretary of State and I agree that this is an area of top priority. We think we need new initiatives with regard to the Alliance for Progress.

I would describe that in this way: I think the difficulty in the past, a well-intentioned difficulty, has been that we have been putting too much emphasis on what we are going to do for Latin America and not enough emphasis on what we are going to do with our Latin American friends. The new Assistant Secretary will attempt to remedy that and we shall attempt to develop new policies.

SENTINEL ABM SYSTEM AND ARMS
CONTROL TALKS

[10.]   Q. Mr. President, the Pentagon announced this morning that Secretary Laird had ordered a temporary halt in the construction of the Sentinel system, pending a high level review. Does that represent a change in policy on our part? Does it indicate that maybe we are getting somewhere with the Russians toward an agreement whereby neither one of us would have to build it?

THE PRESIDENT. Well, Mr. Kaplow

_____

[4] Charles A. Meyer was nominated on March 10, 1969, as Assistant Secretary of State for Inter-American Affairs and U.S. Coordinator, Alliance for Progress. Subsequently he was named to represent the United States on several bodies concerned with special aspects of inter-American affairs (5 Weekly Comp. Pres. Docs., pp. 412, 605, 643, and 726).

[Herbert Kaplow, NBC News], answering the second part of your question first, there has been no progress with regard to the arms control talks with the Russians. I have made it clear in the appointment of Mr. Smith to that position that we are going to put emphasis on those talks, but I do believe we should go forward on settling some of the political differences at the same time.

As far as the decision on the Sentinel is concerned, Secretary Laird and his colleagues at the Defense Department will make decisions based on the security of the United States, and he will announce those decisions and justify them at this point.

U.S. RELATIONS WITH ASIA

[11.]   Q. Mr. President, there has been some apprehension, sir, in Asia that your re-emphasis on U.S. relations with Europe would mean a lessening of U.S. interests in Asia. Would you comment on that, sir?

THE PRESIDENT. This gives me an opportunity to perhaps state my philosophy about emphasis on different parts of the world.

The reason that we have been discussing the Mideast a great deal lately is that it is an area of the world which might explode into a major war. Therefore, it needs immediate attention. That does not mean, however, that we are not going to continue to put attention on Latin America, on Africa, on Asia.

I think you could describe me best as not being a "half-worlder," with my eyes looking only to Europe or only to Asia, but one who sees the whole world. We live in one world and we must go forward together in this whole world.

THE ANTIBALLISTIC MISSILE SYSTEM

[12.] Q. Mr. President, with regard to the ABM [antiballistic missile] system, you know this was planned originally to protect us against the threat of a nuclear attack by Red China early in the 1970's. Does your information indicate that there is any lessening of this threat, or is it greater, or just where do we stand on that?

THE PRESIDENT. First, I do not buy the assumption that the ABM system, the thin Sentinel system, as it has been described, was simply for the purpose of protecting ourselves against attack from Communist China.

This system, as are the systems that the Soviet Union has already deployed, adds to our overall defense capability. I would further say that, as far as the threat is concerned, we do not see any change in that threat, and we are examining, therefore, all of our defense systems and all of our defense postures to see how we can best meet them consistent with our other responsibilities.

PROPOSALS FOR A DEPARTMENT OF PEACE

[13.] Q. Mr. President, as you are aware, I am sure, there has been discussion on the Hill about trying to set up a Department of Peace to include the Peace Corps and the Disarmament Agency and other organizations. I wondered about your reaction to that idea.

THE PRESIDENT. In fact, one of my task forces recommended a Department of Peace. I think, however, that derogates and improperly downgrades the role of the Department of State and the Department of Defense.

I consider the Department of State to be a "Department of Peace." I consider the Department of Defense to be a "Department of Peace," and I can assure you that at the White House level, in the National Security Council, that is where we coordinate all of our efforts toward peace.

I think putting one department over here as a Department of Peace would tend to indicate that the other departments were engaged in other activities that were not interested in peace.

FCC PROPOSAL TO BAN RADIO-TV
CIGARETTE ADVERTISING

[14.] Q. Mr. President, will you support the FCC proposal to ban cigarette advertising on radio and TV?

THE PRESIDENT. Well, as a nonsmoker, it wouldn't pose any problems to me. I, however, have only had that FCC proposal brought to my attention by the late TV reports last night and the morning papers. I have not yet had an opportunity to evaluate it. After I have evaluated it, I will make an announcement as to my position.

ADMINISTRATION POLICY ON SCHOOL
DESEGREGATION

[15.] Q. Mr. President, there has been conflicting speculation about the extent to which your administration will seek to advance school desegregation. Could you tell us what your policy will be on that, specifically including the so-called "freedom of choice" plan?

THE PRESIDENT. That was a subject, as you will recall from having covered me in the campaign, that I addressed myself to on several occasions.

First, as far as freedom of choice is concerned, freedom of choice must be defined in terms of what it does. If freedom of choice is found to be simply a subterfuge to perpetuate segregation, then funds should be denied to such a school system. If a freedom of choice plan, however, is found to be one which actually is bringing an end to segregation, then a freedom of choice plan, in my opinion, is appropriate and should receive funds.

As far as school segregation is concerned, I support the law of the land. I believe that funds should be denied to those districts that continue to perpetuate segregation. I think that what we have here is a very difficult problem, however, in implementing it. One is our desire, a desire that was emphasized by Dr. Allen,[5] to keep our schools open, because education must receive the highest priority. The other is our desire to see to it that our schools are not segregated.

That is why I have, in discussing this with Secretary Finch and with Dr. Allen, urged that before we use the ultimate weapon of denying funds and closing a school, let's exhaust every other possibility to see that local school districts do comply with the law.

AID TO URBAN SCHOOLS

[16.] Q. Mr. President, do you support Dr. Allen's statement of yesterday that he believes massive aid to urban schools is necessary?

THE PRESIDENT. Well, I support the

---

[5] Dr. James E. Allen, Jr., Assistant Secretary-designate for Education in the Department of Health, Education, and Welfare and U.S. Commissioner-designate of Education.

proposition that there needs to be a massive infusion of assistance to education. Let me make one thing very clear in that respect, so that you can get my thinking directly. You will note yesterday that I supported a $10 million increase in the funds for the National Science Foundation, which will go to higher education.

I believe higher education needs more assistance, too. But at the present time the great need is in the area described by educators of "K through 12," kindergarten through the 12th grade—preparing students in those years for the higher education which is now available to virtually every student who is capable of meeting the standards for getting into college.

As far as Dr. Allen's method of doing so, I do not believe that he, sophisticated as he is as the superintendent of a State school system, would suggest that we go around the States. We cannot do that because the cities and the school systems within a State cannot exist without the State government.

However, the area of need is primarily in the city school systems. We will try to meet that problem as best we can.

OIL LEAKAGE IN SANTA BARBARA CHANNEL

[17.] Q. Mr. President, may I ask you two questions about the disaster in Santa Barbara. One, do Secretary Hickel's actions so far accord with your policies; and two, what implications does this disaster have for future conservation policy here?

THE PRESIDENT. Well, answering the second part of your question first, I have found that for 15 years we have not had any updating of our policies with regard to offshore drilling. Secretary Hickel has now initiated a study within the Department for updating those regulations so that this kind of incident will not occur again.

With regard to the action that he has taken, I think he acted promptly in temporarily stopping the drilling and then insisting on very stringent requirements on the Union Oil Company and others involved so that this would not happen.

Looking to the future however, we have got to get at the source of the problem. That means very stringent regulations in offshore drilling, because there isn't any question that if the companies involved will make the necessary expenditures in setting up their wells offshore, there is minimal danger of this kind of an activity.

THE DOCK STRIKE

[18.] Q. Mr. President, we were told yesterday by the congressional leaders,[6] that in dealing with labor disputes, like the dock strike, you preferred a permanent, long-range approach. And yet there seems to be real skepticism on the Hill that anything will be done. Can you give us your views currently on this?

THE PRESIDENT. Well, my view with regard to the dock strike is that for the White House to indicate publicly that we are going to do this and that generally has the effect of telling the parties to do noth-

---

[6] Following a meeting with the President on February 5, 1969, Senate Minority Leader Everett McKinley Dirksen of Illinois and House Minority Leader Gerald R. Ford of Michigan met with reporters at 10:40 a.m. in the Fish Room at the White House for a news briefing (5 Weekly Comp. Pres. Docs., p. 219).

ing. For that reason, I think Secretary Shultz very properly is playing a mediating role but making it very clear that the primary responsibility is on the parties themselves.

Now, long range, I believe that the Taft-Hartley Act's provisions for national emergency strikes, which I helped to write along with other members of the Labor Committee 20 years ago, that those provisions are now outmoded. I do not believe we have enough options in dealing with these kinds of disputes and breakdowns. I have, therefore, asked the Department of Labor to develop some new approaches in this field, and we will submit them by legislation to this Congress.

BLACK CITIZENS AND THE NEW ADMINISTRATION

[19.] Q. Mr. President, do you agree with those who say that you and your administration have a serious problem with distrust among the blacks, and whether you agree that it is one of your more serious problems or not, could you tell us specifically what you are doing to deal with what some consider to be this distrust among the blacks?

THE PRESIDENT. I am concerned about this problem; and incidentally, let me make it very clear that those who have raised this question are not simply those who are political opponents. My Task Force on Education pointed up that I was not considered—I think the words they used—as a friend by many of our black citizens in America.

I can only say that, by my actions as President, I hope to rectify that. I hope that by what we do in terms of dealing with the problems of all Americans, it will be made clear that the President of the United States, as an elected official, has no State constituency. He has no congressional constituency. He does not represent any special group. He represents all the people. He is the friend of all the people.

Putting it another way—as a lawyer—the President is the counsel for all the people of this country, and I hope that I can gain the respect and I hope eventually the friendship of black citizens and other Americans.

RELATIONSHIP BETWEEN THE STATE
DEPARTMENT AND THE NATIONAL
SECURITY COUNCIL

[20.] Q. Mr. President, there has been some confusion this week on the relationship between the National Security Council and the State Department—for example, the Assistant Secretary of State reporting to the NSC. Could you clarify that for us, please?

THE PRESIDENT. Yes. The Secretary of State is my chief foreign policy adviser and the chief agent of this Government in carrying out foreign policy abroad. As one of my very close friends, personally, he advises me independently as well as through the National Security Council.

The question has also, I know, been raised as to who makes the policy and the decisions? Are they made in the National Security Council or are they made in the State Department?

The answer is, neither place. The State Department advises the President. The National Security Council advises the President. The President has the author-

ity to make decisions, and I intend to exercise that authority.[7]

FOREIGN TRADE AND LIMITATION ON
TEXTILE IMPORTS

[21.] Q. Mr. President, during the election campaign, sir, you said that you would seek international agreements to limit the import of certain textiles. Can you tell us when you plan to get around to doing that?

Also, could you give us some idea as to what you feel about the growing feeling of protectionism in Congress?

THE PRESIDENT. Let me start at the second part of the question first. I believe that the interest of the United States and the interest of the whole world will best be served by moving toward freer trade rather than toward protectionism.

I take a dim view of this tendency to move toward quotas and other methods that may become permanent, whether they are applied here or by other nations abroad.

Second, as far as the textile situation is concerned, that is a special problem which has caused very great distress in certain parts of this country, and to a great number of wage earners, as well as those who operate our textile facilities.

For that reason, exploratory discussions have taken place and will be taking place with the major countries involved to see if we can handle this on a volunteer basis

[7] A White House press release of February 7, 1969, announced steps taken by the President since January 20, 1969, designed to revitalize the structure and role of the National Security Council and reorganize its staff. The announcement (5 Weekly Comp. Pres. Docs., p. 232) lists the substantive components of the NSC staff and its personnel.

rather than having to go to a legislation which would impose quotas, and I think would turn the clock back in our objective of trying to achieve freer trade.

THE "PUEBLO" AFFAIR

[22.]   Q. Mr. President, there has been a court of inquiry in the city of Coronado, California for several weeks now on the *Pueblo* [8] seizure. Do you think it is proper for the Navy, in effect, to be sitting in judgment of itself, or do you see any need for any kind of Presidential commission on this?

THE PRESIDENT. Well, as a Navy man, I know that the Navy has procedures which I think very adequately protect the rights of defendants in courts-martial.

Second, I believe those procedures, from my investigation to date, have been very scrupulously followed.

Third, however, because of the great interest in this case, the Secretary of Defense has asked, as you know, Mr. [David] Packard, the Deputy Secretary, to conduct a thorough investigation, not only of the handling of this case, but also an investigation as to how we can avoid this kind of an incident occurring in the future.

I also want to make it clear that I, as the Chief Executive of the Nation, will examine the whole record myself, both with regard to the individual guilt or innocence of the people involved, and also

---

[8] The electronic intelligence ship U.S.S. *Pueblo* and its 83-man crew were seized by North Korean patrol boats January 23, 1968, and taken captive to the port of Wonsan. On December 22, 1968, President Johnson announced the release of the 82 surviving crewmen.

with regard to the even more important objective of seeing to it that this kind of incident can be avoided in the future.

NUCLEAR NONPROLIFERATION TREATY

[23.]   Q. Mr. President, you have now asked the Senate to ratify the Nonproliferation Treaty. On your trip to Europe, do you have any hopes of trying to persuade particularly West Germany and France to move a little closer toward signing that Treaty?

THE PRESIDENT. My view about asking other governments to follow our lead is this: They know what we think, and I am sure that that matter will come up for discussion.

I will make it clear that I believe that ratification of the Treaty by all governments, nuclear and nonnuclear, is in the interest of peace and in the interest of reducing the possibility of nuclear proliferation.

On the other hand, I do not believe that we gain our objectives through heavy-handed activities publicly, particularly in attempting to get others to follow our lead. Each of these governments is a sovereign government. Each has its own political problems. I think in the end, most of our friends in Western Europe will follow our lead. I will attempt to persuade, but I will not, certainly, attempt to use any blackmail or arm-twisting.

WOMEN IN THE NEW ADMINISTRATION

[24.]   Q. [Vera R. Glaser of the North American Newspaper Alliance] Mr. President, in staffing your administration, you have so far made about 200 high-level Cabinet and other policy position appointments, and of these only three have gone to women. Could you tell us, sir, whether we can expect a more equitable recognition of women's abilities, or are we going to remain a lost sex?

THE PRESIDENT. Would you be interested in coming into the Government? [*Laughter*]

Very seriously, I had not known that only three had gone to women, and I shall see that we correct that imbalance very promptly.

SOVIET UNION AND CZECHOSLOVAKIA AND THE NONPROLIFERATION TREATY

[25.] Q. On the Nonproliferation Treaty again, last fall during the campaign, Mr. President, you opposed ratification because of the Soviet invasion of Czechoslovakia. Can you tell me, sir, how you feel that situation has changed since then?

THE PRESIDENT. It has changed in the sense that the number of Soviet forces in Czechoslovakia has been substantially reduced.

It has changed also in the sense that the passage of time tends somewhat to reduce the pent-up feelings that were then present with regard to the Soviet Union's actions.

I want to make it very clear that in asking the Senate to ratify the Treaty, I did not gloss over the fact that we still very strongly disapproved of what the Soviet Union had done in Czechoslovakia and what it still is doing. But on balance, I considered that this was the time to move forward on the Treaty, and have done so.

Merriman Smith, United Press International: Thank you, Mr. President.

NOTE: President Nixon's second news conference was held in the East Room at the White House at 11 a.m. on Thursday, February 6, 1969. It was broadcast on radio and television.

35   Statement on the Forthcoming Visit to Western Europe. *February 6, 1969*

I AM PLEASED to inform you that after consultations with the heads of state and government concerned, I have decided to visit Western Europe late this month. I plan to visit Brussels, London, Bonn, Berlin, Rome, and Paris in that order. The precise schedule will be made available when it is completed.

The purpose of this trip is to underline my commitment to the closest relationship between our friends in Western Europe and the United States. I would like to lift these relationships from a concern for tactical problems of the day to a definition of our common purposes. The Alliance,

held together in its first two decades by a common fear, needs now the sense of cohesiveness supplied by common purpose. I am eager for an early exchange of views on all the important issues that concern us. I favor intimate and frank consultations, and I am delighted that it has proved possible to make this journey so early in my administration. I am going to discuss, not to propose; for work, not for ceremony.

The future of the countries of the West can no longer be an exclusively American design. It requires the best thought of Europeans and Americans alike. I look on this trip as laying the groundwork for a series of meetings to be continued over the months ahead.

While in Paris, I intend also to review intensively the Paris peace talks. To this end, I have set aside a morning to meet with Ambassador Lodge and his staff for a full review of the situation.

36   Remarks to Employees at the Post Office Department. *February* 6, 1969

Mr. Postmaster General, ladies and gentlemen:

From the enthusiasm of your welcome I gather that you probably assume, as a result of the announcement we made yesterday with regard to taking politics out of the appointment of postmasters, that we were going to apply that also to the Postmaster General and that anybody could go up.

But I just do want to say this: that I am very delighted to be here in this Department, one of the oldest, if not the oldest, in terms of its service to the Nation, to this whole country, and one of the most vital, as I will indicate in the remarks that I shall make.

I also should say a word about the Postmaster General. In checking his background before coming over here, I found that he was the first Cabinet officer from the State of Alabama in 72 years.

In view of his record to date, his courage, and his ability to sell this historic decision that we announced at the White House yesterday, I think he is going to be one of the best Cabinet officers in 72 years as Postmaster General.

I got him to take this position only by giving him the assurance that I would back him in the objective of seeing that this Nation had the best postal service in the world.

We all know that we have thousands of dedicated people in the postal service. Except for the few that I have been responsible for appointing, with the approval of the Postmaster General, this room is primarily filled with people who have given their lives to that service.

I know that you are proud of that service. I know that you have been concerned, as I have been concerned and most Americans have been concerned, about the deterioration in service, deterioration which probably was the result of many factors—the growth in population, the increasing costs, morale factors, and the rest.

But I know, too, that when I consider the quality of the people in the career service at the highest levels in this Department, when I consider the thousands of people in the ranks across this country, I know that there is a sense of dedication and purpose which, if only we give the right leadership at the top and the right backing at the top, we can deal with these problems and see that the American people have better postal service so that we can be proud of what we do here and can have that as an example to the world. We want nothing less than that as far as this postal service is concerned.

We therefore need your cooperation. We need your assistance.

I want to say something now, particularly to the Postmaster General, his

Deputy, and the Assistants who are here who are appointees of this administration. I want to make it very clear that the men at the top do make a difference, and each administration appoints its own men at the top.

But I also want to make it equally clear that without the cooperation and the support of the career men and women, such as the men and women in this room, it just isn't possible for the men at the top to carry out their mission.

That is why I am visiting every department of Government. That is why I am making it very clear that while I have every confidence in the men and women that I have appointed to top positions, we need the support of the career service.

I believe in the career service. I know many who have given their lives to Government, who came into Government at an early age, who have not had the financial remuneration they might have had in some other activity, but who came into Government because they wanted that kind of life and also wanted particularly that opportunity to serve.

I feel that there is an opportunity, an opportunity for all of us in this new administration to inspire a new sense of dedication and purpose among those who are in the career service in the Post Office Department and in the other departments of the Government.

In bringing this message to you, I just want to assure you that I am aware of the fact that if we succeed, it will be because of what you do. I am aware of the fact that if we don't succeed, it may be our own failure. But it also may be due to the fact that we have failed to justify the support of those who are in the career service

and who are so essential to seeing to it that any department is run properly.

So, with this visit I am simply trying to underline the conviction that I have that every one of us ought to be proud to be working in the position that we have in the Federal Government.

I think the idea that there is just a little difference if you are in the private sector, that that is a little better than being in Government service, or so on down the line or either way, either approach is wrong, because in our great country, what makes it great is the fact that we have some people who prefer going into private enterprise, others who prefer to go into Government work.

What I wish to make clear is that having spent perhaps most of my adult life in Government rather than in private enterprise, I am proud of my Government service. I am also aware of the fact that there are thousands of people in this Department and millions across the Nation in Government service who can hold their own with anybody in the private sector. That is the way it should be and that is the way we want it to be in this administration.

One final point I would make is that this is going to be a period of change in this Department. We are not going to be able to meet our mission—the mission that I have supported and that the Postmaster General has set—without making some changes.

Some of these changes are going to be difficult. They are going to be difficult politically for us to get across, just like the announcement that was made yesterday. It is always easy when a party is out of power for it to say, "Take politics out of the appointments in the Post Office Department." But when the party in power gives it up, believe me, that is rather hard, as we learned in that meeting we had with the legislative leaders yesterday.

But we have taken the first step. Now we ask your cooperation in helping us to take the other steps that are necessary, steps that may not be a continuation of doing it the way we have always done it, steps that may require a change in personnel policy, steps that may require new policies insofar as automation and a number of other areas that you people are more familiar with than I am.

I am simply saying this: I believe we have in the Postmaster General and his associates a group of dedicated men who are determined to give us the best postal service in the world. I know that in the group in this room you want exactly that and that you will work toward that end.

We have backed and we will continue to back you. We just hope that you will give our group here the same kind of loyalty that they have given to you and will continue to give to you.

Finally, one personal note, in this room are only the leaders. I understand, Red, we have only 150 in this room, the top officials of this great Department. I realize that you represent and that you supervise approximately 750,000.

I would hope that as you talk to the people that you supervise, the word could get down the line, down the line for example, to that underpaid man whom Red Blount spoke to us about the other day who works in a great city and starts at $6,000 a year; if he went to the Sanitation Department, he could get $10,000 a year. Let them know that we in Washington appreciate what they are doing. Let them know that we back them. Let them know that better days are coming. Let them know that we recognize that without their help and their assistance, we cannot do the job that we want to do.

I would hope that when I finish my term in office that we could look back, as far as this Department is concerned, and say that we looked at the problems in the beginning, we examined them fairly in a nonpartisan way, we dealt with them, we had some morale problems up and down the line when we began, but when we finished, every man and woman in this Department, right down to that individual who works as a clerk or a mail carrier at the lowest salary range, that every man was as proud of being in the postal service as men and women were proud to be in that service when Ben Franklin began it before this country became a country.

Thank you very much.

NOTE: The President spoke at 2:17 p.m. at the Post Office Department. His remarks were broadcast on closed circuit television to employees throughout the Nation.

37   Statement Announcing the Nomination of John G. Veneman as Under Secretary of Health, Education, and Welfare. *February 7, 1969*

I AM particularly pleased that Jack Veneman, considered the California Legislature's leading authority in the areas of health care, welfare, and taxation, has agreed to serve as Under Secretary for Health, Education, and Welfare.

During his tenure in the California State Legislature, Mr. Veneman has made significant contributions in building the progressive programs necessary to meet the human needs of the people of California.

Urban problems are certainly the high priority of this administration. In recruiting people for key positions this administration seeks those with the talent to do the job and a sense of social conscience. These are essential if we are to have an impact on the problems besetting the American people today.

38   Remarks to Participants in the 1969 Senate Youth Program.   *February 7, 1969*

Ladies and gentlemen:

It is a very great privilege for me to participate in this closing session of the Senate Student Youth Program.

I want to express appreciation to the Hearst Foundation for making possible what I think is one of the most exciting projects in our Government today.

When I think of all of you from all over the country, from high schools, having the opportunity to come to Washington to be exposed to the great institutions of Government that are here, I think that no greater service could be rendered, not just to you—I mean it is a wonderful experience for you—but to the Nation, because you have the opportunity to go back home now and to tell the people there what government is like. And I hope many of you will be inspired to participate in government in one form or the other. I wouldn't be surprised if some of you will end up in the House or Senate or, who knows, you might be here sometime in the future.

I know you have probably been exposed to a number of statements and a lot of advice during your stay here. I was trying to think, as I presided over the Cabinet meeting—and that is the reason I am late, it ran a little late—I was trying to think of what would be appropriate to say to you that you might not have heard

before. There is not much, really, that can be added.

I know you have heard from Congressmen and Senators, as well as other Government officials.

But perhaps some thoughts that relate to my own experience and background might be of interest to you. During the last campaign there was a very major effort made by both of the major candidates to communicate with the young people of America. And what was really exciting to me was that the young people of America—and I refer not just to college youth, but to high school students—came out in such great numbers and participated as they did in the campaign.

Now let me give you a little background on that. I began in politics before you were born, everybody in this room, because it was 22 years ago that I first ran for the House of Representatives out in California. Incidentally, I had the support of the Hearst Newspapers at that time in that campaign.

Twenty-two years ago, when I ran for office, there was an interest in politics among young people, particularly at the college age, but not at the high school age.

Then I have seen a change occur—a very exciting change. Each year the age limit seems to go down insofar as the interest and understanding of politics is concerned.

You would be surprised, not only at the high school age but I have found even in the grade schools today, particularly in the 6th, 7th, and 8th grades, you will find a high degree of sophistication, a high degree of understanding, about political campaigns. They participate in mock elections. They study about and know more about the world than certainly we knew many, many years ago.

What I am really trying to say is this: When we hear about what is wrong with American youth today, we have to also put it in perspective by realizing what is right.

I have said publicly before and I say it before this group today: As I look at the new generation of Americans of which you are, of course, outstanding examples or you would not have been selected for this program, it is the best educated new generation we have had—young generation; but more than that, it is the most involved, involved in the sense of being interested, not only in how you can get out and make a living, which was our primary concern in the 1930's when making a living was necessary in order to just keep going, but involved in the problems of your neighborhoods and the problems of your Nation and the problems of the world.

Finally, it is a generation which knows more about the problems of the world and knows more about the problems of this country than has any generation in history.

What this means is, very simply, that you are a political force, even though you do not yet have the right to vote. You will

soon have it, of course. I say you will soon have it because you will be 21, or you will soon have it if you are from Kentucky because you will vote when you are 18. Of course, at some time there will be a constitutional amendment.

I have noted that this particular organization, among many others, has indicated its support of that kind of a constitutional amendment.

I want to give you the reason why I believe that 18-year-olds should have the right to vote. Not because, as many say, if you are old enough to fight you are old enough to vote. That is one reason, but not the best reason. The reason that 18-year-olds should have the right to vote is that they are smart enough to vote. They know. They are interested and more involved than were the 21-year-olds of only 20 years ago.

This is a tribute to your teachers. It is a tribute to your parents and it is a tribute to you. I wish that particular message to get home to this group as you complete this particular, very exciting experience that you have had.

Now, a bit of advice—that is what you have to learn to take when you come to these sessions—a bit of advice as to what, if I were your age, I would like to do in terms of preparing for whatever you may go into.

Many of you will, I am sure, go into government. Most of you will end up, probably, in some kind of private activity as lawyers or doctors or businessmen or newspaper men and women, or whatever the case might be. But I would urge that whatever you do, as you go to college, don't specialize too much.

This is an age—those years between 18 and 22 or 17 and 21, as the case might

be, or if you go on to graduate school between 17 and 24 and 25—when you will
have every opportunity to specialize in
the law or in medicine or in some other
profession. But this is the time when your
minds are young, when they can, without
any question, understand more, in which
you can learn faster than at any time in
your life. This is the time to get all of the
broadest possible education that you can.

I don't mean by that that the books
you read in disciplines that are not the
ones that are going to be your profession
will be something that you will remember
later on. But by having that experience
now it means that you create a total environmental background that will serve
you in good stead in the years ahead.

The second point I would make is that
one of the great things about being young
is that young people are impatient. You
want to go to the top very fast.

I have found, for example, that the
young lawyers I interviewed in our office
in New York were asking, "When am I
going to be a partner—tomorrow, the next
day—in the firm?" Of course it takes a
little time in a major law firm for that to
happen.

But impatience, of course, is a good
factor as well. What I am suggesting to
you, however, is this: Not everyone in
this room is going to be the president of a
corporation, is going to be a Congressman
or a Senator, is going to be the top leader
in the field that you choose, but everyone
in this room is going to make a contribution in his particular field that is essential
for the success of whoever may be that top
leader.

Frank Borman and his colleagues were

here in this room just a few days ago. He
made a very interesting point. When I
made an award to him, he said, "I accept
this award on behalf of the 400,000 people who, in one way or another, have
contributed to the success of the Apollo
program." Then he went on to say that in
that Apollo spacecraft there were 2 million parts. Now, if any one of those parts
had gone wrong there was the possibility
that the flight might not have succeeded.

What does this tell us? It tells us that
down the line 400,000 people—there were
workmen who will never get into this
great State Dining Room at the White
House, who will never receive the plau-
dits of the crowd that Frank Borman is
receiving today, but they were essential
to the success of that project.

Now, let us always remember that. Let
us remember as we become leaders—as
most of you will become leaders—that it
takes that team and the efforts of everybody doing his very best in whatever his
assignment is to make sure that we do
have the success that we want.

Then one final point, and I perhaps
speak somewhat from experience here, I
am often asked about my philosophy
about winning and losing insofar as life
is concerned generally, and politics, particularly. I am expert in both, incidentally.
The thing I want to emphasize to you is
this: The important thing for a young
person to remember is not whether you
win or lose, but whether you play the
game. Don't stand aside. Don't be up in
the bleachers when you can be down on
the field. Remember that the greatness
of your life is determined by the extent to
which you participate in the great events

of your time. You are participating in the great events of your time.

As you go through life you are going to find that when you do get in and participate you are going to win some and you are going to lose some. But what you will miss, if you do not get in, is something that you can never recover. It is far more important to get into a battle and fight hard for what you believe in and lose than not to fight at all. It is that kind of philosophy I hope you take with you when you go back to your hometowns because it is that kind of spirit that America needs, that you, as young Americans, can bring to not only the young community, but also you can inspire the older ones as well.

Then, one final point, that is, the time in which we live, and I hope you will not consider what I say in this respect as being simply Pollyanna-ish talking, I am really somewhat of a realist—you have to be a realist to hold the position I do when you see the tremendous problems that America has at home and abroad—but I want all of you to know that as I look at the history of the world and as I look at the world in which we live, that if I were to pick a nation in which to live and a time in which to live, I would pick the United States of America in the year 1969.

We have tremendous problems abroad—no question about that—a war in Vietnam and threats of war in other areas. We have tremendous problems at home—the crisis of our cities, environmental and others. But on the other hand, look at it in terms as young people should look at the problems—not in terms of the threat, but in terms of the opportunity. Never has this Nation, any nation, had

more of an opportunity to do something about its problems, the productivity of our farms, of our factories, and the rest. It is all there if we can only bring it together and get it properly distributed. Also, have this in mind: Have in mind the fact that because you were born in the United States of America and because you live in the United States of America, you in this Nation can play a great role in the affairs of the world—a greater role, actually, than any people in any nation of the world. This is not to downgrade any other great people in the world, because greatness does not come simply from the size of a nation and from the accident of where we happen to be born. But it just does happen that because of the great waves of history that at this time and place the decisions made in the United States of America, as far as the free world is concerned, will determine whether peace and freedom survive in the world.

That is the challenge of young America, looking down to the end of this century. It is an exciting challenge, not a burden to be carried and whimpered about, but one to be accepted with all of the excitement that we have when we meet any kind of new experience, any kind of a challenge.

I can only say as I look at this group, as I realize the intelligence that is here, the dedication that you must have to your education and to your Nation, I have a good feeling about the future of this country. I believe in young America because I know young America. I would say that as you go back to your communities, I trust that each of you, whatever you go into, whatever private occupation you happen to decide on, you will reserve a part of

83

your time for some contribution to public service.

We need you. The Nation needs you. With the help of a young, vigorous American generation we can meet the great challenges that America has to meet in this last third of a century.

Thank you.

NOTE: The President spoke at 12 noon in the State Dining Room at the White House.

The Senate Youth Program provides selected public and private school students from each State and the District of Columbia the opportunity to serve a week's internship in the U.S. Senate and in the Federal Government generally. It operates under a grant approved each year by the trustees of the William Randolph Hearst Foundation.

39   Remarks on Major Appointments in the Department of Transportation.   *February 7, 1969*

Ladies and gentlemen:

The purpose of this particular appearance is to present not only the Secretary of Transportation, but also so that he can meet with you and introduce some of the major appointments in that agency.

These appointments I consider to be especially important to the new administration because the field of transportation offers some of our gravest problems and some of our most exciting opportunities.

We have just had a meeting in my office on these problems and I emphasized my concern that the United States look way ahead in transportation—so that looking ahead 10, 15, or 20 years from now we are not all living on freeways—looking ahead and recognizing that the problems that we see in our great cities here are reflected around the world.

I pointed out that I noted that whether you were in Tokyo, in Rome, in Paris or London, let alone the great cities here— New York, Chicago, Los Angeles—the massive problems of traffic jams choking the cities with traffic and choking the people with smog, that looking at this present problem, if we do not plan for the future we are going to reap some terrible consequences.

What is very encouraging to me is that the team that Secretary Volpe has assembled is made up of men who are thinking about these problems and are not here simply to administer the existing programs, administering the highway program and the others in the same fashion that they have been administered. We need some new approaches.

For that reason I have directed the Secretary to prepare a major report on transportation and a policy for the future.

That will not come tomorrow, and it won't come in a week or a month. We hope that within the next 6 months that report will be available so that we can do some advance planning.

In addition, the Secretary will be able to answer some questions today on the SST and other problems in which you may be interested.

I did want to appear with the group because of the importance of the assignments that they will undertake, and I think we have some high-quality men who have a vision about the future and are not simply going to try to administer the programs of the past.

NOTE: The President spoke at 1:12 p.m. in the Fish Room at the White House. Following his remarks Secretary of Transportation John A.

Volpe introduced to reporters the following Presidential appointees to his Department: James M. Beggs as Under Secretary of Transportation, Dr. Paul Cherington as Assistant Secretary of Transportation for Policy and International Affairs, James D'Orma Braman, as Assistant Secretary for Urban Systems and Environment. Secretary Volpe also announced the appointment of Charles D. Baker to be Deputy Under Secretary of Transportation.

As authorized by the President, Secretary Volpe then announced that an ad hoc interdepartmental committee, to be chaired by Under Secretary of Transportation James M. Beggs, would shortly be formed to conduct, in coordination with the Bureau of the Budget, a complete review of the supersonic transport project, and to make recommendations to the President as to the continuation of the program. An announcement, dated February 27, 1969, formally establishing the committee and listing the membership is printed in the Weekly Compilation of Presidential Documents (vol. 5, p. 329). The committee's recommendations were embodied in a report (30 pp., processed), dated April 1, 1969.

40 Remarks to Employees at the Department of Commerce. *February 7, 1969*

Mr. Secretary, ladies and gentlemen:

In my visits to the various departments I have been impressed by a number of the facilities and by lots of the personnel.

The Secretary told me just before we came into this auditorium, "We have the best auditorium in town." I am sure you have.

He also told me that it was filled with the best people in town. That, of course, is something I am sure we shall all look forward to observing in the years ahead.

In coming to this Department, I first want to say something about Secretary Stans. Everybody here knows of my long, personal association with him, when he was Director of the Budget during the Eisenhower administration, and then he was director of the budget, in effect, for me in my political campaigns. He has been, incidentally, a director of the budget when we lost a campaign in California and when we won one in the country— and that is pretty good, 50 percent. We won the big one, in any event.

I, of course, in all of those activities, learned to not only know him but to respect him and to admire him for his immense capability. When we were able to get him to come into the Cabinet in this position, I think the administration acquired one of the top people for this Secretaryship that we have had in many, many years. That is no reflection on those who have had it before.

I might indicate, too, that when we consider the various Cabinet appointments, this is one that through history has always rated very high.

When Herbert Hoover became Secretary of Commerce he was given his choice, I understand, of any department of the Government. He could have served in almost any of them, except Attorney General—he was not a lawyer—because he had great foreign policy experience during World War I and had experience in a number of other areas.

He chose the Department of Commerce because he thought at that time, in the twenties, that this was the Department where more could be done for the progress of the Nation than anywhere else.

It is also significant to note that the last Cabinet officer to go from the Cabinet to the Presidency was Herbert Hoover, so you see what is in store, possibly, for the Secretary here.

But looking at the Department of Commerce today, I want to emphasize this point: We are thinking of it not simply in terms of the past and not in terms of the traditional activities which are assigned to you, but in terms of new responsibilities that will be given to this Department. This is not the time to discuss those responsibilities.

The Secretary, in the months ahead, will indicate them to you, as I will, in various directives. But it seems to me that the times have changed very greatly since this Department was founded in 1913 and even since the time that Mr. Hoover was Secretary of Commerce.

At the present time we are thinking not only of the traditional functions, the functions in the field of business here and our international trade, but we are thinking also in terms of the role that this Department can play and the major problem that every American is concerned with, that of dealing with the crisis in our cities.

I am very delighted to learn that your new Secretary is one who understands those great forces that are at play in our cities, and also in the country for that matter, and one who recognizes the part that this Department can play.

I am glad that he is one who recognizes that when we speak of business—and the Department of Commerce, I suppose, is the department of business in this country more than any other—that when we speak of business, no longer can we think of it simply in terms of just big business.

We, of course, have never really thought of it only in those terms, but even primarily in those terms, this no longer is possible or is it right. What we must recognize is that every American must know

that he has a chance, if he has what it takes, to have a piece of the action.

You will recall during the recent campaign I referred often to the necessity to build bridges to human dignity. By that I meant in providing for all people in our society the chance not only to be workers, but the chance to become a manager, the chance to become an owner. This does not come overnight. We all know that having an opportunity is not just enough. The individual must be qualified. He must have the training. He must have, certainly, a lot of other activities which are related to the whole problem of becoming a successful owner or manager of a business.

But I want the members of this Department to know that, in addition to all the other many line responsibilities that you have and traditional responsibilities, we are going to look for major leadership, major leadership in building bridges to human dignity and providing opportunity for people to move up and to become— if they have what it takes and if this is what they want—to become owners and managers in this great private enterprise system of ours.

I think one thing we are really fortunate about at the present time is that we have been through an era, I think—I think we have been through it—in which it was not fashionable to be what we call "pro-business."

At the present time I would say the great majority of Americans recognize what a significant part that private business enterprise plays in this Nation. I think that all of us recognize, the great majority of Americans certainly do recognize, that as business becomes more effective in meeting its challenges, this means a better life for all of us.

But, at the same time, we must recognize that we have a responsibility, a responsibility which goes beyond simply "business as usual," a responsibility to see to it that in this Nation everybody has that equal chance—the equal chance at the starting line, the incentives, the motivation to go up, and then the opportunities, the opportunities once he does go up, to go to the very top.

I mention this only because in your departments you perhaps may not have specific assignments as yet in this field, but I mention it particularly because the Secretary of Commerce has spoken to me on this point, quite eloquently. This Department will have a major role in this field and I know you will meet that role and meet it effectively.

One other point I wish to make very briefly: In this room are the top executives of this Department. Immediately in front of me in the first two or three rows are the ones that I appointed, the new, I suppose we call them, political appointees, the ones that change with each administration.

I realize that the success of this Department and the success of this administration will depend, in large part, on the leadership of Secretary Stans and the political appointees who are here. But I also know that they will not be able to succeed unless they have the cooperation and the support of the thousands of career people in the Department who, whatever happens in the top echelons of the Department, are here because they have dedicated their lives to Government service.

I want all of you who are in this room to take this message to heart—and will you carry it back to everybody in your office right down to the secretaries and those who bring the mail in and do all of what are considered to be the rather menial and sometimes boring tasks? In this administration we want the support of the career service.

I believe that every individual should be proud that he works for the Government of the United States. The way that we make him proud is to give the kind of leadership that he can respect, leadership that he will work with rather than against.

I feel, as I talk to you, that we are going to have a successful administration, because I know the dedication of the men and women at the top whom I may have appointed.

But I also believe the administration can be successful, because, as I have moved from department to department, I have been really gratified and it has been most heartening to me to shake hands with and meet hundreds of top career employees of the Government and to have them go through that line and to say, "Well, we have a new administration and we are going to give everything that we can in terms of dedication and hard work to see that it is a successful administration."

If this message could get through that as far as the career servants in this Government, we recognize their importance, they have our support and we want theirs, I think it can have an immense effect on the productivity and on the efficiency of every department of Government.

So, with that, I will just close my remarks with one personal reference. I am proud of all of the members of my Cabinet. I am particularly proud of your Secretary for reasons that I have mentioned, because of our close political association.

Also, I should make mention of one fact for which he, I think, will be famous the rest of his life, and certainly the rest of mine. I always thought that the medium of television was very powerful. I never knew how powerful it was, however, until the name Maurice Stans became a household name because I did not mention him on television.

NOTE: The President spoke at 2:23 p.m. in the Department of Commerce auditorium.

41 Remarks Following a Meeting With the Director of the National Association for the Advancement of Colored People. *February 7, 1969*

Ladies and gentlemen:

This is the first opportunity that I have had since the inauguration to meet with Roy Wilkins, the head of the NAACP.

During the years I was Vice President, and as a Congressman and a Senator, we came to know each other well.

I was remarking that the last time we met and had a chance to talk was in a long plane ride all the way back from Paris to the United States. He had been on a lecture tour, and I had been on a trip abroad involving private business and some conversations with foreign officials.

Mr. Wilkins, of course, will answer your questions with regard to the administration and the conversation we had.

I simply want to say that this is one of a series of meetings that I am trying to have with leaders of the Negro community, as well as representatives of other groups in this country.

I have found through the years that with Roy Wilkins it is possible to have a very direct and candid discussion. We don't always agree, but he gives excellent advice—advice which many times we follow. This is only the first of a series of meetings, and since it was the first I wanted to present him personally to the members of the press, all of whom I am sure know him.

Roy, the floor is yours.

NOTE: The President spoke at 3:55 p.m. in the Fish Room at the White House, after which Mr. Wilkins responded to reporters' questions.

42 Memorandum to the Director, Bureau of the Budget, on the Need for Prompt Release of Statistical Data by Federal Agencies. *February 8, 1969*

Memorandum to Director, Bureau of the Budget:

Although the compilation of statistics by Federal agencies has been conducted on a highly professional basis, that has not always been the case with the release of the figures to the public. In some instances data have been released only after unnecessarily long delay or at irregular intervals. This practice must stop. The prompt release on a regular schedule of official statistics is a matter of vital importance to the proper management of both private and public affairs.

Please direct the departments and agencies of the Executive Branch of the government to review within the next 30 days the publication schedules of all principal weekly, monthly and quarterly statistical series with a view to

(A) reducing to the shortest practicable time the interval between the date to which the figures refer and the date when compilation is completed, and

(B) ensuring that the basic figures are released promptly to the public.

I recognize that some time must be allowed to prepare, review, and reproduce statistical tables, press releases, etc. One or two days for this should be sufficient. The schedules should therefore allow no more than two working days between the time when compilation of the basic figures has been completed and when they are released to the public. In certain special situations, exceptions to this requirement may be necessary, but they must receive prior approval of the Bureau's Office of Statistical Standards. As a rule, new figures should be released through the statistical officer in charge.

Please arrange for the preparation by each statistical agency of a publicly available schedule of future release dates for periodic statistical series covering at least a three-month period ahead.

Each agency should be requested to submit to the Bureau by March 15, 1969, the steps it has taken to assure compliance with your directive.

RICHARD NIXON

NOTE: The memorandum was released at Key Biscayne, Fla. The White House also issued an announcement of the memorandum which appears in the Weekly Compilation of Presidential Documents (vol. 5, p. 249).

43 Letter to the Chairman, Civil Aeronautics Board, on the Transpacific Route Investigation. *February* 11, 1969

Dear Mr. Chairman:

I have received the letter of the Acting Chairman of February 7, transmitting a proposed stay order in the international phase of the *Transpacific Route Investigation,* Docket 16242. I have concluded that the proposed order would be inappropriate, and I therefore decline to approve it.

In accordance with my letter of January 24, 1969, in the *Transpacific Route Investigation* (your Docket 16242 et al.) which rescinded the prior Presidential action and recalled the matter for my further review, please submit for my approval a Board order vacating the Board's order of December 18, 1968, in this case (No. 68–12–105) and the certificates attached thereto.

Sincerely,

RICHARD NIXON

[Honorable John H. Crooker, Jr., Chairman, Civil Aeronautics Board, Washington, D.C. 20428]

NOTE: A memorandum, dated February 10, 1969, from Robert Ellsworth, Assistant to the President, to interested parties in the transpacific air route investigation is printed in the Weekly Compilation of Presidential Documents (vol. 5, p. 250).

An announcement, dated February 14, 1969, that the President had received and approved a Civil Aeronautics Board order vacating previous orders and certificates in the international phase of the transpacific air route investigation, is printed in the Weekly Compilation of Presidential Documents (vol. 5, p. 260).

44 Remarks to Employees at the Department of Transportation. *February* 11, 1969

Mr. Secretary, ladies and gentlemen:

I first want to say that I am delighted to have the opportunity to speak to the key members of this newest Department, and also to tell you, first, that I have great confidence in the new Secretary.

I know him better than most of you do. I know him as a man with great drive, great imagination, a man who will be looking for the new ideas that must come from this Department if it is to meet its mission.

I am sure that in terms of where that running headstart is concerned, that as far as John Volpe, looking at his record is involved, you don't have to worry—he is always going to be running. You just have to run to keep up with him. That, of course, in the Department of Transportation is an essential.

In speaking to you I certainly would not want to impose on your time by trying to describe the mission of this Department adequately. I have had a chance to look at the organization charts in the office of the Secretary. I know the various interests that are represented here, the various departments that have been pulled together in this newest Department of the Government.

But I think speaking from my vantage point, the vantage point of one who sees the problems of the people as a whole, I can very properly bring home to you the immense interest that the people of this country generally have in what you are doing.

I think sometimes in Government we have a tendency to become involved in our problems. The work can get tiring and sometimes seem not too rewarding. We don't get the publicity in some departments that we think we should have and perhaps sometimes we feel that it might not be worth it.

I can assure you from my own experience, if there is one subject that people across this country—regardless of what station in life they come from—one subject they are interested in, it is transportation and all of its aspects.

I recall when that was brought home to me very forcibly very early in the primary campaigns in one of the States I visited last year. I had a question and answer session afterwards. It happened to be in a particular city where there had been some problems with regard to transportation, people not getting into town—the railway had not been running on time, and that sort of thing.

After I had made my opening remarks, I asked for questions and I expected the questions to be on such subjects as Vietnam, the gold flow, and all that sort of thing. The first question right out of the bag was, "What are you going to promise to those of us who don't get to work on time because of the transportation problem?"

In other words, across this country, whether it is the clogged up freeways that we have out in my home State of California, the Long Island Rail Road not running on time to get the commuters into New York City, whether it is the air traffic congestion which many of us experienced last summer during the slowdown, or whether it is the future in terms of what our failure to handle some of our transportation problems with more foresight will mean to us, the American people today are looking to this new Department for some new ideas and for some planning which will make our cities in which most of us will be living—even more of us will be living than at the present time—will make our cities more livable or livable when they may not be at this time or in the future.

So, as you address yourself to your problems—whatever the department may be—I cannot emphasize more the importance of what you do, whether it is in terms of the highway program and its future, whether it is in terms of the development of our railroads, modernizing them not only in terms of freight but also perhaps even passenger capacity, whether it is in terms of rapid transit that affects all of our great urban centers, or whether it is in terms of the exciting new dimensions of air in which over the last 5 years we have seen the number of passengers who fly in a year go from 70 million to 126 million. In the next 5 years it will go from 126 million to 270 million.

In the last 5 years air freight has doubled. In the next 5 years it may double or even triple again. This is only a small indication and always we have found that our estimates have been too low with regard to the breakthroughs in air transportation. That is a small indication of the problem of the future.

As you know, because I knew that he had broad shoulders and liked difficult problems, we have asked the Secretary and, through the Secretary, this Department to give us a recommendation on the SST. This is only one indication of the vital importance of the areas to which you are devoted.

Incidentally, I want to make it very

clear that having referred to railroads and having referred to air transportation and having referred to automobiles, I don't overlook the fact that you have jurisdiction also over a considerable part of our ocean traffic, although the Department of Commerce would argue about some of that in the Maritime Administration.

But what we want from the Secretary and what the Secretary and his top advisers who sit down here in these front rows have indicated that they are going to provide is a new transportation policy which will look forward to what this country is going to be like 10 years from now and 20 years from now. And then rather than just letting it grow like Topsy and having our cities clogged and our airlanes so filled that it is no longer safe to travel by air, or if it is safe, we are delayed too much in getting there because of the traffic, whatever the problem may be, trying to find new answers, better answers for this vital area of transportation.

Because, as we look at the environment that Americans are going to be living in, I think transportation plays as vital a role as any other single entity can play. I am aware of this. I know that you are more aware of it than I am.

What I wanted to bring to this group of the top leaders in this Department is the sense of urgency that I feel and that I believe the American people feel with regard to what you are doing.

Now, one other point that I want to make is something that I tried to say at each one of the departments and that I want to emphasize it here, too. In this room are the leaders. As far as the leaders are concerned, only very few of them have been appointed by the new administration.

I realize that throughout this room the

great majority are people who have given their lives to Government service. They are what are called the career civil servants of the Federal Government. I know that as far as the success of this Department is concerned, it is going to depend upon the kind of leadership that you get from the Secretary, from the Assistant Secretaries, and from the Under Secretaries that have been appointed by this administration.

But I know that no matter how imaginative they are, how creative they are, how bold they are in their thinking, however many new ideas they get, that they cannot succeed without the support, and the enthusiastic support, of the top career leaders who sit behind them in the rows all down here.

Having said that to you, I know that you cannot succeed in carrying out this mission unless you have the support and also the enthusiastic dedication of thousands and tens of thousands of career people that I saw in the halls, the secretaries, the people in the lower grade classifications who are trying to move up in Government and who have given their lives to Government, as you have given yours to Government.

I feel that we need throughout our Federal Government service a new sense of not only dedication to our jobs, but also I think from the very top, let's let every person working with us know that he matters and what he or she does is contributing to not only the better running of this Department, but also to a better Nation for all of us.

I think the best example that I have found and I have used it before, but I think it is worth repeating here because it is in one element of transportation in a sense—the whole area of space. It was

when our astronauts came into my office recently and I was, of course, saying the usual things which we say to them for their amazing exploits.

The response was that they actually could not have done what they had done except for 400,000 people who worked in the Apollo program in one way or another, and also pointing out the fact that 2 million parts were in that Apollo spacecraft—2 million parts.

So what do we see? At the top we see three astronauts going on the exciting voyage around the moon. Then we see 400,000 people, people that most of them, none of them, will ever meet and none of us will have the chance to thank, working on this intricate little part or the other. But the success of the flight is going to depend upon every one of those parts.

I think if there is some way we could get across to all of the people in Government that however boring their job may seem to be, the writing of letters, for example, and getting out forms or running the mimeograph machine or I guess now you do it through a duplicating machine, or whatever the case might be, that all of this matters.

I think if we can have that sense of a new dedication and pride in being an employee of this great Government of ours—the Federal Government—I think if we can instill that, it is going to mean more efficiency, more productivity, and certainly it is going to mean—at the end of whatever our term of office may be— for you or for us, it is going to be a sense of realization that we otherwise would not have had.

I just want to say in conclusion that I spent, as most of you know, a great number of my adult years in the service of the Federal Government. When I was not in the service of the Federal Government it was usually not my own choice. But having been in the service of the Federal Government in the United States Navy for 3½ years, for almost a year and a half in the Office of Price Administration before I went into the Navy, then for 4 years in the House, 2 years in the Senate, and 8 years as Vice President, I always had a sense of pride about it, a sense of pride that I had that opportunity.

I know you will feel that way and particularly those of you who have given your lives to Government service. That is why I am visiting every one of these departments, because I want the top leaders in the department to carry back to the people who work with you and for you and for us the message that everything they do does count, that in this administration we appreciate what they are doing. We are going to support them and we will appreciate their support as well.

Thank you.

NOTE: The President spoke at 2:33 p.m. in the auditorium at the Department of Transportation.

45   Statement on Coastal Oil Pollution at Santa Barbara, California. *February* 11, 1969

THIS MORNING Secretary Hickel and I met and discussed the pollution of the California coastline in the wake of the Santa Barbara tragedy. Our conversation ranged beyond the current situation. It included discussion of how to prevent such occurrences in the future.

Acting at his recommendation, I have today directed the President's Science Adviser, Dr. DuBridge, to bring together at the earliest possible time a panel of scientists and engineers. They will recommend to me ways and means in which the Federal Government can best and most rapidly assist in restoring the beaches and waters around Santa Barbara. They will also submit their views as to how best to prevent this kind of sudden and massive oil pollution.

The obligation to develop our natural resources carries with it the duty to protect our human resources. This country can no longer afford to squander valuable time before developing answers to pollution and oil slicks from wells, tankers, or any other source. Every method in existing technology must be developed to control and remove oil pollution. We must also identify those avenues of research where resources will be most profitably committed in solving this problem. These considerations will be among the issues taken up by the group which Dr. DuBridge will assemble.

Secondly, Secretary Hickel has recommended, and I have endorsed completely, a full-scale review within his department with regard to existing regulations covering such drilling.

His own preliminary review has disclosed there were substantial disagreements in his department as to the adequacy of the existing regulations at the time they were prepared. Questions were also raised as to the wisdom of the original decision to allow drilling to begin off Santa Barbara.

In retrospect those reservations were

right and will be taken into account in the full-scale review the Secretary has initiated.

Its ultimate purpose will be twofold:

To determine the adequacy of existing regulations for all wells licensed in past years now operating off the coast of the United States.

Secondly, to produce far more stringent and effective regulations that will give us better assurance than the Nation now has that crises of this kind will not recur.

The findings of Dr. DuBridge's panel will be made available to Secretary Hickel for inclusion in his review.

NOTE: A White House press release, dated February 13, 1969, announcing the appointment by Dr. Lee A. DuBridge, Science Adviser to the President, of a 14-member panel to study oil spillage problems is printed in the Weekly Compilation of Presidential Documents (vol. 5, p. 257).

The pollution at Santa Barbara was the result of an oil blowout at an off-shore drilling site on January 28, 1969, which created an oil slick covering an area of more than 50 miles.

46   Remarks at the Swearing In of Walter E. Washington as Mayor of the District of Columbia. *February 13, 1969*

Mr. Justice Marshall, ladies and gentlemen:

We are here today for the swearing in of Mayor Washington. I would like to have him step forward and Mrs. Washington step forward with him.

[At this point Thurgood Marshall, Associate Justice of the Supreme Court of the United States, administered the oath of office. The President then resumed speaking.]

Mayor Washington, I congratulate you and I want to make one point that perhaps had not occurred to many people in this room. I am a resident of the city of Washington, and while all over the United States it would probably be recognized that the President is the top citizen, in this city, the Mayor is the top citizen. I am a resident of your city.

At this time, too, I would like to present to this distinguished gathering the three men whose names will be sent to the Sen-ate for confirmation, I trust, as members of the City Council: Gilbert Hahn, as Chairman of the City Council; Sterling Tucker as Vice Chairman; and the Reverend Jerry Moore.

Now, in presenting these three members of the City Council, or members-to-be—we cannot have them sworn in at this time, Mr. Justice, because the Senate would not appreciate my moving before they gave their consent, but I do think it would be appropriate in the presence of the Mayor and the members of the Council to make just a few remarks with regard to the immense importance of the assignments they will be undertaking in the years ahead.

Every day when we pick up our papers or listen to the television and radio, we hear about the crisis of American cities. We would be less than honest if we were not to admit that our cities are in crisis for a variety of reasons that we don't need to go into now.

As we look at the cities and their crises, I can tell you from the brief experience I have already had in the Office of the Presidency that the eyes of the Nation are turned to Washington, first to the Federal Government, and the question that we often—week after week and hour after hour—struggle with in the Executive Office of the President is, "What kind of a Federal program can we develop to handle the problems of the cities?"

I want to make it very clear that the Federal Government will meet its responsibility to assist our cities. The Federal Government will do everything that is appropriate, everything that is possible to help the people of the cities and the governments of the cities meet this crisis.

But also I should emphasize that all of our studies to date and the studies of the previous administrations have led to this conclusion: that the Federal Government could do everything, and unless we have strong local government and unless we have strong home rule, unless we have the support of the people of the cities, it will be nothing—nothing in terms of progress.

That is why, as we look at the city of Washington, while the Federal Government has a greater responsibility here than toward any other city, that here, too, we must recognize that without a strong local government, without real home rule, and without the support of the citizens, the people of Washington, the Federal activities will come to naught.

That is why I am so very happy this morning that we have a strong team, headed by the Mayor and with the members of the City Council and the others who will be in the city organization.

As we move toward home rule in the District of Columbia, the stronger self-government, the stronger home rule we have here, the more progress we can make together toward solving the problems of this city.

As one who has lived in Washington during my adult life, perhaps more than in any other city in the country, I am proud of this city, as is every American who has ever visited here. It is a beautiful city. I think everyone here wants this city to be the model city for all America and a model city for the world.

That is our objective, and with this kind of leadership within the city in the area of home rule and with the assistance that we are going to continue to give on a greater scale than has been in the past at the Federal level, we think we can achieve the goal of making Washington, D.C., a model city for America and the world.

I think we would like to hear from the Mayor. You can speak for your colleagues because they are not confirmed yet and you are.

NOTE: The President spoke at 9:47 a.m. in the East Room at the White House. Following the President's remarks, Mayor Walter E. Washington spoke. His remarks are printed in the Weekly Compilation of Presidential Documents (vol. 5, p. 256).

The three nominees to the Council, introduced by the President, were sworn in on March 13, 1969.

47   Statement on Signing Executive Order Establishing the Office of Intergovernmental Relations.   *February* 14, 1969

TODAY by Executive order I have created a new office, the Office of Intergovernmental Relations, to operate under the immediate supervision of the Vice President. This order provides a center through which one of the most important objectives of this administration can be carried out: the strengthening of Federal, State, and local relations.

By this action the Vice President will become more directly and vitally involved in our effort to move government closer to the people and to make it more responsive to their will.

Specifically, I have asked that, in addition to his other duties, the Vice President undertake responsibility for helping to administer the domestic functions of government in several critical areas.

He is to act as my liaison with the executive and legislative officials of State and local government.

He will encourage the development of maximum cooperation among the various Federal agencies and their State and local counterparts.

He is to help make the Federal executive branch more sensitive and receptive to the views of State and local officials and to serve as the focal point where specific difficulties may be resolved.

He is to work closely with and is to encourage the Advisory Commission on Intergovernmental Relations in its activities.

He is to inform the Council for Urban Affairs regarding general intergovernmental issues so that the Council may readily advise and assist me.

The Office of Intergovernmental Rela-

tions has been established to assist and advise the Vice President in carrying out these important responsibilities. It will aid the Vice President in his liaison responsibility between myself and the State and local officials.

Among its many functions, the Office will assure State and local officials access to the highest offices of the Federal Government, especially those having a direct impact on intergovernmental relations, so that Federal programs, policies, and goals will be more responsive to their views and needs. It will seek to strengthen existing channels of communication and to create new channels among all levels of government.

While aiding in the formulation of proposals to develop a broad and relevant dispersal of authority, the Office will be helping to create many centers of power in the place of one. Thus it will help to establish more decisionmaking authority at the Federal regional offices and will facilitate an orderly transfer of appropriate functions to State and local government.

Under the supervision of the Vice President, the Office of Intergovernmental Relations will have as its overriding objective the bringing together of Federal, State, and local government in order to provide a more balanced system of government.

NOTE: Following the President's signing of Executive Order 11455, Vice President Spiro T. Agnew, in a news briefing released by the White House Press Office, announced the appointment of Nils A. Boe, former Governor of South Dakota, as Director of the Office of Intergovernmental Relations.

A list of officials who attended the signing ceremony in the Cabinet Room at the White House is printed in the Weekly Compilation of Presidential Documents (vol. 5, p. 258).

48   Remarks to Employees at the Department of Health, Education, and Welfare. *February* 14, 1969

Mr. Secretary, ladies and gentlemen:

I am delighted to have the opportunity to come to this Department and to meet the top leaders of the Department, as I have been meeting leaders of the other major departments of Government.

As I stand here, I think back to the time when this Department was born. It is, now, of course, not the newest. As a matter of fact, two others have come into being since it came in.

But I remember at that time when it was set up, so many—it seemed many years ago, and it wasn't many years ago— the real question was whether this new Department, in which were collected what seemed to be the diverse functions of health, education, and welfare, whether it could develop a sense of identity, of unity, of purpose and mission or whether it was simply going to be a conglomerate in the corporate sense.

And I have been very delighted to learn in the few weeks that we have been here that this Department has through the years and is now moving forward with the sense of mission, and unity, and purpose, recognizing what all of us know—that your three great objectives of health, education, and welfare are so interrelated and so important.

I wanted to come here to express my own commitment to your mission. And I wanted to come here, too, to express my confidence in your leadership.

All of you, of course, are aware of my close association with the new Secretary.

I have been reminded on many occasions that he is the youngest of the Cabinet team. As a matter of fact, when I introduced him on television, I found that I added a year to his age. I believe that many years have been added to his age already from being here.

The only thing that I want to say is that in referring to him as the youngest member of our Cabinet team, I don't want him to take it too much to heart in condemning or at least downgrading those who may be a bit older.

I noted that he spoke rather, it seemed to me, in a critical way of the fact that the average age of those in the Office of Education was 58 years. That is only 2 years older than I am. While youth must be served, let's have some place for others of us.

And I would remind you, too, that with all of the Secretary's vibrance and youth and, yes, crewcut and everything else, that this is his 23d wedding anniversary. So he has a little mileage, too.

This is not the occasion to discuss in any detail the subjects in which you are so deeply immersed. I have sent a number of directives to various departments.[1] More have come to HEW than to any other because you have so many functions that are directly related to the problems that we face in the United States today, particularly on the homefront and also, because you are dealing with problems in

---

[1] See Appendix C.

which the jury is still out as to what the best approach is. Very reasonable people, honestly and sincerely motivated about the problems of health, education, and welfare, I have found, reached diametrically different conclusions, and not only will there be two positions but three or four in instance after instance.

That is one of the reasons why in this Department, I would say as much or more than in any department of Government, I expect and will welcome a difference of opinion on these various subjects. We will have to make decisions at the highest levels. We hope they will be the best decisions. But they will be better due to the fact that we did have dissent, due to the fact that we did have a sharp disagreement, as you will have and have had and will continue to have in the years ahead, in how we approach these various problems.

I had a meeting yesterday with a group of college educators and university educators. They happen to be members of the National Science Foundation.

But one of the subjects that came up which directly relates to your field was the new research that can be done in our colleges and universities on a basis that has not adequately been tried out before and the desire on their part that in the allocation of National Science Foundation funds, that an attempt be made to see that this new approach is given an adequate chance for trial.

I am referring to something which all the educators in this room will immediately understand and will know more about it in their sophisticated way than I will—and that is that where a number of disciplines dealing with a particular general subject are brought together in, say, one unit or one college, call it what you

will, to attack a certain problem.

And this is an indication of the kind of exciting new approaches that we can have in the field of education and that have broad ramifications in handling the problems of health and the problems of welfare.

A particular point that was raised during the course of that meeting was the problem with regard to the development of the child, and particularly in the development of the child between the years of 1 to 5.

Research, much of which has only become publicly discussed at any maximum level in the last 5 to 10 years, indicates that what happens to the child from a nutritional standpoint, from an educational standpoint, from an environmental standpoint, in the years between 1 and 5 may affect that child for the balance of his life regardless of what may happen after that time.

Now we have many approaches to that problem as we know in the Office of Economic Opportunity—the Head Start program. I was rather surprised to note that even on that program, one which has bipartisan support in the Congress, one which I have always supported, which the Secretary supports, and we will continue to support enthusiastically, that even as far as that program is concerned we still are not sure that it is the most effective way to deal with this problem.

We know there is a problem. We know we need to get at it. And yet it does indicate that there are no simple answers to these problems in which we have not yet had the adequate research, the adequate trial and error which inevitably we must go through in order to develop a program.

I use this only as an example to demonstrate to the people in this room that in the fields in which you are operating, I recognize there are no simple answers. I recognize that as we look at the programs of the past we don't throw all of them out because some of them haven't worked, and as we look at what we do in the future we don't take some simple, new, exciting program, or exciting and bold, which offers an immediate answer.

I realize that what we need here is that kind of creative, new thought that can only come from a clash of ideas, from discussion, from experiment.

We want that from this Department. That is the only way we are going to get the programs which we will then fund, which will provide for progress in these fields that all of us so very desperately want.

I would like to add, too, that in that connection I have been very much impressed by the work that has been done in this Department under Dr. Robert Choate in the field of nutrition.

I am reminded of the fact that in this country you have to go back only 6 months to find that there was a time when most people assumed that the nutrition problem was not a significant one in the United States. We could see poverty in India, or Bolivia, or Haiti—and I have seen it in all of those countries and many others around the world—but many were not aware of the problem of hunger and poverty, and particularly hunger and malnutrition, in the United States.

And then came along not, incidentally, a Government report, but a CBS television report on the problem of hunger. I referred to this at the Department of Agriculture the other day, and all of you are aware of it. And now the whole Nation is concerned about it.

What we have to do now is to find what the answer is, why these problems of nutrition are ones that have not been adequately dealt with, and what new approaches are needed. Because what we recognize here is that we have the ironical situation where our problem is not the supply, but the distribution; where we can provide all of the nutritional needs for all of the people in this country, and far more, from what we can produce in this country.

And so it gets down to education, it gets down to health, it gets down to diet, and many other things.

So impressive was this report, incidentally, that I have asked that the Secretary send it to the Governors of all the 50 States so it can be one of the subjects for discussion at the Governors' Conference when they are here within the next few weeks.

I will not go further into the various missions of this Department with which you are so deeply involved. I have talked to these two points only to demonstrate that as we consider, as we must, some of the very grave international problems that confront this Nation, that there is no question about our, in the administration at the highest level, putting additional emphasis, not less emphasis, on the problems at home. Because as we solve these problems at home, we are going to be better able to meet the various problems that we have abroad now and may have abroad in the future.

And as we solve them at home we are going to be better able to provide an example, an example which we would hope we could provide for other nations who have similar problems and who will look to us for an example provided we have the quality to provide that kind of leadership.

Finally, one other point that I make at every one of these department visits and which I know will be taken very much to heart by the leaders in this room: I realize that I have appointed very few of the people in this huge Department of 108,000 Government employees.

I have appointed the Secretary and I understand the people in this first row, right across there—maybe not all of them but most of them. As far as the success of the mission of this Department is concerned, it will depend on the quality of the leadership of the Secretary and of the Under Secretary and the Assistant Secretaries and others that will be appointed by the new administration. Without their leadership, the Department will not be able to succeed in its mission as it should.

But the other side of that coin is that they can have leadership, they can have ideas, they can have imagination, they can make the most glowing speeches about what they are going to do, and unless they are backed up by the brains, the ability, and the dedication of the thousands of civil service employees, people who have dedicated their entire lives to Government service, they aren't going to be able to succeed, we aren't going to be able to succeed.

So I simply want all of you in this room to know, those of you who have given your lives to the career civil service, who have given your lives to Government service, that I appreciate what you have done.

I know that many of you in terms of financial income perhaps could have done better had you moved into other fields. I know that you are here because you believe in what you are doing. We need that sense of belief and that sense of dedication. We need your help.

I want you to know that as you provide your help to the new administration, as you back us up, we are going to back

you up. I think this is a message that needs to get across. And I want to go further.

As I walked through the halls a moment ago, I was able to shake hands only briefly with hundreds of the employees down the line, employees that the Secretary, in a Department of 108,000, will probably never meet during the course of his service here.

I want you to let them know that we recognize that the success of any great Department like this depends not just on a few leaders at the top, but it depends also on the dedication and the sense of mission of every individual up and down the line.

I know this sounds like the usual kind of talk you are supposed to make at a pep meeting for Government employees or, if you are in business, to a group of business employees. But I believe it. I am sure you believe it.

And I think I can perhaps demonstrate it best by indicating to you that I recall many years ago when I had a little stint as a Government employee. I was then quite young, I will have to admit. It was just before World War II or at the beginning of World War II when I spent about a year in the Office of Price Administration in the rationing division as a P–3, a Government lawyer, attempting to work on tire rationing regulations.

Now, I can assure you that a P–3—I don't know whether you still have that classification in Government or not— but a P–3 lawyer in OPA in 1942 was a pretty low form of life. I can assure you, too, that the mission that I had, which was to develop the form letters and to write to the thousands of people that were writing to the President of the United States—and, of course, they all write to the President—to tell them why we could not give them an exception as far as their tire rationing requests were concerned. That mission at many times seemed very boring.

It certainly seemed very boring to me and I am sure to my secretary. And I can assure you that as I worked, as many of you work, long hours during the day and on Saturdays and Sundays, there were times that I really wondered if what I was doing really meant anything. Looking back, I realize that it did.

What I am really trying to say is this: that as not just a lawyer, a secretary, a stenographer, or whatever the case might be, our job at the top can only be done if we let it be known to people up and down the line that we know they are there, that

we know why they are there, that we appreciate what they are doing, because we have to remember that whatever they are doing at any time to them is the most important thing in their life.

I believe this from personal experience. You know it from personal experience. And if we can have that kind of a spirit in this great and vital and important Department, if we can have that kind of a spirit, I am sure that you are going forward to not only meet your mission, but to serve this Nation most effectively.

Thank you.

NOTE: The President spoke at 2:25 p.m. in the auditorium at the Department of Health, Education, and Welfare.

49   Remarks to Top Personnel at the Department of the Treasury.   *February* 14, 1969

THE PRESIDENT. Secretary Kennedy just told me that this was historic. He doesn't think a President has ever been in here like this before. I think Presidents have been here before to get their checks, though. [*Turning to Secretary Kennedy.*] You send them over, don't you?

SECRETARY KENNEDY. We'll send them over. [*Laughter*]

THE PRESIDENT. I am delighted to have the opportunity to come here in this way. As a matter of fact, as I look around the room I see many of you that I have met on previous occasions.

Not only Presidents, but even Vice Presidents, you will find, have occasions to come to talk to the Secretary of the Treasury and the Under Secretary, because when you consider this Department and what really makes it distinctive is

that it really serves the whole Government.

I have just come from HEW. Next week I will be in Interior. And of course I have been to Defense, Agriculture, and many other departments. All of them have a special mission and special assignment vitally important to the success of any administration.

But without leadership at the Treasury, nothing else is going to work. I know that. You know that.

I think that is one of the reasons why there has always been a special spirit in the Treasury. I would say this whether this happened to be the administration which I presently head or a previous administration or the next one—a special spirit. Because here in the Treasury the policies have to be developed not just short-range but long-range; long-range for the financial stability of this country, long-range for purposes of trying to maintain the incentives through our tax system and other systems which will keep the country growing, and also long-range, as we all know, in more recent years in terms of the international position of the United States.

I found, for example, that as I prepare for a trip to Europe that I am going to be taking beginning next week, a week from Sunday, that high on the list of papers that I will have to read will be a paper from the Treasury Department on such subjects as balance of payments and controls and the like.

As far as that is concerned, that perhaps has always been a problem that a President would have in taking a trip abroad, but simply looking back only a period of 8 to 10 years, the problem is far more significant today than it was then.

I give you this background only because I want you to know that as one who is your closest neighbor—and the Treasury happens to be the closest neighbor of all the departments, the closest to the White House—that I am aware of the vital importance of your work. I appreciate that importance. I appreciate that that work must be completely beyond any partisan considerations.

I appreciate the fact that that work must have a sense of continuity that perhaps is more apparent here and more needed here than in any other department of Government. I think that sense of continuity is demonstrated by the fact that the three top men that I, as the new President, have appointed, the Secretary of the Treasury and the two Under Secre-taries, all have had service in the Department of the Treasury at one time or another. And this is as it should be.

It is in that spirit that I want to work with this Department, with the Secretary, and the other officials of the Department.

The other point that I would like to make is with regard to some of the immediate missions that you have ahead. I know that many department officials, Cabinet officers, have been somewhat concerned by the number of directives [1] they have been receiving from the White House with dates on them as to "Have this back within a week to 2 weeks." I see a few smiles in the room and I know that many weekends have been spent trying to get those directives adhered to in order to meet the dates that we have set.

The purpose, of course, is to provide for the new administration the well thought-out programs that we can present to the Congress. For that reason, we will appreciate your cooperation and we will appreciate and we thank you for all that midnight oil and those extra hours without doubletime pay that you are going to put in. At least at this level you don't get any doubletime pay, I am sure of that.

But I think, too, that as we look at the Treasury Department, and having spoken of this sense of continuity, perhaps at no time in the history of the country has this Department faced a period when there is a greater need for and a greater prospect for new initiatives and for new approaches in several fields.

I am going to speak very carefully now,

---

[1] See Appendix C.

because I realize that when a Secretary of the Treasury, let alone a President of the United States, says something about tax programs or international monetary matters that it can have the effect of changing the price of gold or, for that matter, changing the price of stocks, and so forth and so on.

What I am suggesting here now is that there will be, that the time comes— these things run in great cycles—the time has come in the history of this country when we must reexamine our whole tax policy. There will be significant recommendations made by the new administration, based on the advice we get from this Department, with regard to tax reform this year. There will be significant recommendations from a longer range standpoint made at a later time. This is the time when the events call for change in this field.

It doesn't mean that in advocating change that we are throwing out all of the approaches of the past. But it does mean that a tax system which has to a certain extent grown like Topsy, and not because this Department was responsible for those decisions, but it has grown like Topsy by necessity. It now needs reevaluation.

I have told the Secretary of the Treasury, and I have been very delighted to learn that he and his top associates share this view, that I want them to think in completely new terms with regard to our tax system. That doesn't mean that we don't retain many of the procedures, many of the approaches of the past. But it does mean that the Congress now, I think, is receptive to significant change.

And what we must do, rather than to be controlled by change, is to help direct the change and the people in this room, those

particularly that have responsibility in the tax field. From the wealth of your experience and your background can come the advice that will see to it that in making changes we do not destroy what is good about what we presently have. That, of course, is the great secret of Government, to have change without destruction. It is, of course, the secret of life.

Another point that I would like to make is that in the international field it is no secret—I pick up the paper every week on a Sunday and read the Sunday review on the financial pages. I don't read it every day. Reading it on Sunday is bad enough. But in any event, I read the reviews.

As I was saying to the Secretary the other day when we were meeting in the National Security Council meeting on preparing our trip to Europe, there are indications that the problems affecting the international monetary system are very possibly going to be a subject not only of major discussion on this immediate trip but also they are going to be a subject of major concern in this next year and perhaps within the next 2 years.

Now is the time to examine our international monetary system to see where its strengths are, where its weaknesses are and then to provide the leadership, leadership which is responsible, not dictatorial, leadership which looks to the good judgment and the good advice that we can get from our friends abroad who will have a similar view about the necessity for a sound international monetary system.

But here in this very old Department with all of its great sense of continuity, a department which usually is thought of as the Department which says, "No, you can't do that because we don't have the money"—I mean you in the Budget

Bureau. But it is somewhat the same, as you know—that here in this Department, I see you here at a time that is very exciting, very exciting, because whether it is in the field of tax reform, whether it is in the field of international monetary policies, there is a need for new approaches.

I want you to know that I look forward to working with you, working of course with the Secretary, and the top people of this Department in attempting to develop those new approaches, approaches that will serve this Nation and in a broader sense will serve the whole world.

Now having said these things, I want to make one thing very clear at the conclusion of my remarks: that I realize that among the people that I have appointed in this Department, very few actually represent the new administration.

Most of the people here have—in this room even you who are the top people in the Department—have served through administration after administration. You have given your lives to Government service.

I am deeply grateful for that. I just want all of those who have not been appointed by the new President upon the recommendation of the Secretary, those who have dedicated their lives to Government service, to know that as I stand here I look back on my own years in Government.

I am proud to have been in Government service in much of my adult life and I appreciate the fact that many have given their whole lives to that. And I wish you would convey that same sense right down the line.

As I walked through the halls here, I was really very touched by the fact that there were hundreds and hundreds of stenographers and others, I suppose secretaries and people that do filing or write form letters, all of the boring, some might call menial tasks, but I don't need to tell you as executives how vital they are to our success.

And sometimes I think we don't convey to them enough our own real appreciation for what they do. Every one of them not only matters, but without their doing a good job, the quality that we do at the top will not be what it should be.

I wish that you could convey as you go back to your offices up and down the line that the new President of the United States has worked at various levels of Government.

I was once a P–3 when they had that. Some of you will remember when they called it that. A P–3 lawyer in the OPA in 1942 was a very low form of life, I can assure you.

I remember then the task that I had of preparing form letters and also preparing congressional mail to be signed by the President of the United States on tire rationing.

It seemed to me to be a very boring job at times. But I do know that what made it mean something was that to me and to all of us who worked under very difficult circumstances in old Tempo-D down on Independence Avenue, since torn down—it should have been torn down even then, but it has been since torn down—what really made it mean something to us was that we felt that we were part of a bigger cause, that by what we did we were helping to make possible success at a very high level of programs that were vital to this country.

If we can just get the people in this Government—I am not referring just to the thousands in Treasury and in all of your departments—but in all the departments of Government, the millions working in the Federal Government, to get a sense of their own importance in a much larger cause, that they do matter, and that we do count on that, I think this can bring a new morale to those serving in Government, a new spirit, more productivity, of course, but more than that, a better life for all of them. And that is something we are interested in.

One final point I want to make—and I do want a chance to meet you before I go back across the street—I, in appointing the Secretary of the Treasury, had a long visit with him.

I met him on other occasions. But I had a long visit with him in the home of Herbert Brownell, an old friend, a mutual friend of ours, and in that discussion we talked about many things. But what really impressed me about him among many other things—I knew that he was a very successful banker. I knew of course of his background in the Treasury. I knew of his leadership in many activities outside simply of his banking experience.

But what impressed me was the fact that here was a man who knew all about money, who knew all about the great forces that determine the value of money and he at least had more than a passing acquaintance with these very sophisticated matters of international finance, taxes, and so forth and so on, but also a man of great heart, a man who understood the prob-

lems of our great cities and in understanding them recognized that it was necessary for us to think in imaginative and new terms about those problems.

I think that is the ideal combination for a man to head this great Department. It is the kind of spirit with which we are approaching the problems. We want a sound administration, one that will provide for a sound currency, one which is stable, one which can have growth without significant inflation.

But also we want an administration that will not be so inhibited in looking to its monetary problems that it cannot solve some of the other problems that confront the Nation, problems that are very serious abroad but also even more serious at home.

And I am delighted that our new Secretary and this whole team has that understanding.

So I simply want to say that I will of course listen when the Secretary says no, as he must from time to time. But I expect that he is going to find a way through the management of our debt, through the new tax reform, and through everything else, so that he can say yes just as often as we want him to say yes to some of the programs we have to deal with.

Thank you.

NOTE: The President spoke at 3:25 p.m. in Room 4125 at the Department of the Treasury.

50   Statement on the Urban Coalition. *February* 17, 1969

THE URBAN AFFAIRS COUNCIL has just had a most productive discussion with Mr. John Gardner of the Urban Coalition. This organization represents the kind of citizen volunteer effort that will help to reinvigorate our cities and our Nation. Its

42 local coalitions reflect the best in grass-roots leadership.

In the Coalition, business, labor, local government, minority groups, and religious leaders work together to repair the grave gaps in communication that have fragmented our cities. These are American citizens who care about their own communities. They seek to end divisiveness and to bind together the conflicting forces within the community and the Nation.

The Urban Coalition is a "bring-us-together" organization, and I congratulate the leaders in American life who have made the Coalition such an effective instrument of citizen volunteer action—men such as Mr. Gardner, Andrew Heiskell, A. Philip Randolph, George Meany, Whitney Young, John Lindsay, and Arthur Flemming.

I urge business leadership throughout the Nation to lend active support to the Urban Coalition, both locally and nationally.

NOTE: The White House also released the list of those in attendance at the Council for Urban Affairs meeting, as follows: John Gardner, chairman of the Urban Coalition and former Secretary of Health, Education, and Welfare; Bayard Rustin, executive director of the A. Philip Randolph Institute, New York, and member of the Urban Coalition steering committee; Andrew Heiskell, chairman of the board

of Time, Inc., and member of the Urban Coalition steering committee and executive committee; James H. J. Tate, mayor of Philadelphia and steering committee member; Max M. Fisher, chairman of the board of Fisher-New Center Co., Detroit, and member of the New Detroit Committee; Arthur Flemming, president of the National Council of Churches, president of Macalester College, St. Paul, Minn., member of the Urban Coalition steering and executive committees, and former Secretary of Health, Education, and Welfare; Frederick Close, chairman of the board of the Aluminum Co. of America, Pittsburgh, and steering and executive committee member; Walter Reuther, president of the United Auto Workers of America, Detroit, and steering and executive committee member; Joseph Allen, president of McGraw-Hill Publishing Co., Inc., member of the steering and executive committees; and M. Carl Holman, vice president for program development of the Urban Coalition.

The President also referred to George Meany, president of AFL–CIO, Whitney M. Young, Jr., executive director of the National Urban League, and John V. Lindsay, mayor of New York City.

The transcript of a news briefing by Chairman Gardner and Dr. Daniel P. Moynihan, Assistant to the President for Urban Affairs, held after the meeting with the President, was also released.

51   Statement Announcing Governor Nelson A. Rockefeller's Mission to Latin America. *February 17, 1969*

BECAUSE of my deep belief in the importance of the special relationship that exists between the United States and the other American Republics, I am happy to announce today that Governor Nelson A. Rockefeller will undertake a Presidential mission to ascertain the views of the leaders in the Latin American nations.

The purpose of this Presidential mission is to listen to the leaders and to consult with them concerning the development of common goals and joint programs

of action, which will strengthen Western Hemisphere unity and accelerate the pace of economic and social development.

Geography, history, and common aspirations have contributed to a very special friendship between the peoples and countries of the Americas. It is because of the importance of this relationship that I have chosen Governor Rockefeller, a distinguished North American who is knowledgeable in government as well as economic and social problems and who has a longtime friendship and association with the peoples of the Latin American Republics.

Governor Rockefeller will visit the individual Latin American countries in a series of trips beginning in April. In the interim the Governor will bring together a staff for intensive preparation relating to the special potentialities and problems of each country in the economic, social, and other fields.

Upon completing his visits, the Governor will report to me personally on his consultations and make recommendations as to how the United States can improve its policies and increase the effectiveness

of its cooperation and support of common objectives.

I want to emphasize that the Governor's trips will be working trips and not ceremonial visits. Governor Rockefeller is going to the individual countries to listen to the Latin American leaders and get their views and ideas.

The Presidential mission will include top advisers in various fields. The schedules for the visits will be worked out through diplomatic consultation with the Latin American countries to be visited. On each week-long journey the mission will hold discussions in four to six countries.

52   Remarks on Presenting Awards of the American Heart Association. *February* 18, 1969

DR. WALTER B. FROMMEYER. Mr. President, as president of the American Heart Association, I bring you greetings from the officers and members of the Association.

THE PRESIDENT. Thank you very much. We are delighted to be here.

DR. FROMMEYER. Mrs. Nixon, it is a pleasure to meet you.

You know, Mr. President, that today we are combining two of the traditional White House events. One has to do with the presentation of the Distinguished Volunteer Service Award of the American Heart Association, this to be conferred by Mrs. Nixon, the Nation's First Lady; and the other award is the Heart of the Year Award, which is to be conferred by you, Mr. President, as President of the United States.

Now regarding the first award, Mrs. Nixon, I would like to tell you briefly what this entails.

Each year the American Heart Association selects an outstanding heart volunteer. And this award, not only being an honor to this individual, also pays homage to the more than 2 million heart volunteers in this Nation who will be distributing educational literature and receiving contributions to the Heart Fund this coming weekend, which is Heart Sunday weekend, February 23.

Our recipient for this year is Dr. Paul Dudley White of Boston, Massachusetts, whom we would like to honor in this regard.

As a physician, as a teacher, as an author, and as a research worker, Dr. White has done much to inspire the people of our Nation to volunteer their services to the American Heart Association and to the Heart Fund.

Mrs. Nixon, as the First Lady of our land, the Heart Association would be grateful to you if you would present the

Distinguished Volunteer Service Award for 1969 of the American Heart Association to that distinguished and lovable Dr. Paul Dudley White.

Mrs. NIXON. It is certainly my pleasure to present this Distinguished Service Award to you, Dr. White, and to just tell you that I am among the millions that worked with you and for you; and heart is really our goal in many ways.

It is my pleasure now to present this.

DR. WHITE. Thank you very much, Mrs. Nixon, Dr. Frommeyer.

THE PRESIDENT. Would you like to respond, Dr. White?

DR. WHITE. No. [*Laughter*]

THE PRESIDENT. Usually Dr. White is not at a loss for words, I can assure you.

DR. WHITE. I would like to remind you, incidentally, of our association in 1954 when you addressed the first assembly of the Second World Congress of Cardiology in Constitution Hall in September of that year, little realizing that a year later we would be together again in Denver.

It is a great pleasure to be here to thank Mrs. Nixon and Dr. Frommeyer for this award, which I accept in honor of the many millions of volunteers who are working so hard for this cause.

We have a lot to do still to control this epidemic which has seized upon the country, and I am sure we can do it with your help.

Thank you.

DR. FROMMEYER. Thank you, Dr. White.

And now, Mr. President, we come to the other award. And, as you know, each year the American Heart Association designates a distinguished individual to receive its Heart of the Year Award.

This particular award is given to an individual who has made important contributions to society, notwithstanding a history of cardiovascular disease. The award, itself, emphasizes the fact that heart disease and stroke are not necessarily barriers to achievement.

The 1969 recipient for the Heart of the Year Award is the distinguished Dr. Irvine H. Page of Cleveland, Ohio, one of the world's leading medical scientists.

I think Dr. Page, Mr. President, rather perfectly exemplifies the purpose of this award. After having suffered an acute coronary heart attack in 1967, Dr. Page, when he recovered, completed his mission as chief of the National Diet-Heart Study.

In the meantime, he continued on with his many vital research activities.

Now, Mr. President, may I ask that you act on behalf of the American Heart Association in conferring the Association's Heart of the Year Award for 1969 on Dr. Irvine H. Page?

THE PRESIDENT. Thank you very much.

Dr. Page, if you will step up here so that all of these cameras can see you.

I am very honored to make this presentation to Dr. Irvine Page of the National Heart of the Year Award, and already the president of the Association has indicated the background of our distinguished recipient.

I can only add that he is what we might call a triple threat man. He is an author, a teacher, and a doctor and a medical scientist as well.

Like so many who have suffered heart attacks it has seemed that he has been able to work even harder after his attack than before, which is something that

Paul Dudley White told me would be the case with General Eisenhower as we flew to Denver together, I recall, in 1955 on an Air Force plane at the time of his heart attack.

In making this presentation I will read the citation:

"Through his faith, courage, and achievement in meeting the personal challenge of heart disease, Dr. Irvine H. Page has set a magnificent example and inspired people everywhere with hope and with the determination to conquer our nation's leading health enemy."

I can only add that the reason I am a bit late coming to this ceremony is perhaps worth mentioning. I had a call from General Eisenhower at the hospital. He is in excellent spirits.

He is recovering from what many thought would be a fatal heart attack after having had one before, several before. He sends his best and his congratulations to you, Dr. Page, and to you, Dr. White, and to all of those who are here.

As I talked to him, I was reminded of the fact that General Eisenhower had a heart attack when he was President in 1955. President Johnson, of course, suffered a heart attack when he was the Majority Leader of the Senate.

Both, after suffering their heart attacks, were, it seemed, able to work even harder and longer than before they had the heart attacks.

I have been trying to figure a way that I could find more hours in the day. I am not suggesting that I am a candidate, understand, for a heart attack.

But I do believe that the example at the highest level—of two Presidents of the United States, the example of Admiral Rickover,[1] of General Norstad,[2] and here now of a distinguished doctor and medical scientist—the example of these men who have recovered from what used to be the kind of disease that was supposed to finish a man for the rest of his life. He was supposed to slow down——

I always thought that until Dr. Paul Dudley White told me it was not the case in 1955, that you were supposed to speed up a bit in order to avoid future ones.

This is certainly a striking example of it and I think the example of your courage, the fact of the contributions you have made after having gone through this experience, just as was the case with President Eisenhower and President Johnson, is a splendid example to the whole Nation.

We congratulate you and we wish you the very best in your continued service to your profession and to the Nation.

Would you like to respond too? You have equal time with Dr. Paul Dudley White.

DR. PAGE. Good! Well, Mr. President, I think you had better have a heart attack because that is what will give us a Republican majority.

My only advice that I can give you is that I got from my baseball cousin, Satchel Paige, who said, "Never look back, something might be gaining on you."

So I think that you are going to hear a great deal about preventive cardiology, we are going to think a great deal more about fatty acids, polyunsaturated fatty acids, and wives are going to have to ask the question do they really want to stay

---

[1] Vice Adm. H. G. Rickover, Director, Division of Naval Reactors.

[2] Gen. Lauris Norstad, former Supreme Commander of Allied Forces in Europe.

with their husbands or not, because if you eat too much saturated fatty acids, you well may not.

So I deeply appreciate the fact you and Mrs. Nixon have taken the time and the trouble to recognize these things which we think are important and will be important to the vast majority, at least 50 percent, of the American citizens.

Thank you, Mr. President.

THE PRESIDENT. As I understand then, the prescription both to avoid a heart attack and recover from one: Not too

much fatty acid and plenty of exercise.

DR. WHITE. And no tobacco.

THE PRESIDENT. And Dr. White said no tobacco. I don't know whether I should get into that or not.

NOTE: The presentation ceremony began at 10:48 a.m. in the Fish Room at the White House. The announcement of the presentations is printed in the Weekly Compilation of Presidential Documents (vol. 5, p. 278).

On January 27, 1969, the President signed Proclamation 3892 proclaiming February as "American Heart Month, 1969."

53 Letter Accepting Resignation of Ray C. Bliss as Chairman of the Republican National Committee. *February* 18, 1969

Dear Ray:

I have read with great personal regret your February 17 letter advising me of your decision to leave the National Chairmanship in mid-April.

In our Party's six score years we have never had a Chairman more dedicated than you have been, more professionally competent, or with a record of greater achievement than yours. It is also true that no Chairman has won more respect throughout our Party's ranks than you have won since you took up the reins of leadership in 1965. You have, therefore, every reason for full satisfaction as you leave this high post. I join our entire Party membership in saluting you for a job extraordinarily well done.

In accepting your decision I must request that you remain available as our counselor despite your retirement, because you offer our Party far too much professional skill to remove yourself entirely from our common cause.

I will, as you suggest, designate a representative to work with you at the Committee, and shortly after my return from Europe I will schedule a meeting for us to discuss the Committee's requirements for the future.

Pat joins me in warmest greetings to Ellen and in congratulations to both of you for having so ably served our Party and our country for so many years.

Sincerely,

DICK NIXON

[Honorable Ray C. Bliss, Chairman, Republican National Committee, 1625 Eye Street, NW., Washington, D.C. 20006]

NOTE: The letter of acceptance was dated February 17, 1969, and released February 18, 1969. Mr. Bliss' letter of resignation, released along with the President's letter, follows:

Dear Mr. President:

While I appreciated very much your suggestion at our January 10 meeting at the Pierre Hotel in New York that I continue as Chairman of the Republican National Committee, I have given it much thought and have concluded that I will retire as Chairman in April and return to my private business.

I am writing to let you know that I will submit my resignation to the Republican National Committee at a meeting in Washington in mid-April, called for the purpose of electing a new Chairman. This will round out four years of service in my present post.

My retirement at that time will provide necessary lead-in time for the new Chairman to prepare for the 1969 and 1970 elections. It will give him the same advance planning period that was available to me on my assumption of the Chairmanship and which I found fully satisfactory.

In order to facilitate an orderly transition, you may find it desirable to appoint a representative of your administration to work closely with me until the new Chairman is elected. Following your return from your most important European trip, I am looking forward to meeting with you and discussing details concerning future political plans for our party and ways I can be most helpful.

The last four years have been the most important and satisfying of my life since they provided me an opportunity to help rebuild the Republican Party and to help elect you President of the United States.

You may be assured of my continued support and dedication to the principles of the Republican Party which you so ably espouse.

With warm regards and high esteem, I am

Sincerely yours,

RAY

54 Message to the Congress Transmitting Annual Report of the National Science Board. *February* 18, 1969

To the Congress of the United States:

I am pleased to submit to the Congress this first Report of the National Science Board, "Toward a Public Policy for Graduate Education in the Sciences," together with a companion volume, "Graduate Education: Parameters for Public Policy," which contains information and discussion supporting the basic Report. These documents have been prepared in accordance with Section 4(g) of the National Science Foundation Act, as amended by Public Law 90–407.

Graduate education is a critically important element in the educational process and one which is entering a particularly difficult period. As the Board points out, graduate enrollments are expected to double and the costs of graduate programs are expected to quadruple during the next decade. Thus it is most important that colleges and universities, state and local authorities, and the interested branches of the Federal Government all re-examine their role with respect to graduate education.

On several occasions, most recently when I increased the expenditure ceiling of the National Science Foundation for the fiscal year 1969, I have emphasized our nation's special debt to its scientists and its special responsibility to maintain an outstanding record in both basic research and technological advance. I emphasize here again that education in general and scientific development in particular will be among the highest priorities in this Administration. One measure of the greatness and vitality of a nation is manifested, I believe, in its readiness to explore the unknown.

The National Science Board has rightly concluded that adequate funding for graduate education and for academic science is only one of the problems we face. Of comparable importance is the need to develop a new strategy for that Federal aid which may be required. I have recently instructed the Secretary of Health, Education, and Welfare to establish an interdepartmental study group to make an overall review of the Federal role in education, including higher education. The Report of the National Science Board will provide a useful resource for that review.

I know that the Congress, like the Executive Branch, will give the Report its careful consideration. I solicit your assistance in developing solutions to the problems which have been identified by this distinguished group of citizens.

RICHARD NIXON

The White House

February 18, 1969

NOTE: The report and its companion volume were printed by the Government Printing Office (63 and 168 pp., respectively). An announcement of their transmittal to the Congress, containing a summary of the report's principal findings and recommendations, is printed in the Weekly Compilation of Presidential Documents (vol. 5, p. 281).

---

55 Special Message to the Congress on the Nation's Antipoverty Programs. *February* 19, 1969

To the Congress of the United States:

The blight of poverty requires priority attention. It engages our hearts and challenges our intelligence. It cannot and will not be treated lightly or indifferently, or without the most searching examination of how best to marshal the resources available to the Federal Government for combatting it.

At my direction, the Urban Affairs Council has been conducting an intensive study of the nation's anti-poverty programs, of the way the anti-poverty effort is organized and administered, and of ways in which it might be made more effective.

That study is continuing. However, I can now announce a number of steps I intend to take, as well as spelling out some of the considerations that will guide my future recommendations.

The Economic Opportunity Act of 1964 is now scheduled to expire on June 30, 1970. The present authorization for appropriations for the Office of Economic Opportunity runs only until June 30, 1969.

I will ask Congress that this authorization for appropriations be extended for another year. Prior to the end of the Fiscal Year, I will send Congress a comprehensive proposal for the future of the poverty program, including recommendations for revising and extending the Act itself beyond its scheduled 1970 expiration.

How the work begun by OEO can best be carried forward is a subject on which many views deserve to be heard—both from within Congress, and among those many others who are interested or affected, including especially the poor themselves. By sending my proposals well before the Act's 1970 expiration, I intend to provide time for full debate and discussion.

In the maze of anti-poverty efforts, precedents are weak and knowledge uncertain. These past years of increasing Federal involvement have begun to make clear how vast is the range of what we do not yet know, and how fragile are projections based on partial understanding. But we have learned some lessons about what works and what does not. The changes I propose will be based on those lessons and those discoveries, and rooted in a determination to press ahead with anti-poverty efforts even though individual experiments have ended in disappointment.

From the experience of OEO, we have learned the value of having in the Federal Government an agency whose special concern is the poor. We have learned the need for flexibility, responsiveness, and continuing innovation. We have learned the need for management effectiveness. Even those most thoroughly committed to the goals of the anti-poverty effort recognize now that much that has been tried has not worked.

The OEO has been a valuable fount of ideas and enthusiasm, but it has suffered from a confusion of roles.

OEO's greatest value is as an initiating agency—devising new programs to help the poor, and serving as an "incubator" for these programs during their initial, experimental phases. One of my aims is to free OEO itself to perform these functions more effectively, by providing for a greater concentration of its energies on its innovative role.

Last year, Congress directed that special studies be made by the Executive Branch of whether Head Start and the Job Corps should continue to be administered directly by OEO, or whether responsibility should be otherwise assigned.

Section 309 of the Vocational Education Amendments of 1968 provides:

"The President shall make a special study of whether the responsibility for administering the Head Start program established under the Economic Opportunity Act of 1964 should continue to be vested in the Director of the Office of Economic Opportunity, should be trans-ferred to another agency of the Government, or should be delegated to another such agency pursuant to the provisions of section 602(d) of the aforementioned Economic Opportunity Act of 1964, and shall submit the findings of this study to the Congress not later than March 1, 1969."

I have today submitted this study to the Congress. Meanwhile, *under the Executive authority provided by the Economic Opportunity Act,* I have directed that preparations be made for the delegation of Head Start to the Department of Health, Education, and Welfare. Whether it should be actually transferred is a question I will take up in my later, comprehensive message, along with my proposals for a permanent status and organizational structure for OEO. Pending a final decision by the Secretary of HEW on where within the department responsibility for Head Start would be lodged, it will be located directly within the Office of the Secretary.

In order to provide for orderly preparation, and to ensure that there is no interruption of programs, I have directed that this delegation be made effective July 1, 1969. By then the summer programs for 1969 will all have been funded, and a new cycle will be beginning.

I see this delegation as an important element in a new national commitment to the crucial early years of life.

Head Start is still experimental. Its effects are simply not known—save of course where medical care and similar services are involved. The results of a major national evaluation of the program will be available this Spring. It must be said, however, that preliminary reports on this study confirm what many have feared: the long term effect of Head Start appears to be extremely weak. This must not discourage us. To the contrary it only demonstrates the immense contribution the Head Start program has made simply by having raised to prominence on the national agenda the fact—known for some time, but never widely recognized—that the children of the poor mostly arrive at school age seriously deficient in the ability to profit from formal education, and already significantly behind their contemporaries. It also has been made abundantly clear that our schools as they now exist are unable to overcome this deficiency.

In this context, the Head Start Follow-Through Program already delegated to HEW by OEO, assumes an even greater importance.

In recent years, enormous advances have been made in the understanding of human development. We have learned that intelligence is not fixed at birth, but is largely formed by the environmental influences of the early formative years. It develops rapidly at first, and then more slowly; as much of that development takes place in the first four years as in the next thirteen. We have learned further that environment has its greatest impact on the development of intelligence when that development is proceeding most rapidly—that is, in those earliest years.

This means that many of the problems of poverty are traceable directly to early childhood experience—and that if we are to make genuine, long-range progress, we must focus our efforts much more than heretofore on those few years which may determine how far, throughout his later life, the child can reach.

Recent scientific developments have shown that this process of early childhood development poses more difficult problems than had earlier been recognized—but they also promise a real possibility of major breakthroughs soon in our understanding of this process. By placing Head Start in the Department of HEW, it will be possible to strengthen it by association with a wide range of other early development programs within the department, and also with the research programs of the National Institutes of Health, the National Institute of Mental Health, and the National Institute of Child Health and Human Development.

Much of our knowledge is new. But we are not on that ground absolved from the responsibility to respond to it. So crucial is the matter of early growth that we must make a national commitment to providing all American children an opportunity for healthful and stimulating development during the first five years of life. In delegating Head Start to the Department of HEW, I pledge myself to that commitment.

The Vocational Education Amendments of 1968 directed the Commissioner of Education to study the Job Corps in relation to state vocational education programs. I have directed the Secretaries of Labor and of Health, Education, and Welfare, and the Assistant Secretary of Labor for Manpower, to work with the Acting Commissioner of Education in preparing such a report for submission to Congress at the earliest opportunity.

One of the priority aims of the new Administration is the development by the Department of Labor of a comprehensive manpower program, designed to make centrally available to the unemployed and the underemployed a full range of Federal job training and placement services. Toward this end, it is essential that the many Federal manpower programs be integrated and coordinated.

Therefore, as a first step toward better program management, the Job Corps will be delegated to the Department of Labor.

For the Department, this will add another important manpower service component. For the Job Corpsmen, it will make available additional training and service opportunities. From the standpoint of program management, it makes it possible to coordinate the Job Corps with other manpower services, especially vocational education, at the point of delivery.

The Department of Labor already is deeply involved in the recruitment, counseling and placement of Job Corpsmen. It refers 80 percent of all male and 45 percent of all female enrollees; it provides job market information, and helps locate Job Corpsmen in the areas of greatest opportunity.

This delegation will also be made effective on July 1, 1969; and the Departments of Interior and Agriculture will continue to have operating responsibility for the Job Corps centers concerned primarily with conservation.

I have directed that preparations be made for the transfer of two other programs from OEO to the Department of Health, Education, and Welfare: Comprehensive Health Centers, which provide health service to the residents of poor neighborhoods, and Foster Grandparents program. In my judgment, these can be better administered at present, or in the near future, within the structure of the Department.

In making these changes, I recognize that innovation costs money—and that if OEO is to continue its effectiveness as an innovating agency, adequate funds must be made available on a continuing basis. Moreover, it is my intent that Community Action Agencies can continue to be involved in the operation of programs such as Head Start at the local level, even though an agency other than OEO has received such programs, by delegation, at the national level. It also is my intent that the vital Community Action Programs will be pressed forward, and that in the area of economic development OEO will have an important role to play, in cooperation with other agencies, in fostering community-based business development.

One of the principal aims of the Administration's continuing study of the anti-poverty effort will be to improve its management effectiveness. When poverty-fund monies are stolen, those hurt most are the poor—whom the monies were meant to help. When programs are inefficiently administered, those hurt most again are the poor. The public generally, and the poor especially, have a right to demand effective and efficient management. I intend to provide it.

I expect that important economies will result from the delegation of the Job Corps to the Department of Labor, and we shall continue to strive for greater efficiency, and especially for greater effectiveness in Head Start.

A Concentrated Management Improvement Program initiated in OEO will be intensified. Under this program, selected Community Action Agencies will be required to take steps to devise improvements in such areas as organizational structure, financial and accounting systems, personnel training and work scheduling. Standards will be applied under the "management improvement program" to evaluate the operations of Community Action Agencies. We intend to monitor these programs actively in order to insure that they are achieving high-level effectiveness and that they are being administered on an orderly basis.

In the past, problems have often arisen over the relationship of State, county and local governments to programs administered by OEO. This has particularly been the case where the State and local officials have wanted to assume greater responsibility for the implementation of the programs but for various reasons have been prevented from doing so. I have assigned special responsibility for working out these problems to the newly-created Office of Intergovernmental Relations, under the supervision of the Vice President.

I have directed the Urban Affairs Council to keep the anti-poverty effort under constant review and evaluation, seeking new ways in which the various departments can help and better ways in which their efforts can be coordinated.

My comprehensive recommendations for the future of the poverty program will be made after the Urban Affairs Council's own initial study is completed, and after I have reviewed the Comptroller General's study of OEO ordered by Congress in 1967 and due for submission next month.

Meanwhile, I would stress this final thought: If we are to make the most of experimental programs, we must frankly recognize their experimental nature and frankly acknowledge whatever shortcomings they develop. To do so is not to belittle the experiment, but to advance its essential purpose: that of finding new ways, better ways, of making progress in areas still inadequately understood.

We often can learn more from a program that fails to achieve its purpose than from one that succeeds. If we apply those lessons, then even the "failure" will have made a significant contribution to our larger purposes.

I urge all those involved in these experimental programs to bear this in mind—and to remember that one of the primary goals of this Administration is to expand our knowledge of how best to make real progress against those social ills that have so stubbornly defied solution. We do not pretend to have all the answers. We are determined to find as many as we can.

The men and women who will be valued most in this administration will be those who understand that not every experiment succeeds, who do not cover up failures but rather lay open problems, frankly and constructively, so that next time we will know how to do better.

In this spirit, I am confident that we can place our anti-poverty efforts on a secure footing—and that as we continue to gain in understanding of how to master the difficulties, we can move forward at an accelerating pace.

RICHARD NIXON

The White House
February 19, 1969

NOTE: On December 30, 1969, the President signed the Economic Opportunity Amendments of 1969 (Public Law 91–177, 83 Stat. 827).

56   Message to the Congress Transmitting Report Relating to the Head Start Program.   *February* 19, 1969

To the Congress of the United States:

Section 309 of the Vocational Education Amendments of 1968 directed the President to make a special study of whether responsibility for administering the Head Start program should be left with the Office of Economic Opportunity, or whether it should be delegated or transferred to another agency. Congress asked that a report of this study be submitted by March 1, 1969.

I am submitting the report herewith.

This report has been prepared in consultation with the heads of the Executive departments and agencies concerned.

The study concludes that Head Start should be delegated to the Department of Health, Education, and Welfare. It leaves for later determination the question of whether the program should eventually be transferred. As I have indicated in a message to Congress today, I will present a set of recommendations before the end of the current fiscal year on a permanent status and organizational structure for the Office of Economic Opportunity. At that time, I will make a recommendation on whether Head Start should be transferred, or whether it should remain a delegated program.

Section 308 of the same Vocational Education Amendments of 1968 directed the Commissioner of Education to make a special study of the means by which the existing Job Corps facilities and programs might, if determined feasible, be transferred to State or joint Federal-State operation. The Commissioner was directed to report his findings to Congress by March 1, 1969.

As my message today indicated, responsibility for administering the Job Corps will be delegated to the Department of Labor effective July 1. The question of State or joint Federal-State operation is a complex one which may well be affected by the over-all manpower-development proposals now being prepared by the Secretary of Labor. In light of these developments, and in order to comply with the intent of Congress, I have asked the Secretaries of Labor and Health, Education, and Welfare, along with the Assistant Secretary of Labor for Manpower, and the Director of OEO, to work with the Acting Commissioner of Education in preparing a report responsive to the Congressional directive to be submitted at the earliest possible time. As directed by Congress, the Acting Commissioner will also consult with other Federal officials, with State officials and with concerned individuals.

In its request for these studies, I recognize the interest of Congress in a constant evaluation and review of the way in which new, experimental programs are being administered, and in the measurement of their results. I welcome that interest, I share it, and I will attempt to be responsive to it.

RICHARD NIXON

The White House

February 19, 1969

NOTE: The report on Head Start (processed, 6 pp. with attachments) was made available with the President's message.

57 Remarks to Employees at the Department of the Interior. *February* 19, 1969

Mr. Secretary, and ladies and gentlemen:

I want to emphasize what the Secretary has said—the fact that this is the last department I have visited does not indicate that it is the last in terms of the importance of your assignment and of my respect for you, those of you who have given so much of your lives to this Department.

I speak with particular feeling about this Department because I, of course, come from the West and although I have lived in most parts of the Nation—and not as much as I would have liked in the West, having come from the West, having known it as a Congressman and as a Senator and also as Vice President, having often spoken of the Western part of the country, its interests which are in many respects the responsibility of this Department—I have an especially close relationship with you.

I was interested to note, as I met some of the people before and as I hope to meet some of you later, that many I had known many years ago in that period when I had the opportunity to work with members of the Interior Department.

As I complete this round of visits to the departments, I want to do here what I have done at every one of the visits: I want to say first a word about your Secretary.

I say this not simply because he had nice things to say about me—after all, he has no choice. The Senate has to give its consent, but I do the picking.

So I do want to say, however, that in speaking of Secretary Hickel and of telling you why I selected him for this post, that his performance since that selection

has borne out, I believe, my decision and the reasons for it.

I knew and you know that filling the post of Secretary of the Interior is not easy. It is not easy in any department, but perhaps in this one, as much as in any and in more than most, it is necessary to take positions at times that will not be agreed with by many very honest people who have reached a different conclusion because they start with different attitudes toward the problem.

I could go down the list of issues in which people are divided as far as the Department of the Interior is concerned.

I know, for example, going back to the time when I was a California Congressman and then a California Senator, how the States of California and Arizona had arguments about water. They are still having arguments about water. And how also with regard to the development of our resources, our oil resources, water resources, and others, that men and women very honestly taking a point of view were in sharp disagreement. Somebody had to make the decision.

So when I picked the Secretary of the Interior, I knew that I would have to find a man, first, who had courage; second, who was an honest man; and, third, a man—and this was one of the things that attracted me to the new Secretary—who had a real love for the land in the deepest sense of the word.

I think Secretary Hickel has demonstrated under fire that he has courage, that he is an honest man, and I know that he loves the land, this whole land, and loves it much.

I got that impression not simply from

seeing him here in Washington as you have, but seeing him in his home State of Alaska and to hear him talk, as he does, about that State and of its resources and of all the possibilities of its development in the future, not just its development for industrial purposes, but its development in the sense of the environment, the beauty of the land, the opportunity for people to come there and live there and enjoy it. I knew from that that he was a man who would understand all of these varying interests that must be reconciled within this Department.

So, under his leadership, I am sure we are going to have a great era of progress and a great era of responsibility as far as the Interior Department is concerned.

Now, a second point I want to make has to do with your responsibility. And it allows me to impose upon you one of my favorite quotations and one that I often use.

Edmund Burke, a great Irish-English philosopher, often used to say that when we speak of patriotism we must look to its root phrases which develop the word. And literally patriotism, when you translate it, means love of country. Then he went on to say that if we are to love our country, our country must be lovely.

I don't think there is any better way to describe the mission of this Department. We all, I know, have a deep feeling of patriotism for this Nation. We all have a deep feeling and sense of history about this Nation, and that feeling of patriotism comes from that.

But if we are to command from the younger generation coming along, and from people generally, that deep feeling of pride and patriotism which we all want, we have to do everything that we can to make our country lovely so that people will love this country and love it very deeply.

They will love this country even when it has some unlovely characteristics. There is no question about that. But how much we can do, how much you can do, as we look to the future 10 years, 20 years, down to the end of this century, how much we can do to see that the America that is built will be a new America, a new America in terms not only of the tremendous concentration of population in our cities—and I have spoken to that point in visits to various departments—how we must plan now for transportation and housing and all of the other areas which will determine the character of our cities in the future, which will be one and a half times as big as they are 15 years from now, but we must also think of the character of that great part of America that is called rural America, the part that you mainly deal with, our water, our land, our resources, everything that really makes America a lovely country, one that gives you a feeling as you move out through the western part of this Nation and up to Alaska and out to Hawaii, a feeling of patriotism, of love of country that goes beyond simply seeing the flag, that goes beyond simply reading our history, that recognizes that we are fortunate to live in a country that was so richly blessed as this country has been blessed with natural resources.

Having said all of that, I realize that I have not decided any of those tough problems you have to work with: making the decisions between whether you develop resources or conserve them.

And I know that sometimes we can talk about conservation and development going along together.

These are decisions that you will have to make, decisions that the Secretary will have to make, decisions on which he will have to advise me.

But in the final analysis, I know that we are all working toward the same goal: to see to it that this great and rich land, more richly blessed when we look at it in terms of our natural resources than any land on earth—and we are fortunate to have it that way—but that this great and rich land will develop in the years ahead, will develop the resources that will enable us to be the best fed and the best clothed and the best housed people in the world, but that will also retain for the generations to come those great areas of beauty and also an environment, clean air, pure water, which will be one that our children will want to live in.

And I can think of no more exciting responsibility than that. So much of that action is right here. We often hear that the action is in the cities and there is a lot of action there; and some would say today that the action is in the universities, and certainly there is a lot of action there.

But there is a lot of action, too, in this Department. I don't need to tell you from what your Secretary went through in his confirmation and also the various decisions that you will be making.

I simply want you to know that knowing what your responsibilities are, knowing what effect your decisions are going to have on the face of America in the years ahead, I don't know of any department that will have more of an effect on what kind of country we are going to have than the Department of Interior.

I wish you well. And in wishing you well, I want to add one further point. I not only wish well those that I have

brought to Washington as members of the new administration team, but also those who serve in the career service, on civil service, those who are here through administrations, those who sometimes are taken for granted, and those without whose support we will be unable to carry out the mission that we have.

I have respect for those who have dedicated their lives to public service. I have spent most of my life actually, my adult life, working in one capacity or another in a public service capacity.

But in speaking of those who are here in the career service, I want you to know that your Secretary, all of those who have been appointed by the new administration depend upon you, and we will appreciate your support and in turn you will have our support, our support for a strong career service which must go on and give continuity to this Government in the years ahead.

Would you pass that message on right down the line? As I came down the halls here, it was very touching to see people gathered in some of the halls and the secretaries and stenographers and others put their hands out. They wanted to shake hands and say hello and the rest.

I thought of how, perhaps for some of them, their jobs must be very routine and sometimes very boring—you know, getting out that last draft of a statement or going through the boring form mail that you have to get out, and all the other things. And if you would just let them know that we in this administration appreciate every person who works in it, because it takes not only the top people that are in this room. You know better than I that we need the cooperation and the support of all of those down the ranks who can, by the quality of their job, make ours that much better.

So with that, I wish you, Mr. Secretary, the very best. You have spoken about whether you are going to be last or first

and I can say the spirit that you have will never be last, and it could well be first.

Thank you.

NOTE: The President spoke at 2:09 p.m. in the auditorium at the Department of the Interior.

58 Special Message to the Congress on Electoral Reform. *February* 20, 1969

To the Congress of the United States:

One hundred and sixty-five years ago, Congress and the several states adopted the Twelfth Amendment to the United States Constitution in order to cure certain defects—underscored by the election of 1800—in the electoral college method of choosing a President. Today, our presidential selection mechanism once again requires overhaul to repair defects spotlighted by the circumstances of 1968.

The reforms that I propose are basic in need and desirability. They are changes which I believe should be given the earliest attention by the Congress.

I have not abandoned my personal feeling, stated in October and November 1968, that the candidate who wins the most popular votes should become President. However, practicality demands recognition that the electoral system is deeply rooted in American history and federalism. Many citizens, especially in our smaller states and their legislatures, share the belief stated by President Johnson in 1965 that "our present system of computing and awarding electoral votes by States is an essential counterpart of our Federal system and the provisions of our Constitution which recognize and maintain our nation as a union of states." I doubt very much that any constitutional amendment proposing abolition or substantial

modification of the electoral vote system could win the required approval of three-quarters of our fifty states by 1972.

For this reason, and because of the compelling specific weaknesses focused in 1968, I am urging Congress to concentrate its attention on formulating a system that can receive the requisite Congressional and State approval.

I realize that experts on constitutional law do not think alike on the subject of electoral reform. Different plans for reform have been responsibly advanced by Members of Congress and distinguished private groups and individuals. These plans have my respect and they merit serious consideration by the Congress.

I have in the past supported the proportional plan of electoral reform. Under this plan the electoral vote of a state would be distributed among the candidates for President in proportion to the popular vote cast. But I am not wedded to the details of this plan or any other specific plan. I will support any plan that moves toward the following objectives: first, the abolition of individual electors; second, allocation to Presidential candidates of the electoral vote of each State and the District of Columbia in a manner that may more closely approximate the popular vote than does the present system; third, making a 40% electoral vote plurality sufficient to choose a President.

The adoption of these reforms would correct the principal defects in the present system. I believe the events of 1968 constitute the clearest proof that priority must be accorded to electoral college reform.

Next, I consider it necessary to make specific provision for the eventuality that no presidential slate receives 40% or more of the electoral vote in the regular election. Such a situation, I believe, is best met by providing that a run-off election between the top two candidates shall be held within a specified time after the general election, victory going to the candidate who receives the largest popular vote.

We must also resolve some other uncertainties: First, by specifying that if a presidential candidate who has received a clear electoral vote plurality dies before the electoral votes are counted, the Vice-President-elect should be chosen President. Second, by providing that in the event of the death of the Vice-President-

elect, the President-elect should, upon taking office, be required to follow the procedures otherwise provided in the Twenty-Fifth Amendment for filling the unexpired term of the Vice-President. Third, by giving Congress responsibility, should both the President-elect and Vice-President-elect die or become unable to serve during this interim, to provide for the selection—by a new election or some other means—of persons to serve as President and Vice-President. And finally, we must clarify the situation presented by the death of a candidate for President or Vice-President prior to the November general election.

Many of these reforms are noncontroversial. All are necessary. Favorable action by Congress will constitute a vital step in modernizing our electoral process and reaffirming the flexible strength of our constitutional system.

RICHARD NIXON

The White House
    February 20, 1969

59   Memorandum to the Secretary of the Interior Reassuming Responsibility for the Nation's Oil Import Policies. *February* 20, 1969

Memorandum for the Secretary of the Interior:

A wide range of complex and highly important issues affecting the nation's oil import policies must be dealt with in the near future. These issues, which have not been examined in depth for a decade, are of such moment to the United States and their impact on national policy is so far-reaching that they require extensive review in detail and in the aggregate.

I am therefore reassuming full responsibility for oil import policies—a responsibility delegated to the Department of the Interior some five years ago—so that there may be full opportunity for the several affected agencies efficiently to coordinate and assert their views.

This undertaking will include a full review of the nation's oil import policies by the Executive Offices of the President.

RICHARD NIXON

60 Statement About the Anniversary of Washington's Birthday. *February* 21, 1969

GEORGE WASHINGTON was the most trusted American. More than any other quality of heroism or wisdom, it was that fact of rocklike trustworthiness that made him "first in the hearts of his countrymen."

If his words were not always eloquent, his word was always good; he projected from his own integrity a concern for a national integrity. He was among the first to speak of a "National Character," and described one of its pillars as the ability of the citizens "to forget their local prejudices and policies, to make those mutual concessions which are requisite to the general prosperity, and in some instances, to sacrifice their individual advantages to the interest of the Community."

Revolutionary times, all great ages of rapid change, call up a need for that bedrock quality of trust. People will accept new departures if they know the men charting the course are men of fundamental principle. The men who earn the people's trust in times of revolutionary change have the most to do with the successful progress of a nation. With the strength that grew out of that trust, Washington forged a new hope for humanity.

There is some irony in issuing a Washington's Birthday message on the eve of a Presidential trip to Europe. We all remember the warning in his Farewell Address to "steer clear of permanent Alliances with any portion of the foreign world."

Yet we must remember that in that farewell, Washington also said this: "Harmony, liberal intercourse with all Nations, are recommended by policy, humanity and interest." The United States, with its purposes of peace and freedom, must accept the opportunity today to widen areas of agreement throughout the world.

In that spirit, together with our friends and ultimately with our adversaries, we can, in Washington's words, "raise a standard to which the wise and honest can repair."

61 Remarks Announcing the Appointment of Donald M. Kendall as Chairman of the National Alliance of Businessmen. *February* 21, 1969

I AM INTERRUPTING the press briefing by Mr. Ziegler for the purpose of making an announcement with regard to the National Alliance of Businessmen.

One of the major objectives of this administration, as you know, is to move people from welfare rolls to payrolls.

The organization in the Nation which has been most effective in a volunteer way in achieving this objective is the National Alliance of Businessmen. If its present goals are realized it may reach the number of 100,000. And beyond that, it already is operating in 50 cities and we are hoping that we may extend this operation to far more cities in the Nation.

In studying this organization and the excellent record it has made up to this point, I have found that what is vitally important is the leadership at the top, the leadership of an individual who knows the volunteer way, who has had the oppor-

123

tunity to practice it and who can inspire others to follow his example.

We have been able to get Mr. Don Kendall to assume this responsibility. Incidentally, his choice has been seconded by the present top people in the Alliance as one who can provide that kind of leadership.

I can only say in speaking of him that in the field of business he has never failed to increase sales throughout his career. In fact, he is generally known among his business colleagues as the man who pours it on. He has agreed that he is going to apply that same vitality and, incidentally, youth to this new assignment.

I am delighted that he is undertaking

it. He will have the full cooperation of the President in this activity.

After I return from my trip abroad, a meeting will be held here of the top officials of the Alliance in order that I may indicate to them my support of this program and my complete backing for Mr. Kendall in carrying it out.

NOTE: The President spoke at 12:05 p.m. in the Fish Room at the White House. Mr. Kendall's response and a statement by the President on the appointment are printed in the Weekly Compilation of Presidential Documents (vol. 5, p. 303).

An announcement, dated February 4, 1969, on the appointment of new metropolitan chairmen for the National Alliance of Businessmen is printed in the Weekly Compilation of Presidential Documents (vol. 5, p. 214).

62 Statement Approving Wider Use of Federal Laboratory Equipment by University Scientists. *February* 21, 1969

THE EQUIPMENT of many Federal laboratories is superb and often unique. This investment should be viewed as a national resource and not one for the exclusive use of the laboratory staff members. While many scientists and engineers from universities now frequently use Federal research facilities, an even closer and more extensive cooperative relation will be productive. I am therefore approving a

policy designed to bring this about. Dr. DuBridge will be able to implement the policy with the help of the Federal Council for Science and Technology, which has recommended its adoption.

NOTE: The statement was made public as part of a White House release announcing that the President had directed his Science Adviser, Dr. Lee A. DuBridge, to monitor the new policy.

63 Memorandum on the Narcotic and Dangerous Drug Traffic in the District of Columbia. *February* 22, 1969

Memorandum for the Attorney General:

In my recent message concerning crime in the District of Columbia, I recognized that illegal traffic in narcotics and dangerous drugs is an acute and growing problem in the District and that it is directly linked to the commission of crimes of

violence. It is therefore imperative that prompt and effective action be taken to combat illegal narcotic and dangerous drug traffic in the District of Columbia. To that end, I request that you immediately direct the Bureau of Narcotics and Dangerous Drugs to concentrate its efforts and channel its available resources to deal with this problem.

The precise steps to be taken must, of course, be determined by you in consultation with the Director of the Bureau of Narcotics and Dangerous Drugs and the District of Columbia Government. But among other possible initiatives, I suggest that you consider the following:

—Employment of additional personnel by the Bureau of Narcotics and Dangerous Drugs for enforcement in the District and those cities which represent the major sources of supply for the District;

—Training programs in detection, apprehension, and treatment of narcotics addicts and drug dependent persons for District law enforcement personnel, school teachers, correction personnel and public health officials;

—Additional technical and scientific assistance to District officials concerned with narcotic addiction and drug abuse.

It is apparent that increased enforcement efforts, educational programs and technical assistance will require additional manpower and funds. Accordingly, you and the Director of the Bureau of the Budget should, if necessary, request additional appropriations from the Congress in order to ensure that these needs can be expeditiously met.

RICHARD NIXON

64 Statement on the Appointment of a Special Coordinator on Relief to Civilian Victims of the Nigerian Civil War. *February 22, 1969*

I KNOW that I speak for all Americans in expressing this Nation's deep anguish for the terrible human suffering in the Nigerian civil war. It is tragic enough to watch a military conflict between peoples who once lived together in peace and developing prosperity. But that tragedy has been compounded, and the conscience of the world engaged by the starvation threatening millions of innocent civilians on both sides of the battle.

Immediately after taking office, I directed an urgent and comprehensive review of the relief situation. The purpose was to examine every possibility to enlarge and expedite the flow of relief. This very complex problem will require continuing study. I am announcing, however, the following initial conclusions of the review:

1. The Red Cross and the voluntary agencies are now feeding nearly 1 million people in areas of the war zone controlled by the Federal Military Government of Nigeria. They fully expect the numbers will grow in magnitude over the coming months. This, therefore, will require additional support for the international relief effort from donor countries, and of course the continued cooperation of Federal authorities.

2. There is widely conflicting information on future food requirements within the Biafran-controlled area, where the relief operation is feeding an estimated 2 million persons. The United States Government therefore is urgently seeking a comprehensive, internationally conducted survey of food needs in that area.

3. Whatever the results of such a survey, it is already clear that the present

relief effort is inadequate to the need in the Biafran-controlled area. The major obstacle to expanded relief is neither money, food, nor means of transport. The main problem is the absence of relief arrangements acceptable to the two sides which would overcome the limitations posed by the present hazardous and inadequate nighttime airlift.

4. The efforts of outside governments to expand relief are greatly complicated by the political and military issues that divide the contestants. Unfortunately, the humanitarian urge to feed the starving has become enmeshed in those issues and stands in danger of interpretation by the parties as a form of intervention. But surely it is within the conscience and ability of man to give effect to his humanitarianism without involving himself in the politics of the dispute.

5. It is in this spirit that U.S. policy will draw a sharp distinction between carrying out our moral obligations to respond effectively to humanitarian needs and involving ourselves in the political affairs of others. The United States will not shrink from this humanitarian challenge but, in cooperation with those of like mind, will seek to meet it.

With the above conclusions in view, I am pleased to announce that Secretary of State Rogers has today appointed Mr. Clarence Clyde Ferguson, Jr., a distinguished American civic leader and professor of law at Rutgers University, as Special Coordinator on relief to civilian victims of the Nigerian civil war. He will be charged with assuring that the U.S. contributions to the international relief effort are responsive to increased needs to the maximum extent possible and that they are effectively utilized. In so doing, he will give particular attention to ways and means by which the flow of relief can be increased to the suffering on both sides of the battleline. He will, of course, work closely with the ICRC [International Committee of the Red Cross] and other international relief agencies, the Organization of African Unity, donor governments, and with the parties to the conflict.

The Special Coordinator will not seek and will not accept a charge to negotiate issues other than those directly relevant to relief.

Nevertheless, the United States earnestly hopes for an early negotiated end to the conflict and a settlement that will assure the protection and peaceful development of all the people involved.

65   Remarks to Reporters on the Forthcoming European Trip.   *February* 22, 1969

THIS LOOKS like a rather sizable number of people who are going on this trip.

As Ron Ziegler has already indicated to you, I thought it might be helpful if I were to talk to you on the record for Sunday release about some of the logistical aspects of the trip which he may not have covered. At least I will elaborate on them and also give you some indications of what I think may be accomplished by the trip and what may not be accomplished by it beyond what I indicated in my press conference a couple of weeks ago.

Let me begin by one assertion that will

put it in context as far as those who have the responsibility of covering this kind of trip.

I am keenly aware of the fact that you have a very difficult problem insofar as the daily news flow is concerned. That is true always on this kind of trip, a Presidential trip. I have talked to many in this room about the problems you have had in traveling with Presidents to summit conferences and the rest, and the thousands of—well, there will be literally thousands of people and sometimes hundreds of reporters who are there with the small amounts of official news items that seem to come out.

This trip will be difficult in that respect because there will be no formal communiques. We are not going for the purpose of negotiating any outstanding differences and so there won't be any spectacular news in that respect.

On the other side of the coin, the trip will be short on that kind of protocol excitement that you usually associate with a trip. There will be, of course, the honors that are usually rendered for a foreign head of state and all that sort of thing.

But you will not have as much of the color and all the other things that sometimes substitute for the hard news.

However, I will do everything that I can during the course of the trip to see that those who go with us from the State Department, from my own staff, brief you on anything of substance that can appropriately be covered. You must have in mind—and I know you all will have in mind—the fact that in the conversations that I have with heads of government or heads of state, it will not be possible to cover those conversations except in the broadest terms insofar as the subjects

that were covered, because the very purpose of that kind of discussion would be destroyed if there were substantial news coverage afterwards of what was discussed. There may be some exceptions that will develop. But that will depend upon conversations that I have.

But I do want you to know that we will be as responsive as possible.

Now, in terms of news also, I will start at the end and then come back to the beginning. We will return, as you know, Sunday night. Monday I will spend here catching up on the signing of documents and so forth, that I understand will be on the desk when I return, on the domestic scene.

Tuesday morning there will be a meeting of the National Security Council in which I will report on various aspects of the trip and it will be discussed.

Then, either Tuesday afternoon or Wednesday morning I will have a meeting with the bipartisan leadership. I am planning then on Thursday to have a press conference, a press conference in this instance which will be different in one respect from the ones we have had previously. It will be my intention to speak at the outset for a few minutes, giving some general observations with regard to what I found in Europe, and then to have questions on a broad range, primarily devoted to that.

It is my plan on that occasion to let the conference go for an hour so that you can get more answers in depth. I think that will serve your purposes more usefully than otherwise.

That will be in lieu of the usual, I say the usual or the sometimes used, technique of coming back and making a nationwide report simply through a speech.

I thought that the press conference would elicit more really substantial information on the trip and on my views and on what I found in Europe than simply to make a statement.

I will make a statement at the outset for a few minutes and then have questions. So much for that.

Now, in terms of the logistics of the trip itself, as you already know, on my part, the substantial amount of time will be spent in the face-to-face discussions with the heads of government and heads of state.

Those conversations will cover, I can now report, a very broad area of subjects. We have heard from each government and, for that matter, each head of government and each head of state, the subjects that they would like generally to discuss.

I have also had discussions at the ambassadorial level and we have had discussions also abroad at the ambassadorial level in that respect.

There are three general categories that should be mentioned. First, I would expect to discuss all bilateral matters of substance which the other government may want to bring up and also those which we might think would be appropriate.

Second, it would be my intention to discuss also multilateral matters, particularly those that involve the Alliance and our relations with other countries in Europe. In each of those countries that we will be visiting we will be bringing up some multilateral matters.

Third, there will be a substantial amount of time spent on subjects that are neither bilateral or multilateral or relating only to Europe. There will be a substantial amount of discussion, from the indications that I have received from the

heads of government and heads of state abroad, on general subjects in the field of foreign affairs in which I will be extremely interested in getting the advice and the best thinking of the leaders abroad on those subjects—East-West relations, for example, arms control. I have already indicated that there will be discussions with our European friends on the possibility and the desirability of having discussions with the Soviet Union on various subjects, discussions of our relations—not only our relations but theirs—with underdeveloped countries, aid programs, for example; discussions also with regard to other areas of the world—Latin America, Africa, and Asia—in which we may have a common interest.

Now, on this latter point, I should emphasize a conviction that has been mine for many years based on what I have learned from previous trips. I have found that it is very valuable for anyone on the American scene in Government to go abroad and talk to leaders abroad, not only in Europe but all over the world, to talk to them with a very broad agenda, not limited to the bilateral matters of hard substance which usually come up. I think this is particularly important now.

We hear it said that the United States is the leader of the free world and because of our wealth and because of our military strength we would have to be described very objectively as being in that position.

But free world leadership, in my view, does not mean dictatorship to the free world. It means consultation with the free world and developing from the leaders of the free world the best possible thinking that we can develop for attacking our common problems.

There may be, for example, instances in

which the United States alone must make decisions which can affect the peace of the world. I want to get the best advice of the European leaders on those decisions.

I can say from experience, and I don't say this simply because I happen to be going to visit these men very shortly, that in previous years I have found there is a great well of knowledge, wisdom, and experience among our European friends; that it is very valuable for an American to go abroad and tap that knowledge, wisdom, and experience.

Consequently, I was delighted to find that when they suggested the agenda items, they were not limited to the bilateral subjects and not limited to the Alliance and their relations to it, but that they were keenly interested in discussing a broad variety of subjects involving world policy—world policy where the United States might have the primary responsibility, but where they, even though they did not have a substantial responsibility, at least might be able to make a contribution, a contribution in thinking as to how the problem could be solved.

Now, as far as the subjects are concerned, there are some, of course, that will be quite generally brought up.

I should begin with the subject of the Mideast. The Mideast will be brought up in all of the visits that I have. I put a high priority on this subject, as on many others, but particularly on this one, because after we complete this trip, it will then be, it seems to me, appropriate for the United States to make a determination as to how talks should go forward on the Mideast.

As you know, preliminary talks are now going forward in the U.N. on the four-power basis, bilaterally first, with the possibility of four-power talks later coming up.

What I want to do is to have direct discussions with all of the European leaders, but particularly with the British and the French, on this subject so that we may be able to find some common principles that will make these talks, which will be coming up, more effective than they otherwise might be and that will move them along at a faster pace.

I should leave here one thought that I have mentioned before, but I emphasize it again now: This is not with the thought that the four powers are going to dictate a settlement in the Mideast. It is with the thought, however, that if the four powers are going to contribute to a settlement that it will be most useful at this time to have these direct discussions, and that subject is on the agenda. We have prepared it very carefully. We know positions that we are prepared to discuss and we will be expecting to discuss that with them.

I use that as an example.

Now, in addition, other matters that will come up in every country are trade and monetary matters in the broadest sense. We will be prepared to discuss such matters. There will be some differences of views there as well as on the Mideast and other subjects. Of course they vary, as all of you are aware, depending upon the country which we may be visiting.

The problems of the Alliance we will be prepared to discuss in depth, and beyond that a number of bilateral subjects that I have already indicated in the East-West relations.

One further thought that perhaps is worth mentioning is that as I go to Europe for this trip, I am reminded of the fact that it was 22 years ago that I first went as a freshman Congressman, as a member of the Herter committee. As I was preparing to come down to meet with you today, I was thinking of how much things had changed in that 22 years.

Twenty-two years ago when we took off for Europe—I remember with Christian Herter, the chairman of the committee, later, as you will recall, our Secretary of State—we went there with the United States in a preeminent position both economically and militarily in the world, and as far as the Europeans were concerned, preeminent in the world militarily because we then had a monopoly on atomic weapons, and economically, the United States was infinitely strong.

The Europeans, of course, economically, militarily, and many of them, spiritually, were on their backs. I recall then that we went to Europe for the purpose of attempting to indicate to them what we would do, what we thought they should do. And they welcomed our leadership. They wanted our leadership. They needed our leadership because they were neither militarily, economically, or politically strong enough to provide it.

I think it was a high act of statesmanship on our part and on theirs that we were able to work out a multilateral arrangement on the aid programs which was effective, as it was.

But today the situation, I am keenly aware, has changed and all of you who have studied it, of course, are perhaps even as much aware of it, if not more.

Today, from an economic standpoint, we go to a Europe with some variations, of course: that is, economically infinitely stronger than it was then, and in some instances they are in a stronger position

with their currency than perhaps we might be, or at least that has been the case sometimes in recent years.

We find a Europe that from a political standpoint has regained political stability and therefore speaks with more independence than was the case previously.

We find, also, that insofar as the military situation is concerned, the world has changed, and as the world has changed, the problems in Europe have changed, not only because of the acquisition of nuclear weapons on the part of the Soviet Union, but because of the development of NATO—of course that was not there at that time.

What this requires us to do now, I think, is to recognize that the United States could make perhaps no greater mistake now than to treat the situation that we find there as it was then.

I am not suggesting that that is a mistake that has been made, but it is one that could be made. That is why I have emphasized that I am not going to Europe for the purpose of lecturing the Europeans, of telling them that we know best, and of telling them to follow us.

We are going there to listen to them, to exchange views, to get their best information and their best advice as to how their problems should be solved and how world problems should be solved. We need their advice and we are going there very honestly trying to seek it.

I think in that spirit we will be able to accomplish several objectives. I said at the outset that you should not expect spectacular news from this trip. I do say, however, that it will be solid news—solid in the sense that as a result of this trip there will be a new spirit of consultation which will result in a new spirit of confidence among our European friends and ourselves.

I believe that this first discussion will lead to others. I believe that the foreign ministers conference that will be held here on the 20th anniversary of NATO will be a more productive conference, looking toward purpose, as I have indicated at my press conference a couple of weeks ago.

I believe also that the meetings that I will expect to have—probably in the United States, with the various leaders that I will be seeing in Europe on this occasion—will be far more useful now that we have started on this kind of basis with my going to Europe first, talking to them, and having long discussions face to face, without feeling the pressure of having to make some kind of settlement of an outstanding crisis problem that comes upon us.

What I am really, perhaps, hoping for most out of this trip is that as a result of it the United States interest in and the United States support of the European-American relationship has never been stronger and has never been more needed if we are going to have a peaceful world.

Secondly, that there will be a new era of consultation, and I mean real give-and-take consultation, between the leaders of the European-American community. We need it, I want it, and I was very happy to find that our colleagues in Europe also want it and need it. I am looking forward to that.

Well, when we return, I will be glad to try to expand on some of these questions that I have not answered in these opening remarks. I would like to just close on one social note.

This is a very large group here and very few of you, maybe half of you, have been on trips with me before. But I am sure that people like Pete Lisagor [Chicago Daily News], and others who have—Bill Theis [Hearst Newspapers], who went on the first one in 1953—will recall that it has always been one of my customs prior to going on a trip to have some sort of a get-together with the members of the traveling press and then afterwards to have a reunion.

I didn't know whether it was possible now that I have moved to this position, but I thought it was worth trying, so I am delighted that you can all come. I won't have the intimate contact that I have always tried to have with the members of the press on such a trip. It isn't possible now, but we will do our best to make it good from a logistical standpoint. I hope that when we return, not only in the more formal press conference, but in the reception which we will hope to have at some time afterwards, I will have a chance to see you all again personally. And now we will move into the State Dining Room if you like and we can chat a bit more.

Thank you.

NOTE: The President spoke at 5:15 p.m. on Friday, February 21, in the East Room at the White House. His remarks were issued in the form of a White House press release on February 22, 1969.

Also released on February 22 were a list of members of the President's party and of the news media representatives accompanying the President on his European trip and background information on previous visits abroad that President Nixon had made.

66   Remarks at Andrews Air Force Base on Departing for Europe.   *February* 23, 1969

Mr. Vice President, Mr. Ambassador and your distinguished colleagues, all of the distinguished Members of the House and the Senate:

I want all of you to know how grateful I am that on this rainy Sunday morning at such an early hour you have come to send me off on this trip to Europe. And as I leave I know that this trip is one which has created a great deal of interest, both in the United States and Europe.

It is a trip, I wish to emphasize, which is not intended and will not settle all of the problems we have in the world. The problems we face are too complex and too difficult to be settled by what I would call the "showboat" diplomacy.

On the other hand, before we can make progress with the problems with which we have differences with our opponents, it is necessary to consult with our friends. And we are going to have real consultation because we seek not only their support but their advice and their counsel on the grave problems that we face in the world—the problem of Vietnam, of the Mideast, monetary problems, all the others that may cause difficulties between nations.

One note I would like to leave with this group before we take off. I have found that many who have written me have expressed concern about the possibility of

demonstrations abroad. And my answer was eloquently given by a letter I received from a friend in Berlin. He said that 95 percent of the people in Berlin were glad that we were coming and 5 percent of the people did not want us to come.

And so it is in the world today. The fact that there are demonstrations or the possibility of demonstrations cannot deter anyone who goes abroad to seek new solutions to the problems that block peace in the world. And I can assure all of our friends abroad that we look forward to their welcome. We will not be deterred by the fact that a few do not want us to come.

We will remember that the great majority of the people here in the United States, as indicated by this bipartisan sendoff, and the great majority of people in Europe and in the world want peace and they want the statesmen of the world to do everything they can to seek peace.

This is the first step in what we hope will be a long series of steps that will take us down the road toward better understanding between nations.

Thank you.

NOTE: The President spoke at 7:47 a.m. at Andrews Air Force Base near Washington, D.C. In his opening words he referred to Ambassador Guillermo Sevilla-Sacasa of Nicaragua, who was Dean of the Diplomatic Corps.

67   Remarks on Arrival in Brussels.   *February* 23, 1969

Your Majesty:

I am most grateful for your very gracious welcome. We in the United States

well recall that Your Majesty's first official trip to another country, after ascending the throne, was made to our country. I am especially pleased, therefore, that my own first trip abroad as President begins in your country.

It was exactly half a century ago this year, in 1919, that one of America's greatest Presidents made an historic postwar visit to what was then a devastated Belgium. That was the last occasion on which an American President set foot on Belgian soil.

Speaking then to the Belgian Parliament, Woodrow Wilson declared on that occasion: "Belgium's cause has linked the governments of the civilized world together. They have realized their common duty. They have drawn together as if instinctively into a league of right. They have put the whole power of organized manhood behind this conception of justice which is common to mankind."

"That," he said, "is the significance of the League of Nations."

Woodrow Wilson's dream collapsed and the League failed, as the people of Belgium know all too tragically. But the search goes on for a durable peace, one that symbolizes and embodies what Wilson then called "this conception of justice which is common to mankind"—or, as I heard Your Majesty describe it so eloquently just 10 years ago, in addressing the United States Congress: "Peace is the tranquility of order. Mere tranquility can be cold war, but the tranquility of order implies justice."

The search for that peace is what brings me now to Europe, to begin the process of consultation with America's allies and gathering their judgment.

It seems altogether appropriate that the first stop on such a trip should be Belgium. Belgium maintains, despite the tragic events of 1914 and 1940, its remarkable spirit, and rebounded from each ordeal with the vigor and resilience of what Your Majesty has just referred to as "a free and ancient land," and not least, a nation that has played so creative a role during the past 20 years in developing the institutions that give substance to the concept of an Atlantic community.

The peoples of our two countries have shared many things. We have been allies in war and partners in peace. But even more important, as we look to the future, are the common ideals that inspire us and that have made the friendship of our peoples so warm and so lasting.

I look forward with great pleasure to the prospect of working in the coming years with Your Majesty, with your government, and with the Belgian people, as together we press toward that peace with justice we all so earnestly seek.

Your Majesty, as I stand here I feel that I stand on hallowed ground for millions of Americans, as well as Belgians. This is the soil that twice in 50 years has been devastated by war. Therefore, it is altogether appropriate that this new search for the peace that will avoid that kind of devastation should begin on this soil. I am proud to be here and to be welcomed by you so graciously. I am confident that at the beginning of this journey, the fact that we start on this soil is a good omen for the future.

Thank you.

NOTE: The President spoke at approximately 9 p.m. at Brussels National Airport in response to welcoming remarks by King Baudouin of Belgium, who spoke as follows:

Mr. President, Belgium is glad to be the first country this side of the Atlantic to receive you on the occasion of the journey by which you have chosen to begin the great task that is involving you in world affairs.

You have come to a free and ancient land which is happy to be the host country of important international organizations, the European Community and NATO.

I have pleasure in welcoming you in Belgium and on our continent. We are delighted at the initiative you are taking, since it aims at coordinating for joint action in the cause of peace the views of the United States of America and those of Europe, which, despite the difficulties accumulated by history, is advancing on the road to unity.

During this year, which will perhaps be that of man's first landing on the moon, we are more than ever conscious of the gulf between the wonderful possibilities open to us and the obligations which burden the world because of war, want, injustice, and inequality.

May your journey and your interviews provide an opportunity for friendly nations better to combine their efforts to solve their problems on which the very future of mankind depends.

May they also make easier a sincere dialogue and sound agreement with those who are governed by other political systems and who share the awe-inspiring responsibility for world peace.

If so, a prayer will be granted.

68   Remarks to the North Atlantic Council in Brussels. *February 24, 1969*

Mr. Chairman and members of the North Atlantic Council:

I thank you for your very thoughtful and generous words of welcome to this Council and it is indeed a very great pleasure for me to be here.

This Council is both symbol and substance of the tie that has joined us as an Atlantic Alliance for nearly 20 years.

On this first trip abroad as President of the United States I find myself thinking back to my first trip to Europe. That was in 1947, in my first year in Congress—my first year, in fact, in public life. I came here then as a member of the Herter committee, which studied Europe's postwar economic needs in order to help lay the foundations for the Marshall Plan. Although I have been back many times, those first impressions remain valid, for 1947 was the starting point of our journey together. What we have built in the past 22 years is a testimony to what can be achieved through common will and a spirit of partnership.

The years since I first visited Western Europe have further confirmed my commitment to the concept of Atlantic partnership.

I should like to take a few minutes today to share with you some of my thoughts about that partnership.

First, as all of us in this room know, partners are not expected always to agree. But they are expected to consult.

I know there have been rumblings of discontent in Europe—a feeling that too often the United States talked at its partners instead of talking with them, or merely informed them of decisions after they were made instead of consulting with them before deciding.

The United States is determined to listen with a new attentiveness to its NATO partners—not only because they have a right to be heard, but because we want their ideas. I believe we have a right to expect that consultation shall be a two-way street.

This point is at the heart of one of the vital problems facing the Alliance. Consultation, simply as a means of getting agreement for unilateral action, is demoralizing. What we need is genuine consultation, a new spirit of cooperation before the fact.

In the course of my campaign last fall, I said: "If our ideals of Atlantic interdependence are to mean anything in practice, it's time we began lecturing our European partners less and listening to them more. What we need is not more proclamations and declarations, but a greater attention to what our allies think." This I deeply believe.

That is why I am here. My visits to some of your capitals—and I wish it could be all of them—and to this Council, are in the nature of a search. I have come for work, not for ceremony; to inquire, not to insist; to consult, not to convince; to listen and learn, and to begin what I hope will be a continuing interchange of ideas and insights.

After 20 years, the Atlantic Alliance must adapt to the conditions brought on by its success. It must replace the unity of a common fear with the community of shared purpose. It must pool not only its arms but also its brains.

One of the greatest values of having an alliance is the chance it provides to share ideas—to broaden the horizons of our thinking, to multiply the resources of experience and perspective we can bring to our problems, not only in our own immediate areas but throughout the world.

Surely one thing we have learned from these difficult years is that no nation has a monopoly on wisdom.

We also have learned that no great nation, and no great group of nations, can view the problems of its own community in isolation.

We are all "riders on the earth together"—fellow citizens of a world community.

In today's world, what kind of an alliance shall we strive to build?

As I see it, an alliance is not the temporary pooling of selfish interests; it is a continuing process of cooperation: "a ship on its passage out, and not a voyage complete."

The purpose of this trip is to help encourage that process, to seek ways to keep the relationship between America and Europe in tune with the times.

A modern alliance must be a living thing, capable of growth, able to adapt to changing circumstances.

To keep the Alliance abreast of the times, we must, I believe, today, ask ourselves some hard questions.

NATO was brought into being by the threat from the Soviet Union. What is the nature of that threat today?

When NATO was founded, Europe's economies were still shattered by war. Now they are flourishing. How should this be reflected by changed relationships among the NATO partners?

We are all grappling with problems of a modern environment, which are the by-products of our advanced technologies—problems such as the pollution of air and water, and the congestion in our cities. Together, we can dramatically advance our mastery of these problems. By what means can we best cooperate to bring this about?

And most fundamental of all—the one thing certain about the next 20 years is that they will be different from the last 20. What do we expect from our alliance in these next 20 years? How shall we adapt our structure to advance our purpose?

The answers to these great questions will not be decided in a week. They deal with the vast sweep of history, they need the most thorough deliberation. But the questions are with us; we cannot evade them; and the fact that we have begun this process of soul-searching is a good augury.

I have said before that we are ending a period of confrontation and entering an era of negotiation. In due course, and with proper preparation, the United States will enter into negotiations with the Soviet Union on a wide range of issues, some of which will affect our European allies. We will do so on the basis of full consultation and cooperation with our allies, because we recognize that the chances for successful negotiations depend on our unity.

I realize that this course has not always been followed adequately in the past. But I pledge to you today, that in any negotiations affecting the interests of the NATO nations, there will be full and genuine consultations before and during those negotiations.

Beyond consulting on those negotiations, and beyond consulting on other policies that directly affect the NATO nations themselves, I intend to consult on a broad range of other matters. I shall not only welcome but actively seek the counsel of America's NATO partners on the questions that may affect the peace and stability of the world, whatever the part of the world in which they arise.

The nations of NATO are rich in physical resources, but they are even richer in their accumulated wisdom, in their experience of the world today. In fashioning America's policies, we need the benefit of that wisdom and that experience.

As NATO enters its third decade, I see for it an opportunity to be more than it ever has been before: a bulwark of peace, the architect of new means of partner-

ship, and an invigorated forum for new ideas and new technologies to enrich the lives of our peoples.

In creating new policy-making machinery in Washington, one of my principal aims has been to shift the focus of American policy from crisis management to crisis prevention. That is one of the reasons why I value NATO so highly. NATO was established as a preventive force—and NATO can be credited with the fact that while Europe has endured its share of crises in these last 20 years, the ultimate crisis that would have provoked a nuclear war has been prevented. Those nations that were free 20 years ago are still free today.

Thus, in its original purpose, NATO has been a resounding success. Europe and America, the old world and the new working together, have proved that the dream of collective security can be made a reality.

But we cannot rest on our laurels; there is no real security in stagnation. The successful strategies of the past two decades are inadequate to the decades ahead.

The tie that binds Europe and America is not the contemplation of danger, to be stretched or tightened by the fluctuations of fear.

The ties that bind our continents are the common tradition of freedom, the common desire for progress, and the common passion for peace.

In that more constructive spirit, let us look at new situations with new eyes, and in so doing, set an example for the world.

NOTE: The President spoke at 9:15 a.m. at NATO Headquarters in Brussels, Belgium. The Chairman of the North Atlantic Council and Secretary General of NATO was Manlio Brosio.

69   Toasts of the President and King Baudouin of Belgium at the Royal Palace in Brussels.   *February* 24, 1969

Your Majesty, Mr. Prime Minister, Mr. Foreign Minister, Mr. Secretary General, Mr. Secretary, Your Excellencies:

In responding to the very gracious toast by His Majesty, I would like to be permitted just a little more length than that, if he will permit me, because I did not want here to be received so graciously and so generously by Your Majesty and Your Majesty the Queen, without indicating what is in the hearts of all of us who come here from the United States on this occasion.

I spoke to that point last night at the airport. I would like to speak, if I might, in more personal terms at this time.

When I met His Majesty 10 years ago, I had a very good chance to talk to him, to know him, and to appreciate him for not only the fact that he was a king, but that he was a man who had a deep sensitivity about the great forces that move the world and a deep concern for his fellow man in the true tradition of the great kings.

As I meet him again on this occasion, I have had the opportunity again to know him, to talk to him, and to hear not only his understanding of those peoples in the world who will never sit at a table like this and his feeling for them which is in his heart, but also his understanding of a great tide in the affairs of nations which affects us all, the search of our young people for a new idealism, a new principle.

It is this kind of thinking, this depth of concern that, clearly apart from the very substantive talks that I have had today with our friends from NATO and that I will be having in the balance of this trip, it is this kind of thinking coming from the head of this state for whom the people of the United States have such a strong feeling, that makes this trip worth while, apart from anything else.

And, having said that, Your Majesty, I am so delighted that while 10 years ago we met only you, that today we meet also Her Majesty the Queen.

We look forward to the time when the two of you will visit us in Washington.

I understand that you will be coming not primarily for that visit, but perhaps to see an Apollo shot. But as you come to see men who may go to the moon, we will look forward to talking to you again in depth about those problems which you can discuss so eloquently of those of us who live on earth.

Finally, I would say that as I stand here in this country, a country that we feel so close to in the United States because of what we have shared together in war and in peace, that I am deeply grateful for your hospitality, for your generous remarks last night, and as I raise my glass in this magnificent hall which reminds us of the past, I am reminded of the fact that a king—an office that often has been considered to be no longer relevant to the great issues of today—that a king in the person of Your Majesty thinks as deeply, with more vision, and with more concern than most of the leaders of the world with whom I have talked.

It is in that spirit, in the spirit of our common affection for the people of your country, of our respect for those people and for all of those at this table, and of our personal respect for you and your gracious Queen that I raise my glass to His Majesty the King.

NOTE: The President spoke at 2:04 p.m. at the Royal Palace in Brussels. In his opening words he referred to King Baudouin, Prime Minister Gaston Eyskens and Foreign Minister Pierre Harmel of Belgium, Manlio Brosio, Secretary General of NATO and Chairman of the North Atlantic Council, and U.S. Secretary of State William P. Rogers who accompanied the President to Europe.

Prior to the President's remarks King Baudouin proposed a toast, as follows:

I ask you to join me in raising my glass and raising your glass to the health of the President of the United States and also to Mrs. Nixon and to the old and lasting friendship between our two countries.

70 Remarks on Departure From Belgium. *February 24, 1969*

I LEAVE Belgium with great regret. This has been much too short a visit, from my standpoint, but a very pleasant and a very productive one.

I leave more convinced than ever that there at the center of the Western Alliance stands a stout-hearted and illustrious people—worthy descendants of those early Celts who gave Caesar's legions no small amount of trouble.

What is certainly one of my most vivid impressions of Belgium is epitomized by your sovereign—an impression of a nation young in spirit. His Majesty's keen interest in space, his desire to involve young people in the revitalizing of society—these are concerns of the future, and concerns that we share.

I have been greatly pleased, also, by my conversations at NATO Headquarters. Under the wise leadership of Secretary General Brosio, our allied representatives are giving careful and intelligent attention to the future of the Alliance, and to the opportunities that can be opened to make it a more effective instrument for peace as it enters its third decade. I might add that my visit persuaded me of another thing: that NATO is indeed fortunate to have its headquarters here, in so delightful and so cosmopolitan a capital.

Brussels was my first stop on this trip, and I have other capitals yet to visit. But I feel encouraged already in my belief that America can work with its European partners in increasing harmony. My talks with President Rey and the Commission of the European Communities have strengthened my convictions as to the high purpose and indispensability of European economic integration. And in all the talks I have had, from all the people I have met, from the vigor and the energy and the graciousness I have seen displayed here in Brussels, I have drawn increased confidence that free people who work together have a right to be optimists about the future.

NOTE: The President spoke at approximately 5 p.m. at Brussels National Airport upon departing for London. During his remarks he referred to King Baudouin of Belgium, Manlio Brosio, Secretary General of NATO and Chairman of the North Atlantic Council, and Jean Rey, President of the Commission of the European Communities.

71   Remarks at the Airport on Arrival in London.
      February 24, 1969

Mr. Prime Minister:

I express to you my very deep appreciation for those eloquent remarks and also for the spirit which was exemplified by your statement that the protocol on this occasion was limited so that we could have more opportunity for the discussions to which we both look forward.

I only know from my previous visits to your country that here the welcome, whether it is one which is filled with protocol or one which is primarily devoted to talk, is one that I have always appreciated and—going back over 22 years I have had the opportunity to meet with British statesmen, with you, and in every instance I have profited by those meetings.

The purpose of this visit, as you have so very accurately indicated, is to discuss our common problems, but beyond that, to discuss the problems of the alliance of which we are a part.

I would add one further dimension, to discuss the problems of the world in which we may not have a direct interest in one country or the other, but in which both of us have responsibilities to adopt those policies which will promote a better way to peace in the world.

On that score, Mr. Prime Minister, I noted with interest the great success of a recent meeting you had with the Commonwealth Ministers. In my travels abroad, going back over those 22 years when I first came here as a young Congressman, I have had the opportunity not only to visit this country many times, but to visit every one of the countries of the Commonwealth and to visit other nations no longer in the Commonwealth, but nations which—like the United States of America—share the language, the same great traditions that we in the United States share with the United Kingdom.

I know the contribution, therefore, the contribution in ideals, the contribution in institutions, the contribution that has been made in so many respects by this nation around the world.

That is why I am looking forward to discussions, not only bilaterally and multilaterally, as they affect our common alliance, but on the problems of the whole world, because I know the wisdom that you and your colleagues can provide— wisdom which is essential for all of us as we attempt to find the solutions to those problems. I believe that the purpose of my visit was perhaps explained, in a different context, best by Woodrow Wilson who was the first American President to visit this country. This is what he told the citizens of Manchester in 1918:

"Friendship must have a machinery. If I cannot correspond with you, if I cannot learn your minds, if I cannot cooperate with you, I cannot be your friend, and if the world is to remain a body of friends, it must have the means of friendship, the means of constant friendly intercourse, the means for constant watchfulness over the common interests."

Winston Churchill called ours a special relationship. He was not referring to legal obligations but to human intangibles. He was referring to the means of communication to which Woodrow Wilson had referred to 50 years ago. And no two nations in the world more commonly and more closely share the means of communication than do the United States and the United Kingdom. We share a common language. We share the common law. We share great institutions of the Parliament. We share other institutions.

Because we share those institutions we enjoy a means of communication which gives us a special relationship. It means, too, that we share something else—a common commitment to a peace that transcends national boundaries and because we are partners in the quest for peace we know that our relationship—that special relationship that we have—is not exclusive because that peace that we seek, the two of us, will be secure only when all nations enjoy the relationship of trust and confidence that unites us.

I believe, as I stand here today, that we can bring about a durable peace in our time. But it cannot come to those who seek it frantically with overnight deals or dramatic gestures. It cannot come to those who pursue it casually, without real help or genuine idealism.

As those in this nation know better than those in our Nation—because of your longer experience—peace will come, I believe, step by step, measured and deliberate, continuing to pursue the goal we seek despite setbacks and disappointments. It is that sense of history that you have, that sense of history that all of us in our country respect and that we seek to emulate. It is from that that we can learn. And so we shall strive on this visit and on many others that we will have over the years that I shall be in office; we shall strive for a mutual trust between our two nations and between all nations, the kind of trust that already exists between your nation and mine.

NOTE: The President spoke at approximately 6 p.m. at Heathrow Airport in response to welcoming remarks by Prime Minister Harold Wilson, which follow:

Mr. President, it is a great pleasure on behalf of Her Majesty's Government, to welcome you to Britain. Equally, my colleagues join with me in welcoming the Secretary of State and your other distinguished colleagues.

You have said, Mr. President, that your purpose in visiting Europe is to work, to observe, and to discuss. For that reason I do not intend, by lengthening my own words of welcome, to defer for more than a few minutes the job that we are to do together while you are our guests.

The weather is cool still, but your welcome from all of those I have the honor to represent is warm. We welcome you personally—a pleasure a number of us have had before. We welcome you as a newly elected President of a great country, our friend and ally. In particular, we welcome your decision, within days after your inauguration, to turn into reality those moving words in your inaugural speech by coming to discuss in this informal way with European heads of government not only the problems of Europe but our mutual hopes and desires for the alliance to which we both belong—not Europe only, not the Atlantic Alliance only, but the problems of the wider world.

There have been those in perhaps both our countries who have been tempted to take these facts of our common purpose and our common alliance too easily for granted because of its success in creating the conditions it set out to create. For those to whom security leads to complacency, the events of last summer represent a call to renewed vigilance, to still stronger solidarity and cohesion.

But equally, Mr. President, on what all of us here in Europe will feel to have been an historic mission, it is right also that our talks should be directed beyond the achieving of security to the most positive ends of the alliance and our common purposes together.

The aim: that from strength on our side we can give on the other side a degree of good will corresponding to that which we are prepared to hold out, moving progressively to a feeling of security, into the path of cooperation and peace.

But, Mr. President, this is not the only lesson that we in Europe drew from the events of last summer. What those events also underlined was a need for still greater unity within Europe, designed not to weaken or disrupt the alliance but to strengthen it: a unity which will enable Europe and each of us as a European country to develop together the great potential of industrial strength and skills which we have, all of us here in Europe; a unity in political and economic terms which will reject narrow, inward-looking attitudes in favor of the wider world concept which you, Mr. President, and we are committed to advance.

For as grows Europe's strength, so grows the strength of the alliance and the thrust of our purposes throughout the world.

Mr. President, you especially asked that with working time so precious, the ceremony and the honors which in other circumstances would be entirely right and fitting for the head of state of your country should be reduced to a minimum. Regard, then, this restricted official welcome as a token only of the welcome which Crown, Parliament, the Estates of the Realm, including industry and labor, and above all, the whole British people, hold out to you—hold out because they feel it in their hearts.

The platform is yours, Mr. President, so that not only those friends but all in whose name we speak can hear from you—and then to work.

72   Letter to the President of the University of Notre Dame on Student Unrest.   *February 24, 1969*

Dear Ted:

I share your concern over the recent disorders that have paralyzed campus after campus across our country in recent weeks, and I want to applaud the forthright stand you have taken.

As you know, the issues raised by the protesting students range from minor reforms within the academic community to major concerns of national policy.

But the means some students—a small, irresponsible minority—have employed reflect an impatience with democratic processes, an intolerance of legitimately constituted authority, and a complete disregard for the rights of others.

Violence and vandalism have marked many of these protests, and the rights of the majority of the students have been grossly abused.

If the integrity of our universities is to be preserved, then certain principles must be re-established and certain basic rules enforced. Intimidation and threats remain outlaw weapons in a free society.

A fundamental governing principle of any great university is that the rule of reason and not the rule of force prevails. Whoever rejects that principle forfeits his right to be a member of the academic community. The university administrator who fails to uphold that principle jeopardizes one of the central pillars of his own institution and weakens the very foundation of American education.

I have directed the Vice President in meetings in Washington this week with the Governors of the fifty states to discuss what action, consistent with the vital importance of maintaining the traditional independence of American universities, might be taken at the state and federal levels to cope with the growing lawlessness and violence on our campuses. I would appreciate it greatly if you would take the time to give him the benefit of your views on this matter.

With warm regards,

Sincerely,

RICHARD NIXON

[Reverend Theodore M. Hesburgh, Notre Dame University, Corby Hall, Notre Dame, Indiana]

NOTE: The letter was dated February 22, 1969, and released February 24, 1969.

73   Special Message to the Congress Proposing Establishment of a New Public Debt Limit.   *February 24, 1969*

To the Congress of the United States:

When I took office as President of the United States, the public debt subject to limit was $364.2 billion—only $800 million below the statutory ceiling of $365 billion. Available projections indicated that borrowings needed to provide the Government with minimum cash balances essential for its operations would place the debt subject to limit at or above the legal ceiling by mid-April.

These projections have now been reviewed and updated on the basis of the latest revenue and expenditure flows. They continue to show inadequate leeway under the debt limit to meet all anticipated cash requirements through the middle of April. These facts permit me only one prudent course of action. I must ask the Congress to revise the debt limit before mid-April. The new limit should provide a reasonable margin for contingencies.

President Johnson foresaw the possible need for such action when he stated in his fiscal year 1970 Budget that "It may be necessary . . . within the next few months to raise the present debt limit."

Continuing high interest rates may add several hundred million dollars to the 1969 expenditures estimated by President Johnson. Other possible increases in outlays, including farm price support payments and a wide variety of past commitments in other programs—such as highways—may be greater than was estimated by the outgoing Administration.

All department and agency heads are now reviewing their programs in a determined effort to reduce costs. But we should not let our hopes for success in this effort deter us from the necessary action on the debt limit. Such cost reductions can have only a minor effect on expenditures in the next month or two, and it is in early March and again in early April that the Treasury will be faced with the heaviest drain on its resources.

Moreover, even if the Budget surpluses for fiscal years 1969 and 1970 were to prove somewhat larger than estimated in the January Budget, the present debt limit would be inadequate for fiscal year 1970. Thus even if an immediate increase in the debt limit could be avoided, an increase cannot be postponed very far into the next fiscal year. My predecessor also noted this fact when he presented his Budget for fiscal year 1970.

The apparent paradox of a need for a higher debt limit in years of anticipated budget surplus is explained mainly by the fact that the fiscal year 1969 and 1970 surpluses reflect substantial surpluses in Government trust funds—projected at $9.4 billion in fiscal year 1969 and $10.3 billion in fiscal year 1970. These surpluses in the trust funds provide cash to the Treasury, but only through the medium of investment in special Treasury issues. The consequent increase in such special issues is subject to the debt limit, under present definitions. Hence, *the debt subject to limit will rise even though borrowing from the public will decline.*

In addition, we must acknowledge the seasonal pattern in Treasury receipts. Net cash requirements prior to the mid-April tax date are regularly very substantial, while after that date the Treasury will be repaying a large amount of debt on a net basis.

While a small, temporary increase in the debt limit might prevent the undue restrictiveness of the present limit in the months immediately ahead, I urge that we now direct our attention to the future and at least through fiscal year 1970.

I believe that the Congress should now enact a debt limit which will serve the needs of our Nation both for the balance of this fiscal year and for the foreseeable future.

In doing so, I also believe that the Congress should take this occasion to redefine the debt subject to limit to bring it into accord with the new unified Budget concept developed by a distinguished Commission that was headed by the present Secretary of the Treasury and included leaders from both Houses of Congress, officials of the previous Administration, and distinguished private citizens. The recommendations of this Commission largely have been adopted in the last two Budget presentations and in the new form of Congressional budget scorekeeping. These have been major forward steps toward better public understanding of the budget. The concept of the debt limit should also be redefined as suggested in the Commission's report.

Under the unified Budget concept, attention is focused on the total receipts and expenditures of the Federal Government, including the trust funds. The surplus or deficit thus reflects the net of revenue and expenditure transactions between the Federal Government and the public, and the net debt transactions between the Government and the public are thus the relevant basis for a proper under-standing of the Federal borrowing requirements. To conform fully with this Budget presentation, only those Federal obligations which are held by the public— all debt except that held by Federally-owned agencies and by the trust funds— should be subject to the statutory limit on the public debt. Debt of Federally-owned agencies held by the public would be included as well as direct Treasury debt.

This change would in no way affect the integrity of the trust funds. This Administration recognizes, as the Commission on Budget Concepts emphasized, the firm obligation of the Government to maintain proper, separate accounting for the trust funds. This can and will be done without including obligations held by the trust funds in the total debt subject to the debt limit.

I therefore propose that the Congress establish a new debt limit defined to accord with the unified Budget concept. On this basis, a limit of $300 billion should be adequate to permit efficient and responsible handling of the Government's financing for the foreseeable future. This compares with an outstanding debt on the unified Budget concept of $293.7 billion on January 21, 1969.

On the present public debt limit concept, the debt outstanding on January 21, 1969 was $364.2 billion as compared with the current debt limit of $365 billion. An increase in that limit to approximately $382 billion would correspond in the next fiscal year to the $300 billion limit I am proposing on the unified budget basis.

RICHARD NIXON

The White House
February 24, 1969

74   Remarks to the Staff at the American Embassy in London.   *February 25, 1969*

Mr. Secretary, Mr. Ambassador, ladies and gentlemen:

I appreciate your very warm welcome as I step for a moment on American soil in this whirlwind trip of Britain and several European countries.

I must not let the remarks of the Secretary of State go by with that reference to being upstaged. I can tell you that we have these little colloquies from time to time because we are old friends going back many, many years.

I can remember a time 10 years ago when I was a young Vice President and he was a young Attorney General of the United States. Now, I suppose it could be said that he is a young Secretary of State and I am an old President.

But I do want you to know that in speaking of your Ambassador and our Ambassador, that when I spoke of the giants I used that term quite objectively and quite deliberately. It is very easy in the diplomatic circuit to use adjectives freely and particularly the adjective "great"—everybody is a "great" man and this was a "great" party and you are a "great" staff, and all that sort of thing.

When I use the word "giant" and apply it to David Bruce, I am simply referring to the fact that in my travels around the world, going back over 22 years, in meeting American Ambassadors in 73 countries of the world, a few stand out.

Virtually all were outstanding and were good representatives of the United States, but a few were men who would be in any post a great credit to this Nation and men who we can ill-afford to lose in the service of the Nation.

When I look back over his service—his service in the post as Ambassador to this country for 8 years, longer than any American Ambassador has ever served as Ambassador to this country; when I look back over his service also as Ambassador to other nations and his work in government over the years, particularly in the foreign policy field—I can certainly subscribe to the fact that, of all those we could describe as giants, he rates very, very high. Not simply because he has been, as he obviously has, a man whom you all respect—you who work for him and with him—but also because through the years, whether it was a Republican President or a Democratic President, whether it was an Eisenhower or a Kennedy or a Johnson or a Nixon or a Truman, we disagreed on some things, but we all agreed that David Bruce was a giant.

Now, having spoken of the giant, I want to speak of the people who make giants possible. I will use an analogy, one not exactly appropriate but one that will illustrate the point.

It has been said that one of the reasons that we can see further than those who went before us is that we stand on the shoulders of the giants who went before us.

And so it is with a man like David Bruce, one who has rendered such distinguished service in so many posts and such distinguished service here. He would be the first to say that his record would not be so outstanding had it not been for the fact that he has in this Embassy one of the outstanding staffs.

I don't refer just to Mr. Kaiser [Deputy Chief of Mission] and to others who are in the top echelons, but I am referring to the people up and down the line. I imagine in this room are people who typed out my schedules—or "sheduels" I should say. [*Laughter*] I can imagine there are those who ran them off on mimeograph machines—oh no, you have got new things where you just push them through like that!

I can imagine that many others have worked overtime in trying to handle the telephone calls, and saying "no" nicely when you said that we could not do this or that. As the visitors come—the VIP's, sometimes a VP, even sometimes a President, and sometimes a Secretary of State—what a tremendous extra burden it puts on a staff.

I know there are hundreds here in this room, in this Embassy, that neither Secretary Rogers nor I will ever be able to thank personally, who helped to make this visit the success that it is from a logistic standpoint. Whether it succeeds from a diplomatic standpoint depends upon us, but I can assure you that what you have done has made our work much more easy because you have handled our arrangements so effectively that we are able to move knowing that everything is arranged in just the way that it should be.

I express my appreciation to each of you who have worked on this trip. But I would like to go beyond that. During the past month and a week that I have served in this office, I have done something that some tell me was unprecedented for a President. I went to each of the departments of Government to pay a visit to the top people in Government—the 400 or 500 who hold the top career posts and appointive posts in the State Department and the other 11 Cabinet departments.

I went there first to get acquainted and second to bring a message to them that I

now want to bring to you. The message is this: that ours is a great country. Our Nation has tremendous responsibilities. Our British friends, as we meet with them—first because they are kind and generous and hospitable, but second, because as pragmatists they realize the fact and point out that the decisions made in the United States, due to our power and our wealth, will affect them and affect the peace of the world for the last third of this century, if not longer.

So as we think of that awesome power, we think of our Government and what our Government does. We think not only of a President and a Secretary of State and an Ambassador and the top officials of his staff, but we think of the 3 million people who work in Government, in all the areas of Government, and we realize that administrations will change and perhaps 400 or 500 people at the top will change, and they will change the policies and perhaps change the direction of an administration, and sometimes they will be rated as successes and sometimes as failures; but whether they succeed, if they do succeed, will depend not only on what they do but it will depend upon the loyalty, the dedication and devotion of thousands, in a case like an embassy as big as this one, and millions, as we look around the world, of Americans working for Government who have given their lives to Government service.

I just want you to know that I know that. I want you to know that I appreciate that.

I want you to know that in my travels around the world—and I mentioned earlier that they have been to 73 countries; I have been entertained by Ambassadors; I have been briefed by briefing officers; I have received the courtesies that are extended to Congressmen, to Senators, and to private citizens—and sometimes I have been a private citizen as I have traveled, not by my own choice—but I have been a private citizen and I can assure you that never have I failed to appreciate the Foreign Service of the United States in the broadest sense, not just the Foreign Service but those who work in USIA and AID, all the programs that are represented.

The point I am trying to get across here is this: that not only in the departments in Washington but in the far-flung agencies of this Government around the world there are millions of Americans in Government service who will determine whether the new leadership, when it finishes its role in Washington, will be a success or a failure and whether, thereby, that new leadership will have contributed to a better world, a more peaceful world, or whether we will have failed in the mission which we have set out to undertake.

So as I recognize our responsibility and what you can contribute, I want you to know that we are deeply grateful, not only for everything you did to make this visit possible, but grateful that you have dedicated your lives to public service.

We recognize that sometimes the jobs you will do will be boring, they seem to be. Sometimes they may seem not to matter. Sometimes you think maybe you don't get the promotion you should get and somebody else goes ahead, and perhaps what you do doesn't count as much as what somebody else does. But I have one illustration that proves my point better than anything else I could say:

You have had a very distinguished visitor to this country, Frank Borman, a few days ago. He made an immense impression here and in the other countries he visited. I recall, when I was at the White House I was congratulating him in a toast for what he and his fellow astronauts had done, his response, in that humility with grace which is his trademark and the trademark of his colleagues, was along these lines: He said, "We appreciate the remarks you have made about us. But," he said, "I want to point out that there are 400,000 Americans who, in one way or another, contributed to the building of the Apollo spacecraft and to this program." He said, "I want to point out that there are 2 million parts in an Apollo spacecraft. So, if something went wrong with one of those parts, which had been created by these 400,000 Americans, that tremendous, exciting journey around the moon could not have been possible."

That, of course, is what government is about. We make decisions at the highest level. Those decisions will depend on the devotion and the dedication of hundreds of thousands of people, yes, millions of people around this world, some of whom will contribute to the making of the decisions, others who will contribute, as you have, to the logistical factors which are so important in a trip like this, and others who will contribute to carrying them out.

I am deeply grateful therefore, as I stand in your presence, for the fact that America is so well represented today by a giant. But I am also grateful for the fact that this giant and all the others like him who have been successful are backed up; as a matter of fact, they become giants because they stand on the shoulders of others like yourselves, dedicated to public service, people we will never be able to thank personally, but people whom, through these words, I want to thank from my heart today. Thank you.

The Ambassador has reminded me that in this room, too, are many who are not

American by background but who are British and who work in our Embassy and in our various missions.

I should also tell you that we are tremendously appreciative of your efforts and just as grateful as we are for the efforts of the others, because without what you do our Americans would not have it so good.

Thank you.

NOTE: The President spoke at 3:55 p.m. at the American Embassy in London following introductory remarks by Ambassador to the United Kingdom David K. E. Bruce and Secretary of State William P. Rogers which are printed in the Weekly Compilation of Presidential Documents (vol. 5, p. 340).

75   Special Message to the Congress on Reform of the Postal Service.   *February* 25, 1969

To the Congress of the United States:

Reform of the postal system is long overdue.

The postal service touches the lives of all Americans. Many of our citizens feel that today's service does not meet today's needs, much less the needs of tomorrow. I share this view.

In the months ahead, I expect to propose comprehensive legislation for postal reform.

If this long-range program is to succeed, I consider it essential, as a first step, that the Congress remove the last vestiges of political patronage in the Post Office Department.

Accordingly, I urge the Congress promptly to enact legislation that would:

—eliminate the present statutory requirement for Presidential appointment and Senatorial confirmation of postmasters of first-, second-, and third-class post offices;

—provide for appointment of all postmasters by the Postmaster General in the competitive civil service; and

—prohibit political considerations in the selection or promotion of postal employees.

Such legislation would make it possible for future postmasters to be chosen in the same way that career employees have long been chosen in the other executive departments. It would not, however, affect the status of postmasters now in office.

Adoption of this proposal by the Congress would assure all of the American people—and particularly the more than 750,000 dedicated men and women who work in the postal service—that future appointments and promotions in this important department are going to be made on the basis of merit and fitness for the job, and not on the basis of political affiliations or political influence.

The tradition of political patronage in the Post Office Department extends back to the earliest days of the Republic. In a sparsely populated country, where postal officials faced few of the management problems so familiar to modern postmasters, the patronage system may have been a defensible method of selecting jobholders. As the operation of the postal service has become more complex, however, the patronage system has become an increasingly costly luxury. It is a luxury that the nation can no longer afford.

In the past two decades, there has been increasing agreement that postmaster appointments should be made on a nonpolitical basis. Both the first and second

Hoover Commissions emphasized the need for such action. So did the recent President's Commission on Postal Organization, headed by Frederick R. Kappel. President Harry S. Truman and many members of Congress from both political parties have proposed legislation designed to take politics out of postal appointments. In the 90th Congress, the Senate, by a vote of 75 to 9, passed a bill containing a provision that would have placed postal appointments on a merit basis. Forty-two such bills were introduced in the House of Representatives during the 90th Congress.

The overwhelmingly favorable public comment that followed my recent announcement of our intention to disregard political consideration in selecting postmasters and rural carriers suggests that the American people are more than ready for legislative action on this matter. The time for such action is now at hand.

The benefits to be derived from such legislation are, I believe, twofold.

First, the change would expand opportunities for advancement on the part of our present postal employees. These are hard-working and loyal men and women. In the past, many of them have not received adequate recognition or well-deserved promotions for reasons which have had nothing to do with their fitness for higher position or the quality of their work. For reasons of both efficiency and morale, this situation must be changed.

Secondly, I believe that over a period of time the use of improved professional selection methods will improve the level of competence of those who take on these important postal responsibilities.

I would not request this legislation without also presenting a plan which insures that the new selection process will be effectively and impartially administered.

The Postmaster General has such a plan.

He is creating a high level, impartial national board to assist him in the future selection of postmasters for the 400 largest post offices in the country. Regional boards, also made up of exceptionally well-qualified citizens, will perform a similar task in connection with the selection of other postmasters. First consideration will be given to the promotion, on a competitive basis, of present postal employees.

The Postmaster General has also initiated action to improve the criteria by which postmasters are selected. The revised criteria will emphasize managerial competence, human relations sensitivity, responsiveness to customer concerns, an understanding of labor relations, and other important qualities.

Proposals for additional legislation dealing with the selection process will be included in the broad program for postal reform that the Postmaster General is now preparing.

Some of the needs of the Post Office clearly require extensive study before detailed solutions can be proposed. Other problems can and should be dealt with now. One objective which can be met promptly is that of taking politics out of the Post Office and I strongly recommend the swift enactment of legislation that will allow us to achieve that goal. Such legislation will be an important first step "towards postal excellence."

RICHARD NIXON

The White House
  February 25, 1969

NOTE: On the same day the White House made public a memorandum, released by Postmaster General Winton M. Blount, setting forth new procedures for selecting postmasters and rural carriers (5 Weekly Comp. Pres. Docs., p. 321).

76 Remarks on Departure From Britain. *February 26, 1969*

Mr. Prime Minister:

This has indeed been a very eventful and rewarding visit for me. Our time together was short, but, in Kipling's words, we filled "the unforgiving minute with 60 seconds' worth of distance run."

We received the typically warm and generous welcome of the British people; we were received by your gracious Queen and Prince Philip; and in the most frank and open manner we were given the opportunity to exchange views with your leaders of government.

I shall always remember the events of yesterday. At Westminster Abbey I was reminded of the splendor of your traditions, the greatness of your history, and I shared the gratitude which General Pershing must have felt when he presented the Congressional Medal of Honor to Britain's unknown soldier.

Yesterday, for the first time in history, a man occupying the Office of President of the United States visited a session of the House of Commons. It was an inspiring and compelling experience, one for which I am deeply grateful. And it was an experience in which I came away with a deep appreciation and respect for the ability of the British parliamentarian to stand up during the question period and answer so effectively.

I believe that your question period is much more of an ordeal than our press conference.

It was a moment which no man who has served in the Congress of the United States can forget, for it was here that representative government was born and it was here that men such as Pitt, Disraeli,

Gladstone, and Churchill turned their genius and eloquence to the challenges of social reform and the defense of freedom.

Yesterday, too, an American President in office was given the opportunity of exchanging views with a representative cross-section of citizens in the nongovernmental sector. This, too, was a very rewarding experience for me and one that I hope may establish a new precedent in visits of this type, that will be made by heads of government and heads of state.

Then, too, as you remarked, the opportunity—an historic opportunity—to meet with members of the British Cabinet not only on points of mutual interest that were bilateral, but more on those subjects that draw together from the beginning time of our own history and of yours where we have been, where we are, where we are going.

This discussion is one that will stay in our memories for all of our lives, because it is centered on how we can best pursue our common purposes—the cause of peace, prosperity, a better life for our young people and for all mankind.

I have never been more certain—and that certainly has been buttressed by my visit here—that the strength of our ideals and purposes, and the collective force that Europe and America have built to safeguard them, are the necessary cornerstones of the lasting peace we both seek.

Let us, Great Britain and America, remember that "United" is our common first name—the United Kingdom, the United States. We know the real meaning of unity—not the unity of the monolith, but the unity that gains strength by encouraging the diversity which is the hallmark of freedom—a diversity that I saw in action around your Cabinet table and that I see in action around mine.

That is the kind of unity we seek within the Western Alliance—a unity creative in its contrasts, flexible in its forms, but above all, powerful in its purpose.

NOTE: The President spoke at 8:40 a.m. at Heathrow Airport in response to farewell remarks by Prime Minister Harold Wilson. An advance text of the President's remarks was also released. Prime Minister Wilson's remarks follow:

Mr. President, as we take our leave of you after this visit, my first thought is to wish you Godspeed as you continue on this mission which you conceived and to which I have said to you on your arrival here, future commentators may well ascribe the phrase "historic."

I told you when you arrived here about 36 hours ago how much we welcomed your decision within days of your inauguration to visit our European Continent.

Allowing for the minimum of sleep which nature requires, I would not have believed that so much constructive discussion could have been crowded into so few hours. The problems of our alliance, the problems of unity in Europe, the problems of a wider world—all these we have discussed against the background of our common purpose—the common purpose of our own society.

These views we have discussed and otherwise examined, not with the idea of reaching firm decisions but with the idea of assuring that they shall be continuously examined in depth, that they shall be examined together.

Together we have given the necessary instructions to insure that what your visit has done will continue. We have established a close relationship and above all, we have established a process of consultation on world affairs.

But as you said on your arrival here, neither of us regards this as an exclusive process, for what views we have discussed must become part of the currency of consultations with all our partners, and this process will continue as you carry forward your discussions with our friends in Germany, in Italy, and in France, and subsequently with our other European partners.

Equally I have in mind—and I doubt if you will forget—that unprecedented, uninhibited exchange of views when last night you sat down with the British Cabinet around the Cabinet table, when we discussed the internal social problems of a modern society, yours, ours, the societies of other countries you will be visiting, problems of urban explosion, problems of race and color, problems of regional participation, and above all, the problems of youth—youth, not only of the articulate, even demonstrative, minority of a nation's youth but the problems of the hard-working and no less sincere sort of our young people seeking to express themselves, seeking the cause, seeking above all, an ideal.

I am glad that we have been able together to give instructions that there will be established fuller consultation between governments and that we have been able to agree that there shall be established equally, insofar as it is in our power to do so, full consultation between Parliament and Congress, indeed between our two societies, on all of these problems.

What we have begun here in London I know you will want to extend in all the other centers you will be visiting—and I believe, instill more widely.

Mr. President, here at Heathrow less than 2 days ago, we both proclaimed our conceptions of the objectives of this visit. Our talks have widened those conceptions and given reality to them.

This is a start and, we both realize, only a start. Both of us look forward to building on what we have begun.

Mr. President, from the British Government and the British people, I wish you Godspeed on your mission of hope.

77   Remarks on Arrival at the Airport in Cologne.
February 26, 1969

Mr. Chancellor:

I wish to express my deep appreciation for that very gracious and eloquent welcome.

I, in return, express to you and to the people of your country our admiration and our respect for what you have accomplished in the years since I first visited this country 22 years ago.

When I first came to this country at that time 22 years ago, I visited Berlin, Essen, Frankfurt, the other great cities of this nation, and I saw them leveled and broken. But one thing was not broken and that was the spirit of the German people.

You have spoken generously of the assistance that the United States has provided for the German recovery, but without the spirit of the German people, without the industry of the German people, there would not have been the miracle which the whole world has admired of German recovery and the strong German nation we see today.

Like so many of my countrymen, I share some of that tradition of the German people. My wife's mother was born in this country and she has that spirit and my two daughters also have that spirit.

But as we speak of the things that have changed over these last 22 years, the miracle of German recovery among them, there are some things that have not changed.

One thing that has not changed is our devotion and dedication to the goal that the German people will again be united. One thing that has not changed is our mutual dedication to the principle of independence and freedom for all of the peoples of Western Europe. And one thing that has not changed is our devotion to the great alliance of which we are a part.

I trust that my visit here and the conversations that I look forward to having with you and members of your government will not only strengthen the relations between our two countries, but also will further strengthen the great alliance of which we are a part.

We stand here together today, heads of our two governments, heads of two great peoples, devoted to the cause of peace, devoted to the cause of freedom, and we will work toward that cause in the talks that we have.

NOTE: The President spoke at 10:16 a.m. at Wahn Airport, Cologne, Germany. His opening words referred to Chancellor Kurt Georg Kiesinger of the Federal Republic of Germany. An advance text of the President's remarks was also released.

Chancellor Kiesinger's welcoming remarks were not made public in the form of a White House press release.

78   Remarks in Bonn Before the German Bundestag.
February 26, 1969

Mr. President, Mr. Chancellor, Your Excellencies, Members of the Parliament:

It is a very great honor for me to appear before this legislative body and to respond to the very generous words of welcome that I have just heard from the presiding officer of this body.

At the outset I regret that I find it necessary to have a translator. I do say, though, that having heard his translation, he had every word right—every word.

Mr. President, you have spoken of some of the great ideals that bind our two nations and our two peoples together. I spoke at the airport this morning of the fact that we in the United States owe so much to our German heritage.

And I can speak personally on that point because the grandmother of my two daughters on their mother's side was born in Germany.

I would like to speak of those principles and ideals that will continue to bind us together in the years ahead. First the great Alliance of which we are a part. This Alliance is strong today and must be maintained in strength in the years ahead.

The success of this Alliance is indicated by the fact that, in the 20 years that it has existed, we have had peace, as far as this part of the world is concerned, and that every one of the nations in the Alliance that was free 20 years ago is free today, including the free city of Berlin.

We are bound together, too, by the economic factors that two great and productive peoples have produced in our two countries. And we know that a strong and productive German economy is essential for a strong free world economy, just as is a strong economy in the United States.

We are bound together, too, by a common dedication to the cause of peace—peace not only for ourselves but for all mankind.

As we enter what I have described as a period of negotiation with those who have been our opponents, we recognize that for those negotiations to succeed it is essential that we maintain the strength that made negotiations possible.

But having spoken of the bonds of national heritage and background, the alliance of the economic factors, those bonds that bring us together, I would add, finally, one that is demonstrated by my presence in this chamber today. We believe, both of our countries and our peoples, in representative government, in free and vigorous debate, and in free and vigorous elections.

And having just been through the ordeal of an election campaign, I wish all of you well in your campaigns. That, as I am sure you will understand, is the international language of politics, being on both sides of the same issue.

Finally, as I stand before this parliamentary body, I realize that we share so many common traditions, and it is to me a very moving experience to report to you that since becoming President of the United States I have not yet had the opportunity to appear before our own Congress, and I have not yet appeared before a legislative body in any other country.

In other words, as I stand here today before this Parliament, this is the first time that I, as President of the United States, have appeared before any legislative body in the whole world.

Mr. President, I will have many honors during the period that I will hold office, but I can assure you that as one who began his political career as a Congressman and served in that post for 4 years, and who then served in our Senate for 2 years, and then served as Vice President of the United States and President of the Senate in the chair where you sit for 8 years, that there will be no honor greater than the one I have today to address my fellow legislators.

NOTE: The President spoke at 6 p.m. before the German Bundestag in Bonn. The President of the Bundestag was Kai-Uwe von Hassel and the Chancellor of the Federal Republic of Germany was Kurt Georg Kiesinger.

On the same day the White House Press Office released a list of distinguished German citizens who met with the President on February 26.

79 Message to the President of Israel on the Death of Prime Minister Levi Eshkol. *February* 26, 1969

Dear Mr. President:

All Americans join me in sending you and the people of Israel our deepest sympathy for your tragic loss. Levi Eshkol was a man of great compassion and a true servant of his people. We shall all be the poorer for his passing.

Sincerely,

RICHARD NIXON

[The Honorable Zalman Shazar, President of Israel]

NOTE: The message was telegraphed to the American Embassy in Tel Aviv from Bonn during the President's visit.

80 Remarks on Arrival at Tempelhof Airport in West Berlin. *February* 27, 1969

Mr. Mayor, Mr. Chancellor:

It is a very great honor for me to be welcomed to this great city in such eloquent and generous terms. I respond to this welcome not only for myself but for all of the people of the United States of America and for all of the people of the free world.

Berlin is known as a four-power city. But there is a fifth power in Berlin. That fifth power is the determination of the free people of Berlin to remain free and the determination of free people everywhere to stand by those who desire to remain free.

I stand here today as a symbol of that fifth power, the power which will not be intimidated by any threat, by any pressure from any direction.

A few days ago, when Mayor Brandt, former Mayor Brandt, now Vice Chancellor, introduced General Lucius Clay [1] at a dinner in New York, he referred to the Berlin airlift as the "cradle of American-German friendship." For 20 years that friendship has grown and flowered.

Today, I declare again that we, the people of the United States, stand with you in the defense of freedom.

That fifth power to which I have referred, the power which is represented by the determination of free men to remain free, is stronger than any other power. It will prevail.

---

[1] Gen. Lucius D. Clay (USA, Ret.) was commander in chief of U.S. forces in Europe and military governor of the U.S. zone of Germany from 1947 to 1949. When, in April 1948, the Soviet military government imposed a land blockade on West Berlin, General Clay's command instituted an Allied airlift which supplied the city with essential food and fuel until the lifting of the blockade in September 1949.

I appreciate the opportunity of visiting Berlin and particularly this special privilege that I have had to review this magnificent contingent of our American Forces in Berlin.

As I speak to you, I only wish that time permitted that I could shake hands with each of you to express the appreciation of your country and my own personal appreciation for the service you are rendering to the country here in this post and in others around the world.

As I am sure you have noted, there have been some changes in Washington in recent months. I will refer briefly to those.

For example, the Washington Redskins have a new coach, Vince Lombardi, and they are looking up. The Washington Senators have a new manager, Ted Williams, and some even believe that they might be going up. And, as you may have noted, there is also a new President in the White House.

There is one thing that I want to assure you that has not changed, and this has been true through the terms of four Presidents. It is true in the term of this President: that is, our pride in the men of our armed services here in Berlin and in Western Europe, around the world, Asia, Vietnam. I have seen the men of our armed services. I know them. I know that whatever we may from time to time read and hear at home about divisions on policy that there is no question about the dedication, the patriotism, the morale of the men who defend the cause of freedom, as you defend it by your presence here.

As I speak to you today, I add one other thought: You are here, it is true, in a land far away from home, but you are also here in a land and in a city which welcomes you and wants you. You are not here as an occupying force. You are not here because the United States of America has designs on any other nation or any other territory.

You are here because of our desire, shared by the people of this country and of this city, to defend their right to be free and that is the American destiny in the world today.

We are a great power. We have obligations around the world. But because of the great changes that have occurred in history, the American mission is different from that of some others who have risen to greatness in their role in the world. We seek no territory. We seek no concessions. All that we want is the right for others that we have for ourselves—the right to be free, the right to choose our own leaders, the right to disagree, and the right to settle our disagreements in a peaceful way.

As I stand here today on one of the first occasions, as a matter of fact the first occasion as the new President of the United States and as the Commander in Chief of the Armed Forces, to review an American force abroad, I want you to know I have never been so proud—proud of you, proud of my country and its role in the world, and humble in the duty that I have to see that the policies that we develop to bring peace are worthy of your dedication to defend peace as demonstrated by your presence here.

Thank you very much.

NOTE: The President spoke at 10:06 a.m. at Tempelhof Airport, West Berlin.

An advance text of the President's remarks was also released.

The President spoke in response to Mayor Klaus Schuetz' welcoming remarks. The Mayor spoke in German. A translation of his remarks follows:

Mr. President, we Berliners are happy to have you here today and to have you with us. The supreme representative of this nation, when coming to Berlin, always comes with friends. We have acquired this friendship in the most difficult situations—during the barricade, during the airlift, during the crucial ultimatum and after that period.

This friendship goes to the American people, but today, Mr. President, it goes very particularly to you. You know this city in East and West. You know the truly indivisible Berlin. Feel at home here, because although you are far away from the White House and the 50 United States of America, an American President, and you, President Nixon, are always at home in this city.

81   Remarks at the Signing of the Golden Book at the Charlottenburg Palace, West Berlin.   *February* 27, 1969

Mr. Mayor, Mr. Chancellor, Mr. Vice Chancellor, Mr. Secretary of State, all of the distinguished guests who are here in this room:

I speak to you at a time when I have experienced a very moving occasion, to travel through this city and to realize again what Berlin means to all the people of the world.

We have seen here a wall. A wall can divide a city, but a wall can never divide a people. A wall can divide physically but it cannot divide Berlin spiritually because the spirit of freedom that I saw on the faces of thousands of Berliners today is the spirit that will continue to survive and will continue to receive support by those who are free throughout the world.

As I went through the city, too, I realized that those who have indicated that this city was a dying city were wrong because I saw the young faces, the children, the workers, smiling—people who realize that this city does have hope, that it does have a future.

Finally, Mr. Mayor, as one who has traveled to many cities in the world and many in the United States, I am somewhat of an expert in looking at crowds and also an expert in the signs that people in the crowds carry.

In some cities in the world and in some cities in the United States I have seen signs that say "Nixon come back" and other signs that say "Nixon go home." But here in Berlin most of the signs that really have meaning, the expression on the faces of people said: "Welcome. We stand with you. We stand for peace. We stand for freedom."

And I well recall that as we were riding in the car the Mayor and the Chancellor translated some of the signs and one in particular seemed to repeat over and over again. It said: *Viel Glueck!* So I say to the people of Berlin: Good luck!

NOTE: The President spoke at 12:15 p.m. in response to remarks by Mayor Klaus Schuetz. An advance text of the President's remarks is printed in the Weekly Compilation of Presidential Documents (vol. 5, p. 342).

The Mayor spoke in German. A translation follows:

Thank you very much, Mr. President and Mr. Chancellor, for coming to Berlin on your first trip after your election—to Berlin, the place where two political worlds look face to face.

You have come here to form your own opinion of the situation. The United States of America is more important to Berlin than to any other city in Europe. They are one of the three protective powers, and that is a very weighty thing.

You said this morning, Mr. President, that Berlin, in your opinion, has been the cradle of German-American friendship after the Second World War. This is where the relationships of our peoples have found a special expression, and this is where their friendship and solidarity spring to the eye and where we find that we can rely on each other.

Six years ago, Mr. President, John F. Kennedy was in this city and, like you, he showed where the American people stand. You, Mr. President, yourself were Vice President when the Honorable Dwight D. Eisenhower and the United States Government helped to overcome and master a very great crisis.

I am glad we have here today among us someone who was then governing Mayor of Berlin, my friend Willy Brandt. He, as all Berliners realized and continue to realize, as we all do, that without the help and support of the American Government, Berlin could not live nor could it live in the future.

We have followed with great attention and sympathy your efforts for peace, Mr. President. You really must know what it is worth to safeguard peace, and we are prepared to make our own convincing contribution to an all-European peace.

Berlin has been and is an advance post for freedom. It has been and wants to be an advance post of peace. You know how shamefully this city is divided, Mr. President, and

you will certainly understand when I say that we here in West Berlin, at this very moment, think very intensively of our fellow citizens in the other part of this city.

Mr. President, this is not an easy place to live, but we are not living at an easy time, either; and the solutions to the problems won't be easy, I suppose.

We are against those who try to propose a simple formula and empty phrases, because we know that these easy-sounding proposals do not solve the problems but rather postpone their solutions.

We are prepared, through hard work, to go all the way. We think we have the right to preserve our freedom, and we want to overcome tensions and safeguard peace.

Mr. President, we are very grateful for the statements you have made about Berlin and we know and appreciate their value. But let me tell you that Berlin has not waited for new guarantees or new promises from the United States, because we know where you stand, as you know where we stand.

Thank you again, very cordially, for coming to visit us; and will you please now give us the honor of signing the Golden Book of the City of Berlin.

82   Remarks at the Siemens Factory, West Berlin. *February 27, 1969*

Mr. Mayor, Mr. Chancellor, Mr. Vice Chancellor, Mr. Secretary of State, distinguished guests, and all of those gathered here in this great, productive factory in Berlin:

I first apologize for the fact that we have kept you waiting. But as we came through the city the crowds were so large that we were unable to keep on our schedule.

So the reason we are here is a demonstration of the truth of what the Mayor has just said: that the people of Berlin are free and that despite a wall this is one city and one people and one nation.

I saw many signs as we came through the streets of the city—some were in English, most were in German. The ones in German, of course, I could not understand. But there was one sign that was a combination that made me feel very much at home. It said "Ho Ha Hay, Nixon is okay."

I first came to this city 22 years ago. At that time most of those that I see here, or many of those, were not yet born. And to many who came here then, Berlin seemed to be a city without hope and without a future. But the pessimists at that period, over 20 years ago, did not know the people of Berlin.

There is no more remarkable story in human history than the creation of this island of freedom and prosperity, of courage and determination, in the center of postwar Europe.

And it is you who have done it.

It is you who have rebuilt this great city; it is you who have stood the shock of crises; it is you who have kept the faith in yourselves and in your allies.

Berlin may look lonely on the map—but it is a vital part of the world that believes in the capacity of man to govern himself with responsibility and to shape his destiny in dignity.

If this is an age of symbols, one of the great symbols of the age is this city. And what you do here is done for free men everywhere throughout the world. You stand for a cause much bigger than yourselves and this is the greatest destiny that a man or a woman can have. Because your will to remain free strengthens the will to freedom of all men; your courage in the face of deliberate and constant challenge fortifies the courage of all those who love liberty.

The presence of an American President in Berlin, following a recent visit by a British Prime Minister, is another kind of symbol. It is a way of demonstrating unmistakably our long-standing commitment to the people of West Berlin.

Let there be no miscalculation: No unilateral move, no illegal act, no form of pressure from any source will shake the resolve of the Western nations to defend their rightful status as protectors of the people of free Berlin.

All the world admires bravery. But there are different kinds of bravery. Bravery in a crisis is expected of those who love freedom; what is much more diffi-

cult, much more rare, is bravery day-by-day—the steady fortitude that resists remorseless pressure and refuses to permit the slow erosion of liberties. That is the remarkable bravery of the Berliner, and it stands as a shining example to people everywhere throughout the world.

The partnership between our two peoples was forged back in the dark days of the blockade when men like Lucius Clay and Ernst Reuter [1] personified our determination to survive as free men. It is appropriate, 20 years after the end of that blockade, that we pay tribute to all who suffered for the ideal of freedom in those days of physical privation and spiritual triumph. As I viewed the progress of this vital city today, I knew that that sacrifice was not in vain.

And to all the people of Berlin today, I bring this message from the heart of America: You have justified the support and the commitment of your friends and, as a result, no city in the world has more friends, or more devoted friends, than has the city of Berlin.

The American responsibility here is derived from the most solemn international agreements. But what we have gone through together in those 24 years has given those agreements a special meaning. Four Presidents before me have held to this principle and I tell you at this time and in this place that I, too, hold fast to this principle: Berlin must remain free.

I do not say this in any spirit of bravado or belligerence. I am simply stating an irrevocable fact of international life.

Our commitment to the freedom of Berlin has never been more steady, never more firm than it is today. For more than a generation we have pledged American

---

[1] Mayor of Berlin 1948–1953.

lives to an ideal and a reality: that Berlin shall be free and that Berlin shall live. For its part, Berlin has remained steadfast.

So have we—and steadfast we shall stay.

No one should doubt the determination of the United States to live up to its obligations. The question before the world is not whether we shall rise to the challenge of defending Berlin—we have already demonstrated that we shall. The question now is how best to end the challenge and clear the way for a peaceful solution to the problem of a divided Germany.

When we say that we reject any unilateral alteration of the status quo in Berlin, we do not mean that we consider the status quo to be satisfactory. Nobody benefits from a stalemate, least of all the people of Berlin.

Let us set behind us the stereotype of Berlin as a "provocation." Let us, all of us, view the situation in Berlin as an invocation, a call to end the tension of the past age here and everywhere.

Our common attitude can best be expressed in a motto of Goethe: "Without haste, but without rest." That is how, step by step, we shall strive together to construct a durable peace.

There were times in the past when Berlin had to stand its ground in defiance of powerful forces that threatened to overwhelm it. Your determination in those times of danger demonstrated beyond the shadow of a doubt that threats and coer-

cion could never succeed. By your fortitude, you have created conditions which may in time permit another kind of determination—a determination that we shall, by negotiation among governments and reconciliation among men, bring an end to the division of this city, this nation, this continent, and this planet.

By your faith in the future you have inspired renewed faith in the hearts of all men. The men of the past thought in terms of blockades and walls; the men of the future will think in terms of open channels. The men of the past were trapped in the gray overcast of cold war; the men of the future, a future toward which we will all work, if only they remember the tragedy and triumph of Berlin, will be free to walk in the warm sunlight of a just peace.

And now one final message from the heart of the people of America to the people of Berlin: Sometimes you must feel that you are very much alone. But always remember we are with you, and always remember that people who are free and who want to be free around the world are with you. In the sense that the people of Berlin stand for freedom and peace, all the people of the world are truly Berliners.

NOTE: The President spoke at 1 p.m. at the Siemens Factory in West Berlin.

An advance text of the President's remarks was also released by the White House Press Office.

83   Remarks on Departure From West Berlin. *February* 27, 1969

Mr. Chancellor:

I am deeply grateful for the eloquent words that you have expressed as I leave

your country and leave this city which is such a vitally important part of your country.

This brief visit that I have made to your country has been valuable in several respects. First, because it allowed me, as the new President of the United States, to develop a basis for very close consultation and cooperation with the members of your government. Cooperation between the German and American Governments is vital and essential if we are to defend the freedom which we both cherish and if we are to achieve the peace which we both seek.

I know now that we have established in this brief visit the basis for that consultation and cooperation which will be so valuable and constructive in seeking our common purposes in the years ahead. This visit also will be memorable to me because it provided my first opportunity to speak before a legislative body at the highest level, and I am proud to have been received as the first foreign visitor to appear before the Bundestag. Also, I am proud that my first appearance was before your Parliament.

Mr. Chancellor, you and I, as political leaders, know that it is essential that the leaders at the top, with executive power, and the legislators who work with them must have an understanding and communication if two nations and two peoples are to work together.

But even more important than Presidents and Chancellors getting along together, and Members of Parliaments and Members of Congress understanding each other, is that the people of two nations share a common spirit and have a common understanding.

Yesterday in Bonn and today in Berlin I saw the German people by the thousands, and I felt, as I saw them, as I heard them, that I was at home among my own people.

We are different people with different languages and different backgrounds, but in a sense we are one people—one people in our dedication to peace and in our dedication to freedom.

Because we are one people in that spirit, we, as leaders of the people, will be able to achieve our goal of a new world in which peoples in nations, in continents, and in the world may live together in peace and in friendship.

NOTE: The President spoke at 2:05 p.m. at Tegel Airport, West Berlin. The Chancellor of the Federal Republic of Germany was Kurt Georg Kiesinger. An advance text of the President's remarks is printed in the Weekly Compilation of Presidential Documents (vol. 5, p. 342).

84   Remarks on Arrival at the Airport in Rome. *February 27, 1969*

Mr. President:

I am most grateful for the generous remarks that you have expressed in welcoming me and the members of my party to your country.

As I stand here I think back 22 years ago when I first visited this country and had the opportunity to know the Italian people. For 2 weeks, at that period, as a new young Congressman, I traveled through this country studying the needs of this nation for the Marshall Plan. I visited Rome, Naples, Milan, Turin, and Trieste.

I had the opportunity to see a nation then in deep economic troubles, a nation which many thought would be unable to recover from those troubles and regain its economic and political strength.

But when I returned to the United States and, along with my colleagues, reported to the Congress, I was confident of the future of Italy because, first, I had seen a great Italian leader, De Gasperi,[1] and I knew that he would provide, with his colleagues, the leadership that this nation needed.

I also reported with great confidence because I had seen a remarkable people, a people who, in adversity had very great strength, a people who had contributed so much to our country and who now, in this land, were to contribute so much to its recovery—and the recovery of Italy, economically and politically—so that it now ranks among the first nations of the world, so that it now stands as one of the strong allies of the Western Alliance.

That recovery is due both to its leaders and to its peoples and I pay tribute to both as I stand here today. Now we look to the future. We look to the future with the new leaders, the leaders that you will provide in your government and that we will provide in ours.

As we look to the future we will look to the new purpose of our alliance and of our association together. As I think of that purpose I think of the words of another American President who visited this nation just 50 years ago. His words were spoken before their time but now their time has come.

Listen to the words of Woodrow Wilson

---

[1] Alcide de Gasperi, Prime Minister of Italy 1945–1953.

spoken in Rome in 1919, 50 years ago: "Our task is to set up a new international psychology, to have a new, real atmosphere where what men once considered theoretical and idealistic turns out to be practical and necessary."

Mr. President, the contribution that you, personally, and that your people have made to the strength of NATO has helped to turn the ideal of collective security into a practical reality.

Now, as we seek a new international atmosphere, the strength of the Western Alliance has never been more necessary. A good ally listens to her partners.

As you pointed out in your remarks, we shall be having discussions with the Soviet Union. But before we have such discussions with the other side we will have discussions and consultations with our allies on this side.

That is the road that leads to Rome today. That is why I appreciate this opportunity to consult with the leaders of your government.

I come here to seek your advice and I am sure I will leave with that, and yet, with something more because we know that great lessons can be learned from people for whom humanity and tolerance are, in truth, a way of life.

That is why our discussion will not be limited to matters just between our two nations. Our talks will extend throughout the structure of our alliance and deal with the great problems of the world.

As an Atlantic partner and as a member of the European Community, Italy is playing a vital and constructive role in world affairs. That is why I am particularly grateful for the opportunity to visit your country at this time, to have the wise counsel of your leaders, and to reaffirm our steadfast friendship and to seek together ways of achieving our high purpose.

NOTE: The President spoke at 4:35 p.m. at Ciampino Military Airport in Rome in response to remarks of welcome by President Giuseppe Saragat of Italy. An advance text of the President's remarks was also released by the White House Press Office.

President Saragat spoke in Italian. A translation follows:

Mr. President, on behalf of the Italian people and on my own it gives me great pleasure to extend my warmest welcome to you and to the distinguished personalities who accompany you.

Your visit confirms the cordiality of Italian-American relations which has its roots in history, in a common civilization, and in the many ties linking our two peoples through the migration of millions of Italians to your great country. Nor are we oblivious to the moral and political significance of this journey which you have wished to undertake at the beginning of your mandate as President of the United States.

Italy is aware, like the other European coun-

tries, of the commitment of the United States, our friend and ally, to search for conditions that would guarantee a just and a lasting peace among all peoples of the world.

Your journey, Mr. President, is therefore of great importance for the future of the relations between the member countries of the Atlantic Alliance and as a basis for the negotiations you will undertake with the Soviet Union.

Europe, however, will be in a position to make a decisive contribution to this great dialogue of peace between East and West only if it finds, through unity, the necessary dimension to master its destiny.

The awareness of sharing the same ideals and the same objectives with the American Nation makes us look with confidence to the talks we are going to have with you in the certainty that they will not only contribute to the strengthening of collaboration within the Western World, but also to build on stronger bases peace and security for all nations.

It is with this hope, Mr. President, that I wish to renew to you our most friendly welcome upon your arrival in this city, ancient site and symbol of a civilization based on the highest human values which are common to all of us.

85 Toasts of the President and President Saragat of Italy. *February* 27, 1969

Mr. President, Your Excellencies:

It is a very great honor for me to be in this magnificent room and to be received in such an eloquent way by the President of this Nation.

I should like to respond to your remarks in both personal terms and then also in the broader terms that you have used in describing the relationship between our two nations.

It was 22 years ago when I first came to this country as a freshman Congressman, and freshmen Congressmen are seldom listened to and seldom survive. I learned much on that journey about this country and our relationship. And when I returned in 1957, as Vice President of the

United States, I spoke to you then in the capacity you held as Vice Premier of this country.

When I returned again to this country in 1963, you were President of the Republic and I was a private citizen.

And so it seemed to me, since you had set the example of going from Vice Premier to President, that I should do likewise.

Mr. President, our relationship and my relationship with the other distinguished guests at this table, many of whom I have met on my previous visits, goes far beyond these personal recollections. It is traditional when an American comes to this country, and particularly when an American President comes and is honored as I am being honored tonight, to speak as you have of what contribution—the magnificent contribution—has been made to the American Nation by the Americans of Italian descent.

We are proud of that tradition—the fact that 20 million Americans are proud to claim their Italian background. And we are proud that going clear back to the days of the American Revolution, Americans of Italian descent have played a very significant part in our history.

It would also be appropriate on an occasion like this for an American President to refer, as I do refer now, to the great debt we owe to this nation and to this people for the history that we feel in this room in which we now meet.

Not just this "Eternal City," but other cities in this country, have an historical background that has a meaning far beyond the relationship between our two countries and which deeply enriches our culture.

But I do not speak today primarily of those usual gracious terms and references that are always appropriate, of our common ties in blood, insofar as our national heritage is concerned, of our history and our culture. I speak, as you do, of not just the past, but primarily of what we can do together in the future.

You have spoken very eloquently, Mr. President, about the dream of a united Europe, a dream which many of us in the United States have also supported.

And while we know that this country, as its productivity increases, is now producing approximately $70 billion in gross national product per year, we also realize that the 300 million people who live in Western Europe produce a total of over $500 billion per year.

We stand here, in other words, in one of the most productive areas of the entire world. But as we think of that, and as I declare again, as I did in my earlier meetings with you and with members of this government, our adherence to and our support of NATO and the Atlantic Alliance, let us also look to how we can further strengthen not only that Alliance, but strengthen the cause of peace in which we are all interested.

There are several pillars in the "Temple of Peace" which we are now constructing. The first is to maintain the strength of the NATO Alliance; the second is to work toward greater unity, not only in military but in other ways for Europe; and, third, we recognize that in this era in which we are now entering, it will be necessary for the United States of America to conduct bilateral negotiations with the Soviet Union, negotiations that will have a massive effect on whether peace survives in the world.

We will enter into those negotiations whenever we think it is appropriate and whenever we think they will serve the cause of peace. But we will remember that before we talk to the other side, it is essential that we consult with and get the advice of our friends on our side.

I indicated, as you pointed out, in my Inaugural Address, that we were entering a new era of negotiation rather than confrontation.

What this trip that I have taken only 6 weeks after being inaugurated as President of the United States means is that we are also entering a new era of full consultation with our allies on all of the matters that may affect the peace of the world.

And I say that, Mr. President, for this reason: We admire this nation and this people for its magnificent cultural background and tradition. We admire this nation for its tremendous economic progress in so many fields. We admire this nation because of the contribution you have made to our Nation in terms of those Americans of Italian descent who have done so much for us.

But there is another reason that we admire and respect this nation. It is one that I can speak personally about because of my own personal experience going back over 22 years.

I have talked to Italian statesmen—to De Gasperi and those who have followed him—and to the men here at this table, not only you, Mr. President, but President Gronchi [1] before you and the many others who are represented around this table.

And I value what each of you has been able to contribute in terms of your experience and background and judgment with regard to the great issues with which the world is confronted.

Speaking quite candidly, Mr. President, it is true that the United States in the free world is the strongest of the free nations. It is true that we are the richest of the free nations. But I would be the last to claim that the United States had a monopoly on the brains and the wisdom in the free nations.

And so I do not visualize an era in which the leader of the United States, with his advisers, alone makes the great decisions that determine the future of Europe, Asia, Africa, and Latin America, but I envision an era in which the leader of the United States talking with, consulting with, getting the best advice of the other leaders in our great alliance, will develop

---

[1] Giovanni Gronchi, President of Italy 1955–1962.

the decisions that will serve our common purpose.

And so, Mr. President, I ask all of your guests tonight to rise and raise their glasses with me, not only to Italian-American friendship, but to the Western civilization which we share together and to the good health of the President of this republic and what he symbolizes in terms of world leadership and cooperation with the United States in the years ahead.

NOTE: The President spoke at approximately 10:30 p.m. in response to a toast proposed by President Giuseppe Saragat at a state dinner in the Quirinale Palace in Rome.

President Saragat spoke in Italian. A translation follows:

Mr. President, it is with a feeling of deep satisfaction and great pleasure that we welcome you today in Rome, only a few months after your election to the Presidency of the United States of America.

Addressing myself to you, the leader of the American Nation, to which we are bound by ties of friendship and alliance, it is gratifying for me to speak first of all of your great country, remembering the hospitality I received there less than 2 years ago and the unforgettable images it has left in my mind.

The Italian Government and the Italian people are indeed keenly aware of the significance of your journey which finds us deeply and spontaneously responsive. Italy, particularly alive and open to the motivations which prompted it, and to the message it conveys, welcomes it, therefore, as a singularly felicitous omen for the future of the relations between the old and the new continent and for the dialogue of peace between East and West.

The Atlantic Alliance unites us in a commitment for defense which guarantees our security and it foreshadows the European-American community, envisaged by the late President Kennedy and outlined recently by you. To the extent to which defense problems are matched by constant initiatives toward detente and peace, we are indeed profoundly convinced that the consolidation and development of such fruitful and freely contracted ties among the peoples who have joined the Atlantic Alliance, far from running counter to the parallel efforts of our countries in order to improve the atmosphere of international relations, and particularly with the East, are a prerequisite for their success. Both, indeed, are complementary factors of a single strategy for peace.

You know well how my country has constantly aimed at a united Europe. We have relentlessly striven and continue to strive toward it, and we do not allow the inevitable obstacles to discourage us in our pursuit.

European unity represents an ever more pressing need in a world where the dimensions and the structures of the past fall short of the demands of the future. Only a united Europe can provide the peoples of our continent with that institution and framework which is indispensable if they are effectively to master their own destiny.

The people of Europe expect to find the friendly American Nation by their side on this road to unity, just as it was by their side in the first hard years following the war when the United States, with generous impulse in the social and economic field and acute political foresight enabled Europe to rise rapidly from the ruins in which war had plunged it.

In your Inaugural Address, Mr. President, you have pointed out that after a period of confrontation we are entering an era of negotiations. This statement cannot but find the full support of my country whose action has always aimed at making such development easier.

We gave a clear proof of this just recently when we signed the Nuclear Nonproliferation Treaty prompted by the fervent hope that this decision would contribute to the consolidation of peace, to the reduction of the existing causes for tension, and to the strengthening of mutual trust among nations.

We are firmly committed to make also in the near future every endeavor so that this trust

which implies strict respect by one and all for the territorial integrity and the independence of each shall find new sources of encouragement and élan in a renewed effort on the part of all of us, so that this community of nations may proceed on a course leading to the ban of the use of force and armaments from international political life.

This is an aim which can be reached only by giving authority and strength to the organization of the United Nations.

Mr. President, we know you are a true friend of Italy and we know you have already had the opportunity of visiting it. We feel sure that returning today to our country you will have readily recognized the face of a nation which in recent years has come through profound changes, but has consistently maintained its loyalty to the ideals of liberty, democracy, and social justice indelibly engraved in its political and social structures.

They are the very same ideals which have always inspired the great American Nation, those which it has defended, as history shows, with generous impulse; those of which America and Europe, in harmonious collaboration, are the prominent bearers in the world today.

The fruitful friendship between the United States and Italy which has its roots in the bonds of common origin and civilization, of which the existence of 20 million American citizens of Italian extraction is one eloquent proof, is a pledge and a guarantee that this historic duty will not be eschewed and its accomplishment will blossom into prosperity and peace for all the nations of the world.

In this belief and with this wish I raise my glass to the success of your mission of peace, to your personal well-being, to that of your family and of the distinguished personalities who accompany you, and to the good fortunes of the noble American Nation and to the future of the friendship between our two peoples.

86 Remarks on Departure From Rome.
February 28, 1969

Mr. Prime Minister and Your Excellencies:

As we leave Rome I want you to know

how deeply grateful I am for the hospitality that has been extended to us on our visit and how reassured I am by our conversations with the President, with you, and with members of your government with regard to the future relations between the United States and Italy, and also with regard to the great possibilities for constructive mutual action on the part of both of our peoples for the cause of peace in the years ahead.

We have discussed the whole range of world problems—the problems of East-West relations, the problems of the Mideast and Mediterranean, financial problems, and trade problems, as well as many others.

It has been very helpful to me to get the counsel and the suggestions that you and the members of your government have with regard to the position the United States should take on these problems, as well as getting your views on our bilateral relationships.

I realized, before I came to this city, that there had been complaints in the past that there has not been enough consultation by the Government of the United States with your government on matters that involve our future peace and security.

Whatever the validity of that complaint may have been in the past, I can assure you that there will be no problem in that respect in the future, because we have established, by this meeting, one consultation on all the major issues with which we are concerned; and, second, a pattern for conferences in the future involving our finance ministers, our trade ministers, the Prime Ministers, the Presidents, whereby on a continuing and regular basis we will discuss the major issues and be sure that we move together toward our common objectives.

As always on my visits to Rome, the climate has been good, the hospitality has been superb, but most important the substance has been solid and we have now developed a new pattern of consultation and progress for the future.

NOTE: The President spoke at 12 noon at Ciampino Military Airport in Rome. An advance text of the President's remarks is printed in the Weekly Compilation of Presidential Documents (vol. 5, p. 345).

Prime Minister Mariano Rumor responded in Italian. A translation follows:

Mr. President, as you are leaving Italy, it gives me great pleasure to convey to you the warmest farewell of the Italian people, of the people, of the government, as well as my own. We are aware of the importance and the significance of your visit to Europe, undertaken at the beginning of your mandate which confirms the common ideals and objectives of freedom and peace binding the United States to the free countries of Europe.

Your visit to our country in particular has once again shown the firmness of the ties of friendship which have for long united the United States and Italy in every field, and which are at the basis of our alliance which remains an essential point of reference of Italian foreign policy.

Moreover, you have been able to realize, Mr. President, that another fundamental basis of this foreign policy is the untiring activity of the Italian Government in the construction of that European unity, with the consent of Europe itself, to undertake a more decisive and determining role in the solution of those problems which harass mankind.

Your visit has also emphasized the importance of an ever closer cooperation between friendly countries and allies so as to strengthen and consolidate that Western solidarity which is one of the fundamental conditions for the enhancement and the acceleration of the pursuit of a detente policy.

The discussions which you, Mr. President, propose to hold with the Soviet Union will be a great contribution toward this end, and for the settlement of the problems which trouble the life of the people and for the construction of a more stable and peaceful international order.

The conversations and the exchange of views which we have had with you and your collaborators represent a further contribution toward our common action which is directed toward reaching ever more effectively the consolidation of peace in freedom and in justice.

This is, in fact, our first objective for the achievement of which we propose to act as we have always done in the conviction that we shall fulfill the highest duty of all those men who are conscious of the future of mankind.

The knowledge that in pursuing this difficult task we can count on the full cooperation of the United States is for us a source of great satisfaction and confidence that all our efforts will bear positive results. It is in the spirit of frankness and friendship that has characterized our meetings that I renew to you, Mr. President, and to the great American Nation, our warmest farewell.

I am happy to add my sincerest wish that your important mission will always be accompanied by every success in the interest of the American people and the people of the friendly countries, and of peace in the world.

87   Remarks on Arrival at the Airport in Paris. *February* 28, 1969

Mr. President, Your Excellencies:

It is a great honor for me to stand here on the soil of the nation that is America's oldest ally and America's oldest friend.

Mr. President, you have spoken eloquently of the relationship that our two countries have had over 200 years. I come here at the conclusion of my European journey for the purpose of underlining our dedication to that relationship and for the purpose of finding those areas in which we can continue to work together in the future.

The problems of the world in which we live are too difficult to repeat the old slogans or discuss the old quarrels. What we seek is to find those new roads which will lead to cooperation and to peace and freedom for all the people of the world.

It is in that spirit that I look forward to the discussions that I shall have with you, Mr. President, and with the members of your government.

Speaking in a personal sense, I look forward to the opportunity to receive from you your judgment, your counsel, not only on the relations between our two countries, but even more on the great problems that divide the world; and your judgment as to how the United States can best fill its role in helping to solve those problems.

We have often talked before and I have always benefited from the wisdom and the experience that you have in such great degree. There has never been a period in the world's history when we need not unilateral decisions on the part of one great power, but when we need the very best wisdom that we can find in finding the policies that will save freedom and maintain peace in the world.

If I could be permitted one personal word as an American coming to France again after many previous visits. We have known this nation as a brave ally in time of war and as a loyal companion in searching the ways of peace. But everyone who has had the privilege of knowing this nation from visiting it, as I have on many occasions, would share the sentiment expressed by Benjamin Franklin many years ago when he said that every man has two homes: "France and his own."

It is in that sentiment, Mr. President, that deep from my heart I say: *Vive la France.*

NOTE: The President spoke at 2:08 p.m. at Orly Airport in Paris in response to welcoming remarks by President Charles de Gaulle of France. An advance text of the President's remarks is printed in the Weekly Compilation of Presidential Documents (vol. 5, p. 346).

President de Gaulle spoke in French. The French Embassy translation follows:

Mr. President, we are delighted to have you visit Paris. It is indeed a visit which in your person the United States of America is cordially paying to France.

For, in the last 200 years, during which every-thing happened, nothing has ever been able to make our country cease to feel the friend of yours. Moreover, you are coming to see us in order that we may define for you our thoughts and our intentions regarding world affairs, and in order that you may enlighten us as to your own views and plans. How could we not attribute the greatest interest and the utmost importance to these exchanges!

Lastly, Mr. President, it is you whom we are welcoming. Allow me to tell you that it is a joy and an honor for us, due to the great esteem that our nation has for the statesman your country has just placed at its head—an esteem to which, on my side, is added, for you, an already tried friendship.

Long live the United States of America.

88   Toasts of the President and President de Gaulle at a Dinner at the Elysée Palace in Paris.   *February* 28, 1969

Mr. President:

On behalf of all of us who are your guests this evening, I express my deep appreciation for your very gracious hospitality and for your eloquent remarks.

As I stand here in this place of honor, in this magnificent room, in the presence of this company, I realize that I stand here at a time in history which will long be remembered. I realize that it was just a few years ago that you entertained another American President, a young man against whom I had run for office and one who came here and sat in the chair that I now occupy. We were members of different parties. We disagreed on some issues. But we were completely agreed on what was important.

We were completely agreed, for example, in the importance of French-American friendship. And we were completely agreed in our dedication to the ideals, the ideals which your country stands for, the ideals that we share with you—ideals of freedom, of equality, of peace and justice for all nations.

And so I speak not just for myself, or for my party, but for the whole American people when I salute you, Mr. President, and your people, and when I say with regard to you that with reference to the fact that the United States is a powerful nation militarily and rich economically, we also recognize that there are other sources of great leadership. And that greatness of leadership can be seen in the character of a great man.

That character can be measured in three ways: the quality of courage, the quality of the ability to convince others of a point of view, and the quality of being able to bring a nation back after that nation has fallen on difficult days.

Mr. President, your life has been an example to millions of your countrymen and to millions throughout the world—an epic of courage, an epic also of leadership seldom equaled in the history of the world, leadership which now has brought this great nation to the rightful place that it should have in the family of nations.

And then there is one other quality we have found always in our visits with you and which we seek now and are finding now, and that is the quality of wisdom and vision—the vision that sees beyond the crisis of the moment, that sees the great forces that are at play in the world and, therefore, is able to have the perspective that leaders need to make the right decisions, the decisions that will stand well in history and not just in the headlines of tomorrow.

And so I ask all of you to raise your glasses to a nation and a people with whom the United States has had the longest uninterrupted friendship—200 years—of any nation in the world, and to a leader who has become a giant among men because he had courage, because he had vision, and because he had the wisdom that the world now seeks to solve its difficult problems: President de Gaulle.

NOTE: The President proposed the toast at 9:30 p.m. in response to a toast by President Charles de Gaulle, who spoke in French. The French Embassy translation follows:

Mr. President, you did very well to come, at all events, it will have been very pleasant and very useful for us. But it so happens that, at this very moment, the tremendous change accomplished by our universe in one generation and those that undoubtedly await it urgently engage the responsibility of the states once each one of them intends to assume its own responsibility. It happens, also, that this is especially true for America, due to the present extent of its power and to the fact that, alone of all the major nations, it has emerged from the two terrible World Wars without major wounds. So, nothing is more natural and more satisfactory than the visits you are paying to several European capitals and, notably, to Paris.

So here you are in the process of exchanging your views with ours in order to serve what we want, you and we, I mean progress and peace. This is being done—is it not true?—in the frankest manner. But that is indeed the manner which is necessary between two countries naturally different in their situation, size, and interests, but which are ever drawn together by a two-centuries-old friendship, as well as by the profound community of a certain human ideal whose flame has often spread more light and warmth in both our countries than anywhere else on our earth.

This means that France, for her part, thanks you warmly for being here.

I raise my glass in honor of Mr. Richard Nixon, President of the United States of America, in honor of the dignitaries accompanying him, in honor of their country, which is always dear to the heart of ours.

89   Toasts of the President and President de Gaulle at a Dinner at the American Ambassador's Residence. *March 1, 1969*

Mr. President and Madame de Gaulle and Your Excellencies:

It is a very great honor for us to have here in the American Embassy residence the President of the French Republic and Madame de Gaulle and the other representatives of the French Government.

On this occasion we would remind the President that we have tried to expose him as much as possible to the products of our country. He will have observed that during the course of the evening we have had several evidences of that type. For example, we have an American Air Force jazz combo which flew in from Wiesbaden for the occasion. And on the menu tonight we had cheese from Wisconsin, asparagus from California, and beef from Kansas City. But there was one very unusual combination: For the first time I have seen on one plate together, plain American baked potato and Russian caviar. There may be some significance in the fact that it took a French chef to bring the two together.

Mr. President, we are deeply grateful for the hospitality that you have extended to all of our party, to the Secretary of State and to me and to the rest of us on this occasion. We are deeply grateful, too, in a broader sense, for the very warm welcome that we have received from the French people.

Before I came to this country I had been reading accounts in our press to the effect that there was an anti-American sentiment among the French people. If ever an answer was needed, we saw it in the faces of thousands of Frenchmen in the last 2 days.

But most of all, we are in your debt for a gift which is the most precious, the gift of your time. The hours that we have spent together in which we have discussed the great problems that we face together in the world have been most helpful to all of us, and we shall always be grateful for the time you have given to that cause.

So, tonight, I feel that this marks, in a sense, the end of one journey and the beginning of another one; the end of a journey that has taken us in a very brief time to the major capitals of Europe, and the beginning of another journey, another journey in which our two peoples will be going forward together toward the same destination, sometimes on different roads, but always in the same direction and motivated by the same ideals and purposes.

I look forward, Mr. President, with great anticipation to working with you and with your country and with your Government for the cause to which you have dedicated your life, the cause of freedom and dignity for nations and for men and for peace and brotherhood for all people.

I ask you to rise and raise your glasses to French-American friendship and to President and Madame de Gaulle.

NOTE: The President spoke at 10:04 p.m. in Paris at the residence of U.S. Ambassador R. Sargent Shriver, Jr. On the same day the White House Press Office released a list of French citizens who met with President Nixon.

President de Gaulle responded in French. The French Embassy translation follows:

Mr. President, if it is not quite true that one learns at every age, it is true that at every age one can see what one knows be confirmed. In thanking you, on behalf of my wife, myself, and all those who accompany us, for your very gracious hospitality, allow me to tell you what has happened to me personally on the occasion of your visit. Yesterday we were saying publicly that the world is undergoing far-reaching changes. But I have been able to note once again, as I have already noted on several memorable occasions throughout my life, that there is one thing that never changes—our French-American friendship.

I have always noted that, when will exists, however difficult the problems that arise before you and before us, Americans and French, we can settle them not only in a climate of frankness and cordiality, but also of mutual confidence.

Another thing that I have been able to confirm, thanks to your visit, is the very deep consideration that I have for you. As I am learning to know you better—and by this visit you have given me that opportunity which I consider historic—I appreciate more the statesman and the man that you are.

90 Remarks at the American Embassy in Paris. *March* 2, 1969

Mr. Ambassador:

I appreciate the opportunity that you have provided for me to greet the Embassy personnel and also some of the members of their families that I see down here in front and also for those that are in this room. There is another group downstairs in the lobby watching on television.

I want to express my regret that we were unable to be able to get everybody in the same room. I was going to say to the Ambassador that we probably needed a larger Embassy. But, who knows? No, I think we have got to speak to Mr. Rooney.[1]

But, nevertheless, on a visit of this type that is so filled with official talks—and I move from here for my last talk during this visit with President de Gaulle and then we go on to see Pope Paul in Rome and then back to Washington tonight. That is just a light day. But we spent the morning on Vietnam.

But, nevertheless, I did not want to leave Paris without expressing to all of those in this Embassy, and all of those who are associated with it in any way, my appreciation for what you have done on this visit, first.

I know what a burden a visit by VIP's places upon an Embassy. I first came to Paris, I remember, 22 years ago in this same building, and then as a Congressman. I know we caused a lot of trouble. I guess that hasn't changed.

But, anyway, then I came back as

a Senator in 1951, and I have been here many times since. I didn't come here as a Vice President, and now I come as a President. They tell me that that is even harder—harder on the staff, I mean.

But I do want you to know that I realize it is hundreds of people, literally hundreds of people, that I will never be able to thank personally or by letter, or to greet personally, who worked on this visit.

I know you worked many hours overtime. And I am speaking now not simply of the officers of the Embassy, the Ambassador, of course, who has been so cooperative, and Bob Blake [Deputy Chief of Mission]. I rather grew up with him in Whittier. He is a little after my time. I should say, I knew his parents.

But, nevertheless, I want you to know that not only the officers, but everybody in all the offices—as I went down the halls today, I saw girls typing out schedules, and I know that you have got to run them through the mimeograph machines and— or, no, you put them through some other kind of a machine now to get them multilithed. And that is just part of it. But the immense amount of logistical detail that is involved in a visit by a President and a Secretary of State is something that places an immense burden on the Embassy. I express appreciation for that.

Beyond that, however, I want to tell you that the visit has been handled in this very brief time that we have been here with great precision.

I have been trying to think of something that I could pick out as a mistake, you know, so that we could do better next time. But I found only one thing: I found

---

[1] Representative John J. Rooney, chairman, Subcommittee on Appropriations for the Departments of State, Justice, Commerce, the Judiciary and Related Agencies.

on one of my schedules—I don't know who happened to prepare this, but nevertheless, the schedule said, with regard to the first dinner, the dinner that President de Gaulle was the host—the second one, as you know, was in Ambassador Shriver's residence, and I was the host there—but at the first dinner where he was the host, he was supposed to make a toast and I was supposed to prepare one to him. On my schedule it said: "President Nixon will speak for 10 minutes and then his speech will be translated into English." I knew I had troubles in communicating, but not that much.

But whether it was my French or English or whatever the case might be, that was the only thing I could find—and we need to have a little humor in a trip. I think it was put in deliberately for that very purpose.

But could I go one step further? Also, in this room are people who have dedicated their lives to the service of the Government of the United States, some in the Foreign Service and some in other branches of the service. You have been in this post; you have been in many others.

I am sure there must be times when you wonder whether you made the right decision. There must be times when the boredom of what your job is, the failure to get the promotion that you think you should have had, the failure to have the responsibility which you think you might be capable of—these are the things we all feel from time to time—all of these things must run through your minds. And, also, perhaps, in the positions that you have you wonder if the country really appreciates people in Government.

I can simply tell you that I, as one who has had the opportunity of traveling now to 73 countries and have seen our em-

bassies abroad and our other missions in most of those countries, I appreciate what you are doing, both as the President of the United States and as an individual.

I know how dedicated you are. I know, in many cases, what a sacrifice it is for you to continue in public service, as you have. I know that many of you probably figure you could have done better economically if you had been in some other branch.

But whatever the case might be, let me give you this one word of reassurance with regard to the decision you made sometime in your life to come into public service.

I firmly am convinced of the fact that all of you are playing a great part in a cause that is much bigger than any of us. All of us have that privilege. And we in America can say that, and it cannot be said in all countries of the world. It can be said frankly in the free world, more in ours than in any other, not because we asked for that responsibility, but because it is ours.

And as we play that great role, I want you to know that sometimes it appears that all that really matters is what a President says or what he does, or what the Ambassador says and what he does—and all of those things are important—or what the Secretary of State may declare in his various remarks or in the statements that he may send out around the world.

But I can assure you that what the men at the top do does have an immense effect on the foreign policy of the United States and whether we have peace and freedom in the world, that the success of a policy depends upon thousands of people around, in an Embassy like this, an establishment like this, and millions around this world—3 million people, maybe 4 million, if you include military and the rest in the service of the United States.

I think I can best bring that home by what Colonel Frank Borman said when I presented an award to him at the White House a few weeks ago, shortly after I was inaugurated. I congratulated him. He accepted the award and he said: I accept it not only for my two colleagues on the voyage to the moon, but for 400,000 Americans who, one way or another, worked on this project.

And then he made a significant point: that in that Apollo there are 2 million parts, and if something went wrong with one of those parts, who knows whether or not the project would have succeeded.

I realize that the success of our efforts at the highest post in Government depends upon how every person in Government does his job. And I am very proud to have the opportunity to serve in the highest post, but I am even prouder to have supporting me, in that search for peace and freedom that we all want, a fine group of career officers and thousands of people like yourselves in this room who have dedicated your life to public service in the Government of the United States.

All of you count—every one. And I know it. And I know that even the tiniest slip on your part might make a difference at the highest level at some point or other, or something that you do may make us do a better job.

Finally, one other point: I realize in this room are some other people who are not American citizens, people who are French by background, but who have worked for this Embassy for many years. We couldn't run it without you. I know that. And I want to thank you for what you have done.

And so, with that, I can only say, again, after having been here for a very busy 48 hours, that the success of the trip, if it was successful, is due, in large part, to the people that I see in front of me. And I thank you for what you have done.

I wish you well in what you do in the future. And when I get back to the States, I will tell them we have a fine team here in Paris under the leadership of Ambassador Shriver.

Thank you.

NOTE: The President spoke at 12:25 p.m. at the American Embassy in Paris. The U.S. Ambassador in Paris was R. Sargent Shriver, Jr.

91 Remarks at Orly Airport on Departure From France. *March 2, 1969*

Mr. President:

I want to express, on behalf of all of the members of our party, our deep gratitude again for the great hospitality you have extended to us and that we have received from the French people.

On this occasion, as I leave this country and go to Rome, and then back to Washington tonight, I am very pleased to announce that President de Gaulle has ac-

cepted an invitation to visit the United States. He will visit Washington sometime in January or February at a time that is mutually convenient for our two schedules.

We look forward to seeing him there again, and I am delighted that he was able to work this visit into his schedule.

NOTE: The President spoke at 2:07 p.m. at Orly Airport near Paris. President Charles de Gaulle responded in French. The French Embassy translation follows:

Mr. President, we are delighted to have had your visit. It is a success, I think, for our two countries, and it is a success for yourself, and we are all pleased by that success.

So, if you wish, until next year.

92   Remarks at a Meeting With Pope Paul VI.
March 2, 1969

Your Holiness:

We are most honored to hear those eloquent words in behalf of our country, and I express my personal appreciation for the time that I have had to talk with you about some of the great issues which divide the world, but issues which, with leadership both by the temporal leaders and the spiritual leaders of the world, we may be able to resolve, and resolve them in an atmosphere of peace.

We all remember, in the United States, your visit, and we remember your coming to the United Nations and your appearance before thousands of Americans in Yankee Stadium, and millions on television. It left a memory that we will always carry very close to our hearts.

We know, as we sit here and consider the difficult material problems that we will have to deal with when we return to our own country, that what the world needs today is the spiritual and moral leadership which Your Holiness has stood for, stood for here in the Vatican and in your arduous travels to other nations in the world.

Your words have inspired us. The fact that we have your prayers will sustain us in the years ahead. We are confident that as we move forward, we shall be able to find those answers that will bring the world to which you have dedicated your life, and that world will be one of peace, and also one of freedom and justice for all people.

NOTE: The President spoke at approximately 5:30 p.m. in the Papal Salon at the Vatican. The remarks of Pope Paul VI, which preceded those of the President, were as follows:

Mr. President, we are very happy and deeply grateful, too, that your courtesy has made this visit possible at the close of your strenuous working journey through Europe.

In the past we have already had the honor of visits from you, but now you come to us in another capacity, with the heavy responsibilities of the President of the United States of America.

It is as such that we greet you, giving expression immediately to a warm and spontaneous wish: May you in your administration experience the deep satisfaction of making a real contribution to the total cessation of those conflicts now unfortunately in progress, and of putting an even more effective stop to the outbreak of new armed struggles, by following the sure way toward a lasting peace and promoting true prosperity by means of a widely based and fruitful understanding.

This is the mission which your great nation, Mr. President, along with the other members of the international community, is called upon to fulfill: a mission of peace, a mission of noblehearted collaboration with all peoples, and particularly with the developing peoples, in mutual esteem, with respect for the fundamental freedoms of men and of nations, and in the promotion of genuine human values.

All peoples are closely bound together, now more than ever before, in a common destiny: the great worldwide effort to build on solid foundations the earthly city in which each individual lives and works.

An exalting and difficult task, this—it is one that calls for foresight, in order that while uncovering the immensity of mankind's needs, it may also realize the no less immense possibilities offered today, especially by science and technology employed in the service of man.

It is also a task that requires good, constructive, and generous ideas, noble desires, moral energy, a clear vision of reality, firm decision, courage to make choices, and persevering constancy in the way that is chosen.

It is therefore a task which has need of an assistance that cannot be physically measured, yet is absolutely indispensable; for unless the Lord builds the house, those who build it will labour in vain. [Ps. 126: 1]

To construct this earthly city in unity, prosperity, wisdom, and concord, the Catholic Church, inspired by the Gospel message, will unfailingly continue to offer her disinterested and active contribution of moral energy and support.

That the serene vision of peace may ever shine in your mind and heart, Mr. President, to inspire and sustain your valiant efforts, our repeated good wishes go with you, and our heartfelt prayer accompanies you, as we invoke upon you and upon the people of the United States of America, who are so dear to us, abundant divine blessings.

93   Remarks to American Priests and Students at the Vatican. *March 2,* 1969

THIS IS INDEED a very great privilege for me to see this very distinguished group of Americans here on this memorable day, and this magnificent place. And when I noted that I was scheduled to visit the North American College—I understand there are some here from the North American College—I became a little concerned, because these days I suppose you could say this is one of the few colleges I could go to without having a demonstration against me. [*Laughter*]

If you will pardon a personal reference—I go back a few years, a few years to the time that I came here as Vice President of the United States in 1957 and Archbishop O'Connor[1] then welcomed me, and then on other occasions, too, he welcomed me—but I remember appearing at the college and meeting so many then.

I did not expect then that I would come back now in the capacity I presently hold. I have been trying ever since then to get through the electoral college, but I finally made it. So here I am.

But I do want you to know Secretary of State Rogers, whom I am sure you can recognize from the picture he had on the cover of Time magazine a few weeks ago. It is more than you can say for me. My pictures don't do me justice.

But as we finish this trip and have this opportunity to meet you, one very serious thought comes to mind: As we have talked in the capitals of Europe with the leaders—with Prime Minister Wilson, with the King of the Belgians and the Prime Minister, with Dr. Kiesinger and members of his government in the Federal Republic, with Prime Minister Rumor and President Saragat in Italy, with President de Gaulle and members of his government in Paris—that over and over again, in addition to the subjects in international relations which are necessarily at the top of our agenda, the subject comes up of youth in the world, in every country and in America.

I spoke facetiously about it a moment ago. I do, however, now speak very seriously on that point. And I speak particularly of the very significant role that I believe you, you who are so young, you

---

[1] Archbishop Martin J. O'Connor, director of the college in 1957.

who have so much to give, you who have such an opportunity to lead the mission that you have in the years ahead, and it is this:

Wherever I went, as I talked to intellectuals, to government leaders and to others—and the Secretary of State confirmed that he had the same experience in the talks that he had—it seems that youth today in the so-called advanced countries have the same problem, those who are demonstrating, and some are, of course, simply demonstrating for the sake of demonstrating, but some deeply believe that their demonstrations are necessary.

The problem they have is that they are against, but too often they do not have anything to be for. And that is the problem of our time.

Here we find, looking at the United States of America, for example, that American youth, I think we could say, never had it so good materially. In terms of being able to get an education, if they have what it takes, they can get it. In terms of being able to get a job after they get the education, they can get them.

This is a seller's market, believe me, because the great companies, the law firms, and all the rest, are out searching for those who have completed their education, trying to bring them into their firms.

But what we find is that at this period when, from a material standpoint, young people never had a better outlook, that they still have, many of them, a sense of frustration, a sense that something is missing. And that is where you come in. It has been so truly written that man does not live by bread alone. And young people today need a sense of purpose, something to be for, a vision and idealism. You provide that. You provide it through the church which you serve and you provide it in a broader sense. We have to provide it also in our own capacities.

I think that as far as American youth is concerned, our purpose needs to be more than simply making our own country one that we can be proud of. We will do that. But it is also to meet our destiny of attempting to lead the world, along with others, on the paths that will bring real peace among nations, and beyond that, in seeing that America, because of its wealth which is unprecedented in the history of nations, does its share in helping the millions of people on this earth who are living at a subsistence level and who, without assistance, will never be able to enjoy even what the very minimum is in the United States.

These are some of the goals that I see for our Nation on the temporal side. There are other problems that we have on the spiritual side.

But all that I am really trying to say is this: We are both going down different roads toward the same destination, and that is to give to the country that we love a sense of mission, a sense of purpose, a sense of idealism, that will inspire the youth of America, make them proud of their country. And I am sure that we are going to do it, and I am sure that you will do it in your capacity.

Thank you very much.

NOTE: The President spoke at 6:08 p.m. in the Salla Clementine at the Vatican.

94   Remarks at Andrews Air Force Base on Returning From Europe.   *March 2, 1969*

Mr. Vice President, Mr. Speaker, all of the distinguished Members of the House, the Senate, and the Cabinet who have come to the airport today:

Over the past week we have had some splendid receptions in the great capitals of Europe, but I can assure you that none means more than to have such a warm welcome on such a cold night as we return to Washington, D.C. I am most grateful for your words which were so generous.

I can only respond at this time by giving you one overall impression of this trip. Later in the week I will be meeting the press and responding in greater detail.

That one impression is, I think, summed up by the word "trust." I sensed, as I traveled to the capitals of Europe, that there is a new trust on the part of the Europeans in themselves growing out of the fact that they have had a remarkable recovery economically and politically, as well as in their military strength, since the devastation of World War II.

Also, I think I sensed a new trust in the United States growing out of the fact that they feel that there are open channels of communication with the United States, and a new sense of consultation with the United States.

Finally, I think that there is developing a new trust in the future, not only on the part of the people of Europe and their leaders, but on the part of the people of

the United States—confidence based on the fact that together we are going to be able to develop some new understandings with those who, in the past, have opposed us on the other side of the world.

I would not want this opportunity to pass without mentioning that while this was a working trip, with most of it devoted to conferences and very few public appearances, there were times, as I rode through the streets of the great capitals of Europe, that I felt that the American people, all of the American people, in the person of their President, were being greeted by the people of Europe.

If you could have been with me as I rode through the streets of Berlin on a snowy, cold day and had seen the thousands of happy and hopeful faces in those crowds on the streets, you would have been proud that America did meet her world responsibilities and has met her world responsibilities in helping others defend their freedom. You would have been proud to be an American at this time in our history.

Thank you very much.

NOTE: The President spoke at approximately 10:10 p.m. at Andrews Air Force Base, Maryland.

The welcoming remarks of Vice President Agnew, which preceded those of the President, are printed in the Weekly Compilation of Presidential Documents (vol. 5, p. 356).

95   Statement Following the Successful Launching of Apollo 9. *March 3,* 1969

THE successful launching of the Apollo 9 spacecraft marks another milestone in the journey of man into space. The hopes and prayers of mankind go with Col. James A. McDivitt, Col. David R. Scott, and Mr. Russell Schweickart on their courageous mission. The genius of the American scientific and technological community, which created and designed the Saturn V, the command ship, and the lunar module, once again stirs the imagination and gratitude of the world.

We are proud of this American adventure, but this is more than an American adventure. It is an adventure of man, bringing the accumulated wisdom of his past to the task of shaping the future.

The 10-day flight of Apollo 9 will, we hope, do something more than bring America closer to the moon; it can serve to bring humanity closer by dramatically showing what men can do when they bring to any task the best of man's mind and heart.

96   Special Message to the Congress on Coal Mine Safety. *March 3,* 1969

To the Congress of the United States:

The workers in the coal mining industry and their families have too long endured the constant threat and often sudden reality of disaster, disease and death. This great industry has strengthened our nation with the raw material of power. But it has also frequently saddened our nation with news of crippled men, grieving widows and fatherless children.

Death in the mines can be as sudden as an explosion or a collapse of a roof and ribs, or it comes insidiously from pneumoconiosis or "black lung" disease. When a miner leaves his home for work, he and his family must live with the unspoken but always present fear that before the working day is over, he may be crushed or burned to death or suffocated. This acceptance of the possibility of death in the mines has become almost as much a part of the job as the tools and the tunnels.

The time has come to replace this fatalism with hope by substituting action for words. Catastrophes in the coal mines are not inevitable. They can be prevented, and they must be prevented.

To these ends, I have ordered the following actions to advance the health and safety of the coal mine workers:

—Increase substantially the number of inspectors, and improve coal mine inspections and the effectiveness of staff performance and requirements.

—Revise the instructions to the mine inspectors so as to reflect more stringent operating standards.

—Initiate an in-depth study to reorganize the agency charged with the primary responsibility for mine safety so that it can meet the new challenges and demands.

—Expand research activities with respect to pneumoconiosis and other mine health and safety hazards.

—Extend the recent advances in human engineering and motivational techniques, and enlarge and intensify education and training functions, for the improvement of health and safety in coal mines to the greatest degree possible.

—Establish cooperative programs between management and labor at the *mine level* which will implement health and safety efforts at the site of the mine hazards.

—Encourage the coordination of Federal and State inspections, in order to secure more effective enforcement of the present safety requirements.

—Initiate grant programs to the States, as authorized but not previously invoked, to assist the States in planning and advancing their respective programs for increased health and safety in the coal mines.

In addition to these immediate efforts under existing law, I am submitting to the Congress legislative proposals for a comprehensive new program to provide a vigorous and multi-faceted attack on the health and safety dangers which prevail in the coal mining industry.

These proposals would:

—Modernize a wide range of mandatory health and safety standards, including new provisions for the control of dust, electrical equipment, roof support, ventilation, illumination, fire protection, and other operating practices in underground and surface coal mines engaged in commerce.

—Authorize the Secretary of the Interior to develop and promulgate any additional or revised standards which he deems necessary for the health and safety of the miners.

—Provide strict deterrents and enforce-

ment measures and, at the same time, establish equitable appeal procedures to remedy any arbitrary and unlawful actions.

—Recruit and carefully train a highly motivated corps of coal mine inspectors to investigate the coal mines, and to enforce impartially and vigorously the broad new mandatory standards.

—Improve Federal-State inspection plans.

—Substantially increase, by direct action, grants and contracts, the necessary research, training, and education for the prevention and control of occupational diseases, the improvement of State workmen's compensation systems, and the reduction of mine accidents.

These legislative proposals, together with other steps already taken or to be taken are essential to meet our obligation to the Nation's coal miners, and to accomplish our mission of eliminating the tragedies which have occurred in the mines.

These proposals are not intended to replace the voluntary and enlightened efforts of management and labor to reduce coal mine hazards, which efforts are the touchstone to any successful health and safety program. Rather, these measures would expand and render uniform by enforceable authority the most advanced of the health and safety precautions undertaken and potentially available in the coal mining industry.

I urge the immediate adoption by Congress of this legislation.

RICHARD NIXON

The White House
    March 3, 1969

97   Message to the Congress Transmitting Reports on the Cash Awards Program for Military Personnel. *March 4, 1969*

To the Congress of the United States:

In accordance with the provisions of 10 U.S.C. 1124, I am forwarding for the information of the Congress reports of the Secretary of Defense and the Secretary of Transportation on awards made during Calendar Year 1968 to members of the Armed Forces for suggestions, inventions, and scientific achievements.

Participation by military personnel in the cash awards program was authorized by Congress in September 1965. The program has proven successful in motivating military personnel to seek ways of reducing costs and improving efficiency. Tangible benefits from suggestions submitted by the Department of Defense and Coast Guard military personnel and adopted during 1968 totalled over $95,000,000, an increase of nearly 50% over the 1967 figures.

In the relatively short period since the program went into effect, tangible first-year benefits derived from the suggestions of military personnel have reached a total of over $214,000,000.

Of 241,090 suggestions submitted by military personnel during 1968, 37,995 were adopted. Cash awards totalled $1,601,265, of which approximately three-fourths were paid to enlisted personnel at Grade E-6 and below.

The cash awards program for military personnel could be justified solely by the net savings which have accrued to the government since the program was initiated. But the benefits of this program are greater than dollars saved. An incentive and a vehicle have been provided for suggestions which effect economies and increase efficiency. Moreover, military personnel now have the assurance that their ideas will not go unheeded in drab suggestion boxes, but will be carefully screened and considered at the highest policy levels of the government. Under the program, every man has an opportunity to forward his ideas and be rewarded for his effort. It is a good program, a sound and wise investment.

RICHARD NIXON

The White House

March 4, 1969

98   The President's News Conference of *March 4, 1969*

THE PRESIDENT'S TRIP TO EUROPE

THE PRESIDENT. [1.] Ladies and gentlemen, as you know, the purpose of this unusually long press conference is to report to the American people on my trip to Europe.

Because I realize that there will probably be a number of questions, some of which may require some rather lengthy answers, I am going to make my opening statement quite brief.

A word about the purpose and also the limitations of a trip like this: I believe all of us in this room have no illusions about the limits of personal diplomacy in settling great differences between nations. A smile or a handshake or an exchange of toasts or gifts or visits will not by themselves have effect where vital interests are concerned and where there are great differences.

On the other hand, I have learned that there is an intangible factor which does affect the relations between nations. I think it was perhaps best described by two of our visitors, those with whom I was talking. One was in the case of Prime Minister Wilson. He used the term mutual trust when he welcomed me. The other, President de Gaulle, when he came to the American Embassy, used the term *confiance*—trust.

When there is trust between men who are leaders of nations, there is a better chance to settle differences than when there is not trust. I think than one of the accomplishments of this trip is that we have established between the United States of America and the major nations of Europe—and, I trust, other nations of Europe as well—a new relationship of trust and confidence that did not exist before.

For example, as we look at the relations with France, they are different today than they were a week ago. Now, how different they are only time will tell. But that they are different and improved, I think, would be a fair assessment of that situation.

We can also say that, as a result of this trip, the United States has indicated its continuing support of the Alliance—the Atlantic Alliance—and that we have also indicated our support of the concept and ideal of European unity.

In addition, we have indicated that we recognize our limitations insofar as European unity is concerned. Americans cannot unify Europe. Europeans must do so. And we should not become involved in differences among Europeans in which our vital interests are not involved.

Finally, a word that I think all of the American people will be gratified to hear. Sometimes we become rather disillusioned with our aid programs around the world, and we look back on our relations with Europe, particularly, and wonder if it was really worth all that we did immediately after World War II, in terms of the Marshall Plan and other programs.

Anyone who saw Europe as I did in that period of devastation after World War II—when I visited all the countries, except Belgium at that time, that I visited on this trip—and then saw it today would realize that it was worth doing, because today a strong, prosperous, free Europe stands there, partly a result of our aid.

It could not have happened without our aid. It also, of course, could not have happened without their great efforts on their own behalf. And so, with that recognition, we now realize that this Alliance deserves our attention, should be the center of our concern, should not be taken for granted. It will not be. That will be a major objective of this administration.

Now, as we go to your questions, I will take questions not only on the European trip but any area of foreign policy, because on the trip I discussed with the leaders of Europe all areas of foreign policy, which was their desire and mine as well.

There will be only one ground rule. I know there will be great interest in what each of the leaders said to me and what

I said to them. I will not divulge the content of these personal conversations because, if we are going to build confidence, we can't build confidence by breaking confidences.

We will go to the questions.

QUESTIONS

AN EAST-WEST SUMMIT MEETING

[2.] Q. Mr. President, we got the impression traveling with you that there was some relationship between your tour and a possible East-West summit at some future time. Could you relate the two?

THE PRESIDENT. Mr. Cormier [Frank Cormier, Associated Press], this tour was a condition precedent to an East-West summit at a later time. I have always indicated that before we had talks with those who have opposed us in the world, it was essential that we had clear understandings with our allies and friends.

I think at times in the past we have not had that kind of consultation. It was essential to have it on this trip. In every visit that I had I discussed East-West relations with the leaders involved—discussed not only what our plans were and what our policies might be but got their views and their advice as to what programs they thought we should handle in any bilateral discussions we had with the Soviet Union.

RELATIONS WITH RED CHINA AND THE
SOVIET UNION

[3.] Q. Mr. President, during the trip, and as recently as the conclusion of the trip Sunday night, you spoke of hoping that with greater unity with our allies,

you would be able to develop new understanding with those who have opposed us on the other side of the world. To follow up on Mr. Cormier's question, of whom are you speaking, sir? We assume the Russians. Are you thinking, for instance, you may be able to reach a better understanding with Red China?

THE PRESIDENT. Looking further down the road, we could think in terms of a better understanding with Red China. But being very realistic, in view of Red China's breaking off the rather limited Warsaw talks that were planned, I do not think that we should hold out any great optimism for any breakthroughs in that direction at this time.

Certainly you are correct in assuming that in referring to those who have opposed us in the world, I was referring primarily to the Soviet Union and to the talks that the United States would be having with the Soviet Union in a number of areas.

Europeans, I found, were greatly concerned by what they called the possibility of a U.S.-Soviet condominium, in which, at the highest levels, the two superpowers would make decisions affecting their future without consulting them.

In fact, one statesman used the term "Yalta." He said: "We don't want another Yalta on the part of the United States and the Soviet Union." Now, whether his assessment was correct about Yalta or not is immaterial.

The point is that Europeans are highly sensitive about the United States and the Soviet Union making decisions that affect their future without their consultation. And that will not happen as a result of this trip.

THE SITUATION IN WEST BERLIN

[4.] Q. Mr. President, would you assess for us, sir, the situation in West Berlin on the eve of the election, how you see it? Do you think it has reached a crisis point?

THE PRESIDENT. Well, the situation in West Berlin at the moment seems to have leveled off. I haven't seen the latest reports. I will have to look at the morning papers to see whether my projection at this point is correct, because it has changed from hour to hour.

I believe that we have made our position quite clear to all the parties involved, as we should. We have made it clear to the West German Government, that if they went ahead with the election, we would support them in that decision, or if they decided that they could gain concessions that they considered significant which would lead them to changing the place for the elections, we would support them in that move.

It is their decision and we are not trying to affect it one way or another. They have a right to have the elections there if they want. Also, we have indicated to the Soviets—to the Soviet Ambassador, Mr. [Anatoly F.] Dobrynin—both Mr. Rogers and I have pointed out that any harassment in West Berlin could jeopardize the progress that we see possible in other areas.

I have reported previously in a press conference that I felt that the Soviet Union did not want to see the West Berlin situation become a cause or even a pretext for any move which would be in retrogression insofar as our bilateral relations are concerned.

At this moment, based on the conversations that I have had myself with various European leaders and also the conversation that I and others have had with the representatives of the Soviet Union, I believe that the Soviet Union does not want to have the situation in West Berlin heated up to the point that it would jeopardize some—what they consider to be—more important negotiations at the highest level with the United States. And because those negotiations, in effect, are in the wings, I think I could predict that the Soviet Union will use its influence to cool off the West Berlin situation, rather than to heat it up.

THE VATICAN

[5.] Q. Do you think, sir, that, from your talks with Pope Paul at the Vatican, there is any possibility that the United States might send an envoy to the Vatican as a permanent representative?

THE PRESIDENT. That possibility has been considered by the State Department and by me, because we have been concerned that we should have the very closest consultation and discussion with the Vatican. I found, for example, my conversation with Pope Paul extremely helpful. It was far ranging, and I received information and also counsel that I considered to be very important. I want that line of communication kept open. Whether we can have it kept open based on the present facilities that are available, I have not yet determined. The matter is still under study. But what is important is that the United States have with the Vatican close consultation on foreign policy matters in which the Vatican has a very great interest and very great influence.

THE COMMUNIST OFFENSIVE IN VIETNAM

[6.] Q. Mr. President, the Communist offensive in Vietnam has aroused speculation that your administration is being tested, particularly as to the understanding that was reached last November 1, which led to the bombing halt. Would you give us your opinion of this, please?

THE PRESIDENT. Well, in speaking of the Communist offensive, I think it is important first to analyze what it is and what its purposes are, compare it with the offensive last year, and then see what that offensive means in terms of the violation of the understanding last October 31 or prior to October 31 at the time of the bombing halt.

When we look at the offensive, we find that in terms of the frequency of attacks it is approximately the same as the offensive of last year. In terms of intensity of attacks, it is less than that of last year. As far as the targets are concerned, it is primarily directed toward military targets, but there are also some very significant civilian targets. Now, as far as the purposes are concerned, we can only guess; but three have been suggested: that it might be directed against the Government of South Vietnam to break its morale and its back; that it might be directed against public opinion in the United States to put more pressure on the administration to move more in the direction of North Vietnam's position at the Paris peace talks; or that it might be directed toward a military victory of sorts, if a military victory of sorts could be accomplished in South Vietnam by the North Vietnamese against our forces there.

Now, this offensive has failed in all three of these areas. It has failed to achieve any significant military breakthrough. It has failed to break the back of the Government of South Vietnam. Far from that, as a matter of fact, in terms of the pacification program, 700,000 were displaced by the Tet offensive last year, and only 25,000 have been displaced by this one. As far as this offensive affecting the United States and its negotiating position in Paris, it could have exactly the opposite effect.

I think that, therefore, we must now analyze the offensive in terms of the understanding of October 31. Now, that understanding was to the effect that continued shelling of, or attacks on, the cities, the major cities of South Vietnam, would be inconsistent with talks toward peace which would be productive in Paris.

Now, we are examining this particular offensive, examining it very carefully, to see whether its magnitude is in violation of that understanding. Technically, it could be said that it is in violation. Whether we reach the conclusion that the violation is so significant that it requires action on our part is a decision we will be reaching very soon if those attacks continue at their present magnitude.

As you know, Secretary Laird is going to South Vietnam tomorrow, and I have asked him to look into the situation and to give me a report after he has been there.

One other factor should be mentioned: I do not want to discount by this analysis the seriousness of these attacks, because the American casualty rate, I note, has doubled during the period of these attacks. Therefore, it is necessary for the American President, in analyzing the attacks, to think not only of the understanding with regard to the attacks on the cities, but also of his obligation to defend American fighting men in Vietnam.

We have not moved in a precipitate fashion, but the fact that we have shown patience and forbearance should not be considered as a sign of weakness. We will not tolerate a continuation of a violation of an understanding. But more than that, we will not tolerate attacks which result in heavier casualties to our men at a time that we are honestly trying to seek peace at the conference table in Paris. An appropriate response to these attacks will be made if they continue.

THE ANTIBALLISTIC MISSILE SYSTEM

[7.]   Q. Mr. President, can you tell me if you, after your consultations overseas, have any reservations or have found any reservations on whether we should deploy an ABM [antiballistic missile] system and whether you share any of the scientific reservations that have been expressed in this country?

THE PRESIDENT. The ABM system was not discussed in any detail in my conversations abroad. As far as the decision is concerned, there will be a meeting of the National Security Council tomorrow, which will be entirely devoted to an assessment of that system.

Then, during the balance of the week, I shall make some additional studies on my own involving the Defense Department and other experts whose opinions I value. I will make a decision and announce a decision on ABM at the first of next week.

THE PRESIDENT'S TRAVEL PLANS

[8.]   Q. Mr. President, there have already been reports that you are already considering another trip abroad, maybe to Latin America or Israel. Would you tell us what your plans are?

THE PRESIDENT. I have no plans for any foreign travel at this time. I have noted that several other travelers have committed me to various trips abroad. I

would like very much at an appropriate time to travel to Latin America again. I was there on a well-publicized trip with some of you in 1958. I was back there again on a less publicized one, but with a much more friendly welcome in 1967.

Such a trip, I think, would be valuable at a later time. But, as you know, Governor Rockefeller is going to Latin America to make an intensive study of our Alliance for Progress programs, a study which is vital because I think we need some changes in our Latin American policy.

THE SITUATION IN THE MIDDLE EAST

[9.]   Q. Mr. President, can you tell us whether or not, as a result of your talks with President de Gaulle and other government leaders in Europe, you are now encouraged about prospects for maintaining peaceful conditions in the Middle East?

THE PRESIDENT. One of the tangible results that came out of this trip was substantial progress on the Middle East. Now, what that progress will be and whether it reaches an eventual settlement—that is too early to predict.

But I know that when I met with you ladies and gentlemen of the press at an earlier time, the question was raised as to the four-power talks, and there were some who thought that I—this administration was dragging its feet on going into four-power talks.

Frankly, I do not believe the United States should go into any talks where the deck might be stacked against us. Now, as a result of the consultations that we had on this trip, the positions of our European friends—the British and the French—are now closer to ours than was the case before. We have a better understanding of their position; they have a better understanding of ours.

And also, we have had encouraging talks with the Soviet Ambassador. The Secretary of State and I have both talked with the Soviet Ambassador with regard to the Mideast. We will continue these bilateral consultations; and if they continue at their present rate of progress, it seems likely that there will be four-power discussions in the United Nations on the Mideast.

Now, I should indicate also the limitations of such discussions and what can come out of them. The four powers—the Soviet Union, the United States, Great Britain, and France—cannot dictate a settlement in the Middle East. The time has passed in which great nations can dictate to small nations their future where their vital interests are involved. This kind of settlement that we are talking about, and the contribution that can be made to it, is limited in this respect.

The four powers can indicate those areas where they believe the parties directly involved in the Mideast could have profitable discussions. At the present time they are having no discussions at all.

Second—and this is even the more important part of it—from the four-power conference can come an absolute essential to any kind of peaceful settlement in the Mideast, and that is a major-power guarantee of the settlement, because we cannot expect the Nation of Israel or the other nations in the area who think their major interests might be involved—we cannot expect them to agree to a settlement unless they think there is a better chance that it will be guaranteed in the

future than has been the case in the past.

On this score, then, we think we have made considerable progress during the past week. We are cautiously hopeful that we can make more progress and move to the four-power talks very soon.

U.S. RESPONSE TO ATTACKS IN VIETNAM

[10.] Q. Mr. President, have you considered an appropriate response if the attacks continue in South Vietnam? Would an appropriate response include resumption of the bombing in the North?

THE PRESIDENT. Well, Mr. Wilson [Richard L. Wilson, Des Moines Register and Tribune], that question is one that I have given thought to but it is one which I think should not be answered in this forum.

I believe that it is far more effective in international policy to use deeds, rather than words threatening deeds, in order to accomplish objectives.

I will only say in answer to that question that the United States has a number of options that we could exercise to respond. We have several contingency plans that can be put into effect.

I am considering all of those plans. We shall use whatever plan we consider is appropriate to the action on the other side. I will not indicate in advance, and I am not going to indicate publicly, and I am not going to threaten—I don't think that would be helpful—that we are going to start bombing the North or anything else.

I will only indicate that we will not tolerate a continuation of this kind of attack without some response that will be appropriate.

CONVERSATIONS WITH PRESIDENT
DE GAULLE

[11.] Q. Mr. President, mindful of your ground rule against revealing contents of your conversations with leaders, I ask you this question: Did the atmosphere of mutual trust generated in your long conversations with General de Gaulle give you any fresh indication, any fresh hope that France could be helpful in the future of NATO, and/or France could be helpful in settling the war in Vietnam, either directly or indirectly?

THE PRESIDENT. Well, on the first point, General de Gaulle said publicly, as you will note, what he has said in the past, that he supported the Alliance. He has withdrawn France's forces from the military side of the Alliance but he supports the Alliance, and he in his conversations backed that up very vigorously.

With regard to whether or not there is a possibility that France could move back into NATO in its military complex, I would not hold out at this time any hope that that might happen.

I would hold out, however, some hope that as our conversations continue, we can find a number of areas for mutual cooperation and consultation on the military side as well as in other respects. I think that beyond that, it would not be appropriate to indicate what General de Gaulle's position is.

As far as Vietnam is concerned, we did discuss it and whether it was Vietnam, or whether it was the Mideast, or whether it was U.S. relations with other countries where the French might be helpful, I re-

ceived from General de Gaulle very encouraging indications that they would like to be helpful where we thought they could be helpful.

I wouldn't go beyond that, but I was very encouraged with the General's attitude. It was one of helpfulness in every respect on all of the major issues.

THE NUCLEAR NONPROLIFERATION
TREATY

[12.] Q. Mr. President, in your conversations with Chancellor Kiesinger, do you believe that you convinced him that his government's reservations against joining in the Nuclear Nonproliferation Treaty were not valid, and that joining in the Treaty would be in West Germany's best interests?

THE PRESIDENT. I think it would be appropriate to say that the German Government has considerable difficulties with regard to ratification of the Treaty—difficulties which we need to understand even though we may not agree with their position.

Their attitude as far as we are concerned is quite well known. They know that I have sent the Treaty to the Senate, that the Senate will probably give its advice and consent and that we will ratify.

They know, too, my position: that it is not only in the interests of the United States but that I believe it is in the interests of all governments, including the West German Government, to ratify.

I did not put pressure on them, publicly or privately, and I will not put pressure on them, publicly or privately. But I believe, that since it is in their interests to ratify the Treaty, that after consideration without pressure the West German Government will at an appropriate time ratify the Treaty.

THE SOVIET UNION AND VIETNAM

[13.] Q. Mr. President, you said in the recent past that you thought the United States might put some pressure, or use the Soviet Union, or seek to enlist the Soviet Union's help in Vietnam. And I wonder whether, since you have become President, you have moved in that respect, trying to get them to alleviate the situation or help solve it?

THE PRESIDENT. Well, Mr. Lisagor [Peter Lisagor, Chicago Daily News], as you know, the Soviet Union is in a very delicate and sensitive position as far as Vietnam is concerned. I do not divulge any confidences from the Soviet Ambassador in indicating that that is the case. You ladies and gentlemen have written it and you are correct, because here you have Communist China aiding North Vietnam; you also have the Soviet Union aiding North Vietnam—each vying for power in the Communist world. And, therefore, what the Soviet Union does in the Vietnamese conflict is a very difficult decision for them as related to that objective—the objective of leadership of the Communist world.

On the other hand, it is well known that the Soviet Union was helpful in terms of getting the Paris peace talks started, that the Soviet Union was helpful in working out the arrangement for the shape of the table; and I think I could say that based on the conversations that the Secretary of State and I have had with the Soviet Ambassador, I believe at this time that the Soviet Union shares the concern of many other nations in the world

about the extension of the war in Vietnam, its continuing. They recognize that if it continues over a long period of time, the possibility of escalation increases. And I believe the Soviet Union would like to use what influence it could appropriately to help bring the war to a conclusion. What it can do, however, is something that only the Soviet Union would be able to answer to, and it would probably have to answer privately, not publicly.

INTERNATIONAL TRADE

[14.] Q. Mr. President, can you tell us what international trade issues came up in your meetings in Europe. Also, specifically, sir, could you tell us whether you discussed the problems of textile and steel imports into this country?

THE PRESIDENT. All international trade issues came up, and I discussed the problem of textile and steel imports in all the countries involved. The Europeans are concerned about some of what they think are our restrictions in the trade area. For example, they talk about the "American selling price," and they talk about the "buy American" programs. I pointed out that many of our congressional people, as well as American businessmen, were concerned about border taxes and other devices which we thought presented a problem.

I also pointed out in our conversations that there were 93 bills in the last session of the Senate alone which were introduced that would have called for quotas in the various products that you mentioned, and others as well, and that unless some voluntary restrictions or restraints were worked out, on textiles particularly, the pressure for legislative quotas would be immense.

I also indicated that I favored freer trade rather than restrictions on trade, but that it would be very difficult to resist that kind of pressure in the event that some action were not taken to deal with the problem.

A final note in this respect: As we look at the whole trade pattern, I think we have to realize that we cannot anticipate in the near future another big round of reductions of tariff barriers. We are going to do well if we can digest what we have on the plate. This is my view, and I found that was the view of our major European friends. I believe that we can make considerable progress in that area. Secretary Stans is going to Europe next month for the specific purpose of discussing trade problems with all of our European friends, with the hope that we can work out some of these differences.

SOVIET AID TO NORTH VIETNAM

[15.] Q. Mr. President, sir, I wonder if you think that the Soviets are anxious to bring the war to an end, or at least not prolong it? I wonder if you have asked them if they will cut off their supplies to Hanoi?

THE PRESIDENT. Well, we have had discussions, as I have already indicated, with the Soviet Ambassador. I do not think it would be appropriate, however, to disclose our discussions with him any more than it is appropriate to disclose our discussions with others that we have dealt with that are supposed to be confidential in nature. I am sure that the Soviet Union is keenly aware of the fact that we would be greatly gratified by anything that they

could do that could pull some of the support away from the Government of North Vietnam. You could probably just guess as to what our conversations were, but I will not indicate what they were.

NEW APPROACHES TO VIETNAM CONFLICT

[16.] Q. Mr. President, Vice President Ky after meeting with you in Paris said you told him that you had new approaches to the war in Vietnam. Is that correct? And, if so, do you think it inappropriate to tell the American people about it at this time?

THE PRESIDENT. What I think Vice President Ky was referring to was new approaches not so much in the military field, but in terms of the diplomatic initiative. In our discussions with him, and also in our discussions with the American negotiating team, we discussed the approaches that might be made that would break the deadlock.

Now, with regard to the Paris negotiations, I think we can now say that we have neared the end of phase one, in which both parties have set out their positions in public forums. Those positions having been set out, we now come to phase two, in which we will have hard bargaining on the major points of difference. Our negotiating team has been given some instructions and will be given more with regard to a variety of approaches, approaches which, in some instances, will also be taken by the Government of South Vietnam.

One point, incidentally, that I was very encouraged by was that Vice President Ky, speaking for his delegation, was most cooperative in indicating his desire to attempt to find and explore new approaches at the conference table, rather than simply resign ourselves to a military decision.

AMERICAN PUBLIC OPINION AND VIETNAM

[17.] Q. Mr. President, you mentioned earlier that the offensive against Saigon might have as its objective an adverse effect upon American public opinion. In light of the experiences of your predecessor, do you feel that you could keep American public opinion in line if this war were to go on for months and even years?

THE PRESIDENT. Well, I trust that I am not confronted with that problem, when you speak of years. Our objective is to get this war over as soon as we can on a basis that will not leave the seeds of another war there to plague us in the future. We have made, we think, some progress. We think that we are going to make some more.

As far as American public opinion is concerned, I think that the American people will support a President if they are told by the President why we are there, what our objectives are, what the costs will be, and what the consequences would be if we took another course of action. It will not be easy. The American people, I can say from having campaigned the country, are terribly frustrated about this war. They would welcome any initiative that they thought could appropriately bring it to an end on some responsible basis.

On the other hand, it is the responsibility of a President to examine all of the options that we have, and then if he finds that the course he has to take is one that is not popular, he has to explain it to the American people and gain their support.

I think I can perhaps be somewhat effective in explaining why we are there and also in keeping the American people informed as negotiations go on. I intend to do so.

WITHDRAWAL OF AMERICAN TROOPS

[18.] Q. Mr. President, President Thieu of South Vietnam has spoken publicly, sir, of the possibility of his expectation of withdrawing up to about 50,000 American troops from South Vietnam this year.

Do you see this possibility of a stage-by-stage withdrawal as a practicality?

THE PRESIDENT. The possibility of withdrawing troops is something that we have, as you know, been considering for some time. There are no plans to withdraw any troops at this time or in the near future.

On the other hand, I have asked for a reexamination of our whole troop level in South Vietnam, and particularly a reexamination of the South Vietnamese effort and the training program of South Vietnamese forces. To the extent that South Vietnamese forces are able to take over a greater burden of the fighting and to the extent, too, that the level of the fighting may decrease, it may be possible to withdraw.

I do not, however, want to indicate at this time that we are going to withdraw 50,000 troops in the near future. I prefer to create the conditions, if we can, where withdrawal can take place and then announce it, rather than to hold up the promise and let people down when it doesn't happen.

ISRAELI-ARAB NEGOTIATIONS

[19.]   Q. Mr. President, on the basis of your conversations, can you foresee a condition under which the Israelis and the Arabs could sit at a negotiating table?

THE PRESIDENT. Not at this time, no. I think we have to recognize that we are far away from the time when the Arabs and the Israelis can sit at a negotiating table. But I believe that by the time we very carefully go down this road of bilateral consultations first, four-power consultations—and incidentally, we are going to consult with the Israelis when they come here—Mr. Eban is going to be here—there will be, I am sure, consultations on the other side as well—I think when we complete our course of action and come up, if we can, with a four-power recommendation for proceeding, that then it might be possible to bring both sides to a conference table. That is our hope.

DISCUSSIONS WITH THE SOVIET UNION

[20.]   Mr. Scali [John Scali, ABC News].

Q. Mr. President, we were told during the trip that at the appropriate moment you were prepared to begin negotiations with the Soviet Union on a broad front and that these negotiations would include not only disarmament but other, possibly political, areas. What problems do you see as ripe for discussion with the Soviets?

THE PRESIDENT. I should first indicate that talks already are going on with the Soviet Union in one sense. The discussions that the Secretary of State and I have had with Ambassador Dobrynin have been substantive and have been talks, in effect, with the Soviet Government, because he had consulted with his own government before he had his talk with me and with the Secretary of State.

The talks on the Mideast would be the first subject in which bilateral as well as multilateral discussions could take place.

The possibility, also, of discussions on strategic arms—this is a possibility for the future.

Let me indicate where it stands now. We have completed our discussions with some of our European friends. We will have more discussions with them as we get our own position developed. We are going forward with the analysis of the American position—of our strategic arms capabilities, of our conventional arms capabilities—so that when we have before us the decision as to whether we go into talks, we will know what our position will be.

Assuming that those studies go forward on schedule, and assuming that we make progress on some of these political areas, like the Mideast, then there is a possibility, a good possibility, that talks could go forward in that area.

I can see those as two areas, and there are others which could develop as well.

THE SOVIET UNION AND THE MIDDLE EAST

[21.]   Q. Mr. President, I believe you have said, although I couldn't give you the direct quote, but the general assumption is that the Soviet Union is interested in peace in the Middle East. But how can this be reconciled with the fact that they have very quickly rearmed and fully rearmed the Arabs?

What evidence do we have, what proof do we have, that the Soviet Union is in fact interested in peace in the Middle East?

THE PRESIDENT. Well, the Soviet

Union's policy in the Mideast and Vietnam—and your question is quite perceptive from that standpoint—is ambivalent.

On the one hand, in Vietnam, they are heating up the war. They furnish 80 percent to 85 percent of the sophisticated military equipment for the North Vietnamese forces. Without that assistance, North Vietnam would not have the capability to wage the major war they are against the United States.

In the Mideast, without what the Soviet Union has done in rearming Israel's neighbors, there would be no crisis there that would require our concern.

On the other hand, at the same time that the Soviet Union has gone forward in providing arms for potential belligerents—potential belligerents in the one area and actual belligerents in another—the Soviet Union recognizes that if these peripheral areas get out of control, the result could be a confrontation with the United States. And the Soviet Union does not want a confrontation with the United States, any more than we want one with them, because each of us knows what a confrontation would mean.

I think it is that overwhelming fact—the fact that if the situation in the Mideast and Vietnam is allowed to escalate, it is that fact that it might lead to a confrontation—that is giving the Soviet Union second thoughts, and leads me to, what I would say, the cautious conclusion at this point: that the Soviet Union will play, possibly, a peacemaking role in the Mideast and even possibly in Vietnam.

I say a cautious conclusion because I base this only on talks that have taken place up to this time. But we are going to explore that road all the way that we can, because, let's face it, without the Soviet Union's cooperation, the Mideast is going to continue to be a terribly dangerous area—if you continue to pour fuel on those fires of hatred that exist on the borders of Israel. And without the Soviet Union's cooperation it may be difficult to move as fast as we would like in settling the war in Vietnam.

U.S. RELATIONS WITH PERU

[22.] Q. Mr. President, you mentioned earlier the deeds rather than words in our international relations. In our relations with Peru and our problems there, is the United States prepared to take action should Peru not respond to our protests over the seizure of the oil company and the attacks on fishing vessels?

THE PRESIDENT. What Peru has done, as you know, in the seizure of our oil company is that under international law they have the right to expropriate a company but they also have the obligation to pay a fair amount for that expropriation.

It is the second point that is at issue, not the right to expropriate. Now if they do not take appropriate steps to provide for that payment, then under the law—the Hickenlooper amendment,[1] as you know—we will have to take appropriate action with regard to the sugar quota and also with regard to aid programs.

I hope that it is not necessary because that would have a domino effect—if I can be permitted to use what is supposed to be an outworn term—a domino effect all over Latin America.

I feel, in my studies in recent days, that we are making some progress in at-

---

[1] For texts of amendments sponsored by Bourke B. Hickenlooper, Senator from Iowa 1945–1969 and former ranking Republican on the Senate Foreign Relations Committee, see 77 Stat. 386 and 79 Stat. 1280.

tempting to get some steps taken by the Peruvian Government to deal with the expropriation matter in a fair way.[2] If they do so then we do not have to go down that road.

PRESIDENT DE GAULLE

[23.] Q. Mr. President, there are some people who think you were a little more fulsome in your praise of General de Gaulle than you were of the other European leaders. Were you conscious of that? Do you have any background you can give us on that?

THE PRESIDENT. I try to have a policy of evenhandedness. I suppose that is a bad word, too—well, it is in the Mideast. In any event, I have the highest regard for all of the leaders that I met. I tried to speak of General de Gaulle with the proper respect that an individual with my background should have speaking to one with his.

After all, of the leaders of Europe, whether we agree or disagree with him, he is the giant, not only in his physical size but in his background and his great influence.

He deserved, I think, the words that I spoke about him. But I can assure you that in speaking of Prime Minister Wilson, Dr. Kiesinger, President Saragat, and Prime Minister Rumor, I intended to speak of all of them with the same feeling, the same affection.

---

[2] The White House on March 11, 1969, announced that President Nixon had appointed John Irwin II, as a special emissary to Peru to explore with the Peruvian Government all factors that would lead to mutually agreeable resolution of differences. See the Weekly Compilation of Presidential Documents (vol. 5, p. 395).

PROBLEMS OF YOUNG PEOPLE

[24.] Q. You demonstrated a great deal of interest, Mr. President, in young people in your discussions, both public and private, abroad. Do you feel that those discussions have given you a better understanding of young people abroad, and are their problems similar to the problems of young people in this country?

THE PRESIDENT. Well, the problems differ, of course, in the different countries. I think they are the same in one respect. The young people abroad, it seems, have somewhat the same problem as many young people here. They know what they are against, but they find difficulty in knowing what they are for. This is not unusual, because this is perhaps something that is common to young people generally. Except that when we look to the revolutions of the past, the revolutionary movements, usually there has been— whether we agreed with those movements or not—there was something, a philosophy, that the young people who supported the revolutions were for. All over Europe this seems to be the case—a young generation against the established institution, against the way the universities are run, and yet not having a sense of purpose, a sense of direction, a sense of idealism.

I feel that that is part of the problem here in the United States, and I think that much of the responsibility rests not on the young people for not knowing what they are for, but on older people for not giving them the vision and the sense of purpose and the idealism that they should have.

In talking—and I talked with every leader about this, every one—all of us are concerned about it. All of us feel that we must find for this great Western family of ours a new sense of purpose and idealism, one that young people will understand, that they can be for.

That is not a satisfactory answer, because I am not able to describe it yet, but, believe me, we are searching for it.

NEW U.S. COMMITMENTS

[25.] Q. Mr. President, there has been some concern in Congress about reports that a general in the Pentagon took the initiative in arranging for the United States to recognize a threat to Spain from North Africa. In your opinion, is this concern merited, and what is the policy of your administration about the carving out of new commitments to other countries by the United States?

THE PRESIDENT. Well, I think as far as commitments are concerned, the United States has a full plate. I first do not believe that we should make new commitments around the world unless our national interests are very vitally involved. Second, I do not believe we should become involved in the quarrels of nations in other parts of the world unless we are asked to become involved and unless also we are vitally involved. I referred earlier to even the quarrels and divisions in Western Europe. I stayed out of most of those up to this point and I intend to in the future.

As far as this report is concerned, with regard to the general on the Spanish bases, I have checked into it, and no commitment has been made. My view is that none should be made. We will, of course, analyze it at the time to see whether our national, vital interests might require me to reassess it.

PRESIDENT DE GAULLE ON AMERICAN INFLUENCE

[26.] Q. Mr. President, there were some interpretations some weeks ago about some of General de Gaulle's actions, as his wanting to have Western Europe free of American influence. Did he address himself to this in talking with you? Did you get any deeper understanding of this?

THE PRESIDENT. I think, Mr. Kaplow [Herbert Kaplow, NBC News], it would be not divulging a confidence to indicate that President de Gaulle completely disassociated his views, which he expressed in great detail to us, on the European Alliance and France's relation to it from any anti-American position.

He believes that Europe should have an independent position in its own right. And, frankly, I believe that, too. I think most Europeans believe that. I think the time when it served our interests to have the United States as the dominant partner in an alliance—that that time is gone. We will be dominant because of our immense nuclear power and also because of our economic wealth.

But on the other hand, the world will be a much safer place and, from our standpoint, a much healthier place economically, militarily, and politically, if there were a strong European community to be a balance basically, a balance between the United States and the Soviet Union, rather than to have this polarization of forces in one part of the world or another.

Now, as far as President de Gaulle's position is concerned, as I understand it, he has talked very eloquently on his desire to have European unity and a separate European identity. He has disagreed, however, with the proposals that currently are supported by most of the other European countries. He believes that it could better be worked out, as he indicated publicly, and he also indicated to me privately, through the major powers reaching an understanding rather than having it done through basically a convention or caucus of all the powers of Europe.

CONDITIONS FOR SUMMIT TALKS

[27.] Q. Mr. President, some of us have been under the impression that you attached important preconditions to summit talks with the Soviets, specifically some prior evidence or showing on their part that they were doing something to improve conditions in either the Middle East or Vietnam. Have those impressions been false or has something happened to your own thinking in this area very recently?

THE PRESIDENT. No, I did not intend to leave the impression that we say to the Soviet Union that unless they do this we will not have talks that they want on strategic arms.

What I have, however, clearly indicated, is that I think their interests and ours would not be served by simply going down the road on strategic arms talks without, at the same time, making progress on resolving these political dif-

ferences that could explode. Even assuming our strategic arms talks were successful, freezing arms at their present level, we could have a very devastating war. It is that point that I have been making.

I should also emphasize that I made this point to every European leader that I talked to, and every one of them—and I do not commit them to the position—every one of them understands the position, because the Europeans have a great sense of history. All of them recognize that most wars have come not from arms races, although sometimes arms races can produce a war, but they have come from political explosions.

Therefore, they want progress, for example, on Berlin; they want progress on the Mideast; they want progress on Vietnam; at the same time that they want progress on strategic arms talks.

So our attitude toward the Soviet is not a highhanded one of trying to tell them: "You do this or we won't talk." Our attitude is very conciliatory, and I must say that in our talks with the Soviet Ambassador, I think that they are thinking along this line now, too. If they are, we can make progress on several roads toward a mutual objective.

Frank Cormier, Associated Press: Thank you, Mr. President.

NOTE: President Nixon's third news conference was held in the East Room at the White House at 9 p.m. on Tuesday, March 4, 1969. It was broadcast on radio and television.

99   Remarks on Presenting the Robert H. Goddard
      Memorial Trophy to the Apollo 8 Astronauts.
      March 5, 1969

MR. MURRAY. On behalf of our National Space Club, Mr. President, we take pride and pleasure to have you present this award to Captain James Lovell.

The Goddard Trophy is something that is endowed by our Club through Mrs. Goddard, presented annually here at the White House and also at the Goddard dinner.

I would like to have the citation read if we may.

THE PRESIDENT. I think we would be interested, for the purpose of our visitors here, in hearing something about the Goddard award, how it came about. I know that it will be covered at the dinner tonight, but I think it would be well to hear it at this ceremony.

MR. MURRAY. The Goddard award came about in 1958. It was felt that for the father of American rocketry that a bust should be designed to endow what he has done for rocketry and astronautics in this country.

Mrs. Goddard may have a few words she'd like to say about this, also.

THE PRESIDENT. Mrs. Goddard, can you tell us something about your husband and this award?

MRS. GODDARD. My husband was dedicated from his 17th birthday to the idea of exploring space. I have been indeed blessed to have lived so long as to see this kind of thing in his honor. Thank you.

THE PRESIDENT. Captain Lovell, I am very honored to present this award to you; honored because of what the award represents and honored because it allows me again to recognize the exploit of our astronauts who took the first historic voyage around the moon.

I am going to let you hold it for a moment. You are stronger than I am. Our spacemen are very strong.

So much has been said about the epic journey into space that I hesitated at first as to whether I should read the citation, but it is such an eloquent citation I think all of us would like to hear it:

"In an epic journey man for the first time in December 1968 soared out of the earth's gravitational field, flew unerringly into a close orbit of the moon, then back to a precise and safe landing. This historic voyage performed at times before the largest television audience in history, and open for coverage by the world's press, reflects the utmost credit on the United States Space Program, Congress, NASA, and thousands of companies and employees in industry representing all these, the courageous, competent crew of Apollo 8."

If I could say a word about Mr. Goddard, who is not here, I think that one of the most impressive memories I have with regard to the dinner that we had with the Apollo crew and their wives at the White House was the statement that was made by a member of the crew to the effect that they had been honored all over the country, but that they realized that they were speaking not just for themselves, but for 400,000 people who at one time or another had played a part in the space program.

They pointed out that there were two million parts in the Apollo spacecraft and of course, we could therefore see how much this was a venture that was symbolized, of course, by the courage of the men who participated in it, but would not have been possible without the support of thousands of others, and also it would not have been possible—and, Mrs. Goddard, this is in relation to your husband—had it not been for the men and women of the past, those who dreamed of what could happen in going to space, those who made the early experiments and who made it possible for us to build on what they have done.

I think perhaps the most appropriate comment I could make with regard to your husband, Mrs. Goddard, is to quote one of my favorite quotations: The reason that we can see further than the ancients is that we stand on the shoulders of the giants who have gone before us.

So the reason that Captain Lovell and his colleagues could see from the moon the earth is that they were able to stand on the shoulders of the giants who had gone before them.

Mr. Goddard was one of the giants. You stood on his shoulders and that is why this award, I think, of all the awards you have received, Captain Lovell, may have a special meaning.

Would you like to say a word?

CAPTAIN LOVELL. Yes, sir. On behalf of Frank Borman, Bill Anders and myself, let me just say that we are very proud and very humble to be here today. It is of special significance for me to be here today, because Dr. Goddard has given me the inspiration to follow the field which I pursued.

I first became interested in rockets around 1943, and during my days as a midshipman at the Naval Academy, I wrote my term paper on rockets and the development of the liquid fuel rocket engine, and my wife had very nicely given me a book called "Rocket Development" which was a compilation of the works Dr. Robert Goddard had done in his experiments out in New Mexico.

So it is a very significant day for me, and again, may I say thank you for the award on behalf of Frank and Bill.

THE PRESIDENT. Now, Dr. Paine, would you step forward, please? I have an announcement to make.

There has been a great deal of interest as to who would be the new head of NASA. I will admit right now that we have searched the country to find a man who could take this program now and give it the leadership that it needs, as we move from one phase to another. This is an exciting period, and it requires the new leadership that a new man can provide.

But after searching the whole country for somebody, perhaps outside the program, we found, as is often the case, that the best man in the country was in the program, and that is why I am announcing today that Dr. Paine, who is now the Acting Director of NASA, will be appointed the Director of NASA.

I know that all of these spacemen will make a talk if they are asked, so go ahead.

DR. PAINE. Mr. President, I am very pleased and very touched by your confidence in me. It has been a tremendously rewarding experience to me to be associated with the fine people in the Space Agency, and I certainly look forward with a great deal of enthusiasm to continuing this association.

I believe in the space program. I believe in this country, and I think that this country should indeed be the preeminent nation in space-faring, and with your help,

Mr. President, I am sure that we can go ahead in the next 4 and then 8 years to really see that the NASA program in the second decade of space will even outperform the accomplishments in the first.

THE PRESIDENT. Thank you very much.

NOTE: The ceremony began at 10:40 a.m. in the Fish Room at the White House. Those taking part included James M. Murray, President of the National Space Club, which sponsored the trophy; Mrs. Robert H. Goddard;

Capt. James A. Lovell, Jr., USN; and Dr. Thomas O. Paine, Acting Administrator of the National Aeronautics and Space Administration.

White House press releases issued on the same day give biographical information on Dr. Paine and background information on the Apollo 8 flight and the three astronauts.

The trophy is given each year to the person or persons selected for great achievement in advancing spaceflight programs contributing to United States leadership in astronautics.

100   Statement About a National Program for Minority Business Enterprise.   *March 5, 1969*

I HAVE often made the point that to foster the economic status and the pride of members of our minority groups we must seek to involve them more fully in our private enterprise system. Blacks, Mexican-Americans, Puerto Ricans, Indians, and others must increasingly be encouraged to enter the field of business, both in the areas where they now live and in the larger commercial community— and not only as workers, but also as managers and owners.

Providing better job training and making more jobs available is only part of the answer.

We must also provide an expanded opportunity to participate in the free enterprise system at all levels—not only to share the economic benefits of the free enterprise system more broadly, but also to encourage pride, dignity, and a sense of independence. In order to do this, we need to remove commercial obstacles which have too often stood in the way of minority group members—obstacles such as the unavailability of credit, insurance, and technical assistance.

Involvement in business has always been a major route toward participation in the mainstream of American life. Our aim is to open that route to potentially successful persons who have not had access to it before.

Encouraging increased minority group business activity is one of the priority aims of this administration.

The Federal Government has long been involved in various programs to support the development of new business enterprises and to help struggling new ones become more stable. By one count, there are now 116 such programs, operated by no less than 21 different departments and agencies. These are largely uncoordinated.

Recently, the Small Business Administration launched a program for the stimulation of minority group enterprise. This program has been well received and deserves continuing support .With better coordination, a broader range of Government resources and assistance can be made available.

Many private, voluntary organizations, and many major corporations, have done outstanding work in assisting the development of new business enterprises among minority groups. Often, however, their efforts have not had the Government support that they deserve.

As recommended by the Urban Affairs Council, I intend to establish within the Department of Commerce an Office of Minority Business Enterprise. Under the leadership of Secretary of Commerce Stans, this new office will be the focal point of the administration's efforts to assist the establishment of new minority enterprises and expansion of existing ones. It will seek to concentrate Government resources, and also to involve the business community and others in order to enlist the full range of the Nation's resources.

This new office will be headed by an Assistant to the Secretary of Commerce, and it will have the direct, personal attention of the Secretary. On its own, it will seek to develop new business opportunities. It will coordinate the efforts of other Government agencies in encouraging minority enterprise. It will mobilize financial and other resources, both public and private. It will provide the centralized leadership which in the past has not been sufficiently evident. It will seek to provide a better focus of Government programs at the local level, in order to give them the impact intended. It will constantly review both existing and possible new programs for the encouragement of minority business enterprise, and will make recommendations for further executive and legislative action as appropriate.

I have today issued an Executive order directing the Secretary of Commerce to coordinate Federal programs related to the strengthening of minority business enterprise, and authorizing him to take the necessary steps to do so effectively. The order also provides for the creation of an Advisory Council for Minority Business Enterprise and for the establishment by the Secretary of Commerce of an information center for the compiling and dissemination of information on successful minority business enterprise programs.

This is not a substitute for the many other efforts that continue to be needed if we are to make headway against the ravages of poverty. It is a supplement, dealing with a special but vital part of the broader effort to bring the members of our minority groups into full participation in the American society and economy. Its success will be measured by tangible results, not by the volume of studies.

What we are doing is recognizing that in addition to the basic problems of poverty itself, there is an additional need to stimulate those enterprises that can give members of minority groups confidence that avenues of opportunity are neither closed nor limited; enterprises that will demonstrate that blacks, Mexican-Americans, and others can participate in a growing economy on the basis of equal opportunity at the top of the ladder as well as on its lower rungs.

NOTE: The national program for minority business enterprise was established by Executive Order 11458.

The White House Press Office released a list of 45 persons involved in various aspects of minority business enterprise who attended the signing of the Executive order.

The text of a news briefing of Secretary of Commerce Maurice H. Stans and Special Assistant to the President Robert J. Brown concerning minority business enterprise was also released.

An announcement of a report to the President on increased job opportunities for minorities was released by the White House on March 20, 1969, and is printed in the Weekly Compilation of Presidential Documents (vol. 5, p. 439).

101   Remarks on Presenting the Medal of Honor to
       Three Members of the United States Army.
       March 7, 1969

Mr. Secretary, General Westmoreland, all of our distinguished guests on this occasion:

I have been honored many times since assuming the Office of the Presidency of the United States, but I can say from my heart that today is the highest honor—the highest honor because I have for the first time the privilege of representing the United States of America in presenting the Congressional Medal of Honor to three of our fine young men who have fought for the cause of freedom and the cause of peace in Vietnam.

The citations will be read by the Secretary of the Army, and they will tell us better than any words I could utter what these men have done beyond the call of duty.

I would like to add just a personal word, a word that I think all of the American people would join me in. We really cannot honor these men, but they have honored America. They have added to the honor of the Nation by what they have done.

They share several things in common: They are men who risked their lives for their fellow man. They are men who faced death and instead of losing their courage they gave courage to the men around them. And, finally, they are young men.

The oldest man is 30; Sergeant Hooper is 30. Sergeant Zabitosky is 26, and Specialist Sasser is 21.

That leads me to give you a conclusion that I reached after studying all of the Congressional Medal of Honor winners in this war. Their average age is 27, which

brings home a thought that we must always remember: When we think of America's younger generation, we sometimes have a tendency to emphasize what is wrong with them, and sometimes young people do get into trouble; sometimes they do not follow the patterns that older people think they ought to follow.

But in the magnificent records of these three young men, they have demonstrated to us that we can be very proud of our younger generation. They are magnificent men, magnificent in their idealism. Idealism is often shown by words, but they have demonstrated their idealism by their deeds.

And because they have made us proud of being Americans and also reminded us that we should be proud of our younger generation, the youth of America, I am honored to be here with them.

Now, Mr. Secretary, if you would read the citations.

[Secretary of the Army Stanley R. Resor read the citations, the texts of which follow.]

The President of the United States of America, authorized by Act of Congress, March 3, 1863, has awarded in the name of The Congress the Medal of Honor to

STAFF SERGEANT JOE R. HOOPER
UNITED STATES ARMY

for conspicuous gallantry and intrepidity in action at the risk of his life above and beyond the call of duty:

Staff Sergeant (then Sergeant) Joe R. Hooper, United States Army, distinguished himself by conspicuous gallantry and intrepidity on 21 February 1968, while serving as squad leader with Company D, 2nd Battalion

(Airborne), 501st Infantry, 101st Airborne Division, near Hue, Republic of Vietnam. Company D was assaulting a heavily defended enemy position along a river bank when it encountered a withering hail of fire from rockets, machine guns and automatic weapons. Staff Sergeant Hooper rallied several men and stormed across the river, overrunning several bunkers on the opposite shore. Thus inspired, the rest of the company moved to the attack. With utter disregard for his own safety, he moved out under the intense fire again and pulled back the wounded, moving them to safety. During this act Staff Sergeant Hooper was seriously wounded, but he refused medical aid and returned to his men. With the relentless enemy fire disrupting the attack, he single-handedly stormed three enemy bunkers, destroying them with hand grenades and rifle fire, and shot two enemy soldiers who had attacked and wounded the chaplain. Leading his men forward in a sweep of the area, Staff Sergeant Hooper destroyed three buildings housing enemy riflemen. At this point he was attacked by a North Vietnamese officer whom he fatally wounded with his bayonet. Finding his men under heavy fire from a house to the front, he proceeded alone to the building, killing its occupants with rifle fire and grenades. By now his initial body wound had been compounded by grenade fragments, yet despite the multiple wounds and loss of blood, he continued to lead his men against the intense enemy fire. As his squad reached the final line of enemy resistance, it received devastating fire from four bunkers in line on its left flank. Staff Sergeant Hooper gathered several hand grenades and raced down a small trench which ran the length of the bunker line, tossing grenades into each bunker as he passed by, killing all but two of the occupants. With these positions destroyed, he concentrated on the last bunkers facing his men, destroying the first with an incendiary grenade and neutralizing two more by rifle fire. He then raced across an open field, still under enemy fire, to rescue a wounded man who was trapped in a trench. Upon reaching the man, he was faced by an armed enemy soldier whom he killed with a pistol. Moving his comrade to safety and returning to his men, he neutralized the final pocket

of enemy resistance by fatally wounding three North Vietnamese officers with rifle fire. Staff Sergeant Hooper then established a final line and reorganized his men, not accepting treatment until this was accomplished and not consenting to evacuation until the following morning. His supreme valor, inspiring leadership and heroic self-sacrifice were directly responsible for the company's success and provided a lasting example in personal courage for every man on the field. Staff Sergeant Hooper's actions were in keeping with the highest traditions of the military service and reflect great credit upon himself and the United States Army.

RICHARD NIXON

The President of the United States of America, authorized by Act of Congress, March 3, 1863, has awarded in the name of The Congress the Medal of Honor to

SERGEANT FIRST CLASS FRED W. ZABITOSKY
UNITED STATES ARMY

for conspicuous gallantry and intrepidity in action at the risk of his life above and beyond the call of duty:

Sergeant First Class (then Staff Sergeant) Fred W. Zabitosky, United States Army, distinguished himself by conspicuous gallantry and intrepidity, at the risk of his life, above and beyond the call of duty in the Republic of Vietnam, on 19 February 1968, while serving as an assistant team leader of a nine-man Special Forces long range reconnaissance patrol. Sergeant Zabitosky's patrol was operating deep within enemy controlled territory when they were attacked by a numerically superior North Vietnamese Army unit. Sergeant Zabitosky rallied his team members, deployed them into defensive positions, and, exposing himself to concentrated enemy automatic weapons fire, directed their return fire. Realizing the gravity of the situation, Sergeant Zabitosky ordered his patrol to move to a landing zone for helicopter extraction while he covered their withdrawal with rifle fire and grenades. Rejoining the patrol under increasing enemy pressure, he positioned each man in a tight perimeter defense and continually moved from man to man, encouraging them and controlling their defensive fire. Mainly due to his example, the outnumbered patrol maintained its precarious position until the arrival of tactical air support and a helicopter extraction team. As the rescue helicopters arrived, the determined North Vietnamese pressed their attack. Sergeant Zabitosky repeatedly exposed himself to their fire to adjust suppressive helicopter gunship fire around the landing zone. After boarding one of the rescue helicopters, he positioned himself in the door delivering fire on the enemy as the ship took off. The helicopter was engulfed in a hail of bullets and Sergeant Zabitosky was thrown from the craft as it spun out of control and crashed. Recovering consciousness, he ignored his extremely painful injuries and moved to the flaming wreckage. Heedless of the danger of exploding ordnance and fuel, he pulled the severely wounded pilot from the searing blaze and made repeated attempts to rescue his patrol members, but was driven back by the intense heat. Despite his own serious burns and crushed ribs, he carried and dragged the unconscious pilot through a curtain of enemy fire to within ten feet of a hovering rescue helicopter before collapsing. Sergeant Zabitosky's extraordinary heroism and devotion to duty were in keeping with the highest traditions of the military service and reflect great credit upon himself, his unit and the United States Army.

RICHARD NIXON

The President of the United States of America, authorized by Act of Congress, March 3, 1863, has awarded in the name of The Congress the Medal of Honor to

SPECIALIST FIVE CLARENCE E. SASSER
UNITED STATES ARMY

for conspicuous gallantry and intrepidity in action at the risk of his life above and beyond the call of duty:

Specialist Five Clarence E. Sasser (then Private First Class) distinguished himself by conspicuous gallantry and intrepidity on 10

January 1968 while assigned to Headquarters and Headquarters Company, 3d Battalion, 60th Infantry, 9th Infantry Division in the Republic of Vietnam. On this date he was serving as a medical aidman with Company A, 3d Battalion, on a reconnaissance in force operation in Ding Tuong Province. His company was making an air assault when suddenly it was taken under heavy small arms, recoilless rifle, machine gun and rocket fire from well fortified enemy positions on three sides of the landing zone. During the first few minutes, over thirty casualties were sustained. Without hesitation, Specialist Sasser ran across an open rice paddy through a hail of fire to assist the wounded. After helping one man to safety, he was painfully wounded in the left shoulder by fragments of an exploding rocket. Refusing medical attention, he ran through a barrage of rocket and automatic weapons fire to aid casualties of the initial attack and, after giving them urgently needed treatment, continued to search for other wounded. Despite two additional wounds immobilizing his legs, he dragged himself through the mud toward another soldier one hundred meters away. Although in agonizing pain and faint from loss of blood, Specialist Sasser reached the man, treated him, and proceeded on to encourage another group of soldiers to crawl two hundred meters to relative safety. There he attended their wounds for five hours until they were evacuated. Specialist Sasser's conspicuous gallantry, extraordinary heroism and intrepidity at the risk of his own life, above and beyond the call of duty, are in keeping with the highest traditions of the military service and reflect great credit upon himself, his unit and the United States Army.

RICHARD NIXON

[Following the reading of the citations the President resumed speaking.]

That concludes the ceremony. We thank you all very much for coming and we are honored that you could be here to participate in this very historic ceremony.

Thank you.

NOTE: The President spoke at 10:10 a.m. in the East Room at the White House.

102   Remarks to Top Personnel at the Central Intelligence Agency.   *March 7, 1969*

Mr. Director, and ladies and gentlemen:

As I stand before you today, this is the first visit I have made to one of the departments that is not represented officially in the Cabinet.

But I must say that after the very warm welcome I received outside and the opportunity, too, to see this really beautiful facility, I am very glad that I came. I want to use the opportunity to express just a few thoughts about this organization, about its Director, and about the people who work in it.

It has been truly said that the CIA is a professional organization. That is one of the reasons that when the new administration came in and many changes were made, as they should be made in our American political system after an election, and a change of parties, as far as the executive branch is concerned, I did not make a change.

I surveyed the field. I checked the qualifications of all of the men, or, for that matter, any women who might possibly be Director of the CIA. That could happen.

I saw the number of women outside of this organization. You have plenty of competition.

But I concluded that Dick Helms was the best man in the country to be Director of the CIA and that is why we have him here.

Now, I am sure that all of you must get a little tired of the jokes about the CIA being an undercover organization, its building being difficult to find, and all that. But I simply can't resist making an allusion to stories that I checked with the Director as we rode in from the helicopter and which I understand have some degree of truth to them.

The first time President Eisenhower came out here to lay the cornerstone, he couldn't find the CIA or the building. So he ordered that a sign be put up, "The Central Intelligence Agency."

Then when President Kennedy came out in 1961 he saw the sign and he ordered it taken down, because, after all, if it is the CIA, the intelligence agency, it should not be so well advertised.

So that leaves me with somewhat of a dilemma to choose.

I usually have said as I have gone to the Department of State, the Department of Defense, the Department of Commerce, the Department of Agriculture, and all the others of the 12, "It is a pleasure to be here."

But the CIA is not supposed to be here. So I suppose that what I am supposed to say now is, it is a pleasure not to be here.

In any event, in speaking of you and your mission, I have perhaps more familiarity with it than some of you might realize. Going back during the 8 years I was Vice President, I sat on the National Security Council and there learned to respect the organization, its Director, and its reports that were made to the Council, and through the Council to the President of the United States.

I know how vitally important the work of this organization is. I also know that this organization has a mission that, by necessity, runs counter to some of the very deeply held traditions in this country and feelings, high idealistic feelings, about what a free society ought to be.

Americans don't like war, of course.

Americans also do not like secrecy. They don't like cold war and consequently, whenever it is necessary in the conduct of our foreign policy, whether in a cold war or whether, as is the situation now, in a hot war, or whether in international tensions, call it a cold war or simply a period of confrontation or even of negotiation, whatever you want to call it, that whenever it becomes necessary to obtain intelligence information by an intelligence organization, many Americans are deeply concerned about this. And they express their concerns. They express them quite violently sometimes, quite directly, as you all know from the experience that this organization has had over the years.

This is a dilemma. It is one that I wish did not exist. But in the society in which we live, as I am sure you, all of you, are so completely aware, it is necessary that those who make decisions at the highest level have the very best possible intelligence with regard to what the facts really are, so that the margin of error will be, to that extent, reduced.

And in a sense, then, I look upon this organization as not one that is necessary for the conduct of conflict or war, or call it what you may, but in the final analysis is one of the great instruments of our Government for the preservation of peace, for the avoidance of war, and for the development of a society in which this kind of activity would not be as necessary, if necessary at all.

It is that that I think the American people need to understand—that this is a necessary adjunct to the conduct of the Presidency. And I am keenly aware of that. I am keenly aware of the fact that many of you at times must have had doubts, perhaps you have not, but perhaps there may have been times when you have had doubts about your mission, the popularity of what you do in the country, and I want to reassure you on that score.

Let me put it another way: This morning I had the greatest honor which has come to me since assuming the Presidency. That honor was to present three Congressional Medals of Honor to three young men who had served in Vietnam.

They had, of course, rendered service far beyond the call of duty. As the citations were read, I realized how fortunate this country was to have produced young men of the idealism—idealism which we saw in their actions in Vietnam.

I realize that in this organization the great majority of you are not in the kind of covert activities which involve great danger, but I also know that some of your colleagues have been involved in such activities and are involved in such activities.

I know, too, that there will be no Purple Hearts, there will be no medals, there will be no recognition of those who have served far beyond the call of duty because by definition where the CIA is concerned your successes must never be publicized and your failures will always be publicized.

So that makes your mission a particularly difficult one. It makes it difficult from the standpoint of those who must render service beyond the call of duty. And I recognize that and I am deeply grateful for those who are willing to make that kind of sacrifice.

In another sense, too, I want to pay proper recognition to great numbers of people that I see in this room and that I saw outside who do not get down to the Cabinet Room to brief me, as does Mr. Helms and his colleagues, who are not in the positions where even private recognition comes too often, but whose work is so absolutely essential to the quality of those little morning briefing papers that I get every morning and read so carefully and that are so important because the decisions I make will be based subconsciously sometimes, other times consciously, on the accuracy of those reports and their findings from around the world.

I think sometimes that all of us know that one of the ironies of life is that it takes more heroism to render outstanding service in positions that are not heroic in character than it does the other way around. What I mean to say is that in an organization like this, gathering facts and information and intelligence, there are literally hundreds and thousands of positions here and around the world that must at times be very boring and certainly frustrating and sometimes without recognition.

I do want you to know that I appreciate that work.

I know how essential it is and I would ask that you as the leaders, you who necessarily and very properly do get more recognition than those down the ranks, that you would convey to them my appreciation for their heroism, heroism in the sense that they have done an outstanding job and are doing an outstanding job to make it possible that the Director is able to do a better job than he otherwise could do in briefing the President of the United States and his colleagues in the National Security Council.

So finally, I would simply say that I understand that when President Truman in 1967 sent a message to the CIA, he put an inscription on it which, as I recall, went something like this: To the CIA, an organization which is an absolute necessity to any President of the United States. From one who knows.

I know. And I appreciate what you do. Thank you.

NOTE: The President spoke at 3:42 p.m. in the auditorium at the Central Intelligence Agency, McLean, Va.

103   Remarks Launching the Easter Seal Campaign. *March 11, 1969*

I AM DELIGHTED to have this opportunity to join with Carol Burnett in kicking off the Easter Seal Campaign. I think we are very fortunate to have this little girl from Florida here, Donna Kay Howell. I think as you look at Donna and also as you listen to her, you can really see what your Easter Seal contribution will mean.

Through Easter Seals 250,000 children and others are helped each year by volunteers. The $32 million that we raise in this campaign between now and April 6 will help them.

Donna is an example. She suffered a very severe stroke at the age of 4 years. She was paralyzed on one side and her speech was affected by it. Her speech is completely cured, as you have heard already. Beyond that, she still is receiving therapy, but here is a very happy and a very healthy child who might not have been this way had it not been for the Easter Seal programs.

So, I join with Carol Burnett in asking all of the American people to support this volunteer program that gives help to children across the country and lets little girls like Donna grow up and be so happy and so pretty and so talkative.

NOTE: The President spoke at 11:03 a.m. in the Fish Room at the White House. Comedienne Carol Burnett, chairman of the 1969 campaign, presented the President with the first issue of 1969 Easter Seals and a book of Easter greetings to the President, drawn by children of the National Easter Seal Society.

Donna Kay Howell, 7, of Tallahassee, Fla., is this year's Easter Seal Child.

The National Easter Seal Society is the oldest and largest voluntary agency serving the handicapped. It has some 2,000 affiliates which maintain 2,500 rehabilitation facilities and programs. These affiliates provide services to some 253,000 patients regardless of race, religion, national background, economic status, or cause of crippling.

104   Message to the Senate Transmitting Conventions for the Protection of Intellectual and Industrial Property. *March* 12, 1969

To the Senate of the United States:

I transmit herewith, for the advice and consent of the Senate to ratification, (1) a copy of the Convention Establishing the World Intellectual Property Organization, signed at Stockholm on July 14, 1967, and (2) a copy of the Paris Convention for the Protection of Industrial Property, as revised at Stockholm on July 14, 1967. I transmit also, for the information of the Senate, the report of the Secretary of State with respect to the Conventions.

The Conventions remained open for signature until January 13, 1968. During that period the Convention Establishing the World Intellectual Property Organization was signed on behalf of 51 States, including the United States, and the Paris Convention was signed on behalf of 46 States, including the United States. Both Conventions remain open for accession.

(1) *Convention Establishing a World Intellectual Property Organization.* Two significant services will be rendered by the new organization. First, it will provide a coordinated administration for the various intellectual property Unions presently administered by the Secretariat, the United International Bureaus for the Protection

of Intellectual Property, and through such administration, render an economical and efficient service to the Member States and the interests protected by the Unions. Second, it will promote the protection of intellectual property, not only for Member States of the intellectual property Unions, but also for the states which, while not members of the Unions, are parties to the World Intellectual Property Organization Convention. This is of particular importance since a forum will thus be provided for the advancement of industrial property and copyright protection on a worldwide basis.

(2) *Revision of the Paris Convention For the Protection of Industrial Property.* Administrative and structural reforms in the Paris Convention have long been overdue, and the modernization of the Union which has been accomplished by the Stockholm revision will be of importance in expanding the protection of industrial property.

A limited amendment to one substantive provision of the Paris Convention was also effected at the Conference. This amendment would accord to applications for inventors' certificates of the Eastern

205

European countries the right of priority presently accorded to patent applications, provided that the Eastern European countries maintain a dual system of both inventors' certificates and patents and that both are available to foreign nationals. Inclusion of this provision is considered helpful to furthering industrial property relations with Eastern European countries.

The Stockholm Act of the Paris Convention and the World Intellectual Property Organization Convention will make a significant contribution to the protection of the foreign intellectual property rights of American nationals. I recommend that the Senate give early and favorable consideration to the Conventions submitted herewith and give its advice and consent to their ratifications.

RICHARD NIXON

The White House
March 12, 1969

NOTE: The texts of the conventions and the report of the Secretary of State are printed in Senate Executive A (91st Cong., 1st sess.).

105 Statement on Reorganization of the Manpower Administration. *March* 13, 1969

A MAJOR AIM of this administration is to eliminate duplication, to consolidate functions, to bring better management to all areas of the Federal Government. Today we are announcing one of the first steps toward that objective: a reorganization of the Department of Labor's Manpower Administration.

If there is one area of Government that should serve as a model for the best use of manpower, it is the Manpower Administration. Accordingly, the Secretary of Labor has moved quickly to overhaul and to modernize operations of this $2 billion per year agency.

The new Manpower Administration will decentralize its functions; a single line of authority from Washington to the field will be established; the regional offices will assume greater responsibility; the overlapping of functions among various bureaus should largely disappear.

This administrative reform opens the door to reorganization of the Job Corps and an elimination of those phases of the program which have proved both inefficient and ineffective in meeting the problem of job training.

In the short run, as well as long run, the reforms will make for a more efficient operation; they will provide more in the way of job training for less in the way of tax dollars.

NOTE: On the same day the White House Press Office released the transcript of a news briefing on the President's statement by Secretary of Labor George P. Shultz, Press Secretary Ronald L. Ziegler, and Arnold R. Weber, Assistant Secretary of Labor for Manpower.

106   Message to the Congress Transmitting First Annual Plan for U.S. Participation in the World Weather Program.   *March* 13, 1969

To the Congress of the United States:

I am pleased to transmit to you, in accordance with Senate Concurrent Resolution 67 of the 90th Congress, the first annual plan for United States participation in the World Weather Program. This document describes the long-range goals of the World Weather Program and the activities in support of that program which have been planned by eight Federal agencies for Fiscal Year 1970. The budget figures shown in this report are consistent with those which appeared in the budget submitted to the Congress on January 15, 1969.

I commend this report to you and hope you will give it your careful attention, for it describes activities which can contribute in important ways to the quality of American life. The World Weather Program promises, for example, to produce earlier and more accurate weather forecasts than we now receive. It is also exploring the feasibility of large-scale weather modifications. Because so much of our social and economic life is significantly influenced by weather conditions, it is important that we encourage those advances in weather prediction and control which our scientists now foresee.

This project, and our role in it, also have great political significance. For the World Weather Program, growing out of United Nations initiatives in the early 1960's has developed into a most impressive example of international cooperation. On a scale never attempted until this decade, scientists and governments in many countries are joining hands across national boundaries to serve the entire human community. Their example should be instructive for all of us as we pursue lasting peace and order for our world.

This report "talks about the weather," but it demonstrates that we can do far more about our weather than merely talk about it. I believe that the plans for American participation which are outlined here reflect the sense of both the Congress and the Executive Branch of our government that the United States should give its full support to the World Weather Program.

RICHARD NIXON

The White House
  March 13, 1969

NOTE: The document is entitled "World Weather Program, Plan for Fiscal Year 1970" (Government Printing Office, 26 pp.).

107   Telegram to the Crew of Apollo 9.   *March* 13, 1969

THE EPIC FLIGHT of Apollo Nine will be recorded in history as ten days that thrilled the world. You have by your courage and your skill helped to shape the future of man in space. The three of you and the great team which enabled you to complete your successful mission have shown the world that the spirit of man and his technological genius are eager to begin an age of adventure, an age which will benefit all the people on this good earth. Knowing that the dining in Apollo Nine, while nourishing, lacked some of the amenities of earth-bound dining, Mrs.

Nixon and I invite you and your wives to have dinner with us at the White House at 8:00 Thursday evening, the twenty-seventh of March.

RICHARD NIXON

108 The President's News Conference of March 14, 1969

DEPLOYMENT OF THE ANTIBALLISTIC MISSILE SYSTEM

THE PRESIDENT. [1.] Ladies and gentlemen, today I am announcing a decision which I believe is vital for the security and defense of the United States, and also in the interest of peace throughout the world.

Last year a program, the Sentinel antiballistic missile program, was adopted. That program, as all listeners on television and radio and readers of newspapers know, has been the subject of very strong debate and controversy over the past few months.

After long study of all of the options available, I have concluded that the Sentinel program previously adopted should be substantially modified. The new program that I have recommended this morning to the leaders, and that I announce today, is one that perhaps best can be described as a Safeguard program.

It is a safeguard against any attack by the Chinese Communists that we can foresee over the next 10 years.

It is a safeguard of our deterrent system, which is increasingly vulnerable due to the advances that have been made by the Soviet Union since the year 1967 when the Sentinel program was first laid out.

It is a safeguard also against any irrational or accidental attack that might occur of less than massive magnitude which might be launched from the Soviet Union.

The program also does not do some things which should be clearly understood. It does not provide defense for our cities, and for that reason the sites have been moved away from our major cities. I have made the decision with regard to this particular point because I found that there is no way, even if we were to expand the limited Sentinel system, which was planned for some of our cities, to a so-called heavy or thick system—there is no way that we can adequately defend our cities without an unacceptable loss of life.

The only way that I have concluded that we can save lives, which is the primary purpose of our defense system, is to prevent war; and that is why the emphasis of this system is on protecting our deterrent, which is the best preventive for war.

The system differs from the previous Sentinel system in another major respect. The Sentinel system called for a fixed deployment schedule. I believe that because of a number of reasons, we should have a phase system. That is why, on an annual basis, the new Safeguard system will be reviewed, and the review may bring about changes in the system based on our evaluation of three major points:

First, what our intelligence shows us with regard to the magnitude of the threat, whether from the Soviet Union or from the Chinese; and, second, in terms of what our evaluation is of any talks that we are having by that time, or may be having, with regard to arms control; and finally, because we believe that since this is a new system, we should constantly examine what progress has been made in the development of the technique to see if changes in the system should be made.

I should admit at this point that this decision has not been an easy one. None of the great decisions made by a President are easy. But it is one that I have made after considering all of the options, and I would indicate, before going to your questions, two major options that I have overruled.

One is moving to a massive city defense. I have already indicated why I do not believe that is, first, feasible, and there is another reason: Moving to a massive city defense system, even starting with a thin system and then going to a heavy system, tends to be more provocative in terms of making credible a first-strike capability against the Soviet Union. I want no provocation which might deter arms talks.

The other alternative, at the other extreme, was to do nothing; or to delay for 6 months or 12 months, which would be the equivalent, really, of doing nothing; or, for example, going the road only of research and development.

I have examined those options. I have ruled them out because I have concluded that the first deployment of this system, which will not occur until 1973—that first deployment is essential by that date if we

are to meet the threat that our present intelligence indicates will exist by 1973.

In other words, we must begin now. If we delay a year, for example, it means that that first deployment will be delayed until 1975. That might be too late.

It is the responsibility of the President of the United States, above all other responsibilities, to think first of the security of the United States. I believe that this system is the best step that we can take to provide for that security.

There are, of course, other possibilities that have been strongly urged by some of the leaders this morning: for example, that we could increase our offensive capability, our submarine force, or even our Minuteman force or our bomber force. That I would consider to be, however, the wrong road because it would be provocative to the Soviet Union and might escalate an arms race.

This system is truly a safeguard system, a defensive system only. It safeguards our deterrent and under those circumstances can, in no way, in my opinion, delay the progress which I hope will continue to be made toward arms talks, which will limit arms, not only this kind of system, but particularly offensive systems.

We will now go to your questions.

QUESTIONS

THE WAR IN VIETNAM

[2.] Mr. Smith [Merriman Smith, United Press International].

Q. Mr. President, the war in Vietnam has been intensifying recently, and if there has been any notable progress in Paris it has not been detectable publicly. Is your patience growing a little thin with these continued attacks, particularly such as came out of the DMZ [demilitarized zone] today?

THE PRESIDENT. Mr. Smith, you may recall that on March 4, when I received a similar question, at an earlier stage in the attacks, I issued what was interpreted widely as a warning. It will be my policy as President to issue a warning only once, and I will not repeat it now. Anything in the future that is done will be done. There will be no additional warning.

As far as the Paris talks are concerned, I have noted the speculation in the press with regard to whether we will have, or should have, or are, for example, approving private talks going forward. I will not discuss that subject. I trust there will be private talks.

I think that is where this war will be settled—in private rather than in public. And this is in the best interests of both sides, but public discussion of what I think is significant progress which is being made along the lines of private talks, I will not indulge in.

THE PRESIDENT'S LEGISLATIVE PROGRAM

[3.] Yes, Mr. Cormier [Frank Cormier, Associated Press].

Q. Mr. President, will you make your own State of the Union Address, and what will your legislative program encompass?

THE PRESIDENT. I do not plan a State of the Union Address in the traditional manner. I will, within approximately a month, however, state a general domestic program. By that time the program will be at the point that I think it should be completely summarized and set forth, not only for the Nation, as to what we have done, but particularly to the Congress as to what we expect for the balance. I would

not like to anticipate now what will be in that program.

CONGRESSIONAL REACTION TO ABM DECISION

[4.] Q. Mr. President, there has been a great deal of criticism in Congress against deployment of any type of antimissile defense system. What kind of reception do you think that your proposal this morning will receive there?

THE PRESIDENT. It will be a very spirited debate, and it will be a very close vote. Debates in the field of national defense are often spirited, and the votes are often close. Many of my friends in Congress who were there before I was there remarked that the vote on extending the draft in 1941 won by only one vote.

This might be that close. I think, however, that after the Members of the House and the Senate consider this program, which is a minimum program, and which particularly provides options to change in other directions if we find the threat is changed, or that the art has changed, or evaluation of the technique has changed, I think that we have a good chance of getting approval. We will, of course, express our views, and we hope that we will get support from the country.

EFFECTIVENESS OF ABM DEPLOYMENT

[5.] Q. Mr. President, I understand that your first construction or deployment of antimissile systems would be around two Minuteman retaliatory operations. Do you think that deploying around these two provides enough deterrent that would be effective?

THE PRESIDENT. Let me explain the difference between deploying around two

Minuteman bases and deploying around, say, 10 cities.

Where you are looking toward a city defense, it needs to be a perfect or near perfect system to be credible because, as I examined the possibility of even a thick defense of cities, I found that even the most optimistic projections, considering the highest development of the art, would mean that we would still lose 30 to 40 million lives. That would be less—half of what we would otherwise lose. But we would still lose 30 to 40 million.

When you are talking about protecting your deterrent, it need not be perfect. It is necessary only to protect enough of the deterrent that the retaliatory second strike will be of such magnitude that the enemy would think twice before launching a first strike.

And it has been my conclusion that by protecting two Minuteman sites, we will preserve that deterrent as a credible deterrent, and that will be decisive and could be decisive insofar as the enemy considering the possibility of a first strike.

RESPONSE TO NORTH VIETNAMESE
OFFENSIVE

[6.] Q. Mr. President, there have been charges from Capitol Hill that you have stepped up the war in Vietnam. Have you?

THE PRESIDENT. I have not stepped up the war in Vietnam. I actually have examined not only the charges, but also examined the record. And I discussed it at great length yesterday with Secretary Laird.

What has happened is this: For the past 6 months, the forces on the other side have been planning for an offensive, and

for the past 6 months they not only have planned for an offensive, but they have been able, as a result of that planning, to have mounted a rather substantial offensive.

Under those circumstances, we had no other choice but to try to blunt the offensive. Had General Abrams not responded in this way, we would have suffered far more casualties than we have suffered, and we have suffered more than, of course, any of us would have liked to have seen.

The answer is that any escalation of the war in Vietnam has been the responsibility of the enemy. If the enemy deescalates its attacks, ours will go down. We are not trying to step it up. We are trying to do everything that we can in the conduct of our war in Vietnam to see that we can go forward toward peace in Paris.

That is why my response has been measured, deliberate, and, some think, too cautious. But it will continue to be that way, because I am thinking of those peace talks every time I think of a military option in Vietnam.

THE ABM SYSTEM AND THE SURCHARGE

[7.] Q. Mr. President, your safeguard ABM system, I understand, would cost about $1 billion less in the coming fiscal year than the plan which President Johnson sent up. Will this give you the opportunity to reduce the surcharge or will the continued high level of taxation be needed for the economy?

THE PRESIDENT. That question will be answered when we see the entire budget. Secretary Laird will testify on the defense budget on Wednesday.

And incidentally, my understanding at this time, and I have seen the preliminary figures, is that the defense budget that Secretary Laird will present will be approximately $2½ billion less than that submitted by the previous administration.

Now whether after considering the defense budget and all the other budgets that have been submitted, we then can move in the direction of either reducing the surcharge or move in the direction of some of our very difficult problems with regard to our cities, the problem of hunger and others—these are the options that I will have to consider at a later time.

U.S. RESPONSE TO INCREASED CASUALTIES IN VIETNAM

[8.] Q. Mr. President, last week you said that in the matter of Vietnam you would not tolerate heavier casualties and a continuation of the violation of the understanding without making an appropriate response.

Is what we are doing in Vietnam now, in a military way, that response of which you were speaking?

THE PRESIDENT. This is a very close decision on our part, one that I not only discussed with Secretary Laird yesterday, but that we will discuss more fully in the Security Council tomorrow.

I took no comfort out of the stories that I saw in the papers this morning to the effect that our casualties for the immediate past week went from 400 down to 300. That is still much too high. What our response should be must be measured in terms of the effect on the negotiations in Paris. I will only respond as I did earlier to Mr. Smith's question. We have issued a warning. I will not warn again. And if we conclude that the level of casualties is higher than we should tolerate, action will take place.

RUSSIAN REACTION TO THE ABM DECISION

[9.] Q. Mr. President, do you have reason to believe that the Russians will interpret your ABM decision today as not being an escalating move in the arms race?

THE PRESIDENT. As a matter of fact, Mr. Kaplow [Herbert Kaplow, NBC News], I have reason to believe, based on the past record, that they would interpret it just the other way around.

First, when they deployed their own ABM system, and, as you know, they have 67 missile ABM sites deployed around Moscow, they rejected the idea that it escalated the arms race on the ground that it was defensive solely in characters; and, second, when the United States last year went forward on the Sentinel system, 4 days later the Soviet Union initiated the opportunity to have arms limitation talks.

I think the Soviet Union recognizes very clearly the difference between a defensive posture and an offensive posture.

I would also point this out, an interesting thing about Soviet military and diplomatic history: They have always thought in defensive terms, and if you read not only their political leaders, but their military leaders, the emphasis is on defense.

I think that since this system now, as a result of moving the city defense out of it, and the possibility of that city defense growing into a thick defense, I think this makes it so clearly defensive in character that the Soviet Union cannot interpret this as escalating the arms race.

ON A FUTURE SUMMIT MEETING

[10.] Q. Mr. President, last week at your press conference you mentioned negotiations with the Russians at the high-est level being in the wings. Could you tell us if since then we have moved any closer to such a summit meeting?

THE PRESIDENT. I should distinguish between negotiations at what you would call the highest level, and what I said was the highest level, and talks. Talks with the Soviet Union are going on at a number of levels at this time, on a number of subjects.

However, those talks have not yet reached the point where I have concluded, or where I believe they have concluded, that a discussion at the summit level would be useful. Whenever those talks, prelimi-nary talks, do reach that point, I anticipate that a summit meeting would take place.

I do not think one will take place in the near future, but I think encouraging prog-ress is being made toward the time when a summit talk may take place.

HOLDOVER APPOINTEES FROM PREVIOUS
ADMINISTRATIONS

[11.]   Q. Mr. President, sir, there have been several reports from your staff mem-bers that Kennedy and Johnson holdover people who made policy have sewn them-selves into civil service status and this may mean some problem for you people in per-sonnel. I wonder if this means that you are going to transfer a lot of these people or abolish jobs?

THE PRESIDENT. Well, I have heard a lot from some of my Republican friends on Capitol Hill on this point, as well as from, of course, Republican leaders in the Nation. It seems that this is a rather com-mon practice, when one administration goes out and the other comes in. We will do what we think will best serve the inter-est of effective government, and if the in-dividual who has been frozen in can do the

job, we are going to keep him.

However, we are moving some out, but we won't do it through subterfuge. We will try to do it quite directly.

EUROPEAN CONTRIBUTIONS TO NATO

[12.]   Q. Mr. President, on your recent European trip, did you find any willing-ness on the part of our allies to increase their military and financial contribution to the Alliance?

THE PRESIDENT. Well, that matter was discussed with all of our allies, and par-ticularly will be a subject for discussion when we have the 20th anniversary meet-ing of NATO here in April.

I think it might be potentially embar-rassing to allies to suggest that we are urging them, any one specifically, to do one thing or another in this field. I think it is best for me to leave it in these terms:

Our allies do recognize the necessity to maintain NATO's conventional forces. They do recognize that they must carry their share or that the United States, and particularly our Congress, representing our people, will have much less incentive to carry our share. I believe they will do their share, but I think we are going to do it best through quiet conversation rather than public declaration.

CONSIDERATION OF THE ABM IN TALKS
WITH THE SOVIET UNION

[13.]   Yes, sir?

Q. In any talks with the Soviet Union, would you be willing to consider abandon-ing the ABM program altogether if the Soviets showed a similar willingness or, indeed, if they showed a readiness to place limitations on offensive weapons?

THE PRESIDENT. Well, Mr. Scali [John

Scali, ABC News], I am prepared, in the event that we go into arms talks, to consider both offensive and defensive weapons. As you know, the arms talks, that at least preliminarily have been discussed, do not involve limitation or reduction. They involve only freezing where we are.

Now, your question goes to abandoning. And on that particular point, I think it would take two, naturally, to make the agreement. Let's look at the Soviet Union's position with its defensive deployment of ABM's. Previously, that deployment was aimed only toward the United States. Today their radars, from our intelligence, are also directed toward Communist China.

I would imagine that the Soviet Union would be just as reluctant as we would be to leave their country naked against a potential Chinese Communist threat. So the abandoning of the entire system, particularly as long as the Chinese threat is there, I think neither country would look upon with much favor.

THE ABM AND THE NUCLEAR NON-PROLIFERATION TREATY

[14.] Q. Mr. President, do you think that deployment of the ABM system by both the Soviet Union and the United States is compatible with the NPT, the Nonproliferation Treaty?

THE PRESIDENT. I considered that problem, and I believe that they are compatible with the NPT. We discussed that in the leaders' meeting this morning, and I pointed out that as we consider this kind of defensive system, which enables the United States of America to make its deterrent capability credible, that that will

have an enormous effect in reducing the pressure on other countries who might want to acquire nuclear weapons.

That is the key point. If a country doesn't feel that the major country that has a nuclear capability has a credible deterrent, then they would move in that direction.

One other point—I wish to make an announcement with regard to the NPT: that I was delighted to see the Senate's confirmation or consent to the Treaty, and this announcement—I hope President Johnson is looking. I haven't talked to him on the phone. I am going to invite President Johnson, if his schedule permits, to attend the ceremony when we will have the ratification of the Treaty, because he started it in his administration, and I think he should participate when we ratify it.

CAMPUS DISORDERS AND FEDERAL AID

[15.] Mr. Lisagor [Peter Lisagor, Chicago Daily News].

Q. Mr. President, I wonder if I could turn you to the campus disorders and unrest. They are continuing and we haven't had an opportunity to ask you your views of them. But particularly, would you favor the cutting off of Federal loans to the offenders?

THE PRESIDENT. Mr. Lisagor, I have asked the Attorney General and the Secretary of Health, Education, and Welfare to examine this problem, particularly in view of a congressional report that 122 of 540 who had been arrested at San Francisco State were direct recipients of Federal funds.

I will have a statement on that that I

will be making either Monday or Tuesday, in detail. I would prefer not to go into it now.

EFFECT ON HANOI OF U.S. RESPONSE
IN VIETNAM

[16.] Mr. Semple [Robert B. Semple, Jr., New York Times].

Q. Mr. President, to follow up Mr. Day's [Anthony Day, Philadelphia Bulletin] question on Vietnam earlier, is there any evidence that your measured response to the enemy attacks in South Vietnam has produced or yielded any results in Paris or in the attitudes of the North Vietnamese leaders in Hanoi?

THE PRESIDENT. Our measured response has not had the effect of discouraging the progress, and it is very limited progress, toward talks in Paris. That is the negative side in answering your question.

As to whether or not a different response would either discourage those talks or might have the effect of even encouraging them is the decision that we now have to make.

PROSPECT OF TROOP WITHDRAWALS IN
VIETNAM

[17.] Q. Mr. President, sir, again on Vietnam, in connection with Secretary Laird's visit, we have heard for some time predictions that American troop levels could be cut as the South Vietnamese capabilities improve, and again last week, while he was in Vietnam, we were getting similar reports from Saigon despite the high level of the fighting that is going on now. Do you see any prospect for withdrawing American troops in any numbers soon?

THE PRESIDENT. Mr. Bailey [Charles W. Bailey 2d, Minneapolis Star and Tribune], in view of the current offensive on the part of the North Vietnamese and the Vietcong, there is no prospect for a reduction of American forces in the foreseeable future.

When we are able to reduce forces as a result of a combination of circumstances— the ability of the South Vietnamese to defend themselves in areas where we now are defending them, the progress of the talks in Paris, or the level of enemy activity—when that occurs, I will make an announcement. But at this time there is no foreseeable prospect in that field.

EFFECT OF ABM PROGRAM ON SHELTER
PROGRAM

[18.] Mr. Theis [J. William Theis, United Press International].

Q. What effect, if any, will your safeguard program have on the shelter program? Can you tell us anything about your long-range plans in this direction?

THE PRESIDENT. Congressman Holifield[1] in the meeting this morning strongly urged that the administration look over the shelter program and he made the point that he thought it had fallen somewhat into disarray due to lack of attention over the past few years.

I have directed that General Lincoln, the head of the Office of Emergency Preparedness—I had directed him previously to conduct such a survey. We are going to look at the shelter program to see what we can do there in order to minimize American casualties.

[1] Representative Chet Holifield of California, Chairman of the Military Subcommittee, Government Operations Committee.

U.S. POSITION ON THE MIDDLE EAST

[19.] Q. Mr. President, if I recall correctly, at the last press conference when you were discussing the meeting with General de Gaulle, and the Middle East situation, you said you were encouraged by what he told you, because he was moving closer to our position.

I wonder if you could tell us what our position is in the Middle East, and if it has changed significantly in the last year?

THE PRESIDENT. We have had bilateral talks not only with the French, but also with the Soviet Union, and with the British, preparatory to the possibility of four-power talks. I would not like to leave the impression that we are completely together at this point.

We are closer together than we were, but we still have a lot of yardage to cover. And until we make further progress in developing a common position, I would prefer not to lay out what our position is.

I don't think that would be helpful in bringing them to the position that we think is the right position.

Merriman Smith, United Press International: Thank you.

NOTE: President Nixon's fourth news conference was held in the East Room at the White House at 12 noon on Friday, March 14, 1969. It was broadcast on radio and television.

109   Statement on Deployment of the Antiballistic Missile System. *March* 14, 1969

IMMEDIATELY after assuming office, I requested the Secretary of Defense to review the program initiated by the last administration to deploy the Sentinel Ballistic Missile Defense System.

The Department of Defense presented a full statement of the alternatives at the last two meetings of the National Security Council. These alternatives were reviewed there in the light of the security requirements of the United States and of their probable impact on East-West relations, with particular reference to the prospects for strategic arms negotiations.

After carefully considering the alternatives, I have reached the following conclusions: (1) the concept on which the Sentinel program of the previous administration was based should be substantially modified, (2) the safety of our country requires that we should proceed now with the development and construc-

tion of the new system in a carefully phased program, (3) this program will be reviewed annually from the point of view of (a) technical developments, (b) the threat, (c) the diplomatic context including any talks on arms limitation.

The modified system has been designed so that its defensive intent is unmistakable. It will be implemented not according to some fixed, theoretical schedule, but in a manner clearly related to our periodic analysis of the threat. The first deployment covers two missile sites; the first of these will not be completed before 1973. Any further delay would set this date back by at least 2 additional years. The program for fiscal year 1970 is the minimum necessary to maintain the security of our Nation.

This measured deployment is designed to fulfill three objectives:

1. Protection of our land-based re-

taliatory forces against a direct attack by the Soviet Union.

2. Defense of the American people against the kind of nuclear attack which Communist China is likely to be able to mount within the decade.

3. Protection against the possibility of accidental attacks from any source.

In the review leading up to this decision, we considered three possible options in addition to this program: a deployment which would attempt to defend U.S. cities against an attack by the Soviet Union; a continuation of the Sentinel program approved by the previous administration; and indefinite postponement of deployment while continuing research and development.

I rejected these options for the following reasons:

Although every instinct motivates me to provide the American people with complete protection against a major nuclear attack, it is not now within our power to do so. The heaviest defense system we considered, one designed to protect our major cities, still could not prevent a catastrophic level of U.S. fatalities from a deliberate all-out Soviet attack. And it might look to an opponent like the prelude to an offensive strategy threatening the Soviet deterrent.

The Sentinel system approved by the previous administration provided more capabilities for the defense of cities than the program I am recommending, but it did not provide protection against some threats to our retaliatory forces which have developed subsequently. Also, the Sentinel system had the disadvantage that it could be misinterpreted as the first step toward the construction of a heavy system.

Giving up all construction of missile de-fense poses too many risks. Research and development does not supply the answer to many technical issues that only operational experience can provide. The Soviet Union has engaged in a buildup of its strategic forces larger than was envisaged in 1967 when the decision to deploy Sentinel was made. The following is illustrative of recent Soviet activity:

1. The Soviets have already deployed an ABM system which protects to some degree a wide area centered around Moscow. We will not have a comparable capability for over 4 years. We believe the Soviet Union is continuing their ABM development, directed either toward improving this initial system, or more likely, making substantially better second-generation ABM components.

2. The Soviet Union is continuing the deployment of very large missiles with warheads capable of destroying our hardened Minuteman forces.

3. The Soviet Union has also been substantially increasing the size of their submarine-launched ballistic missile force.

4. The Soviets appear to be developing a semi-orbital nuclear weapon system.

In addition to these developments, the Chinese threat against our population, as well as the danger of an accidental attack, cannot be ignored. By approving this system, it is possible to reduce U.S. fatalities to a minimal level in the event of a Chinese nuclear attack in the 1970's, or in an accidental attack from any source. No President with the responsibility for the lives and security of the American people could fail to provide this protection.

The gravest responsibility which I bear as President of the United States is for the security of the Nation. Our nuclear forces defend not only ourselves but our allies as well. The imperative that our nuclear deterrent remain secure beyond any possible doubt requires that the United States must take steps now to insure that our strategic retaliatory forces will not become vulnerable to a Soviet attack.

Modern technology provides several choices in seeking to insure the survival of our retaliatory forces. First, we could increase the number of sea- and land-based missiles and bombers. I have ruled out this course because it provides only marginal improvement of our deterrent, while it could be misinterpreted by the Soviets as an attempt to threaten their deterrent. It would therefore stimulate an arms race.

A second option is to harden further our ballistic missile forces by putting them in more strongly reinforced underground silos. But our studies show that hardening by itself is not adequate protection against foreseeable advances in the accuracy of Soviet offensive forces.

The third option was to begin a measured construction on an active defense of our retaliatory forces.

I have chosen the third option.

The system will use components previously developed for the Sentinel system. However, the deployment will be changed to reflect the new concept. We will provide for local defense of selected Minuteman missile sites and an area defense designed to protect our bomber bases and our command and control authorities. In addition, this new system will provide a defense of the continental United States against an accidental attack and will provide substantial protection against the kind of attack which the Chinese Communists may be capable of launching

throughout the 1970's. This deployment will not require us to place missile and radar sites close to our major cities.

The present estimate is that the total cost of installing this system will be $6–$7 billion. However, because of the deliberate pace of the deployment, budgetary requests for the coming year can be substantially less—by about one-half—than those asked for by the previous administration for the Sentinel system.

In making this decision, I have been mindful of my pledge to make every effort to move from an era of confrontation to an era of negotiation. The program I am recommending is based on a careful assessment of the developing Soviet and Chinese threats. I have directed the President's Foreign Intelligence Advisory Board—a nonpartisan group of distinguished private citizens—to make a yearly assessment of the threat which will supplement our regular intelligence assessment. Each phase of the deployment will be reviewed to insure that we are doing as much as necessary but no more than that required by the threat existing at that time. Moreover, we will take maximum advantage of the information gathered from the initial deployment in designing the later phases of the program.

Since our deployment is to be closely related to the threat, it is subject to modification as the threat changes, either through negotiations or through unilateral actions by the Soviet Union or Communist China.

The program is not provocative. The Soviet retaliatory capability is not affected by our decision. The capability for surprise attack against our strategic forces is reduced. In other words, our program provides an incentive for a responsible Soviet weapons policy and for the avoidance of spiraling U.S. and Soviet strategic arms budgets.

I have taken cognizance of the view that beginning construction of a U.S. ballistic missile defense would complicate an agreement on strategic arms with the Soviet Union.

I do not believe that the evidence of the recent past bears out this contention. The Soviet interest in strategic talks was not deterred by the decision of the previous administration to deploy the Sentinel ABM system—in fact, it was formally announced shortly afterwards. I believe that the modifications we have made in the previous program will give the Soviet Union even less reason to view our defense effort as an obstacle to talks. Moreover, I wish to emphasize that in any arms limitation talks with the Soviet Union, the United States will be fully prepared to discuss limitations on defensive as well as offensive weapons systems.

The question of ABM involves a complex combination of many factors:

—numerous, highly technical, often conflicting judgments;

—the costs;

—the relationship to prospects for reaching an agreement on limiting nuclear arms;

—the moral implications the deployment of a ballistic missile defense system has for many Americans;

—the impact of the decision on the security of the United States in this perilous age of nuclear arms.

I have weighed all these factors. I am deeply sympathetic to the concerns of private citizens and Members of Congress that we do only that which is necessary for national security. This is why I am recommending a minimum program essential for our security. It is my duty as President to make certain that we do no less.

NOTE: Appropriations for a modified antiballistic missile system were included in the 1970 Armed Forces appropriation authorization bill approved on November 19, 1969 (Public Law 91–121, 83 Stat. 204).

The text of a letter to the President, dated March 17, 1969, from Dr. Lee A. DuBridge, the President's Science Adviser, on the proposed antiballistic missile system, is printed in the Weekly Compilation of Presidential Documents (vol. 5, p. 430).

110   Remarks at a Luncheon of the National Alliance of Businessmen.   *March* 15, 1969

Mr. Chairman, members of the Cabinet, my fellow presidents, and all the distinguished guests here and supporters of the Alliance:

It is a very great privilege for me to come before this group on one of the very few occasions on which I have left the White House for an appearance outside the White House in Washington or anyplace else.

I realize that some may wonder why.

Well, it seems to me that after trying for so many years to get in, why go out? [*Laughter*]

I am quite familiar with the work of this group, not only with the work that it has done but with the plans that it has for the future, and my remarks will be brief. They will relate to the men who have worked with you in the past, who will be working with you in the future, and also with the mission that I think is yours and is also that of the Nation.

First, a word about Don Kendall. We have several things in common. We were both born in the West. We both played football. We both served in the Navy, and we both made President. He made it a little sooner than I did.

The other thing, however, that I think we have in common is a deep concern about the problems that all of you have been considering during the course of these meetings, during yesterday and today.

In speaking of those problems, I first want to congratulate this Alliance for what it has done. I know that when you first projected your goal, the number of jobs—100,000 by June of 1969—many skeptics wondered whether it could be reached.

You have already reached that. Not only have you reached it before June 1969, but 80,000 of those for whom jobs have been found are still on the jobs, which is a truly remarkable record. I congratulate Henry Ford and all of those who have served so well in providing that kind of leadership for this very exciting project.

I am also aware of the plans you have for the future—the plans to move from 75 cities to 125 cities; the plans also to attempt to get at this whole problem of unemployment, and hard-core unemployment particularly, by moving perhaps as many as 500,000 into jobs—the time, as I understand now, June 1971, but because of the number of new cities, perhaps even sooner.

This is an ambitious project. What I am here to say, and what the members of this Cabinet are here to say, is that it has the complete, unqualified support of this administration, just as it had of the previous administration.

There is no partisanship in this program. All that we want and all that you want is to deal with this basically essential problem in an effective way; to move people from welfare rolls to payrolls. This we want; this you want; and you will have our support in that project.

I have two suggestions. One is to the number of cities. Going from 75 cities to 125 is ambitious. I think it could be more. In meeting with Don Kendall and also in meeting with members of the Chamber of Commerce a couple of days ago, I urged the possibility of considering a number of smaller towns or smaller cities for this particular group to operate in.

I do not know whether that is feasible. But I do know that the spirit is there. I do know that the personnel are there, that the desire is there, and also the problem.

While it would not appear that such massive strides could be made when we talk about smaller towns and smaller cities, certainly it is something that could be considered.

Then, the second area, one that you have already made great progress in, is with regard to youth. I was particularly impressed by the fact that 120,000 young Americans found jobs last summer as a result of what the Alliance did. What I am proposing now is that even more emphasis be put on this youth program.

The Secretary of Labor just recently completed a study that I had requested with regard to unemployment of youth in the United States. I don't need to tell this group of employers that the unemployment rate for youth, of course, is always higher than adults in any country, industrial or otherwise.

In the United States, it is three times as high. But the sad part of the statistic is that unemployment among youth in the

United States is higher than in any industrial country in the world.

This, of course, poses the problem, and it also poses the challenge and the opportunity for this group. I know that under the leadership of Henry Ford, naturally, the slogan of this organization was that this was the group with the "better idea," and I would suggest that under the leadership of Don Kendall this should be the group that "thinks young." [*Laughter*]

In that respect, while I am not, of course, underplaying in any regard the immense responsibility that you have with regard to those in the older-age brackets, I would urge that you particularly concentrate on those programs that deal with unemployment among youth and see that they are folded into the others.

And then finally, one point that I think is a bit sensitive but perhaps needs to be discussed at a meeting like this: At the present time, this administration, like its predecessor, and as will be the case with its successor, is struggling with the problem of welfare.

What do we do about it? What should the level be? Should we have a national standard? Should we raise the standard?

And, as I have been looking at the various proposals with regard to welfare that have come across my desk, a thought has come to my mind that I am sure must come to yours: The word "welfare," I think, is, in a sense, an inaccurate term if we are thinking of the welfare of the individual in the broadest sense. Welfare is necessary—necessary when an individual is unable to get a job, necessary when an individual needs help. But when we think about the welfare of this country and the welfare of an individual, in the best sense, that means a job.

That is truly in the best interest of the welfare of the Nation and the welfare of every individual, because with that job comes dignity, dignity that cannot come, of course, from being on public welfare, no matter how high we are able to raise it, no matter how much we are able to do.

I am not indicating here any intention on the part of this administration not to do what is required and as much as we can do to take care of those who are unable to care for themselves, who cannot find jobs. But I am emphasizing here that when we are speaking of the welfare of an individual, we should not stop in terms of what government can do for him, but we should think in terms of that dignity that can only come from what he does for himself.

That is why what you do is so important. That is why we are supporting this program. That is why we urge you to do more. Because when we look at the history of welfare—it was rather cogently summed up in a recent meeting of the Urban Affairs Council—as we look through the ages, and welfare is not new, we have found that inevitably when such programs continue and escalate in any society, welfare tends to destroy those who receive it and to corrupt those who dispense it. That is why we must move toward the job solution, move toward it effectively, and that is why what you do is an immense contribution not only to the Nation but to the true welfare of every individual who, without what you do, would not have that opportunity to make the contribution to this country and to his own dignity that he could otherwise make.

I want to say to you, Mr. Chairman, that as I speak before many groups over these next few years as President of the United States, I know that many will be important, and the missions that they have will be ones that I will endorse.

I don't know of any one that in terms of concrete progress will serve the public interest and the individual interest of hundreds of thousands of Americans; I don't know of any group that will be more important than this group.

This is a group of very busy people; Governors, mayors, presidents of 300 companies, vice presidents, executive officials. You have taken off to come to Washington to a conference, and I suppose sometimes you wonder "Was this trip worthwhile?" All that I can say is that I know it is worthwhile. I know that without your help we cannot do the job that needs to be done. I know that with your

help there is nothing that we cannot accomplish in this field.

So, I congratulate you and your outgoing chairman on what you have done, and I wish you well, and your new chairman, in what I know you are going to do for the individual and for this Nation.

Thank you.

NOTE: The President spoke at 1:35 p.m. at the Sheraton Park Hotel in Washington at the second annual meeting of the National Alliance of Businessmen. The chairman of the National Alliance of Businessmen was Donald M. Kendall, president and chief executive officer of PepsiCo, Inc. The former chairman of the Alliance was Henry Ford II, president of Ford Motor Co.

The National Alliance of Businessmen, a nonpartisan organization, was formed in 1968 to assist the hard-core unemployed.

111   Remarks at the American Legion's 50th Anniversary Dinner.   *March 15, 1969*

Commander Doyle, and all of the distinguished guests at the head tables, and all of the distinguished guests at this dinner here in Washington, which the American Legion has been giving for so many years to the Members of Congress:

I want you to know that the Commander, having apologized for what he was wearing—what do you think about what I am wearing?

I want to assure you that, as I told the Commander as we were coming in, only the fact that I had agreed several months ago to attend the annual Gridiron dinner, where I am to speak later this evening—and that is a white tie affair over at the Statler Hotel—only that made it impossible for me to be here with you at this dinner. But if you come back next year, I promise this will come first and the

Gridiron will come second.

If I could be permitted just a few brief words before returning to the dinner at the Statler, first a recollection: It is rather hard for me to realize that I have been a member of the American Legion going back to the year 1946, and also hard for me to realize that I have attended—and I think, Commander, you will find this is the case—I have attended 18 of these dinners in Washington, D.C., and I think perhaps have spoken to the American Legion Convention more than any living American at the present time.

I won't make the same speech tonight. But I feel very much at home here. I feel very much at home because I know so many of you. I visited your States. I know what you stand for. I know your strong convictions. And right now, incidentally,

I want to express my appreciation for some resolutions that you passed today supporting my national defense policy—our national defense policy.

And having spoken of that policy, could I say a word with regard to the very moving ceremony that I have just participated in?

Fifty years ago this organization was founded, and through 50 years it has served the Nation well, served it in so many ways that many Americans are not aware, but particularly in a way that I am particularly aware, and that is in the cause of keeping the Nation strong—strong militarily, strong spiritually, strong in every way—so that America could lead in the cause for peace.

I think sometimes we fail to understand that only through strength can this great Nation lead for peace, and it is that kind of strength that we want.

As I tried to emphasize, as I was announcing the very difficult decision, one that many with great honesty disagreed with me on, perhaps some in this room, a decision with regard to the antiballistic missile, the purpose of our strength was not in any sense a threat to any other nation, but I know that the strength of America is so essential for those who will be meeting with others in various parts of the world over these next few years in conferences that will determine whether we have war or peace.

My friends, I simply want to say this: Whoever is President of the United States, whether it is the man standing before you today, or whether it is his successor, let us be sure that whenever our President sits at a conference table with any other nation that the United States is never a second-rate military power.

This is not said with any belligerence. It is only said in the sense that a strong nation can speak of its beliefs and what it is willing to do in order to protect those beliefs and to stand for them.

And now a word about that ceremony. A few years ago, as Vice President of the United States, I participated in the occasion when the Unknown Soldier from World War II and the Unknown Soldier from Korea were buried at the Tomb of the Unknowns.

I will never forget that day and the thoughts that ran through my mind on that occasion. And then on my recent trip to Europe, I laid a wreath on behalf of all the American people at a Tomb of an Unknown Soldier in London, and another one at the Tomb of an Unknown Soldier in Rome, and another at the Tomb of an Unknown Soldier at the Arc de Triomphe in Paris.

I thought of all of them and of all of ours. And I realized how great our responsibility was, yours and mine, to see to it that this great Nation meets its responsibility in the world to maintain our strength so that we can negotiate the differences between nations that may possibly avoid another war, and thereby see to it that the day will come when it will not be necessary for us to bring home men, whether unknown or known, bring them home after having fought and died in a nation's wars. We feel that way particularly about our own.

But also we as Americans feel that about every other person in the world. When you think of a young man, and I have seen them in Korea, 18, 19, 20, so young, all their hopes and their ideals and all their lives ahead of them and then that life snuffed out; whether it is an American

223

boy, or a French boy, or an Italian boy, or a Russian boy—whoever that boy is—we want the kind of a world that he can grow up in in peace with all the other peoples of the world.

That is what I believe. That is what the Legion stands for. That is why you are for strength. And I pledge to you that backed by the strong positions that you have taken, we will maintain America's military strength and from that position of strength, not with arrogance, not with belligerence, we will attempt to develop those new channels which can lead to peace in the world. I believe it is possible.

So I thank you for the opportunity to be here to share with you briefly these thoughts and to tell you that when I joined the Legion—and I was young then, in 1946, I ran for Congress that year—I was proud to be a member of the Legion. I have been proud of my membership ever since. And I will be proud to be with you at your convention next year.

Thank you.

NOTE: The President spoke at 9:02 p.m. at the Sheraton Park Hotel in Washington. William C. Doyle was National Commander of the American Legion.

Prior to his remarks, President Nixon pressed a remote control button activating a new lighting system for the Tomb of the Unknowns at Arlington National Cemetery. The $100,000 system and the $25,000 to maintain it were the Legion's 50th anniversary gift to the Nation.

112 Statement on St. Patrick's Day. *March* 17, 1969

IT HAS been said that on Saint Patrick's Day everyone is an Irishman. As one whose ancestors came to America from Ireland, I wish all the Irish—including those who are Irish for only today—a happy and memorable Saint Patrick's Day.

The life of this national hero and great saint is filled with the power of love. Having been a slave for 6 years, he knew what it was to love liberty. He loved his country and its people. And he devoted his life to bringing God's word to the Irish.

These three loves—of liberty, of country, and of God—have been the heritage of the Irish people wherever they have been. This heritage has enriched the world, but it has particularly enriched the United States of America. In labor, in politics, in industry, in religion, in law, in military service, the Irish who have made this country their home have contributed greatly to the building of a strong and free nation.

Not to be forgotten is the great cleansing gift of Irish laughter, a gift needed today more than ever before. Recently Father Theodore Hesburgh, president of Notre Dame University, suggested that we in the United States should not be afraid to laugh at ourselves and at our troubles. The Irish have shown through the centuries that a people can be strengthened and sustained by the gift of laughter. They have shown the world that men can be serious without always being solemn.

Saint Patrick has long been recognized as representing the spirit of the Irish people. It is in this spirit, in the spirit of liberty and laughter and love of country and of God, I say to all Irishmen today, whatever their country, *Eireann Go Bragh.*

113   Message to the President of Ireland on St. Patrick's Day.
      March 17, 1969

ON THIS Saint Patrick's Day, the American people and I extend our warmest greeting to you and the people of Ireland. Proud of my own and of my wife's Irish heritage and proud of the contributions made by the Irish to the United States and to the cause of freedom everywhere, I look forward to a continuation of that spirit of cooperation and friendship which has for so long existed between your country and mine.

RICHARD NIXON

[The Honorable Eamon de Valera, President of Eire]

114   Remarks at a Meeting With the Irish Ambassador.
      March 17, 1969

Mr. Ambassador:

This is a very special and happy occasion for us, and I understand an annual occasion here at the White House—the celebration of St. Patrick's Day.

We welcome you, and, of course, every successful administration in this country has a bit of Irish in it.

I should point out that in our family, Mrs. Nixon's father was Irish, and on my side my mother was Irish. So between the two you have one. And of course this is the day that we celebrate as her birthday, St. Patrick's Day.

Both of us having visited your country, we feel very close to you and on this day we are so delighted to welcome you here so that you can speak to all Americans who on this day have a little bit of Irish in them.

AMBASSADOR FAY. Mr. President, it is a very great honor and privilege that you do me. May I say a word?

THE PRESIDENT. Yes, sir, more than one word.

AMBASSADOR FAY. Well, we are supposed to be garrulous, Mr. President, but I shall restrain myself, I hope, to a very few words. But I must say something of the privilege and pleasure it is for me to be received by you and Mrs. Nixon on this occasion.

We, too, are happy that the Irish have been able to contribute, we believe, something to this great country. And on this day, the Irish at home join themselves to the Irish in the United States in wishing you and Mrs. Nixon and all the people of this great country our very best wishes.

And in pledge of that, may I have the privilege of presenting to you some shamrock contained in a specially designed and engraved vase made by Waterford Glass in Ireland.

It has an engraving of the White House on it, which, as one of your predecessors, President Kennedy, remembered when he visited us, had been designed by an Irish architect, and he was pleased to remember that the house the architect in question had designed, which is now our National Parliament, is Leinster House in Dublin.

Mr. President, may I ask you to accept this shamrock from me—to put a little in your buttonhole, if I can manage it.

THE PRESIDENT. Does it work?

AMBASSADOR FAY. I hope so.

THE PRESIDENT. Thank you very much.

I do want to say, incidentally, that on our last trip—the trip that we just took to Europe—we were unable to include Ireland. But I want you to know that sometime during this administration, Mrs. Nixon and I are hoping that we can pay a visit to Ireland.

AMBASSADOR FAY. Well, Mr. President, you will do us great pleasure and great honor.

May I at the same time take this occasion, as I have been instructed to do by my Government, to say that we wish to invite you quite formally as and when it pleases you to come and visit us. And you are always welcome.

THE PRESIDENT. Thank you.

While we are here, I think this is also a very special occasion in another sense, that I have nominated today the new Ambassador from the United States to Ireland, Mr. John Moore.

Mr. Moore, would you like to come over and join the ranks of the ambassadors, with the consent of the Senate, I trust?

Are you Irish by any chance, Mr. Ambassador?

MR. MOORE. By any chance, indeed, Mr. President. My father, when we were young, told us to say we were 100 percent Americans and 100 percent Irish descent.

THE PRESIDENT. Well, we also have an Irish setter, you see.

Thank you very much.

NOTE: The President spoke at 11:52 a.m. in the Roosevelt Room at the White House at a meeting with William P. Fay, Ambassador to the United States from Ireland, and John D. J. Moore of Short Hills, N.J., president of W. R. Grace and Co., U.S. Ambassador-designate to Ireland.

On March 12, 1969, the Fish Room in the West Wing of the White House was renamed the Roosevelt Room.

A White House announcement of the appointment of Mr. Moore is printed in the Weekly Compilation of Presidential Documents (vol. 5, p. 428).

---

115 Remarks on Presenting the Medal of Honor Posthumously to Pfc. Melvin E. Newlin, USMC. *March 18, 1969*

Ladies and gentlemen:

The purpose of this meeting this morning is for the award of the Medal of Honor posthumously to Mr. Newlin.

The Secretary of the Navy will read the citation.

[Secretary of the Navy John H. Chafee read the citation, the text of which follows.]

The President of the United States in the name of The Congress takes pride in presenting the Medal of Honor posthumously to

PRIVATE FIRST CLASS MELVIN E. NEWLIN
UNITED STATES MARINE CORPS

for service as set forth in the following

CITATION:

For conspicuous gallantry and intrepidity at the risk of his life above and beyond the call of duty while serving as a machine gunner attached to the First Platoon, Company F, Second Battalion, Fifth Marines, First Marine Division, in the Republic of Vietnam on 3 and 4 July 1967. Private Newlin, with four other marines, was manning a key position on the perimeter of the Nong Son outpost when the enemy launched a savage and well coordinated mortar and infantry assault, seriously wounding him and killing his four comrades. Propping himself against his machine gun, he poured a deadly accurate stream of fire into the charging ranks of the Viet Cong. Though repeatedly hit by small arms fire, he twice repelled enemy attempts to overrun his position. During the third attempt, a grenade explosion wounded him again and knocked him to the ground unconscious. The Viet Cong guerrillas, believing him dead, bypassed him and continued their assault on the main force. Meanwhile, Private Newlin regained consciousness, crawled back to his weapon, and brought it to bear on the rear of the enemy causing havoc and confusion among them. Spotting the enemy attempting to bring a captured 106 recoilless weapon to bear on other marine positions, he shifted his fire, inflicting heavy casualties on the enemy and preventing them from firing the captured weapon. He then shifted his fire back to the primary enemy force, causing the enemy to stop their assault on the marine bunkers and to once again attack his machine gun position. Valiantly fighting off two more enemy assaults, he firmly held his ground until mortally wounded. Private Newlin had singlehandedly broken up and disorganized the entire enemy assault force, causing them to lose momentum and delaying them long enough for his fellow marines to organize a defense and beat off their secondary attack. His indomitable courage, fortitude, and unwavering devotion to duty in the face of almost certain death reflected great credit upon himself and the Marine Corps and upheld the highest traditions of the United States Naval Service.

RICHARD NIXON

[Following the reading of the citation, the President resumed speaking.]

Mrs. Newlin, there is very little I can add to that citation, but we do want you to know that the people of this country are grateful for the sacrifice of your son.

They are also aware of the fact that this kind of remarkable courage never occurs as an accident. Only if a young man had a fine family, mother and father, would he have acted as he did.

Therefore, we present this for him. But we also present it to you because you, his mother and father, contributed so much to this fine young man in the background that you provided for him.

NOTE: The President spoke at 11 a.m. in his office at the White House at the presentation of the Medal of Honor to Mr. and Mrs. Joseph L. Newlin of Wellsville, Ohio, parents of Private Newlin.

At private ceremonies on four separate occasions later in 1969, President Nixon presented posthumous Medals of Honor to the families of the following servicemen:

M. Sgt. Charles E. Hosking, Jr., USA, and Sp4c. Don L. Michael, USA, on May 23, 1969 (5 Weekly Comp. Pres. Docs., p. 732).

Sgt. Paul H. Foster, USMCR, Cpl. Larry E. Smedley, USMC, and Cpl. William T. Perkins, Jr., USMC, on June 20, 1969 (5 Weekly Comp. Pres. Docs., p. 884).

Platoon Sgt. Bruce A. Grandstaff, USA, S. Sgt. Frankie Z. Molnar, USA, and Pfc. Leslie A. Bellrichard, USA, on July 10, 1969 (5 Weekly Comp. Pres. Docs., p. 969).

Sp5c. Edgar L. McWethy, Jr., USA, Sp4c. Carmel B. Harvey, Jr., USA, and Sp4c. Dale E. Wayrynen, USA, on October 16, 1969 (5 Weekly Comp. Pres. Docs., p. 1423).

116   Letter to the Head of the U.S. Delegation at the Conference of the Eighteen-Nation Disarmament Committee. *March* 18, 1969

Dear Ambassador Smith:

In view of the great importance which I attach to the work of the Eighteen-Nation Disarmament Conference in Geneva, I wish to address directly to you, as the new Director of the Arms Control and Disarmament Agency and the head of our delegation, my instructions regarding the participation of the United States in this conference.

The fundamental objective of the United States is a world of enduring peace and justice, in which the differences that separate nations can be resolved without resort to war.

Our immediate objective is to leave behind the period of confrontation and to enter an era of negotiation.

The task of the Delegation of the United States to the disarmament conference is to serve these objectives by pursuing negotiations to achieve concrete measures which will enhance the security of our own country and all countries.

The new Administration has now considered the policies which will help us to make progress in this endeavor.

I have decided that the Delegation of the United States should take these positions at the Conference.

First, in order to assure that the seabed, man's latest frontier, remains free from the nuclear arms race, the United States delegation should indicate that the United States is interested in working out an international agreement that would prohibit the implacement or fixing of nuclear weapons or other weapons of mass destruction on the seabed. To this end, the United States Delegation should seek discussion of the factors necessary for such an international agreement. Such an agreement would, like the Antarctic Treaty and the Treaty on Outer Space which are already in effect, prevent an arms race before it had a chance to start. It would ensure that this potentially useful area of the world remained available for peaceful purposes.

Second, the United States supports the conclusion of a comprehensive test ban adequately verified. In view of the fact that differences regarding verification have not permitted achievement of this key arms control measure, efforts must be made towards greater understanding of the verification issue.

Third, the United States Delegation will continue to press for an agreement to cut off the production of fissionable materials for weapons purposes and to transfer such materials to peaceful purposes.

Fourth, while awaiting the United Nations Secretary General's study on the effects of chemical and biological warfare, the United States Delegation should join with other delegations in exploring any proposals or ideas that could contribute to sound and effective arms control relating to these weapons.

Fifth, regarding more extensive measures of disarmament, both nuclear and conventional, the United States Delegation should be guided by the understanding that actual reduction of armaments, and not merely limiting their growth or spread, remains our goal.

Sixth, regarding the question of talks between the United States and the Soviet Union on the limitation of strategic arms, the United States hopes that the international political situation will evolve in a way which will permit such talks to begin in the near future.

In carrying out these instructions, the United States Delegation should keep in mind my view that efforts toward peace by all nations must be comprehensive. We cannot have realistic hopes for significant progress in the control of arms if the policies of confrontation prevail throughout the world as the rule of international conduct. On the other hand, we must attempt to exploit every opportunity to build a world of peace—to find areas of accord—to bind countries together in cooperative endeavors.

A major part of the work of peace is done by the Eighteen-Nation Disarmament Committee. I expect that all members of the United States Delegation will devote that extra measure of determination, skill, and judgment which this high task merits.

I shall follow closely the progress that is made and give my personal consideration to any problems that arise whenever it would be helpful for me to do so.

Please convey to all your colleagues my sincere wishes for success in our common endeavor. Over the years, their achievements at the Eighteen-Nation Dis-

armament Conference have been outstanding. I am confident that in the future our efforts, in cooperation with theirs, will be equal to any challenge and will result in progress for the benefit of all.

Sincerely,

RICHARD NIXON

[Honorable Gerard Smith, United States Representative, Eighteen-Nation Disarmament Conference, Geneva, Switzerland]

NOTE: The letter was dated March 15, 1969, and released March 18, 1969.

On March 13, 1969, the White House announced that Mr. Smith would hold the personal rank of Ambassador during his tenure as head of the U.S. delegation to the Conference of the Eighteen-Nation Disarmament Committee to convene in Geneva on March 18, 1969.

117   Remarks on Presenting the Boy of the Year Award. *March* 19, 1969

TODAY I am most honored to present the award to the Boy of the Year of the Boys' Clubs. This award is presented annually, but I have a special interest in it because I served as chairman of the Boys' Clubs of America before coming to the office which I presently hold.

On several occasions over those 5 years that I served as chairman of the Boys' Clubs I presented this award. It is a great honor for me to present it here at the White House to the Boy of the Year.

I hand you the plaque and I will read the citation here:

"Presented to Perry Joseph Ludy, chosen from the more than 800,000 members of the Boys' Clubs of America as Boy of the Year for 1969 in recognition of superlative service to his home, church, school, community, and Boys' Club. Perry typifies juvenile decency in action."

Now, that plaque reads very well, but I would like to add just an informal word with regard to Perry and his remarkable record. He is 17 years of age. He was president of his junior class and has been a leader in school activities in his high school. He was all-State in both basketball and track. He teaches a Sunday school class. He helps his mother in handling many of the household duties and giving leadership to the younger members of the family.

In addition to that he has participated in a number of activities in his community whenever he is called upon, not only the Boys' Clubs, where he has served in a number of very important positions, but also in drives for other volunteer organizations in his city of Oxnard.

Now, with all of this Perry has managed to be in the top 5 percent of his class

229

in high school. You can see, therefore, why he is the Boy of the Year, not only for Oxnard, California, but for the United States of America. We congratulate him. And with this award, not only goes the plaque but a $1,000 scholarship from the Reader's Digest; and I am sure that in view of that athletic accomplishment, you will probably get another scholarship, too.

MR. LUDY. Thank you, Mr. President. I would like to make this presentation to you, Mr. President. It is a life honorary membership to the Boys' Clubs of America, and also this is a replica of California, and it is presented by the Oxnard Boys' Club of Oxnard, California.

THE PRESIDENT. Well, thank you very much. We wish you the very best. Where are you going to college? Have you de-

cided yet?

MR. LUDY. No, sir, I have not decided. I have cut my list down to about six schools now. I am interested in pre-med.

THE PRESIDENT. You are going to be a doctor perhaps?

MR. LUDY. I hope so, yes.

THE PRESIDENT. You have cut your list down to six? For the boys at the top of their class with leadership capabilities this is a seller's market right now, isn't it? I can see that they would all want you. And we wish you the best.

NOTE: The President spoke at 11:50 a.m. in the Roosevelt Room at the White House. A White House release giving additional information on Mr. Ludy is printed in the Weekly Compilation of Presidential Documents (vol. 5, p. 438).

118   Remarks at the Swearing In of Donald L. Jackson as a Member of the Interstate Commerce Commission. *March* 20, 1969

BEFORE you have the swearing in, would you please sit down? I would like to indicate to all of those who are our guests here that it is not usual for the President to be present for the swearing in of a member of one of the Commissions. It seemed that there is always a reason for an exception, and since Don Jackson and I came from almost neighboring districts in California to the Congress 22 years ago, campaigned together—he in my district and I in his—and have been friends and associates through those years, that as he moves now to the Interstate Commerce Commission I wanted to be present.

I am very confident he will do a very effective job as a member of that Commission, just as he was one of the exceptional Members of the Congress beginning

in the 80th Congress, and as a member of the Foreign Affairs Committee. Since he is an expert in foreign affairs, he will now concentrate on commerce within the United States.

[At this point, the oath of office was administered by Attorney General John N. Mitchell. The President then resumed speaking.]

I have never heard the press applaud so much before. They are some of your colleagues, Mr. Jackson.

NOTE: The President spoke at 12:04 p.m. in the Roosevelt Room at the White House at the swearing in of Donald L. Jackson, Representative from California 1947–1961.

Following the President's remarks, Mr. Jackson spoke. The text of his remarks is printed in the Weekly Compilation of Presidential Documents (vol. 5, p. 440).

119 Remarks at Van Horn High School, Independence, Missouri. *March* 21, 1969

I AM DELIGHTED to have the opportunity, with Mrs. Nixon, to stop for a moment on our way out to see President Truman. It occurred to me that it would be worth reminding all of you that in just a month or so we will be celebrating the 20th anniversary of the NATO Alliance.

Most or all of you were born since that happened, but when that happened, when President Truman was President, I was a freshman Congressman, and as a Republican, I supported this concept which was developed by a Democratic President.

What I am trying to say to you today is that this visit, shortly before President Truman's 85th birthday, is a demonstration of the fact that where the strength of America is concerned and policies that will keep the peace of the world so that you young people will not have to be involved in any wars in the future, that

we are not Republicans or Democrats, we are Americans. That is what this visit is all about.

So, we thank you very much. We wish you the very best in your work, not only in high school, but in whatever endeavor you select in the future.

I can say that I have a particular understanding and affection for not only those who are students in high school, because two of our daughters have just been through that experience and then gone on to college, but also because my wife, when I met her, was a high school teacher. So treat your teachers real well.

Thank you.

NOTE: The President spoke at 11:16 a.m. at Van Horn High School, Independence, Mo. Following his remarks the President went to the Truman home and then accompanied former President and Mrs. Truman to the Truman Library.

120 Remarks at the Truman Library During a Visit With the Former President. *March* 21, 1969

Mr. President and Mrs. Truman, ladies and gentlemen:

I have a very special purpose and honor today and that is to present to President Truman the piano that he used when he was in the White House during the years he was in Washington.

To show you the special affection he had for this instrument, I have checked its history and I find that it was one of the few pieces of furniture that he moved from the White House to Blair House and had it in Blair House while the White House was being renovated, and then moved it, of course, back to the White

House. Then when President Truman left the White House, the instrument which the Steinway Company had loaned to the White House was kept there, and has been there for the last 16 years.

It seemed to me that since, in addition to the many other great contributions to the Nation President Truman has made, that he is certainly the most distinguished and accomplished pianist, that his piano from the White House ought to be in his library, and here it is, Mr. President.

PRESIDENT TRUMAN. I appreciate it very, very, very much.

I love piano music, but I can't play.

PRESIDENT NIXON. I have heard differently.

I would also like to say that, as I said a moment before, Mr. President, to the schoolchildren, I have just finished a trip to Europe. I met with the leaders of the great nations of Europe, and all of us were talking about the 20th anniversary of NATO, which will be celebrated in April in Washington. We hope you can come with Mrs. Truman.

I want to say, looking back to that day when NATO came into being, when I was a freshman Congressman and you were President of the United States, I am proud of the fact that, along with many other Republicans, I supported the Marshall Plan and the Turkish aid program; but particularly, I think, it is important to point out that without your leadership of the United States and the free world at that time, setting up this great Alliance, we would not have had the strength which has avoided a world war since that time.

I think that for a Republican President to say that about a man who served as President when he was in the Congress shows that where the defense of the United States is concerned, or peace is concerned, we are not Republicans or Democrats, but Americans.

PRESIDENT TRUMAN. That is true. Thank you very, very much.

MRS. TRUMAN. Aren't you going to play something?

PRESIDENT NIXON. I will play something for the President. I play everything in the key of G, Mr. President, by ear.

NOTE: The President spoke at 12:09 p.m. at the Harry S. Truman Library in Independence, Mo.

The President played "The Missouri Waltz," a song long associated with former President Truman.

121   Remarks on Arrival at Point Mugu Naval Air Station, Oxnard, California.   *March* 21, 1969

Commander Whipple, all of the distinguished guests here, and all of you who have welcomed us so graciously to California:

I want you to know that it is very good to be here, back in my home State, and also to have this opportunity to welcome back the Mobile Construction Battalion 3 from Vietnam.

We were remarking just as we got off the airplane that the Secretary of State and I both served in the Navy in World War II, and so consequently we have a special feeling toward this naval base and I for the Seabees, for a reason that I will mention.

The Secretary of State, when he was in the Pacific, was stationed on carriers. I was stationed on land as an administrative officer—an operations officer for a Marine transport air group. In that capacity I had the responsibility of selecting the particular mess that the very small detachment which I headed was to use.

I tried them all, as we went up through the chain of islands in the Solomons. I tried the Army. I tried the Marines. I tried the Air Force, and I tried the Navy—the regular Navy, that is. Finally I tried the Seabees, and that is what we settled on.

I can tell you that I don't say for one moment that the Marines and the Army and the Air Force don't serve this country well and don't present for the country some great fighting men, but I found during World War II that when it came to good food, the Seabees had the best in the Pacific—back 25 years ago before most of the men in this battalion were born.

That, of course, doesn't seem very important as you come back from your tour in Vietnam. I think what particularly is important to mention at this time is that over half the men in this battalion have had two tours in Vietnam, and a number of you have had three tours.

As you return we welcome you, we express appreciation for what you have done. This unit has had one of the most outstanding records of any unit in service in Vietnam.

As we express appreciation for what you have done in Vietnam, we want to pledge to you—I as President, the Secretary of State, all of us in this administration—that we, on our part, will assume our responsibility to do everything that we can to bring the war in Vietnam to an honorable conclusion; and by an honorable conclusion I mean the kind of conclusion so that we can have a better chance to live in a peaceful world, not have another war, so that your sons will not be fighting at another period in another war in the future.

In concluding, I simply want to say that as we look at that war and all of the sacrifices it has meant to so many families in America, it has been controversial here in the United States and in the world, but I, having been there many times, having seen what our fighting men have done, am proud of the young Americans that have been there—proud as an American, proud now as President and Commander in Chief.

I think that as I recognize what you have done, the sacrifices you have made, that I can assure you we will do everything we possibly can to see that those sacrifices were not in vain, and that we can build a world in which nations and peoples can live together in peace.

Thank you very much.

NOTE: The President spoke at 2:59 p.m. at Point Mugu Naval Air Station near Oxnard, Calif. Commander Caryll R. Whipple was the commanding officer of Mobile Construction Battalion 3.

The Battalion had been awarded the Vietnam Service Medal, the National Defense Service Medal, and had participated in the Navy Unit Commendation awarded to the 30th Naval Construction Regiment.

122   Remarks Following Inspection of Oil Damage at Santa Barbara Beach.   *March* 21, 1969

Mr. Mayor, Senator Lagomarsino, and all of the other people who have conducted me on this tour:

I appreciate the opportunity to see the damage and, secondly, to hear your very strong convictions with regard to what ought to be done to avoid this happening in the future.

I think that the State of California is very fortunate to have the Senator, to have a man who is very vigorously speaking up for the idea that all of us are concerned about here: to see that this area, one of the most beautiful areas of California, and the people of this area who have a special concern about this, will never be subjected to this kind of disaster in the future.

I was particularly interested in the

Senator's resolution which suggests that, whatever Federal regulations are adopted, there might be a joint State and Federal supervision of those regulations to be sure that they are adhered to. I will present this to the Committee when I go back.

SENATOR LAGOMARSINO. I might say, Mr. President, that this is the present situation on the onshore Federal property, Bureau of Land Management.

THE PRESIDENT. So you are simply suggesting that this be the case with regard to rights.

As all of you are aware, the Secretary of the Interior yesterday issued regulations that cover this area and also offshore drilling generally that are far more stringent than any that ever existed before.

That only indicates that the previous ones in the past have been inadequate.

Had the regulations which the Secretary issued yesterday been in effect at the time this disaster occurred, it would not have happened. I am, however, aware of the fact that the Mayor and Senator and others have suggested that this particular area is one that opposes any drilling whatever by the State or the Federal Government because of not only what has happened here, but because of the tremendous concern that this area be preserved for the future, not only the physical beauty we see in front of us, but also the potential beauty of the sea and all the beaches.

I shall, of course, consider this proposal. I will discuss it with the Secretary of the Interior and others who are concerned.

I can only say in conclusion that speaking as a Californian—and speaking as one who, when I was in high school and college and used to drive along these beaches, and in fact before my wife and I were married, when we used to drive all the way up from Whittier and down to Santa Bar-

bara and down these beaches—that I have a special feeling in my heart for this part of the State and of the Nation.

I recognize the tremendous interest of the people here to preserve this beauty, and it will be our responsibility to see that the regulations that the Federal Government adopts are adequate.

I believe that the Secretary of the Interior has gone a long way and, I trust, far enough to deal with the problems. The representatives of the city and the county believe it is not as far as it should be. I will take that into consideration, too.

One other point I should add: What is involved here, and it is sad that it is necessary that Santa Barbara has to be the example that had to bring this to the attention of the American people, but what is involved is something much bigger than Santa Barbara; what is involved is the use of our resources of the sea and the land in a more effective way and with more concern for preserving the beauty and the natural resources that are so important to any kind of society that we want for the future.

I don't think we have paid enough attention to this. All of us believe that, all of us who have watched America grow as it has grown so explosively since World War II.

Looking toward the end of the century in the next 25 years—and the decisions we make now will affect the next 25 years—that is why I have set up within the Cabinet a Cabinet group for the environment [1] which will consider not only problems like this, but the broader problems like the use of our resources in a way that

---

[1] The Environmental Quality Council and the Citizens' Advisory Committee on Environmental Quality were established by Executive Order 11472 of May 29, 1969.

will see that we have all the material progress that we need, but that we have that material progress not at the cost of the destruction of all those things of beauty without which all the material progress is meaningless.

This is what we believe, and I think that the Santa Barbara incident has frankly touched the conscience of the American people. It made headlines in Santa Barbara. I can assure you it made headlines in Washington and New York and all over this Nation.

As a result of that, we are all thinking,

in this administration, of this problem and we are going to do a better job than we have done in the past. It is up to the Federal Government to provide the leadership, and I know in the State here we will have all the cooperation of the State and the city.

NOTE: The President spoke at 3:55 p.m. on the beach near Santa Barbara, Calif. The mayor of Santa Barbara was Gerald Firestone. Robert J. Lagomarsino was California State senator for the 24th district.

The President's visit included an aerial tour of the damaged area.

123   Statement on Campus Disorders. *March* 22, 1969

THIS WEEK the Secretary of Health, Education, and Welfare has sent a letter [1] to the presidents of the institutions of higher education in the Nation calling attention to the provisions enacted in law by the 90th Congress which provide for the withdrawal of various forms of Federal support to students found guilty of violation of criminal statutes in connection with campus disorders.

He did this in the exercise of his responsibility as the Cabinet officer chiefly charged with the routine enforcement of Federal laws pertaining to education. However, the state of our campuses has for some time been anything but routine.

I should like to take this occasion to make some more general comments which I hope may be of some assistance in moderating the present turmoil.

First, a measure of perspective is in order with regard to the action of the previous Congress. The new regulations are

---

[1] Printed in the Congressional Record of March 25, 1969 (E 2538).

moderate, and they are justified. It is one of the oldest of the practices of universities and colleges that privileges of various kinds are withdrawn from students judged to have violated the rules and regulations of their institution. Congress has done no more than to withdraw Federal assistance from those students judged, not by university regulations, but by courts of law, to have violated criminal statutes. Almost by definition, given the present tactics of disruption, anyone so convicted may fairly be assumed to have been assaulting the processes of free inquiry which are the very life of learning. Any society that will not protect itself against such assault exhibits precious little respect for intellect, compared to which the issue of public order is very near to *de minimis*.

For there is a second issue, of far greater concern to me, and, as I believe, to the Congress, to the American people generally, and the faculties and students of American colleges and universities especially. That is the preservation of the

235

integrity, the independence, and the creativity of our institutions of higher learning.

Freedom—intellectual freedom—is in danger in America. The nature and content of that danger is as clear as any one thing could be. Violence—physical violence, physical intimidation—is seemingly on its way to becoming an accepted, or, at all events, a normal and not to be avoided element in the clash of opinion within university confines. Increasingly it is clear that this violence is directed to a clearly perceived and altogether too conceivable objective: not only to politicize the student bodies of our educational institutions but to politicize the institutions as well. Anyone with the least understanding of the history of freedom will know that this has invariably meant not only political disaster to those nations that have submitted to such forces of obfuscation and repression, but cultural calamity as well. It is not too strong a statement to declare that this is the way civilizations begin to die.

The process is altogether too familiar to those who would survey the wreckage of history: assault and counterassault, one extreme leading to the opposite extreme, the voices of reason and calm discredited. As Yeats foresaw: "Things fall apart; the center cannot hold. . . ." None of us has the right to suppose it cannot happen here.

The first thing to do at such moments is to reassert first principles. The Federal Government cannot, should not—must not—enforce such principles. That is fundamentally the task and the responsibility of the university community. But any may state what these principles are, for they are as widely understood as they are cherished:

First, that universities and colleges are places of excellence in which men are judged by achievement and merit in defined areas. The independence and competence of the faculty, the commitment, and equally the competence of the student body, are matters not to be compromised. The singular fact of American society, the fact which very likely distinguishes us most markedly from any other nation on earth, is that in the untroubled pursuit of an application of this principle we have created the largest, most democratic, most open system of higher learning in history. None need fear the continued application of those principles; but all must dread their erosion. The second principle—and, I would argue, the only other—is that violence or the threat of violence may never be permitted to influence the actions or judgments of the university community. Once it does, the community, almost by definition, ceases to be a university.

It is for this reason that from time immemorial expulsion has been the primary instrument of university discipline. Those who would not abide the rules of the community of learning have simply been required to leave it, for any other form of coercion would cause that community to change its fundamental nature.

The difficulty of this moment, as of most times when fundamental principles are challenged, is that many of those posing the challenges, and even more of those supporting them, are responding to very basic problems. To reassert, in the face of student protest, the first principles of academic freedom, while ignoring the issues that are foremost in the minds of those students, is less than inglorious: it is slothful and dishonest, an affront to those principles and, in the end, futile.

Students today point to many wrongs which must be made right:

—We have seen a depersonalization of the educational experience. **Our** institutions must reshape themselves lest this turn to total alienation.

—Student unrest does not exist in a vacuum but reflects a deep and growing social unrest affecting much of our world today. Self-righteous indignation by society will solve none of this. We must resolve the internal contradictions of our communities.

—There must be university reform including new experimentation in curricula such as ethnic studies, student involvement in the decisionmaking process, and a new emphasis in faculty teaching.

I have directed the Department of Health, Education, and Welfare to launch new initiatives toward easing tensions in our educational community.

This administration will always be receptive to suggestions for constructive reform. But the forces of separation and nonreason must be replaced by vigorous, persuasive, and lawful efforts for constructive change.

124   Remarks of Welcome at the White House to Prime Minister Trudeau of Canada.   *March* 24, 1969

Mr. Prime Minister, and ladies and gentlemen:

As most of you are aware, the Prime Minister is the first official visitor since the new administration assumed office.

In welcoming him personally today and also in welcoming him representing his country, I do so saying first that it is altogether appropriate that he should be the first official visitor to this country. Because as we look at the relations between your country and my country, Mr. Prime Minister, we recognize many factors that are often spoken about in the classroom and in the press and on television: We share the longest common border of all nations. We share the common law. We share a common language. We share many common characteristics with regard to our history. And, in addition to that, we share a very precious asset, the asset of friendship.

In describing that friendship, however, I would emphasize a characteristic about it that somteimes we forget. That characteristic is that the friendship that Canada and the United States have enjoyed for so many years is not characterized by that total unanimity of view which destroys creativity, but it is characterized by a lively diversity and through that diversity we have the hallmark of freedom.

As the Prime Minister and I will be talking, and as his associates will be talking with the Secretary of State and their opposite numbers, we will find most areas in which we are in agreement. We will find other areas in which we find that we have differences. But those differences are ones that, between friends, we will be able to discuss and find, in most instances, a common ground which is perhaps superior to the position that either of us had before.

This is the mark of true friendship. And it is why in speaking to you today, Mr. Prime Minister, I welcome you in behalf of all of the American people, so many of us who have known and enjoyed your country.

I can only add this: I only hope we can make you feel as much at home here in the United States as my wife and I, and so many hundreds of thousands of Americans, have been welcomed in your country when we have visited there as private citizens.

NOTE: The President spoke at 10:04 a.m. in the East Room at the White House. Earlier, Prime Minister Pierre Elliott Trudeau of Canada was given a formal welcome with full military honors at the North Portico.

See also Items 126 and 127.

Prime Minister Trudeau responded as follows:

Mr. President, ladies and gentlemen:

On behalf of my colleagues and myself, I want to thank you for your very cordial welcome.

I am very happy to be here. I feel very honored that you should have extended your welcome to me, sir, so early in the days of your new administration.

We have, as you say, very many ties which link us, ties of friendship and ties of common interest. And, especially, we have a common outlook on the world. We have the same values and we tend to face the issues in a common way.

It is because of this, Mr. President, that I am looking forward to our discussions, discussions of matters of mutual interest. And I am looking forward to listening to your views on world problems, on the information, and the wisdom that you will want to impart upon me in your talks.

For these reasons, I am very glad to be here. Like so many Canadians, I always look forward to a visit to the United States with great pleasure. I have great pleasure in being here and I am looking forward to my stay with great anticipation.

Thank you very much, sir, for your welcome.

125   Statement on Bank Holding Companies. *March* 24, 1969

THE Secretary of the Treasury, with my approval, has today transmitted to the Congress proposed legislation on the further regulation of bank holding companies.

Legislation in this area is important because there has been a disturbing trend in the past year toward erosion of the traditional separation of powers between the suppliers of money, the banks, and the users of money, commerce and industry.

Left unchecked, the trend toward the combining of banking and business could lead to the formation of a relatively small number of power centers dominating the American economy. This must not be permitted to happen; it would be bad for banking, bad for business, and bad for borrowers and consumers.

The strength of our economic system is rooted in diversity and free competition; the strength of our banking system depends largely on its independence. Banking must not dominate commerce or be dominated by it.

To protect competition and the separation of economic powers, I strongly endorse the extension of Federal regulation to one-bank holding companies and urge the Congress to take prompt and appropriate action.

126   Toasts of the President and Prime Minister Trudeau of Canada.   *March* 24, 1969

Mr. Prime Minister, and our distinguished guests:

In any new administration, every moment becomes a historical moment when it occurs. And this, Mr. Prime Minister, is a historical moment in this room because this is the first State dinner that has been held in this room since the new administration came to office.

We are very proud and honored that we can honor you and the people of Canada through this dinner.

In speaking in that vein, I also would like to point out that we have a number of reasons that you have a special place in our hearts, not only your people, but you, personally.

As I sat here in this room, I thought of the many moments that I have been here before, and I have heard on occasions President Eisenhower toast Winston Churchill and President de Gaulle, Konrad Adenauer, Prime Minister Nehru, the leaders of great nations all over the world.

Each of those was a very special occasion and each of those men and each of those nations had a special place in our hearts. But none has the really unique relationship that we have with our guests tonight.

I was thinking, for example, of the fact that during the years I was Vice President, along with my wife, I visited many countries on official visits, about 30 or 35. And I pointed out to the Prime Minister I had never made an official visit to Canada.

The reason was that I was only sent to those countries where we had trouble. And at that time, at least, we did not seem to have troubles that were so significant as to require my presence—or maybe they thought that if I went we would create troubles that were not ever there.

But despite the fact that we have missed the official visit, going back over the years, as I imagine every person in this room from the United States will probably be able to say: "We recall the times we have been to Canada and the warm welcomes we have received in Vancouver, in Quebec, Montreal, St. John's, Toronto, and Ottawa." And as we recall those moments and those associations, we realize how fortunate we are to have such good friends and neighbors along the longest boundary in the world.

I could speak more of the relationships of our two countries, but that will be covered in other speeches and communiqués and the rest.

I can only say that in this room tonight, Mr. Prime Minister, are people from all walks of life, from business and from labor, from the field of education, from the field of politics, Democrats and Republicans. But they are all as one in their affection for your country and in the respect for you.

And now, if it will not be embarrassing to the Prime Minister, I would like to say a personal word about him. And don't be worried. I can assure you that having sometimes been in this position myself of wondering what was coming up next, I will be careful with what I say.

But I was thinking of those many accolades that as an American, and particularly as an American political leader, we could pass on to you. I can refer to the fact that you are a distinguished political philosopher. I could refer to the fact that you are a distinguished member of the bar, eminently successful.

But since this is a room in which there are many from political life, what is the most impressive factor in your achievements to date is your political leadership.

When I think that the Prime Minister entered politics in 1965 and within 4 years became the head of government, believe me, for one for whom it took 22 long years to get here, we have, sir, for you the greatest respect for that political leadership which you have provided.

I do not need to say—and I do not say this simply because you are here—that you have been for your own people a very exciting personality, and you have been for the people of the United States.

We are glad to get to know you better. We are happy to exchange views with you. We particularly appreciate the opportunity to get the benefit of your thinking not only on the bilateral problems which we usually work out effectively and successfully, but on the great problems that will determine the future of all of us who live on this planet.

I was delighted in the long talk that I had with the Prime Minister today to find that here was a man who had the vision to see beyond the net election and to see what kind of continent we would have 25 years from now, 30 years from now. And on that great issue there can be no difference, fundamentally, in the goals that we seek—the people of the United States and the people of your country.

And so to all of our friends tonight, I would ask you to rise and to join me, as is the custom, in two toasts: first, Canada, as one of the strong members of the British Commonwealth, Her Majesty, The Queen; and then to our honored guest this evening, the Prime Minister of Canada.

NOTE: The President proposed the toast at 9:58 p.m. in the State Dining Room at the White House at a dinner in honor of Prime Minister Pierre Elliott Trudeau of Canada.

See also Items 124 and 127.

Prime Minister Trudeau responded as follows:

Mr. President and Mrs. Nixon, distinguished guests:

You do me great honor, Mr. President, in drinking my health. And the kind words you have spoken about me are all the more welcome and moving that they come not only from the head of the country which is Canada's best friend and ally, but they come from a man who has shown through his years in politics, 22, you said, Mr. President—that is about six times longer than myself, but then your country is ten times greater so it probably works out— a man who has shown that he could occupy many of the elective offices of his land and who now holds the highest elective office in his country, your country, the greatest, the most powerful on earth, a man who has served his country well with devotion, with knowledge, with wisdom, with fortitude, with courage, a man who has been persistent, a man who has been sincere and faithful.

For these reasons, sir, I thank you for your welcome. And I want to say that being one of Gallic descent, I have particular affinity for things American as I think the Americans have for things French and Gallic.

There is a saying, I know, in your land that every good American when he dies goes to Paris. I would suggest, Mr. President, that many of your fellow countrymen have not waited until they die nor until they be good to find Paris.

But I would be remiss in my duty if I didn't suggest that there is a very easy and pleasant alternative much closer at hand, Montreal, which welcomes all Americans and which would welcome you, Mr. President.

I hope you will be visiting our country as soon as your office permits. I can assure you you will be very welcome there. I can't guarantee that there will be no trouble. I can't guarantee it for myself. But as one new politican to a more mature one, I can tell you that we will take our chances together. And I think that the Canadian people will show you how much they respect and admire the President of the United States of America.

Every year many Americans come to Canada and the same number, more or less, of Canadians come to the United States—70 million border crossings last year, Mr. President.

We all come to the United States in pursuit of happiness of one kind or another. When I was a student and a younger man I pursued a different kind of happiness.

We come here, though, also to seek knowledge, to learn from your greater technology, from your great advances in science, from your great universities; we learn also from the hospitality of your people and from the great ideals and institutions that the leaders of your country have set up as models for humanity over the years.

We learn these things and we respect you for that. As one man who is a former Harvard graduate and coming to Washington at the beginning of a new administration, I can promise that I will stay less long than some others.

But I will say that many of the things that I learned in one of your great schools was about this fine sense of balance that the Americans had shown in their ideals and in their institutions and how from the very early days they tackled and solved this problem of eternal conflict between liberty and the rule of law, between the need for authority and the need for individual freedoms, how they tackled the problem of the individual wanting to be alone and yet needing society, and how over the decades and over the years your country has been able to adapt and meet these changes.

And I think all foreign students of your country come to admire most this great vitality, this toughness, this resilience of your great society and how rather than be too influenced by its mother country—of course you had a rather violent parting with your mother country, Mr. President. But we are perhaps in Canada a little bit too inclined to borrow from England and borrow from France. But you went out on your own and you invented this great institution of modern federalism, and you found this balance in your institutions between freedom and order.

That is why today when we see the mighty upheavals in your society we know you will meet them. We know you will find solutions and because you are so far ahead of other industrial societies we know that we will be able to learn from the lessons that you will give other nations who are trying to acquire this great industrial status.

We will learn from your errors. We will learn from your successes. And we know we will always have a helping hand in the United States.

There have been for so many years now, Mr. President, no tensions between our countries. It was your first President, George Washington, in his farewell address, who said that passionate relationships between one country and another engendered a host of evils.

Well, for a long time there have been no passionate relationships between our countries. There have been relationships based on discussion, on reason, on, as you put it this morning, sir, in welcoming me, the excitement of diversity. But always we have solved these through discussion, through reasonable men getting together and sometimes reasonable women getting together asking ourselves about our problem and seeking the best solution for everyone concerned.

And we know this will be the way of the future. I have learned in our discussions this morning, Mr. President, and this afternoon. I have seen how this will still be the pattern of relationship between our countries, a pattern based on wisdom rather than passion, a pattern based on a desire to understand rather than to dominate.

It was a Frenchman, de Tocqueville, who first described I think in a very able way the kind of delicate balance that the United States ideals and institutions were able to put forward. And he had a phrase, *si vous me permettez de traduire un peu librement,* which went about like this: That you don't receive truth from your enemies and your friends are rarely willing to offer it. "It is for this reason," he said, "that I have written these books."

Well, Mr. President, we are the kind of friends who do tell the truth to each other. We have told it this morning. I am sure we will tell it in the future.

We find that this kind of relationship is the only basis on which nations of the world can live in peace together—in understanding.

I want to say also how grateful I am to you, Mrs. Nixon, for your very gracious hospitality, for the wonderful food, the lovely flowers, and the exciting music. I feel almost as though I am among old friends. I hope we will become such.

But I do want to, in thanking you, ask the ladies and gentlemen assembled to drink your continued good health, sir, to drink the health of not only Canada's closest neighbor, the head of state which is Canada's closest neighbor, our longstanding ally, but also the health of a friend, President Nixon of the United States.

127   Remarks at the Conclusion of the Visit of Prime Minister Trudeau of Canada.   *March* 25, 1969

Mr. Prime Minister and ladies and gentlemen:

We have just completed a series of meetings, first a private talk between the Prime Minister and myself, and also a number of meetings at other levels of government between members of his party and members of the administration.

I think it could be said without fear of contradiction that this is one of the most successful meetings of this type—successful in the sense of the number of subjects covered and the progress which has been made in the solution of those subjects— ever held between the two countries.

We have issued to the press a joint statement [1] which will indicate the subjects that were discussed and the positions that were taken and several future meetings that are planned.

I have only two other brief things to add before the Prime Minister will have a chance to indicate his reactions to some of the subjects we discussed.

Your visit, Mr. Prime Minister, has provided us here an opportunity to know intimately the problems of your country, but also to know you. This we deeply appreciate.

I have been impressed by the candor and also by the restraint of the statements, the conversations that we have had.

As we work together in the years ahead, I am confident that the relationship will be a close one; it will be an honest one; it will be one where we will find some areas of disagreement, but far more areas of agreement.

We are so delighted that you came here so that we had the opportunity to know you in this way.

Finally, the Prime Minister has invited me to pay a visit to Canada. Mrs. Nixon and I are delighted to accept that invitation. We will arrange a time convenient to both the Prime Minister and ourselves at some later time.

But apart from that visit, I think that the members of the press should know that we have established several channels of communication; some existed before, new ones have been added at all Cabinet levels where there are common interests.

We found several new areas in which communications could go forward. As far as the Prime Minister is concerned, we will not talk only on official visits of this type, or like the one I will pay to his country; we will be in communication by tele-

---

[1] See the joint news briefing by Press Secretary Ronald L. Ziegler and Romeo LeBlanc, Press Secretary to the Prime Minister, printed in the Weekly Compilation of Presidential Documents (vol. 5, p. 467).

phone, of course, as well as through the diplomatic channels, because this is a new era of consultation and, we hope, cooperation between our countries who share so much together.

Thank you.

NOTE: The President spoke at 12:10 p.m. in the Rose Garden at the White House.

Prime Minister Pierre Elliott Trudeau of Canada responded as follows:

Mr. President, ladies and gentlemen:

I essentially want to state my agreement with what you just said, Mr. President. This has been 2 days of agreement in many areas, and I agree wholeheartedly with your summary of our meetings.

We have laid the groundwork, the foundations for consultation between our two countries, as you put it, in many areas, in my meetings with yourself, sir, with the Vice President, and with most ministers of your Cabinet.

We have covered a great deal of ground and we have established—I repeat your words—the channels through which very many of our bilateral problems can be tackled and solved.

We discussed at great length the problems of wheat and problems of oil, which are very important in our Canadian West. We discussed trade problems generally, and our approach to them in the world.

I find that we reached agreement, especially when we were looking outward, on the kind of value in which we believe, and I can only repeat what I said to you, sir, the admiration I have for the place you have put so early in your administration on consultation with your European friends, and then with us, that you should have taken such time so soon to state your points of views, to ask us questions, and to answer ours, is to us a guarantee, a symbol of the kind of warm relationships we will have.

It is appropriate that yesterday was kind of a rainy day, in which we did a lot of work, and today it is warming up and we can now—we have, in French, an expression: *L'important, c'est la rose.*

Well, the important thing is that we should be saying this in a rose garden under the sun, and this augurs well, I am sure, for all future relationships between yourself and us Canadians.

When I arrived, I brought you the greetings of the Canadian people, and I am proud now to go back and report to Parliament the cordiality of your welcome, sir, and the candid and sincere quality which you brought into all discussions, whether bilateral or looking outward towards the world.

I thank you very much for your hospitality. I will be looking forward to your visit and Mrs. Nixon's visit to Canada at a time when you can conveniently arrange it.

Thank you again so much.

128   Remarks at the Presentation of the Walt Disney Commemorative Medal.   *March* 25, 1969

Mrs. Disney, members of the Disney family, ladies and gentlemen, and all of our younger guests here today:

Many ceremonies are held in this White House, but none that I think will have more meaning to all of us, young and old, than this one today, because it is my great privilege to present to Mrs. Walt Disney, on behalf of the Congress of the United States, by reason of a joint resolution, and on behalf of all the people of the United States and, I think, of the world, a gold medal; a gold medal honoring Walt Disney for his service through so many years not only to the people of the United States, but to the people of the world.

The medal and the resolution will speak for themselves, but in making this presentation, and before I do so, I would like to just add a word that I know all of you would want to say to Mrs. Disney and to her children and to Walt Disney's brother, Roy Disney, and their family who are here today.

It is very hard to describe our feelings about Walt Disney. I say our feelings, because my wife and I had the opportunity of knowing him personally. He was just as exciting and interesting personally as he was in all of those wonderful movies that we remember through the years, starting with the cartoons and then the real-life ones and then "Mary Poppins," and all of the rest.

To know this man was to know that we had been fortunate to have a spirit with us that perhaps comes once in a generation to a fortunate people.

But I think we are all very lucky that we still have Walt Disney with us. We have him in his movies; we see him on television sometimes when we see those wonderful creations rerun, and of course, those of us who have the chance can go to Disneyland in California or Disneyland in Florida when it is completed, and there it all is, this man so creative, so imaginative, so fine.

You know in these days of entertainment when we do have on television and sometimes in the movies some kinds of entertainment that many think are not perhaps too constructive and too healthy—I was talking to Senator Pastore about this problem in my office yesterday—we are very fortunate to have had a Walt Disney, a Walt Disney who recognized that what was important was to make people happy.

You have heard some music today, and the theme of that music was "Dreams Coming True." If you think back about all of the music, the soundtracks from the Walt Disney films, looking ahead, dreams were coming true.

That is why he leaves for us a very special place in our hearts. And in our hearts that means a very special place in our hearts for you, Mrs. Disney, and for your family.

I once asked Walt Disney how I should describe him when we went out and dedicated the monorail at Disneyland. He said that he was an "imagineer," which means he was an engineer with imagination.

But he was more than that. He was a great artist. He was a perfectionist. He was a wonderful human being.

All of that he shared with us, not just with his family who loved him because they knew him, but he shared it with the world, and the world is a better and a happier and more joyful place in which to live because he was there.

Could I say a word to the children that are here? Most people, when they think of Walt Disney, think that he created his various movies and cartoons and the rest, and Disneyland just for children. But he didn't think that at all.

I once asked him about that, and he said, "Oh, that isn't true." He said: "I don't create just for children. I never talk down to them."

The reason he was successful, you see, was that he respected children—young people of all ages—and because he respected them he was able to communicate not only with the young people, but with the older people as well.

Perhaps that is what we all need today. When we talk about the problem of the generation gap, and how we are able to communicate with our children, we can learn from Walt Disney, a man who could communicate because he had that one quality which is so important. He had respect for an individual no matter how young he was, or how old.

So with those words, Mrs. Disney, I am

244

honored, on behalf of the Congress, to present this gold medal to you, and also to make presentations of bronze medals to the members of your family and also the Members of the House and the Senate who are here, who sponsored the joint resolution.[1]

In addition, I want to tell you that the sales of these commemorative medals will go to a very good purpose, and that is for the California Institute of the Arts, which will further the very programs that Walt Disney had such a vital interest in.

Thank you very much.

MRS. WALT DISNEY. I am very grateful to be here, and to see all of you wonderful children who knew him and loved him, too. I think this is a wonderful time in our life.

Thank you.

THE PRESIDENT. Thank you.

I think that since Senator Murphy is the ranking Member of the House and Senate that sponsored this resolution, we would like to hear a word from Senator Murphy. He knew and loved Walt Disney.

George, would you say a word?

SENATOR MURPHY. I would be very honored to. I think that the story of Walt Disney and Walt Disney's feeling for people and understanding has been very well expressed by the President this morning.

I, too, had the privilege of knowing him, knowing him quite well. He was one of the most wonderful individuals I think probably that ever lived.

---

[1] Senator George Murphy and Representatives Del Clawson, Bob Wilson, and Richard T. Hanna cosponsored the enabling legislation.

As you said so well, Mr. President, we are fortunate in this generation to have known him. We are particularly fortunate to have so many of his accomplishments and his works recorded on film and existing in the Disneyland parks, so that not only this generation, but generations to come can have the same enjoyment and the same privilege.

Thank you very much, Mr. President.

THE PRESIDENT. This is Walt's partner and brother, Roy Disney.

Thank you very much for coming. We are particularly happy to welcome all of our guests from California, and all of the schoolchildren from the Washington area. We hope that you will all get a chance to go to Disneyland sometime.

How many of the schoolchildren here have been to Disneyland? You see, quite a few, but not enough. We hope you all go either to the one in California or the one in Florida, because it is a wonderful treat.

How many of the adults have been to Disneyland? You are missing something.

Thank you very much.

NOTE: The President spoke at 11:05 a.m. in the State Dining Room at the White House. Some 200 third and fourth grade Washington area schoolchildren were invited to the White House for the ceremony followed by a party in the East Room.

The commemorative gold medal, authorized by Public Law 90–316 (82 Stat. 130) and struck by the U.S. Mint in Philadelphia, bears a likeness of Walt Disney on one side and Walt Disney's famous cartoon character, Mickey Mouse, on the other.

The text of a White House release describing the medal and the ceremony is printed in the Weekly Compilation of Presidential Documents (vol. 5, p. 469).

129 Remarks at the Convention of the National Association of Broadcasters. *March 25, 1969*

Mr. President, all distinguished guests at the head table, Mr. Pace, and all of the distinguished members of this audience:

As you know, I am an added starter today, and I was just saying to Frank Pace that I would not infringe too much on his time, because I know he is your scheduled speaker.

I sometimes have been in the position where somebody else came and infringed on my time, so I understand how this goes.

As I stand before you today, I have spoken in this room many times before, before many distinguished audiences. It isn't just because you are here, but only because it is a matter of fact and a statement of truth that this is without question one of the most powerful groups that I could address in the Nation.

I speak both from an objective standpoint, as I analyze the great influence that your organizations can have on the thinking of the American people, and I speak from a personal standpoint. Certainly I am the world's living expert on what television can do for a candidate, and what it can do to a candidate as well.

Having spoken of television, I don't mean to downgrade radio. We found it a very useful medium in the last campaign. While that is not the purpose of my remarks here today, I can only say that, looking to the future, I can only see growth and excitement in the tremendously interesting ventures in which you are engaged.

It occurred to me that what might be useful for you in brief remarks of this type would be for me to share some of the problems that a President has in attempting to run what we call an open administration, and in attempting to be candid and honest with regard to the great issues in which you are vitally interested.

I think if we were to pick one issue of all the others that the American people have an interest in, it is Vietnam. On that issue, on television, on radio, and in the newspapers, day after day, we hear speculation. We read it, about what is happening in Vietnam, what is happening on the battlefield, but more important, what is happening at the negotiating tables.

I want you to know what my belief is about the conduct of this war, about the negotiations, and about the prospects. What I say will not give you, perhaps, as much hope as you might like to hear. But what I say, I believe, is in the best interests of the result, and the result is ending the war on a basis that will promote real peace in the Pacific.

I could stand before you today and talk rather optimistically about the prospect of bringing boys home from Vietnam at a time when a Communist offensive is at a high peak. I can tell you that it will be the objective of this administration to bring men home from Vietnam just as soon as the military situation, the diplomatic situation, and the training of the South Vietnamese forces will enable us to do so.

But I can also tell you that I think it is not in the interests of the Nation for the President of the United States to stand before any audience and to raise hopes and then disappoint them. So I will only tell you today what our objective is.

I will tell you, looking toward the future, I think we are going to achieve that objective of a peace that will be one that will not just be for the year or 2 years, but for the foreseeable future in the Pacific and in the world—that kind of peace.

But in talking of what we do with regard to our troop strength there, I think all of you know that at this particular time as an offensive is going on, and as negotiations are beginning, it is vitally important that the United States maintain its position of strength until we have reason to believe that a reduction on our part would also have a major contribution in bringing about a reduction on their part.

So while I would like to make news here, while I would like to leave impressions that would go flashing out across the country about what is going to happen, in a hopeful way, I can only say—and I do not say this in any partisan sense, because I have been one that has supported, as you know, as a Republican, the efforts of our Nation in Vietnam—that I believe there has been too much of a tendency to speak of peace being just around the corner, the boys may be coming home in a matter of a few months, and thereby raising those optimistic feelings in the minds of people without justification, and then dashing them.

We shall not do this in this administration. We may not make the headlines of today, but what we are interested in are the results of tomorrow. I believe that is what you are interested in, and that is why we are going to follow this very candid and honest discussion insofar as our hopes are concerned.

Now I realize that in this room are not the broadcasters and the reporters—I mean by that the commentators and the reporters and all of the rest—but you are the managers, the people on the business side of the great television and radio installations around the country. I think all of you will understand the next point that I will make particularly well.

Two or three weeks ago, I noted considerable criticism of the administration because we had not, at the time that I was in Paris, announced that we were starting private talks with the enemy in order to negotiate those areas of difference and bring the day of peace closer.

Now let me be quite candid. As far as any negotiated peace is concerned, it will come from private rather than public talks because where both sides—and I am referring now particularly to the North Vietnamese and the South Vietnamese—have a problem of prestige and a problem of face among many others involved, that kind of negotiation cannot take place in a goldfish bowl with communiqués every day, because there the tendency always is to speak to their people at home, but more than that to the people of the world, and to simply repeat the old rhetoric.

Most of the progress that has been made today in bringing about talks in a public forum has come from private talks.

So, I can tell you that it is our conviction and our belief that it is through private talks with the North Vietnamese and others involved that real progress toward peace will be made.

But, if private talks are to be private, they must be private. Consequently, if I am asked—and this is true of the Secretary of State and it is true of the Secretary of Defense, and my instructions to everybody in this administration—as to whether private talks have begun, as to when they will begin, as to what has occurred, we will say nothing. Because the moment we tell you, any of you—and let me say the questions are always proper, sometimes the answers would not be appropriate on our part—but I can only say that if we are to make progress in private talks they must be private.

Therefore, to disclose when and where and what and how in any degree would not serve the interests of peace. Now, again, I realize that it would raise hopes. It would make a good headline, and a good first 2 minutes on the evening show, if I were to indicate that we were proceeding in private talks or what was going on.

But let me say that that would not serve the long-range interests of bringing peace. I can only assure you that there is no objective of this administration that is higher—and let me say this was also true of the other administration, but we are proceeding in different ways—than to bring this war to a conclusion at the earliest possible time in a manner that will promote real peace.

We think we are on the right track but we are not going to raise false hopes. We are not going to tell you what is going on in private talks. What we are going to do is to do our job and then a few months from now, I think you will look back and say we did what was right. If we did what was wrong then it doesn't make any difference, the headline that we have made today. So, this will be our policy in that respect.

Again, I think that you as negotiators will recognize the validity of that position. Much as we want an open administration, there are times when it is necessary to have those quiet conversations without publicity in which each side can explore the areas of difference and eventually reach an agreement which then, of course, publicly will be announced.

If Frank Pace will indulge me just a little longer, I understand there has been some interest in the ABM Safeguard sys-

tem which I have talked about. I am not here to twist your arms or to attempt to influence you one way or another. All of you, as far as that system, the defense of the country, in all of these matters, must examine the evidence and then make your own decisions with regard to what is in the best interests of the Nation.

But I would like to share with you briefly the considerations that went into that decision—not an easy decision. In fact, the easy decision would have been not to make it. The easy decision would have been to put it off, to have research and development, or to indicate that there was no significant threat, or that it wouldn't work, or that it really didn't matter.

But I can tell you that these were the factors that we were confronted with and which we had to deal with, and which made it necessary for us to announce a hard decision rather than an easy one. We hope it is the right one. We think it is. That is for you to judge. It is for the American people to appraise.

I found when I came to office that in 1962, when the Cuban confrontation occurred, that the balance of power between the United States and the Soviet Union was approximately four or five to one in our favor. Because of that balance of power in our favor, the President of the United States in a very courageous decision was able to act in the best interests of the United States and avoid a missile installation 90 miles from our shore.

If the United States had not had that kind of assurance—not only the assurance of our power but also a recognition that those who threatened our security at that time, the Soviet Union, had a recognition on their part that we had that kind of strength—if that had not been the case that decision might not have been made or it would have been much more dangerous to make.

Now, what has happened from 1962 to 1969? Since that time the Soviet Union has widened the gap in conventional weapons which they have always had in Western Europe. They have rapidly closed the gap in naval strength, particularly in the Mediterranean, and they have substantially closed the gap in strategic weapons. So, we look at that situation today. And in describing it, let me lay to rest one point of view that I saw expressed in some reaction to Secretary Laird's testimony. In describing this, this is no cause for fright.

The United States is still infinitely strong and powerful. We are still able to meet any potential threat. But the problem that the President of the United States faces as the Commander in Chief and as the one who has the responsibility to see that our defenses are adequate to make peaceful diplomacy possible, the responsibility that he has is to examine not only what the situation is now but what it will be 4 or 5 years from now. And the decision that I made here and the decisions I will be making on all defense matters, I can assure you, will have one consideration only.

I do not believe that the United States should threaten any other nation. We are not interested in aggression. I do believe, however, that without the power of the United States the great hundreds of millions of people who live in the free world would not have had the assurance of freedom that they have had. In other words, it is the power of the United States that has avoided a world war and a world confrontation.

And whether it is in my administration or in the next, I never want the President of the United States, when he sits down at a conference table, to be in a second-rate position as far as the strength of the United States is concerned. [*Applause*]

I am not suggesting that that means we embark on an arms race. I am not suggesting that that means that we go forward in order to regain the four or five to one superiority that we once had. That will not happen. But I am suggesting that when we look at those facts, there are some limited actions that the United States, I think, should take.

One involves the ABM Safeguard system. What this system will do, first, is to provide some protection for our deterrent capability, our Minuteman sites. That means our second strike capability. This was necessary because we found that the Soviet Union had developed new weapons with greater accuracy, the SS9, that could take out our hardened Minuteman sites, and thereby reduce the credibility of our second strike capability.

The credibility of the American second strike is essential, diplomatically and also in the long range as far as preserving peace in the world. In addition to that, the ABM Safeguard system provides an area defense of the entire United States for any attack by the Chinese Communists within the next 10 years, or any other nuclear power which might acquire such weapons in that period.

Let me emphasize what Safeguard does not do. There is no way at this time that we can safeguard all of the American people through antiballistic missiles against an attack by a sophisticated major nuclear power like the Soviet Union. But we can increase the credibility of our second strike force by defending our Minuteman sites.

On the other hand, when we look at a

less developed nuclear power with fewer missiles, it is possible to develop the area defense which will be effective. So, those were the two purposes of making that decision.

Now, many questions arise. First, will it work? Those for whom I have great respect, including perhaps beyond others the Deputy Secretary of Defense, Mr. [David] Packard, an expert in this field, say that it will. And some indication that it must have some meaning is that the Soviet Union has deployed 66 of this type of defense around Moscow and are now covering not only the threat from the West but also from Communist China.

But in order to guard against plunging into a program that would be a boondoggle, we have made the decision on a phase basis.

Every year we will examine this new system with the minimal appropriations for this year, which you are aware of, with three things in mind:

One, progress that may be made on arms talks.

Two, progress that may be made on the state of the art, whether or not it proves that it is something that we can do or that we cannot do.

And finally, we shall always examine this system in terms of the overall capability of the United States and our responsibilities in the world which I have described up to this time.

Let me conclude with this final thought: Any of you, and I know many of you have been exposed to briefings on the massive destructive power of nuclear weapons, must sometimes wonder why enough isn't enough.

As some have put it, with regard to the potential of a Chinese threat, why should we be concerned, because assuming 8 or 10 years from now they have 60 or 70 or 80 missiles, and assuming that is the case, no rational man who was the leader of that country would launch an attack against the United States knowing that our immense retaliatory power would destroy half of the population of Communist China.

I agree with that analysis. But when we examine history, we find within the last third of a century that sometimes decisions by great powers, as well as small, are not made by rational men. Hitler was not a particularly rational man in some of his military decisions.

So it is the responsibility of the President of the United States not only to plan against the expected, and against what normal and rational men will do, but within a certain area of contingency to plan against the possibility of an irrational attack.

To do all this, having in mind maintaining the necessary balance between security and freedom which is so essential, this we have tried to do. I think the decision was a correct one.

In presenting it to you in this way today, as I have presented it previously, I can only say and repeat what I have said earlier, that all of us, whatever our partisan affiliations, have one primary goal in mind. That is peace in the world—peace in the world which is the real peace that comes from the kind of security that only the United States can provide.

I have just met with the Canadian Prime Minister. I have just completed meetings with the heads of government of the major European powers. And I have been reminded again of this fundamental fact: Without the power of the

United States of America, the rest of the world would be, in effect, at the mercy of potential diplomatic aggression, and that is really what is at stake here.

We have a responsibility. We have met it ever since World War II, and I believe that now it is our destiny to continue to meet it, while at the same time— and I can assure you we are exploring this other road—to pursue every path toward peace, and to pursue every path toward

arms limitations, so that we can divert our resources to other areas than those of destruction.

Thank you.

NOTE: The President spoke at 1:25 p.m. in Sheraton Hall at the Sheraton-Park Hotel in Washington. Vincent T. Wasilewski was president of the National Association of Broadcasters, and Frank Pace, Jr., was chairman of the board of the Corporation for Public Broadcasting.

130   Remarks on Accepting the "Sword of Hope" of the American Cancer Society Crusade.   *March* 25, 1969

I THANK YOU very much. We are very happy to have this sword among our mementos here at the White House, and when we see it we will think of you and your mother and father.

In accepting this sword and also in responding to the remarks that have been made, I think it is very appropriate to open this National Cancer Month with some statistics.

I was frankly surprised at what had happened, the progress that had been made, because, like most laymen, I have always felt that when we hear about cancer, it was assumed that it was incurable. I find that 1½ million have been cured. I recall that when I came to the Congress 20 years ago, when I first met Mr. Elmer Bobst, one of the founders of the national Cancer Society, at that time one out of four were cured.

Since that time, and that is only 20 years, it is now down to one out of three have been cured of cancer. I understand that if the American Cancer Society's programs and other programs for getting people to take checkups and also for going forward in research are successful,

that one out of every two who get cancer can be cured. That is the objective of this program and that is the program we are all supporting.

I think you have a very good slogan, too. As I understand it, it says that the people of the United States are told to help fight cancer by getting a checkup and sending your check.

In speaking of the checkups, too, I found another interesting statistic that I think will be of great interest to the American people, and particularly to the men who are listening to this program. I find that as far as checkups are concerned, 46 percent of all women get annual checkups, but only 13 percent of the men.

This is the great deficiency, a gap which exists there, as far as the checkups are concerned, which reminds me it is about time I got my checkup.

We do, by participating in this ceremony, want to indicate the Nation's support as well as the Government's support of this volunteer effort. Over 2 million volunteers will be distributing the booklets of the American Cancer Society, telling people the very simple things they can do

251

to get a checkup.

This kind of volunteer activity and the fighting of this dread disease is a wonderful example for all of us who are working in government or in other fields. We thank you for coming—for reminding us of it.

I understand that Mrs. Nixon is the honorary chairman of the drive. You will have her complete support as well as mine.

NOTE: The President spoke at 4 p.m. in the Roosevelt Room at the White House. Tele-

vision personality Virginia Graham, 1969 Crusade Chairman, introduced former cancer patient, 9-year-old Dyana Butler of East Point, Ga., who presented the symbolic "Sword of Hope" to the President. The President also received the first copy of an educational leaflet entitled, "If You Ignore It."

On March 25, 1969, the President signed Proclamation 3903 "Cancer Control Month, 1969."

An announcement of the ceremony inaugurating the drive is printed in the Weekly Compilation of Presidential Documents (vol. 5, p. 476).

---

131 Message to the Senate Transmitting Broadcasting Agreements With Mexico. *March* 25, 1969

To the Senate of the United States:

With a view to receiving the advice and consent of the Senate to ratification, I transmit herewith two separate but related agreements between the United States of America and the United Mexican States signed at Mexico City on December 11, 1968, namely:

(1) an agreement concerning radio broadcasting in the standard broadcasting band (535–1605 kHz), and

(2) an agreement concerning the operation of broadcasting stations in the standard band (535–1605 kHz), during a limited period prior to sunrise ("pre-sunrise") and after sunset ("post-sunset").

I transmit also, for the information of the Senate, the report of the Secretary of State with respect to the two agreements.

Since the end of 1967, when the broadcasting agreement of January 29, 1957 ceased to be in force, there has been no agreement governing the relations between the United States and Mexico in the use of the standard broadcasting band.

Relations of the United States with other major countries in the North American Region in the broadcasting field continue to be governed by the North American Regional Broadcasting Agreement of November 15, 1950, to which Mexico is not a party.

The two agreements with Mexico have been concluded after negotiations extending over a period of more than two years between United States and Mexican delegations, with representatives of the United States broadcasting industry participating as advisers to the United States delegation. The Federal Communications Commission and the Department of State express the opinion that the best interests of the United States would be served by ratification and entry into force of both agreements, the substance of which is understood to be generally satisfactory to broadcasting interests in the United States.

The first-mentioned agreement, referred to as the broadcasting agreement, contains detailed provisions designed to resolve many engineering and allocation problems between the United States and Mexico, as explained more fully in the report of the Secretary of State.

The other agreement, referred to as the pre-sunrise/post-sunset agreement, is tied to the broadcasting agreement in the sense that it can be effective only so long as the broadcasting agreement remains in effect. The regulations therein for station operation with daytime facilities for limited periods of time before the sunrise-to-sunset period heretofore prescribed will enable the Federal Communications Commission to implement plans for pre-sunrise operation of United States daytime stations, so that, for the first time, it will be possible for a large number of such stations, now operating on seven clear (I–A) channels accorded to Mexico in the broadcasting agreement, to have uniform starting times throughout the year. Whereas the United States would gain

from the provisions for pre-sunrise operation, Mexico would gain from the post-sunset provisions.

The two agreements would be brought into force by the exchange of instruments of ratification and would remain in effect for a term of five years and indefinitely thereafter unless replaced by a new agreement or unless terminated by a one-year written notice from either party to the other party.

I recommend that the Senate give early and favorable consideration to the two agreements with Mexico.

RICHARD NIXON

The White House
    March 25, 1969

NOTE: The treaties were favorably considered by the Senate on June 19, 1969, and the President signed the instrument of ratification on July 2, 1969. The texts of the treaties and the report of the Secretary of State are printed in Senate Executive B (91st Cong., 1st sess.).

132   Special Message to the Congress on Fiscal Policy. *March 26, 1969*

To the Congress of the United States:

Clearly this Nation must come to grips with the problem of an inflation that has been allowed to run into its fourth year. This is far too long, and it has already caused substantial distortions in our economy.

Inflation is a form of economic aggression against the very young and the very old, the poor and the thrifty. It is these Americans who are largely defenseless against the kind of price increases for food, clothing, medicine, housing and education that have swept over the Nation in the last few years.

Government has two major instruments

for dealing with this problem. One is monetary policy, which should continue its program of restraint. The other is fiscal policy—the management of the Federal budget—which must turn away from budgets which have propelled the inflation, and turn instead to one with a strong surplus that will help to curb it.

The prospect of a thin budget surplus or a return to deficits would again nudge monetary policy off course. The result, as always, would be further increases in interest rates, a dangerously overheated economic engine, and the threat of accelerating the advance of the price level. Because the problem of inflation was neglected far too long, we cannot risk even a neutral budget policy of narrow balance.

Only a combined policy of a strong budget surplus and monetary restraint can now be effective in cooling inflation, and in ultimately reducing the restrictive interest rates forced on us by past policies. This is fundamental economics, and we intend to deal with fundamentals.

We are determined to keep faith with America's wage earners, farmers and businessmen. We are committed to take every necessary action to protect every American's savings and real income from further loss to inflation.

The budget for the year beginning July 1, 1969, submitted in January, estimates the surplus at $3.4 billion. However, current examination of this budget reveals that some of its estimates of expenditures were low. For example, interest on the Federal debt will be far more than was estimated. This, along with such items as an underestimate of farm price support payments and a substantial overestimate of offshore oil lease receipts, means that a current analysis of the budget submitted in January shows a reduction in the surplus of $1.3 billion for this fiscal year and $1.7 billion for the fiscal year 1970.

Thus, half of the projected 1970 surplus has disappeared before the year begins. Similarly, more than half of this year's projected surplus of $2.4 billion will not be realized—and for the same reasons.

On the Matter of Cutting Expenditures

To produce a budget that will stop inflation, we must cut expenditures while maintaining revenues. This will not be easy. Dealing with fundamentals never is.

I intend to submit budget revisions which will reduce Federal spending in fiscal 1970 significantly below the amount recommended in January, even before those previous figures have been adjusted to reflect current conditions.

On the Matter of Maintaining Revenues

I am convinced that the path of responsibility requires that the income tax surcharge, which is expected to yield $9½ billion, be extended for another year. As I have said before, the surcharge is a temporary tax that must be ended as soon as our commitments in Southeast Asia and economic conditions permit. Because of budget and economic conditions, I reaffirm my support of the recommendation President Johnson made last January that the surcharge be extended, and I am transmitting to the Congress a request that this be done.

In addition, the scheduled reductions in the telephone and passenger car excise taxes must be postponed, and user charges equal in revenue yield to those now in the budget should be enacted. Together, these will produce close to $1 billion in revenue next year.

On the question of tax reform, this Administration remains committed to a more equitable and more efficient tax structure. In the coming month, the first specific proposals of that reform will be coming up to the Congress from the Treasury Department.

Taken together, these actions to reduce spending and maintain revenues will produce the strong budget surplus urgently needed to meet the inflationary threat.

Moreover, by proving Government's serious intent to counter the upward spiral of prices and wages, we will create conditions which will encourage the private sector to stop assuming a high rate of inflation in long-range planning.

Courageous Government action will modify the inflationary psychology which now afflicts business, labor and consumers generally. It is particularly hard on small business, and those of modest means in the management of their incomes and savings.

This ordering of our economic house—distasteful as it is in many respects—will do much to slow down the rise in the cost of living, help our seriously weakened

position in international trade, and restore the sound basis for our on-going prosperity.

RICHARD NIXON

The White House
  March 26, 1969

NOTE: A White House release issued the same day, summarizing the President's supplemental appropriations requests for fiscal year 1969, is printed in the Weekly Compilation of Presidential Documents (vol. 5, p. 479).

133   Letter to a Student Concerning the Miami Teen-Age Rally for Decency.   *March* 26, 1969

Dear Mike:

I was extremely interested to learn about the admirable initiative undertaken by you and 30,000 other young people at the Miami Teen-age Rally for Decency held last Sunday.

This very positive approach which focused attention on a number of critical problems confronting society strengthens my belief that the younger generation is our greatest natural resource and therefore of tremendous hope for the future.

I hope that you will express my appreciation to everyone involved and my congratulations on the success of their efforts.

Sincerely,

RICHARD NIXON

[Mr. Mike Levesque, 401 To-To-Lo-Chee Drive, Hialeah, Florida 33000]

NOTE: The letter was dated March 25, 1969, and released March 26, 1969. Mike Levesque, 17, senior at Miami Springs High School, was the organizer of the rally.

134   Statement on Establishing Common Regional Boundaries for Agencies Providing Social and Economic Services.   *March* 27, 1969

THE REORGANIZATION ACT which the Congress has passed and which I am signing today [1] gives the President important tools in his effort to make the machinery of government work more effectively. As a part of that same effort, I am announcing today certain structural changes which I am making in the systems through which the Government provides important social and economic services.

It was possible for me to take these particular actions without the authority extended under the Reorganization Act. I announce them at this time, however, because they provide specific illustrations of ways in which we can make significant improvement in the quality of government by making it operate more efficiently.

This restructuring expresses my concern that we make much greater progress in our struggle against social problems. The

---

[1] Public Law 91–5 (83 Stat. 6).

best way to facilitate such progress, I believe, is not by adding massively to the burdens which government already bears but rather by finding better ways to perform the work of the Government.

That work is not finished when a law is passed, nor is it accomplished when an agency in Washington is assigned to administer new legislation. These are only preliminary steps; in the end the real work is done by the men who implement the law in the field.

The performance of the men in the field, however, is directly linked to the administrative structures and procedures within which they work. It is here that the Government's effectiveness too often is undermined. The organization of Federal services has often grown up piecemeal; creating gaps in some areas, duplications in others, and general inefficiencies across the country. Each agency, for example, has its own set of regional offices and regional boundaries; if a director of one operation is to meet with his counterpart in another branch of the Government, he often must make an airplane trip to see him. Or consider two Federal officials who work together on poverty problems in the same neighborhood, but who work for different departments and, therefore, find themselves in two different administrative regions, reporting to headquarters in two widely separated cities.

Coordination cannot flourish under conditions such as that. Yet without real coordination, intelligent and efficient government is impossible; money and time are wasted and important goals are compromised.

This is why I said in the campaign last fall that "the need is not to dismantle government but to modernize it." The systematic reforms I announce today are

designed to help in that modernization process. I would discuss those reforms under three headings: rationalization, coordination, and decentralization. It should be recognized, of course, that the three elements are interdependent. Without one the others would be meaningless.

I. The first concern is to rationalize the way our service delivery systems are organized. I have therefore issued a directive which streamlines the field operations of five agencies by establishing, for the first time, common regional boundaries and regional office locations. This instruction affects the Department of Labor; the Department of Health, Education, and Welfare; the Department of Housing and Urban Development; the Office of Economic Opportunity; and the Small Business Administration. The activities of these agencies—particularly in serving disadvantaged areas of our society—are closely related. Uniform boundaries and regional office locations will help assure that they are also closely coordinated.

The eight new regions and the locations of the new regional centers are as follows:

Region I (Boston)—Connecticut, Maine, Massachusetts, New Hampshire, Rhode Island, and Vermont;

Region II (New York City)—New York, New Jersey, Puerto Rico, and the Virgin Islands;

Region III (Philadelphia)—Delaware, District of Columbia, Kentucky, Maryland, North Carolina, Pennsylvania, Virginia, and West Virginia;

Region IV (Atlanta)—Alabama, Florida, Georgia, Mississippi, South Carolina, and Tennessee;

Region V (Chicago)—Illinois, Indiana, Minnesota, Michigan, Ohio, and Wisconsin;

Region VI (Dallas-Fort Worth)—Arkansas, Louisiana, New Mexico, Oklahoma, and Texas;

Region VII (Denver)—Colorado, Idaho, Iowa, Kansas, Missouri, Montana, Nebraska, North Dakota, South Dakota, Utah, and Wyoming;

Region VIII (San Francisco)—Alaska, Arizona, California, Guam, Hawaii, Nevada, Oregon, and Washington.

I am asking all other Federal agencies to take note of these instructions, and I am requesting that any changes in their field organization structures be made consistent with our ultimate goal: uniform boundaries and field office locations for all social or economic programs requiring interagency or intergovernmental coordination.

My directive also asks that the five departments and agencies involved provide high-level representation in cities where regional offices do not exist. Such physical relocations as are required will be made over the next 18 months, with special efforts to minimize disruptions to the programs, the employees, and the communities involved.

II. The second step in this reform process emphasizes coordination. It calls for an expansion of the regional council concept from the four cities where it presently operates (Chicago, New York, Atlanta, and San Francisco) to all eight of the new regional centers. The regional council is a coordinating body on which each of the involved agencies is represented. It offers an excellent means through which the various arms of the Federal Government can work closely together in defining problems, devising strategies to meet them, eliminating friction and duplications, and evaluating results. Such councils can make it possible for the Federal Government to speak consistently and with

a single voice in its dealings with States and localities, with private organizations, and with the public.

III. The third phase of this systematic restructuring of domestic programs focuses on decentralization. I am asking the Director of the Bureau of the Budget to join with the heads of nine departments and agencies in a review of existing relationships between centralized authorities and their field operations. Participating in the review will be the Departments of Agriculture; Commerce; Health, Education, and Welfare; Housing and Urban Development; Labor; Transportation; Justice; the Office of Economic Opportunity; and the Small Business Administration.

This review is designed to produce specific recommendations as to how each agency: (1) can eliminate unnecessary steps in the delegation process, (2) can develop organizational forms and administrative practices which will mesh more closely with those of all other departments, and (3) can give more day-by-day authority to those who are at lower levels in the administrative hierarchy. Decentralized decisionmaking will make for better and quicker decisions; it will also increase cooperation and coordination between the Federal Government on the one hand and the States and localities on the other. Those Federal employees who deal every day with State and local officials will be given greater decisionmaking responsibility.

Again, this action is a concrete manifestation of a concern I expressed during the campaign: "Business learned long ago that decentralization was a means to better performance. It's time government learned the same lesson."

Some of the reforms which I am announcing today have been urged for many years, but again and again they have been thwarted. This inertia must be overcome. Old procedures that are inefficient, however comfortable and familiar they may seem, must be exchanged for new systems which do the job as it must be done.

The particular reforms I have discussed here are part of a broad and continuing process of restructuring the basic service systems of government. The reorganization of the Manpower Administration in the Department of Labor, announced on March 13, is another example of this process. So are the reforms which are being made in the postal system and in the Office of Economic Opportunity.

I have established both the Urban Affairs Council and the Office of Intergovernmental Relations in part so that the Government could be better advised on additional improvements in service systems. Further systematic restructuring is on the way. Each reform, I believe, will

have a major impact on the quality of American government—an impact which will benefit all of our citizens, in all parts of our country—well beyond the lifetime of this administration.

The Federal Government has been assigned many new responsibilities in the last several decades, many of which it carries and many of which it fumbles. Many of the disappointments and frustrations of the last several years can be blamed on the fact that administrative performance has not kept pace with legislative promise.

This situation must be changed. The actions I announce today are important steps toward achieving such changes. By rationalizing, coordinating, and decentralizing the systems through which government provides important social and economic services, we can begin at last to realize the hopes and dreams of those who created them.

135 Statement Announcing Appointment of the President's Commission on an All-Volunteer Armed Force. *March 27, 1969*

TO ACHIEVE the goal of an all-volunteer force we will require the best efforts of our military establishment and the best advice we can obtain from eminent citizens and experts in many related fields of national endeavor. For this purpose, I have today appointed an advisory Commission on an All-Volunteer Armed Force under the chairmanship of the Honorable Thomas S. Gates, Jr., former Secretary of Defense.

I have directed the Commission to

develop a comprehensive plan for eliminating conscription and moving toward an all-volunteer armed force. The Commission will study a broad range of possibilities for increasing the supply of volunteers for service, including increased pay, benefits, recruitment incentives, and other practicable measures to make military careers more attractive to young men. It will consider possible changes in selection standards and in utilization policies which may assist in eliminating the need for inductions. It will study the estimated costs and savings resulting from an all-volunteer force, as well as the broader social and economic implications of this program.

The transition to an all-volunteer armed force must, of course, be handled cautiously and responsibly so that our national security is fully maintained. The Commission will determine what standby machinery for the draft will be required in the event of a national emergency and will give serious consideration to our requirements for an adequate reserve forces program.

I have instructed the Department of Defense and other agencies of the executive branch to support this study and provide needed information and assistance as a matter of high priority.

The Commission will submit its report to me in early November 1969.

NOTE: Press Secretary Ronald L. Ziegler announced that William Meckling, dean of the College of Business Administration of the University of Rochester, New York, would serve as Executive Director of the Commission. A list of the members of the Commission is printed in the Weekly Compilation of Presidential Documents (vol. 5, p. 482).

136   Memorandum on Equal Employment Opportunity in the Federal Government.   *March* 28, 1969

Memorandum to Heads of Departments and Agencies:

SUBJECT: Equal Employment Opportunity

The concept of nondiscrimination is inherent in the Civil Service Act of 1883, which calls for a Federal service based on merit and fitness alone. "Nondiscrimination" was broadened by President Eisenhower to "equal employment opportunity" with his issuance of Executive Order 10590 in 1955. In the years that followed, other Executive Orders designed to insure equal opportunity in the employment, development, advancement and treatment of employees of the Federal Government have been issued. This series of Presidential directives reflects continuing support for this program at the highest levels of Government.

I want to emphasize my own official and personal endorsement of a strong policy of equal employment opportunity within the Federal Government. I am determined that the Executive Branch of the Government lead the way as an equal opportunity employer.

Although under the leadership of the Civil Service Commission significant progress has been made towards the goal of equal employment opportunity, much remains to be done. Accordingly, I have directed the Chairman of the Commission to make a thorough review of all present efforts to achieve equal employment opportunity within the Federal Government and to report back to me on or before May 15, 1969, with recommendations for desirable policy and program changes in regard to those efforts.

Meanwhile, I want every reasonable

259

effort made to insure that the Federal Government is an equal opportunity employer. I further urge you, if you have not already done so, to communicate your

personal support for this program to all officials and employees of your agency.

RICHARD NIXON

137 Statement on the Death of General Eisenhower. *March 28, 1969*

GENERAL EISENHOWER held a unique place in America's history, and in its heart, and in the hearts of people the world over.

For a quarter of a century he spoke with a moral authority seldom equaled in American public life. This was not only because he held the Nation's highest military rank and its highest civilian office, but more importantly because of the kind of a man he was. He was a man of great strength, wisdom, and compassion. But it always seemed to me that two qualities stood out above all in both his public and his private life: one was an unwavering sense of duty; the other was that whatever he did, he did because he believed it was right.

The measure of Dwight Eisenhower's place in history is that we have to reach back two centuries, to the first days of our Republic, to find another American who was a citizen, "first in war, first in peace, and first in the hearts of his countrymen."

One key to the character of General Eisenhower was revealed in a message he prepared but never had to deliver. Just before D-Day, he wrote a statement in the event of disaster: "Our landings in the Cherbourg-Havre area have failed to gain a satisfactory foothold and I have withdrawn the troops. My decision to attack at this time and place was based upon the best information available. The troops,

the air, and the Navy did all that bravery and devotion to duty could do. If any blame or fault attaches to the attempt it is mine alone."

The landing was successful, and the message filed away. But that was a man ready to take the consequences of decision. That was Eisenhower.

Dwight Eisenhower was selfless. He was devoted to the common cause of humanity, to his beloved country, and to his family and friends. He was both a great man and a good man. To millions the world over, he was a symbol of decency and hope.

As President, I salute him for his services as a soldier, statesman, and peacemaker. As the one who was privileged to serve for 8 years as his Vice President, I pay tribute to him as an inspiring leader and a great teacher. As a person who is proud to have been his friend, and who has happily seen our families united, I join with my fellow Americans in mourning his death and in offering my condolences.

A grateful nation stands in his debt, and those of us who knew him, or who shared this period of history with him, will always warmly cherish his memory.

NOTE: Former President Dwight David Eisenhower died of heart failure on March 28, 1969, at the age of 78 at the Walter Reed Army Medical Center in Washington, D.C.

138   Special Message to the Congress on the Death of General Eisenhower.   *March 28, 1969*

To the Congress of the United States:

It is my sad duty to inform you officially of the death of Dwight David Eisenhower, the thirty-fourth President of the United States.

We have lost a great leader, a great friend and a great man. I know there are many members of the Congress who had the privilege of serving under his military leadership, and who later, during his eight years as President, shared with him in the building of a better America. He had a profound respect for the traditions, the institutions and the instruments of our nation. He leaves to the Congress and to all Americans the spirit of patriotism and statesmanship beyond party which marked his entire career. As we grieve at his death, we all will recall that spirit, which can guide and sustain us in our tasks ahead. He has been an inspiration to us all, and ours is a better government because he walked among us.

RICHARD NIXON

The White House
March 28, 1969

139   Proclamation 3907, Announcing the Death of Dwight David Eisenhower.   *March 28, 1969*

By the President of the United States of America a Proclamation

To the People of the United States:

I have the sad duty to announce officially the death of Dwight David Eisenhower, the thirty-fourth President of the United States, on March 28, 1969.

In London, in 1945, this great soldier received the Freedom of the City of London. At that time, he said: ". . . . we should turn to those inner things, call them what you will—I mean those intangibles that are the real treasures free men possess."

As a soldier, he was guided by those inner things. As a President, he was strengthened by their wisdom and by the knowledge that the ancient virtues, intangible but unconquerable, could offer comfort and solace even during the darkest hours.

And so it should be with us who today mourn his death. The memory of his greatness is now one of those "real treasures free men possess;" it belongs now to all Americans, and in its simplicity, its devotion, its courage, and its compassion, his life will shape the future as it shaped our time.

As long as free men cherish their freedom, Dwight Eisenhower will stand with them, as he stood during war and peace; strong, confident, and courageous. Even in death he has left us a great spirit that will never die.

Now, THEREFORE, I, RICHARD M. NIXON, President of the United States of America, in honor and tribute to the memory of this great and good man, and as an expression of public sorrow, do hereby direct that the flag of the United States be displayed at half-staff at the White House and on all buildings, grounds, and Naval vessels of the United States for a period of thirty days from the day of death. I also direct that for the same length of time the representatives of the United States in foreign countries shall make similar arrangements for the display of the flag at half-staff over their Embassies, Legations, and other facilities abroad, including all military facilities and stations.

I hereby order that suitable honors be rendered by units of the Armed Forces under orders of the Secretary of Defense on the day of the funeral.

I also do appoint Monday, March 31, 1969 to be a National Day of Mourning throughout the United States. I earnestly recommend that the people assemble on that day in their respective places of divine worship, there to bow down in submission to the will of the Almighty God, and to pay their homage of love and reverence to the memory of President Eisenhower. I invite the people of the world who share our grief to join us in this day of mourning and rededication.

IN WITNESS WHEREOF, I have hereunto set my hand this twenty-eighth day of March in the year of our Lord nineteen hundred and sixty-nine and of the Independence of the United States of America the one hundred and ninety-third.

RICHARD NIXON

NOTE: On the same day the President signed Executive Order 11462 "Providing for the closing of Government departments and agencies on March 31, 1969, and for the granting of administrative leave on March 28, 1969."

140   Eulogy Delivered at the Capitol During the State Funeral of General Eisenhower.   *March 30, 1969*

Mrs. Eisenhower, Your Excellencies, friends of Dwight David Eisenhower in America and throughout the world:

We gather today in mourning, but also in gratitude.

We mourn Dwight Eisenhower's death, but we are grateful for his life.

We gather, also, conscious of the fact that in paying tribute to Dwight Eisenhower, we celebrate greatness. When we think of his place in history, we think, inevitably, of the other giants of those days of World War II; and we think of the qualities of greatness and what his were that made his unique among all.

Once, perhaps without intending to do so, he, himself, put his finger on it. It was 1945, shortly after VE-Day, at a ceremony in London's historic Guildhall. The triumphant Supreme Commander of the Allied Forces in Europe was officially given the Freedom of the City of London.

In an eloquent address that day, Dwight Eisenhower said: "I come from the heart of America."

Perhaps no one sentence could better sum up what Dwight Eisenhower meant to a whole generation of Americans. He did come from the heart of America, not only from its geographical heart, but from its spiritual heart.

He exemplified what millions of parents hoped that their sons would be: strong and courageous and honest and compassionate. And with his own great qualities of heart, he personified the best in America.

It is, I think, a special tribute to Dwight Eisenhower that despite all of his honors, despite all of his great deeds and his triumphs, we find ourselves today thinking, first, not of his deeds but of his character. It was the character of the man, not what he did, but what he was that so captured the trust and faith and affection of his own people and of the people of the world.

Dwight Eisenhower touched something fundamental in America which only a man of immense force of mind and spirit could have brought so vibrantly alive. He was a product of America's soil and of its ideals, driven by a compulsion to do right and to do well; a man of deep faith who believed in God and trusted in His will; a man who truly loved his country and for whom words like "freedom" and "democracy" were not clichés, but they were living truths.

I know Mrs. Eisenhower would permit me to share with you the last words he spoke to her on the day he died. He said: "I have always loved my wife. I have always loved my children. I have always loved my grandchildren. And I have always loved my country." That was Dwight Eisenhower.

He was a man who gave enormously of himself. His way of relaxing from the intense pressures of office or command was to do something else intensely, whether as a fierce competitor on the golf course or executing one of those hauntingly beautiful paintings that he did with such meticulous care. But even more than this, he gave enormously of himself to people. People loved Dwight Eisenhower. But the other side of this coin was that he loved people.

He had the great leader's capacity to bring out the best in people. He had the great humanist's capacity to inspire people, to cheer them, to give them lift.

I remember, for example, just a few months ago when I asked all of the members of the Cabinet to go out and call on him. And each of them returned with wonder and admiration and said: "You know, I went out there to cheer him up and instead I found he cheered me up."

His great love of people was rooted in his faith. He had a deep faith in the goodness of God and in the essential goodness of man as a creature of God.

This feeling toward people had another side. In the political world, strong passions are the norm and all too often these turn toward personal vindictiveness. People often disagreed with Dwight Eisenhower, but almost nobody ever hated him. And this, I think, was because he, himself, was a man who did not know how to hate.

Oh, he could be aroused by a cause, but he could not hate a person. He could disagree strongly, even passionately, but never personally.

When people disagreed with him, he never thought of them as enemies. He simply thought: "Well, they don't agree with me."

I remember time after time, when critics of one sort or another were misrepresenting him or reviling him, he would sit back in his chair and with that wonderful half-smile and half-frown, he would say: "I am puzzled by those fellows." And he was genuinely puzzled by frenzy and by hate. Because he was incapable of it himself, he could never quite understand it in others.

The last time I saw him that was what he talked about. He was puzzled by the hatreds he had seen in our times. And he said the thing the world needs most today is understanding, an ability to see the other person's point of view and not to hate him because he disagrees.

263

That was Dwight Eisenhower.

And yet, of course, he was more than all that. He had a side more evident to those of us who worked with him than to the rest of the world. He was a strong man. He was shrewd. He was decisive.

Time and again I have seen him make decisions that probably made the difference between war and peace for America and the world.

That was always when he was at his best. No matter how heated the arguments were, he was always then the coolest man in the room.

Dwight Eisenhower was that rarest of men, an authentic hero.

Wars bring the names of many men into the headlines and of those some few become national or even international heroes. But as the years then pass, their fame goes down.

But not so with Dwight Eisenhower. As the years passed, his stature grew: Commander of the mightiest expeditionary force ever assembled, receiver of the surrender of the German Armies in World War II, president of Columbia University, Supreme Commander of NATO, 34th President of the United States. The honors, the offices were there in abundance. Every trust that the American people had it in their power to bestow, he was given.

And, yet, he always retained a saving humility. His was the humility not of fear but of confidence. He walked with the great of the world, and he knew that the great are human. His was the humility of man before God and before the truth. His was the humility of a man too proud to be arrogant.

The pursuit of peace was uppermost in his mind when he ran for the Presidency. And it was uppermost in his conduct of that office. And it is a tribute to his skill and determination that not since the 1930's has the Nation enjoyed so long a period of peace, both at home and abroad, as the one that began in 1953 and continued through his Presidency.

As Commander of the mightiest allied force ever assembled, he was the right man at the right place at the right time. And as President, once again he was the right man at the right place at the right time.

He restored calm to a divided nation. He gave Americans a new measure of self-respect. He invested his office with dignity and respect and trust. He made Americans proud of their President, proud of their country, proud of themselves. And if we in America were proud of Dwight Eisenhower, it was partly because he made us proud of America.

He came from the heart of America. And he gave expression to the heart of America, and he touched the hearts of the world.

Many leaders are known and respected outside their own countries. Very few are loved outside their own countries. Dwight Eisenhower was one of those few. He was probably loved by more people in more parts of the world than any President America has ever had.

He captured the deepest feelings of free men everywhere. The principles he believed in, the ideals he stood for, these were bigger than his own country.

Perhaps he himself put it best again in that Guildhall speech in 1945. He said then: "Kinship among nations is not determined in such measurements as proximity, size and age. Rather, we should turn to those inner things—call them what you will—I mean those intangibles that are the real treasures free men possess.

"To preserve his freedom of worship, his equality before law, his liberty to speak and act as he sees fit, subject only to provisions that he trespass not upon similar rights of others—a Londoner will fight. So will a citizen of Abilene.

"When we consider these things, then the Valley of the Thames draws closer to the farms of Kansas and the plains of Texas."

Some men are considered great because they lead great armies or they lead powerful nations. For 8 years now, Dwight Eisenhower has neither commanded an army nor led a nation. And, yet, he remained through his final days the world's most admired and respected man—truly, the first citizen of the world.

As we marvel at this, it leads us once again to ponder the mysteries of greatness. Dwight Eisenhower's greatness derived not from his office, but from his character, from a unique moral force that transcended national boundaries, even as his own deep concern for humanity transcended national boundaries.

His life reminds us that there is a moral force in this world more powerful than the might of arms or the wealth of nations. This man who led the most powerful armies that the world has ever seen, this man who led the most powerful nation in the world, this essentially good and gentle and kind man—that moral force was his greatness.

For a quarter of a century to the very end of his life Dwight Eisenhower exercised a moral authority without parallel in America and in the world. And America and the world are better because of it.

And so today we render our final salute. It is a fond salute to a man we loved and cherished. It is a grateful salute to a man whose whole extraordinary life was consecrated to service. It is a profoundly respectful salute to a man larger than life who by any standard was one of the giants of our time.

Each of us here will have a special memory of Dwight Eisenhower.

I can see him now standing erect, straight, proud, and tall 16 years ago as he took the oath of office as the 34th President of the United States of America.

We salute Dwight David Eisenhower standing there in our memories, first in war, first in peace, and, wherever freedom is cherished, first in the hearts of his fellow men.

NOTE: The President delivered the eulogy at 5:25 p.m. at the Rotunda of the Capitol.

On the following evening President and Mrs. Nixon held a reception in the Blue Room at the White House for heads of government and foreign representatives in Washington to attend the funeral. The White House Press Office issued a list of guests invited to the reception, and a list giving the order of guests received.

141   Statement on the Balance of Payments. *April 4,* 1969

IN MY fiscal message to the Congress on March 26, I called for a strong budget surplus and monetary restraint to curb an inflation that has been allowed to run into its fourth year. This is fundamental economics, and I pointed out that we intend to deal with fundamentals.

Similarly, the problem of regaining equilibrium in the U.S. balance of payments cannot be solved with expedients that postpone the problem to another year. We shall stop treating symptoms and start treating causes, and we shall find our solutions in the framework of freer trade and payments.

Fundamental economics call for:

—creating the conditions that make it possible to rebuild our trade surplus.

—ultimate dismantling of the network of direct controls which may seem useful in the short run but are self-defeating in the long run.

The U.S. balance of payments showed a surplus last year. But this surplus included an unusually high and probably unsustainable capital inflow. Our trade surplus, which reached a peak of $6.5 billion in the mid-sixties, declined sharply and all but disappeared.

That trade surplus must be rebuilt, and it can only be rebuilt by restoring stable and noninflationary economic growth to the U.S. economy. Inflation has drawn in a flood of imports while it has diminished our competitiveness in world markets and thus dampened our export expansion.

This is why our program of fiscal and monetary restraint is as necessary for our external trade as for restoring order in our domestic economy.

Building on the solid base of a healthy, noninflationary economy—a base that only the fundamentals of fiscal and monetary restraints now can restore—we are planning a sustained effort in several key areas:

—*In export expansion,* we have tentatively set an export goal of $50 billion to be achieved by 1973. This compares with 1968 exports of about $34 billion. This is primarily the task of American private enterprise, but government must help to coordinate the effort and offer assistance and

encouragement. We must also call on the productivity and ingenuity of American industry to meet the competitive challenge of imported goods.

—*In trade policies,* we will be working with our major trading partners abroad to insure that our products receive a fair competitive reception.

—*In defense activities,* we will also work with our friends abroad to insure that the balance of payments burden of providing for the common defense is shared fairly.

—*In travel,* we will encourage more foreign travel to the United States. Here, as in other areas, we will be relying heavily on the support of the private community. We seek no restrictions on the American tourist's freedom to travel.

—*In international investment,* we will review our own regulations and tax policy to assure that foreign investment in the U.S. is not discouraged; for example, we move now to eliminate from our laws the prospective taxation of interest on foreign-held bank deposits.

—*In the international financial area,* we will be continuing to work with our friends abroad to strengthen and improve the international monetary system. An expanding world economy will require growing levels of trade with adequate levels of reserves, and effective methods by which countries can adjust their payments imbalances. In particular, we look forward to ratification by the International Monetary Fund members of the Special Drawing Rights plan and its early activation.

I am confident that measures in these

areas, coupled with the cooling of the economy through fiscal-monetary restraint, will move us in an orderly manner toward true balance-of-payments equilibrium. Accordingly, I have begun, gradually but purposefully, to dismantle the direct controls which only mask the underlying problem.

Specifically:

First, I have today signed an Executive order [11464] reducing the effective rate of the interest equalization tax from 1¼ percent to ¾ of 1 percent. This measure was designed to close a large gap—which has now narrowed—between foreign and domestic interest rates. I shall, however, request the Congress to extend the President's discretionary authority under the interest equalization tax for 18 months beyond its scheduled expiration in July.

Second, I have approved a recommendation to relax somewhat the foreign direct investment program of the Department of Commerce. This means that most firms investing abroad will have substantially more freedom in planning these investments.

Third, I have been informed by Chairman Martin of modifications in the Federal Reserve program which will provide more flexibility for commercial banks, particularly smaller and medium-sized banks, to finance U.S. exports.

These are prudent and limited steps that recognize the realities of our present balance-of-payments situation.

The distortions created by more than 3 years of inflation cannot be corrected overnight. Nor can the dislocations resulting from a decade of balance-of-payments deficits be corrected in a short time.

But the time for restoring the basis of our prosperity is long overdue. We shall continually direct America's economic policy, both foreign and domestic, at correcting the root causes of our problems, rather than covering them over with a patchwork quilt of controls.

By facing up to fundamental economic needs, the inflationary tide and the trade tide can be turned and the U.S. dollar continued strong and secure.

NOTE: The statement was released at Key Biscayne, Fla.

142 Remarks of Welcome at the White House to King Hussein I of the Hashemite Kingdom of Jordan. *April 8,* 1969

Your Majesty:

As you can tell from the reception you have received today, you are among friends. We welcome you again as one who has visited our country before and we say as you come again that we think you come at a very appropriate time.

As we all know, the area of the world in which you rule is one that presently has some very explosive problems. And in order to solve those problems, leadership is required—leadership from within that area. The kind of leadership that is required I would describe as having three qualities: the quality of courage, the quality of wisdom, and the quality of moderation.

And it is those three qualities that we in this country have seen in you, Your Majesty, through the years. You have been a man of courage and you have captured the imagination of our people because of that courage. You have been a man of wisdom and you have been a man of moderation.

And for that reason, we look forward to the conversations we will have with you and with members of your Government in attempting to find new avenues that could lead to permanent peace in that troubled area of the world.

We welcome you, then, today as an old friend. We welcome you, too, as one with whom we look forward to searching together for a new period of peace and understanding in the Middle Eastern area of the world.

NOTE: The President spoke at 10:08 a.m. on the South Lawn at the White House where King Hussein was given a formal welcome with full military honors.

The King responded as follows:

Mr. President:

I wish to thank you most sincerely for your kind and warm words of welcome. It is indeed a privilege for me to be here once again. And I know that I am amongst friends.

Sir, it was on my first visit to the United States in 1959 during the term of office of one

of the greatest men of our times—President Eisenhower—that I had the privilege of meeting you. And since then I have been proud of the fact that you are my friend.

The relations between our two countries were never as strong as they were during that period and it is our sincere hope and desire that they grow now stronger than they ever were in the past.

The area from which I come, sir, is a troubled area. Thus, I feel the weight of responsibility even more as I come here to meet with you, sir, to discuss the problems of that area. For within the very near future we can either move towards our objective—a just and honorable peace in that area—or we might, indeed, lose the chance and the opportunity to establish peace, a just and lasting peace, there.

I really hope that we will move in the direction of peace because the situation, as explosive as it is, holds many dangers, not only to those involved in the area, but to the world as a whole.

And what we have sought and what we are seeking always is the establishment of a just and durable peace in the area; that all our energies and resources be diverted towards building the better future that we seek and we feel is the right of all in that area.

I thank you very, very much, indeed, sir, for your kindness and I am really so very proud and happy to be with you here again.

Thank you, sir.

143   Statement Announcing a Program for Rehabilitation of Urban Areas Damaged by Riots.   *April 8, 1969*

THE NEIGHBORHOODS of our cities torn by the disturbances of last spring and before still bear the marks of violence and destruction. Little rehabilitation or reconstruction has taken place. Months, and in some cases years, have passed—months of planning, argument, and frustration—but the wreckage of the riots remains: fire-scarred, boarded-up buildings, vacant retail stores, and rubble-strewn vacant lots.

This is the overwhelming evidence of a survey, recently undertaken by Secretary George Romney at my request, of those cities which have suffered riot damage. More than 20 cities were surveyed. The 10 with the worst remaining damage are Newark, Baltimore, Washington, Boston, Pittsburgh, Cleveland, Detroit, Chicago, Kansas City, and Los Angeles. I have directed Secretary Romney to assemble a program designed to initiate and coordinate prompt Federal, State, local, and private action in as many as possible of these 20 cities. I have made funds available to do so.

The idea for such an effort grew out of my visit to 7th and T Streets, Northwest, in Washington, D.C., earlier in the year. I was shocked by the sight of those rotting, boarded-up structures, barely 30 blocks from the White House. I had ordered a program of immediate Federal aid using HUD's interim assistance and neighborhood development grants for the District of Columbia. I wondered how many of our other cities across the country were in a similar state, and I directed Secretary Romney to do this survey, with representative photographs, which I present to you today.

This is a pictorial essay on the impotence of modern government at all levels. No wonder our citizens are beginning to question government's ability to perform. There could be no more searing symbol of governmental inability to act than those rubble-strewn lots and desolate, decaying buildings, once a vital part of a community's life and now left to rot.

Little has changed—and not always, or even chiefly, for lack of Federal aid as such. The survey shows that many of the riot-scarred, burnt-out areas are included within designated and planned Model Cities and Neighborhood Development program areas. Much of the damaged property is privately owned. But almost all sectors of the community seem paralyzed by a combination of obstacles, some federally imposed, which forestall action.

The program to be announced by Secretary Romney will combine Federal, State, local, and private efforts to initiate projects to improve the physical environment and meet the needs of our riot-trou-

bled neighborhoods. Following working consultations with the cities, the Federal Government will make available $9 million in interim assistance, which can be used in those cities which qualify, to provide temporary playgrounds, parks, clean-up services, repairs to public buildings and streets, where now there is charred rubble. Under this program, cities receiving such aid must undertake to provide one-third matching funds. This is a short-range, immediate effort.

In addition, local projects under various other HUD programs have been recently approved or are pending and likely to be approved which exceed $200 million and which can bring needed facilities and services to these riot-troubled cities. HUD will offer assistance to these cities in accelerating the delivery time of those programs which relate to riot-troubled neighborhoods.

I must emphasize that the above measures cannot erase overnight the problems of riot-troubled neighborhoods, much less the problems of our cities. They are limited measures designed to begin the business of revitalizing and rebuilding these neighborhoods.

Finally, I have directed the Secretary to present to me, within 60 days after funds for the next fiscal year have been appropriated by the Congress, a specific plan for channeling an appropriate amount of funds into a concentrated effort to accelerate the renewal and revitalization of our riot-troubled cities. This would call on all the tools at our command—including, for example, neighborhood facilities grants, Model Cities, accelerated urban renewal, and aids to housing and social services.

The program I announce today is a start, a beginning, to bring aid to the victims of these riots—the vast majority who fought or fled the burning and now must live among its remains. Especially, it is a program for the young, who play among littered glass and gutted buildings.

NOTE: The photographs referred to in the statement were on display at a White House news briefing on the program by Dr. Daniel P. Moynihan, Assistant to the President for Urban Affairs, Richard C. Van Dusen, Under Secretary, and Lawrence M. Cox, Assistant Secretary for Renewal and Housing Assistance, Department of Housing and Urban Development.

144 Statement Announcing the Establishment of the Office of Child Development. *April 9, 1969*

IN MY MESSAGE to the Congress of February 19th on the Economic Opportunity Act, I called for a "national commitment to providing all American children an opportunity for healthful and stimulating development during the first five years of life." I again pledge myself to that commitment.

No such commitment has ever before been asked in our Nation. No such pledge has ever been given.

Two fundamental developments bring it about.

The first is one of the most characteristic developments of the modern age: new knowledge, new facts. We know today—and with each day our knowledge grows more detailed—that the process of human development is in certain fundamental ways different from what it has been thought to be. Or perhaps it is the case that mothers have always understood, but that only men have failed to take notice.

We have learned, first of all, that the process of learning how to learn begins very, very early in the life of the infant child. Children begin this process in the very earliest months of life, long before they are anywhere near a first grade class, or even kindergarten, or play school group. We have also learned that for the children of the poor this ability to learn can begin to deteriorate very early in life, so that the youth begins school well behind his contemporaries and seemingly rarely catches up. He is handicapped as surely as a child crippled by polio is handicapped, and he bears the burden of that handicap through all his life. It is elemental that, even as in the case of polio, the effects of prevention are far better than the effects of cure.

Increasingly we know something about how this can be done. With each passing year—almost with each passing month, such is the pace of new developments in this field of knowledge—research workers in the United States and elsewhere in the world are learning more about the way in which an impoverished environment can develop a "learned helplessness" in children. When there is little stimulus for the mind, and especially when there is little interaction between parent and child, the child suffers lasting disabilities, particularly with respect to the development of a sense of control of his environment. None of this follows from the simple fact of being poor, but it is now fully established that an environment that does not simulate learning is closely associated in the real world with poverty in its traditional forms. As much as any one thing it is this factor that leads to the transmission of poverty from one generation to the next. It is no longer possible to deny that the process is all too evidently at work in the slums of America's cities, and that is a most ominous aspect of the urban crisis.

It is just as certain that we shall have to invent new social institutions to respond to this new knowledge.

Elementary school, kindergarten, even Head Start appear to come too late for many of those children who most need help. This is no ground for despair, but to the contrary, a clear challenge to our creativity as a great urban, democratic society. Ways of reaching and helping the very young and their mothers—when they need such help—must be found. There must be ways that protect the privacy of that relationship, and the sacred right of parents to rear their children according to their own values and own understandings. But they also bear a solemn responsibility to insure that the full potential of those children is enabled to come forth. Finding a balance between these imperatives will test our moral wisdom as much as our scientific knowledge. But it can be done, and it must.

The delegation of Head Start to the Department of Health, Education, and Welfare was the first step in fulfilling my commitment to the first 5 years of life. In HEW, this program can be supported and supplemented by other Federal programs dealing with children in the early years.

The second step, which I announce today, is the creation of an Office of Child Development, reporting directly to Secretary Finch's office. This Office must take a comprehensive approach to the development of young children, combining programs which deal with the physical, social, and intellectual.

Preliminary evaluations of this program

indicate that Head Start must begin earlier in life, and last longer, to achieve lasting benefits. Toward this end, Secretary Finch has decided to expand the Parent and Child Center and Follow Through programs, while reducing summer programs.

We must remember that we are only beginning to learn what works, and what does not, in this field. We are on the verge of exciting breakthroughs, but much more must be learned before we can prepare a successful nationwide preschool program.

There are any number of urban problems that can be dealt with promptly—and should be. Others can be approached in terms that admit of clear results in 2, 3, and 4 years. But some matters take longer. Above all, the process of a child's maturing is one of slow and steady growth that will not be speeded up for all our scientific knowledge.

America must learn to approach its problems in terms of the timespan those problems require. All problems are pressing; all cry out for instant solutions; but not all can be instantly solved. We must submit to the discipline of time with respect to those issues which provide no alternative.

The process of child development is such a matter.

Our commitment to the first 5 years of life will not show its full results during my administration, nor in that of my successor. But if we plant the seeds and if we respond to the knowledge we have, then a stronger and greater America will surely one day come of it.

NOTE: Also released by the White House Press Office was the text of a news briefing by Dr. Daniel P. Moynihan, Assistant to the President for Urban Affairs, and officials of the Department of Health, Education, and Welfare including Secretary Robert H. Finch, Deputy Assistant Secretary for Intergovernmental Affairs, Robert E. Patricelli, and Acting Chief of the Children's Bureau and Director of the Office of Child Development, Jule M. Sugarman.

145   Address at the Commemorative Session of the North Atlantic Council.   *April* 10, 1969

Mr. Secretary, Mr. President, Mr. Secretary General, Your Excellencies, and our distinguished guests:

As we gather here today, we celebrate a momentous anniversary.

We celebrate one of the great successes of the postwar world.

Twenty years ago, as has already been mentioned, a few dedicated men gathered in Washington to cement an Atlantic partnership between the older nations of Europe and their offspring in the New World—and in this very room the North Atlantic Treaty was signed. Some of the men who were here then are here today—and I would like to suggest that those who were here then and who are here today stand for a moment. [*Applause*]

Gentlemen, with our hindsight, we now have saluted your foresight at that time. In referring to that event, I thought I should share with you the conversation that I had with some of the founders in the room prior to coming to this meeting.

Secretary Acheson [1] recalled that before the signing of the treaty the Marine Band played "We've Got Plenty of Nothing" and "It Ain't Necessarily So."

Certainly what has happened in those 20 years proved that as far as the music was concerned, it was not prophetic.

As we sit here today we also look back on those 20 years, what has happened, and we think, as the previous speakers have indicated, of all of those who have contributed to the Alliance and particularly to the one who commanded the armies that liberated Europe, the first Supreme Commander of the forces of NATO, the American President who did so much to bring NATO to its strength and to give life to its principles—to Dwight David Eisenhower.

His life demonstrated that there is a moral force in the world which can move men and nations. There is a spiritual force lodged in the very roots of man's being.

As for NATO, it is precisely because it has always been more than a military alliance that its strength has been greater than the strength of arms. This Alliance represents a moral force which, if we marshal it, will ennoble our efforts.

Dwight Eisenhower was a great humanist. He was also a great realist. If he were with us today, he would have recognized that together, as men of the Old World and of the New World, we must find ways of living in the real world.

As we know too well, that real world today includes men driven by suspicion, men who would take advantage of their neighbors, men who confuse the pursuit of happiness with the pursuit of power.

It also is peopled with men of good will, with men of peace and with men of hope and with men of vision.

No nation, and no community of nations, is made up entirely of one group of men or another. No part of the world has a monopoly on wisdom or virtue.

---

[1] Dean Acheson, Secretary of State 1949–1953.

Those who think simply in terms of "good" nations and "bad" nations—of a world of staunch allies and sworn enemies—live in a world of their own. Imprisoned by stereotypes, they do not live in the real world.

On the other hand, those who believe that all it takes to submerge national self-interest is a little better communication, those who think that all that stands in the way of international brotherhood is stubborn leadership—they, too, live in a world of their own. Misled by wishful thinking, they do not live in the real world.

Two decades ago, the men who founded NATO faced the truth of their times; as a result, the Western world prospers today in freedom. We must follow their example by once again facing the truth—not of earlier times, but of our own times.

Living in the real world of today means recognizing the sometimes differing interests of the Western nations, while never losing sight of our great common purposes.

Living in the real world of today means understanding old concepts of East versus West, understanding and unfreezing those concepts, but never losing sight of great ideological differences that still remain.

We can afford neither to blind our eyes with hatred nor to distort our vision with rose-colored glasses. The real world is too much with us to permit either stereotyped reacting or wishful thinking to lay waste our powers.

Let us then count ourselves today among the hopeful realists.

In this same spirit of hopeful realism, let us look at NATO today.

We find it strong but we find it challenged. We find disputes about its structure, political divisions among its members, and reluctance to meet prescribed force quotas. Many people on both sides of the Atlantic today find NATO anachronistic, something quaint and familiar and even a bit old-fashioned.

As the Alliance begins its third decade, therefore, there are certain fundamentals to be reaffirmed:

First, NATO is needed; and the American commitment to NATO will remain in force and it will remain strong. We in America continue to consider Europe's security to be our own.

Second, having succeeded in its original purpose, the Alliance must adapt to the conditions of success. With less of the original cement of fear, we must forge new bonds to maintain our unity.

Third, when NATO was founded, the mere fact of cooperation among the Western nations was of tremendous significance, both symbolically and substantively. Now the symbol is not enough; we need substance. The Alliance today will be judged by the content of its cooperation, not merely by its form.

Fourth, the allies have learned to harmonize their military forces; now, in the light of the vast military, economic, and political changes of two decades, we must devise better means of harmonizing our policies.

Fifth, by its nature, ours is more than a military alliance; and the time has come to turn a part of our attention to those nonmilitary areas in which we all could benefit from increased collaboration.

Now, what does all this mean for the future of the Western Alliance?

To deal with the real world, we cannot respond to changing conditions merely by changing our words. We have to adapt our actions.

It is not enough to talk of flexible response, if at the same time we reduce our flexibility by cutting back on conventional forces.

It is not enough to talk of relaxing tension, unless we keep in mind the fact that 20 years of tension were not caused by superficial misunderstandings. A change of mood is useful only if it reflects some change of mind about political purpose.

It is not enough to talk of European security in the abstract. We must know the elements of insecurity and how to remove them. Conferences are useful if they deal with concrete issues which means they must, of course, be carefully prepared.

It is not enough to talk of detente, unless at the same time we anticipate the need for giving it the genuine political content that would prevent detente from becoming delusion.

To take one example, a number of America's Western partners have actively supported the idea of strategic arms control talks with the Soviet Union. I support that idea. When such talks are held, we shall work diligently for their success.

But within our Alliance we must recognize that this would imply a military relationship far different from the one that existed when NATO was founded. Let's put it in plain words. The West does not today have the massive nuclear predominance that it once had, and any sort of broad-based arms agreement with the Soviets would codify the present balance.

How would progress towards arms control affect the nature of consultation within our Alliance?

Up to now, our discussions have mainly had to do with tactics—ways and means of carrying out the provisions of a treaty drawn a generation ago. We have discussed clauses in proposed treaties; in the

negotiations to come, we must go beyond these to the processes which these future treaties will set in motion. We must shake off our preoccupation with formal structure to bring into focus a common world view.

Of course, there is a diversity of policies and interests among the Western nations; and, of course, those differences must be respected. But in shaping the strategies of peace, these differences need not block the way—not if we break through to a new and deeper form of political consultation.

To be specific, the forthcoming arms talks will be a test of the ability of the Western nations to shape a common strategy.

The United States fully intends to undertake deep and genuine consultation with its allies, both before and during any negotiations directly affecting their interests. That is a pledge I shall honor— and I expect to consult at length on the implications of anything that might affect the pattern of East-West relations.

In passing that test together, this Alliance will give new meaning to the principle of mutual consultation.

To seize the moment that this opportunity presents, we would do well to create new machinery for Western political consultation, as well as to make greater use of the machinery that we have.

First, I suggest that deputy foreign ministers meet periodically for a high-level review of major, long-range problems before the Alliance.

Second, I suggest creation of a special political planning group, not to duplicate the work now being done by the Council or by the senior political advisers, but to address itself specifically and continually to the longer-range problems we face.

274

This would by no means preclude efforts to develop a fuller European cooperation. On the contrary, we in the United States would welcome that cooperation. What ties us to Europe is not weakness or division among our partners but community of interest with them.

Third, I strongly urge that we create a committee on the challenges of modern society, responsible to the deputy ministers, to explore ways in which the experience and resources of the Western nations could most effectively be marshaled toward improving the quality of life of our peoples.

That new goal is provided for in Article II of our treaty, but it has never been the center of our concerns. Let me put my proposal in concrete terms and in personal terms. On my recent trip to Europe I met with world leaders and private citizens alike. I was struck by the fact that our discussions were not limited to military or political matters. More often than not our talks turned to those matters deeply relevant to our societies—the legitimate unrest of young people, the frustration of the gap between generations, the need for a new sense of idealism and purpose in coping with an automating world.

These were not subjects apart from the concerns of NATO; indeed they went to the very heart of the real world we live in. We are not allies because we are bound by treaty; we bind ourselves by treaty because we are allied in meeting common purposes and common concerns.

For 20 years, our nations have provided for the military defense of Western Europe. For 20 years we have held political consultations.

Now the alliance of the West needs a third dimension.

It needs not only a strong military dimension to provide for the common defense, and not only a more profound political dimension to shape a strategy of peace, but it also needs a social dimension to deal with our concern for the quality of life in this last third of the 20th century.

This concern is manifested in many ways, culturally and technologically, through the humanities and the sciences.

The Western nations share common ideals and a common heritage. We are all advanced societies, sharing the benefits and the gathering torments of a rapidly advancing industrial technology. The industrial nations share no challenge more urgent than that of bringing 20th century man and his environment to terms with one another—of making the world fit for man, and helping man to learn how to remain in harmony with the rapidly changing world.

We in the United States have much to learn from the experiences of our Atlantic allies in their handling of internal matters: for example, the care of infant children in West Germany, the "new towns" policy of Great Britain, the development of depressed areas programs in Italy, the great skill of the Dutch in dealing with high density areas, the effectiveness of urban planning by local governments in Norway, the experience of the French in metropolitan planning.

Having forged a working partnership, we all have a unique opportunity to pool our skills, our intellects, and our inventiveness in finding new ways to use technology to enhance our environments, and not to destroy them.

The work of this committee would not be competitive with any now being carried on by other international agencies. Neither would it be our purpose to limit this cooperation and the benefits that flow from it to our own countries. Quite the opposite; our purpose would be to share both ideas and benefits, recognizing that these problems have no national or regional boundaries. This could become the most positive dimension of the Alliance, opening creative new channels to all the rest of the world.

When I visited the North Atlantic Council in Brussels I posed the question: "In today's world, what kind of an alliance shall we strive to build?"

Today I have sketched out some of the approaches that I believe the Alliance should take.

I believe we must build an Alliance strong enough to deter those who might threaten war, close enough to provide for continuous and far-reaching consultation, trusting enough to accept the diversity of views, realistic enough to deal with the world as it is, and flexible enough to explore new channels of constructive cooperation.

Ten years ago, addressing the North Atlantic Council in this same room, President Eisenhower spoke of the need for unity. Listen to his words: There is not much strength in the finger of one hand, he said, but when five fingers are balled into a fist, you have a considerable instrument of defense.

We need such an instrument of defense and the United States will bear its fair share in keeping NATO strong.

All of us are also ready, as conditions change, to turn that fist into a hand of friendship.

NATO means more than arms, troop levels, consultative bodies, and treaty commitments. All of these are necessary. But what makes them relevant to the future is what the Alliance stands for. To discover what this Western Alliance means today, we have to reach back, not across two decades, but through the centuries to the very roots of the Western experience.

When we do, we find that we touch a set of elemental ideals, eloquent in their simplicity, majestic in their humanity, ideals of decency and justice and liberty and respect for the rights of our fellow men. Simple, yes; and to us they seem obvious. But our forebears struggled for centuries to win them and in our own lifetimes we have had to fight to defend them.

These ideals are what NATO was created to protect. It is to these ideals, on this proud anniversary, that we are privileged to consecrate the Alliance anew. These ideals—and the firmness of our dedication to them—give NATO's concept its nobility, and NATO's backbone its steel.

NOTE: The President spoke at 2:26 p.m. in the Departmental Auditorium in Washington. In his opening words he referred to Secretary of State William P. Rogers, Honorary President of the North Atlantic Council Vice Chancellor Willy Brandt of the Federal Republic of Germany, and Secretary General of the North Atlantic Treaty Organization Manlio Brosio.

146 Joint Statement Following Discussions With King Hussein I of Jordan. *April* 10, 1969

H.M. KING HUSSEIN, King of the Hashemite Kingdom of Jordan, visited Washington at President Nixon's invitation April 8, 9, and 10. During this time, His Majesty and members of his delegation had friendly and constructive discussions on matters of mutual interest and common concern with the President, the Secretaries of State and Defense and other senior United States Government officials.

The principal topic of the discussion was the common United States and Jordanian desire for a just and durable peace in the Middle East. The United States informed the Government of the Hashemite Kingdom of Jordan of its efforts, bilateral and multilateral, to help bring about peace in the Middle East.

H.M. the King explained that the explosive nature of the situation in the Middle East is caused by the continued occupation of Jordanian and other Arab territories, and expressed his conviction that peace can only be achieved by the early withdrawal of the forces of occupation in the context of the Security Council Resolution of November 22, 1967.

For its part, the United States called to the attention of the Government of Jordan and reaffirmed the statement made by Secretary Rogers on this point and on other points before the Senate Foreign Relations Committee on March 27.

Both the United States and Jordan reaffirmed their strong support for Ambassador Jarring's mission and for all the principles and provisions of the Security Council Resolution. Both Governments recognize the compelling need to seek actively a just and lasting peace in the area.

The United States reaffirmed its support for the political independence and territorial integrity of the Hashemite Kingdom of Jordan.

The discussions renewed and deepened the close and friendly relations which exist between the two countries.

His Majesty the King extended an invitation to President Nixon to visit the Hashemite Kingdom of Jordan. The President expressed his gratitude for the invitation and said he hoped to be able to make this visit at an appropriate time.

NOTE: Gunnar Jarring was Swedish Ambassador to the Soviet Union and United Nations mediator in the Middle East dispute.

147 Letter to the Chairman, Civil Aeronautics Board, on the Transpacific Route Investigation. *April* 11, 1969

Dear Mr. Chairman:

I have concluded my review of the international phase of the Transpacific Route Investigation (your Docket 16242). Based upon considerations of foreign relations and national security, I have concluded that the international route structure which was tentatively established by President Johnson last December must be modified as follows:

(1) Awards of Great Circle routes to the Orient from California points are not approved.

(2) Pan American's authorization to provide service from the Pacific Northwest to the Orient over a Great Circle route is not approved.

(3) The second carrier route to the South Pacific should bypass the California gateway. On this aspect of the case, I ask

the Board to recommend a carrier to serve U.S. East Coast and Midwest coterminal points.

(4) The new American Samoa-Okinawa route segment should be deferred, and considered by the Board in the pending *Pacific Islands Local Service Investigation.*

(5) The award to Hawaii via Mexico to carry stopover passengers is disapproved.

(6) The use of so-called satellite airports in this case appears unwise and should not be required.

Otherwise, President Johnson's deci-

sion of last December is approved.

I desire the Board to submit immediately for my approval an order effectuating these conclusions.

Sincerely,

RICHARD NIXON

[The Honorable John H. Crooker, Jr., Chairman, Civil Aeronautics Board, Washington, D.C.]

NOTE: In a news briefing on April 24, Presidential Press Secretary Ronald L. Ziegler announced that the President had received and approved a Civil Aeronautics Board order drafted in compliance with his request in the last paragraph of the above letter.

148   Statement on Proposed Changes in the 1970 Budget. *April* 12, 1969

THE ADMINISTRATION'S first full review of the Federal budget for the fiscal year 1970 is now complete. As a result, beginning next week I shall send a series of budget amendments to the Congress.

Amendments for most agencies will go forward within a few days. The overall totals are now being made available.

The budget that we inherited from the previous administration in January stated the estimated expenditures for the fiscal year 1970 at $195.3 billion. Our examination of that budget reveals that some of these estimates—notably those for interest on the Federal debt and farm price support payments—are turning out to be too low. After making the necessary adjustments to cover these underestimated items, we find that the actual expenditures budget submitted by the previous administration is $196.9 billion.

I am proposing new reductions in Federal spending of $4.0 billion, reducing the overall spending figures for the coming

fiscal year to $192.9 billion. I am also recommending to the Congress cuts totaling $5.5 billion in appropriations requests and other budget authority—thereby reducing significantly the future spending obligations of the Federal Government.

Our proposals mean not only a substantial cutback in the spending of tax dollars in the coming year, but a substantial reduction in claims against future tax dollars and future budgets. With this approach, we believe we have made a necessary and significant beginning toward bringing the Federal budget under closer Presidential control; we have taken the reins firmly in hand.

We recognize, however, the responsibility for budget control is a continuing one. For the past 8 years—the sole exception being the current year—our Government has run an uninterrupted string of budget deficits. Our actions now, we believe, have brought an end to the era of the chronic budget deficit.

278

As a result of this review and these cutbacks, we are proposing the largest budget surplus in 18 years—and the fourth largest in our history—a surplus of $5.8 billion dollars for fiscal year 1970.

We believe that a surplus of this magnitude will speak louder than any words to the business and labor communities in this country and to the world that the United States is determined to bring a halt to the inflationary spiral which has seriously affected our economy these last 4 years.

In the last 36 months, inflation has seriously eroded the value of every pay raise won by the average wage earner; it has done unquestionable harm to the economic welfare of the very poor in our society and those millions of Americans living on pensions and social security; it has weakened our international payments position; it has sapped foreign and domestic confidence in the American dollar.

Inflation is the most disguised and least just of all the taxes that can be imposed; and we intend to lift that hidden tax off the backs of an overtaxed people.

These reductions in spending cannot be achieved effortlessly or without making some very difficult decisions as to our priorities. But they can be achieved by an administration and a Congress dedicated to eliminating the crushing burden of inflation and committed to the responsible control of the Federal budget. They can be achieved if this Government is willing to impose upon itself the same new discipline that inflation and rising taxes have imposed upon the American wage earner and his family.

Some of the decreases in the budget will require legislation; others will result from smaller appropriation requests; still others will come from executive actions that I have directed be taken. In sum, these reductions constitute my best judgment as to where to reduce this budget to bring the acceleration of Federal spending under control.

But even in the wake of these cuts—which we believe to be in the best interest of all Americans—great resources remain at our disposal to do the work that needs to be done in our society.

For example, I am proposing for fiscal year 1970 a level of spending for our domestic problems $6½ billion higher than the figure for the fiscal year 1969.

This administration will never turn its back upon the growing needs of the American people. That is why domestic spending in the coming year—even after these cuts—will far exceed that for any other year in American history.

We have come into office convinced that there are better ways than the old ways to solve new problems; and we intend to explore these more hopeful approaches.

With regard to specific cuts, the Secretary of Defense has already identified reductions in defense budget outlays of $1.1 billion. We believe these cuts will enhance our economic security without risk to our national security. Information with regard to other specific cuts will be released by the Bureau of the Budget on Tuesday.

As part of the budget review, I have directed that a substantial reduction be made in the level of Federal employment recommended by the preceding administration. As a result, full-time employment in the executive branch, by the close of the coming fiscal year, will be more than 45,000 below that recommended in the January budget.

These reductions will not be made

"across the board," but selectively, since manpower for vital needs such as crime control will have to be increased.

Consistent with these objectives, I will ask Congress for repeal of section 201 of the Revenue and Expenditure Control Act, which imposes restrictions on hiring in the executive branch. I am in full accord with the objective of that legislation. However, that objective is best achieved, not through some arbitrary limitation, but through leadership determined to reduce personnel and willing to make the difficult decisions as to where the cuts should come.

Just as we have made the judgments as to where the Federal budget should be cut, so we ask for the authority to determine those areas where the reduction of personnel can most beneficially be made.

Although the officials of this administration have worked long and hard conducting this review of Federal expenditures and employment, the 1970 budget is not yet a finished effort.

Conditions affecting the budget change constantly.

What will remain constant, however, is our determination to rein in this rising cost of living and to spend the tax dollars of the American people with a full awareness of the personal effort and labor they represent.

NOTE: Transcripts of two related news briefings by Budget Director Robert P. Mayo and Presidential Press Secretary Ronald L. Ziegler were released by the White House Press Office on April 12 and 15.

Additional discussion of the budget occurred in a news briefing on April 15 by Mr. Ziegler and Representative Gerald R. Ford of Michigan, House Minority Leader. The text is printed in the Weekly Compilation of Presidential Documents (vol. 5, p. 561).

As recommended by the President in his statement, section 201 of the Revenue and Expenditure Control Act of 1968 was repealed by section 503 of the Second Supplemental Appropriations Act of 1969 (Public Law 91–47, 83 Stat. 83), which was approved on July 22, 1969.

149   Remarks to the Assembly of the Organization of American States.   *April* 14, 1969

Mr. President, Your Excellencies, my fellow Americans:

I can use that term, "my fellow Americans" and cover everybody in this room. And this is the only international group in which I can do so.

As I speak to my fellow Americans today, I first want to thank the President of this organization for his very warm and friendly comments. And in responding to those comments, I first want to establish a personal bond of communication with all of you here—or should I say reestablish it with you.

As I came into this building today, I re-

called those many occasions when my wife and I were here and when you were gracious enough to allow us to use your home as the Vice President's place to entertain distinguished visitors from abroad.

My memory went back to not only many visits to this building, but visits to every one of the countries in this hemisphere.

Of all the international organizations that I have addressed, including the NATO Ministers, this statement can only be made with regard to the Organization of American States.

I am very fortunate to have had the

opportunity to know each of the countries represented here personally from having visited each of those countries. And I only hope that in the years that I am in office I shall have the opportunity to return and to visit many or, I hope, all of those countries in the future.

But as I speak to you today, I want, too, to speak from my heart with regard to the feeling that I have personally insofar as our American family is concerned.

I come from the State of California. I was born in a little town of Yorba Linda. It had, of course, not only a Spanish name but a great Spanish tradition and background.

My wife and I, in the year 1940—as you see her now she must have been a child bride—we took our honeymoon in Mexico. And 25 years later we returned with our two daughters for our anniversary trip to Mexico.

During the years that I have visited each of your countries, I have had some very interesting experiences. I know that the international press has tended to build up those experiences that have at times been difficult. But I can assure everyone in this room that my memories and the memories of my wife are not of those few who may have been unfriendly, but of the thousands of friendly faces we saw; and that we shall always take with us and we shall always remember as we attempt to develop our new policies for the future.

But having spoken, as I have deliberately done so warmly, about my personal affection for the countries represented in this room and the people represented in the countries among our neighbors to the south, I now want to speak very candidly and very honestly about some of the problems with which we are presently confronted.

I think there has been a tendency, in examining the relations of the United States with our friends to the south, to smother the problems that we have with fine slogans, beautiful rhetoric, and sometimes with *abrazos*.

I think there is a place for a fine slogan and always there is a place for eloquent language. And I would not underplay, certainly, the importance of that kind of relationship on a dignified basis between nations and the leaders of nations.

But at the present time, the problems we confront in this hemisphere are too serious to be glossed over simply by the usual slogans and the words and the gestures of the past. What we need is a new policy. What we need are new programs. What we need are new approaches.

I would like to describe those policies today, not with a new slogan, because I have none—none that I think would be appropriate to the challenge that we face.

But I would like to describe our approach in this way: Sometimes the new administration has been described as an open administration. I hope we can live up to that particular description. But if I were to set forth the objectives for our approach to the problems of this hemisphere, it would be in these words: I want our policies to be ones which are derived from open eyes, open ears, open minds, and open hearts.

Let me be specific on each of those particular items. When I speak of open eyes, I mean that it is necessary for us to look at our common problems without any of the prejudices that we may have had in the past and without being imprisoned by the policies of the past or without perpetuating the mistakes of the past.

The President of this organization has referred to Governor Rockefeller and the trip that he will be taking—or several trips, I should say—to this hemisphere in the months ahead.

On that trip, as Governor Rockefeller will tell each of the Ambassadors assembled here today, he is going with open eyes and open ears. He is not going there to tell the people in the various countries that he will visit what the United States wants them to do. But he is going there to listen to them and to hear what they believe we can do together.

I think there has been too much of a tendency in the past for the discussion to get down to this point: What will the United States do for Latin America?

The question, otherwise, I think should be put—and this is the approach of the Rockefeller mission, it is the approach of the Secretary of State, the new Assistant Secretary of State, Charles Meyer. Our approach is this: Not what do we do for Latin America, what do we do with Latin America? What do we do together?

We want, therefore, to have open eyes and we also have open ears. We want to hear from our friends in each of the countries represented what you think is wrong with our policy, but also what you think you can do with us to develop a better policy.

And we, fortunately, approach this problem with no preconceived notions as to the policies of the past.

One of the reasons that we must also have open minds is that there sometimes is a tendency to become wedded to a program because it has a popular connotation. I speak of the Alliance for Progress, a great concept.

And as I examined the effect of the Alliance for Progress on my last trip to Latin America, in which I covered most of the countries in that continent in 1967, I saw many areas where the Alliance for Progress had done much good.

On the other hand, when I looked at the overall statistics as to what has happened to the rate of growth in Latin America during the period of the Alliance for Progress as compared with the period immediately preceding the Alliance, and when I compared that rate of growth with the rates of growth in other areas of the world, I found a very disconcerting result.

And it very simply is this: The rate of growth is not fast enough. It has been approximately the same during the period of the Alliance as it was before the Alliance.

But even more significant, the rate of growth in Latin America overall—and of course there are some individual countries that are far ahead—but overall the rate of growth is less than the rate of growth in non-Communist Asia, and it is less, even, than the rate of growth in Communist Eastern Europe.

This is a result which we cannot tolerate. We must do better. We must find the ways and the means whereby we can move forward together in a more effective way.

And that is why I emphasize that we will have open eyes and open ears and open minds in attempting to find the answer.

But I emphasize at the last the most important element: We shall have open hearts—open hearts because no one can come here today, as my wife and I have, and to have sensed again the warm reception, the feeling that comes from the heart any time you come to an assemblage of this sort, no one can visit the countries of Latin America as we have on so many occasions without realizing how close our bonds are.

We are all part of the New World. We are all part of the American family. We come from the same traditions. We share the same concerns.

Simón Bolívar said 150 years ago that the "freedom of the New World is the hope of the universe." That was true then. I believe it is even more true today.

But then we have to make this freedom in the New World something which can be more meaningful to the millions of people not only in America, but in all the countries in this hemisphere so that there will be hope where there is now despair, so that there will be opportunity where there is now no chance for millions who simply want a chance—a chance not to receive but a chance simply on their own to make their own contribution both to their own welfare and to their country's welfare.

And as we think of this problem in that context, as we think how close our bonds are, I try to put it in the perspective of history. I think how long this organization has been in operation. And I look ahead just 33 years to the end of this century, less than that, 32 years, and I think of what this hemisphere—the New World—will be like at the end of this century. And I realize that if the present rates of growth that we have in the United States and in the balance of the hemisphere are not changed, at the end of this century the per capita income in the United States of America will be 15 times as high as that of the per capita income of our friends, our neighbors, the members of our family in the balance of the hemisphere.

This is something we cannot allow to happen. And it will require the best minds, it will require the best ideas that all of us can produce together.

So, Mr. President, as I come here today, let me say I was tempted simply to respond to your very gracious remarks with the response that I had in my heart, to express my appreciation for your welcome.

But I want you to know that we do consider the problems of this hemisphere to be of the highest priority. We do consider that whatever progress we have made has not been enough and for that reason we come here today asking your assistance in working with us so that we can find better solutions for those problems that we mutually have throughout the hemisphere.

Again, to all of you, my fellow Americans, our gratefulness for your warm reception, and I hope that this meeting may mark the beginning of a new era of cooperation, of consultation, but most important, of progress for all the members of our great American family.

Thank you.

NOTE: The President spoke at 11:14 a.m. at Pan American Union headquarters in Washington on the occasion of the Pan American Day Meeting of the OAS Assembly. In his opening words he referred to Carlos Holguin, representative of Colombia and Chairman of the Council of the Organization of American States. Charles A. Meyer was Assistant Secretary of State for Inter-American Affairs and United States Coordinator, Alliance for Progress.

39-861—71——22

150   Special Message to the Congress on Forthcoming
Legislative Proposals Concerning Domestic Programs.
April 14, 1969

To the Congress of the United States:

As the members of Congress know, I have had under consideration the question of whether to send to the Congress this year a message on the State of the Union. I have decided against doing so. However, to assist Congress in formulating its plans, I would like to indicate at this time some of the principal legislative proposals that I will be sending in the weeks immediately ahead, and to report on the development of Administration plans and priorities as they relate to domestic programs.

The first twelve weeks of the new Administration have been devoted intensively to the pursuit of peace abroad, and to the development of new structures and new programs for the pursuit of progress at home.

Peace has been the first priority. It concerns the future of civilization; and even in terms of our domestic needs themselves, what we are able to do will depend in large measure on the prospects for an early end to the war in Viet Nam.

At the same time, the first days of this Administration have afforded us a unique opportunity to study the nation's domestic problems in depth, and to overhaul and re-tool the complex machinery of the Executive Office.

A systematic review of domestic programs and policies has led to a series of recommendations which I will begin sending to Congress this week. Among those recommendations will be:

—An increase in Social Security benefits, to take account of the rise in living costs.

—New measures to combat organized crime, and to crack down on racketeers, narcotics traffickers and peddlers of obscenity.

—A program of tax credits, designed to provide new incentives for the enlistment of additional private resources in meeting our urgent social needs.

—A program to increase the effectiveness of our national drive for equal employment opportunity.

—A comprehensive reorganization of the Post Office Department.

—A program for the District of Columbia, including home rule and Congressional representation.

—A start on sharing the revenues of the Federal government, so that other levels of government where revenue increases lag behind will not be caught in a constant fiscal crisis.

—A far-reaching new program for development of our airways and airports, and our mass transit systems.

—A comprehensive labor and manpower program, including job training and placement, improvements in unemployment insurance, and proposals to help guarantee the health and safety of workers.

—Reform of the tax structure. The burden of taxation is great enough without permitting the continuance of unfairness in the tax system. New legislation will be proposed to prevent several specific abuses this year, and plans will be set in motion for a comprehensive revision of our tax structure by 1970, the first since 1954.

The legislative proposals of the next

few weeks are a beginning. They form part of a responsible approach to our goal of managing constructive change in America.

This is not law we seek in order to have it "on the books," but law that we need in action. It is designed, not to look appealing in the record, but to take effect in our lives.

It will be the goal of this Administration to propose only legislation that we know we can execute once it becomes law. We have deliberated long and hard on each of these measures, in order to be sure we could make it work. Merely making proposals takes only a typewriter; making workable proposals takes time. We have taken this time.

In other areas, where more time is needed, we will take more time. I urge the Congress to join with this Administration in this careful approach to the most fundamental issues confronting our country. Hasty action or a seeking after partisan advantage either by the Congress or Executive Branch can only be self-defeating and aggravate the very ills we seek to remedy.

For example, one area of deep concern to this Administration has to do with the most dependent constituency of all: the child under five. I have announced a commitment to the first five years of life as one of the basic pledges of this Administration. Head Start was one promising idea for bettering the environment and nutrition of young children; there also are many others. We have already begun enlarging the scope of our commitment in this vital field, including the establishment of an Office of Child Development within the Department of Health, Education, and Welfare. We hope that this enlarging commitment will be ac-

companied by an enlarging of the base of knowledge on which we act. We are not beginning with "massive" programs that risk tripping over their own unreadiness. Rather, our proposals will include step-by-step plans, including careful projections of funding requirements. Equally important, though Federally supported, they will embrace a network of local programs that will enlist voluntary participation.

These legislative proposals are, of course, being prepared within the context of other Administration actions which bear on domestic program development.

On taking office, I could see that whether measured in terms of its ability to respond, to decide or to implement, the Executive Branch simply was not structured to meet the emerging needs of the 1970s. Therefore my first moves were organizational.

The National Security Council was revitalized. The Urban Affairs Council was created, so that the problems of our cities could be approached in the broader perspective they now require. A Cabinet Committee on Economic Policy was established, to bring greater coherence to the management of our nation's economic prosperity. The system of Federal regional offices was reorganized so that for the first time, related agencies will have common regional headquarters and common regional boundaries. An Office of Intergovernmental Relations was set up, to smooth the coordination of Federal, State and local efforts.

In specific operational areas, we removed postmasterships from politics, started an overhaul of the Office of Economic Opportunity and its programs, and streamlined the administration of the various manpower programs.

One purpose of this early emphasis on organizational activity was to get the decision-making process in order before moving to the major decisions.

At the same time, I sent more than 100 directives [1] to the heads of the various departments and agencies, asking their carefully considered recommendations on a wide range of domestic policy issues. The budget was submitted to an intensive review, and throughout the Administration we addressed ourselves to the critical question of priorities.

One priority that has emerged clearly and compellingly is that we must put a halt, swiftly, to the ruinous rise of inflationary pressures. The present inflationary surge, already in its fourth year, represents a national self-indulgence we cannot afford any longer. Unless we save the dollar, we will have nothing left with which to save our cities—or anything else. I have already outlined certain steps that will be required:

—Continuation of the monetary policies the Federal Reserve authorities are now pursuing.

—A reduction of fiscal year 1970 expenditures by $4 billion below the best current estimate of the budget expenditures recommended by the last Administration.

—Continuation of the income tax surcharge for another year.

—Postponing of the scheduled reductions in telephone and passenger car excise taxes.

—Enactment of user charges equal in revenue to those now in the budget.

—An increase in postal charges.

These steps are not pleasant medicine.

---

[1] See Appendix C.

Medicine to combat inflation is never pleasant. But we can no longer delay taking it.

Another priority is the control of crime. On January 31, I announced a detailed plan for combatting crime in the District of Columbia, recognizing that the Federal city should be made a model of law observance and law enforcement. The crime-control package soon to be submitted to Congress will make clear the Federal Government's commitment, nationwide, to assisting local authorities in protecting the lives, rights and property of their citizens.

An equally pressing priority is the entire complex of needs that we commonly group under the heading, "the problems of the cities"—but which in fact reach beyond the cities, and include the distresses of rural America as well.

Our policy review has strengthened my conviction that in approaching these problems, America needs a new direction— not a turning away from past goals, but a clear and determined turn toward new means of achieving those goals.

One example is hunger and malnutrition. The failure of past effort to combat these problems has been made shockingly clear. Our new programs will be both vigorous and innovative.

Another example is welfare. Our studies have demonstrated that tinkering with the present welfare system is not enough. We need a complete re-appraisal and re-direction of programs which have aggravated the troubles they were meant to cure, perpetuating a dismal cycle of dependency from one generation to the next. Therefore, I will be submitting to Congress a program providing for the reform of the welfare system.

286

In the field of social legislation, we now have a hodge-podge of programs piled on programs, in which too often the pressure to perpetuate ill-conceived but established ones has denied needed resources to those that are new and more promising.

We have learned that too often government's delivery systems have failed: though Congress may pass a law, or the President may issue an order, the intended services never reach the intended recipients. Last week, for example, in announcing a $200 million program for rebuilding riot-torn areas, I noted that after two, three and even four years nothing had been done, and cited this as evidence of the growing impotence of government. The crucial point here is that whereas in the past, "leave it to the states" was sometimes a signal for inaction by design, now "leave it to Washington" has become too often a signal for inaction by default. We have to design systems that go beyond "commitment," and guarantee performance.

If there is one thing we know, it is that the Federal Government cannot solve all the nation's problems by itself; yet there has been an over-shift of jurisdiction and responsibility to the Federal Government. We must kindle a new partnership between government and people, and among the various levels of government.

Too often, Federal funds have been wasted or used unwisely—for example, by pouring them into direct grants, when more money could have been made available at less cost by the use of incentives to attract private funds.

The programs I will submit have been drawn with those principles in mind. Among their aims are:

—To supplement Federal funds with private funds, through the use of "seed money" devices such as tax credits and loan guarantees.

—To enlist the great, vital voluntary sector more fully, using the energies of those millions of Americans who are able and eager to help in combatting the nation's ills.

—To help rebuild state and local institutions, so that they both merit and gain a greater measure of confidence on the part of their own citizens.

—To streamline the administration of Federal programs, not only for efficiency and economy, but to improve the certainty of delivery and to cut away the clouds of confusion that now surround not only their operation, but often their purposes.

—To make maximum use of the new knowledge constantly being gained, as, for example, in our commitment to the first five years of life.

These programs will not carry extravagant promises. The American people have seen too many promises, too many false hopes raised, too much substitution of the easy slogan for the hard performance.

Neither will they carry large price-tags for the coming fiscal year. We must recognize, however, that in the long run progress will not come cheaply; and even though the urgency of controlling inflation dictates budget cuts in the short run, we must be prepared to increase substantially our dollar investment in America's future as soon as the resources become available.

This Administration will gladly trade the false excitement of fanfare for the abiding satisfaction of achievement. Con-

solidation, coordination and efficiency
are not ends in themselves; they are necessary means of making America's government responsive to the legitimate demands
for new departures.

Quietly, thoughtfully, but urgently, the
members of this Administration have

moved in these first few months to redirect the course of the nation. I am confident of the direction, and convinced
that the time to take it has come.

RICHARD NIXON

The White House
April 14, 1969

151   Message to the Senate Transmitting United States-Canadian Agreements.   *April* 14, 1969

To the Senate of the United States:

With a view to receiving the approval
of the Senate, I transmit herewith the texts
of two notes, signed and exchanged at
Washington on March 21, 1969, constituting an agreement between the Government of the United States of America and
the Government of Canada, providing for
additional temporary diversions from the
Niagara River for power production
purposes.

It is provided in the agreement that it
will enter into force upon notification that
the exchange of notes has been approved
by the Senate of the United States. The
agreement requires Senate advice and
consent to approval because it would authorize a departure from the limitations
prescribed in the Niagara River Treaty of
February 27, 1950 in regard to minimum
flows.

An agreement with Canada providing
for the construction of a temporary
cofferdam above the American Falls at
Niagara was concluded by an exchange
of notes on the same date. Copies of those
notes are transmitted herewith for the information of the Senate. This cofferdam
agreement is deemed to be a "special
agreement" of the kind expressly author-

ized by the Boundary Waters Treaty of
January 11, 1909 with Canada. It is
stipulated in this agreement that it enters
into force immediately upon the exchange
of notes.

I also transmit for the information of
the Senate a report by the Secretary of
State explaining more fully the background and purposes of the two
agreements.

I urge that the Senate give early and
favorable consideration to the agreement
authorizing additional temporary diversions from the Niagara River for power
production purposes.

RICHARD NIXON

The White House
April 14, 1969

NOTE: The agreement concerning Niagara
River diversions was favorably considered by
the Senate on May 13, 1969, and after ratification entered into force on May 20, 1969. It was
proclaimed by the President on May 27, 1969.
The text is printed, together with the related
exchange of notes on the temporary cofferdam,
in United States Treaties and Other International Agreements (20 UST 726). The complete exchange of notes, together with the above
message and the report of the Secretary of
State, is also printed in Senate Executive C
(91st Cong., 1st sess.).

152   Statement on the Life Insurance Industry's Pledge
of Additional Investment Capital for Urban Core
Areas.   *April* 15, 1969

THE PLEDGE made by the life insurance companies to provide a second billion dollars of investment capital for urban core areas is most heartening. It demonstrates again the depth of their concern about the problems of our cities, and it will provide an effective way to bring more jobs and better housing to many Americans who need them.

Because this action represents a continuation of a program which began in 1967, the industry will be able to draw upon a great deal of experience. Our urban problems require intelligent planning as well as additional money, after all, and the life insurance industry is increasingly able to provide the needed skills. In the first billion-dollar program, the industry financed specific projects in 227 cities in 42 States, the District of Columbia, and Puerto Rico. They also financed 63,000 units of better housing for low-income families and invested in core area business enterprises and community services which created 30,000 permanent jobs.

The continuing commitment of the life insurance companies illustrates the effectiveness of volunteer business efforts in meeting social needs. It is no surprise that many of these companies are also involved in programs like the National Alliance of Businessmen and Plans for Progress. The men and women who are responsible for such initiatives are truly pioneers, breaking new ground and setting a pace which

other groups and individuals can be expected to follow.

With such cooperation, government can work effectively by entering into a creative partnership with the private sector. The life insurance executives can be sure that this administration will cooperate fully in making their program as effective as possible. We realize, too, that government can do more than it has done in the past to encourage further efforts of this sort by private investors.

The program of the insurance industry will have an impact far beyond what is directly accomplished by this particular investment. The effectiveness of that investment will be multiplied many times by providing economic stimulation, by inspiring further investments, and by encouraging greater cooperation between private and public institutions.

The Nation deeply appreciates the farsightedness and the sense of responsibility of the life insurance companies. On its behalf, I congratulate them for this significant decision.

NOTE: The pledge of funds was made by a group of life insurance executives to the President at a White House meeting.

Also released was the transcript of a news briefing by George W. Romney, Secretary of Housing and Urban Development, Francis E. Ferguson, Chairman of the Joint Committee on Urban Problems of the American Life Convention and the Life Insurance Association of America, Hilary Sandoval, Jr., Small Business Administrator, and Ronald L. Ziegler, Press Secretary to the President.

153   Message to the Senate Transmitting the Convention on Conduct of Fishing Operations in the North Atlantic. *April* 16, 1969

To the Senate of the United States:

With a view to receiving the advice and consent of the Senate to ratification, I transmit herewith a certified copy of the Convention on Conduct of Fishing Operations in the North Atlantic, done at London, June 1, 1967. The Convention has been signed on behalf of seventeen governments, including the United States of America, which represent the great majority of vessels engaged in the fisheries in the area.

For the information of the Senate, I also transmit the report by the Secretary of State with respect to the Convention.

The Convention establishes a generally uniform system of identification, marking, light signals, conduct, and enforcement for fishing vessels and support vessels in a large part of the North Atlantic. The Convention is sufficiently flexible that it might be extended to other areas of the Atlantic if developments in the fishery pattern make this desirable.

Many European fishing vessels have followed a code of conduct laid down in the 1882 Convention for Regulating the Police of the North Sea Fisheries, even though many of the European governments did not actually become party to the Convention. This code was gradually extended throughout the Northeast Atlantic as congestion on the fishing grounds gradually spread beyond the North Sea. Eventually, the code extended to the Northwest Atlantic.

Since foreign fishermen rarely operated close to our Atlantic coast, such a code was of little direct concern to our fishermen. This situation has changed dramatically during the past few years. Complaints of harassment or impaired operating freedom due to congestion on the fishing grounds have become frequent. As a result, our fishermen have called for a modern code of conduct to assist them. Their needs in this respect were made known to our negotiators.

I believe that the requirements of American fishermen in dealing with problems caused by the heavy concentration of vessels on the fishing grounds in the Convention area are substantially met by the terms of the Convention. The Convention will also assist us in our continuing effort to promote harmony in the international fisheries through agreements with other governments.

Proposed legislation to carry out the provisions of the Convention will be submitted.

I recommend that the Senate give early and favorable consideration to the Convention.

RICHARD NIXON

The White House

April 16, 1969

NOTE: The convention was favorably considered by the Senate on October 22, 1969, and ratified by the President on November 12, 1969. The text of the convention and the report of the Secretary of State are printed in Senate Executive D (91st Cong., 1st sess.).

154   Remarks at the 17th Annual Republican Women's Conference. *April 16, 1969*

Mary Brooks, Senator Dirksen, all of the distinguished guests at the head table, all of the distinguished guests in the audience, both in this room and downstairs:

I stopped in the overflow room before and I can tell you that there is just as much excitement and just as much enthusiasm there as there is here.

As Senator Dirksen has indicated, I don't think I have ever seen so many women in one place and I have seen them upstairs and downstairs.

I want you to know, too, as I stand here before you, I realize that over these past few days you have heard from a number of representatives from the new administration. I have not spoken to you. I will speak to you tonight briefly.

I am going to make a promise, though, with regard to what I will do next year. That will come later. But before referring to that, I want to say just a few words about those whom you are honoring tonight. As I understand it, you are honoring women generally. First I want to tell you how proud I am of the women that we have in the present administration. I am not going to name any one of them by name, except for Mary Brooks. She is typical of them and all that I can say is we wish we had more. We need more like Mary Brooks in this administration.

I would like to also tell you how proud I am of the women in this administration who do not hold office, but who hold the hands of their husbands who do hold office. I refer to our Cabinet wives.

I wonder if both downstairs, where they are carrying this on closed circuit television, and upstairs will the Cabinet wives please stand so that you can all see them, those who are in the Cabinet?

I want you to know that I am—I was going to say "an expert on wives." I don't mean that. But I have seen not only many women in government, but I have seen the wives of government officials and I have had the opportunity to see the wives of the members of the new Cabinet. I want to tell you first I am proud of every member of that Cabinet. It is a fine team. It is one of the best teams we have ever had.

But I can tell you that I have had an unusual experience, as you probably noted. We have done two things that have never been done before. We have had two meetings. Immediately before the Inauguration we had a meeting of all of the Cabinet, with the wives, an all-day meeting in which they were briefed along with the members of the Cabinet on the major issues that we would be facing.

Then just this last week we had another meeting. We are going to have one every quarter, because we believe that in government, when men have to make these very important decisions, if the member of the Cabinet happens to be a man, he needs not only the sympathy of his wife; he needs her advice, her understanding.

I can tell you that as I have seen those Cabinet women around that table, as I have seen them at dinners, state dinners at the White House, as I see them tonight, we have one of the finest groups of Cabinet wives I have ever seen. I am very proud of them, too.

Having spoken of our Cabinet family, I want to speak also of our Republican family—Republican women. As we were having a reception just the other day for a group that was in the White House, the National Committee, several came through the line and said, "We thank you for inviting us to the White House." I know that, as I read the statistics that Mary Brooks just handed me, yesterday in the White House there were 4,762 women who consumed 24,500 cookies, 235 gallons of punch, and came over in 44 buses.

I simply want to say this: To those of you who expressed thanks to me and to my wife Pat for inviting you to the White House, we want to thank you for making it possible that we could invite you to the White House. I know that Ev Dirksen will back me up in what I say. Without your help, we couldn't have done it; and with your help, we are going to continue to do it.

I think you should know that the first Women's Conference actually occurred in 1953. That was the first one, 17 years ago. Mrs. Eisenhower hosted the women at that conference. That was the first time in 20 years that the Republican Women had been visitors at the White House in that capacity. This year Pat Nixon hosted you. We hope to make it an annual event for as many years as you will allow us to do so.

Now if I could express a personal word—I can't often do this at home—but I understand that you are going to honor my wife and my two daughters for their role in the campaign. Believe me, they deserve it. Any wife who can do as my wife has, listen to my speeches through campaigns, at home and abroad in over 60 countries for 23 years, and sit there transfixed, as if she is hearing it for the first time, believe me, that is service far beyond

the call of duty.

But beyond that, I want you to know that in this last campaign I was proud of what all the Republican women did, the marvelous work you did all over this country. I was proud of what the women of my family did, my wife making appearances on her own in so many places, as did the wives of the Cabinet who are up here today, and my two daughters going out and making appearances all over the country.

People ask me about the fan mail we get. We get more for them than we do for me, believe me. We get more invitations for them, I think, than we do for me. That is fine.

I am reminded of a lesson that I have never forgotten: I remember in 1952, right after being nominated for Vice President, naturally, as a young Senator and a young candidate for Vice President—the youngest in history except for one up to that time—I felt, you know, rather puffed up about it, and I was put in my place at one of the first receptions. I remember it was in Nebraska. It was one of those long handshakers, and people came through the line over and over again saying, "Congratulations. This was fine," and so forth and so on.

Then one fellow came through the line. He said that he came from a farm and had driven over 200 miles to that meeting. He put it quite directly. He said, "Dick, I want to tell you something"—because he had seen me out there before when I had spoken as a Congressman and as a Senator. If there is any place I have not spoken, you name it. But believe me, he said to me, "I just want you to know that as I stand here and shake hands with you, I congratulate you for what you did. But never forget this: You are controversial, but everybody likes Pat."

So you see, I know the asset of the women in my family. I know what assets the Cabinet wives and all of the women in this administration are to this administration. I know what each of you has done in this campaign, and I thank you for it.

Now, if I could speak briefly about what you campaigned for, where we stand on it, and what I hope to be able to report next year. There were many great issues in the last campaign. Among those that I think stood out most in the minds of the women workers and the women voters to whom I talked in such great numbers were these:

First, the desire to bring peace in the world again. That was uppermost in the minds of women voters across this country, not the illusory peace that comes from simply ending a war, but the kind of a peace that is lasting, ending a war on a basis that will discourage other wars.

The women wanted that kind of leadership. They weren't satisfied with the past leadership. They voted for new leadership. That, therefore, was a major issue.

A second major issue was the desire upon the people of this country, among them, to stop the rise in taxes and stop the rise in prices. Women particularly were concerned about that issue because women have the responsibility for the family budget, and having the responsibility for the family budget, they know that unless we deal effectively in handling the problems of the Federal budget, you are not going to be able to balance the family budget.

They voted for new leadership to stop the rise in prices and stop the rise in taxes so that millions of Americans would do a better job and have a better chance to balance that family budget.

Then there is another great issue that I found—whether it was in the North, the East, the West, or the South—that women particularly were interested in, and that was to stop the rise in crime and reestablish respect for law and order throughout the United States.

This administration has been in office for almost 3 months. I know that many are quite impatient, perhaps, or might be impatient as to why we don't have peace, why we haven't stopped inflation, and why we haven't stopped the rise in crime and reestablished respect for law with justice and order throughout this country.

I could stand here and tell you that it had been done. That would not be true. I could stand here and promise you when it would be done. But that would not be responsible.

But I will tell you this: There are no three issues that have a higher priority in this administration than those three. I can tell you that on this day, for example, not only in the morning but throughout the afternoon, and when I leave this meeting to return to the White House for further meetings tonight, those were the three great issues on which my time was being spent.

I will tell you that I am going to make a pledge tonight. I ask not to speak formally to this group this year. Next year I am going to ask for an invitation to make a speech to the Republican Women's Conference when you come back. I ask the women in this audience to hold me and all of my Cabinet colleagues responsible on those three great issues. I will make this promise:

Next year I will be able to report to you and to the American people that we have made real progress toward bringing peace in the world, reestablishing law and order at home, and also in stopping the rise in taxes and inflation in the United States.

This is our goal. We are not over-promising. But I can assure you we have the programs, we have the men, and we have the women, I believe, that can bring success to those programs.

Now, finally, I had a thought. Mary Brooks said, "Tell us what we can do." There is no election this year, unless you happen to live in Virginia or New Jersey, and if you do, we wish you good luck in those States, believe me. But there is something else that you can do that goes beyond whether you happen to be a Republican, as all of you are, or a Democrat. It involves the mission of all the women in this country above everybody else.

I read a very disturbing report the first of this week. It was from the British Institute of Strategic Studies.[1] Many of you probably read it, too. What made the headlines in this report was its appraisal of American strength in the world compared with that of the Soviet Union.

It pointed out some facts that we found were accurate when we came into office. First, that over the past few years in terms of conventional weapons, the Soviet Union has been moving at a much faster pace than the United States; and that in terms of strategic weapons of the nuclear type, that in the year 1969 some estimates indicate that the Soviet Union might pass the United States. That compares with what the situation was in 1962 when there was at least a 4 to 1 advantage of the United States over the Soviet Union.

I mention those statistics because they have been publicly printed, not to frighten

anybody, because we need not be afraid. We still have major advantages in several areas. But I bring you those statistics simply to indicate that in the field of military strength we have the responsibility and we shall see to it that the United States, as we attempt to negotiate with other nations, as we are going to be willing to and desire to, as we negotiate to bring peace, we shall always negotiate from strength and never from weakness. That we pledge we will do.

Also, we have the responsibility in this administration for maintaining the economic strength of this country. We think we have programs that will do that.

But getting back to the study of the London Institute, it made one other point in which you have a special responsibility. It raised a question as to whether the year 1969 might mark the period in the history of the Western world when the United States not only lost the military superiority that it had, but more significantly, lost the will and the determination to be a major power and to play a major role in the world.

The study didn't go into it in detail, but the clear implication was that as far as the United States was concerned, a grave question now existed as to whether this great Nation, the Nation on whom the hopes for peace and freedom of the whole free world ride—the question was raised not simply with regard to our military strength, something that your administration takes responsibility for, but with regard to our moral strength, with regard to our will, with regard to our determination.

I simply want to say to the women in this audience, and to the women of America, through you, that will, that determination, cannot be brought by any

[1] The Strategic Survey, 1968–1969, an annual report issued by the Institute for Strategic Studies, London, England.

President to the people. It must come from the home. It must come from the families. It must come from our churches, from our schools throughout the Nation, and I can tell you that having spoken across this Nation for so many years, I am not pessimistic about that will.

This is a great country. I have traveled all the nations of the world and I know the criticisms of America. But I can tell you that when I come back to the United States, I realize that this Nation not only is militarily strong and will remain so, not only is it the richest Nation and will remain so, but that as a great nation, we are going to meet the challenge of our time because we do have the character and we do have the moral stamina that this country requires and that the world requires today. This I believe.

All that I ask is this: that as you return to your homes, we instill that spirit—a spirit of pride, a spirit of patriotism in the very best sense of the word, a spirit of what America has always stood for to the world, not bent on aggression, but recognizing that freedom, meaning as much as it does to us, that we have a responsibility to hold that standard high for all the world to see.

This is the charge that I leave with you tonight, and I am confident, as I have talked to you and as I have received reports from this meeting—I am confident that you are going to meet it.

A few days ago when I delivered the eulogy to President Eisenhower, I referred to the fact that in his eloquent and memorable speech at London's Guildhall, he made the statement: "I come from the heart of America." And he truly did, from the geographical heart and the spiritual heart of America.

I simply want to say that as I see a great group of Americans like this, not just because you are Republicans—I like that—but as I see you vitally interested in your country, concerned about the issues, making this trip to Washington, going back and carrying the word back to the precincts throughout this country, as I see you, I am going to leave this meeting knowing that the heart of America is good because you are going to keep it good and strong. I am sure you will.

Thank you.

NOTE: The President spoke at 9:39 p.m. at the Sheraton Park Hotel in Washington. Mary Thomas Brooks, retiring assistant chairman of the Republican National Committee, was nominated by the President as Director, Bureau of the Mint on March 28, 1969.

155 Remarks at a Reception Commemorating the 50th Anniversary of the League of Women Voters of the United States. *April 17, 1969*

Ladies and gentlemen:

In this great East Room of the White House many ceremonies are held, but perhaps none that symbolizes a great change in the political life of this country more than this one today.

A year before the 19th amendment was adopted the League of Women Voters was founded, and that organization, in the past 50 years, has played a major role in this Nation on a nonpartisan basis of stimulating creative thought, new ideas, discussion on the great issues confronting the American people.

I have a special relationship to the League which Mrs. Benson, the present president, and Mrs. Gundersen [1] would not know about. But it happened that when I first ran for Congress—and I am sure that as I see other Members of the Congress around here today they have probably had similar experiences—when I first ran for Congress the first joint appearance I had with my congressional opponent was before a candidates' meeting set up by the League of Women Voters of Pasadena, California. It was called a debate, incidentally. And I won that debate.

But through the years all of us who are here—and I see so many Senators and Congressmen in this room—have appeared on forums sponsored by the League. We know the nonpartisan character. We know the tremendous interest of the organization in all of the great issues. I speak for all of my colleagues who have been candidates in thanking you for making it possible for us to reach more people to present our points of view, as you have.

Also, in speaking today about this 50th anniversary, I should tell you I was rather surprised when I walked into the reception room and found Mrs. Benson and Mrs. Gundersen—Mrs. Gundersen is from Wisconsin; Mrs. Benson, incidentally, has something in common with my daughter, Julie; she is a Smith girl married to an Amherst man—but also John Gardner, the former Secretary of HEW and now the head of the Urban Coalition.

I asked John Gardner how he was able to work into this group—and incidentally, Senator Fulbright was also there; I found

that he was there just covering all the bases—but John Gardner pointed out that he had the very special responsibility this year to head the fundraising drive for the League of Women Voters. Now, when a man takes on the responsibility of raising money for the women, believe me, that is the kind of, shall we say not "bipartisanship," but you can call it something else, that we need in this country.

Now, at this point I would like to add perhaps one word of perspective about the role of women in politics in America. Last night I spoke to 4,000 Republican women who were here in Washington, D.C. Their Democratic counterparts will also be here in the months ahead and through the years we have seen, particularly, I would say, since about 1947, a tremendously escalating role of women in politics in the United States.

We all know the important role that women play as Members of the Senate, Members of the House, members of State legislatures. We all know of the appointments that they have carried out with great distinction in various government positions, the Federal Government, the State government, the city government. We know, too, of the role that they play in political action and, of course, most are in that field, virtually all are, as a matter of fact.

I often say that men do the talking and women do the working in campaigns and that often happens as we get into our campaigns and find that those great groups of women workers will make the difference in a close election; who has more; who has the greatest excitement among them. All this we know.

Then, of course, as we look at the past 50 years we wonder what could happen in the next 50 years. Now, I can speak

---

[1] Mrs. Alfred Gundersen, chairman of the 50th anniversary committee.

with some sense of—shall we say "complacency"—on that score as far as my own position is concerned at this time. But as I look around the world and as I find that India has a woman Prime Minister, Ceylon has a woman Prime Minister, Israel has a woman Prime Minister, certainly in the next 50 years we shall see a woman President—maybe sooner than you think.

Whatever the case might be, whether that happens or not, and I notice that polls have been taken recently by Gallup and Harris indicating that that is something that very well might happen in the United States in the near future, what is even more important is not to think in terms of whether a woman could or should be President, but I think we should all say that by reason of the role women have played in politics in America a woman can and should be able to do any political job that a man could do. That I know and that you know.

But what is more important is what the League of Women Voters stands for. What is more important is to have this tremendous participation, this motivation, involvement, which the League of Women Voters has brought not only to women, but also to men, in their first 50 years. I just hope it continues. That is what the country needs.

We have so many issues that are not partisan in character. The issue of peace in the world is not a partisan issue. The issue of making our cities more livable, not only in terms of the enforcement of the law and the safety of our streets, but also in terms of the total environment of our cities—that is not a partisan issue.

The problem of holding down the cost of living and taxes, that is not a partisan issue. The problem of how we progress to the kind of life we want—all of these is-

sues we find Republicans and Democrats not breaking down on strictly partisan lines, but breaking down on the basis of their honest convictions with regard to that issue.

As I know the League of Women Voters, that is the way you approach the problems—not on the basis of partisanship, but on the basis of the facts of what the best interests of the Nation may be. Then you encourage your members to participate in the parties of their choice and to be active in working for whatever side of an issue that particular individual honestly believes in. That is the American system.

That is the way it works best. It is because the League stands for that, perhaps as much or more than any political organization that I know in America, that I have issued a proclamation today,[2] a proclamation asking the people of the United States to join the League of Women Voters in commemorating this 50th anniversary.

Now with that, since I often, around the dinner table, have deferred to a girl from Smith, I now turn this microphone over to the president of the League of Women Voters, Mrs. Benson, a graduate of Smith College.

[At this point Mrs. Bruce B. Benson spoke. The President then resumed speaking.]

Believe me, I have never been lobbied more graciously than that. Even though he doesn't know that I am going to call on him, I do think that we would like to hear from John Gardner, a distinguished educator and a distinguished leader of the Nation in so many ways.

John, would you say a word to us?

Before the Secretary—I call him the Secretary because once a Cabinet officer,

---

[2] Proclamation 3909.

always one. In any event, the one rule we have in the White House is that, generally speaking, we do not have fundraising dinners or anything of that sort because that would have a partisan context, but we shall break that rule and if you want to make a fundraising pitch here to those television cameras, you may do so, or even for the Urban Coalition, if you like.

[At this point Mr. Gardner, chairman of the League's national sponsors committee, spoke. The President then resumed speaking.]

We have so many distinguished guests here today that I do not want to pick them out by name, but I wonder if all of those who are members of the Supreme Court would please stand. I see one of the Justices here, at least. Justice White represents all of the Court very well right here in this room today. [*Applause*]

Then I see several Members of the Senate. I wonder if the Members of the Senate would please stand. [*Applause*]

As you know, we will go all the way from Massachusetts to Hawaii here, so we have a very good representation there.

Are there any Members of the House here? [*Applause*]

Again, a broad cross section.

Thank you very much. We hope you all enjoy your visit to this house. You can stay and look around—and coffee—but don't take anything else, please.

NOTE: The President spoke at 10:10 a.m. in the East Room at the White House.

The remarks of Mrs. Benson and Mr. Gardner are printed in the Weekly Compilation of Presidential Documents (vol. 5, p. 569).

156 The President's News Conference of *April* 18, 1969

QUESTIONS

NORTH KOREA'S ATTACK ON U.S. RECONNAISSANCE FLIGHT

[1.] Q. Mr. President, the question on all of our minds is where do we go from here with the incident of the shooting down of the plane? [1] What further action might you contemplate diplomatically and militarily?

THE PRESIDENT. Mr. Cormier [Frank Cormier, Associated Press], first, I think a word with regard to the facts in this case: As was pointed out in the protest that was filed at Panmunjom yesterday and also in the Defense Department statement, the

---

[1] On April 15, 1969, in the Sea of Japan, some 100 miles off the Korean coast.

plane involved was an unarmed Constellation, propeller-driven.

The mission was a reconnaissance mission which at no time took the plane closer to the shores of North Korea than 40 miles. At the time the plane was shot down, all of the evidence that we have indicates that it was shot down approximately 90 miles from the shores of North Korea while it was moving outward, aborting the mission on orders that had been received. We knew this, based on our radar.

What is also even more important, the North Koreans knew it, based on their radar. Therefore, this attack was unprovoked. It was deliberate. It was without warning. The protest has been filed. The North Koreans have not responded.

Now a word with regard to why we

have such missions in the Sea of Japan. As you ladies and gentlemen are aware, there are 56,000 American troops stationed in South Korea. Those 56,000 men are the responsibility of the President of the United States as Commander in Chief.

In recent weeks and months, in fact going back over the last 2 or 3 years, but particularly in recent weeks and months, North Korea has threatened military action against South Korea and against our forces in South Korea. The number of incidents has increased.

It is the responsibility of the Commander in Chief to protect the security of those men. That is why, going back over 20 years and throughout the period of this administration being continued, we have had a policy of reconnaissance flights in the Sea of Japan similar to this flight. This year we have had already 190 of these flights without incident, without threat, without warning at all.

Now the question is: What do we do about these flights in the future? They were discontinued immediately after this incident occurred.

I have today ordered that these flights be continued. They will be protected. This is not a threat; it is simply a statement of fact.

As the Commander in Chief of our Armed Forces I cannot and will not ask our men to serve in Korea, and I cannot and will not ask our men to take flights like this in unarmed planes without providing protection. That will be the case.

Looking to the future, as far as what we do will depend upon the circumstances. It will depend upon what is done as far as North Korea is concerned, its reaction to the protest, and also any other developments that occur as we continue these flights.

OUTLOOK FOR PEACE IN SOUTHEAST ASIA

[2.] Mr. Smith [Merriman Smith, United Press International].

Q. Mr. President, now that you have had about 3 months in a position of Presidential responsibility, do the chances of peace in Southeast Asia seem to come any closer at all, or has the situation, the outlook for peace, improved or deteriorated since your inauguration?

THE PRESIDENT. Mr. Smith, the chances for peace in Southeast Asia have significantly improved since this administration came into office. I do not claim that that has happened simply because of what we have done, although I think we have done some things that have improved those chances; and I am not trying to raise false hopes that peace is just around the corner, this summer or this fall.

But a number of developments clearly beyond the Paris peace talks have convinced me that the chances for bringing this war to a peaceful conclusion have significantly improved.

One factor that should be mentioned, that I note has not been covered perhaps as much as others, is the fact that South Korea has significantly improved its own capabilities. The way we can tell this has happened is that the South Korean President has taken an attitude with regard to the make-up of a government after peace comes that he wouldn't have even considered 6 months ago, and he has done this because South Korean—I am sorry, South Vietnamese forces; it is natural that you transplant these two words, I find, in discussing these two subjects—South Vietnamese forces are far better able to handle themselves militarily, and that program is going forward on a much more intensive basis than it was when this administration came into office.

Second, political stability in South Vietnam has increased significantly since this administration came into office. The trend had begun before, but it has continued and escalated since that time.

As a result of these two factors, it means that South Vietnam is able to make a peace which I think will give a better opportunity for negotiating room for their negotiators and ours at the Paris conference. That is one of the reasons for my feeling somewhat optimistic, although we still have some hard ground to plow.

CONSIDERATION OF TROOP WITHDRAWALS

Yes, sir.

[3.] Q. To follow that up, then, are you considering now the unilateral withdrawal of American troops from South Vietnam?

THE PRESIDENT. I am not. If we are to have a negotiating position at the Paris peace talks, it must be a position in which we can negotiate from strength, and discussion about unilateral withdrawal does not help that position. I will not engage in it, although I realize it might be rather popular to do so.

It is the aim of this administration to bring men home just as soon as our security will allow us to do so. As I have indicated previously, there are three factors that we are going to take into consideration: the training of the South Vietnamese, their ability to handle their own defense; the level of fighting in South Vietnam, whether or not the offensive action of the enemy recedes; and progress in the Paris peace talks.

Looking to the future, I would have to say that I think there are good prospects that American forces can be reduced, but

as far as this time is concerned, we have no plans to reduce our forces until there is more progress on one or all of the three fronts that I have mentioned.

LEVEL OF COMBAT ACTIVITY IN SOUTH VIETNAM

[4.] Q. Mr. President——

THE PRESIDENT. Mr. Lisagor [Peter Lisagor, Chicago Daily News], yes.

Q. Could I ask you whether you have ordered that the level of American combat activity in South Vietnam be reduced in order to reduce the casualties?

THE PRESIDENT. No, Mr. Lisagor, the casualties have been reduced, as you have noted in your question, but the reason that American casualties are down is because the level of offensive action on the part of the enemy has receded.

An analysis—and I have studied this quite carefully because I have noted the great interest in this country on this subject as to whether or not our casualties are the result of our action or theirs. What we find is that the level of casualties substantially increased during the spring offensive. That spring offensive at this time either has run its course or is in a substantial lull. Because that offensive is in that status at this time, our level of casualties is down.

I have not ordered and do not intend to order any reduction of our own activities. We will do what is necessary to defend our position and to maintain the strength of our bargaining position in the Paris peace talks.

THE TAX SURCHARGE AND TAX REFORM

[5.] Q. Mr. President, do you foresee the possibility or the likelihood that after the Vietnam war ends, the 10 percent income tax surcharge will be continued indefinitely to help pay for what you call this country's compelling domestic needs?

THE PRESIDENT. No, I do not foresee that likelihood and that will not be the objective of this administration. I indicated during the campaign that I thought that taxes were too high. I still believe that. And I believe that the surcharge, the so-called "war tax," which some describe it, that that tax should be reduced and removed just as soon as we are able to do so, either because of Vietnam or for other reasons.

I will also indicate that at this time the administration's interim tax reform package will be submitted to the Congress early next week, either Monday or Tuesday. The Secretary of the Treasury, or the Treasury Department, is testifying on Tuesday. I have already approved the message. It will have some information on this and other matters that will be of interest to all of you.

THE ABM SYSTEM

[6.] Mr. Theis [J. William Theis, Hearst Newspapers].

Q. Mr. President, it has been suggested that you may go directly to the country on the ABM issue to further clarify and support your case. Can you tell us of any plans you have in that direction, perhaps today?

THE PRESIDENT. No, I have no plans at this time to go to the country, as you have suggested. As a matter of fact, I consider a press conference as going to the country. I find that these conferences are rather well covered by the country, both by television, as they are today, and also by the members of the press.

With regard to the ABM decision, however, I wish to emphasize again the point that I made when I announced that decision in this room a few weeks ago.

I made that decision after I considered all the options that were before me with regard to what was necessary to maintain America's defenses, and particularly the credibility of our national security and our diplomacy throughout the world.

I analyzed the nature of the threat. I found, for example, that even since the decision to deploy the ABM system called Sentinel in 1967, the intelligence estimates indicated that the Soviet capability with regard to their SS-9's, their nuclear missiles, was 60 percent higher than we thought then; that their plans for nuclear submarines were 60 percent greater than we had thought then.

Under these circumstances, I had to make basically a command decision as to what the United States should do if we were to avoid falling into a second-class or inferior position vis-à-vis the Soviet Union.

I had a number of options. We could have increased our offensive forces in various directions. I determined that this limited defensive action, limited insofar as the Soviet Union is concerned, to defend our Minuteman missile sites, was the best action that could be taken.

I still believe that to be the case. I believe it is essential for the national security, and it is essential to avoid putting an American President, either this President or the next President, in the position where the United States would be second rather than first, or at least equal to any potential enemy.

The other reason, and I emphasize this strongly, is that the Chinese Communists, according to our intelligence, have not moved as fast recently as they had over the past 3 to 4 years, but that, nevertheless, by 1973 or 1974 they would have a significant nuclear capability which would make our diplomacy not credible in the Pacific unless we could protect our country against a Chinese attack aimed at our cities.

The ABM system will do that, and the ABM Safeguard system, therefore, has been adopted for that reason.

CONSULTATION ON PROTECTION OF RECONNAISSANCE FLIGHTS

[7.] Q. Mr. President, has there been any consultation with our allies or with Japan on sending armed planes along to guard the reconnaissance craft? Is it necessary?

THE PRESIDENT. There has been no consultation up to this point. I can only say in answer to that question that when I refer to protecting these flights, I am not going to go beyond that at this time. I am simply indicating that they will be protected.

If we think that consultation is necessary, we will have consultation.

PARTISANSHIP AND THE ABM ISSUE

[8.] Q. Mr. President, on the ABM issue, as you know, there are a number of Republican Senators who oppose your views on the ABM.

Do you think that they should support you because you are a Republican President even though they oppose the principle?

THE PRESIDENT. I certainly do not. I want to make it crystal clear that my decision on ABM was not made on the basis

of Republican versus Democrat. It was made on the basis of what I thought was best for the country.

I talked, for example, just yesterday, with Senator Cooper [Senator John Sherman Cooper of Kentucky]. He is one of those who opposes me as a Republican. He honestly and sincerely believes that this is not the best step to take.

I respect that belief, and I respect others who disagree with me on this. I also respect the beliefs of Senator Jackson, Speaker McCormack, Senator Stennis, and Senator Russell, and a number of Democrats, who believe that this is the right step to take.

This issue will be fought out, as it should be fought out, on the basis of what is best for the Nation. It will not be fought out on partisan lines.

I am going to fight as hard as I can for it because I believe it is absolutely essential to the security of the country. But it is going to be fought on the basis of asking each Senator and Congressman to make his own decision, and I am confident, incidentally, that that decision will be in favor of the system when they know all the facts.

INVESTMENT TAX CREDIT

[9.] Q. Mr. President?

THE PRESIDENT. Yes, sir.

Q. Democrats in the House have voted to repeal the 7 percent investment tax credit. What is your position on this, sir?

THE PRESIDENT. The position of the administration on this will be announced in the tax reform measure that will be submitted on Monday or Tuesday of next week. I will not discuss it further at this time.

MISSILE CAPABILITY OF THE SOVIET UNION

[10.]   Q. Mr. President?

THE PRESIDENT. Yes, Mr. Scali [John A. Scali, ABC News].

Q. Secretary [of State William P.] Rogers said at a recent news conference that if and when we begin talks with the Soviets on missiles, one of the first questions to be asked them is why they find it necessary to build a big missile with a 25 megaton warhead.

Since the Russian decision to proceed to build such an enormous missile is one of the major factors in your going ahead with the ABM, the question is: Why are we waiting to ask that question for the beginning of negotiations? Why don't we ask it now?

THE PRESIDENT. Well, Mr. Scali, in a sense I think Secretary Rogers probably asked the question by stating it as he did in a press conference. As you know, because you have covered these diplomatic matters for many years, in dealing with the Soviet Union or any other nation, this type of question is not always asked simply on a formal basis in a diplomatic conference.

Sometimes the best way to handle it is to state the position publicly. As far as Secretary Rogers' statement is concerned, I share his puzzlement as to why the Soviet Union is moving so heavily in this direction. As far as the Soviet Union's intentions are concerned, and I want to clarify one point that is made, the question as to their intentions is not something that I am going to comment upon. I don't know what their intentions are.

But we have to base our policy on their capabilities and when we project their SS–9 plans to 1972 or 1973, if we allow those plans to go forward without taking any action on our part, either offensively or defensively, to counteract them, they will be substantially ahead of the United States in overall nuclear capability. We cannot allow that to happen.

I would remind the members of this press corps—I am here at a time when the United States faces a threat, not of the magnitude that President Kennedy faced at the time of the Cuban missile crisis—but I would remind the members of this press corps that at that time all of the professional experts agreed that the U.S. superiority was at least 4 to 1 and maybe 5 to 1, over the Soviet Union in terms of overall nuclear capability.

Now we don't have that today. That gap has been closed. We shall never have it again because it will not be necessary for us. Sufficiency, as I have indicated, is all that is necessary. But I do say this: I do not want to see an American President in the future, in the event of any crisis, have his diplomatic credibility be so impaired because the United States was in a second-class or inferior position. We saw what it meant to the Soviets when they were second. I don't want that position to be the United States in the event of a future diplomatic crisis.

SOVIET ROLE IN THE PLANE INCIDENT

[11.]   Q. Mr. President, could you tell us what the Soviet role has been in the plane incident, and could you go beyond that and tell us what were some of the other elements that figured in your deliberations on how to properly respond to the downing of the plane?

THE PRESIDENT. The Soviet role in the plane incident, first, is one of being of assistance to the United States in recovering the debris and looking for survivors. We are most grateful to the Soviet Union for helping us in this respect.

Our intelligence and, of course, no one can be sure here, indicates that the Soviet Union was not aware that this attack was to be made. North Korea is not a nation that is predictable in terms of its actions. It is perhaps more than any other nation in the Communist bloc completely out of the control of either the Soviet Union or, for that matter, Communist China. That, at least, is our intelligence estimate at this time.

Now, as far as other matters that entered into this interim decision, and I emphasize it as an interim decision, I have concluded that the United States must face up to the fact that intelligence gathering—intelligence gathering that does not involve overflights, that does not involve interdiction of another nation's air space, or moving into its waters—here where intelligence people are involved, we recognize that they are necessarily subject to whatever action can or should be taken by another nation to defend itself.

But when planes of the United States, or ships of the United States, in intelligence gathering, are in international water or in international air space, they are not fair game. They will not be in the future. I state that as a matter of fact, and that was the basis for this interim decision.

DR. LONG'S POSITION ON THE ABM SYSTEM

[12.] Q. Mr. President, on the question of dissent on the ABM, can you tell us, sir, did you or did you not block the appointment of Dr. Long [Dr. Franklin A. Long, vice president, Cornell University] as head of the NSF [National Science Foundation] because he disapproved of your position on the ABM?

THE PRESIDENT. Dr. Long's potential appointment was not discussed with me until after he had had a conversation with Dr. DuBridge on this matter.

The determination was made by members of the White House Staff that his appointment, in view of his very sincere beliefs opposing the ABM, would not be in the best interests of the overall administration position.

I wish to make it clear that we have vigorous dissent and discussion within our National Security Council on this and other matters. But to have at this time made an appointment of a man who quite honestly and quite sincerely—a man of eminent credentials, incidentally—disagreed with the administration's position on a major matter of this sort, we thought this would be misunderstood. My staff thought that and, under the circumstances, I approved of their decision not to submit the recommendation to me.[2]

---

[2] On April 28 the President met with representatives from the National Science Board and the Council of the National Academy of Sciences. At his news briefing following the meeting, Press Secretary Ronald L. Ziegler announced that the President had asked the National Science Board to submit new nominations for the position of National Science Foundation Director.

On June 19 the White House announced the President's intention to nominate as Director, Dr. William D. McElroy, chairman of the Department of Biology at Johns Hopkins University in Baltimore (5 Weekly Comp. Pres. Docs., p. 877). Dr. McElroy was confirmed on July 11 and took office on July 14.

THE PLANE INCIDENT AND THE "PUEBLO"
ATTACK

[13.] Q. Mr. President, how do you
assess the motives of the North Koreans
in this attack and do you see any parallel
or pattern in this attack and also the one
on the *Pueblo?*

THE PRESIDENT. Well, the *Pueblo* incident was quite different in two respects.
One, there was some uncertainty for some
time as to where the *Pueblo* was. Present
indications are that the *Pueblo* was in
international waters. But there was a
more uncertain factor.

There was no uncertainty whatever as
to where this plane was, because we know
what their radar showed. We, incidentally, know what the Russian radar
showed. And all three radars showed exactly the same thing.

Let me also say that there is no question
of what they claim as their air space.
Some of you, of course, know the confusion and, as a matter of fact, the confrontation we are having with Peru about the
200-mile limit.[3] North Korea claims only
12 miles as its limit, so we were at least
28 miles away at the very closest point.

Also, with regard to the *Pueblo,* in the
case of the *Pueblo* the North Koreans had
warned and threatened the *Pueblo* for a
period of several weeks before they seized
it. In the case of these flights, they have
been going on, as I have indicated, for
years, and during this administration,
without incident, 190 of them have
occurred this year.

---

[3] On February 14 and again on March 19,
1969, Peruvian naval units seized or damaged
a total of four American-owned fishing vessels.
Fines totaling $27,000 were assessed against
them for illegal fishing.

Under these circumstances, it was a
completely surprise attack in every sense
of the word and, therefore, did not give
us the opportunity for protective action
that I would have taken had it been
threatened.

ELECTORAL REFORM

[14.] Mr. Bailey [Charles W. Bailey 2d,
Minneapolis Star and Tribune].

Q. Mr. President, it appears that the
House Judiciary Committee is going to
report out an electoral reform bill providing for direct popular election of the
President, perhaps with a provision delaying the effectiveness of this until past the
next election. Will you support this?

THE PRESIDENT. Mr. Bailey, if the
House and the Senate approve a direct
election proposal for amending the Constitution, it will have my support. It is my
judgment that that kind of proposal will
have far less chance to get the requisite
number of States to approve it than the
proposal that I favor, the proportional system. But my view is that, first, the present
system must be modified. As far as I am
concerned, the proportional system, the
congressional district system, or the direct
election system would be preferable to the
present system. That is my conviction as
far as my judgment.

As to what the House and the Senate
ought to do, I have expressed my view as
to the practical political realities. If the
Members of the House and Senate conclude that they can get the three-fourths
of the States for the direct election system,
and if they pass and can agree in conference that that is what they will approve,
then that modification, that amendment,

305

will have my enthusiastic support; however with some doubts as to whether it will succeed.

CIVIL RIGHTS

[15.] Q. Mr. President, Roy Wilkins of the NAACP, on Wednesday, characterized the civil rights record of your administration thus far as mixed, citing the textile mills case in the Department of Defense and also the resignation of Clifford Alexander.[4]

How would you characterize your administration's civil rights record?

THE PRESIDENT. Well, the intent of our administration is to enforce the laws of this land and to develop a coordinated program in which there will be standards that everybody will understand so that we will not be subject to this criticism of our record being mixed.

Now, the reason for Roy Wilkins' criticism, and he has expressed this to me personally, too, the reason for it is well-founded as far as the implementation is concerned.

As all of you know, the number of agencies involved in civil rights compliance means that in these gray areas in which close cases come up, you will get different men coming up with different conclusions.

You mentioned the textile cases. The three South Carolina cases involved the Defense Department and Defense contracts and the Compliance Section inter-

---

[4] Clifford L. Alexander, Jr., resigned as Chairman of the Equal Employment Opportunity Commission on April 9, 1969, but continued as a Commissioner. He was succeeded in the chairmanship by William H. Brown III on May 6, 1969.

preting how compliance could be obtained for that contractual provision.

The North Carolina case, which was brought by the Department of Justice, did not involve compliance with a Defense contractor but it involved a mill with no Government contracts and since compliance could not be negotiated, suit had to be brought.

That can be called "mixed" but nevertheless, I think you can see how that kind of result could be attained.

PROBLEMS IN RESPONDING TO AGGRESSION

[16.] Q. Mr. President, you have addressed yourself many times in the past, sir, to the danger and the consequences of aggression against our country by a minor military power.

It seems to me what we have seen developed here is a kind of new rules of warfare which we certainly have not agreed to and obviously the Soviet Union hasn't.

In your present circumstances, sir, can you tell us of some of the problems that you have faced in making a proper response?

THE PRESIDENT. The problems with regard to a proper response are quite obvious: the question as to what reaction we could expect not only from the party against whom we respond but other parties that might be involved, and also putting it in the larger context, how responding in one area might affect a major interest of the United States in another area, an area like Vietnam, Vietnam being the top priority area for us.

Now, in answering the question in that way, I do not want to leave the implication that the announcement of the re-

newal of and the continuation of reconnaissance flights is the final action that
can or will be taken here.

Our action in this matter will be determined by what happens in the future.

THE SOVIET UNION AND CZECHOSLOVAKIA

[17.] Looking at the Soviet Union, it
seems to me that had it not been for this
incident the major story that I would have
been asked about today was what happened in Czechoslovakia. I suppose that
my reaction to that would be to condemn
the Soviet Union for what it did.

The Soviet Union is aware of our disapproval of that action. All Americans,
in fact all people in the free world, see
this as perhaps the final chapter in the
great tragedy of the Czechoslovak people
under Communist rule.[5]

---

[5] On April 17, 1969, Alexander Dubcek,
first secretary of the Czechoslovak Communist
Party and leader of Czechoslovakia's liberaliz-

We hope it is not the final chapter. We
hope that some vestiges of freedom will
remain. Yet, the Soviet Union has acted
there and acted quite decisively. They
have to consider now, in terms of any
future action, how that might affect their
relations with the United States and with
the Western world.

What I am trying to do in answering
your question is to pose the problem that
great powers confront when they take actions involving powers that are not in that
league.

We must always measure our actions
by that base.

Merriman Smith, United Press International: Thank you, Mr. President.

NOTE: President Nixon's fifth news conference
was held in the East Room at the White House
at 11:32 a.m. on Friday, April 18, 1969. It
was broadcast on radio and television.

---

ing movement was ousted due to Soviet pressure. The central committee of the Czechoslovak Communist Party named the more
conservative Gustav Husak to succeed Dubcek.

157   Memorandum on Employment of the Handicapped. *April* 18, 1969

To Heads of Executive Departments and Agencies:

Subject: Policy for Federal Employment
of the Handicapped

It is the policy of this Administration, in
staffing the Federal service, to give full
consideration to the employment and
selective placement of the handicapped.

Administrations of both parties, since
World War II, have set examples of national leadership in opening the Government's doors to more than one-quarter

million citizens who, though handicapped, have nonetheless been occupationally qualified. Today throughout the
economy we find general acceptance of
the reminder: "Hire the Handicapped—
It's Good Business."

I have personally observed the mutual
benefits that derive from hiring the handicapped, and I want this "good business"
to continue and prosper.

Therefore, I ask each of you to make a
commitment to removing any remaining
barriers to the Federal employment of

307

—the *physically impaired* who are not occupationally handicapped when assigned to the right jobs.

—the *mentally restored* whose only handicap is that they once suffered an emotional illness.

—the *mentally retarded* who can demonstrate ability to perform the simple and routine tasks that need

doing in all organizations, regardless of size.

The Civil Service Commission will provide leadership and direction for the overall Federal effort in carrying out this policy.

I am confident that you will give this policy and the Commission your earnest support.

RICHARD NIXON

158   Letter to the President of the American Bar Association, Requesting an Appraisal of the Federal Trade Commission.   *April 18, 1969*

Dear Mr. Gossett:

As you may be aware, this Administration is conducting an extensive review of the Federal Government's activities in the field of consumer protection. Consumer protection has become a matter of major public concern, in part it appears, because existing agencies charged with the protection of consumer interests may have failed to discharge their obligations satisfactorily.

The Federal Trade Commission has broad consumer protection responsibilities under the Federal Trade Commission Act and several more specialized statutes as well as important responsibilities in the field of anti-trust.

The American Bar Association has a number of eminent experts who are familiar with the Federal Trade Commission and its work. It would be of great assistance to this Administration if the Bar Association would undertake a professional appraisal of the present efforts of the Federal Trade Commission in the field of consumer protection, in its enforcement of the anti-trust laws, and of the allocation of its resources between these two

areas. I would hope that such a study would make recommendations for the future activities and organization of the Commission.

It would be most helpful if the report could be made available to me by September 15 so that I may consider it together with a review of consumer protection activities of the Executive Branch now in progress.

May I express in advance my great appreciation for your cooperation in this important effort.

Sincerely yours,

RICHARD NIXON

[William T. Gossett, Esq., President, American Bar Association, American Bar Center, Chicago, Illinois]

NOTE: The letter was dated April 17, 1969 and released April 18, 1969. Mr. Gossett's letter to the President, agreeing to undertake the appraisal is printed in the Weekly Compilation of Presidential Documents (vol. 5, p. 576).

The "Report of the ABA Commission to Study the Federal Trade Commission" (American Bar Association, 119 pp.), was submitted to the President on September 15, 1969, by chairman Miles W. Kirkpatrick.

159   Remarks at the Swearing In of Virginia H. Knauer as Special Assistant to the President for Consumer Affairs. *April* 19, 1969

Ladies and gentlemen:

You have already met Mrs. Knauer when she had her press conference on the occasion of her being named as the Assistant to the President for Consumer Affairs.

My remarks, therefore, today, will be very brief, since she has already covered the responsibilities that she will have.

I think the point I particularly wish to emphasize is that her appointment is based solely on merit and qualification for the job. It happens that she is a woman, and a very attractive woman.

It also happens, however, that of all the people in the United States who are expert in the field of consumer affairs, she had the experience, the background, and the dedication in this subject that we thought qualified her for the top position in the Federal Government on consumer affairs.

As head of the Pennsylvania Bureau of Consumer Protection, she set a record that won her acclaim throughout America at the State level.

Senator [Hugh] Scott and others from the State of Pennsylvania will back me up when I make that statement.

Consequently, we think, having proved herself at the State level and with all her experience in many other areas as well, that she now can assume the major responsibility at the Federal level.

I note that one of the first questions that she was required to answer at her news conference was with regard to her age. She didn't dodge that question, as do some of us, and, as is said, do most women.

I would only say that any woman who would very honestly give her age certainly will be able to get manufacturers in this country to tell the truth about their products.

Holding the Bible for her swearing in will be her granddaughter, Nancy Knauer. Judge Kelly of the District Court of Appeals will administer the oath.

NOTE: The President spoke at 11:20 a.m. in the Rose Garden at the White House. The oath of office was administered by Associate Judge Catherine B. Kelly of the District of Columbia Court of Appeals.

For the announcement of Mrs. Knauer's appointment on April 9, see the Weekly Compilation of Presidential Documents (vol. 5, p. 535). Released at the same time was the transcript of a news conference she held following the announcement.

160   Remarks Announcing the Nomination of Representative Donald Rumsfeld as Director, Office of Economic Opportunity. *April* 21, 1969

Ladies and gentlemen:

I have an announcement to make today that has already been, as usual, anticipated by the press.

As Director of the Office of Economic Opportunity, I am naming Don Rumsfeld, Congressman from Illinois. This, of course, is subject to Senate confirmation.

We expect, however, no troubles in the Senate in getting confirmation.

A release has already been given to the members of the press giving the background with regard to Congressman Rumsfeld's appointment, how it is worked out logistically and the like.

I will summarize it briefly in this way: He will have as his primary responsibility that of running the Office of Economic Opportunity as Director of the Office of Economic Opportunity. He will have, also, the rank of Assistant to the President and he will have Cabinet rank.

He will be a member of the Urban Affairs Council, of which Mr. [Daniel P.] Moynihan is the Director.

All of these responsibilities, I think, fit into the decision that Mr. Rumsfeld has made.

I was saying to him in our meeting in the office just before coming in here, that I remember when I was his age, 36 years of age, in 1949, I made the hardest political decision of my life. That decision was to give up a safe seat in the Congress—I had won both nominations in the election immediately preceding—and to run for the Senate.

Don Rumsfeld, today, is "crossing the Rubicon" to an extent. He is making what, for him, may have been his hardest and most important political decision. He is giving up one of the safest seats in the Congress of the United States to take on one of the most important agencies, one of the most controversial agencies in the entire Government.

This, to me, displays unusual courage, and it is an indication of his great dedication to this problem, the problem of finding the answers to poverty in America.

Don Rumsfeld in the Congress specialized in this problem and now he will have the opportunity to operate—operate at the very highest level—in helping to solve the problem.

The fact—and I think the singular fact—that he was willing to give up a seat in the Congress to assume this responsibility gives great promise to what he will be able to do.

In my view, despite his relatively young years, he has the experience, he has the judgment, but as he has demonstrated by this decision, he has the courage to handle this immensely important assignment.

I am very happy to present him to the members of the press. You will be seeing him quite often in the years ahead.

He will speak briefly to you now and answer questions before going down for his Senate confirmation later in the week.

NOTE: The President spoke at 9:42 a.m. in the Roosevelt Room at the White House.

Statements by the President and Representative Rumsfeld are printed in the Weekly Compilation of Presidential Documents (vol. 5, pp. 585 and 586). Also released was the transcript of a news conference held by Mr. Rumsfeld following his statement.

161 Special Message to the Congress on Reform of the Federal Tax System. *April* 21, 1969

To the Congress of the United States:

Reform of our Federal income tax system is long overdue. Special preferences in the law permit far too many Americans to pay less than their fair share of taxes. Too many other Americans bear too much of the tax burden.

This Administration, working with the Congress, is determined to bring equity to the Federal tax system. Our goal is to take important first steps in tax reform legislation during this session of the Congress.

The economic overheating which has brought inflation into its fourth year keeps us from moving immediately to reduce Federal tax revenues at this time. Inflation is itself a tax—a cruel and unjust tax that hits hardest those who can least afford it. In order to "repeal" the tax of inflation, we are cutting budget spending and have requested an extension of the income tax surcharge.

Although we must maintain total Federal revenues, there is no reason why we cannot lighten the burden on those who pay too much, and increase the taxes of those who pay too little. Treasury officials will present the Administration's initial group of tax reform proposals to the Congress this week. Additional recommendations will be made later in this session. The overall program will be equitable and essentially neutral in its revenue impact. There will be no substantial gain or loss in Federal revenue, but the American taxpayer who carries more than his share of the burden will gain some relief.

Much concern has been expressed because some citizens with incomes of more than $200,000 pay no Federal income taxes. These people are neither tax dodgers nor tax cheats. Many of them pay no taxes because they make large donations to worthy causes, donations which every taxpayer is authorized by existing law to deduct from his income in figuring his tax bill.

But where we can prevent it by law, we must not permit our wealthiest citizens to be 100% successful at tax avoidance. Nor should the Government limit its tax reform only to apply to these relatively few extreme cases. Preferences built into the law in the past—some of which have either outlived their usefulness or were never appropriate—permit many thousands of individuals and corporate taxpayers to avoid their fair share of Federal taxation.

A number of present tax preferences will be scaled down in the Administration's proposals to be submitted this week. Utilizing the revenue gained from our present proposals, we suggest tax reductions for lower-income taxpayers. Further study will be necessary before we can propose changes in other preferences, and as these are developed we will recommend them to the Congress.

Specifically, the Administration will recommend:

—*Enactment of what is in effect a "minimum income tax" for citizens with substantial incomes by setting a 50% limitation on the use of the principal tax preferences which are subject to change by law.*

This limit on tax preferences would be a major step toward assuring that all Americans bear their fair share of the Federal tax burden.

—*Enactment of a "low income allowance," which will remove more than 2,000,000 of our low income families from the Federal tax rolls and assure that persons or families in poverty pay no Federal income taxes.*

This provision will also benefit students and other young people. For example, the person who works in the summer or throughout the year and earns $1,700 in taxable income— and now pays $117 in Federal income taxes—would pay nothing.

The married couple—college students or otherwise—with an income of $2,300 and current taxes of $100 would pay nothing. A family of four would pay no tax on income below $3,500—the cutoff now is $3,000.

The "low income allowance," if enacted by the Congress, will offer genuine tax relief to the young, the elderly, the disadvantaged and the handicapped.

Our tax reform proposals would also help workers who change jobs by liberalizing deductions for moving expenses and would reduce specific preferences in a number of areas:

—taxpayers who have certain non-taxable income or other preferences would have their non-business deductions reduced proportionately.

—certain mineral transactions (so-called "carved out" mineral production payments and "ABC" transactions) would be treated in a way that would stop artificial creation of net operating losses in these industries.

—exempt organizations, including private foundations, would come under much stricter surveillance.

—the rules affecting charitable deductions would be tightened—but only to screen out the unreasonable and not stop those which help legitimate charities and therefore the nation.

—the practice of using multiple subsidiaries and affiliated corporations to take undue advantage of the lower tax rate on the first $25,000 of corporate income would be curbed.

—farm losses, to be included in the "limitation on tax preferences,"

would be subject to certain other restrictions in order to curb abuses in this area.

I also recommend that the Congress repeal the 7% investment tax credit, effective today.

This subsidy to business investment no longer has priority over other pressing national needs.

In the early 60's, America's productive capacity needed prompt modernization to enable it to compete with industry abroad. Accordingly, Government gave high priority to providing tax incentives for this modernization.

Since that time, American business has invested close to $400 billion in new plant and equipment, bringing the American economy to new levels of productivity and efficiency. While a vigorous pace of capital formation will certainly continue to be needed, national priorities now require that we give attention to the need for general tax relief.

Repeal of the investment tax credit will permit relief to every taxpayer through relaxation of the surcharge earlier than I had contemplated.

The revenue effect of the repeal of the investment tax credit will begin to be significant during calendar year 1970. *Therefore, I recommend that investment tax credit repeal be accompanied by extension of the full surcharge only to January 1, 1970, with a reduction to 5% on January 1.* This is a reappraisal of my earlier recommendation for continuance of the surcharge until June 30, 1970 at a 10% rate. If economic and fiscal conditions permit, we can look forward to elimination of the remaining surtax on

162 Message to the Congress Transmitting the Annual Report of the National Capital Housing Authority. *April 21, 1969*

To the Congress of the United States:

I herewith transmit the Annual Report for 1968 of the National Capital Housing Authority. During the past year, the jurisdiction of the Authority has grown to include over 10,000 public low-rent housing units. But the housing needs of low-income families in the Nation's Capital still exceed the supply.

I am pleased to report that the Authority is beginning to place greater emphasis than it has in the past on working with the private sector in building and acquiring decent housing for the people of the District. It is pioneering in the use of the "Turnkey" method, in which a private developer builds or acquires a project and later turns it over to the Authority. It is also placing new emphasis

on offering social services to the residents of these dwellings—often in cooperation with groups of volunteer citizens—and on managing and maintaining the properties in an enlightened manner, sometimes through private management firms.

These and other initiatives—many of them still in their trial stages—will help the Authority make important progress toward its goal of providing safe, clean, and economical housing for the low-income families of this city.

RICHARD NIXON

The White House

April 21, 1969

NOTE: The report is entitled "Annual Report 1968, National Capital Housing Authority, For the Fiscal Year Ended June 30, 1968" (Government Printing Office, 24 pp.).

163 Message to the Congress Transmitting the Annual Report on the Food for Peace Program. *April 22, 1969*

To the Congress of the United States:

I am pleased to transmit the report for 1968 on the Food for Peace Program under Public Law 480—a program which over the years has helped provide better diets for millions of people in more than 100 nations. In addition to its primary humanitarian aspects, Food for Peace contributes significantly to the maintenance of export markets for U.S. agricultural commodities and to the U.S. balance of payments position.

While this is my first official report on the program as President, I have been

closely associated with it since its beginning. This great humanitarian effort began in 1954 during the Presidency of Dwight D. Eisenhower. As Vice President at the time, I was keenly interested in the program and have followed its development and accomplishments ever since.

It is evident that the battle against hunger must continue, both in the United States and in the world at large, through programs such as Food for Peace. The present Administration eagerly accepts this challenge and dedicates itself to dealing effectively with the problems of hunger and malnutrition at home and abroad.

RICHARD NIXON

The White House
April 22, 1969

NOTE: The report is entitled "The Annual Report on Activities Carried Out Under Public Law 480, 83d Congress, As Amended, During the Period January 1 Through December 31, 1968" (157 pp. and appendixes, processed).

164   Letter of Congratulations to President Zalman Shazar on the 21st Anniversary of the State of Israel. *April 22, 1969*

Dear Mr. President:

My warmest congratulations go out to you and your people on the occasion of the twenty-first anniversary of the State of Israel.

As so many of my fellow Americans, I deeply admire the accomplishments your country has realized in the course of its young life. Adversity has been your challenge as you have pressed forward in the face of overwhelming odds toward progress and well-being for your citizens.

But as so many peace-loving men and women throughout the world, I, too, am deeply disturbed and saddened by the conflict that has marred the great success you have attained.

So on this anniversary, as I share your satisfaction in the continuing achievements of your nation, I also join with you—and with all men of goodwill—in the fervent hope that peace may soon accompany the prosperity you enjoy.

Sincerely,

RICHARD NIXON

[His Excellency Zalman Shazar, President of Israel]

165   Special Message to the Congress on a Program To Combat Organized Crime in America. *April 23, 1969*

To the Congress of the United States:

Today, organized crime has deeply penetrated broad segments of American life. In our great cities, it is operating prosperous criminal cartels. In our suburban areas and smaller cities, it is expanding its corrosive influence. Its economic base is principally derived from its virtual monopoly of illegal gambling, the numbers racket, and the importation of narcotics. To a large degree, it underwrites the loan-sharking business in the United States and actively participates in fraudulent bankruptcies. It encourages street crime by inducing narcotic addicts to mug and rob. It encourages housebreaking and burglary by providing efficient disposal methods for stolen goods. It quietly continues to infiltrate and corrupt organized labor. It is increasing its enormous holdings and influence in the world of legitimate business. To achieve his end, the organized criminal relies on physical terror and psychological in-

315

timidation, on economic retaliation and political bribery, on citizen indifference and governmental acquiescence. He corrupts our governing institutions and subverts our democratic processes. For him, the moral and legal subversion of our society is a life-long and lucrative profession.

Many decent Americans contribute regularly, voluntarily and unwittingly to the coffers of organized crime—the suburban housewife and the city slum dweller who place a twenty-five cent numbers bet; the bricklayer and college student who buy a football card; the businessman and the secretary who bet illegally on a horse.

Estimates of the "take" from illegal gambling alone in the United States run anywhere from $20 billion, which is over 2% of the nation's gross national product, to $50 billion, a figure larger than the entire federal administrative budget for fiscal year 1951. This wealth is but one yardstick of the economic and political power held by the leaders of organized crime who operate with little restriction within our society.

Organized crime's victims range all across the social spectrum—the middle-class businessman enticed into paying usurious loan rates; the small merchant required to pay protection money; the white suburbanite and the black city dweller destroying themselves with drugs; the elderly pensioner and the young married couple forced to pay higher prices for goods. The most tragic victims, of course, are the poor whose lack of financial resources, education and acceptable living standards frequently breed the kind of resentment and hopelessness that make illegal gambling and drugs an attractive escape from the bleakness of ghetto life.

BACKGROUND

For two decades now, since the Attorney General's Conference on Organized Crime in 1950, the Federal effort has slowly increased. Many of the nation's most notorious racketeers have been imprisoned or deported and many local organized crime business operations have been eliminated. But these successes have not substantially impeded the growth and power of organized criminal syndicates. Not a single one of the 24 Cosa Nostra families has been destroyed. They are more firmly entrenched and more secure than ever before.

It is vitally important that Americans see this alien organization for what it really is—a totalitarian and closed society operating within an open and democratic one. It has succeeded so far because an apathetic public is not aware of the threat it poses to American life. This public apathy has permitted most organized criminals to escape prosecution by corrupting officials, by intimidating witnesses and by terrorizing victims into silence.

As a matter of national "public policy," I must warn our citizens that the threat of organized crime cannot be ignored or tolerated any longer. It will not be eliminated by loud voices and good intentions. It will be eliminated by carefully conceived, well-funded and well-executed action plans. Furthermore, our action plans against organized crime must be established on a long-term basis in order to relentlessly pursue the criminal syndicate. This goal will not be easily attained. Over many decades, organized crime has extended its roots deep into American society and they will not be easily extracted. Our success will first depend on the support of our citizens who must be informed of the dangers that organized crime poses. Success also will require the help of Congress and of the State and local governments.

This Administration is urgently aware of the need for extraordinary action and I have already taken several significant steps aimed at combating organized crime. I have pledged an unstinting commitment, with an unprecedented amount of money, manpower and other resources to back up my promise to attack organized crime. For example—I have authorized the Attorney General to engage in wiretapping of organized racketeers. I have authorized the Attorney General to establish 20 Federal racketeering field offices all across the nation. I have authorized the Attorney General to establish a unique Federal-State Racket Squad in New York City. I have asked all Federal agencies to cooperate with the Department of Justice in this effort and to give priority to the organized crime drive. I have asked the Congress to increase the fiscal 1970 budget by $25 million, which will roughly double present expenditures for the organized crime effort.

In addition, I have asked the Congress to approve a $300 million appropriation in the 1970 budget for the Law Enforcement Assistance Administration. Most of these funds will go in block grants to help State and local law enforcement programs and a substantial portion of this assistance money will be utilized to fight organized crime. I have had discussions with the State Attorneys General and I have authorized the Attorney General to cooperate fully with the States and local communities in this national effort, and to extend help to them with every means at his disposal. Finally, I have directed the Attorney General to mount our Federal anti-organized crime offensive and to coordinate the Federal effort with State and local efforts where possible.

ASSISTANCE TO STATES AND LOCAL GOVERNMENTS

Through the Law Enforcement Assistance Administration, and other units of the Department of Justice, the Attorney General has already taken some initial steps:

1. A program is being established so that State and local law enforcement people can exchange recent knowledge on the most effective tactics to use against organized crime at the local level.

2. The Justice Department is furnishing technical assistance and financial help in the training of investigators, prosecutors, intelligence analysts, accountants, statisticians—the professional people needed to combat a sophisticated form of criminal activity.

3. The Justice Department is encouraging municipalities and States to re-examine their own laws in the organized crime area. We are also encouraging and assisting in the formation of State-wide organized crime investigating and prosecuting units.

4. A computerized organized crime intelligence system is being developed to house detailed information on the personalities and activities of organized crime nationally. This system will also serve as a model for State computer intelligence systems which will be partially funded by the Federal Government.

5. We are fostering cooperation and coordination between States and between communities to avoid a costly duplication

of effort and expense.

6. We are providing Federal aid for both State and local public information programs designed to alert the people to the nature and scope of organized crime activity in their communities.

These actions are being taken now. But the current level of Federal activity must be dramatically increased, if we expect progress. More men and money, new administrative actions, and new legal authority are needed.

EXPANDED BUDGET

There is no old law or new law that will be useful without the necessary manpower for enforcement. I am therefore, as stated, asking Congress to increase the Fiscal Year 1970 budget for dealing with organized crime by $25 million. This will roughly double the amount spent in the fight against organized crime during Fiscal Year 1969, and will bring the total Federal expenditures for the campaign against organized crime to the unprecedented total of $61 million. I urge Congress to approve our request for these vital funds.

REORGANIZATION OF THE CRIME EFFORT

I have directed the newly appointed Advisory Council on Executive Organization to examine the effectiveness of the Executive Branch in combating crime—in particular organized crime.

Because many departments and agencies of the Executive Branch are involved in the organized crime effort, I believe we can make lasting improvement only if we view this matter in the full context of executive operations.

FEDERAL RACKETEERING FIELD OFFICES

The focal center of the Federal effort against organized crime is the Department of Justice. It coordinates the efforts of all of the Federal agencies. To combine in one cohesive unit a cadre of experienced Federal investigators and prosecutors, to maintain a Federal presence in organized crime problem areas throughout the nation on a continuing basis, and to institutionalize and utilize the valuable experience that has been gained by the "Strike Forces" under the direction of the Department of Justice, the Attorney General has now established Federal Racketeering Field Offices in Boston, Brooklyn, Buffalo, Chicago, Detroit, Miami, Newark, and Philadelphia. These offices bring together, in cohesive single units, experienced prosecutors from the Justice Department, Special Agents of the FBI, investigators of the Bureau of Narcotics and Dangerous Drugs, the finest staff personnel from the Bureau of Customs, the Securities and Exchange Commission, the Internal Revenue Service, the Post Office, the Secret Service and other Federal offices with expertise in diverse areas of organized crime.

The Racketeering Field Offices will be able to throw a tight net of Federal law around an organized crime concentration and through large scale target investigations, we believe we can obtain the prosecutions that will imprison the leaders, paralyze the administrators, frighten the street workers and, eventually, paralyze the whole organized crime syndicate in any one particular city. The Attorney General plans to set up at least a dozen additional field offices within the next two years.

FEDERAL-STATE RACKET SQUAD

Investigations of the national crime syndicate, La Cosa Nostra, show its membership at some 5,000, divided into 24 "families" around the nation. In most cities organized crime activity is dominated by a single "family"; in New York City, however, the lucrative franchise is divided among five such "families."

To deal with this heavy concentration of criminal elements in the nation's largest city, a new Federal-State Racket Squad is being established in the Southern District of New York. It will include attorneys and investigators from the Justice Department as well as from New York State and city. This squad will be directed by the Department of Justice, in conjunction with a supervisory council of officials from State and local participating agencies, who will formulate policy, devise strategy and oversee tactical operations. Building on the experience of this special Federal-State Racket Squad, the Attorney General will be working with State and local authorities in other major problem areas to determine whether this concept of governmental partnership should be expanded to those areas through the formation of additional squads.

NEW LEGISLATION

From his studies in recent weeks, the Attorney General has concluded that new weapons and tools are needed to enable the Federal government to strike both at the Cosa Nostra hierarchy and the sources of revenue that feed the coffers of organized crime. Accordingly the Attorney General will ask Congress for new laws, and I urge Congress to act swiftly and

favorably on the Attorney General's request.

WITNESS IMMUNITY

First, we need a new broad general witness immunity law to cover all cases involving the violation of a Federal statute. I commend to the Congress for its consideration the recommendations of the National Commission on Reform of Federal Criminal Laws. Under the Commission's proposal, a witness could not be prosecuted on the basis of anything he said while testifying, but he would not be immune from prosecution based on other evidence of his offense. Furthermore, once the government has granted the witness such immunity, a refusal then to testify would bring a prison sentence for contempt. With this new law, government should be better able to gather evidence to strike at the leadership of organized crime and not just the rank and file. The Attorney General has also advised me that the Federal Government will make special provisions for protecting witnesses who fear to testify due to intimidation.

WAGERING TAX AMENDMENTS

We shall ask for swift enactment of S. 1624 or its companion bill H.R. 322, sponsored by Senator Roman Hruska of Nebraska and Congressman Richard Poff of Virginia respectively. These measures would amend the wagering tax laws and enable the Internal Revenue Service to play a more active and effective role in collecting the revenues owed on wagers; the bills would also increase the Federal operator's tax on gamblers from $50 annually to $1000.

CORRUPTION

For most large scale illegal gambling enterprises to continue operations over any extended period of time, the cooperation of corrupt police or local officials is necessary. This bribery and corruption of government closest to the people is a deprival of one of a citizen's most basic rights. We shall seek legislation to make this form of systematic corruption of community political leadership and law enforcement a federal crime. This law would enable the Federal Government to prosecute both the corruptor and the corrupted.

ILLEGAL GAMBLING BUSINESSES

We also shall request new legislation making it a Federal crime to engage in an illicit gambling operation, from which five or more persons derive income, which has been in operation more than thirty days, or from which the daily "take" exceeds $2000. The purpose of this legislation is to bring under Federal jurisdiction all large-scale illegal gambling operations which involve or affect inter-state commerce. The effect of the law will be to give the Attorney General broad latitude to assist local and state government in cracking down on illegal gambling, the wellspring of organized crime's financial reservoir.

This Administration has concluded that the major thrust of its concerted anti-organized crime effort should be directed against gambling activities. While gambling may seem to most Americans to be the least reprehensible of all the activities of organized crime, it is gambling which provides the bulk of the revenues that eventually go into usurious loans, bribes

of police and local officials, "campaign contributions" to politicians, the wholesale narcotics traffic, the infiltration of legitimate businesses, and to pay for the large stables of lawyers and accountants and assorted professional men who are in the hire of organized crime.

Gambling income is the lifeline of organized crime. If we can cut it or constrict it, we will be striking close to its heart.

PROCEDURAL LAWS

With regard to improving the procedural aspects of the criminal law as it relates to the prosecution of organized crime, the Attorney General has been working with the Senate Subcommittee on Criminal Laws and Procedures to develop and perfect S. 30, the "Organized Crime Control Act of 1969." As Attorney General Mitchell indicated in his testimony on that bill, we support its objectives. It is designed to improve the investigation and prosecution of organized crime cases, and to provide appropriate sentencing for convicted offenders. I feel confident that it will be a useful new tool.

DEVELOPMENT OF NEW LAWS

Finally, I want to mention an area where we are examining the need for new laws: the infiltration of organized crime into fields of legitimate business. The syndicate-owned business, financed by illegal revenues and operated outside the rules of fair competition of the American marketplace, cannot be tolerated in a system of free enterprise. Accordingly, the Attorney General is examining the potential application of the theories underlying our anti-trust laws as a potential new weapon.

The injunction with its powers of contempt and seizure, monetary fines and treble damage actions, and the powers of a forfeiture proceeding, suggest a new panoply of weapons to attack the property of organized crime—rather than the unimportant persons (the fronts) who technically head up syndicate-controlled businesses. The arrest, conviction and imprisonment of a Mafia lieutenant can curtail operations, but does not put the syndicate out of business. As long as the property of organized crime remains, new leaders will step forward to take the place of those we jail. However, if we can levy fines on their real estate corporations, if we can seek treble damages against their trucking firms and banks, if we can seize the liquor in their warehouses, I think we can strike a critical blow at the organized crime conspiracy.

Clearly, the success or failure of any ambitious program such as I have outlined in this Message depends on many factors. I am confident the Congress will supply the funds and the requested legislation, the States and communities across the country will take advantage of the Federal capability and desire to assist and participate with them, and the Federal personnel responsible for programs and actions will vigorously carry out their mission.

RICHARD NIXON

The White House
April 23, 1969

NOTE: White House announcements concerning the establishment and membership of the President's Advisory Council on Executive Organization are printed in the Weekly Compilation of Presidential Documents (vol. 5, pp. 530 and 789).

166   Message of Congratulations on the Fifth Anniversary of the Interracial Council for Business Opportunity. *April 24, 1969*

IT IS A PLEASURE for me to congratulate the members of the Interracial Council for Business Opportunity as you celebrate your fifth anniversary and the launching of your sixth year.

Giving minorities a bigger and better "piece of the action" in our private enterprise system has been a major thrust of this administration's program during its first 90 days.

The distinguished past achievements of your organization in encouraging large industry to voluntarily share its training and experience with the struggling new minority-owned businesses of our inner cities will serve as an invaluable reference point and road map for us as we attempt to expand and solidify the gains and needs in this area. I am informed, for example, that you have already helped over 2,000 businesses in your reasonably young existence, and that your plans for the future include even bolder and more imaginative programs. In these efforts, I wish you continued success.

It is my firm hope that by providing additional incentives for the movement of private capital and assistance into the disadvantaged areas of our country, this administration will accelerate the establishment of minority business institutions. And with the ready assistance of groups such as yours, I am convinced that we will achieve this goal.

NOTE: The message, dated April 23, 1969 and released April 24, 1969, was read by Robert J. Brown, Special Assistant to the President, at the Council's annual dinner at the Hotel Americana in New York City.

The Interracial Council for Business Opportunity was formed on October 30, 1963, by a group of New York business and professional people under the sponsorship of the Urban League of Greater New York and the Metropolitan Council of the American Jewish Congress. Its aim is to stimulate the growth of successful business enterprise by Negroes and members of other minority groups.

167   Special Message to the Congress Proposing Postal Rate Increases To Reduce the Postal Deficit. *April 24, 1969*

To the Congress of the United States:

The Post Office Department faces a record deficit in Fiscal Year 1970, one which will reach nearly $1.2 billion. This unhappy fact compels me to recommend to the Congress that it increase postal rates for first, second, and third class mail.

The increases that I am proposing will reduce the postal deficit in Fiscal Year 1970 by over $600 million. If rates were not raised, that sum would have to be added to the already considerable burdens of our taxpayers. But if these recommendations are adopted, the costs of postal service will be borne more adequately by those who use the service most.

That is the way it should be if the Post Office is to become an example of sound business practices. That is also what the law requires. The Postal Policy Act stipulates that postal rates should produce revenue which is approximately equal to the cost of operating the postal establishment—after the costs of such special public services as the Congress may designate are deducted. It is in accordance with both general principle and specific law, then, that I make the following recommendations:

1. First class mail—I propose that the rates for letters and postcards be increased one cent, to seven and six cents respectively, on July 1, 1969. Air mail postage rates would remain unchanged.

2. Second class mail—The rates for newspapers and magazines which circulate outside the county in which they are published would go up by 12 percent on July 1, 1970. This increase would constitute an addition to the 8 percent increase for second class mail which is already scheduled to take effect on January 1 of next year.

3. Third class mail—Bulk rates are already scheduled for increase on July 1, 1969. I suggest that there be a further increase on January 1, 1970, so that the overall level at that time would be some 16 percent above present levels. Further, I recommend that the minimum single piece third class rate be increased by one cent on July 1, 1969.

I regret the need to raise postal rates. I can suggest, however, that these increases can help our country achieve two important goals. First, the proposal can help in our efforts to control inflation by bringing federal revenues and expenditures into better balance. Secondly, rate increases will make it easier for the Postmaster General and his associates to provide better postal service. After carefully reviewing the fiscal 1970 Post Office budget submitted by the previous administration, we have been able to achieve reductions of net outlays equal to $140 million. A comprehensive review of all postal operations is now underway; modern management techniques are being introduced and efficiency is being increased.

Further improvements will take time— and during that time it is essential that financial pressures should not impair or reduce available services.

I would add one further comment: this Administration is determined that the cycle of greater and greater postal deficits and more and more rate increases will be broken. The only way to break that cycle is through effective, long-range reforms in the way the postal system operates. Some of these reforms can be implemented by the Postmaster General; others will require Congressional action.

We will be submitting specific proposals for such reform to the Congress within the next forty-five days.

Postal reform will not be achieved easily; there are always many obstacles to even the most necessary change. But we remain confident that we can, with your cooperation, move boldly toward our three goals: better postal service, improved working conditions for all employees, and a reduction of the recent pressure for frequent increases in postal rates.

Proposed legislation to effect the revenue increases which I have recommended here will be sent to the Congress shortly.

RICHARD NIXON

The White House
April 24, 1969

168   Remarks at the Azalea Festival in Norfolk, Virginia. *April* 26, 1969

Mr. Mayor; Your Majesty, Queen Tricia; all of the princesses in this magnificent court; Your Excellencies, the Ambassadors and other representatives of the NATO nations; Your Excellency, the Governor; distinguished guests in this wonderful audience here today:

I want you first to know that on this my first visit to Norfolk which is completely nonpolitical in character, I could not have had a greater honor than to crown my daughter the Queen of the Azalea Festival.

This is the first occasion of this type that I have participated in since assuming the Office of President, and I am glad that it was here and on this particular occasion for these reasons:

I have a special feeling for this city, because of my Navy background. The mayor told me just before the ceremony that he often had a friendly argument with the mayor of San Diego as to whether San Diego or Norfolk was the Navy capital of the United States.

Well, at least when I am in Norfolk, Norfolk is the naval capital of the United States.

And then I am honored to be here because you not only have honored my daughter, but you have honored these other lovely princesses. I think you will agree with me that any one of them could be the queen of this festival. They are all really queens as well as princesses.

And finally, on a serious note, I am glad

the day is a beautiful day, and that the azaleas are in such magnificent, full bloom with all their beauty.

I would point out to this great assembly that this festival which now is in its 16th year, is one that reminds us of a great truth. It is a festival which celebrates beauty but at the same time celebrates freedom.

I think all of us as Americans, and all of us as members of the NATO community of free nations, realize that only in freedom can we truly enjoy the fullness of beauty.

We see beauty around us, but NATO—that great alliance of free nations—makes it possible for us as Americans to enjoy beauty with freedom.

Let us always be thankful for that great truth.

And, finally, I will make no other comments on the great problems confronting the world. I will only say that on my recent trip to Europe, to the NATO na-tions—to some of them—that I met queens, prime ministers, ambassadors, admirals, and generals, and the conversation was always on the great subjects of weighty discussion among nations.

Now here, what do we find? A queen, together with 15 princesses, a Governor, a mayor, admirals, generals. And what do we discuss? We very appropriately discuss beauty—the beauty of this place, of the Azalea Festival.

I am honored to be here for that kind of meeting and that kind of discussion.

Thank you very much for allowing me to participate.

NOTE: The President spoke at 3 p.m. at the Amphitheater in the Azalea Gardens in Norfolk, Va. The mayor of Norfolk was Roy B. Martin, Jr., and the Governor of Virginia was Mills E. Godwin, Jr.

The festival is sponsored annually by the city of Norfolk and the Norfolk Chamber of Commerce in tribute to the naval command of the North Atlantic Treaty Organization located there. The princesses represented each of the NATO nations.

169   Remarks Presenting the National Teacher of the Year Award.   *April 28, 1969*

I AM very honored today to present to Barbara Goleman the award of Teacher of the Year.

And I think back to the year 1953 when I first helped to make this award. I was then Vice President of the United States and it is a particular pleasure to make it today to Barbara Goleman.

She is obviously an extraordinary teacher, as are all of those who have won this award before. Her three students—I can see their smiles—must agree that she is.

I looked into her record and she would perhaps be not willing to brag so much as to disclose what her students say about her. But they say that she cares and she makes them glad to be alive.

What an inspirational teacher she must be. It is this kind of inspiration that we have among hundreds of thousands of our teachers around this Nation that here at the White House today we honor.

Sometimes we talk about our schools and our teachers in terms that are very critical, and sometimes we fail to appreciate these very dedicated people who have devoted their lives to teaching.

I would like to say to you, Miss Goleman, an interesting thing: I found in studying history that six Presidents, before they became President, were teachers, including, incidentally, President Johnson. He was a teacher before he became President.

While I cannot claim that, my wife, Mrs. Nixon, was a teacher before I married her. So I have, therefore, a special feeling about teachers, both because of being in the Office that I hold and the personal relationship.

So we congratulate you. We congratulate your students for speaking so highly of you so that you receive this award.

Also, I want to congratulate your student, Mr. Mayland. I understand that he has been selected as valedictorian of his class of 542.

So we have an outstanding student and the teacher who made him that way.

NOTE: The President spoke at 10:12 a.m. in the Rose Garden at the White House. The "Teacher of the Year," Miss Barbara Goleman, is head of the English department at Miami Jackson High School, Miami, Fla. She was accompanied to the presentation ceremony by Kenneth T. Mayland and two of her other students.

The "Teacher of the Year" is chosen from finalists selected by a screening committee of national educational leaders. The award is sponsored by Look magazine in cooperation with the Council of Chief State School Officers, an organization of State superintendents and commissioners of education.

Miss Goleman's response accepting the award is printed in the Weekly Compilation of Presidential Documents (vol. 5, p. 614).

170 Messages of Sympathy on the Death of President Barrientos of Bolivia. *April 28, 1969*

Dear Mrs. Barrientos:

Mrs. Nixon joins me in sending you our deepest sympathy and condolence during this time of sorrow. We were all shocked to hear of the tragic and untimely death of your husband. His loss will be particularly felt by his countrymen, for whom he worked so hard. The memory of his brilliant leadership will, however, remain a source of inspiration and encouragement to all his friends, countrymen and fellow Americans.

Our thoughts are with you and your family and we pray God may now give you the same strength and courage that earned your husband the esteem of his countrymen.

RICHARD NIXON

[Mrs. Rose Marie Barrientos]

Dear Mr. President:

On behalf of my fellow countrymen, may I extend to you, Mr. President, and to the people of Bolivia our deepest sympathy for the untimely death of President Barrientos. A tragic accident has silenced a dynamic leader, and his loss will be deeply mourned by all who knew him. But the example of his leadership and his accomplishments will remain as a lasting legacy for all of his fellow Americans, and especially for his countrymen for whom he worked so hard. All who knew him are the richer for his memory, and Bolivia can be justly proud of his leadership and his life.

RICHARD NIXON

[His Excellency Luis Adolfo Siles Salinas, President of Bolivia.]

NOTE: President René Barrientos Ortuño was killed on April 27, 1969, in the crash of his helicopter near Cochabamba, Bolivia.

171   Letter to General Charles de Gaulle on the Announcement of His Resignation as President of France.   *April 28, 1969*

Dear Mr. President:

It is with deep regret that I have learned of your resignation as President of France. I have greatly valued the frank and comprehensive exchanges of views it has been my privilege to have with you, both as a private citizen and as Vice President and President of the United States. Nor shall I forget the courtesy of your welcome and the wisdom of your counsel during my recent visit to Paris. Our talks proved the occasion for a new departure in friendly cooperation between our two nations.

We in the United States will not forget what you have done for France, both at home and abroad, and for the world, both in war and in peace.

Mrs. Nixon joins me in sending you and Madame de Gaulle our warm personal regards and best wishes for the future.

RICHARD NIXON

[His Excellency Charles de Gaulle, President of the French Republic]

172   Special Message to the Congress on the District of Columbia.   *April 28, 1969*

To the Congress of the United States:

Carved out of swampland at our country's birth, the Nation's Capital city now sets a new test of national purpose. This was a city that men dared to plan—and build by plan—laying out avenues and monuments and housing in accordance with a common rational scheme. Now we are challenged once again to shape our environment: to renew our city by rational foresight and planning, rather than leaving it to grow swamp-like without design.

At issue is whether the city will be enabled to take hold of its future: whether its institutions will be reformed so that its government can truly represent its citizens and act upon their needs.

Good government, in the case of a city, must be local government. The Federal Government has a special responsibility for the District of Columbia. But it also bears toward the District the same responsibility it bears toward all other cities: to help local government work better, and to attempt to supplement local resources for programs that city officials judge most urgent.

My aim is to increase the responsibility and efficiency of the District of Columbia's new government, which has performed so ably during its first perilous years. Early in this Administration, we recommended proposals that would increase the effectiveness of local law enforcement and provide the resources needed by local officials to begin revitalizing the areas damaged during the civil disturbance. Those proposals, however, cover only a part of the program which will be essential for the District Government to respond to the wishes of its people.

I now present the second part of this program, worked out in close consultation with the District Government, and based upon the needs articulated by the Mayor and the City Council.

This program will provide:

—An orderly mechanism for achieving self-government in the District of Columbia.

—Representation in Congress.

—Added municipal authority for the City Council and the Mayor.

—Additional top management positions to bring new talents and leadership into the District Government.

—A secure and equitable source of Federal funds for the District's budget.

—An expanded rapid rail transit system, linking the diverse segments of our Capital's metropolitan region.

The Federal Government bears a major responsibility for the welfare of our Capital's citizens in general. It owns much of the District's land and employs many of its citizens. It depends on the services of local government. The condition of our Capital city is a sign of the condition of our nation—and is certainly taken as such by visitors, from all the states of the Union, and from around the globe.

However, this Federal responsibility does not require Federal rule. Besides the official Washington of monuments and offices, there is the Washington of 850,-000 citizens with all the hopes and expectations of the people of any major city, striving and sacrificing for a better life— the eighth largest among the cities of our country.

Self-Government

Full citizenship through local self-government must be given to the people of this city: The District Government cannot be truly responsible until it is made responsible to those who live under its rule. The District's citizens should not be expected to pay taxes for a government which they have no part in choosing—or to bear the full burdens of citizenship without the full rights of citizenship.

I therefore ask Congress to create a Commission on Self-Government for the District of Columbia, to be charged with submitting to Congress and the President a proposal for establishing meaningful self-government in the District.

In order for any government to be accountable to the people, responsibilities must be clearly pinpointed, and officials must have the powers they need to carry out their responsibilities. The Commission would recommend how best to augment and allocate the legislative and executive authorities with respect to governing the city.

The members of this Commission would be partly appointed by the President, partly designated by the Congress, and partly chosen in a city-wide election by the citizens of the District. They would be given an adequate but strictly defined time period to formulate their plan. I would hope that the Commission would be established promptly, so that its report could be submitted to Congress and the President in time for the 1970 legislative session. With adequate funding, they would be able to draw on the wisdom of consultants throughout the country—men who know firsthand the art of the possible, as well as those who study government—in addition to their own staff.

The Commission members must give thorough consideration to the many alternative plans for self-government which have been presented over the years. But they must also make use of new knowledge we have gained about the problems of existing local governments around the country—in finance, management, urban development, citizen participation and many other areas. They must seek the sentiment of the District's citizens from the earliest stages of their work.

There also is a Federal interest that must be respected. The normal functions of the Federal agencies must be guaranteed and their vital operations protected. There must be continued Federal jurisdiction over public buildings and monuments and assurance of well-being for the men and women who work in them or come to visit. The rights of the national government must be protected, at the same time as the rights of the city's residents are secured. There must be respect for the responsibilities with regard to the District which the Constitution places in the Congress.

To establish a new government in so diverse and active a city as the District is certainly no easy task. There are dangers in setting up new governments, as well as opportunities. Congress has been rightly concerned that the plan for self-government must insure responsible elections, effective executive leadership, protection of individual liberty and safeguards for District of Columbia employees. Self-government must be extended in a timely and orderly manner.

It is especially important that the Commission go beyond the issue of self-government as such, and concern itself with the effective functioning of government in the District of Columbia. Under the existing government structure the City Council finds itself without the power to deal with many crucial problems because of the conflicting and divided authorities that now reside in independent agencies.

But there is no cause for delay: Self-government has remained an unfulfilled promise for far too long. It has been energetically supported by the past four Presidents—Harry S. Truman, Dwight D. Eisenhower, John F. Kennedy, and Lyndon B. Johnson. The Senate approved measures to provide it during the 81st, 82nd, 84th, and 86th Congresses. We owe the present lack of local elections to the Reconstruction period, when Congress rescued the District from bankruptcy but suspended the voting franchise. Congress established the Commission form of government in 1874 as a temporary "receivership," but the Commissioners' government persisted for over 90 years—and today, even after reorganization in 1967, the District remains under Federal control.

The history of failure for self-government proposals shows the need for a new plan strong enough to stand up against the old questions or criticisms. Myriad different plans have been offered—and will be offered again this year. But each will have its own doubters as well as its supporters. A Commission must examine all of them, combining old and new ideas in a proposal that will at last win the broad-based respect necessary for final acceptance, and that will carry the authority of a disinterested group of men whose vocation is government—jurists, political leaders and scholars, as well as other citizens, investing the wisdom of their life's work in a truly new government.

Recognizing both the solemn right of the District's citizens to self-government and the Federal interest, I ask Congress to act promptly on proposed legislation to establish a *Commission on Self Government for the District of Columbia,* which will be transmitted shortly.

CONGRESSIONAL REPRESENTATION

I also urge Congress to grant voting representation in Congress to the District of Columbia. It should offend the democratic senses of this nation that the 850,-000 citizens of its Capital, comprising a population larger than eleven of its states, have no voice in the Congress.

I urge that Congress approve, and the States ratify, an amendment to the Constitution granting to the District at least one representative in the House of Representatives, and such additional representatives in the House as the Congress shall approve, and to provide for the possibility of two Senators.

Until such an amendment is approved by Congress and ratified by the States, *I recommend that Congress enact legislation to provide for a nonvoting House delegate from the District.*

STRENGTHENING THE CITY COUNCIL AND MAYOR

While working for self-government and Congressional Representation for the future, I recommend that Congress take certain measures this session to strengthen the present District Government, in both authority and efficiency.

The Reorganization Plan which established the present government left to Congress many mundane municipal functions which are burdensome chores to it but important functions for good local government. At present, Congress must allot a portion of its legislative calendar to set-

ting ordinances for the District of Columbia, in effect performing the duties of a local City Council for the Capital. It thus deals with matters which are of little or no importance to the nation as a whole— the setting of a fee, for example, to redeem a dog from the city pound. The concerns of the District are frequently shunted aside to allow for higher-priority legislative business. "No policy can be worse than to mingle great and small concerns," argued Augustus Woodward, one of the founders of our city, when Congress considered establishing a territorial form of government in 1800. "The latter become absorbed in the former; are neglected and forgotten."

Legislation will be proposed to transfer a number of specific authorities to the District Government—including authority to change various fees for user charges now fixed by statute, waive license fees for new businesses, for persons whose businesses have been burnt out in a civil disturbance and modernize the licensing of various businesses, occupations and professions.

In addition, I recommend that the Mayor be given certain local responsibilities now exercised by Federal departments or agencies. Reorganization plans will be submitted in the coming weeks to transfer local functions now operated by the Federal Government—and frequently paid for by the District—to the Executive Branch of the District Government. Local services should be operated by local government. Such responsibilities are only an extra burden for the Federal departments, which should rightly devote their energies to the welfare of the entire nation.

I will also submit other reorganization plans to transfer certain independent or quasi-independent District agencies to the Mayor's jurisdiction. These actions will strengthen the executive direction of the City's administration and complement the continuing reorganization and strengthening of the District's administrative structure.

Granting new authority to the Mayor and City Council would in no way prejudice the ultimate form or degree of Self Government. It would provide them with powers which any good local government, however chosen, should exercise. By initiating this process now, we thus build the strength of local institutions even as we make them more responsible, formally, to their citizens.

More High Level Civil Servants

Good government is the product of able and dedicated people working together. The District Government needs the very best urban managers and experts this nation has to direct the Capital's growth and apply its resources, and it must be able to attract such public servants at realistic salary rates.

Adding to the number of top management positions is vital to the effective carrying out of District Government reorganization—the creation of new departments recently announced by the Mayor, and other steps planned for the future. Such reorganization, streamlining the chain of command, is one of the most promising achievements of the Mayor's first years.

Accordingly, I urge Congress to enact legislation to increase the number of supergrade positions available to the District Government.

The Federal Payment

The District of Columbia cannot achieve strong and efficient government unless it has ample and dependable sources of financing. Sound financing can be achieved only if the Federal Government pays its appropriate share.

I therefore recommend that the Congress authorize a Federal payment formula, fixing the Federal contribution at 30 percent of local tax and other general fund revenues.

This formula would equitably reflect the Federal interest in the District of Columbia at this time with respect to:

—the 217,000 Federal employees who work in the District, about one-third of the local work force.

—the more than 10 million Americans who visit their nation's Capital each year.

—the embassies and nationals of the foreign governments.

—the land and buildings owned by the Federal Government which cannot be taxed but comprise more than 40 percent of the District's land value.

Enactment of a formula approach would be a significant step toward effective government in the District. It would tie the level of Federal aid to the burden of local taxes on the District's citizens. It would also provide the District with a predictable estimate for use in the annual budget process, thus allowing it to plan its expenditures more accurately and imaginatively for the growing needs of its population. A similar formula, dealing with District borrowing authorization, was enacted by the Congress more than a year ago—and has already proven its worth in improved budgetary planning.

The proposed Federal payment formula would not involve an automatic expenditure of Federal funds. The Federal payment would still have to be appropriated by Congress.

By authorizing the Federal payment at 30 percent of all District general fund revenues, the Congress would allow a payment of $120 million in fiscal 1970, an increase of $30 million above the present fixed authorization. This payment is incorporated in the District's 1970 budget request.

BALANCED TRANSPORTATION SYSTEM

The National Capital needs and deserves a mass transit system that is truly metropolitan, unifying the central city with the surrounding suburbs. As a part of its responsibility for the National Capital Region, the Federal Government should support deliberate action, based upon effective planning, to meet the future transportation needs of the Region. The surrounding areas in Maryland and Virginia, as Congress rightly recognized, include the most rapidly growing areas of population and job opportunities, potentially of rich benefit to the inner city.

Mass transit must be part of a balanced transportation network. A subway will not relieve local governments of the duty to modernize and improve their highway systems and other forms of transportation, so that all citizens have an adequate choice as to how they travel. Clearly, the impasse that has arisen between proponents of road and rail transportation in the Washington metropolitan area has contributed little to the progress of either. There are,

however, hopeful signs that a fair and effective settlement of these issues will be reached in the near future. It is in the interest of all those involved—central city dwellers, suburbanites, shoppers, employees, and visitors alike—that this be done.

The Washington Metropolitan Area Transit Authority, in consultation with the District Government and other local jurisdictions, has prepared legislation which would extend the presently authorized 25-mile rapid rail transit system to a 97-mile regional system. The expanded system would provide rapid transit between the downtown and outlying areas. It would facilitate the free flow of resources and labor, and would benefit all eight jurisdictions involved in its planning and approval.

The proposed legislation fulfills the Congressional mandate in a 1966 Act, which directed the Washington Metropolitan Area Transportation Authority to plan, develop, finance and provide for the operation of a full regional rapid rail system for the National Capital area.

The 97-mile system would relieve downtown congestion; increase employment; make educational, cultural and recreational facilities more accessible; reduce air pollution; stimulate business, industry, and tourism; broaden tax bases; and promote orderly urban development of the Nation's Capital.

The cost of the expanded system is estimated to be some $2.5 billion. Fare box receipts would pay for $835 million. The remaining cost of $1.7 billion (the net project cost) would be divided equitably among all the governments concerned on a ⅔–⅓ sharing basis between Federal and local governments.

The local governments concerned have already passed bond referenda or taken other appropriate action to finance their contributions of $347 million. But action by Congress is needed to authorize grants sufficient to cover the $1.1 billion Federal (⅔) share of the net project cost and capital contributions of $216 million for the District's portion of the local (⅓) share.

I urge that Congress promptly enact the necessary authorizing legislation for the 97-mile system.

PENNSYLVANIA AVENUE

Finally, we come to the Washington that so many millions flock to visit; the Washington that stands as a proud physical symbol of our Nation's liberties and its hopes.

Pennsylvania Avenue should be one of the great Avenues of our Republic—as in the original vision of our Capital City—and will be so if the Pennsylvania Avenue Commission presses forward with its present plans. Already, in accordance with the Commission's plans, construction of the Presidential Building at 13th Street has been completed; construction is continuing on the new Capitol Reflecting Pool, as well as buildings for the Federal Bureau of Investigation and the Labor Department. Planning is going forward for the Federal Triangle, a new Municipal Center at Judiciary Square, and an extension of the National Gallery. Our ultimate goal must be the Avenue of L'Enfant's Plan, a grand route connecting the Congress and the President's House, the vital center of the City, monumental in importance but designed for the Citizens of this Nation to enjoy at all hours for work or pleasure. I will encourage the development of this plan and submit legislation at the appropriate time.

One of the most significant additions to Pennsylvania Avenue will be an international center for scholars, to be established as a living memorial to Woodrow Wilson in the area just north of the National Archives. There could hardly be a more appropriate memorial to a President who combined a devotion to scholarship with a passion for peace. The District has long sought, and long needed, a center for both men of letters and men of affairs. This should be, as it was first proposed, "an institution of learning that the 22nd Century will regard as having influenced the 21st."

The renewal of Pennsylvania Avenue is an enterprise which two Presidents have supported. Their vision was the great vision of Pierre L'Enfant, George Washington, and Thomas Jefferson, whose plans embodied the ageless ideal of a Capital City. It is a vision which links Presidents, as it links the citizens of the District, in the love of this city. And I am proud to join them.

A GREAT ENTERPRISE

It is a noble aim—this planning of a Capital City. It encompasses a drive which must apply to areas of rebuilding beyond a single Avenue, and to areas of need beyond physical renovation. It infuses our knowledge of human want with a new urgency. It tests our vision of man, and of the future of his cities.

I ask the Congress, and the American people, to join in this great enterprise, knowing that if we govern with wisdom in this Capital City, it will be a proud symbol of the quality of American life and the reach of America's aspirations.

RICHARD NIXON

The White House

April 28, 1969

NOTE: The present District of Columbia Government was established by Reorganization Plan 3 of 1967.

Of the legislation proposed in this message, the following was enacted during 1969:

Additional supergrade positions for certain District officials were included in a comprehensive measure adding to the supergrade positions in the Federal Executive (Public Law 91–187, 83 Stat. 850).

Federal payments to the District Government were authorized by title VII of the District of Columbia Revenue Act of 1969 (Public Law 91–106, 83 Stat. 180) and the District of Columbia Appropriation Act of 1970 (Public Law 91–155, 83 Stat. 428).

A 97-mile rapid rail transit system for Washington was authorized by the National Capital Transportation Act of 1969 (Public Law 91–143, 83 Stat. 320), and funds for the system were provided by title II of the Department of Transportation and Related Agencies Appropriation Act of 1970 (Public Law 91–168, 83 Stat. 461).

173   Letter to the Chairman, President's Commission for the Observance of Human Rights Year 1968, on the Commission's Final Report. *April* 29, 1969

Dear Governor Harriman: [1]

I have received the Final Report of the President's Commission for the Observance of Human Rights Year 1968, and I thank you for it. You, the other members of the Commission, and those who worked on its staff are to be commended for your diligent and consistent effort in response to the request of the United Nations General Assembly that its members commemorate the twentieth anniversary of the Universal Declaration of Human Rights.

Your concern that Americans speak as one when they seek to promote the cause of human rights is fully shared by this Administration. We wholeheartedly agree

---

[1] Mr. Harriman served as Governor of New York from 1955 to 1959.

with your statement that our moral position in the world reflects our devotion to these fundamental principles.

Our government and, I am confident, our people remain committed to continuing action for human rights. I commend you for the many contributions you have made to this vital process.

Sincerely,

RICHARD NIXON

[Honorable W. Averell Harriman, Chairman, The President's Commission for the Observance of Human Rights Year 1968, Department of State, Washington, D.C. 20520]

NOTE: The letter was dated April 28, 1969, and released April 29, 1969. The report is entitled "To Continue Action for Human Rights, Final Report, The President's Commission for the Observance of Human Rights Year 1968" (Government Printing Office, 62 pp.).

174   Remarks at the Annual Meeting of the Chamber of
Commerce of the United States.   *April* 29, 1969

*Members of the Chamber of Commerce,
and your guests:*

Things have changed in Washington, but let the record show that you still have a President from Texas. [*Laughter*]

President Shivers tells me that there is a new one coming in tonight, from Oklahoma.

It is a very great privilege for me to speak to you, even though briefly, today, and to reminisce a bit about the other appearances I have made before this organization over the years.

I suppose except for President Johnson, I am the only other individual who has spoken to the national meetings of the Chamber of Commerce as a Congressman, as a Senator, as Vice President, and, finally, as President.

I am here a little later than I expected in the last capacity.

I remember through the years those meetings, some of them at dinners and some of them at occasions like this. I cherish the friendships that I have had throughout the country with your local organizations and with your national officers.

I have noted with great interest and appreciation that you have scheduled several representatives from the new administration to address you. I notice, for example, one of the panels is going to be on budget and taxes. If you find any answers, please let me know.

Certainly on that score, I will not say what our Budget Director and members of the Council of Economic Advisers will say much better when they appear later.

I know, too, from having talked to your president and those who have planned your program, that you have considered a number of other subjects during the course of this meeting.

Consequently, I have decided to speak briefly on a subject of very great concern to all of you, of very great concern to me and, I will say, to all Americans at this time. I refer to the problems of education in the very broadest sense in the United States.

I am not going to cover that subject in all of its ramifications. That is something that the Secretary of Health, Education, and Welfare and Dr. Allen could do much more ably than I. But there are phases of it that I think do require, at this time, a statement by the President of the United States, amplifying a statement I made earlier on a problem that deeply concerns us all.

That is the problem of what I would call the new revolutionary spirit and new revolutionary actions that are taking place on the campuses of many of our colleges and universities and also that may begin to take place, and also are taking place, I understand, in some of the high schools of this country.

Now I am not going to speak to that problem in the way that you might usually expect. It is easy to be against some of the actions that have occurred. All of us are concerned by those actions. We are against them. The question is to refine our discussions to some simple issues and some simple principles. I am going to state some opinions now that are my own.

Some will not agree with them. But I think they are opinions that are in accord with the great traditions of free education in America. I think they need to be stated by the President of the United States and if you share them, I hope that when you go back to your communities you will state them and I would hope also, to the extent that you have opportunities in official or other capacities, school boards, or as trustees, or faculty members, if you are that, you will be able, perhaps, to implement them.

First, with regard to that great problem of dissent on the college and university campuses, let us recognize that this is a very healthy force when we consider it at its best. We do not want, in America, an educational system which becomes ingrown, stultified, loses the ability to develop the new ideas to keep pace with the change in our very fast-changing society.

Consequently, we can be thankful today that we do have a younger generation which is, as I have often said, with all of the faults that we may see in it, the best educated younger generation that we have ever had, more deeply motivated than any that we have ever had, one that deeply cares about America, about our system, and about our educational system. We may not agree with them, but they do care.

Now having said that, I now indicate what I think are some principles in which dissent must properly be expressed. One is this: As far as our colleges and universities are concerned, I think that young people, students, are correct in asking that they have a voice, a voice in determining what the courses should be, a voice in determining what the rules should be. But then I say that while they should have a voice, under no circumstances should they be given control of the colleges and the universities. That is something else again.

I suppose some could quarrel with that qualification. But I would suggest that we can always learn from history, not only the history of our own country, but the history of countries throughout the world who have gone through similar revolutions. The philosopher Santayana once wrote that, "Those who cannot remember the past are condemned to repeat it."

Look to the countries to the south of us, our closest neighbors, our closest friends—very proud countries, many great and old universities. Those universities, most of them, went through a revolution similar to ours 100 years ago.

The students won. They won not only a voice but they won control in many of those universities, the right to hire and fire the professors and to determine the courses. And the result is that the educational system as far as higher education is concerned, in Latin America generally, is one of the most inferior in the world. I say let us not let it happen here in the United States of America.

So our answer here is not to deny the voice. We must listen, and certainly where that voice expresses views that ought to be implemented, we should implement them. But on the other hand, remember that it is the responsibility of faculties and boards of trustees to provide the leadership for educational institutions.

Then we come to the second point: that is the method of dissent. Here again, we have some fine lines that need to be drawn and some principles that we must have in mind.

There are those who believe that any means are justified if the end is worthwhile. And all of us, again, if we remember the past, will, of course, agree that we can never adopt that principle, because when we adopt that principle of any means to the end, the end eventually becomes the means.

335

So we look at our college campuses and our university campuses today and we see some things which concern us. We see, first, the dissent. That we accept, we welcome, and we encourage, provided it is the peaceful kind of dissent within the rules of an institution and of our society.

And, second, we also—and I presently today proclaim, as I have previously, the principle that we do not want to have the Federal Government of this country running our institutions. We do not want them interfering with our colleges and our universities. It is their responsibility to provide education in an independent, free way in the American tradition.

But, third, we have another factor that we must face. That is this: When we find situations in numbers of colleges and universities which reach the point where students, in the name of dissent and in the name of change, terrorize other students and faculty members, when they rifle files, when they engage in violence, when they carry guns and knives into classrooms, then I say it is time for faculties, boards of trustees, and school administrators to have the backbone to stand up against that kind of lawlessness in our society.

What I am simply suggesting here is this: We do not want government control of our great educational institutions. We want to have that freedom which comes from the independence of a great university and college community. But as we look at the situation today, I think all of those who have a responsibility for providing educational leadership must recognize that there can be no compromise with lawlessness and no surrender to force if free education is to survive in the United States of America.

Now, on the positive side, may I make another suggestion? Yesterday, I had a very pleasant duty, and that was to participate in making an award to the Teacher of the Year, selected by Look magazine in an annual event that has been going on for the past 15 years—a very attractive teacher in high school from Lakeland, Florida.

After that award ceremony, I was discussing its meaning with Dr. Allen, the new head of the Office of Education. He knew that I was going to speak to this organization today. And he made a suggestion that I think has a great deal of merit, which we are going to consider implementing at the national level next fall, but which I would urge that all of you in your community programs might consider discussing and possibly implementing during the next year.

And it is this: We hear so much these days of what is wrong with education and all of our problems. And we tend too often, I am sure, to blame teachers, or students for that matter, but when we find a good teacher—and there are thousands of them, hundreds of thousands of them around this country—when we find them doing a dedicated job, isn't it really time that we provide for them the backing? Isn't it time for us to provide the honor and the respect which the best salary in the world cannot certainly compensate for?

What I am saying is this: We are doing a better job than we were doing 20 years ago, when I first appeared before the Chamber of Commerce in Washington, D.C., as a Congressman, in paying our teachers. But when it comes to respect for a job well done, honoring this great and honored profession, perhaps, particularly where our public schools are concerned and our private schools as well, we have not shown the respect which we might.

That can come from the community. It can come from a Chamber of Commerce or a service club. And that is why I think we might consider the Teacher of the Year Award in every community of this Nation, so that we can get the positive side of education on the platter as well as the negative.

Then, finally, while I am speaking of a positive note, may I leave this thought with you: I can imagine that you came to Washington even in perhaps the most beautiful spring that Washington has had in many years and you are here just at the right time, when the Chamber of Commerce has put on the best flower display we have ever had. And I suppose that when you come here and hear all of the weighty subjects of government discussed, when you consider our problems abroad, a war which is still not concluded in Vietnam, when you consider our problems at home—the educational problem that I mentioned is only one—the problem of our cities with which you are so deeply concerned is another, and the problem of hunger in America is another one, as you know. It has been in our headlines.

All of these must sometimes lead some to the conclusion that this is a rather difficult time to be in a position of responsibility, whether in your city or whether in government at the State or national level.

I just want to give you my own philosophy in a word, as I conclude. We do have tremendously difficult problems in this country. But what really, it seems, should give us inspiration today, as you bring your convention to a conclusion, is this: We can do something about our problems.

To the extent that we have hunger in America, we have the food to deal with and to stop that particular problem. To the extent that our cities need to be rebuilt, we can rebuild them. To the extent that we have any problem any place in this Nation, America is so strong and so rich that we have what it takes to deal with the problem.

What we need is what you are providing and what we trust government can help to provide with you.

That is the effort not only of a government, but the effort of a community, of all the people of this Nation, working together.

I simply want you to know that as I look at America today and its place in the world, I do not have that lack of faith that some seem to have. If I were to pick a time and a place in which to live, I would pick the United States of America right today, 1969.

You could call that Chamber of Commerce talk. But I can assure you that the very fact that this country is rich enough to solve its problems and that the decisions that are made in the United States, of all the nations of the free world, will determine whether peace or freedom survives in this world in this last third of the century—this means that no people in the history of the world have had a greater challenge and no people in the history of the world have had more resources to meet that challenge.

That is why this is an exciting time to be alive. That is why it is a very great inspiration for me to speak to you, recognizing that your program of Forward America means that we have throughout this Nation hundreds of thousands, yes, millions of Americans, who in their private capacities are going to work with government for the solution of our problems.

I say to you, my friends, when you leave Washington, go with the renewed sense of faith in this country and faith in its future. It will be a good future because we are going to help make it so.

Thank you.

NOTE: The President spoke at 3:01 p.m. at the Sheraton Park Hotel in Washington. Allan Shivers of Texas was incoming chairman of the Executive Committee of the Chamber of Commerce, and Jenkin Lloyd Jones of Oklahoma was incoming president.

175 Toast of the President at a Dinner Honoring Duke Ellington. *April* 29, 1969

TO ALL of our guests here this evening, I think you would be interested to know that many years ago, the father of our guest of honor, in this very room, serving as one of the butlers in this White House, helped to serve state dinners.

Tonight, in honoring his son, I was trying to think of something that would be appropriate, something that has not been more adequately said, I think very well, by the music that we have heard. We have tried to convey our affection for Duke Ellington through that music, and later on in the East Room, when I will make the first presentation in this administration of the Medal of Freedom to Duke Ellington, I will have more to say in more extended remarks about what this day means to us

and what it means to this House.

But in this room, at this time, for these special guests, it occurred to me that the most appropriate thing for me to say would be this: I, and many others here, have been guests at state dinners. I have been here when an emperor has been toasted. I have been here when we have raised our glasses to a king, to a queen, to presidents, and to prime ministers.

But in studying the history of all of the great dinners held in this room, never before has a Duke been toasted.

So tonight I ask you all to rise and join me in raising our glasses to the greatest Duke of them all, Duke Ellington.

NOTE: The President spoke at 10:02 p.m. in the State Dining Room at the White House.

176 Remarks on Presenting the Presidential Medal of Freedom to Duke Ellington. *April* 29, 1969

Ladies and gentlemen:

As you can probably surmise, this is a very unusual and, for us, a special evening at the White House in this great room.

Before the entertainment begins, we have a presentation to make. I was looking at this name on here. It says, "Edward Kennedy Ellington."

For the first time during this administration, I have the honor of presenting the Presidential Medal of Freedom. I

think it is most appropriate that that medal be presented to Duke Ellington.

When we think of freedom, we think of many things. But Duke Ellington is one who has carried the message of freedom to all the nations of the world through music, through understanding, understanding that reaches over all national boundaries and over all boundaries of prejudice and over all boundaries of language.

Because he has an unusual gift, a gift that he has shared with us, his own fellow citizens, and with the citizens of the world, we believe that this citation fits him particularly well. I will read it to you.

"The President of the United States of America awards this Presidential Medal of Freedom to Edward Kennedy Ellington. Edward Kennedy Ellington, pianist, composer, and orchestra leader, has long enhanced American music with his unique style, his intelligence, his impeccable taste. For more than 40 years he has helped to expand the frontiers of jazz, while at the same time retaining in his music the individuality and freedom of expression that are the soul of jazz. In the royalty of American music, no man swings more or stands higher than the Duke."

MR. ELLINGTON. Thank you very much, Mr. President. Thank you, ladies and gentlemen.

This is the Presidential Medal of Freedom. And the word "freedom" is one, coincidentally, that we are using at the moment in our sacred concert.

And, of course, we speak of freedom of expression and we speak of freedom generally as being something very sweet and fat and things like that. In the end when we get down to the payoff, what we actually say is that we would like very much to mention the four major freedoms that my friend and writing-and-arranging composer, Billy Strayhorn, lived by and enjoyed.

That was freedom from hate, unconditionally; freedom from self-pity; freedom from fear of possibly doing something that may help someone else more than it would him; and freedom from the kind of pride that could make a man feel that he is better than his brother.

THE PRESIDENT. Ladies and gentlemen, please don't go away. Duke was asking earlier if I would play, and I said I had never done so yet in the White House. But it did occur to me as I looked at the magnificent program prepared for us that one number was missing.

You see, this is his birthday. Now, Duke Ellington is ageless, but would you all stand and sing "Happy Birthday" to him. And, please, in the key of G. [*Laughter*]

[At this point the President played the piano and sang along with the guests in honor of Mr. Ellington's 70th birthday.]

NOTE: The President spoke at 10:36 p.m. in the East Room at the White House.

177 Statement on Government Support of Voluntary Action. *April 30, 1969*

ONE of the great, distinguishing characteristics of the American people is their readiness to join together in helping one another. The principle of voluntary action is not something lately grafted onto America's ways; it goes back as far as the Nation's founding.

Today, we find that the Nation has grown enormously in wealth, and that its wealth is more widely distributed than ever before. Yet need persists: human need, personal need, which government can help to meet but which it cannot meet alone. The very magnitude of everything, government included, increases the need for that direct, human dimension that only the concerned individual can provide. More than ever, America needs the enlistment of the energies and resources of its people—not as substitutes for government action, but as supplements to it. People can reach where government cannot; people can do what government cannot. Today, more than ever, America needs the hearts and hands of its people, joined in those common enterprises, small as well as large, that are the mark of caring and the cement of community.

There is no lack of will. Millions of Americans stand ready to serve and to help, eager to know what they can do and how they can do it. One of the chief aims of this administration is to help in matching up the willing hands with the tasks that need doing.

Voluntary efforts already are contributing enormously to our national well-being, but they have had neither the assistance nor the recognition that they deserve.

In the past, government has sometimes been the jealous competitor of private efforts. From now on, it will offer encouragement and support.

Toward this end, I have taken or am taking four preliminary steps:

—On the Government side of the effort, I will, by Executive order,[1] form a Cabinet Committee on Voluntary Action. Its Chairman will be Secretary Romney of the Department of Housing and Urban Development, who scored impressive successes in stimulating voluntary action during his terms as Governor of Michigan. Its other members will be the Secretaries of Commerce, of Labor, of Agriculture, and of Health, Education, and Welfare, the Attorney General, and the Director of the Office

of Economic Opportunity.

—I have asked Secretary Romney to establish an Office of Voluntary Action in his Department.

—I have asked Max M. Fisher of Detroit to serve as my Special Consultant on Voluntary Action and to work with Secretary Romney and the Cabinet Committee. Mr. Fisher has brought together small groups of private leaders for informal consultation on the most effective means by which the Government can assist in stimulating voluntary activities. He will have continuing responsibility for the important aspect of this program which involves nongovernmental organizations and individuals. Mr. Fisher is currently chairman of the New Detroit Committee, the United Foundation of Detroit, and president of the United Jewish Appeal.

—I have directed the Secretary of Housing and Urban Development to establish a clearinghouse for information on voluntary programs, and on government programs designed to foster voluntary action. Eventually this clearinghouse will be a function of the private sector.

The Cabinet Committee will report directly to the Cabinet and the President. It will foster cooperation among the various departments and agencies on programs related to voluntary action, and will seek to promote more widespread reliance on and recognition of voluntary activities. In addition, it will serve voluntary organizations by providing a focal point through which they can better make their needs and concerns known to the administration, and by clearing away governmental roadblocks to the effective employment

---

[1] Executive Order 11470.

of voluntary resources. It will be a prime mover in developing new Federal initiatives for encouraging voluntary action.

The Office of Voluntary Action in the Department of Housing and Urban Development will seek the development and implementation of voluntary action programs for solving problems of urban living and poverty. It will provide for the development and operation of the information clearinghouse, and will make use of both Government vehicles and nongovernment channels to help expand and multiply innovative voluntary action programs. Consistent with law, it will coordinate Federal voluntary action programs for dealing with urban and poverty problems. It will cooperate with private groups and citizens, and will be available to assist Mr. Fisher.

Mr. Fisher is already counseling with representatives of a wide range of different kinds of private and voluntary organizations:

—Private social service, health, and welfare organizations.

—Private economic organizations—business, labor, and agriculture.

—Fraternal service, professional, and religious organizations.

—Foundations.

—Civic and community organizations.

—Youth, women's, and minority group organizations.

—Communications media and their organizations.

Representatives of State and local governments will also be consulted because of their own great potential for stimulating voluntary action.

The response of the groups Mr. Fisher has consulted with thus far has been enthusiastic. Many of them have offered to make staff available full-time to work with the Office of Voluntary Action during its initial stages.

The information clearinghouse will fill a need long recognized but never met. It will serve government, private organizations, and individuals.

At one time or another, millions of Americans have asked themselves or others, "What can I do? How can I help?" One of the chief aims of this new effort will be to make answers readily available. It is a remarkable and little-appreciated fact that for practically every one of the great social ills that plagues us, solutions have been found somewhere—*by citizen volunteers,* who have devised programs that actually work in their own community. In nearly every case, the experience can be helpful to those who are concerned with similar problems elsewhere.

The four steps I have outlined today are a beginning. As we consider further steps, we will develop them in the closest possible collaboration with the leaders of voluntary activities themselves. All of us involved in this effort are keenly aware that this is an area in which Government initiatives must not be imposed, and that a too-tight Federal embrace could smother the voluntary principle. I will not allow that to happen. Our effort will be to assist, not to control; to encourage, not to coerce.

Our aim is not to substitute Federal leadership for the dedicated private leadership that already exists in our voluntary organizations. Rather, we will seek to help in every way possible in order that these groups can better realize their larger ambitions for public service.

Within the limits of this caution, however, I am convinced that an enriched partnership—a creative partnership—is possible.

The measure of a government's performance is not only its capacity to deliver services to its citizens, but also its capacity to inspire them to contribute their own efforts.

From the time our Nation's first settlers struggled together against a wilderness, voluntary action for mutual help and community betterment has been a hallmark of the American way. Free men and women have worked with one another and aided one another. That spirit is vigorously alive today, and the encouragement of that spirit is needed if our Nation is to become what it has the capacity to be.

NOTE: On the same day the White House released a news briefing on the program by George W. Romney, Secretary of Housing and Urban Development, Max M. Fisher, Special Consultant to the President on Voluntary Action, and Ronald L. Ziegler, Press Secretary to the President.

178 Message of Congratulations to Newly Elevated American Cardinals. *April 30, 1969*

PLEASE accept my warm congratulations on your elevation to the rank of Cardinal.

Your fellow countrymen are proud of the international recognition that you have gained for the continuing contributions you make to our society—and to all mankind.

America's religious leaders guard more than just the sacred tenets of the faith they preach. You personify the spirit of human brotherhood and charity that form the cornerstone of peace and understanding among men and nations. Your distinguished decades of religious service— both individually and collectively—equip you well for a dynamic role in our challenging and changing times. And you are accompanied in your noble mission by our prayers and those of all men of goodwill.

RICHARD NIXON

NOTE: The message was addressed to Bishop James Hickey, Rector of the North American College at the Vatican in Rome, who read the message at a luncheon honoring Terence Cardinal Cooke, Archbishop of New York; John Cardinal Dearden, Archbishop of Detroit; John Cardinal Carberry, Archbishop of St. Louis; and John Cardinal Wright, Archbishop of Pittsburgh.

179 Special Message to the Congress on Consolidation of Federal Assistance Programs. *April 30, 1969*

To the Congress of the United States:

In the administration of Federal programs, one of the principal needs today is to improve the delivery systems: to ensure that the intended services actually reach the intended recipients, and that they do so in an efficient, economical and effective manner.

As grant-in-aid programs have proliferated, the problems of delivery have grown more acute. States, cities, and other recipients find themselves increasingly faced with a welter of overlapping programs, often involving multiple agencies and diverse criteria. This results in confusion at the local level, in the waste of time, energy and resources, and often in frustration of the intent of Congress.

As a major step toward improved administration of these programs, I urge that Congress enact a Grant Consolidation Act.

Under our present fragmented system, each one of a group of closely related categorical grants is encumbered with its own individual array of administrative and technical requirements. This unnecessarily complicates the planning process; it discourages comprehensive planning; it requires multiple applications, and multiple bookkeeping both by the Federal agencies and by State and local governments.

The legislation I propose would be patterned in part after procedures used successfully for the past 20 years to reorganize Executive Branch functions. It would give the President power to initiate consolidation of closely related Federal assistance programs, and to place consolidated programs under the jurisdiction of a single agency. However, it would give either House of Congress the right to veto a proposed consolidation within 60 days, and it would establish stringent safeguards against possible abuse.

In order to make consolidation possible, it would be necessary in many cases to make changes in the statutory terms and conditions under which individual programs would be administered. Formulas, interest rates, eligibility requirements, administrative procedures, and other terms and conditions of the various programs being consolidated would have to be brought into harmony. The proposed legislation would empower the President to do this in drawing up his consolidation plans—but only within carefully defined limits. For example:

—Only programs in closely related functional areas could be consolidated.

—Terms and conditions could be changed only to the extent necessary to achieve the purposes of the consolidation plan.

—In setting new terms and conditions, the President would be limited by the range of those already provided in the programs being consolidated. Thus, if a program providing for a 10 percent State matching share were being merged with one providing a 20 percent matching share, he would have to propose a matching share between 10 and 20 percent.

—No consolidation plan could continue any program beyond the period authorized by law for its existence.

—No plan could provide assistance to recipients not already eligible under one of the programs being merged.

—Responsibility for the consolidated program could not be vested in an agency or office not already responsible for one of those being merged.

The effect of these limits would be to safeguard the essential intent of Congress in originally establishing the various programs; the effect of consolidation would be to carry out that intent more effectively and more efficiently.

The number of separate Federal assistance programs has grown enormously over the years.

When the Office of Economic Opportunity set out to catalogue Federal assistance programs, it required a book of more than 600 pages even to set forth brief descriptions. It is an almost universal complaint of local government officials that the web of programs has grown so tangled that it often becomes impermeable. However laudable each may be individually, the total effect can be one of government paralysis.

If these programs are to achieve their

intended purposes, we must find new ways of cutting through the tangle.

Passage of the Grant Consolidation Act would not be a substitute for other reforms necessary in order to improve the delivery of Federal services, but it is an essential element. It would be another vital step in the administrative reforms undertaken already, such as establishing common regional boundaries for Federal agencies, creating the Urban Affairs Council and the Office of Inter-governmental Relations, and beginning a streamlining of administrative procedures for Federal grant-in-aid programs. Its aim, essentially, is to help make more certain the delivery and more manageable the administration of a growing complex of Federal programs, at a time when the problems they address increasingly cross the old jurisdictional lines of departments and agencies.

This proposal would permit rapid action, initiated by the President, while preserving the power of Congress to disapprove such action. It would benefit the intended beneficiaries of the programs involved; it would benefit State and local governments, which now have to contend with a bewildering array of rules and jurisdictions; and it would benefit the American taxpayer, who now bears the cost of administrative inefficiencies.

RICHARD NIXON

The White House
April 30, 1969

---

180   Statement on the Death of Washington Newspaperman Jeremiah O'Leary.   *May* 1, 1969

I WAS SADDENED to learn of the death yesterday of Jerry O'Leary. For 47 years, until his retirement in 1964, Mr. O'Leary served with great distinction as a reporter for the Washington Star.

He was a reporter who covered the Senate and the political scene with fairness and insight, and his passing is mourned by all those in journalism and government who value the quality of integrity he so richly possessed.

---

181   Special Message to the Congress on Obscene and Pornographic Materials.   *May* 2, 1969

To the Congress of the United States:

American homes are being bombarded with the largest volume of sex-oriented mail in history. Most of it is unsolicited, unwanted, and deeply offensive to those who receive it. Since 1964, the number of complaints to the Post Office about this salacious mail has almost doubled. One hundred and forty thousand letters of protest came in during the last nine months alone, and the volume is increasing. Mothers and fathers by the tens of thousands have written to the White House and the Congress. They resent these intrusions into their homes, and they are asking for federal assistance to protect their children against exposure to erotic publications.

The problem has no simple solution. Many publications dealing with sex—in a way that is offensive to many people—are protected under the broad umbrella of the First Amendment prohibition against any law "abridging the freedom of speech, or of the press."

However, there are constitutional means available to assist parents seeking to protect their children from the flood of sex-oriented materials moving through the mails. The Courts have not left society defenseless against the smut peddler; they have not ruled out reasonable government action.

Cognizant of the constitutional strictures, aware of recent Supreme Court decisions, this Administration has carefully studied the legal terrain of this problem.

We believe we have discovered some untried and hopeful approaches that will enable the federal government to become a full partner with states and individual citizens in drying up a primary source of this social evil. I have asked the Attorney General and the Postmaster General to submit to Congress three new legislative proposals.

The first would prohibit outright the sending of offensive sex materials to any child or teenager under 18. The second would prohibit the sending of advertising designed to appeal to a prurient interest in sex. It would apply regardless of the age of the recipient. The third measure complements the second by providing added protection from the kind of smut advertising now being mailed, unsolicited, into so many homes.

PROTECTING MINORS

Many states have moved ahead of the federal government in drawing distinctions between materials considered obscene for adults and materials considered obscene for children. Some of these states, such as New York, have taken substantial strides toward protecting their youth from materials that may not be obscene by adult standards but which could be damaging to the healthy growth and development of a child. The United States Supreme Court has recognized, in repeated decisions, the unique status of minors and has upheld the New York Statute. Building on judicial precedent, we hope to provide a new measure of federal protection for the young.

I ask Congress to make it a federal crime to use the mails or other facilities of commerce to deliver to anyone under 18 years of age material dealing with a sexual subject in a manner unsuitable for young people.

The proposed legislation would not go into effect until the sixth month after passage. The delay would provide mailers of these materials time to remove from their mailing lists the names of all youngsters under 18. The federal government would become a full partner with parents and states in protecting children from much of the interstate commerce in pornography. A first violation of this statute would be punishable by a maximum penalty of five years in prison and a $50,000 fine; subsequent violations carry greater penalties.

PRURIENT ADVERTISING

Many complaints about salacious literature coming through the mails focus on advertisements. Many of these ads are designed by the advertiser to appeal exclusively to a prurient interest. This is clearly a form of pandering.

I ask the Congress to make it a federal crime to use the mails, or other facilities of commerce, for the commercial exploitation of a prurient interest in sex through advertising.

This measure focuses on the intent of the dealer in sex-oriented materials and his methods of marketing his materials. Through the legislation we hope to impose restrictions on dealers who flood the mails with grossly offensive advertisements intended to produce a market for their smut materials by stimulating the prurient interest of the recipient. Under the new legislation, this form of pandering could bring a maximum penalty of 5 years imprisonment, and a fine of $50,000 for a first offense and 10 years and a fine of $100,000 for subsequent offenses.

INVASION OF PRIVACY

There are other erotic, sex-oriented advertisements that may be constitutionally protected but which are, nonetheless, offensive to the citizen who receives them in his home. No American should be forced to accept this kind of advertising through the mails.

In 1967 Congress passed a law to help deal with this kind of pandering. The law permits an addressee to determine himself whether he considers the material offensive in that he finds it "erotically arousing or sexually provocative." If the recipient deems it so, he can obtain from the Postmaster General a judicially enforceable order prohibiting the sender from making any further mailings to him or his children, and requiring the mailer to delete them from all his mailing lists.

More than 170,000 persons have requested such orders. Many citizens however, are still unaware of this legislation, or do not know how to utilize its provisions. Accordingly, I have directed the Postmaster General to provide every Congressional office with pamphlets explaining how each citizen can use this law to protect his home from offensive advertising. I urge Congress to assist our effort for the widest possible distribution of these pamphlets.

This pandering law was based on the principle that no citizen should be forced to receive advertisements for sex-oriented matter he finds offensive. I endorse that principle and believe its application should be broadened.

I therefore ask Congress to extend the existing law to enable a citizen to protect his home from any intrusion of sex-oriented advertising—regardless of whether or not a citizen has ever received such mailings.

This new stronger measure would require mailers and potential mailers to respect the expressed wishes of those citizens who do not wish to have sex-oriented advertising sent into their homes. These citizens will put smut-mailers on notice simply by filing their objections with a designated postal authority. To deliberately send such advertising to their homes would be an offense subject to both civil and criminal penalties.

As I have stated earlier, there is no simple solution to this problem. However, the measures I have proposed will go far toward protecting our youth from smut coming through the mails; they will place new restrictions upon the abuse of the postal service for pandering purposes; they will reinforce a man's right to privacy in his own home. These proposals, however, are not the whole answer.

The ultimate answer lies not with the government but with the people. What is required is a citizens' crusade against the obscene. When indecent books no longer find a market, when pornographic films can no longer draw an audience, when obscene plays open to empty houses, then the tide will turn. Government can maintain the dikes against obscenity, but only

people can turn back the tide.

RICHARD NIXON

The White House

   May 2, 1969

NOTE: The White House Press Office also released the text of a news briefing held by John W. Dean III, Associate Deputy Attorney General, and David A. Nelson, General Counsel, Post Office Department, on the President's message.

182   Remarks in Columbia, S.C., During a Visit With Former Governor and Mrs. James Byrnes.   *May 3,* 1969

IF I COULD HAVE your attention for just a moment:

It has been a very great honor and privilege for Mrs. Nixon, for me, and for the Members of the Senate and the House, to come here to join in this tribute to Governor Byrnes and to Mrs. Byrnes.

I think, really, the character of this wonderful family is indicated when the Governor said, as we came into the house and wished him happy birthday, that he wanted to make clear that the main purpose of this day was not to celebrate his birthday, but the 63d wedding anniversary with Mrs. Byrnes.

So we honor that wonderful family relationship.

I understand the Governor's secret, and Mrs. Byrnes told it to me. We asked, did they ever have an argument in 63 years, and she said, "Yes, now and then," but they always had a rule that before the day ended they kissed and made up.

I want to leave one thought with regard to the Governor as we honor him:

I look back over the men that I have known around the world and in this country, and I have known great Congressmen, Senators, Governors, Justices of the Supreme Court of the United States, Sec-

retaries of State, and men who have served in wartime as the top advisers to the President of the United States. But never in American history has one man held more high offices with more distinction than Governor Byrnes of South Carolina.

NOTE: The President spoke at 12:43 p.m. in Columbia, S.C., at the home of former Governor James F. Byrnes. He and Mrs. Nixon stopped en route to Louisville, Ky., for the Kentucky Derby to congratulate the Governor and Mrs. Byrnes on their 63d wedding anniversary and the Governor's 90th birthday.

Governor Byrnes served as Representative 1911–1925, Senator 1931–1941, Governor of South Carolina 1951–1955, Justice of the United States Supreme Court 1941–1942, Head of the Office of Economic Stabilization 1942–1943, Director of the Office of War Mobilization 1943–1945, and Secretary of State 1945–1947.

Following the President's remarks, Governor Byrnes spoke as follows:

Mr. President:

I address you as Mr. President because last fall I told you that I hoped when you came again to South Carolina I could greet you as "Mr. President."

I do so today.

I thank you from the bottom of my heart for your honoring me by coming to visit my home. I will never forget this day; I will never forget you.

183 Messages on the Death of President Zakir Husain of India. *May* 3–4, 1969

Dear Mr. President:

All Americans join me in sending you and the people of India our deep sympathy for your great loss. We mourn with you on this sad occasion. Zakir Husain was a man of courage and integrity whose loss will be long felt.

Sincerely,

RICHARD NIXON

[V. V. Giri, Acting President of India]

India has lost a great statesman. We mourn the death of Zakir Husain, a man admired by all for his service to humanity. You and your people have my deepest sympathy in this time of sadness.

Sincerely,

RICHARD NIXON

[Mrs. Indira Nehru Gandhi]

NOTE: President Zakir Husain died at the age of 72 in New Delhi, India.

The message to Acting President Giri was dated May 3 and the message to Prime Minister Gandhi was dated May 4.

184 Remarks at the Swearing In of Joseph H. Blatchford as Director of the Peace Corps. *May* 5, 1969

Ladies and gentlemen:

The purpose of this occasion is to swear in, as Director of the Peace Corps, Joe Blatchford.

I think this appointment is a particularly good one for reasons that go beyond the fact that he, like myself, is a native Californian. In checking the statistics in the Peace Corps, I found the greatest number of volunteers in the whole country have come from the State of California. It has caught the imagination of the Nation, but particularly of the western part of the United States and the State of California.

Joe Blatchford, throughout his private career, has had a tremendous interest in this kind of activity, particularly in Latin America.

He brings to this position an enthusiasm and some new ideas which he will be glad to discuss with members of the press after he is sworn in.

I am very privileged to have him as a member of the administration in this vitally important function. He has the responsibility, despite his very young years, to come up with new ideas. He has the opportunity to develop new programs and those programs will receive the very highest priority within the administration.

Judge Hart, of the District Court, will conduct the ceremony.

NOTE: The President spoke at 10:11 a.m. in the Rose Garden at the White House.

The oath of office was administered by Judge George L. Hart, Jr., of the United States District Court for the District of Columbia.

The text of a news briefing held by Mr. Blatchford following the ceremony was released by the White House Press Office on the same day. A release containing biographical information on Mr. Blatchford is printed in the Weekly Compilation of Presidential Documents (vol. 5, p. 435).

185   Message to the Senate Transmitting the Vienna
        Convention on Consular Relations and the Optional
        Protocol Concerning the Compulsory Settlement of
        Disputes. *May* 5, 1969

To the Senate of the United States:

With a view to receiving the advice and consent of the Senate to ratification, I transmit herewith a certified copy of the Vienna Convention on Consular Relations and a certified copy of the Optional Protocol Concerning the Compulsory Settlement of Disputes, signed at Vienna under date of April 24, 1963. The Convention and Protocol entered into force on March 19, 1967.

I transmit also, for the information of the Senate, the report which the Secretary of State has addressed to me in regard to the matter, together with the enclosures thereto.

The convention is the first agreement envisaging the regulation of consular relations on a world-wide basis and represents the culmination of eight years of work. Based on a draft convention prepared by the International Law Commission, it was concluded at a United Nations Conference of 92 States, one of a series of Conferences having the aim, in the words of the United Nations Charter, of "encouraging the progressive development of international law and its codification". A previous United Nations Conference in the series formulated the 1961 Vienna Convention on Diplomatic Relations, which was approved by the Senate on September 14, 1965.

Account has been taken of the interests and views of new and old nations and of nations with varied political and economic systems in the codification and development of consular law as contained in the present Convention, and the Convention is considered to be an important contribution to friendly relations between States. I recommend that the Senate give early and favorable consideration to the Convention and Protocol submitted herewith and give its advice and consent to their ratification.

RICHARD NIXON

The White House
May 5, 1969

NOTE: The convention was favorably considered by the Senate on October 22, 1969, and after ratification entered into force on December 24, 1969. The texts of the convention and optional protocol, as well as the report of the Secretary of State, are printed in Senate Executive E (91st Cong., 1st sess.).

186   Remarks at the Swearing In of William H. Brown III as
        a Member of the Equal Employment Opportunity
        Commission. *May* 6, 1969

WE ARE here today for the swearing in of the member of the Commission, and then I will make an announcement after that about Mr. Brown's appointment.

He will be sworn in by an old friend, Judge Hyde.

Mrs. Brown, would you hold the Bible and stand here?

[At this point, Judge DeWitt S. Hyde of the District of Columbia Court of General Sessions administered the oath of office. The President then resumed speaking.]

Now, if the Senators and others would come here, all of you who would like to congratulate Mr. Brown, then I will say a word and leave him to the press.

In making the appointment of Mr. Brown to this Commission, I did so with the full knowledge that he was a man who was uniquely qualified for it. He comes from Philadelphia. I suppose we could describe him as a Philadelphia lawyer, because he is a lawyer. But he is a Philadelphia lawyer in a much broader sense than we usually think of that term.

He knows the law. He is an expert in the law. But he also has what I would call a spirit of brotherly love which the city of Philadelphia has been so long associated with.

Combining that legal expertise with a deep dedication to the principle of equality of opportunity for all people in this country, an equal chance for all people, I think these are the unique attributes that we need, not only as a member of the Commission, but as Chairman of the Commission.

I am delighted to be able to appoint a man so well qualified, so full of dedication, to this very important position.

We wish him and the members of the Commission well. I know that, having had a chance to talk to him, he will provide the leadership that this administration wants in this vitally important field.

Now, I will leave you for your first press conference as Chairman of the Commission here in this very pleasant place.

NOTE: The President spoke at 4:15 p.m. in the Rose Garden at the White House.

An announcement on March 13, 1969, of Mr. Brown's nomination to the Commission is printed in the Weekly Compilation of Presidental Documents (vol. 5, p. 400).

The text of a news conference held by Chairman Brown following the ceremony was released on the same day.

187   Special Message to the Congress Recommending a Program To End Hunger in America.   *May 6, 1969*

To the Congress of the United States:

We have long thought of America as the most bounteous of nations. In our conquest of the most elemental of human needs, we have set a standard that is a wonder and aspiration for the rest of the world. Our agricultural system produces more food than we can consume, and our private food market is the most effective food distribution system ever developed. So accustomed are most of us to a full and balanced diet that, until recently, we have thought of hunger and malnutrition as problems only in far less fortunate countries.

But in the past few years we have awakened to the distressing fact that despite our material abundance and agricultural wealth, many Americans suffer from malnutrition. Precise factual descriptions of its extent are not presently available, but there can be no doubt that hunger and malnutrition exist in America, and that some millions may be affected.

That hunger and malnutrition should

persist in a land such as ours is embarrassing and intolerable. But it is an exceedingly complex problem, not at all susceptible to fast or easy solutions. Millions of Americans are simply too poor to feed their families properly. For them, there must be first sufficient food income. But this alone would only begin to address the problem, for what matters finally is what people buy with the money they have. People must be educated in the choosing of proper foods. All of us, poor and non-poor alike, must be reminded that a proper diet is a basic determinant of good health. Our private food industry has made great advances in food processing and packaging, and has served the great majority of us very well. But these advances have placed great burdens on those who are less well off and less sophisticated in the ways of the modern marketplace. We must therefore work to make the private food market serve these citizens as well, by making nutritious foods widely available in popular forms. And for those caught in the most abject poverty, special efforts must be made to see that the benefits of proper foods are not lost amidst poor health and sanitary conditions.

The Council for Urban Affairs has for the past three months been studying the problem of malnutrition in America, and has assessed the capacities of our present food and nutrition programs. As a result of the Council's deliberations, I am today prepared to take the following actions:

1. FAMILY FOOD ASSISTANCE PROGRAMS

The Federal government presently provides food assistance to nearly seven million needy Americans through the Food Stamp and Direct Distribution programs.

Though these programs have provided welcome and needed assistance to these persons, both are clearly in need of revision.

The present Food Stamp program also can be greatly improved. I shall in a short period of time submit to the Congress legislation which will revise the Food Stamp program to:

—provide poor families enough food stamps to purchase a nutritionally complete diet. The Department of Agriculture estimates this to be $100 per month for a typical family of four.

—provide food stamps at no cost to those in the very lowest income brackets.

—provide food stamps to others at a cost of no greater than 30% of income.

—ensure that the Food Stamp program is complementary to a revised welfare program, which I shall propose to the Congress this year.

—give the Secretary of Agriculture the authority to operate both the Food Stamp and Direct Distribution programs concurrently in individual counties, at the request and expense of local officials. This will permit the Secretary to assist counties wishing to change from Direct Distribution to Food Stamps, and to meet extraordinary or emergency situations.

It will not be possible for the revised program to go into effect until sometime after the beginning of the calendar year 1970, that is to say after the necessary legislative approval and administrative arrangements have been made. The requested appropriations will then permit the establishment of the revised program

351

in all current Food Stamp counties before the end of the fiscal year, as well as a modest expansion into Direct Distribution counties, and some counties with no current programs.

This program, on a full year basis, will cost something in excess of $1 billion per year. (Precise estimates will only become available over time.) This will be in addition to the $1.5 billion for food for the hungry which I have requested for the forthcoming fiscal year, making a total program of $2.5 billion. In the meantime, $270 million is being reprogrammed within the forthcoming budget to permit the program to begin as soon as legislative and administrative arrangements can be made and other necessary measures taken.

While our long-range goal should be to replace direct food distribution with the revised Food Stamp program, the Direct Distribution program can fill many short-range needs. Today there are still over 440 counties without any Family Food Assistance program, and this Administration shall establish programs in each of these counties before July 1970. The Direct Distribution program will be used in most of these counties. In these and other Direct Distribution counties, the most serious criticism of the program will be met by ensuring that all counties offer the full range of available foods.

To strengthen both current Family Food Assistance programs, efforts will proceed on a high priority basis to establish more distribution points, prompter and simpler certification, financing arrangements, mailing of food stamps, and appeal mechanisms.

2. SPECIAL SUPPLEMENTAL FOOD PROGRAM

Serious malnutrition during pregnancy and infancy can impair normal physical and mental development in children. Special effort must be made to protect this vulnerable group from malnutrition.

The Special Package program, which provides needy women and mothers with packages of especially nutritious foods, was designed to meet this need. But the program has encountered logistical problems which have severely limited its success. I am therefore directing that a substantial portion of the Fiscal Year 1970 budget for this program be used to establish pilot programs that make use of the private food market. Under these programs, needy pregnant women and mothers of infants will be issued vouchers, redeemable at food and drug stores for infant formulas and other highly nutritious special foods. If such a program seems workable, and the administrative problems are resolved, the program will be expanded later on the basis of that experience.

3. ADMINISTRATION OF FOOD PROGRAMS

I am directing the Urban Affairs Council to consider the establishment of a new agency, the Food and Nutrition Service, whose exclusive concern will be the administration of the Federal Food programs. Presently the food programs are operated in conjunction with numerous other unrelated programs. The creation of a new agency will permit greater specialization and concentration on the effective administration of the food programs.

4. PRIVATE SECTOR INVOLVEMENT

I shall shortly announce a White House Conference on Food and Nutrition, involving executives from the nation's leading food processing and food distribution companies and trade unions. I shall ask these men to advise me on how the private food market might be used to improve the nutritional status of all Americans, and how the government food programs could be improved. I shall also call on these men to work with the advertising industry and the Advertising Council, to develop an educational advertising and packaging campaign to publicize the importance of good food habits.

5. INTER-AGENCY EFFORTS

Although most of the current food and nutrition programs are administered by the Department of Agriculture, other agencies are critically involved. I am therefore establishing a sub-Cabinet working committee of the Urban Affairs Council to promote coordination between the food and nutrition programs and other health, educational, and anti-poverty programs.

At the present time, I am directing the Secretary of Health, Education, and Welfare and the Director of the Office of Economic Opportunity to take a number of immediate steps.

I am asking the Secretary of HEW to:
—work with state agencies to ensure that the Medicaid program is fully coordinated with the Special Package and pilot voucher programs for pregnant women and infants, so that vitamin and mineral products can be made available to those diagnosed as suffering from nutrient deficiencies.
—expand the National Nutrition Survey, presently being conducted by the Public Health Service, to provide us with our first detailed description of the extent of hunger and malnutrition in our country.
—initiate detailed research into the relationship between malnutrition and

mental retardation.
—encourage emphasis by medical schools on training for diagnosis and treatment of malnutrition and malnutrition-related diseases.

The Office of Economic Opportunity, with its exclusive commitment to the problems of poverty and its unique "outreach" among the poor themselves, has an especial role to play. I am asking the Director of OEO to:
—work with the Secretaries of Agriculture and HEW to establish a greatly expanded role for the Community Action Agencies in delivering food stamps and commodity packages. Volunteers working in the VISTA program will also aid in the delivery and outreach process, supplementing the efforts of the Agricultural Extension Service.
—redirect OEO funds into the Emergency Food and Health Service program to increase its food, health, and sanitation services for our most depressed areas. Presently, health and sanitary conditions in many of our most depressed counties are so poor that improved food services alone would have little impact on the nutritional health of the population. The Emergency Food and Health Service has provided invaluable services in aiding these areas, and its good work should be substantially expanded.

More is at stake here than the health and well-being of 16 million American citizens who will be aided by these programs and the current Child Food Assistance programs. Something very like the honor of American democracy is at issue. It was half a century ago that the "fruitful plains" of this bounteous land were first called on to a great work of humanity, that of feeding a Europe exhausted and bleeding from the First World War. Since then on one occasion after another, in a succession of acts of true generosity—let those who doubt that find their counterpart in history—America has come to the aid of one starving people after another. But the moment is at hand to put an end to hunger in America itself. For all time. I ask this of a Congress that has already splendidly demonstrated

its own disposition to act. It is a moment to act with vigor; it is a moment to be recalled with pride.

RICHARD NIXON

The White House
May 6, 1969

NOTE: On November 13, 1969, the President approved a bill to increase the appropriation authorization for the food stamp program for fiscal year 1970 (Public Law 91–116, 83 Stat. 191).

188 Toasts of the President and Prime Minister John G. Gorton of Australia. *May 6, 1969*

Mr. Prime Minister, Mrs. Gorton, and our friends:

Tonight is a very special evening for all of us in this room because, as I noted when you were passing through the receiving line, at least two-thirds of the guests had been to Australia or personally knew the Prime Minister and Mrs. Gorton.

As I was thinking of something that would be appropriate to say, I was reminded of what I think was one of the most eloquent greetings that a visitor can receive when he travels around the world—as has the Prime Minister, and as I have on occasion, and as will the Secretary of State be traveling in just a few days—in this country, at least in that part of the Midwest from which my mother and father came, the common expression is "Make yourself at home." In Latin America the expression is quite different. It means the same thing. They say *"Está usted en su casa,"* which means "you are in your own home."

I was reminded of the fact that tonight as we received the Prime Minister and Mrs. Gorton and the members of their party that of all the countries of the world

that my wife and I have visited, and there are over 70, that there is no country in the world when we thought we were in our own home more than Australia.

I suppose part of this is due to the fact that we are from the West, from California, and we get the feeling when we are in Melbourne and in Sydney, that north and south or south and north reverse, San Francisco versus Los Angeles, and also because as you see that great country with all of its magnificent cities and yet the tremendous possibilities for development for the future, you realize that this is one of the great new frontiers, some would say last frontiers, geographically, at least. But there is another reason that has more to do than geography or size of cities or the like. It has to do with people.

I have felt from the time we were first there in 1953 and through the years since then when we have been there, and I know many of you tonight have this same feeling, that we have a special kinship with our friends from Australia. We see the world as they see it. They are among those who understand, as I think most of us in this room understand, how much rides on what happens in the Pacific. They are a Pacific power, as we are; and at a time when most of the world, whatever they may think privately, will not speak up publicly with regard to what the United States is doing in the Pacific. And as indicated in the very difficult war in Vietnam, our friends in Australia know why we are there and why they are there, and we know that they are there with us.

They know why and beyond that, they are willing to say why. At a time when we sometimes wonder if our policies are understood or appreciated, at such times we are most grateful to have such good friends, friends who have been friends of ours over the years and who remember those days we read about in World War I. Those of us who were in World War II, the Secretary and myself, in the Pacific, we served with Australians and we feel that they are so much like us or we are like they are.

Now tonight we have a man who represents this country, who has all of the vital energy that we think of when we think of Australia, who can see the tremendous possibilities of development there, who knows the great role that his country can play, that ours must play, and who has that courage that we all admire so much— the courage to speak up when sometimes it might be perhaps more political to say nothing, or at least to say something else.

So tonight, as I ask you to rise, I am going to do so not simply in the usual protocol way. We could toast his country, we could toast his office, but I suggest we raise our glasses to a man and that great new country, a new country with an old tradition, but the country of the future and a man who stands for all the hopes and aspirations that it represents.

To the Prime Minister.

NOTE: The President spoke at 9:59 p.m. in the State Dining Room at the White House.

Prime Minister Gorton responded as follows:

Mr. President, ladies and gentlemen:

This is a speech, sir, to which it is very difficult easily to reply. I think it is true that there are, between the people of the United States and the people of my own country, some particular bonds which are not of recent birth, but which have matured over the years.

True it is, that in our own country we reached self-government by means of evolution and you by revolution. But nevertheless, in some degree we think of you as being responsible for it. I know a lot of other countries do that, too. [*Laughter*] Because it was only after the Declaration of Independence and a certain amount of unpleasantness which culminated at Yorktown, following that, that Great Britain looked to another outlet, if I may put it that way. But it gave us the first impetus to the growth of Australia and so, perhaps in that indirect way, sir, you have helped us in our beginnings.

But that was just at the beginning. Since then we have stood together in many struggles; the First World War, fought far away from our shores and yours, but fought for the same reasons by our soldiers and yours, the Second World War, the Korean war where Australians were within the first week in action with the United States forces and the first country so to be in action. And now, the Vietnam war.

I don't know why it is—or perhaps I do— but I am not sure why it is that when countries talk, as you and I are talking, of the bonds which unite and have united them, so often one turns to wars and to struggles in which one has been together. Because, after all, a successful war does not gain anything new. What it does do, if it is successful, is prevent the imposition of something bad and obtain an opportunity for new building on a proper basis and a proper foundation of freedom and participation and peace.

Perhaps it is because men have for so long had to struggle and probably always will have to struggle against the idea of absolute and arbitrary power, against the idea of the secret police and the hangman, against the philosophy that in order to be free and live in peace one must subject one's self to the rule—

without law—of dictatorship. Perhaps it is because the fainthearted all through the years have been prepared to say: "If you wish to eat you must sell your immortal soul. If you wish peace you must submit to dictatorship." Perhaps it is because there is in the human spirit a refusal to accept this that one talks of nations standing together in war not because it is in war, but because of the objectives sought by such struggles.

You, sir, are bearing today a burden, greater, I think, than that borne by any other man in the world I know. And in a way, here, history is repeating itself because as I look up there and see a former Republican [*indicating portrait of Abraham Lincoln*]—I hope no Democrats would be up there—I see a former Republican looking down upon us, my mind goes back to those times and that burden and the turmoil in this country in that period.

Too often do we now look back at Lincoln and tend to think the speeches he made were well received and tend to think the ideals he professed were accepted by all the people of the United States. But not enough do we look back and think of the burden for 5 long years he bore during a period when the United States lost more dead than it had in any of the many wars since. And he bore the burden.

During a period when Copperheads were inciting riots in order to bring peace; during the period when the Horace Greeleys and others of the press were attacking not only his ideas, but him personally; during the period when regiments from the Army of the Potomac had to be brought back to quell draft riots in New York—that was a burden. But it was one carried like a man.

There would be no United States today. There would be—who knows? There would

have been, at any rate, a slave autocracy of the South and what that, in conjunction with South America, could then have led to in the world no one can tell. But there would have been no United States.

So the bearing of these burdens and the successful consummation of these struggles is something which is not for that time alone or for this time alone, but which, having been successful in that time, led to the United States being able to be what it is today, which, if it is successful in this time, will lead to there being able to be throughout the world an opportunity for us, when we next speak, when we next meet, or at least communicate or whatever it may be, to talk not of war but of the other progress which is the other part of which you spoke, sir, of which the United States and ourselves, you helping us economically, building us, helping us to build ourselves, the other part may be the real outcome of success in this situation. I think it will be.

I think that we will stand together in the future as we have in the past, we the small, the apparently small, but fired by the same motives, resolute in the same way.

I hope that this will be true. It has been true and I believe it will be true. And for our part, speaking for Australians, wherever the United States is resisting aggression, wherever the United States or the United Kingdom or any other country is seeking to insure that there will be a chance for the free expression of the spirit of man from himself and not from dictatorship from above; wherever there is a joint attempt to improve not only the material but the spiritual standards of life of the peoples of the world, then, sir, we will go "Waltzing Matilda With You."

189 Statement Following the Visit of Prime Minister Gorton of Australia. *May* 7, 1969

IT HAS been a great pleasure to welcome Prime Minister and Mrs. Gorton to Washington. Mrs. Gorton is of course returning to the land of her birth, so we always have a special greeting for her. Prime Minister Gorton is no stranger to our shores either,

and he has come as the head of government of one of our closest friends and allies in the world. We will always be delighted to see them both.

This visit has been most useful for me and, I think, for other officers of this Government. It has given us a chance to get acquainted with an outstanding statesman with whom we expect to be working very closely in the future.

Australia is a member of ANZUS and SEATO, two alliances which are fundamental to our strategy and position in Southeast Asia. As between us, ANZUS, with its provisions for mutual aid in developing our individual and collective capacity to resist armed attack, and its declaration that "no potential aggressor should be under the illusion that any of them (Australia, New Zealand or the United States) stand alone in the Pacific area," is of great importance to both our countries. Australian troops are fighting beside ours and those of other free world nations to help South Vietnam preserve its independence. Australian forces are stationed in Malaysia and Singapore as part of the Commonwealth Strategic Reserve, and Prime Minister Gorton has recently announced that these forces will remain after the British forces withdraw in 1971, to continue making their important contribution to the security of that area. This is a historic and farseeing decision, and needless to say, it has our full understanding and the decision has our support.

Australia is also making an outstanding contribution to peaceful cooperation and economic development in its part of the world. It participates wholeheartedly in the Colombo Plan, the Asian Development Bank, and many other regional activities. In percentage of national income devoted to foreign aid, Australia ranks second in the world. This is a record of which any nation can be proud.

All things considered, I think Australia and the United States can both be proud of the contribution we are making, as partners, to the security and progress of the Pacific region to which we both belong. That partnership and that contribution will continue.

These two days have provided opportunities for us to discuss a whole range of subjects, including of course Vietnam and regional security generally, but including also a number of topics outside the security field. Australia is geographically closer to some of these problems than we are, and Prime Minister Gorton has been in office a year longer than I have, so I have very much appreciated the opportunity to exchange views with him. I have obtained a number of new insights, but fundamentally, I find the perspective from "down under" is very much the same as it is from Washington.

This visit has been both profitable and enjoyable for us. I hope that you can say the same, Mr. Prime Minister, and that you and your charming wife will come and see us again.

190   Remarks on the Departure of Prime Minister Gorton of Australia. *May* 7, 1969

Mr. Prime Minister:

As you leave the White House—and you are not leaving the country yet, because we hope you will stay here for a few more days—I want you to know how grateful

I am for your returning to the United States after having been here at the time of President Eisenhower's funeral, and for giving us the opportunity to have a very full discussion of the major issues that are not really between us so much as they involve our common interests for peace and security in the Pacific area.

This talk has been most helpful, as far as I am concerned, and as far as the Secretary of State and the Secretary of Defense are concerned. We have opened a line of communication which will be used very extensively in the months and years ahead in pursuing our mutual purposes and goals in the world.

I want to say, finally, that as one who has been to your country on two occasions, I hope to visit there again. And, like all Americans, I have a very deep personal feeling of respect for your country, for your people, and for the leadership that you have provided for your people.

We are very proud to have been your allies and friends in great struggles in the past and to be your allies and friends as we deal with the problems of the future.

NOTE: The President spoke at 12:45 p.m. in the Rose Garden at the White House.

Prime Minister Gorton responded as follows:

Thank you very much, Mr. President.

I feel that the written statement which you have made, and which was agreed to between us, gives a clear indication of those matters of common concern which we were able to discuss in such depth.

I think that we have reached an arrangement for close and constant consultation between our two selves on matters which may arise in the future and that this will be of great advantage to both our countries.

I can only express gratitude to you for the hospitality that you have extended, for the complete openness of your talks with me, and a belief that not only the talks but the underlining of the importance of the ANZUS Treaty to both our countries which has evolved from the talks are of considerable significance to Australia and to Australia's future and I believe that that, in turn, is of some significance to the United States and to the nations of the free world as a whole.

Thank you.

191   Remarks at the Swearing In of Lt. Gen. Robert E. Cushman, Jr., as Deputy Director, Central Intelligence Agency. *May 7, 1969*

THE PURPOSE of our ceremony today is the swearing in of the Deputy Director of the CIA.

I will have some remarks about him in just a moment.

But at this point we will go forward with the ceremony and he will be sworn in by Judge Sirica of the U.S. District Court of the District of Columbia, and General Cushman's wife will hold the Bible.

[At this point Judge John J. Sirica administered the oath of office.]

Ladies and gentlemen, I want to say a personal word with regard to General Cushman.

Usually, as you know, I am not present except for the swearing in of the chairmen or the top directors of the agencies, but this is a special case and an exception for reasons that all of you will understand.

Back in the year 1957, on the basis of a recommendation of Admiral Radford,[1] General Cushman, then Colonel Cush-

---

[1] Adm. Arthur W. Radford, USN, Chairman, Joint Chiefs of Staff 1953–1957.

man, came to my office as Vice President as my Executive Assistant. At that time there was no allocation in the funds for the Vice President for that kind of staff work. So I gave him the responsibility as my Executive Assistant and particularly in the field of national security affairs.

He did that job in a very effective way. And as a result of doing it so effectively, I gave him his added responsibilities, that of running my office and a few other things which, of course, he will well remember.

But I think you will note that he has a very distinguished career in the Marine Corps and World War II, then in Vietnam where he has been our top commander of the Marines in the I Corps area near the DMZ [demilitarized zone].

He is one of America's most distinguished men who has served us both in war and in peace and now he takes on a new assignment in the field of intelligence—new for him in the sense of this particular duty, but not new for him in the sense of his past experience, because in the Marine Corps he had a lot of valuable experience, as Director Helms pointed out, in the intelligence field.

What really convinced me, however, that he was fitted for this responsibility, was not his service in World War II, which was distinguished, not his work with me simply in the national security field, which was distinguished, and not his work in the Vietnam war area, but a personal factor entered into it.

I recall I had a very difficult assignment at one point when I was Vice President. There came a time when it was necessary to move half of my small staff from one building to another, from the Senate Of-

fice Building over to the Capitol. As is usually the case, half the staff that had to be moved didn't want to be moved.

I knew that I was not able to handle that very, very difficult task of forcing them to move, and knowing that General Cushman, then Colonel Cushman, as a Marine had had experience in tough tasks, I just turned it over to him; I delegated it to him.

He accomplished it, but he came in to see me afterwards and wiped his brow and said that he had carried out the orders and that he just had one observation to make: that it was more difficult to move six secretaries from the Senate Office Building to the Capitol than it was to move a whole division of Marines across the Pacific.

With that kind of experience and knowing the great number of fine secretaries that you have, Mr. Helms, in the agency, I know we have here a topnotch administrator with a fine background in the military and also in intelligence.

This organization, the CIA, has a distinguished record of being bipartisan in character. It is a highly professional group. It will remain that in this administration, and General Cushman is one who is in the great tradition of service to his Nation without regard to any partisan considerations.

I am delighted that he is going to work with Mr. Helms in this capacity.

NOTE: The President spoke at 4:11 p.m. in the Rose Garden at the White House.

General Cushman's response to the President's remarks and an announcement of his nomination are printed in the Weekly Compilation of Presidential Documents (vol. 5, p. 666 and p. 374).

192   Remarks at the Republican Victory Dinner. May 7, 1969

Senator Tower, all of the distinguished guests in the audience:

I can assure you, first, that that book will have a very special place in my library, and the names of everyone in that book will have a very special place in my heart and in the hearts of our family, because we know that without the support of those in this room we could not be where we are today.

I speak now of the whole new family that is in Washington. Not only the family that is living in the White House, but the Cabinet officers and all the rest. We thank you from the bottom of our hearts for what you have done and what you are doing tonight, and for all those things you will do in the future, for the cause which was so well described by Everett Dirksen and Jerry Ford before.

As all the introductions were being made, and particularly as the members of the Cabinet were being introduced, I thought how much had changed in Washington just as a result of an election. That change seems to have infected the whole city.

It has been really the most beautiful spring, they tell me, we have had in Washington for many years. And thanks to Bill Middendorf [Treasurer of the Republican National Committee] we have tulips, which are an indication of that spring. Those tulips I see, incidentally, every day in the Rose Garden of the White House. I look out on them and realize what that change means to me.

Also it has really infected other segments of the society in Washington. The Washington Senators are doing better.

I am a baseball fan, and you prove it by being for the Senators, believe me.

I was reminded of the fact that they may be doing better primarily because they have a new manager. And I was also reminded of the fact before I came in here that that new manager almost didn't make it. Everett Dirksen was going to stop him in the Senate.

When Ev heard that some fellow by the name of Ted was going to take over his Senators, his hair stood right on end.[1] [*Laughter*]

But it did occur to me tonight that in all the introductions that were made, there was one part that was missed, and I have the privilege of participating in that introduction. The Congressmen, the Senators, the members of the Cabinet, and other distinguished guests were introduced, but those that were not introduced were those who make it possible for all of us to be where we are; the ones who campaigned with us, who listened to our speeches, who encouraged us when we were down, and who kept us moving forward when we were moving too slowly.

I think we would like to see tonight, too, those in every family, our great Republican family here, who have participated in the victory that we celebrate tonight.

I would like, first, to suggest that all of the wives of the Members of Congress please stand so that we can applaud you.

Now if all of the wives of the Members of the Senate would please stand so that we can applaud you.

---

[1] The President was alluding to Ted Williams, new manager of the Washington Senators baseball team and to Senator Edward "Ted" Kennedy, newly elected Senate majority whip.

And now, a very special group of women, as far as my official family is concerned. Will all of the wives of the members of the Cabinet please stand?

And two very special people—Mrs. Ray Bliss and Mrs. Rogers Morton.[2] Will you please stand, right up here at table five?

I have been speaking about the changes in Washington. I can assure you there have been some changes in the decorations at the White House. The chief decorator, Pat Nixon, will you please stand?

Now the script calls for me to talk. Just like Ev Dirksen and Jerry Ford, I am limited to 4 minutes, but they doubled my time. And I will not impose upon your time too long, but there are some things I would like to say with regard to some of the problems we are confronting, have confronted, and that we hope to have action on in the years ahead.

I did not have as much time to prepare as I would have liked this evening. The days have been long. As you have noted from the appointments schedule, it has been rather heavy this week.

Just before coming over here, I made a call over to an old friend in the Cabinet who has had some political experience, Bob Finch, and asked if he had any ideas. He said that he would be glad to send me over some guidelines. [*Laughter*] I told him not to bother; I would just use my own outline.

But nevertheless, I do want you to know that I realize that you have been reading in the papers and hearing on television and radio about the fact that we have passed the first 100 days of this administration and that we are well along

---

toward the first 4 months.

Naturally, and understandably, there are those who are impatient about what has happened. Some believe we should have moved faster in some areas—for example on appointments—and others think that we should have moved faster in finding the solutions to the great problems with which we were confronted.

Tonight I want to tell you how I look at this situation. We deliberately have not attempted to make the kind of a record that looked awfully good in the headlines of today and that made very bad history in the books 3 or 4 years from now. We want a solid achievement we can all be proud of.

It would have been very easy, I can assure you, on the first day after the inauguration, for me to have announced that we were immediately going to bring all the men home from Vietnam; that immediately the solution of the problem of inflation and others that we had inherited were to be found.

I could not say that. I could not say that because I knew we could not produce.

I can assure you of one thing: We will make our mistakes. We have made some, and we will make some more in the future. But as far as this administration is concerned, we are going to lay it on the line with the American people. We are never going to promise something we cannot produce. I think that is the kind of government that you want.

Now, I think Ev Dirksen and Jerry Ford have well described the great issues that brought us here. There are really three that stand out above all the others, the ones that stood out during the election campaign, and the ones that are on the minds and in the hearts of every person in this audience.

The first is peace, the desire to have the kind of a peace that will give us a chance not only to end the war in which we presently are engaged, but a chance to avoid other wars of that type, or any type, in the years ahead. So that goal, the goal of peace—the American people who have not known peace for 4 years—is one that they want the new administration to achieve.

The second goal is the goal closely related to the problem of peace abroad, and that is the problem of peace at home. The American people want to stop the rise in crime, as Ev Dirksen and Jerry Ford indicated, and they want to restore respect for law in this country. That was the second great issue of the last campaign.

Then the third goal that the American people want achieved by their new administration is to stop the rise in taxes and the rise in prices, and to have the orderly progress, prosperity without inflation, that the American people are entitled to.

Now there are other issues, of course, local issues and some national. But these are the three great issues that seemed to be on the minds of most of the people during the campaign, and from my mail and from my discussions with Congressmen and Senators, these are the issues that the American people are going to judge the new administration by.

I want to tell you about these various issues. If I could paraphrase Winston Churchill, I cannot tell you tonight that in finding a solution to the problem of peace abroad and peace at home, and restoration of respect for law, and stopping inflation, that we had reached the point where we could say that it was the

beginning of the end of those problems, but I can say that we have reached the point that it is the end of the beginning.

We have had the opportunity—an opportunity that we think we have used well—to get control of this Government, of the vast administrative machinery; to develop the plans and the programs over these past 3½ months which will enable us to make progress on these issues.

Now that it is the end of the beginning, I think the American people will begin to see the results of that progress. I mean results in terms not of a flashy headline, not of a promise that cannot be kept, but results in the kind of progress that is solid, that is achievable, and that the American people can count on.

On that score, I want to tell all of you that when you get together, as I am sure most of you will, a year from now, in this room, I want you to look back on this year. I want you to look at what this administration has achieved, and I think you will find that in terms of bringing peace abroad, in terms of restoring respect for law at home, in terms of stopping inflation and stopping the rise in taxes, this administration will have made the progress that you wanted. This we can do and this we pledge to you.

Now, that brings me to a very sensitive point. As I was signing autographs here a few moments ago, and meeting people from all over the country, I thought of those many hundreds of invitations that I have been unable to accept to address fundraising dinners and political meetings all over the country. I would like to do it.

As I am sure some of you recall, going back over 22 years, I have been in virtually every city in this country on some occasion or another. I have not been able to in these first 3½ months. As a matter of fact, this is one of the first major political meetings that I have attended, and I must tell you that I will not be able to in the next few months because, I think that as far as this group is concerned, what you want from the new President of the United States is his complete dedication and devotion to solving these problems so that the money that you are putting up will bring the dividends.

So I pledge to you we will provide that devotion and that dedication. We will provide some good speakers for you, too, from our Cabinet team, and from among the Senators and the House Members, but above everything else, we want to give you a record which you can be proud of, a record that our candidates for the House and Senate and Governors will be proud to run on. This is what we are working toward, and believe me, every effort will be made to achieve that goal and not to disappoint you.

Then one final thought. Three hours ago at the White House, I received in the Rose Garden the members of the finance committee of the Republican National Committee, about 150 people. What a splendid group of people they were. I looked across that group there standing in that garden and I saw people who, going back over 20 years, have raised money for this party in good years and bad, for my campaigns, but more than that, for the campaigns of Republicans every place, and I regretted the fact that time was such, that my appointments schedule was so heavy, that even with that small a group I was unable to thank each one of them personally for what he had done. Here tonight, 1,600 people, $1,000 a plate. Believe me, if you don't think there

is inflation, think of that price! But nevertheless, my wife and I are able only to thank a few of you.

I just want you to know as I stand here and as I see this great sea of faces before me, I am deeply grateful, we are all deeply grateful, those of us who are in Washington because of what you have done, for the contributions you have made, for your support of this dinner.

Speaking in a very personal sense, I know, as the one who was described by Jerry Ford a few moments ago—a little boy in California, growing up in Yorba Linda, listening to the one train a day go by—I know that in those contests that I had to participate in—as did so many Members of the House, first for the House, and then for the Senate, then the Vice Presidency and then the Presidency—that it all would not have been possible without the help of hundreds of people that I know, but thousands of people like yourselves who contributed, that I have never really had a chance to speak to and to thank adequately.

I hope over the years that we are here in Washington we can express our personal appreciation to each and every one of you, but tonight I can tell you this is a great moment for us, a great moment for Pat, my wife, and for myself. We know that in this room are the people without whose support we could not have achieved the goal which we finally realized.

We can assure you that in the years that we are here, we will always remember what you have done; and we will do everything in our power not only not to let you down, but to make you proud of what you have done, to make you proud of our party, but more than that, proud of our country and proud of the great role that

America can and will play in the world for the rest of this century.

Thank you.

NOTE: The President spoke at 10:03 p.m. at the Washington Hilton Hotel. In his opening words he referred to Senator John G. Tower of Texas, chairman of the Republican Senatorial Campaign Committee, who presented him with a book containing the names of the contributors to the fundraising dinner.

193 Remarks Prior to the Departure of Governor Nelson A. Rockefeller for Latin America. *May 11, 1969*

Ladies and gentlemen:

Governor Rockefeller and members of his party, Mrs. Rockefeller and others, have stopped here at Key Biscayne on the first leg of the continental tour they are taking through Latin America.

They will be in Mexico for a late luncheon, a few hours from now, and then will go to all of the countries in Central America before returning to Washington and to New York.

After that there will be several other trips to Latin America over the next 3 to 4 months which the Governor will be glad to describe.

As I have indicated previously, I consider this to be one of the most vitally important missions ever undertaken by an independent group in behalf of the Government of the United States.

If you look at the members of the Governor's party, some of whom are standing here with us—Mr. Watson, Mr. Woods, and others—it is a group of experts which has never been equaled in terms of qualifications and the broad base of experience. It is a group which is going to Latin America not for the purpose of studying the problem—as the Governor was saying to me a few moments ago, and he is an expert in this field because he first visited Latin America 35 or 40 years ago—Latin America has been stud-ied over the years, and all kinds of study recommendations have been made—but this has the unusual and, I think, very necessary purpose of listening to the leaders of Latin America and coming back to Washington and making recommendations for new directions and new policies.

The group goes with no preconceived prejudices against existing programs, but it has an open mind with regard to new approaches.

The Governor now will be glad to answer any questions insofar as he can on the mission. I want to say that we are grateful that he could take the time to make this trip at this point. It will be vitally important to not only the new relations and a better relationship between the United States and our friends in Latin America, but toward developing new policy directions in this critical area of the world.

Good luck.

NOTE: The President spoke at 12:03 p.m., at Key Biscayne, Fla. Arthur K. Watson was president of the IBM World Trade Corp., and of the International Chamber of Commerce. George D. Woods was director and consultant to the First Boston Corporation and former President of the International Bank for Reconstruction and Development.

A list of advisers who accompanied Governor Rockefeller to Latin America was released by the White House Press Office on May 8, 1969.

The text of Governor Rockefeller's news briefing following the President's remarks is printed in the Weekly Compilation of Presidential Documents (vol. 5, p. 681).

On May 27 a news briefing by Governor Rockefeller on the second of four visits to Latin America was released by the White House.

194   Special Message to the Congress on Reforming the Military Draft.   *May* 13, 1969

To the Congress of the United States:

For almost two million young men who reach the age of military service each year—and for their families—the draft is one of the most important facts of life. It is my conviction that the disruptive impact of the military draft on individual lives should be minimized as much as possible, consistent with the national security. For this reason I am today asking the Congress for authority to implement important draft reforms.

Ideally, of course, minimum interference means no draft at all. I continue to believe that under more stable world conditions and with an armed force that is more attractive to volunteers, that ideal can be realized in practice. To this end, I appointed, on March 27, 1969, an Advisory Commission on an All-Volunteer Armed Force. I asked that group to develop a comprehensive plan which will attract more volunteers to military service, utilize military manpower in a more efficient way, and eliminate conscription as soon as that is feasible. I look forward to receiving the report of the Commission this coming November.

Under present conditions, however, some kind of draft will be needed for the immediate future. As long as that is the case, we must do everything we can to limit the disruption caused by the system and to make it as fair as possible. For one's vision of the eventual does not excuse his inattention to the immediate. A man may plan to sell his house in another year, but during that year he will do what is necessary to make it livable.

Accordingly, I will ask the Congress to amend the Military Selective Service Act of 1967, returning to the President the power which he had prior to June 30, 1967, to modify call-up procedures. I will describe below in some detail the new procedures which I will establish if Congress grants this authority. Essentially, I would make the following alterations:

1. Change from an oldest-first to a youngest-first order of call, so that a young man would become less vulnerable rather than more vulnerable to the draft as he grows older.

2. Reduce the period of prime draft vulnerability—and the uncertainty that accompanies it—from seven years to one year, so that a young man would normally enter that status during the time he was nineteen years old and leave it during the time he was twenty.

3. Select those who are actually drafted through a random system. A procedure of this sort would distribute the risk of call equally—by lot—among all who are vulnerable during a given year, rather than arbitrarily selecting those whose birthdays happen to fall at certain times of the year or the month.

4. Continue the undergraduate student deferment, with the understanding that

the year of maximum vulnerability would come whenever the deferment expired.

5. Allow graduate students to complete, not just one term, but the full academic year during which they are first ordered for induction.

6. In addition, as a step toward a more consistent policy of deferments and exemptions, I will ask the National Security Council and the Director of Selective Service to review all guidelines, standards and procedures in this area and to report to me their findings and recommendations.

I believe these reforms are essential. I hope they can be implemented quickly.

Any system which selects only some from a pool of many will inevitably have some elements of inequity. As its name implies, choice is the very purpose of the Selective Service System. Such choices cannot be avoided so long as the supply of men exceeds military requirements. In these circumstances, however, the Government bears a moral obligation to spread the risk of induction equally among those who are eligible.

Moreover, a young man now begins his time of maximum vulnerability to the draft at age nineteen and leaves that status only when he is drafted or when he reaches his twenty-sixth birthday. Those who are *not* called up are nevertheless vulnerable to call for a seven-year period. For those who *are* called, the average age of induction can vary greatly. A few years ago, when calls were low, the average age of involuntary induction was nearly twenty-four. More recently it has dropped to just about twenty. What all of this means for the average young man is a prolonged time of great uncertainty.

The present draft arrangements make it extremely difficult for most young people to plan intelligently as they make some

of the most important decisions of their lives, decisions concerning education, career, marriage, and family. Present policies extend a period during which young people come to look on government processes as particularly arbitrary.

For all of these reasons, the American people are unhappy about our present draft mechanisms. Various elements of the basic reforms which I here suggest have been endorsed by recent studies of the Selective Service System, including that of the Marshall Commission of 1967,[1] the Clark panel [2] of that same year, and the reports of both the Senate and the House Armed Services Committees. Reform of this sort is also sound from a military standpoint, since younger men are easier to train and have fewer family responsibilities.

My specific proposals, in greater detail, are as follows:

1. *A "youngest-first" order of call.* Under my proposal, the government would designate each year a "prime age group," a different pool of draft eligibles for each consecutive twelve-month period. (Since that period would not necessarily begin on January 1, it would be referred to as a "selective service year.") The prime age group for any given selective service year would contain those registrants who were nineteen years old when it began. Those

[1] The National Advisory Commission on Selective Service under the chairmanship of Burke Marshall. Its report is entitled "In Pursuit of Equity: Who Serves When Not All Serve?" (Government Printing Office, 219 pp.).

[2] The Civilian Advisory Panel on Military Manpower Procurement, chaired by Gen. Mark W. Clark. Its report to the House Committee on Armed Services is dated March 28, 1967 (Committee Print, 90th Cong., 1st sess., 30 pp.).

who received deferments or exemptions would rejoin the prime age group at the time their deferment or exemption expired. During the first year that the new plan was in operation, the prime age group would include *all* eligible men from nineteen to twenty-six, not deferred or exempt, so that no one would escape vulnerability simply because of the transition.

2. *Limited vulnerability.* Each individual would experience maximum vulnerability to the draft only for the one selective service year in which he is in the prime age group. At the end of the twelve-month period—which would normally come sometime during his twentieth year—he would move on to progressively less vulnerable categories and an entirely new set of registrants would become the new prime age group. Under this system, a young man would receive an earlier and more decisive answer to his question, "Where do I stand with the draft?" and he could plan his life accordingly.

3. *A random selection system.* Since more men are classified as available for service each year than are required to fill current or anticipated draft calls, Selective Service Boards must have some way of knowing whom to call first, whom to call second, and whom not to call at all. There must be some fair method of determining the sequence of induction for those available for service in the prime age group.

In my judgment, a fair system is one which randomizes by lot the order of selection. Each person in the prime age group should have the same chance of appearing at the top of the draft list, at the bottom, or somewhere in the middle. I would therefore establish the following procedure:

At the beginning of the third month after Congress grants this authority, the first of a sequence of selective service years would begin. Prior to the start of each selective service year, the dates of the 365 days to follow would be placed in a sequence determined by a random method. Those who spend the following year in the pool would take their place in the draft sequence in the same order that their birthdays come up on this scrambled calendar. Those born on June 21st, for example, might be at the head of the list, followed by those born on January 12th, who in turn might be followed by those born on October 23rd. Each year, a new random order would be established for the next year's draft pool. In turn those who share the same birthday would be further distributed, this time by the first letter of their last names. But rather than systematically discriminating against those who come at the front of the alphabet, the alphabet would also be scrambled in a random manner.

Once a person's place in the sequence was determined, that assignment would never change. If he were granted a deferment or exemption at age nineteen or twenty, he would re-enter the prime age group at the time his deferment or exemption expires, taking the same place in the sequence that he was originally assigned.

While the random sequence of induction would be nationally established, it would be locally applied by each draft board to meet its local quota. In addition to distributing widely and evenly the risk of induction, the system would also aid many young men in assessing the likelihood of induction even before the classification procedure is completed. This would reduce uncertainty for the individual registrant and, particularly in times of low draft calls, simplify the task of the draft boards.

4. *Undergraduate student deferments.* I continue to believe in the wisdom of college deferments. Permitting the diligent student to complete his college education without interruption by the draft is a wise national investment. Under my proposal, a college student who chooses to take a student deferment would still receive his draft sequence number at the time he first enters the prime age group. But he would not be subject to induction until his deferment ended and he reentered a period of maximum vulnerability.

5. *Graduate Student Induction.* I believe that the induction of men engaged in graduate study should be postponed until the end of the full academic year during which they are first called to military service. I will ask the National Security Council to consider appropriate advice to the Director of the Selective Service to establish this policy. At present, graduate students are allowed to delay induction only to the end of a semester. This often means that they lose valuable time which has been invested in preparation for general examinations or other degree requirements. It can also jeopardize some of the financial arrangements which they made when they planned on a full year of schooling. Induction at the end of a full academic year will provide a less damaging interruption and will still be consistent with Congressional policy.

At the same time, however, the present policy against general graduate deferments should be continued, with exceptions only for students in medical and allied fields who are subject to a later special draft. We must prevent the pyramiding of student deferments—undergraduate and graduate—into a total exemption from military service. For this reason the postponement of induction should be possible only once for each graduate student.

6. *A review of guidelines.* The above measures will reduce the uncertainty of young men as to when and if they may be called for service. It is also important that we encourage a consistent administration of draft procedures by the more than 4,000 local boards around the country. I am therefore requesting the National Security Council and the Director of Selective Service to conduct a thorough review of our guidelines, standards and procedures for deferments and exemptions, and to report their findings to me by December 1, 1969. While the autonomy of local boards provides valuable flexibility and sensitivity, reasonable guidelines can help to limit geographic inequities and enhance the equity of the entire System. The 25,000 concerned citizens who serve their country so well on these local boards deserve the best possible framework for their decisions.

Ultimately we should end the draft. Except for brief periods during the Civil War and World War I, conscription was foreign to the American experience until the 1940's. Only in 1948 did a peacetime draft become a relatively permanent fact of life for this country. Now a full generation of Americans has grown up under a system of compulsory military service.

I am hopeful that we can soon restore the principle of no draft in peacetime. But until we do, let us be sure that the operation of the Selective Service System is as equitable and as reasonable as we can make it. By drafting the youngest first, by limiting the period of vulnerability, by randomizing the selection process, and by reviewing deferment policies, we can do much to achieve these important interim goals. We should do no less for the youth of our country.

RICHARD NIXON

The White House

May 13, 1969

NOTE: Following a meeting with the President on May 13, Representative Gerald R. Ford of Michigan held a news briefing which touched upon the President's draft reform proposals. The text of the news briefing is printed in the Weekly Compilation of Presidential Documents (vol. 5, p. 683).

195 Address to the Nation on Vietnam. *May 14, 1969*

Good evening, my fellow Americans:

I have asked for this television time tonight to report to you on our most difficult and urgent problem—the war in Vietnam.

Since I took office 4 months ago, nothing has taken so much of my time and energy as the search for a way to bring lasting peace to Vietnam. I know that some believe that I should have ended the war immediately after the inauguration by simply ordering our forces home from Vietnam.

This would have been the easy thing to do. It might have been a popular thing to do. But I would have betrayed my solemn responsibility as President of the United States if I had done so.

I want to end this war. The American people want to end this war. The people of South Vietnam want to end this war. But we want to end it permanently so that the younger brothers of our soldiers in Vietnam will not have to fight in the future in another Vietnam someplace else in the world.

The fact that there is no easy way to end the war does not mean that we have no choice but to let the war drag on with no end in sight.

For 4 years American boys have been fighting and dying in Vietnam. For 12

months our negotiators have been talking with the other side in Paris. And yet the fighting goes on. The destruction continues. Brave men still die.

The time has come for some new initiatives. Repeating the old formulas and the tired rhetoric of the past is not enough. When Americans are risking their lives in war, it is the responsibility of their leaders to take some risks for peace.

I would like to report to you tonight on some of the things we have been doing in the past 4 months to bring true peace, and then I would like to make some concrete proposals to speed that day.

Our first step began before inauguration. This was to launch an intensive review of every aspect of the Nation's Vietnam policy. We accepted nothing on faith, we challenged every assumption and every statistic. We made a systematic, serious examination of all the alternatives open to us. We carefully considered recommendations offered both by critics and supporters of past policies.

From the review, it became clear at once that the new administration faced a set of immediate operational problems:

—The other side was preparing for a new offensive.

—There was a wide gulf of distrust between Washington and Saigon.

—In 8 months of talks in Paris, there had been no negotiations directly concerned with a final settlement.

Therefore, we moved on several fronts at once.

We frustrated the attack which was launched in late February. As a result, the North Vietnamese and the Vietcong failed to achieve their military objectives.

We restored a close working relationship with Saigon. In the resulting atmosphere of mutual confidence, President Thieu and his Government have taken important initiatives in the search for a settlement.

We speeded up the strengthening of the South Vietnamese forces. I am glad to report tonight that, as a result, General Abrams told me on Monday that progress in the training program had been excellent and that, apart from any developments that may occur in the negotiations in Paris, the time is approaching when South Vietnamese forces will be able to take over some of the fighting fronts now being manned by Americans.

In weighing alternate courses, we have had to recognize that the situation as it exists today is far different from what it was 2 years ago or 4 years ago or 10 years ago.

One difference is that we no longer have the choice of not intervening. We have crossed that bridge. There are now more than a half million American troops in Vietnam and 35,000 Americans have lost their lives.

We can have honest debate about whether we should have entered the war in Vietnam. We can have honest debate about how the war has been conducted. But the urgent question today is what to do now that we are there.

Against that background, let me discuss first, what we have rejected, and second, what we are prepared to accept.

We have ruled out attempting to impose a purely military solution on the battlefield.

We have also ruled out either a one-sided withdrawal from Vietnam, or the acceptance in Paris of terms that would amount to a disguised American defeat.

When we assumed the burden of helping defend South Vietnam, millions of South Vietnamese men, women, and children placed their trust in us. To abandon them now would risk a massacre that would shock and dismay everyone in the world who values human life.

Abandoning the South Vietnamese people, however, would jeopardize more than lives in South Vietnam. It would threaten our long-term hopes for peace in the world. A great nation cannot renege on its pledges. A great nation must be worthy of trust.

When it comes to maintaining peace, "prestige" is not an empty word. I am not speaking of false pride or bravado—they should have no place in our policies. I speak rather of the respect that one nation has for another's integrity in defending its principles and meeting its obligations.

If we simply abandoned our effort in Vietnam, the cause of peace might not survive the damage that would be done to other nations' confidence in our reliability.

Another reason for not withdrawing unilaterally stems from debates within the Communist world between those who argue for a policy of confrontation with the United States, and those who argue against it.

If Hanoi were to succeed in taking

over South Vietnam by force—even after the power of the United States had been engaged—it would greatly strengthen those leaders who scorn negotiation, who advocate aggression, who minimize the risks of confrontation with the United States. It would bring peace now but it would enormously increase the danger of a bigger war later.

If we are to move successfully from an era of confrontation to an era of negotiation, then we have to demonstrate—at the point at which confrontation is being tested—that confrontation with the United States is costly and unrewarding.

Almost without exception, the leaders of non-Communist Asia have told me that they would consider a one-sided American withdrawal from Vietnam to be a threat to the security of their own nations.

In determining what choices would be acceptable, we have to understand our essential objective in Vietnam: What we want is very little, but very fundamental. We seek the opportunity for the South Vietnamese people to determine their own political future without outside interference.

Let me put it plainly: What the United States wants for South Vietnam is not the important thing. What North Vietnam wants for South Vietnam is not the important thing. What is important is what the people of South Vietnam want for South Vietnam.

The United States has suffered over a million casualties in four wars in this century. Whatever faults we may have as a nation, we have asked nothing for ourselves in return for those sacrifices. We have been generous toward those whom we have fought. We have helped our former foes as well as our friends in the task of reconstruction. We are proud of

this record, and we bring the same attitude in our search for a settlement in Vietnam.

In this spirit, let me be explicit about several points:

—We seek no bases in Vietnam.

—We seek no military ties.

—We are willing to agree to neutrality for South Vietnam if that is what the South Vietnamese people freely choose.

—We believe there should be an opportunity for full participation in the political life of South Vietnam by all political elements that are prepared to do so without the use of force or intimidation.

—We are prepared to accept any government in South Vietnam that results from the free choice of the South Vietnamese people themselves.

—We have no intention of imposing any form of government upon the people of South Vietnam, nor will we be a party to such coercion.

—We have no objection to reunification, if that turns out to be what the people of South Vietnam and the people of North Vietnam want; we ask only that the decision reflect the free choice of the people concerned.

At this point, I would like to add a personal word based on many visits to South Vietnam over the past 5 years. This is the most difficult war in America's history, fought against a ruthless enemy. I am proud of our men who have carried the terrible burden of this war with dignity and courage, despite the division and opposition to the war in the United States. History will record that never have America's fighting men fought more bravely for more unselfish goals than our men in Vietnam. It is our responsibility to see that they have not fought in vain.

In pursuing our limited objective, we insist on no rigid diplomatic formula. Peace could be achieved by a formal negotiated settlement. Peace could be achieved by an informal understanding, provided that the understanding is clear, and that there were adequate assurances that it would be observed. Peace on paper is not as important as peace in fact.

And so this brings us to the matter of negotiations.

We must recognize that peace in Vietnam cannot be achieved overnight. A war that has raged for many years will require detailed negotiations and cannot be settled by a single stroke.

What kind of a settlement will permit the South Vietnamese people to determine freely their own political future? Such a settlement will require the withdrawal of all non-South Vietnamese forces, including our own, from South Vietnam, and procedures for political choice that give each significant group in South Vietnam a real opportunity to participate in the political life of the nation.

To implement these principles, I reaffirm now our willingness to withdraw our forces on a specified timetable. We ask only that North Vietnam withdraw its forces from South Vietnam, Cambodia, and Laos into North Vietnam, also in accordance with a timetable.

We include Cambodia and Laos to ensure that these countries would not be used as bases for a renewed war.

Our offer provides for a simultaneous start on withdrawal by both sides, for agreement on a mutually acceptable timetable, and for the withdrawal to be accomplished quickly.

The North Vietnamese delegates have been saying in Paris that political issues should be discussed along with military issues, and that there must be a political settlement in the South. We do not dispute this, but the military withdrawal involves outside forces, and can, therefore, be properly negotiated by North Vietnam and the United States, with the concurrence of its allies.

The political settlement is an internal matter which ought to be decided among the South Vietnamese themselves, and not imposed by outsiders. However, if our presence at these political negotiations would be helpful, and if the South Vietnamese concerned agreed, we would be willing to participate, along with the representatives of Hanoi, if that also were desired.

Recent statements by President Thieu have gone far toward opening the way to a political settlement. He has publicly declared his Government's willingness to discuss a political solution with the National Liberation Front, and has offered free elections. This was a dramatic step forward, a reasonable offer that could lead to a settlement. The South Vietnamese Government has offered to talk without preconditions. I believe the other side should also be willing to talk without preconditions.

The South Vietnamese Government recognizes, as we do, that a settlement must permit all persons and groups that are prepared to renounce the use of force to participate freely in the political life of South Vietnam. To be effective, such a settlement would require two things: first, a process that would allow the South Vietnamese people to express their choice, and, second, a guarantee that this process would be a fair one.

We do not insist on a particular form

of guarantee. The important thing is that the guarantees should have the confidence of the South Vietnamese people, and that they should be broad enough and strong enough to protect the interests of all major South Vietnamese groups.

This, then, is the outline of the settlement that we seek to negotiate in Paris. Its basic terms are very simple: mutual withdrawal of non-South Vietnamese forces from South Vietnam and free choice for the people of South Vietnam. I believe that the long-term interests of peace require that we insist on no less, and that the realities of the situation require that we seek no more.

And now, to make very concrete what I have said, I propose the following specific measures which seem to me consistent with the principles of all parties. These proposals are made on the basis of full consultation with President Thieu.

—As soon as agreement can be reached, all non-South Vietnamese forces would begin withdrawals from South Vietnam.

—Over a period of 12 months, by agreed-upon stages, the major portions of all U.S., allied, and other non-South Vietnamese forces would be withdrawn. At the end of this 12-month period, the remaining U.S., allied, and other non-South Vietnamese forces would move into designated base areas and would not engage in combat operations.

—The remaining U.S. and allied forces would complete their withdrawals as the remaining North Vietnamese forces were withdrawn and returned to North Vietnam.

—An international supervisory body, acceptable to both sides, would be created for the purpose of verifying withdrawals, and for any other purposes agreed upon between the two sides.

—This international body would begin operating in accordance with an agreed timetable and would participate in arranging supervised cease-fires in Vietnam.

—As soon as possible after the international body was functioning, elections would be held under agreed procedures and under the supervision of the international body.

—Arrangements would be made for the release of prisoners of war on both sides at the earliest possible time.

—All parties would agree to observe the Geneva Accords of 1954 regarding South Vietnam and Cambodia, and the Laos Accords of 1962.

I believe this proposal for peace is realistic, and takes account of the legitimate interests of all concerned. It is consistent with President Thieu's six points. It can accommodate the various programs put forth by the other side. We and the Government of South Vietnam are prepared to discuss the details with the other side.

Secretary Rogers is now in Saigon and he will be discussing with President Thieu how, together, we may put forward these proposed measures most usefully in Paris. He will, as well, be consulting with our other Asian allies on these measures while on his Asian trip. However, I would stress that these proposals are not offered on a take-it-or-leave-it basis. We are quite willing to consider other approaches consistent with our principles.

We are willing to talk about anybody's program—Hanoi's 4 points, the NLF's

[National Liberation Front] 10 points—provided it can be made consistent with the very few basic principles I have set forth here tonight.

Despite our disagreement with several of its points, we welcome the fact that the NLF has put forward its first comprehensive program. We are studying that program carefully. However, we cannot ignore the fact that immediately after the offer, the scale of enemy attacks stepped up and American casualties in Vietnam increased.

Let me make one point clear. If the enemy wants peace with the United States, that is not the way to get it.

I have set forth a peace program tonight which is generous in its terms. I have indicated our willingness to consider other proposals. But no greater mistake could be made than to confuse flexibility with weakness or of being reasonable with lack of resolution. I must also make clear, in all candor, that if the needless suffering continues, this will affect other decisions. Nobody has anything to gain by delay.

Reports from Hanoi indicate that the enemy has given up hope for a military victory in South Vietnam, but is counting on a collapse of American will in the United States. There could be no greater error in judgment.

Let me be quite blunt. Our fighting men are not going to be worn down; our mediators are not going to be talked down; and our allies are not going to be let down.

My fellow Americans, I have seen the ugly face of war in Vietnam. I have seen the wounded in field hospitals—American boys, South Vietnamese boys, North Vietnamese boys. They were different in many ways—the color of their skins, their religions, their races; some were enemies; some were friends.

But the differences were small, compared with how they were alike. They were brave men, and they were so young. Their lives—their dreams for the future—had been shattered by a war over which they had no control.

With all the moral authority of the Office which I hold, I say that America could have no greater and prouder role than to help to end this war in a way which will bring nearer that day in which we can have a world order in which people can live together in peace and friendship.

I do not criticize those who disagree with me on the conduct of our peace negotiations. And I do not ask unlimited patience from a people whose hopes for peace have too often been raised and then cruelly dashed over the past 4 years.

I have tried to present the facts about Vietnam with complete honesty, and I shall continue to do so in my reports to the American people.

Tonight, all I ask is that you consider these facts, and, whatever our differences, that you support a program which can lead to a peace we can live with and a peace we can be proud of. Nothing could have a greater effect in convincing the enemy that he should negotiate in good faith than to see the American people united behind a generous and reasonable peace offer.

In my campaign for the Presidency, I pledged to end this war in a way that would increase our chances to win true and lasting peace in Vietnam, in the Pacific, and in the world. I am determined to keep that pledge. If I fail to do so, I expect the American people to hold me accountable for that failure.

But while I will never raise false expectations, my deepest hope, as I speak to you tonight, is that we shall be able to look back on this day, at that critical turning point when American initiative moved us off dead center, and forward to the time when this war would be brought to an end and when we shall be able to devote the unlimited energies and dedication of the American people to the exciting challenges of peace.

Thank you and good night.

NOTE: The President spoke at 10 p.m. in the Theater at the White House. His address was broadcast on radio and television.

On the same day, the White House Press Office released an advance text of the President's address to the Nation on Vietnam.

196   Remarks Following a Meeting With Ambassador Henry Cabot Lodge on Vietnam and the Paris Peace Talks.   *May* 15, 1969

Ladies and gentlemen:

Ambassador Lodge, Ambassador Walsh, and Mr. Habib were here for the meeting of the Cabinet and the Security Council, and helped to brief the Council on the situation in Vietnam and in Paris.

They are the senior members of our negotiating team in Paris, and immediately after this meeting will be flying to Paris for the plenary session of the Paris meeting, which will take place tomorrow.

Ambassador Lodge does have time to answer a few questions before he leaves, and I will present him to you now.

Mr. Ambassador.

[At this point Ambassador Lodge answered questions from reporters.]

NOTE: The President spoke at 11:55 a.m. in the Rose Garden at the White House. Ambassador Lawrence E. Walsh was Deputy Chief and Philip C. Habib was chief adviser of the U.S. delegation to the Paris meetings on Vietnam.

The text of Ambassador Lodge's news briefing is printed in the Weekly Compilation of Presidential Documents (vol. 5, p. 699).

197   Letter Accepting the Resignation of Abe Fortas as Associate Justice of the Supreme Court of the United States.   *May* 15, 1969

Dear Mr. Justice Fortas:

I have received your letter of resignation and I accept it, effective as of its date.

With sincere personal regards,

RICHARD NIXON

[Mr. Justice Abe Fortas, United States Supreme Court, Washington, D.C.]

NOTE: Justice Abe Fortas' letter of resignation, dated May 14, 1969, and released by the White House Press Office along with the President's letter on May 15, 1969, read as follows:

My dear Mr. President:

For the reasons expressed in a letter of this date which I have written to the Chief Justice, a copy of which, with his permission, I enclose, I wish hereby to tender my resignation as an Associate Justice of the Supreme Court, which, with your approval, will be effective as of this date.

I have appreciated the opportunity to serve the country and the Court during these past years as an Associate Justice.

Very truly yours,

ABE FORTAS

198   Statement on the Control of Inflation.
May 15, 1969

THIS ADMINISTRATION is committed to a policy that comes to grips with the problem of inflation. That policy is based firmly on three propositions.

First, this long-sustained erosion in the purchasing power of the dollar has been causing serious economic and social damage, and it must be curbed. The rise in the price level last year approximated 5 percent—a pace that would double the general price level in 15 years. This inflation has been harder on the average man than on the sophisticated investor. It has produced the highest interest rates of a century, posing difficult problems for home buyers. And it has had an adverse effect on our balance of payments and the strength of the dollar internationally.

Second, we can cool inflation only if we deal with fundamentals. Statements that set guidelines and generate headlines have not worked. The inflation that erupted after 1965 was caused by excessively expansive economic policies—such as the $25 billion deficit in fiscal year 1968—that kept our economy in a chronically overheated condition. Our first actions, therefore, had to be getting these fiscal and monetary policies back on course. Accordingly we have reviewed every program in the budget, cutting $4 billion out of projected expenditures for the 1970 fiscal year. I have also proposed a program of tax measures that will give us revenues needed to cover these outlays. This includes extension of the full surcharge through December, and at half the present rate to the end of the next fiscal year. These tax recommendations are crucial to an orderly economy at home, and to a strong dollar in the world

economy. It is essential that there be early and favorable action in the Congress on the tax measures we need for a sound budget.

Third, to cool inflation, we must curb "inflation psychology." When people understand what is behind the sharply rising cost of living, they see that tax measures essential for a strong budget are better than the cruel tax of inflation. When the public fully believes the Government is determined to slow inflation, there will be less tendency to automatically include the assumption of continuing inflation in decisions about prices, investments, and wages. Preachments about restraint are not credible unless basic economic policies of Government create economic conditions that make this restraint in the prudent self-interest of the consumer, the union, or the business.

In view of all this, I indeed welcome the program of public education being sponsored by the Advertising Council, the Joint Council on Economic Education, and the Chamber of Commerce of the United States. Only with a better informed public can we build a sound basis for prosperity in the months and years ahead.

Private enterprise, far more than Government spending, is the impetus behind sound economic growth. The voluntary effort of the men and women of private enterprise is needed now, as never before, to enlist the support of the American people in the fight against inflation.

NOTE: The President's statement was released following a meeting with representatives of the Chamber of Commerce of the United States, the Joint Council on Economic Education, and the Advertising Council, Inc. The representatives presented a voluntary action program to develop public understanding of inflation control and economic stability.

The text of a news briefing by Secretary of the Treasury David M. Kennedy and others following the meeting with the President concerning inflation control was released by the White House Press Office on the same day.

199   Letter to Private Dennis Ray Roberts on Serving in the Army.   *May* 16, 1969

Dear Private Roberts:

It was gratifying to receive your recent letter regarding your sense of pride and dignity as a soldier in the United States Armed Forces particularly since our nation honors our Armed Forces this week.

Letters such as yours are most reassuring that there are young men throughout our nation and the Armed Forces who stand ready in our quest for peace for all mankind. As President and Commander-in-Chief, I appreciate your expression of dedication and willingness to share in the responsibilities of maintaining our freedom and security as a nation.

My best wishes for your success.

Sincerely,

RICHARD NIXON

[Private Dennis R. Roberts, B–7–2, United States Army Training Center, Fourth Platoon, Fort Benning, Georgia]

NOTE: Private Roberts' letter, dated May 4, 1969, and released by the White House Press Office along with the President's letter on May 16, 1969, read as follows:

Dear Mr. President:

I'm writing this letter to you to let you know just how I feel about the two years I'll be in The United States Army.

Mr. President, I know you will never see this letter nor will you read it, but I'm sure there must be many guys like myself who just want you to know their feelings toward you and the United States. Mr. President, I'm proud to serve my country in the best way possible—that by being in the Armed Forces of the United States, and Mr. President, I'm very proud to be under your leadership and guidance. I know there is a lot more hardships to face than what our country has faced in the past but I will do whatever I can for my country and for you, Mr. President. You don't have to answer this letter. I know there is a lot more work that's more important than answering a letter from a soldier, so do that work and maybe, I pray, we won't need all the soldiers we have now in the United States Armed Forces.

So, Mr. President, do your work because that's the only answer I want.

Cordially yours,

PVT. DENNIS RAY ROBERTS

P.S. Maybe, Mr. President, one day I can meet you and tell these words to you and not send them to you on paper.

200   Remarks on Presenting the Medal of Honor to CWO Frederick E. Ferguson and Sp4c. Thomas J. Kinsman, USA.   *May* 17, 1969

Ladies and gentlemen:

This is a proud day for the men who have received the highest award that this Nation can give to a man in the Armed Forces.

It is a proud day for their parents, for

the Armed Forces, for this Nation, and for me personally, and also in my official capacity as President of the United States of America.

This is Armed Forces Day, and all over America today Americans will be reminded of what we owe to the young men who serve in the Armed Forces of the United States.

These two men symbolize that service because they have rendered service in the highest tradition, far beyond the call of duty.

But as I make these awards to them, and as I stand here in the presence of their families, I want to say that I personally and, I think, all of the people who witnessed this ceremony on this magnificent day on the White House lawn are proud to be Americans as we see these men and the families that helped to produce them.

We are proud to be Americans because, first, we recognize that only a fine family and a fine background could produce men who, under the very gravest circumstances, rose to the heights of bravery.

We are proud also for another reason, for what these men were fighting for; not for glory, not for conquest, not for an inch of territory or a concession, or for conquering any other people, but for the cause of peace with freedom, which has been the cause for which young Americans have fought and died in World War I, in World War II, in Korea, and now in Vietnam.

Sometimes we forget this. Sometimes, as we hear critics of all wars, and particularly of this war, comment upon America's role in the world, we forget that the American goal is a very great goal, an unselfish goal.

Yes, we are concerned about our own freedom and we recognize that our freedom and our peace is very closely tied with the freedom and peace for others.

We recognize that what happens in Vietnam, halfway around the world, and whether Americans meet their responsibility there, may affect the future of not only Vietnam, not only the other nations in the Pacific, but the future of America itself.

Therefore, on this Armed Forces Day, I simply say to Warrant Officer Ferguson and to Specialist Kinsman, thank you for being such great Americans under fire, and for reminding us of the fact that we sometimes forget—that Americans in this century have had to go into war not because we wanted war, but because we wanted peace.

We have had to go into war not because we wanted conquest but because we didn't want it; because we wanted every nation in this world to be and to have the right to choose its own way without conquest and without aggression.

What a great goal you have fought for. What a great example you have set for us. You have made us proud to be Americans, proud of our flag, and, of course, proud of you.

Thank you.

Incidentally, when their parents and our two award winners came into my office, I asked each father who was primarily responsible for the fact that these men had developed into such fine Americans. And in each case, they said, "Mother was responsible."

[The texts of the two citations follow.]

THE PRESIDENT of the United States of America, authorized by Act of Congress, March 3, 1863, has awarded in the name of The Congress the Medal of Honor to

CHIEF WARRANT OFFICER FREDERICK E.
FERGUSON
UNITED STATES ARMY

for conspicuous gallantry and intrepidity in action at the risk of his life above and beyond the call of duty:

Chief Warrant Officer Frederick E. Ferguson, United States Army, distinguished himself by conspicuous gallantry and intrepidity while serving with Company C, 227th Aviation Battalion, 1st Cavalry Division (Airmobile) at Hue, Republic of Vietnam. On 31 January 1968, Chief Warrant Officer Ferguson, commander of a resupply helicopter, monitoring an emergency call from wounded passengers and crewmen of a downed helicopter under heavy attack within the enemy controlled city of Hue, unhesitatingly volunteered to attempt evacuation. Despite warnings for all aircraft to stay clear of the area due to heavy anti-aircraft fire, Chief Warrant Officer Ferguson began a low-level flight at maximum airspeed along the Perfume River toward the tiny, isolated South Vietnamese Army compound in which the crash survivors had taken refuge. Coolly and skillfully maintaining his course in the face of intense, short range fire from enemy occupied buildings and boats, he displayed superior flying skill and tenacity of purpose by landing his aircraft in an extremely confined area in a blinding dust cloud under heavy mortar and small arms fire. Although the helicopter was severely damaged by mortar fragments during the loading of the wounded, Chief Warrant Officer Ferguson disregarded the damage and, taking off through the continuing hail of mortar fire, he flew his crippled aircraft on the return route through the rain of fire that he had experienced earlier and safely returned his wounded passengers to friendly control. Chief Warrant Officer Ferguson's extraordinary gallantry, determination and intrepidity saved the lives of five of his comrades. His actions are in the highest tradition of the military service and reflect great credit on himself and the United States Army.

THE PRESIDENT of the United States of America, authorized by Act of Congress March 3, 1863, has awarded in the name of The Congress the Medal of Honor to

SPECIALIST FOUR THOMAS J. KINSMAN
UNITED STATES ARMY

for conspicuous gallantry and intrepidity in action at the risk of his life above and beyond the call of duty:

Specialist Four Thomas J. Kinsman (then Private First Class) distinguished himself by gallantry and intrepidity in action on the afternoon of 6 February 1968 while serving as a Rifleman with Company B, 3rd Battalion, 60th Infantry, 9th Infantry Division, on a reconnaissance in force mission near the City of Vinh Long, in the Republic of Vietnam. As his company was proceeding up a narrow canal in armored troop carriers, it came under sudden and intense rocket, automatic weapons and small arms fire from a well entrenched Viet Cong force. The company immediately beached and began assaulting the enemy bunker complex. Hampered by exceedingly dense undergrowth which limited visibility to ten meters, a group of eight men became cut off from the main body of the company. As they were moving through heavy enemy fire to effect a link-up, an enemy soldier in a concealed position hurled a grenade into their midst. Specialist Kinsman immediately alerted his comrades of the danger, then unhesitatingly threw himself on the grenade and blocked the explosion with his body. As a result of his courageous action, he received severe head and chest wounds. Through his indomitable courage, complete disregard for his personal safety and profound concern for his fellow soldiers, Specialist Kinsman averted loss of life and injury to the other seven men of his element. Specialist Kinsman's conspicuous gallantry and extraordinary heroism at the risk of his own life, above and beyond the call of duty, are in keeping with the highest traditions of the military service and reflect great credit upon himself, his unit, and the United States Army.

NOTE: The Presiden spoke at 10:43 a.m. on the South Lawn at the White House.

A White House release issued on May 16, 1969, announcing the Medal of Honor presentation ceremony is printed in the Weekly Compilation of Presidential Documents (vol. 5, p. 703).

201 Remarks on Armed Forces Day Aboard the
U.S.S. *Saratoga*. *May* 17, 1969

I APPRECIATE the opportunity to speak to the officers and men of the United States Fleet. As I met many of you a few moments ago and thought back to the time—almost 30 years ago—when I was in the Navy in World War II, I never thought then that I would outrank an admiral.

I can assure you that the opportunity to be here is a very proud one for me, and a particularly proud one because of the chance I have had for the first time to see a coordinated operation such as I have witnessed over the past 2 hours.

There are some things that impressed me very much by what I saw. First, the magnificent teamwork, the teamwork that is so essential for an operation of this type. I realize that when we see a pilot or a captain of one of our very sophisticated, great airplanes, we see a man whose opportunities to do his job are only made possible by hundreds of men on the ground or on the flight deck, working together as a team.

When I saw that teamwork, it made me feel very confident of the Armed Forces of this country and of the United States Navy and the various functions that it must carry out.

Another thing that impressed me was what happened as we were looking down on the flight deck from up above there, and we saw the number one catapult have troubles and for about 15 or 20 minutes they could not get off. The Admiral was saying to me that those men on that catapult team were probably somewhat embarrassed about it. Let me say, I was very impressed by what I saw, because when you really prove yourself is not

when everything goes right but when something goes wrong and you make it right. What a great job it was to get that catapult back on and have those planes going off of it, just like the others.

And one other thing I would like to add is this: Earlier today—this being the Armed Forces Day in which the people of the United States pay honor and tribute to the 3 million men who are in our Armed Forces—I presented two Medals of Honor to two of our fighting men from Vietnam. It was a very moving ceremony for me to see these young men who had displayed such great courage under tremendous challenge in that battlefield so far away. The ceremony was held on the South grounds of the White House. Those of you who have visited the White House will recall how it looks. The great balcony of the White House overlooks it. All the tourists were in Washington in such great numbers in this beautiful spring—I suppose 3,000 or 4,000 were gathered there.

I escorted the two Medal of Honor winners with their families—each had his mother and father there—I escorted them from my office over to the residence of the White House and the platform, which was constructed, from which the honor guard was reviewed and the medals were officially presented.

As we walked along, most of the people were cheering and clapping their hands as these magnificent men were there to receive their honors, and, as is sometimes the case these days, one individual in the crowd shouted out: "Peace, peace, peace."

I would like to say a word about not what that individual said, but what you stand for, and what those two Medal of Honor winners stand for, and what our Armed Forces stand for in America. We today honor the Armed Forces of the United States. To me you are the peace forces of the world because without the strength of the United States of America there would not be peace in the world and there could not be the survival of freedom in the world.

That is the proud duty you have. I repeat what I said on television on Wednesday night [1] and again this morning: that in four wars in this century—World War I, World War II, Korea, and now Vietnam—young Americans have fought not for conquest, not for the glory of battle, but because they believe in peace and because they believe in freedom, and they want it for themselves and their children, and they want it permanently and not just for the moment.

So, as I address the magnificent men of the Atlantic Fleet today, and, through you, all the Armed Forces of the United States of America around this world, just let me say this: When you hear the criticism sometimes of the "military complex" in this country, when you hear what is wrong with the United States and particularly what is wrong with our Armed Forces and what we are necessarily doing

---

[1] See Item 195.

in the cause of peace and freedom in Vietnam and every place else in the world, just remember that history will record that never has a great nation had military forces more dedicated to peace, and whose activities made a greater contribution to peace than the Armed Forces of the United States.

By what you do, by what you are, we will achieve peace in Vietnam and the Pacific and we are going to be able to keep peace in the world.

I am proud to be here as the one who has been elected to lead this country and particularly proud to stand in the presence of the men over whom I am Commander in Chief.

Thank you very much. My very best wishes to the peace forces of the United States and the world.

NOTE: The President spoke at 3:11 p.m. on the flight deck of the U.S.S. *Saratoga* following a 2-hour demonstration of naval training maneuvers by the Atlantic Fleet. The demonstration, staged 50 miles off Norfolk, Va., included 16 warships, approximately 10,000 men, and six kinds of jet warplanes. Also displayed were five varieties of guided missiles and numerous rockets and high explosive bombs launched from the air, the surface, and from under the sea by a nuclear submarine.

The President was accompanied during the demonstrations by Adm. Thomas H. Moorer, USN, Chief of Naval Operations and Adm. Ephraim P. Holmes, Commander in Chief, United States Atlantic Fleet.

202   Remarks on Presenting Scholastic Achievement Awards to Blind College Students. *May* 19, 1969

I HAVE two awards to present today to two of the most outstanding young men in America and, I would say, in the world.

This is the Scholastic Achievement Award from the Recording for the Blind

organization, with which many of you are familiar.

It is to James Winford Selby III, in recognition of outstanding academic performance in attaining the degree of bachelor of arts from Tulane University.

Congratulations.

I should point out, too, that not only was his performance outstanding; he was first in his class with a 3.8 average. That is a magnificent achievement. You have set a fine standard and example for all of the rest of us.

And the second award, the Scholastic Achievement Award, to David Steven Mischel, in recognition of outstanding academic performance in attaining the degree of bachelor of arts from Trinity College.

Again, an outstanding record in every respect, the 3.8 average, first in his class, with great competition, and again a man that we all admire, not only for that high scholastic achievement, but also for the example that he has set for all the rest of us.

Congratulations.

Now, if I could say a word with regard to the work of the organization, the scholastic Recording for the Blind. This is one of several organizations in this field, but it is one that deserves support of all Americans. Except for the contributions that are made by private citizens, by corporations, and others voluntarily, it would not have been possible to record these books so that these young men—who

could not see but who could hear and thereby could understand—it would not have been possible for them to learn and achieve this academic excellence for which they are being rewarded today.

And to all who may be listening to this program, I only say this: that having, many years ago, gone through the experience of competing in college and then in law school for high academic achievement, it is very difficult to get near the top of the class or anywhere near it when you have every ability to read and to see. But to have a boy go clear to the top when he was not able to see, this is certainly a magnificent achievement for that boy, but a wonderful example for all the rest of us. And particularly it makes us all realize that we should, to the extent that we can, give assistance through our contributions to organizations like Recording for the Blind so that they will be able to help others—others who are not as fortunate as we are, but who have the capability to go clear to the top if they just get that little bit of help.

Thank you very much.

NOTE: The President spoke at 10:12 a.m. in the Rosevelt Room at the White House. The awards are made annually by Recording for the Blind, Inc., a national nonprofit organization which provides free recorded textbooks for college students.

203   Message to the Congress Transmitting the Annual Report of the Board of Actuaries for the Retired Serviceman's Family Protection Plan.   *May* 19, 1969

To the Congress of the United States:

Pursuant to Section 1444 (b), title 10, United States Code, transmitted herewith is the Fourteenth Annual Report of the Board of Actuaries for the Retired Serv-

iceman's Family Protection Plan, covering the administration of the Plan for Calendar Year 1967.

The Plan, inaugurated in November 1953, provides that members of the uniformed services may elect reduced retired pay during their lifetime in order to provide survivor annuities for their widows and children. The basic principle underlying the Plan is that reductions in retired pay shall be computed by the actuarially-equivalent method using actuarial tables selected by the Board. Thus, the Plan is to be self-supporting, imposing no added cost to the Federal Government, beyond administrative costs.

RICHARD NIXON

The White House
   May 19, 1969

NOTE: The report, dated December 30, 1968, is entitled "Board of Actuaries for the Retired Serviceman's Family Protection Plan, Fourteenth Annual Report, Calendar Year 1967" (processed, 117 pp.).

204   Remarks at the Presentation of the World Trade "E" Awards.   *May* 19, 1969

Ladies and gentlemen:

The purpose of this ceremony is for the presentation of the "E" Awards. The Secretary of Commerce will read the citations for the awards. But before he does so, since he has just returned from a trip to the Far East, which had to do with some of our export and import problems in addition to many other problems, I would simply like to say this:

One of the developments in the United States that has occurred in the past few years that is very disturbing is the dwindling of our export surplus. Eight years ago it was $5 billion a year. Now it is down to approximately $800 million a year.

We are trying to change that. When I say we are trying to change it, I speak not just of a government, but I speak more of those in private enterprise who by their practices will be able to win the markets abroad.

And the 10 companies that will be honored today are companies that have shown the initiative, and they have shown the imagination that is essential to compete in the export markets. And the ability to compete in the export markets is something that is, I think, particularly noteworthy today when we consider the fact that American workmen are paid by far the highest wages in the world. And when an American businessman paying those highest wages can still go in and compete in an export market, that means he deserves an award for excellence and excellence for export.

Mr. Secretary, if you will read the citations.

NOTE: The President spoke at 5:23 p.m. in the Roosevelt Room at the White House. Following his remarks, the citations were read by Secretary of Commerce Maurice H. Stans.

The President's "E" awards were established by Executive Order 10978 of December 5, 1961, entitled "Establishing Presidential Awards for Significant Contributions to the Export Expansion Program" (3 CFR, 1959–1963 Comp., p. 498). The order states that the awards "may be made to persons, firms, and organizations engaged in the marketing of products who make significant contributions to the expansion of the export trade of the United States. It shall consist of a flag having a field of white upon which will appear a blue 'E.'"

Recipients of the awards are chosen by the Secretary of Commerce after considering the recommendations of an interagency awards committee.

A White House press release of May 16, 1969, listing this year's award winners with further information on the award, is printed in the

Weekly Compilation of Presidential Documents (vol. 5, p. 719).

205   Remarks on Accepting the Hope Chest Award of the National Multiple Sclerosis Society. *May 20, 1969*

Ladies and gentlemen:

I am very honored to receive this award, and I welcome the opportunity to state again my support for the National Multiple Sclerosis organization, for the work it has done and for the work it will be doing under the program that has just been outlined by the chairman.

I think it is quite significant that the drive for funds for this organization begins on Mother's Day and ends on Father's Day. And that allows me to make a point that is perhaps often overlooked.

Multiple sclerosis affects young people 20 to 40 years of age. The great tragedy of mothers and fathers and families having young people in their families, children who contract this disease, a disease that up until the time this society was founded, was without hope, but that now has some hope—it seems to me that this brings home very eloquently why we should all support the fundraising drive.

The fact that half a million Americans are volunteers working in this cause, the fact that half a million young Americans have contracted this disease and need this hope—all of this again brings home the message that we would like to convey through receiving this award.

Finally, one personal note that I think is related: I remember the first major league ball game I saw in the year 1936. I came from Duke University Law School, where I was attending. We were in Washington, D.C. It was a doubleheader in old Griffith Stadium.

On that occasion I recall what a thrill it was to see Lou Gehrig play. He, at that time, was playing for the Yankees. As I recall in that doubleheader, he hit at least one home run, possibly two.

We all know the great tragedy of Gehrig. Now, he did not die of multiple sclerosis; it was lateral sclerosis, a related disease. Here we saw a man who was an idol of young Americans. He was a young man himself and in the prime of life. His hope, as far as future activity was concerned, completely disappeared.

When we think of a man like that, I think it brings home to us what these dedicated volunteers—from business and others—what they are doing, and we thank you for what they are doing, and we wish you well in your activities.

MRS. BLACK. Mr. President, may I say a couple of words?

THE PRESIDENT. Yes, you are always welcome.

[At this point Mrs. Shirley Temple Black, National Chairman of Volunteers for the National Multiple Sclerosis Society, spoke. The President then resumed speaking.]

Well, I can only say that the participation of executives like Mr. Haughton, and people like Shirley Temple Black, as volunteers, and all of the rest who are here, that in itself is an inspiration.

I think it is very important that you brought home the point that while we have our political differences in the world, and while the world may be divided between the East and the West, and the East is divided within itself, and the West has its divisions, too, that when we talk about these diseases that afflict all people, and when we talk about the human suffering that occurs—not just to the individuals who have the disease, but within the families, the parents—that this is something that crosses all the political lines and all the geographical lines and whatever discoveries are made are going to help the whole world.

That is why I think this is a cause far

bigger than this little ceremony that we have here. It is as big as the whole world itself.

Thank you.

NOTE: The President spoke at approximately 11 a.m. in the Roosevelt Room at the White House. Daniel J. Haughton, president of the National Multiple Sclerosis Society, presented the Hope Chest Award to the President. Remarks of Mr. Haughton and Mrs. Shirley Temple Black are printed in the Weekly Compilation of Presidential Documents (vol. 5, p. 722).

The ceremony marked the formal start of a 5-year program to raise $10 million to further research programs of the National Multiple Sclerosis Society.

206   Toasts of the President and King Baudouin of Belgium.   *May* 20, 1969

Your Majesty and our guests:

On my recent trip to Europe, the first stop, as many of you will recall, was Belgium. I think it was particularly appropriate that that stop was selected, first because there is no country in Europe, or for that matter the world, that has a more special place in the hearts of Americans than the country of Belgium. That is because of what we knew of it during World War I and the Second World War; a people who had courage, a people who had suffered much, and a people who came back.

Americans, therefore, developed a special admiration for the people of Belgium, for those who represent them in the council of work.

So, subsequently, we are very honored today to have again in this house, as our very special guest, His Majesty the King of Belgium.

I can speak of him in many ways, of his interest in space. Along with the Queen,

he has just witnessed the space shot,[1] something, incidentally, I have never done. I have never gone to Cape Kennedy, and I hope to go, perhaps for the next shot,[2] after hearing their description of how exciting this one was.

But I speak of him more than that, not only the leader of his country, its chief of state, but as one who has a deep concern for people all over the world. All of us who know him personally know of that concern. Whether it be the people of Africa or Asia or Latin America or any of the underdeveloped areas, I know of no leader who speaks more eloquently or feels more deeply about the problems of those less fortunate people than does His Majesty the King.

Also, I think we are very honored to

---

[1] Apollo 10, launched May 18, 1969.

[2] The President watched the July 16, 1969, launch of the Apollo 11 on television in his office in the White House but was present for the completion of the mission at splashdown and recovery in the Pacific.

385

have him here because he represents the cause of peace which has been so important to his people in the history of his country, the history I referred to earlier today.

He spoke of that history 10 years ago when he addressed the Congress in this very month. He said then that it takes 20 years or more of peace to make a man, and it takes only 20 seconds of war to destroy him.

So, it is altogether appropriate that NATO—the greatest peacekeeping force that the world has ever seen—has its home in his country and that he and his people have welcomed it there and provided the support for it, not only in their capacity as members, but also in their capacity as the home of the NATO offices.

Now, another reason we are very honored to have His Majesty back with us is that something has been added to his visit this time that was not here before.

I remember sitting by him in the White House on that occasion—President Eisenhower sat in this chair, the King sat in that chair, and I think I was in the one next to it. But Queen Fabiola was not with him then because she was not his wife at that time. But I think you will note the character of the music today, with the Spanish overtones. She reminded me, as did His Majesty, of the luncheon menu: the first item—and you will pardon my pronunciation—*l'Andalouse,* which is of course the province in which Her Majesty the Queen grew up in Spain; and then of course we have *veau bruxelloise*—I will not try to pronounce it the way it read here, but to cap the meal off today we have had *mousse Fabiola.* However the mousse tastes and however beautiful, I am sure you will agree that the Queen is much more lovely.

For these and many other reasons we are delighted to welcome Their Majesties here today, and I know that you will be pleased to rise with me and raise our glasses to Their Majesties, the King and Queen of Belgium.

NOTE: The President proposed the toast at 2:30 p.m. in the State Dining Room at the White House.

King Baudouin responded as follows:

Mr. President:

My gratitude for the charming words you have just addressed to me. I would like to be able to express myself as graciously, to let you know how we feel in our hearts toward our hosts.

Two days ago we had the privilege to live the tremendous experience of the Apollo shot. I promise you, it inspired us beyond words. We appreciate the President's kind invitation, your generous hospitality. With this, you have added yet to the warm welcome.

It is for us a rare pleasure to be received by you and Mrs. Nixon in such a select and nice company. For all this, we thank you greatly.

Ladies and gentlemen, I raise my glass to the President of the United States and Mrs. Nixon, to their family, and to the happiness of the people of the United States of America.

207 Remarks at the Swearing In of Robert Ellsworth as United States Permanent Representative to NATO. *May* 21, 1969

Members of the Congress, members of the diplomatic corps, ladies and gentlemen:

We are here today for the purpose of swearing in Mr. Robert Ellsworth as the American Permanent Representative to the North Atlantic Treaty Organization.

Judge Hart of the District Court will administer the oath and Mrs. Ellsworth will hold the Bible.

[At this point, Judge George L. Hart, Jr., of the United States District Court for the District of Columbia administered the oath of office. The President resumed speaking, as follows:]

Ladies and gentlemen, as Mr. Ellsworth now has officially taken the oath, he is Ambassador Ellsworth and I would like to say a word with regard to the significance of this appointment.

He came to the Congress in 1961 and served there for 6 years. While he was in the Congress he showed a particular interest in and understanding of the problems of the North Atlantic Alliance, and after he left the Congress in the year 1967, he traveled with me to Europe in a major factfinding trip that I made at that time.

As you know, he has been an Assistant to the President on the White House Staff for the past 4 months. His appointment should signify to all of those in the North Atlantic Treaty Organization, and also to the people of the United States the deep personal interest that I, as President of the United States, have in the NATO Alliance.

He is a close personal friend and associate, but more than that, he is one who is deeply interested in the Alliance and he is one that I know will represent this country well in terms of our interest, but even more important, who will represent to the President of the United States, from the members of the Alliance, their views and provide that indispensable consultation which is vitally important if we are to have a continuing strong NATO Alliance.

I am sure Mr. Ellsworth would like to say a word before he undertakes his responsibilities.

NOTE: The President spoke at 10:10 a.m. in the Rose Garden at the White House. Ambassador Ellsworth's response is printed in the Weekly Compilation of Presidential Documents (vol. 5, p. 725).

208   Statement on the Realignment of Regional Boundaries of Certain Federal Agencies. *May 21, 1969*

ON March 27 I announced a series of steps being taken to streamline the structure and processes of Federal agencies in the field. I am confident that these changes will greatly improve the effectiveness of Federal social and economic services.

The first of these actions was the establishment of a common pattern of regional boundaries and headquarters for the Department of Labor, the Department of Health, Education, and Welfare, the Department of Housing and Urban Development, the Office of Economic Opportunity, and the Small Business Administration.

Since the announcement we have met with congressional, State, and local interests from many areas of the country and received from them a great deal of valuable information on implementing this plan.

After considering this information, I have concluded that the level of Federal service which would be required of the planned subregional offices in Kansas City and Seattle warrants their elevation to full regional status.

Three other changes are desirable. With the establishment of the new Seattle region, it is appropriate to shift Idaho to that region from the Denver region. Also, after reviewing the situation, I have concluded that the States of North Carolina and Kentucky would be better served from Atlanta than from Philadelphia.

In summary, the new alignment for the regions is as follows:

Region I (Boston)—Connecticut, Maine, Massachusetts, New Hampshire, Rhode Island, and Vermont;

Region II (New York City)—New York, New Jersey, Puerto Rico, and the Virgin Islands;

Region III (Philadelphia)—Delaware, District of Columbia, Maryland, Pennsylvania, Virginia, and West Virginia;

Region IV (Atlanta)—Alabama, Florida, Georgia, Kentucky, Mississippi, North Carolina, South Carolina, and Tennessee;

Region V (Chicago)—Illinois, Indiana, Minnesota, Michigan, Ohio, and Wisconsin;

Region VI (Dallas-Fort Worth)—Arkansas, Louisiana, New Mexico, Oklahoma, and Texas;

Region VII (Kansas City)—Iowa, Kansas, Missouri, and Nebraska;

Region VIII (Denver)—Colorado, Montana, North Dakota, South Dakota, Utah, and Wyoming;

Region IX (San Francisco)—Arizona, California, Hawaii, and Nevada;

Region X (Seattle)—Alaska, Idaho, Oregon, and Washington.

209   Remarks Announcing the Nomination of Judge Warren Earl Burger To Be Chief Justice of the United States.   *May 21, 1969*

Mr. Vice President, members of the Cabinet, ladies and gentlemen:

I have invited you to the White House tonight for an historic announcement, the nomination of the next Chief Justice of the United States.

This announcement is one that I have considered for many months, since I knew that I would have the responsibility even before I became President. I say this with due respect to the great responsibilities held by all the members of the Cabinet here: I believe that the most important nomination that a President of the United States makes during his term of office is that of Chief Justice of the United States.

I say this for several reasons. The Chief Justice is the guardian of the Constitution of the United States. Respect for law in

a nation is the most priceless asset a free people can have, and the Chief Justice and his associates are the ultimate custodians and guardians of that priceless asset.

When we consider what a Chief Justice has in the way of influence on his age and the ages after him, I think it could fairly be said that our history tells us that our Chief Justices have probably had more profound and lasting influence on their times and on the direction of the Nation than most Presidents have had. You can see, therefore, why I consider this decision to be so important.

I have nominated a man who I think is superbly qualified to serve as Chief Justice.

His education is one that he got the

hard way. He went to law school at night and worked during the daytime, but he made a brilliant academic record. He was eminently successful in the practice of law.

He was appointed by President Eisenhower as an Assistant Attorney General of the United States in 1953 and since 1956 has served on the Circuit Court of Appeals for the District of Columbia.

I have known him for 21 years and I would evaluate him as being qualified intellectually, qualified from the stand-point of judicial temperament, qualified from the standpoint of his legal philosophy, and above all, qualified because of his unquestioned integrity throughout his private and public life.

I am very proud tonight to nominate as the 15th Chief Justice of the United States, Judge Warren Burger.

NOTE: The President spoke at 7 p.m. in the East Room at the White House. Judge Burger's remarks in response are printed, together with biographical information concerning him, in the Weekly Compilation of Presidential Documents (vol. 5, p. 727).

210   Conversation With Newsmen on the Nomination of the Chief Justice of the United States.   *May* 22, 1969

THE PRESIDENT. Let me take a moment to tell you what I thought would be useful for you on this occasion. We have never done this before. Some of you may remember the days when the custom was to have the press conferences in this room, and when the custom also was to have the President quoted indirectly in the third person.

Since we have not announced a press conference, I don't, of course, want the people who are not White House regulars to feel that they have been cut out of something, but I want to try this as an experiment which, from time to time, on a major issue, we may try again.

What I would suggest as the format would be this: That we will make, for those of you who are taking notes, we are going to record it all and Mr. Ziegler will have it run immediately so you will have a complete transcript of what I am saying, and of course, of your questions and the answers as well.

However, as far as the way you write it, I would like for you to write it as: "In an informal meeting with members of the White House press corps in his office, the President discussed the appointment of the Chief Justice, and the President said this, he said that, he said that," but do not use it as a Q and A, a direct quote procedure.[1]

Q. You want us to use third person then?

THE PRESIDENT. Third person, right. But you can use everything I say; everything is on the record. But if you could put it in the third person, that the President said that political clearances were not involved in the Supreme Court, then a reporter asks whether or not he had talked to the Chief Justice-designate before, and the President said that he talked to him for the first time, as I will indicate—like that.

---

[1] The text of these remarks was later released for publication in this volume.

389

If you could cover it all that way, I think that will give it to you all right.

As to the time for release, let me say, this is not a hot news story in the sense of immediate news, and I think it is one that you will want to get the full text to work on, and I would like to suggest that we make it just a flat Friday a.m. release.

Q. 6:30 p.m.?

THE PRESIDENT. 6:30 tonight. In other words, the people who have recordings can run it on that and the newspapers and wires, 6:30 a.m. release. Not to tell you about your business, but for the most part, you will find probably in the Q and A also, what I would say, matters that would be of great interest in think pieces for maybe a couple of days after that, but that is for you to judge.

All of it is for release, to the extent you think it is worth releasing, at 6:30. Some of you, I am sure will find that this does not, however, have immediate news impact. It is more, shall we say, color and background.

Let me begin by trying to spell out the processes that I went through in making the decision. As you know, at the time of the exchange of letters with the Chief Justice, before the inauguration, I knew that I would have this decision to make.

I also knew at that time that I did not have to make it in a hurry. In fact, I thought it was very wise not to make it too soon, because I thought that it would not be a proper mark of respect for the Court and for the Chief Justice to have a nomination go down, say, in February or March, and then have possibly the Senate hearings and the like at a time that the Court was sitting.

So, from the beginning, while I did not pick any certain deadline date, I felt that the decision should be made before the term of Court ended so that the new Chief Justice could be indoctrinated in effect about the rules of the Court and so forth, by the outgoing Chief Justice. But this turned out to be the right time. That is why it came in the middle of May, although it could have come May 1. I have always thought between May 1 and June 1, but that is how this came about.

Now, my thinking with regard to the kind of man that should be Chief Justice, I spelled out in the campaign. I want to differentiate two things here: There is a different standard for a Chief Justice than there is for a Justice, not in terms of intellectual qualifications, not in terms of knowledge of law, not in terms of the character, and that sort of thing, but in terms of what I describe as a leadership quality. The Chief Justice is the leader of the Court. He is the chief administrative officer of the Court.

In talking to Chief Justice Warren, for example, I find that there is an enormous amount of administrative responsibility which rests with the Chief Justice. So the Chief Justice must be a man who can be an equal to all the other Justices in terms of education, and above all else, however, have that, if I may use the term, that special quality in addition, of commanding the respect and being able to lead the Court.

He cannot always, as we know, get unanimity, and let us get one thing very clear: the Warren Court is not the first one that had 5 to 4 decisions. When I was studying law in 1930, we all remember there were 5 to 4 decisions, when four dissented and five voted the other way.

But this leadership quality is a factor I was looking for, beyond the bare essentials, which I or anybody would look for in appointing a judge to the Supreme

Court of the United States.

There are several things that I think should be clarified at the beginning. There were no political clearances in this case, and there will be none for any judges to the Supreme Court that I appoint. By a political clearance, I mean that we do not clear—I think Judge Burger comes from Minnesota and now lives in Virginia—we did not inform or clear with either the Minnesota or Virginia Senator. They knew nothing about it and we will not do that with any others.

With regard to Circuit Court and District Court judges, we do clear; that is the custom. I think the custom has varied with the Supreme Court, but I feel very strongly that Supreme Court Justices should be appointed by the President without going through the political processes.

I say that because I think the Supreme Court must be above politics. Now, this does not mean that the Supreme Court judges are not Republicans, as was Mr. Burger when he was named, or Democrats, as, let us say was Justice [Hugo L.] Black when he was appointed. But I think it is very important that once they are appointed, and once they sit on the Court, that they sit there without owing that appointment to any political clearance process.

So there was no clearance with any Senators, no clearance with the National Committee, and there will be none as far as any other judges I appoint.

There was also no ABA clearance. Now, this is a technical fact which I suppose somebody here that covers the Supreme Court knows about. The American Bar Association is in town now. There had been some noises made to the effect that the ABA Committee should be consulted, as they are, as you know, on Circuit Court

and District Court judges. We run it by the ABA, as I understand.

There was some talk, particularly after the Fortas thing came up last year,[2] that the ABA ought to be consulted on Supreme Court appointments. I decided against that. I do not think this is a matter that should be submitted to the American Bar Association, and I did not have it submitted.

I think that another factor that should be discussed is this: I noticed Arthur Goldberg's[3] statement with regard to whether or not there was to be—as some members described it—a Jewish seat on the Court. I subscribe to Arthur Goldberg's conclusion. I do not consider that there is a Jewish seat or a Catholic seat or a Negro seat on the Court. I made this appointment and I will make other ones based on the consideration of their competence. I will see to it, of course, that judges or people who might be qualified, representing all segments of the country, come before me, but in the final analysis the Court will not be used for the purpose of racial, religious, or geographical balance, at least not while I am here.

Now, because of the Fortas matter, I determined that the appointee should not be a personal friend. I determined also that if possible, I should avoid appointing somebody who would be a political friend or, using the Washington vernacular, "crony."

I felt it was vitally important that it be a man who, if possible, could be approved by the Senate without violent controversy,

---

[2] See Public Papers of the Presidents, Lyndon B. Johnson, 1968–69, Item 339 [2], et seq.

[3] Arthur J. Goldberg, former Associate Justice of the Supreme Court of the United States, and former U.S. Representative to the United Nations.

and if possible, with a strong—well, not unanimous—but a strong vote of approval.

It seemed to me that the Court, at this time, needs to have, particularly at the Chief Justice level, a man who has wide support in the Nation and wide support in the Senate. This does not mean that you could find any man who would satisfy that great spectrum of views in the Senate on economic and social philosophy or even legal philosophy, but I do feel that in this appointment I have been able to find a man who will command respect in these areas that I think are so important.

Now, during the campaign, I set forth, as some of you may remember, my own philosophy with regard to what the role of a judge should be, a judge particularly of the Supreme Court, and for that matter, of other courts where they interpret constitutional matters, where they rule on constitutional cases, as distinguished from simply civil cases involving parties that don't have constitutional issue.

I said, and I think I used the term, that I was a strict constructionist. Let me explain that in terms of this appointment, and also in terms of my study of the Court for years. I think one of the best examples to prove that point is the career of Mr. Justice [Felix] Frankfurter. Mr. Justice Frankfurter was a liberal and was widely known as a liberal and adviser to Presidents in that respect, and of course, as a teacher at the Harvard Law School.

When he went on the Court, his first decisions—and it was only something that happened, the way it happened—the first decisions that came down involved the Federal Government expanding through the Congress its legislative activity in fields where individuals raised the constitutional question as to whether the

Congress had the right to go that far.

Mr. Justice Frankfurter upheld the right in several of those cases, for the Congress to legislate. It happened that those cases for the most part involved the Congress legislating in a liberal direction.

Then later in his career, as the trend of the cases before the Court turned in other directions, a number of cases came before the Court involving State governments moving in a conservative area, State legislations passing legislation which basically had conservative overtones.

Mr. Justice Frankfurter, to the great surprise of many who had cheered him as a liberal Justice, then proceeded to uphold those laws, also.

That is the kind of a judge that I was looking for here. I am not concerned about whether the man is a liberal or conservative in his economic or social philosophy. My interest is how does he regard his role with regard to the Constitution.

I happen to believe that the Constitution should be strictly interpreted, and I believe, as did Mr. Justice Frankfurter— and I just use him only as an example, because most of the judges in our courts through the years have held this philosophy—Mr. Justice Frankfurter felt it was his responsibility to interpret the Constitution, and it was the right of the Congress and the right of the State legislatures to write the laws and have great leeway to write those laws, and he should be very conservative in overthrowing a law passed by the elected representatives of the people at the State or Federal level. I use this as an example.

Now, before coming to Mr. Burger, specifically, his philosophy and what it is, let me tell you, we will give you the blow-by-blow as to when it was decided. You are all entitled to know this.

First, the only man that I discussed the appointments to the Supreme Court with in any detail was the Attorney General. This was quite deliberate. I told all the Members of the Senate and the House, Democrat and Republican, and many of my personal friends who were lawyers around the country, and nonlawyers who wrote me, that I wanted them to submit their recommendations and their arguments to the Attorney General for his evaluation.

The Attorney General, however, had the responsibility not to recommend a man but to submit the case for each man to me and then I made the decision. I did this because I did not want to become personally involved in the contest, the very lively contest among several very well-qualified people for this position.

Every President works differently, but as you notice I kind of like to be detached and stand back from it and decide as coolly and objectively as possible.

Now, I think you will be interested to know what happened with regard to several of those that you speculated about very properly.

For example, a man who was perhaps my closest friend among all of those who are considered was Charley Rhyne.[4] He went to law school with me, as you know, and was head of our citizens in '60 and '68 and has argued cases before the Supreme Court; a very distinguished constitutional lawyer.

But he was a personal friend and I felt

---

[4] Charles F. Rhyne, former president of the American Bar Association and head of Citizens for Nixon Committees in the 1960 and 1968 presidential campaigns.

that the appointment of a personal friend to the Supreme Court, particularly at this time in our history, would not be in the best interests of the Court.

Then something that I think should be reported to you with regard to four other men who were under consideration and what they did and how, on their own initiative, they affected my decision.

Incidentally, in these times I think it is quite a tribute to each of these men in its own way. I would characterize the four as four men who, at this time in their lives, each one of them would probably rather be Chief Justice than President of the United States. So that shows you how much they would have wanted to be Chief Justice. And yet each one of them asked me not to consider them, either directly or indirectly.

Some of them I did not talk to personally. I will not indicate which, except for one I did talk to personally. Each one of them let me know they did not feel they should be considered because they felt it would not be best for the Court for any one of them—for the individual—to be on the Supreme Court.

The first I will mention is Herbert Brownell [U.S. Attorney General 1953–1957]. You all know my high regard for him. You know he was the man, next to Attorney General Mitchell, who was my closest adviser in selecting the Cabinet. I think he would have made a superb Chief Justice. But former Attorney General Brownell said, quite directly in that candid way of his, that he thought if he were nominated that there would be a controversy in the Senate—not because of any personal criticism of him, but because of the roles he played when he was Attorney General.

I told him on that score that I was sure that the Senate would approve the nomination, but he felt it would not be in the interest of the Court to have a sharp partisan or personal controversy and, therefore, asked not to be considered.

Tom Dewey [Governor of New York 1943–1955]. Tom Dewey wrote himself out because of age. He said that he felt the man who should be Chief Justice should be able to serve at least 10 years in that position. And there may have been other considerations. I did not discuss this with him directly, but his name had been mentioned and he ruled himself out.

Mr. Justice [Potter] Stewart. You may have noted he was on my appointment list recently—I guess he was. Well, he did come in. What is the matter with Ziegler, anyway? [*Laughter*]

He asked to come to see me. This was 2 or 3 weeks ago. It was really quite a moving experience for me to see this young man—I say young man, he is 45— who knew that he had tremendous support for this position, to come in and he said that he felt that it would not be in the best interest of the Court to appoint a sitting judge on the Court to Chief Justice.

He went over the history of the Court and said on only two occasions has it happened. I don't recall the two, incidentally. But he said that, generally speaking, because of the special role that the Chief Justice has to play as the leader of the Court, it would be very difficult to take a man from the Court and put him above the others. He said it would be better to bring a man from the outside rather than one from the Court. And with that he took himself out and asked me not to consider him.

For a man to do that, and I use three examples of men ruling themselves out— and the fourth man is Attorney General Mitchell.

Attorney General Mitchell had very great support from the beginning when we first discussed it. He said he did not want himself considered.

And, incidentally, he is superbly qualified in my view. He is my closest adviser, as you know, on all legal matters and on many other matters as well. I would say that I don't know of any man in the administration whose views on the law are closer to mine than Attorney General Mitchell's.

But he said quite bluntly that it would not be good for the Court to have a political friend, as distinguished from a personal friend in the case of Charley Rhyne, appointed as Chief Justice at this time. So that was that.

Now, we came to the situation with regard to Mr. Justice Burger. I have felt for a long time that we should elevate Circuit or District Court judges who have proved themselves on the line of battle, on the firing line, to be capable, able judges who have a track record.

I think it is well, when they are qualified, to elevate them to higher courts— from the District Court to the Circuit Court or a Circuit Court judge to the Supreme Court. It has been done in some cases, but more often than not Circuit Court judges do not go to the Supreme Court and very, very seldom does a judge of the Circuit Court go to the Chief Justice. I think this is one of the first times.

Looking over all the Circuit Court judges in terms of age, 61 or 62, but in terms of what I mentioned last night, his legal qualifications, in terms of his background, integrity, I determined over the weekend at Camp David, I gave a lot of thought to it, that we should move toward Mr. Chief Justice—well, who will be Mr. Chief Justice—toward Judge Burger.

This will be hard for you to believe, but at no time over these past few months up until 3 minutes before we went downstairs to meet the press did I talk to Judge Burger. He did not know that I was considering him.

The first conversation that I had with him was when he came upstairs to meet me prior to our walking down to be introduced to the press.

As far as the decision being made, on Monday morning I called the Attorney General. I also called him from Camp David to discuss it. And I said that quietly I wanted him to begin the investigation processes that are necessary—I am referring to the FBI investigation that was made and also the investigation of other matters which might come up in a Senate hearing.

The Attorney General made that investigation and then on Wednesday at approximately 12:30 the Attorney General had then met, was meeting at that time at my request, with Judge Burger. And he called here and said that Judge Burger would be prepared to accept the appointment.

It was then that I made the decision that we would announce it at the press conference that evening and you were informed, of course, at that point.

The only others who were informed—I should point this out. I did not discuss this appointment with any members of the White House Staff, not with Ehrlich-man, not with Haldeman, not with Burns[5] or any of the others that might be interested, and with no Cabinet officers except with the Attorney General. As far as others who were informed, only these were informed.

Naturally, the Attorney General, in making the investigation, while he did not inform Mr. Hoover [Director of the Federal Bureau of Investigation] that Mr. Burger was being considered for Chief Justice, he did ask him to make an investigation and, naturally, Mr. Hoover, I guess, would probably surmise that we were thinking in those directions.

Then in the afternoon, at my direction, the Attorney General informed the Chief Justice, Chief Justice Warren, of our decision and he informed the Vice President. He informed Governor Dewey and he informed Mr. Brownell.

As a matter of fact, I informed Mr. Brownell. I called Mr. Brownell. And he informed Mr. Dewey and the Chief Justice.

We did not inform other members of the Court because we felt it was only proper to inform the Chief Justice under the circumstances.

One final point, and I know you will have some questions, a number of Senators and Congressmen did let their views be known to me—Senator Allen, Congressman Arends, Senator Griffin[6]—but more in general terms, and I referred them to the Attorney General.

---

[5] John D. Ehrlichman, Counsel to the President, H. R. Haldeman, Assistant to the President, and Arthur F. Burns, Counsellor to the President.

[6] Senator James B. Allen of Alabama, Representative Leslie C. Arends of Illinois, and Senator Robert P. Griffin of Michigan.

The final point I wish to make is with regard to the relationship I now have with Judge Burger, and I think it will show why I did not want to see him beforehand. While my study of his opinions and my knowledge of his views would indicate that we happen to share many views, I think it is vitally important that the Chief Justice and all judges of the Supreme Court know that they are absolutely independent of the Executive and Legislative.

He will owe his appointment to the fact that I appointed him, but he is to sit there and consider these decisions, these great questions, without any pressure from the White House, without any understanding as to what is expected from him.

I suppose because I am a lawyer and have had minimal experience, but some, before the Supreme Court on a couple of occasions, that I feel perhaps more strongly on this than maybe some other Presidents. But because I feel so strongly, I want the relationship between the President and the Chief Justice and the other judges to be one which is cordial but at arm's length and that is why prior to this time I did not sit down with Judge Burger and go over—well, "How do you stand on this?" and "How do you feel about this?" and "What do you think about this?" What I was interested in was his background, his general legal philosophy, which, as I said, to me is close to mine.

And now, if he is confirmed by the Senate, he will be his own man which I think is the right thing.

Q. Mr. President, the second criteria you mentioned in the campaign had to do with general views on criminal law and the rights of the accused. How did that figure in this?

THE PRESIDENT. Judge Burger has, in the Circuit Court of Appeals of the District of Columbia, has written some opinions and also he has written articles and made speeches that I think reflect what is now the minority view or has been the minority view of the Supreme Court. It happens to be my view. I would hope it would become the majority view. But when he gets to the Supreme Court, he will be his own man.

Q. Mr. President, did that figure in it? Aside from you going along with the strict constructionists, this is the law, isn't it?

THE PRESIDENT. When I talk about the legal philosophy of the judge, I am referring to his whole legal background, his opinions in all fields. He is a strict constructionist as far as the Constitution is concerned; and incidentally, when you talk about these criminal law cases, that involved strict constructionists because that involves the extent to which the Constitution—what an individual's views are with regard to the Constitution, whether or not you interpret that in a, shall we say, in a very liberal way or a more strict way.

I would say that Judge Burger, in these 5 to 4 decisions, would have been with the four, rather than the five—well, he said so.

Q. Mr. President, have Mr. Mitchell, Mr. Rhyne, and Mr. Brownell, by reason of their close personal friendship with you, also been eliminated from consideration of the seat left vacant by the resignation of Justice Fortas?

THE PRESIDENT. I think so, yes. I have not told them this, but I think that the Supreme Court at this time needs the infusion of judges of which there will be no question of personal friendship, strictly political considerations, or great controversy. For that reason they are not under consideration.

Q. Mr. President, are you considering the other one, the Fortas seat?

THE PRESIDENT. Very deliberately. I would say with all deliberate speed; but I believe it is important to have the Chief Justice considered and acted upon before we move on the other one, so I think that is the only thing I will say. I don't want to get the two matters mixed up.

Q. Mr. President, do you anticipate that you might have an appointment before the new term of the Court in October; all things being equal do you think that?

THE PRESIDENT. Oh, I have to, yes. We would have to, because they would not want a vacancy. But on the other hand, I would expect confirmation to come in June—I would hope it would—and after that I will then sort out the second spot that has to be filled.

Q. When you said the Court needs an infusion of judges, did you mean that literally; that the next appointee would come from the Appellate or District Court?

THE PRESIDENT. No. Well, Appellate or District Court—without completely fencing myself in—Appellate or District Court experience, in my view, is a very strong recommendation, but I am also considering individuals who are not on the Appellate or District Court, but who have substantial constitutional law credibility.

In other words, as you can imagine, you have people in the law schools who are legal scholars of the first rank, and you have some constitutional lawyers in private practice, so I am not ruling that out,

but as you can tell from this appointment, naturally I would say that Appellate and District Court experience gives an individual an edge, but not necessarily the job.

Q. Mr. President, you spoke of Mr. Justice Stewart excluding himself from any possible consideration because of his feeling that a sitting Justice should not be made Chief.

I am not quite clear on whether you shared that feeling and whether that was a factor.

THE PRESIDENT. Yes, I did. I think, as I look at the Court—let me go back to this. You see, you also do these things in terms of your background. I think of the great judges that I remember—Holmes, Brandeis, Cardozo—I think each of those was a great judge. I don't think any one of them would have been a great Chief Justice. They were individuals and usually dissenters, which was to their credit, in my view.

I happen to agree with most of the Holmes-Brandeis dissents in those periods, but on the other hand, they were men who were so individualistic that they could not have brought the Court together, to coalesce, to lead. Incidentally, let me say, whatever disagreement I may have expressed or others may have expressed with previous Chief Justices—take Warren. When you look at them—Warren, Stone, Hughes, all of them—each in his way, apart from his individual views in the law, had a leadership quality which enabled him to lead the Court.

Now, let me say how that relates to Potter Stewart. If Potter Stewart had been in the Circuit Court, you could have taken him then and elevated him. But when he has worked with these men, as an equal, you see, and he has been in all this period

397

June 30, 1970.

I am convinced, however, that reduction of the surtax without repeal of the investment tax credit would be imprudent.

The gradual increase in Federal revenues resulting from repeal of the investment tax credit and the growth of the economy will also facilitate a start during fiscal 1971 in funding two high-priority programs to which this Administration is committed:

—Revenue sharing with State and local governments.

—Tax credits to encourage investment in poverty areas and hiring and training of the hard-core unemployed.

These proposals, now in preparation, will be transmitted to the Congress in the near future.

The tax reform measures outlined earlier in this message will be recommended to the House Ways and Means Committee by Treasury officials this week. This is a broad and necessary program for tax reform. I urge its prompt enactment.

But these measures, sweeping as they are, will not by themselves transform the U.S. tax system into one adequate to the long-range future. Much of the current tax system was devised in depression and shaped further in war. Fairness calls for tax reform now; beyond that, the American people need and deserve a simplified Federal tax system, and one that is attuned to the 1970's.

We must reform our tax structure to make it more equitable and efficient; we must redirect our tax policy to make it more conducive to stable economic growth and responsive to urgent social needs.

That is a large order. Therefore, I am directing the Secretary of the Treasury to thoroughly review the entire Federal tax system and present to me recommendations for basic changes, along with a full analysis of the impact of those changes, no later than November 30, 1969.

Since taxation affects so many wallets and pocketbooks, reform proposals are bound to be controversial. In the debate to come on reform, and in the even greater debate on redirection, the nation would best be served by an avoidance of stereotyped reactions. One man's "loophole" is another man's "incentive." Tax policy should not seek to "soak" any group or give a "break" to any other—it should aim to serve the nation as a whole.

Tax dollars the Government deliberately waives should be viewed as a form of expenditure, and weighed against the priority of other expenditures. When the preference device provides more social benefit than Government collection and spending, that "incentive" should be expanded; when the preference is inefficient or subject to abuse, it should be ended.

Taxes, often bewailed as inevitable as death, actually give life to the people's purpose in having a Government: to provide protection, service and stimulus to progress.

We shall never make taxation popular, but we can make taxation fair.

RICHARD NIXON

The White House
April 21, 1969

of time, I think it is—and we talked about it at some length—I think it is very difficult for them to move him from that position to the first among equals.

Q. Mr. President, if you get that 5 to 4, have the minority turned into the majority on such things as these criminal cases we were just discussing, would it be your hope that some of these previous decisions like the Mallory case and the Durham case could be rewritten or overturned?

THE PRESIDENT. I wouldn't get into that, because when I talk about 5 to 4 decisions, I should point out that the Court is not that easy to predict. I think the piece that Kilpatrick [James J. Kilpatrick, syndicated columnist] had recently shows that the Court is quite individualistic. Take Potter Stewart, John [M.] Harlan, Black, for example, has moved to a strict constructionist in some cases.

I don't think this appointment should in any way be interpreted as saying it has been 5 to 4 one way and now it is going to be 5 to 4 the other way. But every President naturally, by his appointment to the Court, affects the direction of the Court. He affects it in a certain way, but he does not affect the individual decisions. He cannot do that because I cannot emphasize too strongly, that when lawyers begin to consider facts, they are very unpredictable.

Could I add one thing for the ladies here? I was sure somebody would ask me this: "What did he say when he came in?" Well, he came upstairs, and he is really very nice. I hope you get to know him. He and Chief Justice Warren are alike, very decent men and good men.

I first got to know him, strangely enough, in 1948. I said 21 years—well, that was the year. Some of you may remember there was a convention in Philadelphia, and he and George [E.] MacKinnon, who is now on the Circuit Court and was on the Labor Committee—they were great [Harold E.] Stassen men.

So I was there as a Congressman attending the convention and got to know him. In 1952 he helped to bring the Stassen delegation over to Eisenhower. But, nevertheless, I have only seen him off and on, never socially, through the years. When I say socially, except in a large group, although he has written me, and I have written him on occasion. In fact, I wrote him when I thought he made a good speech a couple of years ago. So much for that.

So I had not talked to him at all about this, and I remember I walked out of the Oval Room upstairs and he was just coming out of the elevator. It was three minutes until game time. [*Laughter*] He stood there and I walked over, and I said, "Well, will you take the job?"

He thought a moment, and incidentally, he is a humble man, but he said, "You know, I know that question is somewhat facetious, but as I thought about it this afternoon, I had some concern."

Of course he was going to do it. He had said he would do it, but he recognizes the enormous importance of it. He said, "Sometime when we have more time to talk, I want to thank you for this."

Then I apologized to him, and I said, "You know we will have you and your wife up to meet the members of the Cabinet and their wives, and have a cup of coffee right after the ceremony." I said, "I wanted to apologize for the fact that we couldn't have you to dinner because it would be too many."

He said, "Don't worry about that. After

what I've been through this afternoon, I am just going home to go to bed." And I think he did.

Reporter: Thank you.

NOTE: The conversation with newsmen began at 11:43 a.m. in the President's office at the White House.

211   Remarks at a Concert by the University of Minnesota Band. *May* 23, 1969

Ladies and gentlemen:

On behalf of all of you who have had the opportunity to hear this splendid program, I wish to express our appreciation and the appreciation of the Nation for this fine musical organization.

I think that as we conclude the program you would like to know and to meet, at least, some of the other distinguished guests who are here in addition to the distinguished guests who are part of this musical organization.

First, I should say that when you hear a band like this play so well, including somebody playing a tuba like I didn't think a trumpet could be played, when you hear that you wonder, are they really amateurs, are they really students, and I have news for you—one in the band is a ringer. The one in the band who is a ringer, incidentally, is the second flutist, who is Mrs. Bencriscutto,[1] because the second flutist who is playing in that position has just been drafted. So she ought to be introduced. Will you please stand up.

We will do our very best to get him back to school as quickly as we can.

Then, too, I think you would like to meet the president of the university. I take special pleasure presenting him to you, because for 8 years he was here with President Eisenhower in a top capacity, as one of the assistants to the President; as

---

[1] Mrs. Frank A. Bencriscutto, wife of the conductor of the University of Minnesota Band.

an adviser to the President. He is one of the great educators of this country, a political scientist, a political philosopher, but also one who has had a deep interest in international relations, Dr. Malcolm Moos.

Dr. Moos, I think since you are back where you used to work for so long for so little—I mean in money, of course—that you might be permitted a word or two.

[At this point Dr. Moos spoke briefly. The President then resumed speaking.]

I understand today we have several representatives from the Congress from Minnesota to honor the band. I think Senator Nelsen [Representative Ancher Nelsen of Minnesota] is here? Senator [Eugene J.] McCarthy? No? Well, at least we have a Congressman here, I know. Al [Representative Albert H. Quie of Minnesota].

Having spoken of both the Senators—and I know that only their duties on Capitol Hill made it impossible for them to be here—let me say that this seems to be the year of Minnesota, because last year, in the year 1968, two of the major Presidential candidates, of course, came from Minnesota—Vice President [Hubert H.] Humphrey and Senator McCarthy—and this year the next Chief Justice of the United States [Warren E. Burger] comes from Minnesota, but I would say standing taller than all the rest today is the band from Minnesota, the concert band.

I am sure that we would all like to see the man who played a major role in helping to make these arrangements and who represents his country with such distinction here in Washington, Ambassador Dobrynin.

Mr. Ambassador, would you like to come up and say a word?

[At this point Soviet Ambassador Anatoly F. Dobrynin spoke, recalling the tour of his country by the University of Minnesota Band. The President then resumed speaking.]

Ten years ago—and it was just 10 years ago that Mrs. Nixon and I went to the Soviet Union on an official visit—our host on that occasion was the man mentioned a moment ago by Ambassador Dobrynin, one of the most distinguished representatives of the Foreign Service of the United States, one who has served in major posts throughout the world, and who has just completed his diplomatic career, but is going on in other careers, and still serving the Nation in special capacities, Ambassador Thompson. Would you come up and say a word, too?

[At this point former U.S. Ambassador to the Soviet Union Llewellyn E. Thompson spoke. The President then resumed speaking.]

I would like to conclude this very heartwarming and exciting performance here in the Rose Garden with a response to the remarks of our two Ambassadors, Ambassador Thompson and Ambassador Dobrynin, and to say a word with regard to the itinerary of this band.

Here in the United States we all, of course, know of Moscow and Leningrad, the great cities that are so often visited and are so often in the news, but very few Americans have had the opportunity to visit and to know the other parts of this

country and those parts this band had the opportunity to visit, and I think this is of interest to all of us.

I noticed on their itinerary is Novosibirsk, a great city in the heart of Siberia. I recall that when we were there in 1959 we saw the Novosibirsk Ballet Company put on a performance of Swan Lake that was, I think, almost up to the Bolshoi. Some said it was better. But in any event, it indicated what was going on in the other parts of the country.

In addition to that, this musical organization went to Alma-Ata, which is down in what is called the Asian part of the Soviet Union. It is only about 100 miles from the Chinese border. It is a very different part of the country. It is called the country where the apples grow.

Then, in addition, they went to the storied and famous city of Samarkand, where you can see the magnificent blue temples for miles and miles before you get there, glistening there in the sunlight.

Then, as I was reading, before the band came this morning, some background with regard to Samarkand, in the year 327 Alexander the Great took it by storm, and in the year 700 the Arab forces had to conquer it by siege. Then 700 years ago, in the year 1200, Genghis Khan again conquered Samarkand, but only after a siege.

I think, Mr. Ambassador, you will agree that this musical organization, without firing a shot, took Samarkand easily on this trip by the reception they received there.

But if I could indicate the thrust of my remarks directly to what the Ambassador has said, any of us who have traveled in the Soviet Union know, as we meet the Russian people in all of the farflung areas of that country, that the Russian people and the American people are not natural enemies. The Russian people and the American people, on the contrary, are natural friends.

We have somewhat the same sense of humor, as the Ambassador so well demonstrated a few moments ago. We like much of the same kind of music. We respect each other.

Now it is true that in terms of our diplomatic problems today we have some very great differences to which the Ambassador alluded, and those differences it is the responsibility of statesmen and diplomats to resolve without having them escalate into armed conflict.

But I think that the hope of all of us today, as we hear this magnificent musical organization, and as we think of those things we have in common, is this: that the time will come when the Russian people and the American people and the Soviet Nation and the American Nation will continue to be rivals, as good friends can be; and we shall continue to compete,

as friends can compete; but we shall compete in how each of us can enrich life rather than destroy it, how we can enrich life through our music, through our culture, through our economic progress, through all of those areas in which the people of the world, wherever they may live, have a vital interest in the quality of life.

I think this is the lesson this band brings to us here today. I hope this will only be the beginning of more exchanges where the Russian people and the American people will know each other better so that we can realize as statesmen what a responsibility that we have to see to it that these two great peoples can live together— yes, in rivalry, but in rivalry with the peaceful competition which can only be good for both of us.

Thank you.

NOTE: The President spoke at 10:26 a.m. in the Rose Garden at the White House.

Remarks of Dr. Moos, Ambassador Thompson, and Ambassador Dobrynin are printed in the Weekly Compilation of Presidential Documents (vol. 5, pp. 730 and 731).

212 Message to Members of the Armed Forces on Memorial Day. *May 23, 1969*

ON MEMORIAL DAY, the American people unite to pay tribute to the many brave men and women who have given their lives in the service of their country. We pause to reflect upon the courage and sacrifice of those who responded when their nation called, who left home and family to take up arms on distant shores to ensure to posterity the blessings of peace and freedom. We render our thanks and express our gratitude, for we have not

forgotten what they did or the price they paid.

On this Memorial Day, a great American army is in the field in Vietnam, and other American forces stand guard on the frontiers of freedom throughout the world. These young men and women are responding just as bravely today as their forefathers did on previous occasions when the call to duty came. Their sense of purpose, their personal courage, their professionalism, and their loyalty are an inspiration to all.

For the heroism and sacrifice displayed by the American fighting man, past and present, we are indeed filled with pride and gratitude.

RICHARD NIXON

NOTE: The message was dated May 9, 1969 and released May 23, 1969.

213   Remarks at a Reception Marking the Sixth Anniversary of the Organization of African Unity.
May 25, 1969

Ambassador Peal and Mrs. Peal, all of the distinguished Ambassadors from the African nations and the other distinguished Ambassadors that are here, and Members of the Congress, and other distinguished guests:

I am very honored to be here to participate in the sixth anniversary of the formation of the Organization of African Unity.

As I was listening to Ambassador Peal describe the problems of Africa and also of my relationship to those problems, both privately and now officially, I simply want to bring the proper bipartisan note into this occasion. I hope that on this occasion we carve up neither elephants nor donkeys.

We are glad that today we have our Democratic and Republican Representatives and Senators present, because there is one thing that I can assure all of our guests here: And that is that in this country, when it comes to support of the great goals that the Ambassador has described in his eloquent remarks of unity, of prosperity, and of the progress that we all want, that we in the United States, regardless of party, share your desires. We want to help you. We want to work with you. And this is true whether it is a Republican administration or a Democratic administration.

Having said that, I would like also to remind some of our hosts here today that while I do not know Africa as well as I would like to, that I have had the privilege of visiting more African countries than any man who has ever been President of the United States.

Now, for fear that my alleged very good memory—which I derived from my elephant association—might fail me, I will try to name those countries. If I leave one out, I trust someone in the audience will remind me.

But on those two trips—the one in 1957 where the Assistant Secretary of State, now the Assistant Secretary of State for African Affairs, Joseph Palmer, accompanied me, and then in another one, which came as a private citizen 10 years later—I learned to know this continent, to know its people, through visiting what few of the countries I was able to visit: Morocco, Tunisia, Libya, the Sudan, and Ethiopia, in the northern and central part of the continent, and then in 1957 to the independence celebration for Ghana, and then to Liberia, Uganda, and then in 1967 again returning on that occasion, I visited the Congo, Zambia, Ivory Coast, and Kenya. I think I have mentioned 12 countries. If there is another one, I may have made some airport stops.

I mentioned these countries not for the

purpose of demonstrating any ability to memorize, but more to make a point. There are 41 nations in Africa. The Ambassador has spoken of the great hopes for African unity which were there 6 years ago when this organization was set up and which are there today.

And I would like to speak quite candidly and directly about African unity and unity in this world in which we live and to speak about it in terms of what we can expect and what we cannot expect.

First, one thing I learned about Africa is that we have a tendency in this Nation, particularly those of us who have not had the opportunity to know the continent well, to think of Africa as just one great continent very much the same.

Now, of course, any even unsophisticated observer knows that North Africa is different from Central Africa, and that is different from South Africa. But on the other hand, what I have found, as I traveled through Africa, whatever the place might be, that the diversity of the continent was what was impressive. Not one of the countries is the same.

The costumes are different. There are different religions. There are different traditions. There are different governments.

So when we talk about unity, the kind of unity that will be meaningful for the continent of Africa, it does not mean a unity in which all will be the same. It does mean the unity which will allow the diversity. Let me put it another way.

When ours was a very young country and we still are a young country by most standards, I suppose, but when we were a very young country, George Washington reminded the American people as he was finishing his second term as President of the United States that the new nation would find itself in great difficulty or greater difficulty as the glow of winning the War of Independence began to go away; and that then what the Nation had to guard against was the disunity that might follow.

The United States did have problems in that respect. And we survived those problems.

But I would simply say that as we look at the new nations of Africa, as we see the problems that are there, it is, of course, very natural to expect that a new country, a young country, starting with new programs dealing with great, great problems cannot be expected overnight to have the unity either within a country and certainly not the kind of a unity which covers a whole continent.

This should not be discouraging. It is only a challenge.

I would add another point. As we look back on our own history and as each of you look back on your history, we tend and you tend to think of those who led the revolutions. They are our great heroes. I would suggest that perhaps the more difficult task is not for those who lead a revolution, as difficult and as challenging as that is, but those who build a nation after the revolution is won.

And that is one problem that you have—the Ambassadors who are here, your governments at home. It is not as exciting. It sometimes may be very, very difficult and tortuous and sometimes almost dull. But this kind of work, the challenging job, day-in and day-out, of building rather than destroying, building a nation rather than destroying one, this is the true test of a people.

And all over this great continent, particularly in the newer countries, the people of Africa are meeting that test.

And then another point I would make with regard to the Organization for African Unity, I would emphasize that we would not want and you would not want to see that unity destroy the differences that can enrich the whole life of a continent and the life of this world.

What we want is the kind of unity which allows the diversity, which enriches a nation or a continent and avoiding the disunity which destroys.

As we consider that, we think, therefore, of the future of Africa, at this time, on the sixth anniversary of a very young organization, but an organization with tremendous responsibilities in the years ahead.

And I simply want to say that speaking as one who has visited several of your countries, speaking as one who knows that the problems of building a new government, building a new society, are perhaps infinitely greater than those of simply changing it through revolution, that I admire and respect those who are working in this difficult task.

I do not expect and no one should expect that that task will be achieved overnight. And I would say that what we all are privileged today to commemorate is the fact that people so diverse, so different over this great continent with 300 million people and all the potential for the future, that the people there are working in their different way toward the same goal, the unity which will avoid that destruction which comes from war, but also the diversity which will allow for the creative freedom which we all know leads to progress and prosperity.

Mr. Ambassador, I want you to know that Mrs. Nixon and I are privileged to be here in this house, to be here on this bit of African soil. As we are here, we want you to know, all of you from every one of the countries represented, that with all the grave problems we have in the world, the problems of Asia and Vietnam, of Europe, of Latin America, that you do have in the President of the United States a man who knows Africa, not as well as he should, but he knows it, he believes in its future, and he wants to work with you for that greater future.

Thank you.

NOTE: The President spoke at approximately 7:10 p.m. at the Liberian Embassy in Washington following welcoming remarks by Liberian Ambassador S. Edward Peal. The Ambassador's remarks are printed in the Weekly Compilation of Presidential Documents. (vol 5, p. 744).

214   Remarks at the Swearing In of Donald Rumsfeld as Director, Office of Economic Opportunity. *May 26, 1969*

Mr. Vice President, members of the Cabinet, Mayor Lindsay, Mayor Washington, ladies and gentlemen:

This is another one of our swearing-in ceremonies and one of very great importance to this administration and also to the Nation.

Don Rumsfeld will, after his swearing in, assume several responsibilities: one is an Assistant to the President; second, as

Director of the Office of Economic Opportunity; and, third, as a member of the Cabinet by designation of the President.

He will be the youngest member of the Cabinet, but one very experienced in all of the responsibilities that he will have.

You have already met him. I have already introduced him at the time that his

nomination was sent to the Senate.

Now, he will be sworn in. Judge [Austin L.] Fickling, of the Circuit Court of Appeals of the District of Columbia, will administer the oath and Mrs. Rumsfeld will hold the Bible.

NOTE: The President spoke at 10:12 a.m. in the Rose Garden at the White House.

215   Remarks About the Special Message to the Congress on Postal Reform.   *May* 27, 1969

Ladies and gentlemen:

As you know, for the past several weeks we have been considering in the leadership meetings and in other areas, reform of the postal system.

Those studies have now been completed, and I am sending to the Congress today a message incorporating the recommendations made by the Postmaster General. This is the most significant reform bill ever sent to the Congress, ever offered by an administration in this area.

The Postmaster General will answer your specific questions, but I would summarize these points:

First, it will dramatically improve the working conditions for the 750,000 men and women who work in the postal service.

Second, we believe it will, without question, increase the efficiency and reduce the cost, eventually, of postal service in the United States.

Third, it continues the progress toward a goal we set for ourselves early in this administration, of completely removing the Post Office Department from political control.

As a matter of fact, this is the first message, I believe, sent by a President to the

Congress in which the President is recommending, with the concurrence of his Cabinet officer, that the Cabinet position be abolished, because the Postmaster General, assuming that we are able to get approval of this program, substantially, the Postmaster General will no longer hold the Cabinet rank that he presently has.

I believe this message is one of the most significant proposals that will be made during the entire period of this administration. I think it will have a very significant effect on not only this Government but particularly the future of the Nation insofar as the postal service affects it.

It has my complete backing, and I think the Postmaster General is to be congratulated for getting the support that he has on a bipartisan basis—as he will explain to you in his speaking before you—on a bipartisan basis from the Congress and in the country for the message up to this time.

The Postmaster General—at least we call you that until this program is adopted.

NOTE: The President spoke at 9:40 a.m. in the Roosevelt Room at the White House. Also released was the transcript of a news briefing by Postmaster General Winston M. Blount immediately following the President's remarks.

216   Special Message to the Congress on Postal Reform.
May 27, 1969

To the Congress of the United States:

Total reform of the nation's postal system is absolutely essential.

The American people want dependable, reasonably priced mail service, and postal employees want the kind of advantages enjoyed by workers in other major industries. Neither goal can be achieved within the postal system we have today.

The Post Office is not keeping pace with the needs of our expanding population or the rightful aspirations of our postal workers.

Encumbered by obsolete facilities, inadequate capital, and outdated operation practices, the Post Office Department is failing the mail user in terms of service, failing the taxpayer in terms of cost, and failing the postal worker in terms of truly rewarding employment. It is time for a change.

Two years ago, Lawrence F. O'Brien, then Postmaster General, recognized that the Post Office was in "a race with catastrophe," and made the bold proposal that the postal system be converted into a government-owned corporation. As a result of Mr. O'Brien's recommendations, a Presidential Commission was established to make a searching study of our postal system. After considering all the alternatives, the Commission likewise recommended a government corporation. Last January, President Johnson endorsed that recommendation in his State of the Union message.

One of my first actions as President was to direct Postmaster General Winton M. Blount to review that proposal and others.

He has made his own first-hand study of the problems besetting the postal service, and after a careful analysis has reported to me that only a complete reorganization of the postal system can avert the steady deterioration of this vital public service.

I am convinced that such a reorganization is essential. The arguments are overwhelming and the support is bipartisan. Postal Reform is not a partisan political issue, it is an urgent national requirement.

CAREER OPPORTUNITIES AND WORKING CONDITIONS

For many years the postal worker walked a dead-end street. Promotions all too often were earned by the right political connections rather than by merit. This Administration has taken steps to eliminate political patronage in the selection of postal employees; but there is more—much more—that must be done.

Postal employees must be given a work environment comparable to that found in the finest American enterprises. Today, particularly in our larger cities, postal workers labor in crowded, dismal, old fashioned buildings that are little short of disgraceful. Health services, employee facilities, training programs and other benefits enjoyed by the worker in private industry and in other Federal agencies are, all too often, unavailable to the postal worker. In an age when machines do the heavy work for private companies, the postal worker still shoulders, literally, the burden of the nation's mail. That mail fills more than a billion sacks a year; and the men and women who move those sacks need help.

Postal employees must have a voice in determining their conditions of employment. They must be given a stake in the quality of the service the Department provides the public; they must be given a reason for pride in themselves and in the job they do. The time for action is now.

HIGHER DEFICITS AND INCREASING RATES

During all but seventeen years since 1838, when deficit financing became a way of life for the Post Office, the postal system has cost more than it has earned.

In this fiscal year, the Department will drain over a billion dollars from the national treasury to cover the deficit incurred in operating the Post Office. Over the last decade, the tax money used to shore up the postal system has amounted to more than eight billion dollars. Almost twice that amount will be diverted from the Treasury in the next ten years if the practices of the past are continued. We must not let that happen.

The money to meet these huge postal deficits comes directly out of the taxpayer's pocket—regardless of how much he uses the mails. It is bad business, bad government, and bad politics to pour this kind of tax money into an inefficient postal service. Every taxpayer in the United States—as well as every user of the mails—has an important stake in seeing that the Federal Government institutes the kind of reform that is needed to give the nation a modern and well managed postal system. Without such a system Congress will either have to raise postage rates far above any level presently

contemplated, or the taxpayers will have to shoulder the burden of paying postal deficits the like of which they have never seen before.

Neither alternative is acceptable. The nation simply cannot afford the cost of maintaining an inefficient postal system. The will of the Congress and the will of the people is clear. They want fast, dependable and low-cost mail service. They want an end to the continuing cycle of higher deficits and increasing rates.

QUALITY POSTAL SERVICE

The Post Office is a business that provides a vital service which its customers, like the customers of a private business, purchase directly. A well managed business provides dependable service; but complaints about the quality of postal service under existing procedures are widespread. While most mail ultimately arrives at its destination, there is no assurance that important mail will arrive on time; and late mail—whether a birthday card or a proxy statement—is often no better than lost mail.

Delays and breakdowns constantly threaten the mails. A complete breakdown in service did in fact occur in 1966 in one of our largest cities, causing severe economic damage and personal hardship. Similar breakdowns could occur at any time in many of our major post offices. A major modernization program is essential to insure against catastrophe in the Post Office.

A modern postal service will not mean fewer postal workers. Mail volume—tied as it is to economic activity—is growing at such a rate that there will be no cutback in postal jobs even with the most dramatic gains in postal efficiency. Without a modernized postal system, however, more than a quarter of a million new postal workers will be needed in the next decade simply to move the growing mountain of mail. The savings that can be realized by holding employment near present levels can and should mean more pay and increased benefits for the three quarters of a million men and women who will continue to work in the postal service.

Opportunity Through Reform

While the work of the Post Office is that of a business enterprise, its organization is that of a political department. Traditionally it has been run as a Cabinet agency of the United States Government—one in which politics has been as important as efficient mail delivery. Under the present system, those responsible for managing the postal service do not have the authority that the managers of any enterprise must have over prices, wages, location of facilities, transportation and procurement activities and personnel policy.

Changes in our society have resulted in changes in the function of the Post Office Department. The postal system must be given a non-political management structure consistent with the job the postal system has to perform as a supplier of vital services to the public. Times change, and now is the time for change in the postal system.

I am, therefore, sending to the Congress reform legislation entitled the Postal Service Act of 1969.

Postal Service Act of 1969

The reform that I propose represents a basic and sweeping change in direction; the ills of the postal service cannot be cured by partial reform.

The Postal Service Act of 1969 provides for:

* removal of the Post Office from the Cabinet
* creation of an independent Postal Service wholly owned by the Federal Government
* new and extensive collective bargaining rights for postal employees
* bond financing for major improvements
* a fair and orderly procedure for changing postage rates, subject to Congressional review
* regular reports to Congress to facilitate Congressional oversight of the postal system
* a self-supporting postal system.

The new government-owned corporation will be known as the United States Postal Service. It will be administered by a nine-member board of directors selected without regard to political affiliation. Seven members of the board, including the chairman, will be appointed by the President with the advice and consent of the Senate. These seven members will select a full-time chief executive officer, who will join with the seven others to select a second full-time executive who will also serve on the board.

Employees will retain their Civil Service annuity rights, veterans preference, and other benefits.

The Postal Service is unique in character. Therefore, there will be, for the first time in history, true collective bargaining in the postal system. Postal employees in every part of the United States will be given a statutory right to negotiate directly with management over wages and working conditions. A fair and impartial mechanism—with provision for binding arbitration—will be established to resolve negotiating impasses and disputes arising under labor agreements.

For the first time, local management will have the authority to work with employees to improve local conditions. A modernization fund adequate to the needs of the service will be available. The postal worker will finally take his rightful place beside the worker in private industry.

The Postal Service will become entirely self-supporting, except for such subsidies as Congress may wish to provide for specific public service groups. The Postal Service, like the Tennessee Valley Authority and similar public authorities, will be able to issue bonds as a means of raising funds needed for expansion and modernization of postal facilities and other purposes.

Proposals for changes in classes of mail or postage rates will be heard by expert rate commissioners, who will be completely independent of operating management. The Board of the Postal Service will review determinations made by the Rate Commissioners on rate and classification questions, and the Presidentially appointed members of the board will be empowered to modify such determinations if they consider it in the public interest to do so.

Congress will have express authority to veto decisions on rate and classification questions.

The activities of the Postal Service will be subject to Congressional oversight, and the Act provides for regular reports to Congress. The Postal Service and the rules by which it operates can, of course, be changed by law at any time.

TOWARD POSTAL EXCELLENCE

Removing the postal system from politics and the Post Office Department from the Cabinet is a sweeping reform.

Traditions die hard and traditional institutions are difficult to abandon. But tradition is no substitute for performance, and if our postal system is to meet the expanding needs of the 1970s, we must act now.

Legislation, by itself, will not move the mail. This must be done by the three-quarters of a million dedicated men and women who today wear the uniform of the postal service. They must be given the right tools—financial, managerial and technological—to do the job. The legislation I propose today will provide those tools.

There is no Democratic or Republican way of delivering the mail. There is only the right way.

This legislation will let the postal service do its job the right way, and I strongly recommend that it be promptly considered and promptly enacted.

RICHARD NIXON

The White House
May 27, 1969

217   Remarks of Welcome to Prime Minister de Jong and Foreign Minister Luns of the Netherlands. *May 27, 1969*

Mr. Prime Minister, Mr. Foreign Minister:

On this beautiful day we are very honored to welcome you to Washington, D.C., our Nation's Capital, as the first official visitor from a Western European country.

It is appropriate that you should be the first visitor in several respects. Next year the United States marks the 350th anniversary of the Pilgrims arriving in the New World. It was from a Dutch port that the Pilgrims embarked from the Old World to come to the New World.

Through that 350 years, your country and ours have been so closely associated in friendship and in good causes. We are not unaware of the fact that you were one of the first of the major countries to recognize the new Nation in 1782. Then, through the period that has passed since then, we have worked together, we have shared problems together, and today we are strong partners in the North Atlantic Treaty Alliance.

You also have given to our country so many of your own people and we are proud of the Americans of Dutch heritage who have added so much to our culture and who have enriched our land.

Today, as you arrive for this official visit, we want you to know that we hope that we can continue to work with your people and your government in the pursuit of peace which has been a cause to which you and your people have been so greatly devoted.

I think all of our guests here today would be interested to note that the Government of the Netherlands is one of the very few countries of the world that has earmarked a portion of its armed forces for U.N. peacekeeping duties. This is an indication of foresight and an indication also of the kind of cooperation that the United States desires to have with other free peoples throughout the world.

Mr. Prime Minister and Mr. Foreign Minister, you are most welcome. We trust that the sun will shine on you during this visit and all of the years ahead in your own country as it does today.

NOTE: The President spoke at 10:55 a.m. on the South Lawn at the White House where Prime Minister Petrus J. S. de Jong and Foreign Minister Joseph M. A. H. Luns were given a formal welcome with full military honors. Prime Minister de Jong responded as follows:

Mr. President, on behalf of my colleague, the Minister of Foreign Affairs, and myself, allow me to say a few words of thanks for your warm words of welcome.

When we approached your shores yesterday, we received the happy news of the safe arrival and the splashdown of the astronauts. Before I say anything, I want to extend my most warmest and sincerest congratulations to you and the American people on this magnificent performance. The whole world followed the voyage of the astronauts with bated breath. I think all mankind rejoices with you in this glorious victory of mind over the limitations. A very great performance.

As we proceeded, Mr. President, by way of contrast, to Williamsburg, we had an interesting experience of going back to the 18th century. We saw where George Washington and so many of your American patriots of global fame have lived. The name of the town itself perpetuates in your history the idea of King William the Third, the Prince of Orange, who as Stadtholder of the Netherlands, became at the same time King of England in what in British history is known as "The Glorious Revolution."

From those days, Mr. President, the first alliance between your country and ours was forged. In 1776, just half a year after the Declaration of Independence was written, the first time the Stars and Stripes were saluted by a foreign power was by a Dutch fortress at St. Eustatius, one of the Windward Islands in the Caribbean, now forming part of the Netherland Antilles.

In 1780, the English declared war on us and gave as the principal war reason the fact that we gave too great a support to the American cause for independence.

In 1782, we concluded a formal treaty of friendship between the United States and the then Republic of the United Netherlands.

But as we crossed the Atlantic yesterday, Mr. President, in a few hours and in, incidentally, more comfortable circumstances than our ancestors did, I felt the same words could still apply, that the very first Minister to the United States spoke in the Congress of Princeton in 1783, when he said, "We know the value of independent freedom, and we appreciate the greatness of your aims. We will do all that is in our power to help you further the ties of friendship and further the alliance as much as we can."

I don't think, Mr. President, there are very many countries in the world which share such long ties of friendship as your country and ours. The efforts and the sacrifices of the United States for the liberation of Europe and the reconstruction afterwards have not been forgotten by my country. With you we share a continued dedication to the ideals of peace, freedom, and democracy. Those ideals will guide us during the talks we hope to have together.

Thank you.

218   Special Message to the Congress on Foreign Aid. *May* 28, 1969

To the Congress of the United States:

Americans have for many years debated the issues of foreign aid largely in terms of our own national self-interest.

Certainly our efforts to help nations feed millions of their poor help avert violence and upheaval that would be dangerous to peace.

Certainly our military assistance to allies helps maintain a world in which we ourselves are more secure.

Certainly our economic aid to developing nations helps develop our own potential markets overseas.

And certainly our technical assistance puts down roots of respect and friendship for the United States in the court of world opinion.

These are all sound, practical reasons for our foreign aid programs.

But they do not do justice to our fundamental character and purpose. There is a moral quality in this Nation that will not permit us to close our eyes to the want in this world, or to remain indifferent when the freedom and security of others are in danger.

We should not be self-conscious about this. Our record of generosity and concern for our fellow men, expressed in concrete terms unparalleled in the world's history, has helped make the American experience unique. We have shown the world that a great nation must also be a good nation. We are doing what is right to do.

A Fresh Approach

This Administration has intensively examined our programs of foreign aid. We have measured them against the goals of our policy and the goad of our conscience. Our review is continuing, but we have come to this central conclusion:

411

U.S. assistance is essential to express and achieve our national goals in the international community—a world order of peace and justice.

But no single government, no matter how wealthy or well-intentioned, can by itself hope to cope with the challenge of raising the standard of living of two-thirds of the world's people. This reality must not cause us to retreat into helpless, sullen isolation. On the contrary, this reality must cause us to redirect our efforts in four main ways:

We must enlist the energies of private enterprise, here and abroad, in the cause of economic development. We must do so by stimulating additional investment through businesslike channels, rather than offering ringing exhortations.

We must emphasize innovative technical assistance, to ensure that our dollars for all forms of aid go further, and to plant the seeds that will enable other nations to grow their own capabilities for the future.

We must induce other advanced nations to join in bearing their fair share— by contributing jointly to multilateral banks and the United Nations, by consultation and by the force of our example, and by effective coordination of national and multilateral programs in individual countries.

We must build on recent successes in furthering food production and family planning.

To accomplish these goals, this Administration's foreign aid proposals will be submitted to the Congress today. In essence, these are the new approaches:

I. ENLISTING PRIVATE ENTERPRISE

I propose the establishment of the Overseas Private Investment Corporation.

The purpose of the Corporation is to provide businesslike management of investment incentives now in our laws so as to contribute to the economic and social progress of developing nations.

The majority of the Board of Directors, including its President, will be drawn from private life and have business experience.

Venture capital seeks profit, not adventure. To guide this capital to higher-risk areas, the Federal government presently offers a system of insurance and guaranties. Like the Federal Housing Administration in the housing field here at home, the Overseas Private Investment Corporation will be able to place the credit of the United States Government behind the insurance and guaranties which the Corporation would sell to U.S. private investors.

The Corporation will also have a small direct lending program for private developmental projects. It will carry out investment survey and development activities. And it will undertake for A.I.D. some of the technical assistance required to strengthen private enterprise abroad. The financial performance of OPIC will be measurable: It is expected to break even or to show a small profit.

The Overseas Private Investment Corporation will give new direction to U.S. private investment abroad. As such, it will provide new focus to our foreign assistance effort.

Simultaneously, I propose a mandate for the Agency for International Development to direct a growing part of its capital, technical and advisory assistance to improving opportunities for local private enterprise in developing countries—on farms as well as in commerce and industry.

We do not insist that developing countries imitate the American system. Each nation must fashion its own institutions to its own needs. But progress has been greatest where governments have encouraged private enterprise, released bureaucratic controls, stimulated competition and allowed maximum opportunity for individual initiative. A.I.D.'s mandate will be directed to this end.

2. EXPANDING TECHNICAL ASSISTANCE

I propose a strong new emphasis on technical assistance.

Over one-fifth of the funds requested for fiscal year 1970 are for technical assistance activities. Imaginative use of these funds at the points where change is beginning can have a gradual but pervasive impact on the economic growth of developing nations. It can make our dollars for all forms of aid go further.

Technical assistance takes many forms. It includes the adaptation of U.S. technical knowledge to the special needs of poor countries, the training of their people in modern skills, and the strengthening of institutions which will have lives and influence of their own. The main emphases of technical assistance must be in agriculture, education and in family planning. But needs must also be met in health, public administration, community action, public safety and other areas. In all of these fields, our aim must be to raise the quality of our advisory, training and research services.

Technical assistance is an important way for private U.S. organizations to participate in development. U.S. technical assistance personnel serving abroad must increasingly come from private firms, universities and colleges and non-profit service groups. We will seek to expand this broad use of the best of our American talent.

A.I.D. is preparing plans to reorganize and revitalize U.S. technical assistance activities. A new Technical Assistance Bureau headed by an Assistant Administrator will be created within A.I.D. to focus on technical assistance needs and ensure effective administration of these activities. The bureau will devise new techniques, evaluate effectiveness of programs, and seek out the best qualified people in our universities and other private groups.

To make it possible to carry through these plans most effectively, I am requesting a two-year funding authorization for this part of the A.I.D. program.

3. SHARING THE ASSISTANCE EFFORT

I propose that we channel more of our assistance in ways that encourage other advanced nations to fairly share the burden of international development.

This can be done by:
—Increasing jointly our contributions to international development banks.
—Increasing jointly our contributions to the United Nations technical assistance program.
—Acting in concert with other advanced countries to share the cost of aid to individual developing countries.

Most development assistance—from other advanced nations as well as the United States—is provided directly from one country to another. That is understandable. Such bilateral programs provide assistance in accordance with each country's own standards, make the source more visible to the recipient's people and can reflect historical political ties.

But assistance through international development banks and the United Nations is approaching a fifth of total world-wide aid for development and should be expanded. Multilateral programs cushion political frictions between donors and recipients and bring the experience of many nations to bear on the development problem. Moreover, they explicitly require shared contributions among the advanced nations. This calls for funds in addition to those which I am proposing today.

I appreciate the prompt response by the Congress to my earlier proposal authorizing the United States to join with others in the second replenishment of the International Development Association. I urge early passage of appropriations for this contribution so that we may meet our pledge.

I reaffirm my request for appropriations in Fiscal 1970 of $20 million for the ordinary capital of the Asian Development Bank, and $300 million for our scheduled contribution to the Fund for Special Operations of the Inter-American Development Bank.

In separate legislation I will submit a new proposal for a U.S. contribution of $25 million to the Special Fund of the Asian Development Bank in FY 1970. I am convinced that a fairly-shared Special Fund, to enable the Bank to provide concessional financing for priority needs, is a necessary supplement to the Bank's ordinary lending facilities. The United States should join with other donor countries in establishing this Special Fund, and strengthen the Bank so that it can better deal with Asia's current development problems and future needs.

The United States will consult with the management of the African Development Bank and with other potential donors, to identify the most appropriate way we can support the objectives of African development and assist in meeting the needs of that continent.

Today's proposed legislation includes a 43 per cent increase in the U.S. contribution to multilateral technical assistance through the United Nations Development Program. Our contribution will be on the same sharing basis as in the past.

4. FURTHERING FOOD PRODUCTION AND FAMILY PLANNING

This Administration, while moving in the new directions I have outlined, will apply the lessons of experience in our foreign aid programs.

One basic lesson is the critical importance of releasing the brakes on development caused by low agricultural productivity. A few years ago, mass starvation within a decade seemed clearly possible in many poor nations. Today they stand at least on the threshold of a dramatic breakthrough in food production. The combination of the new "miracle" seeds for wheat and rice, aid-financed fertilizer, improved cultivation practices, and constructive agriculture policies shows what is possible. They also demonstrate the potential for success when foreign aid, foreign private investment and domestic resources in developing countries join together in a concerted attack on poverty.

The experience of this decade has also shown that lower rates of population growth can be critical for speeding up economic development and social progress. An increasing number of countries have adopted national family planning programs to attack the problem. At least another decade of sustained hard work will be needed if we are to win the battle between economic development and population. But our assistance to voluntary family planning programs and support for the work of the United Nations and other international organizations in this field must continue to have high priority, as will our support of efforts to increase food production.

Another important lesson is that our aid programs need better means of continuous management inspection. We are creating a new position of Auditor-General in the Agency for International Development. His job will be to make sure that A.I.D.'s funds are used for their intended purpose and that A.I.D.'s operations are managed as tightly and efficiently as possible. He will report directly to the A.I.D. Administrator.

LEGISLATIVE AND BUDGET REQUESTS

The proposed legislation revises that part of the present Foreign Assistance Act which deals with economic aid, to reflect the priorities of this Administration. The proposals are designed to accomplish the following:

—Create the Overseas Private Investment Corporation and authorize its programs for an initial five years.
—Strengthen A.I.D.'s mandate to use official aid to stimulate private initiative in development.
—Expand the role of technical assistance under consolidated legislation and a two-year authorization.

The proposed budget includes new appropriation of $2,210 million for A.I.D., $138 million below the January budget request of the previous Administration. In addition, the budget includes $75 million to augment existing reserves for guaranties to be issued by the proposed Overseas Private Investment Corporation.

The appropriation request for economic assistance will support these regional programs:

—For Latin America, $605 million.
—For the Near East and South Asia, $625 million.
—For Africa, $186 million.
—For East Asia, $234 million.
—And for Vietnam, $440 million.

In order to protect the U.S. balance of payments at the same time we are providing assistance abroad, goods and services will be purchased in the United States wherever practicable. Over 90 per cent of all A.I.D. expenditures and virtually all purchases of goods will be made in the United States. The remaining funds that are spent abroad are mainly for living expenses of U.S. personnel and for other local expenditures in support of technical assistance programs.

For military assistance, the proposed budget includes $375 million, the same as in the January budget. Maintenance of a climate of international security still calls for military strength sufficient to deter aggression. Seventy-seven per cent of the total amount available for the military assistance program will be allocated to four of our long-standing allies—Korea, the Republic of China, Turkey and Greece. The balance of the request will be used to provide modest amounts of training and equipment to 44 other countries where our security and foreign policy interests are partially met by this form of assistance. We are negotiating a renewal of our base agreement with Spain. If these negotiations succeed, we shall then need to request an amendment to this authorization asking for additional funds to cover our year's needs for Spain.

The United States will continue to provide military assistance from the U.S. Armed Services budget to Vietnam, Laos and Thailand.

I am also asking in separate legislation for $275 million for credit necessary to facilitate the purchase of essential military equipment by countries now able to buy all or a growing part of their defense requirements. These funds will be returned to the United States during the next few years as the purchasing countries meet their repayment obligations.

PLANNING FOR THE 70S

I believe these proposals for fiscal year 1970 are sound—and necessary to make clearly desirable improvements in our foreign aid program.

But we need to learn more about the role which foreign assistance can play in the development process, and the relationship between development and overall U.S. foreign policy.

I am therefore establishing a task force of private citizens to make a comprehensive review of the entire range of U.S. aid activities, to consider proposals of the United Nations bodies and international commissions, and to help me determine what our national policies should be toward the developing countries in the decade of the 1970's. I will look to the task force's report in developing the program next year, in my response to the Javits Amendment[1] to the Foreign Assistance Act, and in considering the recommendations of the internationally-sponsored

Pearson Commission report to be published in the fall.[2]

TOWARD A WORLD OF ORDER

Foreign aid cannot be viewed in isolation. That is a statement with a double meaning, each side of which is true.

If we turn inward, if we adopt an attitude of letting the underdeveloped nations shift for themselves, we would soon see them shift away from the values so necessary to international stability. Moreover, we would lose the traditional concern for humanity which is so vital a part of the American spirit.

In another sense, foreign aid must be viewed as an integral part of our overall effort to achieve a world order of peace and justice. That order combines our sense of responsibility for helping those determined to defend their freedom; our sensible understanding of the mutual benefits that flow from cooperation between nations; and our sensitivity to the desires of our fellow men to improve their lot in the world.

In this time of stringent budgetary restraint, we must stimulate private investment and the cooperation of other governments to share with us in meeting the most urgent needs of those just beginning to climb the economic ladder. And we must continue to minimize the immediate impact on our balance of payments.

---

[1] The amendment of Senator Jacob K. Javits of New York, requires a comprehensive reappraisal of United States foreign assistance programs and a report to the Congress on such findings. It is included in section 501 of the Foreign Assistance Act of 1968 (Public Law 90–554, 82 Stat. 960).

[2] The report of the Commission on International Development, chaired by Lester Pearson, former Prime Minister of Canada, is entitled "Partners in Development" (Praeger Publishers, New York City, 399 pp.).

This request for foreign economic and military assistance is the lowest proposed since the program began. But it is about 900 million dollars more than was appropriated last year. I consider it necessary to meet essential requirements now, and to maintain a base for future action.

The support by the Congress of these programs will help enable us to press forward in new ways toward the building of respect for the United States, security for our people and dignity for human beings in every corner of the globe.

RICHARD NIXON

The White House
May 28, 1969

NOTE: On the same day the White House released the transcript of a news briefing on the foreign aid message by Dr. John A. Hannah, Administrator, and Rutherford Poats, Deputy Administrator, of the Agency for International Development.

219　Remarks on the Departure of Prime Minister de Jong and Foreign Minister Luns of the Netherlands. *May 28, 1969*

Mr. Prime Minister and Mr. Foreign Minister:

As this visit concludes, I wish to tell you how much we have been honored having you here as the first official visitors from Western Europe, and also as the first visitor from your country at the Prime Minister level on an official visit.

We think that the discussions that we have had have been most helpful on a bilateral basis, but I would like to say further that they have been for me most constructive, as we have discussed some of the broader problems we have, not only with regard to Western Europe, but internationally.

It is this kind of exchange between leaders who have responsibilities to our countries which is most valuable, most valuable in helping us in each of our respective capacities, to make decisions that are not parochial, not provincial, and not limited to those bilateral matters that may concern our two countries, but see the whole world and not just part of the world.

I would say, finally, that one of the things that has always impressed me about my friends from the Netherlands is that they look outward, they think in international terms, and therefore, it is always helpful to me to talk to leaders from the Netherlands and to get that broad world perspective which we sometimes lose sight of as we sit in our office thinking of the immediate problems that we have.

I conclude with one personal thought. The Prime Minister and the Foreign Minister reminded me that I had not visited the Netherlands. It is true, although my wife and daughters have. I remember during the days I was Vice President, I visited many countries, but I usually went to countries where we had problems, and it is because we seem to have no serious problems with the Netherlands that I never have gotten there. I hope to correct that oversight during my term of office, and to be able to return this visit that you so gracefully have paid to us.

We wish you bon voyage.

PRIME MINISTER PETRUS J. S. DE JONG. Ladies and gentlemen, I really have nothing to add to what the President has said.

As regards the invitation on the official side, one expects, between countries with such good relations, to be received pleasantly, but I must say we have been struck by the warmth of the welcome and the genuine friendliness—the style of the reception.

As regards the talks we had, the thing we appreciate most in you is that we come directly, with very open and honest talks, to the crux of the matter, and are able to talk together and exchange views on the whole world.

We have been very pleased with the results of our talks and I, for one, am much better informed, and I hope a slightly wiser man on return than when I arrived here.

We are, I must say, very pleased that you, Mr. President, are willing to accept our invitation to visit the Netherlands whenever your very busy schedule allows you to do so.

Thank you once again very much for a very, very nice reception.

THE PRESIDENT. Mr. Foreign Minister, you may say something, if you wish.

FOREIGN MINISTER JOSEPH M. A. H. LUNS. It would be very presumptuous for me to make a long statement, so I won't talk much longer than 2 to 5 minutes after the President and Prime Minister. I would only confirm what the Prime Minister said a moment ago, that we are pleased with the results of our bilateral talks and the results of the talks on multilateral matters.

There were some rather tricky problems which, to our great satisfaction, have now been solved. And I think we owe a debt to the President of the United States and to the Acting Secretary of State [Elliot L. Richardson] for the way these talks were prepared and for the way we came, in 2 days, to solutions which will be worked out—I am thinking of air matters—and which I feel sure will be hailed in the Netherlands as a result which was more than worthwhile.

So this ceremonial visit was at the same time a working visit and I am very grateful to the President of the United States that we got so much of his time and that he devoted so much of his energy and knowledge to this discussion of these problems.

THE PRESIDENT. I would just like to add one thing for all of those who cover the Washington scene. This does mark a special occasion in another sense. We have all, those of us who have been here, have known the Ambassador from the Netherlands to the United States [Carl W. A. Schurmann], have known him and his family, and have realized how much he has contributed to good relations between our two countries and also to the very distinguished ambassadorial corps that we have in this city.

This year I learned that he is retiring from diplomatic service. This is one of his last official appearances. Mr. Ambassador, we thank you for your years of service to your country, to the cause of good relations between our two countries, and we wish you the very best in whatever you undertake.

Ambassadors deserve a little credit for these visits, too.

NOTE: The exchange of remarks began at 12:51 p.m. in the Rose Garden at the White House.

220   Remarks at the Graduation Exercises of the FBI
        National Academy.   *May* 28, 1969

*Mr. Attorney General, Director Hoover,
all of the distinguished guests, members of
the graduating class, Your Excellencies,
the Ambassadors from the foreign nations
who are represented in the graduating
class, and all of the families and friends
of those who are here in the class:*

I am very privileged and honored that
this graduation ceremony is being held
here in the White House, which belongs to
all of the people of America; and I don't
think that there could be any more appropriate use of this great room, the East
Room, where so many ceremonies are
held, than to have law enforcement at its
highest level respected in the way that we
respect it today.

I want to express my appreciation, too,
to Mr. Hoover for giving me an honorary
membership in the FBI and that allows
me to tell a little story which he would
have told, I am sure, if he had not thought
it might be perhaps a bit presumptuous.

But he remembers, and I remember
very well, that in 1937 I graduated from
law school, during the depression years,
just as did the Attorney General. In 1937
when I was graduating from law school,
the Federal Bureau of Investigation then,
as now, was doing some recruiting in the
law schools and, along with three or four
other members of the class, I submitted
an application to become a member of
the FBI and I never heard anything from
that application. [*Laughter*]

Now, years later, after I became Vice
President of the United States, I asked
Mr. Hoover what happened to my application. He did not know that I had submitted one because, after all, there were

many law school graduates in those
depression years, I am sure, that were not
able to be received into the FBI, whatever their qualifications might have been,
because there were more applicants than
there were positions.

So, he said, as he would always do, "I
will check the files." Sure enough, he
found my application. I don't know
whether this part of the story is true or
not, although Mr. Hoover always tells the
truth but, nevertheless, he said that what
had happened was that actually I had
been approved as an agent of the FBI and
that I would have been made a member of
the FBI except for one fact: that the Congress did not appropriate the necessary
funds requested for the Bureau in the
year 1937. [*Laughter*]

I just want to say in Mr. Hoover's presence and in Mr. Mitchell's presence that
that will never happen again.

There is very little that I can add to the
words of the Attorney General on law enforcement and the words of Mr. Hoover,
but I do think that it is appropriate in this
room for me to say very briefly what I
think the Nation feels about this class and
what you represent.

As we consider America at this time in
our history, we know we have problems.
We have the problem of war abroad. We
also have the problem of a great crisis of
respect for law at home.

We have never really had the latter
problem, respect for law, certainly not in
this magnitude, in our history before. And
difficult as it is to find an answer to end
the war abroad, and to keep the peace
abroad, difficult as that problem is, a

problem which is my primary responsibility, perhaps even more difficult is that of establishing and maintaining respect for law at the highest level all over the United States.

We have been doing a lot of thinking about that in this administration. I have been doing a lot of thinking about it because of my own background in the law, and I have talked with the Attorney General and Mr. Hoover at great length about it, as they will tell you.

I do have some observations with respect to that problem that I think are quite appropriate to this occasion.

First, if we are going to have respect for law in the United States, we have to have law that deserves respect.

That means something more than the laws, the written laws on the books, being fair and equitable. That is the responsibility of the Congress, the State legislatures and also the municipal legislative bodies.

But it also means the man who enforces the law. He must be strong, he must be competent, he must be efficient, he must be fair. And that is what the FBI has stood for. That is what law enforcement, as represented by the graduates of this class all over America, I know, has stood for in the past, and will stand for even more in the future.

And so, our problem at this time is to see to it that all over America our laws, the written laws, deserve respect of all Americans, and that those who carry out the law, who have that hard, difficult, grueling, sometimes dangerous task of enforcing the law—that they carry out their responsibilities in a way that deserves respect.

I do not know of any one function or, I should say, any one man or one organiza-

tion that has done more to establish respect for law in the best sense than the Director of the FBI, Mr. Hoover, and the FBI organization.

Now, a further word: During the last presidential campaign, you heard from all of the major candidates discussion of the problem of enforcement of law and respect for law in this Nation. And I am sure that many people in the country may have received the impression that the primary responsibility was at the Federal level.

There is a great deal of responsibility at the Federal level—what a President can do and an Attorney General, the Members of the Congress in the passing of laws, and the Federal courts. But the men in this room know what is really the truth, that is, that 85 percent of the job, as far as enforcement of the law is concerned, is not done by the Federal Government and its agencies, but by local government.

That is what you represent. That is why it is so important that the kind of training that you have received is going to go back all over America and to some other countries as well.

And I think that the fact that this ceremony pays tribute to the men in the city and in the town and in the county and in the State who day by day carries on law enforcement responsibilities is something that the Nation needs to be reminded of.

That allows me to make two other points: The Attorney General referred to the matter of compensation. Compensation for law enforcement officials is inadequate. It is inadequate not in all cities, but in most; not in all towns, but in most.

And when we talk about the men who have these responsibilities, I would strongly urge that all of the local legislative bodies recognize that if we are going to be able to have within our law enforcement bodies the kind of men and the kind of women who can meet the high standards that we expect, the standards that you men represent, it is absolutely essential that they be adequately compensated.

That is one part of the problem. But then there is another part of the problem. And this is something that money can't buy. No matter how well we pay our law enforcement officials, it isn't going to mean much to them unless they also have some respect from the community, from the State, from the Nation for the job that they are doing.

It has become quite fashionable in recent years to look upon the man, the policeman, the sheriff, the representatives of various law enforcement agencies, as a second-class citizen. It has become quite fashionable to downgrade him and every time there is a conflict involving the law on the one side and those charged with breaking the law on the other side, the automatic reaction is to take the side of those who may have been charged with breaking the law.

Now we all know that sometimes one side may be right and sometimes the other side may be right. But we also know that in this country, unless we have not only respect for our laws, but for the men and women who are doing their very best to carry them out fairly and equitably, we are not going to continue to survive as a free country.

As a matter of fact, the greatest guarantee against the emergence of a police state in America is a competent, effective, just police force throughout our Nation. That is what we are talking about.

That is the challenge that the members

of this class have and all of your colleagues across the country.

And that brings me to my final observation: When I sometimes read and hear about criticism of those in the police forces who are doing a fair job—underpaid but, nevertheless, giving it everything that they have, who are doing their very best, and, nevertheless, receive the condemnation of those who are so quick to criticize—I think particularly on a day like this of their families. And I see their wives here, and I see their children.

And I wonder what they must feel when they pick up the papers or look at television and hear law enforcement described in the deriding terms that it is so often described.

What I am not suggesting here is that law enforcement should be above criticism, because it is through criticism that we all do a better job in any particular assignment that we may have. But I am simply saying here to you, the members of this class, to the members of your families, and to the American people: Let us, whenever our law enforcement officials are wrong, criticize them so that they may improve and do what is right.

But when they are right, when they are protecting our society from those who would injure it or destroy it or endanger it, let us back them up. Let us give them the encouragement. Let us pay them adequately.

But above everything else, let us give them respect, respect that money cannot buy, but which they deserve by what they are doing.

Thank you.

NOTE: The President spoke at 3:42 p.m. in the East Room at the White House before presenting diplomas to 100 graduates of the 83d session of the Academy.

An announcement of the ceremony and a list of the graduates are printed in the Weekly Compilation of Presidential Documents (vol. 5,

pp. 670 and 769).

The text of the remarks by Attorney General Mitchell was also released.

221 Statement Announcing the Creation of the Environmental Quality Council and the Citizens' Advisory Committee on Environmental Quality. *May 29, 1969*

"THE CONSERVATION of our natural resources and their proper use constitute the fundamental problem which underlies almost every other problem of our national life," Theodore Roosevelt said in 1907. When men talked about conservation in his time, they usually singled out the wild lands, plant and animal life, and valuable minerals, for in these areas they saw the threat of scarcity. Resources such as the air or the water or the countryside itself were of less concern, for the supply and the quality of such things seemed invulnerable.

I am sure that Roosevelt and his associates of sixty and more years ago would be most surprised if they knew that in our time technological development threatens the availability of good air and good water, of open space and even quiet neighborhoods. Yet that is exactly what is happening. Each day we receive new evidence of the declining quality of the American environment.

Because the quality of American environment is threatened as it has not been threatened before in our history, I am creating today, by Executive order, the Environmental Quality Council. This new body will be a Cabinet-level advisory group which will provide the focal point for this administration's efforts to protect all of our natural resources.

The Council, the structure of which in some respects parallels that of the National Security Council and the Urban Affairs Council, will have as its Executive Secretary the Science Adviser to the President, Dr. Lee A. DuBridge. My Executive order also creates a 15-member Citizens' Advisory Committee on Environmental Quality, which will be chaired by Laurance S. Rockefeller.

I am asking the new Council, with the assistance of the Citizens' Advisory Committee, to examine the full range of variables which affect environmental quality. I expect the group to review existing policies and programs and to suggest ways of improving them. Its members must project the impact of new technologies and encourage scientific developments which will help us protect our resources.

I am hopeful that the Environmental Quality Council will foster greater cooperation in this problem area between our Government and the governments of other nations, between the various levels of American government, and between governmental and relevant nongovernmental organizations.

Finally, I would suggest that this new body must anticipate new problems even as it focuses on present ones. It is not enough that it provide answers to the questions we are asking today. It must also pose the new questions which will face us tomorrow.

The deterioration of the environment is in large measure the result of our inability to keep pace with progress. We have become victims of our own technological genius. But I am confident that the same energy and skill which gave rise to these problems can also be marshaled for the purpose of conquering them. Together we have damaged the environment and together we can improve it.

As I said during last fall's campaign: "We need a high standard of living, but we also need a high quality of life. . . . We need a strategy of quality for the seventies to match the strategy of quantity of the past." I am pleased to announce the creation of the Environmental Quality Council, for I believe it will provide us with that strategy and will give us the means for implementing it.

NOTE: Executive Order 11472 established the Environmental Quality Council and the Citizens' Advisory Committee on Environmental Quality.

Also released was a news briefing by Dr. Lee A. DuBridge, Science Adviser to the President and Director of the Office of Science and Technology, and Dr. John L. Buckley, staff member of the Science Advisory Committee, concerning the establishment of the Environmental Quality Council.

An announcement concerning a report to the Council on university contributions in solving environmental problems and an announcement of a review by the Council of a report by the Commission on Pesticides on the regulation of pesticides are printed in the Weekly Compilation of Presidential Documents (vol. 5, pp. 1558, 1632).

The statement was released at Key Biscayne, Fla.

222   Statement About Teacher Remembrance Day.   *May* 31, 1969

NO GROUP is more deserving of national recognition and gratitude than America's teachers.

By your selfless dedication to our sons and daughters in classrooms across the country, you help ensure a successful future by cultivating our most precious resources, and by strengthening the educational system which equips young Americans to become good citizens and leaders in their communities.

Teachers are among the most critically needed, yet least celebrated, members of our society. So it is most fitting that Teacher Remembrance Day provides us the opportunity to recognize the vital contributions you make to our legacy and lives throughout each school year.

I know that Americans everywhere join me in offering special congratulations to the admirable men and women who, with patience and perseverance, develop and direct the talents of America to their fullest potential.

Both individually and as members of a most noble, rewarding profession, you enrich our Nation more than any of us can ever say. And although there is no adequate measure for the daily good you do, I hope that you may always share the satisfaction and joy that accompany a lifetime of service to others.

NOTE: The statement was released at Key Biscayne, Fla.

223 Statement on Proposals Concerning the Office of Economic Opportunity. *June 2, 1969*

IN A MESSAGE to Congress on February 19, I stated that "the blight of poverty requires priority attention," and pledged a "searching examination of how best to marshal the resources available to the Federal Government for combatting it."

The examination already has produced a series of concrete actions and recommendations. Among them:

—a tax reform that would exempt those in the lowest income brackets entirely from Federal income taxes,

—an expanded campaign against hunger and malnutrition,

—revision and improvement of the Model Cities program,

—new efforts for the encouragement of minority business enterprise,

—the beginning of a new Federal effort to assist and encourage voluntary activity aimed at helping the needy.

Another major step forward was taken last week, with the swearing in of Donald Rumsfeld as the new Director of the Office of Economic Opportunity. I have every confidence that Mr. Rumsfeld will proceed with energy and imagination in strengthening OEO, in terms of both management and programs.

In doing so, he will have my full support. I believe deeply in the importance of an effective antipoverty effort, and I share his determination to see this effort succeed.

Toward this end, I will request an extension of the authorization for OEO appropriations from June 30, 1969, to June 30, 1971; and I will ask that the Economic Opportunity Act of 1964 be extended from June 30, 1970, to June 30, 1972.

This represents a change from my earlier intention. In my February 19 message, I stated that I planned to ask for a 1-year extension of the authorization for OEO appropriations, and I indicated that by the end of the current fiscal year I would send to the Congress a comprehensive proposal for the future of the antipoverty program.

I have now concluded, however, that a 2-year extension would provide a better framework within which the necessary improvements in the antipoverty program can be made. This will not preclude asking for legislative changes to take effect before the act's expiration, but it will establish a stable environment in which those changes can be considered.

A 2-year extension will have a number of advantages. From a management standpoint, by allowing longer-range planning it will make possible a more orderly and efficient allocation of funds. From a recruiting standpoint, it will guarantee to those whose talents are needed that the Nation's commitment is a continuing one. Furthermore, an innovative agency has a special need for both continuity and flexibility. It is in the nature of experiments that some succeed, and some fail; a 2-year extension will give greater assurance to those whose function it is to experiment that even though a particular program may fail, the lessons learned will be put to use, and that the larger effort of which it is a part will continue.

We already have set in motion a number of changes.

In my February 19 message, I indicated that I believed the primary role of the

Office of Economic Opportunity should be innovative: to search out new knowledge and initiate new programs, serving as an "incubator" for experimental efforts. I also made clear that I would insist on more rigorous management standards, and I announced the delegation of the Job Corps to the Department of Labor and of Head Start to the Department of Health, Education, and Welfare. The effective date of these delegations will be July 1, 1969. They represent program funds of over $500 million, approximately one-fourth of the OEO budget. The delegations of operating responsibility for Head Start and the Job Corps will free OEO to concentrate more fully on its innovative role.

Under the leadership of the new OEO Director, a comprehensive review and analysis of antipoverty efforts will continue during the coming months. Its purpose will be not only to evaluate existing programs and improve their operation, but also to determine what new programs

should be initiated. Many of the improvements most immediately needed fall within the management authority of the present law. For example, planning procedures can be improved, program analysis strengthened, internal reorganization accomplished, and more rigorous management and fiscal controls instituted. New experimental programs can also be launched.

If we are to make lasting, significant headway against poverty, there still is a great deal to be learned about what works and what does not. This administration is committed to search for that knowledge, and to use it. We are committed to the continuation of an agency whose special concern is the poor; and we are determined to make the Nation's antipoverty efforts function more efficiently and serve the poor more effectively.

NOTE: Provisions incorporating the President's proposals were enacted in the Economic Opportunity Amendments of 1969 (Public Law 91–177, 83 Stat. 827).

224 Address at the Dedication of the Karl E. Mundt Library at General Beadle State College, Madison, South Dakota. *June 3, 1969*

Senator and Mrs. Mundt, Governor and Mrs. Farrar, all of the distinguished guests on the platform, and all of the very gracious guests in the audience:

I first want to begin with a personal note, responding to the very gracious remarks that have been made to me and about me by the Governor and by Karl Mundt, and, as I respond to them I want you to know that I feel very much at home here.

I feel at home here because I, too, grew up in a small town. I attended a

small college, about the size of this one; and when I was in law school, at a much larger university, one of the ways that I helped work my way through that law school was to work in the law school library.

So I feel very much at home here before a great, new library, on the campus of a small college which is growing larger, and in a small town in the heartland of America.

I would like to relate what I have said a little more, perhaps, closely to this State.

425

I suppose the best thing I could say would be that I was born in South Dakota. I was not. I was born in California. I could also say, possibly, that Mrs. Nixon was born in South Dakota. She was not. She was born in Nevada.

But I can go very close to that, because my wife's mother and father, Mr. and Mrs. Thomas [William] Ryan, were married and lived in their early years, before they moved to Nevada, in Lee, South Dakota. So we have a South Dakota background.

I should also point out that in the small estate that her father left was a mining claim in the Black Hills of South Dakota. We paid taxes on that in California for many, many years, and so we were South Dakota taxpayers.

No gold was ever discovered there, but when I returned to South Dakota as a candidate in 1960, I was presented with some Black Hills gold cuff links, and I am wearing them today to show my relationship to South Dakota.

Now an occasion like this does call for more than the usual informal remarks which, I think, are usually quite welcomed by an audience.

This is a solemn occasion. It is the beginning of a new institution as part of a larger institution.

I think as we dedicate this beautiful, new library, that this is the time and place to speak of some very basic things in American life. It is the time, because we find our fundamental values under bitter and even violent attack all over America. And it is the place, because so much that is basic to America is represented right here where we stand.

Opportunity for all is represented here.

This is a small college, not rich and famous like Yale and Harvard, and not a vast State university like Michigan and Berkeley. But for almost 90 years it has served the people of South Dakota, opening doors of opportunity for thousands of deserving young men and women. Like hundreds of other fine small colleges across this Nation, General Beadle State College—soon to be known as Dakota State College—has offered a chance to people who might otherwise not have had a chance for an education. And as one who had such a chance at a small college, I know what that means.

The pioneer spirit is represented here, and the progress that has shaped our heritage. Because here in South Dakota we still can sense the daring that converted a raw frontier into part of the vast heartland of America. The vitality of thought is represented here.

A college library is a place of living ideas; a place where timeless truths are collected to become the raw materials of discovery. In addition, the Karl E. Mundt Library will house the papers of a wise and dedicated man who for 30 years has been at the center of public events. Thus, more than most, this is a library of both thought and action, containing and combining the wisdom of past ages with a uniquely personal record of the present time.

So today, as we dedicate this place of ideas, I think we should reflect on some of the values we have inherited and which are now under challenge.

We live in a deeply troubled and profoundly unsettled time. Drugs and crime, campus revolts, racial discord, draft resistance—on every hand we find old standards violated, old values discarded, old precepts ignored. A vocal minority of our young people are opting out of the process by which a civilization maintains its continuity: the passing on of values

426

from one generation to the next. Old and young across the Nation shout across a chasm of misunderstanding, and the louder they shout, the broader the chasm becomes.

As a result of all this, our institutions in America today are undergoing what may be the severest challenge of our history. I do not speak of the physical challenge, the force and threats of force that have racked our cities and now our colleges. Force can be contained. We have the power to strike back if need be, and we can prevail. The Nation has survived other attempts at insurrection. We can survive this one. It has not been a lack of civil power, but the reluctance of a free people to employ it, that so often has stayed the hand of authorities faced with confrontation.

But the challenge I speak of today is deeper—the challenge to our values and to the moral base of the authority that sustains those values.

At the outset, let me draw a very clear distinction. A great deal of today's debate about "values," or about "morality," centers on what essentially are private values and personal codes: patterns of dress and appearance, sexual mores, religious practices, the uses to which a person intends to put his own life.

Now these are immensely important, but they are not the values I mean to discuss here today.

My concern and our concern today is not with the length of a person's hair, but with his conduct in relation to the community; not with what he wears, but with his impact on the process by which a free society governs itself.

I speak not of private morality, but of public morality—and of "morality" in its broadest sense, as a set of standards by which the community chooses to judge itself.

Some critics call ours an "immoral" society because they disagree with its policies, or they refuse to obey its laws because they claim that those laws have no moral basis. Yet the structure of our laws has rested from the beginning on a foundation of moral purpose. That moral purpose embodies what is, above all, a deeply humane set of values—rooted in a profound respect for the individual, for the integrity of his person, for the dignity of his humanity.

At first glance, there is something homely and unexciting about basic values as we have long believed in them. And we feel apologetic about espousing them; even the profoundest truths become clichés with repetition. But these truths can be like sleeping giants: slow to rouse, but magnificent in their strength.

So today let us look at some of those values—so familiar now, and yet once so revolutionary in America and in the world:

— liberty, recognizing that liberties can only exist in balance, with the liberty of each stopping at that point at which it would infringe the liberty of another;

— freedom of conscience, meaning that each person has the freedom of his own conscience, and therefore none has the right to dictate the conscience of his neighbor;

— justice, recognizing that true justice is impartial and that no man can be judge in his own cause;

— human dignity, a dignity that inspires pride, is rooted in self-reliance, and provides the satisfaction of being a useful and respected member of the community;

427

—concern, concern for the disadvantaged and dispossessed, but a concern that neither panders nor patronizes;

—the right to participate in public decisions, which carries with it the duty to abide by those decisions when reached, recognizing that no one can have his own way all the time;

—human fulfillment, in the sense not of unlimited license, but of maximum opportunity;

—the right to grow, to reach upward, to be all that we can become, in a system that rewards enterprise, encourages innovation, and honors excellence.

In essence, these are aspects of freedom. They inhere in the concept of freedom; they aim at extending freedom; they celebrate the uses of freedom. They are not new, but they are as timeless and as timely as the human spirit, because they are rooted in the human spirit.

Our basic values concern not only what we seek, but how we seek it.

Freedom is a condition; it is also a process. And the process is essential to the freedom itself.

We have a Constitution that sets certain limits on what government can do, but that allows wide discretion within those limits. We have a system of divided powers, of checks and balances, of periodic elections, all of which are designed to insure that the majority has a chance to work its will but not to override the rights of the minority, or to infringe the rights of the individual.

What this adds up to is a democratic process, carefully constructed, stringently guarded. Now it is not perfect. No system could be. But it has served the Nation well, and nearly two centuries of growth and change testify to its strength and adaptability.

They testify, also, to the fact that avenues of peaceful change do exist in America. And those who can make a persuasive case for changes they want can achieve them through this orderly process.

To challenge a particular policy is one thing; to challenge the government's right to set that policy is another—for this denies the process of freedom itself.

Lately, however, a great many people have become impatient with this democratic process. Some of the more extreme even argue, with a rather curious logic, that there is no majority, because the majority has no right to hold opinions that they disagree with. Scorning persuasion they prefer coercion. Awarding themselves what they call a higher morality, they try to bully authorities into yielding to their "demands." On college campuses they draw support from faculty members who should know better; in the larger community, they find the usual apologists ready to excuse any tactic in the name of "progress."

It should be self-evident that this sort of self-righteous moral arrogance has no place in a free community in America, because it denies the most fundamental of all the values we hold—respect for the rights of others. This principle of mutual respect is the keystone of the entire structure of ordered liberty that makes freedom possible.

The student who invades an administration building, roughs up the dean, rifles the files, and issues "nonnegotiable demands" may have some of his demands met by a permissive university administration. But the greater his "victory," the more he will have undermined the security of his own rights. In a free society, the rights of none are secure unless the rights of all are respected. It is precisely the structure of law and custom that he has chosen to violate—the process of freedom—by which the rights of all are protected.

We have long considered our colleges and universities citadels of freedom, where the rule of reason prevails. Now both the process of freedom and the rule of reason are under assault. At the same time, our colleges are under pressure to reduce our educational standards, in the misguided belief that this would promote "opportunity."

Instead of attempting to raise the lagging students up to meet the college standards, the cry now is to lower the standards to meet the students. This is the old, familiar, self-indulgent cry for the easy way. It debases the integrity of the educational process because there is no easy way to excellence, no shortcut to the truth, no magic wand that can produce a trained and disciplined mind without the hard discipline of learning. To yield to these demands would weaken the institution; more importantly, it would cheat the student of what he comes to college for, a good education.

Now, no group, as a group, should be more zealous defenders of the integrity of academic standards and the rule of reason in academic life than the faculties of our great colleges and universities. But if the teacher simply follows the loudest voices, parrots the latest slogan, yields to unreasonable demands, he will have won not the respect but the contempt of his students; and he will deserve that contempt. Students have some rights. They have a right to guidance, to leadership, and direction; they also have a right to expect their teachers to listen and to be reasonable, but also to stand for something—and most especially, to stand for the rule of reason against the rule of force.

Our colleges and universities have their weaknesses. Some have become too impersonal, or too ingrown, and curricula have lagged. But let us never forget that for all its faults, the American system of higher education is the best in this whole imperfect world, and it provides in the United States today a better education for more students of all economic levels than ever before anywhere in the history of the world.

And I submit this is no small achievement. We should be proud of it. We should defend it and we should never apologize for it.

Often the worst mischief is done in the name of the best cause. In our zeal for instant reform we should be careful not to destroy our educational standards and our educational system along with it, and not to undermine the process of freedom on which all else rests.

The process of freedom will be less threatened in America, however, if we pay more heed to one of the great cries of our young people today. I speak now of their demand for honesty: intellectual honesty, personal honesty, public honesty. Much of what seems to be revolt is really little more than this: an attempt to strip away sham and pretense, to puncture illusion, to get down to the basic nub of truth.

We should welcome this. We have seen too many patterns of deception in our lives:

—in political life, impossible promises;

—in advertising, extravagant claims;

—in business, shady deals.

In personal life, we all have witnessed deceits that ranged from the "little white lie" to moral hypocrisy; from cheating on income taxes to bilking the insurance company.

In public life, we have seen reputations destroyed by smear, and gimmicks paraded as panaceas. We have heard shrill voices of hate shouting lies and sly voices of malice twisting facts.

Even in intellectual life, we too often have seen logical gymnastics performed to justify a pet theory, and refusal to accept facts that fail to support it.

Of course, absolute honesty, on the other hand, would be ungenerous. Courtesy sometimes compels us to welcome the unwanted visitor, and kindness leads us to compliment the homely girl on how pretty she looks. But in our public discussions we sorely need a kind of honesty that too often has been lacking: the honesty of straight talk, a careful concern with the gradations of truth, a frank recognition of the limits of our knowledge about the problems we have to deal with. We have long demanded financial integrity in private life. We now need the most rigorous kind of intellectual integrity in public debate.

Unless we can find a way to speak plainly and truly, unselfconsciously, about the facts of public life, we may find that our grip on the forces of history is too loose to control our own destiny.

The honesty of straight talk leads us to the conclusion that some of our recent social experiments have worked and some have failed and that most have achieved something—but far less than their advance billing promised. This same honesty is concerned not with assigning blame, but with discovering what lessons can be drawn from that experience in order to design better programs next time. Perhaps the goals were unattainable; perhaps the means were inadequate; perhaps the program was based on an unrealistic assessment of human nature.

We can learn these lessons only to the extent that we can be candid with one another. We have and we face enormously complex choices. In approaching these, confrontation is no substitute for consultation; and passionate concern gets us nowhere without dispassionate analysis. More fundamentally, our structure of values depends on mutual faith, and faith depends on truth.

The values we cherish are sustained by a fabric of mutual self-restraint woven of ordinary civil decency, respect for the rights of others, respect for the laws of the community, and respect for the democratic process of orderly change. The purpose of these restraints, I submit, is not to protect an "establishment," but to establish the protection of liberty; not to prevent change, but to insure that change reflects the public will and respects the rights of all.

This process is our most precious resource as a nation, and it depends on public acceptance, public understanding, and public faith.

Whether our values are maintained depends ultimately not on government, but on people.

A nation can only be as great as the people want it to be.

A nation can only be as free as its people insist that it be.

A nation's laws are only as strong as the

people's will to see them enforced.

A nation's freedoms are only as secure as the people's determination to see them maintained.

And a nation's values are only as lasting as the ability of each generation to pass them on to the next.

We often have a tendency to turn away from the familiar because it is familiar, and turn to the new because it is new.

To those intoxicated with the romance of violent revolution, the continuing revolution of democracy may sometimes seem quite unexciting. But no system has ever liberated the spirits of so many so fully. Nothing has ever "turned on" man's energies, his imagination, his unfettered creativity, the way the ideal of freedom has. We can be proud that we have that legacy and that we celebrate it today.

Now there are some who see America's vast wealth and protest that this has made us materialistic. But we should not be apologetic about our abundance. We should not fall into the easy trap of confusing the production of things with the worship of things. We produce abundantly, but our values turn not on what we have but on what we believe.

And what we believe very simply is this: We believe in liberty, in decency, and the process of freedom. On these beliefs we rest our pride as a nation. In these beliefs we rest our hopes for the future. And by our fidelity to the process of freedom we can assure to ourselves and our posterity the blessings of freedom.

I have spoken today of these basic values on this occasion because of the man we honor and also because of the place in which I stand. I know that many in this audience have shared the concern that I have shared, that in recent years, due to the fact that the spotlight has been turned on some public officials who have not reached the standard of integrity that we think they should have reached, we have tended to lose faith in the integrity of all of our institutions.

Let me, as one who for almost a quarter of a century has had the opportunity to meet Governors and Congressmen and Senators and State legislators and judges and public officials all over this land—as a matter of fact, I have probably met more than any living American—just let me say something based on my own observation.

There are men, some, who fail to meet the standards of integrity which should be met by a public servant, but I want this audience to know that as I look at the men who served in public life during my own generation, the great majority of Congressmen and Senators and Governors and State legislators and mayors and judges are honest, dedicated, decent men. And Karl Mundt represents that kind of honesty, decency, and honor. His public life stands for these values about which I have spoken. I am proud to have known him for 22 years. I am proud to have had his friendship and support in victory and also in defeat. And I am proud today to join with you in honoring him by dedicating in his name a library which will preserve those values for which and about which he has spoken so eloquently in 30 years of public life.

NOTE: The President spoke at 2:57 p.m. at the open-air dedication of the Karl E. Mundt Library before an audience of approximately 10,000 persons.

Frank Farrar was Governor of South Dakota.

225   Address at the Air Force Academy Commencement Exercises in Colorado Springs, Colorado.   *June 4,* 1969

General Moorman, Governor Love, Senator Allott, Senator Dominick, General McConnell, Secretary Seamans, all the distinguished guests on the platform, members of the graduating class, and this great audience here in Falcon Stadium:

Before addressing the members of the graduating class, I would like to be permitted a personal word to the people of Colorado and to the people of this city. I want to thank you for the very warm and gracious welcome you gave to me and the members of our family.

I well remember the conversations that I had with General Eisenhower in the months before he died. He often reminisced about the past and among his fondest memories were his visits to Colorado. These were some of the happiest days of his life.

Yesterday when we arrived in Colorado Springs, we stepped out of the aircraft; we breathed this wonderfully fresh air; we looked off across to the mountains 50 miles away; and as we stood there we knew what he meant when he spoke of Colorado, its people, and also the climate—everything that all of you who live here know and love so much.

I should just like to give you one impression that shows you there is some continuity in history. Dwight David Eisenhower II, the grandson of General Eisenhower, and his namesake, as he saw this beautiful country and looked to the mountains off to the distance, said, "Gee, this is great country." I want you to know that I agree, and I congratulate the Air Force for having the good judgment to locate the Air Force Academy here in Colorado Springs.

One other personal note: I had the opportunity before coming to this stadium to take a tour of some of the campus facilities and particularly the chapel. Now, there has been some controversy about that chapel. This is the first time that I have seen it. I am not an architectural expert, but I think it is magnificent, and I think you can be very proud of that chapel at the Air Force Academy.

Now, if I could address the members of the graduating class. For each of you, and your parents, and your countrymen, this is a moment of quiet pride. After years of study and training, you have earned the right to be saluted.

But you are beginning your careers at a difficult time in military life. On a fighting front, you are asked to be ready to make unlimited sacrifice in a limited war. On the home front, you are under attack from those who question the need for a strong national defense, and indeed see a danger in the power of the defenders.

You are entering the military service of your country when the Nation's potential adversaries abroad have never been stronger and when your critics at home have never been more numerous.

It is open season on the Armed Forces. Military programs are ridiculed as needless if not deliberate waste. The military profession is derided in some of the so-called best circles of America. Patriotism is considered by some to be a backward fetish of the uneducated and the unsophisticated. Nationalism is hailed and applauded as a panacea for the ills of every nation—except the United States of America.

This paradox of military power is a

symptom of something far deeper that is stirring in our body politic. It goes beyond the dissent about the war in Vietnam. It goes behind the fear of the "military-industrial complex."

The underlying questions are really these: What is America's role in the world? What are the responsibilities of a great nation toward protecting freedom beyond its shores? Can we ever be left in peace if we do not actively assume the burden of keeping the peace?

When great questions are posed, fundamental differences of opinion come into focus. It serves no purpose to gloss over these differences, or to try to pretend that they are mere matters of degree. Because there is one school of thought that holds that the road to understanding with the Soviet Union and Communist China lies through a downgrading of our own alliances and what amounts to a unilateral reduction of our arms in order to demonstrate our "good faith."

They believe that we can be conciliatory and accommodating only if we do not have the strength to be otherwise. They believe that America will be able to deal with the possibility of peace only when we are unable to cope with the threat of war.

Those who think that way have grown weary of the weight of free world leadership that fell upon us in the wake of World War II. They argue that we—that the United States is as much responsible for the tensions in the world as the adversaries we face.

They assert that the United States is blocking the road to peace by maintaining its military strength at home and its defenses abroad. If we would only reduce our forces, they contend, tensions would disappear and the chances for peace would brighten.

America's powerful military presence on the world scene, they believe, makes peace abroad improbable and peace at home impossible.

Now we should never underestimate the appeal of the isolationist school of thought. Their slogans are simplistic and powerful: "Charity begins at home. Let's first solve our problems at home and then we can deal with the problems of the world."

This simple formula touches a responsive chord with many an overburdened taxpayer. It would be easy, easy for a President of the United States to buy some popularity by going along with the new isolationists. But I submit to you that it would be disastrous for our Nation and the world.

I hold a totally different view of the world, and I come to a different conclusion about the direction America must take.

Imagine for a moment, if you will, what would happen to this world if America were to become a dropout in assuming the responsibility for defending peace and freedom in the world. As every world leader knows, and as even the most outspoken critics of America would admit, the rest of the world would live in terror.

Because if America were to turn its back on the world, there would be peace that would settle over this planet, but it would be the kind of peace that suffocated freedom in Czechoslovakia.

The danger to us has changed, but it has not vanished. We must revitalize our alliances, not abandon them.

We must rule out unilateral disarmament, because in the real world it wouldn't work. If we pursue arms control

433

as an end in itself, we will not achieve our end. The adversaries in the world are not in conflict because they are armed. They are armed because they are in conflict, and have not yet learned peaceful ways to resolve their conflicting national interests.

The aggressors of this world are not going to give the United States a period of grace in which to put our domestic house in order—just as the crises within our society cannot be put on a back burner until we resolve the problem of Vietnam.

The most successful solutions that we can possibly imagine for our domestic programs will be meaningless if we are not around to enjoy them. Nor can we conduct a successful peace policy abroad if our society is at war with itself at home.

There is no advancement for Americans at home in a retreat from the problems of the world. I say that America has a vital national interest in world stability, and no other nation can uphold that interest for us.

We stand at a crossroad in our history. We shall reaffirm our destiny for greatness or we shall choose instead to withdraw into ourselves. The choice will affect far more than our foreign policy; it will determine the quality of our lives.

A nation needs many qualities, but it needs faith and confidence above all. Skeptics do not build societies; the idealists are the builders. Only societies that believe in themselves can rise to their challenges. Let us not, then, pose a false choice between meeting our responsibilities abroad and meeting the needs of our people at home. We shall meet both or we shall meet neither.

That is why my disagreement with the skeptics and the isolationists is fundamental. They have lost the vision indispensable to great leadership. They observe the problems that confront us; they measure our resources and then they despair. When the first vessels set out from Europe for the New World these men would have weighed the risks and they would have stayed behind. When the colonists on the eastern seaboard started across the Appalachians to the unknown reaches of the Ohio Valley, these men would have counted the costs and they would have stayed behind.

Our current exploration of space makes the point vividly; here is testimony to man's vision and to man's courage. The journey of the astronauts is more than a technical achievement; it is a reaching-out of the human spirit. It lifts our sights; it demonstrates that magnificent conceptions can be made real.

They inspire us and at the same time they teach us true humility. What could bring home to us more the limitations of the human scale than the hauntingly beautiful picture of our earth seen from the moon?

When the first man stands on the moon next month every American will stand taller because of what he has done, and we should be proud of this magnificent achievement.

We will know then that every man achieves his own greatness by reaching out beyond himself, and so it is with nations. When a nation believes in itself—as Athenians did in their Golden Age, as Italians did in the Renaissance—that nation can perform miracles. Only when a nation means something to itself can it mean something to others.

That is why I believe a resurgence of

American idealism can bring about a modern miracle, and that modern miracle is a world order of peace and justice.

I know that every member of this graduating class is, in that sense, an idealist.

However, I must warn you that in the years to come you may hear your commitment to the American responsibility in the world derided as a form of militarism. It is important that you recognize that strawman issue for what it is, the outward sign of a desire by some to turn America inward and to have America turn away from greatness. I am not speaking about those reponsible critics who reveal waste and inefficiency in our defense establishment, who demand clear answers on procurement problems, who want to make sure new weapons systems will truly add to our defense. On the contrary, you should be in the vanguard of that movement. Nor do I speak of those with sharp eyes and sharp pencils who are examining our post-Vietnam planning with other pressing national priorities in mind. I count myself as one of those.

But as your Commander in Chief, I want to relay to you as future officers of our Armed Forces some of my thoughts on these great issues of national moment.

I worked closely with President Eisenhower for 8 years. I know what he meant when he said: ". . . we must guard against the acquisition of unwarranted influence, whether sought or unsought, by the military-industrial complex."

Many people conveniently forget that he followed that warning with another: ". . . we must also be alert to the equal and opposite danger that public policy could itself become the captive of a scientific-technological elite."

We sometimes forget that in that same farewell address, President Eisenhower spoke of the need for national security. He said: "A vital element in keeping the peace is our military establishment. Our arms must be mighty, ready for instant action, so that no potential aggressor may be tempted to risk his own destruction." [1]

I say to you, my fellow Americans, let us never forget those wise words of one of America's greatest leaders.

The American defense establishment should never be a sacred cow, but on the other hand, the American military should never be anybody's scapegoat.

America's wealth is enormous, but it is not limitless. Every dollar available in the Federal Government has been taken from the American people in taxes, and a responsible government has a duty to be prudent when it spends the people's money. There is no more justification for wasting money on unnecessary military hardware than there is for wasting it on unwarranted social programs.

There can be no question that we should not spend unnecessarily for defense. But we must also not confuse our priorities.

The question, I submit, in defense spending is a very simple one: "How much is necessary?" The President of the United States is the man charged with making that judgment. After a complete review of our foreign and defense policies I have submitted requests to the Congress for military appropriations. Some of these are admittedly controversial. These requests represent the minimum I believe essential for the United States to

---

[1] "Public Papers of the Presidents, Dwight D. Eisenhower, 1960–61," Item 421.

meet its current and long-range obligations to itself and to the free world. I have asked only for those programs and those expenditures that I believe are necessary to guarantee the security of this country and to honor our obligations. I will bear the responsibility for those judgments. I do not consider my recommendations infallible. But if I have made a mistake, I pray that it is on the side of too much and not too little. If we do too much it will cost us our money. If we do too little, it may cost us our lives.

Mistakes in military policy today can be irretrievable. Time lost in this age of science can never be regained. America had months in order to prepare and to catch up in order to wage World War I. We had months and even years in order to catch up so we could play a role in winning World War II. When a war can be decided in 20 minutes, the nation that is behind will have no time to catch up.

I say: Let America never fall behind in maintaining the defenses necessary for the strength of this Nation.

I have no choice in my decisions but to come down on the side of security, because history has dealt harshly with those nations who have taken the other course.

So, in that spirit, to the members of this graduating class, let me offer this credo for the defenders of our Nation:

I believe that we must balance our need for survival as a nation with our need for survival as a people. Americans, soldiers and civilians, must remember that defense is not an end in itself; it is a way of holding fast to the deepest values known to civilized men.

I believe that our defense establishment will remain the servants of our national policy of bringing about peace in

the world and that those in any way connected with the military must scrupulously avoid even the appearance of becoming the master of that policy.

I believe that every man in uniform is a citizen first and a serviceman second, and that we must resist any attempt to isolate or separate the defenders from the defended. So you can see that in this regard, those who agitate for the removal of the ROTC [Reserve Officers' Training Corps] from college campuses contribute to an unwanted militarism.

I believe that the basis for decisions on defense spending must be "What do we do; what do we need for our security?" and not "What will this mean for business and employment?" The Defense Department must never be considered as a modern WPA [Work Projects Administration]. There are far better ways for government to help insure a sound prosperity and high employment.

I feel that moderation has a moral significance only in those who have another choice. The weak can only plead. Magnanimity and restraint gain moral meaning coming from the strong.

I believe that defense decisions must be made on the hard realities of the offensive capabilities of our potential adversaries, and not on the fervent hopes about their intentions. With Thomas Jefferson, we can prefer "the flatteries of hope" to the gloom of despair, but we cannot survive in the real world if we plan our defense in a dream world.

I believe we must take risks for peace—but calculated risks, not foolish risks. We shall not trade our defenses for a disarming smile or charming words. We are prepared for new initiatives in the control of arms in the context of other specific moves to reduce tensions around the world.

I believe that America is not going to become a "garrison state," or a "welfare state," or a "police state"—simply because the American people will defend our values from those forces, external or internal, that would challenge or erode them.

And I believe this above all: That this Nation shall continue to be a source of world leadership, a source of freedom's strength, in creating a just world order that will bring an end to war.

Members of the graduating class and your colleagues in the Academy, a President shares a special bond with the men and women in the Nation's Armed Forces. He feels that bond strongly at moments like these, facing all of you who have pledged your lives, your fortunes, and your sacred honor to the service of your country. He feels that bond most strongly when he presents the Medal of Honor to an 8-year-old boy who will never see his father again. Because of that bond, let me say this to you:

In the past generation, since 1941, this Nation has paid for 14 years of peace with 14 years of war. The American war dead of this generation has been far greater than all of the preceding generations in America's history. In terms of human suffering, this has been the costliest generation in the two centuries of our history.

Perhaps this is why my generation is so determined to pass on a different legacy. We want to redeem that sacrifice. We want to be remembered, not as the generation that suffered in war, but as the generation that was tempered in its fire for a great purpose: to make the kind of peace that the next generation will be able to keep.

This is a challenge worthy of the idealism which I know motivates every man who will receive his diploma today.

I am proud to have served in the Armed Forces of this Nation in a war which ended before the members of this class were born.

It is my deepest hope and my belief that each of you will be able to look back on your military career with pride, not because of the wars in which you have fought, but because of the peace and freedom which your service will make possible for America and the world.

NOTE: The President spoke at 9:52 a.m. in Falcon Stadium at the Air Force Academy in Colorado Springs, Colo. In his opening words he referred to Lt. Gen. Thomas S. Moorman, Superintendent, U.S. Air Force Academy; Governor John A. Love, Senator Gordon Allott, and Senator Peter H. Dominick, all of Colorado; Gen. John P. McConnell, Chief of Staff of the U.S. Air Force; and Secretary of the Air Force Robert C. Seamans, Jr.

On the same day the White House Press Office released an advance text of the President's remarks.

226   Declaration of Amnesty for Air Force Academy Cadets.   *June 4, 1969*

WHEREAS, it is customary and traditional that a visiting Head of State at the United States Air Force Academy grant reprieve to those cadets who unfortunately are required to perform extra duty or suffer punishment for violation of United States Air Force Academy regulations;

And whereas, it is now desired that

amnesty be granted on the occasion of this state visit to the United States Air Force Academy;

Therefore, I do proclaim amnesty for all cadets who have committed minor violations of United States Air Force Academy regulations.

RICHARD NIXON

NOTE: The declaration was released at Colorado Springs, Colo.

227   Remarks Introducing Donald E. Johnson, Nominee for Administrator of Veterans Affairs.   *June* 5, 1969

Ladies and gentlemen:

We first want to welcome the members of the press to California, those of you who are traveling with us. This is our first appearance here at what will be the summer White House in August.

We will have a rather full schedule, both today and tomorrow, and during the month of August we will have, for the press, a schedule which will be the same intensity of the kind you would have in Washington, D.C.

The purpose of this meeting today is to introduce to the members of the press the man whom I have nominated for the Director of the Veterans Administration.

This agency, as all of you know, is the largest of the independent agencies, with a budget of over $7 million a year. I suppose it could be said that of all the independent agencies—and frankly, you could include a number of Cabinet positions as well—there is none that has a greater impact on more Americans than does the Veterans Administration, because the veteran population from World War I, World War II, Korea, and now Vietnam, runs into the millions; and the Veterans Administration has the primary responsibility for dealing with the needs of all veterans.

In selecting Mr. Johnson, I wanted a man who, first, was a veteran, and therefore knew the problems of veterans; a man, second, who had the business experience which would qualify him to handle the immense administrative problems involved in the Veterans Administration; and third, a man who would administer this agency without regard to any partisan considerations.

Don Johnson meets the test in all respects. He has a distinguished record in World War II. He is a former Commander of the American Legion. He has the business background which qualifies him for administration, and he has a deep devotion to country, which goes completely beyond any partisan consideration, although he does happen to be a Republican.

Finally, as we have already indicated, one of his primary immediate responsibilities will be to develop a new program for our veterans from Vietnam. We believe that the programs of World War II are not adequate for the new generation of veterans coming out of Vietnam.

I was, frankly, not only surprised, but I would say shocked, to find that the number of veterans from Vietnam who were applying for benefits under the GI bill of rights to allow them to go to college was much lower than in either World War II or in Korea.

This means there is something wrong— something wrong that the veterans returning from Vietnam are not taking advantage of the opportunity to go on to college. We think we have to find a new answer. We have to find new ways to motivate these veterans so that they can come back and be competitive with their contemporaries who did not serve in the Armed Forces. And Don Johnson is going to take this responsibility on his broad shoulders right at the beginning and give it special priority, as well as the other responsibilities involved in managing this immensely important Administration.

Mrs. Johnson is here, too, and I present both the new director and Mrs. John-son, and he will be glad to answer your questions. Thank you.

I won't congratulate you yet, because the Senate has to approve you—and that's premature. I'm sure you'll make it though.

NOTE: The President spoke at 11:58 a.m. at Newport Beach, Calif. On the same day the White House Press Office released the text of a news conference of Donald E. Johnson on his nomination.

The announcement of intention to nominate Mr. Johnson as Administrator is printed in the Weekly Compilation of Presidential Documents (vol. 5, p. 803).

228 Statement on Benefits for Vietnam Veterans. *June* 5, 1969

AMERICANS have long known that those who defended the great values of our Nation in wartime are of great value to the Nation when the war is over. It is traditional that the American veteran has been helped by his Nation so that he can create his own "peace story," a story of prosperity, independence, and dignity.

Initially, this help took the form of health and old age benefits. With the enactment of the GI bill in the Second World War—a bill, in effect, reenacted for Korean veterans in 1952 and for Vietnam veterans in 1966—a major transformation took place. The education and training of the veterans became a matter of the most immediate concern.

Veterans benefit programs have therefore become more than a recognition for services performed in the past; they have become an investment in the future of the veteran and of his country.

The time has come for a careful reevaluation of this investment. Just as there is a difference between the kinds of battles fought in Normandy in 1944 and in South Vietnam in 1969, so there is also a difference in the kinds of problems faced by the returning veterans of these battles. Therefore, we must be certain our programs are tailored to meet the needs of today's veterans.

We are proud of the existing programs that now are available to our veterans. What we must do is to seek and find ways in which the efforts of the Veterans Administration and the Federal Government in general can be improved and made available to the largest possible number of Vietnam veterans.

I am, therefore, appointing today the President's Committee on the Vietnam Veteran. This Committee will be chaired by the Administrator of the Veterans Administration and will consist of the Secretary of Defense, Secretary of Labor, Secretary of Health, Education, and Welfare, the Director of the Office of Economic Opportunity, and the Chairman of the Civil Service Commission.

The staff of the Committee will be drawn from the respective Departments, the Executive Office of the President, the Veterans Administration, and the Office of Economic Opportunity. The Committee will consult with representatives from business, labor groups, veterans organizations, and veterans themselves.

I have directed the Committee to report to me on the present stage of benefits for returning veterans and recommendations on how these provisions can be improved or redirected.

In connection with the formation of this Committee, I have directed the Bureau of the Budget to undertake a general study of returning veterans with emphasis upon those coming from disadvantaged backgrounds. I am convinced that this study will be of service to the Committee in its efforts to determine what assistance such veterans are getting and what further assistance they may need.

I expect that the Committee will provide answers to three major questions:

1. How can we help more veterans to benefit from existing programs?

2. How can we design programs to help those veterans who need help the most—the undereducated, ill-trained, hitherto unemployed or underemployed?

3. How can we improve the overall program of veterans benefits so that it meets the specific challenges of our society and the needs of the veterans?

It is our hope that there will come a day when the benefits of peace will convince men and nations of the folly of war; until then, we must make certain that the benefits we offer reflect our pride in our veterans and our gratitude for their sacrifices.

NOTE: "The President's Committee on the Vietnam Veteran Interim Report" and its letter of transmittal, dated October 21, 1969, are printed in the Weekly Compilation of Presidential Documents (vol. 5, p. 1450).

Also on October 21, the White House Press Office released the text of a news briefing by the Administrator of Veterans Affairs Donald E. Johnson concerning the report.

The President's statement was released at San Clemente, Calif.

229 Statement on Establishing Nationwide Youth Advisory Committees to the Selective Service System. *June 6,* 1969

IT REMAINS my firm conviction that the military draft should be abolished and the Armed Services of the United States manned entirely by volunteers. Unfortunately, it is not possible to effect this change under present international circumstances.

Until the time when a volunteer armed force can become a reality, we must exert every effort to make the Selective Service System as fair and equitable as possible. Toward this end, I recently sent to the Congress a message on draft reform proposing legislation which would reduce the period of uncertainty that young men face in connection with the draft from 7 years to 1 and would establish a fairer, random selection.

Today, I am pleased to announce another step in our effort to improve the Selective Service System.

For some time now the System has used advisory panels for many purposes. On the local level it has medical advisers,

advisers for registrants, and appeal agents. On the national and State level there are some advisory groups that help in selecting physicians and dentists, and others that advise on manpower needs and occupational deferments. But one thing we have not had in the past is an advisory group made up of young people. This administration believes that this deficiency should be corrected. We believe that those who administer our draft laws should systematically seek advice from young people about young people.

We are therefore establishing a nationwide system of Youth Advisory Committees to the Selective Service System.

The young people with whom I am meeting today represent those who have participated in the experimental phase of this new program. In a sense, they have been the test pilots for this new project. It is because of their success that we are now expanding this arrangement from five States to 50 States, with separate programs in the District of Columbia, New York City, the Virgin Islands, Puerto Rico, the Canal Zone, and Guam as well. Each of the new committees will work through a State director of the Selective Service System, contributing their views and recommendations on the way in which the Selective Service System conducts its operations.

Established institutions of all varieties are under attack today—especially from young people—for being distant and unresponsive. The Selective Service System has been a major target for such criticism, for it is particularly important in the lives of young people and yet often seems to be particularly remote from their influence. It is my hope that a system of Youth Advisory Committees will result in a better informed and more responsive draft mechanism. And I hope, too, that it will answer questions and dispel illusions about the conscription process which are now held by many of our younger citizens.

It is the essence of democratic government that those who are most directly affected by a decision of the government should have their views represented in the process by which that decision is made. The Youth Advisory Committee program will not give young people control over the decisions of the Selective Service System, but it will give them a channel for communication and for influence. It will provide a way in which young people can help to shape government policies in which they have a very special stake.

NOTE: Along with the President's statement, the White House released an announcement of the establishment of the nationwide system. The text is printed in the Weekly Compilation of Presidential Documents (vol. 5, p. 807).

The White House also released the text of a news briefing by members of the five pilot Youth Advisory Committees to the Selective Service System.

The President's statement was released at San Clemente, Calif.

230   Remarks at Honolulu Enroute to a Meeting With President Nguyen Van Thieu of the Republic of Vietnam at Midway Island. *June* 7, 1969

WE WANT to express our appreciation to all of you who have come out and given us such a warm welcome to Hawaii.

I also want to express my thanks to the Honor Guard—some of their children are here, I am sure—for their splendid symbolism of our Armed Forces here in Hawaii.

I can say from a personal standpoint that we have been looking forward to returning to this State. I only regret that it is for such a brief time.

I remember that when Mrs. Nixon and I visited here in the year 1951, we reached virtually all of the islands, and we took away memories that we have with us still, and Hawaii has always had a special place in our hearts as it has for everyone who has a chance to come here.

In that connection, I would like you to know that we are very happy that our two daughters, Tricia and Julie, could be with us, and David Eisenhower. None of them have been to Hawaii, and so I know that in 2 days they will learn to love this State as we learned to love it so many years ago.

I would like to say to those on the other islands who might be listening to this broadcast that I know that Oahu, of course, is the island that everybody comes to; but we remember Hawaii, the big island, and Kauai, the garden island, and Maui No-Ka-Oi—with all of those memories in mind we only hope there will be a time when all of us can return for perhaps a vacation and to see them.

Now on a very serious note, as you know, this is one journey that will take me tomorrow to Midway. The purpose of that meeting has been well described in the press. I will not elaborate on it now, except to make this comment which is quite relevant to this State and the people in it.

From my own observation, there is no State and no people in any one of our States that has a greater interest in and a greater stake in the overall problem of

peace in the Pacific than the people of Hawaii.

You know how tremendously important it is that we find a way to bring an end to the war in which we are now engaged in Vietnam and bring an end to that war in a way that it will promote the cause of real peace in the Pacific and not plant the seeds for another war.

We believe that this meeting in Midway will be one step in that direction—a very important step, as will be indicated by the results of that meeting and other events that will follow.

I only want to say, as I conclude, that when I think of this great Pacific State of ours, when I think of the people that are here and all that you represent, the feeling of good will, of people from all backgrounds living together in peace and in friendship, that is what we want to see all over this great Pacific area, that is the cause that we are going to Midway for. And we know that you wish us well and that your prayers are with us as we go.

Thank you very much.

I also want to say, I tried to get them up here for the picture; but I am particularly appreciative of the fact that not only did Hiram Fong and Mrs. Fong come out to welcome us, but Governor Burns and all of the members of the congressional delegation, the two Senators and two Congressmen from the State of Hawaii. This is true bipartisanship. It proves that the cause of peace knows no partisanship, not in this State or any place in America.

NOTE: The President spoke at 1:15 p.m. at Hickam Field, Honolulu. Hiram L. Fong was United States Senator from Hawaii and John A. Burns was Governor of Hawaii.

231   Remarks Following Initial Meeting With President
       Thieu at Midway Island. *June* 8, 1969

Mr. President:

I want to take this opportunity officially to welcome you to this meeting at Midway and to tell you how much I have appreciated the opportunity to talk with you again.

We met on two occasions in your country. This is the first time we have had the chance to talk in our present capacities as heads of our Governments and Chiefs of State.

Our meeting this morning has taken approximately 2 hours. We will continue our private discussion through the noon hour, before meeting the larger group, including the Secretary of State, and their opposite numbers, for approximately an hour and a half, later in the afternoon.

The communiqué at the end of the day, which will be issued at approximately 4, will cover the wide range of subjects that the President and I have discussed. Among those this morning were these: the progress of the talks in Paris; the situation in Vietnam in a number of areas; the pacification program, where I received a very encouraging report from the President; the plans for what seems to me a very important land reform program, which will be implemented in South Vietnam by President Thieu and his Government; and the progress insofar as the conduct of the war is concerned.

In addition to these subjects, all of which will be covered in the communiqué which will be given to you later this afternoon, the President and I had a substantial discussion with regard to the present situation insofar as the training of South

Vietnamese Armed Forces are concerned. And as a result of that discussion, we reached a decision which I should like to report to you now, and President Thieu will also express his views with regard to this decision.

President Thieu informed me that the progress of the training program and the equipping program for South Vietnamese forces had been so successful that he could now recommend that the United States begin to replace U.S. combat forces with Vietnamese forces. This same assessment was made by General Abrams when he reported to me last night and this morning.

As a consequence of the recommendation by the President and the assessment of our own commander in the fields, I have decided to order the immediate redeployment from Vietnam of a division equivalent of approximately 25,000 men.

This troop replacement will begin within the next 30 days and it will be completed by the end of August. During the month of August and at regular intervals thereafter, we shall review the situation, having in mind the three criteria that I have previously mentioned with regard to troop replacement:

First, the progress insofar as the training and equipping of South Vietnamese forces; second, progress in the Paris peace talks; and third, the level of enemy activity.

I will announce plans for further replacements as decisions are made. As replacement of U.S. forces begins, I want to emphasize two fundamental principles:

39–861—71——32

No actions will be taken which threaten the safety of our troops and the troops of our allies; and second, no action will be taken which endangers the attainment of our objective, the right of self-determination for the people of South Vietnam.

It is significant to note that it was just 27 years ago that the Battle of Midway, which history records as one of the major turning points in World War II, came to a conclusion. I believe that the decision made at Midway today, and which we are announcing at this time, marks a significant step forward in achieving our goal of protecting the right of self-determination for the people of South Vietnam, and in bringing lasting peace to the Pacific.

President Thieu, I know that the members of the press would like to hear your views on our discussions as well.

NOTE: The President spoke at 12:40 p.m. at the residence of Capt. Albert S. Yesenky, Commanding Officer of the U.S. Naval Station on Midway Island.

Following the President's remarks, President Nguyen Van Thieu of South Vietnam spoke as follows:

Thank you, Mr. President.

Once again I would like to thank you most sincerely for your very kind words and your cordial welcome. It is a great pleasure for me to meet with President Nixon on this island in the middle of the Pacific.

It's our honest hope that the Pacific will become a vast community of free nations living in peace, prosperity, and brotherhood.

Ladies and gentlemen, as everyone knows, this ocean was named after peace because the first navigators were fortunate enough to sail over peaceful waves. But other navigators subsequently found out that this name can be at times only a pious hope. They knew they had to rely on their strength, determination, and perseverance when they run into stormy weather.

But after the tempest and typhoon, the sun always rises over the immense stretch of the blue waters.

We are, therefore, always confident of the bright and beautiful tomorrow.

So, Mr. President, once again I look forward very much to my exchange of views with you on our common efforts to establish a long-lasting peace and freedom in Vietnam and in Southeast Asia.

Now, I come to a more substantial matter, that is, what President Nixon just said to you.

As you know, ladies and gentlemen, as I have announced many times in the past 12 months, it has been the constant purpose of the Government of the Republic of Vietnam to shoulder an increasing share in the struggle to defend freedom in Vietnam and to alleviate the burden nobly assumed by the United States in participating with us in this struggle. We have made continued efforts in that direction.

And in the past months the strengthening of the Vietnamese Armed Forces through general mobilization, and the rapid progress on the pacification and the rural development, have made it possible for me to inform President Nixon that the Armed Forces of Vietnam are now able to start the process of the replacement of the American forces.

And the equivalent of one U.S. combat division will be replaced by Vietnamese troops. That first replacement will start in July and will be completed the end of August. Further replacements of American troops will be considered at regular intervals in the light of the three criteria that President Nixon has decided. That means the progress in training and equipment of Vietnamese Armed Forces; secondly, the level of Communist hostility; and thirdly, the progress which can be made in Paris talks.

Ladies and gentlemen, on this occasion I would like, once again, in the name of the Vietnamese people, to express our deep gratitude for the sacrifice generously accepted by the American people in joining us in the defense of freedom in Vietnam.

Thank you.

232   Joint Statement Following the Meeting With President Thieu.   *June* 8, 1969

PRESIDENT Nguyen Van Thieu of the Republic of Vietnam and President Nixon of the United States met on Midway Island on June 8, 1969. The meeting was at the invitation of President Nixon.

The principal purpose of the meeting was to permit the two Presidents to review a broad range of matters of mutual interest. These included developments in Vietnam—political, economic, and military—the Paris talks, and the general situation in Southeast Asia. Their day-long discussions were chiefly private though they drew on the assistance and counsel of senior members of their respective governments. Though it marked their first meeting as Chiefs of State, the occasion offered President Thieu and President Nixon the opportunity to renew a friendship dating from 1965.

The two Presidents examined in detail the military situation in Vietnam and received a briefing from Vietnamese and American military commanders. They agreed that the failure of the other side to achieve its objectives should convince it of its inability to gain a victory by military means. They expressed the hope that the other side will realize the futility and dangers of its efforts and that it will accept a solution based on the principle of self-determination for the people of South Vietnam. They agreed that application of the principle of self-determination requires that the people be able to choose without interference or terror. They rejected communist attempts to pre-determine the outcome of future elections before they are held.

The two Presidents confirmed their conviction that the form of government under which the people of South Vietnam will live should be decided by the people themselves. They reiterated their common resolve to reject any attempt to impose upon the Republic of Vietnam any system or program or any particular form of government, such as coalition, without regard to the will of the people of South Vietnam. They declared for their part they will respect any decision by the people of South Vietnam that is arrived at through free elections.

The two Presidents agreed that it would be appropriate to offer guarantees and safeguards for free elections. Provisions for international supervision could be written into the political settlement.

The two Presidents reviewed with particular attention the steps being taken to modernize and improve the Vietnamese armed forces. President Thieu referred to the principle of replacement of American by Vietnamese troops which he had first enunciated in his address to the nation of December 31, 1968, and he expressed pleasure in informing President Nixon that the armed forces of the Republic of Vietnam were now reaching the point where they can assume an increasingly large share of the burden of combat.

President Nixon welcomed this development. He and President Thieu thereafter made an announcement regarding the replacement program. Both Presidents agreed that the replacement program

445

should be carried out in consonance with the security situation prevailing at the moment.

President Thieu explained his plans for further strengthening the local forces and asked for additional assistance for that program. President Nixon said he would give this request sympathetic consideration.

The two Presidents then discussed the negotiations taking place in Paris. They reviewed carefully the positions each had recently enunciated—President Thieu on March 25, when he made the offer to talk directly with the "National Liberation Front," the six points he presented on April 7, and President Nixon's May 14 speech. The two Presidents are convinced that the proposals they have put forward represent a reasonable basis for peace. They took note of the 10-point proposal tabled by the other side in Paris on May 8, and observed that despite the fact that it contained certain unacceptable provisions, there were certain points which appear not too far from the positions taken by the Government of the Republic of Vietnam and the United States.

The two Presidents expressed their intention to seek a just settlement to the conflict in the spirit of patience and good will. President Thieu reiterated his Government's willingness to talk directly to the NLF about moves relating to a peaceful settlement.

The two Presidents reviewed and reaffirmed the positions taken in concert by the allies at the recent seven-nations conference of ministers in Bangkok. They reiterated in particular the allied position concerning mutual withdrawals of non-South Vietnamese forces, agreeing that withdrawals could commence simultaneously and proceed expeditiously on the basis of a mutually acceptable timetable; that all externally introduced forces would have to be withdrawn not only from South Vietnam but also from Laos and Cambodia; and that the further introduction of forces into these countries must be prohibited. They agreed that the essential element of any arrangement on withdrawal of non-South Vietnamese forces is that there be adequate assurances and guarantees of compliance with the terms of the arrangement.

President Thieu informed President Nixon that his Government was devoted to the principle of social and political justice for the people of South Vietnam. The policy of national reconciliation had been adopted with this in mind. His offer to negotiate directly with the "National Liberation Front"—without conditions—had been inspired by this principle. If the other side is genuinely interested in finding peace, it should be possible to create an atmosphere in South Vietnam in which all of the people of South Vietnam can participate in the life of a free, viable, and prosperous state.

The two Presidents discussed the progress that has been made in economic and political development in Vietnam despite the present conflict, including the installation of the supreme court and the inspectorate provided for by the Constitution, the wide-spread holding of village and hamlet elections, and the extension of security in rural areas. President Thieu outlined his Government's plans for additional village and hamlet elections, and he laid particular stress on his pursuit of a vigorous land redistribution program that would give the land to those who work it. President Nixon expressed gratification at this progress, expressed special interest in the new concepts of land distribution developed by President Thieu and offered American cooperation to help achieve it.

Finally, the two Presidents reviewed the plans now being formulated by the Republic of Vietnam for the post-war development of the country. They expressed gratification that, despite the continuation of the conflict, plans were going forward. Given the substantial natural and human resources available, the prospects are excellent for conversion to a peace-time economy, job opportunities, increased domestic production in agriculture and industry, as well as exports. President Nixon pledged his country's assistance to this end. Economic self-sufficiency could be achieved in a decade of peace. The two Presidents looked forward, after the termination of hostilities, to an era of peace and the economic and national development of Southeast Asia.

President Thieu asked President Nixon to convey to the American people the deep gratitude of the people of South Vietnam for the sacrifices they have made and the assistance they have given the Republic of Vietnam in its struggle to maintain its freedom. President Nixon assured President Thieu of the determination of the American people to assist their South Vietnamese allies to realize the basic objectives of the two nations. He acknowledged the trust placed in the American people by the people of the Republic of Vietnam and promised that this trust will be honored.

The two Presidents agreed to meet again and review developments in the near future.

NOTE: The joint statement was released at Midway Island.

233   Remarks at the Conclusion of Discussions With President Thieu.   *June 8*, 1969

Mr. President:

As we complete our talks, I wish to express my appreciation to you for your frankness and candor in discussing the problems that we mutually face in Vietnam, and I know that you share with me the sentiments that were expressed in our communiqué which has already been distributed to members of the press.

I believe that that communiqué indicates the progress that has been made and the progress we can expect in the future toward a resolution of this struggle which has torn apart the people of North Vietnam, which has cost your people so much in men, in lives, and has cost our people as well.

I would like to say, finally, this one personal word. You have a long journey. You will be back in Saigon tonight because of the time change. You will be speaking to the people of South Vietnam when you arrive.

Would you extend to the people of South Vietnam from the people of the United States our good wishes. We know how they have suffered. We share with them the tragedy of war. We want for them what we have for ourselves—the blessings of peace within our own country and within your own country.

We know—and I speak personally in this respect—that the people of your country are a peaceful people, a hard-working people; that if only you have the opportunity, Vietnam can be one of the

447

most powerful, constructive forces for peace and progress and economic development in all of Southeast Asia and the Pacific.

This is what I feel from having been there many times before. This is what your people are fighting for. It is the goal which we all seek.

We wish you well, personally; more than that, the people of the United States wish your people well. We look forward to the day when they can live in peace together.

NOTE: The President spoke at 3:49 p.m. at the base theater on Midway Island.

Following the remarks of the President, President Thieu spoke as follows:

Mr. President, I thank you very much for your very comfortable words. I can say that our first meeting here in Midway is very useful. It is not like some speculation before I arrived here that there would be some difference between President Nixon and President Thieu and I had to come here to dissipate or to discuss again those differences. It is not true.

I come here for more understanding and closer cooperation, for more common position between President Nixon and I; not for difference, because we have had no difference before.

You may mention about the eight-point program of President Nixon for peace. I ask you to remember that immediately after President Nixon had his speech, I said it was consistent with the position of Vietnam and very consistent with my six points.

So, we have close consultation before, and we have a very close understanding on that. So I come here to discuss with President Nixon, to have better cooperation, and to have a better common position.

I think in the future, when the circumstance demands and when we have an opportunity, we may agree together to meet again, so I think this is the best way to have closer cooperation between two governments and two people.

Now, for you ladies and gentlemen of the press, I think that this morning President Nixon and I, we have announced—and what I consider good news for the American people—that the Vietnamese forces replace the U.S. combat forces to an equivalent of one combat division.

I would like to emphasize again, it is a constant duty of Vietnamese people to take over more responsibility and to alleviate the burden of U.S. people to support us to defend the freedom in Vietnam.

We never forget that the blood and human life are precious to anyone, to any people, at any time.

So I think, once again, we are very grateful and the whole Vietnamese people are very grateful for the sacrifice that the United States people have accepted and continue to accept to join us in defense of freedom and defend the common cause of the free world.

But, once again, I say that we will do our best—our best—from now on to alleviate the burden of the American people. We have to do our best to deserve the noble sacrifice that the American people have accepted for Vietnamese people.

Once again—I hope you understand well my English—I am ready to leave for Saigon and I sincerely thank President Nixon for the useful talks, for the heartfelt welcome, the hospitality of the people in Midway Island. It is the first time I know this island and it is very interesting.

I think you may join us to share the success of this meeting. Thank you.

234   Remarks on Departure From Midway Island. *June 8, 1969*

Captain Yesensky and all of the officers and men and families here in Midway:

I first want to say how much all of us

in our party have appreciated the courtesy that has been extended to us on our short visit to Midway.

It happens that for most of us this is the first time we have been to this island. We have read about it for years, and now we finally have come and seen it. We have been most impressed by the splendid American group that is here.

I also know that many of you probably wonder about many of the others in our party, and I think you would like to know who they are. You see the two Presidents, and now I think you would like to meet a man who, like myself, got his World War II experience in the Navy, the Secretary of State, Mr. Rogers.

You know your CINCPAC, Admiral McCain,[1] a submariner. Commander of our forces in Vietnam, and one of the great military men of our generation, General Abrams. One of the most distinguished members of our diplomatic corps who has taken a number of very difficult assignments and has handled them with great distinction around the world, Ambassador Bunker.[2] The man who was my running mate when I ran for President in 1960, and who now is serving as our chief negotiator in Paris, Ambassador Henry Cabot Lodge.

If I could add just one personal word before we go. As I stand here and see so many of you who are serving your country, and your wives and children and families who are with you, I can imagine that sometimes you must have those moments when you wonder about whether you should have entered the armed services. For some of you it was, perhaps, a voluntary action; for others, it may have been the necessary service that so many of our

---

[1] Adm. John S. McCain, Jr., Commander in Chief, U.S. Forces in the Pacific.

[2] Ellsworth Bunker, U.S. Ambassador to South Vietnam.

young people are undertaking at this time.

Particularly, I think it is difficult to serve in an area like this, so far away from the great cities, and for that matter, so far away from the battlefront. I have often thought that serving in what is called a rear area when there is any kind of action going on is more difficult than to be in the area where the action is.

Also, in these periods, I know that you must have read and heard about some of the concern that has been expressed about America's role in the world, and the role of our military. I had something to say about that a few days ago, when I spoke at Colorado Springs.

I simply want, in personal terms, to express my feelings about you who are serving in our Armed Forces. Without the power of the United States of America in places like Midway and around the world, there would be no chance for millions of people on this earth to have peace and freedom.

Now, I know you hear those terms so often they sound like clichés. But that is the fact. Without the presence that you help to create and the power that you have helped to establish, other nations, other peoples in the world, would not have the opportunity that they now have, a chance to choose their own way and not to be dominated by a foreign power.

Speaking of Vietnam, this has been a terribly difficult war. It has deeply divided the people of Vietnam, and it has divided the people of the United States.

But I think we can see in that war something that makes us very proud of the American role in the world. When that war comes to a conclusion, the United States will not have a base; we won't have any economic concessions; we won't have any territory.

We will have gained nothing for ourselves except the possibility that the people of South Vietnam will be able to live in peace and choose their own way without any foreign domination. And this is the American role in the world.

It could have been otherwise. We are the most powerful nation in the world. We are the most powerful, by far, of all the free world nations. The United States could have played, I suppose, a role in which we tried to embark on conquests around the world. We chose not to do so.

I say to you that we as Americans should be proud of our Armed Forces, proud of the role we play in the world. We want, for ourselves and for the world, peace, freedom, and we are willing to make the sacrifices to achieve that goal.

Twenty-seven years ago today, the Battle of Midway came to a conclusion. It was the turning point in World War II.

What this meeting at Midway means, only history will record. But I will say this: That I am confident that as I stand here on this historic island that Americans can

be proud of their role in World War II and what men did in that battle and so many others.

And I am confident that in the years ahead Americans can look back on this period of our history with all of the difficulties that have been presented to us, and we are going to be proud that we played a great role in the world; that we did not back away from the challenges that were presented to us; and that as a result of what we did, as a result of the sacrifices that Americans made, the world was a better place for everybody to live in. That is something you can be proud of.

And I certainly want you to know that for all of us who work with you, those men who were standing with me on this platform, we hope that the policies we develop will be worthy of the fine sacrifices all of you are making in your service to the United States of America.

Thank you.

NOTE: The President spoke at 4:16 p.m. at the air terminal at the U.S. Naval Station on Midway Island. Capt. Albert S. Yesensky was Commanding Officer of the U.S. Naval Station at Midway Island.

235   Remarks on Return From Meeting With President Thieu at Midway Island.   *June 10, 1969*

Mr. Vice President, Mr. Speaker, Members of the Cabinet, members of the diplomatic corps, Members of the Congress, of the House and of the Senate, and all of our friends here in Washington, D.C.:

After a very long journey that took us to the middle of the Pacific, it is good to be home again and to be received so warmly by all of you who have been so kind to come out here and greet us.

As all of you know from having heard the reports from our meetings in the

Pacific, it was just 27 years ago that a great battle took place at Midway, which historians now recognize was one of the turning points, a decisive battle, in World War II.

I know that all of you will be interested in an appraisal of the meaning of Midway today. I am going to meet, immediately after addressing you, with the legislative leaders in order to brief them. But prior to that time, let me briefly tell you what I think is the meaning of the meeting that we had in Midway.

First, that meeting brought home the message that the forces of South Vietnam have now been trained and equipped to the point that they are able to take over a substantial portion of combat activities presently being borne by Americans.

Second, that meeting means that President Thieu completely approves and supports the eight-point peace program which I set forth in my May 14 speech to the Nation. There is no disagreement between us on that program.

And, third, that meeting means that after 5 years in which more and more Americans have been sent to Vietnam, we finally have reached the point where we can begin to bring Americans home from Vietnam.

This does not mean that the war is over. There are negotiations still to be undertaken. There is fighting still to be borne until we reach the point that we can have peace.

But I do think, in conclusion, that this observation is worth making: By the May 14 speech that I made setting forth an eight-point program for peace, and by our action in withdrawing 25,000 American combat forces from Vietnam, we have opened wide the door to peace.

And now we invite the leaders of North Vietnam to walk with us through that door, either by withdrawing forces, their forces, from South Vietnam as we have withdrawn ours, or by negotiating in Paris, or through both avenues.

We believe this is the time for them to act. We have acted and acted in good faith. And if they fail to act in one direction or the other, they must bear the responsibility for blocking the road to peace and not walking through that door which we have opened.

Finally, on a personal note, I haven't had much chance to follow the newspapers. at least from the standpoint of local news, since leaving Washington. But there was one byproduct of my trip abroad which I am sure of. No one can say what history will say about this meeting for sure, until perhaps a few months or even years later.

But I found that in the week or so that I was away from Washington, the Senators finally began to win and are now at .500.

One of the first things I am going to do when I do have a little time off, when they return from the road trip, is to go out and see them play. I hope I am not bad luck for them when I see them.

Thank you very much.

NOTE: The President spoke at 4:51 p.m. on the South Lawn at the White House.

236 Statement on the White House Conference on Food, Nutrition, and Health. *June 11, 1969*

IN APPOINTING Dr. Jean Mayer as Special Consultant to the President, I would like to emphasize the importance of the responsibility he is assuming. The White House Conference on Food, Nutrition, and Health will be an event of great significance.

Over the years, no country has been as closely associated with the science of nutrition as the United States: Pioneers such as Lafayette B. Mendel of Yale, E. V. McCollum of [Johns] Hopkins, Joseph

Goldberger of the United States Public Health Service, and Conrad Elvehjem of Wisconsin were founders of the science. No country has ever undertaken such a gigantic and successful task of raising food as was done by this country in World War II. No country has succeeded in providing such a high standard of diet to so many millions of citizens while assisting millions more in less fortunate countries. In calling the White House Conference on Food, Nutrition, and Health, we are both reaffirming our commitment to a full and healthful diet for all Americans and exploring what we yet need to know and do to achieve that goal.

For despite our achievements much remains to be done. All of us have been shocked as we have become more aware that millions of Americans are malnourished because they are too poor to purchase enough of the right kinds of foods. We also know that many Americans who have enough money to afford a healthful diet do not have one. Many of our youngsters have erratic diets which may be deficient in certain nutrients. Many more of us eat not wisely but too well.

The White House Conference on Food, Nutrition, and Health is intended to focus national attention and national resources on our country's remaining—and changing—nutrition problems. It will assemble the Nation's best minds and expertise, from our business, labor, and academic communities. I shall ask them to consider the following questions:

1. How do we ensure continuing surveillance of the state of nutrition of our citizens?

2. What should be done to improve the nutrition of our more vulnerable groups—the very poor, pregnant and nursing mothers, children and adolescents, the aged, and those such as Indians for whom we have a direct and special responsibility?

3. As we develop new technologies of food production, processing, and packaging, how do we monitor the continued wholesomeness and nutritional value of our foods and ensure that the poor, and indeed all Americans, obtain the greatest amount of nutrients for their money?

4. How do we improve nutrition teaching in our schools—from Head Start to medical schools; and what programs of popular education do we need to better inform the public of proper food buying and food consumption habits?

5. What should be done to improve Federal programs that affect nutrition, either directly as in the Armed Forces and the Veterans Administration, or indirectly through programs such as the food stamp, commodity distribution, and school lunch programs?

I shall ask the Conference to prepare specific goals in response to these questions, goals for private industry, for government policy, and for needed research. Its conclusions and its goals will not be neatly bound and placed on a library shelf and forgotten. They will be the basis for action by this administration and the beginning of a national commitment—to put an end to malnutrition and hunger among the poor, to make better use of our agricultural bounty and nutritional knowledge, and to ensure a healthful diet for all Americans.

NOTE: On the same day the White House Press Office released an announcement of the appointment of Dr. Jean Mayer as Special Consultant to the President with responsibility for planning the White House Conference on Food, Nutrition, and Health. The text of the release is printed in the Weekly Compilation of Presidential Documents (vol. 5, p. 829).

The text of a news briefing on the Conference by Dr. Daniel P. Moynihan, Assistant to the President for Urban Affairs, and Dr. Mayer was also released.

237   Remarks of Welcome at the White House to President Lleras of Colombia. *June* 12, 1969

Mr. President:

I am very honored to welcome you and the members of your party here to Washington today in three capacities: first, as the representative of your country, which I have had the privilege of visiting; second, as the representative of a great continent; and third, as an individual.

As a representative of your country, it is very appropriate to note that you were the first state visitor to the United States from the American family to the south. It is very appropriate that you should be the first, coming as you do from Colombia, because we all recall the great events in which your country played such an important role in developing the organizations which created the American family that we know today.

It was in 1948 in Bogotá that the Organization of American States was set up. It was in 1960 that the Act of Bogotá was adopted, which became the foundation for the Alliance for Progress.

And just a month ago—and incidentally, primarily through your leadership— the Andean Common Market had its birth in Bogotá.

So, the role that Colombia has played in the greater problems of the hemisphere in developing the spirit of the American family, we honor today in receiving you in Washington, D.C.

We also welcome you today in your capacity as an individual. We know your background, going back over many years in the field of government, in the field of education, in the field of politics in the very broadest sense.

And we know that you have contributed, through your thought, to the ideas, the exciting ideas, which we are going to need, if we, in this American hemisphere, develop the programs which are adequate to the tremendous challenges that we face.

I am looking forward to the talks we will have, not only in the bipartisan and also bilateral context in which they will be conducted—because it is bipartisan in this country whenever we speak of foreign policy, but particularly whenever we speak of the American family—but also because, in the broader sense, we believe that you are one of the new voices speaking for the American family that needs to be heard.

We know that your ideas will be ideas that should be considered in developing new policies which will meet the common goals that we all want to achieve for the Americas.

So, because you represent a great country, a country with which we have had such friendly relations, because you represent a great continent, a continent so close to us, not only geographically, but in our hearts, and because, as an individual, you represent ideas that we need to hear and that we want to discuss with you, we welcome you most warmly today to the United States.

NOTE: The President spoke at 10:47 a.m. on the South Lawn at the White House, where President Carlos Lleras Restrepo was given a formal welcome with full military honors.

See also Items 240 and 242.

President Lleras responded as follows:

Mr. President:

Thank you, Mr. President, for your generous words of welcome. They are an admirable reflection of the traditionally warm friendship that exists between Colombia and the United States, of your special interest in inter-American affairs, and your own personal awareness of the issues and problems pertinent to the common welfare of the hemisphere.

Several years ago I had the honor of greeting you and Mrs. Nixon in Bogotá. As Vice President of the United States you were providing at that time ample proof of your desire to obtain firsthand information on all the foreign policy matters concerning your country.

Today, as I arrive in response to your kind invitation, you are burdened with the full weight of the supreme responsibility for the direction of United States foreign policy as head of state.

You have shouldered that burden, Mr. President, with admirable decision and courage. You have understood that the leadership role of the United States requires no less. You have considered useful for the relations between our peoples and our Governments an exchange of ideas; and I greatly appreciate this opportunity to express to you, with frankness, my viewpoints.

I am grateful for your kind references to the achievements of the Colombian Government, the Colombian people, and to my personal contribution in that task. I have tried to be consistent with my belief that a man that has chosen public service as a career must dedicate all his energy and all his time, as you have done, to the welfare of his fellow men.

This is my only merit, and the words with which you have enhanced my efforts are, Mr. President, a further demonstration of your friendship.

You have mentioned Colombia's contribution to the economic integration of the Andean countries. This is, I hope, another step toward a closer economic union of Latin America as a whole and to a more comprehensive economic relationship with the other countries of this hemisphere.

I look forward to our talks with interest and hope, in the firm conviction that they will be fruitful. They will be inspired by our common ideals of fraternity between nations and by mutually shared awareness of the problems of mankind.

The days which my wife, my companions, and myself will spend here will undoubtedly be very pleasant. I believe that they will also be useful for a more complete understanding of our problems and for the strengthening of the links which have traditionally existed between our countries.

Please accept, Mr. President, the most cordial and friendly greeting on behalf of the people of Colombia.

238   Statement on the Death of John L. Lewis. *June 12, 1969*

THE DEATH of John L. Lewis takes away from the American scene one of the giants of our time, a man who helped to shape modern America. His talents were great, his energies prodigious. Few men in contemporary American life have been as controversial; few men possessed the proud heart and the passionate mind to engage in such large-scale controversies. His impact on the coal-mining industry, on organized labor, and on the entire range of the American economy cannot be exaggerated. Mrs. Nixon joins me in extending deepest sympathy to his family.

NOTE: John L. Lewis, President of the United Mine Workers of America for 40 years, died on June 11, 1969, at the age of 89.

239   Remarks at the Graduation Ceremony of the Capitol Page School.   *June* 12, 1969

Ladies and gentlemen:

I understand that not only those among the graduating class, but many of their parents are here.

This is a very special occasion for this White House Rose Garden. The roses come later in the season, fellows, if you miss them.

I remember the first time I handed out diplomas for the Capitol Page School was in 1953, about the year that some of the members of this class probably were born.

And through the years, going back clear to 1947, I recall those occasions when pages have rendered superb service, first in the House and then in the Senate.

I particularly appreciate the opportunity to participate in this ceremony today because, of all the graduating classes across this country from the secondary schools of America, I would say that the percentage chance that one of the members or more, or any member of this class, could become a Member of the House or Senate or even higher is higher among the Capitol pages than any other group.

As you know, it has been traditional for many years that people who serve as Capitol pages, while they may get very tired of it, it gets into their blood; and they enter political life at a later time. Some of them run for office. All of them participate in politics in their own communities.

I simply want to say in this brief address to you, because I know you have been submitted to a great deal of speaking in these last 3 days of these ceremonies, that we appreciate the work that you have rendered during your service in the House.

I know that all of you will now go on to higher education and, also, I hope that many of you will have gotten just enough taste of politics and political life to continue in that field in the years ahead.

We wish you the very best. We congratulate you. We congratulate your parents for having the foresight to have you become Capitol pages.

Thank you.

NOTE: The President spoke at 5:28 p.m. in the Rose Garden at the White House. Following his remarks he presented diplomas to graduating members of the Capitol Page School.

240   Toasts of the President and President Lleras of Colombia.   *June* 12, 1969

Mr. President, Señora Lleras, amigas y amigos:

I suppose that many of you wondered, among the repertoire of the [Strolling] Strings, what that delightful number was, the third one that they played, the second from the end.

Señora Lleras tells me that is the *bambuco,* which is the great Colombian dance, and in playing that number we were trying, through music, to express a sentiment that I will try to express in my very limited Spanish, a sentiment that everyone in this room feels.

Mr. President, in this room, as you know from having met them in the receiving line, we have young and old; we have Republicans and Democrats; we have businessmen; we have people from government and other areas; but they are alike in one respect, in their affection for your country, the people of your country, and their respect for you and your family who are with you.

And we want you to know that as you come to this house today, that many distinguished visitors have come, but none who receives a warmer reception from us and the best way that I can express that sentiment is not through the way we would say it in English: "Make yourself at home," but the way it is said in Spanish when you arrive in a Spanish home: *"Haga usted esta su casa."* And to everybody in this room, we say, you are in your own house tonight.

Mr. President, on this occasion I could speak of many things: of the matters that I spoke of when we welcomed you on the White House lawn earlier today, of the role that your country and that you have played in the problems of this hemisphere and, particularly, in terms of the American family and the friendship that we want to develop within that family among the nations that are members of it.

But, I think that our guests tonight, since this is truly a personal dinner in honor of you and of your wife and your family, that they would like for me to speak of you, what you stand for, what you stand for in your country, what you stand for in this continent, in this hemisphere.

First, you have our respect because of your background. We know that at a very early age you entered the field of politics, and you were very successful in that area.

You not only have been successful in the field of politics, but you are quite unusual among politicians. You are a

scholar, also.

I do not mean that politicians may not be scholars sometimes, but not always.

We are aware of the fact that you are an economist and a very distinguished economist with a world reputation. And when we hear of that, we are reminded that the study of economics is called, "the dismal science."

I suppose it acquired that description because in the days of Malthus, all economists had a dismal prediction about the future. They predicted then that population would outrun the production of food in the world.

Well, several hundred years have passed, and it has not yet happened, although we still have an enormous problem, both with regard to hunger in the world and in regard to population.

But while you are an economist, I would say that you are an economist in a new tradition, the tradition of pragmatism coupled with idealism and optimism; an economist with a philosophical view of the great problems of your country and the great problems of the world.

And that is one of the reasons why you have been so successful in the political leadership of your country, one of the reasons why your ideas about how we can better develop together with the great natural and human resources of this hemisphere, why your ideas have spread far beyond your country, are respected all over this hemisphere, and are particularly respected here in the United States.

That is one of the reasons why your coming here, as the first official visitor to this country from the Latin American area, I think, is particularly appropriate, apart from the fact that your country has meant so much in terms of its background, insofar as the development of the Latin

456

American institutions are concerned: the development of the Organization of American States, the Act of Bogotá, the other matters to which I referred earlier today.

But, speaking quite directly and simply to you, Mr. President, we respect you today as a man who has devoted your life to the service of your people, to the service of your country, and to the service of a cause that is bigger than either of our countries, as big as this whole hemisphere, as big as the whole world itself.

We live in a very troubled time. We all know that, and the problems that you have are quite similar to the problems we have within our own country.

And I was very interested to note that the national motto of Colombia is "Liberty and Order." And I don't know of any man among the world leaders that it has been my privilege to meet who more symbolizes and represents that kind of leadership in the world than our guest of honor tonight.

Liberty and order—we all know that that is the art of politics. We realize that liberty in itself and by itself, if we have it without order, means that we can have, in effect, anarchy. And we know that if we have order without liberty, we have dictatorship.

And it is only that delicate balance between the two which you have maintained in your country and in your leadership which we try to maintain here. It is that liberty and order, liberty with order, that provides the basis for progress.

So we respect you for that kind of leadership. We hope we can learn from you and that we will all profit from this visit that you have paid to us.

So, tonight, I know that all of you around this table will want to join me in raising their glasses to you and in doing so, I am reminded of the crop that is very famous in Colombia, among many others, the crop of coffee, and the advertisement that the Pan American coffee group had a few years ago.

They said: "Coffee is like friendship. It is rich, and it is very strong and very warm."

And I would like to reverse it by saying tonight that we speak to you in friendship, friendship between the United States and Colombia, friendship that is rich and warm and very strong. And your visit has helped to make it richer and warmer and stronger.

And so to the friendship of our two countries, and to you and your family, I ask all of you to raise your glasses to the President of Colombia.

NOTE: The President spoke at 10:10 p.m. at a dinner in the State Dining Room at the White House.

See also Items 237 and 242.

President Carlos Lleras Restrepo responded as follows:

Mr. President, Mrs. Nixon, ladies and gentlemen:

I cordially thank you, Mr. President, for your gracious toast. It expresses, once more, the friendliness that has surrounded my wife and daughter, my companions and myself from the very moment of our arrival in this country. It also shows your great interest in Latin America and the particular attention you give to those matters concerning the relations between our two countries. In spite of the ponderous legacy of world conflicts and complex domestic situations that your Government has to confront, you have recognized that this hemisphere should have a high priority in the framework of United States foreign policy. Your invitation to me reflects, I believe, this priority. It also shows your understanding of Colombia's internal and international policies: democratic, progressive, friendly, and independent.

I have struggled, Mr. President, as you have, throughout a lifetime in the political arena, maintaining, thereby, close contact with public affairs. We belong to a generation that has witnessed unprecedented change: some of us as astonished spectators; some as victims; some as voluntary or as unwilling actors. Now, in one of the most contradictory moments of history, we feel bound to examine the world situation with an open mind, trying to see clearly through the clouds that encircle us without any prejudice and also without allowing ourselves to become bewitched followers of new myths or cowardly deserters from principles which are vital to organized society.

It is not easy, indeed, to abandon ideas, attitudes, aspirations that at one time or another were respected and cherished and that have become obsolete in the present erratic world. It is difficult sometimes to sacrifice certain economic interests that fight to survive even when they contradict the more essential needs of larger human groups or international solidarity. It is not easy either to know whether some beliefs and ideals must be considered as unrealistic or unattainable. Are we not often mistaking our own human inconstancy and skepticism for an obsolescence of rightful social concepts? Are we looking carefully enough to discover all the rich realities that are concealed behind some discouraging facts or apparent failures?

These reflections come to me as I review in my mind the history of the inter-American system and of the many efforts directed towards the achievement of a higher degree of cooperation in the hemisphere.

Simón Bolívar's "Letter from Jamaica" initiated the ideological process of union then confined to the Latin American countries. The circular letter addressed also by Bolívar, from Lima in 1824, already contained the main juridical and political elements which we are still trying to apply after nearly a century of inter-American conferences. There, that great man outlined the organization of an assembly that could give us its advice whenever a conflict should arise and arrange for consultation in case of danger, act as an arbiter or judge for the resolution of eventual differences, and provide the proper interpretation of treaties. Colombia and Mexico then sought to associate

the United States within the projected system, but without positive results.

The long evolution that followed is well known, and its different aspects are too complex to be summarized tonight. They include such subjects as the relations between the regional organization and the United Nations; the nature of the inter-American system itself; and the cooperation of all the members for the economic, social, and cultural development of the Americas, a cooperation considered essential for the common welfare and prosperity. No agreement, of course, can be so perfect as to cover the infinite number of contingencies that may arise in the internal life or the international links of so many countries, living in great diversity of material and institutional conditions. Still, the Protocol of Buenos Aires, signed in 1967, leaves little room for new declarations of principles concerning relations between the member states. Almost all the matters that need to be agreed upon in general terms have already been discussed, shaped, and stipulated in writing. We know, nevertheless, that neither today, nor in the past, have the great principles of the inter-American system been faithfully observed.

No practical man, therefore, regards today the great questions of the continent simply through Alice's mirror of statutes and declarations. Of course, we do not want to break the mirror. We will always have to base our daily conduct upon written rules, freely arrived at, inspired by equity and human solidarity. But now the most important task seems to be to advance further in the useful and effective implementation of already accepted policies. Let us translate into simple, day to day practices those images that still remain nebulous in the magic glass.

We cannot and should not underestimate the magnitude and significance of what has already been achieved. Neither can we ignore the existence of a system capable, if properly oriented, of gradually fulfilling the better part of our common hopes. The peaceful solution of political and juridical differences, the narrowing of the dangerous gaps that divide nations and societies, are well within the power of the present inter-American organization, provided all the necessary support from the member states is forthcoming. Unfortunately, no one could assert that this support has always been given with an identical degree of conviction and enthusiasm.

I trust the inter-American system. It is the best instrument for the defense and promotion of what has been from the beginning the ideological patrimony of this continent: liberty, equality, and justice. It constitutes the full recognition of human solidarity as the source of international law. The Americas were once called the "land of hope" and I am sure this title can and should be preserved as the symbol and guide of our common conduct.

Still, Mr. President, we must not disregard the great material, psychological, and political obstacles already apparent and those that are emerging with dreadful implications. The future is full of ominous dangers, open to sudden eruptions. It could be disturbed by new and more serious misunderstandings.

You, Mr. President, were already familiar with inter-American affairs when, during the Eisenhower administration, you played such a constructive role in the proceedings that led to the Act of Bogotá. This document was the prelude to the Alliance for Progress. It is a well known fact that in the following years you have maintained a lively interest in Latin American problems and in their possible solutions.

During the presidential campaign, you pointed out some grim facts and disappointing figures concerning the pace of development in Latin America. You enunciated also some new means of action and attractive solutions. Reviewing your speeches I find in them an objective recognition of hard realities, coupled with a strong faith in our ability to change them. This is the same spirit with which I view the problems of the hemisphere.

Recently the Ministers of Foreign Affairs, on behalf of the Latin American states, described some of these obstacles and enunciated practical rules to facilitate commercial and financial relations in the hemisphere. The document signed in Viña del Mar, which collects the results of many experiences and technical studies, has already been delivered to you.

I am sure you have received it as a positive contribution for the improvement of inter-American relations. Working together on the subjects contemplated therein, the Latin American countries and the United States surely could generate new patterns of trade and

remove harmful practices and irritating stipulations. We must avoid as much as possible whatever can disrupt the efforts to develop Latin America economically and socially within an atmosphere of understanding and cordiality. This common effort can influence also, in the right direction, the economic relations with other continents, and put an end to the existing discriminations against Latin America.

I would emphasize the importance of sharing science and technology for the development of the hemisphere, an issue which is also analyzed in the above mentioned document.

A new demonstration of the interest with which you want to study and to conduct a continental policy has been provided by the special mission entrusted to Governor Nelson Rockefeller. I can assure you that, in the case of Colombia, an almost unanimous welcome was extended to your representative. The fruitful exchange of information and opinions covered a wide spectrum, and left behind a warm and friendly memory. I thank you for having given us this opportunity to discuss our common problems with such an enlightened friend.

Colombia is facing its great political, economic, and social challenges with resolution and, I venture to say, with a bold and comprehensive policy. The diagnosis of our specific situation is not difficult and is already well known, as are the factors that can be considered common to most of the developing countries. This is not the occasion to make a new analysis of matters that, furthermore, have been a part of our dialogue. But I should like to assert that Colombia is fulfilling the conditions that the Alliance for Progress requires from her.

If these efforts have been great, so has the cooperation rendered by the United States and by the international organizations. I wish to reaffirm tonight that Colombia fully values and deeply appreciates that support.

It is regrettable that this support, as well as our hard work, has been at times partially frustrated, mainly by the inequities of the world economic mechanism and by unjust patterns of trade. On the other hand the views of the Colombian Government and those of our partners in the Alliance have not always coincided. But, as the head of a nation determined to promote its development, both through its own efforts and joint international action, my message is not one of complaint. I speak the language of resolute realism, a realism inspired by attainable goals but aware of the obstacles that must be overcome.

If ever my perseverance should lag or my confidence in the future fail, I would look back upon your kind words tonight for encouragement and inspiration.

Before raising my glass to propose a toast

to the Government and the people of the United States, to our kind host and Mrs. Nixon, and to Colombian-American friendship, let me pray that, in the words of Whitman, democracy may sing in the future throughout the Americas: "Come, I will make the continent indissoluble."

241   Statement on the Merger of the National Alliance of Businessmen and Plans for Progress. *June* 13, 1969

THIS MORNING, in the Urban Affairs Council meeting, Mr. Donald Kendall, Chairman of the National Alliance of Businessmen, and Mr. Roger Lewis, who has been serving as Chairman of Plans for Progress, presented reports on the roles of their organizations.

Both of these organizations, one of them now 8 years old and the other less than 2, have as their goal the employment of our disadvantaged and minority group Americans.

Plans for Progress, which was formed in 1961, now has 441 cooperating corporations, which employ a total of over 10 million persons in more than 22,000 plants across the country. The organization cooperates closely with the Federal Equal Employment Opportunity Commission, and seeks to foster voluntary adoption by American business of plans to hire more minority group members and upgrade their skills.

The Plans for Progress organization has met with important success in these efforts, for more than 10 percent of the total employed by member organizations come from minority groups, and, since 1965, two out of every seven jobs in companies which have adopted Plans for Progress have been filled by minority group members.

The National Alliance of Businessmen has concentrated the attention of the business community on the high unemployment rates in our inner cities, and has mounted an impressive attack on the predicament of the hard-core unemployed. Some 15,000 participating companies have about 102,000 formerly hard-core unemployed persons on the job. The NAB has pledged that by June 1970, it will have found jobs for 218,000 persons, and the hope is that over 600,000 will be generated by June 1971.

In many respects, the purposes of the two organizations have been related if not identical. Some of the programs sponsored by the Plans for Progress organization, such as their Vocational Guidance Institutes, have now consciously been established in many of the 125 cities in which the National Alliance of Businessmen is organized.

Both organizations represented an attempt by the American corporate and financial community to contribute in efforts to break the cycle of unemployment and dependency. Both represent efforts to reduce the barriers to employment opportunities which for so long stood in the way of many simply because of their accident of birth.

Today, Mr. Kendall and Mr. Lewis

told the Urban Affairs Council that their respective boards of directors have approved a merger of the two organizations. To both the members of the Urban Affairs Council and myself, the merger seems an appropriate means of rationalizing and focusing the attack by American business on the problems of unemployment and minority group employment.

The merged organization will permit some of the Nation's most public spirited companies to combine their efforts so that there is a single thrust and focus—total employment and advancement opportunities—throughout every level of industry for members of minority groups and the hard-core unemployed.

Mr. Kendall will be Chairman of the merged organization which will take the name of the National Alliance of Businessmen. Mr. Lewis will serve with him as

Vice Chairman. Mr. Lynn Townsend also will serve as Vice Chairman.

To insure that the Federal Government puts its full resources behind the important work of this organization, I have asked that Vice President Agnew work closely with the Alliance, and that future meetings of the NAB board will be held at the White House.

NOTE: A news briefing concerning the merger was held at the White House on the same day by Dr. Daniel P. Moynihan, Assistant to the President for Urban Affairs, Donald M. Kendall, Chairman of the National Alliance of Businessmen, and Roger Lewis, Chairman of Plans for Progress.

An announcement on March 13, 1969, naming Lynn Townsend as Vice Chairman and Paul W. Kayser as Executive Vice Chairman of the National Alliance of Businessmen is printed in the Weekly Compilation of Presidential Documents (vol. 5, p. 399).

242   Remarks on the Departure of President Lleras of Colombia.   *June* 13, 1969

Mr. President, Mr. Foreign Minister, and gentlemen:

As you, Mr. President, complete your official visit here, I want you to know first how much we have enjoyed knowing you and your family personally and how much we have profited from the opportunity of exchanging views with you, not only on the bilateral matters which we have discussed and on which we have made considerable progress, I believe—as I understand you will cover some of those matters in your own statements, both here and when you return—but also in terms of the broader aspects of the policies of the United States in the American Hemisphere.

You are the first visitor, as we have

pointed out, from Latin America during this new administration. We recognize the urgency of this problem. We recognize the need for new ideas. We recognize the need for new programs, and we want those new ideas and those new programs to be ones that we share together in which we not just talk, but in which we listen and in which we learn.

In our wide ranging discussions, not only of our bilateral problems, but in a broader sense, of the problems of the hemisphere, I cannot think of any leader in Latin America who could have contributed more to our own thinking.

I think your visit will mark a major step forward in the development of new policies by the United States in its relationship with our friends in Latin America. And I think that next week at the Economic Conference [Inter-American Economic and Social Conference] that is being held in Trinidad we will see some of the first fruits of those new directions and certainly the credit for these new departures—they will be modest to begin with, but the promise for the future will be very great—the credit will go to you and to this visit. Without your visit we might not have moved as fast as we should have.

NOTE: President Nixon spoke at 12:03 p.m. in the Rose Garden at the White House. The Minister of Foreign Affairs of Colombia was Alfonso López Michelsen.

See also Items 237 and 240.

President Carlos Lleras Restrepo responded as follows:

Mr. President, gentlemen:

The talks which President Nixon and I held during my visit to Washington were fruitful and comprehensive. They have reaffirmed the traditionally warm friendship which exists between Colombia and the United States. They have given us an opportunity to review the principal issues on the inter-American agenda. I believe they will contribute to the new era of hemispheric cooperation, which Latin America, as well as the United States, is looking

forward to.

I have found an open and understanding attitude everywhere, in the White House and at all levels of the United States Government, towards the problems that confront the hemisphere.

Both President Nixon and I are convinced of the need to continue the inter-American dialogue in an atmosphere of cordiality and friendship and of the urgency of implementing adequate solutions.

Our discussions covered such topics as the improvement of financial and commercial relationships within the hemisphere, basic commodities with special references to coffee, the physical integration of the Americas, including the accelerated completion of the Pan American Highway, the transfer of science and technology and, of course, the ways and means of working together in close collaboration on these issues.

I am certain that this exchange between our two Governments on matters of mutual interest will strengthen our bilateral relations and will lead to the enhancement of the Americas' role in the world.

I wish to express my heartfelt thanks to President Nixon and the United States Government for the warmth and friendship extended to me, my family, and my fellow Colombians.

Seldom in my public life have I encountered a comparable open-mindedness or a more pleasant human relationship.

243   Message of Congratulations to President-Elect Georges Pompidou of France.   *June* 16, 1969

Dear Mr. President-Elect:

Please accept my warm congratulations on your victory and my best wishes for your success as you prepare to take up the responsibilities and challenges of your high office.

As you embark upon your new responsibilities, I wish to assure you and the people of France of the continued friendship and sympathetic interest of the

American Government and people.

I look forward to working with you not only to develop closer relations between our countries but also to concert our efforts in the cause of peace and the brotherhood of all peoples.

Sincerely,

RICHARD NIXON

[The Honorable Georges Pompidou, President-elect of France]

244   Special Message to the Congress Proposing
      Improvements in the Air Transportation
      System.   *June* 16, 1969

To the Congress of the United States:

PREPARING FOR THE FUTURE OF AIR
TRANSPORTATION

Years of neglect have permitted the problems of air transportation in America to stack up like aircraft circling a congested airport.

The purpose of air transportation is to save time. This purpose is not served when passengers must wait interminably in terminals; when modern jet aircraft creep at five miles per hour in a long line waiting for takeoff; when it takes longer to land than it takes to travel between cities; or when it takes longer for the air traveler to get to an airport than it does to fly to his destination.

In the tenth year of the jet age, more intercity passenger miles were accounted for by air than by any other mode of common carriage. In 1968, scheduled airlines logged over 150 million passenger trips, triple that of a decade ago; at the same time, the non-airline aircraft fleet almost doubled and the use of air freight quintupled. That rate of increase is likely to continue for the next decade—but it can be accommodated only if we prepare for it now.

The growth in the next decade must be more orderly. It must be financed more fairly. It must be kept safe. And it must not permit congestion and inadequate facilities to defeat the basic purpose of air transportation: to save time.

Air travel is a convenience hundreds of thousands of people take for granted—a means of commerce that millions depend upon for their goods and services. In a nation as large as ours and in a world grown suddenly small, flight has become a powerful unifying force. The ability to transport people and products by air—safely, surely and efficiently—is a national asset of great value and an international imperative for trade and travel.

That ability is being challenged today by insufficiencies in our nation's airports and airways. The demand for aviation services is threatening to exceed the capacity of our civil aviation system. Unless relieved, this situation will further compromise the convenience of air transportation, erode its efficiency and—ultimately—require more regulation if the enviable safety record of the airplane as a means of public and private transportation is to be preserved.

The challenge confronting us is not one of quality, or even of technology. Our air traffic control system is the best in the world; our airports among the finest anywhere. But we simply do not have the capacity in our airways and airports ample to our present needs or reflective of the future.

Accordingly, the Secretary of Transportation is submitting to the Congress today legislative proposals to provide the resources necessary to the air transportation challenges facing us. These proposals are responsive to the short-term as well as the long-range opportunities for civil aviation progress.

IMPROVING OUR AIRWAYS

To provide for the expansion and improvement of the airway system, and for a high standard of safety, this Administration proposes that *the program for construction of airways facilities and equipment be increased to about $250 million annually* for the next ten years. This is in sharp contrast to the average of $93 million appropriated in each of the past ten years, and is responsive to the *substantial expansion in the operation and maintenance of the air traffic system in the next decade.*

While this will provide for the needs of the '70s, development for the 1980s and beyond cannot be neglected. Technology is moving rapidly and its adaptation to provide future solutions must keep pace. Consequently, this program includes a provision for a doubling of development funds.

BUILDING AND IMPROVING AIRPORTS

The proposed airport program consists of both an expanded planning effort and the provision of additional Federal aid for the construction and improvement of airports. The airport systems planning we contemplate at both the Federal and local level will begin a new era of Federal, State and local cooperation in shaping airport development to meet national and local needs.

I propose Federal aid for airport development in fiscal 1970 of $180 million and in fiscal 1971 of $220 million, with continued expansion leading to a total of two and one-half billion dollars in the next ten years. Together with matching grants on a 50–50 basis with State and local governments, this strongly increased

program will permit financing of *five billion dollars in new and expanded airfield facilities.*

The proposed fiscal year 1970 program of $180 million would help finance the development of airfield facilities, the conduct of airport systems planning, and airport planning and development activities carried on by States.

Of the $180 million,

—$140 million would be available for grants to air carrier and general aviation airports, with a primary objective of alleviating congestion in the most heavily used air terminals.

—$25 million in grants would be available to aid in the development of airfields used solely by general aviation.

—$10 million would be available in grants to planning agencies to assist them in conducting airport systems planning.

—$5 million would be available for grants to States to carry on airport planning and development activities.

Airport terminal buildings are a responsibility of local airport authorities. The Administration's legislative proposal suggests ways in which those authorities can meet that responsibility.

IMPROVING THE ENVIRONMENT OF TRANSPORTATION

In all planning for airways and airports, it will be the policy of this Administration to consider the relation of air transportation to our total economic and social structure.

For example, existing jetports are adding to the noise and air pollution in our urban areas. New airports become a nucleus for metropolitan development. These important social and conservation considerations must be taken into greater account in future air systems development.

In addition, airport planners must carefully consider the opportunity for business growth and the availability of labor supply. The presence of airport facilities is both a follower of and a harbinger of business and job development.

Most important, government at all levels, working with industry and labor, must see to it that all aviation equipment and facilities are responsive to the needs of the traveler and the shipper and not the other way around. Transportation to airports, whether by public conveyance or private vehicle, is as much a part of a traveler's journey as the time he spends in the air, and must never be viewed as a separate subject. A plane travels from airport to airport, but a person travels from door to door. I have directed the Secretary of Transportation to give special attention to all the components of a journey in new plans for airways and airports improvements.

FINANCING AIR TRANSPORTATION FACILITIES

The Federal Government must exert new leadership in the development of transportation, in the integration of the various modes, and in supporting programs of national urgency.

However, the added burden of financing future air transportation facilities should not be thrust upon the general taxpayer. The various users of the system, who will benefit from the developments, should assume the responsibility for the costs of the program. By apportioning the costs of airways and airports improvements among all the users, the progress

of civil aviation should be supported on an equitable, pay-as-we-grow basis.

At present, the Treasury obtains revenues, generally regarded as airways user charges, from airline passengers who pay a five per cent tax on the tickets they buy, and from the operators of aircraft who pay a tax at the effective rate of two cents a gallon on aviation gasoline. The revenues obtained from these taxes are not applied directly to airways expenditures. They are either earmarked for other purposes or go into the general fund of the Treasury.

I propose that there be established a revised and expanded schedule of taxes as follows, the revenues from which would be placed in a Designated Account in the Treasury to be used only to defray costs incurred in the airport and airway programs:

—A tax of eight percent on airline tickets for domestic flights
—A tax of $3 on passenger tickets for most international flights, beginning in the United States
—A tax of five per cent on air freight waybills
—A tax of nine cents a gallon on all fuels used by general aviation.

This new tax schedule would generate about $569 million in revenues in fiscal year 1970, compared with the revenues of $295 million under existing taxes.

To sum up:

—For the airline passenger, the proposed legislation would save his time and add to his safety.
—For the air shipper, it would expedite the movement of his goods, thereby permitting him to improve his services.
—For the private aircraft owner, it

465

would provide improved facilities and additional airports.

—For the airline, it would permit greater efficiencies and enable the carrier to expand its markets by providing greater passenger convenience.

In short, the airways and airports system which long ago came of age will come to maturity. Those who benefit most will be those who most bear its cost, and the nation as a whole will gain from aviation's proven impetus to economic growth.

The revenue and expenditure programs being proposed are mutually dependent and must be viewed together. We must act to increase revenues concurrently with any action to authorize expenditures; prudent fiscal management will not permit otherwise.

These proposals are necessary to the safety and convenience of a large portion of our mobile population, and I recommend their early enactment by the Congress.

RICHARD NIXON

The White House
June 16, 1969

245 Remarks on Announcing Appointment of the White House Fellows for 1969–1970. *June 16, 1969*

Dr. Flemming and all of our distinguished guests here in the State Dining Room at the White House:

We are very honored at this occasion because it marks one of those historic opportunities that a President has—to announce the new White House Fellows.

I say "historic"—this program is only 5 years old.[1] But I think that Dr. [Arthur S.] Flemming would agree that the man who was one of his successors in the position of the Secretary of Health, Education, and Welfare, Dr. John Gardner, showed tremendous foresight and perception in developing this program.

At the time that it was developed 5 years ago, it was generally thought that those who would be selected as Fellows from around the country would have an opportunity to broaden their perspective; having been scholars in their particular fields, they would now have the opportunity to work in various agencies dealing with those subjects which they had studied.

What we have found—I think this has been true certainly of this administration and I would imagine it has been true of the other administrations as well—what we have found is that the presence of the White House Fellows in the departments has broadened our perspective.

I can give you a very good example. A few weeks ago we were considering, in the Cabinet Committee on Urban Affairs, the problem of hunger in America. It was a very big meeting. All of the members of the Committee were there and there were staff members and experts completely surrounding the members of the Committee and filling the room to its

---

[1] See "Public Papers of the Presidents, Lyndon B. Johnson, 1963–64," Book II, Item 622.

capacity.

During the long discussion, which took about 3 hours, one of the major problems which had to be considered was the problem of nutrition, the problem of proper diet, to what extent that contributed to the general problem not only of the poor but of all Americans insofar as their health was concerned.

I noted that participating in the conversation on several occasions, not simply voluntarily but because she was often called upon by the Secretary of Agriculture and the Secretary of Health, Education, and Welfare, was a woman who was sitting immediately back of the Secretary of Agriculture, a young woman, obviously very intelligent and obviously the one in that room who knew more about nutrition than all the people in government and all the others in the back. She was one of the White House Fellows, a graduate of the Harvard Medical School.[2]

And afterwards I spoke to her and I found that in this particular area there is a need in the medical profession for far more emphasis than we presently have. So my perspective was broadened as a result of having her participate in that meeting. She made a contribution that might not have been made had not she been in Washington at that time serving in that year's program. That is an idea of what all of the Fellows can contribute in their various fields, not perhaps as dramatically as she did but certainly in every way.

I simply want to say that today it is a very great privilege for me to stand here with the new members of the Commission and Dr. Flemming, the Chairman of the Commission. I understand they worked practically the whole weekend, day and night, in making these selections because the competition was so keen.

I understand, too, that in addition to those who are the winners, we also have those who were the finalists.

I asked what the difference between a winner and a finalist was and apparently a finalist is one who came in second. I imagine they feel something like Deane Beman and Bob Rosburg[3] must feel today. [*Laughter*]

Having come in second a couple of times myself, I know how you feel, too. [*Laughter*]

If I can paraphrase the Biblical injunction: The second shall be first. Who knows?

I also want you to know that I recognize that among those who have been selected we have the great universities, prestigious institutions from all over this country represented. I note that such great, prestigious universities as Harvard, Columbia—and Whittier—are in the group.

I have spoken long enough and now I know that you are all most interested to know who are the White House Fellows for the year 1969–1970.

Dr. Flemming will present them to you.

DR. FLEMMING. Thank you, Mr. President.

Mr. President, I know that I express the feelings of all of the members of the Commission and all who have partici-

---

[2] Caro Elise Luhrs, a White House Fellow in 1968–69.

[3] Runners-up in the 1969 U.S. Open Golf tournament.

pated in this program when I say to you, thank you so much for being with us in order to greet the winners.

I think that I should warn you, however, that I have discovered today that there has already been organized an alumni association of White House Fellows. I understand they have already passed a couple of resolutions which are to be presented to me. But you helped a great deal because in appointing the Commission you did appoint one of the graduates of the White House Fellows program.

THE PRESIDENT. If I could interrupt you, Dr. Flemming, being a member of an alumni group connected with the White House is a very great responsibility. If I know alumni groups, you will have to, each year, be dunned to help us with our deficit. [*Laughter*]

DR. FLEMMING. Now it is my pleasure to present to you, Mr. President, the winners.

[At this point Dr. Flemming introduced each of the White House Fellows by name. He then resumed speaking.]

That is the group, Mr. President, and I know that the members of the Commission feel that the persons who have just been presented to you will render very outstanding service to the Government in the months that lie ahead.

At this time I would like to introduce the members of the Commission who are here.

First of all, one Mr. Patrick J. Buchanan [Special Assistant to the President].

Dr. W. Glenn Campbell, director of the Hoover Institute for War and Peace at Stanford University.

Francis L. Dale, president and publisher of the Cincinnati Enquirer.

You know Secretary Finch could not be with us for this weekend. He is a member of the Commission also.

Mrs. Vera Glaser, Washington bureau chief of the North American Newspaper Alliance.

Dr. Mason W. Gross, president of Rutgers University.

Mr. H. R. Haldeman [Assistant to the President], who was unable to be present, but was ably represented by Mr. Kenneth Cole [Special Assistant to the President] over the weekend.

Miss Doris Kearns, assistant professor of government, Harvard University and a member of the White House Fellows Alumni Association.

Mr. Roy E. Lieuallen, who is chancellor of the Oregon State System of Higher Education from Eugene, Oregon.

And finally, Hobson R. Reynolds, the Grand Exalted Ruler of the Elks.

We regard it as a real pleasure and privilege to serve in this capacity and thank you for the opportunity.

THE PRESIDENT. Thank you very much, Dr. Flemming. I again want to congratulate collectively all of the winners who are standing behind me. Some of their superiors—we should not call them that, but some of those who will be giving them their assignments—the Cabinet officers are here and the Under Secretaries and Deputies in the various Cabinet positions. That is an indication of the importance we attach to the work they will be doing. We know you will have an interesting year in Washington, and we hope when you leave next year things will be better than they are today. Thank you.

NOTE: The President spoke at 3:07 p.m. in the State Dining Room at the White House. An announcement listing the 1969–70 White House Fellows is printed in the Weekly Compilation of Presidential Documents (vol. 5, p. 866).

246   Message to the Congress Transmitting Annual Report Comparing Federal and Private Enterprise Salaries. *June* 17, 1969

To the Congress of the United States:

I forward herewith the annual comparison of Federal salaries with the salaries paid in private enterprise, as provided by section 5302 of title 5, United States Code.

The report, prepared by the Director of the Bureau of the Budget and the Chairman of the Civil Service Commission, compares the present Federal statutory salary rates with average salary rates paid in private enterprise for the same levels of work, as reported in the Bureau of Labor Statistics Bulletin No. 1617, *National Survey of Professional, Administrative, Technical, and Clerical Pay, June 1968.*

Also transmitted is a copy of an Executive order promulgating the adjustments of statutory salary rates to become effective on the first day of the first pay period beginning on or after July 1, 1969. These adjustments were developed in the joint report from the Director and Chairman, and in accordance with the directions of section 212 of Public Law 90–206, the Federal Salary Act of 1967.

Public Law 90–206 provides that comparable adjustments shall be made, by administrative action of appropriate officers, in the salary rates of employees of the judicial and legislative branches and those of Agricultural Stabilization and Conservation County Committee employees.

RICHARD NIXON

The White House

June 16, 1969

NOTE: The message was dated June 16, 1969, and released June 17, 1969. The report is printed as House Document 131 (91st Cong., 1st sess.).

Executive Orders 11474 and 11475 of June 16, 1969, adjust, respectively, Federal civilian and military pay rates.

247   Remarks at the Presentation of the Young American Medals for Bravery and Service. *June* 17, 1969

Mr. Solicitor General, Mr. Hoover, ladies and gentlemen:

We are here today to make some awards that have been presented by the President of the United States since the year 1950. The Young American Awards are unique among those that are presented by the President in that they go to young people, in this case to teenagers, selected from all over the United States.

If I were to use a term to describe the people who are receiving these awards, I think I could use the term "bravery" in its broadest sense. By "bravery" we often think of the personal bravery where an individual faces up to a challenge that involves himself, but "bravery" in the broadest sense is that that involves courage in serving some larger cause, serving someone else.

Each of those who receives an award today, as you will note, has shown bravery in this larger sense, in serving his community, serving his family, serving the Nation.

The Solicitor General will present each of the award winners. Mr. Hoover will hand the medal to them, and I will be here to make the presentation.

Mr. Solicitor General.

NOTE: The President spoke at 11:09 a.m. in the Roosevelt Room at the White House.

He presented gold medals for service to Gail Ann Budlow, 17, of West Allis, Wis., for her work with the aged and with retarded children; and to Janette Ann Litten, 20, of Alhambra, Calif., who headed various charitable drives for Alhambra High School including a Christ-mas drive for a Navajo Indian mission in Arizona and served as a companion to elderly patients at a sanatorium in Rosemead, Calif.

He presented gold medals for bravery to Ronald Clark Lee, 20, and his brother Randy, 19, of Stanley, Wis., who rescued their mother and two younger brothers from their burning house.

The winners were chosen from among 55 nominations submitted from 18 States, Guam, and the District of Columbia. Members of the Young American Medals Committee who judged the nominations were Director of the Federal Bureau of Investigation J. Edgar Hoover, Solicitor General Erwin N. Griswold, and Clifton F. Sessions, former Director of Public Information, Department of Justice. The awards were for 1967 and make a total of 31 medals for bravery and 16 for service awarded since the establishment of the program under the Department of Justice by the Congress in 1950 (Public Law 638, 64 Stat. 397). The selections were made during 1968.

Remarks by Solicitor General Griswold on introducing the winners to the President are printed in the Weekly Compilation of Presidential Documents (vol. 5, p. 875).

248   The President's News Conference of June 19, 1969

THE PRESIDENT. Won't you be seated, please?

QUESTIONS

ACTION AGAINST THE RISING COST OF LIVING

[1.] Mr. Smith [Merriman Smith, United Press International].

Q. Mr. President, I ask this question against the background of a continually heating economy. Now with your tax package seemingly on its way through Congress, are you giving any concern to doing something else—some new moves against rising prices and the rising cost of living as they are reflected monthly in the Federal indices?

THE PRESIDENT. Mr. Smith, it is true that we have rising prices, a rising cost of living, and also rising interest rates at 8½ percent at the last report. However, in looking at an economy, we find that there is usually a lead time of about 6 months from the time decisions are made on the economy from a fiscal standpoint within Government and the effect of those decisions on it.

Now, this administration has made some decisions—decisions in cutting the budget, decisions in asking for an extension of the surtax, and we expect it to be extended, and other decisions with regard to tightening of credit. We believe that the decisions that we have made will begin to have effect within a matter of 2 to 3 months. If our projection proves to be wrong, then we will have to look to other courses of action, because we cannot allow prices to continue to go up, interest to go up, and the other factors which you have described to continue.

NEW YORK CITY ELECTIONS

[2.] Mr. Cormier [Frank Cormier, Associated Press].

Q. Could you tell us whom you favor for Mayor of New York at this point?

THE PRESIDENT. I think the people of New York have had some difficulty in that respect lately.

I will follow the practice as President of the United States and as leader of the Republican Party of endorsing all Republican nominees. Therefore, I will endorse Senator Marchi[1] and the other Republican nominees on the city ticket in New York.

However, I will also follow the practice that has been my practice during my entire political career of campaigning and participating in only national and State elections. I will not participate in, and I

---

[1] New York State Senator John J. Marchi defeated New York City Mayor John V. Lindsay on June 17, 1969, in the mayoral primary election for the Republican nomination.

will not comment upon, city or local elections, including the election in New York.

THE PARIS PEACE TALKS

[3.] Q. Mr. President, on the Midway trip, we were told by an official of your administration that he felt the time had come for substantive negotiations to begin at Paris. Do you agree with this assessment, and, if so, what evidence is there to point it up?

THE PRESIDENT. I agree with the conclusion that the time has come for some substantive negotiations in Paris. As far as evidence that such negotiations have begun, there is no substantial evidence, publicly, to report.

However, I am not pessimistic about the outcome. As you may recall when these questions were first raised, when the talks in Paris were beginning, I pointed out that it would be a long, hard road after we got over the procedural points.

When this administration came in, all that had been decided was the shape of the table. Now we are down to substance. The two sides are far apart. But we believe that the time has come for a discussion of substance and we hope within the next 2 to 3 months to see some progress in substantive discussions.

MR. CLIFFORD'S ARTICLE ON VIETNAM

[4.] Q. Mr. President, former Defense Secretary Clark Clifford has suggested that 100,000 American troops ought to be out by the end of this year and we ought to say that all ground troops will be out by the end of 1970. I wonder if you think that is a realistic timetable?

THE PRESIDENT. Well, I noted Mr. Clifford's comments in the magazine Foreign Affairs,[2] and, naturally, I respect his judgment as a former Secretary of Defense.

I would point out, however, that for 5 years in the administration in which he was Secretary of Defense in the last part, we had a continued escalation of the war, we had 500,000 Americans in Vietnam; we had 35,000 killed; we had over 200,000 injured.

And, in addition to that, we found that in the year, the full year, in which he was Secretary of Defense, our casualties were the highest of the whole 5-year period and, as far as negotiations were concerned, all that had been accomplished, as I indicated earlier, was that we had agreed on the shape of the table.

This is not to say that Mr. Clifford's present judgment is not to be considered because of the past record. It does indicate, however, that he did have a chance in this particular respect, and did not move on it then.

I believe that we have changed that policy. We have started to withdraw forces. We will withdraw more. Another decision will be made in August. I will not indicate the number, because the number will depend upon the extent of the training of the South Vietnamese, as well as developments in Paris, and the other factors that I have mentioned previously.

As far as how many will be withdrawn by the end of this year, or the end of next year, I would hope that we could beat Mr. Clifford's timetable, just as I think we have done a little better than he did

---

[2] Issue of July 1969, pp. 601–622.

when he was in charge of our national defense.

Q. Mr. President, Mr. Clifford goes on to urge that you order our military commanders to cease the policy of applying maximum military pressure against the enemy and switch, instead, to a policy of reducing the level of combat operations. Do you intend to issue any such instructions?

THE PRESIDENT. Mr. Scali [John A. Scali, ABC News], I have checked the situation with regard to our operations as compared with the enemy's since this administration took over. I find that our casualties are in direct ratio to the level of enemy attacks.

We have not escalated our attacks. We have only responded to what the enemy has done.

As far as Mr. Clifford's suggestion is concerned, it implies that the United States is at the present time responsible for the level of fighting. It takes two in order to reduce the level of fighting, and I would only suggest that if the enemy now will withdraw forces, one-tenth of its forces, as we have withdrawn one-tenth of our combat forces, that would tend to reduce the level of fighting.

As far as the orders to General Abrams are concerned, they are very simply this: He is to conduct this war with a minimum of American casualties. I believe he is carrying out that order with great effectiveness in the field.

NORTH VIETNAMESE REACTION TO
U.S. TROOP WITHDRAWAL

[5.] Q. Mr. President, have you had any response from the North Vietnamese

472

or the Vietcong either in Paris or on the battlefield to the withdrawal of the first 25,000 American troops?

THE PRESIDENT. No, we have not.

STRATEGIC ARMS LIMITATION TALKS WITH THE SOVIET UNION

[6.] Q. When and where do you expect to begin arms talks with the Soviet Union, and do you favor suspension of the testing of multiple warheads in the meantime?

THE PRESIDENT. We are just completing our own strategic review, and as a matter of fact, the National Security Council meeting dealing with our position on the SALT talks, as they are described—the first was held this last Friday, and the second will be held on Wednesday. Consultation with our allies will then proceed through the balance of June and through July.

We have set July 31st as a target date for the beginning of talks, and Secretary [of State] Rogers has so informed the Soviet Ambassador. We have not had a reply from them.

Assuming that our consultations are completed, and that the Soviets find this date is acceptable to them, I would say that sometime between July 31st and the 15th of August there would be a meeting. As far as the place of the meeting is concerned, it could be Vienna; it could be Geneva. We are open on that question.

VIETCONG ANNOUNCEMENT OF PROVISIONAL GOVERNMENT FOR SOUTH VIETNAM

[7.] Q. Mr. President, the Vietcong and/or Hanoi recently announced the creation of a new provisional government

for South Vietnam. There have been many interpretive reports of what that may mean for the political stability or instability of South Vietnam and its portent on the international scene for progress toward peace. Could you give us an assessment of the new government?

THE PRESIDENT. The new government is simply a new name for the same activity that was there previously, the NLF or National Liberation Front, as it was called. There is no new blood in it. It has no capital. As a matter of fact, I do not know where ambassadors would present their diplomatic credentials because it has no major city or town which it controls in South Vietnam.

As far as the changed situation is concerned, however, I would make this suggestion: President Thieu has offered to have internationally supervised elections to let the people of South Vietnam determine whether they want his government or some other government.

It would seem that if the provisional government which also claims to represent the people of South Vietnam really means that, that they would accede to this request and agree to internationally supervised elections.

As far as the United States is concerned, we will accept any decision that is made by the people of South Vietnam, but we think that the provisional government should join with the Government of South Vietnam, and any other political parties in South Vietnam, in participating in supervised elections.

CONSIDERATION OF MORATORIUM ON MIRV TESTS

[8.] Q. Mr. President, referring to an earlier question by Mr. Valeriani [Richard Valeriani, NBC News], do you regard further testing of MIRV's [multiple independently targetable reentry vehicles] as an obstacle to reaching an arms control agreement?

THE PRESIDENT. I am sorry, Mr. Semple [Robert B. Semple, Jr., New York Times], I forgot the last half of his question. I am glad you brought it back.

As far as the further testing is concerned, this suggestion was made to me by Senator Brooke [Senator Edward W. Brooke of Massachusetts] and by others in the Senate. I know that it is certainly a very constructive proposal insofar as they, themselves, are thinking about it. We are considering the possibility of a moratorium on tests as part of any arms control agreement.

However, as far as any unilateral stopping of tests on our part, I do not think that would be in our interest. Only in the event that the Soviet Union and we could agree that a moratorium on tests could be mutually beneficial to us, would we be able to agree to do so.

VIEWS ON CEASE-FIRE IN VIETNAM

[9.] Q. Mr. President, several prominent Americans have urged you to propose a cease-fire in Vietnam as a means of reducing American casualties. Why does that idea not commend itself to you?

THE PRESIDENT. Well, the idea of a cease-fire, Mr. Lisagor [Peter Lisagor, Chicago Daily News], does commend itself to me. But I do not want us to cease and have the other side continue to fire, because, basically, as I have pointed out in a previous press conference, where we have a conventional war, cease-fire is very relevant; then we know that the guns have stopped firing.

In the case of a guerrilla war, unless you have an international force or some outside force to guarantee it, a cease-fire is a grave disadvantage to those forces that are in place.

I should point out, however, that in my May 14th speech, I advocated supervised cease-fires. That is the position of this administration. It is the position also of Mr. Thieu.

We want cease-fires, but we want them supervised. We don't want us to cease fire and the other side to continue to kill our men.

THE FBI AND ELECTRONIC SURVEILLANCE

[10.] Q. Mr. President, against the background of a controversy involving Mr. Hoover, J. Edgar Hoover [Director, Federal Bureau of Investigation], a controversy which revolves around electronic surveillance and in which one newspaper, at least, has called for his resignation, may I ask you two questions: One, does Mr. Hoover continue to enjoy your complete confidence; and, two, has there been any decision concerning his tenure?

THE PRESIDENT. Mr. Hoover does enjoy my complete confidence, and there has been no discussion with regard to his tenure as far as the future is concerned.

I should add, further, that with regard to the controversy on electronic surveillance, that I checked personally into the matter as to whether or not that surveillance which had been discussed had been conducted by him and the FBI, by themselves, or whether it had been, as is supposed to be the case, always approved by the Attorney General.

I found that it had always been approved by the Attorney General, as Mr. Hoover testified in 1964 and 1965. As far as this administration is concerned, our attitude toward electronic surveillance is that it should be used very sparingly, very carefully, having in mind the rights of those who might be involved, but very effectively to protect the internal and external security of the United States.

A NEW RECONSTRUCTION FINANCE CORPORATION

[11.] Q. Mr. President, sir, the small business people of this country are suffering and much more so now because of the high interest rates. I wonder if you have given any thought to organizing a Reconstruction Finance Corporation again?

THE PRESIDENT. I know that the high interest rates have caused great concern, particularly to the small business people.

I do not believe, however, that a new RFC would necessarily be the approach that would be effective to deal with it. I think the way to get at high interest rates is to get at the cause, as I answered the earlier question put by Mr. Smith.

CONGRESSIONAL REPORT ON CAMPUS UNREST

[12.] Q. What is your answer, sir, to the report presented to you yesterday by the group of Republican Senators on campus unrest? [3]

THE PRESIDENT. It was a very thoughtful report by men who do not have the problem of the generation gap. They are young men, vitally interested in these problems, and they gave me a lot of information that is essential for this administration to have in mind as it develops

---

[3] The text of the report entitled "Report of the Brock Campus Tour" is printed in the Congressional Record (June 25, 1969, E 5237).

a program to deal with campus unrest.

With regard to what our position is, I would like to point out, however, that I cannot support the legislative proposals in the House of Representatives which would simply cut off funds from any college or university in which there was a demonstration. This would be cutting off our nose to spite our face, and it would be just what the demonstrators wanted, because we do not want the Federal Government interfering in and responsible for discipline in every college and university in this country.

The responsibility for discipline in colleges and universities should be on the college administrators. That is why I have asked the Attorney General to develop, if he can, new legal remedies that might be available to college administrators to use where violence or lawlessness does occur on the campus. The responsibility should be theirs. The Government's role should be to help them meet that responsibility.

ASSISTANT SECRETARY OF HEW

[13.] Q. Mr. President, Secretary Finch very much wants Dr. John Knowles to be Assistant Secretary of Health. Evidently Senator Dirksen very much doesn't want him to be. Are you going to support your Secretary against your Senate leader?

THE PRESIDENT. I have heard of this controversy from some people. As you well know, the President of the United States, under the Constitution, makes nominations with the advice and consent of the Senate. I have found in my short term of office that it is very easy to get advice and very hard to get consent.

But with regard to this particular matter, Secretary Finch has the responsibility

475

for selecting those who will be his Assistant Secretaries. When he makes a recommendation, after he has made every effort to clear it with the Senators involved, I will support that recommendation.[4]

PRESIDENT THIEU OF SOUTH VIETNAM

[14.] Q. Mr. President, you expressed the hope earlier for substantive talks on Vietnam, perhaps in the next 3 months. I wonder, sir, in this process, and before elections are held in Vietnam, are we wedded, to whatever degree, to the government of President Thieu?

THE PRESIDENT. When you use the term "wedded to the government of President Thieu," I would not say that the United States, insofar as any government in the world is concerned, is wedded to it in the sense that we cannot take any course of action that that government does not approve.

On the other hand, I do not want to leave any doubt on this score: President Thieu is the elected President of Vietnam. He is cooperating with the United States in attempting to bring this war to a conclusion. He has made a very forthright offer and has supported our position that we have made, and I know will be making an offer of his own with regard to a political settlement. Under those circumstances, there is no question about our standing with President Thieu.

I would also say further that insofar as our offers are concerned, we are not going

to accede to the demands of the enemy that we have to dispose of President Thieu before they will talk. That would mean a surrender on our part, a defeat on our part, and turning over South Vietnam to the tender mercies of those who have done a great deal of damage, to those in North Vietnam.

FURTHER COMMENT ON MR. CLIFFORD'S ARTICLE

[15.] Q. Mr. President, although not all of his recommendations were accepted, Mr. Clifford did reverse himself while in office, a rather rare thing for a public official to do. My question to you is perhaps somewhat philosophical: How do you keep from being locked in on a decision involving something as pressurized as Vietnam? How do you determine once a policy is adopted that it continues to be right?

THE PRESIDENT. This is one of my major concerns, and it is one of the reasons why I perhaps allow more controversy and, frankly, even open dissent, as I note from reading all the newspapers, within our administration than any in recent years.

I believe that a President must constantly reexamine the policies, and I am reexamining our policy on Vietnam every day. I am examining the military policy. I am examining the political policy, our diplomatic options, and I will not be frozen in.

With regard to my comment on Mr. Clifford, I do not mean to suggest that because he, in a very difficult position, was unable to do anything about it, that his words should not now be given some weight. They should be given some weight, and a man should be given credit

---

[4] A White House announcement on June 28, 1969, of the President's intention to nominate Dr. Roger O. Egeberg as Assistant Secretary of Health, Education, and Welfare for Health and Scientific Affairs is printed in the Weekly Compilation of Presidential Documents (vol. 5, p. 926).

for changing his mind if the facts have changed.

But I am only suggesting that, as I make up my own mind at this time, I have to look at the facts as they are presented to me today, and as they are presented to me today I think we are on the right road in Vietnam.

We have started toward the withdrawal that Mr. Clifford has advocated and, I hope, as I said earlier, that we will be able to beat his timetable and that we will not be in Vietnam as long as he suggests we will have to be there.

CONSULTATION WITH
PRESIDENT JOHNSON

[16.] Q. Mr. President, your predecessor in office used to quite often solicit the advice of one of his predecessors, General Eisenhower, particularly with respect to foreign policy. Have you solicited Mr. Johnson's advice, and have you got any that is comparable to Clifford's, and does he back your policy?

THE PRESIDENT. I have talked to Mr. Johnson on the telephone, Mr. Potter [Philip Potter, Baltimore Sun], on two occasions, and he has been regularly briefed by members of the National Security Council, by Dr. Kissinger, and also by our Economic Advisers, and those briefings, of course, have provided an occasion for him to give his ideas to us. He has been very helpful in terms of advice and I think he will be more helpful in the future.

ELECTIONS IN LOS ANGELES, NEW YORK,
AND MINNEAPOLIS

[17.] Mr. Kaplow [Herbert Kaplow, NBC News].

Q. Mr. President, what do you make of the recent election results in the mayors' races in Los Angeles, New York, and Minneapolis? What do you think the voters are saying?

THE PRESIDENT. Well, I think the snap reaction to the election in Los Angeles, which was understandable, may have been wrong. The snap reaction to that election, because it was a white man against a black man, was that it was simply a white-black vote.

And yet when you see Minneapolis, where there is only a 4 percent black constituency, coming up with a 62 percent vote for a candidate against the Republican candidate for mayor, and then in New York City where you see conservative candidates, that is the label that has apparently been given to both of them, in both the Democratic and Republican primaries, winning over the liberal candidates, it seems to me we have to take a different view.

What I feel is this: I do not believe the great majority of the American people in our cities are anti-Negro. I do not believe they are anti-poor, or anti-welfare, or reactionary, or members of hate groups.

I do believe, however, this, and this is the message that comes through rather loud and clear from these elections: The American people in our cities, in our small towns, and in this country are fed up to here with violence and lawlessness and they want candidates who will take a strong stand against it. I think that is the message for the candidates in the future.

HEW APPOINTMENTS

[18.] Q. Mr. President, the Surgeon General [William H. Stewart] said today

477

that your administration faces what he called a crippling lack of leadership in its top health offices. You earlier indicated that you are staying out of the Dirksen-Finch controversy for now. Will there come a time when you feel that you must intervene as the nominating officer for those jobs?

THE PRESIDENT. I think that I can go even further than that. I will not have to intervene, because Mr. Finch will make a decision on that next week.

PRESIDENTIAL POWERS

[19.] Q. Mr. President, what do you think of the Fulbright [Senator J. William Fulbright of Arkansas, Chairman of the Senate Foreign Relations Committee] proposal that would limit the Presidential power to act militarily in an emergency?

THE PRESIDENT. Well, I understand the sentiment behind the proposal. When I was a Member of the Senate and a Member of the House, I will have to admit that I felt that there should be more consultation with the Senate, and that Presidents should not have unlimited power to commit this Nation, militarily as well as politically.

On the other hand, as I now assume the responsibilities of power, I, of course, see it from a different vantage point. And for a President of the United States to have his hands tied in a crisis in the fast-moving world in which we live would not be in the best interests of the United States.

As President, I intend to consult with the Senate, with Senator Fulbright and with his colleagues on the Foreign Relations Committee and the Armed Services Committee before taking any action when-

ever I can.

But look, for example, at President Eisenhower in 1958. He had to move very fast in order to save the situation in Lebanon.[5] There was no time to consult, and also it would have tipped off the enemy.

Look at President Johnson when he sent in airplanes to save the missionaries in the Congo in 1964.[6] He had to move fast. He had no time to consult.

I don't think a President of the United States should be tied down by a commitment which will not allow him to take the action that needs to be taken to defend American interests and to defend American lives where there is no time to consult.

THE MIDDLE EAST

[20.] Q. Mr. President, 5 months ago at your first news conference you described the Middle East as a dangerously explosive situation in need of defusing. In the 5 months since that time, do you think there has been any defusing that you can measure, or do you think the situation has become acutely worse?

THE PRESIDENT. I would have to admit that I see very little defusing. The situation is better only from the standpoint that we do have some four-power talks going, and we would trust that from those talks we might get some basis of

---

[5] See "Public Papers of the Presidents, Dwight D. Eisenhower, 1958," Items 172, 173, and 176.

[6] See "Public Papers of the Presidents, Lyndon B. Johnson, 1963–64," Book II, Item 780 [2, 10, 16].

communication between the two sides, and particularly that we might get all parties involved, including the Soviet Union, to use their influence to defuse a crisis. The talks will serve that interest if they serve no other interest.

Also in that connection, I would like to say that I, as you know, have met already with the King [Hussein] of Jordan, and I am hoping to meet sometime within the next month with the Prime Minister [Golda Meir] of Israel.

We intend to have bilateral talks, multilateral talks—anything that we can do—to attempt to defuse the situation.

EXTENSION OF THE SURTAX

[21.] Q. Mr. President, you said earlier that you feel that the income surtax will be extended by the Congress. However, it expires in just 11 days. If the Congress does not act or does not act in time, what economic situation will you be faced with, and what realistic policy options will you be considering?

THE PRESIDENT. Despite the fact that the surtax will expire, and that has happened before, the Congress will pass a resolution which will allow the forms to go out and the collections to proceed. What is important is not that the Congress pass the tax before it expires, but that the general public and the world knows that the tax will eventually be passed. That has a psychological effect.

In my belief, due to the bipartisan support—and it has been really statesmanlike support that we received from the Democratic leadership as well as the Republican leadership—due to that support, it will pass the House and I then think will pass the Senate.

GOVERNOR ROCKEFELLER'S VISITS TO LATIN AMERICA

[22.] Q. Mr. President, due to Governor Rockefeller's difficulties on his Latin American jaunt, do you see any usefulness coming out of the trips, and could you tell us what it might be?

THE PRESIDENT. A great deal of usefulness. For example, in my conversations with President Lleras, the talking paper that President—Governor Rockefeller; a Freudian slip—the talking paper that Governor Rockefeller gave me was extremely helpful, extremely helpful because it gave me the background of his conversation with President Lleras.

I would say further that the very fact that there are these rather explosive demonstrations indicates that such a trip was necessary. The United States can't be penned up within our borders simply because of the fear of demonstrations.

I remember very well when I planned my trip to Europe there were several editorials to the effect that I shouldn't take the trip because of the possibility of demonstrations. As those of you who were with me will remember, there were demonstrations in every major city which I visited. Yet the trip was worthwhile.

As far as I am concerned, I am very happy that Governor Rockefeller has made this trip. He is getting valuable information which we needed to get.

I would add one further thought: We must not interpret these demonstrations as reflecting the will of the people of Latin America. The few demonstrators, violent as they are, in Latin America, no more represent the 200 million people of Latin America than the Black Panthers represent the 11 million law-abiding Negro citizens of this country. That is what we have to get across.

THE SAFEGUARD SYSTEM

[23.] Q. Mr. President, when you proposed the Safeguard antiballistic system, you said it was vital to the interests of the United States. Nevertheless, reports persist that it is in trouble, the program is in trouble in the Senate, and there is now talk of a possible compromise in our program. What is your position on Safeguard, and what do you intend to do to win passage for the program?

THE PRESIDENT. On March 8th, before I announced my decision on Safeguard, a story appeared in the Washington Post indicating that the count at that time was 20 Senators for it, 46 against it, with the rest undecided.

The latest count I have seen indicates that there are 50 or 51 for it, 46 against it, and the rest undecided. We will win the fight on Safeguard. It will not be necessary to compromise.

I don't mean by that that every section of the bill as presented to the Armed Services Committee has to be kept as it is. That is up to the Committee and to the

Chairman [Senator John Stennis of Mississippi] to work out.

But in recommending Safeguard, I did so based on intelligence information at that time. Since that time new intelligence information with regard to the Soviet success in testing multiple reentry vehicles—that kind of information, has convinced me that Safeguard is even more important. Because however we may argue about that intelligence, as to whether it has an independent guidance system as ours will have, there isn't any question but that it is a multiple weapon and its footprints indicate that it just happens to fall in somewhat the precise area in which our Minutemen silos are located.

This would mean that by the year 1973, in the event the Soviet Union goes forward with that program, that 80 percent of our Minutemen would be in danger. ABM is needed particularly in order to meet that eventuality.

Merriman Smith, United Press International: Thank you, Mr. President.

NOTE: President Nixon's sixth news conference was held in the East Room at the White House at 7 p.m. on Thursday, June 19, 1969. It was broadcast on radio and television.

---

249   Remarks at the Swearing In of Warren E. Burger as Chief Justice of the United States.   *June 23, 1969*

Mr. Chief Justice, may it please the Court:

I am honored to appear today, not as President of the United States, but as a member of the bar admitted to practice before this Court.

At this historic moment I am reminded of the fact that while this is the last matter that will be heard by the Chief Justice

of the United States, the first matter to be heard by this Court when he became Chief Justice was the occasion when, as Vice President of the United States on October 5, 1953, I moved the admission of Warren Olney III, and Judge Stanley Barnes to be members of this Court.

I have also had another experience at this Court. In 1966, as a member of the bar, I appeared on two occasions before the Supreme Court of the United States. Looking back on those two occasions, I can say, Mr. Chief Justice, that there is only one ordeal which is more challenging than a Presidential press conference, and that is to appear before the Supreme Court of the United States.

On this occasion, it is my privilege to represent the bar in speaking of the work of the Chief Justice and in extending the best wishes of the bar and the Nation to him for the time ahead.

In speaking of that work, I naturally think somewhat in personal terms of the fact that not only is the Chief Justice concluding almost 16 years in his present position, but that today he concludes 52 years of public service to local, State, and national government—as District Attorney in Alameda County, as Attorney General of the State of California, as Governor of the State of California, the only three-term Governor in the history of that State, as Chief Justice of the United States of America.

The Nation is grateful for that service.

I am also reminded of the fact that the Chief Justice has established a record here in this Court which will be characterized in many ways. In view of the historical allusion that was made in the opinions just read, may I be permitted an historical allusion?

Will Rogers, in commenting upon one of the predecessors of the Chief Justice, Chief Justice William Howard Taft, said that "It is great to be great. It is greater to be human."

I think that comment could well apply to the Chief Justice as we look at his 52 years of service. One who has held high office in this Nation, but one who, in holding that office, always had the humanity which was all-encompassing, the dedication to his family—his personal family, to the great American family, to the family of man.

The Nation is grateful for that example of humanity which the Chief Justice has given to us and to the world.

But as we consider this moment, we also think of the transition which will shortly take place. We think of what it means to America, what it means to our institutions.

Sixteen years have passed since the Chief Justice assumed his present position. These 16 years, without doubt, will be described by historians as years of greater change in America than any in our history.

And that brings us to think of the mystery of government in this country, and for that matter in the world, the secret of how government can survive for free men. And we think of the terms "change" and "continuity." Change without continuity can be anarchy. Change with continuity can mean progress. And continuity without change can mean no progress.

As we look over the history of this Nation, we find that what has brought us where we are has been continuity with change. No institution of the three great institutions of our Government has been more responsible for that continuity with change than the Supreme Court of the United States.

Over the last 16 years there have been great debates in this country. There have been some disagreements even within this Court. But standing above those debates has been the symbol of the Court as represented by the Chief Justice of the United States: fairness, integrity, dignity. These great and simple attributes are, without question, more important than

481

all of the controversy and the necessary debate that goes on when there is change, change within the continuity which is so important for the progress which we have just described.

To the Chief Justice of the United States, all of us are grateful today that his example, the example of dignity, the example of integrity, the example of fairness, as the chief law official of this country, has helped to keep America on the path of continuity and change, which is so essential for our progress.

When the historians write of this period and the period that follows, some with a superficial view will describe the last 16 years as the "Warren Court" and will describe the Court that follows it as the "Burger Court."

I believe, however, that every member of this Court would agree with me when I say that because of the example of the Chief Justice, a selfless example, a nonselfish example, that this period will be described, not only his but that of his successor, not as the Warren Court, not as the Burger Court, not in personal terms, but in this hallowed moment in this great Chamber, the Supreme Court. It was always that way; may it always be that way. And to the extent that it is, this Nation owes a debt of gratitude to the Chief Justice of the United States for his example.

NOTE: The President spoke at 10:17 a.m. at the Supreme Court. The oath of office was administered by retiring Chief Justice Earl Warren.

250 Remarks at the House of Representatives "Gymnasium Dinner." *June 25, 1969*

I WANT to tell you how much I have enjoyed this brief visit to the gymnasium party. It always makes me realize how much time has passed when I come to such a party as this and then start to reminisce about the "old days."

I remember first coming to the House Gym in 1947 and the fellow then who was the meanest guy in paddleball—he was the guy that you always wanted with you—was [Olin E.] Tiger Teague. I am still sore, believe me.

Tiger, let me ask you, do you still hit other people as much as the ball?

Well, I also, of course, think back to those days when all of the other great stars in the House were playing there. I used to play quite regularly. I don't take exercise any more but I took enough then. I banked it for all the time now.

In a very serious vein, I am just delighted that the House has had the good sense and the Senate has had the good sense to have adequate facilities here in the gymnasium. I understand you even have a swimming pool. Sometime I will bring my surfboard down and try it.

As you probably have read, or you might have read, I like to go to Florida now and then and sometimes to California, and I particularly like salt water rather than fresh water.

But when I come to a party like this and see the good fellowship—Republicans and Democrats having a good time—I realize that looking back on those House years, and I was in the House for 4 years, that they were really very great years.

I just hope, as I particularly talk to the younger men here, I mean the very new men, young in the sense of being here one term or two terms, that they will remember that these are the best years of their lives, because there is a certain comradeship in the House that you will never have in any other organization and there is a place where you will feel it more than any place else and that is in the gymnasium—and I don't mean just here.

Also, I would only like to say that I trust that as you do exercise between now and next Monday, and also as you enjoy this good food—and I address this remark, of course, only to the Republicans—please keep enough strength that if we need your votes you can walk down to the well of the House and vote.

Thank you very much.

NOTE: The President spoke at 6:50 p.m. in the cafeteria at the Longworth House Office Building following introductory remarks by Representative Carl Albert of Oklahoma, House Majority Leader. The dinner, sponsored annually by the House Gymnasium Association, is open to the entire membership of the House of Representatives.

251   Remarks at a Ceremony Commemorating the 10th Anniversary of the St. Lawrence Seaway. *June 27, 1969*

Mr. Prime Minister, Governor Rockefeller, all of the distinguished guests, the Governors, the Members of the Cabinets of both Nations, the Members of Congress from the Senate and from the House, and all of the other distinguished guests and those who have gathered here today for this very special ceremony:

I want to express, first, my appreciation to Governor Rockefeller for his very generous and warm welcome. It is good to be here in New York State again.

It is good to see this wonderful turnout in the interest of international friendship. And I particularly was glad to note that when the Secretary of State was introduced that the people from Norfolk [New York] were here to welcome him. Because I think, as you may know, Secretary Dulles [1] also came from northern New York; Secretary Rogers was born in Norfolk and grew up in northern New York State. I think you will be interested to note that while we commemorate 10 years for the Seaway today, this is also the 33d wedding anniversary of Secretary and Mrs. Rogers. So we give them our special greetings today.

Now, on this occasion, I realize, too, that we think of the closeness of our two countries, Canada and the United States. We think also of the speed of change, the fact that 10 years ago we were celebrating the opening of a Seaway, and that within a month we hope to see the landing of the first man on the moon.

I would only suggest that when Governor Rockefeller made his introductions, that perhaps he may have been a bit prophetic. Our two Nations are indeed close together. And when he presented Mrs. Trudeau, she might be out there on the American side here in this audience.[2]

On this occasion, in trying to think of

---

[1] John Foster Dulles, Secretary of State 1953–1959.

[2] Prime Minister Trudeau was not married.

what would be appropriate to say in presenting to you the Prime Minister of Canada, I think that the inscription which appears on the great installation in which we met just a few minutes ago is one to which I can refer.

Ten years ago when Queen Elizabeth, on this very day, met with me, after having met with President Eisenhower the preceding day on the Canadian side, she unveiled a plaque and that plaque set forth the common purposes of our two countries.

It pointed out that our frontiers are the frontiers of friendship; our ways are the ways of peace; and, our works are the works of progress and of freedom.[3]

I think that as we stand here today, and we think of the United States and Canada—frontiers of friendship, ways of freedom, works of peace—that what we have done in this great cooperative venture is certainly an example for the world to follow in terms of the relations between nations.

Sometimes we just take for granted the fact that we have the longest unguarded frontier between two nations in the world. Sometimes we just take for granted the fact that our two countries have had a period in which we have fought together in war, in which we have worked together in peace, and in which we have been joined in really true friendship for over a century and a half.

---

[3] The inscription, which appears on the international peace monument at the Robert Moses-Robert Saunders Power Dam, reads: "This stone bears witness to the common purpose of two nations whose frontiers are the frontiers of friendship, whose ways are the ways of freedom and whose works are the works of peace."

But we should not take for granted these magnificent accomplishments. And this Seaway, which opened the heartland of Canada and the heartland of America, this Seaway which was conceived by men who dreamed of great things and was put into being by men who were able to produce them, the practical engineers, this is an indication of what can happen when nations can work together, when they can be at peace with each other.

And today, as I walked with Prime Minister up this Avenue of Flags, with the flags of all the nations, and then the flags of Canada on the one side and the flags of the United States on the other, I was proud to be an American citizen.

I was proud, also, of the relations between our two countries and I am particularly proud today to present to you the man who heads the Government of our neighbor to the north.

It was altogether appropriate that the first official visitor to the United States of America, after my inauguration as President, was Prime Minister Trudeau, because our two countries are so close in the ways that I have mentioned.

And on that visit, he made a great impression on our Government officials and also on the American people. We are glad to have him back here today on what is, in effect, a semi-official occasion.

We welcome the Prime Minister to the American shore just as he will welcome me in a few moments to Canada.

And we can only say in welcoming him that we look forward to that continuing friendship which has produced so much in the way of progress in peace and freedom for the American Continent and the Northern Hemisphere of the great continent in which we live.

I am proud to present to this audience of Americans and Canadians, the Prime Minister of Canada.

NOTE: The ceremony began at 1:50 p.m. at the Dwight D. Eisenhower Lock on the Seaway at Massena, N.Y.

The President spoke following introductory remarks by Gov. Nelson A. Rockefeller of New York. The Governor's remarks are printed in the Weekly Compilation of Presidential Documents (vol. 5, p. 922).

The remarks of Prime Minister Trudeau follow:

Mr. President, Governor Rockefeller, distinguished guests, ladies and gentlemen:

I want to thank you, particularly Governor Rockefeller, for having invited us, so many Canadians both on and off the platform, to visit the State of New York.

This is a unique occasion. It is the first half of a ceremony, the second half of which will take place in Montreal, and which celebrates a truly unique event.

President Nixon reminded us that it was the 10th anniversary of the opening of the Seaway, but, also, the 10th anniversary to the day of his meeting with Queen Elizabeth on the Canadian-U.S. border 10 years ago.

The dream of a Seaway permitting the ships of the world to sail into the heart of the American Continent was a dream in the minds of men in these lands for many centuries; and, also, the dream, no doubt because of their industry, because of their inventiveness, the dream of harnessing the falling water from the Great Lakes falling towards the seas, this tremendous source of energy, which could be harnessed for the use of both nations.

This dream was realized thanks to the cooperation, not only of the Governments of two great countries, and of several of the Provinces and States therein, but thanks to the cooperation of the people of these countries and of the many institutions, public and private, on both sides of the border.

And, now today, 10 years later, we see the benefits of this—those who live along these shores see the ships of many nations. Ships of over 30 nations, I am told, will go through these locks and up and down these waters from far-away lands of Japan and Thailand and the Soviet Union, bearing cargoes as diverse as Scotch whiskey and soybeans.

This also resulted in the development of industries and, also, because the creators of this vast work were careful to preserve its beauty in the development of the tourist trade and more and more intensified exchanges between the people of the United States and the people of Canada.

But more than showing cooperation between two people for economic benefits, I think this great work, as the President said, has given spirit and imagination to the people of these two lands.

I remember when I was a boy in Montreal we used to say that Montreal was the harbor which was the sea-going harbor which was further inland of any sea-going harbor in the world, some thousand miles inland. And now I am sure it is the school boys and girls of the cities of Duluth and of the lake head, who are saying that of their cities some 2,000 miles away from the sea.

And this tremendous work of engineering, this tremendous work built on cooperation by two countries, symbolizes the unity and friendship between our two countries.

And I think it is proper that this ceremony should take place beside the lock named after General Eisenhower, because General Eisenhower will long be remembered in esteem by Canadians, those who remember the ceremony 10 years ago, and more still by those Canadians who followed him as the General to victory in Europe.

Another American we will remember, an American who is well-known, a poet, Robert Frost, who wrote a poem called "Mending Wall," and in which he tells of two neighboring farmers bringing stones from their lands and replacing them on the wall that has been a bit damaged by the frost swells during the winter. And they talked and one feels that perhaps they don't need a wall so strong, so long, because they are friends. But one says to the other, perhaps to justify his work, "Good fences make good neighbors."

Perhaps it is also true, Mr. President, that good ditches make good neighbors.

And this day is one which permits us to

celebrate the opening of this Seaway which unites our countries, and which is truly a marvelous ditch.

And may that ditch long run between our countries and insure the friendship of the people of the United States of America and of the people of Canada.

252 Remarks at the International Exhibition "Man and His World" in Montreal, Canada. *June 27, 1969*

Mr. Prime Minister, all of the distinguished guests on the platform, and all of the very friendly audience here in Canada:

I express my deep appreciation to the Prime Minister and to his colleagues here in Canada for the very gracious words of welcome that they have uttered on this occasion.

As I noted the bilingual characteristics of the remarks that have preceded me, I realized that I, perhaps, have a responsibility in that respect that I might not be able to fill as well as I would like.

However, whatever my pronunciation may be, what I now say will come from the heart. *Je suis très heureux d'être au Canada dans la Belle Province de Québec.*

And if you understood that, give the credit to a senior at McGill University who just before me said that meant I am very happy to be in Canada in the beautiful Province of Quebec.

Now, on this occasion, we celebrate the 10th anniversary of the Seaway. Earlier, on the United States side, we pointed out the significance of that celebration.

But the Seaway has meant to the United States what it has meant to Canada, what it has meant to all the nations of the world whose flags are there before us in the breeze.

We also spoke of what the Seaway has meant in a larger sense, as a lesson as to how two nations can work together; how they can dream together and make those dreams come true.

And if I have one thought today to leave with this great audience, it is this: I believe that the spirit that built this Seaway is the spirit that the world needs today to bring the people of the world together.

Second, I would like to express, on behalf of all of us from the United States side, the great pleasure that is ours to be here at the site of Expo '67, which, as I understand from Mayor Drapeau,[1] will go on and on and on, Expo '68 and Expo '69.

I was thinking of the heritage of Expo '67. My family and I were not as fortunate as some to visit it then, and we are so fortunate to have seen it today, and we are glad you kept it so we could see it today. And that heritage is in many ways the millions of people, 50 million who came that first year in 1967, most of them from the United States, and as a result of having come here took away with them an understanding of and an affection for Canada and the people of Canada that they will carry with them the rest of their lives.

And, second, Expo '67 will live on, not only in the physical environment that we see here, but also, of course, in the Expos

---

[1] Jean Drapeau, Mayor of Montreal.

who now play in the National League.

I should point out to you that I am somewhat of a baseball fan. I know the record of the Expos to date. Some of my friends in Montreal and in Canada have expressed some concern about that record. But I have noted that despite the place in the standings that the Expos presently occupy, the attendance of the fans from Montreal is still at an all-time high for any new team in the League.

And to those who may have any question about the future, just let me say, I speak from experience. For 14 years in Washington, I rooted for the Washington Senators and they were in the cellar every year. And now they are out of the cellar, and so will the Expos be, if you just stick with them as I know the fans in Montreal will in the years ahead.

But now, on a more serious subject, serious in the sense that it transcends all of the interests that we have already spoken of, the Seaway, the field of sports, and it is what this exposition stands for today, "Man and His World." And we all think what a great and profound theme that truly is—not the Canadian and his world, not the American and his world, not the Russian and his world, but "Man and His World."

And here at this exposition, we get a feeling of what that really means to all of us. We recognize here in this Place of Nations that within a month when the first man lands on the moon, it will happen that he will be an American.

But it is significant to note that when he lands there, he will come in peace and he will come from all the world and not just the American part of the world.

And so, today, as we think of what our two great countries have done together in building this Seaway, as we think of the

record of peace and friendship that we have built together over 150 years, as we think of what we can do together in the future, in working for the cause of progress and freedom and peace in the world, I think that we will leave this occasion, not with the sense of desperation about the admittedly difficult problems the Prime Minister has referred to that we have, that you have, and other nations have, but with the sense of hope, a sense of hope because in a moment like this, we realize that those great principles and those great desires and those great dreams that unite men are infinitely stronger than those that divide them.

And as we learn to dream together, we shall learn to work together, we shall live in peace together, as Canada and America have always lived in peace together and will for the time that we can see ahead.

Thank you.

NOTE: The President spoke shortly after 4:20 p.m. at the Place des Nations Stadium on the site of "Man and His World" in response to remarks by Canadian Prime Minister Pierre Elliott Trudeau who spoke in French. A translation of his remarks follows:

Mr. President, Governor Rockefeller of the State of New York, Representatives of the Governments of Quebec and Ontario, distinguished guests, ladies and gentlemen:

It is fitting, Mr. President, that we should meet at this site to celebrate the tenth anniversary of the great work which our two peoples have built together. For several centuries, the inhabitants of North America, the settlers from Europe and before them the Indians, considered this great river as a waterway opening into the mysterious and the unknown, and from the beginning, explorers have plied it from the ocean to its most distant sources.

It is truly a fine thing that this river has, like the open arms of a continent, drawn to the interior peoples ever eager to discover unimaginable beauties and unhoped-for wealth. It is these people who have enabled our two countries to develop and it is this river which has made it possible for our countries to go to the source; it has truly been the path of progress—the path of physical progress, but also the path of material, social, and economic progress. All these villages, towns, and cities extending along its course actually served as a link between those who were pressing onwards and those who were planting roots and developing their country.

And it is for this reason that we are happy to welcome you here, Mr. President, and to salute the great work which our peoples have undertaken together. It is proof not only that the economic progress which resulted from it was essential to the happiness of men, but also that this waterway which nature has given us, laboured upon by men working together, can serve not as a barrier between peoples but as a path of welcome, of progress, and of access. And in this way, the symbol of our river, the symbol of the Seaway, this gigantic and marvelous work, symbolizes friendship and cooperation between our two peoples.

[At this point the Prime Minister continued speaking in English]

Mr. President:

It is a great pleasure, Mr. President, to welcome you here with Mrs. Nixon and with members of your family. And it is truly appropriate on this, the first visit to Canada since your election, that the meeting should take place here at the Place des Nations.

This open forum, which knows no division, was during the year of Expo '67 the meeting place of peoples of many lands who came here to share knowledge, friendship, acquaintances,

in a spirit of brotherhood and understanding.

I know this lesson, Mr. President, of men building together with what nature has given them so that they should be freer and more prosperous. This lesson is one that we will all remember and imitate.

And I am very happy to welcome you here and I am very pleased that you should have come with Mrs. Nixon and with members of your family and with many of your colleagues.

I remember well when I was in Washington in March, the welcome that Mrs. Nixon extended to me at the White House, the charm, the warmth of the welcome, and I am very glad that you came with her today. Because we are told—at least, I have heard—that wives have a great influence on the travel plans of their husbands and I hope that Mrs. Nixon will impress on you the warm welcome that we will always have in the heart of Canadians whenever you come to visit us.

You are the head of state of a very great nation, Mr. President—a nation which has immense resources, and extraordinary people, which always knows great difficulties, which we know that your people, your Government, is attempting to solve in a spirit of friendship and equity and we realize the difficulty of the problem.

But we want to say to you, not only that you are welcome here, but that we understand, that we want to share in the spirit of friendship that is in the hearts of the American people.

It is my great privilege to introduce to you today the head of state of Canada's closest friend and ally, and to introduce also the members of the First Family.

Mr. President.

253 Remarks at a Ceremony Marking the 30th Anniversary of the Executive Office of the President. *June 30, 1969*

I AM DELIGHTED to have the opportunity to attend this birthday party, not just for the Bureau of the Budget, because it is much older than 30 years, but because of the time 30 years ago when the Executive Office of the President was set

up and the Bureau of the Budget became an integral part of that office.

I should say that this is the first time since becoming President that I have been in this room, the Indian Treaty Room, and I was reminded by the Budget Director, who, of course, knows everything—everything about history and everything else—almost everything—that President Eisenhower used to have his press conferences here.

This will not be a press conference, but I do want to speak quite directly to those who work in the Bureau of the Budget and also to pay a tribute to the former Budget Directors who are here, and to all of those who have something directly or indirectly to do with Budget, including the Secretary of the Treasury, who is here.

First, as one of the guests at the White House worship services last Sunday, the Director of the Budget, Mr. [Robert P.] Mayo, as I presented him to the distinguished man who had delivered the sermon that day, Rabbi Finkelstein, the Director of the Budget said, "I am known as the meanest man in town." I guess Budget Directors earn that by what they do and what they have to do.

I know that all of you who work in the Bureau of the Budget in this great historic building, as you make the decisions, the very hard ones you must make day after day, you must sometimes wonder if there could not be a more popular job to have than to say "no" nicely. That is what those who are in the Budget Bureau have to learn to do. At times you can say "yes" and, of course, that is one of those times you will appreciate.

But I realize that there is no department of this Government and no group working in the Office of the President that has a more difficult responsibility than those in the Bureau of the Budget. It is not simply a case of saying "no" when the amount that is requested is too great from a department, but it is also a case of attempting to have an orderly way of running a government in these days when many

are wondering whether government as we know it today may have gotten to the point that it can no longer deliver what it is supposed to deliver.

I don't think any of us would go as far as Peter Drucker did when he said that Government had now become so inefficient that all it could really do was to inflate the currency and wage war, and there is some doubt as to whether it can wage war.

But certainly as far as the currency is concerned there seems to be little doubt about that at the present time. But what Peter Drucker did say in that article and in that book,[1] which I know many of you have read, was quite relevant to the problem we have today, and I would like to emphasize it on the occasion of this birthday party.

Your job is bigger than simply determining how much. Your job has to do with the whole organization of government, how we do things, how this delivery system can be made to work.

The Congress must make the great decisions as to what the legislation will be. The President must make decisions and recommendations to the Congress with the hope they will execute them, but here at the Bureau of the Budget you have to take the various programs and see how they fit into this complex machinery of government, and your recommendations will have an enormous effect on whether those programs will work.

We know that government is much better than what many of its critics have suggested. But we do know that particularly in dealing with the problems of our

---

[1] Peter F. Drucker, "Sickness of Government," The Public Interest, Winter 1969; and "The Age of Discontinuity: Guidelines to Our Changing Society" (Harper and Row, 1969).

cities, dealing with the great domestic crisis of our time, that the problem is not simply how much, but the problem is whether we are going to be able to develop a program that will work.

Men of very good intentions will vote for programs spending billions of dollars, and then at the end of those programs we look back and see that they have failed. So that is why your advice on not only how much, but how—how we can get away from the overlapping and all of the other inefficiencies, why that advice is very valuable to the President, very valuable to the Congress, and very valuable to the country.

I know that hanging in the Budget Director's office is the statement by Charles Dawes, who was the first Budget Director in 1921, to the effect that those who work in the Bureau of the Budget are like those who stoke the furnaces in a ship. The President and the Congress up on the bridge determine which way the ship will go, but those down there who stoke the furnaces in the Budget Bureau determine how far it will go.

Certainly there is another way that we could say that. There is an analogy between those who stoke the furnaces of a

ship and those who work in the Bureau of the Budget. You take plenty of heat and so do they.

But I simply want you to know that as one who does not get over to this office where you work as often as I should, but as one who sees your Director and the others in the Budget Bureau many times in the Cabinet Room, I appreciate what you have done. All of us in Government know that your job is necessary; it is essential to the orderly working of Government. And on this 30th birthday party of your being part of the Executive Office of the President, you can be sure that the President of the United States, speaking for the people of the United States, is indeed grateful for the dedicated people, regardless of party, who year after year do the fine work that the Bureau of the Budget has done and is doing for this present administration. Thank you very much.

NOTE: The President spoke at 4:50 p.m. in the Indian Treaty Room in the Executive Office Building.

The Executive Office of the President was established under the authority of the Reorganization Act of 1939 (53 Stat. 561) by Reorganization Plans I and II of 1939 (3 CFR, 1938–1943 Comp., pp. 1288–1298).

254   Message to the Eighteen-Nation Disarmament Committee Meeting in Geneva. *July* 3, 1969

I HAVE FOLLOWED closely the activities of the spring session of the Disarmament Committee, and Ambassador [Gerard C.] Smith has reported to me on the prospects for progress in the near future.

As the Conference resumes its work after a recess of 6 weeks, I would like to

address the following thoughts to the members of the Committee:

First, the ground has been prepared for concrete arms control negotiations. In addition to the valuable suggestions by many members of the Committee, draft agreements have been submitted by the United States and by the Soviet Union to prevent an arms race on the seabeds.[1] Although differences exist, it should not prove beyond our ability to find common ground so that a realistic agreement may be achieved that enhances the security of all countries.

The framing of an international agreement to apply to more than 100 million square miles of the earth's surface lying under the oceans is a high challenge to our vision and statesmanship. I ask the participants in this Committee to join with us in elaborating a measure that is both practical and significant. With good will on all sides and a fair measure of hard work, we may achieve agreement in the course of this session. With each passing day the seabed becomes more important for the security and well-being of all nations. Our goal should be to present a sound seabed arms control measure to the 24th General Assembly of the United Nations.

Second, the Secretary General of the United Nations has just issued his study on the effects of chemical and biological warfare.[2] Experts from many countries have contributed to this important work. I am pleased that an expert from the United States, Dr. Ivan Bennett, has also played a role in the study. We welcome the Secretary General's study, since it will draw the attention of all mankind to an area of common concern. The specter of chemical and biological warfare arouses horror and revulsion throughout the world.

The delegation of the United States is prepared to examine carefully, together with other delegations, any approaches that offer the prospect of reliable arms control in this field.

Third, in my letter to Ambassador Smith on March 18 at the opening of the first session of this Committee, I reaffirmed United States support for the conclusion of a comprehensive test ban adequately verified; I stated my conviction that efforts must be made toward greater understanding of the verification issue. I am pleased that, during your first session, serious exploration of verification problems took place. The United States delegation will be prepared to continue to participate in efforts towards greater understanding of this key issue. It is only by means of careful study, with due regard for all of the relevant technical and political considerations, that progress can be made.

Fourth, I recently announced that the United States hopes to be able to commence talks with the Soviet Union on strategic arms limitations around July 31 or shortly thereafter. When these talks begin, which I hope and trust will be soon, they will of necessity be bilateral negotiations between the United States and the Soviet Union. The United States Government is, however, deeply conscious of its responsibilities to its allies and to the community of nations.

While these talks progress, it is particularly important that multilateral negotiations continue in this Committee in an atmosphere of determination and promise. Arms control is without dispute a subject of direct concern to all nations, large and small. The wisdom, the advice, and the informed concern of many nations

---

[1] Background information and a draft of the treaty banning emplacement of nuclear weapons on the seabed are printed in the Department of State Bulletin (vol. 60, p. 520).

[2] The 100-page report, dated July 1, 1969, is entitled "Chemical and Bacteriological [Biological] Weapons and the Effect of Their Possible Use" (United Nations sales publication number E. 69. I. 24).

are needed in a continuing body such as this to ensure that no opportunities are missed to achieve genuine progress.

This Committee clearly is the world's preeminent multilateral disarmament forum. Its record of accomplishment, which needs no recital here, is greater than that of any other disarmament committee in history. I trust that your Committee will continue its efforts with all of the combined skill and dedication which its members have demonstrated in the past.

The negotiation of sound arms control and disarmament, like all work contributing to peace, must be an integrated and comprehensive effort. Progress in the tasks of your Committee will be a contribution to a world of peaceful international cooperation, a world where fear and conflict are supplanted by the honest give-and-take of negotiation aimed at meeting the legitimate aspirations of all.

The United States will work in every way to bring us closer to such a world.

NOTE: The President's message was released at Key Biscayne, Fla.

255 Statement on Naming Members to the American Revolution Bicentennial Commission. *July 3, 1969*

IN THE LIFE of a person, no birthday is ever quite like the one before it. The same is true of a nation. Each Fourth of July America is 1 year older, 1 year's growth larger, 1 year richer in knowledge and experience.

As we celebrate this Fourth, it is appropriate that we look not only back, but also ahead. Only 7 years from now, the United States will celebrate its 200th birthday. Already, these two centuries have been a time of unparalleled human achievement. The next 7 years—beginning with man's first footstep on the moon—promise to be a time of momentous events. But as we look forward to that 200th anniversary, our aim is not to catalogue laurels to rest on, but to discover lessons to build on.

America's bicentennial can be an immensely important occasion, not only for the United States, but also for people everywhere who cherish liberty. Those who led America's Revolution spoke to their time, and to all time; their words

ring as fresh and as true today as when they were written. They captured an ideal, and gave it life.

Three years ago, Congress provided for the creation of an American Revolution Bicentennial Commission "to plan, encourage, develop, and coordinate the commemoration of the American Revolution. . . ."[1] The Commission's charter is broad; its responsibility is great. The bicentennial is more than a ceremonial occasion. The way in which we as a Nation choose to celebrate that 200th anniversary will have an important bearing on what we learn from it, and on the inspiration we draw from it.

I have today named 17 distinguished Americans to be members of that Commission. In doing so, I repose in them a high trust: to reach back to our Nation's founding and distill those themes that can illumine its future, and to devise the kinds of activities that can best bring alive for

---

[1] 80 Stat. 259.

today's generations what that Revolution has meant for America and for mankind.

The bicentennial celebrates more than the events of the Revolution. It belongs not only to the Thirteen Original States, but equally to the newest and the farthest from those 18th-century battlefields. It is a national celebration, a national anniversary; it challenges each of the 50 States, and every community, to look to its heritage and its hopes.

We have forged one Nation from an extraordinary diversity of people, cultures, and traditions. Each generation has mastered new problems and discovered new opportunities. All this is part of the rich treasure of experience on which we must draw for the bicentennial; and our goal must be to marshal this experience so as to launch the Nation's third century with a new "Spirit of '76" that matches the first.

NOTE: A release issued by the White House Press Office contains the names of 17 members of the American Revolution Bicentennial Commission and is printed in the Weekly Compilation of Presidential Documents (vol. 5, p. 932).

The President's statement was released at Key Biscayne, Fla.

256 Message to Thor Heyerdahl and the Crew of Expedition Ra. *July* 4, 1969

YOUR message and your mission remind the leaders and the peoples of all nations that we are all travelers together on this ancient ship called Earth. You are pursuing two of the noblest aims of man— the quest for knowledge of his past and the hope for peace in his future. May your courageous voyage bring you safely to port and may your eminent example contribute to greater cooperation among all nations for all that is best for mankind.

NOTE: The expedition led by Thor Heyerdahl, Norwegian explorer and anthropologist, left Morocco on May 17, 1969, aboard the *Ra*, a 60–70 foot boat of woven papyrus. They traveled 2,600 miles to within 600 miles of Barbados before being forced to abandon the craft. Although partially submerged, the *Ra* drifted on alone to South America.

On July 3, 1969, the President received a radio message from Thor Heyerdahl in mid-Atlantic. The President radioed his message in reply to the crew of the *Ra* on the following day. The message from Thor Heyerdahl follows:

Seven men from seven nations, attempting to cross the widest span of the Atlantic Ocean from Morocco in Africa to the New World in a replica of an ancient Egyptian papyrus ship, take pleasure in sending you, Mr. President, our message of best wishes upon having covered 2,000 miles and thus completed half our voyage. Our objective is to investigate whether or not it might have been possible for ancient civilizations in the Mediterranean area to bring cultural impulses to the original populations of the New World.

Simultaneously, it is our desire to experiment in small scale with international cooperation under difficult and stressed conditions and thus to test the unity of mankind both in time and space. Our expedition has the privilege to sail under the flag of the United Nations, together with the flags of each nation represented on board, which are: the United States represented by Norman Baker, the Soviet Union by Yuri Senkevich, Italy by Carlo Mauri, Chad by Abdoulaye Djibrime, Egypt by Georges Sourial, Mexico by Santiago Genoves, and Norway by the undersigned.

Having found in our little world of floating

papyrus bundles that cooperation of men of different national, racial, linguistic, religious, and political backgrounds can be readily accomplished and highly fruitful to the common cause, we take the liberty to extend symbolically the sincere wish that the captains of greater vessels, like the large and small powers, shall have success in every effort made to encourage friendship and cooperation between the different peoples of the world in the true spirit of the United Nations.

Respectfully yours,

THOR HEYERDAHL

257 Remarks of Welcome at the White House to Emperor Haile Selassie I of Ethiopia. *July* 8, 1969

Your Majesty, Your Excellencies, and our friends here in the White House:

Your Majesty, this historic house has witnessed many historic occasions, but as all of our guests here today I am sure will agree, and as those who are listening on television and radio will understand, no visit to this house has a greater historical significance than your visit to the White House again.

First, because in all the world today you, as Chief of State, have served longer—53 years—than any Chief of State in the world, and we honor you for that.

Second, because I am the fourth President of the United States to have the honor of receiving you here in the White House as an official state visitor. In the whole history of the United States, over 190 years, this has not been the case with any official visitor. You broke the record with four Presidents today.

Third, because you are the first visitor, official visitor, to this country since my inauguration as President of the United States from the great continent of Africa, to which you have offered such outstanding leadership.

For these reasons we honor you today, and also for others that I will mention briefly.

We honor you because of the personal leadership that you have provided for your country, an ancient land, a proud people, but one which under your leadership has moved forward in the field of economic and social progress dramatically in these last years.

Second, because in this great continent of Africa, a very old continent with many new nations, you have provided the counsel and the guidance and the leadership to the new nations, to the new leaders, which was so essential, and also the example for unity, unity which transcends differences in the continent. The fact that the Organization of African Unity is in your capital city is an indication of that leadership.

But finally, to all of us who are here, those of us who go back a few years, we welcome you as one who appealed to and inspired the whole conscience of the world in 1936, when you, standing virtually alone, spoke out against aggressive totalitarianism; and as a result of speaking out, you gave an example, an example which should have been followed then, but an example which today, historians will recall, provided inspiration to leaders and people throughout the world.

As we look back over your life, as we look back over your leadership, we can truly say that no chief of state or head of government can be welcomed to the

United States of America who really touches our hearts more than you touch our hearts, because you stand for those great principles, principles of independence, principles of national dignity, principles of unity which transcend differences between nations.

You stand for those principles and have stood for them through the years, in difficult years, as well as those in which you have had perhaps a better opportunity than in times past.

So today we welcome you. We regret that our weather last night was difficult so that you were unable to be received by the great throngs who wanted to welcome you if we could have had this ceremony outside. But I can assure you that small though our numbers may be because of the restrictions of this room, that the hearts of all Americans—200 million Americans—are full with respect as you return again to this country, and we look forward to our conversations with you and we wish you good health.

We wish you, also, a good visit here, and we wish you the very best for the years of leadership which we know you will provide, not only to your nation, not only to your continent, but to those who cherish and honor freedom throughout the world.

NOTE: The President spoke at 10:29 a.m. in the East Room at the White House following a formal welcome with full military honors for His Imperial Majesty Haile Selassie I at the North Portico. The arrival had been scheduled for the preceding afternoon but was delayed by inclement weather.

See also Items 259 and 260.

His Imperial Majesty spoke in Amharic and his remarks were translated from notes by Ambassador Minasse Haile of Ethiopia.

His Imperial Majesy responded as follows:

Your Excellency, President Nixon, ladies and gentlemen:

Mr. President, first of all I wish to take this opportunity to thank you for the most kind words you have uttered about my country and myself.

I also wish to take this opportunity to thank you for extending an invitation for me to come and visit the United States of America once more. I hope in my brief sojourn to this country I will have the opportunity of renewing old acquaintances as well as making new friends.

As you have said, Mr. President, the relations between the United States and Ethiopia are not new ones. We have, for many decades, maintained the most friendly relations. We have manifested this friendship not merely by words, but in terms of specific, concrete, and joint efforts and sacrifices we have made.

Our friendship has been based on certain solid common interests which, as time goes on, rather than being weakened are strengthening themselves each day.

Mr. President, I am happy today to be here, particularly to meet you again in your own country. I have vivid recollections of your visit to Ethiopia and the extensive exchange of views we have had concerning the bilateral relations between the United States and Ethiopia, as well as multilateral relations and questions affecting international peace and security.

I am glad that my arrival here in the United States yesterday is affording me another opporunity to exchange views with you, Mr. President, with a view toward strengthening further the good and friendly relations that have long remained as the basis of the relations between Ethiopia and the United States.

I also wish to emphasize that the friendship between our two countries has not been solely confined to relations between us, such as my visit here or President Nixon's visit to Ethiopia; but many people in different walks of life, both from Ethiopia as well as from the United States, visit each other's country, and we consider this to be indispensable in strengthening already existing friendly ties.

Mr. President, you have mentioned African problems. You have mentioned the Organization of African Unity, an organization which the people of our vast continent have established with a view to performing certain specific tasks.

Briefly speaking, the Organization is established for the purpose of protecting in a better fashion the independence of African states. It is also meant to expedite the economic and social progress through cooperation of African peoples.

It also has the important task of assisting in the maintenance of international peace and security. Because this very principle for which that Organization is established is in accord with the basic policy of the Government of the United States, the Organization has had ample support on the part of the people and Government of this country.

I hope that in the time to come the United States Government and people would find it possible to come to even a greater assistance of that Organization, for the principles for which it stands are of universal value and never changing ones.

Mr. President, I hope, as I see it, as a result of my visit and exchange of views I will have the pleasure of having with you, the relations between our two countries will be strengthened further.

In this time of a fast changing world, where new things come about and so forth, it is essential for leaders to come together to exchange and consider views to see by what joint effort they will be able to strengthen that relation.

I hope that as a result of the broad general understanding we are going to arrive at during my visit here, our understanding will be reflected in the kind of policy that will follow and the kind of consideration and attitude we will have regarding each other's vital problems.

I hope in broad terms, as I see it, the good relation between our two countries will be further broadened, not to the exclusive advantage of one party, but with a view toward bringing forth mutual benefits and mutual advantage.

I wish to thank you again, Mr. President, for the very kind words you have said. I also wish to thank the people and the Government of the United States for giving me such a cordial reception.

Thank you very much.

258 Special Message to the Congress on the Unemployment Insurance System. *July 8, 1969*

To the Congress of the United States:

The best time to strengthen our unemployment insurance system is during a period of relatively full employment.

The Secretary of Labor is sending to the Congress today proposed legislation to extend unemployment insurance to 4,800,000 workers not now covered; to end the shortsighted restrictions that stand in the way of needed retraining efforts; and to add a Federal program automatically extending the duration of benefits in periods of high unemployment.

There are three principles to be considered as we move to make the unemployment insurance system responsive to our times.

Unemployment insurance is an earned benefit. When a man covered by unemployment insurance is working, the em-

ployer pays a tax on his wages to insure against the day when the employee may be between jobs. That insurance is like a mandatory fringe benefit; it is insurance bought in the employee's behalf, and the worker therefore is entitled to the benefits he receives when he is unemployed. Accordingly, there is no demeaning of human dignity, no feeling of being "on the dole," when the insured worker receives benefits due.

Unemployment insurance is one of the foremost examples of creative Federal-State partnership. Although the system was created by Federal law, most decisions about the nature of the program are left to the States, which administer the system with State employees. This makes the system far more flexible and attuned to local needs and special circumstances of local economies.

Unemployment insurance is an economic stabilizer. If, for example the economy were ever to slow and unemployment were to rise, this program automatically would act to sustain personal income. This would help prevent a downturn from gathering momentum resulting from declines in purchasing power. When employment is at a high level, and greater stimulation of consumer demand is unwanted, relatively little money flows into the economy from unemployment insurance.

With these principles in mind, I am making these recommendations for both Federal and State action:

1. We should act together to extend unemployment protection to more employees, including many highly vulnerable to layoffs who are not now covered.

2. The States should make certain that workers throughout the United States receive enough money for a long enough period of time to sustain them while they seek new jobs.

3. We should end the restrictions imposed by almost half the States on payments to unemployed workers undergoing retraining and, instead, follow the lead of those States which encourage retraining.

4. We should better protect the investment made on behalf of the insured by seeing to it that the funds are paid only to those who should receive them.

5. We should increase the responsiveness of the system to major changes in national economic conditions.

6. We should strengthen the financing of the system which presently discriminates against the low-wage worker and the steady employer.

1. PROTECTING MORE EMPLOYEES

Over 57 million workers are protected by unemployment insurance. However, almost 17 million are not covered: more than half of these are employees of State and local governments. The last extension of coverage was enacted during the Eisenhower Administration, when 6 million additional workers were included; there is a clear social need today to cover as many more employees as we can.

I propose that an additional 4.8 million workers be covered by unemployment insurance. These include:

—1,600,000 workers in *small firms* with less than four employees;

—400,000 on large farms employing four or more workers in each of 20 weeks;

—200,000 in *agricultural processing* activities;

—1,800,000 in *non-profit organizations;*

—600,000 in *State hospitals* and *universities;*

—200,000 salesmen, delivery tradesmen, and others who are not currently defined as employees.

These 4,800,000 workers are in real need of protection against unemployment. Many of them are low wage workers with little job security and no prospect of termination pay if they are laid off.

The present gaps in coverage work a disproportionate hardship on minority workers, since a higher percentage of the 4,800,000 are nonwhite, compared to the entire labor force.

To cushion the immediate impact of this extension on employers, I recommend that States be permitted to lower the tax rates on newly covered employers

497

until such time as a record of employment experience can be compiled to determine what their true rate should be.

With the passage of this legislation, the majority of those remaining uncovered will be employees of State and local governments. I urge the States and localities to take action, in the light of their local circumstances, to include their own employees in unemployment insurance coverage.

2. MAKING BENEFITS ADEQUATE

The basic purpose of the Unemployment Insurance Program is to pay weekly benefits high enough to prevent a severe cut in a worker's standard of living when he is between jobs. The principle is generally accepted that it takes at least 50% of the worker's wage to meet this purpose.

Almost every State subscribes to this general principle, but benefit ceilings in their legislation have in fact made this principle largely ineffective, especially for the family breadwinner. At least two out of five claimants currently fail to get a benefit equal to one-half their wages.

In 1954, President Eisenhower recommended to States that they provide a maximum high enough to permit the great majority of covered workers to receive one-half their wages. This means that at least 80% of insured workers should be able to receive a benefit of one-half their wages if unemployed.

Men are most adversely affected by the limit on weekly benefits. In one large industrial State, for example, only 23% of the men receive benefits equal to as much as one-half their weekly wages.

If the program is to fulfill its role, it is essential that the benefit maximum be raised. A maximum of two-thirds of the average wage in the State would result

in benefits of 50% in wages to at least 80% of insured workers.

Up to now, the responsibility for determining benefit amounts has been the responsibility of the States. There are advantages in States having that freedom. However, the overriding consideration is that the objective of adequate benefits be achieved. I call upon the States to act within the next two years to meet this goal, thereby averting the need for Federal action.

3. ENCOURAGING RETRAINING

During the present decade, many manpower programs were launched in the United States. We have seen how unemployed workers can be equipped with new skills and started on new careers. When the decade began, only three States permitted workers who enrolled in retraining programs to continue to receive benefit payments. All the rest disqualified them upon entry into training.

During the early 1960's, many States recognized the potential of training for employment rehabilitation, and by 1969 twenty-five States, plus Puerto Rico and the District of Columbia, had removed such restrictive requirements.

However, twenty-five States continue to discourage retraining by denying benefits to workers in such programs on the theory that they are not "available for work." On the contrary, the workers are trying to keep themselves available by learning new techniques and technologies, and government should certainly stop penalizing them for doing something that government, business and labor all want to encourage.

I propose a requirement that the remaining States permit workers to continue to receive benefits while enrolled in train-

ing programs designed to increase their employability.

4. PROTECTING THE INSURANCE SYSTEM

We must also be sure that benefits are going only to those people the system is designed to protect. The funds must not be dissipated.

Attachment to the Labor Force. The unemployment insurance system is designed to protect workers whose attachment to the labor force is more than casual. A worker's attachment is measured by both his past employment history and his present situation. He must be ready, willing and able to work and trying to find work while he is claiming benefits; and he must have had at least a certain amount of employment in the recent past. Generally, from fourteen to twenty weeks of work is required, depending on the employment patterns of the State and the minimum duration of benefits.

A few States, however, measure past employment by a flat dollar amount. This discriminates against the low-wage worker, because it means he must work for a longer period to be eligible. Also, it permits other high wage workers to become eligible on the basis of very short seasonal work. *I recommend that a standard based on a minimum period of 15 weeks' employment be required as a condition of benefit eligibility, and that no flat dollar amount be permitted as the only yardstick.*

Workers on Strike. The unemployment tax we require employers to pay was never intended to supplement strike funds to be used against them. A worker who chooses to exercise his right to strike is not in-voluntarily unemployed.

In two States, workers on strike are paid unemployment insurance benefits after a certain period. This is not the purpose of the unemployment insurance system.

I propose a requirement that this practice of paying unemployment insurance benefits to workers directly engaged in a strike be discontinued.

5. IMPROVING RESPONSIVENESS TO ECONOMIC CONDITIONS

Difficult times are far less likely to occur in nations that take the trouble to prepare for them. The presence of a strong, anti-recessionary arsenal will in itself help prevent the need for its ever being used.

In normal times, the duration of benefit payments may be adequate. Most State programs now provide around twenty-six weeks of benefits; for the great majority of claimants, this is enough to see them through to another job. However, if the economy were ever to falter, the number of persons exhausting benefits would grow rapidly.

In each of the last two periods of high unemployment, the President proposed, and the Congress enacted, legislation to extend the duration of benefits temporarily. However, while this process was taking place, many workers were without income, and the economy was exposed to sharp declines in personal income due to unemployment.

I am proposing legislation that would automatically extend the length of time benefits are paid in all States when the national jobless rate of those covered by insurance equals or exceeds 4.5% for three consecutive months. If periods of high unemployment were ever to occur, individuals would receive benefits for an additional period up to 13 weeks; this extension would end when the national unemployment rate of those in the system (currently 2.2%) fell back below 4.5%, and when the number exhausting their benefits in a three-month period dropped below 1% of those covered. These additional payments would be financed out of that portion of the unemployment tax that is now retained by the Federal government.

6. STRENGTHENING AND REFORMING FINANCING

We must enable the Federal government to finance its share of the improvements proposed in this message, along with the costs of administering the Employment Security System. In addition, there will be a need to improve the ability of States to finance the higher benefit levels I am urging.

I propose that the taxable wage base be raised over a five-year period to $6,000 and thereafter be reviewed periodically to make certain the adequacy of financing.

In the majority of States, the taxable wage base for the Unemployment Insurance Tax is the first $3,000 of wages— exactly what it was three decades ago. In that same period, average wages in employment covered by the system have increased almost five-fold. The low tax base places obstacles in the way of hiring low-wage workers because a substantially higher proportion of their wage is taxed. In addition, the impact of the tax tends to encourage use of overtime rather than adding workers.

The higher base will have the desirable effect of allocating costs more equitably among employers. Particularly at the State level, overall benefit costs will represent a lower percent of taxable wages, and allow rates to reflect employer experience more accurately.

An Anchor to Windward. Unemployment insurance was begun as an answer to the human need for sustenance of the unemployed workingman seeking another job. It was designed to reduce the element of economic panic in job-hunting.

But as we move now to extend that insurance and meet that need more fully, we discover—not quite by accident—the bonus of serendipity. Here is insurance purchased through a tax on the employers of America in behalf of their employees that can be a potent counter to a downturn in the business cycle. This proves that well-conceived social legislation can be a great boon to business and to all Americans affected by the state of the economy.

The success of this system can be a great example in the relationship between the States and the Federal government.

The Federal government brought this unemployment insurance system into being—but the States have rightly adopted it as their own. The Federal government has traditionally established minimum coverage—but many States have expanded that coverage to fit their own needs.

Now the Federal-State system of unemployment insurance should move to provide adequate benefits in accordance with the goal that has been set and with full recognition of the diversity of economic conditions among States. Such action is most important to protect the individual and to achieve the anti-recessionary potential of unemployment insurance.

The Federal and State actions recommended will help advance the economy of each State and in protecting the economy of the nation. In human terms, the recommended changes will better enable a worker to weather the adversity of unemployment and to find a suitable job.

I urge that the Congress and the States

enact the legislation proposed to carry out these improvements.

RICHARD NIXON

The White House
July 8, 1969

NOTE: On the same day the White House Press Office released the text of a news briefing by Secretary of Labor George P. Shultz on the unemployment insurance message.

259   Toasts of the President and Emperor Haile Selassie I of Ethiopia. *July 8, 1969*

Your Imperial Majesty and our guests this evening:

As we welcome His Majesty again to this house, our thoughts must go back to the many events that have occurred in this room, because no one can be in the presence of His Majesty without thinking of all the history which he has seen and which he has made.

So tonight we honor him as the leader of a great country with whom the United States is very fortunate to have the most cordial and close relations.

We honor him as the leader and counselor and adviser to the great new nations of Africa in which he has played such a significant role, and we honor him also for his world leadership with which all of us are familiar.

I have been trying to think of something that would be appropriate to say that has not already been said about His Majesty on what is now the fourth occasion that he has been in this room as the official guest of a President of the United States.

As I pointed out when we welcomed him in the White House this morning, this is a record that has never been equaled before and may never be equaled again, the head of state being received by four

different Presidents as an official guest.

Those things that occur to me I am sure occur to all of you. He is a respected leader of his own country. He is a respected leader of a great continent and he is a respected leader of the world.

But he is more than that, and will be remembered by all of us, not only in this country but throughout the world, for more than those things, because that could be said about many of the official guests who are honored in this room.

I can think of the fact that His Majesty, of course, is a descendant of Solomon. If I can recall the Biblical phrase correctly, when King David died and the Lord asked Solomon what he wanted most, Solomon said, "Lord, give me an understanding heart." And because he asked for that, he received great wisdom, a long life and, of course, he had an understanding heart.

So it is with His Majesty. He has wisdom. He has had a long life, and, I know from personal experience, an understanding heart.

I share that with you for one moment. I had the great privilege, which some in this room have enjoyed, of visiting his country in 1957. My wife and I were received as royal guests at that time and treated royally. I returned again to his country in 1967, holding no office, having no portfolio whatever. I was received again as a royal guest and treated royally. This is a man with an understanding heart. [*Laughter*]

So tonight we honor him for what he has been to his country, to his continent, and to the world. We honor him also for what he means to history. What he means to history is something more than that of national leader or continental leader or world leader. What he means is a spirit— a spirit that in these days we sometimes think is lost, the spirit that does not give up when all the odds seem too difficult to overcome, the spirit that will not compromise when there is no compromise which would not destroy that in which he believed, the spirit that inspired us all in 1936, when we saw him standing tall and proud before the League of Nations talking for what all of the pragmatists, all of the realists said was a lost cause.

But because he spoke so strongly and proudly and vigorously for what was said to be a lost cause he was victorious, his nation was victorious. But what was more important, the cause of freedom, of strong men who refuse to be overcome by the odds and by the difficulties—that survived.

What His Majesty leaves, that heritage, on the pages of the history books of the world means more than the leadership of a nation, or a continent, or, for that matter, of the world. And for that moment of inspirational leadership we are all in his debt.

And tonight therefore, I know that all of you will welcome the opportunity to join with me, as has been the occasion on four different times, as I have indi-

cated before, in this room, to drink to his health; and in drinking to his health, I have found that there is a phrase in his country, a phrase of salutation, which I think is particularly appropriate. Translated from the Amharic it reads as follows: "May he live long for our glory."

I think there is nothing more appropriate that we can say to His Imperial Majesty tonight than that we trust he may live long for our glory.

Let us raise our glasses to His Imperial Majesty, Haile Selassie.

NOTE: The President spoke at 10:05 p.m. in the State Dining Room at the White House.

See also Items 257 and 260.

His Imperial Majesty Haile Selassie I spoke in Amharic and his remarks were translated from notes by Ambassador Minasse Haile of Ethiopia as follows:

Mr. President, Mrs. Nixon, distinguished guests:

I wish to express our heartfelt gratitude to Your Excellencies, to you, the Government, and the people of the United States of America, for the very warm welcome and cordial hospitality accorded to me ever since my arrival to this great and friendly country.

The kind and generous words which you have just addressed to me and my people are deeply appreciated. As you have rightly said, the friendship existing between us is of long standing and goes far back to when you were the Vice President of the United States of America.

The discussions and the exchange of views which I have had with you during your two visits to our country have certainly helped in strengthening this friendship.

This is not the first time, as I said today, for us to visit this great land. Upon the invitations that have been previously extended to us by your predecessors to visit this country, we have come here and learned at firsthand how much the American people treasure the friendship of our people.

This friendship has been tested in times of war and peace, and it has proven to be a firm and lasting one.

Thirty-three years have lapsed since our innocent and defenseless people suffered the agonies and atrocities of Fascist aggressors whose action irked and aroused the consciences of men and women everywhere.

It was following this most brutal aggression, as you have already mentioned this evening and this morning, that we made our appeal to the League of Nations to condemn this inexcusable aggression and to support Ethiopia's just cause.

Though the League of Nations failed us, we continued to seek its support, because we were convinced that only through this world body could this aggression be checked in time before the whole world was engulfed in a great catastrophe.

Our warnings were not heeded. However, we were proven right in the ensuing years. The moral force of our cause and the refusal of friendly countries like the United States of America to recognize the annexation of Ethiopia by force helped to sustain us and our gallant people in the struggle for total liberation of Ethiopia.

I, myself, and our people, are most grateful for this contribution of the United States. Ever since Ethiopia liberated herself from enemy occupation, the Government and the people of the United States of America have generously contributed to our effort of reconstruction and development.

Ethiopia, like other developing countries, has numerous problems in the field of education, public health, agriculture, communication, and other things related to development.

With regard to education, the people of the United States of America have given invaluable assistance by building schools in Ethiopia and by providing teachers. They have further granted scholarships to Ethiopian students to pursue their higher education in the United States of America, and have also given assistance to the Haile Selassie University, the first university.

One of the principles of American assistance to Ethiopia has also been in the field of communications. The friendly Government of the United States of America continues to participate in Ethiopia's efforts to modernize its agriculture and improve the health of its people.

We wish to express our appreciation and heartfelt thanks for the continued assistance given to us by the American people in our endeavor to maintain the security and territorial integrity of our nation.

In the field of international relations, the United States and Ethiopia have similar interests and objectives which give more reason for our two countries and peoples to increase that area of cooperation.

The age-old friendship existing between Ethiopia and the United States of America, we believe, has flourished as a result of our close cooperation both in the interest of our two peoples and in the general cause of world peace. It is our belief that our two countries should continue to cooperate even more closely.

Ethiopia is a nation fully committed to African unity and to the greater cause of world peace and subsequently shall continue to support and strengthen the Organization of African Unity which was established as an African instrument for peace and progress.

The Organization of African Unity, consulting its Committee on Nigeria, of which I have the honor of being chairman, has so far done its utmost to find ways and means of ending the tragic war in Nigeria. Without despair, we shall continue to exert our efforts with a view to finding an acceptable formula for peace.

It was very gratifying for me when I read the fact that you, Mr. President, have selected a competent individual to represent you in the humanitarian effort of the United States in Nigeria. I have had the privilege of talking with your representative and I am glad to report that our ideas about relief operations are very close and coincide on many points.

The history of the Ethiopian people is a history of a peace-loving nation. The annals of history are proof of the general stand of Ethiopia in this regard. However, there are still certain quarters who seek to compromise the territorial integrity and unity of our country. Such a sinister attitude will only strengthen our determination to safeguard the freedom and independence of our nation.

The reality of our position has impressed upon us the need to remain strong in all aspects of defense, a measure which can only be realized through the accelerated development of our nation. We are confident that the friendly peoples and Government of the United States of America will continue to give Ethiopia their usual encouragement and support in our determination to advance the good and well-being of our people in a climate of peace and stability.

Mr. President, Mrs. Nixon, and distinguished guests: I would like to ask all present here to join me in a toast to the good health and happiness of President and Mrs. Nixon, and to the continued well-being and prosperity of the American people, and to the lasting friendship between the people of the United States and the people of Ethiopia.

260   Remarks at the Conclusion of the Visit of Emperor Haile Selassie I of Ethiopia.   *July* 9, 1969

Your Imperial Majesty:

As you leave the White House I want to thank you for coming to the United States and for giving us the opportunity to meet with you again. I thank you first personally as an old friend and I appreciated the chance that has been provided to renew our personal acquaintance.

I want to thank you, too, because it provided the opportunity to discuss the bilateral problems that we have between our two countries. Certainly those were easy problems to discuss, easy because our traditional friendship led to the constructive type of solutions which we both expected when our conversations began.

But beyond that, I want to express to you my appreciation for your coming to this country because you gave the opportunity for all of us who met you to see not only the relations between Ethiopia and the United States in a better light, but to see the problems of the continent of Africa and of the whole world from the long perspective of history which you have and also from the understanding of the whole world which has always been yours.

Our discussions covered, as you know, the problems of the new nations of Africa and U.S. policy toward those nations, the agony of Nigeria and Biafra and what steps might be taken by this country and steps that could be taken by you to bring a solution to that problem, and also the problems of the Mideast which are so much in our minds as well as in yours.

This type of opportunity that it has provided, for discussion at the highest level of problems that affect the future of both of our countries, but beyond that, the future of a whole continent and the whole world, is one that made this visit very worthwhile, certainly from my standpoint and from the standpoint of my colleagues in government, and I hope from yours and your colleagues'.

As you leave, I say again, as I said last night, that perhaps the most appropriate words are the words from a greeting from your own language which, as I understand, literally translated to the English means, "May you live long for our glory."

We all feel that. We feel it in our hearts. May you live long, live long not just for yourself, not just for your people, but for the greater service that you can render to the cause of peace and progress in the continent of Africa, in the Mideast, and in the whole world.

NOTE: The President spoke at 12:20 p.m. in the Rose Garden at the White House.

Following the President's remarks, His Imperial Majesty spoke in Amharic. His remarks were translated from notes by Ambassador Minasse Haile of Ethiopia, as follows:

Mr. President, as I have already said, this is not the first visit I am paying to the United States. Each time I have come to this country I have been impressed by the friendship that has been manifested to me by responsible American officials as well as by the people in all walks of life that I have encountered.

I am happy to have gotten another opportunity to come to the United States with a view to discussing problems of common concern with the President of the United States and other distinguished officials of this Government.

In our discussions, Mr. President, as you have indicated, we have considered the possibility of expanding the relations between Ethiopia and the United States on a bilateral basis. We have also considered problems affecting our region as well as problems affecting international peace and security.

I am confident that as the result of the discussions I have had that the relations between our two countries will be strengthened further. There are many matters regarding which we have achieved a measure of understanding, and

the details about how to implement specific ideas will be left to officials, both of Ethiopia and the United States Government, who will be working on the details.

Mr. President, I also wish to take this opportunity of publicly extending to you an invitation to visit our country for a third time. This is an opportunity which I, myself, and the people of my country will be looking forward to.

I am sure that in accordance with the general understanding and views we have expressed and understanding we have achieved, the detailed consideration of problems will also be satisfactory. The discussion has been most rewarding to me, and I am satisfied with the opinions which have been expressed and with the meeting of minds that has been achieved.

Mr. President, may God bless you, your family, and may God bless the American people. Thank you.

261   Remarks at a Briefing on the Nation's Health System. *July* 10, 1969

Ladies and gentlemen:

When this administration came into office in January, we initiated a major study of the Nation's health care problems and programs. That study has now been completed and the report, which has been already distributed to members of the press, provides the directions which this administration will move toward in the months ahead.

In indicating those directions, I will say first that I realized when the administration came in, in January, that we had a major problem with regard to health care, that the problem was primarily one of enough doctors, the quality of the doctors, enough hospital beds to take care of the massively increasing demands in this field.

The report [1] that I have received from

Secretary Finch and from Dr. Egeberg indicates that the problem is much greater than I had realized. We face a massive crisis in this area; and unless action is taken, both administratively and legislatively, to meet that crisis within the next 2 to 3 years, we will have a breakdown in our medical care system which could have consequences affecting millions of people throughout this country.

I don't think I am overstating the case. I am simply indicating that we are aware of the problem and that we are now prepared to take the administrative and legislative action to deal with it.

Secretary Finch and Dr. Egeberg will be here to answer your questions and to further elaborate.

I simply want to say, finally, that the Department of Health, Education, and Welfare, and Dr. Egeberg, in his activities as our new Assistant Secretary, once the Senate confirms him, as it will very

---

[1] The text, "A Report on the Health of the Nation's Health Care System," July 10, 1969, is printed in the Weekly Compilation of Presidential Documents (vol. 5, p. 967).

shortly,[2] have my complete and unqualified support in this program which is now
being initiated.

NOTE: The President spoke at 12 noon in the
Roosevelt Room at the White House. Following

─────────────

[2] Dr. Egeberg's nomination was confirmed
on July 11, 1969.

his remarks, Secretary Robert H. Finch, Assistant Secretary-designate for Health and Scientific Affairs Dr. Roger O. Egeberg, and Under Secretary John G. Veneman, all of the
Department of Health, Education, and Welfare,
held a news briefing concerning health care.
The text of the news briefing is printed in the
Weekly Compilation of Presidential Documents
(vol. 5, p. 964).

262   Remarks on Presenting the Distinguished Service Medals of the Army, Navy, and Air Force to General Lyman L. Lemnitzer. *July 11, 1969*

*Mr. Secretary, General and Mrs. Lemnit-
zer, all of the distinguished guests here in
the Rose Garden this morning:*

This is a very historic occasion, as are
many of the occasions in the White House,
historic because we honor a man today
who completes over 50 years of service to
his country in the Armed Forces of the
United States, and historic because at this
time General Lemnitzer will receive the
Distinguished Service Medal of the Army,
the Navy, and the Air Force.

Now, others have received all three of
those awards, but for the first time in
history, a man who has served the Nation
so well in so many different capacities will
receive all three at the same time, and
finally, because it allows an opportunity
for me, not only as President of the United
States, but also as an individual who has
worked with General Lemnitzer, going
back over 15 years, to speak of his work
and to say what it means.

He is a distinguished, professional
soldier, and I say that as a compliment.
He is a professional soldier in the great
tradition of the American Armed Forces,
a man who is proud of wearing the uniform of his country, but a man who
respects the civilian authority.

He is one who could best be described
as a work horse rather than a show horse.
He served in World War II; he served in
Korea; he served as our Supreme Commander in Europe, and in all of these
capacities when something had to be done
that required hard, diligent work without
the publicity and, I suppose, all of the
glamour that goes with the other types of
assignments, General Lemnitzer was a
man we so often turned to.

And because of these capacities, I
would say that in all of our Armed Forces
today there is probably no man who is
more respected by all the services for
his professional capacity than General
Lemnitzer.

Finally, I would say, not only do we
respect him here in this country, but he is
respected abroad. I noted that he has
received at least 13 decorations from
foreign governments, including, I noted,
one from Thailand, the Order of the
White Elephant.

And as far as that Order is concerned,
General, I can assure you that we will
impute to it no political considerations
today.

Now the citation will be read by the
Secretary of Defense.

[Secretary of Defense Melvin R. Laird read the citation, the text of which follows.]

THE UNITED STATES ARMY
DISTINGUISHED SERVICE MEDAL
(THIRD OAK LEAF CLUSTER)

THE UNITED STATES NAVY
DISTINGUISHED SERVICE MEDAL

THE UNITED STATES AIR FORCE
DISTINGUISHED SERVICE MEDAL
TO
GENERAL LYMAN L. LEMNITZER
UNITED STATES ARMY

General Lyman L. Lemnitzer distinguished himself by exceptionally meritorious service to the United States Government and to the North Atlantic Treaty Organization (NATO) in positions of great responsibility as Supreme Allied Commander Europe (SACEUR) from 1 January 1963 to 1 July 1969, and as Commander in Chief, United States European Command (CINCEUR) from 1 November 1962 to 5 May 1969.

Evidencing an unshakable faith in the principles and objectives upon which NATO was founded, General Lemnitzer sacrificed the privileges and freedom of retirement which he had long since merited in order that he might further serve the Alliance by assuming the duties of SACEUR/CINCEUR. Remaining in uniform for an additional six and one-half years, he tirelessly and selflessly contributed to the cause of NATO and thereby to the security interests of the United States and the Free World. Among his notable contributions during that period were his persuasive efforts to encourage the member nations of Allied Command Europe to produce and maintain the forces necessary to make their deterrent credible and their capability to defend Europe unquestionable; his translation of strategic guidance from the North Atlantic Council into realistic defensive plans for the Alliance; his direction and guidance of the required relocation from France of some 100,000 personnel and more than one million tons of supplies and equipment; the development of a new $35 million headquarters complex to accommodate SHAPE in Belgium.

These singularly distinctive accomplishments clearly established General Lemnitzer as a truly outstanding officer of international status and culminated more than 50 years of continuous uniformed service with more than 27 years service as a general officer. A grateful nation recognizes that General Lemnitzer's long and distinguished career continues the finest traditions of the military service and reflects the highest credit upon himself, the Armed Forces of the United States, and the United States of America.

NOTE: The President spoke at 10 a.m. in the Rose Garden at the White House.

The remarks of General Lemnitzer, following the reading of the citation, are printed in the Weekly Compilation of Presidential Documents (vol. 5, p. 972).

263 Statement on the July 11 Speech of President Thieu of the Republic of Vietnam. *July 11, 1969*

PRESIDENT THIEU has put forward a comprehensive, statesmanlike, and eminently fair proposal for a political settlement in South Vietnam. It deserves the support of all who seek peace in that tortured land.

President Thieu's proposal would establish a set of procedures and guarantees to ensure that the political future of South Vietnam would reflect, as accurately and as fairly as possible, the will of the people of South Vietnam—including those whose allegiance is to the other side as well as those whose allegiance is to his own government.

In my television address of May 14, I said: "What the United States wants for South Vietnam is not the important thing.

39–861—71——36

What North Vietnam wants for South Vietnam is not the important thing. What is important is what the people of South Vietnam want for South Vietnam."

I believe President Thieu's proposal is in this spirit, and that it would genuinely give the people of South Vietnam—all of them—the opportunity to determine their own fate for themselves. If the other side is prepared for serious negotiations, and willing to abide by the free choice of the South Vietnamese people, this should open the way at last for a rapid settlement of the conflict.

President Thieu has proposed elections in which all political parties and groups can participate—specifically including the National Liberation Front. He has offered to set up special guarantees to ensure fairness:

—establishment of an election commission, on which the NLF and all other parties would be represented,

—empowering this commission to assure all candidates equal opportunity to campaign, and all parties equal opportunity to participate in watching the polls and in supervising the counting of ballots,

—establishment of an international body to supervise the elections.

Beyond this, President Thieu has indicated his willingness to discuss with the other side the timetable and details of these elections. He has declared that his government will abide by the results of such elections, and has asked that the other side do the same. He also has renewed his offer of private talks with the NLF without preconditions.

President Thieu's offer marks the culmination of a long series of steps by the South Vietnamese and American Governments, all of which together demonstrate

clearly the sincere desire of our two Governments to negotiate an honorable and rapid settlement of the war.

Let us look at the record:

Prior to January 20, the United States had halted the bombing of North Vietnam and agreed to sit down at the conference table with the NLF, as well as with the Governments of Hanoi and Saigon. We have remained at that table and refrained from a resumption of the bombing despite Hanoi's shelling of South Vietnam's major cities, its violation of the Demilitarized Zone, and its refusal to deal with the Saigon Government.

On March 25, President Thieu offered to meet with the NLF for private talks without preconditions on a political settlement. This was refused.

On May 14, with the full support of President Thieu, I put forward an eight-point plan for peace. In this plan, I renounced reliance on a military solution. I offered a withdrawal of U.S. and allied forces within 12 months. I suggested placing the process of mutual withdrawal under international guarantees. I said that we sought no military bases, and no military ties, but only to secure the right of the people of South Vietnam to determine their own future without outside interference.

On June 8, at Midway, with the agreement of President Thieu, I announced the withdrawal of 25,000 American troops. The fact that the troops being withdrawn are actual combat forces, not logistical units, should underscore the fact that our desire is to reduce violence and achieve a negotiated peace. The program of replacing U.S. forces with South Vietnamese will be reviewed again in August.

At that same Midway meeting, President Thieu and I declared our readiness to accept *any* political outcome which is arrived at through free elections.

President Thieu has now offered a concrete program by which free elections can be held and the will of the South Vietnamese people can be determined. He has challenged the other side to test its claims to popular support at the polls. He has offered means by which the other side can participate in developing election procedures and by which the elections themselves can take place under international supervision.

If the other side genuinely wants peace, it now has a comprehensive set of offers which permit a fair and reasonable settlement. If it approaches us in this spirit, it will find us reasonable. Hanoi has nothing to gain by waiting.

I also want to repeat to the American people what I said in my speech of May 14: "Nothing could have a greater effect in convincing the enemy that he should negotiate in good faith than to see the American people united behind a generous and reasonable peace offer."

We and the South Vietnamese Government have made such an offer.

I call upon the leaders of the other side to respond in a spirit of peace, and let the political issues be resolved by the political process.

264   Exchange of Letters With Harold K. Bell of the District of Columbia.   *July* 11, 1969

Dear Harold:

It was good to hear from you again after so many years and I am glad to know you have almost completed your college program, and are working here in the District with the Department of Recreation.

Your reflections on our late evening golf at Burning Tree brought back wonderful memories, and I well remember our discussions at the time. Like too many youngsters you had to begin your working career early and were forced to bypass the good times and games that most boys and girls your age were able to enjoy. What makes me very proud of you is that you have returned to the young people whose lives today resemble your own early years, and that you are dedicated to giving them help along the difficult road of life. They sorely need the inspiration and the example that you are able to give them.

It is my prayer as President that the hope for something better will always be with all our boys and girls as it was with you. You may have been suffering, but you were determined not to let it get you down. I am glad you are there to help maintain the spark of hope for these youngsters and I promise you I shall always work to keep that hope alive and to make progress possible for all of our people.

I would enjoy seeing you again and I hope it will not be too long before we have a chance to say hello.

With warm personal regards,

Sincerely,

RICHARD NIXON

[Mr. Harold K. Bell, 1204–42nd Place NE., Washington, D.C. 20019]

NOTE: The letter was dated June 25, 1969, and released July 11, 1969. Mr. Bell, accompanied by his wife, visited the President at the White House on the afternoon of July 11, 1969.

Mr. Bell's letter, which was dated May 12, 1969, and released by the White House Press

Office along with the President's letter on July 11, 1969, read as follows:

Dear Mr. President:

It has been a little more than ten years ago since we last met and there might be some doubt as to my identity. Mr. President, my name is Harold K. Bell, I was your golf caddy at the Burning Tree Golf Course. I remember staying out of sight from Mr. Elbin until you and Mr. Rogers arrived for one of your late evening rounds of golf. I would then pop up, hoping that Mr. Elbin would call me for the bags and he always did. I think he knew what was going on, but he never said anything.

Things were pretty tough for me then and I don't quite know where I got the strength to keep going, but I am thankful that I did. I think that some of the strength came from our conversations as we rode to catch my bus at Wisconsin and Massachusetts Avenues, NW. I am saying all this because I feel everyone needs to know that there is someone who cares, whether it be the Vice President or the newspaperman on the corner. Mr. President, I was not at all surprised at your recent appearance on Seventh Street. I expected nothing less, because I know that you do care about the welfare of your fellow man.

Since I left Winston-Salem College in North Carolina in 1963, I have been working with youths. My present position is that of a Roving Leader (GS–9) for the Department of Recreation, serving the Cardozo area. At this time, I need only a semester to complete my B.A. degree and I plan to continue my education this summer at D.C. Teachers College. My career has provided me with many opportunities, but the greatest satisfaction I have had is to be able to show other disadvantaged youths that there is a brighter road, and that there are people who want to help them if they are willing to help themselves. I have first hand knowledge of this, as I can remember the moments of frustration in my life which centered around the agony of poverty.

Sir, I have never been a backslapper or handshaker, but I felt an impulse to write and let you know that I am pleased to see you back in the Nation's Capital as our country's President. Most Negroes in the United States are not aware of your past, which surely was not a bed of roses. If they were, I am most certain that they would come to realize that you, as an individual, have had time to accumulate more of an insight into America's problems than any Chief Executive before you.

I am writing this letter, Mr. President, to tell you that if the people give you a chance, and I don't mean blacks and whites, but all the people, they will find out, as I did what a great person you are. Everyone seems obsessed with this racial thing, and talking about black power and white power, but what we need is people power, individuals pulling together to make this a stronger Nation. So here is wishing you all the luck and success there is in the world.

I have enclosed some newspaper clippings which relate to my work as a Roving Leader.

Respectfully yours,

HAROLD K. BELL

Enclosures

P.S. You must be shooting in the low 70's now (smile) H.K.B.

[The President, the White House, Washington, D.C. 20500]

265 Statement on the Establishment of the National Goals Research Staff. *July* 12, 1969

IN 7 short years, the United States will celebrate its 200th anniversary as a nation. It is time we addressed ourselves, consciously and systematically, to the question of what kind of a nation we want to be as we begin our third century.

We can no longer afford to approach the longer-range future haphazardly. As the pace of change accelerates, the process of change becomes more complex. Yet at the same time, an extraordinary array of tools and techniques has been developed by which it becomes increasingly possible to project future trends—and thus to make the kind of informed choices which are necessary if we are to establish mastery over the process of change.

These tools and techniques are gaining widespread use in business, and in the social and physical sciences, but they have not been applied systematically and comprehensively to the science of government.

The time is at hand when they should be used, and when they must be used.

Therefore, I have today ordered the establishment, within the White House, of a National Goals Research Staff. This will be a small, highly technical staff, made up of experts in the collection, correlation, and processing of data relating to social needs, and in the projection of social trends. It will operate under the direction of Leonard Garment, Special Consultant to the President, and will maintain a continuous liaison with Dr. Daniel P. Moynihan in his capacity as Executive Secretary of the Council for Urban Affairs, and with Dr. Arthur Burns, Counsellor to the President, in his capacity as head of the Office of Program Development. The functions of the National Goals Research Staff will include:

—forecasting future developments and assessing the longer-range consequences of present social trends;

—measuring the probable future impact of alternative courses of action, including measuring the degree to which change in one area would be likely to affect another;

—estimating the actual range of social choice—that is, what alternative sets of goals might be attainable, in light of the availability of resources and possible rates of progress;

—developing and monitoring social indicators that can reflect the present and future quality of American life

and the direction and rate of its change;

—summarizing, integrating, and correlating the results of related research activities being carried on within the various Federal agencies, and by State and local governments and private organizations.

I would emphasize several points about this new unit:

—It is not to be a substitute for the many other research activities within the Federal Government; rather, it is intended to help us make better use of the research now being done by bringing together, at one central point, those portions of it that relate directly to future trends and possibilities. It will make accessible what has too often been fragmented.

—It is not to be a "data bank." It might more accurately be referred to as a key element in a management information system. For the first time, it creates within the White House a unit specifically charged with the long perspective; it promises to provide the research tools with which we at last can deal with the future in an informed and informative way.

Since taking office as President, one of my major objectives has been to improve the processes by which our Nation is governed. It has long since become clear that the old ways are no longer adequate, and that much of the old machinery is obsolescent if not obsolete. It also has become clear that one of the principal requirements is for new mechanisms which can enable government to respond to emerging needs early enough so that the response can be effective.

Out of the studies undertaken by the new administration over the past several months, a number of conclusions have emerged that bear directly on the creation of this new unit:

—There are increasing numbers of forecasting efforts in both public and private institutions, which provide a growing body of information upon which to base judgments of probable future developments and of the choices available.

—There is a need to synthesize the results of these efforts, and to analyze the interrelationships of the various kinds of change they represent. The lack of such analysis is a shortcoming of most present forecasting efforts.

—Despite the recent rapid increase of such activity, there are many areas in which a longer-range perspective is still needed.

—There is an urgent need to establish a more direct link between the increasingly sophisticated forecasting now being done, and the decision-making process. The practical importance of establishing such a link is emphasized by the fact that virtually all the critical national problems of today could have been anticipated well in advance of their reaching critical proportions. Even though some were, such anticipation was seldom translated into policy decisions which might have permitted progress to be made in such a way as to avoid—or at least minimize—undesirable longer-range consequences.

—We have reached a state of technological and social development at which the future nature of our society can increasingly be shaped by our own conscious choices. At the same time, those choices are not simple. They require us to pick among alternatives which do not yield to easy, quantitative measurement.

Only by focusing our attention farther into the future can we marshal our resources effectively in the service of those social aims to which we are committed, such as eliminating hunger, cleaning up our environment, providing maximum opportunity for human development during the critical first 5 years of life, maintaining and improving standards of education and medical care, reducing welfare dependency, and making our cities livable for all.

Only by marshaling the facts can we know how to marshal our resources.

We should expect this look into the future to be both exciting and sobering: exciting, because it will show how great is the reach of the possible; sobering, because it also will show that there are some problems against which the best will in the world can produce only painfully slow progress. The important thing is that we know—that we know both the reach and the limits of what can be done, and the probable consequences, so that our choices can be informed by this knowledge.

The first assignment of this new research group will be to assemble data that can help illumine the possible range of national goals for 1976—our 200th anniversary. It will prepare a public report, to be delivered by July 4 of next year, and annually thereafter, setting forth some of the key choices open to us, and examining the consequences of those choices. It is my hope that this report will then serve as a focus for the kind of lively widespread public discussion that deserves to go into decisions affecting our common future. The key point is this: it will make such discussion possible while there still is time to make the choices effective.

Instead of lamenting too late what might have been, it will help give us, as a people, both the luxury and the responsibility of conscious and timely choice.

Only shortly beyond the Nation's 200th anniversary lies the year 2000. These dates, together, can be targets for our aspirations. Our need now is to seize on the future as the key dimension in our decisions, and to chart that future as consciously as we are accustomed to charting the past.

NOTE: On July 11, 1969, Dr. Daniel P. Moynihan, Assistant to the President for Urban Affairs, held a news briefing at 3:50 p.m. in the Roosevelt Room at the White House concerning the establishment of the National Goals Research Staff. The text of the briefing is printed in the Weekly Compilation of Presidential Documents (vol. 5, p. 985).

266   Special Message to the Congress on Control of Narcotics and Dangerous Drugs. *July* 14, 1969

To the Congress of the United States:

Within the last decade, the abuse of drugs has grown from essentially a local police problem into a serious national threat to the personal health and safety of millions of Americans.

A national awareness of the gravity of the situation is needed; a new urgency and concerted national policy are needed at the Federal level to begin to cope with this growing menace to the general welfare of the United States.

Between the years 1960 and 1967, juvenile arrests involving the use of drugs rose by almost 800 percent; half of those now being arrested for the illicit use of narcotics are under 21 years of age. New York City alone has records of some 40,000 heroin addicts, and the number rises between 7000 and 9000 a year. These official statistics are only the tip of an iceberg whose dimensions we can only surmise.

The number of narcotics addicts across the United States is now estimated to be in the hundreds of thousands. Another estimate is that several million American college students have at least experimented with marihuana, hashish, LSD, amphetamines, or barbiturates. It is doubtful that an American parent can send a son or daughter to college today without exposing the young man or woman to drug abuse. Parents must also be concerned about the availability and use of such drugs in our high schools and junior high schools.

The habit of the narcotics addict is not only a danger to himself, but a threat to the community where he lives. Narcotics have been cited as a primary cause of the enormous increase in street crimes over the last decade.

As the addict's tolerance for drugs increases, his demand for drugs rises, and the cost of his habit grows. It can easily reach hundreds of dollars a day. Since an underworld "fence" will give him only a fraction of the value of goods he steals, an addict can be forced to commit two or three burglaries a day to maintain his habit. Street robberies, prostitution, even the enticing of others into addiction to drugs—an addict will reduce himself to any offense, any degradation in order to acquire the drugs he craves.

However far the addict himself may fall, his offenses against himself and society do not compare with the inhumanity of those who make a living exploiting the weakness and desperation of their fellow men. Society has few judgments too severe, few penalties too harsh for the men who make their livelihood in the narcotics traffic.

It has been a common oversimplification to consider narcotics addiction, or drug abuse, to be a law enforcement problem alone. Effective control of illicit drugs requires the cooperation of many agencies of the Federal and local and State governments; it is beyond the province of any one of them alone. At the Federal level, the burden of the national effort must be carried by the Departments of Justice, Health, Education, and Welfare, and the Treasury. I am proposing ten specific steps as this Administration's initial counter-moves against this growing national problem.

I. Federal Legislation

To more effectively meet the narcotic and dangerous drug problems at the Federal level, the Attorney General is forwarding to the Congress a comprehensive legislative proposal to control these drugs. This measure will place in a single statute, a revised and modern plan for control. Current laws in this field are inadequate and outdated.

I consider the legislative proposal a fair, rational and necessary approach to the total drug problem. It will tighten the regulatory controls and protect the public against illicit diversion of many of these drugs from legitimate channels. It will insure greater accountability and better recordkeeping. It will give law enforcement

stronger and better tools that are sorely needed so that those charged with enforcing these laws can do so more effectively. Further, this proposal creates a more flexible mechanism which will allow quicker control of new dangerous drugs before their misuse and abuse reach epidemic proportions. I urge the Congress to take favorable action on this bill.

In mid-May the Supreme Court struck down segments of the marihuana laws and called into question some of the basic foundations for the other existing drug statutes. I have also asked the Attorney General to submit an interim measure to correct the constitutional deficiencies of the Marihuana Tax Act as pointed out in the Supreme Court's recent decision. I urge Congress to act swiftly and favorably on the proposal to close the gap now existing in the Federal law and thereby give the Congress time to carefully examine the comprehensive drug control proposal.

II. State Legislation

The Department of Justice is developing a model State Narcotics and Dangerous Drugs Act. This model law will be made available to the fifty State governments. This legislation is designed to improve State laws in dealing with this serious problem and to complement the comprehensive drug legislation being proposed to Congress at the national level. Together these proposals will provide an interlocking trellis of laws which will enable government at all levels to more effectively control the problem.

III. International Cooperation

Most of the illicit narcotics and high-potency marihuana consumed in the

United States is produced abroad and clandestinely imported. I have directed the Secretary of State and the Attorney General to explore new avenues of cooperation with foreign governments to stop the production of this contraband at its source. The United States will cooperate with foreign governments working to eradicate the production of illicit drugs within their own frontiers. I have further authorized these Cabinet officers to formulate plans that will lead to meetings at the law enforcement level between the United States and foreign countries now involved in the drug traffic either as originators or avenues of transit.

IV. SUPPRESSION OF ILLEGAL IMPORTATION

Our efforts to eliminate these drugs at their point of origin will be coupled with new efforts to intercept them at their point of illegal entry into the United States. The Department of the Treasury, through the Bureau of Customs, is charged with enforcing the nation's smuggling laws. I have directed the Secretary of the Treasury to initiate a major new effort to guard the nation's borders and ports against the growing volume of narcotics from abroad. There is a recognized need for more men and facilities in the Bureau of Customs to carry out this directive. At my request, the Secretary of the Treasury has submitted a substantial program for increased manpower and facilities in the Bureau of Customs for this purpose which is under intensive review.

In the early days of this Administration, I requested that the Attorney General form an inter-departmental Task Force to conduct a comprehensive study of the problem of unlawful trafficking in narcotics and dangerous drugs. One purpose of the Task Force has been to examine the existing programs of law enforcement agencies concerned with the problem in an effort to improve their coordination and efficiency. I now want to report that this Task Force has completed its study and has a recommended plan of action, for immediate and long-term implementation, designed to substantially reduce the illicit trafficking in narcotics, marihuana and dangerous drugs across United States borders. To implement the recommended plan, I have directed the Attorney General to organize and place into immediate operation an "action task force" to undertake a frontal attack on the problem. There are high profits in the illicit market for those who smuggle narcotics and drugs into the United States; we intend to raise the risks and cost of engaging in this wretched traffic.

V. SUPPRESSION OF NATIONAL TRAFFICKING

Successful prosecution of an increased national effort against illicit drug trafficking will require not only new resources and men, but also a redeployment of existing personnel within the Department of Justice.

I have directed the Attorney General to create, within the Bureau of Narcotics and Dangerous Drugs, a number of special investigative units. These special forces will have the capacity to move quickly into any area in which intelligence indicates major criminal enterprises are engaged in the narcotics traffic. To carry out this directive, there will be a need for additional manpower within the Bureau of Narcotics and Dangerous Drugs. The budgetary request for FY 1970 now pending before the Congress will initiate this program. Additional funds will be requested in FY 1971 to fully deploy the necessary special investigative units.

VI. EDUCATION

Proper evaluation and solution of the drug problem in this country has been severely handicapped by a dearth of scientific information on the subject—and the prevalence of ignorance and misinformation. Different "experts" deliver solemn judgments which are poles apart. As a result of these conflicting judgments, Americans seem to have divided themselves on the issue, along generational lines.

There are reasons for this lack of knowledge. First, widespread drug use is a comparatively recent phenomenon in the United States. Second, it frequently involves chemical formulations which are novel, or age-old drugs little used in this country until very recently. The volume of definitive medical data remains small—and what exists has not been broadly disseminated. This vacuum of knowledge—as was predictable—has been filled by rumors and rash judgments, often formed with a minimal experience with a particular drug, sometimes formed with no experience or knowledge at all.

The possible danger to the health or well-being of even a casual user of drugs is too serious to allow ignorance to prevail or for this information gap to remain open. The American people need to know what dangers and what risks are inherent in the use of the various kinds of drugs readily available in illegal markets today. I have therefore directed the Secretary

of Health, Education, and Welfare, assisted by the Attorney General through the Bureau of Narcotics and Dangerous Drugs, to gather all authoritative information on the subject and to compile a balanced and objective educational program to bring the facts to every American—especially our young people.

With this information in hand, the overwhelming majority of students and young people can be trusted to make a prudent judgment as to their personal course of conduct.

VII. RESEARCH

In addition to gathering existing data, it is essential that we acquire new knowledge in the field. We must know more about both the short- and long-range effects of the use of drugs being taken in such quantities by so many of our people. We need more study as well to find the key to releasing men from the bonds of dependency forged by any continued drug abuse.

The National Institute of Mental Health has primary responsibility in this area, and I am further directing the Secretary of Health, Education, and Welfare to expand existing efforts to acquire new knowledge and a broader understanding in this entire area.

VIII. REHABILITATION

Considering the risks involved, including those of arrest and prosecution, the casual experimenter with drugs of any kind, must be considered at the very least, rash and foolish. But the psychologically dependent regular users and the physically addicted are genuinely sick people.

While this sickness cannot excuse the crimes they commit, it does help to explain them. Society has an obligation both to itself and to these people to help them break the chains of their dependency.

Currently, a number of federal, state and private programs of rehabilitation are being operated. These programs utilize separately and together, psychiatry, psychology and "substitute drug" therapy. At this time, however, we are without adequate data to evaluate their full benefit. We need more experience with them and more knowledge. Therefore, I am directing the Secretary of Health, Education, and Welfare to provide every assistance to those pioneering in the field, and to sponsor and conduct research on the Federal level. This Department will act as a clearinghouse for the collection and dissemination of drug abuse data and experience in the area of rehabilitation.

I have further instructed the Attorney General to insure that all Federal prisoners, who have been identified as dependent upon drugs, be afforded the most up-to-date treatment available.

IX. TRAINING PROGRAM

The enforcement of narcotics laws requires considerable expertise, and hence considerable training. The Bureau of Narcotics and Dangerous Drugs provides the bulk of this training in the Federal government. Its programs are extended to include not only its own personnel, but State and local police officers, forensic chemists, foreign nationals, college deans, campus security officers, and members of industry engaged in the legal distribution of drugs.

Last year special training in the field of narcotics and dangerous drug enforcement was provided for 2700 State and local law enforcement officials. In fiscal year 1969 we expanded the program an estimated 300 percent in order to train some 11,000 persons. During the current fiscal year we plan to redouble again that effort—to provide training to 22,000 State and local officers. The training of these experts must keep pace with the rise in the abuse of drugs, if we are ever to control it.

X. LOCAL LAW ENFORCEMENT CONFERENCES

The Attorney General intends to begin a series of conferences with law enforcement executives from the various States and concerned Federal officials. The purposes of these conferences will be several: first, to obtain firsthand information, more accurate data, on the scope of the drug problem at that level; second, to discuss the specific areas where Federal assistance and aid can best be most useful; third, to exchange ideas and evaluate mutual policies. The end result we hope will be a more coordinated effort that will bring us visible progress for the first time in an alarming decade.

These then are the first ten steps in the national effort against narcotic marihuana and other dangerous drug abuse. Many steps are already underway. Many will depend upon the support of the Congress. I am asking, with this message, that you act swiftly and favorably on the legislative proposals that will soon be forthcoming, along with the budgetary requests required if our efforts are to be successful. I am confident that Congress shares with me the grave concern over this critical problem, and that Congress will do all that is necessary to mount and continue a new and effective federal pro-gram aimed at eradicating this rising sickness in our land.

RICHARD NIXON

The White House
July 14, 1969

---

267   Telegram to the Apollo 11 Astronauts on the Eve of the Launch. *July* 15, 1969

ON the eve of your epic mission, I want you to know that my hopes and my prayers—and those of all Americans—go with you. Years of study and planning and experiment and hard work on the part of thousands have led to this unique moment in the story of mankind; it is now your moment and from the depths of your minds and hearts and spirits will come the triumph all men will share. I look forward to greeting you on your return. Until then, know that all that is best in the spirit of mankind will be with you during your mission and when you return to earth.

NOTE: The President also telephoned the crew members, Neil A. Armstrong, Col. Edwin E. Aldrin, Jr., and Lt. Col. Michael Collins, at 6 p.m. on the evening preceding the launch. In describing the conversation, Press Secretary Ronald L. Ziegler reported that the President told the astronauts, ". . . as you lift off to the moon, you lift the spirits of the American people as well as the world." He also quoted the President as saying, "You carry with you a feeling of good will in this greatest adventure man has ever taken," and "I am particularly impressed by the fact that all three of you have the attitude of quiet and serene confidence, confidence that comes from superb training, preparation, and the inner strength of character which is characteristic and a common attitude of all our astronauts."

---

268   Proclamation 3919, National Day of Participation Honoring the Apollo 11 Mission. *July* 16, 1969

By the President of the United States of America a Proclamation

Apollo 11 is on its way to the moon. It carries three brave astronauts; it also carries the hopes and prayers of hundreds of millions of people here on earth, for whom that first footfall on the moon will be a moment of transcendent drama. Never before has man embarked on so epic an adventure.

In the words of the plaque the Apollo astronauts expect to leave on the moon, they go "in peace for all mankind." The adventure is not theirs alone, but every-one's; the history they are making is not only scientific history, but human history. That moment when man first sets foot on a body other than earth will stand through the centuries as one supreme in human experience, and profound in its meaning for generations to come.

In past ages, exploration was a lonely enterprise. But today, the miracles of space travel are matched by miracles of space communication; even across the vast lunar distance, television brings the moment of discovery into our homes, and makes all of us participants.

As the astronauts go where man has never gone, as they attempt what man has never tried, we on earth will want, as one people, to be with them in spirit; to share the glory and the wonder, and to support them with prayers that all will go well.

In order that as many as possible can have the opportunity to share as fully as possible in this surpassing occasion, I, RICHARD NIXON, President of the United States of America, do hereby proclaim Monday, July 21, 1969, to be a National Day of Participation; and I invite the Governors of the States and the Commonwealth of Puerto Rico, and officials of other areas subject to the jurisdiction of the United States to issue similar proclamations.

All executive departments, independent establishments, and other governmental agencies, including their field services, shall be closed on the National Day of Participation, and all of their employees (except employees of the Department of State, the Department of Defense, or other agencies who in the judgment of their

agency heads should be at their posts of duty for national security or other public reasons), shall be excused from duty on that day. And I direct that the flag of the United States be displayed on all public buildings on that day.

I urge the Governors of the States, the mayors of cities, the heads of school systems, and other public officials to take similar action. I also urge private employers to make appropriate arrangements so that as many of our citizens as possible will be able to share in the significant events of that day. And, finally, I call upon all of our people, on that historic day, to join in prayer for the successful conclusion of Apollo 11's mission and the safe return of its crew.

IN WITNESS WHEREOF, I have hereunto set my hand this sixteenth day of July, in the year of our Lord nineteen hundred and sixty-nine, and of the Independence of the United States of America the one hundred and ninety-fourth.

RICHARD NIXON

---

269   Remarks on Presenting the Distinguished Service Medal to General John P. McConnell. *July* 17, 1969

General and Mrs. McConnell, Mr. Secretary, all of our distinguished guests from the Congress, ladies and gentlemen:

We are here again for one of those historic ceremonies which all of us will remember, and particularly, I think, has special meaning for this Nation.

General McConnell, who retires today, is one who began his service 40 years ago, and as I was thinking of the historic flight to the moon which is now in process, it occurred to me that General McConnell's service in the Air Force really spans a

great period in the whole history of flight, because he entered the service just a year after Charles Lindbergh flew across the Atlantic.

We all remember the immense reaction—those of us who are old enough—remember the immense reaction we had in this country when that occurred, and now General McConnell completes his service as man now makes the great breakthrough of going to the moon.

On this occasion we think of the service he has rendered, in war and in peace. I think "in peace" should be particularly emphasized, because I believe that General McConnell's whole life, his service in the Joint Chiefs—and I have sat with him in meetings of the National Security Council and know whereof I speak—his whole life bears out what General Twining [1] once said, that if our air forces are never used, they have served their finest purpose. That is what the men in the Air Force, the men in the Army, the men in the Navy, all the Armed Forces truly believe in this country. We maintain our strength, but we maintain it for peace.

I think as this flight goes to the moon today we have one, what to me is a very moving and touching aspect of it that I would like to report to you now.

Our astronauts will be taking with them the flags of the 50 States and a number of other items of great interest which they will bring back. They will also be taking with them the medals that were given to three of our astronauts who were killed in the Apollo flight, and they will leave on the moon the patches from those medals.

They also will be taking with them two other medals. When Frank Borman was in the Soviet Union he was presented two medals from the wives of the cosmonauts, the Russian cosmonauts, who lost their lives in their space program. And at the request of their wives we will leave those medals on the moon.

I think this symbolic act of leaving on the moon in the one case the aspects of the medals of those who lost their lives in our space program, and the medals of the Soviet cosmonauts, indicates the true spirit of the American Armed Forces. We

maintain strength, but we maintain it because we want peace, peace with all countries.

It is in that spirit today that I am very happy to participate in honoring a man whose life has been dedicated to peace, dedicated to peace even when he had to fight in war, and dedicated to peace as he has maintained the air forces and their strength in times of peace.

Now Secretary Laird will read the citation.

[Secretary of Defense Melvin R. Laird read the citation, the text of which follows.]

CITATION TO ACCOMPANY THE AWARD OF
THE DISTINGUISHED SERVICE MEDAL
(FIRST OAK LEAF CLUSTER)

TO

JOHN P. M'CONNELL

The President of the United States of America, authorized by Act of Congress July 9, 1918, awards the Distinguished Service Medal to General John P. McConnell, for exceptionally meritorious service in a duty of great responsibility. General McConnell distinguished himself as Chief of Staff, United States Air Force, from 1 February 1967 to 31 July 1969. In the highest military office of the Air Force, which position he assumed initially in February 1965, and as a member of the Joint Chiefs of Staff, General McConnell consistently manifested an untiring devotion to duty, combining outstanding professional knowledge with leadership and integrity of the highest calibre. Throughout a period of continuing threats to the security and vital interests of the United States and the Free World, General McConnell's extensive knowledge, managerial skill, and diplomacy greatly enhanced the capability of the Air Force and Department of Defense to meet expanding world-wide military commitments. His personal concern for the welfare of Air Force men and women led to significant improvements in pay, housing, promotion, and medical care for Air Force Personnel. During a period of major advance-

---

[1] Gen. Nathan F. Twining, Air Force Chief of Staff 1953–1957 and Chairman, Joint Chiefs of Staff 1957–1960.

ments in the technological development of the Air Force, his foresight and leadership added materially to the preservation of aerospace power as a potent factor in the attainment of world peace. The singularly distinctive accomplishments of General McConnell culminate a long and distinguished career of more than 37 years of service to his country, and reflect the highest credit upon himself, the Armed Forces of the United States, and the United States of America.

RICHARD NIXON

NOTE: The President spoke at 10:04 a.m. in the Rose Garden at the White House.

The remarks of General McConnell, following those of the President, are printed in the Weekly Compilation of Presidential Documents (vol. 5, p. 998).

270   Statement About Honoring American and Russian Space Heroes During the Apollo 11 Mission.   *July* 17, 1969

THE TWO MEN we hope will set foot on the moon represent all mankind.

Their achievement will be the world's achievement. It is fitting, therefore, that the first lunar explorers carry with them some recognition of the sacrifice made by other space pioneers who helped to blaze their trail.

There is no national boundary to courage. The names of Gagarin and Komarov, of Grissom, White, and Chaffee, share the honor we pray will come to Armstrong, Aldrin, and Collins.

In recognizing the dedication and sacrifice of brave men of different nations, we underscore an example we hope to set: that if men can reach the moon, men can reach agreement.

NOTE: The Apollo 11 crew carried with them two Soviet commemorative medals, one Apollo 204 crew patch, and three Apollo 204 commemorative medals.

The Soviet medals, which were awarded posthumously, were brought back to the United States by Col. Frank Borman, Commander of Apollo 8, who received them in Moscow from the widows of Russian cosmonauts Col. Yuri Gagarin and Col. Vladimir Komarov. Colonel Gagarin was killed on March 27, 1968, when his jet plane crashed northeast of Moscow during a routine training flight. Colonel Komarov was killed while completing a 2-day orbital flight when his Soyuz I spacecraft became tangled in its parachute cords after reentering the earth's atmosphere.

271   Special Message to the Congress on Problems of Population Growth.   *July* 18, 1969

To the Congress of the United States:

In 1830 there were one billion people on the planet earth. By 1930 there were two billion, and by 1960 there were three billion. Today the world population is three and one-half billion persons.

These statistics illustrate the dramatically increasing rate of population growth. It took many thousands of years to produce the first billion people; the next billion took a century; the third came after thirty years; the fourth will be produced in just fifteen.

If this rate of population growth continues, it is likely that the earth will contain over seven billion human beings by the end of this century. Over the next thirty years, in other words, the world's

521

population could double. And at the end of that time, each new addition of one billion persons would not come over the millenia nor over a century nor even over a decade. If present trends were to continue until the year 2000, the eighth billion would be added in only five years and each additional billion in an even shorter period.

While there are a variety of opinions as to precisely how fast population will grow in the coming decades, most informed observers have a similar response to all such projections. They agree that population growth is among the most important issues we face. They agree that it can be met only if there is a great deal of advance planning. And they agree that the time for such planning is growing very short. It is for all these reasons that I address myself to the population problem in this message, first to its international dimensions and then to its domestic implications.

In the Developing Nations

It is in the developing nations of the world that population is growing most rapidly today. In these areas we often find rates of natural increase higher than any which have been experienced in all of human history. With their birth rates remaining high and with death rates dropping sharply, many countries of Latin America, Asia, and Africa now grow ten times as fast as they did a century ago. At present rates, many will double and some may even triple their present populations before the year 2000. This fact is in large measure a consequence of rising health standards and economic progress throughout the world, improvements which allow more people to live longer and more of their children to survive to maturity.

As a result, many already impoverished

nations are struggling under a handicap of intense population increase which the industrialized nations never had to bear. Even though most of these countries have made rapid progress in total economic growth—faster in percentage terms than many of the more industrialized nations— their far greater rates of population growth have made development in per capita terms very slow. Their standards of living are not rising quickly, and the gap between life in the rich nations and life in the poor nations is not closing.

There are some respects, in fact, in which economic development threatens to fall behind population growth, so that the quality of life actually worsens. For example, despite considerable improvements in agricultural technology and some dramatic increases in grain production, it is still difficult to feed these added people at adequate levels of nutrition. Protein malnutrition is widespread. It is estimated that every day some 10,000 people—most of them children—are dying from diseases of which malnutrition has been at least a partial cause. Moreover, the physical and mental potential of millions of youngsters is not realized because of a lack of proper food. The promise for increased production and better distribution of food is great, but not great enough to counter these bleak realities.

The burden of population growth is also felt in the field of social progress. In many countries, despite increases in the number of schools and teachers, there are more and more children for whom there is no schooling. Despite construction of new homes, more and more families are without adequate shelter. Unemployment and underemployment are increasing and the situation could be aggravated as more young people grow up and seek to enter the work force.

Nor has development yet reached the stage where it brings with it diminished family size. Many parents in developing countries are still victimized by forces such as poverty and ignorance which make it difficult for them to exercise control over the size of their families. In sum, population growth is a world problem which no country can ignore, whether it is moved by the narrowest perception of national self-interest or the widest vision of a common humanity.

INTERNATIONAL COOPERATION

It is our belief that the United Nations, its specialized agencies, and other international bodies should take the leadership in responding to world population growth. The United States will cooperate fully with their programs. I would note in this connection that I am most impressed by the scope and thrust of the recent report of the Panel of the United Nations Association, chaired by John D. Rockefeller III.[1] The report stresses the need for expanded action and greater coordination, concerns which should be high on the agenda of the United Nations.

In addition to working with international organizations, the United States can help by supporting efforts which are initiated by other governments. Already we are doing a great deal in this field. For example, we provide assistance to countries which seek our help in reducing high

---

[1] The 57-page report, dated May 1969, is entitled "World Population, A Challenge to the United Nations and Its System of Agencies." The report was issued by the National Policy Panel established by the United Nations Association of the U.S.A.

birthrates—provided always that the services we help to make available can be freely accepted or rejected by the individuals who receive them. Through our aid programs, we have worked to improve agricultural production and bolster economic growth in developing nations.

As I pointed out in my recent message on Foreign Aid, we are making important efforts to improve these programs. In fact, I have asked the Secretary of State and the Administrator of the Agency for International Development to give population and family planning high priority for attention, personnel, research, and funding among our several aid programs. Similarly, I am asking the Secretaries of Commerce and Health, Education, and Welfare and the Directors of the Peace Corps and the United States Information Agency to give close attention to population matters as they plan their overseas operations. I also call on the Department of Agriculture and the Agency for International Development to investigate ways of adapting and extending our agricultural experience and capabilities to improve food production and distribution in developing countries. In all of these international efforts, our programs should give further recognition to the important resources of private organizations and university research centers. As we increase our population and family planning efforts abroad, we also call upon other nations to enlarge their programs in this area.

Prompt action in all these areas is essential. For high rates of population growth, as the report of the Panel of the United Nations Association puts it, "impair individual rights, jeopardize national goals, and threaten international stability."

IN THE UNITED STATES

For some time population growth has been seen as a problem for developing countries. Only recently has it come to be seen that pressing problems are also posed for advanced industrial countries when their populations increase at the rate that the United States, for example, must now anticipate. Food supplies may be ample in such nations, but social supplies—the capacity to educate youth, to provide privacy and living space, to maintain the processes of open, democratic government—may be grievously strained.

In the United States our rate of population growth is not as great as that of developing nations. In this country, in fact, the growth rate has generally declined since the eighteenth century. The present growth rate of about one percent per year is still significant, however. Moreover, current statistics indicate that the fertility rate may be approaching the end of its recent decline.

Several factors contribute to the yearly increase, including the large number of couples of childbearing age, the typical size of American families, and our increased longevity. We are rapidly reaching the point in this country where a family reunion, which has typically brought together children, parents, and grandparents, will instead gather family members from *four* generations. This is a development for which we are grateful and of which we can be proud. But we must also recognize that it will mean a far larger population if the number of children born to each set of parents remains the same.

In 1917 the total number of Americans passed 100 million, after three full cen-

turies of steady growth. In 1967—just half a century later—the 200 million mark was passed. If the present rate of growth continues, the third hundred million persons will be added in roughly a thirty-year period. This means that by the year 2000, or shortly thereafter, there will be more than 300 million Americans.

This growth will produce serious challenges for our society. I believe that many of our present social problems may be related to the fact that we have had only fifty years in which to accommodate the second hundred million Americans. In fact, since 1945 alone some 90 million babies have been born in this country. We have thus had to accomplish in a very few decades an adjustment to population growth which was once spread over centuries. And it now appears that we will have to provide for a third hundred million Americans in a period of just 30 years.

The great majority of the next hundred million Americans will be born to families which looked forward to their birth and are prepared to love them and care for them as they grow up. The critical issue is whether social institutions will also plan for their arrival and be able to accommodate them in a humane and intelligent way. We can be sure that society will *not* be ready for this growth unless it begins its planning immediately. And adequate planning, in turn, requires that we ask ourselves a number of important questions.

Where, for example, will the next hundred million Americans live? If the patterns of the last few decades hold for the rest of the century, then at least three quarters of the next hundred million persons will locate in highly urbanized areas. Are our cities prepared for such an influx? The chaotic history of urban growth suggests that they are not and that many of their existing problems will be severely aggravated by a dramatic increase in numbers. Are there ways, then, of readying our cities? Alternatively, can the trend toward greater concentration of population be reversed? Is it a desirable thing, for example, that half of all the counties in the United States actually lost population in the 1950's, despite the growing number of inhabitants in the country as a whole? Are there ways of fostering a better distribution of the growing population?

Some have suggested that systems of satellite cities or completely new towns can accomplish this goal. The National Commission on Urban Growth has recently produced a stimulating report on this matter, one which recommends the creation of 100 new communities averaging 100,000 people each, and ten new communities averaging at least one million persons.[2] But the total number of people who would be accommodated if even this bold plan were implemented is only twenty million—a mere one-fifth of the expected thirty-year increase. If we were to accommodate the full 100 million persons in new communities, we would have to build a new city of 250,000 persons each month from now until the end of the century. That means constructing a city the size of Tulsa, Dayton, or Jersey City every thirty days for over thirty years. Clearly, the problem is enormous, and we must examine the alternative solutions very carefully.

Other questions also confront us. How, for example, will we house the next hundred million Americans? Already econom-

[2] The report issued by the National Committee on Urban Growth Policy, an ad hoc group of Urban America, Inc., is included in the book, "The New City," published by Praeger and edited by Donald Canty.

ical and attractive housing is in very short supply. New architectural forms, construction techniques, and financing strategies must be aggressively pioneered if we are to provide the needed dwellings.

What of our natural resources and the quality of our environment? Pure air and water are fundamental to life itself. Parks, recreational facilities, and an attractive countryside are essential to our emotional well-being. Plant and animal and mineral resources are also vital. A growing population will increase the demand for such resources. But in many cases their supply will not be increased and may even be endangered. The ecological system upon which we now depend may seriously deteriorate if our efforts to conserve and enhance the environment do not match the growth of the population.

How will we educate and employ such a large number of people? Will our transportation systems move them about as quickly and economically as necessary? How will we provide adequate health care when our population reaches 300 million? Will our political structures have to be reordered, too, when our society grows to such proportions? Many of our institutions are already under tremendous strain as they try to respond to the demands of 1969. Will they be swamped by a growing flood of people in the next thirty years? How easily can they be replaced or altered?

Finally we must ask: how can we better assist American families so that they will have no more children than they wish to have? In my first message to Congress on domestic affairs, I called for a national commitment to provide a healthful and stimulating environment for all children during their first five years of life. One of the ways in which we can promote that goal is to provide assistance for more parents in effectively planning their families. We know that involuntary childbearing often results in poor physical and emotional health for all members of the family. It is one of the factors which contribute to our distressingly high infant mortality rate, the unacceptable level of malnutrition, and the disappointing performance of some children in our schools. Unwanted or untimely childbearing is one of several forces which are driving many families into poverty or keeping them in that condition. Its threat helps to produce the dangerous incidence of illegal abortion. And finally, of course, it needlessly adds to the burdens placed on all our resources by increasing population.

None of the questions I have raised here is new. But all of these questions must now be asked and answered with a new sense of urgency. The answers cannot be given by government alone, nor can government alone turn the answers into programs and policies. I believe, however, that the Federal Government does have a special responsibility for defining these problems and for stimulating thoughtful responses.

Perhaps the most dangerous element in the present situation is the fact that so few people are examining these questions from the viewpoint of the whole society. Perceptive businessmen project the demand for their products many years into the future by studying population trends. Other private institutions develop sophisticated planning mechanisms which allow them to account for rapidly changing conditions. In the governmental sphere, however, there is virtually no machinery through which we can develop a detailed understanding of demographic changes

and bring that understanding to bear on public policy. The federal government makes only a minimal effort in this area. The efforts of state and local governments are also inadequate. Most importantly, the planning which does take place at some levels is poorly understood at others and is often based on unexamined assumptions.

In short, the questions I have posed in this message too often go unasked, and when they are asked, they seldom are adequately answered.

COMMISSION ON POPULATION GROWTH
AND THE AMERICAN FUTURE

It is for all these reasons that I today propose the creation by Congress of a Commission on Population Growth and the American Future.

The Congress should give the Commission responsibility for inquiry and recommendations in three specific areas.

First, *the probable course of population growth, internal migration and related demographic developments between now and the year 2000.*

As much as possible, these projections should be made by regions, states, and metropolitan areas. Because there is an element of uncertainty in such projections, various alternative possibilities should be plotted.

It is of special importance to note that, beginning in August of 1970, population data by county will become available from the decennial census, which will have been taken in April of that year. By April 1971, computer summaries of first-count data will be available by census tract and an important range of information on income, occupations, education, household composition, and other vital considerations will also be in hand. The Federal government can make better use of such demographic information than it has done in the past, and state governments and other political subdivisions can also use such data to better advantage. The Commission on Population Growth and the American Future will be an appropriate instrument for this important initiative.

Second, *the resources in the public sector of the economy that will be required to deal with the anticipated growth in population.*

The single greatest failure of foresight—at all levels of government—over the past generation has been in areas connected with expanding population. Government and legislatures have frequently failed to appreciate the demands which continued population growth would impose on the public sector. These demands are myriad: they will range from preschool classrooms to post-doctoral fellowships; from public works which carry water over thousands of miles to highways which carry people and products from region to region; from vest pocket parks in crowded cities to forest preserves and quiet lakes in the countryside. Perhaps especially, such demands will assert themselves in forms that affect the quality of life. The time is at hand for a serious assessment of such needs.

Third, *ways in which population growth may affect the activities of Federal, state and local government.*

In some respects, population growth affects everything that American government does. Yet only occasionally do our governmental units pay sufficient attention to population growth in their own planning. Only occasionally do they consider the serious implications of demographic trends for their present and future activities.

Yet some of the necessary information is at hand and can be made available to all levels of government. Much of the rest will be obtained by the Commission. For such information to be of greatest use, however, it should also be interpreted and analyzed and its implications should be made more evident. It is particularly in this connection that the work of the Commission on Population Growth and the American Future will be as much educational as investigative. The American public and its governing units are not as alert as they should be to these growing challenges. A responsible but insistent voice of reason and foresight is needed. The Commission can provide that voice in the years immediately before us.

The membership of the Commission should include two members from each house of the Congress, together with knowledgeable men and women who are broadly representative of our society. The majority should be citizens who have demonstrated a capacity to deal with important questions of public policy. The membership should also include specialists in the biological, social, and environmental sciences, in theology and law, in the arts and in engineering. The Commission should be empowered to create advisory panels to consider subdivisions of its broad subject area and to invite experts and leaders from all parts of the world to join these panels in their deliberations.

The Commission should be provided with an adequate staff and budget, under the supervision of an executive director of exceptional experience and understanding.

In order that the Commission will have time to utilize the initial data which results from the 1970 census, I ask that it be established for a period of two years. An interim report to the President and Congress should be required at the end of the first year.

OTHER GOVERNMENT ACTIVITIES

I would take this opportunity to mention a number of additional government activities dealing with population growth which need not await the report of the Commission.

First, increased research is essential. It is clear, for example, that we need additional research on birth control methods of all types and the sociology of population growth. Utilizing its Center for Population Research, the Department of Health, Education, and Welfare should take the lead in developing, with other federal agencies, an expanded research effort, one which is carefully related to those of private organizations, university research centers, international organizations, and other countries.

Second, we need more trained people to work in population and family planning programs, both in this country and abroad. I am therefore asking the Secretaries of State, Labor, Health, Education, and Welfare, and Interior along with the Administrator of the Agency for International Development and the Director of the Office of Economic Opportunity to participate in a comprehensive survey of our efforts to attract people to such programs and to train them properly. The same group—in consultation with appropriate state, local, and private officials—

should develop recommendations for improvements in this area. I am asking the Assistant to the President for Urban Affairs to coordinate this project.

Third, the effects of population growth on our environment and on the world's food supply call for careful attention and immediate action. I am therefore asking the Environmental Quality Council to give careful attention to these matters in its deliberations. I am also asking the Secretaries of Interior, Agriculture, and Health, Education, and Welfare to give the highest priority to research into new techniques and to other proposals that can help safeguard the environment and increase the world's supply of food.

Fourth, it is clear that the domestic family planning services supported by the Federal Government should be expanded and better integrated. Both the Department of Health, Education and Welfare and the Office of Economic Opportunity are now involved in this important work, yet their combined efforts are not adequate to provide information and services to all who want them. In particular, most of an estimated five million low income women of childbearing age in this country do not now have adequate access to family planning assistance, even though their wishes concerning family size are usually the same as those of parents of higher income groups.

It is my view that no American woman should be denied access to family planning assistance because of her economic condition. I believe, therefore, that we should establish as a national goal the provision of adequate family planning services within the next five years to all those who want them but cannot afford them. This we have the capacity to do.

Clearly, in no circumstances will the activities associated with our pursuit of this goal be allowed to infringe upon the religious convictions or personal wishes and freedom of any individual, nor will they be allowed to impair the absolute right of all individuals to have such matters of conscience respected by public authorities.

In order to achieve this national goal, we will have to increase the amount we are spending on population and family planning. But success in this endeavor will not result from higher expenditures alone. Because the life circumstances and family planning wishes of those who receive services vary considerably, an effective program must be more flexible in its design than are many present efforts. In addition, programs should be better coordinated and more effectively administered. Under current legislation, a comprehensive State or local project must assemble a patchwork of funds from many different sources—a time-consuming and confusing process. Moreover, under existing legislation, requests for funds for family planning services must often compete with requests for other deserving health endeavors.

But these problems can be overcome. The Secretary of Health, Education and Welfare—whose Department is responsible for the largest part of our domestic family planning services—has developed plans to reorganize the major family planning service activities of his agency. A separate unit for these services will be established within the Health Services and Mental Health Administration. The Secretary will send to Congress in the near future legislation which will help the Department implement this important program by providing broader and more precise legislative authority and a clearer source of financial support.

The Office of Economic Opportunity can also contribute to progress in this area by strengthening its innovative programs and pilot projects in the delivery of family planning services to the needy. The existing network of O.E.O. supported community groups should also be used more extensively to provide family planning assistance and information. I am asking the Director of the Office of Economic Opportunity to determine the ways in which his Agency can best structure and extend its programs in order to help achieve our national goal in the coming years.

As they develop their own plans, the Secretary of Health, Education and Welfare and the Director of the Office of Economic Opportunity should also determine the most effective means of coordinating all our domestic family planning programs and should include in their deliberations representatives of the other agencies that share in this important work. It is my intention that such planning should also involve state and local governments and private agencies, for it is clear that the increased activity of the Federal government in this area must be matched by a sizeable increase in effort at other levels. It would be unrealistic for the Federal government alone to shoulder the entire burden, but this Administration does accept a clear responsibility to provide essential leadership.

FOR THE FUTURE

One of the most serious challenges to human destiny in the last third of this century will be the growth of the population. Whether man's response to that challenge will be a cause for pride or for despair in the year 2000 will depend very much on what we do today. If we now begin our work in an appropriate manner, and if we continue to devote a considerable amount of attention and energy to this problem, then mankind will be able to surmount this challenge as it has surmounted so many during the long march of civilization.

When future generations evaluate the record of our time, one of the most important factors in their judgment will be the way in which we responded to population growth. Let us act in such a way that those who come after us—even as they lift their eyes beyond earth's 'bounds—can do so with pride in the planet on which they live, with gratitude to those who lived on it in the past, and with continuing confidence in its future.

RICHARD NIXON

The White House
July 18, 1969

272   Telephone Conversation With the Apollo 11 Astronauts on the Moon. *July* 20, 1969

HELLO Neil and Buzz, I am talking to you by telephone from the Oval Room at the White House, and this certainly has to be the most historic telephone call ever made from the White House.

I just can't tell you how proud we all are of what you have done. For every American this has to be the proudest day of our lives, and for people all over the world I am sure that they, too, join with Americans in recognizing what an immense feat this is.

Because of what you have done the heavens have become a part of man's world, and as you talk to us from the Sea of Tranquility, it inspires us to redouble our efforts to bring peace and tranquility to earth.

For one priceless moment in the whole history of man all the people on this earth are truly one—one in their pride in what you have done and one in our prayers that you will return safely to earth.

ASTRONAUT ARMSTRONG. Thank you, Mr. President. It is a great honor and privilege for us to be here representing not only the United States, but men of peaceable nations, men with an interest and a curiosity, and men with a vision for the future. It is an honor for us to be able to participate here today.

THE PRESIDENT. Thank you very much, and I look forward, all of us look forward, to seeing you on the *Hornet* on Thursday.

ASTRONAUT ARMSTRONG. Thank you. We look forward to that very much, sir.

NOTE: The President spoke at 11:49 p.m. in the Oval Room at the White House with Apollo 11 astronauts Neil A. Armstrong and Col. Edwin E. (Buzz) Aldrin, Jr., at Tranquility Base on the moon.

On July 21, 1969, the White House Press Office released the text of the news briefing of Col. Frank Borman, Press Secretary Ronald L. Ziegler, and others concerning the Apollo 11 mission.

273   Remarks to American Field Service Students. *July 22, 1969*

WE WERE DELAYING because we understand that there were about a thousand more who were expected to attend but apparently there is a bus strike and they could not get here. But I understand that in this great audience here on the South Lawn of the White House there are 2,000 students from 60 countries.

THE AUDIENCE. Three thousand.

THE PRESIDENT. Two thousand here. One thousand are in the buses. But we know that there are 3,000 who are in this great program, and I want you to know that in the 6 months that I have been in the White House, I have been in many occasions welcoming chiefs of states, heads of governments, prime ministers, kings, emperors here on this South Lawn, but no group has been more inspiring than yours.

Incidentally, I expect, and I say this with great conviction, that as I look at this group, as I know that you come from all of these 60 countries represented and will be going back to your own countries, and I know, too, that you would not be here unless you had a great interest in political affairs, and I am very sure that from this group at some time a future President will be welcoming a prime minister or a president, I am sure, from some other country abroad.

I see we have plenty of candidates.

Also, could I say, as you know, I am leaving tonight on a trip myself, one that will take me around the world, not to all of the 60 countries—and I think I have visited 50 of the 60 that are represented here—but to many others. Just to get an idea, I wonder if there are any here today from the first country that I will visit, which will be the Philippines. Anybody from the Philippines?

THE AUDIENCE. Yes!

THE PRESIDENT. Anybody from Indonesia? How about Thailand?

THE AUDIENCE. Yes!

THE PRESIDENT. India?

THE AUDIENCE. Yes!

THE PRESIDENT. Pakistan?

THE AUDIENCE. Yes!

THE PRESIDENT. I will also be in Britain.

THE AUDIENCE. Yes!

The PRESIDENT. That is an indication of the countries that will be covered.

THE AUDIENCE. Brazil!

THE PRESIDENT. There is a future President of Brazil right there, I'm sure.

THE AUDIENCE. Chile!

THE PRESIDENT. I have been there, too.

THE AUDIENCE. Peru!

THE PRESIDENT. Right. Romania?

THE AUDIENCE. Honduras!

THE PRESIDENT. Well, if I mentioned Honduras, how about El Salvador?

THE AUDIENCE. Yes!

THE PRESIDENT. Costa Rica, San José; Afghanistan, Kabul?

THE AUDIENCE. Yes!

The PRESIDENT. Denmark, Copenhagen? Yes. Vietnam? Yes, I have been there. Colombia? Yes.

Well, you can see if I called the roll

that we would take all the time.

Could I speak seriously to you for just a moment as I welcome you to the White House and in effect say goodby to you as you return to your own countries?

I want to say first that my only regret is that our family could not have had some of you visit us in our homes during this last year. Of course, in this last year I have been a little busy, but nevertheless, we have so many friends who have had the privilege of having students from this group in their homes and many of them have said that it was really the best thing that ever happened in their lives.

We thank you all for giving so many Americans the privilege of knowing your countries through you, the youth of your countries. This is a great privilege; it is a privilege that many American families have never had before and we are very grateful for that.

Second, I want you to know that as I meet you and realize your ages and all the years ahead of you, I think what a wonderful time it is for you to be alive. I suppose that that sounds rather strange these days when we read of some of the problems in the world—problems in Latin America, Africa, Asia, and the Mideast, and the like, a war in Vietnam, all of these problems—but let us look at it, if we can, for a moment, without being Pollyannish, but look at it with the true realism that an idealist must have, looking at the facts, but also looking beyond them as we really should, to the future, which you can help to build.

You could not find a more exciting time to be born; you could not find a more exciting time to finish high school and then go on to college and then pick your profession, because when you are my age or perhaps a little younger than I am, in the year 2000, and you celebrate the new year that comes once in a thousand years, look at what you look back on and look at what you will see then and what you will look forward to in the 21st century.

We think of those men who are returning from the moon. Wasn't that a great thing to see? In the year 2000 I believe, and I am sure that those in this audience who are so young and so full of life and so full of optimism, will agree with me, in the year 2000 we will, on this earth, have visited new worlds where there will be a form of life.

I know this will happen, and I want to tell you as I look forward and dream about that future, as I am sure you look forward to it and dream about it, this is the kind of world I would like to see and the kind of exploration of that new world that I know all Americans want.

I hope that when the next great venture into space takes place that it will be one in which Americans will be joined by representatives of other countries so that we can go to the new world together. I know from the telegrams that I have received around the world that the spirit of all the people of the world was with those three brave men. They are not just Americans; they represented all of mankind. That is why as we look at the future adventures into the free world, let them not be adventures of conquest, but adventures of exploration which tend to unite us all into one people which we truly are, and we feel that today in a crowd like this.

What those new worlds will be like, whether on Mars or Venus or any of the other areas we may be able to explore, no one can presently say, but let me say a word about what this world can be like and what you can make it like.

Sometimes we get very pessimistic about problems. We see the population curve going up. We see the food production not going up as fast, and we look at great areas of the world in Asia and Africa and Latin America and wonder if those two curves are going to pass and the dire prediction of Malthus, made a century or two centuries ago, may prove true in our time—later than he thought, but yet prove true. I don't think so, because I am convinced that we have the genius— genius represented by young people in this group, but genius represented by people all over the world—so that we can produce the food and the clothing, the health care, the housing, the shelter, all the things that we need to keep ahead of population and continue to progress.

That is the challenge you have; it is the challenge you, I am very confident, are going to meet.

I think, too, that, as we look to the future, we think of the possibilities not only of the new worlds, what may not be or may be on the Moon or Mars or Venus, but we think of what that moon achievement means in terms of what we can do on this earth.

So often we hear: "This cannot be done. The problem is too great." But when I saw, or at least heard and saw the simulation of those two space vehicles traveling at 4,500 miles an hour, coupling together in space, let alone landing on the moon and the takeoff on the moon, but saw that take place out there in outer space, as I realized all of the scientific genius and the technical ability, let alone the human factors that went into that decision, I realized that this is no time for the pessimists; this is the time for the optimists and the idealists.

Be optimistic and idealistic about the future. I realize the kind of teamwork, the kind of scientific achievement, the kind of idealism that we saw in that space shot, that landing on the moon. If we could just bring all that to bear on the problems here on earth, the problems of our environment, the problems of adequate food, health, and shelter, and progress, a fair share for everybody in this earth—if that can be done, what a world we can create.

Let me look just a little further ahead in another way. I thought one of the, shall we say, rather sad things about that great day on Monday when man first stepped on the moon was that while most of the peoples of the world saw it on television or participated in it on television or radio, that there was approximately one-half the world that did not see it, the whole of Communist China, and the world of the Soviet Union.

I thought how sad that was, sad not in terms of East-West conflict, because this is no time to discuss that, but sad in terms of the people involved, because you see I know the Russian people. I have visited them. They are a great people. And their young people are like you people.

And I know the Chinese people. I have never seen them on the mainland of China, but I have seen them in Taiwan and I have seen them in Manila and I have seen them in Indonesia and I have seen them in Thailand and I have seen them in New York and I have seen them in San Francisco, and I want the time to come when the Chinese people and the Russian people and all the peoples of this world can walk together and talk together.

I want to say to you that in the time that I am in this office, however long it will be, that the major goal that I will have will be to bring peace to this world, real peace, and also to hasten the day when we can have a truly open world, open cities, open borders, open countries, open minds, open hearts, open ideas. That is what we want. That is what you want. And that is what we are going to build for us.

Now I suppose that when we look at the world today and those great political differences that divide us and the war that goes on, we sometimes perhaps would be pessimistic and say, "Well, you are just dreaming." I don't think so. I want you to know that as I see you today, as I realize the experience that you have, as I know the spirit you will carry back to your own countries, you are going to help to make these dreams come true; and I would simply add to that great slogan that I understand all of you have of walking together and talking together. Let's add to it. Let's dream together, too. Let's dream about the future.

I know of no group of young people in the world who can help more to make those dreams come true than all of you, and I ask all of you as you leave the United States of America—remember, of course, the differences that you saw here, have in mind the problems you saw here, and try to avoid them in your own countries—but remember above everything else: The American people are with you in their hearts. They want for you what we want for ourselves: the right to be free, the right to move ahead, the right to talk together and walk together and to dream together.

All of these things you believe in and all of these things, I am sure, the world believes in, if the leaders of the world simply have the ability to allow the people of the world to let their views be felt and their views to prevail.

So, to my good friends, and some of you I hope to meet in some of my future journeys around the world, I can only say: Thank you for coming to America. As one who was born in this country, I love my country, and I think it is a great country; but I can tell you, as one who has visited over 60 countries in the world, I think every people in this world is a great people, and a great country. If we think that way we are going to go a long way.

Thank you.

NOTE: The President spoke at 11:06 a.m. on the South Lawn at the White House to approximately 3,000 exchange students attending a 3-day American Field Service Conference. The students, ages 16 to 18 years, had all spent the previous year living with a family in the United States. The American Field Service is a private educational organization which seeks to promote peace through understanding among peoples of the world.

274   Message to the Congress Transmitting Reorganization Plan for the Interstate Commerce Commission. *July 22, 1969*

To the Congress of the United States:

The Interstate Commerce Commission, oldest of the Federal regulatory agencies, has jurisdiction over 17,000 carriers—rail and motor, water and pipeline, express companies and freight forwarders. Its decisions help shape the scope and character of the Nation's transportation system.

But, as important as the Commission is, as extensive as its jurisdiction is, it is hampered by:

1. *Lack of continuity:* The Chairman of the Commission serves only a year, selected by annual rotation from among the eleven Commissioners. In no other major Federal regulatory agency is the President without the power to designate the Chairman.

2. *Lack of leadership:* The Chairman does not have vested in him by law the executive and administrative functions of the Commission. As a result there is no firm and clear legal responsibility for the management of the Commission's day-to-day affairs.

To change this situation, I am sending to the Congress today Reorganization Plan No. 1 of 1969, prepared in accordance with chapter 9 of title 5 of the United States Code.

1. CONTINUITY

The Chairman of the Interstate Commerce Commission is the Commission's spokesman, its key link to other agencies and the industry, the supervisor of its staff, and director of its internal operations. Yet today, despite the need for sustained leadership, the Chairman of this agency serves only one year. I know of no modern business that would tolerate the practice of annually rotating its chief executive.

To provide the necessary continuity of leadership in the conduct of the Commission's administrative affairs, *I propose that the President be authorized to designate the Chairman of the Commission from among its members.* This principle of good management has already

been taken with respect to most other major Federal regulatory agencies. The time has come to apply it to the Interstate Commerce Commission.

2. LEADERSHIP

The administrative powers of the Chairman must be strengthened.

In 1961, the Commission delegated its administrative powers to its Chairman. However, unless and until the administrative powers are vested in the Chairman by law, statutory authority will remain dispersed among the Commissioners.

Almost 20 years ago the Hoover Commission emphasized that "Administration by a plural executive is universally regarded as inefficient." It then recommended that all administrative responsibility be assigned the chairmen of these regulatory agencies.

That recommendation is as sound today as it was then. It has already been applied to almost every other major Federal regulatory agency. *I propose that administrative authority be vested in the Chairman of the Interstate Commerce Commission.*

In sum, the reorganization plan provides continuity of leadership and vests responsibility for internal administrative functions in a chairman designated by the President, with safeguards to ensure that the Commission retains full control over policy and the direction of its regulatory programs. This does not affect the statutory provisions governing the exercise of quasi-legislative and quasi-judicial powers by the Commission and its employees to whom it has delegated the responsibility of hearing and deciding cases.

Each reorganization included in the plan is necessary to accomplish one or more of the purposes set forth in section 901(a) of title 5 of the United States

Code. In particular, the plan is responsive to section 901(a)(1), "to promote the better execution of the laws, the more effective management of the executive branch and of its agencies and functions, and the expeditious administration of the public business;" and section 901(a)(3), "to increase the efficiency of the operations of the Government to the fullest extent practicable." This plan will help achieve those ends.

This plan should result in more efficient operation of the Commission. To itemize or aggregate resulting expenditure reductions under the plan is not practicable. I shall continue to explore other ways to

make the Commission structure more effective.

I strongly recommend that the Congress permit this necessary reorganization plan to become effective.

RICHARD NIXON

The White House
July 22, 1969

NOTE: Reorganization Plan 1 of 1969 became effective on October 11, 1969, except section 3 which became effective on January 1, 1970.

Also on July 22, 1969, the White House Press Office released the text of a news briefing held by Press Secretary Ronald L. Ziegler and Assistant to the President Peter M. Flanigan concerning Reorganization Plan 1 of 1969.

275 Statement on the 1970 Budget.
July 22, 1969

I HAVE today signed into law the final supplemental appropriations bill for the fiscal year ended June 30. In addition to providing budget authority for the operation of the Federal Government, the measure removes a restriction that had been placed on Federal hiring by the Revenue and Expenditure Control Act of 1968.

Written into the law is another ceiling—on Federal spending during the fiscal year 1970, the one we have just entered. This new ceiling is set at $191.9 billion—one billion dollars below my own fiscal 1970 expenditure recommendations of last April.

However, the Congress has made this new ceiling somewhat flexible. There are a number of categories in the Federal budget—such as medicare, interest on the public debt, social insurance benefits, and farm price supports—where costs can rise without new appropriation action. Congress has determined that increases

in these items—up to $2 billion—will be exempt from the $191.9 billion ceiling.

There are other outlays such as military expenditures in Southeast Asia, public assistance, Medicaid benefits, and veterans benefits, where it is also very difficult to budget a precise figure. Any additional appropriations the Congress votes, in these categories, above our 1970 revised budget estimates, will result in an upward adjustment of that $191.9 billion ceiling.

There is another aspect to the proposal. If, after voting this new lower ceiling, Congress fails to cut the budget to fit under it, the President must take over and finish the job. On the other hand, if Congress should cut the budget below $191.9 billion, that new lower figure automatically becomes a new ceiling. The latter hypothesis does not appear at this point to be a strong probability.

In making the new ceiling somewhat flexible, the Congress has acted wisely.

However, the new ceiling will be of little help in keeping Federal spending under control if the Congress that imposed it does not cooperate fully with the administration in meeting it.

Last April I presented a revised 1970 budget to the Congress. That budget contained specific reductions totaling $4 billion from the budget left by the previous administration. It brought the proposed Federal spending figure for this fiscal year down to $192.9 billion, a figure I still believe reflects a responsible fiscal policy in our highly inflationary environment. If we hold the line on that spending figure, as I intend to, and if the requisite revenues are provided, this fiscal year will produce the kind of budget surplus needed to cool off an economy that was dangerously overheated before we assumed office.

Three months have passed since the administration's revised budget was sent to the Congress. We are already 3 weeks into the 1970 fiscal year, and the Congress has not completed its action on a single regular 1970 appropriations bill. It seems apparent that it will not be known until the late fall just how much of a contribution the Congress intends to make toward meeting the spending ceiling Congress itself has imposed.

In the meantime, since April, the budget picture has worsened. We now anticipate further increases of approximately $2.5 billion in expenditure for such uncontrollable items as interest on the public debt, Medicare, social security, civil service retirement benefits, reduced receipts from offshore oil leases, public assistance, and veterans benefits.

In addition, congressional action to date has been inconsistent with a number of my proposals in April. For example, Congress has not acted on my recommendation for a postal rate increase to be effective July 1. Nor has it terminated the special milk and agricultural conservation programs as I recommended. Instead of reducing aid to schools in impacted areas, it is moving to increase such aid. These, and similar actions, could add at least another billion dollars net to Federal spending in 1970.

Thus our current estimate of fiscal 1970 spending has risen to $196.4 billion even though we in the administration have done nothing in the way of discretionary action to add to our earlier $192.9 billion estimate.

Given our commitment to hold Federal spending to the April figure of $192.9 billion there is only one course of action open to the administration, and we are taking it. I am directing the heads of all departments and agencies to reduce spending in the fiscal year just begun by an additional $3.5 billion, the amount necessary to bring current estimates back in line with the $192.9 billion target figure we set in April.

No Federal program is above scrutiny. Some highly desirable programs will have to be stretched out, others reduced. The dollar reductions will be accompanied by a further lowering of the personnel ceilings established last April.

I know the Congress shares my determination to make the budget an effective instrument against the inflation that has wrought so much damage to the income and savings of millions of Americans. If the Congress did not share that commitment, it would not have imposed this spending ceiling. However, this general expression of support for fiscal restraint must now be matched by specific acts of the Congress.

The Congress should also recognize that

if it approves further increases above the April budget estimates, we cannot live within the $192.9 billion figure unless more offsetting cuts are made.

I would prefer that the Congress make these offsetting cuts in programs it considers of lesser priority, if it votes increases over my April budget for activities it considers essential. If it does not do so, the duty of making such cuts clearly becomes mine.

NOTE: As enacted, the Second Supplemental Appropriations Act of 1969 is Public Law 91–47 (83 Stat. 49).

On the same day the White House Press Office released the text of a news briefing by Robert P. Mayo, Director of the Bureau of the Budget, concerning the President's statement on the 1970 budget.

276 Remarks at the Baseball All-Star Reception. *July 22, 1969*

Mr. Commissioner and ladies and gentlemen:

I want you all to know that of the many receptions that have been held in this room, this is one of the most exciting of all; exciting because like so many who never made the team, I am always awed in the presence of people who have made the team and are the champions.

On this particular occasion I know that last night at the dinner there were many references to the 100 years of baseball, the baseball centennial, and also to the recognition on that occasion that was given to the great heroes of baseball through the years.

I am not going to try to top what was said then. I certainly am not going to top what I hope to see tonight. Incidentally, just to give you an indication of how much I think of this game, they wanted me, in order to get out of San Francisco tonight and get a night's sleep before going out to the splashdown in the Pacific the next day, they said I could leave at the fifth inning. I'll tell you, I never leave in the middle of a game because I know what happens in baseball.

I was just trying to think—you know, on an occasion like this you try to show off

a little about your baseball knowledge—I can't pretend to be the expert that Shirley Povich [1] and some of the other experts around here are, but I should point out that my first recollection as far as World Series were concerned, one of the freshest in mind, involved a year that most of the people in this room, particularly those who came from the field that you used to be in, Mr. Commissioner, the field of finance, the year of the big crash, 1929, but I remember that Series so well, because I had always followed the Philadelphia Athletics and the great Connie Mack.

I recall the great pitchers that team had. I was thinking what the Senators would do if we had those three in addition to Joe Coleman and a couple of others. You remember that year he could have started with Lefty Grove or Rube Walberg, two great left-handers, or George Earnshaw, who had won over 20 games with a right hand, and then on the other hand he came up with Howard Ehmke, who fanned 14 men and they won the first game.

But the reason that I learned—and of course all of this was through sports pages

---

[1] Sports editor for the Washington Post.

in those days before the days of television—that you never left a game—I had never seen a World Series game before that time—was that in one of the games in that Series, I think it was October 12, the Cubs were ahead 8 to nothing going into the eighth inning and the Athletics with, of course, a great murderers' row, [Jimmy] Foxx, [Al] Simmons and all the rest, scored 10 runs and won the game, 10 to 8. I stayed all the way through every game after that experience.

So much for that. There are other memories that flash through, of course, the ones that are written about so often. Charlie Root, of course, was a favorite of mine because he came up from Los Angeles which used to be the Cubs' farm team back in the days when they played at Wrigley Field.

He was pitching, you recall, in 1932 in Chicago. The Cubs had done pretty well up to that point. Babe Ruth, pointing to that fence and then hitting one right over the fence against a really great pitcher. Those events come to mind.

We think of catches and stealing and the rest—Carew stealing home—the great ones through the years, and we have some pretty good base stealers and pretty good stealers in other places, too—not in Washington.

But in any event, I think of Pepper Martin going down to second base against one of the great catchers of all time, Mickey Cochrane, and that made an indelible impression in my mind and nothing perhaps could ever equal that, because you remember those days more than you remember the present days.

But I should not say that, because to prove that I am a baseball fan. I have always been for the Senators and, believe me, you have to be a baseball fan to have

been for the Senators in those days. Of course there were years, and this year is one of those, when you can be for the Senators and have a better than 50–50 chance that they can win, but it was not always that way, I can assure you.

Bobo Newsom comes to mind, pitching against the Yankees. He was a hero. He always lost, but he was a hero, I can assure you, because he did so well against a very great team in those years. And of course, Roy Sievers.

I have to mention some of our Washington baseball heroes. A fellow who you may recall had a bad arm because he ran into a fence trying to catch a fly ball, but he could still hit the long ball, and was the best that Washington had and one of the greatest in the American League in his period, and so on through the years.

So when we get to the present time, and I think of the relationship of baseball to politics, I think of the fact, for example, that some of the great political columnists started out as sports columnists. Now I don't know if that is going up or down, but in any event, Bill Henry of the Los Angeles Times used to write sports and Scotty Reston of the New York Times used to write sports, and, of course, Bob Considine used to write sports and now they write politics. As far as I am concerned I just want you to know that I like the job I have, but if I had to live my life over again, I would have liked to have ended up as a sports writer.

I also want to make it clear that if I had been in Boston, I would not have been against Ted Williams, either, as a sports writer.

I have talked enough about my own recollections, but these recollections will tend to bring home the message that I think all of you can get through loud and

39–861—71——38

clear. I didn't see a major league game until the year 1936. I was in law school then and came up to Washington and saw a double-header on July 4 between the Yankees and the Senators and the Yankees won both games—they would with Gehrig and all that great group that they had with them at that time—but I knew baseball, knew it through what I had read. So I pay tribute today to those who have written baseball so well that those of us who never saw a game could learn to like it as well as we did.

Today we see it on television, and, of course, that has enormously increased the baseball audience. So I pay tribute to the poor sports writers, and I also have in mind the fact that they also might become political writers later. So, I will pay that tribute to them.

Secondly, I want to pay tribute too, before going to the players, to the owners and those who run the league and to those who have the toughest job of all. I of course refer to the umpires, and to men like Bowie Kuhn—and I have known many commissioners through the years— who have given to this game in the minds of millions of fans who never see it except on television or hear about it on radio or read about it in the newspapers, have given to it a credibility that is beyond reproach. Baseball is great because anything can happen through the ninth inning. It is great also because everybody knows it is an honest game. And it is great, too, because the men who play it and the men who are in it—and I should say now looking at the owner of the Mets,[2] the women who are in it—that as far as baseball is concerned, those who are in base-

ball are people we can look up to, that our young people look up to. I think that is something we are all very proud of.

I want to say to all the baseball players who are here and all of the former baseball players, that I am proud to be in your company. I am one of your fans, and even though I didn't make the team, I am with you in spirit and I am going to be delighted to meet each and every one of you here today.

Thank you very much.

MR. GILES. I want to try and wean you to the National League. You have spoken entirely about the American League. But the National League proudly extends to you the courtesy of all its grounds during your lifetime.

THE PRESIDENT. Thank you very much. I appreciate that so much. The way the dollar is going, I had better keep this gold.

COMMISSIONER KUHN. Mr. President, may I say a word? I came here today, among other things, to make a presentation to the President, and when you see what the presentation is you will see why I felt it desirable to talk about what a wonderful baseball fan the President is. I had planned to make a somewhat elaborate statement, with the President's permission, about what a fine fan he is. But I think after what we have heard today, I am not going to say another word. I don't think another word is necessary to demonstrate to all of us here in this room, indeed to all America, that I have standing at my left America's number one baseball fan.

It is a great pleasure for me, under these circumstances, Mr. President, to present to you the exact award that we presented last evening, to the greatest baseball players of all time, and we present it to you as baseball's number one fan.

---

[2] Mrs. Charles (Joan) Payson, director and president of the New York Mets.

THE PRESIDENT. Well, it took a lot of years, but I finally made it.

COMMISSIONER KUHN. Mr. President, I might say, we think you are very much on the team.

THE PRESIDENT. Mr. Commissioner, I am most grateful, and this award will have a very proud place in the Presidential Library.

Now, I know that we have got to get to the game on time, so let's get this reception going.

NOTE: The President spoke at 4:43 p.m. in the East Room at the White House.

Warren Giles, president of the National League, presented the President with a gold, lifetime pass to all National League games. Baseball Commissioner Bowie K. Kuhn presented him with a gold trophy inscribed to "Baseball's Number One Fan."

The All-Star game which the President had planned to attend at Robert F. Kennedy Stadium was postponed because of heavy rains. Vice President Spiro T. Agnew represented the President at the game the following day.

277   Remarks to Apollo 11 Astronauts Aboard the U.S.S. *Hornet* Following Completion of Their Lunar Mission. *July* 24, 1969

Neil, Buzz, and Mike:

I want you to know that I think I am the luckiest man in the world, and I say this not only because I have the honor to be President of the United States, but particularly because I have the privilege of speaking for so many in welcoming you back to earth.

I can tell you about all the messages we have received in Washington. Over 100 foreign governments, emperors, presidents, prime ministers, and kings, have sent the most warm messages that we have ever received. They represent over 2 billion people on this earth, all of them who have had the opportunity, through television, to see what you have done.

Then I also bring you messages from members of the Cabinet and Members of the Senate, Members of the House, the space agency, from the streets of San Francisco where people stopped me a few days ago, and you all love that city, I know, as I do.

But most important, I had a telephone call yesterday. The toll wasn't, incident-

ally, as great as the one I made to you fellows on the moon. I made that collect, incidentally, in case you didn't know. But I called three, in my view, three of the greatest ladies and most courageous ladies in the whole world today—your wives.

From Jan, Joan, and Pat, I bring their love and their congratulations. We think it is just wonderful that they have participated at least in television in this return. We are only sorry they couldn't be here.

Also, I will let you in on a little secret. I made a date with them. I invited them to dinner on the 13th of August, right after you come out of quarantine. It will be a state dinner held in Los Angeles. The Governors of all the 50 States will be there, the Ambassadors, others from around the world and in America. They told me that you would come, too. All I want to know is: Will you come? We want to honor you then.

MR. NEIL A. ARMSTRONG. We will do anything you say, Mr. President, anytime.

THE PRESIDENT. One question, I think, that all of us would like to ask: As we saw you bouncing around in that float out there, I wonder if that wasn't the hardest part of the journey. Did any of you get seasick?

MR. ARMSTRONG. No, we didn't, and it was one of the hardest parts, but it was one of the most pleasant, we can assure you.

THE PRESIDENT. Well, I just know that you can sense what we all sense. When you get back now—incidentally, have you been able to follow some of the things that happened since you have been gone? Did you know about the All-Star Game?

COL. EDWIN E. ALDRIN, JR. Yes, sir. The capsule communicators have been giving us daily reports.

THE PRESIDENT. Were you American League or National League?

COL. ALDRIN. National League.

MR. ARMSTRONG. Neither one.

THE PRESIDENT. There is the politican in the group.

MR. ARMSTRONG. We are sorry you missed that.

THE PRESIDENT. You knew that, too?

MR. ARMSTRONG. We heard about the rain. We haven't learned to control the weather yet, but that is something we can look forward to.

THE PRESIDENT. Well, I can only summarize it because I don't want to hold you now. You have so much more to do. You look great. Do you feel as great as you look?

MR. ARMSTRONG. We feel great.

THE PRESIDENT. Frank Borman feels you are a little younger by reason of having gone into space. Is that right? Do you feel a little bit younger?

MR. ARMSTRONG. We are younger than Frank Borman.

THE PRESIDENT. He is over there.

Come on over, Frank, so they can see you. Are you going to take that lying down?

ASTRONAUTS. It looks like he has aged in the last couple weeks.

COL. FRANK BORMAN. They look a little heavy.

Mr. President, the one thing I wanted—you know, we have a poet in Mike Collins. He really gave me a hard time for describing the words "fanstastic" and "beautiful." I counted them. In 4 minutes up there, you used four "fantastics" and three "beautifuls."

THE PRESIDENT. Well, just let me close off with this one thing: I was thinking, as you know, as you came down, and we knew it was a success, and it had only been 8 days, just a week, a long week, that this is the greatest week in the history of the world since the Creation, because as a result of what happened in this week, the world is bigger, infinitely, and also, as I am going to find on this trip around the world, and as Secretary Rogers will find as he covers the other countries in Asia, as a result of what you have done, the world has never been closer together before.

We just thank you for that. I only hope that all of us in Government, all of us in America, that as a result of what you have done, can do our job a little better.

We can reach for the stars just as you have reached so far for the stars.

We don't want to hold you any longer. Anybody have a last—how about promotions? Do you think we can arrange something?

MR. ARMSTRONG. We are just pleased to be back and very honored that you were so kind as to come out here and welcome us back. We look forward to getting out of this quarantine and talking without having the glass between us.

THE PRESIDENT. Incidentally, the speeches that you have to make at this dinner can be very short. If you want to say "fantastic" or "beautiful," that is all right with us. Don't try to think of new adjectives. They have all been said.

Now, I think incidentally that all of us, the millions who are seeing us on television now, seeing you, would feel as I do, that, in a sense, our prayers have been answered, and I think it would be very appropriate if Chaplain Piirto, the Chaplain of this ship, were to offer a prayer of thanksgiving. If he would step up now.

NOTE: The President spoke at 8:55 a.m. aboard the U.S.S. *Hornet* near the splashdown site in the Pacific. The prayer offered by Lt. Comdr. John A. Piirto, USN, Chaplain of the *Hornet* follows:

Let us pray.

Lord God, our Heavenly Father, our minds are staggered and our spirits exultant with the magnitude and precision of this entire Apollo 11 mission. We have spent the past week in communal anxiety and hope as our astronauts sped through the glories and dangers of the heavens.

As we tried to understand and analyze the scope of this achievement for human life, our reason is overwhelmed with the bounding gratitude and joy, even as we realize the increasing challenges of the future. This magnificent event illustrates anew what man can accomplish when purpose is firm and intent corporate.

A man on the moon was promised in this decade, and though some were unconvinced, the reality is with us this morning in the persons of the astronauts: Armstrong, Aldrin, and Collins. We applaud their splendid exploits, and we pour out our thanksgiving for their safe return to us, to their families, to all mankind.

From our inmost being, we sing humble yet exuberant praise. May the great effort and commitment seen in this Project Apollo inspire our lives to move similarly in other areas of need. May we, the people, by our enthusiasm and emotion and insight move to new landings in brotherhood, human concern, and mutual respect. May our country, afire with inventive leadership and backed by a committed followership, blaze new trails into all areas of human care.

Speed our enthusiasm and bless our joy with dedicated purpose for the many needs at hand. Link us in friendship with peoples throughout the world as we strive together to better human conditions. Grant us peace beginning in our own hearts and a mind attuned with good will toward our neighbors.

All this we pray as our thanksgiving rings out to Thee in the name of our Lord, Amen.

278   Remarks on Arrival at Guam International Airport. *July* 25, 1969

THANK YOU very much. Mrs. Nixon and I want you to know how very much we appreciate your wonderful welcome here at Guam.

As I stand here and think of what happened today, the completion of that historic flight to the moon and the landing on the moon, I can say that I am sure all of us—all of the American citizens around the world—are proud today of what has happened, and all the people in Guam join with all of us in that.

After such a warm welcome as this, I would, of course, remember this visit to Guam, brief as it is, in any event, but I will remember it particularly, and my wife will remember it, because on the day that our astronauts came back from the moon, we stayed in Guam, and we are glad we are here with you. We only wish we had the time to meet each and every one of you, but we have a fairly heavy schedule while we are here, and then on tomorrow to the Philippines.

I simply want to say in conclusion that when we come here, when we see this great crowd of people, all of whom are deeply devoted to our country far across the Pacific, we realize what a great challenge those of us have who are in positions of leadership to develop the programs that will bring peace and progress to all the world, and particularly we feel that when we see these literally thousands of chil-

dren. We want them to grow up in a world of peace.

I can assure you that coming here has given us a real inspiration. We thank you for your welcome. We look forward to meeting at least some of you before we leave, and all of you, if we don't meet you personally, at least we hope we do sometime in the future.

Thank you.

NOTE: The President spoke at 4:45 p.m. at the International Airport, Agana, Guam.

279 Informal Remarks in Guam With Newsmen. *July 25, 1969*

THE PRESIDENT. [1.] As Ron Ziegler [Press Secretary] has already told you, the remarks today will be for attribution but not direct quotation, and for background.[1]

For your further information in that respect, Marshall Green [Assistant Secretary of State for East Asian and Pacific Affairs] will brief the members of the press who desire to have background on the Philippines and Indonesia. He will be with us through those two stops. For the balance of the stops, Henry Kissinger will be available to brief you if you desire him to do so.

Insofar as the plans are concerned, there are no changes in schedule to announce; I have seen some speculation about changes in schedule. I have no present plans to go to Vietnam. I should say, however, that Ambassador Bunker[2] will be coming to Bangkok along with the Ambassadors from the other Asian countries that we will not be visiting, and I intend

to have a conversation with him there which will be apart from the conversation I will have with the other Ambassadors on the general situation in the area.

There is also a possibility that General Abrams will be able to come over with Ambassador Bunker to Bangkok for that meeting.

UNITED STATES ROLE IN ASIA

[2.] Now, insofar as this phase of the trip is concerned, and I will speak first to the Asian phase and then later and briefly to the Romanian phase, I think that the backgrounder that you have already had from Henry Kissinger and the general statements that have been made from the State Department have covered it pretty well. I think what would be of greatest interest to you before we go to your questions is to give you the perspective that I have with regard to Asia and America's role in Asia.

As you know, my background here goes back a few years. It was in 1953 that I first visited this area. That trip was very

---

[1] The text of these remarks was later released for publication in this volume.

[2] Ellsworth Bunker, U.S. Ambassador to the Republic of Vietnam.

extensive, with the usual 4 days in each country, a so-called state visit in each country. It provided an opportunity to meet the leaders, but more than that to know the countries in a very effective way.

In the 16 years that have passed, however, since that time, the changes have been very dramatic. I have returned to Asia, as you know, on a number of occasions since then, and particularly to the countries that we will be visiting on this trip. Consequently, I have kept up with later developments and also, with the exception of President Yahya [Gen. Agha Muhammad Yahya Khan] in Pakistan, I know each of the Asian leaders that I will be meeting and will be able to speak to them from that background.

Insofar as the general purpose of a trip like this, I can understand some of the speculation to the effect that: Why does a President of the United States think he learns anything by spending 1 day each in an Asian country—or, for that matter, as we did earlier, in a European country?

The answer is, and I might indicate what will be my general policy for the balance of my service in the White House, that I think a 1-day trip is just as valuable as 4 days. In other words, if you take a 1-day trip, and concentrate, as I do, on very little protocol and a great deal of face-to-face conversation, an individual, in meeting the leader of the other country, will gain as much as if he stretches it out over a period of 4 days. I have been through both experiences and, therefore, am somewhat knowledgeable in that respect.

I feel, too, that when one considers the time that is available to a President in these periods, that it is essential, in order to cover all the ground that needs to be covered, to limit, first, the amount of travel and the amount of time that is taken for each one of the stops. I mention that only as some of the reasoning that has gone into my decision with regard to covering a great deal of ground in a very short period of time—in this case, going around the world and, in the space of about 8 days, after the moon shot, covering a number of countries.

Now, insofar as the individuals are concerned, having met all of these leaders previously, I suppose the question could be raised, and with good reason, that once you know a leader then contact with ambassadors would be sufficient. However, I have found it in my previous travels in Asia, and in Europe as well, that as these situations change it is vitally important to have a renewed contact with the leader in each of the countries involved, a renewed contact because his attitudes may change. And in that way, when I read, as I do read day after day, the cables that come in from all over the world, I can have a much better understanding of what those cables mean, the nuances, if I have more recently had a direct contact, face-to-face, with the individual involved, the individual leader involved.

That is one of the reasons why I am a great believer in visits of this sort, where they are consistent with and can be taken at a time that will fit in with other very demanding parts of our schedule.

Now, a word about what is a very consuming interest in Asia. A consuming interest, I say, because it is one that I have had for a number of years, and one that now, as I look at the perspective of history, becomes even more imperative.

The United States is going to be facing, we hope before too long—no one can say how long, but before too long—a major decision: What will be its role in Asia and in the Pacific after the end of the war in Vietnam? We will be facing that decision, but also the Asian nations will be wondering about what that decision is.

When I talked to Prime Minister Gorton [of Australia], for example, he indicated, in the conversations he had had with a number of Asian leaders, they all wondered whether the United States, because of its frustration over the war in Vietnam, because of its earlier frustration over the war in Korea—whether the United States would continue to play a significant role in Asia, or whether the United States, like the French before, and then the British, and, of course, the Dutch—whether we would withdraw from the Pacific and play a minor role.

This is a decision that will have to be made, of course, as the war comes to an end. But the time to develop the thinking which will go into that decision is now. I think that one of the weaknesses in American foreign policy is that too often we react rather precipitately to events as they occur. We fail to have the perspective and the long-range view which is essential for a policy that will be viable.

As I see it, even though the war in Vietnam has been, as we all know, a terribly frustrating one, and, as a result of that frustration, even though there would be a tendency for many Americans to say, "After we are through with that, let's not become involved in Asia," I am convinced that the way to avoid becoming involved in another war in Asia is for the United States to continue to play a significant role.

I think the way that we could become involved would be to attempt withdrawal, because, whether we like it or not, geography makes us a Pacific power. And when we consider, for example, that Indonesia at its closest point is only 14 miles from the Philippines, when we consider that Guam, where we are presently standing, of course, is in the heart of Asia, when we consider the interests of the whole Pacific as they relate to Alaska and Hawaii, we can all realize this.

Also, as we look over the historical perspective, while World War II began in Europe, for the United States it began in the Pacific. It came from Asia. The Korean war came from Asia. The Vietnamese war came from Asia.

So, as we consider our past history, the United States involvement in war so often has been tied to our Pacific policy, or our lack of a Pacific policy, as the case might be.

As we look at Asia today, we see that the major world power which adopts a very aggressive attitude and a belligerent attitude in its foreign policy, Communist China, of course, is in Asia, and we find that the two minor world powers—minor, although they do have significant strength as we have learned—that most greatly threaten the peace of the world, that adopt the most belligerent foreign policy, are in Asia, North Korea and, of course, North Vietnam.

When we consider those factors we, I think, realize that if we are thinking down the road, down the long road—not just 4 years, 5 years, but 10, 15 or 20—that if we are going to have peace in the world, that potentially the greatest threat to that peace will be in the Pacific.

I do not mean to suggest that the Mideast is not a potential threat to the peace of the world and that there are not problems in Latin America that concern us, or in Africa and, of course, over it all, we see the great potential conflict between the United States and the Soviet Union, the East-West conflict between the two super powers.

But as far as those other areas are concerned, the possibility of finding some kind of solution, I think, is potentially greater than it is in the Asian area.

Pursuing that line of reasoning a bit further then, I would like to put it in a more positive sense: When we look at the problems in Asia, the threat to peace that is presented by the growing power of Communist China, the belligerence of North Korea and North Vietnam, we should not let that obscure the great promise that is here.

As I have often said, the fastest rate of growth in the world is occurring in non-Communist Asia. Japan, in the last 10 years, has tripled its GNP [gross national product]; South Korea has doubled its GNP; Taiwan has doubled its GNP; Thailand has doubled its GNP. The same is true of Singapore and of Malaysia.

The record in some of the other countries is not as impressive. But consider the Philippines where there are very grave problems, as you will learn when you are there, political problems and others. One of the brighter spots is that when I was in the Philippines in 1953, it was a major importer of rice. Today, as a result of "miracle rice," it no longer has to import it. Some progress is being made in an area like that.

When we look at India and Pakistan and the terribly difficult and traumatic experience they have had, because of their conflict with each other more than with the problems they have had from the outside, the picture tends to be rather black.

But India's rate of growth as a result of 2 good crop years, and a reasonably good one this year, has been at 6 percent. If we can get the population problem—if they

can—under better control the promise for the future, of course, is rather bright.

As far as Pakistan is concerned, they are emphasizing growth in manufacturing. They are growing at the rate of 10 percent per year in manufacturing and from 1965 to 1970 their agricultural production will go up 21 percent.

When you visit these two countries, even in the brief visits that we have, when you see the poverty which strikes you in the face, if you have not seen it before, with a tremendous impact, you will wonder whether there is a great deal to hope for. But all I can say is that having seen what it was in 1953 and seeing what it was again in 1967, the amount of progress that has taken place, even in those countries where the rate has not been as high as others, is a very, very formidable thing to see.

So, what I am trying to suggest is this: As we look at Asia, it poses, in my view, over the long haul, looking down to the end of the century, the greatest threat to the peace of the world, and, for that reason the United States should continue to play a significant role. It also poses, it seems to me, the greatest hope for progress in the world—progress in the world because of the ability, the resources, the ability of the people, the resources physically that are available in this part of the world. And for these reasons, I think we need policies that will see that we play a part and a part that is appropriate to the conditions that we will find.

Now, one other point I would make very briefly is that in terms of this situation as far as the role we should play, we must recognize that there are two great, new factors which you will see, incidentally, particularly when you arrive in the Philippines—something you will see there that we didn't see in 1953, to show you how quickly it has changed: a very great growth of nationalism, nationalism even in the Philippines, vis-à-vis the United States, as well as other countries in the world. And, also, at the same time that national pride is becoming a major factor, regional pride is becoming a major factor.

The second factor is one that is going to, I believe, have a major impact on the future of Asia, and it is something that we must take into account. Asians will say in every country that we visit that they do not want to be dictated to from the outside, Asia for the Asians. And that is what we want, and that is the role we should play. We should assist, but we should not dictate.

At this time, the political and economic plans that they are gradually developing are very hopeful. We will give assistance to those plans. We, of course, will keep the treaty commitments that we have.

But as far as our role is concerned, we must avoid that kind of policy that will make countries in Asia so dependent upon us that we are dragged into conflicts such as the one that we have in Vietnam.

This is going to be a difficult line to follow. It is one, however, that I think, with proper planning, we can develop.

TRIP TO ROMANIA

[3.] One word about Romania. Let me just answer some of the speculation about Romania by pointing out that this trip to Romania is not directed toward the Chinese or toward the Russians, but toward the Romanians.

I do not believe that the President of the United States should be able to accept an invitation to visit a Western European country, but should automatically have to decline an invitation to visit an Eastern European country.

I have said that this is an era, I hope, of negotiation rather than confrontation. It will be more difficult, of course, to develop the communication with Eastern European Communist countries than with the Western European countries, but I think it is time that a beginning be made.

We will have discussions of bilateral issues with President [Nicolae] Ceausescu, the problems of Europe, East-West relations. But this trip under no circumstances should be interpreted as an affront to the Soviet Union or as a move toward China.

It will, if it works out, I trust, set the stage for more openings of this type with countries in Eastern Europe where it would be mutually beneficial to the United States and the other country involved.

QUESTIONS

U.S. MILITARY RELATIONSHIPS IN ASIA

[4.] Q. Mr. President, sir, on the question of U.S. military relationships in Asia, if I may ask a hypothetical question: If a leader of one of the countries with which we have had close military relationships, either through SEATO or in Vietnam, should say, "Well, you are pulling out of Vietnam with your troops, we can read in the newspapers. How can we know that you will remain to play a significant role as you say you wish to do in security arrangements in Asia?" What kind of an approach can you take to that question?

THE PRESIDENT. I have already indicated that the answer to that question is not an easy one—not easy because we will be greatly tempted when that question is put to us to indicate that if any nation desires the assistance of the United States militarily in order to meet an internal or external threat, we will provide it.

However, I believe that the time has come when the United States, in our relations with all of our Asian friends, be quite emphatic on two points: One, that we will keep our treaty commitments, our treaty commitments, for example, with Thailand under SEATO; but, two, that as far as the problems of internal security are concerned, as far as the problems of military defense, except for the threat of a major power involving nuclear weapons, that the United States is going to encourage and has a right to expect that this problem will be increasingly handled by, and the responsibility for it taken by, the Asian nations themselves.

I believe, incidentally, from my preliminary conversations with several Asian leaders over the past few months that they are going to be willing to undertake this responsibility. It will not be easy. But if the United States just continues down the road of responding to requests for assistance, of assuming the primary responsibility for defending these countries when they have internal problems or external problems, they are never going to take care of themselves.

I should add to that, too, that when we talk about collective security for Asia, I realize that at this time that looks like a weak reed. It actually is. But looking down the road—I am speaking now of 5 years from now, 10 years from now—I think collective security, insofar as it deals with internal threats to any one of the countries, or insofar as it deals with a threat other than that posed by a nuclear power, I believe that this is an objective which

free Asian nations, independent Asian nations, can seek and which the United States should support.

INTERNAL THREATS TO ASIAN COUNTRIES

[5.] Q. Mr. President, when you speak of internal threats, do you include threats internally assisted by a country from the outside, such as we have in Vietnam?

THE PRESIDENT. Generally speaking, that is the kind of internal threat that we do have in the Asian countries. For example, in Thailand the threat is one that is indigenous to a certain extent to the northeast and the north, but that would not be too serious if it were not getting the assistance that it was from the outside. The same is true in several of the other Asian countries.

POSSIBILITY OF SUMMIT MEETING WITH SOVIET UNION

[6.] Q. Mr. President, you mentioned that you hoped that your meetings in Romania would open the way to other meetings involving Eastern Europe. Is it your hope that you would eventually be invited to Moscow to talk with the Russians perhaps within the next 6 months or so?

THE PRESIDENT. As far as any meeting with the Soviet Union is concerned, summit meeting, I have stated my position previously. And I think it would be well to restate it again.

I do not believe that any summit meeting with the Soviet Union is useful unless a subject of major interest to both powers is to be discussed with some promise of finding a solution or at least making progress on that particular problem.

I believe, for example, as I look over the history of summitry with the Soviet Union, that while, in all administrations, we have had the best of intentions, that summitry has not been particularly helpful. I would say this with regard to the spirit of Geneva, the spirit of Camp David, the spirit of Vienna, and the spirit of Glassboro.

I feel that where the Soviet Union is concerned, for example, today, there are three major areas where a summit meeting could be useful. If, for example, the time had come when we could make a breakthrough in the Mideast and a summit meeting with the Soviet Union would play a significant part, I think that could be considered. I do not anticipate that, incidentally. We are too far apart at this time to suggest that that is on the way.

The second area, of course, is in the field of arms control. I had, as you know, a long discussion with Mr. [Gerard C.] Smith just a few days ago, just before leaving, the day before leaving. As far as arms control is concerned, at this time, the place and the forum in which the discussion should take place is at the ambassadorial level. There may come a time when a summit meeting may be the device which will make the breakthrough that we need to make on arms control. And in that case, I would, of course, favor an arms control.

Then at the top of the list, of course, I would put the problem of Vietnam where, if a summit meeting would serve a useful purpose insofar as Vietnam is concerned, naturally we would welcome that opportunity. That poses, as we all know, however, a very significant problem because whether the Soviet Union can be of assistance in Vietnam is somewhat dependent on its evaluation of whether such

assistance should be so publicly provided as a summit, of course, would indicate.

RELAXATION OF RESTRICTIONS WITH COMMUNIST CHINA

[7.] Q. Mr. President, it has been suggested that we have relaxed trade and travel restrictions to China as a backdrop to your Asian trip, and that this may cause some disquiet in those countries which fear Communist China. Can you say whether there was any connection between your trip and those relaxations, and what accounted for the timing of them?

THE PRESIDENT. No. As a matter of fact, suggestions for relaxing restrictions vis-à-vis Communist China—incidentally, suggestions going considerably beyond those that I adopted have been before the National Security Council for the past 3 months. As far as these two matters that you refer to, one, of course, as you know, dealt simply with the purchase by tourists of commodities of $100 or less; the more significant one dealt with the travel restrictions. I have always felt that with Communist China or with any country in the world, that an exchange of persons is very valuable for us, and I would trust also for them.

This is a policy I have announced previously, and it is one that I was simply implementing at this time. It had no relationship to the timing of this trip. I see no reason why any of the countries should be concerned.

PROSPECTS FOR ADDITIONAL TROOP REPLACEMENTS

[8.] Q. Mr. President, as a background to your thinking on Vietnam, even though we recognize it is not to be a major subject of discussion, could you tell us what sort of reports you had from General Wheeler about the prospects for additional replacement of American troops, and on the question of whether the fighting has eased to the point where we can make some deescalation move ourselves?

THE PRESIDENT. I would rather not comment on that at this time. If, after my conversations with Ambassador Bunker and possibly with General Abrams, I feel that some comment would be appropriate, I will make it then.

But I should, Mr. Scali [John A. Scali, ABC News], correct one impression which I should not have left, and that is that Vietnam will not be a major subject for discussions. In each of the Asian countries I am going to raise with the Asian leaders the question of the extent to which they would be willing to participate in the international supervisory bodies for elections in South Vietnam and for the policing of cease fires provided we are able to get any kind of acceptance on the part of the North Vietnamese and the VC [Vietcong] on our May 14th proposal.

I believe, for example, that the international supervisory bodies which, as you know, Mr. Thieu has also agreed to—that they should primarily be made up of and come from Asian nations, and the Asian nations that I visit I know will all be interested in this subject. I want to get their views on that.

U.S. WITHDRAWAL AND ASIAN SECURITY

[9.] Q. Mr. President, do you anticipate in that connection that during your talks with the Asian leaders you are going to have to spend any significant amount of time perhaps convincing them that your plan for withdrawal of American forces

from Vietnam will pose no threat to their security?

THE PRESIDENT. Well, one of the reasons for this trip is to leave no doubt in the minds of the leaders of non-Communist Asia that the United States is committed to a policy in the Pacific—a policy not of intervention but one which certainly rules out withdrawal—and regardless of what happens in Vietnam that we intend to continue to play a role in Asia to the extent that Asian nations, bilaterally and collectively, desire us to play a role.

I think that some reassurance is needed because Vietnam is on the minds of all the Asian leaders. I believe, incidentally, that I will not have difficulty in providing that reassurance because from the report that I did get from General Wheeler, he tells me that the troop withdrawals have been accepted by the Thieu Government and by the military in South Vietnam with not only very good grace, but that they have responded very effectively in meeting their own requirements and in handling their own defense. I think that I can give some reassuring comments to those Asian leaders who might raise the question.

FUTURE INVOLVEMENT IN ASIA

[10.] Q. Mr. President, you mentioned that you felt that perhaps 5 years or 10 years from now the Asian nations could collectively take care of their regional security problems. What is our policy to be in the meantime if a Vietnam-type situation does occur?

THE PRESIDENT. Well, I would rather not speculate about one occurring. Each of these countries, as you, of course, know from your studying the background materials and as you will note when you visit it, poses an entirely different question. I would simply say we are going to handle each country on a case-by-case basis but attempting to avoid that creeping involvement which eventually simply submerges you—incidentally, I don't say that critically of how we got into Vietnam, but I do know that we can learn from past experience, and we must avoid that kind of involvement in the future.

Let me put it this way. I recall in 1964 some advice that I got from Ayub Khan, who was then the President of Pakistan. This was before the United States had any significant troop commitment in Vietnam. I asked him what his view was as to what our role should be. He said, "Well, the role of the United States in Vietnam or the Philippines or Thailand or any of these countries which have internal subversion is to help them fight the war but not fight the war for them." Now, that, of course, is a good general principle, one which we would hope would be our policy generally throughout the world.

TROOP WITHDRAWALS FROM THAILAND

[11.] Q. Mr. President, the last time we met with you, you mentioned that it was your hope that we might be able to withdraw all our combat troops, ground combat troops, in South Vietnam by the end of next year. In the light of that, I wonder if you have any plans for withdrawing the troops that we now have, or some percentage of them, from Thailand, and could you tell us what you are going to tell the Thais about that?

THE PRESIDENT. Well, I would tell the Thais first. But it is certainly, of course, a proper question.

We are reviewing, as you know, not only our civilian personnel abroad, where I announced a cut a few weeks ago, but our

military personnel abroad, including Thailand.

This is a matter, however, which will be discussed with the Thais, but it would not be appropriate to make any announcement as to what we were going to do until we have discussed it.

MILITARY AND ECONOMIC ASSISTANCE IN ASIA

[12.] Q. Mr. President, in looking at the situation post-Vietnam, and in countries other than Vietnam, would it seem to you that in terms of our military strength, the military men that we put into these other countries to help them, or military assistance or economic assistance, that in Asia, generally, we would have more or less of this type of assistance and aid in the years down the road than we have now?

THE PRESIDENT. Less. Yes. If I get your question correctly, you mean more or less a military type of assistance?

Q. Both in the military and the non-military. There are really two parts to this assistance problem, the economic part and the military part. And I was wondering from your discussion whether you would see us having a greater expenditure and a greater involvement in those respects or a lessened involvement as we look down the road.

THE PRESIDENT. What I would see would be that the military involvement, the military assistance, military aid programs and the rest, and particularly the commitment of military personnel—that that type of program would recede.

However, as far as economic programs are concerned, and particularly those of a multilateral character—and here we have some new ideas that we will be expanding on in the months ahead—I would say that the level of U.S. activity would be adequate to meet the challenge as it develops, because it is very much in our interest in terms of economic assistance, economic assistance through loans and other programs, to help build the economies of free Asia.

Let us consider, for example, what has happened to South Korea, what has happened to Taiwan, what has happened to Thailand, what has happened to Japan, all of whom we have assisted enormously economically. All of them now, or virtually all, are on their own feet, at least from an economic standpoint, and are very good customers of ours.

Let us consider Indonesia for just one moment. Indonesia has been through a terribly difficult experience as we all know.

Incidentally, I found in reading my statistics here that in 1965 the rate of inflation was 635 percent in Indonesia and it is zero now. I want to find out from Mr. Suharto [President of Indonesia] how he did it.

But, nevertheless, here is Indonesia with 117 million people, and the greatest, richest resources of any country in Asia. It is very much in the interest of the United States, which has a minimal economic program in Indonesia, to participate in some way in the economic development of Indonesia. That will give you an indication of my thinking.

EXISTENCE OF SECRET DEFENSE AGREE-
MENT WITH THAILAND

[13.] Q. Mr. President, there has been quite a bit of speculation in the papers lately, both in Washington and in Thailand, as to whether or not there exists some sort of secret defense agreement between the U.S. and Thailand.

I was wondering, could you shed any light on the existence or nonexistence of such a thing and whether we have any similar arrangements with any other countries that might commit us beyond what your hopes might be?

THE PRESIDENT. There is no secret defense agreement with Thailand. We, of course, as you know, have the SEATO Treaty. We will keep our commitments under that treaty. We had the Rusk-Thanat Khoman communiqué [3] which simply spelled out the treaty. We will, of course, keep our commitments set forth there as well.

But as far as any secret commitments are concerned, we not only have none in any of these nations, I can assure you, and I will make none—incidentally, I told Senator Fulbright [J. William Fulbright of Arkansas] that the other day, too—reassured him.

USE OF COUNTERINSURGENCY TACTICS

[14.] Q. Mr. President, on the question of creeping involvement and the advice that Ayub Khan once gave you, could you tell us if there is any future in Asia for American counterinsurgency tactics as they have developed since 1960?

THE PRESIDENT. Well, there is a future for American counterinsurgency tactics only in the sense that where one of our

[3] Secretary of State Dean Rusk and Minister of Foreign Affairs for Thailand Thanat Khoman were delegate leaders to the 13th meeting of the Council of Ministers of the Southeast Asia Treaty Organization. The text of the final communiqué issued on April 3, 1968, at the close of the 2-day meeting is printed in the Department of State Bulletin (vol. 58, p. 515).

friends in Asia asks for advice or assistance, under proper circumstances, we will
provide it. But where we must draw the
line is in becoming involved heavily with
our own personnel, doing the job for them,
rather than helping them do the job for
themselves.

Now, I know I begged the question
with that answer but I intend to do so.
I intend to do it because I think that there
is one American trait which we saw in
Korea, we have seen it in Vietnam, and we
see it pretty much around the world: We
do things, we think, rather well. And particularly in the military field, where we
are pretty advanced, we think that we
can do it better than to try to teach somebody else to do it.

That may be the easy answer at the
outset, but it is the wrong answer in the
long run. I want to be sure that our
policies in the future, all over the world,
in Asia, Latin America, Africa, and the
rest, reduce American involvement. One
of assistance, yes, assistance in helping
them solve their own problems, but not
going in and just doing the job ourselves
simply because that is the easier way to
do it.

MR. ZIEGLER. This will have to be the
last question.

ECONOMIC AND POLITICAL CAPABILITY OF
COMMUNIST CHINA

[15.] Q. Mr. President, could you give
us your impression or evaluation——

THE PRESIDENT. We will take another
5 minutes. I don't mean the question will
be 5 minutes. [*Laughter*]

Q. I will make it very short.

THE PRESIDENT. No, no. That is all
right.

Q. Could you give us your evaluation
of Red China's economic-political capability of inspiring further wars of liberation in the Asian nations? Are they able
to continue that?

THE PRESIDENT. Red China's capacity
in this respect is much less than it was
5 years ago, even 10 years ago. Because
of its internal problems, Red China is
not nearly as effective in exporting revolution as it was then. I think a pretty good
indication of that is the minimal role that
Red China is playing in Vietnam as compared with the Soviet Union.

Three years ago, Red China was furnishing over 50 percent of the military
equipment, the hardware, for the North
Vietnamese. Now it is approximately
80–20 the other way around.

There may be other reasons for that
coming about, but part of it is that Red
China has enough problems within.

Another point I would make in that
respect that bears on this, how things have
changed in Asia: In 1953, in country after
country that I visited—and I was in every
one that we are visiting here and all the
others as well, the ones that Secretary
[of State William P.] Rogers is going to
visit on that trip—among most of the
intellectual leaders and among many government leaders, there was a real question
as to what was the best path for progress,
a question as to whether communism, as
it was developing in Red China, a Communist system, was a better way to progress, or whether a non-Communist system
was the better way.

Now, one of the significant developments that has occurred over these past
16 years, with all the bad things that have
occurred, including the war in Vietnam,
has been that that situation has reversed

itself. The appeal of the Communist philosophy, for example, in Pakistan, in India, in Indonesia, in Japan, in any one of these countries, is less today than it was 16 years ago, 10 years ago, 5 years ago.

On the other hand, I would have to say that the effectiveness of subversive activities in many of these countries has not abated to the same extent. It can be on the upgrade. But as we look at the whole of Asia today, it is significant to note that what we have going for us more than anything else is this enormous rate of growth in non-Communist Asia as compared with Communist Asia. You compare Hong Kong with Communist China, you compare Taiwan with Communist China, you look at Japan with 100 million people, with a greater GNP than China with 700 million people, looking clear around the perimeter, from Japan through India, we find that free Asia's record of growth is a very significant factor in affecting the thinking of those who have to make the determination as to which path they are going to take.

AVOIDING FUTURE WARS IN ASIA

[16.] Q. Mr. President, sir, when you say that the United States is going to continue to play a major role in Asia, that this is one message that you intend to take with you on this trip, my impression, from the thrust of your remarks today, is that another message is no more Vietnams. Is that impression correct, sir?

THE PRESIDENT. Certainly the objective of any American administration would be to avoid another war like Vietnam any place in the world. You may recall—and, of course, it was called campaign oratory, I said it and so did my opponent, Mr.

[Hubert H.] Humphrey, during the campaign—that we should develop a policy that would avoid other Vietnams.

I realize it is very easy to say that. I will be quite candid when I admit that to develop the policies to avoid that is taking an enormous amount of my time and those of my associates.

But what we can do is to learn from the mistakes of the past. I believe that we have, if we examine what happened in Vietnam—how we became so deeply involved—that we have a good chance of avoiding that kind of involvement in the future.

ANNOUNCEMENT OF TROOP WITHDRAWALS IN AUGUST

[17.] Q. Mr. President, do you intend to make it clear to the Asian leaders that if the lull in Vietnam continues, you will announce a substantial withdrawal of U.S. forces in August?

THE PRESIDENT. No, I will not make any announcement of, and no decision on, troop withdrawals on this trip, and, of course, I would not make any disclosures of plans in that respect to Asian leaders prior to the time that we had discussed it with the Government of South Vietnam and then made the announcement jointly.

As you do know, we are reexamining, as I indicated we would, our whole troop commitment in Vietnam during the month of August, and we hope to be able to make an announcement sometime during the month of August with regard to troop withdrawal.

But that is one of the matters that I have still under study, under consideration, that I will be discussing with Ambassador Bunker, that I did discuss with

General Wheeler, and that I may discuss with General Abrams.

MILITARY TACTICS IN VIETNAM

[18.] Q. Mr. President, is there also a pending question as to whether your administration will change its policy of maintaining maximum military pressure on the enemy in Vietnam?

THE PRESIDENT. We have been re-examining, since the time this administration came into office, our military tactics in Vietnam, and one of the subjects that I have discussed at great length with General Wheeler and General Abrams has been the character of our commitment and the tactics that should be used. I defer, naturally, to military men as to the conduct of a war because they are more expert than I am in this field.

However, when we are in the process of negotiations, then military tactics become part of the negotiations and, therefore, we are reevaluating our tactics in Vietnam, having in mind the fact that we have a parallel action going along in the negotiating field.

If we have any changes in this respect, I, of course, will announce them.

Reporter: Thank you, Mr. President.

NOTE: The President spoke at 6:30 p.m. at the Top O' The Mar Officers' Club in Guam.

280 Remarks on Departure From Guam. *July 26, 1969*

BEFORE we take off for Manila I wanted to just say a very few words to tell you how greatly we appreciated the very warm welcome we received on this brief visit to Guam. I know that many of you who live here, and perhaps even some of you who are stationed here, perhaps consider that those who stop at Guam do so only as a fuel stop on the way to someplace else. But for us it was a stop that meant a great deal in itself. It meant a great deal because we realized it was 25 years ago that the liberation of Guam took place and that the festivities had just concluded. And also because we had the opportunity to see so many thousands of people at the airport, on the roads, as we went through the cities and realized that where the day begins for America there is a lot of feeling as citizens of the United States for all the people that are here and we appreciate that very much.

Also I'd like to say I heard that there was a great storm the day before we arrived and that then there was a massive cleanup campaign before the arrival. We thank you for that and we hope that the weather will be good, that you'll have some smooth sailing and smooth flying, and above all, a good life in the time ahead.

And as I leave I think of an inscription that I saw on the photograph that Admiral Nimitz left in his quarters where we stayed last night: an inscription in his own handwriting, in the year 1945, when he returned from Guam to the United States mainland. It goes like this:

He says, "To my successor who may live in these quarters, I hope you may find the calm, peaceful rest and relaxation which will enable you to face your problems with confidence."

And I can say that our stay in Guam

this one day and that fine evening last night and this wonderful welcome gave us the calm, peaceful rest and relaxation which will enable us to face the problems of this great Nation with confidence.

Thank you very much.

NOTE: The President spoke at 12:15 p.m. at the Naval Air Station in Agana, Guam. Fleet Adm. Chester W. Nimitz was Commander in Chief of the U.S. Pacific Fleet and Pacific Ocean Area in World War II from June 1944 to August 1945.

281   Remarks on Arrival at Manila, the Philippines. *July* 26, 1969

President Marcos, Mrs. Marcos, all of the distinguished guests who are assembled here, and all of the members of this tremendous welcoming party at the airport:

I have been deeply moved by the words that have been expressed by President Marcos in his welcoming and also by the numbers of you that are here today. And as one who has visited the Philippines many times, I can say that I have looked forward to this return visit, as every American looks forward to returning to the Philippines once he knows the people of this country, knows them and has the affection for them, and the respect for them and the admiration for them that I have as an American citizen.

I think it is significant to note that the first world capital that I am visiting, after having greeted the first men to have set foot on the moon, is Manila, the capital of the Philippines.

And that, it seems to me, is appropriate from a number of circumstances, but particularly so because now we speak not just of our world, but of the universe.

And I am not unaware of the fact that a very lovely lady from the Philippines, Miss Gloria Diaz, has been named Miss Universe.

Also, the first Asian capital that I am visiting on this trip which takes me around the world is very appropriately Manila and the country is the Philippines. The reasons for that have already been mentioned by President Marcos.

I would like to add to what he has said in just a few words.

As we think of that great venture into space, as we think of the first man setting foot on the moon, we realize the meaning that that has, clearly apart from the technical achievement, we realize that if man can reach the moon, that we can bring peace to the earth. And that should be the great lesson of that great space journey for all of us.

This mission, which begins here, is in the quest of peace, peace in the Pacific, peace in Asia, peace in the world.

I come here because the Philippines— the leaders of this country have played and will play a great role in bringing that peace. And, it seems to me, that we must think of the Pacific and of Asia in terms of the past, of the present, and the future.

I noted, for example, that the commander of the honor guard, which I just had the privilege of reviewing, was one of the veterans of Bataan. He was the commander of the honor guard when I visited this country in 1956 on the 10th anniversary of the Philippines. That brought home to me the close relationships between our two countries, but par-

557

ticularly the stake that the Philippines and the United States have together in peace in the Pacific.

We went through World War II together. We have gone through Korea together. We now have a war in Vietnam. And when we look at the possibilities of potential war, down to the end of this century, perhaps we would have to say that the greatest danger exists in Asia and in the Pacific.

But that also presents the greatest challenge. And the challenge I think can be met—it must be met.

And I want to speak very candidly to my friends in the Philippines, because I know you like straight talk. I know that in your political campaigns you have a lot of straight talk, just as we have in the United States.

But if peace is to come from Asia— and I emphasize this point—the United States will play its part and provide its fair share. But peace in Asia cannot come from the United States. It must come from Asia. The people of Asia, the governments of Asia, they are the ones who must lead the way to peace in Asia.

That is why I compliment the leaders of the Philippines in playing a role in Asian cooperation, economically, politically, and otherwise, to bring about the peace that we all seek.

And then in another vein, we realize, as we look at that great venture into space, the larger meaning that it has for all of us in terms of seeking peace.

A great French philosopher once said that true friendship comes not when we look at each other, but when we look outward together in the same direction. And for just a few moments, the whole world looked outward together in the same direction toward the moon.

And as we did that, we were brought closer together.

Your own great President Quezon [1] put it very eloquently when he said that nationalism can be a very constructive force in the world, but that nationalism is most constructive when we remember that we are all part of the great human family; that being part of that great human family, the greatest role that any nation can play is the role of serving the interests of all mankind and of, therefore, serving the interests of peace.

I speak in these general terms today because it is appropriate to do so on this first welcome after that historic exploit into space, on my first visit to an Asian capital [on a journey] that will take me clear around the world.

But, as I conclude, I want to speak very directly, too, about the relations between our two countries, relations that I have a very strong feeling about, as I am sure that everybody here, be he Filipino or American, has a strong feeling about. Let me be quite candid.

It is true that our relations with the Philippines go back further than that with any Asian nation. It is true that the people of the United States feel closer to the people of the Philippines than we do to the people of any Asian nation. This is because of those things that we have shared together.

It is also true that our relations have been strained, strained recently for a variety of reasons. We are still very good friends, but even among friends, it is possible to have strained relations.

And I want everybody here to know that as I come to the Philippines in this

---

[1] Manuel L. Quezon, President of the Commonwealth of the Philippines 1935–1941.

brief stay, I hope that we can initiate a new era in Philippine-American relations, not returning to the old special relationship, because the winds of change have swept away those factors, but building a new relationship, a new relationship which will be based on mutual trust, on mutual respect, on mutual confidence, on mutual cooperation.

That is what we want, and that is what I think the people of the Philippines and of the United States will support.

So, Mr. President, in that spirit and in the spirit of your very eloquent remarks, again, I thank you for this wonderful welcome.

In that spirit, also, I say from the bottom of my heart to all of our friends in the Philippines, *mabuhay* [greetings, good wishes].

NOTE: The President spoke at approximately 1 p.m. at Manila International Airport in response to welcoming remarks by President Ferdinand E. Marcos. An advance text of the President's remarks was also released by the White House Press Office on July 26, 1969.

President Marcos spoke as follows:

Mr. President and Mrs. Nixon, members of his party:

In the name of the Filipino people, I bid you and Mrs. Nixon welcome to the Philippines, to this country which has welcomed you before with open arms, and to whom you are no stranger.

Gratefully we remember one of your previous visits. As Vice President of the United States you came to solemnly affirm your Government's recognition of Philippine ownership and sovereignty over the American bases on our soil.

Today you honor us again by coming to these shores as the President of the United States. And you come at a time when the imagination of the whole world has been fired by America's historic achievement in space exploration.

It is for us significant that the Philippines should be your first stop in your journey through Asia after witnessing two of three American astronauts on the moon and their return, a feat unparalleled in implications, in radicalism, and in the prospects of hope it promises man in the entire history of human achievement.

Your visit too makes us feel ourselves to be part of this meaningful triumph, vicariously a partner in the conquest of a new frontier, just as over 60 years ago the Philippines became the first major involvement of the United States in Asian affairs.

At that time we could not join in any celebration, but changing circumstances enable us today to stand straight and strong, thanks also to the great country, the United States of America, to join them in applauding this feat not of arms but of mind and fortitude. Even as we do this, we are mindful that yours is a triumph also of Asians as well as of all mankind. For today, every human being, every nation, all humanity, partake of the labor, of the hope, and of the responsibility that goes into the invention or discovery of whatever is new.

In recalling the beginning of the association between our two peoples on this, the occasion of America's victory in outer space, we are also reminded that many things remain to be achieved in the mutual relations between our two countries. But I am confident that in any future history, it shall not be said that America was a success in all its undertakings except in the sphere of human and social relations. I trust it shall not be said that America successfully breached the frontiers of space and technology, but failed in matters close to the heart and mind, the relations of man with other men.

I am certain this will not be so, because increasingly today, technology and science are bound up with the things that concern the welfare and the happiness of human beings, as the negative example of war has shown us. It is my hope, one that is shared by all of my countrymen regardless of partisan belief, that the powerful thrust of technology and science shall be applied, not only by the United States but by all countries, on unresolved problems of human misery and unhappiness everywhere. Let this present triumph be the springboard for a more vigorous attack on these problems in this region.

Your visit to the Philippines gives us the distinct honor of being able to be the first to personally congratulate you on this historic achievement, which we very much appreciate. It also affords us the opportunity, during your

559

brief stay with us, to resume our discussions on outstanding issues affecting our two countries' relations in Southeast Asia, and to advance our countries' interests, but not at the expense of the others.

It is hoped that out of these discussions a new consensus can be achieved between us whose basis will be a dignified and self-respecting mutual regard for each other. For this I voice the hope of millions of my countrymen for the coming of a new era of peace and prosperity not only in the Philippines but for all of Asia, which they believe these great events which you lead portend.

Let your coming, therefore, signal the start of a new series of constructive breakthroughs in the relations between us and among the countries of the Pacific and Asia, and let your courageous astronauts symbolize our quest for peace and partnership for global welfare and prosperity among all peoples, a goal worthy of our utmost dedication. On the ethics of generosity and of responsibility, America's record is clear that it has been exemplary both in its commitment and its fulfillment.

In the list of Presidents who have flashed through the brilliant pages of America's history, you are to us in Asia the most knowledgeable about the problems and the aspirations of the countries and of the peoples of Asia. To Asia you are no stranger; to the Philippines you are more than a friend, for you first came as a guarantor of the sovereign rights of the Filipino people. By a fortunate coincidence this triumph of American science and spirit comes at a time, during your administration, when the United States is anxious to reexamine her national purposes in relation to the rest of the world.

Thus, as you commence this visit, its manifold meanings will not be lost to Asia and to all who long for peace and prosperity. For you come, we trust, not only to reinforce the traditional guarantees that bind your world to ours; you come also to proffer new gifts that science can bring to all mankind; and you come, we are certain, to forge in the smithies of the world, because of your courage, your vision, your statesmanship, a brilliant new role for America, and history will remember you as its wise and far-seeing architect.

In this spirit, I bid you once again welcome to the Philippines and to Asia.

282 Toasts of the President and President Marcos at a State Dinner in Manila. *July 26, 1969*

President Marcos, Mrs. Marcos, all the distinguished guests at this very distinguished dinner tonight:

I first wish to express, on behalf of all of us who are here as your guests, our appreciation for this dinner, and for the opportunity to be with you on such an historic occasion.

You have spoken most eloquently, Mr. President, about the accomplishment of the moon landing. I would only want to be sure that we all recognize that what happened there belongs not just to the three men who were in the vehicle and the two who set foot on the moon, or even to those who had preceded them in the Apollo missions, nor did it belong alone to the American people, because nations around the world participated.

I know, too, that the hopes and the prayers of the people in nations all over the world went with those first men from earth to land on the moon.

I know that as we drove through the streets of Manila today, the first capital we have visited since that landing occurred, that the unprecedented size of that welcome and the wonderful warmth that we felt in that crowd was in great part due to the fact that the people of the Philippines, too, shared in that moon venture, and their prayers and their hopes went with our astronauts. We are most grateful for those hopes and those prayers as they were rendered.

As I met those—at least some of those—who are here at this head table tonight, I realized how many years my own experience in the Philippines covered, because of those who have served as President of this country, several are here, and I have had the opportunity to think back to the other visits that we have had.

The first was in 1953, the next in 1956—when we were present with President Magsaysay [1] at the 10th anniversary of the independence for the Philippines, and a crowd of three-quarters of a million people were gathered in what is now Rizal Park, and then as a private citizen in 1964, and then in 1966 and 1967 and, finally, today, I return again.

This is the first time I have been here as President of the United States, but to give you an indication of what I feel about this country, what I remember is—whether I came as Vice President or as private citizen—the welcome was just as warm as it was when I was President of the United States. For that I am grateful.

I suppose that tells us something about the relations between our two countries, relations of which you have spoken so warmly.

We do have ties that go back over many years. We have fought together in war; we have worked together in peace. Today we look to the future realizing that what we do together will have a great effect not only on our two nations, but on the future of peace and freedom in Asia and in the world.

In that respect, I would like to refer just briefly to the time which your career, Mr. President, has spanned, and my own

as well, although I am a bit older than you.

You served in World War II, as I did. Since that time we have seen in one generation World War II and two smaller wars, one in Korea and now one in Vietnam—all of them affecting Asia. We trust that the war in Vietnam can be brought to a successful conclusion. When that time comes, it will then be our opportunity to see what statesmanship can produce for the next quarter of a century.

Now I happen to be an optimist, an optimist in one sense, indicated by this moon landing. When I planned this trip, I planned it on the basis that we would take off immediately after the splashdown for a trip around the world. I was asked by some friends if we had any contingency plans in the event that the landing failed. I want you to know we had no contingency plans. We had faith that it would succeed.

But looking to the future, and what it means to all of us, I realize, as all of us in this room realize, that if war is to come, it is most likely to come again from the Pacific and from Asia in the last third of this century. But the other side of that rather pessimistic outlook is that if peace is to come, it must come primarily from the initiatives of those who live in Asia and from the United States, because we who live on the rim of the Pacific have within our hands the power to avoid another war in Asia, to bring peace, and, if we have that peace, then we can see the exciting possibilities for progress in this last third of a century.

Population will double. But, more than that, the development of the resources that we will see in a time of peace can mean progress such as men have never dreamed of before.

---

[1] Ramon Magsaysay, President of the Republic of the Philippines 1953–1957.

It is this dream—this dream of what peace in the Pacific, peace in Asia, can really be—it is this dream for which we are all living today.

When we think of the Philippines and the United States, of the wars through which we have lived, of the trials that we have had, of the progress that we have made, I think we all realize in this room that we stand now at the beginning of what could be a new era, a new era in which peace will come, as it will come, to Asia and the Pacific, and, therefore, to the world. And then we shall be able to keep that peace and have the progress that we all want, not only for ourselves but for our children in this very exciting period, a period in which we explore not just the earth, but the heavens—and by exploring the heavens we learn better how to develop the resources on earth—a period in which we learn to live together in progress and live together in peace as you have already described.

I would not want this evening to end without also paying tribute to one other at this table who has indicated the great power in this country of what we have learned in the United States: the power of the wife of a political man in the field of politics.

I can only say that Mrs. Nixon spent the afternoon with Mrs. Marcos. She had read, as I have, about her various achievements—the volunteer activities in which she has worked. And without becoming involved in what I know is an upcoming political campaign, all that I can say is this: After having spoken to Mrs. Marcos tonight, knowing of how she has campaigned with her husband, if I am ever in a campaign, I don't want her on the other side. [*Laughter*]

And if I may be permitted a self-serving statement, I never want my wife on the other side in a campaign either. [*Laughter*]

Here I pay tribute to all the women in this room—all who have worked with their husbands in helping them in their careers. Too often the men make the speeches and take the bows where the women should have the credit.

Tonight, let us be sure that we all recognize how important in our lives those who are the women in this room have been in helping us to whatever successes we have had.

One final point: When Mrs. Marcos visited the United States in May of 1968, in her party was a young Filipino who indicated a great interest in our space program and a great knowledge of it. As a result, the Protocol Department of the State Department sent him with an escort down to Cape Kennedy to evaluate the space program and have an opportunity to see how it was working.

After he looked it over, he said that he would like to put in a request to be the first Filipino to go to the moon.

I, tonight, have an announcement to make. That announcement is that on the first vehicle that carries passengers that goes to the moon, Bong Bong will be on that space vehicle. [*Laughter and applause*]

This is just to make it official: Here he is.

If, because of age, he will not be able to go to the moon, maybe we can have him go on the first vehicle to Mars.

Tonight, my friends, in the spirit of all that has been said tonight, let me ask you to join me in raising your glasses to the friendship of our two countries, the Philippine and the American people, and to the parents of Bong Bong—President and

Mrs. Marcos.

NOTE: The President spoke at approximately 10:30 p.m. in Malacanang Palace in Manila in response to a toast proposed by President Ferdinand E. Marcos. "Bong Bong" was Ferdinand E. Marcos, Jr., 13-year old son of President and Mrs. Marcos.

President Marcos spoke as follows:

President and Mrs. Nixon, distinguished guests, Your Excellencies of the diplomatic corps, ladies and gentlemen:

Seldom has it been given in the history of man for one to be allowed the privilege of participating in the celebration of one of the most outstanding achievements of mankind, especially one who represents a small and humble nation like the Philippines, in an achievement like the exploration of the moon attained by the great American Nation under the leadership of our guest tonight.

This is my privilege, in representation of the Filipinos and the Republic of the Philippines, as we have as our guests some of those who were principally responsible for this achievement of American courage and American genius.

If we turn back the pages of history, nay even that of unrecorded history, artifact, and legend, which show and document the aspiration and ascension of man to his rightful heritage as the prime creature on earth, thus, the neolithic scientist who discovered the fashioning of the wheel, and recently the man who discovered the internal combustion engines, and the voyages of discovery—including that of our forebears, the Polynesians—the radio, the airplane, the field of relativity, and closer to the ultimate secret of life, the theory of DNA—all these tend to show the dominance of man over his environment and over the universe.

And, as I have said, we participate in the celebration of this achievement as man aspires for the stars, the stars outside of this world and the stars within himself and within his spirit.

It is the hope of humanity, as it is the hope of the Philippines, that this vision and this genius, this courage and this ingenuity shall be utilized for the solution of man's problems.

For while man claims the dominance of the universe, still he must grovel at the feet of his ancient enemies in some places of our own earth. The enemies: disease, ignorance, and war. We trust that our guest, the leader of the great American Nation, will know how to meet these dreaded enemies.

We, in the Philippines, have reason to appreciate the generosity and the courage of the American Nation, and it is, perhaps, fitting and proper that the President and Mrs. Nixon have seen fit to make the Philippines their first stop and visit after their first success in the exploration of space, because, indeed, the Philippines was created after the great American Republic, and here in the Philippines is a test of the success of a democracy in a small developing nation.

Our observers say if democracy cannot succeed in the Philippines, perhaps it cannot succeed anywhere else in Asia.

So, as we play host to President and Mrs. Nixon, we remember our past. We remember that because of the ties that bind us, we stand firm on the side of freedom and resolute against anyone who should threaten to subvert our free institutions; and that we have demonstrated this capability to stand for our freedoms and for our institutions as in the past.

We are a small country but when our Republic was thought to be subverted by a Communist rebellion, our people stood as one and overwhelmed and overcame such a rebellion without the aid of any alien soldier.

The Philippine troops met the enemy, fought them in every battlefield, and won. Today, the threat that seeks to destroy our Republic has dwindled, and it is my privilege, however, to acknowledge publicly that while the Philippine soldier accomplished this, he did so with the aid and support of armaments, equipment, and supplies coming from our great ally, the United States of America.

Today, small Asian nations like the Philippines again are met by similar dangers, for it is not external aggression that we fear, but internal subversion. It is our resolution and belief that if there ever should be any attempt again to subvert our free institutions and our Republic, that our country, this small Asian country, the Philippines, can stand alone, can fight alone, and win alone, and sustain our freedoms and our liberties.

But it is our hope that the great American

Nation, in accordance with its solemn treaties between our two countries, will extend its aid and support, not in the form of ground troops and soldiers, but with equipment and supplies in accordance with the solemn agreements between our two countries.

We have, as our guest, my friends, the leader of a nation that may also be in crisis. He has met with problems graver than we have ever come to know and as he meets these problems, this Nation, the Nation—the United States of America—compassionate as it is, still bears upon its shoulders the burden of the whole world, and there is not anything, perhaps, that the leader of America, President Nixon, does or does not do which does not affect the life of any man on earth. This is the cross that he must bear.

And so, Mr. President comes to us, not merely as the President of the United States of America, representing America's national interest, but more than this, he comes to us symbolizing all the longings, the dreams, and hopes of all of mankind. He comes to us perhaps as a trustee of all of mankind. And he comes to us seeking to solve not only the problems of other countries and other nations, but to solve perhaps even the greater problems of the equality of races, and of justice within his own country and, therefore, he embodies all the noblest aspirations of humanity.

Therefore, it is my privilege and honor, my friends, to request you to stand up with me and join me in a toast to felicitate President and Mrs. Nixon for the success of the moon exploration and for the continued health and prosperity of the great American Nation.

283 Statement on the Asian Development Bank. *July 27, 1969*

ON THIS FIRST TRIP which I have made to Asia as President of the United States, I will be able to visit only five nations. I am particularly happy, therefore, to have this opportunity to address a statement to the Asian Development Bank. For in that way, I can, on behalf of my countrymen, express my appreciation to all 20 of the Asian nations which belong to the Bank.

The United States firmly supports the cause of economic development in Asia. And we therefore support the work of the Asian Development Bank, for we believe that this Bank will play a critical role in that development. That is why I requested in May that our Congress appropriate $20 million for the ordinary capital of the Asian Development Bank, and $25 million to its special fund during the next fiscal year.

The Asian Development Bank was born because its founders recognized the importance of international cooperation—both within Asia and between this continent and the rest of the world—in achieving economic progress.

This Bank—with its 33 member nations—exemplifies such cooperation. When our Secretary of the Treasury attended the Bank's Board of Governors meeting in Sydney this past April, he underscored this point. The Asian Development Bank can "point the way to even greater cooperation among nations . . ." he said, and he described it, therefore, as a "unique and inspiring step in the history of man." I wholeheartedly endorse his statement.

In addition, the Asian Development Bank is a prime example of what President Marcos has called "Asian solutions to Asian problems." It is above all else an Asian institution, with its headquarters in a key Asian commercial and economic center, and with a requirement that the

564

Bank's president, seven of its 10 directors, and 60 percent of its capital must come from Asia. This is as it should be. Only a great sense of commitment and cooperation among the Asian peoples themselves can make this institution successful and bring the development that all of us seek. The United States and other non-Asian nations can play a certain role within that framework, but the leadership must always come from Asia.

The future of the Bank is Asia's potential—and Asia is on the move. A number of Asian countries have experienced economic growth rates in excess of 10 percent annually over the last 5 years. Taiwan's trade has quadrupled since 1958, and its GNP has doubled. Korea, whose exports were only $16 million in 1958, exported 20 times that much—$320 million—in 1967. Like Taiwan, its increased exports

were from new industries: The traditional agricultural exports have given way to a wide variety of industrial products, most of which are exported to developed countries. The Philippines has developed new high yield strains of rice which are now being planted in India, Indonesia, and Laos. Singapore, like Hong Kong, is changing from a center of transit trade to a center of industry.

This astonishing growth in the past few years of trade, industry, agricultural production, and the exchange of ideas is only a beginning. I applaud the Bank's accomplishments and extend my best wishes as it serves as a catalyst to this exciting new Asian dynamism. I also take this opportunity to extend my personal regards to the Bank's president, Mr. [Takeshi] Watanabe.

NOTE: The statement was released in Manila.

284 Statement on Departure From the Philippines. *July 27, 1969*

IT HAS BEEN a great pleasure for me to visit again the Philippine Republic. For all you have done to make this visit such a pleasant and valuable experience, I express my sincere appreciation and say to you—with all the warmth which this word traditionally conveys in your language: *Mabuhay.*

I am reminded as I leave the Philippines that yours was a country and a people to which our late President Eisenhower felt particularly close. He lived here for 4 years in the late 1930's, and here his son grew into manhood. When he returned in 1960, President Eisenhower told your Congress that he felt he was "revisiting an old home." And so he was. And so it has been for so many Americans who have

come to know and love these islands and their people. So it has been for me this week.

This visit has been important in many ways. It has enabled us to renew and extend our acquaintance with you, Mr. President, and with the members of your government. It has allowed us to consult with an allied government about the war in Vietnam. It has afforded us an occasion for discussing the future of Asia, especially after the Vietnam war is over.

I have expressed the conviction that the United States has the same wishes as the Philippine Republic concerning the future relationship between our two countries. You want the Philippines to be strong, self-reliant, and independent in every sense. So do we. You want the United States to be a good and loyal friend. That, too, is our desire.

I have also conveyed the firm belief that the United States has the same wishes you have concerning the future of Asia. We both want Asia to develop economically. We both understand—in the words of President Marcos—that the people of Asia must seek "Asian solutions to Asian problems." It is in that framework that my country can best contribute to Asia's peaceful development.

We have met at a time when the imagination of all mankind has been fired by the success of man's first landing on the moon. We are reminded by that event of the great capacity of the human spirit to overcome all obstacles and break all barriers as it pursues the future. It is that same human spirit, applied in different circumstances, which is even now bringing economic and social progress in this part of the world. It is that same spirit which even now is hastening the day when the Pacific Ocean will truly be the peaceful place which its name suggests it should be—and which the people who live near it so earnestly want it to be.

Again, my thanks and good wishes. *Mabuhay* [greetings, good wishes].

NOTE: The statement was released at Manila.

285 Remarks on Departure From the Philippines. *July 27, 1969*

Mr. President, Mrs. Marcos, distinguished members of the diplomatic corps and of the Philippine Cabinet, other distinguished guests:

I begin by saying that the eloquent remarks that President Marcos has just uttered are ones that I subscribe to, because they, in a very definitive way, sum up the conversations that we have had during the period that we have been together.

I would also say that if this trip—which will take me to several other Asian nations as well as to two European nations—if this trip were to have included only the Philippines, our coming here, the conversations that we have had, the welcome that we have received, would have made it all worthwhile. We are deeply grateful to those of you who have welcomed us so warmly, and also to the President and to Mrs. Marcos for their very gracious hospitality.

I believe that, as one who has been here in that period of time when so many changes have occurred in Asia, I can really evaluate what has happened, and what will happen in the future.

When I was first here in 1953, the countries of Asia were moving out of a period of colonialism. They had a new sense of independence—a new sense of independence but not the ability and, in some instances, not the means, the desire, to use that independence to create the self-reliance which true independence requires.

Then after moving from the period of colonialism to independence there came an uneasy period of dependence upon others for their security, and also for their progress.

Now we reach a new period—a period in which there will continue to be assistance and cooperation, particularly from the United States of America as a Pacific power, and the economic and other developments that are going forward in this exciting part of the world, and in which there will continue to be, insofar as any intervention by major powers, a military presence as far as the United States is concerned so that these nations can have that independence which they have fought so hard to get—where our desire is like the desire of the people of the Philippines, and I am sure of the other peoples of the other great nations that we will visit, that each of them can now acquire a new sense of independence in the most complete sense that we can describe it.

I mean the independence that comes with economic strength, with political stability, and also with the means insofar as any threat internally that may occur in those countries—the ability to handle those internal problems without outside assistance, except that kind of assistance which is limited to material support and which, of course, would therefore exclude the kind of support which would involve a commitment of manpower.

This is a goal. It is a goal that we can now achieve. It is a goal that all the nations of Asia want to achieve, and it is one that we, the people of the United States and the Government of the United States, want to work with them to achieve. Certainly there is no country in Asia, than the country which I am now leaving, which more symbolizes the truth of what I have said than the Philippines.

We have a special relationship with the Philippines which will always be in our hearts. But we also recognize that the Philippines, which was once in a colonial status as far as the United States is concerned, and then in a dependent status, is now feeling, as it should feel, that sense of self-reliance, that sense of construc-

tive nationalism, as President [Manuel] Quezon has described it so many years ago, which is so, it seems to me, the wave of the future in Asia, and also in all of the world in which nations have gone through these same phases.

It is good that we came here first, good that we saw our oldest friends and our closest friends first; got their advice as we did on these subjects that I have described, and also on the complicated problems of Vietnam, bringing peace to Vietnam, how that peace then can be achieved in the balance of Asia, what U.S. policies should be in Asia after Vietnam—all of these, as well as the many bilateral subjects, were those that were covered in our conversations.

Finally, I would like to add one personal note. At the magnificent dinner that was given last night for us and the members of our party, Mrs. Marcos pointed out that the room in which it was held was one which previously had been used for various offices, and that she had had reconstructed so that they would have the room for such a large gathering. And she pointed to one corner of the room and said that in that very corner President Eisenhower, as a young officer, once had his office.

I thought of all of the history that was implicit in that remark. The young Major Eisenhower of that period, serving under General [Douglas] MacArthur, developing here in the Philippines understanding of military tactics but, beyond that, even more important, of the great political forces which move the world, and I thought, too, of his return to this country in 1960 and what he said before the Philippine Congress.

He said then he felt that he was returning to his old home, because he had lived here for 4 years with his wife, and his son had gone to school here, and they had so many pleasant memories.

I cannot say that Mrs. Nixon and I have lived here for any length of time, but we have had the privilege of being here before; we have had the privilege of knowing many, many friends in the Philippines; and every time we return, the welcome we receive makes us feel as if we were returning to our own home.

We thank you for that, and we will carry from this visit many memories—the memories of our conversations and the constructive activities that will come from them. But above everything else, we will remember yesterday, that drive into the city, the hundreds of thousands of people that lined the streets, and particularly the faces of the children, the children of the Philippines, the children of Asia, the children of all mankind, smiling, happy, looking to the future.

The President and I share one thing in common. We are both lawyers. Today I would say that we could say, as Woodrow Wilson once said, that we have only as our clients the children of the world, the children of this country, of our country, and of all the others of the world, because what we do in these years ahead will determine the future of those wonderful children that we saw yesterday.

This is the sentiment that I take away in my heart today. We thank you for giving us that warm welcome and this great send-off on the balance of a trip that will take us on around the world.

NOTE: The President spoke at approximately 11 a.m. at Manila International Airport in response to farewell remarks by President Ferdinand E. Marcos, who spoke as follows:

Mr. President, Mrs. Nixon, members of the party of the American President, Your Excel-

lencies and members of the diplomatic corps, distinguished guests, my friends:

The time has come for us, the Philippine people, to say goodby to our friend from the great American Nation, their leader and President, President Richard Nixon. It is with a heavy heart that we do say goodby.

But we have, I hope, been able to present to them a country that, since the beginning of the century, has welcomed them with open arms.

I believe you go to your other destinations, Mr. President, with the same thought that we have, that is, that there are no friends like old friends.

We are indeed honored and pleased that you came to visit with us. More than the importance of the subject or the specific issues that may have been taken up in the conversations between the two heads of state, is the fact that there have been consultations, and that the leader of the greatest power on earth, at the height of its greatest triumph, the success of space exploration, should see fit to come and consult with the nations of Asia, not only about policy but about the future of Asia.

We must, indeed, say that the candor, frankness, and the openness being shown in these conferences and consultations have led us to clear all the doubts that we had about the policies of the United States of America; for before you came, Mr. President, I was not alone in feeling dread and doubt about the emerging policies of the United States in Asia. You have met us with frankness, and from these conversations I can now announce to our people that while before we dreaded the possibility that the United States was going to abandon Asia completely, and on the other extreme that there might be, again, reestablished the policy of colonial dominance over the Asian countries, the President of the United States has made it clear, first, that he encourages nationalism in each and every Asian country, including that of the Philippines.

We are happy to note that in accordance with the libertarian traditions of the United States of America, he recognizes the need for the treatment of his Asian allies and friends with dignity. It is, indeed, gratifying to note, too, that while treating Asia wtih the policy of encouragement of nationalism, independence, and freedom, he does not intend to abandon Asia; that while we are moving toward what we have always hoped for, through political and economic independence, he supports the idea of Asian countries being able to defend themselves alone if necessary, and helping them and supporting them with whatever aid he can extend to them in these particular tasks.

We are happy, Mr. President, that you have come to us, to consult with us on matters that involve Asia. I have said before that the Philippines feel that the greatest danger to it is not external aggression but internal subversion.

Our history indicates that we are capable of meeting internal subversion with our own troops, and that we do not intend to call upon any foreign power to help us with foreign troops. We have demonstrated this in fighting the Hukbalahaps [Communist guerrillas], and we intend to protect and defend our free institutions with our lives, alone if necessary. But we are happy that you guarantee to us that the treaties that we have entered into shall be complied with, and that you are an ally, indeed, who understands our problems.

So, Mr. President, may I repeat what the Asians say in saying goodby. I die a small death, we die a small death, as you go and we say goodby; but it is our hope that we shall live continuously in the friendship and affection that we have for each other.

We hope, Mr. President and Mrs. Nixon, that you have a happy voyage and happy landings, and that your trips to other nations will be as productive as your trip to the Philippines. Thank you.

286 Remarks on Arrival at Djakarta, Indonesia. *July 27, 1969*

Mr. President, Madame Suharto, Your Excellencies, ladies and gentlemen:

As I stand here in Djakarta on this beautifully brilliant day, I realize that this is a very special occasion for me and for my wife, and, in a sense, in the relations between our two countries.

Because it was 16 years ago that I first visited Indonesia, and Indonesia's was the first Asian capital that I visited as Vice President of the United States. I remember the warm welcome we received all over the country on that occasion, and we have always wanted to return.

Then again in 1967 I had the privilege of returning as a private citizen, and at that time, Mr. President, it was my privilege to meet you and to talk to you, and to others in your Government.

Now as I stand here today, I realize that for the first time in history, a President of the United States of America is visiting Indonesia. This is a privilege for me, to be the President at this time—at this time in the history of our country, of your country, and the history of civilization—because this is a momentous time, a time that we will always remember.

We realize that just a few days ago the first men from earth set foot on the moon, and all of our ideas about the heavens and the limitations that we have on earth thereby were changed.

We have a saying in our country: The sky is the limit. And up until the time that these two men set foot on the moon, that was the ultimate that anyone could say— the sky is the limit.

And now no longer is the sky the limit. Because of what happened—not simply because two Americans set foot on the moon, but because two men who represented all mankind, all the people on earth, set foot on the moon—the sky is no longer the limit. And if we can soar beyond the sky, certainly we can find the way to bring peace and progress to those who live beneath the sky on this earth.

That is the lesson for all of us of this great adventure in which we have shared.

As I stand here in Indonesia today, I realize what a great part this country will play in that great adventure for the future, not only because it is a major country in Asia and in the Pacific, not only because it is one of the great and most populous democracies in all the world, but because this country has its future before it.

It has a great past—a past full of tradition, tradition which I was able to see along with Mrs. Nixon when we traveled over the country.

But as one that has moved from colonial status to independent status, and now looks to the future, as a nation with great numbers of people, with unbounded natural resources, Indonesia is a nation that excites the imagination of all the peoples of the world.

Mr. President, I want you to know, the members of your Government and all the people of your country to know, that the people of the United States wish to share with you in this adventure in progress— share in this way: We know you want to be independent, and we understand that. We know that you wish to be self-reliant, and we understand that. We know, too, that there is much in the way of resources that needs to be developed, and to the extent that we and other nations on a multilateral basis, or a bilateral basis, can be of assistance, we want to play our fair part.

So I look forward to the talks that we will have—talks that I trust will bring a better understanding between our two countries, between Indonesia and the United States of America—talks that will promote the cause of peace in the Pacific,

and that means in the world—and talks that, above all, will provide for the future of this great country and of all the countries in the world the progress, the peace, the independence, and the right to choose their own way that all people want.

With these thoughts in mind, I thank you again, Mr. President, for your welcoming remarks. It is very good to return for the third time to this great country.

Thank you.

NOTE: The President spoke at 2:48 p.m. at Kemajoran International Airport in Djakarta in response to remarks of welcome by President Suharto. On the same day the White House Press Office released an advance text of President Nixon's remarks and a translation of those of President Suharto, who spoke in Indonesian. The translation follows:

Your Excellency Mr. President and Mrs. Nixon:

First of all, in the name of the Government of Indonesia, of the whole people of Indonesia, and on my own behalf, allow me to extend to you, Mr. President, and to the distinguished members of your party, a warm welcome.

This moment and the recent past are extremely memorable to the relation between the United States of America and Indonesia, to the Americans themselves, and to the future of mankind.

Your Excellency has previously visited Indonesia, but today, for the first time a President of the United States of America pays a visit to the Republic of Indonesia.

A few days ago, three brave American astronauts, the first human beings, set their feet on the moon; they are now safe and sound back in this world. Once again, on behalf of the people of Indonesia and on my personal behalf, I would like to congratulate the United States of America for their extraordinary achievement and as a member of the community of nations, we take pride in your brilliant success. I am sure that in essence, the objective of the United States of America and other advanced countries is part of the efforts in attaining greater happiness for men in a peaceful world.

Likewise, I am convinced that your visit to this country and to several others is to pave the way towards the realization of men's welfare and to strengthen the foundations of that peaceful world.

We know the United States of America not merely as the richest country in the world, nor for their extraordinary technological potentiality, but rather as a nation which strives for equality of all mankind.

As a free nation, we are also very grateful to the United States of America, which left us a profound impression, because the United States of America is one among many other nations which comprehended our national aspirations at the time when the Republic of Indonesia proclaimed its independence almost a quarter of a century ago.

At present, we are implementing our development program as a sequel to replenishing it. We highly appreciate that during the difficult early stages of our development, the United States of America, as a friendly country, has once again shown its understanding and provided Indonesia with the necessary assistance.

Mr. President, I hope that during your present visit you may observe closely the determination and the efforts of the people of Indonesia in building their future.

I also expect that our forthcoming discussions will be extremely valuable in exchanging views relating various problems toward world peace and a more extensive people's welfare, precisely because today the nations in the world, particularly in Asia, are still alarmed by war, by the threat of war which menaces world peace. All of us, without exception, should safeguard mankind.

It is my ardent desire, and I am sure it will be also cherished by Your Excellency, that this momentous visit constitutes a new page to foster mutual understanding, strengthen friendly relations, and to expand cooperation between both our countries.

We wholeheartedly welcome Your Excellency, Mrs. Nixon, and members of your party, and we hope that you will enjoy your stay in our country among the people of Indonesia.

I thank you.

287   Toasts of the President and President Suharto at a State Dinner in Djakarta.   *July* 27, 1969

Mr. President, Mrs. Suharto, all of these very distinguished guests this evening:

I first wish to express on behalf of those who are your guests from the United States our grateful appreciation for this beautiful dinner and also for the kind remarks that you have just made about our country, and particularly about our astronauts whose great feat, as I mentioned earlier today, we considered as one that was beyond the achievement of a nation, but which belonged to all mankind.

Also, on this occasion I realize that the position that I am in is a unique one— one that will not come again—because since I am the first American President ever to pay a state visit to Indonesia, the next American President who comes here will not be in the position I presently find myself in.

Consequently, I would like to respond to your very gracious remarks by trying to relate our policy as I understand it to the hopes and desires of your great people.

You have spoken very properly of the fact that we in many ways have similarities in background; the fact that we both were once colonies and had revolutions.

Ours is older than yours by almost 200 years, but we went through many of the same problems that your nation has gone through and is going through today. And because we are a nation that has an immense interest in all the developments in the world, we have followed what has happened in Indonesia. We have followed it because this is one of the major

571

countries of the world. What happens here, the future of the 115 million people of Indonesia, will have an enormous effect on the future of peace in the Pacific and, therefore, on peace in the world.

We, therefore, are interested in Indonesia for that reason, but we are also interested in Indonesia for another one, because those of us who have had the privilege—a privilege that I have had—of visiting this country, of knowing your people, realize how rich this country is in its resources and, more important, how rich it is in its people.

Today, again, we were reminded of that wealth as we visited the Djakarta Fair. We saw many, many people. But we saw represented there, too, all of the country, the customs and the culture of the past, and the diversity of this country which gives it such wealth.

But we saw also the plans for the future—the exciting 5-year plan which your Government has initiated.

As I thought of those things, the past and the plans for the future, I realized that our country is privileged to play a part with you in helping to achieve those plans, those ideals, and those goals. I say privileged, because sometimes we think of the assistance that we provide to other countries as being a burden. I do not consider it that way.

As I see it, only when it is mutually helpful to us both is such assistance something that either of us would want.

As I consider Indonesia and all that it means to peace in the Pacific and in the world, as I consider the possibilities for progress in this country in the years ahead—possibilities that probably are as exciting as for any nation in the world today—then I realize that the United States of America should welcome the role

of being of some assistance in achieving that goal.

Let me be also quite precise in another respect.

You referred in your remarks to the fact that when our astronaut first set foot on the moon that he uttered the historic words that it was: ". . . one small step for a man, one giant leap for mankind." And so it was.

But you also very appropriately referred to the fact that here on earth too often the steps for mankind are very, very small, if at all.

That is why, as we consider your country, all the countries of Asia that I will visit, we will be thinking of how those steps can be larger; how they can become, finally, a giant leap for mankind on earth at a time that we have made a giant leap for mankind in expanding his knowledge beyond the earth—toward the heavens.

I would like to say in this connection that we have admired, Mr. President, your policies—admired them because, as we study the history of nations, it can truly be said that while a revolution is very difficult—difficult and costly in men, in treasure, and in lives—that many times the more difficult part of a nation's development is what comes after a revolution: that hard, daily drudgery of building again after the revolution has necessarily destroyed some of the institutions of the past.

So we see you engaging in that task, you and your colleagues represented in this room today. We saw evidences of it at the fair, and your 5-year plan.

I have seen it quite precisely in an issue that we are trying to deal with in the United States. I noted that 3 years ago Indonesia had one of the highest rates of inflation in the whole world, and today it is one of the lowest.

If you would tell us the secret, that would be very helpful for me to take back to the United States.

But as we look at that achievement, as we look at the stability, the strength, the political stability, the economic stability, that you have provided to this country during the time that you have been present—you and your colleagues—we have confidence that Indonesia now is ready to move forward—move forward not with just small steps, but bigger and bigger steps, so that in the end it will mean a giant leap forward.

We want to be with you. We want to assist you in any way that you think is appropriate—we along with other nations who have the capacity to do so.

For that reason, it is a very great privilege for me to return to this country for the third time, to return in an official capacity as President of my country, and to reaffirm the ties of friendship which sometimes, as you have indicated, have been strained, but which, fortunately, today are very, very strong.

If there is one goal that the administration, which I now heard in Washington, will have, it will be to see that the ties of friendship, and cooperation, and mutual trust and assistance between Indonesia and America will be stronger and stronger, because this is in our interest as well as in yours. It is in both of our interests because what happens here, as I have indicated earlier, may well determine whether peace and independence survive in the Pacific and, therefore, in the world.

And so I ask all of you to join me in raising your glasses to the President and Mrs. Suharto, and to the great Indonesian people, to their prosperity, their progress, their independence, and the peace that we will all enjoy.

NOTE: The President spoke at 9:58 p.m. at Negara Palace in Djakarta in response to a toast proposed by President Suharto, who spoke in Indonesian. A translation of his toast follows:

Your Excellency Mr. President and Mrs. Nixon, Excellencies and distinguished members of the Presidential party, ladies and gentlemen:

It is for me a great privilege that this evening I have the opportunity of holding a banquet in honor of the President of the United States of America. But beyond this formal banquet, leaders of both our countries assembled here at this moment are delegates representing the friendship of our two countries.

Mr. President, although this is not your first visit to Indonesia, as I stated earlier this afternoon, your present visit is very important to us and also to the relation of both our countries. In addition to being the first American Presidential visit to Indonesia, it also coincides with the early stages of the implementation of our Five Year Development Plan. I hope that Your Excellency will discern the differences, the alterations, and the spirit of the Indonesian people today as compared to 2 years ago.

The target of our development is very simple indeed. This is not owing to our lack of higher aspirations, but because we have to admit our limited potentiality. This does not reflect a lamentation either, but rather a consciousness coupled with full responsibilities. This reality and potentiality are still far away from our ideals. The Indonesian people, through a planned and progressive development, are working hard to change the present shortcomings, which hamper us in realizing our high aims.

Food, clothing, infrastructure, building materials, the extension of labor facilities and spiritual welfare are the prime targets of our Five Year Development Plan. It aims at raising the people's standard of living and at the same time at establishing solid bases for subsequent developments.

We have labored and lived tightly for almost 3 years, so that we are now able to create the basis of future developments on the remnants of a deplorable past. Lamentable, owing either to the negligence of economic problems, or to aberrations of political ideologies, reaching their climax with the G–30–S/PKI [30th of September movement of the Indonesia Communist Party (PKI)] putsch in 1965, which was quelled by the Indonesian people themselves.

We believe that we will be successful in our great tasks to develop our country, because we have already succeeded in our great struggles, which are full of sufferings in the past, that is, to maintain Indonesia's independence based on a solid political ideology, the Pantjasila.

Similar to the American Nation about two centuries ago, this national independence represents our very capital and our greatest honor. Based on this asset, we have to attain physical and spiritual welfare for the 115 million inhabitants of Indonesia, the number of which increases annually, and which stretches from Sabang to Merauke, possessing a democratic way of life, politically and economically, based on the Pantjasila. Our national ideals go beyond the boundaries of our territory. As a member of the community of nations, we are responsible in establishing a lasting peace in the world, in a friendly atmosphere, based on mutual respect and assistance, in order to create a veritable welfare of mankind.

We do not neglect our responsibility toward world peace; however, in order to give effective contribution to it, we have to be strong at home, we have to possess national endurance in all fields, in ideology, politics, social-economy, in defense and security. We are now concentrating on the economic potentiality, which is indeed very pressing. We fulfill our other obligations, internal or external, in harmony with our potentiality in this economic field.

Mr. President, ladies and gentlemen, our world today seems to be dotted with controversial realities, toward annihilation on the one hand, and toward welfare on the other. On the one side a strong spirit of nationalism and independence is flourishing, on the other, wanton wishes of certain forces to impose their will on other nations.

Aspirations toward peace are contending against a limited war, which is terrifying and threatening world peace. On the one side, a number of nations owing to their backwardness have to strive to build their countries, but due to their limited potentialities, they feel that they have made but a slow progress; whereas on the other, capital, energy, and other elements in large quantities are utilized for an armament race which obviously will lead to disaster.

Mankind, the world over, is actually for peace and prosperity. However, it seems that there exists a widening gap between nations in this world.

The synchronization of efficiency, with advanced technology, capital, and extraordinary courage, has enabled American astronauts to land on the moon. Man is now able to pass a tremendous distance in the outer space and to surmount delicate journeys. But, ironically, our hearts in this world are still far apart and sometimes the distance stretches even further. The gap between advanced countries and the developing ones is still great. On the one side there are nations living in abundance furnished with computers; on the other, millions of people lead an existence full of fear, work with primitive implements; there are even those who still live in a stone age.

Mr. President, I underline Mr. Armstrong's momentous enunciation, when he, as the first human being, put his feet on the moon, declaring: "That's one small step for a man, one giant leap for mankind." This leap has occurred in the outer space, a very expansive space full of mysteries, but it has not taken place in this world of ours, which seems to be contracting and is relatively simpler. The flags of all nations, representing peace and unity of mankind, have been planted on the moon. It is the task of all nations in this world to realize peace and unity.

I believe that your visit to our country and to other countries having different social and political systems, will promote world peace, close in the relations among nations, master their rupture arising from bias and prejudice, enhance closer cooperation among nations in order to flatten this gap between advanced and developing countries, and create instead a more equitable prosperity.

Yesterday all men followed anxiously and prayed for the safety of three American astronauts. Today the world is witnessing very closely your steps during your journey and further measures which will be taken by the great American people.

Mr. President, during our struggle for independence in 1945, we were set afire by the American spirit and independence. In the course of our patriotic war, slogans like "A government from the people, by the people and for the people," "For existence, for freedom and for happiness," were written everywhere—on walls, trains, vehicles in Djakarta up to the remotest villages; they are even rooted deep in our heart. I see similarities between the Declaration of the Independence of America and the Preamble of the 1945 Constitution of Indonesia. Both contain a promise and solemn determination of free and responsible nations, either to ourselves or to the world at large.

The relations between our two countries have indeed passed through delicate periods; it was even very tense several years ago. Thank God that we have passed those difficult moments. We have opened a new page in our friendly relation full of expectations.

I earnestly hope that your present visit constitutes the zenith of a friendly manifestation, of a mutual understanding and assistance beneficial to both our countries or to the welfare of mankind. We will not stop at this pinnacle, because there is quite a lot to do and our aims are still distant.

On this occasion, on behalf of the people of Indonesia, I would like to express our highest appreciation and our heartfelt thanks for the understanding and the effective assistance rendered to us by the Government and the people of America. Those aids are very significant and of great use to our efforts in developing Indonesia's economy.

Once again, I wholeheartedly welcome you and members of your party. Your visit is a great honor to us.

In conclusion, allow me to invite you all to raise our glasses and propose a toast to the health and happiness of Mr. President and Mrs. Nixon and to the welfare and glory of the people of America.

Thank you.

288   Remarks on Departure From Indonesia. *July* 28, 1969

Mr. President, Mrs. Suharto, all of the distinguished members of the Cabinet, the diplomatic corps, and those who are gathered here at the airport today:

This is the third time that I have said goodby at this airport to the people of this country. As I leave, I leave with the most pleasant memories of a wonderfully warm reception every place that we were. I only wish that we could have stayed longer. I look forward to the time that we can return.

Also, as I leave, I leave with the conviction that the future of this country is in good hands, and that the chances for a great breakthrough for progress, economically, are better than they have ever been before in the history of this country.

I am confident that is the case because of my meetings with the leaders of this nation, and also because of what I have seen insofar as the 5-year plan and the other policies that have been adopted by your Government, Mr. President. I can only say that the future of Indonesia is, of course, important to the 115 million people who live in Indonesia, but it is also vital to the future of the billions of people who live on this earth and particularly who live in the Pacific and the Asian area, because what happens here will have a dramatic effect on what happens every place else.

So we in the United States are proud that we have the opportunity to not only visit your country but, to the extent that you desire, to work with you in building that new future, to work with you always with the idea that we will work together, but always also with the idea that you choose your own way, and you develop your own policies; that there will never be any domination; that there will always be the freedom, the *merdeka* that means so much to the hearts of all the people of this country.

And, Mr. President, I can say that I am particularly pleased that you may be able to come to the United States. We want you to come on a return visit, at a time that will be convenient for you, and we only hope that we can give you and Mrs. Suharto and the members of your party as warm a welcome, as friendly a welcome, that all of us found every place that we were on this visit. I can say, in conclusion, that I have appreciated the great numbers of people that we have seen, and the very friendly signs that we have seen from place to place, some in English and some in your language. I have learned a little of your language while I have been here. One word I learned from you, and I heard it on several occasions. I repeat it as I leave. *Hidup* [long live] President Suharto, *Hidup* Indonesian and American friendship.

NOTE: The President spoke at 12:24 p.m. at Kemajoran International Airport in Djakarta in response to farewell remarks by President Suharto, who spoke in Indonesian. A translation of his remarks follows:

Your Excellency Mr. President and Mrs. Nixon, distinguished members of the Presidential party:

In a few moments you are leaving Indonesia.

Although your visit is very brief, you have, nonetheless, left us with a profound impression.

You have held discussions with leaders of Indonesia; you have also had the opportunity to mingle among the people of the capital and talked with some of them. I am sure that you have a clearer picture on our ideals, on our views with regard to world problems in general, as well as on our current issues, on our working programs and our firm determination in building a better future.

The frank discussion held in an understanding atmosphere, the desire to enhance friendly relations in a sincere and straightforward manner, are indeed very fruitful to us.

I greatly value your comprehension with regard to our identity. On behalf of the people of Indonesia, I would like also to express our appreciation to the United States of America, which is constantly disposed to assist us in building our future in harmony with our principles, aspirations, and our own ways.

This mid-20th century is characterized by the emergence of nations having their own identities. Every nation which has earlier gained independence should understand and accept this reality. One cannot evade this obligation because it constitutes a guarantee to world peace.

Mr. President, on this occasion, I would like to express my thanks for your kind invitation to visit the United States of America. God willing, I will gladly honor it at an appropriate time.

You have added some pillars to the "bridge" of friendly relations between our two countries; it is our common duty to foster and strengthen it further. We should launch on it a closer cooperation, beneficial to both our countries, which may contribute to the welfare of a new Southeast Asia, to world peace, and to the prosperity of mankind.

I wish, with your intermediary, Mr. President, to extend a warm greeting from the people of Indonesia to the great people of America. The whole people of Indonesia and I personally wish you and Mrs. Nixon a great success in your journey to other countries, and a safe homecoming in the United States of America.

Have a nice trip and till we meet again.

May God the Almighty perpetually bless all mankind.

289   Remarks at a Welcoming Ceremony in Bangkok, Thailand. *July* 28, 1969

Your Majesties, Mr. Lord Mayor, Your Excellencies, and all of the citizens of Bangkok and those from the United States who are gathered here today:

I want to express my deepest appreciation for receiving the key to this city—a city that I have known and, like anyone who knows this city, I have come to love.

As I think back on the many occasions that I have been here, I realize why this city means so much to so many people, not only in Thailand but throughout the world.

Some of you who are listening to me today may recall that not long ago an article appeared in an American magazine in which I was asked to describe among all the great cities of the world I had visited the one that I would recommend first and above all to any tourist, and I chose the city of Bangkok.

I did so for a number of reasons: first, because it is truly a beautiful city; and, second, because here, as much as any city in the world, we have combined the old with the new, a great sense of history with all of the monuments that remind us of a magnificent past, and yet all of the progress of a modern city.

But there was a deeper reason that I chose this city, as I called it the perfect city, if I were to pick one, of all the cities of the world that I would like to visit again.

It is because of the people of this city and the people of this nation. They are a people who command respect from all those who know them. They are a people who have a proud tradition of freedom. This is truly the land of the free. And they are also a people who have a capacity for hospitality that is unequaled anywhere in the world.

I speak deeply from my heart when I say that to have this key will be a treasured possession—a treasured possession as President of the United States, but, more than that, as a citizen of the United States and as a citizen of the world who knows most of the great cities and who comes back to this city with a deep feeling of affection.

I would like to add one other thought. As we drove in through the streets from the airport and saw the thousands of people gathered there, including many of the schoolchildren, we were reminded again of the association between the American people and the Thai people, association in war and association in peace.

We were reminded, too, of that when we came by the SEATO Treaty Building, and realized that the SEATO organization has its offices here.

That leads me to say that everyone knows that Thailand and the United States are signatories of that treaty. We are bound together by that treaty.

A treaty can have many meanings. It can be just a scrap of paper with no meaning at all. But as far as Thailand and the United States are concerned, a treaty means far more, because we share common ideals; because what we want for Asia and the world is the right of freedom which Thailand enjoys for all peoples here; because we have been willing to fight for that as we are fighting for it together in Vietnam; because of these deep spiritual and ideological ties that bind us.

The treaty that we have with Thailand means that it is not just another treaty, not just another piece of paper, but that it is one that has a significance far beyond that—a significance which I have indicated time and again in public statements, and I indicate today in my first public statement as I visit Bangkok and this country.

We will honor our obligations under that treaty. We will honor them not simply because we have to, because of the words that we have signed, but because we believe in those words, and particularly believe in them in the association that we have with a proud and a strong people— the people of Thailand.

We have been together in the past. We are together at the present. And the United States will stand proudly with Thailand against those who might threaten it from abroad or from within.

So, again, Mr. Lord Mayor, I thank you for presenting the key to the city. I can only say that I hope that on many occasions in the future, both in a public capacity and a private capacity, I will have the opportunity to use this key and to return again to Bangkok, the great city for all the tourists and for others in the world.

Thank you.

NOTE: The President spoke at approximately 5 p.m. at the Phan Fah Bridge Pavilion in Bangkok. In his opening words he referred to King Bhumibol Adulyadej and Queen Sirikit of Thailand and Chalit Kulkanthorn, Lord Mayor of Bangkok, who presented him with the key to the city. The Lord Mayor's remarks, which preceded the President's, follow:

Mr. President, Madame Nixon:

The citizens of Bangkok consider today as a wonderful occasion in the history of the city of Bangkok, for it is a great honor for us to welcome you once again.

Mr. President, you have honored us with five previous visits over the past 15 years: first as Vice President of the United States and more recently as a private citizen. You know of the great and rapid changes in our capital and of the rapid progress of our country during these years. Together with the material progress evident, we are fast developing our latent abilities in order that we may secure maximum benefit in the near future. These developments have been enhanced through various sources and one is the strong cooperation which we have received from your country. We owe a great deal to the United States. We have changed for the better since your first visit, Mr. President.

That great respect and admiration with which we greeted you previously also has developed into something greater, at once a profound friendship and an unshakable trust. We look to you as the leader of the peace-seeking nations. We are deeply honored by your presence in our city.

To indicate the warmth of our welcome, may I present to you, sir, the key to our city. Never was a key more symbolic than this, for the gates of our city already are open wide to you, Mr. President.

290 Statement on the President's Visit to Thailand. *July 28, 1969*

IN RETURNING once again to Thailand, I am deeply conscious of the fact that Thailand has a special interest in the strength of America's determination to honor its commitments in Asia and the Pacific. We will honor those commitments—not only because we consider them solemn obligations, but equally importantly because we fully recognize that we and the nations of Southeast Asia share a vital stake in the future peace and prosperity of this region.

Both geography and common interest link the United States with the nations of Southeast Asia. We recognize the Pacific Ocean not as a barrier, but as a bridge. We recognize also that whether peace can be maintained in Asia and the Pacific will determine whether peace can be maintained in the world, and we recognize here in Asia the beginnings of patterns of dynamic development that can be of enormous significance.

Our determination to honor our commitments is fully consistent with our conviction that the nations of Asia can and must increasingly shoulder the responsibility for achieving peace and progress in the area. The challenge to our wisdom is to support the Asian countries' efforts to defend and develop themselves, without attempting to take from them the responsibilities which should be theirs. For if domination by the aggressor can destroy the freedom of a nation, too much dependence on a protector can eventually erode its dignity.

What we seek for Asia is a community of free nations able to go their own way and seek their own destiny with whatever cooperation we can provide—a community of independent Asian countries each maintaining its own traditions and yet each developing through mutual cooperation. In such an arrangement, we stand ready to play a responsible role in accordance with our commitments and basic interests.

Seven centuries ago the great Thai King Rama Kamheng, father of the Thai alphabet, had his belief inscribed in the new written language: "In the water there are fish; in the fields there is rice ... Whoever wants to trade in elephants so trades. Whoever wants to trade in horses so trades; whoever wants to trade in silver and gold so trades."

These words expressed the philosophy that a nation, like a man, should be free to seek its own destiny. In Korea, and again in Vietnam, Thailand has been in the forefront of those nations actively engaged in protecting this principle. The Thai contribution to the struggle to preserve the independence of South Vietnam has been of great significance—as befits a nation that places so high a value on its own long history of independence. As a nation which has shared so generously in the burdens of war, Thailand has a special interest in the strategy for achieving a durable peace—that is, one which guarantees to the people of South Vietnam the right to determine their own future without outside coercion. In developing this policy, the government of Thailand has been fully consulted, and will continue to be so in the future.

I believe that the greatest problem before us is not the war in Vietnam, but the bringing about of a dynamic set of international relationships which guarantee peace and progress. This cannot be done by the United States alone. It must be a cooperative effort. We must contribute to relationships by which the peoples of the area can master their challenges and shape their future.

Thailand is one of the foremost examples of the promise that the future holds in Asia—in terms of its economic development, its commitment to advancing the welfare of its people, and its larger view of new patterns of regional cooperation that can benefit all the nations and peoples of Asia. We are proud to consider

Thailand our friend.

In this spirit, I see the vision of King Rama coming true not only for Thailand, but for all of Asia.

NOTE: The statement was released at Bangkok, Thailand.

291 Toasts of the President and King Bhumibol Adulyadej at a State Banquet in Bangkok. *July* 28, 1969

Your Majesties, Your Excellencies, ladies and gentlemen:

As I stand here in this room, I realize what a very great privilege it is for me to answer the eloquent remarks that have been spoken by His Majesty, and, of course, to point out that insofar as the achievement of our astronauts is concerned, that it belongs not to just one nation, but to the knowledge that came through the generations and, yes, through the centuries, so that finally this pinnacle could be achieved.

But, also, as I stand here, I am reminded of other things, reminded not only of what that achievement means for the future, the excitement of it all, but, also, of the fact that we are very fortunate in this great room tonight in the presence of this company to think of the past, and how that past can be blended with the present in order to build a greater future.

And there is no leader in the world, and no nation in the world, in which that is being better accomplished than in this nation and in this leadership.

If you will permit a personal recollection. In the year 1953, when I was a young Vice President and His Majesty was a very young King—of course, he is still a young King—I recall asking him a question that I asked of 18 leaders of Asia on a trip that Mrs. Nixon and I took as representatives of President Eisenhower through the Asian areas. The question at that time, in 1953 when the world was

wondering which way Asia would turn, and what the prospects were for peace and freedom and progress in this area, the question was: If you were to pick out one single factor that was more important than all the others, what would you choose for the essential ingredient for progress?

In many other nations, some had said economic development, others had spoken of the necessity for military strength to deal with their internal problems, but this very young and, as I described him in a speech which I made when I returned to the United States and spoke to the Nation's editors, one of whom is here tonight, and present at this dinner, what he said was to me very revealing.

He said, "What we need, what we need in Asia, and what we need in the world, is understanding above everything else."

I did not realize then what that word "understanding" really meant, because I knew what it meant in English. But I have only since learned the deeper meaning that it has in the Thai language. And "understanding" in the Thai language means literally "enter the heart."

And certainly I would say, as I look back over the past 16 years in which we have seen war and difficulty and violence around the world, that those words and that opinion stand up very, very well. The world needs understanding, understanding which penetrates deep into the hearts of all of us, understanding which realizes that the achievement of going to the moon is almost miraculous when we think of it, and, therefore, deserves our respect; but understanding which also recognizes what we have learned from the past, how much we owe to those that have gone before us.

As one philosopher has put it, the reason that we can see further than the ancients is that we stand on the shoulders of those who have gone before us. And here in this land, a land that has been free for 1,000 years, a land which has maintained, as we see in this room tonight, the tradition, the culture of the past, and, yet, has been able to blend that with the modern programs which mean the tremendous progress that we see in this city and over this land today.

This, I say, is the kind of understanding that each nation and each people in the world needs.

And, so, tonight as I reflect with you on these things, I simply want to conclude with this thought: that we are fortunate in this room on this occasion to be reminded by His Majesty of the great promise of the future and of the technological achievement that made that promise possible, but we are also fortunate to be reminded that that progress would not have been possible had not we built on the sound foundations of all the learning, of the culture and the tradition and the discipline of the past.

And right here in this room we feel it, we see it, we hear it all.

Your Majesty, this is the sixth time that I have visited your country, and each time I have been overwhelmed with the courtesy that we have received, the hospitality that has been extended.

Tonight, at this beautiful dinner, and particularly as we drove through the streets to see the most spectacular display of lights that I have ever seen, even at Christmastime in our own country, I realize that we were very fortunate again to come to this land of the free and to be your guests.

So, I know all of you would like to join me in raising our glasses to Their Majesties, the King and Queen of Thailand, and to that understanding which enters the hearts of all men, so that we can really have true peace and freedom in the world.

NOTE: The President spoke at 10:35 p.m. in the Chakri Throne Hall of the Grand Palace in Bangkok in response to a toast proposed by King Bhumibol, who spoke in Thai. A translation of his remarks follows:

Mr. President:

On behalf of the Thai Nation, the Queen and I take particular pleasure in extending to you and Mrs. Nixon, as well as to the members of your party, a warm and cordial welcome to Thailand.

I consider it an auspicious omen that under your eminent leadership, Mr. President, the unqualified success of man's first landing on the moon and the subsequent safe return of the astronauts to earth have been achieved. For this momentous occasion, the Thai Nation joins me in offering Your Excellency and the American people our heartfelt congratulations. Last week's breathtaking achievement of Apollo 11 and its brave American crew cannot be measured solely in scientific terms, for it also indicates man's ability to look beyond his earthbound problems, and to set his sights on new horizons in quest of wider knowledge and deeper understanding of himself and his environment.

It is both significant and gratifying for me to realize that, in the face of this epoch-making achievement of the American people, of whom you are the leader, you, Mr. President, have not lost sight of and are still deeply concerned with the more mundane human affairs both inside your own country and elsewhere, as evidenced by your visit to Asia and to this country. It is my hope that your efforts in this field meet with all the success that they deserve.

Your visit to this country, Mr. President, will

do much to cement and further the traditional ties of friendship between our two peoples, who are today more firmly linked as never before in the cause of peace, freedom, and human progress. Although we are now living in the days of changing policies and broadening political horizons, the people of Thailand are still determined to work for that cause. Allow me to reassure you, Mr. President, that as long as it remains within your policy to foster peace and uphold freedom in this part of the world, we shall cooperate with you to the fullest measure for the benefit of our peoples.

Ladies and gentlemen, may I invite you to join me in drinking a toast to the good health and continued success of His Excellency the President of the United States of America and Mrs. Nixon, and to the friendship and cooperation between our two countries and people.

292 Remarks to Employees at the American Embassy in Bangkok. *July* 29, 1969

Mr. Ambassador and my fellow Americans:

As I make this stop in Bangkok on a trip around the world, this is the only occasion I will have to speak to members of the American community, and I think it is good that we selected Bangkok because this is one of our larger installations with so many Americans here from the Foreign Service, from the Armed Services, from our other missions abroad.

I just want you to know that while, of course, this kind of a trip is tremendously exciting, to meet all the leaders of the world and see the hundreds of thousands of people that I have seen in Manila, Djakarta, and then in Bangkok, that it is always good to feel at home right here in the United States among a great number of American citizens.

I particularly feel at home when I find here that somebody read that I had received in the White House the other day an insignia from the Commissioner of Baseball indicating that I was the Number 1 baseball fan. So here is the cap for it. It is certain our Americans can leave the United States, but you can never take baseball out of an American boy. I see a great number of them over there. I only wish that I had the time to see one of your games.

I would like to just say one serious word to you, if I could. I realize that our people have been stationed in some instances many months and perhaps even many years away from home. If you are going to be outside the United States in a foreign city or a foreign country—and I have been to over 60 now—I can assure you that this is one of the best places in the world to be, right here in Thailand.

I also want you to know that I realize that, from my trips abroad, it is difficult for families to be abroad, to be away from home, to go to schools that are different from the ones they are used to at home, although I might note that the American schools and the other schools that you go to here are among the best that you can find in the world.

I know, too, that you tend to get homesick. I am sure you do for your own hometowns and for the people that you have known back home. Just let me say, as one who appreciates—as an American citizen, as President of the United States—the service that you are rendering, all of you in every capacity, that we live in a period in which what the United States does in this country and in other countries abroad will probably determine whether peace and freedom survive in the world.

That is very big talk, I know. It is not said in any sense of braggadocio. It is just said in a sense of recognizing what the facts are. Sometimes we have many frustrations—frustrations in fighting a very difficult war in Vietnam, frustrations in our foreign policy, our foreign aid programs, and many of the others. You know those as well as I do.

But just let me say this: that for a man or a woman to be able to play a role at this time in the history of the world, in the history of the United States, to be able to play a role that might make a difference in determining whether this country, the millions that live here and the millions that live throughout this world, will have

a better chance to grow up in peace and freedom—that is an exciting thing to do. I think we are all privileged to be able to play a role in that respect.

I want you to know that I am very proud of all of the Americans who are serving the United States, in whatever capacity. I want to thank you for your service. I only hope that those of us who have to make the decisions in Washington will be worthy of the dedication and the hard work of the people out here in the field.

Thank you very much.

NOTE: The President spoke at 4:03 p.m. The U.S. Ambassador to Thailand was Leonard Unger.

293   Remarks at a Reception at Santi Matri Hall, Government House, Bangkok, Thailand. *July* 29, 1969

Your Royal Highnesses, Mr. Prime Minister, Your Excellencies, and ladies and gentlemen:

In responding to the very generous remarks of the Prime Minister, I can only add to what I tried to say yesterday on arriving at this city again; that is, that having been here many times before, I always especially look forward to returning.

As Mrs. Nixon and I walked around the room and met our friends from Thailand, and then also some from the United States who were here, and who have the same affection for this country that we have, because they have the opportunity of living here, we realize how very deep our friendship is, how far back it goes, and how important it is to see that that friendship continues in the years ahead.

Mr. Prime Minister, you referred to the

war in Vietnam, and the fact that in both the case of the American Nation and in the case of Thailand, that we are participating in that war. I think it is well for all of us here who are Americans, and there are a number of Americans, to be reminded of the fact that Thailand is a country that not only stands on its own two feet, handling its own problems, dealing with subversive forces in this country—which are particularly difficult to deal with in the north and northeast—but in addition to that, Thailand has furnished armed forces to fight beside those of South Vietnam and the United States and other Asian countries in Vietnam.

This can only mean one thing: that it would be easy for this government and the people of Thailand to say simply that their problems are enough, and that if they can defend their own freedom without asking for outside manpower—a point which the Prime Minister has made in the talks that we have had today—that they should not be asked to undertake in addition the burden of sending troops to Vietnam.

But the fact that the people of Thailand value freedom so much for themselves that they are willing also to fight for it for others is an indication of why this country has a special meaning to us who visit you from the United States, or Americans who may live here.

This is truly the land of the free, and it is this same sense of self-reliance, of freedom, of willingness to fight for freedom both at home and abroad that we wish to develop all over the world as something we are very proud to be associated with, with our friends from Thailand.

Finally, as I think of the remarks that you have made, Mr. Prime Minister, with regard to our astronauts, we, of course, are proud of them because they were young Americans who went very high, higher than men have ever gone before, but we think of them also as brave men who represent the best of all the men on this earth. The men who went to the moon could have been Thais. They happened to be Americans. They represented a spirit that is bigger than the United States. It is as big as the whole world itself.

As a matter of fact, it could really be said that the spirit which took those men to the moon is truly a universal spirit, a spirit of peace and a spirit of friendship, and as we stand here in Thailand, a spirit of freedom which we cherish, as you cherish, where we stand with you, stand by your side, both of us recognizing that if freedom is to survive, we must not only keep it at home, but we sometimes must make sacrifices to help others to keep it abroad.

So with those thoughts in mind, I simply will conclude by saying that I speak for all of the Americans in telling you that we have appreciated the warm welcome we have received. We will always remember these few hours that we have been here, and remembering them can only mean that we will return, as I have returned so many times.

So now, your Royal Highnesses, Mr. Prime Minister, Your Excellencies, ladies and gentlemen: I ask you to raise your glasses to His Majesty, the King, and to the Prime Minister of Thailand, and to that spirit of freedom which Thailand stands for and which Americans also believe in. The King.

NOTE: The President spoke at 7:04 p.m. In his opening words he referred to King Bhumibol Adulyadej, Queen Sirikit, and Prime Minister Thanom Kittikachorn.

The Prime Minister's remarks were not made public in the form of a White House release.

294   Statement on Arrival at Saigon, Republic of Vietnam. *July* 30, 1969

I AM HAPPY that the moon landing, which in its universality signifies a symbolic drawing together of all mankind, has provided an occasion for me to meet with President Thieu in the capital of his country.

We have reviewed the developments which have taken place since Midway:

—the steady progress in pacification, involving the people in greater political participation and in decisions about their future;

—the elections of village and hamlet officials, and in training for more effective local administration;

—the improving performance of the Vietnamese armed forces, and in their equipment and training, and their determination to take over an increasing share of the burden of the conflict;

—the plans for a revolutionary land reform program;

—and most importantly, the moves we together have made toward peace.

Our purpose is peace.

We have repeatedly come forward with proposals which could lead to the beginning of the end of this tragic conflict.

On March 25th President Thieu offered to talk with the NLF [National Liberation Front] without preconditions.

In the six points of his speech of April 6 he proposed a basis on which those opposed to the government would be welcomed as full members of the national community.

On May 14 I proposed eight points which could lead to the withdrawal of all non-South Vietnamese forces, a ceasefire, and elections under international supervision.

On July 11 President Thieu undertook

another major step in his six point proposal through which all the people of South Vietnam could exercise their right of self-determination through internationally supervised elections, in which they can genuinely express their choice, free from fear and coercion. An electoral commission in which all political parties would be represented would assure equal opportunities to all candidates.

The GVN [Government of Vietnam] has offered to abide by the results of the elections, whatever they may be.

On July 20, President Thieu made the offer to North Vietnam for direct discussions toward reunification through free and internationally supervised elections.

President Thieu, after his return from Midway said "everything is negotiable."

We have gone as far as we can or should go in opening the door to negotiations which will bring peace. It is now time for the other side to sit down with us and talk seriously about ways to stop the killing, to put an end to this tragic war which has brought so great destruction to friend and foe alike. We have put forward constructive proposals to bring an end to the conflict. We are ready to talk with the other side about their proposals. Let us, with determination and good will, seek to put an end to the destruction and suffering which the people of Vietnam, North and South, have borne so long.

NOTE: The statement was released at Saigon.

295   Remarks Following a Meeting With President Thieu in Saigon. *July* 30, 1969

Mr. President:

I wish to express my appreciation to you and to Madame Thieu for the very warm welcome you have given to Mrs. Nixon and me on our visit to Saigon.

I have been here before, the first time

in 1953, and this makes the eighth visit to Saigon and other parts of Vietnam.

As I evaluate the situation today, I wish first to point out that what happens in Vietnam, the kind of peace that we are able to achieve in Vietnam, will have an enormous impact on the future of peace and freedom in all of Asia. I say this based on what I have been told by the leaders of the countries I have already visited on my Asian trip.

So the stakes here, important as they are for the people of North and South Vietnam, are important also to all the people of the Asian area and, of course, the people of the world. That is why the sacrifices that your people, our people, and other allied forces have been making in Vietnam are so important—so important beyond simply the vitally important object of seeing that the people of South Vietnam have the right to choose their own future.

I also wish to point out that when I first came here in 1953, I had the opportunity not only of visiting Saigon, but also Hanoi. Since then, the country has been divided. But as I think back over those 16 years, and as I think of your statement pointing out that for 20 years you have been engaged in what is all of the difficulty of war in this now divided country, I realize how much suffering the people of South Vietnam have gone through, and also the people of North Vietnam. The time has come to stop that suffering.

Mrs. Nixon today, accompanied by Mrs. Thieu, has visited an orphanage. The children in that orphanage are there because their parents, both mother and father, were killed in this war.

These tragedies, whether they are in North or South Vietnam, have been going on long enough, and it is time to bring

an end to the war, but to bring an end to the war in a way that will not encourage another war; bring an end to the war in a way which will provide the right to choose the kind of government they want for the people of South Vietnam, and in providing that right, make it more possible for the other nations in Southeast Asia to retain that same right for themselves.

I say to you, too, Mr. President, that as I look over the period that has elapsed since the time I became President of the United States, I believe the record is clear as to which side has gone the extra mile in behalf of peace. We have stopped the bombing of North Vietnam. We have withdrawn 25,000 American troops. They have been replaced by South Vietnamese. We have made, and you have made, a peace offer which is as generous as any ever made in the history of warfare. It is a peace of reconciliation that is offered, a peace in which the people will decide, a peace that is just for both sides, a peace which is fair to both sides, a peace which offers an equal chance to both sides.

We have gone as far as we can or should go in opening the door to peace, and now it is time for the other side to respond. Otherwise, the other side must assume the responsibility for the continuing suffering among a people who have already suffered much too long both in South and North Vietnam.

And finally, Mr. President, I can say that as I leave Saigon on this very short visit, I go away with, again, the admiration for the brave men who have fought for their freedom and, in fighting for their freedom have helped the cause of freedom and peace for all of their neighbors in the Pacific area, and I go away with a deep appreciation for the hospitality that you and Madame Thieu have extended to

Mrs. Nixon and me on this occasion.

NOTE: The President spoke at 3:06 p.m. at the Independence Palace in Saigon.

A statement by President Thieu following the meeting with President Nixon is printed in the Weekly Compilation of Presidential Documents (vol. 5, p. 1053).

296   Remarks to American Troops of the 1st Infantry Division in Vietnam. *July* 30, 1969

YOU ARE doing your duty and, I am sure, producing what will eventually be the basis for a lasting peace in the Pacific area.

I would like to say just a word about this war.

I know that you have had all of this indoctrination. I know that some of you, all of you, probably, read in the newspapers and hear on television and radio a debate over this war, why we got into it, how it is being conducted, and how are we going to end it.

I simply want to say to you that, as we all know, any war is difficult, particularly difficult for that man who is out there fighting. This war is the most difficult war any army has ever fought. Certainly, it is the most difficult war any army of the United States of America has fought. Because this is the first time in our history when we have had a lack of understanding of why we are here, what the war is all about, where we have had real division at home.

This is why I say that the men who have fought in this war, who fight courageously, who do their duty, day after day—they really deserve the thanks of the United States.

Because I think you know why you are here, and I would just like to summarize it in a word in the broadest sense before meeting some of you personally.

I just visited three countries in Asia, and in each of those countries I can tell you they are watching Vietnam. What happens in Vietnam, how this war is ended, may well determine what happens to peace and freedom in all of Asia.

I am not suggesting that each of three countries will go Communist in the event this war is not brought to a successful conclusion. I am saying this: If we can bring this war to an end, and an early end, and that is our goal, and if that war is ended in a way that the people of South Vietnam have a right to choose their own way, and that is all we are asking—if we do that, then the chance for all of the people of Asia to have a chance to have real peace in Asia, the possibility that we can discourage aggression and reduce the chances of more wars in the future—that is what we want to accomplish.

I have long believed this. I believe it now. I simply want you to know that I only hope that those of us who are the political leaders can be worthy of the men out here in the fighting line so that we can bring this war to a conclusion—bring it to a conclusion in a way that will be worthy of your service, of your sacrifices, of your—it seems to me for all of you—your great activity beyond the call of duty. I would say that to each and every man here whether he receives a medal or not.

And one final word. I suppose out here, as is always the case, you perhaps get tired of lectures. I don't mean to lecture now. But I do want you to know that we are going to record sometime the history of this time, and in that history it is going to be one of the most exciting periods in all the history of man—the landing on the moon, those three brave men who landed there.

But also out here in this dreary, difficult war, I think history will record that this may have been one of America's finest hours, because we took a difficult task and we succeeded.

You are doing your job. I can assure you we are going to try to do ours to see that you didn't fight in vain.

Thank you.

NOTE: The President spoke at Headquarters, 2d Brigade, 1st Infantry Division at Di An, 13 miles north of Saigon.

297 The President's Toast at a Dinner Given by Prime Minister Thanom Kittikachorn of Thailand. *July 30, 1969*

Mr. Prime Minister:

Responding to your very gracious and warm toast, I would like to say that I feel very gratified that on this visit to Thailand we have been received officially in such a warm manner and, also, that we have the opportunity to come to your home and to be received again here.

You all know how deeply grateful I am for the previous visits that I have had to Thailand. I seem to come back year after year. And I hope that will always be the case in the future. I particularly appreciate the fact that you have suggested that our daughters come. I can tell you that I have already recommended to them that they come to Thailand.

We may not be able to come with them, but I can assure you that probably before we return that our older daughter, Patricia, her mother's namesake, and our younger daughter, Julie, and her husband, David Eisenhower, will be visiting Thailand. And we know that they will love it as much as we have.

Speaking from a personal standpoint, I would like to say this: that as I arrived in the city—it seems in a way just a short time ago and in other ways a very long time ago because so many nice things have happened since we arrived—we arrived in the city and saw the wonderful welcome of the crowds, the city all lighted up as I have never seen a city lit up before; we both thought that no welcome could be more outstanding than this one.

But I should like to point out that I will also remember that when I came to this country on several occasions, when I held no office at all, I was not President, I was not Vice President, I was just an American citizen, that I was received by the people around this table, I was received by you, Mr. Prime Minister, and welcomed in your home then just as you welcome me tonight. That is true friendship. I am deeply grateful for that expression of friendship. It is the kind of friendship that we feel for you and all of you around this table.

So to that kind of friendship, which our many good friends in Thailand seem to have in such great abundance, we are particularly pleased to raise our glasses tonight. And in doing so, I suggest that and urge that all of you stand and we raise our glasses to the Prime Minister and Mrs. Thanom.

NOTE: The President spoke at 10:05 p.m. at Rangong House in Bangkok. The Prime Minister's toast was not issued in the form of a White House press release.

298   Remarks on Arrival in New Delhi, India. *July* 31, 1969

Mr. President, Your Excellencies, ladies and gentlemen:

It is a very great honor for me to return to India for the third time and to extend to all of the people of India from all of the people of the United States our warm good wishes. As I return, Mr. President, I, too, have the regret that you alluded to in your remarks, that my visit is so short.

A friend asked me, when he learned of this trip, how I could possibly know India in one day, and my response is: It would be impossible to know a country as populous, with such a diverse history, tradition, culture, going back through the generations, the centuries—it would be impossible to know such a country in a week, a month, a year, or a lifetime. But as far as this day is concerned, I believe it will serve one purpose to which we are all deeply devoted.

It was just 16 years ago that I was privileged as Vice President of the United States to visit India and to be received then by Prime Minister Nehru.[1] I asked him what he believed was the greatest need for India and her neighbors in Asia. He responded: What we need above everything else is a generation of uninterrupted peace.

That was true then. It is even more true now. We did not succeed over these past 16 years in beginning that generation

of uninterrupted peace and our major goal will be to try to succeed now in the dream that he had then—a generation of peace for India, for Asia, for the world.

Also, as I come here, Mr. President, I am keenly aware of the fact that the people of this great nation desire to choose their own way to progress. I respect that, as do all Americans. I would say that we want to work with you to the extent that you feel we can and should, for the goals that you believe are best for India, and not for the goals that we may think are best for India; provided, of course, always that we bear in mind those principles in which we both believe—peace for the world, independence for all nations, progress, justice, and freedom for all people in those nations.

Mr. President, you have referred very generously to the fact that three very brave Americans landed on the moon. We are very proud, of course, of that achievement, but proud not in any simply nationalistic sense, but because we believe this was a venture in which all mankind was represented by those three brave men.

I want to say now that as we begin our new administration in Washington that our goal—and I know the goal of all the American people—is simply this: We want our generation to be remembered as the one in which man first set foot on the moon, and as the one in which for the first time in the 20th century we had un-

---

[1] Jawaharlal Nehru, Prime Minister of India 1947–1964.

interrupted peace, with justice and freedom for man on earth.

Mr. President, I am sure that the meetings that I will have with the Prime Minister and members of the government will serve that great goal in which I know the people of India and the people of the United States are as one.

Thank you.

NOTE: The President spoke at 12:48 p.m. at Palam Airport in New Delhi.

Acting President Mohammed Hidayatullah's remarks of welcome were not issued in the form of a White House press release.

299 Statement on the President's Visit to India. *July 31, 1969*

IT IS a privilege and a pleasure for me to return for my third visit to India, the largest nation in free Asia. I first came here in 1953, as Vice President of the United States, and since then I have followed with particular interest the steady progress that has been made in this land that has the sublime combination of great tradition, deep philosophical and religious insight, and enormous progressive spirit.

The first principle of the relationship between India and the United States is that our two countries share fully the basic objective of peace in Asia and peace in the world.

Only in peace can Asian nations devote their full energy and attention to the most important problem they face: the grave human problem of meeting the expectations of men, women, and children to share in all the benefits of modern science and technology. Mankind has reached the moon. Now we must improve the quality of life here on earth.

India's leaders have a vision—a vision of Asian nations working together bilaterally and in regional groupings reflecting shared interests.

The United States shares that vision. The United States will support efforts toward that goal—when we are asked and when our contribution can be significant.

The United States respects the determination of Indians—and of their Asian neighbors—to work out their destiny and their security in their own way. We respect India's way, emphasizing national independence while accepting the interdependence of nations. We firmly believe that Asian problems must be resolved by the people of Asia. But we stand ready to help.

We stand ready to help because of our friendship and human concern for the people of Asia and because we have our own interest in helping. The United States has an important stake in the stability of Asia, and the United States knows that the changes taking place in Asia in the last third of this century will have an impact on the history of the world over the next several centuries. As we apply the scientific, technological, agricultural, and industrial achievements of this age to all of our national and human problems, Asia can be the area of greatest opportunity. India will be a leader in that Asian future.

The United States is proud of the role it has played, through economic assistance, in India's economic progress. We honor the people and leaders of India for what they have achieved with their own resources and their own hard work—their genuine revolution in agriculture and their progress in industry. But Indian leaders know, as do we, that problems—large problems—remain to be solved.

Coming to India, I find this a time to remember the words of President Eisenhower when he addressed a joint session of the Parliament of India in 1959:

"Before us we see long years of what can be a new era; mankind in each year reaping a richer harvest from the fields of the earth—gaining a more sure mastery of elemental power for human benefit—sharing an expanding commerce in goods and in knowledge and in wisdom—dwelling together in peace."

The new era spoken of by President

Eisenhower 10 years ago is within our reach. Let us cooperate to grasp it, knowing that peace is not only the absence of war, but a process of creative order, of orderly change.

I am certain that this new era will be one in which the ancient goal of dwelling together in peace finds inspiration in the title of a collection of the writings of Mahatma Gandhi: *All Men Are Brothers*.

It is in this spirit that I come to New Delhi and it is in this spirit that I look forward to fruitful discussions with Prime Minister Gandhi and the other leaders of this bastion of democracy in Asia.

NOTE: The statement was released in New Delhi.

300   Toasts of the President and Acting President Hidayatullah at a State Dinner in New Delhi.   *July* 31, 1969

Mr. President, Your Excellencies, and our friends from India and the United States:

I want to thank you first, Mr. President, for your very gracious and generous remarks, and to tell you, indeed, though this visit is a short one, that Mrs. Nixon and I have already felt the warmth of the friendship of the people of India.

We regret that we have only this brief time to be here, but we think that had we only planned this trip to come to India for one day, it would have been worthwhile—worthwhile because of the opportunity that was provided to see and know this country again; but, more important, for the opportunity that was provided to see and know the people of India and the leaders of India, and to talk to them face to face about some of the great problems that we face together.

It was appropriate that you spoke of

peace and progress and cooperation. As you noted, this journey that I am now on is a journey in quest of peace. This afternoon I had a very great privilege, that of laying a wreath, a memorial, to a great man of peace, one of the truly great men of all time and of all nations.

It was an honor for me, a great honor, to pay homage to Mahatma Gandhi, in this, his centennial year.

In responding to your remarks, Mr. President, I find myself reflecting on the lessons of Gandhi. If I would not presume before this audience that knew him much better than I, I would like to talk about those lessons, what they mean to me, what they mean to the world.

Forty years ago, speaking from a personal standpoint, when I was graduated from high school, my grandmother, who was a devout Quaker and a deeply be-

591

lieving pacifist, gave me as a graduation present a biography of Gandhi. I learned to know him through that book.

And since then I, of course, like many throughout the world who never met him, knew him through his writings, knew him for what he stood for. Gandhi's life was inspired by truths which know no boundary of space or time, because they are eternal truths.

There is a greatness which transcends the ordinary meaning of that word, a greatness at once mysterious and self-evident, a greatness beyond the trappings of power, beyond the opinions of men, a greatness of the spirit. Such a greatness was his.

He was, above all, a man of peace, who knew both the need for peace and the power of peace. He once wrote: "Love is the strongest force the world possesses and yet it is the humblest imaginable." Love was at the center of his greatness: a love of India, a love of mankind, a love of peace; and he forged it into a power that moved nations and transformed the world.

As we reflect on his greatness, it is appropriate that we reflect also on the nature of peace.

The concept of peace is as old as civilization, but the requirements of peace change with a changing world. Today we need a new definition of peace—one which recognizes not only the many threats to peace, but also the many dimensions of peace.

Peace is much more than the absence of war and, as Gandhi's life reminds us, peace is not the absence of change. Gandhi was a disciple of peace. He also was an architect of profound and far-reaching change. He stood for the achievement of change through peaceful methods; for belief in the power of con-science; for faith in the dignity and grace of the human spirit, and in the rights of man.

In today's rapidly changing world, there is no such thing as a static peace or a stagnant order. To stand still is to build pressures that are bound to explode the peace; and more fundamentally, to stand still is to deny the universal aspirations of mankind. Peace today must be a creative force, a dynamic process, that embraces both the satisfaction of man's material needs and the fulfillment of his spiritual needs.

The pursuit of peace means building a structure of stability within which the rights of each nation are respected: the rights of national independence, of self-determination, the right to be secure within its own borders, to be free from intimidation.

This structure of stability can take many forms. Some may choose to join in formal alliances; some may choose to go their own independent way. We respect India's policy of nonalignment, its determination to play its role in the search for peace in its own way. What matters is not how peace is preserved, but that it be preserved; not the formal structure of treaties, but the informal network of common ideals and common purposes that together become a fabric of peace. What matters is not whether the principles of international behavior these represent are written or unwritten principles, but rather that they are accepted principles.

Peace demands restraint. The truest peace expresses itself in self-restraint—in the voluntary acceptance, whether by men or by nations, of those basic rules of behavior that are rooted in mutual respect and demonstrated in mutual forbearance.

When one nation claims the right to

dictate the internal affairs of another, there is no peace.

When nations arm for the purpose of threatening their weaker neighbors, there is no peace.

There is true peace only when the weak are as safe as the strong; only when the poor can share the benefits of progress with the rich; and only when those who cherish freedom can exercise freedom.

Gandhi touched something deep in the spirit of man. He forced the world to confront its conscience, and the world is better for having done so. Yet we still hear other cries, other appeals to our collective conscience as a community of man.

The process of peace is one of answering those cries—yet doing so in a manner that preserves the right of each people to seek its own destiny in its own way, and strengthens the principles of national sovereignty and national integrity on which the structure of peace among nations depends.

However fervently we believe in our own ideals, we cannot impose those ideals on others and still call ourselves men of peace. But we can assist others who share those ideals, and who seek to give them life. As fellow members of the world community, we can assist the people of India in their heroic struggle to make the world's most populous democracy a model of orderly development and progress.

There is a relationship between peace and freedom. Because man yearns for peace, when the people are free to choose, their choice is more likely to be peace among nations; and because man yearns for freedom, when peace is secure, the thrust of social evolution is toward greater freedom within nations.

Essentially, peace is rooted in a sense of community, in a recognition of the common destiny of mankind, in a respect for the common dignity of mankind, and in the patterns of cooperation that make common enterprises possible. This is why the new patterns of regional cooperation emerging in Asia can be bulwarks of peace.

In the final analysis, however, peace is a spiritual condition. All religions pray for it. Man must build it by reason and patience.

On the moon, now, is a plaque bearing these simple words: "We came in peace for all mankind."

Mahatma Gandhi came in peace to all mankind.

In this spirit, then, let us all together commit ourselves to a new concept of peace:

—A peace that combines continuity and change, stability and progress, tradition and innovation.

—A peace that turns the wonders of science to the service of man.

—A peace that is both a condition and a process; a state of being and a pattern of change; a renunciation of war and a constructive alternative to revolution.

—A peace that values diversity and respects the right of different peoples to live by different systems—and freely to choose the systems they live by.

—A peace that rests on the determination of those who value it to preserve it, but that looks forward to the reduction of arms and the ascendancy of reason.

—A peace responsive to the human spirit, respectful of the divinely-inspired dignity of man; one that lifts the eyes of all to what man in brotherhood can accomplish, and that now, as man crosses the threshold of the heavens, is more necessary than ever.

It is, then, in a spirit of peace, in a spirit of brotherhood, and in a spirit of confident hope, that I ask you to join me in a toast to the Acting President, the Prime Minister, and the people of India, a nation rich in spirit, proud of its heritage, advancing toward a future bright with promise, and marked by destiny to play an historic role in man's progress toward that peace we all so fervently seek.

NOTE: The President spoke at approximately 10 p.m. in the Banquet Hall at Rashtrapti Bhavan in response to a toast proposed by Acting President Mohammed Hidayatullah. The Acting President's remarks follow:

Mr. President, Mrs. Nixon, Your Excellencies, ladies and gentlemen:

Your visit, Mr. President, though very brief, brings the United States of America close to India. Such visits are helpful in promoting international understanding. It would be a better world if all the sovereign states came close in harmony and became interdependent. It is fortunate that the advance of science and technology has conquered space, and nations far apart are yet near enough for their leaders to get together and frame policies. We value this opportunity to welcome you and to be able to exchange thoughts on subjects of great moment.

Mr. President, you come to us after your country and particularly your space men have blazed a new trail. The epic flight to the moon and back by three of your countrymen has amazed the world and marks a new stage in science and technology. On behalf of the Government and people of India, and myself, I congratulate you and, through you, the people of your country on this historic occasion.

This achievement is symbolic of the restless spirit of man and his desire to widen the horizons. We are glad to know that you are sharing the knowledge you have gained with the rest of the world and this leads us to hope that the new knowledge of science and technology will always be shared between the more advanced and the less developed countries of the world.

We, of course, wish that you and Mrs. Nixon had spent some more time in our country, traveled in it, and seen the problems we face and the efforts we are making to overcome those problems and the measure of our success. This would have also given you an opportunity to sense and feel the warmth of our friendship and the depth of our good will for you and the people of your great country. We can only hope that you and Mrs. Nixon will come to India again soon and for a longer visit. You will be most welcome.

Mr. President, your journey to India and some other countries of Asia in the wake of peaceful exploration of our satellite may be described as a journey in quest of peace. We sincerely appreciate it. We firmly believe that peace and security, progress and stability, particularly in the developing countries, can only come by waging a ceaseless war on poverty, hunger, ignorance and disease.

Asian countries can have security and stability only if the economic conditions are healthy. Political stability is tied to economic well-being.

Most of the countries of Asia have won their independence recently and they desire to achieve stability and economic self-sufficiency under their own leadership. They do not want to work alone, but in cooperation with other friendly countries in Asia and outside.

In this behalf, your country, Mr. President, has a distinguished record of economic aid to and cooperation with many countries in this region. We ourselves have received much assistance from your country, for which we are grateful.

We have, however, many difficult problems, which we are trying to solve in our own way and according to our own traditions and convictions. Our policy of nonalignment and peaceful coexistence is not a mere slogan but stems from our history, traditions, and beliefs and from our determination to remain independent and to exist in peace and friendship with others. As Jawaharlal Nehru said: Our freedom and independence are but a part of freedom and independence of all nations.

594

Mr. President, I believe this world is now entering a new era. It has already learned the hard way that slogans must be mistrusted and seldom relate to the complex realities of changing situations. Decisionmaking today requires thinkers and intellectuals who share the hopes and aspirations of the masses and feel with them, thus winning their willing consent.

Our two countries have a very similar system of government and we have adopted a social organization which is based on the cornerstones of individual liberty, democracy, and security.

We, in India, are at the same time face to face with the problem of ensuring that the weaker elements in our society are not made victims of uncontrolled economic forces. For this purpose we believe that capital, which is scarce, must often be employed in certain priority sectors for the nation's collective good.

We are apt to hear that ours is a mixed economy but our economy, by reason of our situation, is incapable of being interpreted in strict ideological terms. The real and practical problem in India today is how to increase production and attain equitable distribution of wealth with equal opportunity for all. Our Constitution emphasizes these as the directive principles in the governance of the country.

In many ways, your country, Mr. President, was a pioneer in what we are ourselves trying to achieve but in more difficult circumstances and in a comparatively shorter time.

We, in Asia, are facing major changes, more fundamental than elsewhere in the world. It is no coincidence that everywhere there is a call for a fresh look at old presumptions. The traditional concepts of friend and enemy, of war and peace, of spheres of influence and balance of power, have to be modified.

In Asia we have to remove the basic causes of tension and insecurity. The discontent of a deprived and underprivileged people is a more potent danger than any that an enemy can devise. The people must have rights to protect and happiness to defend. If they have these, they will gladly share responsibilities and make sacrifices.

There are tensions, both national and international, which arise from basic factors—economic, social, and political. They are not amenable to simple explanations of power politics and power vacuum. A military solution cannot remove the main causes of weakness and tension.

The emphasis must, therefore, shift from a military solution to peaceful settlement, to economic and social development, so that people may have adequate food and shelter, health and education, employment and leisure, with peace and freedom.

Mr. President, we are making, in India, a concerted effort both to improve the lot of our people and build friendships with our neighbors and with others. We are glad that relations between most Asian nations are better today than before. Certain tensions and conflicts remain still but they can and must be resolved only through peaceful means and not by force.

Your country, Mr. President, has a deep and abiding interest in the peace and progress of this region. The prestige and potential of America can be of great help in strengthening the framework of economic cooperation in this area. We in this country have admiration for the high sense of responsibility and earnestness and the new and realistic approach to Asia which has been shown by your administration.

We hope that your visit to India and other countries will open a new era of friendships. We also hope that your visit, brief though it is, will enable you to have a glimpse of the immense good will and friendship that exists in India for your country. Though sometimes there have been differences, they are but natural between friendly sovereign and independent countries. These differences are not in the aims and objectives but only in the means to achieve them.

It is our hope, Mr. President, that India and the United States can go forward together in friendship and cooperation for their mutual benefit and for the benefit of Asia and the world community.

Excellencies, ladies and gentlemen, may I request you to join me in a toast to the health of the President and Mrs. Nixon, to the happiness and welfare of the people of the United States of America, and to the growing friendship between our two countries, and peace in the world. To your health, Mr. President, and to the prosperity and greatness of the American people.

39–861—71——41

301 Remarks on Departure From India. *August 1, 1969*

Mr. President, Your Excellencies, ladies and gentlemen:

As I leave India after this third visit, I leave with a sense of destiny, and also with a greater confidence than ever before about the future—the future for this country—and because this country's future is one that will have such an enormous effect on all of Asia and the world, confidence in the future of the world.

My talks with the Prime Minister, with you, Mr. President, with members of the Government, have been most helpful in establishing a new channel of communication, a new attitude with regard to the relations between our two countries, that I believe means our working together more effectively than in the past for interests that transcend any national concerns, but that go to our desires that we mutually share for peace and friendship, freedom, justice, all of these great principles that go far beyond any country, far beyond any continent, that go throughout the world.

I want to say finally, Mr. President, that Mrs. Nixon and I are most grateful for the warm hospitality that we have re-

ceived on every side, not only at the magnificent state dinner last night, but also from the hundreds of thousands of people that we saw lining the streets on a hot day, in the middle of the day. To this we certainly want to say our thanks, because we know that this means that we have friends here, personal friends, as well as those who may be friends because of our official position.

We hope to return some day, not only to see this country and its leaders, but to see again our many friends in India. Thank you.

NOTE: The President spoke at 10:45 a.m. at Palam Airport in New Delhi. Acting President Mohammed Hidayatullah's, remarks follow:

Mr. President, it has been a pleasure and privilege to have you and Mrs. Nixon visit us, even though your visit was so brief. You have seen for yourself, in a small measure, the great warmth of feeling and friendship that my government and people entertain for you both and for your people. Your visit, Mr. President, as I have no doubt, helped in further strengthening our friendly relations and our mutual understanding and will, I am sure, lead to greater cooperation between our two countries.

I should like to take this opportunity of wishing you bon voyage, happy landings, and success in your quest for peace. Thank you.

302 Remarks on Arrival at Lahore, Pakistan. *August 1, 1969*

Mr. President, Your Excellencies, ladies and gentlemen:

This is the sixth time I have had the privilege of visiting Pakistan. And, as I stand here, I am aware of some of the impressions that were deeply imbedded in my mind on those previous visits.

First, of a people with great courage;

second, of a people with great vitality; third, of a people with a great idealism and great confidence insofar as their future is concerned; and, fourth, of a people in terms of hospitality who cannot be exceeded by any people in the world.

And I come, Mr. President, here today in a different capacity than on previous occasions; the first two times as Vice President of the United States, the next three times as a private citizen, and now, in an official capacity as President of the United States.

And as I speak today, I want the people of this country to know, and I want those with whom I will be talking to know, that I come not just as the political leader, the head of state of my country, but I come as a friend of Pakistan. I value the friendships that I have had here over the years, and that my wife has had on those occasions that she has accompanied me.

I know, too, that, as you have indicated, there have been some strains in our relationships over recent years. And I do not suggest that on one visit that all differences will be resolved.

But I do know this: that what we can do and what we intend to do on this visit is to restore a relationship of friendship based on mutual trust which is so essential to good relations between two countries. That is what we will do.

And so, in that spirit, I welcome the opportunity to visit this country again, to meet with you, and the colleagues, your colleagues in government, and to extend to all of the people of Pakistan from all of the people of the United States our warm good wishes and our friendship as a people from one great people to another great people.

Thank you.

NOTE: The President spoke at 11:55 a.m. at Lahore International Airport in response to the remarks of President A. M. Yahya Khan which follow:

President Nixon, Mrs. Nixon, ladies and gentlemen:

It gives me great pleasure to welcome Your Excellency and Mrs. Nixon, and the members of your distinguished party, to Pakistan.

In your person, Mr. President, we are not only welcoming you as the head of a great and friendly country, but also an old friend, whose abiding interest in Pakistan and its people is demonstrated by several visits over the years. We still remember your first visit in 1953, when you came as your country's Vice President. That was the beginning of a new era of cooperation and mutual collaboration between our two countries.

The pattern of our relations has changed somewhat since then but there is no diminution in our mutual regard, nor, I am happy to say, in your country's interest in Pakistan's wellbeing. The United States' contribution to Pakistan's development efforts has been very substantial and will always be remembered with gratitude.

Your visit, Mr. President, is taking place at a critical time. It will provide us with an opportunity to get to know each other and exchange views on mutual interests.

The city of Lahore is happy to receive you on its historic soil and to share your joy at the most recent and the most memorable triumph of human courage, determination, and scientific skill which was achieved by your astronauts when they were the first to land on the moon.

I hope during your all-too-brief stay, Mr. President, you and Mrs. Nixon will have a glimpse of Lahore's unique character and its traditional hospitality.

I wish you and Mrs. Nixon, and your party, a pleasant stay, Mr. President.

303   Statement on the President's Visit to Pakistan. *August 1, 1969*

IT IS A GREAT PLEASURE for me to visit Pakistan, where I always have found a warm welcome from a great and friendly people. It is a special pleasure for me to return on this, my sixth visit, but my first as President.

This will be a working visit, during which I look forward to discussing many matters of mutual interest with Pakistan's leaders. At the outset, however, there are several points I would like to emphasize.

First, I want to convey the sense of friendship and respect that the people of my country feel for the people of Pakistan and that my Government feels for the Government of Pakistan. This is a feeling that has existed between our countries for many years and under a variety of circumstances. There have been good times and there have been some difficult times. There have been times when we have not understood each other as well as we might and there have been other times when we have worked very closely together. But through all of these experiences, the basic feeling of friendship and respect has not been lost. I come here today to reexpress that feeling—and to reaffirm the stable and cordial relationship between our nations which that feeling makes possible.

Second, a stable and cordial relationship must be built on a clear understanding by each of our governments of the interests and viewpoints of the other, and of the way in which the other sees important problems. I look forward, on this visit, to our sharing in candor our respective assessments of our national interests and informing each other of our views on a wide variety of subjects.

Third, I want to stress the continuing interest of the United States in the progress of Pakistan and all of Asia. Just as the historic trip to the moon has opened a new era in human history, so the dra- matic changes taking place in this part of the world will have an enormous impact on men everywhere. The United States will continue to give strong encouragement to Asian development.

Fourth, I wish to communicate my Government's conviction that Asian hands must shape the Asian future. This is true, for example, with respect to economic aid, for it must be related to the total pattern of a nation's life. It must support the unique aspirations of each people. Its purpose is to encourage self-reliance, not dependence. And this it has done in Pakistan.

Fifth, I want to say that we share your concern for the well-being of the great numbers of individuals who form the backbone of our societies. Governments are at their best when they look not just to the overall well-being of the nation but to the opportunity of individual men, women, and children. That is where the strength of a nation lies.

Finally, it is our hope that Asians will work more closely with each other in a variety of constructive bilateral and regional projects. The Regional Cooperation for Development organization in which Pakistan participates with Iran and Turkey is one encouraging example of such activity.

I mention all these points because I believe these policies represent the best way of bringing peace and progress to Asia. I am confident that our talks here in Lahore will advance that common goal.

NOTE: The statement was released at Lahore, Pakistan.

304   Remarks on Accepting the Nishan-e-Pakistan.
       August 1, 1969

Mr. President:

I wish to express my deep appreciation to you and the Government of Pakistan and the people of Pakistan for honoring me this way.

I think you would be interested to know that for me this is the first time since becoming President of the United States— this is the first citation of this type or any decoration that I have received. I am proud of it.

I want you to know, too, that the citation, the eloquent words that were expressed, I only hope that I can be worthy of those words, of those sentiments, and also to say finally that I accept this award as President of the United States for the American people, but also I accept it in another sense, for more personal reasons, as one who has been, is, and always will be a friend of Pakistan.

NOTE: The President spoke at 6:20 p.m. in the Grey Room at Government House in Lahore. The medal was presented to him by President A. M. Yahya Khan and the citation was read by Pakistani Chief of Protocol M. Anwar Khan, as follows:

Mr. President, the Government and people of Pakistan have the highest regard for your constant efforts to strengthen the ties of friendship and cooperation between Pakistan and the United States of America.

For your personal contribution in bringing about a closer understanding between the peoples of our two countries, and for the deep interest you have shown in Pakistan during your previous visits to our country, for the way in which you have upheld the right of individual freedom and dignity, for your constant efforts to promote greater collaboration between the industrially advanced and developing nations of the world, for your education in the advancement of science and technology that has led to the attainment of new frontiers in human knowledge, and for your unfailing support of the Charter of the United Nations to serve as a bulwark for peace and a just order in the world.

In recognition of these contributions, I, on behalf of the Government and people of Pakistan, give expression to our sentiments of deep regard by presenting to you, Mr. President, the Nishan-e-Pakistan, which is the highest civilian award in our country.

305   Toasts of the President and President Yahya Khan
       of Pakistan at a State Dinner in Lahore.
       August 1, 1969

Mr. President, and our friends from Pakistan and the United States:

I have the privilege of responding to the very gracious and eloquent words of the President on this occasion, and in doing so, I want to respond for all of those from the United States that are here, and for the many who are friends of Pakistan in the United States who could not be here.

Mr. President, I can say that this has been a very memorable day for all of us, and particularly for me and for Mrs. Nixon; memorable from the time that we arrived at the airport, when we saw the very friendly people who welcomed us as we drove through the roads on the way here to this residence, and then the very constructive talks that we had during the afternoon, the truly magnificent presentation on the grounds where we saw not only the dances, but in addition, the splendid—I perhaps should say the best—bagpipe group that probably exists in the world.

Then tonight this dinner, one that we shall always remember because of the historic setting in which it takes place, because of the good company that is here, and because of the really superb way in which this dinner has been presented.

In that connection, if I could be permitted one personal comment, we have particularly enjoyed the music, the chance alternately to appreciate and understand the music of Pakistan and then the music of the United States. We are most grateful to the orchestra and we thank you for that.

I learned something interesting about the music, incidentally, when one number was being played. I found that it was a wedding number and I was told that wedding numbers quite often are melancholy in Pakistan because it is a sad time to have the bride leave the family and go, of course, away from home to someone else. When we had met the lovely ladies from Pakistan here tonight, we well understood why that would have been the case.

But if I may turn to what are more serious thoughts for a moment, earlier this evening in the reception, one of your guests pointed out that on this occasion our stay in Pakistan would be exactly 22 hours, which happens to coincide with the exact number of hours that the two astronauts spent on the moon.

I think there is a lesson in that, a lesson in it that I would like to expand on very briefly. This journey came about due to the fact that I wanted to be present when our astronauts came back from the moon. It was truly a very exciting experience—after having talked to them on the telephone when they were on the moon—to be

there in the Pacific when they completed that successful journey.

Now, with this visit to Pakistan, we complete the Asian phase of our journey around the world. It is true that the visits have been brief, only one day in each country, except for a longer stay in Bangkok, where we had 2 days. But in that period of time, it gave us the opportunity, and particularly me the opportunity, to revisit a number of countries that I had known before, to talk to a number of leaders that I had met before and to meet some that I had not had the opportunity to talk to before, but beyond that, putting it in the perspective of that 22 hours on the moon, and the 22 hours that we are spending in Pakistan, it brings home this one thought:

Unfortunately—I say unfortunately because all around this table, I am sure, would like to participate in the high adventure of being the first to go to the moon or the first to go to Mars, provided we had an absolute, guaranteed, free ticket, whatever the case might be—but we all know that that is not possible, that none of us here will be in that experience, although we will share in it, share in it through the medium of television and radio and communication, which now brings the world together as it has never been brought together before.

On the other hand, while that was a very great adventure, and as the President very generously has pointed out, an achievement of which we are very proud, I think that what we have seen in this less than a week in Asia is also adventure of the very highest order.

I visited all of these countries 16 years ago. Many problems have developed since that time, and I know that there are still many problems today. But looking at the perspective of 16 years, I know that virtually all of the nations that I visited then have moved forward substantially from where they were. That is true of Pakistan. It is true in terms of your economic development. It is true in terms of your industrial development. Despite whatever other problems may have occurred in the meantime, keeping it in the long perspective of history, this is something we must always have in mind as a symbol of hope for the future.

But looking further down the road, in the countries we have visited and the area that we have covered, what we see are one and a half billion people in Asia. In 25 years there will be 3 billion people in Asia. And from this part of the world will either come the greatest progress, and thereby the peace that we all want in the Pacific and in the world, or the greatest destruction that the world has ever known.

I do not think I am overstating in putting it that way. So we look at these countries, we look at the hope, and we look also at the problems. We can see that all of our hopes are bound together. We have our differences, yes, between nations in the area, on this policy or that policy, but looking toward the future, it is essential, absolutely essential, that we have a generation of peace for Asia and the world.

We in the United States want to play our part in attempting to begin that generation by ending a war in which we are presently engaged on a basis that will promote that real peace that we all want, and then to work on for peaceful policies all over the world in the future.

But beyond that, and responding particularly to what the President has said, as we consider this explosion in population from 1½ billion to 3 billion people over 25 years, the greatest explosion that has ever occurred in the history of the world, it means that there must be an increase in agricultural production, in industrial production, and also the ability to handle this period of tremendous change in a peaceful way.

What I am really trying to say is, as great and exciting as was the accomplishment of those men landing on the moon, those of us who have the opportunity and the responsibility and the challenge of dealing with this problem also have an exciting and, it seems to me, great adventure, because what we do—what we do day by day in making the decisions that will determine whether peace and freedom and justice and progress go forward together in Asia and the world—what we do can affect the future of not just a billion and a half, not just 3 billion, but of the 4½ to 5 billion people that will live on this earth 25 years from now.

Talking in such big numbers I am sure seems to raise the whole problem beyond the ability to comprehend. But, again, we get back to the moon.

Who would have thought 25 years ago that two men from earth would stand on the moon? It was too much to comprehend. But it happened. It happened because men worked together and they planned together, and as a result, they achieved success.

And I say that that kind of planning and working, that kind of genius, it is not limited to one nation, but that comes from all peoples all over the world, that that kind of genius applied to these enormous problems and these enormous challenges that we see, particularly in Asia.

We can have a period of peace, uninterrupted peace, for a generation. And that can mean the progress that we want for this area and for all the world.

And I just want to say, finally, Mr. President, I came here, as everybody around this table knows, as one who has long been a friend of Pakistan. You were generous to state that while I was Vice President of the United States, I played some role in seeing that the friendship between our two countries remained strong and became stronger.

Now that I am President of the United States, with somewhat more influence than I had as Vice President, I can assure you that I am going to continue to work for a cause that is very close to my heart, the friendship, the friendship between two great peoples, so that we can work together in the solutions of these great problems, work together possibly not in going to the moon or to Mars, although we can participate also in those great ventures in one way or another, but in working together in the equally exciting adventure that I have described, of the future, the future of the hundreds of thousands, yes, I would say millions of children that I have seen on the streets of the cities of Asia over these past 6 days.

And, so, with that, I conclude simply by saying that I am proud to be in this room to respond to this toast in this way, in a country where I have been received so often officially in such a generous way, and when I came as a private citizen in just as hospitable a way.

Mr. President, I ask that all here stand and raise their glasses to the President of Pakistan and to the continuing and increasing friendship between the people of Pakistan and the people of the United States.

NOTE: The President spoke at approximately 10:30 p.m. at Government House in Lahore

in response to the following toast proposed by President A. M. Yahya Khan:

Mr. President, Mrs. Nixon, ladies and gentlemen:

It gives me immense pleasure to extend a most hearty welcome on behalf of the Government, the people of Pakistan, and on my own behalf to an old and esteemed friend of Pakistan, His Excellency, Mr. Richard M. Nixon, President of the United States of America, his charming wife, and the distinguished members of their party who have come to Pakistan.

We recall, with pleasure, your several visits to Pakistan, commencing in 1953 when you were your country's Vice President, and your key role in establishing close, friendly links between our two countries. Your continued interest in Pakistan over the years is reflected in the compliment you paid us by visiting our country several times even when you were no longer in office. Your election last year to the highest public office in the United States was a source of great satisfaction to your friends and admirers, among them Pakistan, and today we are happy to welcome you as a friend, as a world statesman, and as the head of the great United States.

We are glad, Mr. President, that you decided to undertake your present tour and thus afforded us this early opportunity to meet you and some of your distinguished officials for an exchange of views on important questions of the day.

Our discussions today were wide-ranging. They were marked with cordiality and frankness, and I found them very useful. I trust, as a result, both of us understand each other's viewpoint on bilateral, regional, and world affairs a little bit better. We were greatly interested to know how you viewed the current situation in this region, the intraregional problems and the shape of things after, as everyone hopes, peace comes to the troubled land of Vietnam. We are grateful to you, Mr. President, for giving us your assessment.

It is natural that in the course of our discussions we should have covered our bilateral relations. We attach great importance to continued friendly and meaningful relations with the United States.

We are grateful for the generous assistance

your country has given us in the past, and your own personal initiative and role, Mr. President, therein is remembered with gratitude and appreciation. We hope that we shall continue to receive this assistance of which in the past we have made excellent use.

As you know so well, we are at a critical stage in our efforts to attain the takeoff stage for self-sustaining economic growth. While endeavoring to sustain a high rate of economic growth, we must insure that progress in the social sector goes hand in hand with economic development and does not lag behind.

With the demands of the social sector being accorded high priority, our main hope for preventing the rate of development from slipping below the rate of population growth lies in the continued adequate availability of aid from friendly countries like the United States.

Mr. President, the world is passing through deeply troubled times. There is hardly a country which is not going through an excruciating self-examination over domestic conflicts or tormented by one aspect or another of the international situation. We, in Pakistan, are convinced that peace is mankind's most urgent need of the day. Nations need peace at home and peace abroad.

As a developing country, we regard peace among nations as the most essential prerequisite of progress. It is out of this conviction that we actively seek, and not merely desire, durable friendly relations with all countries, especially our neighbors.

It is for this reason that we have always been urging that the basic disputes between India and Pakistan be resolved and got out of the way so that the two of us can live in peace and amity and bend all our energies for the betterment of our people.

This also explains our deep concern over the dangerous situation in the Middle East and over the Vietnam conflict. We know, Mr. President, how strongly you and your countrymen feel on the peace issue. We earnestly hope that through your policies and your administration's endeavors a way will be found to reduce tensions everywhere and to bring peace to the embattled lands.

Your countrymen have just performed what may be rightly regarded as man's most outstanding feat in science, technology, and high adventure. While sharing your joy and pride in this historic achievement, it is our fervent hope that this feat, and the many further triumphs that await man, will be used solely in the service of man and for peace and prosperity of the human race.

Ladies and gentlemen, I would request you now to join me in a hearty toast to the health and happiness of our distinguished guest, His Excellency, Mr. Richard M. Nixon, President of the United States, and Mrs. Nixon, and to the lasting friendship between Pakistan and the United States.

306   Remarks on Departure From Pakistan.
August 2, 1969

Mr. President:

We want to express our grateful appreciation to you for the very heartwarming welcome we have received here and although, as you have said, the weather here may not be as good as it might be at some other time of year, we can only say that as far as the welcome was concerned, it was as warm a welcome as we have ever received on our visit to Pakistan or to any other country. For that we are grateful.

The talks we have had have been most helpful in giving me a better understanding of the problems of Pakistan, of our bilateral relations, but beyond that, of the problems of Asia as they relate to our overall goal of peace and progress in the world.

I feel as I leave Pakistan and complete what is now this phase of this journey, my trip through Asia, that Asia is on the road to a new era of progress, a new era of self-reliance, of independence, but that all this depends upon whether the leaders of the world will be able to produce peace— peace which will see that what is created by the hardworking people we have seen on the streets of Lahore, by the government officials who are working night and day on programs—to see that that progress which is so created is not destroyed by war. To that goal I have dedicated our administration, and that goal you also share. As I leave, I can say to you we look forward to a period of better relations between our two countries, based on mutual trust and friendship, and we look forward also to a period in which we can have real peace in Asia and thereby create the conditions which could lead to a lasting peace in the world. Thank you.

NOTE: The President spoke at 8:50 a.m. at Lahore International Airport in response to farewell remarks by President A. M. Yahya Khan, who spoke as follows:

President Nixon, Mrs. Nixon:

We bid you a goodby on the conclusion of your brief visit to Pakistan. We wish you a very pleasant homeward journey. We are happy to have had the opportunity to welcome again an esteemed friend in our midst, and trust that your next visit to Pakistan will be a little longer.

The charms of Lahore are not exhausted in a day, Mr. President. There are other places in Pakistan with feelings of warmth for honored guests like you. As the weather goes this is not the best time of the year, but I hope that you and Mrs. Nixon, and your party, have enjoyed your stay.

We are especially appreciative of Mrs. Nixon's interest in social welfare projects. Her visit yesterday to the Society for Rehabilitation of the Disabled and to the APWA School, an institution for the needy, was heartwarming for the social workers of Lahore. It was a happy thought on her part to have decided to accompany her distinguished husband in his travels. All that I can say to her: Come again. Farewell. God bless you.

307   Remarks on Arrival at Bucharest, Romania. *August 2,* 1969

Mr. President, Your Excellencies, ladies and gentlemen:

Speaking on behalf of all of the American people, I wish to express my deep appreciation for the very warm welcome that you have extended to us on this occasion, and I bring with me the warm good wishes and feelings of friendship from all of the American people to all the people of Romania.

As you pointed out, this is not my first visit to your country. I recall with pleasure that first visit. It was at the very end of winter, at the beginning of a new spring, and I had very useful talks with you at that time, and other Romanian Government officials. I recall vividly the warm

welcome extended to me by the people of Romania.

This is an historic occasion. While this is not my first visit to your country, it is the first visit of a President of the United States to Romania, the first state visit by an American President to a socialist country or to this region of the continent of Europe.

Mr. President, this significant moment in the history of relations between our two countries coincides with a great moment in the history of the human race. Mankind has landed on the moon. We have established a foothold in outer space. But there are goals that we have not reached here on earth. We are still building a just peace in the world. This is a work that requires the same cooperation and patience and perseverance from men of good will that it took to launch that vehicle to the moon.

I believe that if human beings can reach the moon, human beings can reach an understanding with each other on the earth.

If we are to make progress in this lifetime effort, we must see the world as it is— a world of different races, of different nations, of different social systems—the real world, where many interests divide men and many interests unite them.

Our meetings represent, I am sure, the desire of the Romanian people and of the American people that we do not allow our differences to prevent a deeper understanding of our national points of view. Yours is a European country and your most direct concern is, therefore, with the security of this continent. I come from another continent, but from a country that twice in this century has shed the blood of its sons in the pursuit of that European security.

We are prepared to do our part, also, in this era of negotiations so that all in Europe can pursue the fulfillment of their just aspirations for a better life, free from the fear of war or threats of war, and in constructive cooperation with others, near and far.

Let us agree at the outset to be frank with each other. Our differences are matters of substance; indeed, no nation's range of interests are identical to any other nation's. But nations can have widely different internal orders and live in peace. Nations can have widely differing economic interests and live in peace.

The United States believes that the rights of all nations must be equal, but we do not believe that the character of all nations must be the same.

My country has already undertaken new initiatives to reduce the tensions that exist in the world. We stand ready to respond firmly and positively to sincere and concrete initiatives that others may take. Every nation, of whatever size and whatever region of the world, will find us receptive to realistic new departures on the path to peace.

The purpose of your invitation, Mr. President, and the purpose of my visit here, is to improve communications between our two nations. This is a useful and a peaceful purpose.

In that spirit of realism and of open-mindedness, I look forward to our talks. I thank you for your hospitality.

Traiasca prietenia Romano-Americana. [Long live Romanian-American friendship.]

NOTE: The President spoke at approximately 12:40 p.m. at Otopeni Airport in Bucharest in response to welcoming remarks by President Nicolae Ceausescu. An advance text of President Nixon's remarks was also released by the White House Press Office. A translation of President Ceausescu's remarks follows:

Dear Mr. President, dear Mrs. Nixon, ladies and gentlemen:

I am pleased to extend to you, the first President of the United States of America ever visiting Romania, the cordial greetings of the Council of State and of the Government, to express the feelings of sympathy of the Romanian people towards the American people whose contribution to the cause of world progress and civilization is unanimously appreciated in this country.

I hope that your visit to Romania, though a short one, will enable you to get more closely acquainted with the endeavors made by the Romanian people for the development of economy, science, and culture, their determination to build a dignified, free, and prosperous life, and also with their aspirations for peace and cooperation with all of the states of the world, irrespective of their social system.

Personally, I recall with satisfaction, Mr. President, the meeting we had together 2 years ago, the spirit of frankness and sincerity during our discussions at that time, and I have no doubt that the same spirit will characterize the exchange of views we are going to have together these days.

We believe that in the complex conditions of international affairs today, the development of relations between states on the basis of the principles of peaceful coexistence and respect for the independence, sovereignty, equal rights, and noninterference in the internal affairs, represents the safe way towards promoting a climate of confidence and understanding among peoples, and of peace and security in the world.

In this direction an important contribution can be made through the contacts, meetings, and discussions between the leaders of states. We are confident that your visit and the talks we shall have will contribute towards the development of relations between our two countries, that they will prove useful and fruitful for the cause of cooperation between nations for general peace.

It is with these feelings and convictions that we welcome you in Romania today, Mr. President, with the traditional greeting of our people: *"Bine ati venit"* [welcome].

308 Toasts of the President and President Ceausescu at an Official Dinner at the Council of State in Bucharest. *August 2, 1969*

Mr. President, Mrs. Ceausescu, Your Excellencies, ladies and gentlemen:

Before I make my formal reply to the very eloquent remarks of the President, I would like to say that for all of us today, the wonderful welcome we have received here in Bucharest, in Romania, has touched our hearts, and we are most grateful for the reception we have received.

I have traveled to many countries in the world and have gone through the great capital cities of the world, but perhaps never in all of the years I have traveled have we received a warmer welcome, and we are most grateful to the people of Romania for the warmth of your hearts.

This visit to your country is a brief one and I regret that it is not longer, for though your country is smaller geographically than ours, we share many of the same qualities of diversity.

You have magnificent valleys and great mountains and seashores and forests and farm lands.

In addition, several peoples make up the Romanian nation, just as the American Nation is made up of many different peoples who came to our country from different lands.

Indeed, one bond we share is that of ancestry. Today almost a quarter of a million Americans can claim one or both parents born in Romania.

While our visit here is brief, we will have the opportunity to view some of your nation's natural beauty and also some visible manifestations of your economic progress in recent years.

From my previous visit in 1967, and also because of our information, we are aware in the United States of the strides your nation has made in building a modern industrial society. We welcome the opportunity to see examples of that progress, as we will tomorrow, and we wish you more progress in the future.

When I arrived, I spoke of a cause very close to the hearts of the American people, the cause of a just peace, a peace among peoples of differing races and differing beliefs about the nature of man and of God, a peace among nations of different interests and vastly different social systems.

Of this one thing we are sure: We know mankind cannot build a just and lasting peace until all nations recognize and respect the sovereignty and rights of other nations, large and small. There are great similarities between the United States and Romania, but as I have mentioned, there are also great differences. Our political and social systems are different. Our economic policies are different. We do not share each other's views on many issues about the nature of our world and the shape of the future. But having mentioned the differences, let us look at some of those areas where we agree.

Both Romania and the United States are members of the family of nations, and we both enjoy the rights of all nations. Each of us wishes to preserve its national institutions and unique national character in a shrinking world. Each of us wishes to advance the economic well-being of its own people. Each of us seeks peaceful solutions to international disagreements. Each believes in better understanding and greater communication between those who disagree—and that is why these meetings are being held.

Mr. President, your country pursues a policy of communication and contact with all nations—you have actively sought the reduction of international tensions. My country shares those objectives.

We are seeking ways of ensuring the security, progress, and independence of the nations of Asia, for, as recent history has shown, if there is no peace in Asia, there is no peace in the world. My country will bear the proper share of the burdens in that part of the world.

In Europe, we are prepared to consider all concrete and promising possibilities of removing tensions. We favor negotiations on disputed issues—not just for the sake of negotiations, but for the sake of resolving the disputes in order to improve the existing situation and advance the security of all nations.

We are prepared to negotiate seriously on the crucial and complex problem of strategic arms, and will consider any arrangement that equitably protects the security of all concerned while bringing the qualitative and quantitative growth of arsenals under control.

We seek a stable peace in the Middle East, a peace in which all the countries of the region, and those outside of it, can repose confidence—and a peace which no one, whether inside the region or outside, will seek to exploit for narrow purposes.

Mr. President, as I told you today in our meetings, we seek normal relations with all countries, regardless of their domestic systems. We stand ready to reciprocate the efforts of any country that seeks normal relations with us.

We are flexible about the methods by which peace is to be sought and built. We see value neither in the exchange of polemics nor in a false euphoria. We seek the substance of détente, not its mere atmosphere.

We seek, in sum, a peace not of hegemonies, and not of artificial uniformity, but a peace in which the legitimate interests of each are respected and all are safeguarded.

Mr. President, as we came into the city today, I noticed a number of people holding up signs with a picture of the three astronauts on them. More than a billion people around the world saw and heard the landing on the moon. And thoughtful men all over the world saw the earth in a new perspective—as the home of a human family whose similarities and common interests far outweigh their differences.

Because all nations must search for understanding, I value the very frank discussions we had today, and I look forward to those that we will have tomorrow. I note the growth of bilateral relations between us in recent years; our bilateral ties in many fields have expanded, and as a result of our talks they will continue to grow.

And now, Mr. President, I wish to express again to you, on behalf of all of the members of our party, our appreciation for this superb dinner tonight, for the magnificent music, and for the warm welcome you have extended to us.

I know that the welcome we received, as we rode in from the airport, was not for me or for my wife individually, but for our country, for the American people, and for all of the American people we express our appreciation. And speaking for the American people, I want you to know that we respect and admire your national independence and sovereignty. We wish you success and prosperity in the development of your country.

In the United States, as you may know, if you followed our inaugural ceremonies, we have occasionally used the phrase "Forward together." I have discovered that that concept is not original with me. And for my toast tonight, may I, therefore, use the words of a great Romanian poet, Mihai Eminescu: "May your sons go forward, brothers hand in hand."

And so I ask you all to join me in raising your glasses to the President of Romania and to Romanian-American friendship.

NOTE: The President spoke at 9:30 p.m. in response to a toast proposed by President Nicolae Ceausescu of Romania. An advance text of President Nixon's remarks was also released by the White House Press Office. A translation of President Ceausescu's remarks follows:

Dear Mr. President, dear Mrs. Nixon, ladies and gentlemen:

I am glad to be in a position to greet you, high representatives of the American people, at this dinner. The welcome given to you, Mr. President, by the citizens of our capital reflects the feelings of appreciation and esteem which our two peoples have for each other, it expresses our people's desire to live in peace and friendship with the American people, with all the peoples of the world. It is an undisputed fact that the presence in Romania, for the first time in history, of the President of the United States of America, has a special significance for the development of the relations between our two states.

At the same time this visit mirrors the favorable changes which have taken place in the modern world and bears proof to the vitality of the policy of peaceful coexistence, which asserts itself in international affairs ever more strongly.

It is well known that Romania and the United States are two countries with different systems and therefore our views on the social and political development of the world also differ. We believe, however, that the existing difference between social systems should not prevent the development of relations and cooperation between nations; on the contrary, this very fact calls for active work to promote in international affairs the policies of peaceful coexistence, a realistic, sober, and constructive policy, the wide cooperation of all countries with an aim to consolidate peace and security.

Your visit to Romania, Mr. President, takes place on the eve of the anniversary of a quarter-century since the liberation of our people from the Fascist yoke. Taking its fate in its own hands and energetically proceeding along the path of a free and independent life, the Romanian people were able, during a short period in history, to change the country's image, from the very foundations, to develop the economy, science, and culture, to build a new system, the paramount goal of which is the well-being and happiness of those who work. Our people are determined to continue with intensity their vast, peaceful, and creative work, to ensure the steady and many-sided progress of the nation to turn Romania into an advanced country of the world. It is on this basis that it participates more and more actively in the exchange of material and spiritual assets of the contemporary world.

In our country the outstanding achievements of your people in the field of economy, science, technology, and culture are well-known. The magnificent space voyage of the American astronauts—the first inhabitants of the earth who stepped on the moon and brought back to our planet fragments of matter from another celestial body—was a source of joy for us for it represents a brilliant victory of human genius and of universal knowledge. This event shows once more how necessary it is to establish peaceful coexistence and cooperation between all nations on our own planet. We express our hope that this achievement of the human mind will contribute not only to the progress of science and technology, but also to the development of cooperation between peoples, in the interest of peace and civilization.

We appreciate the fact that the relations between Romania and the United States—two countries between which there are no interstate disputes—have seen an upward trend of development. During our talks it has been put into evidence that the stage reached by the cooperation between our two countries is still far from exhausting the existing opportunities, and a mutual desire has been expressed to explore new ways of expanding our economic, scientific, technological, and cultural exchanges and cooperation. I express my firm belief that your visit to Romania, Mr. President, will prove to be a significant step in the development of many-sided, mutually advantageous relations between our two countries.

We also appreciate favorably the fact that our talks have outlined some possibilities to broaden our cooperation in the world arena, in the interest of the cause of peace. Naturally, in the course of our discussions different opinions were also voiced on certain problems pertaining to the present international situation, but this can not inhibit joint action along the way of détente and the search for new ways of improving the world political atmosphere. Romania proceeds from the idea that all the countries of the world, big and small, bear the responsibility for the fate of peace, for the development of international relations, and that they are dutybound to contribute to the settlement of the thorny issues of contemporary life and to the establishment of confidence and cooperation between nations.

Being a socialist country, Romania places in the center of her foreign policy the many-sided cooperation with the socialist countries, to which she is bound by a common social system. At the same time, she steadily develops fruitful relations in all the fields with the other countries of the world. In our opinion, when more and more new nations assert themselves in the world arena, showing their firm desire to step as independent entities on the way to progress and civilization to secure the conditions enabling each nation to decide its own future and the road of its social and political development is the essential imperative requirement of international life. In our view, at present the condition sine qua non of peace is to establish in the relations between all states the principles of independence and national sovereignty, to liquidate once and for all the policy of domination and interference in the internal affairs of others, to instate the full equality among nations. These principles acquire an ever wider international recognition, they assert themselves more and more strongly in the relations between countries and enjoy broad adhesion from public opinion everywhere. The infringements upon these principles endanger world security, breed tension, conflicts, and new hotbeds of war.

In this connection, we cannot fail to express our concern, which is indeed the concern of the whole world, about the continuation of the war in Vietnam. During our discussions we explained our position on this problem. We hope that the negotiations in Paris will lead to the cessation of the war and the withdrawal of troops from Vietnam, thus creating the conditions for the Vietnamese people to decide by itself the course of its economic and social development, in an independent way, without any interference from outside. Romania also believes that it is necessary that all efforts should be made to solve the conflict in the Middle East in the spirit of the Security Council resolution of 1967, aiming to bring about the withdrawal of the Israeli troops from the occupied territories and to ensure the right of every state in the area to independent existence, to development and progress.

Romania believes that one of the crucial problems of the international affairs today, the solution of which could make a radical contribution to the strengthening of peace, is to achieve disarmament, nuclear disarmament in the first place, to carry out concrete measures aimed at reducing and liquidating the thermonuclear danger. To this effect, the liquidation of the present division of the world into military blocs confronting each other, the dissolution of the North Atlantic Treaty Organization and, concurrently, of the Warsaw Treaty, the liquidation of the foreign military bases and the withdrawal of all troops within their national boundaries would be of particular importance.

An important progress in the direction of détente would be achieved, in our opinion, by the establishment of lasting security on the European continent. European security can be accomplished only by proceeding from the realities established as a result of World War II, from the existence of the two German states, from the recognition of the inviolability of the postwar frontiers, including the frontier on Oder-Neisse. A favorable impact would be produced by holding a European conference, a desideratum expressed by an increasing number of states. The accomplishment of security on this continent is a matter in which not only the European peoples are vitally interested, but also all the peoples of the world; the attainment of this objective would exert a particularly favorable influence on the political climate, on all countries.

I express my firm belief, Mr. President, that the meeting and the talks we had together, our determination to develop the cooperation between Romania and the United States, will make a substantive contribution to the cause of peace and international cooperation, to the ever wide promotion of the principles of peaceful coexistence in the world.

Our meeting, taking place only a few days after the accomplishment of the millenary dream of mankind to voyage on celestial bodies, gets a particular significance. It symbolizes the possibility for peoples to live in peace and mutual understanding on this planet—the ancient cradle of their existence—to unite their efforts for the achievement of the other millenary dream: a world without war, without destruction, a world of cooperation and progress. We are confident that this meeting and our talks signify a decisive moment in expanding the many-sided cooperation and collaboration between Romania and the United States, between our two peoples. At the same time we would like this visit, which is appreciated by the public opinion as an outstanding event of the international life, to mark a progress on the way of improving the relations between all nations of the world, free and equal in rights.

Allow me to propose this toast to the triumph of peace, this grand ideal of human beings on all continents regardless of their race, creed, political and philosophical beliefs.

To your health, Mr. President, to your health, dear Mrs. Nixon, to the health of our other guests, to the health of all here present.

309   Toasts of the President and President Ceausescu at a Luncheon at Government Guest House in Bucharest. *August 3, 1969*

Mr. President, ladies and gentlemen:

As we near the end of our brief visit to Romania, we only regret that we were unable to entertain the President and the members of the Romanian Government at the American Embassy. I recall in 1967, when Ambassador [Richard H.] Davis had a luncheon for me at the Embassy, that it was rather difficult to get more than 25 or 30 in the room. So regardless of whatever else comes out of these talks that we have had, and much good will come from them, one decision I have made: We will build a new embassy residence so that we can have this party next time in the embassy residence.

After seeing the splendid Titan housing project, I am sure we can find a good architect for the residence.

Mr. President, it is very difficult on this occasion to tell you how deeply we have appreciated the courtesies that you have extended to us, and also to tell you how deeply moved we have been by the reception we have received from the people of Bucharest on this visit.

We have tried on this occasion to bring as much of the United States to Bucharest as we could. The placecards, the matches, and the menus were all printed in the United States. The beef came from Kansas City; the peas came from California; the tomatoes came from Florida; and the hearts of palm came from Hawaii. But one thing we could not bring were the flowers, because no place in the world can you go and find more beautiful flowers than in Bucharest.

So, consequently, I simply want to conclude by saying that we have had very exhaustive talks, but they have not been exhausting because talk is exhausting only when it is boring, and when President Ceausescu and I talk, it is never boring. We have discussed matters of tremendous importance to relations between the United States and Romania, and also the whole problem of world peace. I know that from the talks we have had that much good will come in terms of bringing closer the day when we can have world peace.

One final point I would make on a personal note: We also brought our music. Even though we had magnificent music

last night, we thought you would like to hear from a typical American combo. The young men who have played for you are from our Air Force from Wiesbaden, and in mentioning that, I did not intend to bring in the Warsaw-NATO pact, because for us, music is the language of peace and not the language of war.

But I think you should know that one of the selections played today at the request of the First Lady of Romania was "My Fair Lady," so in proposing a toast today, I would like to propose it not only to the President, but to our fair ladies who are here, and to that friendship which I know is going to be even warmer and closer in the years ahead between the peoples of Romania and the United States.

To my fair lady and the President.

NOTE: The President proposed the toast at 2:45 p.m. President Ceausescu responded in Romanian. A translation of his remarks follows:

Mr. President, ladies and gentlemen:

I should like first of all to express on behalf of all of my associates present here our thanks for the warm welcome, for the good welcome, given to us, and particularly for the things you have treated us with, brought over from the United States.

Listening to President Nixon saying that beef, matches, cigarettes, wine, champagne, were all brought over from the United States, a thought crossed my mind: that it is unjust when people say that Romanians are nationalistic. I see that United States representatives are able to go faster than we do in this field, too.

Secondly, I should beg to apologize to Mrs. Nixon and the President for the fact that we organized a tough program for them and left no time for them to have a rest during the visit.

As to the talks we had yesterday and today, it is true that they covered a broad range of subjects. Some parts of our discussion were rather lively, but I have to say that they were always civilized and constructive. Of course, not on all problems did we share the same point of view, but I wonder that if the representatives of states had the same point of view on all things, on all problems, then they would certainly meet much less frequently than they do now.

We hope, however, that notwithstanding the differences of views even on such problems, our two sides would work together toward finding appropriate solutions in order to strengthen cooperation between peoples and bring about peace to the world.

I should also like to express my gratitude to the President for having especially brought over the band of the Air Force, bypassing at the same time both NATO and the Warsaw treaty.

It is true that music is called upon to serve friendship between peoples and peace. It might be a good thing in order that music should not follow roundabout ways in order to get to places, and just to dismantle the military blocs in order to let music free. We could turn both the Warsaw Pact and the NATO into instruments of international cooperation in the field of music, for instance, and let us have competition between the two blocs then.

PRESIDENT NIXON. I agree.

PRESIDENT CEAUSESCU. May I be permitted to propose this toast to the President of the United States and to Mrs. Nixon, who has already promised to come again to Romania one day: To the friendship between the United States and Romania; to the peace in the world.

310   Remarks on Departure From Romania. *August 3, 1969*

Mr. President, ladies and gentlemen:

It has been my privilege to visit over 60 countries in the world, and of all the countries I have visited, there has been none that has been more memorable than the visit to Romania. This is true not only because of the very substantive talks you, Mr. President, and I have had on issues—talks which I am convinced history will record will serve the cause of peace—but it is true also because of the wonderfully heartwarming welcome we have received from the people of Romania every place we have gone.

Mr. President, I am convinced, after this visit, as I am sure you are, that regardless of the differences in policies, the peoples of the world are determined to be one and, Mr. President, from the bottom of my heart, as I leave your country, I want to say, in your own language as well as I can: *Traiasca prietenia noastra. La revedere* [Long live our friendship. Until we meet again].

NOTE: The President spoke at 3:53 p.m. at Otopeni Airport in Bucharest. President Ceausescu responded in Romanian. A translation of his remarks follows:

Mr. President, ladies and gentlemen, dear comrades:

As President Nixon has already said, in the brief period of time he spent, together with Mrs. Nixon and accompanying persons, in the territory of Romania, I should also like to mention that the conversations we had together were focused on the concern for the development of relations between our two countries, and also for finding new avenues to contribute to the cause of cooperation among peoples and peace in the world.

The welcome extended to you, Mr. President, by the population of the city of Bucharest is an expression of the feelings of friendship our people have for the American people and it mirrors the hospitality of the Romanian people and the desire to live in friendship and peace with the people of America, with all the nations of the world.

Upon your return to your homeland, sir, I should like you to convey, on my own behalf, on behalf of the Romanian people, our friendly greeting to the people of America, our best wishes for prosperity and peace. And now allow me to bid you bon voyage.

311   Remarks on Arrival at Mildenhall Air Force Base,
England.   *August 3, 1969*

Mr. Prime Minister, ladies and gentlemen:

I wish to express to you, Mr. Prime Minister, my grateful appreciation for those very warm words of welcome, and to tell you that though this is but a brief stop, I welcome the opportunity that is provided to talk with you again about some of the problems that we mutually face in the world, and to discuss them in the context of the trip that I am now bringing to a conclusion.

You have graciously mentioned the adventure which took three Americans to the vicinity of the moon, and two to step on the moon. I found that as I traveled all over the world, in every nation, whether it was in Asia or in Eastern Europe, this was uppermost in the minds of all people, leaders and people that I met from all walks of life.

I think that in this is perhaps a lesson for all of us. There are differences that divide the world today—very deep differences. But as we saw very dramatically and very movingly in Bucharest today and yesterday, those things which unite men and women in the world are much stronger than those which divide us.

I can assure all who are listening to me now that while the path to peace may seem very difficult, and preserving the peace is, of course, a task which we have found to be tremendously arduous and hazardous over these past few years, that the people of the world deep in their hearts want peace.

They are on the side of peace. That is the message that comes from all over Asia; it comes from Eastern Europe; and I sense it again as I step here on British soil.

It is the responsibility of leaders—leaders like those that I had the privilege of meeting on this trip, leaders, Mr. Prime Minister, like yourself—it is our responsibility to develop those policies that will reflect the deep yearning of people to be together rather than apart, to communicate rather than being denied the opportunity to know each other.

It is this great goal to which we are dedicated.

I believe that this trip may have served a useful purpose in bringing us closer to that goal. I am confident that our conversations will also further that purpose as they have in the past.

Finally, I say again, it is always a great privilege to come here, to be welcomed here on British soil, and I can only say that I wish my stay were longer but there will be another day. On this occasion, at least, for this one hour, we can talk about the world and perhaps develop some constructive thoughts that would further that cause of peace to which we are all so deeply dedicated.

Thank you.

NOTE: The President spoke at 6:29 p.m. in response to remarks of welcome by Prime Minister Harold Wilson, which follow:

Mr. President, it is a very real pleasure for me to welcome you and Mrs. Nixon this evening as you touch down on British soil, currently here in a very real sense Anglo-American soil, at the last stage of a round-the-world tour which I hope you, Mr. President, feel has been as rewarding as it has been arduous, and which, when its full implications have been worked out, may well prove to have been historic.

While your mind must be teeming, Mr. President, with the accumulated thoughts of your talks and your welcome in seven different countries, I am sure that even these will not have displaced your memory of seeing the splashdown after the momentous and successful Apollo mission.

This evening gives me the opportunity to extend to you, and this time without the aid of a hot line, the congratulations of Her Majesty's Government and of the whole British people on what has been achieved.

Meanwhile, and immediately, you, Mr. President, and I seek to make the maximum use of the short time that you are here with us. While we have kept in the closest touch since your visit in February, I look forward to this chance of hearing from you, firsthand, your first impressions of your discussions on your world tour; equally, to exchange views on the subjects of our informal agenda, for both of us are conscious of the possible developments, challenges, and opportunities that lie ahead as we pursue our common tasks together.

312   Remarks at Andrews Air Force Base on Returning From the Global Tour.   *August 3, 1969*

Mr. Vice President, Members of the Cabinet, Members of the Senate and House, members of the diplomatic corps, and all of our friends who have been so kind to come to the airport on this rainy evening:

It seems the way to get weather is for me to return from either Europe or Asia. When I returned from Europe it snowed and when I returned from Asia it rained. So that means from now on I will be called "Nixon the Rainmaker." That is better than being called a "troublemaker."

I do want to say in response to your very warm remarks of welcome that we had some wonderful receptions around the world in seven countries. I knew those receptions were not for me as an individual, but for what this Nation stands for.

America has millions of friends in this world and we can be proud of America, and I was proud to represent America as I visited these nations and saw friendship for America in the eyes of people on the streets of cities in the seven countries that you have mentioned.

Also I would like to point out that on this trip the theme was as pretty well stated as it could be, by the Acting President of India, when he proposed a toast a few nights ago, that it was a trip in quest of peace. And that was the theme of this trip.

What we were trying to do was to bring this message to the world that the United States wants to bring peace to the world and that we want to do our fair share in working with others to maintain peace in the world. That feeling, believe me, is shared by people all over this world.

Another thought that occurs to me is with regard to the visit to Bucharest. This was the most moving experience that I have had in traveling to over 60 countries in the world, not that all the other countries were not also extremely exciting and interesting and receptive, but here in this country in which we have an entirely different political philosophy from our own, people were out by the hundreds of thousands, not ordered by their government, but cheering and shouting—not against anybody—but simply showing their affection and friendship for the people of the United States.

This means to me one simple thing: that deep differences in political philosophy cannot permanently divide the peoples of the world. This has a great meaning to the future. It means that we can live in peace in the world, live in peace with other nations who may have different political philosophies.

Finally, another thought occurs to me. I

want to bring this to a conclusion because I know this has been a long day for you and this is the end of a 24-hour day for me. It is raining, so under the circumstances, I do want to leave, however, one final thought that you touched upon.

In Bucharest I noted that so many, particularly of the young people, held up a newspaper picture of the astronauts landing on the moon, and everywhere we went it was the same. Some way, when those two Americans stepped on the moon, the people of this world were brought closer together.

As I stand here today, I really feel in my heart that it is that spirit, the spirit of Apollo, that America can now help to bring to our relations with other nations. The spirit of Apollo transcends geographical barriers, and political differences. It can bring the people of the world together in peace.

Thank you and good night.

NOTE: The President spoke at 11:23 p.m. at Andrews Air Force Base in response to the following remarks of welcome by Vice President Spiro T. Agnew:

Mr. President, it is indeed a privilege to welcome you back. This return from a successful trip in Asia in many ways represents a repetition of a return from a successful trip earlier this year in Europe. There is one distinct difference that I appreciate very much, and that is that the runway is not icy.

However, as successful as both those trips were, Mr. President, this one has a significant difference in that it began on a soaring of the spirit as you stood on the deck of the carrier *Hornet* and watched the astronauts return to safety again.

We could see mirrored in your face, sir, a reaction that was within each one of us, of pride and indeed, in awe, that man has come to this great accomplishment.

Mr. President, I think that spirit accompanied you on your trip throughout the Asian nations, to the Philippines, to Indonesia, to Thailand, and then that trip to Vietnam, where you visited our battleline troops. I think it was reflected on the faces of the troops and on the faces of the people of Asia, as they heard you say what I thought was your most significant remark, that we are not going to treat the Pacific Ocean as a barrier, but as a bridge.

Then after Vietnam, your visits to India and Pakistan and finally that wonderful experience that each of us shared with you when you went to Romania and received that tremendous outpouring of spirit that could not conceivably be arranged by any nation under any circumstances. It assured us that there is a brotherhood of man—a brotherhood of man that indicates that there is a brotherhood for peace— peace for all nations—and we should all strive for this.

We should all be determined that the people can prosper and grow together as long as the people's wishes are being met and I think that basically is the message that you so successfully put around the world, and we are so pleased to have you back and so proud of what you have accomplished.

313   Message to the Congress Transmitting Annual Report on the Operation of the International Coffee Agreement. *August 5, 1969*

To the Congress of the United States:

I transmit herewith the 1968 report on the operations of the International Coffee Agreement.

This treaty, in force since 1963, is vital to the economic well-being of many friendly developing countries in Latin America and Africa. It has provided them stable and predictable earnings from their principal export crop and thus has encouraged their economic development. The United States consumer in turn has benefitted from stable prices considerably below the peaks reached before the Agreement entered into force. I hope to see the Agreement continued and strengthened. I reaffirm our support of the Coffee Diversification Fund, designed to encourage a shift of resources away from the production of surplus and unneeded coffee. Discussions with the Coffee Fund on the terms and conditions of a United States loan to the Fund are expected to begin fairly soon.

The report reviews the operations of the International Coffee Agreement in 1968.

On April 30, 1969 agreement was reached with the Brazilian Government regarding Brazilian soluble coffee exports. This has obviated any immediate need for United States' action.

RICHARD NIXON

The White House
August 5, 1969

NOTE: The report, entitled "1968 Annual Report of the President to the Congress on the International Coffee Agreement" (12 pp. plus annexes), was published by the Department of State.

The text of the April 1969 agreement with Brazil is printed in the Department of State Bulletin (vol. 60, p. 455).

314   Message to the Congress Transmitting Annual Report of the Atlantic-Pacific Interoceanic Canal Study Commission.   *August 6, 1969*

To the Congress of the United States:

I am transmitting the fifth annual report of the Atlantic-Pacific Interoceanic Canal Study Commission. The report covers the period July 1, 1968 to June 30, 1969.

The Commission has now completed its data collection activities on all of the five sea-level canal routes under investigation. Field operations have been terminated, and all facilities and equipment not removed from the routes have been turned over to host-country governments under the terms of the survey agreements.

Within the United States the office and laboratory evaluations of route data are well-advanced, as are the Commission's studies of the diplomatic, economic, and military considerations that bear on the feasibility of a new, sea-level canal constructed by conventional or nuclear excavation. The Commission will render its final report not later than December 1,

1970, pursuant to its authorizing legislation.

During the year the Atomic Energy Commission conducted the third of its planned series of nuclear excavation experiments in support of the canal investigation. Although all the now planned nuclear cratering experiments will not be completed soon enough for full evaluation by the Commission, it is expected that the Commission will be able to reach general conclusions as to the feasibility of employment of nuclear explosives for canal excavation.

This anniversary sees the canal investigation entering its final phase, and I take great pleasure in forwarding the Commission's fifth annual report to the Congress.

RICHARD NIXON

The White House
August 6, 1969

NOTE: The report, dated July 31, 1969, is entitled "Fifth Annual Report of the Atlantic-Pacific Interoceanic Canal Study Commission" (13 pp. and appendixes).

315 Special Message to the Congress on Occupational Safety and Health. *August 6, 1969*

To the Congress of the United States:

Technological progress can be a mixed blessing. The same new method or new product which improves our lives can also be the source of unpleasantness and pain. For man's lively capacity to innovate is not always matched by his ability to understand his innovations fully, to use them properly, or to protect himself against the unforeseen consequences of the changes he creates.

The side effects of progress present special dangers in the workplaces of our country. For the working man and woman, the byproducts of change constitute an especially serious threat. Some efforts to protect the safety and health of the American worker have been made in the past both by private industry and by all levels of government. But new technologies have moved even faster to create newer dangers. Today we are asking our workers to perform far different tasks from those they performed five or fifteen or fifty years ago. It is only right that the protection we give them is also up-to-date.

There has been much discussion in recent months about the quality of the environment in which Americans live. It is important to note in this regard that during their working years most American workers spend nearly a quarter of their time at their jobs. For them, the quality of the workplace is one of the most important of environmental questions. The protection of that quality is a critical matter for government attention.

Few people realize the extent of needless illness, needless injury, and needless death which results from unsafe or unhealthy working conditions. Every now and then a major disaster—in a factory or an office building or a mine—will dramatize certain occupational hazards. But most such dangers are realized under less dramatic circumstances. Often, for example, a threat to good health will build up slowly over a period of many years. To such situations, the public gives very little attention. Yet the cumulative extent of such losses is great.

Consider these facts. Every year in this country, some fourteen thousand deaths can be attributed to work-related injuries or illnesses. Because of accidents or diseases sustained on the job, some 250 million man-days of labor are lost annually. The most important consequence of these losses is the human tragedy which results when an employee—often the head of a family—is struck down. In addition, the economy loses millions of dollars in unrealized production and millions more must be used to pay workmen's compensation benefits and medical expenses. It is interesting to note that in the last five years, the number of man-days lost because of work-related injuries has been ten times the number lost because of strikes.

What have we done about this problem? The record is haphazard and spotty. For many decades, governmental responsibility for safe workplaces has rested with

617

the States. But the scope and effectiveness of State laws and State administration varies widely and discrepancies in the performances of State programs appear to be increasing. Moreover, some States are fearful that stricter standards will place them at a disadvantage with other States.

Many industries and businesses have made commendable progress in protecting worker health and safety on their own. Some, in fact, have managed to reduce the frequency of accidents by as much as 80 or 90 percent, demonstrating what can be accomplished with the proper effort. But such voluntary successes are not yet sufficiently widespread.

There are some other positive signs. Collective bargaining agreements often include safety and health provisions; many professional organizations have suggested voluntary standards; groups like the National Safety Council have worked to promote better working conditions. But the overall record is still uneven and unsettling.

The Federal role in occupational safety and health has thus far been limited. A few specific industries have been made subject to special Federal laws and limited regulations have been applied to workers in companies who hold certain government contracts. In my message to Congress last March on Coal Mine Safety, I outlined an important area in which further specific Federal action is imperative. But something broader is also needed, I believe. I am therefore recommending a new mechanism through which safety and health standards for industry in general can be improved.

The comprehensive Occupational Safety and Health Act which the Secretary of Labor will soon transmit to the Congress will correct some of the important deficiencies of earlier approaches. It will go beyond the limited "accident" orientation of the past, giving greater attention to health considerations, which are often difficult to perceive and which have often been overlooked. It will separate the function of setting safety and health standards from the function of enforcing them. Appropriate procedures to guarantee due process of law and the right to appeal will be incorporated. The proposal will also provide a flexible mechanism which can react quickly to the new technologies of tomorrow.

Under the suggested legislation, maximum use will be made of standards established through a voluntary consensus of industry, labor, and other experts. No standard will be set until the views of all interested parties have been heard. This proposal would also encourage stronger efforts at the State level, sharing enforcement responsibility with states which have adequate programs. Greater emphasis will also be given to research and education, for the effects of modern technologies on the physical well-being of workers are complex and poorly understood. The Public Health Service has done some important groundwork in the field of occupational health, but we still need much more information and understanding.

Our specific recommendations are as follows:

1. Safety and health standards will be set by a new National Occupational Safety and Health Board. The five members of the Board will be appointed by the President with the advice and consent of the Senate to five-year terms; one member of the Board will change each year. At least three members of the Board must

have technical competence in the field of occupational safety and health.

The Board will have the power to promulgate standards which have been established by nationally-recognized public or private standard-setting organizations. Thousands of these standards have been carefully worked out over the years; the Board will adopt such a "national consensus standard" when the standard-setting organization possesses high technical competence and considers the views of all interested parties in making its decisions.

If the Secretary of Labor (in matters of safety) or the Secretary of Health, Education and Welfare (in matters of health) objects to any such "national consensus standard," they may bring that objection before the Board. The Board can then set a new standard after giving the matter a full public hearing. When national consensus standards do not exist, the Board will have the power to break new ground after full hearings. If the Secretary of Labor or the Secretary of Health, Education and Welfare object to the Board's action, they can delay its implementation until at least three of the Board members reconfirm their original decision.

2. The Secretary of Labor will have the initial role in enforcing the standards which the Board establishes. The Secretary will ask employers whom he believes to be in violation of the standards to comply with them voluntarily; if they fail to do so, he can bring a complaint before the Occupational Safety and Health Board which will hold a full hearing on the matter. If the Board determines that a violation exists, it shall issue appropriate orders which the Secretary of Labor can then enforce through the Court system. In emergency situations, the Secretary can go directly to the courts and petition for temporary relief.

3. The State governments will be encouraged to submit plans for expanding and improving their own occupational safety and health programs. Federal grants will be available to pay up to 90 percent of the cost of developing such plans. When a State presents a plan which provides at least as much protection to the worker as the Federal plan, then the federal standard administration will give way to the State administration, with the Federal government assuming up to 50 percent of that State's costs.

4. The Secretary of Health, Education and Welfare will be given the specific assignment of developing and carrying out a broad program of study, experiment, demonstration, education, information, and technical assistance—as further means of promoting better safety and health practices in the workplace. The Secretary will be required to submit a comprehensive report to the President and the Congress, including an evaluation of the program and further recommendations for its improvement.

5. A National Advisory Committee on Occupational Safety and Health will be established to advise the Secretary of Labor and the Secretary of Health, Education, and Welfare in the administration of the Act.

Three years ago, following its study of traffic and highway safety, the Congress noted that modern technology had brought with it new driving hazards, and, accordingly, it enacted the National Traffic and Motor Vehicle Act and the Highway Safety Act. With the advent of a new workplace technology, we must now give similar attention to workplace safety and health.

The legislation which this Administration is proposing can do much to improve the environment of the American worker. But it will take much more than new government efforts if we are to achieve our objectives. Employers and employees alike must be committed to the prevention of accident and disease and alert to every opportunity for promoting that end. Together the private and public sectors can do much that we cannot do separately.

RICHARD NIXON

The White House
August 6, 1969

NOTE: The text of a news briefing on the message by James D. Hodgson, Under Secretary of Labor, and Laurence H. Silberman, Solicitor of the Department of Labor, was released on the same day by the White House Press Office.

316 Remarks of Welcome to Chancellor Kiesinger of the Federal Republic of Germany. *August 7, 1969*

Mr. Chancellor, ladies and gentlemen:

I want to take this opportunity to extend, on behalf of 200 million Americans, a very warm welcome to the Chancellor of the Federal Republic to our country, and particularly a warm welcome of the millions of Americans who are proud of their German background, including, incidentally, my wife, whose mother was born in Germany, and our two daughters, who, therefore, are one-fourth German.

Mr. Chancellor, as you come here today, this visit is tremendously significant because the discussions that now are taking place on East-West relations revolve around the problem of Europe and the heart of the problem of Europe is the Federal Republic.

I know from our previous discussions, and from my analysis of events in Europe, that your country has almost inevitably been the focus of not only discussion, but sometimes of violent attack. Sometimes, I am sure, that you and your colleagues and those who live in the Federal Republic and those who live in Berlin must think that you are somewhat lonely with all of the attacks that are made on you, at least verbally.

We just want you to know that here in the United States we proudly stand with you as friends and allies. Here in the United States we are proud to welcome you as the leader of your country to our Nation.

I know that the talks that we will have will continue—as did our talks in February, when I visited your country—to advance the cause of our mutual defense; but beyond that, to expand the great alliance, of which we are a part, into one which will deal not only with those problems that result from fear, but with the more exciting problems in which we can make progress toward the peace and the understanding in all areas which people throughout this world so deeply seek.

Finally, I would add that having come so recently from a visit to Eastern Europe, knowing, therefore, that what seems to divide Eastern Europe from Western Europe may be a barrier which seems insurmountable at times, that deep down the peoples of all of Europe—of all of the world, for that matter—are determined to be together, together in their search for peace and together in their determination to have progress.

Having seen all this, I know that the spirit of our talks and the result of our

620

talks will be most helpful, most helpful because you, coming from the Federal Republic are so keenly aware of what it means to live in a divided country.

Mr. Chancellor, finally, I simply want to say to you that I will always remember the warm welcome that we received on our visit to your country, in Bonn and Berlin. I can assure you that every place you go in the United States you will receive an equally warm welcome from all of your friends in America.

NOTE: The President spoke at 10:38 a.m. on the South Lawn at the White House where Chancellor Kurt Georg Kiesinger was given a formal welcome with full military honors.

See also Items 318, 320, and 321.

The Chancellor responded in German. A translation of his remarks follows:

Mr. President, ladies and gentlemen:

First of all, thank you very much, Mr. President, for these very kind words of welcome that you have extended to us on your own behalf and on behalf of the American people.

I, for my part, would like to extend to you the cordial and respectful greetings of the German people living in the Federal Republic of Germany, and I know that I could extend this to mean and include the entire German people.

You have mentioned, Mr. President, the ties that exist between our two nations, through the fact that many Germans have come over here to America, and in that way, Mr. President, they are participating. My two grandchildren today are citizens of the United States, and in fact, citizens of Washington, and I should like to say that they rejoice in this relationship, this direct tie that exists. We have had, several times, the opportunity of talking to each other and exchanging our views.

I am gladly remembering your stay in Bonn, when you came at the time as a private citizen, and you came to me and spoke to me about your ideas concerning the situation in the world and the situation of the United States. I must say that you spoke very clearly.

Now in these 2 past years since I have been here at this place last time, and at that time greeted by President Lyndon B. Johnson, in these 2 years a lot of things have happened in the world. You, Mr. President, have been elected President of the United States and very soon after having taken that very high office, you have come to Germany.

I will never forget the very overwhelming impression during the long drive from Tempelhof Air Field in Berlin to Charlottenburg Castle, the drive of many miles where hundreds of thousands of Berliners cheered you and expressed to you their confidence and trust in your personality and in your policy.

I was here again, for a sad occasion, participating in the funeral of that great son of the United States, President Eisenhower, and at that occasion also, we had the opportunity of exchanging views. I say a lot has happened during these 2 years. A lot has happened in the world, a lot that causes us concern in Europe, too.

I just recall the events in Czechoslovakia, and the military intervention of the Soviet Union.

We know, Mr. President, that you are undertaking every effort in order to secure peace and consolidate peace in this world. In that undertaking of yours, you enjoy the wholehearted support and sympathy of the German people and the wholehearted support of my government, any support that we are capable to give.

It is not an easy task and it is not one that one will resolve overnight. What is required is patience and that power of endurance which many people in our hectic times unfortunately no longer have. But I know that you, Mr. President, have that patience and that power.

We wish you luck, and wherever you are directing these efforts, be it in Vietnam, be it in your efforts to finding a solution to the Middle East conflict, be it in your attempt to improve the situation with Europe, you can be sure that wherever we can we will cooperate with you in these efforts.

We are looking forward to the attempts. We are closely following and sympathetically following all the attempts you are undertaking in this respect, and especially in these days when you try to get into contact with the Soviet Union in trying to improve the situation in and around Berlin and between the two parts of Germany.

Let me tell you that we are grateful to you, to the United Kingdom, and to France for taking that initiative and that we hope that that initiative will be successful. Without illusion, but with a firm determination never to slacken in our efforts toward peace in this world, we shall continue to support and join our efforts with those of your administration.

May you, the representative of the great leaders of the Western World, succeed, and as I said, we shall do our share in contributing to that. May you succeed in securing to the nations and to the world the achievement of their long aspiration to enjoy the happiness of freedom and the blessings of peace.

What human beings are capable of doing, I think, has been most strikingly demonstrated to us by Americans in these very weeks. That great event, the landing of the first human beings on the moon, has proved what humans are capable of doing. This feat should encourage us to try and join our forces, the forces of all mankind. I think if all mankind join forces we would be living the days where we would really be able to experience what the combined efforts of men of good will are capable of achieving.

Thank you again, Mr. President, for this very kind and honoring reception, and I am now looking forward to exchanging views with you.

317   Special Message to the Congress on Public Transportation.   *August 7, 1969*

To the Congress of the United States:

Public transportation has suffered from years of neglect in America. In the last 30 years urban transportation systems have experienced a cycle of increasing costs, decreasing funds for replacements, cutbacks in service and decrease in passengers.

Transit fares have almost tripled since 1945; the number of passengers has decreased to one third the level of that year. Transit industry profits before taxes have declined from $313 million in 1945 to $25 million in 1967. In recent years 235 bus and subway companies have gone out of business. The remaining transit companies have progressively deteriorated. Today they give their riders fewer runs, older cars, and less service.

Local governments, faced with demands for many pressing public services and with an inadequate financial base, have been unable to provide sufficient assistance.

This is not a problem peculiar to our largest cities alone. Indeed, many of our small and medium-sized communities have seen their bus transportation systems simply close down.

When the Nation realized the importance and need for improved highways in the last decade, the Congress responded with the Highway Act of 1956. The result has been a magnificent federally-aided highway system. But highways are only one element in a national transportation policy. About a quarter of our population lack access to a car. For these people—especially the poor, the aged, the very young and the handicapped—adequate public transportation is the only answer.

Moreover, until we make public transportation an attractive alternative to private car use, we will never be able to build highways fast enough to avoid congestion. As we survey the increasing congestion of our roads and strangulation of our central cities today, we can imagine what our plight will be when our urban population adds one hundred million people by the year 2000.

We can not meet future needs by concentrating development on just one means of transportation. We must have a truly balanced system. Only when automobile transportation is complemented by adequate public transportation can we meet those needs.

THE PUBLIC TRANSPORTATION PROGRAM

I propose that we provide $10 billion out of the general fund over a 12-year period to help in developing and improving public transportation in local communities. To establish this program, I am requesting contract authorization totaling $3.1 billion for the first five years starting with a first year authorization of $300 million and rising to $1 billion annually by 1975. Furthermore, I am asking for a renewal of this contract authorization every two years so that the outstanding contract authorization will never be for a shorter period than three years. Over the 12-year period, $9.5 billion is programmed for capital investments and $500 million for research and development.

The program which I am recommending would help to replace, improve and expand local bus, rail and subway systems. It would help to develop and modernize subway tracks, stations, and terminals; it would help to build and improve rail train tracks and stations, new bus terminals, and garages.

The program would authorize assistance to private as well as public transit systems so that private enterprise can continue to provide public services in urban transportation. It would give State governments an opportunity to comment on project applications in order to improve intergovernmental coordination. It would require local public hearings before any major capital construction is undertaken. And it would permit localities to acquire rights-of-way in advance of system construction in order to reduce future dislocation and costs.

Fares alone cannot ordinarily finance the full cost of public transit systems, including the necessary capital investments. Higher fares usually result in fewer riders, taking much of the "mass" out of mass transit and defeating the social and economic purpose of the system.

One problem with most transit systems operating today is that they rely for revenues on people who *must* use them and make no appeal to those who have a choice of using them or not. Thus we have the self-defeating cycle of fewer riders, higher fares, lower revenues, worse facilities, and still fewer riders.

The way to break that cycle is to make public transit truly attractive and convenient. In this way, more riders will provide more revenues, and fares can be kept down while further efficiencies can be introduced.

In addition to assistance for capital improvements, I am proposing substantial research and technology efforts into new ways of making public transit an attractive choice for owners of private cars. These would include:

—Advanced bus and train design to permit easier boarding and dismounting.

—Improved interiors in bus and trains for increased convenience and security for riders.

—New traffic control systems to expedite the flow of buses over streets and highways.

—Tracked air cushioned vehicles and automated transit.

—Flexible bus service based on computer-forecast demands.

—New bus propulsion systems which would reduce noise and air pollution as well as cost.

—Systems such as moving sidewalks and capsules to transport people for short distances within terminals, and other major activity.

In summary, this public transportation program I am recommending would give State and local governments the assurance of Federal commitment necessary both to carry out long-range planning and to raise their share of the costs. It would meet the challenge of providing resources that are adequate in amount and it would assure adequate duration of their availability.

The bus rider, train commuter and subway user would have better service. The car driver would travel on less congested roads. The poor would be better able to get to work, to reach new job opportu-

nities and to use training and rehabilitation centers. The centers of big cities would avoid strangulation and the suburbs would have better access to urban jobs and shops.

Most important, we as a Nation would benefit. The Nation which has sent men to the moon would demonstrate that it can meet the transportation needs of the city as well.

RICHARD NIXON

The White House

August 7, 1969

NOTE: On the same day the White House Press Office released a news briefing on the message by Dr. Daniel P. Moynihan, Assistant to the President for Urban Affairs, James M. Beggs, Under Secretary of Transportation, and Carlos Villarreal, Administrator of Urban Mass Transportation, Department of Transportation.

318 Toasts of the President and Chancellor Kiesinger of Germany. *August 7, 1969*

Mr. Chancellor and our friends:

This is for all of us a very special occasion, because it is the first visit of the Chancellor of the Federal Republic to this country since the new administration came into office.

It also, incidentally, is a first in another respect that I know the Chancellor, as a lawyer, will appreciate my mentioning. It is the first time that the new Chief Justice of the United States has ever attended a state dinner as Chief Justice. Coming, as he does, from St. Paul, with so much German-American background, I think it is altogether appropriate that this is the first dinner that he was able to attend.

Our thoughts tonight go to many things,

and above all I would say to the makeup of the company that is here to honor the Chancellor and the members of his party. I look around this room and I see two former Secretaries of State, Secretary Acheson and Secretary Rusk, and I know of their devotion to the same principle that all of us have held—the close alliance and friendship between our two countries.

I see Jack McCloy, who has served as [U.S.] High Commissioner [for Germany], and think of his service. Then, of course, I see General Lucius Clay,[1] whose name is legend still in Berlin and will always be,

---

[1] Commander in Chief of U.S. Forces in Europe and Military Governor, U.S. Occupation Zone in Germany 1947–1949.

because of what he did and what he stood for in that period.

I mention these names because they cover both political parties and they indicate something that is very deep in the American spirit, regardless of party. There is a recognition of the tremendous importance of the Federal Republic and the United States having the closest relations, the importance of our recognizing that the survival of the Federal Republic as a strong and vital country in the heart of Europe is important in the highest degree to the survival of freedom in Europe and in the world. This we know and this company knows—those who are here all share that view.

Also, from a personal standpoint, Mr. Chancellor—we welcome you here as the head of government of a great friend and ally, and we welcome you here as the leader of a great people—but from a personal standpoint, we also have other bonds. I have been delighted to have a chance to talk to your daughter [Mrs. Volkmar Wentzel], who now lives among us and to hear of your two grandchildren whom you mentioned this morning, both American citizens, which bring us to a point that we Americans all are very proud of—the great contribution that is made to the United States of America by peoples from so many countries and particularly the contribution that has been made by people of German descent.

I am reminded of that when I think of the great dinners that must have been held in this room, some of which I attended, many of which I did not. One in particular, where Winston Churchill, early in World War II in 1941 was here, honored by Franklin Roosevelt, the then President of the United States.

After the dinner he went down to speak to the Congress of the United States and he made a statement that was of great impact in that Congress and it will always be remembered. He said, "I cannot say that this is my fatherland, but this is my mother's land."

I could say that, if my wife, who has just completed a long journey with me and who stood up in the heat of Asia much better than I did, were to go and speak at the Parliament of Bonn. She could say, "This is not my fatherland, but it is my mother's land," because like so many Americans, she has that background. Her mother was German and her father was Irish and Chancellor [Konrad] Adenauer once said that that combination made the very best—right in this very room he told me that.

Well, so much for the personal references.

I would like to leave just one thought that I think is very appropriate and timely to mention on this occasion. As we speak of what this country is, our country, the United States of America, where it came from, and all of the genius that we have, to the extent we have genius, we, as Americans, all know that we came from all of the nations of the world, and that we owe something to all the peoples of the world.

I think of some of our guests tonight. I will not go into all of their national backgrounds; that would take one hundred to describe. But I think of Edward Teller [pioneer nuclear physicist] of Hungary. He was one of my first and earliest advisers in some of the very difficult problems that we confronted in the fifties.

I think of Wernher von Braun.[2] I re-

---

[2] Director, George C. Marshall Space Flight Center, Huntsville, Ala.

member the first Sputnik, when it went up, the first man who came to see me then—I was then Vice President—and talked about the challenges of space and what the United States and other countries could do, was Wernher von Braun.

There were many others who followed. But that is an indication of the broad spectrum that the United States represents and all of the genius and the ability and dedication that went into the exploration of the moon that has caught the imagination of the world. That is why, as I spoke around the world, I could truly say that we were proud of it as Americans, but we recognized that this was an accomplishment for all men; that all mankind some way was able at that particular time, at that particular place, to combine in one great venture, and in so combining to raise the sights of the world, to bring the world, in a sense, closer together.

Finally, that brings us to our two countries, what we have done, where we are and where we are going. It is essential, as we said earlier today, both in our public conversations and in our private conversations, that our two countries continue to be close friends and allies.

It is also essential for us to realize how much we can do together—the genius of the German people combined with the genius and ability of the American people—together what a tremendous power, not just for defense against any threat, a power that was set up and has been very effective over the last 20 years, but a genius which can be so effective and powerful for good, for creativity.

This is what we can think of as we look down over the next 20 years. I know that the people of your country—from my visit in February, and the exciting welcome we received every place we went, in Berlin

and Bonn and all the other places—I know that they share this view. And I know as we meet here today that everybody in this room, whether they be United States citizens or German citizens, recognizes that so much rests in our hands; that the kind of policies we develop, the firmness, the strength, the intelligence, will determine whether freedom will survive in Europe, western civilization—this great source of strength which is so important for the future of mankind.

Mr. Chancellor, we have been gratified to have had the opportunity to know you and have worked with you during your years of service, and I can only say that looking to the future we look forward to the opportunity to work with you and your colleagues, for that German-American friendship which is so essential and absolutely indispensable to the survival of peace and to the achievement of freedom with peace and justice in Europe and in the world.

So with that, I know all of you will want to rise and raise your glasses to the Chancellor of the Federal Republic and to the friendship of the people of the Federal Republic of Germany and the people of the United States.

To the Chancellor.

NOTE: The President proposed the toast at 10 p.m. in the State Dining Room at the White House.

See also Items 316, 320, and 321.

Chancellor Kiesinger responded in German, as translated by his interpreter, as follows:

Mr. President, Madam, Mr. Chief Justice, Excellencies, ladies and gentlemen:

Thank you, Mr. President. I am moved to the bottom of my heart for this fine and festive occasion that you have prepared for myself and my party. I would like to extend this heartfelt thanks also on behalf of my daughter and son-in-law, who I know particularly enjoy this event.

I remember that last time I had the opportunity of saying a few words in this room I quoted a saying by Goethe, the famous one, that runs along these lines: America, you are better off than that old and ancient Europe. And he thought in terms of the fact that we are laden with the heavy traditions while America is free and easy in choosing its path into the future, and he was right in thinking along these lines.

That was the great chance that this country had, and now look what this country has been able to make of it. I think that this is one of the greatest chapters of human history, of the history of mankind, the history of what has happened to this America and in this America since the first settlers came over from the Old World, and I know how then they were all looking toward Europe.

I also find a word by Jefferson that says: "Our difficulties are indeed great, but when viewed in comparison to those of Europe, we are like the joys of paradise." I know, Mr. President, you would not be prepared and willing any longer to apply these words to the present situation.

Nowadays, we are all living on this dwindled planet, living together, confronted with the same dangers, but also confronted with the same great opportunities that the modern world offers to us. I have been active in the political life of my country for some 20 years.

I never thought I would ever become head of government of my country and even becoming a minister was too high an aim at that time. But I remember, I don't know what made the then High Commissioner in Germany, Mr. John McCloy, one day call a number of young members of Parliament—it was then very early—as early as 1950—to come and meet him for dinner, and we were all looking at each other wondering what he had in store for us, what his intentions about us were, and those he had convened were people called Brentano, Schroder, Blank, Strauss, and I, myself, had the honor of being in that group.

I must say that somehow he gave proof of a very strong prognostic power, because afterwards we found that all of those he had invited at the time fulfilled an important task in rebuilding our country.

Now in those 20 years in which I have been active in the political life of my country there has never been any doubt in the free part of Germany, in the Federal Republic of Germany, and never any difference of opinion that the great and overwhelming majority of our people about the necessity that we have to secure peace and security and freedom in Europe in closest cooperation and friendship with these United States of America.

We all are deeply indebted to the United States for what they have done for us. Gathered in this room there are many men who have made historic contributions during those 20 years.

You, Mr. President, have mentioned some of them. I could add quite a number of names to your list, but I really would not know where to begin and where to end in quoting them. But let me tell all of them that they can be convinced that what I say is not only what Chancellor Kiesinger thinks, but it is the opinion and conviction of my people.

We believe that the wise and determined policy of these 20 years—and we have just been celebrating a few months ago the 20th anniversary of the North Atlantic Alliance and that Alliance has secured the peace and freedom of our nations and we all know that it is because of that policy that we have been successful and that is why we want also in the future to stay and stick firmly to the Alliance, an alliance as necessary today as it was when it was founded.

Now this does not mean that we should not try and find ways in which we could ease conditions, ease situations, and move towards a better peace, a peace that will be eventually durably secure. But this effort presupposes that taking the world as it is without any illusions we should, nevertheless, not renounce the hope that human beings after all are born to be reasonable and that when all is said and done human beings will be reasonable and that reason will prevail.

In all the talks I had with you, Mr. President, I felt that we were both firmly unanimous in that opinion. I have had several opportunities of meeting with you and talking with you. The first one was back in 1954 during my first visit to the United States. Then in recent years we had several other occasions and I am very glad about them and they have provided the basis of not only my confidence, but really the basis of the confidence of the entire German people, the trust in your policy, a policy under wise leadership.

We consider NATO to be more than a purely defensive alliance. We think that that alliance affords us the opportunity as free partners with the United States and together with others to jointly work towards securing peace.

Now, if we look back we find that there are many things that have happened in these very few years. Just very recently in a small and very forlorn Tyrolean village I was able to witness a great event, that fact of human beings setting foot, human beings, Americans, setting foot for the first time on the moon.

I would say it is nearly impossible to incorporate this fact into our human vision of history and nobody as yet will be able to say what this will lead to. But you, the American people, can be proud about that grand achievement and you can be sure that we all rejoice with you.

I may repeat what I said 2 days ago in New York, that the amazing precision with which this achievement was prepared and executed, this enormously complicated undertaking, fills the statesman with envy and he would only wish that these down-to-earth affairs with which we have to deal could be planned as exactly and precisely as this great achievement was. We know only too well that this is not possible

and that this world continues to be a puzzling and uncertain one, full of dangers, but also full of opportunities. And in order to take advantage of those opportunities it is absolutely necessary that we be together.

The more dangerous this world is, the less calculable this world is. The more we need to join our efforts in facing the common dangers and to join our forces to use fully the opportunities offered to us.

Mr. President, you can be sure that the German people are ready to do that. We are not only thinking in terms of our own problems, but we shall in the future have an open mind for all the problems of the world, together with you, the leader of the Western World. We are aware of our responsibilities and we know we have ourselves to contribute our share.

I am sure that if the free nations of this world stand together, that they will be eventually able to secure freedom and to secure peace and that is my wish for the American people, for the German people, for all the peoples on this earth.

It is in that spirit of gratitude and of friendship that the Chancellor raised his glass to the further consolidation over the years to come of that existing friendship and he asked his friends to drink with him to the President of the United States of America.

319   Remarks at a Surprise Celebration on the Anniversary of the President's Nomination.   *August 8, 1969*

THANK YOU very much, Mr. Chairman.

Well, I think that after the references that the chairman has very appropriately made to Mrs. Nixon, that she ought to come up here, too.

The chairman has made reference to that trip abroad, and except, of course, for Romania, we were in countries where it was very warm. As a matter of fact, when I was speaking to Prime Minister Gandhi in India, she said to me, "You came at

the wrong time of day"—we motorcaded through New Delhi at noon—"and the wrong time of year, the hottest time of year." Yet hundreds of thousands of people stood there in 115-degree heat.

Well, I just want you to know that it was easy for me because once we finished the motorcade, I went into meetings in air-conditioned rooms, and my wife, Pat, went out to the hospitals, the children's homes, and so forth, in the stifling heat. That really showed, it seems to me, that

628

the women in our family have a lot more stamina than the men in the family, because they did it.

Also, as I listened to Chairman Morton speak about how we got here, I was very interested in that letter that was written, as he said, in Les Arends' office, and that he and others signed. He said that Les wrote it. I thought I had written it. [*Laughter*]

I do want you to know, though, that as far as his speech today was concerned, his very generous remarks, I did not write that, and I am most grateful, and I am most grateful for all of you being here.

I look across this crowd. I see members of the Cabinet. I see Governors. I see people who worked in the campaign office. I just wish I could thank all of you personally again for that long year, not only the year after August 8th—what has happened in that year—but the period before.

I see a few who started in the snows of New Hampshire and went through Wisconsin, Nebraska, and Oregon, in all that primary period. I see, of course, others who were with us during those long days of the campaign.

However difficult you may think, and however much strain there is on a 9-day trip around the world to seven countries, there is nothing that equals the excitement, there is nothing that equals the satisfaction, and there is nothing, also, that equals the strain of a presidential campaign.

We went through it; we survived; we won. Now, it was close. I seem always to be involved in things that are close. But I can assure you, and I want to say something in the presence of the Members of the House and the Senate, that we won a close election. We did not win the House

or the Senate. We had a 3 to 2 majority against us in both. But since that, we haven't lost any. We have won the close ones, and we are going to continue to win the close ones, and we are going to win them even bigger in the years ahead.

Finally, if I could add simply these words, many times when some of you have been at the White House you have thanked me and you have thanked Pat, my wife, for inviting you. We just say that we want to thank you for making it possible for us to invite you to the White House.

We also want you to know that from the time of that convention, when we stood there before that huge audience and recognized that we were going to carry the banner of one of the great political parties in the campaign, through a very exciting period of traveling to States across this Nation, and now from an additionally exciting period of traveling all over this land, we are very proud that we have had the backing of such fine people.

There isn't anybody here who has asked for anything as a result of that backing. I have asked you to do things and you have done them. That is in a tradition that is at the very highest level of American political life.

I would simply say finally that, in addition to those things that Rogers Morton has mentioned, some of which we will take credit for and some of which probably will be credited to others, but however it may be, we are glad that they happened if they are for the good.

One thing that really can't be measured in words, can't be measured in programs, has happened to America and to America's position in the world that we can all be thankful for, and I don't take credit for it personally. Perhaps it is simply the fact that I was here at a time when America's position in the world was bound to change.

When we came in, America had deep problems in the world. We still have many of those problems. We are trying to solve them. But one of the problems in the world was that Americans, particularly those in leadership positions, found it difficult to go abroad—difficult without running into very serious demonstrations.

As I look at this recent trip, as I look to the visit to Manila, Djakarta, Thailand, Saigon, India, Pakistan, and then to Romania in the heart of Eastern Europe, as I look at all of Asia and to the center of Eastern Europe and think of the hundreds of thousands—yes, millions—of people that we saw, not once in that period of time was there a significant demonstration of hostility to the United States of America. This makes us very proud.

This is not just due to a man. It is not just due to a new administration. It is due to a new spirit that we may have helped to create, but also a new spirit that we are very proud to represent. We are proud to be here representing a great party, representing the United States of America at this time in history.

I can only say that on August 8th I realized we carried a great responsibility to live up to the high hopes that all of you had for us. Now we are going to continue that responsibility, to make America worthy of the trust that millions in this world have in it, millions all over the world; the trust that they have in our leadership, because without our leadership there cannot be real peace in the world, there cannot be the survival and the chance for freedom in the world; and also to make us live up to, at home, the trust

that millions here have in their leadership in the White House.

We haven't satisfied all. Some are disgruntled. Some believe we should do more. Some believe we should do less in some fields. But I can assure you we are going to do our best, and with the kind of support we have had, we are going to succeed—succeed in making all of us proud of our country and proud of our party, and of that day a year ago where it all began.

Thank you very much.

They said I should open the present. Has it been checked by the Secret Service? [*Laughter*] It is rather heavy.

That is my badge. [*Laughter and applause*]

Does that mean that I am a permanent delegate to national conventions from now on?

REPRESENTATIVE ROGERS C. B. MORTON. Yes, sir.

Mr. President, the delegate from our host State of Florida at the Miami convention also has something. I don't think you have to unwrap it.

CONGRESSMAN WILLIAM C. CRAMER. Mr. President, as chairman of the Host Committee, I want to present you a souvenir which I have been waiting for a year to do because you are the one person who didn't get one, of the thousands who were there. I am making up for it today.

Come back again.

THE PRESIDENT. Thank you. We were glad of the convention and so glad that Florida came through in 1968 as it did—also in 1960 and in 1956 and 1952.

CONGRESSMAN CRAMER. We are looking forward to the next one.

THE PRESIDENT. Thank you very much. We do appreciate your coming. Who thought of these balloons?

[*Laughter*] Ev, it is like Kankakee.[1]

Thank you very much.

NOTE: The President spoke at approximately 10:20 a.m. in the Rose Garden at the White House.

During the ceremony Representative Morton, chairman of the Republican National Committee, presented the President a clock with a 1968 convention badge and ribbon on the dial. Representative Cramer presented him with a china plate containing the Florida flag and State seal and the signatures of Governor Claude R. Kirk, Jr., of Florida, William Murfin, Florida Republican State chairman, and himself.

Introductory remarks by Chairman Morton follow:

Mr. President, distinguished Members of the Cabinet, distinguished Members of the Congress, honored guests:

A year ago today we were, most of us here, in Miami working diligently and totally for your nomination to become the Republican candidate for the Presidency of the United States.

Later that evening, our mission was accomplished, and we achieved a great goal.

This has been a very exciting year for you and for us. You have united our party as it has never been united before and, Mr. President, your actions since you have become President have continued to bring us closer together.

In November, the great hopes and dreams of the Republican Party came true as you were elected the 37th President of the United States. Your election, sir, is perhaps one of the great political achievements in the history of our country.

But I would like to pause just for a moment, if I may, in paying a special tribute to one of the principal architects of your campaign, of your great victory; a tribute to a very brilliant, a very wonderful man—our good friend, your 1968 campaign manager and now the Attorney General of the United States, John Mitchell.

---

[1] The President, directing his final remarks to Senator Everett McK. Dirksen of Illinois, was referring to some balloons released from the roof of the gallery bordering the Rose Garden just as they had been at rallies during the President's campaign in 1968.

It has been a long time since Les Arends sat down next to some of us in the House of Representatives and said, "Let's write Dick a letter. I think he ought to be President." I would like to pay my personal thanks to Les Arends, who sat down next to me and suggested that we write this letter. Les was a tireless worker, as were other Members of the Congress throughout the campaign.

Mr. President, we did share a victory of a year ago, but we also are now sharing other victories, current victories, victories of the day. The success on the extension of the surtax, the bringing of the tax reform bill to the surface and passing it through the House of Representatives is an example of the kind of victory that I am talking about.

There are many other successes and accomplishments. Your recent highly successful visit to Romania, as well as your earlier trip to Europe, accomplished a great step forward in the relations of our country with the rest of the world. Through your calm approach, through your rectitude, through your great personal example of leadership, and through your deliberate action against some of the most difficult problems of our time, you have raised the prestige of the United States throughout the world, and the feeling of well-being among its people to the highest level it has been in many years.

In Vietnam, our troops are beginning to return. You have taken courageous action to curb inflation. We have a balanced budget.

Under your leadership order is being restored, not through force and fear, but through justice and understanding. You have made great strides, Mr. President, toward the essential reorganization of the government.

Tonight you will present to the Nation your plan for a comprehensive program of redesign for a confused welfare system, for a greater utilization of the Nation's manpower, for a concept we have all long believed in, for revenue sharing with the States, for a drastic and meaningful reorganization of the Office of Economic Opportunity.

These are bold, new steps toward a new Federalism, a new participation of the people of this great country in the pluralism that is essential to our democracy. These steps will bring a life on this planet into higher order.

Personally, Mr. President, you have brought

great dignity to the Presidency. Your family, sir, is a model for the Nation. Mrs. Nixon's historic visit to Vietnam is a source of inspiration and example to the mothers and families of this great country. Your determination to be open and straightforward with the American public has established an unparalleled degree of credibility in this country.

With your life, which you are dedicating to us, your fellow Americans, there is a prime example of what man can be and what man can achieve when he has faith in God, faith in his country, and faith in the destiny of mankind.

Mr. President, those who are here commemorating your nomination in Miami, and who have made a personal commitment to the service of your administration, have been richly rewarded. It is with a great sense of pride, sir, that I have the opportunity to speak for mil-

lions of Republicans, bringing their deep appreciation to you and to Mrs. Nixon.

We look forward with confidence and excitement to the days ahead, and to the anniversary which we will celebrate here year after year through August 8, 1976.

Mr. President, I am sorry that your running mate in Miami, my former Governor and close friend, is not here. He is out working for you and for the country. But we who participated in the convention at Miami have also here a present, a token of our esteem and appreciation, to our great friend, to your able Vice President, Ted Agnew.

We give you this token of our affection and esteem from those of us who participated and those who were so excited about your nomination a year ago.

320   Joint Statement Following Discussions With Chancellor Kiesinger of Germany.   *August 8, 1969*

PRESIDENT NIXON and Chancellor Kiesinger issued the following joint statement at the conclusion of their meeting at the White House on August 8:

The President and Chancellor Kiesinger are very pleased to have had the opportunity to meet together during the past two days and to continue their personal consultations on important issues which they had begun during President Nixon's visit to Germany in February. They agreed that the meetings just concluded were extremely useful. They were characterized by an atmosphere of warm friendship and mutual confidence which is an important element in relations between the United States of America and the Federal Republic of Germany.

During their meetings President Nixon and Chancellor Kiesinger agreed on the importance of staying in close communication with one another. In order to assure that they will be able to communi-

cate rapidly in case of emergency, the President and the Chancellor have agreed to the establishment of a "hot line" between the White House and the Chancellor's office. The line will be installed as soon as technical arrangements are completed.

The Chancellor and the President exchanged views on the international situation. In particular, they discussed the full range of issues affecting relations between East and West, including prospects for strategic arms limitation talks and broadening discussions on European security. They agreed on the desirability of continuing efforts to bring existing international conflicts to a just end, to achieve progress toward disarmament and to seek to eliminate the causes of tensions in Europe. The President and the Chancellor agreed that negotiations to this end are desirable. The Chancellor welcomed the opportunity for full consultation in NATO on the strategic arms limitation talks and on issues affecting European security. The President assured the Chancellor that the United States would take full account of the interests of its Allies in the strategic arms limitation talks. They were of the opinion that progress in strategic arms limitation is interrelated with a climate favorable for dealing with long-existing European problems.

President Nixon took the opportunity during the meetings to give Chancellor Kiesinger a detailed account of the impressions he gained during his recent trip to Asia and Romania.

Chancellor Kiesinger reported on developments in Berlin and Germany which have occurred since the last meeting between the Chancellor and the President. Chancellor Kiesinger and President Nixon share the hope that the Soviet Union will respond in a constructive manner to the tripartite initiative aimed at improving the situation in and around Berlin and between the two parts of Germany. President Nixon expressed his strong support of the efforts of the Federal Republic of Germany to alleviate the hardships that result from the division of Germany.

The Chancellor and the President reaffirmed their conviction that the North Atlantic Alliance is an essential instrument in the maintenance of peace and stability in the North Atlantic area. They agreed that the proposed NATO committee on the challenges of modern society would add a new dimension to the Alliance and give it a direct part in the challenging task of marshalling resources of member nations to improve the quality of life for all people.

The President and the Chancellor welcomed the recently-concluded offset agreement between the United States and the Federal Republic which they regarded as symbolic of the determination of the two governments to cooperate in the maintenance of a sound defense posture within the necessary framework of economic stability.

The Chancellor and the President expressed satisfaction over the agreement envisioned on Special Drawing Rights which is one important step to an orderly development of the international monetary system. The President and the Chancellor are confident that agreement on SDR's will facilitate the continued advance of world trade and investment. President Nixon outlined his Government's resolve to bring inflation under control and to strengthen the position of the dollar as a world currency. In the interest of international trade and monetary developments, the Chancellor and the President agreed on the continued necessity of maintaining closest cooperation between the United States and Germany. Both opposed additional barriers to international trade.

Chancellor Kiesinger reported to the President on recent developments in the European Community and on prospects for future development. The President affirmed that the United States has consistently supported European unity, and expressed his conviction that European nations will move forward in a way which will meet their interests and at the same time contribute to an international climate of cooperation and prosperity.

On the subject of bilateral technological cooperation, the President and the Chancellor welcomed the progress made, especially in the field of space research, where the joint Project Helios is of great importance. They agreed to continue and to widen this cooperation.

The Chancellor extended the invitation to the astronauts of Apollo 11 to visit Germany as his guests in the near future.

At the conclusion of their talks the President and the Chancellor expressed their renewed conviction that the close understanding and harmony of interests between the United States and the Federal Republic provide a sound basis for continuing constructive cooperation between the two countries and, beyond that, constitute a very important element of strength in the search for the resolution of international problems and the achievement of a just and lasting peace to which both countries are dedicated.

321   Remarks on the Departure of Chancellor Kiesinger From the White House.   *August 8, 1969*

Mr. Chancellor, ladies and gentlemen:

I want to express on behalf of all of us who have had the opportunity to talk to you and your colleagues our appreciation for your making this journey and for paying us this visit.

Our talks in February in Bonn were extremely useful, and our talks here in Washington have been equally useful—even more so, because we were able to go into matters that then we could only touch upon at the beginning. We were further along and we were able to get into more depth and more detail.

As we complete these talks, I would say first that the joint statement that has been issued sets forth some of the substance. Beyond that, I would add that the bilateral relations between our two countries have never been closer. They will continue to be close, because we are friends, we are allies, and each country is proud of that alliance and of that friendship and will seek to maintain it.

However, clearly beyond our bilateral relations, we are glad that you came, because it was very valuable for me to get your views on the situation in Europe generally, and in the world. It is vitally important that we recognize that the best thinking of the world's statesmen must be applied to the terribly difficult problems we face in the world.

Finally, I would say that when I speak of our alliance, it is truly an alliance in the very best sense. It threatens no one. It is an alliance which is strong enough to defend ourselves, but also strong enough to negotiate with those who might oppose us, negotiate as freely, as candidly, as openly as we possibly can with the thought that we can reduce those tensions that divide the world; that we can bring down the barriers that divide the world and that divide Europe. This is our goal, and I believe we have made progress in achieving that goal.

Thank you.

NOTE: The President spoke at 12:13 p.m. in the Rose Garden at the White House.

See also Items 316, 318, and 321.

Chancellor Kiesinger responded in German. A translation of his remarks follows:

Mr. President, ladies and gentlemen:

May I say first that I and my countrymen who are here are deeply impressed by the cordiality and generosity of the hospitality we found here, which you gave us, and likewise deeply impressed by the results of our consultations.

I was very glad that we had no difficult bilateral problems to talk about, so we found time to cover all the field of world politics.

I must confess, Mr. President, that you, in a masterful way, portrayed this picture of world politics which impressed me deeply. It is a very sound policy. I just said to you, listening to you when you summarized the results of our discussions, that I should have wanted our people to listen, to be able to listen to you, because I am quite sure that that would have been most valuable because they would have seen

that the leading power of the West is led by a statesman of clear and realistic outlook.

I am glad to say that I fully agree with what you said in our talks, and that is not only a polite formula. I am quite sure that this visit will contribute to strengthening the bonds of friendship and cooperation between our two countries, within NATO and outside NATO.

I wish you full success, Mr. President, in whatever you have started to do. Thank you.

322   Memorandum on Equal Employment Opportunity in the Federal Government.   *August 8, 1969*

Memorandum for Heads of Departments and Agencies:

In my memorandum to you of March 28, 1969, I reaffirmed the Government's policy of providing equality of opportunity for all citizens in Federal employment. At the same time I directed the Chairman of the Civil Service Commission to review present efforts in the Government to achieve equal employment opportunity and give me recommendations for desirable policy and program changes.

The Civil Service Commission has given me its report. Because I believe the report and its recommendations are of vital importance to the Government, I am attaching a copy for your personal review. I completely endorse the new program directions which it outlines, and I look for positive results from these new efforts.

No more serious task challenges our nation domestically than the achievement of equality of opportunity for all our citizens in every aspect of their lives regardless of their race, color, religion, national origin or sex. This includes the opportunity for all persons with full recognition of their dignity as individuals, to seek and to achieve their highest potential and pro-

ductivity in employment situations. Discrimination of any kind based on factors not relevant to job performance must be eradicated completely from Federal employment. In addition, we must, through positive action, make it possible for our citizens to compete on a truly equal and fair basis for employment and to qualify for advancement within the Federal service. We must search for new ways to provide the necessary encouragement, assistance and training opportunities, where appropriate, so that all employees may utilize their capabilities to the fullest extent in meeting the manpower needs of Federal agencies.

There are several points in Chairman Hampton's report which I want to emphasize:

—Assuring equal employment opportunity in a Federal department or agency is the responsibility of the organization's head. It must have his continuing high priority attention and that of all agency executives.

—Equal employment opportunity must become an integral part of the day-to-day management of Federal agencies and interwoven with every action which has an effect on employees. This is the road to true equal employment opportunity.

—While we must continue to search out qualified personnel from all segments of our population, we must now assure the best possible utilization of the skills and potential of the present work force. Employees should have the opportunity to the fullest extent practicable to improve their skills so they may qualify for advancement. Those who have potential to serve at the supervisory level and above should be identified and given the opportunity to develop to their fullest capability. Programs are underway and new efforts are being developed to achieve this end.

—Special efforts must be made to assure that opportunities in the Federal Government at the professional levels are made known to men and women of all races, religions and ethnic backgrounds so that positions of leadership in the future can be assumed by persons from all segments of our population.

—Every possible step must be taken by agency heads to make sure that each manager and supervisor in the Government understands and implements the objective of equal employment opportunity for all Americans. Our supervisors' performance must in every way support equality of opportunity for all employees.

—In addition to assuring equal employment opportunity for all persons, the Government, as a responsible employer, must do its part along with other employers to provide special employment and training programs to those who are economically or educationally disadvantaged. We must hold out a helping hand and imaginatively use the facilities of the Government to prepare such persons for useful and productive employment.

I have asked the Civil Service Commission to work closely with agencies and other interested organizations in the implementation of these program directions and to keep me informed of progress. Interagency consultation and coordination will hasten our progress and assure common understanding of our goals and the Commission will have the direct support of my staff in this effort. I request that you and your staffs cooperate fully in this urgent undertaking and move forward energetically in the direction outlined in the Civil Service Commission's report.

At the same time, I have issued a new Executive Order [11478] on equal employment opportunity in the Federal Government. This Order clearly states the policy of this Administration in this critical area and demonstrates the continuing Federal commitment to equal employment opportunity.

I look forward to receiving the Commission's progress reports on a regular basis. They will have my personal attention.

I suggest that every supervisor have an opportunity to see this memorandum.

RICHARD NIXON

NOTE: The memorandum report to the President from Civil Service Commission Chairman Robert E. Hampton is printed in the Weekly Compilation of Presidential Documents (vol. 5, p. 1100).

323   Statement on the Tax Reform Bill Following Passage
      by the House of Representatives.   *August* 8, 1969

IN MY MESSAGE to Congress on April 21, I stated that "we shall never make taxation popular, but we can make taxation fair."

The tax reform bill just passed by the House of Representatives is a long step in that direction. Not only did the House adopt, in essence, the administration's proposed minimum income tax and low income allowance, but it also added many constructive reforms to the 16 we proposed initially.

I am much aware of the many hours of cooperative labor that went into the preparation of this bill. To me this is further proof that the administration and the Congress, even in a time of politically divided government, can work constructively together to advance the national interest.

While the administration will have some suggestions in the Senate on certain specifics of this bill, I strongly endorse its passage by the House and commend the principal architects of the bill on the House Ways and Means Committee.

324   Address to the Nation on Domestic Programs.
      August 8, 1969

Good evening my fellow Americans:

As you know, I returned last Sunday night from a trip around the world—a trip that took me to eight countries in 9 days.

The purpose of this trip was to help lay the basis for a lasting peace, once the war in Vietnam is ended. In the course of it, I also saw once again the vigorous efforts so many new nations are making to leap the centuries into the modern world.

Every time I return to the United States after such a trip, I realize how fortunate we are to live in this rich land. We have the world's most advanced industrial economy, the greatest wealth ever known to man, the fullest measure of freedom ever enjoyed by any people, anywhere.

Yet we, too, have an urgent need to modernize our institutions—and our need is no less than theirs.

We face an urban crisis, a social crisis—and at the same time, a crisis of confidence in the capacity of government to do its job.

A third of a century of centralizing power and responsibility in Washington has produced a bureaucratic monstrosity, cumbersome, unresponsive, ineffective.

A third of a century of social experiment has left us a legacy of entrenched programs that have outlived their time or outgrown their purposes.

A third of a century of unprecedented growth and change has strained our institutions, and raised serious questions about whether they are still adequate to the times.

It is no accident, therefore, that we find increasing skepticism—and not only among our young people, but among citizens everywhere—about the continuing capacity of government to master the challenges we face.

Nowhere has the failure of government been more tragically apparent than in its efforts to help the poor and especially in its system of public welfare.

TARGET: REFORMS

Since taking office, one of my first priorities has been to repair the machinery of government, to put it in shape for the 1970's. I have made many changes designed to improve the functioning of the executive branch. And I have asked Congress for a number of important structural reforms; among others, a wide-ranging postal reform, a comprehensive reform of the draft, a reform of unemployment insurance, a reform of our hunger programs, a reform of the present confusing hodge-podge of Federal grants-in-aid.

Last April 21, I sent Congress a message asking for a package of major tax reforms, including both the closing of loopholes and the removal of more than 2 million low-income families from the tax rolls altogether. I am glad that Congress is now acting on tax reform, and I hope the Congress will begin to act on the other reforms that I have requested.

The purpose of all these reforms is to eliminate unfairness; to make government more effective as well as more efficient; and to bring an end to its chronic failure to deliver the service that it promises.

My purpose tonight, however, is not to review the past record, but to present a new set of reforms—a new set of proposals—a new and drastically different approach to the way in which government cares for those in need, and to the way the responsibilities are shared between the State and the Federal Government.

I have chosen to do so in a direct report to the people because these proposals call for public decisions of the first importance; because they represent a funda-

mental change in the Nation's approach to one of its most pressing social problems; and because, quite deliberately, they also represent the first major reversal of the trend toward ever more centralization of government in Washington, D.C. After a third of a century of power flowing from the people and the States to Washington it is time for a New Federalism in which power, funds, and responsibility will flow from Washington to the States and to the people.

During last year's election campaign, I often made a point that touched a responsive chord wherever I traveled.

I said that this Nation became great not because of what government did for people, but because of what people did for themselves.

This new approach aims at helping the American people do more for themselves. It aims at getting everyone able to work off welfare rolls and onto payrolls.

It aims at ending the unfairness in a system that has become unfair to the welfare recipient, unfair to the working poor, and unfair to the taxpayer.

This new approach aims to make it possible for people—wherever in America they live—to receive their fair share of opportunity. It aims to ensure that people receiving aid, and who are able to work, contribute their fair share of productivity.

This new approach is embodied in a package of four measures: First, a complete replacement of the present welfare system; second, a comprehensive new job training and placement program; third, a revamping of the Office of Economic Opportunity; and fourth, a start on the sharing of Federal tax revenues with the States.

Next week—in three messages to the Congress and one statement—I will spell out in detail what these measures contain. Tonight I want to explain what they mean, what they are intended to achieve, and how they are related.

WELFARE

Whether measured by the anguish of the poor themselves, or by the drastically mounting burden on the taxpayer, the present welfare system has to be judged a colossal failure.

Our States and cities find themselves sinking in a welfare quagmire, as caseloads increase, as costs escalate, and as the welfare system stagnates enterprise and perpetuates dependency.

What began on a small scale in the depression 30's has become a huge monster in the prosperous 60's. And the tragedy is not only that it is bringing States and cities to the brink of financial disaster, but also that it is failing to meet the elementary human, social, and financial needs of the poor.

It breaks up homes. It often penalizes work. It robs recipients of dignity. And it grows.

Benefit levels are grossly unequal—for a mother with three children, they range from an average of $263 a month in one State, down to an average of only $39 in another State. Now such an inequality as this is wrong; no child is "worth" more in one State than in another State. One result of this inequality is to lure thousands more into already overcrowded inner cities, as unprepared for city life as they are for city jobs.

The present system creates an incentive for desertion. In most States a family is denied welfare payments if a father is present—even though he is unable to support his family. Now, in practice, this is what often happens: A father is unable to find a job at all or one that will support his children. And so, to make the children eligible for welfare, he leaves home—and the children are denied the authority, the discipline, the love that come with having a father in the home. This is wrong.

The present system often makes it possible to receive more money on welfare than on a low-paying job. This creates an incentive not to work, and it also is unfair to the working poor. It is morally wrong for a family that is working to try to make ends meet to receive less than a family across the street on welfare. This has been bitterly resented by the man who works, and rightly so—the rewards are just the opposite of what they should be. Its effect is to draw people off payrolls and onto welfare rolls—just the opposite of what government should be doing. To put it bluntly and simply—any system which makes it more profitable for a man not to work than to work, or which encourages a man to desert his family rather than to stay with his family, is wrong and indefensible.

We cannot simply ignore the failures of welfare, or expect them to go away. In the past 8 years, 3 million more people have been added to the welfare rolls—and this in a period of low unemployment. If the present trend continues, another 4 million will join the welfare rolls by 1975. The financial cost will be crushing; and the human cost will be suffocating.

That is why tonight I, therefore, propose that we will abolish the present welfare system and that we adopt in its place a new family assistance system. Initially, this new system will cost more than welfare. But, unlike welfare, it is designed to correct the condition it deals with and, thus, to lessen the long-range burden and cost.

Under this plan, the so-called "adult categories" of aid—aid to the aged, the blind, the disabled—would be continued, and a national minimum standard for benefits would be set, with the Federal Government contributing to its cost and also sharing the cost of additional State payments above that amount.

But the program now called "Aid to Families with Dependent Children"—the program we all normally think of when we think of "welfare"—would be done away with completely. The new family assistance system I propose in its place rests essentially on these three principles: equality of treatment across the Nation, a work requirement, and a work incentive.

Its benefits would go to the working poor, as well as the nonworking; to families with dependent children headed by a father, as well as to those headed by a mother; and a basic Federal minimum would be provided, the same in every State.

What I am proposing is that the Federal Government build a foundation under the income of every American family with dependent children that cannot care for itself—and wherever in America that family may live.

For a family of four now on welfare, with no outside income, the basic Federal payment would be $1,600 a year. States could add to that amount and most States would add to it. In no case would anyone's present level of benefits be lowered. At the same time, this foundation would be one on which the family itself could build. Outside earnings would be encouraged, not discouraged. The new worker could keep the first $60 a month

of outside earnings with no reduction in his benefits; and beyond that, his benefits would be reduced by only 50 cents for each dollar earned.

By the same token, a family head already employed at low wages could get a family assistance supplement; those who work would no longer be discriminated against. For example, a family of five in which the father earns $2,000 a year—which is the hard fact of life for many families in America today—would get family assistance payments of $1,260, so that they would have a total income of $3,260. A family of seven earning $3,000 a year would have its income raised to $4,360.

Thus, for the first time, the government would recognize that it has no less an obligation to the working poor than to the nonworking poor; and for the first time, benefits would be scaled in such a way that it would always pay to work.

With such incentives, most recipients who can work will want to work. This is part of the American character.

But what of the others—those who can work but choose not to?

Well, the answer is very simple.

Under this proposal, everyone who accepts benefits must also accept work or training provided suitable jobs are available either locally or at some distance if transportation is provided. The only exceptions would be those unable to work and mothers of preschool children.

Even mothers of preschool children, however, would have the opportunity to work, because I am also proposing along with this a major expansion of day-care centers to make it possible for mothers to take jobs by which they can support themselves and their children.

This national floor under incomes for

working or dependent families is not a "guaranteed income." Under the guaranteed income proposal, everyone would be assured a minimum income, regardless of how much he was capable of earning, regardless of what his need was, regardless of whether or not he was willing to work.

Now, during the presidential campaign last year, I opposed such a plan. I oppose it now and I will continue to oppose it, and this is the reason: A guaranteed income would undermine the incentive to work; the family assistance plan that I propose increases the incentive to work.

A guaranteed income establishes a right without any responsibilities; family assistance recognizes a need and establishes a responsibility. It provides help to those in need and, in turn, requires that those who receive help work to the extent of their capabilities. There is no reason why one person should be taxed so that another can choose to live idly.

In States that now have benefit levels above the Federal floor, family assistance would help ease the State's financial burdens. But in 20 States—those in which poverty is most widespread—the new Federal floor would be above present average benefits and would mean a leap upward for many thousands of families that cannot care for themselves.

MANPOWER TRAINING

Now I would like to turn to the job training proposals that are part of our full opportunity concept. America prides itself on being a "land of opportunity." I deeply believe in this ideal, as I am sure everyone listening to me also believes in this ideal.

Full opportunity means the chance for upward mobility on every rung of the economic ladder—and for every American,

no matter what the handicaps of birth.

The cold, hard truth is that a child born to a poor family has far less chance to make a good living than a child born to a middle-income family.

He is born poor; he is fed poorly; and if his family is on welfare, he starts life in an atmosphere of handout and dependency; often he receives little preparation for work and less inspiration. The wonder of the American character is that so many have the spark and the drive to fight their way up. But for millions of others, the burdens of poverty in early life snuff out that spark.

The new family assistance would provide aid for needy families. It would establish a work requirement and a work incentive, but these in turn require effective programs of job training and job placement—including a chance to qualify not just for any jobs, but for good jobs, that provide both additional self-respect and full self-support.

Therefore, I am also sending a message to Congress calling for a complete overhaul of the Nation's manpower training services.

The Federal Government's job training programs have been a terrible tangle of confusion and waste.

To remedy the confusion, arbitrariness, and rigidity of the present system, the new Manpower Training Act would basically do three things.

—It would pull together the jumble of programs that presently exist, and equalize standards of eligibility.

—It would provide flexible funding—so that Federal money would follow the demands of labor and industry, and flow into those programs that people most want and most need.

—It would decentralize administration,

gradually moving it away from the Washington bureaucracy and turning it over to States and localities.

In terms of its symbolic importance, I can hardly overemphasize this last point. For the first time, applying the principles of the New Federalism, administration of a major established Federal program would be turned over to the States and local governments, recognizing that they are in a position to do the job better.

For years, thoughtful Americans have talked of the need to decentralize Government. The time has come to begin.

Federal job training programs have grown to vast proportions, costing more than a billion dollars a year. Yet they are essentially local in character. As long as the Federal Government continues to bear the cost, they can perfectly well be run by States and local governments, and that way they can be better adapted to specific State and local needs.

The Manpower Training Act will have other provisions specifically designed to help move people off welfare rolls and onto payrolls:

—A computerized job bank would be established to match job seekers with job vacancies.

—For those on welfare, a $30 a month bonus would be offered as an incentive to go into job training.

—For heads of families now on welfare, 150,000 new training slots would be opened.

—As I mentioned previously, greatly expanded day-care center facilities would be provided for the children of welfare mothers who choose to work. However, these would be day-care centers with a difference. There is no single ideal to which this administration is more firmly commit-

ted than to the enriching of a child's first 5 years of life, and thus, helping lift the poor out of misery at a time when a lift can help the most. Therefore, these day-care centers would offer more than custodial care; they would also be devoted to the development of vigorous young minds and bodies. As a further dividend, the day-care centers would offer employment to many welfare mothers themselves.

OFFICE OF ECONOMIC OPPORTUNITY

One common theme running through my proposals tonight is that of providing full opportunity for every American. A second theme is that of trying to equip every American to play a productive role and a third is the need to make Government itself workable—which means reshaping, reforming, innovating.

The Office of Economic Opportunity is basically an innovative agency, and thus it has a vital place in our efforts to develop new programs and apply new knowledge. But in order to do so effectively what it can do best, OEO itself needs reorganization.

This administration has completed a thorough study of OEO. We have assigned it a leading role in the effort to develop and test new approaches to the solving of social problems. OEO is to be a laboratory agency where new ideas for helping people are tried on a pilot basis. When they prove successful, they can be spun off to operating departments or agencies—just as the space agency, for example, spun off the weather satellite and the communications satellite when these proved successful. Then OEO will be free to concentrate on breaking even newer ground.

The OEO reorganization to be announced next week will stress this innovative role. It also will stress accountability, a clear separation of functions, and a tighter more effective organization of field operations.

REVENUE SHARING

We come now to a proposal which I consider profoundly important to the future of our Federal system of shared responsibilities. When we speak of poverty or jobs or opportunity or making government more effective or getting it closer to the people, it brings us directly to the financial plight of our States and cities.

We can no longer have effective government at any level unless we have it at all levels. There is too much to be done for the cities to do it alone, for Washington to do it alone, or for the States to do it alone.

For a third of a century, power and responsibility have flowed toward Washington, and Washington has taken for its own the best sources of revenue.

We intend to reverse this tide, and to turn back to the States a greater measure of responsibility—not as a way of avoiding problems, but as a better way of solving problems.

Along with this would go a share of Federal revenues. I shall propose to the Congress next week that a set portion of the revenues from Federal income taxes be remitted directly to the States, with a minimum of Federal restrictions on how those dollars are to be used, and with a requirement that a percentage of them be channeled through for the use of local governments.

The funds provided under this program will not be great in the first year. But the principle will have been established, and the amounts will increase as our budgetary situation improves.

This start on revenue sharing is a step toward what I call the New Federalism. It is a gesture of faith in America's State and local governments and in the principle of democratic self-government.

With this revenue sharing proposal we follow through on a commitment I made in the last campaign. We follow through on a mandate which the electorate gave us last November.

In recent years, we all have concentrated a great deal of attention on what we commonly call the "crisis of the cities." These proposals I have made are addressed in part to that, but they also are focused much more broadly.

They are addressed to the crisis of government—to adapting its structures and making it manageable.

They are addressed to the crisis of poverty and need, which is rural as well as urban. This administration is committed to full opportunity on the farm as well as in the city; to a better life for rural America; to ensuring that government is responsive to the needs of rural America as well as urban America. These proposals will advance these goals.

I have discussed these four matters together because together they make both a package and a pattern. They should be studied together, debated together, and seen in perspective.

Now these proposals will be controversial, just as any new program is controversial. They also are expensive. Let us face that fact frankly and directly.

The first-year costs of the new family assistance program, including the child care centers and job training, would be

643

$4 billion. I deliberated long and hard over whether we could afford such an outlay. I decided in favor of it for two reasons: First, because the costs will not begin until fiscal year 1971, when I expect the funds to be available within the budget; and second, because I concluded that this is a reform we cannot afford not to undertake. The cost of continuing the present system, in financial as well as human terms, is staggering if projected into the 1970's.

Revenue sharing would begin in the middle of fiscal 1971, at a half-year cost of a half billion dollars. This cuts into the Federal budget, but it represents relief for the equally hard-pressed States. It would help curb the rise in State and local taxes which are such a burden to millions of American families.

Overall, we would be spending more—in the short run—to help people who now are poor and who now are unready for work or unable to find work.

But I see it this way: Every businessman, every workingman knows what "start-up costs" are. They are a heavy investment made in early years in the expectation that they will more than pay for themselves in future years.

The investment in these proposals is a human investment; it also is a "start-up cost" in turning around our dangerous decline into welfarism in America. We cannot produce productive people with the antiquated, wheezing, overloaded machine we now call the welfare system.

If we fail to make this investment in work incentives now, if we merely try to patch up the system here and there, we will only be pouring good money after bad in ever-increasing amounts.

If we do invest in this modernization, the heavily burdened taxpayer at least will

have the chance to see the end of the tunnel. And the man who now only looks ahead only to a lifetime of dependency will see hope—hope for a life of work and pride and dignity.

In the final analysis, we cannot talk our way out of poverty; we cannot legislate our way out of poverty; but this Nation can work its way out of poverty. What America needs now is not more welfare, but more "workfare."

The task of this Government, the great task of our people, is to provide the training for work, the incentive to work, the opportunity to work, and the reward for work. Together these measures are a first long step in that direction.

For those in the welfare system today who are struggling to fight their way out of poverty, these measures offer a way to independence through the dignity of work.

For those able to work, these measures provide new opportunities to learn work, to find work.

For the working poor—the forgotten poor—these measures offer a fair share in the assistance given to the poor.

This new system establishes a direct link between the Government's willingness to help the needy and the willingness of the needy to help themselves.

It removes the present incentive not to work and substitutes an incentive to work; it removes the present incentive for families to break apart and substitutes an incentive for families to stay together.

It removes the blatant inequities and injustices and indignities of the welfare system.

It establishes a basic Federal floor so that children in any State can have at least the minimum essentials of life.

Together, these measures cushion the

impact of welfare costs on States and localities, many of which have found themselves in fiscal crisis as costs have escalated.

They bring reason, order, and purpose into a tangle of overlapping programs, and show that Government can be made to work.

Poverty will not be defeated by a stroke of a pen signing a check, and it will not be reduced to nothing overnight with slogans or ringing exhortations.

Poverty is not only a state of income. It is also a state of mind, a state of health. Poverty must be conquered without sacrificing the will to work, for if we take the route of the permanent handout, the American character will itself be impoverished.

In my recent trip around the world, I visited countries in all stages of economic development; countries with different social systems, different economic systems, different political systems.

In all of them, however, I found that one event had caught the imagination of the people and lifted their spirits almost beyond measure: the trip of Apollo 11 to the moon and back. On that historic day, when the astronauts set foot on the moon, the spirit of Apollo truly swept through this world. It was a spirit of peace and brotherhood and adventure, a spirit that thrilled to the knowledge that man had dreamed the impossible, dared the impossible, and done the impossible.

Abolishing poverty, putting an end to dependency—like reaching the moon a generation ago—may seem to be impossible. But in the spirit of Apollo, we can lift our sights and marshal our best efforts. We can resolve to make this the year not that we reached the goal, but that we turned the corner—turned the corner from a dismal cycle of dependency toward a new birth of independence; from despair toward hope; from an ominously mounting impotence of government toward a new effectiveness of government, and toward a full opportunity for every American to share the bounty of this rich land.

Thank you and goodnight.

NOTE: The President delivered the address on nationwide radio and television at 10 p.m.

The advance text of the President's address is printed in the Weekly Compilation of Presidential Documents (vol. 5, p. 1103).

325 Statement on Announcing the Nomination of Mrs. Helen D. Bentley as a Member of the Federal Maritime Commission. *August 9, 1969*

IN NOMINATING Helen Bentley as a member of the Federal Maritime Commission, I am conscious of the fact that in one way at least, this nomination is unique.

Mrs. Bentley has earned a very strong position for herself in what most of us would feel to be "a man's world"—the world of maritime affairs. As maritime editor of the Baltimore Sun, she has won the respect of all segments, labor and management alike, in this field and has established a record of professional excellence unsurpassed by any maritime expert in the country.

Although we are at the beginning of the age of space, it is good to be reminded that the United States is a sea power, a nation that has grown and prospered over the years because of our maritime trade with every corner of the earth and because our ports have been recognized as some of the best in the world.

Helen Bentley knows the world of maritime trade. She has not only reported it from a desk at the Baltimore Sun, she has traveled all over the world to the great seaports, she has sailed on ships and learned much of their operations at first hand. She knows that maritime trade, which has played such an important part in the development of civilization in ages past, is still an important area today.

She knows—perhaps better than anyone else—the complex and profoundly important world of the sea and its influence on the strength and growth of our Nation.

Although Mrs. Bentley is well aware that she is being nominated to this post solely on her very considerable merits as a maritime expert, it would be less than candid of me not to say how gratified I am to be able to nominate a woman to such an important position.

There was once a time when, I suppose, there was a bit of condescension involved in appointing a woman to an important position. That day is gone. Mrs. Bentley is

representative of the extremely well-qualified women we have been able to bring into Government service. As a knowledgeable lady in a man's world, she has gained a reputation for being the best there is. That, in the long run, is what we are looking for in any position, and I am doubly glad that in Mrs. Bentley we find that the best there is also just happens to be a charming and wonderful lady.

And now I would like to add one important point: Upon Mrs. Bentley's confirmation by the Senate, it is my intention to designate her as Chairman of the Maritime Commission.

NOTE: Mrs. Bentley was confirmed by the Senate as a member of the Commission on October 3, 1969. On October 6 she was designated by the President as Chairman of the Commission, and the oath of office was officially administered to her by Commission Secretary Thomas Lisi on October 10. On October 27 Mrs. Bentley was ceremonially sworn in by Vice President Spiro T. Agnew.

A White House announcement, released with the President's statement, contains biographical details concerning Mrs. Bentley. It is printed in the Weekly Compilation of Presidential Documents (vol. 5, p. 1113).

326 Remarks on Arrival at the Orange County Airport, Santa Ana, California. *August 9, 1969*

WE WANT to thank all of you for giving us such a wonderful welcome home to California and to my home county, Orange County.

I am sure you have noted that we have been traveling a bit lately, and we have had some wonderful welcomes all around the world—in the Philippines, in Guam, in Djakarta, Indonesia, in Thailand, in India, in Pakistan, and then in Bucharest, Romania, then in England, and, finally, in Washington, D.C.

But I can tell you that however great they were, there is nothing like coming home and being welcomed by a group of friends from California.

I want you to know, too, that I heard about the little debate that developed over whether or not this plane could land at the Orange County Airport. I have had to make quite a few decisions in the last few days. This was one of the toughest.

The pilot came in and said, "No plane of this size has ever landed at the Orange

County Airport. Do you want to try?"

I thought about it and I said, "Well, if Neil Armstrong could land on the Sea of Tranquility, we will take Air Force One into Orange County Airport."

I also want you to know that during the month—it will be not quite a month—we will be here, we will be having Cabinet meetings, and a number of people from all over the country will be coming to San Clemente and to Orange County. We know they will get the same warm welcome that you have given us.

Of all of the things that have happened since we have had the high privilege of being in Washington, D.C., in the White House, I can tell you that to bring the summer White House back to my home county, that is one of the finest things of all.

Thank you very much.

I have been trying to find a couple of others.

We brought George Murphy with us. Where is he? Senator Murphy. We can't find him. He is out campaigning right over there.

And how about Congressman Utt? He is with us here, too.

And, also, the Attorney General of the United States, Attorney General Mitchell, is with us. Come here, Mr. Attorney General.

I think you should know that one of the announcements we will be making this week will be the announcement of another

Justice of the Supreme Court. There are only two people in the United States who know at this time who that man is going to be. The Attorney General is one. I will let you guess as to who the other is. [*Laughter*]

I think you should know that when the Attorney General came in on the plane today with his daughter and wife, I asked them what they wanted to do. We were chatting a bit about it. The Attorney General says he understands people in Orange County are for law and order. He is, too. [*Laughter*]

Here is Marty and Mrs. Mitchell.

So I asked her what she wanted to do. You know what? She has grown up in New York, and she has been to Florida, and she has never been to California. And, most important, she has never been to Disneyland, and she is going.

And we are glad to have the Disneyland Band and the Santa Ana High School Band. We certainly appreciated their coming out here today.

Incidentally, if you want to ask what I am going to be doing, I am going to be walking the beach during those times that we are not working. But if somebody wants to borrow a surfboard, I have got a good one. [*Laughter*]

NOTE: The President spoke at 4:45 p.m. at the Orange County Airport in Santa Ana, Calif.

A description of the President's residence in San Clemente, Calif., was released by the White House on August 11, 1969.

327   Special Message to the Congress on Reform of the Nation's Welfare System.   *August* 11, 1969

To the Congress of the United States:

A measure of the greatness of a powerful nation is the character of the life it creates for those who are powerless to make ends meet.

If we do not find the way to become a

working nation that properly cares for the dependent, we shall become a Welfare State that undermines the incentive of the working man.

The present welfare system has failed us—it has fostered family breakup, has provided very little help in many States and has even deepened dependency by all-too-often making it more attractive to go on welfare than to go to work.

I propose a new approach that will make it more attractive to go to work than to go on welfare, and will establish a nationwide minimum payment to dependent families with children.

I propose that the Federal government pay a basic income to those American families who cannot care for themselves in whichever State they live.

I propose that dependent families receiving such income be given good reason to go to work *by making the first sixty dollars a month they earn completely their own, with no deductions from their benefits.*

I propose that we *make available an addition to the incomes of the "working poor,"* to encourage them to go on working and to eliminate the possibility of making more from welfare than from wages.

I propose that these payments be made upon certification of income, with demeaning and costly investigations replaced by simplified reviews and spot checks and with *no eligibility requirement that the household be without a father.* That present requirement in many States has the effect of breaking up families and contributes to delinquency and violence.

I propose that all employable persons who choose to accept these payments be required to register for work or job training and *be required to accept that work*

or *training,* provided suitable jobs are available either locally or if transportation is provided. Adequate and convenient day care would be provided children wherever necessary to enable a parent to train or work. The only exception to this work requirement would be mothers of pre-school children.

I propose *a major expansion of job training and day care facilities,* so that current welfare recipients able to work can be set on the road to self-reliance.

I propose that we also *provide uniform Federal payment minimums for the present three categories of welfare aid to adults*—the aged, the blind and the disabled.

This would be total welfare reform—the transformation of a system frozen in failure and frustration into a system that would work and would encourage people to work.

Accordingly, we have stopped considering human welfare in isolation. The new plan is part of an overall approach which includes a comprehensive new Manpower Training Act, and a plan for a system of revenue sharing with the States to help provide all of them with necessary budget relief. Messages on manpower training and revenue sharing will follow this message tomorrow and the next day, and the three should be considered as parts of a whole approach to what is clearly a national problem.

NEED FOR NEW DEPARTURES

A welfare system is a success when it takes care of people who cannot take care of themselves and when it helps employable people climb toward independence.

A welfare system is a failure when it takes care of those who *can* take care of themselves, when it drastically varies payments in different areas, when it breaks up families, when it perpetuates a vicious cycle of dependency, when it strips human beings of their dignity.

America's welfare system is a failure that grows worse every day.

First, it fails the recipient: In many areas, benefits are so low that we have hardly begun to take care of the dependent. And there has been no light at the end of poverty's tunnel. After four years of inflation, the poor have generally become poorer.

Second, it fails the taxpayer: Since 1960, welfare costs have doubled and the number on the rolls has risen from 5.8 million to over 9 million, all in a time when unemployment was low. The taxpayer is entitled to expect government to devise a system that will help people lift themselves out of poverty.

Finally, it fails American society: By breaking up homes, the present welfare system has added to social unrest and robbed millions of children of the joy of childhood; by widely varying payments among regions, it has helped to draw millions into the slums of our cities.

The situation has become intolerable. Let us examine the alternatives available:

—We could permit the welfare momentum to continue to gather speed by our inertia; by 1975 this would result in 4 million more Americans on welfare rolls at a cost of close to 11 billion dollars a year, with both recipients and taxpayers shortchanged.

—We could tinker with the system as it is, adding to the patchwork of modifications and exceptions. That has been the approach of the past, and it has failed.

—We could adopt a "guaranteed mini-

mum income for everyone," which would appear to wipe out poverty overnight. It would also wipe out the basic economic motivation for work, and place an enormous strain on the industrious to pay for the leisure of the lazy.

—Or, we could adopt a totally new approach to welfare, designed to assist those left far behind the national norm, and provide all with the motivation to work and a fair share of the opportunity to train.

This Administration, after a careful analysis of all the alternatives, is committed to a new departure that will find a solution for the welfare problem. The time for denouncing the old is over; the time for devising the new is now.

RECOGNIZING THE PRACTICALITIES

People usually follow their self-interest.

This stark fact is distressing to many social planners who like to look at problems from the top down. Let us abandon the ivory tower and consider the real world in all we do.

In most States, welfare is provided only when there is no father at home to provide support. If a man's children would be better off on welfare than with the low wage he is able to bring home, wouldn't he be tempted to leave home?

If a person spent a great deal of time and effort to get on the welfare rolls, wouldn't he think twice about risking his eligibility by taking a job that might not last long?

In each case, welfare policy was intended to limit the spread of dependency; in practice, however, the effect has been to increase dependency and remove the incentive to work.

We fully expect people to follow their

self-interest in their business dealings; why should we be surprised when people follow their self-interest in their welfare dealings? That is why we propose a plan in which it is in the interest of every employable person to do his fair share of work.

THE OPERATION OF THE NEW APPROACH

1. *We would assure an income foundation throughout every section of America for all parents who cannot adequately support themselves and their children.* For a family of four with less than $1,000 income, this payment would be $1600 a year; for a family of four with $2,000 income, this payment would supplement that income by $960 a year.

Under the present welfare system, each State provides "Aid to Families with Dependent Children," a program we propose to replace. The Federal government shares the cost, but each State establishes key eligibility rules and determines how much income support will be provided to poor families. The result has been an uneven and unequal system. The 1969 benefits average for a family of four is $171 a month across the Nation, but individual State averages range from $263 down to $39 a month.

A new Federal minimum of $1600 a year cannot claim to provide comfort to a family of four, but the present low of $468 a year cannot claim to provide even the basic necessities.

The new system would do away with the inequity of very low benefit levels in some States, and of State-by-State variations in eligibility tests, by establishing a Federally-financed income floor with a national definition of basic eligibility.

States will continue to carry an important responsibility. In 30 States the Federal basic payment will be less than the present levels of combined Federal and State payments. These States will be required to maintain the current level of benefits, but in no case will a State be required to spend more than 90% of its present welfare cost. The Federal government will not only provide the "floor," but it will assume 10% of the benefits now being paid by the States as their part of welfare costs.

In 20 States, the new payment would exceed the present average benefit payments, in some cases by a wide margin. In these States, where benefits are lowest and poverty often the most severe, the payments will raise benefit levels substantially. For 5 years, every State will be required to continue to spend at least half of what they are now spending on welfare, to supplement the Federal base.

For the *typical "welfare family"*—a mother with dependent children and no outside income—the new system would provide a basic national minimum payment. A mother with three small children would be assured an annual income of at least $1600.

For the *family headed by an employed father or working mother,* the same basic benefits would be received, but $60 per month of earnings would be "disregarded" in order to make up the costs of working and provide a strong advantage in holding a job. The wage earner could also keep 50% of his benefits as his earnings rise above that $60 per month. A family of four, in which the father earns $2,000 in a year, would receive payments of $960, for a total income of $2,960.

For the *aged, the blind and the disabled,* the present system varies benefit levels from $40 per month for an aged person in one State to $145 per month for the blind in another. The new system would establish a minimum payment of $65 per month for all three of these adult categories, with the Federal government contributing the first $50 and sharing in payments above that amount. This will raise the share of the financial burden borne by the Federal government for payments to these adults who cannot support themselves, and should pave the way for benefit increases in many States.

For the *single adult* who is not handicapped or aged, or for the *married couple without children,* the new system would not apply. Food stamps would continue to be available up to $300 per year per person, according to the plan I outlined last May in my message to the Congress on the food and nutrition needs of the population in poverty. For dependent families there will be an orderly substitution of food stamps by the new direct monetary payments.

2. *The new approach would end the blatant unfairness of the welfare system.*

In over half the States, families headed by unemployed men do not qualify for public assistance. In no State does a family headed by a father working full-time receive help in the current welfare system, no matter how little he earns. As we have seen, this approach to dependency has itself been a cause of dependency. It results in a policy that tends to force the father out of the house.

The new plan rejects a policy that undermines family life. It would end the substantial financial incentives to desertion. It would extend eligibility to *all* dependent families with children, without regard to whether the family is headed by a man or a woman. The effects of these changes upon human behavior would be an increased will to work, the survival of more marriages, the greater stability of families. We are determined to stop passing the cycle of dependency from generation to generation.

The most glaring inequity in the old welfare system is the exclusion of families who are working to pull themselves out of poverty. Families headed by a non-worker often receive more from welfare than families headed by a husband working full-time at very low wages. This has been rightly resented by the working poor, for the rewards are just the opposite of what they should be.

3. *The new plan would create a much stronger incentive to work.*

For people now on the welfare rolls, the present system discourages the move from welfare to work by cutting benefits too fast and too much as earnings begin. *The new system would encourage work by allowing the new worker to retain the first $720 of his yearly earnings without any benefit reduction.*

For people already working, but at poverty wages, the present system often encourages nothing but resentment and an incentive to quit and go on relief where that would pay more than work. The new plan, on the contrary, would provide a supplement that will help a low-wage worker—struggling to make ends meet—achieve a higher standard of living.

For an employable person who just chooses not to work, neither the present system nor the one we propose would support him, though both would continue to support other dependent members in his family.

However, a welfare mother with preschool children should not face benefit reductions if she decides to stay home. It is not our intent that mothers of pre-school children must accept work. Those who

651

can work and desire to do so, however, should have the opportunity for jobs and job training and access to day care centers for their children; this will enable them to support themselves after their children are grown.

A family with a member who gets a job would be permitted to retain all of the *first $60 monthly income,* amounting to $720 per year for a regular worker, *with no reduction of Federal payments.* The incentive to work in this provision is obvious. But there is another practical reason: Going to work costs money. Expenses such as clothes, transportation, personal care, Social Security taxes and loss of income from odd jobs amount to substantial costs for the average family. Since a family does not begin to *add* to its net income until it surpasses the cost of working, in fairness this amount should not be subtracted from the new payment.

After the first $720 of income, the *rest* of the earnings will result in a systematic reduction in payments.

I believe the vast majority of poor people in the United States prefer to work rather than have the government support their families. In 1968, 600,000 families left the welfare rolls out of an average caseload of 1,400,000 during the year, showing a considerable turnover, much of it voluntary.

However, there may be some who fail to seek or accept work, even with the strong incentives and training opportunities that will be provided. It would not be fair to those who willingly work, or to all taxpayers, to allow others to choose idleness when opportunity is available. Thus, they must accept training opportunities and jobs when offered, or give up their right to the new payments for themselves. No able-bodied person will have a "free ride" in a nation that provides opportunity for training and work.

4. *The bridge from welfare to work should be buttressed by training and child care programs.* For many, the incentives to work in this plan would be all that is necessary. However, there are other situations where these incentives need to be supported by measures that will overcome other barriers to employment.

I propose that funds be provided for expanded training and job development programs so that an additional 150,000 welfare recipients can become jobworthy during the first year.

Manpower training is a basic bridge to work for poor people, especially people with limited education, low skills and limited job experience. Manpower training programs can provide this bridge for many of our poor. In the new Manpower Training proposal to be sent to the Congress this week, the interrelationship with this new approach to welfare will be apparent.

I am also requesting authority, as a part of the new system, to provide child care for the 450,000 children of the 150,000 current welfare recipients to be trained.

The child care I propose is more than custodial. This Administration is committed to a new emphasis on child development in the first five years of life. The day care that would be part of this plan would be of a quality that will help in the development of the child and provide for its health and safety, and would break the poverty cycle for this new generation.

The expanded child care program would bring new opportunities along several lines: opportunities for the further involvement of private enterprise in providing high quality child care service; opportunities for volunteers; and opportunities for *training and employment in child care centers of many of the welfare mothers themselves.*

I am requesting a total of $600 million additional to fund these expanded training programs and child care centers.

5. *The new system will lessen welfare red tape and provide administrative cost savings.* To cut out the costly investigations so bitterly resented as "welfare snooping," the Federal payment will be based upon a certification of income, with spot checks sufficient to prevent abuses. The program will be administered on an automated basis, using the information and technical experience of the Social Security Administration, but, of course, will be entirely separate from the administration of the Social Security trust fund.

The States would be given the option of having the Federal government handle the payment of the State supplemental benefits on a reimbursable basis, so that they would be spared their present administrative burdens and so a single check could be sent to the recipient. These simplifications will save money and eliminate indignities; at the same time, welfare fraud will be detected and lawbreakers prosecuted.

6. *This new departure would require a substantial initial investment, but will yield future returns to the Nation.* This transformation of the welfare system will set in motion forces that will lessen dependency rather than perpetuate and enlarge it. A more productive population adds to real economic growth without inflation. The initial investment is needed now to stop the momentum of work-to-welfare, and to start a new momentum in the opposite direction.

The costs of welfare benefits for fam-

ilies with dependent children have been rising alarmingly the past several years, increasing from $1 billion in 1960 to an estimated $3.3 billion in 1969, of which $1.8 billion is paid by the Federal government, and $1.5 billion is paid by the States. Based on current population and income data, the proposals I am making today will increase Federal costs during the first year by an estimated $4 billion, which includes $600 million for job training and child care centers.

The "start-up costs" of lifting many people out of dependency will ultimately cost the taxpayer far less than the chronic costs—in dollars and in national values—of creating a permanent underclass in America.

FROM WELFARE TO WORK

Since this Administration took office, members of the Urban Affairs Council, including officials of the Department of Health, Education and Welfare, the Department of Labor, the Office of Economic Opportunity, the Bureau of the Budget, and other key advisers, have been working to develop a coherent, fresh approach to welfare, manpower training and revenue sharing.

I have outlined our conclusions about an important component of this approach in this message; the Secretary of HEW will transmit to the Congress the proposed legislation after the summer recess.

I urge the Congress to begin its study of these proposals promptly so that laws can be enacted and funds authorized to begin the new system as soon as possible. Sound budgetary policy must be maintained in order to put this plan into effect—especially the portion supplementing the wages of the working poor.

With the establishment of the new approach, the Office of Economic Opportunity will concentrate on the important task of finding new ways of opening economic opportunity for those who are able to work. Rather than focusing on income support activities, it must find means of providing opportunities for individuals to contribute to the full extent of their capabilities, and of developing and improving those capabilities.

This would be the effect of the transformation of welfare into "workfare," a new work-rewarding system:

For the first time, all dependent families with children in America, regardless of where they live, would be assured of minimum standard payments based upon uniform and single eligibility standards.

For the first time, the more than two million families who make up the "working poor" would be helped toward self-sufficiency and away from future welfare dependency.

For the first time, training and work opportunity with effective incentives would be given millions of families who would otherwise be locked into a welfare system for generations.

For the first time, the Federal government would make a strong contribution toward relieving the financial burden of welfare payments from State governments.

For the first time, the Federal government—family in America would be encouraged to stay together, free from economic pressure to split apart.

These are far-reaching effects. They

cannot be purchased cheaply, or by piecemeal efforts. This total reform looks in a new direction; it requires new thinking, a new spirit and a fresh dedication to reverse the downhill course of welfare. In its first year, more than half the families participating in the program will have one member working or training.

We have it in our power to raise the standard of living and the realizable hopes of millions of our fellow citizens. By providing an equal chance at the starting line, we can reinforce the traditional American spirit of self-reliance and self-respect.

RICHARD NIXON

The White House
August 11, 1969

APPENDIX

PROPOSED BENEFIT SCHEDULE

[Excluding all State Benefits]

Earned income	New benefit	Total income
$0	$1,600	$1,600
500	1,600	2,100
1,000	1,460	2,460
1,500	1,210	2,710
2,000	960	2,960
2,500	710	3,210
3,000	460	3,460
3,500	210	3,710
4,000	0	4,000

(For a four-person family, with a basic payment standard of $1,600 and an earned income disregard of $720.)

NOTE: A welfare reform fact sheet of background material containing charts and additional statistical tables, dated August 8, 1969, was made available by the White House Press Office.

328 Statement on the Office of Economic Opportunity.
August 11, 1969

WE LIVE in an exciting and difficult time. We possess great strength and skill; yet we are often unable to harness our

strength in the service of our ideals. We sense new possibilites for unlocking the full potential of every individual; yet our institutions too often are unresponsive to our needs. We dream of what we might be able to make of our society; but we have not yet learned to achieve that dream.

Our Nation will attain its social objectives, I believe, only if we develop a new spirit of adventure in their pursuit. We must become pioneers in reshaping our society even as we have become pioneers in space. We must show a new willingness to take risks for progress, a new readiness to try the untried.

Such an innovative spirit should characterize all of our institutions and all agencies of Government. But it is in the Office of Economic Opportunity that social pioneering should be a specialty. It is the OEO that should act as the "R and D" [research and development] arm for Government's social programs.

When I sent a message to the Congress on OEO last February, I offered several preliminary comments about the agency. Since that time, the new Director of the Office has made a thorough review of its operations. On the basis of our discussions, I have reached a number of further conclusions about the direction of OEO and the way it does its work.

The following are among the specific changes in OEO which I am announcing today:

—Creation of a new Office of Program Development.

—Revamping and strengthening the Office of Planning, Research, and Evaluation.

—Strengthening and upgrading the Office of Health Services and the Office of Legal Services.

—Creation of a new Office of Program Operations to improve the administration of activities in the field.

These and other specific changes, in turn, are based on a number of general principles which will help set new directions for OEO.

SETTING NEW DIRECTIONS

It has been said frequently in the past few weeks that if our country can marshal resources so effectively that we can travel to the moon, then we should also use our power and knowledge to better advantage in solving social problems on our own planet. I share this view. But if we are to make a better response to social challenges, then we will have to act with the same clear commitment to well-defined goals, the same freedom to undertake bold experiments, the same managerial discipline, and the same spirit of teamwork that has characterized our accomplishments in space.

A Clear Commitment. This administration believes that every American should have the opportunity to participate in our Nation's economic life to the full extent of his abilities. The Office of Economic Opportunity will make this objective its highest priority. It will address itself to unanswered and difficult questions: What determines an individual's capacity for growth and achievement? What can be done to awaken this capacity and develop it? How can we be sure that these capacities, when they are available, will be fully used and properly rewarded?

It is important that OEO concentrate its energies on causes rather than symptoms, that it help people become productive participants in the economy rather than focusing on the conduct of income support or other ameliorative activities. These latter functions should belong instead to efforts such as the new family assistance program, a revised unemployment compensation system, improved plans for food distribution, and various benefit payment programs.

We see today a healthy determination on the part of our people to continuously examine and update national priorities so that the energy and resources of our country can be properly allocated to solve domestic problems. But our people have also learned that the challenge of bringing unproductive people into active economic roles is more difficult than many had thought. We know now that the amount of money we spend in this effort will mean little unless the approach is right. The Office of Economic Opportunity will help us develop needed new approaches to this problem. It will translate our general commitment to provide full opportunity to all Americans into specific programs which will help us use our resources to the greatest effect.

Bold Experimentation. The freedom to try out a wide variety of ideas, to test them fully both in theory and in practice, to move boldly on several fronts, to thoroughly master and carefully apply the results of this experimental process—these are capacities which are as instrumental to social progress as they are to advances in science.

Since OEO is to be the cutting edge by means of which government moves into unexplored areas, the experimental temper will be vital to its success. The agency should marshal the most creative minds in the country, both to ask new questions and find new answers. It should be free to take creative risks. It should set up a variety of demonstration projects, carefully test their effectiveness, and systematically assess the results.

Just as NASA developed weather satellites and communication satellites and then spun them off, transferring them to the Department of Commerce and to ComSat, so OEO should concentrate on the experimental stage of domestic programs. When a program has proven successful in the domestic area, it too may be transferred to other agencies or other levels of the government or even to the private sector if that seems desirable. This approach will leave OEO free to break still newer ground.

Managerial Discipline. Too often the lines of responsibility in OEO programs have been badly blurred; too often there has been no method for determining whether a program has succeeded or failed and what is responsible for failure and success. Too often the same individuals or groups, at both the national and local level, have found themselves wearing many hats: coordinating old programs, doing new research, setting up demonstration projects, evaluating results, and serving as advocates before the government on behalf of the poor. Precisely because each of these functions is important, each should be assigned to specific offices wherever that is possible, and they, in turn, should be held strictly accountable for the way in which their work is performed.

A Spirit of Teamwork. Finally, our social programs will require a greater sense of common endeavor among our people. Close cooperation between the private sector and government, for example, can be a key in assisting the economically disadvantaged as it has been a key to success in space. Moreover, we should be certain that the fears or suspicions which sometimes separate races or economic groups are diminished by our activities and not accentuated. We must avoid words and actions which drive people apart and emphasize instead the common stake of all Americans in extending economic opportunity.

These are some of the new directions which will define the scope of OEO and give new focus to its work. The specific organizational reforms we are making in the agency will help us move in these new directions; they will make OEO a stronger and more flexible instrument in the struggle for human dignity.

Specific Reforms

1. *Office of Program Development.* This new unit will be responsible for most of the experimental efforts which OEO will now emphasize and will include within it both totally new programs and some existing activities which previously were distributed throughout the agency. The Office of Program Development will seek new ways of bringing services to the poor, helping them to increase their skills, educate their children, improve their homes, protect their health, and develop their communities. It will try to find new methods of increasing their business and employment opportunities.

2. *Office of Planning, Research, and Evaluation.* The Office of Planning, Research, and Evaluation will be reorganized and strengthened. Reporting straight to the Director, it will have responsibility for reviewing existing social programs, for comparing the results of projects with the objectives which have been set for them, for commenting on the adequacy with which both programs and objectives are formulated, and for recommending alterations in existing programs as well as new experiments. It will seek to establish more precise standards for measuring performance than OEO has used in the past. The Office of Planning, Research, and Evaluation will provide a regular source

for that independent appraisal of Federal social programs which often is not available at present.

3. *Office of Health Services.* A strengthened Office of Health Services will also report directly to the Director of OEO. Many of the problems of the poor are the product of ill health and many have serious medical consequences. We have already begun to develop new mechanisms for helping the poor pay medical costs. But now we must further improve our methods of delivering health services so that all the poor will have ready access to doctors, diagnosis, treatment, and hospital care. The Neighborhood Health Center program is one experimental effort which is working in this direction; OEO will initiate other activities in this area. The 1970 budget will also show increases in food and nutrition programs, family planning services, and other health related activities.

4. *Office of Legal Services.* The Office of Legal Services will also be strengthened and elevated so that it reports directly to the Director. It will take on central responsibility for programs which help provide advocates for the poor in their dealings with social institutions. The sluggishness of many institutions—at all levels of society—in responding to the needs of individual citizens is one of the central problems of our time. Disadvantaged persons in particular must be assisted so that they fully understand the lawful means of making their needs known and having those needs met. This goal will be better served by a separate Legal Services program, one which can test new approaches to this important challenge.

5. *Office of Program Operations.* More attention must be given to the way in which OEO policies are carried out at the

local, State, and regional level. A new Office of Program Operations will work to improve the quality of field operations; it will be able to define more clearly the purposes for which grants and contracts are given and to apply higher standards of effective management. Training and technical assistance funds for those who run OEO-supported programs will be increased. We also plan to raise allocations to State Economic Opportunity offices.

It is particularly important that the management of community action agencies be improved. The goals of community action are desirable ones and the work of these agencies deserves our support. Unfortunately, many of these local agencies have suffered from a proliferation of duties and from a confusion of roles. While some progress has been made in correcting these problems, the activities of community action agencies must be further clarified and such agencies must more clearly assign priorities among their various functions.

One of the important strengths of the community action program has been its ability to involve local citizens in planning and carrying out its projects. This value should not be lost. Community organizations, close to the people, can play an important role in delivering government programs on a local and individual level.

OTHER PROGRAMS

Following the belief that the Office of Economic Opportunity should be an innovative agency, this administration has already moved the Job Corps to the Department of Labor and the Head Start program to the Department of Health, Education, and Welfare. In addition, I am suggesting in my manpower training proposals that several OEO-funded manpower programs which have been administered by the Department of Labor be transferred to that Department. These are on-going programs which have passed the trial stage and should now be seen as parts of our established manpower strategy.

Some proven programs which are national in scope should, however, remain in OEO because they can help us develop new experiments and because of the agency's special identification with the problems of the poor. The VISTA program is one example; it will make a greater effort to attract people with specific technical and professional skills to its ranks.

Mankind is presently entering a new era of exploration and fulfillment. We are able to move beyond the limits which once confined us, both in our travels beyond this planet and in our efforts to shape our life upon it. Now we must use this ability to explore on earth, as we have explored in space, with intelligence and courage, recognizing always how little we really know and how far we still must go.

I believe that the goal of full economic opportunity for every American can be realized. I expect the Office of Economic Opportunity to play a central role in that achievement. With new organizational structures, new operating procedures, and a new sense of precision and direction, OEO can be one of the most creative and productive offices in the government. For here much of our social pioneering will be done. Here will begin many of our new adventures.

NOTE: The statement was released at San Clemente, Calif.

329   Special Message to the Congress on Manpower
       Training. *August* 12, 1969

To the Congress of the United States:

A job is one rung on the ladder of a lifelong career of work.

That is why we must look at manpower training with new eyes: as a continuing process to help people to get started in a job and to get ahead in a career.

"Manpower training" is one of those phrases with a fine ring and an imprecise meaning. Before a fresh approach can be taken, a clear definition is needed.

Manpower training means: (1) making it possible for those who are unemployed or on the fringes of the labor force to become permanent, full-time workers; (2) giving those who are now employed at low income the training and the opportunity they need to become more productive and more successful; (3) discovering the potential in those people who are now considered unemployable, removing many of the barriers now blocking their way.

Manpower training, in order to work on all rungs of the ladder, requires the efficient allocation by private enterprise and government of these human resources. We must develop skills in a place, in a quantity and in a way to ensure that they are used effectively and constantly improved.

Today, government spends approximately 3 billion dollars in a wide variety of manpower programs, with half directly devoted to job training; private enterprise spends much more on job training alone. The investment by private industry—given impetus by the profit motive as well as a sense of social responsibility—is the fundamental means of developing the nation's labor force. But the government's investment has failed to achieve its potential for many reasons, including duplication of effort, inflexible funding arrangements and an endless ribbon of red tape. For example:

—*A jobless man* goes to the local skill training center to seek help. He has the aptitudes for training in blue collar mechanical work, but no suitable training opportunities are available. At the same time, vacancies exist in a white collar New Careers project and in the Neighborhood Youth Corps. But the resources of these programs cannot be turned over to the training program that has the most local demand.

—*A 17-year old boy wants to take job training.* The only manpower program available to him is the Job Corps, but its nearest camp is hundreds of miles away. With no other choice, he leaves home; within 30 days he has become homesick or feels his family needs him; he drops out of the Corps and has suffered "failure" which reinforces his self-image of defeat.

—*A big-city Mayor* takes the lead in trying to put together a cohesive manpower program for the entire labor market area—tying together jobless workers in the inner city with job openings outside the "beltway." He finds it difficult to assemble a coherent picture of what's going on. Manpower programs funded by different agencies follow different reporting rules, so that the statistics cannot be added up. Moreover, there is no single agency which maintains an inventory of all currently oper-

39–861—71——45

ating manpower programs. He knows that help is available—but where does he turn?

—*An unemployed high school drop-out* in a small town wants to learn a trade in the electronics field. His local employment office tells him that there is not enough demand in his town for qualified technicians to warrant setting up a special training class in a local public school. He is also told that "administrative procedures" do not lend themselves to the use of a local private technical institute which offers the very course he wants. This youngster walks the streets and wonders what happened to all those promises of "equal opportunity."

This confused state of affairs in the development of human resources can no longer be tolerated. Government exists to serve the needs of people, not the other way around. The idea of creating a set of "programs," and then expecting people to fit themselves into those programs, is contrary to the American spirit; we must redirect our efforts to tailor government aid to individual need.

This government has a major responsibility to make certain that the means to learn a job skill and improve that skill are available to those who need it.

Manpower training is central to our commitment to aid the disadvantaged and to help people off welfare rolls and onto payrolls. Intelligently organized, it will save tax dollars now spent on welfare, increase revenues by widening the base of the taxpaying public, and—most important—lift human beings into lives of greater dignity.

I propose a comprehensive new Manpower Training Act that would pull to- *gether much of the array of Federal training services and make it possible for State and local government to respond to the needs of the individual trainee.*

The Nation must have a Manpower System that will enable each individual to take part in a sequence of activities— tailored to his unique needs—to prepare for and secure a good job. The various services people need are afforded in laws already on the books. The need today is to knit together all the appropriate services in one readily available system. By taking this step we can better help the disadvantaged gain control and direction of their own lives.

A first step was taken in this direction in March when I announced the reorganization of the Manpower Administration of the U.S. Department of Labor. This reorganization consolidated the agencies that had fragmented responsibility for carrying out most of the Nation's manpower training program. We must now complete the job by streamlining the statutory framework for our manpower training efforts.

In specific terms, the Act which I propose would:

1. *Consolidate major manpower development programs* administered by the Department of Labor—namely, the Manpower Development and Training Act and Title I–A (Job Corps) and I–B (Community Work and Training Program) of the Economic Opportunity Act. These programs, operated in conjunction with strengthened State manpower agencies, will provide training activities in a cohesive manpower services system. The Office of Economic Opportunity, without major manpower operational responsibilities, will continue its role in research work

and program development working with the Department of Labor in pioneering new manpower training approaches.

2. *Provide flexible funding* of manpower training services so that they can be sensitive to and focused on local needs; this will ensure the most efficient use of available resources.

3. *Decentralize administration of manpower services* to States and metropolitan areas, as Governors and Mayors evidence interest, build managerial capacity, and demonstrate effective performance. This process will take place in three stages. First, a State will administer 25 per cent of the funds apportioned to it when it develops a comprehensive manpower planning capability; second, it will exercise discretion over 66⅔ per cent when it establishes a comprehensive Manpower Training Agency to administer the unified programs; and, third, it will administer 100 per cent when the State meets objective standards of exemplary performance in planning and carrying out its manpower service system.

The proposed Act will assure that equitable distribution of the manpower training dollars is made to the large metropolitan areas and to rural districts, working through a State grant system.

By placing greater reliance on State and local elected officials, the day-to-day planning and administration of manpower programs will become more responsive to individual job training needs. A dozen States have already taken steps to reshape administrative agencies and to unify manpower and related programs.

To qualify for full participation under the proposed Act, each State and the major cities in a State would unify its manpower administration under State

and local prime sponsors. These agencies would administer the programs funded by the Federal Government; be responsible for other State and local activities to help people secure employment; help employers find manpower; and work in close liaison with State and local vocational education, vocational rehabilitation and welfare programs, for which leadership will be provided at the national level by the Department of Health, Education, and Welfare.

In addition, the State and local prime sponsors would establish advisory bodies, including employees, employers and representatives of the local populations to be served, to assist in developing local policy. In this manner, the units of government would be able to benefit continually from the experience and counsel of the private sector.

4. *Provide more equitable allowances for trainees,* simplifying the present schedule to provide an incentive for a trainee to choose the training best suited to his own future, and not the training that "pays" most.

As an incentive to move from welfare rolls to payrolls, the allowance to welfare recipients who go into training would be increased to $30 per month above their present welfare payments. These increased training allowances carefully dovetail into the work incentives outlined in my message to the Congress regarding the transformation of the welfare system. As the welfare recipient moves up the ladder from training to work, the first $60 per month of earnings would result in no deductions from Federally-financed payments.

5. *Create a career development plan for trainees,* tailored to suit their individ-

ual capabilities and ambitions.

Eligible applicants—in general, those over 16 who need training—would be provided a combination of services that would help them to train, to find work, and to move on up the ladder. These services will include counseling, basic vocational education, medical care, work experience, institutional and on-the-job training, and job referral. Manpower services will also be available for those who are presently employed but whose skill deficiencies hold them in low-income, dead-end jobs.

6. *Establish a National Computerized Job Bank* to match job seekers with job vacancies. It would operate in each State, with regional and national activities undertaken by the Secretary of Labor, who would also set technical standards.

The computers of the Job Bank would be programmed with constantly changing data on available jobs. A job seeker would tell an employment counselor his training or employment background, his skills and career plans, which could be matched with a variety of available job options. This would expand the potential worker's freedom of choice and help him make best use of his particular talents.

7. *Authorize the use of the comprehensive manpower training system as an economic stabilizer.* If rising unemployment were ever to suggest the possibility of a serious economic downturn, a countercyclical automatic "trigger" would be provided. Appropriations for manpower services would be increased by 10 percent if the national unemployment rate equals or exceeds 4.5 percent for three consecutive months. People without the prospect of immediate employment could use this period to enhance their skills—and the productive capacity of the nation.

I proposed a similar measure in my message to the Congress on expansion of the unemployment insurance system.

The proposed comprehensive Manpower Training Act is a good example of a new direction in making Federalism work. Working together, we can bring order and efficiency to a tangle of Federal programs.

We can answer a national need by decentralizing power, setting national standards, and assigning administrative responsibility to the States and localities in touch with community needs.

We can relate substantial Federal-State manpower efforts to other efforts in welfare reform, tax sharing and economic opportunity, marshaling the resources of the departments and agencies involved to accomplish a broad mission.

We can meet individual human needs without encroaching on personal freedom, which is perhaps the most exciting challenge to government today.

With these proposals, which I strongly urge the Congress to enact, we can enhance America's human resources. By opening up the opportunity for manpower training on a large scale, we build a person's will to work; in so doing, we build a bridge to human dignity.

RICHARD NIXON

The White House
August 12, 1969

NOTE: The White House Press Office also released the text of a news briefing on the President's message, held in San Clemente, Calif., by George P. Shultz, Secretary of Labor, Arnold R. Weber, Assistant Secretary of Labor for Manpower, and Ronald L. Ziegler, White House Press Secretary.

The message was released at San Clemente, Calif.

330   Memorandum on the Joint Financial Management
      Improvement Program.   *August* 12, 1969

Memorandum for the Heads of Departments and Agencies:

In charting the goals of this Administration, I have emphasized the need to improve the decision-making processes of the Federal Government. We must make our system for delivering program services more effective.

Therefore, I am giving full support to the Joint Financial Management Improvement Program, an indispensable project with a charter to sharpen some of the tools of management.

Under the leadership of the Comptroller General, the Secretary of the Treasury, the Budget Director, and the Chairman of the Civil Service Commission, the Joint Program has promoted many far-reaching improvements in the past. I want to see achievements in the future that will make management of Government operations more responsive and efficient.

To get full measure from the resources available to us, we must have all the necessary management information. We must have financial systems that illuminate every level and stage of decision-making: from the first-line supervisor to the President and the Congress, from the long-range forecast to the critical post-audit.

Nothing less will let us go forward with programs that provide the most benefit for the taxpayer's dollar.

I have previously asked for a vigorous effort to convert to the accrual basis for stating budget revenues and expenditures. That high priority goal dovetails with the objective of developing effective financial system, including budgeting, accounting, reporting, and auditing.

I direct the head of each department and agency to join Comptroller General Elmer B. Staats, Secretary of the Treasury David M. Kennedy, Budget Director Robert P. Mayo, and Civil Service Chairman Robert E. Hampton, under the Joint Financial Management Improvement Program, to make the development of effective financial systems a high priority in strengthening administrative practices. Without this effort, our ability to cope with the needs of the 1970's will be seriously impaired.

The challenge is there. I call upon each Federal manager to accept it as a personal challenge. Demand better financial information and use it.

RICHARD NIXON

NOTE: The memorandum was released at San Clemente, Calif.

331   Statement on House Action on the Recommended
      Budget for the Department of Health, Education,
      and Welfare.   *August* 12, 1969

THE House of Representatives recently added more than $1.1 billion to the budget which I had recommended for the present fiscal year for the Department of Health, Education, and Welfare. I regard this action as inconsistent with the intent of the Congress a week earlier when it imposed a ceiling on spending for the current fiscal year.

In enacting the ceiling, the Congress reflected the concern of the citizens of this Nation with inflation and excessive Federal expenditures. Because of this same concern, I stated my intention when I signed the Second Supplemental Appropriation Act to restrict expenditures in this fiscal year to $192.9 billion, the same figure transmitted to Congress in April. Estimates made then for some of the uncontrollable programs—such as interest on the national debt, Medicare, social security, public assistance, and veterans' benefits—have already risen by some $2.5 billion. This increase, plus another billion dollars of added expenditures arising from congressional action or inaction to date other than on HEW, requires an offsetting reduction of $3.5 billion in other programs. I have ordered that cut.

Congressional action to date on my revenue recommendations also has been disappointing. In the aggregate, congressional policies thus far add up to taxing less and spending more. Appealing as this may be at the moment, it promises long-term grief for the people.

Most of the spending increases in the HEW bill are for education programs. I share the concern of all Americans for improved quality of our education system. But I am also mindful of the needs of this Nation for improved housing, more readily available health care, more adequate nutrition, better training for jobs and job placements, increases in social security benefits, welfare reform, and improvements in other social programs. We must demonstrate the discipline to hold down inflation, which continues to work a special cruelty upon the very poor, those on pensions and fixed incomes, and home buyers who pay increasing prices and high interest rates.

In the interest, therefore, of those who most need our help, we must act responsibly to hold down National Government spending in the present economic environment.

Present circumstances plainly require a point of predictable firmness and responsibility in dealing with these budgetary problems.

I shall serve as that point in the interest of the American people.

Let me reiterate my intention not to spend in this fiscal year any funds appropriated in excess of my budgetary estimates of April this year. No commitments will be made to spend these additional appropriations until the Congress has completed action on all appropriation bills and revenue measures.

At that juncture we will be in a position to measure the economic circumstances we confront, to determine which programs must be cut by the executive to accommodate increases made available by the Congress and which programs have received compensatory cuts by the Congress to offset the increases. Then, consistent with my obligation under the Constitution and the laws, I will not spend funds in excess of the expenditure ceiling.

In short, I have pledged fiscal responsibility. The Congress has imposed an expenditure ceiling; I have myself accepted the spirit of the ceiling and pledged this administration to respect a ceiling for this fiscal year of $192.9 billion.

Let the Congress and the country understand that I shall keep that commitment. I trust that the future actions of Congress will be consistent with its own commitments to fiscal responsibility.

NOTE: The statement was released at San Clemente, Calif.

332   Special Message to the Congress on Sharing Federal Revenues With the States.   *August* 13, 1969

To the Congress of the United States:

If there is a single phenomenon that has marked the recent history of nations, large and small, democratic and dictatorial, it has been rise of the central government.

In the United States, revenues of the Federal government have increased ninety-fold in thirty-six years. The areas of our national life where the Federal government has become a dominant force have multiplied.

The flow of power from the cities and States to Washington accelerated in the Depression years, when economic life in America stagnated, and an energetic national government seemed the sole instrument of national revival. World War II brought another and necessary expansion of the Federal government to marshal the nation's energies to wage war on two sides of the world.

When the war ended, it appeared as though the tide would be reversed. But the onset of the cold war, the needs of a defeated and prostrate Europe, the growing danger and then the reality of conflict in Asia, and later, the great social demands made upon the Federal government by millions of citizens, guaranteed the continued rapid growth and expansion of Federal power.

Today, however, a majority of Americans no longer supports the continued extension of federal services. The momentum for federal expansion has passed its peak; a process of deceleration is setting in.

The cause can be found in the record of the last half decade. In the last five years the Federal government enacted scores of new Federal programs; it added tens of thousands of new employees to the Federal payrolls; it spent tens of billions of dollars in new funds to heal the grave social ills of rural and urban America. No previous half decade had witnessed domestic Federal spending on such a scale. Yet, despite the enormous Federal commitment in new men, new ideas and new dollars from Washington, it was during this very period in our history that the problems of the cities deepened rapidly into crises.

The problems of the cities and the countryside stubbornly resisted the solutions of Washington; and the stature of the Federal government as America's great instrument of social progress has suffered accordingly—all the more so because the Federal government promised so much and delivered so little. This loss of faith in the power and efficacy of the Federal government has had at least one positive impact upon the American people. More and more, they are turning away from the central government to their local and State governments to deal with their local and State problems.

As the Federal government grew in size and power, it became increasingly remote not only from the problems it was supposed to solve, but from the people it was supposed to serve. For more than three decades, whenever a great social change was needed, a new national program was the automatic and inevitable response. Power and responsibility flowed in greater and greater measure from the state capitals to the national capital.

Furthermore, we have hampered the effectiveness of local government by constructing a Federal grant-in-aid system of staggering complexity and diversity. Many of us question the efficiency of this intergovernmental financial system which is based on the Federal categorical grant. Its growth since the end of 1962 has been near explosive. Then there were 53 formula grant and 107 project grant authorizations—a total of 160. Four years later on January 1, 1967, there were 379 such grant authorizations.

While effective in many instances, this rapid growth in Federal grants has been accompanied by:

—Overlapping programs at the State and local level.

—Distortion of State and local budgets.

—Increased administrative costs.

—Program delay and uncertainty.

—A decline in the authority and responsibility of chief executives, as grants have become tied to functional bureaucracies.

—Creation of new and frequently competitive state and local governmental institutions.

Another inevitable result of this proliferation of Federal programs has been a gathering of the reins of power in Washington. Experience has taught us that this is neither the most efficient nor effective way to govern; certainly it represents a radical departure from the vision of Federal-State relations the nation's founders had in mind.

This Administration brought into office both a commitment and a mandate to reverse the trend of the last three decades—a determination to test new engines of social progress. We are committed to enlist the full potential of the private sector, the full potential of the voluntary sector and the full potential of the levels of government closer to the people.

This week, I am sending to Congress for its approval for Fiscal Year 1971, legislation asking that a set amount of Federal revenues be returned annually to the States to be used as the States and their local governments see fit—without Federal strings.

Because of budget stringencies, the initial fund set aside to start the program will not be great—$500 million. The role of the Federal government will be re-defined and re-directed. But it is my intention to augment this fund annually in the coming years so that in the Fiscal Year beginning in mid-1975, $5 billion in Federal revenues will be returned to the states without Federal strings. Ultimately, it is our hope to use this mechanism to so strengthen State and local government that by the end of the coming decade, the political landscape of America will be visibly altered, and States and cities will have a far greater share of power and responsibility for solving their own problems. The role of the Federal Government will be re-defined and re-directed toward those functions where it proves itself the only or the most suitable instrument.

The fiscal case for Federal assistance to States and localities is a strong one. Under our current budget structure, Federal revenues are likely to increase faster than the national economy. At the local level, the reverse is true. State and local revenues, based heavily on sales and property taxes, do not keep pace with economic growth, while expenditures at the local level tend to exceed such growth. The result is a "fiscal mismatch," with potential Federal surpluses and local deficits.

The details of this revenue sharing program were developed after close consultation with members of the Congress, governors, mayors, and county officials. It represents a successful effort to combine the desirable features of simplicity and equity with a need to channel funds where they are most urgently needed and efficiently employable.

The program can best be described by reviewing its four major elements.

First, the size of the total fund to be shared will be a stated percentage of personal taxable income—the base on which Federal individual income taxes are levied. For the second half of Fiscal Year 1971, this will be one-third of one percent of personal taxable income; for subsequent fiscal years this percentage will rise to a regular constant figure. In order to provide for the assured flow of Federal funds, a permanent appropriation will be authorized and established for the Treasury Department, from which will be automatically disbursed each year an amount corresponding to the stipulated percentage.

Second, the allocation of the total annual fund among the 50 States and the District of Columbia will be made on the basis of each State's share of national population, adjusted for the State's revenue effort.

The revenue effort adjustment is designed to provide the States with some incentive to maintain (and even expand) their efforts to use their own tax resources to meet their needs. A simple adjustment along these lines would provide a state whose revenue effort is above the national average with a bonus above its basic per capita portion of revenue sharing.

Third, the allocation of a State's share among its general units of local government will be established by prescribed formula. The total amount a State will share with all its general political sub-divisions is based on the relative roles of State and local financing in each State. The amount which an individual unit of general local government will receive is based on its share of total local government revenue raised in the State.

Several points should be noted about these provisions for distribution of a State's portion of revenue sharing.

—The distribution will be made by the State.

—The provisions make allowance for State-by-State variations and would tend to be neutral with respect to the current relative fiscal importance of State and local governments in each State.

—In order to provide local flexibility, each State is authorized to develop an alternative distribution plan, working with its local governments.

Fourth, administrative requirements are kept at a minimum. Each State will meet simple reporting and accounting requirements.

While it is not possible to specify for what functions these Federally shared funds will provide—the purpose of this program being to leave such allocation decisions up to the recipient units of government—an analysis of existing State and local budgets can provide substantial clues. Thus, one can reasonably expect that education, which consistently takes over two-fifths of all state and local general revenues, will be the major beneficiary of these new funds. Another possible area for employment of shared funds, one most consistent with the spirit of this program, would be for intergovernmental cooperation efforts.

This proposal marks a turning point in Federal-State relations, the beginning of decentralization of governmental power,

667

the restoration of a rightful balance between the State capitals and the national capital.

Our ultimate purposes are many: To restore to the States their proper rights and roles in the Federal system with a new emphasis on and help for local responsiveness; to provide both the encouragement and the necessary resources for local and State officials to exercise leadership in solving their own problems; to narrow the distance between people and the government agencies dealing with their problems; to restore strength and vigor to local and State governments; to shift the balance of political power away from Washington and back to the country and the people.

This tax-sharing proposal was pledged in the campaign; it has long been a part of the platform of many men in my own political party—and men in the other party as well. It is integrally related to the national welfare reform. Through these twin approaches we hope to relieve the fiscal crisis of the hard-pressed State and local governments and to assist millions of Americans out of poverty and into productivity.

RICHARD NIXON

The White House
    August 13, 1969

NOTE: The message was released at San Clemente, Calif.

On the same day the White House Press Office released the text of a news briefing on the President's message, held in San Clemente, Calif., by Dr. Arthur F. Burns, Counsellor to the President.

On July 8, 1969, the White House Press Office released the text of a news briefing on revenue sharing by Dr. Burns, Gov. Daniel Evans of Washington, and Mayor Jack D. Maltester of San Leandro, Calif., and County Executive Edwin G. Michaelian of Westchester County, N.Y., both members of the Advisory Commission on Intergovernmental Relations.

333   Remarks at the Swearing In of John Wilks as Deputy Assistant Secretary of Labor for Compliance and Director of the Office of Federal Contract Compliance. *August 13, 1969*

BEFORE the Secretary handles the swearing-in ceremony, we already have issued a release on this appointment. But I want to at least leave a personal note.

I am very happy that we have come all the way to California to find the man to take on this appointment that I have indicated my support of in a statement on August 8.

The Office of Federal Contract Compliance is one of the major offices that is part of this administration's whole equal opportunity program.

And we, therefore, wanted to find a man with broad experience, broad experience on both the management side and the labor side in all areas, to take over this assignment.

The Secretary of Labor assures me that Mr. Wilks, who happens to be now a Californian, but who has lived in Boston, in New York, in West Virginia, and was born in South Carolina, has the broad national understanding, but also the experience in this field to be the top man in the country to handle this assignment.

He will have my complete support as well as the support of the Secretary of Labor in carrying out his general purpose, the purpose that all of us share, and that is that where Federal funds are used for Federal contracts, that every American should have an equal opportunity to have the employment that those funds may be able to produce.

There may be argument in this country on this whole problem of equality of opportunity, but there can be absolutely no compromise and no argument on that score. And this is the assignment that Mr. Wilks and I have discussed. It is one that he is undertaking.

The Secretary will now swear him in.

[The oath of office was administered by Secretary of Labor George P. Shultz. Mr. Wilks then spoke.]

NOTE: The President spoke at 12:50 p.m. at San Clemente, Calif. He referred to a Labor Department news release of August 6, 1969, giving biographical information on John Wilks.

Mr. Wilks' remarks are printed in the Weekly Compilation of Presidential Documents (vol. 5, p. 1147).

334   Remarks at a Dinner in Los Angeles Honoring the Apollo 11 Astronauts.   *August* 13, 1969

THANK YOU, Governor Reagan, for that very gracious and generous welcome to California to our astronauts and also to all of our guests who have come a long way, not as far as they have come, but a long way to this dinner.

And before we make some of the official awards on this historic occasion, I thought that all of the people in this great audience here and those millions who are listening on television, or seeing on television, would like to know some of the people that are here. All should be introduced in this distinguished group. All cannot be. But I am sure that we should have some.

And except for those that will later participate in the program, I wish that those that I will now name will stand and their wives with them as they are named so that those on television and those in this audience can know who have come to honor our astronauts.

First, the Chief Justice of the United States and Mrs. Burger.

The former Vice President of the United States and Mrs. Humphrey.

There are 50 Members of the House and Senate of the United States present. Will all of the Members of the House and Senate of the United States and their wives please stand so that we may honor you?

There has never been a White House dinner in which so many Governors have been present, because there can only be 100 seated at a White House dinner. There are 44 Governors here present. Will the 44 Governors and their wives please stand and be honored?

Also, there are more members of the Cabinet present than are usually present at a Cabinet meeting. [*Laughter*] Will the 14 members of the Cabinet please stand and be honored?

And now, there are 83 countries represented here tonight by their ambassadors or other representatives. This is the greatest representation at a state dinner ever held in the United States of America. Will the 83 countries represented, the ambassadors and chargés, please stand and be honored?

Our astronauts had a great welcome in New York and later in Chicago and now in Los Angeles. And I can tell them that when they go abroad they will also there receive a welcome, because Mrs. Nixon and I have just returned from a trip around the world. It took us to eight countries in 9 days. And in every one of those nations, every country, the streets of Manila and Djakarta and New Delhi and Bangkok and Bucharest, wherever we went, the words, the deeds, what the astronauts meant to the world, that was everything that we heard.

And I do think of the moment, a very moving moment in Bucharest, just a little over a week ago, when almost a million people were on the streets. And on the other side of the Iron Curtain, thousands of those people held up a picture of the three astronauts. This was certainly one way to bring the world together there in Bucharest, Romania a week ago.

Now, tonight, we honor three very brave men. They would be the first to tell us that what they achieved would not have been possible had it not been for the assistance they received from many thousands of others who will also be honored tonight and, also, by others who preceded them in the work that now has reached the pinnacle of success.

When we think of those who have gone before, it reminds us that the reason we can see further than those of yesterday is that we have the privilege sometimes of standing on the shoulders of the giants who have gone before us. Many giants have gone before these three great men we honor tonight.

January 27, 1967, was a day that all Americans will remember, a day of sadness and a day of shock, but it is a day tonight that we wish to remember in a

different way.

On that day, three of the giants who made possible this achievement died. And the names of Grissom and White and Chaffee will live forever in the annals of brave men, brave men who through their exploration and their sacrifice made possible the magnificent achievement we honor tonight.

And, therefore, tonight, I would like to ask Dr. Paine, the Director of NASA, to step forward and to read a citation to these three men, a posthumous award of NASA's highest decoration, the Distinguished Service Medal.

Dr. Paine.

[Dr. Thomas O. Paine, Administrator of NASA, read the posthumous citation which was awarded separately to the three astronauts, Lt. Col. Virgil I. Grissom, Lt. Col. Edward H. White, 2d, and Lt. Comdr. Roger B. Chaffee, who died in a fire in their Apollo 204 spacecraft at Cape Kennedy. The three citations, which were identical except for the name of the recipient, read as follows:]

THE NATIONAL AERONAUTICS AND
SPACE ADMINISTRATION
AWARDS TO
VIRGIL I. GRISSOM
(POSTHUMOUSLY)
THE
NASA DISTINGUISHED SERVICE MEDAL

For professional skill, courage, and dedication to duty in Project Apollo. He gave his life in this country's historic undertaking to realize the goal of landing men on the moon and returning them safely to earth.

Signed and sealed at Washington, D.C.
this eleventh day of August
Nineteen Hundred and Sixty-Nine

T. O. PAINE
Administrator, NASA

[The President resumed speaking.]

Ladies and gentlemen, tonight in this audience are two very brave women. The men who explore the unknown are men of courage and the women who stay behind, their wives, are gallant women, women of courage. And tonight I would like to ask Mrs. Betty Grissom and Mrs. Pat White to step forward to receive the medals that their husbands have just been awarded.

When we think of the achievements of our astronauts, we also are aware of what we have often been told by those who have been on flights before.

And I recall that over and over again, the same theme runs through what they say. The theme is that it wouldn't have been possible except for all of those who worked on the ground.

Four hundred thousand, perhaps over 400,000, men and women made possible the success of the space flights.

So, tonight, we not only want to honor the men who made this great achievement, but we also want to honor those who helped them make it possible.

And we are honoring them through a citation, a Group Achievement Award, which will now be read, a citation by Dr. Paine.

[Dr. Paine read the following citation:]

THE NATIONAL AERONAUTICS AND
SPACE ADMINISTRATION
PRESENTS THE
GROUP ACHIEVEMENT AWARD
TO
APOLLO 11 MISSION OPERATIONS TEAM

For exceptional service in planning and exemplary execution of mission operational responsibilities for Apollo 11—the first manned lunar landing mission. The distinguished performance of this team was decisive in the success of this first extraterrestrial exploration mission, a major milestone in the advancement of mankind.

Signed and sealed at Washington, D.C.
this eleventh day of August
Nineteen Hundred and Sixty-Nine
T. O. PAINE
Administrator, NASA

[The President then resumed speaking.]

Anyone who has visited Houston or who has had an opportunity to visit some of the other installations of our space program is enormously impressed by the men and women who work in it. We are impressed by their intelligence, by their dedication, and when I was in Houston I was greatly impressed by their youth.

The man that has been selected tonight to receive this Group Achievement Award for the whole 400,000, who, in one way or another, have contributed to the success of this program, is a young man, 26 years of age. But Steve Bales, who was the Flight Control Engineer on this project, made a critical decision just before Eagle [1] landed on the Sea of Tranquility that could have made the difference between success or failure. And if he would step forward to receive this Group Achievement Award, representing all of those on the ground who made the venture to the moon possible.

This is the young man, when the computers seemed to be confused and when he could have said "Stop," or when he could have said "Wait," said, "Go."

And now, we reach the moment in the day, a long day for our astronauts, which we have all been looking forward to here and all the Nation has been awaiting, when the Nation tries in the highest way we know possible to honor these men for what they have done.

We are, therefore, awarding them tonight the Medal of Freedom, the highest

---

[1] The Eagle was the lunar excursion module which took astronauts Armstrong and Aldrin down to the moon's surface on July 20, 1969, and then carried them back into lunar orbit to rendezvous with the command ship, Columbia.

civilian honor that we can present to an American citizen. And to read those citations, the Vice President of the United States, who is Chairman of the Space Council, will now come to the rostrum.

[Vice President Spiro T. Agnew read the text of the citations which were awarded separately to the Apollo 11 astronauts, Neil A. Armstrong, Col. Michael Collins, and Col. Edwin E. Aldrin, Jr. The three citations which were identical except for the name of the recipient read as follows:

THE PRESIDENT OF THE UNITED STATES OF
AMERICA
AWARDS THIS
PRESIDENTIAL MEDAL OF FREEDOM
WITH DISTINCTION
TO
NEIL A. ARMSTRONG

As a member of the crew of the United States Spacecraft Apollo Eleven, he participated directly in a unique and profoundly important adventure. The accumulated scientific knowledge and technological ability of mankind made man's first step on the moon practicable; the courage and skill of men like Neil Armstrong made it possible. His contribution to this great undertaking will be remembered so long as men wonder and dream and search for truth on this planet and among the stars.

RICHARD NIXON

The White House
Washington, D.C.
    August 13, 1969

[The President then resumed speaking.]

Now, ladies and gentlemen, it says here, "remarks by the President." Don't worry, I won't try to top what we have just witnessed and felt.

But I do know that all of us here, even after a long day, would like to hear briefly from each of our astronauts.

COL. COLLINS. Mr. President, here stands one proud American, proud to be a member of the Apollo team, proud

to be a citizen of the United States of America—which nearly a decade ago said that it would land two men on the moon and then did so, showing along the way, to the world, both the triumphs and the tragedies—and proud to be an inhabitant of this most magnificent planet.

As I looked at it from nearly a quarter of a million miles away, 3 weeks ago, the people of New York, of Chicago, and of Los Angeles were far from my mind, frankly. [*Laughter*]

But tonight, they are very close to my mind. I wish that each and every one of you could have been with us today to see their enthusiasm and the magnificent greeting which they gave us upon our return.

And, of course, now the Freedom Medal. I simply cannot express in words what that means to me. But I would like to say thank you very much.

THE PRESIDENT. Colonel Aldrin.

COL. ALDRIN. Thank you, Mr. President. I feel that the honor you have given us goes not just to us as a crew but to countless thousands of others. Some are here tonight. Many cannot be.

It goes to hundreds of thousands of Government and industry people who have strived over 8 long years on Apollo. Their success and the steppingstones of Apollo 7, 8, 9, and 10, gave us the opportunity to take Apollo 11 to the moon and land.

It is an honor, in a sense, that goes to all Americans who believed, who persevered with us.

Across this country today, we saw how deeply they believed. We saw it by their spontaneous enthusiasm and warmth of greeting for us.

Our flight was your flight. We flew

Eagle and Columbia with your hands helping us on the controls and your spirit behind us.

When Neil and I saluted the flag, all Americans, I think, saluted it with us.

We hope that the proud emblem of the American Eagle, carrying the olive branch to the moon, may inspire a new generation.

The words you spoke to us, Mr. President, that incredible night on the moon, summed up many of the feelings which we have felt today from the people of this great country.

What Apollo has begun we hope will spread out in many directions, not just in space, but underneath the seas and in the cities, to tell us unforgettably that we can do what we will and must and want to do.

Never before have travelers been so far removed from their homelands as we were. Yet, never before have travelers had so many human beings at their right hand.

There are footprints on the moon. Those footprints belong to each and every one of you, to all of mankind, and they are there because of the blood, the sweat, and the tears of millions of people.

These footprints are a symbol of the true human spirit.

Thank you, Mr. President.

THE PRESIDENT. The first man to set foot on the moon, Neil Armstrong.

MR. ARMSTRONG. We were privileged to leave on the moon a plaque endorsed by you, Mr. President, saying "for all mankind."

You, too, took a trip, as you pointed out, around the world and carried that message to all mankind. Perhaps in the third millennium a wayward stranger will read that plaque at Tranquility Base and let history mark that this was the age in which that became a fact.

I was struck this morning in New York by a proudly-waved, but uncarefully scribbled sign. It said, "Through you, we touched the moon." Through you, we touched the moon.

It was our privilege today across the country to touch America.

I suspect that perhaps the most warm, genuine feeling that all of us could receive came through the cheers and shouts and, most of all, the smiles of our fellow Americans.

We hope and think that those people shared our belief that this is the beginning of a new era, the beginning of an era when man understands the universe around him, and the beginning of the era when man understands himself.

Thank you.

THE PRESIDENT. Will you please remain standing for a moment?

Ladies and gentlemen, it is my high honor and privilege at this point to propose a toast. And in doing so, I want to say very simply to our three astronauts, we thank you for your courage. We thank you for raising our sights, the sights of men and women throughout the world to a new dimension—the sky is no longer the limit.

And we thank you, too, for the men that you are, you and all of your colleagues, what fine men, what fine examples to young America and young people all over the world.

It has been my privilege in the White House, and also in other world capitals, to propose toasts to many distinguished people, to emperors, to kings, to presidents, to prime ministers, and, yes, to a duke; and tonight, this is the highest privilege I could have, to propose a toast to America's astronauts.

Let's raise our glasses to America's astronauts.

NOTE: The exchange of remarks began at 10:30 p.m. in the Los Angeles Room at the Century Plaza Hotel, Los Angeles, Calif.

The remarks of Governor Ronald Reagan, who introduced the President, are printed in the Weekly Compilation of Presidential Documents (vol. 5, p. 1148).

An announcement on August 12, 1969, of the dinner and biographic information on the three astronauts is printed in the Weekly Compilation of Presidential Documents (vol. 5, p. 1141). On the same day a release containing a partial list of those attending the dinner was also issued. On August 13, 1969, a more complete guest list was issued by the White House Press Office.

335 Statement on the Guaranteed Student Loan Program. *August 14, 1969*

IT IS regrettable that a parliamentary impasse prevented the Congress from completing action, before its recess, on legislation needed to assure the continued success of the Guaranteed Student Loan Program during the academic year which opens soon.

Since its inception in the fall of 1965, this program has become an important element in the series of student aid programs supported by the Federal Government. For the fiscal year just ended, more than 738,000 students borrowed a total of $670 million from 19,000 lending institutions. For the present year, it has been estimated that the number of students benefiting would rise to 920,000 and the loan volume to $800 million.

It has become apparent, however, that with a fixed interest rate of 7 percent, these student loans would not be competitive in a money market where the prime rate is now 8½ percent. There are indications that without some adjustment in the rate, at least 200,000 students depending on these loans for the coming school year would not be able to obtain them. Accordingly, this administration recommended legislation which would

permit a market adjustment allowance of up to 3 percent, in addition to the fixed interest of 7 percent to be paid by the Federal Government to lending institutions.

This incentive allowance was approved August 12 by the Senate, and while it was not brought to a vote in the House, it has already been approved by the appropriate House committee.

I have congressional assurances that favorable action will be completed soon after Congress returns from its summer recess. This would be consistent with the action taken last year in increasing the interest rate from 6 percent to 7 percent when a similar problem existed. Certainly, this administration will lend the full weight of its support to prompt approval of the adjustment allowance, and it is inconceivable to me that the Congress would turn its back on 200,000 young Americans who need these loans for their education.

Meanwhile, with the start of the school year rapidly approaching, I strongly urge the lenders to proceed with the loans to avoid further indecision and delay, and I have directed the Secretary of Health,

Education, and Welfare to communicate with the leading lending institutions of our Nation. The legislation before the Congress, I should point out, provides that the interest adjustment payments above the 7 percent figure would be made retroactively at least to August 15, so loans made for the school term beginning this fall would be fully covered.

I have every confidence that Congress will do its part to see that no deserving student is forced to give up his education because he cannot obtain a loan for which he qualifies. I trust that the lending institutions across the land will be equally responsive to this clear national need.

NOTE: The Emergency Insured Student Loan Act of 1969 was approved on October 22, 1969 (Public Law 91–95, 83 Stat. 141).

The statement was released at San Clemente, Calif.

336   Statement on Signing Bill Designating the Ventana Wilderness, California.   *August* 19, 1969

I HAVE approved S. 714, which designates 98,000 acres in the Los Padres National Forest in the State of California as the Ventana Wilderness.

The Wilderness Act of September 3, 1964, declared it to be the policy of the Congress to secure for the American people of present and future generations the benefits of an enduring resource of wilderness, and for that purpose the act established a National Wilderness Preservation System. I wholeheartedly endorse this concept.

Wilderness, unspoiled by man, is deeply rooted in American history and tradition. In the past, our task was to conquer it. Today we must struggle to preserve remaining wilderness areas that still offer the rewards of solitude and unmarred natural grandeur. The steps that have been taken over the years to preserve wilderness areas are a monument to Americans with vision and an awareness of Americans' deepest needs.

Today we take another important step along this historic path with the approval of the Ventana Wilderness, and I am particularly gratified that this addition to the Wilderness System under my administration involves a wilderness area right here in California.

Encompassing 98,000 acres, the Ventana Wilderness contains superb mountain scenery and unusual species of wild animals and trees, including the bristlecone or Santa Lucia fir which grows only here in the Santa Lucia Mountains. It offers a striking and unspoiled setting for hikers, horseback riders, and the trout fisherman, in an area located near large centers of population.

The Congress still has many other wilderness proposals under consideration. I hope that I will have the opportunity to approve a number of these in the coming months so that our wilderness preservation system may continue to grow and pay dividends, intangible but nevertheless real, for countless years ahead.

NOTE: As enacted, the bill (S. 714), approved on August 18, 1969, is Public Law 91–58 (83 Stat. 101).

The statement was released at San Clemente, Calif.

337   Remarks of Welcome in San Francisco to President Chung Hee Park of South Korea.   *August* 21, 1969

Mr. President:

It is a very great honor for me to welcome you and Mrs. Park and the members of your party to the United States of America.

And it is particularly significant that you are being welcomed in the State of California and in the city of San Francisco. I am proud that, as President of the United States, the first welcome to a head of state outside of Washington, D.C., is in my home State of California for the President of Korea.

It is particularly appropriate that this should be so, because California looks to the Pacific; and San Francisco, for over 100 years, has been known as the Gateway to the Orient. But your visit to our country has significance far beyond these historical and geographical considerations.

It was 16 years ago that the war, in which Americans fought side by side with Republic of Korea soldiers, came to an end. I visited Korea in the winter of 1953, and I saw there a country where 25 percent of the people were homeless and where many outside observers thought that the people of Korea could never come back.

But in these 16 years, we have seen a remarkable progress which has excited the admiration and respect of the people of the United States and all the people of the world.

The Republic of Korea maintains armed forces that are strong enough to assume the major share of the responsibility for defending Korea against the threat from the north.

And we are also keenly aware of the fact that the Republic of Korea, next to the United States of America, furnishes more men fighting in South Vietnam than any other nation, except for the South Vietnamese themselves.

We are grateful for the sacrifices that are made there by the 50,000 men from South Korea. But we also have tremendous respect for the fact that despite the military burdens that the Republic of Korea must bear that economic progress has moved forward at a dimension no one thought was possible.

The Republic of Korea has received aid from the United States of America, but the people of Korea are determined that they will stand on their own feet and their economy has moved forward to the point where they can look to the day where they will be able to stand on their own feet without outside aid.

And so, Mr. President, because of this record, because of our association together in war, because of our working together in peace, and because the people of the Republic of Korea have demonstrated a spirit, a courage in war and peace, which has brought admiration from our people and people throughout the world, we welcome you especially with a warm heart on this very beautiful day in San Francisco.

We are proud to have stood together with a strong, self-reliant people in the past, and we shall be proud to stand together with you and your people in the future.

NOTE: The President spoke at approximately 11:45 a.m. at Crissy Field, San Francisco, Calif., where President Chung Hee Park of

South Korea was given a formal welcome with full military honors.

An advance text of the President's remarks is printed in the Weekly Compilation of Presidential Documents (vol. 5, p. 1168).

President Park responded as follows:

Mr. President, Mrs. Nixon, distinguished guests, ladies and gentlemen:

On behalf of the Government and the people of the Republic of Korea, I wish to express my deep appreciation to President and Mrs. Nixon for the kind invitation extended to Mrs. Park and me. I would also like to thank the Mayor and the citizens of this beautiful city of San Francisco for their warm welcome. And I have particular pleasure in again visiting this great country which has so recently succeeded in placing the first men on the moon.

I think it very significant that our meetings will take place in the city of San Francisco, the birthplace of the United Nations, a city which has knitted a special relationship with Asia and the Pacific, a city which has developed such close historical ties with Korea as to be mentioned frequently in the history of our independence movement.

Mr. President, I am pleased to say that we are in accord with the Asian policy which you have recently put forth. I am sure the meetings here will provide us with an excellent opportunity for a full exchange of views concerning Korea and Vietnam, both of which remain under constant Communist threat, and also concerning problems of Asia and the Pacific as a whole.

Citizens of the United States who are here to welcome us, I wish to take this opportunity to convey the deep appreciation of the Korean people to you for the genuine friendship and unsparing support which you have extended to the Korean people in our efforts to defend ourselves and to achieve economic reconstruction of our homeland, the Republic of Korea.

Thank you.

338 Toasts of the President and President Park at a State Dinner in San Francisco. *August* 21, 1969

Mr. President, Mrs. Park, all of the distinguished guests in this very distinguished audience tonight:

As I am sure most of you realize, this is an historic occasion not only because of the visit that the President of the Republic of Korea is paying to the United States in an official capacity—because this is the first time in this administration and probably in any administration that a state dinner is being given by the President of the United States for the head of the government of another State, in this case the Republic of Korea, and I am honored that it is in my own State of California and here in the great city of San Francisco.

We have tried to create to an extent the atmosphere which you would find in the White House. The President was pointing out that when he was at the White House at a state dinner there that the audience was not as large, because only 110 could be seated at a White House state dinner.

The wines are from California, the record will show. The flowers are from California, and much of the audience is from California. But the Marine Orchestra, which for 100 years has been the President's orchestra in the White House, was brought from Washington, and the Strolling Strings from the Army came from Washington. We brought them here because we want you to hear them, because one of mine and my wife's most pleasant memories and fondest memories of Korea was in the year 1953 when we became acquainted with the great love of music of the Korean people.

Tonight, in attempting to bring to those in this audience who come from California and all over the Nation something of the feeling of Korea that I have and that I believe the people of the United States do have and should have so they will know the facts, I would like to speak, not simply in my capacity as head of state and head of government, officially welcoming another head of state and head of government, whose friendship we value, but I would like to speak from the hearts of all of the American people to the people of Korea.

And I would like to tell this audience what Korea means, what it means to me, what I think it means to America and to the world.

Korea, first, is a land much like California, a thousand miles of mountains and rivers and valleys. Korea is a land which is very varied in its climate, and in its phyiscal conditions.

Korea, to many in the United States, means a war, a war that was difficult, a war that cost casualties, a war that was controversial. But we should think of Korea tonight in a different sense, because as President Park has often reminded us each time he comes to the United States, he speaks of a different Korea.

Korea today should mean to America and to the world these things: One, it means courage. In all of the world, and I have been to most of the countries of the world, there are no people more courageous than the people of Korea.

They proved their courage fighting for their own freedom in a war that ended 16 years ago. They are proving it by fighting alongside the persons of the United States and those of South Vietnam and other countries in the war in Vietnam with 50,000 Koreans there. And they prove it by maintaining one of the largest armed forces in the world in order to meet the

threat which is posed against them in the north.

And this kind of courage Americans admire. Korea means courage, therefore, to us.

Korea also means friendship and alliance in the deepest sense, not the friendship and alliance simply of words, but the friendship and alliance which goes beyond that, and which involves cooperation not just in a war in Vietnam, but in building the new collective arrangements in Asia, which are so important to peace in the Pacific.

And as all of the people in this audience, particularly from California, will realize. peace in the Pacific is essential if we are going to have peace in the world. Because we must remember that the wars that we have been engaged in in the last quarter of a century on three occasions came from the Pacific.

But, finally, Korea today means something else that we need to be reminded of. It means self-reliance. It means self-respect. It means independence. You see it in the faces of the Korean people when you go to that country.

You see it in the faces of that wonderful children's choir, the orphans' choir, when they come to America and sing so beautifully that the tears come to your eyes when you think of what they have been through, and yet how happy they can be despite all that.

And you see it when you realize, as I realized on every occasion today, that Korea is a country which has received aid from the United States, but a country that wants to develop the ability to stand on its own feet. On occasion after occasion, the President and Mrs. Park have expressed the appreciation of the Korean people for the aid they have received from the United States.

And my answer is this: We have aided over 100 countries over the last 25 years. Some of those programs have been successes. More of them have been failures.

But there is one great lesson. All of the aid in the world will not help the people who are unable or unwilling to help themselves. And the people of Korea are not only willing to help themselves, they insist on helping themselves.

And despite their immense military budget, they are developing economically in a remarkably effective way so that the time is now nearing when they will proudly be able to stand on their own two feet economically without any assistance from the United States or any other nation.

So these qualities are what we think of or I think of when I think of Korea: courage, true friendship and alliance, and self-reliance, self-reliance which is so important for the character of a great people.

In proposing a toast to the President of Korea, I have been reminded that there is a saying in Korea which goes like this: The times in which we live are most trying, but may the time come when peace and prosperity will finally come to those thousand miles of mountains and rivers on which we live.

That is what we feel about Korea tonight. We want peace and prosperity for Korea, for all the nations of the world; and, so, from our hearts, I know all will want to join me tonight in raising our glasses to that peace and prosperity for the people of Korea and to the President of Korea and to Mrs. Park—to the President.

NOTE: The President spoke at 10:31 p.m. at the St. Francis Hotel in San Francisco, Calif.

President Chung Hee Park of South Korea responded as follows:

Mr. President, Mrs. Nixon, distinguished guests, ladies and gentlemen:

It is a great honor for me to have received such warm and splendid welcome and hospitality here in this beautiful city of San Francisco today. And I would like to express my highest admiration again to the American people for their greatest achievement of all, the landing of the first men on the moon.

My heartfelt congratulations are also extended to President Nixon for the remarkable diplomatic success he has achieved for world peace through his recent visit to a number of countries of the world.

On behalf of the Government and people of the Republic of Korea, I would like to take this opportunity to express my deep appreciation to the Government and people of the United States for their unfailing support to the cause of freedom, independence, security, and prosperity in Korea.

I am most pleased to inform you that your officers and men in Korea are discharging their duties in the most superb way today as in the past, standing guard side by side with my fellow countrymen in uniform along the demilitarized zone.

I extend my personal thanks and highest praise to those American youths for their distinguished service in Korea. At this very moment, the Republic of Korea is striving hard for its own progress, while guarding the defense line along the demilitarized zone.

All Koreans are working vigorously toward strengthening the national defense on the one hand, and the realizing of the economic self-sufficiency on the other.

The remarkable progress achieved so far by the Republic of Korea is the result of efforts of the Korean people who are receiving assistance coupled with the friendship of the American people who are rendering assistance.

I think that this is not only a matter of pride for the Korean people, but also that for the American people. And we are happy with and proud of the fact that we have demonstrated the immense strength which has been generated from the close cooperation between our two countries.

Ladies and gentlemen, we are, however, still faced with certain elements who, out of jealousy of our splendid achievement, threaten to destroy, at every opportunity, what we have accomplished through our joint efforts.

They are the very aggressive North Korean Communists who continue to commit belli-cose acts of provocation and infiltration, con-stantly seeking an opportunity for renewed aggression.

The bellicose North Korea has gained not even an inch of our free land despite their cease-less attempts.

It is because, in my belief, of the staunch anti-Communist stance of the Korean people, together with the firm determination of the United States to defend Korea, that we have prevented this.

I take this opportunity to pay my sincere tribute to the memory of those young officers who have sacrificed themselves for the peace in Korea and its neighboring areas.

My deepest sympathy goes to their bereaved families. I have no doubt that the noble sacri-fices for peace will shine increasingly brighter in the pages of history of mankind and be long remembered by us all.

Ladies and gentlemen, it is our fervent desire that peace must be restored as early as possible, not only in Korea, but in every corner of the world, especially in Vietnam.

This is the reason why I have deep under-standing of, and give full support to, the en-deavors of President Nixon to settle the Viet-namese conflict and to restore peace in Vietnam as early as possible.

And this is why the Republic of Korea spares no effort in cooperating in the cause of peace.

Frankly speaking, I realize through my own experience that, as far as Communists are concerned, there can be no peace as we under-stand it. Theirs in reality is no more than a peace in disguise during which they prepare for a larger-scale aggression.

Through my own long experience in dealing with Communists in Asia, I am firmly con-vinced that the only, and the best, way to restore peace in the region is to convince the Communists of our superior strengths which they cannot defeat, so that they may abandon their futile theme of aggression.

It is because of this belief that at every opportunity I have emphasized the importance of the principle of responsive actions in our dealings with the Communists.

I can only hope that our honest effort for peace will eventually be accepted in good faith by the Communists and that they will abandon their usual method.

Ladies and gentlemen, today there is an up-surging trend toward self-determination and self-dependence among free nations in Asia, who are endeavoring to attain progress and prosperity through their own initiatives and efforts.

This outlook and vigorous effort on the part of the Asian people are throwing a brilliant new light on the paths toward a new era in Asia. They are giving greater hope and encourage-ment to the prospect of world peace.

Despite such a new hope in Asia, however, there still lie serious obstacles in the way. And these are, I must point out once again, the Com-munist threats.

Under these circumstances, the time has now come for free nations in Asia to unite and work together for the common objective of prosperity. I believe that it is now time for you to take resolute action toward this end.

I am convinced that regional security and prosperity can be achieved by the nations of the region themselves, if they unite, cooperate, and endeavor together more closely for the attainment of these common objectives.

I believe what President Nixon has em-phasized in his new Asian policy is this very spirit of self-dependence in Asia which calls for the initiative of Asians themselves in shap-ing their own destiny—Asia for Asians.

And the United States will not abandon Asia, but continue to remain there as an Asian and Pacific power to assist Asians in their own effort for the development of their region and will honor the commitment made to the area.

This underlying theme of President Nixon's policy, will, I am pleased to say, have our wholehearted support.

In my view, the President's policy has laid emphasis on the two aspects: the responsibility of the Asians themselves and the role of the United States in regional cooperation. And I firmly beleive that this policy will contribute positively to self-dependence of Asia and will help Asians realize well-being in the region through a higher degree of cooperation.

I think the Asians as well as the United States people should bear in mind that only when the initiatives and efforts of the Asians themselves and the United States cooperation are well coordinated and balanced together, so as to meet the needs of Asia in an effective way, can we expect a great effect from the new approach of the United States for the stability and progress of this region.

But should these efforts become imbalanced for want of a positive effort on the part of either side, new disturbances and threats will inevitably recur in this region.

Citizens of the great United States who have sent men to the moon, I would like to ask you to join me now in a toast to the continued good health and happiness and success of the President and Mrs. Nixon.

339   Joint Statement Following Discussions With President Park of South Korea.   *August* 22, 1969

AT THE invitation of His Excellency President Richard Nixon of the United States of America, His Excellency President Park Chung Hee of the Republic of Korea and Mrs. Park visited San Francisco August 21 and 22, 1969. The meetings of the two Presidents took place in an atmosphere of warm cordiality reflecting the close and long-standing relationship between the United States and the Republic of Korea.

The two Presidents agreed that a new era is beginning in Asia marked by the increasing strength and prosperity of most Asian countries. They affirmed that these countries are increasingly contributing to the security of the East Asian and Pacific region as well as to their own security. They agreed on the desirability of strengthening existing organizations and institutions for East Asian and Pacific regional cooperation.

President Park gave an account of continuing acts of aggression committed by the North Korean communist regime against the Republic of Korea. The two Presidents agreed that Republic of Korea forces and American forces stationed in Korea must remain strong and alert and the two Presidents reaffirmed the deter-

mination of their Governments to meet armed attack against the Republic of Korea in accordance with the Mutual Defense Treaty between the Republic of Korea and the United States.

President Nixon and President Park took note of the newly formed Homeland Reserve Defense Force as a contribution to the security and stability of Korea. They agreed that support for the Homeland Reserve Defense Force should be continued.

The two Presidents recognized the necessity for long term efforts to lessen the causes of tension on the Korean peninsula.

The two Presidents agreed that allied nations should continue to work toward securing an honorable and lasting peace in Vietnam and they reaffirmed the right of the Vietnamese people to determine their own future without external interference or intimidation. President Park expressed agreement with the proposals put forth by President Nixon on May 14, 1969. President Nixon expressed appreciation to President Park for the contribution which the valiant troops of the Republic of Korea are making in Vietnam and agreed that the United States would continue to consult closely with the Republic of Korea and its other allies concerning the situation in Vietnam.

President Park expressed the gratitude of his countrymen for the consistent efforts of the United States on behalf of Korea's independence, freedom and economic reconstruction both in war and peace.

President Park conveyed to President Nixon the congratulations of the Korean people for the great achievement of Apollo 11 which marked a new chapter in the history of mankind by landing men on the moon and expressed his desire that this accomplishment would add new momentum to the common efforts of all nations in realizing a better world where all mankind would enjoy lasting peace and prosperity.

President Nixon expressed his admiration for the rapid and remarkable progress of the Republic of Korea in economic, social and other fields in recent years under President Park's leadership. President Park reaffirmed that Korea's economic goal is self-sufficiency and President Nixon expressed the intention of the United States Government to continue to cooperate with the Government of the Republic of Korea in its efforts to promote international trade and to attain an even higher level of economic development. President Nixon affirmed the readiness of the United States Government to continue to extend technical cooperation for further development of science and industry in the Republic of Korea. The two Presidents recognized that investment in Korea of United States private capital and joint ventures between United States and Korean enterprises are mutually beneficial.

The two Presidents pledged themselves to a continuation of the close cooperation which has characterized relationships between the two Governments in keeping with the mutual friendship forged on the fields of battle, first in Korea and now in Vietnam.

President Park expressed his deep appreciation to President Nixon, the Government of the United States and the Mayor and citizens of San Francisco for the warmth of their reception and for the courtesies extended to him and his party during the visit.

President Park cordially invited President Nixon to visit the Republic of Korea and President Nixon accepted the invitation with pleasure. They agreed that the visit would take place at a time of mutual convenience.

NOTE: The joint statement was released at San Francisco, Calif.

340   Remarks on the Departure of President Park of South Korea.   *August 22, 1969*

WELL, Mr. President, as we complete our talks, I wish to express appreciation to you for coming to the United States and for giving me the benefit of your views, not only on the relations between our two countries, but also on United States policy generally in the Pacific and in the Asian area.

I have found these talks most helpful. And I am sure that not only are we going to continue to have the relations, the good relations, we have had in the past between the Republic of Korea and the United States, but that U.S. understanding of the great forces now at play in Asia, forces that will shape the future for the last third of this century, that that understanding has been increased as a result of having the benefit of your views.

And finally, I want to say that I look forward, during my term of office, at some time of returning to Korea and of visiting your country again and of seeing you and Mrs. Park again at that time.

NOTE: The President spoke at 10:50 a.m. at the St. Francis Hotel in San Francisco, Calif.

President Chung Hee Park responded as follows:

I wish to take this opportunity once again to express my most sincere appreciation to President and Mrs. Nixon for their cordial invitation and also to express my wholehearted appreciation for the warm welcome which has been extended by the President and Mrs. Nixon and the citizens of the United States.

During my talks with President Nixon, and the talks between our ministers concerned, we have been able to exchange most candid views of the matters of mutual concern and interest. I am very pleased and satisfied with the conference and discussion we have had so far. And I am sure this meeting will even further strengthen the cordial and amicable relationship which we have enjoyed in the past. I am very glad that President Nixon has accepted my invitation to visit the Republic of Korea, where I could have the opportunity to reciprocate the hospitality that we have been accorded during our visit here in San Francisco.

And I hope that you gentlemen here would also accompany President Nixon when he visits Korea and we would like to reciprocate the courtesy to you also. Thank you very much.

341   Conversation With Bob Hope During the Red Cross Telethon in Mississippi. *August* 24, 1969

MR. HOPE. Mr. President, I wish you could be here to see this crowd.

THE PRESIDENT. Oh, it sounds great. But I must say that I have had the reports, of course, of this terrible disaster. General Lincoln [Director, Office of Emergency Preparedness] and Vice President Agnew have both been down there. They told me that it is probably the worst natural disaster we have had in this century.

But just from hearing that crowd, I can see that the spirit of the people down there is great, is that right?

MR. HOPE. Oh, it is fantastic. We are really having a ball. I know you can feel it. You can't see this crowd, but this coliseum is just jammed to capacity and they are just ready. The whole State is coming forth.

THE PRESIDENT. Bob, you can't say this, but as one of your old friends and fellow Californians we are mighty proud that you are down there, too. I think you are doing a great job for the country and for the people there.

MR. HOPE. We have a lot of people here, Mr. President. We have the Gold-diggers.[1] There are an awful lot of people here. The Governor [John Bell Williams] is standing right here. I think everybody in the State is jammed into this coliseum tonight.

THE PRESIDENT. That is wonderful.

MR. HOPE. The people who are not here are watching and so far they have raised $1 million.

THE PRESIDENT. A million dollars— that is wonderful. As you know, Bob, we are doing everything we can through the Government facilities, but I think what is

---

[1] A group of television entertainers.

done through this kind of activity where people from all over the country volunteer not only their money, but also their help, and through organizations like the Red Cross they come to the help of others who are in difficulty—this is really the true American spirit because this comes from the heart. This is something that money can't buy.

MR. HOPE. Well, it sure is, and everybody is leaning towards this effort, and I am sure they are going to take care of all the people.

Naturally everybody is very grateful for your fast action and the action of the Government. You heard that applause when you were announced, and it was just tremendous. That is the kind of crowd we have here.

THE PRESIDENT. Well, I can just say this one thing, that I speak to the people down there and to all of those who are sending in their contributions, not just as President of the United States in a govern-

mental capacity, but as one of their fellow Americans, I am very proud to be an American when Americans come through in a crisis like this. With this kind of a heart, America is going to do all right in the years ahead. There is no question about that. It is coming through in a crisis that proves that a country has what it takes.

Bob, you must have a great audience there.

MR. HOPE. Thank you, Mr. President. You heard them.

THE PRESIDENT. You have a great audience. We will see you when you get back. I hope you get back before I leave California. Goodby.

MR. HOPE. Wonderful, thank you very much.

NOTE: President Nixon spoke by telephone at 6:45 p.m., from San Clemente, Calif., with comedian Bob Hope who was conducting a telethon in Jackson, Miss., to raise funds for the victims of Hurricane Camille.

342 Statement About Labor Day, 1969.
August 26, 1969

ABRAHAM LINCOLN described working men as "the basis of all governments." Woodrow Wilson said that working people were "the backbone of the nation." And even Calvin Coolidge, who on one occasion suggested that the business of America was business, also declared when he was President that "America recognizes no aristocracy save those who work."

I am sure these sentiments are shared by all Americans as the nation observes another Labor Day. The workers of America have assumed important responsibilities and have carried them out faithfully.

It is important now that the nation fully carry out its responsibilities to them. It is essential, for example, that the wages of working people be protected against inflation. This administration has made the fight against inflation a matter of highest priority. We have already succeeded in our effort to cut federal spending, an important anti-inflationary move. We believe that, with the cooperation of all Americans, we can prevent another wage-price spiral and restore stability to our economy.

It is important, too, that the chance

to hold a good job be extended to the many Americans who do not enjoy this opportunity at present. More jobs must be provided—good jobs which provide dignity for the worker and security for his family. Only a strong and growing economy can adequately achieve this goal.

We must also be sure that those who seek employment are prepared for the jobs which will exist. It is encouraging to note in this regard that the number of job training opportunities for disadvantaged Americans will increase by some 80,000 during the coming year—so that the total will be more than one million. But even this increase is in adequate. This Administration has therefore proposed a new, comprehensive manpower program, one which will improve and extend job counseling, training, and placement services. The proposed program would transfer greater administrative responsibility for manpower projects to the Mayors and Governors, officials who are well equipped to tailor projects to meet local requirements.

We have also developed a new approach to welfare, one which will provide incentives for the recipients to seek training and employment. Our plan is designed to reward labor; under our new scale of benefits, it would always pay to work.

Because we believe in the dignity of work, we also believe that work opportunities should be made *equally* available to all Americans. We have proposed stronger government efforts to protect equal opportunity in employment—even as we have moved to bring greater fairness to the hiring practices of the Federal Government.

The health and safety of our workers also requires immediate attention. Each

year, more than 14,000 people are killed and more than two million are incapacitated because of work-related illnesses or accidents. We have therefore proposed to the Congress a new national Occupational Safety and Health Act under which we would establish and enforce nationwide standards for safe and healthful work places. We have suggested special legislation of this sort for the coal industry.

As we renew our commitment to the general well-being of the working man, we also reaffirm our faith in sound collective bargaining. In an increasingly complex society, one in which so many elements depend so heavily on one another, the process of collective bargaining must be strong and effective and exercised with self-restraint on all sides. But the process cannot work unless the participants are free to reach their own decisions. This Administration will always respect that freedom.

I mention these particular concerns because they are of special importance to the working people of this country. In the weeks ahead, we will move forward in each of these areas. We will also make progress in other fields which have a direct impact on workers' lives: tax reform, for example; crime control; and, of course, the pursuit of peace. And we will proceed toward all of these goals with greater confidence because we know that the labor force of this country shares our commitment and supports these efforts.

This nation has always been dedicated to the proposition that honor lies in honest toil. We believe that the strength and well-being of American working people is central to the strength and well-being of the nation. And we are convinced that the genius of America lies in the energy and perseverance with which millions of Americans do their daily work.

Labor Day, 1969, is an appropriate time for all of us to reaffirm these important precepts. I am pleased to join my country-men in expressing admiration and appreciation to the working men and women of America.

RICHARD NIXON

NOTE: The statement was released at San Clemente, Calif.

343 Remarks on the Arrival in California of Former President and Mrs. Johnson. *August 27, 1969*

WE ARE here, as I know all of you know, for a very special occasion. We are going into the redwoods to dedicate a park.

And I think it is most significant that in the whole history of this country there has perhaps been no First Lady who, in the field of beautification and in the field of dedication to the conservation of the natural beauty of our country, has done more than Lady Bird Johnson—Mrs. Johnson.

We are here to dedicate these magnificent redwoods to Mrs. Johnson under the name of Lady Bird Johnson Grove.

But also we are here, it happens by coincidence, on another day. It happens that President Johnson and I have several things in common. We both were born in small towns. We both served in the House. We both served in the Senate of the United States. We both served as Vice President, and we have both served as President of the United States. And we both are very fortunate in the fact, we think, that we married above ourselves to Mrs. Johnson and Mrs. Nixon.

But also today, I know you want to join us in wishing President Johnson a happy birthday. This is his 61st birthday. How about that!

[At this point, "Happy Birthday" was sung to former President Johnson.]

This is President Johnson's first visit to this part of California; I know that you would all like to hear from him.

PRESIDENT JOHNSON. *Mr. President and Mrs. Nixon, Governor Reagan, Congressman Clausen, Senator Murphy:*

I want to express the appreciation of the Johnson family to the President and the First Lady for their generosity and their thoughtfulness today.

Since the President has let out how old I am, I just want to say that I don't know of any one of the 61 birthdays that I have had where I have been happier or where people have done more to try to make me happy. When you come to a good congressional district, a beautiful place in a beautiful State and a beautiful land, you are naturally appreciative.

When the President and the First Lady of the United States recognize and honor the work of what I believe to be a great woman, that is the best birthday present I could have.

Thank you very much.

NOTE: The President spoke at 3 p.m. at Arcata Airport in Eureka, Calif., where he and Mrs. Nixon greeted former President and Mrs. Johnson prior to their flight to Redwood National Park for the dedication of the Lady Bird Johnson Grove.

The remarks were released at Arcata Airport in Eureka, Calif.

344   Remarks at the Dedication of Lady Bird Johnson
      Grove in Redwood National Park in California.
      August 27, 1969

President and Mrs. Johnson, Governor Reagan, Secretary Hickel, Congressman Clausen, Dr. Graham, all of the distinguished guests here on the platform and in the audience:

My participation in this program will be brief, but it is very necessary because the time now comes for the signing of a proclamation, the proclamation that Don Clausen referred to earlier whereby in one instance through the stroke of a pen we can accomplish something we want to accomplish.

I do want to say, however, before signing the proclamation which is here on this redwood table appropriately beside me— I do want to say that I think that Congressman Clausen deserves a great deal of credit for not only his support of this great redwood forest, the support that he gave to it, that Tom Kuchel as Senator, gave to it, and others who are present here, but also for his idea; and it was his idea that this grove be appropriately named for the First Lady, Mrs. Lady Bird Johnson, who has done more in the field of beautification than any First Lady in history.

Now there is very little that I can add to what her record already says to all of us. That record is well known: 5 years of traveling this country, going into the parks all over the country, and also to other areas which are not parks, but for the purpose of seeing what could be done to make the country a more beautiful country, one that we could all be proud of.

I simply want to say, as I stand here in this magnificent grove of redwoods, that

President Johnson and I happen to share a number of things in common. I mentioned them briefly at the airport at Arcata. We both served in the House, in the Senate. We both served as Vice President, and we both served as President of the United States.

And there is one other thing I find that we have in common. We both have a great admiration for Theodore Roosevelt who was the President of the United States who first showed an immense interest in the whole field of conservation.

I am on vacation now, if a President ever takes a vacation. I am on vacation down in San Clemente, California. Sometimes in the evenings I have a chance to read, and President Johnson noted, as he was looking over the library, that the book I currently was reading was one of the biographies of Theodore Roosevelt that happened to be there at this time.

In reading that biography, one point came through to me very clearly: that he, as President of the United States, found that he always received renewed strength from going to the great outdoors. He, of course, was known as the President that believed in the strenuous life.

I am not sure that I can go as far as he went in that respect—I won't even ride a surfboard. On the other hand, he was one who liked to come to great groves like this. He came always to the West. He was renewed by going to the West and then going back to the awesome duties that he had in the White House.

The duties that he had at the turn of the century from 1900 to 1908 were very,

very heavy. The duties that a President of the United States today has perhaps would have to be described as even heavier.

But certainly to stand here in this grove of redwoods, to realize what a few moments of solitude in this magnificent place can mean, what it can mean to a man who is President, what it can mean to any man or any woman who needs time to get away from whatever may be the burdens of all of our tasks, and then that renewal that comes from it—to stand here makes us realize the great service that a President of the United States, Theodore Roosevelt, rendered when he put so much emphasis on conservation; that these Congressmen and Senators and Governors have rendered by their support of conservation and that our very honored guest, Mrs. Lyndon B. Johnson, Lady Bird Johnson, has rendered in her work for beautification, and particularly her work with regard to this very grove in which we stand.

So today I sign this proclamation as President of the United States, but I sign it for all of the people of California, for all the people of the United States, in admiration and respect for a great First Lady: Lady Bird Johnson.

[At this point, the President signed Proclamation 3925. He resumed speaking, as follows:]

Now, ladies and gentlemen, it is my great privilege to present to you Mrs. Lyndon B. Johnson, Lady Bird Johnson, for whom this magnificent grove of redwoods has now been named.

MRS. JOHNSON. Thank you, Mr. President. You have given me a day to treasure always, and I am grateful. I am grateful, too, to another President who in his time, along with many, many people, did what

he could to insure that these trees would be here for all the tomorrows.

Conservation is indeed a bipartisan business because all of us have the same stake in this magnificent continent. All of us have the same love for it and the same feeling that it is going to belong to our children and grandchildren and their grandchildren—I am coming to understand that a lot better these days—the same opportunity to work in our time to see that it stays as glorious.

So, President Nixon, I am very grateful to you for associating me with this part of it for all the tomorrows, and I thank you very much, as all my family does, and thank you, Congressman Clausen, too.

PRESIDENT NIXON. We are now going to unveil the plaque on this site.

Incidentally, our musical group is the Humboldt County A Cappella Choir. We are very happy to have them here today.

If I could be permitted one personal local reference. This occasion has been particularly memorable for all of us to have a chance to come to this beautiful redwood forest, but it is also appreciated in this respect: This is the first time I have had a chance to be in Humboldt County for 7 years, and I am glad to be back here today for this occasion.

And now, ladies and gentlemen, while this is not on the official program, I know that all of you would like to hear a word from—I don't know whether you say the first person in the family or the second on such a day as this—but I will simply say this: that as you do know, this happens to be President Johnson's birthday. I have been trying to think of how we could wish him a happy birthday, and I was studying some of the background with regard to the age of these trees.

I find that the average age of the trees

in this grove is 500 years, and I find that the oldest trees are 2,500 years—as [Rev. William F.] Billy Graham pointed out in his eloquent invocation—before Christ.

So I suppose that what we could best say to President Johnson on this, his birthday, may he live as long as these trees, and, of course, in some countries they say: "May you live 1,000 years." But at least in expressing it that way—may he live as long as these trees—that means we are giving him every benefit of every chance to live as long as he possibly can.

So I am very proud to present to my fellow Californians the man who served in the office that I now hold for a period of 5 years—served with distinction and with great courage over that period of time: President Lyndon B. Johnson.

PRESIDENT JOHNSON. *Mr. President, Mrs. Nixon, Mrs. Johnson, Secretary Hickel, Governor Reagan, Dr. Graham, Congressman Clausen, Senator Murphy, Congressman and Mrs. Boggs, my dear friends of California:*

It is such a wonderful way to spend one's birthday and all the Johnson family feel deeply in the debt of President and Mrs. Nixon for bringing us here to this beautiful setting, away from the 105° temperature that we are having down in Texas, and showing us the beauties of nature that abound in this great, beautiful State.

President Nixon was talking to you about some of his political heroes, and I guess I might be pardoned if I also mentioned a Roosevelt. While Theodore Roosevelt was one of our great Presidents, one of our great progressive leaders, there was another Roosevelt who had something in common with Theodore, and that was most strikingly noted in the field of conservation.

Presidents have many things in common, as President Nixon pointed out. My father said to me one time when I was a little boy: "Son, you will never know what it is to be a father until you are a father." And one never knows what it is to be a President until you are a President.

Mr. President, Mrs. Johnson and I are all the more grateful because we are so aware of the burdens that you and your gracious wife carry on behalf of this great Nation and that you would take the time to come here and pay this honor to this great lady is something that we will always cherish and always remember.

The last month I was in the White House I read a book about Theodore Roosevelt and the contributions that he made to this land. As I was telling the President coming up, I read a document published by the Franklin D. Roosevelt Library on his contributions in the field of conservation.

I was amused in reading that document about letters that he wrote as a State Senator of the State of New York—long before he became its distinguished Governor or Assistant Secretary of the Navy of the Nation or the President of our country—in attempting to develop a State park policy and to preserve some of the playgrounds and parks for the people of the great State of New York.

So, if I could express a hope today—I know that the hope that President Nixon expressed that I might live to be as old as these trees, I will never realize that, but I might realize this one—I would hope that future generations might look down the history of our past and look at the great conservation leaders and that some of my children and my grandchildren and if I am fortunate, even myself, could read not only what both President Nixon and

I read about the works of Theodore Roosevelt and his leadership in the field of conservation and Franklin D. Roosevelt and what he had done to conserve this Nation, but that soon we might have a book from the Richard M. Nixon Library that would join with the great names of Roosevelt, the great name of Richard Nixon; because if I am a prophet—one that can see the beauties that abound in this State where he grew up and where he enjoyed coming to the forests and building a fire and talking about the glories of this State—it could well be and should be extended to the rest of the Nation and the other States.

Since Presidents do have things in common, I remember that on President Truman's 61st birthday he was in the White House, and he sat down and wrote his mother a letter. Presidents are lonely people, and the only ones they are really sure of all the time are their womenfolk. President Nixon and I have something else in common. We can always depend on our womenfolk. Just as Mrs. Johnson has been by my side every step of the way, so has Mrs. Nixon.

President Truman wrote to his mother and sister Mary, and said: "I slept in the President's room and Churchill woke me at daylight and said he wanted to jump the gun on an announcement that we had agreed would be made in Washington at 9 o'clock and London at 3 o'clock and Moscow at 4 o'clock."

So, President Truman, on his 61st birthday, had his timing problem, too. He said he had to tell Mr. Churchill that he could not do that, that they had agreed it would be simultaneous. It was great news for the world. It was the announcement of V–E Day.

I cannot make any announcement like that today, and President Nixon can't either. But I am sure if we both could announce what is in our hearts and what we want to announce more than anything else in the world it would be that there would be peace among men throughout this world.

So, President Truman concluded his letter by saying to his mother and his sister that he hoped that they could come and visit with him and they could come at a time when he did not have his timing problems.

Well, I didn't have Churchill call me at daylight and wake me up, but for some reason or other one of the few times in our 35 years of married life, Mrs. Johnson waked up first this morning and she must have had this occasion on her mind because she had our daughter, who lives in Washington, and our son-in-law come down and bring our granddaughter, and I don't know why they chose me, but they brought in my young granddaughter with two teeth, about 9 months old, and deposited her on my stomach and told me to play with her for a while while the ladies went to the hairdresser.

When they came back both of the ladies were rushing me to get dressed so that we could be on time with President Nixon. I said: "Well, you have asked me to keep the baby and I have had her on my lap for an hour. I have had no time to dress and now you want to walk out with me in my pajamas to get out to the redwoods." That shows how much she loves the beauty of this country and this Nation.

It also shows that while I did not have problems with Churchill, I did have problems with my wife. But if all my problems were as simple as those I have with her, what a wonderful life this would be.

President Nixon, I want to conclude by

690

saying to you that we are most thankful to be Americans. We are very grateful that we can live in a country that is strong and vital and still has the spirit of adventure that this Nation has.

We are very proud to stand behind you and to support you in your earnest quest for peace in the world and for prosperity at home.

Of one thing I am absolutely sure, of the 37 Presidents that have come, and 36 have gone on, I feel sure from what I have read and studied about their lives that their greatest problem was never doing what was right; their greatest problem was knowing what was right.

No man occupied the place that you occupy who didn't want to do the best he could, and some have succeeded and some have had less success. But of this you can be sure: If all of your days are as successful as today in bringing happiness to your predecessor, you will have a most successful Presidency.

Thank you from the bottom of our hearts.

NOTE: The exchange of remarks took place at 4:05 p.m. at the dedication of the Lady Bird Johnson Grove in the Redwood National Park, Calif.

The text of the remarks was released at Arcata Airport, Eureka, Calif.

345   Remarks on Arrival at Colorado Springs To Address the National Governors' Conference.   *September 1, 1969*

General McKee, Governor Love, Senator Allott, Senator Dominick, all the distinguished guests, and all of this wonderful crowd here in Colorado Springs:

Mrs. Nixon and I wish to express our appreciation for your wonderful welcome on this beautiful day. General McKee told me the weatherman was cooperating as usual, that the storm would wait until after we had completed our inspection, and he was right.

But we do want you to know that as the plane was circling the area to come down for its landing, we saw all the cars parked, and we realized what a chore it really is for people to get in their cars, drive to the airport, walk to the area where you now stand, stand there for a half hour beforehand, or longer.

The General says some were here at 8:30 this morning. Well, we thank all of you, whenever you came, for giving us such a wonderful welcome to Colorado.

As you know, we are here for two purposes: one, the Governors' Conference tonight, where I will have the opportunity to meet with Governor Love and his colleagues at this very, very important meeting of all the Governors of all the States; and second, for the purpose of inspecting the NORAD establishment here in Colorado Springs.

I simply want to say one thing to all of you before we go on for the inspection, and that is this: As you know, we returned just a few weeks ago from a trip that took us around the world after the astronaut landing in the Pacific. We saw many great cities. We saw also many magnificent crowds. And we have a great respect for all of the nations abroad that we visited, for the Continent of Asia, and for the Continent of Europe, Africa, whatever the case may be.

But as I stand here in Colorado Springs,

here where we have represented the United States of America and Canada, I simply want to say that those of us who have the privilege of living in the North American Continent are indeed fortunate.

This is great country. It is the country of hope for many people all over the world. We only trust that we will be worthy of those hopes in all the years ahead; hopes for peace, hopes for new roads to progress and prosperity, hopes that all of you have for your children and for the future.

Again, we thank you very much for welcoming us to Colorado Springs. As a matter of fact, we receive such a wonderfully warm welcome every time we come, we always want to come back. We will be back again.

Thank you.

NOTE: The President spoke at 1:27 p.m. at Peterson Field near Colorado Springs, Colo. Gen. Seth McKee, USAF, was Commander in Chief, North American Air Defense Command (NORAD) and Continental Air Defense. John A. Love was Governor of Colorado, and Gordon Allott and Peter H. Dominick were U.S. Senators from Colorado.

346   Toasts of the President and Governor Love at a Dinner in Colorado Springs.   *September 1, 1969*

Governor Love, Mrs. Love, and all of the distinguished Governors and their guests and our guests tonight:

I very much appreciated those very warm words and the welcome that I have received, along with my wife, on this occasion.

Naturally, after hearing such words, I tend to think of the last time I attended a Governors' Conference, and none of you were there. Because I understand that the senior Governor of all the Governors here is the Governor of the State of New York, Nelson Rockefeller, and I know where he was in 1954 [1]—he was in Washington with me.

At that time you will remember that we developed the Federal highway program and President Eisenhower had a death in his family,[2] and I had the responsibility of going to the Governors' Conference, which was held in New York State that year, and presenting that program, the Federal highway program.

So it has been 15 years since the Governors have invited me back. I appreciate being invited back. We have a very high regard for Governors in this administration. We have a Governor as Vice President. We have three Governors in the Cabinet,[3] and certainly if any Governors are interested in other positions, we have those, too.

So tonight I could talk about Governors, as I will a little later when we get into what I understand is the formal speech that you have to listen to.

I think that on this occasion that all of you would agree that perhaps a brief re-

---

[1] Governor Rockefeller was Special Assistant to President Eisenhower 1954–1955.

[2] President Eisenhower's sister-in-law, Mrs. Milton S. Eisenhower, died July 10, 1954.

[3] Secretary of the Interior Walter J. Hickel of Alaska, Secretary of Housing and Urban Development George W. Romney of Michigan, and Secretary of Transportation John A. Volpe of Massachusetts.

mark with regard to others who are so responsible for our success might be in order.

I have been sitting here at a table with the wife of the Governor of Colorado on one side and the wife of the Governor of Virginia [Mrs. Mills E. Godwin] on the other. And in a completely bipartisan way, I have learned, really again, how much the first ladies of the States and the first ladies in our families mean to any man in a political career.

I was talking to Mrs. Love. I tried to get in on some of her secrets. I said: "What do you do when somebody calls, and the man is sitting right there, and says, 'Is he in?' "

She is a very smart wife, I can assure you. Because she said: "I begin by saying, he is not in. Who is calling?" Now if it is a dumb wife, she says, "Who is calling?" and then says, "He is not in."

Virtually all of the wives here have to be of very great intelligence to know how to handle those calls. Of course that is only the smaller part of it; the correspondence, making the arrangements for such a beautiful party like this, and then having those two delightful children— I say children, teenagers—hand out the favors for the evening.

I know and you know, as Governors, how much time went into planning this party, and I think that all of the wives deserve our special appreciation. They deserve our appreciation for first being married to a man who is in politics. That is hard enough.

Then they deserve appreciation for the fact that they have campaigned with us through the years. I say this for our Republican and Democratic colleagues here tonight because, believe me, the lot of man is hard enough. He has to make all

those speeches. The wife has to listen to them, and that is harder.

But in any event, above everything else, we all know, that apart from the listening to the speeches and the handling of the social engagements and the answering of the correspondence and picking up that telephone, that our wives in a very special way in America today have a life all their own. They are the ones who attend functions that we are unable to attend and functions on their own, who stimulate activities and interests in government, who really give heart to the First Family, give heart by their sympathy and interest in all the problems of state.

So you see what I am trying to get at. I could propose a toast tonight to the Governors, but I think that at this beautiful dinner and on an occasion when we all realize how much we owe to our wives who have served in so many ways in our campaigns, that we should think of them.

I recall the book that I wrote— incidentally, I will never write another one—but I recall the book[4] that I wrote and I dedicated it in the flyleaf, "To Pat, she also ran." That was after the election of 1960. If you think it is hard when you win, you should think how it is when you lose.

So what I am simply saying tonight, with a full heart, I know all of you will join me in raising our glasses to the first ladies of the 50 States.

GOVERNOR LOVE. And to the First Lady of the United States.

THE PRESIDENT. Just so we don't show any discrimination, because we must have equality of opportunity for all, I think we ought to drink to the outgoing chairman

---

[4] "Six Crises" (Doubleday and Co., Inc., New York, 1962).

of the Governors' Conference, Governor [Buford] Ellington [of Tennessee].

I don't know how the vote is coming out, but I have a few proxies in my pocket. I think we will drink to the incoming chairman, Governor Love.

NOTE: The President spoke at 8:45 p.m. in the Penrose Room of the Broadmoor Hotel in Colorado Springs in response to a toast proposed by Governor John A. Love of Colorado, chairman of the National Governors' Conference.

Governor Love's toast follows:

Ladies and gentlemen:

It is my very great privilege to propose a toast to our guest of honor this evening.

Mr. President, we are delighted to have you back in the great, beautiful State of Colorado again, and it is a greater honor for Ann and me to be able to host and entertain you in our own hometown in Colorado Springs.

For the Governors, we are most grateful that for the first time in your administration and as President you are participating in a National Governors' Conference. We have been discussing, in all the conferences that I know about, the problems of strengthening the States and revitalizing our Federal system, and we are most heartened with the recent program pronouncements that you have made. I think I can speak for all of us in saying, we pledge to you our complete support in the goals that you have enunciated.

We wish for you and to you and your leadership for our beloved Nation, continued success and progress.

Ladies and gentlemen, the President of the United States.

347 Address at the National Governors' Conference.
September 1, 1969

Vice President and Mrs. Agnew, Governor Ellington, Governor Love, all of the distinguished Governors and their first ladies who are here, and all the distinguished members of this audience:

I first want to express my appreciation to Governor Ellington for his eloquent introduction and very generous introduction, and I hope that in my remarks tonight I can respond in the same spirit.

I also want to express my appreciation to the Governors of the 50 States for their service to this Nation, whether they be Republicans or Democrats, for inviting me to address them on this occasion.

I speak somewhat with humility whenever I address a group of Governors. If you will permit a personal reference at the outset, as many of you are aware, I have run for many offices in my political career. Twenty-three years ago I ran for the House and 4 years later for the Senate, and then for Vice President and then for President, and then for Governor and then for President. The only office that I have sought and have never won is that of Governor, so, therefore, I respect the Governors who are here tonight.

To show that respect, as a demonstration of it, we have in our administration not only the Vice President, who served as the Governor of Maryland, but three other members of the Cabinet, who hold their respective posts with great distinction.

I suppose that one of the reasons this administration feels so strongly about the relationships between the Federal Government and the various States, the necessity to have a new relationship to which I will refer tonight, is that we have that strong representation, the strong voice of those who have served as Governors and who, therefore, know what the problems are.

We are meeting here tonight at a time of great and fundamental change in America—of changes more far-reaching than have ever been seen in the span of a single lifetime.

These changes summon all of us—the Federal Government, the States, the counties, the cities, and towns—each person everywhere—to a high adventure in human advancement.

We stand on the threshold of a time when the impossible becomes possible—a time when we can choose goals that, just a generation ago, would have seemed as unreachable as the moon seemed to be unreachable then. We can reach those goals.

The Spirit of Apollo gave us a brief, glittering glimpse of how far we can stretch. Thousands of minds, thousands of hands, all were marshaled in selfless dedication in achieving a great human dream—and the dream came true.

Today, we in America can afford to dream—but we have to put drive behind those dreams.

This requires that we turn—now—to a new strategy for the seventies—one that enables us to command our own future by commanding the forces of change.

Only 7 years from now, in 1976, America will celebrate its 200th birthday as a nation. So let us look ahead to that great anniversary in the Spirit of Apollo—and discover in ourselves a new Spirit of '76.

Let us resolve that what we can do, we will do.

When a great nation confronts its shortcomings, not angrily, but analytically; when it commits its resources, not wantonly but wisely; when it calms its hatreds, masters its fears, and draws together in a spirit of common endeavor, then the forces of progress are on the march.

The central race in the world today is neither an arms race nor a space race. It is the race between man and change. The central question is whether we are to be the master of events, or the pawn of events.

If we are to win this race, our first need is to make government governable.

When the new administration took office last January, we confronted a set of hard and unpleasant facts. I cite these facts not in a partisan way; they are not the fault of any one administration or of any one party. Rather, they are part of our common experience as a people, the result of an accumulating failure of government over the years to come to grips with a future that soon overtook it.

We confronted a legacy of Federal deficits that has added $58 billion to the burden of public debt in the past 10 years.

We confronted the fact that State and local governments were being crushed in a fiscal vise, squeezed by rising costs, rising demands for services, exhaustion of revenue sources.

We confronted the fact that in the past 5 years the Federal Government alone has spent more than a quarter of a trillion dollars on social programs—over $250 billion. Yet far from solving our problems, these expenditures had reaped a harvest of dissatisfaction, frustration, and bitter division.

Never in human history has so much

been spent by so many for such a negative result. The cost of the lesson has been high, but we have learned that it is not only what we spend that matters, but how we spend it.

Listen to Professor Peter Drucker analyze the problem of government today: "There is mounting evidence that government is big rather than strong; that it is fat and flabby rather than powerful; that it costs a great deal but does not achieve much. . . . Indeed, government is sick—and just at the time when we need a strong, healthy, and vigorous government." [1]

The problem has not been a lack of good intentions, and not merely a lack of money. Methods inherited from the thirties proved to be out of date in the sixties. Structures put together in the thirties broke down under the load of the sixties.

Overcentralized, overbureaucratized, the Federal Government became unresponsive as well as inefficient.

In their struggle to keep up, States and localities found the going increasingly difficult.

In the space of only 10 years, State and local expenditures rose by two and a half times—from $44 billion in 1958 to $108 billion in 1968.

States alone have had to seek more than 200 tax increases in the past 8 years.

You know—you as Governors—and I know, that simply piling tax on tax is not the long range solution to the problems we face together.

We have to devise a new way to make our revenue system meet the needs of the seventies. We have to put the money where the problems are, and we have to

get a dollar's worth of return for a dollar spent.

Our new strategy for the seventies begins with the reform of government:
  —overhauling its structure;
  —pruning out those programs that have failed or that have outlived their time;
  —ensuring that its delivery systems actually deliver the intended services to the intended beneficiaries;
  —gearing its programs to the concept of social investment;
  —focusing its activities not only on tomorrow, but on the day after tomorrow.

This must be a cooperative venture among governments at all levels, because it centers on what I have called the "New Federalism"—in which power, funds, and authority are channeled increasingly to those governments that are closest to the people.

The essence of the New Federalism is to help regain control of our national destiny by returning a greater share of control to State and local governments and to the people.

This in turn requires constant attention to raising the quality of government at all levels.

The new strategy for the seventies also requires a strategy for peace—and I pledge to you tonight that we will have an effective strategy for peace.

Let me tell you what that strategy means and what it does not mean. It means maintaining defense forces strong enough to keep the peace, but not allowing wasteful expenditures to drain away resources we need for progress.

It means limiting our commitments abroad to those we can prudently and realistically keep. It means helping other

---

[1] Peter F. Drucker, "The Age of Discontinuity: Guidelines to Our Changing Society" (Harper and Row, 1969), p. 212.

free nations maintain their own security, but not rushing in to do for them what they can and should do for themselves.

It does not mean laying down our leadership. It does not mean abandoning our allies. It does mean forging a new structure of world stability in which the burdens as well as the benefits are fairly shared—a structure that does not rely on the strength of one nation but that draws strength from all nations.

An effective strategy for peace abroad makes possible an effective strategy for meeting our domestic problems at home. To place this new domestic strategy in concrete terms, I would like to cite a few examples we in the new administration have made or proposed since taking office.

We have proposed, as all of you know because you have discussed it in this conference, the first major reform of welfare in the history of welfare.

This would abolish the discredited Aid to Families With Dependent Children program, and launch in its place a new system that for the first time would insure a minimum income for every family with dependent children—and at the same time provide a coordinated structure of work requirements, work incentives, and training designed to move people off the welfare rolls and onto payrolls in the United States.

Now I realize that some object to some of these proposals—understandably—as seeming to favor one region over another, or because they give the rich States more or less than they give to poorer States. I considered these arguments, rejected them, because, as Buford Ellington indicated in his introduction, we are one country. We must think in terms of the people and their needs—wherever they are. We must meet our problems where

the problems are. Because, unless we act to meet the problems of human need in the places where they exist, the problems and troubles of rural America today will be the problems of urban America tomorrow.

Consider for a moment the name of this Nation: the United States of America. We establish minimum national standards because we are united; we encourage local supplements because we are a federation of States; and we care for the unfortunate because this is America.

We have proposed the first major restructuring of food programs for the needy in the history of food programs.

Let's face it, for years, food programs were designed as much to get rid of surplus commodities as to feed hungry people, and now, for the first time, we propose that every American family shall have the resources, in food stamps, commodities, and other assistance, to obtain a minimum nutritious diet, with free food stamps for those with very low incomes.

We have declared the first 5 years of a child's life to be a period of special and specific Federal concern.

New knowledge recently acquired has shown that these earliest, formative years are crucial to a child's later development. Yet with only random exceptions, no provision has previously been made to insure the welfare of children during these years. With an eye to the next generation, we have made it our business to fill this void.

We have proposed the first major reform of the income tax system in nearly 20 years, to remove millions of the poor from the tax rolls entirely, to close loopholes that have allowed many of the rich to escape any taxation at all, and to make the entire structure more balanced and more equitable.

697

We have proposed the most fundamental reform of the unemployment insurance system in the history of unemployment insurance.

We have proposed the first reform in the fiscal structure of federalism since the 1930's.

In proposing to begin the sharing of Federal tax revenues with the States—to be spent as the States see fit—we are putting our money where our principles are. The power to tax is the power to destroy; but the sharing of tax revenues provides the power to build.

We have proposed, for the first time in history, a comprehensive and effective delegation of Federal programs to State and local management.

The Comprehensive Manpower Act would turn over to State and local direction a major Federal program which clearly has to be nationwide in scope and federally funded, but which can most effectively be managed at the State and local level.

We have begun the first overall reform of the organization of the Federal Government since the Hoover Commission.

By establishing common headquarters and common regional boundaries for the various Federal agencies, we have made decentralized administration possible—and made it possible for Governors and mayors to do their business with those agencies at one time and in one place.

In speaking to one of the Governors tonight, Governor [James A.] Rhodes of Ohio, he mentioned the fact that in his State, for some Federal programs, the welfare programs, approximately 40 percent of the payroll was for the purpose of filling out the federally required forms.

Let me say that we would welcome from the Governors your suggestions as to how we can reduce that kind of a load that has been imposed upon you by the Federal Government.

For the first time, machinery has been created to raise the problems of the cities and the problems of the environment to the level of formal, interdepartmental, Cabinet-level concern, with the creation of an Urban Affairs Council and the Council on the Environment.

For the first time, machinery has been created within the White House for a coordinated system of forward planning of needs and resources. With establishment of the National Goals Research Staff, we have built into the budgetary and program operations of the National Government a systematic assessment of future needs and the resources available for meeting those needs.

There is another reform I have asked for, and to which I attach special priority as a matter of the highest principle: reform of the draft.

Until peacetime conditions make a shift to an all-volunteer armed force possible—and while the draft remains necessary—it is imperative that we make it as nearly fair as possible, and that we reduce to a minimum the unnecessarily long period of uncertainty that now hangs over the lives of millions of our young people. We shall have some directives that will be issued in the very near future that will accomplish some of those results.

In summary, the 24 legislative proposals—the major ones—that I have sent to Congress, have also included proposals ranging from an overhaul of foreign aid to the most wide-ranging reform of the postal service in history; from a new program of mass transit aid to new measures for the combatting of narcotics, pornography, and organized crime.

Taken together, these measures are sweeping in their implications. I admit, too, they are controversial, as any new programs are. They also represent fundamental new directions in national policy. But to those who say they are controversial, to those who criticize them for what they are, I make this one suggestion: We have been on a road for a long time that is leading us to disaster, and when you are on the wrong road, the thing to do is get off and get onto a new road and a new progress.

These programs represent a comprehensive, concerted effort to make Government work, to make it work fairly, to make it responsive, and to gear it to the early anticipation of emerging needs, rather than belated response to crises that could have been avoided.

Now I would like for all of us to look at these measures in a larger framework.

Exactly 4 months from today, we will enter the decade of the seventies. And as we look ahead toward that 200th anniversary of American independence in 1976, we have a target to shoot for.

What kind of a nation we will be on that momentous anniversary is ours to determine by what we do or fail to do now.

As conditions are changing, so we must change.

The reforms I have proposed in these legislative recommendations are not partisan changes. They are positive changes. They have no special constituency of region or class or interest group. Their constituency is tomorrow.

It already is painfully clear that many hard choices will have to be made. Dreams of unlimited billions of dollars being released once the war in Vietnam ends are just that—dreams. True, there will be additional money, but the claims on it already are enormous. There should be no illusion that what some call the "peace and growth dividend" will automatically solve our national problems, or release us from the need to establish priorities.

There are hard budget and tax decisions ahead. These involve your interests as Governors; they involve the interests of all of us as citizens.

In order to find the money for new programs, we are going to have to trim it out of old ones. This is one reason why I regard the reforms I have proposed as essential. We can no longer afford the luxury of inefficiency in Government. We cannot count on good money to bail us out of bad ideas.

Equally important, continued improvement of governments at the State and local levels is essential to make these new concepts work.

If the delegation of funds and authority to the State and local governments under the Comprehensive Manpower Act is successful, this can then be a model for more delegations in the future. But we can only toss the ball; the States and localities have to catch it and they have to carry it.

I am confident that you can.

For a long time, as all of us know, the phrase "States rights" was often used as an escape from responsibility—as a way of avoiding a problem, rather than of meeting a problem.

But that time has passed.

I can assure you of this: We are not simply going to tell you the States have a job to do; we are going to help you find the funds, the resources, to do that job well.

We are not simply going to lecture you on what you should do. We are going to examine what we can do together.

699

One of the key points I want to make tonight is, in a sense, very similar to one I made on my recent visits to our NATO partners and to our friends in Asia. Washington will no longer try to go it alone; Washington will no longer dictate without consulting. A new day has come, in which we recognize that partnership is a two-way street, and if a partnership is to thrive, that street has to be traveled—both ways.

This poses a new challenge to the States—not only to administer programs, but to devise programs; not only to employ resources, but to choose the things for which they should be used.

In my talks with many Governors and other State officials, I have found them ready to rise to that challenge. And I have become convinced that States today are ready for a new role.

The New Federalism also recognizes the role of people—of individuals doing and caring and sharing. The concept of voluntary action, of community action, of people banding together in a spirit of neighborliness to do those things which they see must be done, is deeply rooted in America's character and tradition. As we have swept power and responsibility to Washington, we have undercut this tradition. Yet when it comes to helping one another, Washington can never bring to the task the heart that neighbors can. Washington can never bring the sensitivity to local conditions, or the new sense of self-importance that a person feels when he finds that some one person cares enough to help him individually.

In encouraging a new birth of voluntary action, I intend to look not only to the Federal Government, but also to the States, for inspiration and encouragement. Each State has its own pattern of experience, its own examples of how people have successfully helped people. By sharing these examples, they can be multiplied.

As we look toward 1976 and beyond, our range of possible choices is truly breathtaking: how we manage our growing abundance, how we make real our ideals of full opportunity, how we clean up our air and our water, how we balance our systems of transportation, how we expand our systems of education and health care—the list could go on and on indefinitely.

As only one dimension to the new task we face, the best estimates are that America's population will increase by 100 million between now and the year 2000—30 years from now. This means that 30 years from now there will be half again as many people in America as there are today. It means that in this short span of time we have to build 50 cities the size of Philadelphia today.

Or to put it another way, the [National] Committee on Urban Growth Policy has recommended that we should begin planning now for 100 new cities of 100,000 each, and 10 new cities of 1 million each—and yet even if we did this, it would accommodate only 20 percent of the added population we have to plan for—for the year 2000.[2]

Yet the other side of this coin of challenge is an enormous opportunity.

Growth on such an heroic scale offers an unprecedented opportunity to shape that growth so that our cities and communities enhance man himself.

More than anything else, it is these new tasks of the future—not the distant future, but the immediate future—that give

---

[2] The Committee's recommendations appear in their study entitled "The New City" (Frederick A. Praeger, Inc., 1969).

urgency to the need to reform government today.

We can command the future only if we can manage the present.

The reforms I have proposed are designed to make this possible.

Only if we clean out the unnecessary can we focus on the necessary.

Only if we stop fighting the battles of the thirties can we take on the battles of the seventies.

These reforms represent a New Federalism, a new humanism, and, I suggest also, a new realism.

They are based not on theoretical abstractions, but on the hard experience of the past third of a century.

They are addressed to the real problems of real people in a real world—and to the needs of the next third of a century.

They represent not an end but a beginning—the beginning of a new era in which we confound the prophets of doom, and make government an instrument for casting the future in the image of our hopes.

That task requires the best efforts of all of us together.

It requires the best thinking of all of us together, as we choose our goals and devise the means of their achievement.

But the future that beckons us also holds greater promise than any man has ever known. These reforms are steps in the direction of that promise—and as we take them, let us do so confident in the strength of America, firm in our faith that we can chart our destiny to the abundant spirit of a great and resourceful people. This spirit has been our strength. Marshaled in a new Spirit of '76, giving force to our purposes and direction to our efforts, it can be our salvation.

And now to those of you who are Governors here present tonight, I would like to add one personal note. Governor Ellington already indicated we come from different parties, from different parts of the country, we represent different religions, different backgrounds. But we are all the same in one respect: We are men, we are women in the great field of politics.

Sometimes as I consider that field of politics and particularly as I talk to the wives of some of those who have chosen the field of politics, I realize how very difficult that particular assignment can seem to be.

But, I think we have to look at this all in terms of the perspective of the times in which we live. As all of you know, I have had the opportunity of traveling both to Europe and to Asia during the first 7 months of my term of office. I visited the leaders in the great countries of both Europe and Asia. I have seen great civilizations and great governments and great peoples.

When I returned to the United States, after meeting with these leaders, one truth always comes back home to me, and it is this: This is the period of time in which whether peace or freedom survives in the world will depend upon what happens in the United States of America. And it depends not only on what a President will do, but it depends on what we do in all areas, government and nongovernmental. And particularly in the field of government, it depends not only on what we do on the Federal level, but the State and local level as well. Because, if the United States is going to meet the challenge which is ours, to preserve peace and freedom in the world, to bear our fair share in this period, if we are going to be able to deserve that mantle of leadership which is ours, whether we want it or not, we are going to have to first demonstrate that we can handle our problems at home.

I submit to all of you tonight, no men, no women, could have a more exciting challenge than this. Yes, the task is a great one. It is one that at times may seem frustrating. But I want to say to all of you that as we look toward the challenge of the last third of the century, as we look toward the decade of the seventies, and as we look toward that 200th anniversary of the American Declaration of Independence, 1976, I have great confidence in that future, confidence in it because I know that there are men and women in this country in the field of politics, in the field of government, who are determined to make government work, who are determined that this time in our history that we will not fail in the challenge that is ours.

Let me put it in historical perspective. When this Nation was founded in 1776—13 colonies, 3 million people, very weak militarily, poor economically—the men who founded this Nation said: "We act not just for ourselves, but for the whole human race."

That was a presumptuous thing for them to say then. But some way that Spirit of '76 appealed to all the world.

Today the United States of America, because of its power, because of its wealth, because of what we stand for, does act for the whole human race. And that is the challenge that we face, and that is the challenge that I know that we can meet.

I am proud to work with the Governors of the 50 States, Republican and Democrat alike, to see that America deals effectively with its problems at home, so that we can provide the example of leadership which will enable us to meet the challenges of keeping peace and freedom abroad.

NOTE: The President spoke at 10 p.m. at the International Center in the Broadmoor Hotel at Colorado Springs, Colo.

348   Remarks on Reform of the Nation's Postal System. *September 2, 1969*

Ladies and gentlemen:

I am flanked this morning by a bipartisan group which is gathered together for what I consider to be one of the top priority measures of this administration.

Several months ago you will recall my meeting with the press in Washington, along with Postmaster General Blount, and indicating the complete support of this administration for postal reform, the setting up of a Government corporation in place of the present system.

Within the next 2 weeks a major decision will be made in the House of Representatives by the Post Office and Civil Service Committee with regard to the bill which will be reported to the House. This will be the first round in a very significant battle as to whether we are to continue a system which has proved that it is inefficient, inadequate to meet the tremendous responsibilities that we have today, or whether we are to have a new system that will give this country what it deserves—fast, efficient postal service.

This is a bipartisan measure, bipartisan in the sense that it was first recommended by President Johnson, and as indicated today, it is supported not only by the administration and the Postmaster General, but by two former chairmen of the National Committees, the former Democratic national chairman, Mr. [Lawrence F.] O'Brien, and the former Republican national chairman, Senator [Thruston B.] Morton.

And also, Mr. O'Brien, I should say, has had the position Mr. Blount has had, Postmaster General, and is enthusiastically for this legislation.

I simply want to say in conclusion, before they submit to your questions, that I believe that postal reform is high on the list of those items which I indicated in my speech last night needs a new approach, an approach that will be adequate to the seventies.

Our present postal system is obsolete; it has broken down; it is not what it ought to be for a nation of 200 million people, and a nation that will be 300 million within 30 years. And now is the time to act. We are very happy to have the bipartisan support that we have, as indicated by this meeting this morning.

The Postmaster General will take over, and I understand all three of you will answer questions—either on the Post Office or political.

NOTE: The President spoke at 10:45 a.m. in the Conference Room at the Western White House in San Clemente, Calif.

The White House Press Office released the text of a news briefing held by Postmaster General Blount, Mr. O'Brien, and Senator Morton following the President's remarks.

349   Statement on the Jewish High Holy Days. *September 3, 1969*

IN THIS SEASON of the Jewish High Holy Days, my warmest New Year's wishes are extended to all my fellow Americans of the Jewish faith. I share your hope that the eve of September 12, which ushers in a New Year on your calendar, may mark the beginning of an era which will bring new blessings of peace and prosperity for all mankind.

Inspired by this year's triumphant demonstration of man's capacity to master the technology and intellectual challenge of our age, may all men of good will join their efforts toward the achievement of well-being here on earth. Out of the glory we have witnessed and before which we stand in awe, may man's terrestrial as well as his celestial life be fortified and enriched.

The holy season you celebrate particularly reminds us of the urgent need for self-examination and for rededication to the imperatives of justice and mercy. It stirs the conscience of men throughout the world to right the wrongs and alleviate the suffering that mar the progress we have realized. And it brings us all together in the prayer that the words of the prophet Isaiah may gain fulfillment in our lifetime, and that nation shall not lift up sword against nation.

The American Jewish community has throughout the history of our Nation been in the forefront of the search for true equality, dignity, and decency for all. But at this time, we are especially reminded of the enduring contributions you have made to the unrelenting search for a real

703

brotherhood of man under the Fatherhood of God. Our thoughts are with you as you begin these solemn days of worship, and our hearts are filled with gladness as we extend to each of you the traditional Hebrew greeting, *Shanah Tovah*: A Happy New Year.

NOTE: The statement was released at San Clemente, Calif.

350 Letter to Governor Rockefeller on Receiving His Report on His Latin American Mission. *September 3, 1969*

Dear Nelson:

As you know, it was my conviction from the earliest moment of my Administration that our policies toward Latin America and the way in which we conceived of our relationships with the other nations of this hemisphere needed a fresh and comprehensive re-examination. It was evident during the past several years that the area had been experiencing profound change which had deeply affected institutions, attitudes and relationships, and had set in motion new dynamics of which we were only beginning to be aware. Yet the assumptions and conceptions that guided our policy had remained relatively static during this same period.

I concluded, therefore, that it would be advisable to send a mission to the other American Republics to consult with leaders and people, to listen to their points of view and then to recommend to me measures that we could take to develop new policies, and more effective relationships. As you know, during my first day in office, I discussed the question of U.S.-Latin American relations with Galo Plaza, Secretary General of the OAS [Organization of American States], and he suggested that you be asked to head such a mission.

I cannot express to you adequately enough my appreciation and admiration for the dedicated, courageous and efficient way in which you and your associates carried out this trust. I consider this inconvenience and sacrifice of time to have been tremendously useful and worthwhile. It has dramatized our concern with the relationships that unite us with our sister Republics, it has focused attention on the problems and concerns of our neighbors and it has provided the Administration with an informed and fresh perspective of our relationships and policies.

I consider your mission in all of its aspects—both the personal contacts and the analysis and recommendations you are now submitting—to have constituted a signal contribution to our Latin American policy. Your report and its recommendations will be a central point of reference in the formulation of new policies toward the other nations of the hemisphere. I will submit your report and its proposals very promptly to the National Security Council for its study and appropriate action, and I am confident that these recommendations will play a vital part in the construction of sensitive new concepts and programs.

Please accept again my very sincere gratitude and appreciation for all that you have done, and for the devotion and dedication which you brought to this task. Please express my appreciation as well to your staff and to the advisors who also gave so generously and unselfishly of their time and energy.

With warmest personal regards,

RICHARD NIXON

[Honorable Nelson A. Rockefeller, Governor of the State of New York, Albany, New York]

NOTE: The letter was released at San Clemente, Calif.

351 Statement on Appointing Nancy Hanks as Chairman, National Endowment for the Arts. *September 3*, 1969

ONE OF THE IMPORTANT goals of my administration is the further advance in the cultural development of our Nation. We build on strong foundations; in almost every artistic field our country has had monumental achievement in this century. But the Federal Government has a vital role as catalyst, innovator, and supporter of public and private efforts for cultural development and its specific agency for this purpose is the National Endowment for the Arts, to which I have today appointed Miss Nancy Hanks of New York as Chairman. I anticipate that soon she will be joined by a deputy of equal stature.

Miss Hanks has my full confidence and will have my full cooperation.

The concept of the National Endowment for the Arts accords with the administration's policy of stimulating State action through Federal incentive. It is to be noted that a most important part of the national arts program is support of the arts councils of the various States. One major result of the activities of the Endowment is that every State now has an arts council.

Also, the Endowment seeks to assist both public and private cultural activities worthy of its support which would otherwise fall below the margin of feasibility. This cooperation with public entities on State and local levels and with private

activities is another tenet of this administration.

Finally, the Endowment is designed to give special attention to areas of the country which would not otherwise be adequately reached by modern development in arts, theater, design, and other cultural activities; and this again—the broadening and deepening of the intellectual and cultural life of all areas of our country—is a fundamental objective of this administration.

It is my expectation that the States, colleges and universities, civic groups, and public cultural institutions at every level will both see and seize this new, historic opportunity for realizing the finest qualities of artistic creativity and enjoyment throughout our country. I shall hope to give leadership to this effort and urge the Congress to do the same, so that we may have the full benefit of what is for us a relatively new governmental activity in the cultural field but which has vital importance for the welfare of our people and the future of our Nation.

NOTE: The statement was released at San Clemente, Calif., together with a White House announcement of the appointment containing biographical information on Miss Hanks, and the text of a news conference she held on September 3, 1969.

Miss Hanks was confirmed by the Senate on October 2, 1969.

352 Statement on the Construction Industry. *September 4, 1969*

THE COST of building a home or an apartment house has become exorbitant.

The Housing Act of 1968 sets as a goal 26 million houses in the next decade. Unless fundamental action is taken now to reduce the rise in housing prices, the Nation will fall far short of that goal. Low income groups, and a large share of Americans who are better off as well, face the danger of being priced out of the housing market.

Moreover, the rapidly rising costs of housing are a particular cause for major concern when we are striving to bring the forces of inflation under control.

Artificial means of holding down housing prices—whether through persuasion or coercion—cannot be effective in the long run. *We must take action that will directly affect construction supply and demand, which is what really determines prices.*

The *demand* for construction is clearly here and must be met; this means that government must move to affect supply—specifically, to enlarge the industry's capacity and thereby reduce the upward pressure on the cost of construction of new housing.

The great construction industry today accounts for almost 10 percent of our entire national output. Besides providing us with housing, this industry constructs the industrial and commercial complexes that enlarge job opportunities, and it meets government needs—from post offices to our far-flung highway system.

The entire construction industry has been laboring under demands that have strained its capacity. And these heavy demands will continue.

It is clear, therefore, that two types of action are now needed: For the near term, we must take steps to relieve immediate strains in the industry. And for the long term, we must take actions now to accelerate the growth in this industry's basic capacity to build.

Accordingly, I am taking action today that will help us get started toward more orderly building for the 1970's.

First, I am directing all agencies of the Federal Government to put into effect immediately a 75 percent reduction in new contracts for Government construction. This limitation, which will continue until conditions ease, will still permit projects of the highest social priority to be carried forward.

Although this action will cause some hardships, it will also release resources for home building where the need is great and where severe strains are already being felt.

Second, I strongly urge the State and local governments to follow the example of the Federal Government by cutting back temporarily on their own construction plans. The degree and promptness with which they respond to this plea for partnership in action will be watched carefully. If the response proves insufficient, I shall need to restrict the commitments for construction that can be financed through Federal grants. Should this step become unavoidable, the States and localities will, of course, be given due notice, so that they can adjust their affairs properly.

Third, I also urge businessmen to reappraise their current construction plans, and to postpone projects that are not immediately essential.

Fourth, I am directing the Secretaries of Labor and Health, Education, and Welfare to move promptly to provide for manpower training and vocational education in order to achieve a major increase in needed skilled labor for the construction industry. A shortage of skilled manpower is at the root of many problems faced by this industry.

Fifth, I am today establishing a Cabinet Committee on Construction. This Committee will be responsible for reviewing the vast range of Federal activities affecting the industry in order to assure that Government is not in its own programs and policies a major source of problems for the industry. It will also appraise the Nation's needs for construction, trends in resources available for building and financing, developments in wages and other costs and prices, problems of seasonality and technology, labor-management problems, and other matters pertinent to assuring that the Nation's on-going construction needs are served in an orderly and efficient manner.

The members of the Committee will consist of the Secretaries of Commerce, Labor, Housing and Urban Development, Transportation, the Postmaster General, and the Chairman of the Council of Economic Advisers, who will also act as Chairman of this Cabinet Committee.

The Committee will consult regularly with representatives of industry, unions, and the public. In this connection, I am directing the Secretary of Labor to explore the establishment of a mechanism to facilitate cooperation with union and employer groups in the solution of collective bargaining and related problems.

I shall direct the Cabinet Committee to report regularly to me on development in the industry and on their recommendations for actions to improve its performance.

With such actions we shall lay the foundation for orderly market conditions and ample productive resources in the construction industry. For this next decade, which may very well call for over $1 trillion of new construction, we are preparing for another great chapter in the building of our Nation.

NOTE: The statement was released at San Clemente, Calif., together with the text of a news briefing on the President's statement by Dr. Arthur F. Burns, Counsellor to the President.

353 Statement on the Death of Senator Everett McKinley Dirksen of Illinois. *September 7, 1969*

EVERETT DIRKSEN was one of a kind—and a remarkably likable man. To politics and government he brought a dedication matched by few and a style and eloquence matched by no political leader in our time.

He had his greatest moments as the leader of the loyal opposition. In the history of that role in the Congress, he had unequaled influence and accomplishment.

He will be remembered as a giant in the history of Congress and as one who on the great issues always placed the Nation first. I mourn the loss of this great American— a legislator of matchless skills, and my warm personal friend since my first days in the Congress 22 years ago.

NOTE: Senator Dirksen died on September 7,

1969, at Walter Reed Army Medical Center following a cardiac and respiratory arrest at the age of 73.

He served in the House of Representatives from 1933 to 1949, in the Senate from 1951 until the time of his death, and as Minority Leader of the Senate since 1959.

The President on September 8 and 10 issued Executive Orders 11479 and 11481 ordering flags to be flown at half-staff in honor of the late Senator.

The statement was released at San Clemente, Calif.

354 Remarks at the Dedication of the Amistad Dam on the Rio Grande. *September* 8, 1969

Mr. President, Señora Diaz Ordaz, Your Excellencies, and our friends from Mexico and the United States:

As I stand here today on this historic site, I think back to another day. In 1953, the first year of his administration, President Eisenhower traveled to the Mexican-American border to meet with President [Adolfo] Ruìz Cortines to dedicate the new Falcón Dam on the Rio Grande. And that structure, he said at that time, was a "living testimony to the understanding and the cooperation binding our two peoples."

Now, in 1969, in the first year of my administration, I, too, come to Mexico. I come to talk with President Diaz Ordaz and to dedicate another new dam along that same river, a complement to the Falcon Dam, and one which was built as a direct result of an agreement which President Eisenhower signed in 1960, his last full year in office.

Like the Falcón Dam, the new Amistad Dam also testifies to the spirit of understanding and cooperation which binds our two countries. In fact, its very name describes better than any other single word the special spirit of our relationship.

How that name came about is an interesting story. In October 1959, President Eisenhower at Camp David met with President López Mateos. The dam then

was to be known as the Diablo Dam. President Eisenhower thought that was a rather ominous name for a dam and President López suggested that the name be changed to Amistad.

So today we have a name which to millions of my countrymen who speak Spanish means "friendship," and friendship for my countrymen is a word which carries a special meaning and a special warmth. As we dedicate this dam today, we also rededicate ourselves to the furtherance of an ideal friendship.

Mr. President, we meet today on an international border. It is a beautiful place where we gather, beautiful for natural reasons and beautiful, too, because we see here what two great countries can accomplish when they work together.

This dam is an impressive achievement in many ways. First of all, it is an impressive physical achievement. It will contribute to the conservation and regulation of water supplies and will provide a fine recreational resource for both our people.

It is also an impressive diplomatic accomplishment, the result of complex and determined efforts which have stretched over a period of many years.

And finally, this achievement is impressive in human terms, impressive because of what it says about the special relationship which has grown up between the people of Mexico and the people of the United States.

It is a relationship based on a full understanding, for each of our countries knows the other way. It is a relationship based on mutual trust, for each of our countries has confidence in the other's good will. And it is a relationship based on mutual respect. Each of us recognizes the sovereignty and independence of the other and the right of each to reach different conclusions in matters of mutual interest without impairing our basic friendship.

Mr. President, while our visit today is a brief one, this great dam which we dedicate will continue to bear witness to our relationship day in and day out, year in, year out. It stands as a persuasive example to all the people of the world of the advantages which can come from peaceful cooperation between nations. And it will remain always a tangible monument to the spirit of friendship and partnership between our two peoples and our two nations.

NOTE: The President spoke at 1:45 p.m. at the Amistad Dam on the Rio Grande between Del Rio, Texas, and Ciudad Acuña, Mexico.

Following President Nixon's remarks President Diaz Ordaz responded in Spanish. A translation follows:

Mr. President, Mrs. Nixon, ladies and gentlemen:

It is very satisfactory to have this first contact with you, Mr. President, and it is especially satisfactory to have it under the name of this dam—Amistad, friendship.

I certainly hope that this first contact between us will help to establish and continue the friendship between us. It is a good thing President López Mateos and President Eisenhower gave this name to this dam. Can you imagine what might have happened if we had remained with the old name?

We are two countries with a long frontier between us and, consequently, with many problems between us. Fortunately, none of these problems is important enough, is serious enough, so that it cannot be solved by mutual comprehension and within the law, and none of them can or will become a barrier between us.

This frontier is not just a frontier between two different countries but between two different worlds, two different languages, two different cultures, two different forms of life.

On this line is where Latin America ends. Because of this we have two special tasks. One is to be faithful to ourselves as Mexicans and the other is to be faithful to ourselves as Latin Americans.

Taking into account the great complexity of the relations between our two countries, our relations are the best that we have ever had in our history and I believe that with your cooperation we two together can make them even better.

How is it possible that with so many obstacles our peoples have managed to establish friendship, to maintain it, and to make it ever closer? It is only as you, yourself, have just said, Mr. President: with comprehension, with friendship, and within the law. Whatever unites two that do not respect each other can be called anything except friendship.

We have made efforts through the years to understand and accept that we have two different nations that have different forms of expression and each one of which has its own sovereignty. All the peoples of the world have the right to choose their own road, to construct their own way of life which will lead them to liberty and the prosperity of their inhabitants. We have made every effort to remain within the rule of law.

It took us 100 years to achieve an agreement on the Chamizal. On the other hand, the Los Indios bank, which the river took from one side of the border in 1967, has been already returned to us, and we have already made the canals necessary to clear from salt the flow of water into this river.

You and I, Mr. President, are not only officers of our countries, we are also lawyers. And we know that the application of law is what brings about justice. That is why we both know that any problems that may arise in the future must be resolved within a spirit of comprehension, with mutual respect, and within the rule of law that you mentioned a few moments ago.

We are united here by a very special ceremony. We are about to inaugurate this dam which is important in itself by the economic effort it implies and also by the capacity of our technicians and our workers.

But it is even more important because of its significance. One is the one that lies in its name and the other which you yourself have just mentioned is the demonstration of what two friendly countries can do together.

Thus, this dam is only one more part of the road that we have walked together and we will walk further together in order to respect our-

selves and to maintain our friendship.

This dam is not only to hold back the waters of the Rio Bravo or to show that nature can be held back, but it is also a bridge, one more bridge, constructed between our two peoples.

I am very glad to invite you and Mrs. Nixon to inaugurate, together with me, this new dam and bridge. You are awaited by the land of the State of Coahuila, the fountain of our revolution that saw the birth of Francisco I. Madero and Venustiano Carranza, one who initiated our social revolution and the other who consolidated it in our present Constitution in 1917.

Mr. President, to you and your party, we open our arms, the arms of cordiality. You are very welcome to our homeland, to Mexico.

355   Toasts of the President and President Diaz Ordaz at a Luncheon in Mexico. *September 8,* 1969

Mr. President, Señora Diaz Ordaz, Your Excellencies:

On this occasion I first want to express the grateful appreciation of all of the members of the American party for this superb luncheon that you have extended to us.

We came here for what was described simply as a ceremony, the dedication of a dam. But with your flowers, the music, the dancing, and also with your words, you have touched our hearts.

We want you to know that as we meet here in Mexico, this happens to be the first visit that I have paid as President of the United States to any of the countries in Latin America. It is right that this should be so, because of our long association in the past and also because it has afforded an opportunity for us to discuss some of the problems on which our mutual thinking can be helpful to find solutions.

This is the first occasion that I have had to meet and talk with the President of Mexico, and I found in him a kind man,

a compassionate man, and a very wise man in his understanding of the problems of the people of the world.

I hope that this will be only the first of many discussions that we will have on the problems on which we can work together.

Now, on this very happy occasion and very festive occasion, I would like to add a personal note. One of the songs that was presented a few moments ago by the group that presented the record to us was composed on the 30th wedding anniversary of President and Señora Diaz Ordaz just 2 years ago. Two days from now they will celebrate their 32d wedding anniversary in Mexico City, and on that occasion their son will be married.

Mr. President, we appreciate your taking the time to come here to greet us on this occasion, but with the wedding coming up, even where it is the mother of the groom, we particularly appreciate Señora Diaz Ordaz coming here. I can only say, from recent experience, had it been the mother of the bride, that would not have been possible at all.

That allows me to refer to the fact that in the official background that was prepared for me for this visit, it was pointed out that I had visited Mexico on three previous occasions: in 1952 as Vice President-elect when I attended the inauguration of [Adolfo Ruiz] Cortines as President; in 1955 when I was on a visit to Mexico and to Central America, when I traveled as Vice President; and in 1967 when I was received very warmly and graciously by several of those here, including Mr. Carrillo Flores,[1] as a private citizen.

But the official background left out the two most important things. In 1940, my wife and I visited Mexico for 2 weeks on our wedding trip. In 1965 we returned again on our 25th wedding anniversary with our two children, and again spent a week in Mexico.

I say this only to indicate that from all the words that we have spoken to date, you can be sure that the new administration has a strong feeling of affection for the Government of Mexico, and for the people of Mexico.

But on my part, and speaking also for my wife, that feeling is not just official; it is very personal for reasons that I have now described. Mexico has a special place in our hearts and you can be sure that in all the years ahead we shall look forward to more visits like this, either here or in Washington, or perhaps even in California.

Now I would ask you all to rise and to raise your glasses to the continued friendship of the people of Mexico and the people of the United States, and even more important, to the President of Mexico, to

---

[1] Antonio Carrillo Flores, Secretary of Foreign Affairs for Mexico since 1964.

Señora Diaz Ordaz, to their happiness in all the years ahead and to the happiness of their children.

NOTE: The President spoke at 4:30 p.m. in the Banquet Room at El Mirador, Coahuila, Mexico, in response to a toast by President Gustavo Diaz Ordaz. President Diaz Ordaz spoke in Spanish. The translation follows:

Mr. President, ladies and gentlemen:

In the very real conversation President Nixon, Mrs. Nixon, and myself have had, President Nixon has been kind enough to accept the invitation we have made to the three astronauts who went to the moon to start their trip around the world in Mexico.

Thank you very much, Mr. President. We will make our best efforts to receive these three intrepid heroes as they deserve to be received.

Thank you also because you permitted us to participate in a way, because the astronauts definitely left the messages of other countries—among them Mexico—which now remain forever in this natural satellite of ours.

I repeat our heartfelt congratulations to the Government and to the people of the United States for this most extraordinary of all time and epic voyage, and our warmest homage to those three men who went to the moon, Armstrong, Aldrin, and Collins, whose names will be repeated by schoolboys throughout the rest of time.

The United States gave proof of its greatness when it achieved this great triumph, but it became even greater when they understood it and accepted it as a triumph of all humanity.

In that moment, in millions of men throughout the earth, a new sentiment of human immortality was born, when Armstrong put his foot on the surface of the moon.

It is impossible to understand today individual feats such as Charles Lindbergh crossing the Atlantic alone. Behind these three men there were those of others, scientists, technicians, workers, and not only the efforts of those who directly participated in making this trip possible, but when they were alone up in the heights, they were accompanied by a sentiment of solidarity by humans throughout the world.

I toast to the people who made this feat possible. I toast the people of the United States on their road to liberty and prosperity in my

own name and that of Mrs. Diaz Ordaz and that of the Government officials and visitors who accompany me. I toast this great people

in the person of President Nixon, who is here beside me, and Mrs. Nixon.

356 Remarks on Departure From Mexico.
September 8, 1969

MR. PRESIDENT, as the time comes to say goodby, we want to express our deep appreciation for the wonderful welcome you have given us on this visit to Mexico, and the warm hospitality, the wonderful entertainment, the beautiful luncheon. The words that you have spoken have only meant to us that we look forward to the time that we can return for a longer visit.

At the luncheon the President made an announcement that I think all of those here would like to hear as well. Our astronauts are going to take a trip around

the world, beginning in about 2½ weeks. They have been invited to most of the countries of the world, including an invitation, a very gracious invitation, from Mexico.

The President of Mexico has issued such an invitation and the first stop on their world trip will be in Mexico City on September 29 or 30.

NOTE: The President spoke at 5:10 p.m. at El Mirador, Coahuila, Mexico, near the Amistad Dam. He referred to Apollo 11 astronauts Neil A. Armstrong, Col. Edwin E. Aldrin, Jr., USAF, and Col. Michael Collins, USAF.

357 Remarks on Departure From Texas.
September 8, 1969

BEFORE we fly on to Washington, with a stop in Mississippi to look at the flood damage in between, I just wanted to take this opportunity to express, on behalf of Mrs. Nixon and myself, our appreciation for all of you for giving us such a warm welcome. I am not speaking of the weather. I am speaking of the welcome that you have given us by coming out here to the airstrip as we arrived and when we take off.

I understand that most of the people here are, one way or another, with the Laughlin Air Force Base. You serve in the Air Force or you are dependents of Air Force families.

Having just traveled around the world with my wife on a world trip in an Air

Force plane, a pretty good one, incidentally, and having also traveled to Europe and all over the United States, I know many of the top Air Force personnel in that capacity, but also I have seen them in our bases around the world.

I am really tremendously proud of the men and the women who serve in the Armed Forces of the United States, proud of them for the job they do abroad and proud of them for the job they do here in bases like this in the United States.

We often hear a lot of criticism of our Armed Forces these days. I can only say that as far as those who are serving in the Armed Forces, you can look at your service with pride. You can recognize that by reason of what you do the United States of America is able to maintain a position of world leadership which is so essential if peace is to be brought to this world, and if we are going to have peace with freedom in the world.

That is the goal of any President. It is the goal of any diplomat. That goal cannot be achieved without the strong Armed Forces strength which the Air Force makes a great contribution to.

With those words, let me say again, thank you so much for coming out and welcoming us. We wish you the very best and we look forward to seeing you again, perhaps in Washington, or some other base, or at your hometown, wherever that may be.

Thank you very much.

NOTE: The President spoke at 5:30 p.m. at Laughlin Air Force Base, Tex.

358   Remarks Following Aerial Inspection of Damage Caused by Hurricane Camille in Mississippi. *September 8, 1969*

Governor Williams, Senator Eastland, Senator Stennis, Chairman Colmer, the other distinguished Members of the Congress, the other distinguished guests here on the platform, and all of this magnificent crowd here in Gulfport, Mississippi:

I want to express appreciation to you for giving me and my wife such a warm welcome and to tell you that as I flew over the damage today in Mississippi, I could see that the facts that have been given to me before could not adequately state that damage.

As you know, this is the worst storm that has been recorded in 100 years of recording storms in the United States and that means that it probably is the worst in terms of damage, physically, that any State or any area has ever suffered.

As you know, thousands have been made homeless, hundreds are dead, hundreds of millions of dollars in property damage—all of this I saw before me as we flew over Mississippi today.

Then, for a few moments, as the plane landed and as we stepped out on the platform and looked at this huge crowd, I realized that whatever had happened to

Mississippi from the standpoint of physical destruction, the spirit of the people of Mississippi is still high and it will continue to be high.

I am very proud as I stand before you as an American, not just as President of the United States but as an American speaking to my fellow Americans, to see such a wonderful spirit despite the adversity which you have suffered.

I do not want to sound now as if all that happened to you could turn out to be for the best. But could I for a moment remind this great audience of some of the lessons of history?

Throughout history we have found that great natural disasters have either made or broken civilization, and the same can be said of a man or a woman, a disaster can make or break him.

Also, throughout history we have found that when a people are able to survive a disaster that they then develop a greatness that otherwise they never would have had or never knew that they had, because what was required of them was to develop a new approach and a new spirit and a new way of life which they other-

713

wise might never have discovered.

I refer, for example, to my own State of California. One of the most beautiful cities in the world is San Francisco, and yet San Francisco 60 years ago was leveled by an earthquake and a fire. It came back more beautiful than ever.

I refer in more recent times to Anchorage, Alaska. I saw the destruction there in that earthquake 5 years ago. Yet, Anchorage, Alaska, has come back and it is going to be a greater city and the people of Anchorage will have a greater challenge and will be a greater people than ever before.

I predict today that the people of Mississippi and particularly those that have suffered damage will come from this destruction and you will rise from it and be a greater people than was the case before. And we congratulate you for that kind of a spirit.

On the part of your Federal Government, I can certainly pledge to you a continuation of the interest that we have already shown, an interest that is not partisan—it represents all the people of this country; an interest in terms of all the departments of Government, all the agencies in Government; an interest which is shared by the Members of the House and the Senate, led by your own House and Senate delegation.

I can pledge to you, too, that what has happened in Mississippi, and also to the neighboring State of Louisiana and areas there, has touched the heart of the Nation and volunteer organizations are making their contributions.

I was touched on the night when I called the Bob Hope telethon to hear that over $1 million had been raised that very night from all over the Nation for the people here who suffered in Mississippi.[1]

I know, too, that here in this State, under the leadership of your Governor and working with the Members of the House and the Senate, and also the State legislature, that you have set up an unprecedented group of private citizens and government officials to work together for a new kind of cooperation, a plan in which you will not just rebuild as it was, what was old, but in which you will build a new area, not only new buildings, but new ideas and new opportunities for all of the people of this great State. What a challenge that is.

I am confident you are going to meet it. I am confident because of the words that I have heard during these past few minutes from the leaders of your State, both at the State level and your representatives in Washington, D.C.

But I am confident for another reason, for what I see before me here today, thousands of people. I saw your cars lined up for miles and I hear that some of you have been here since 2 o'clock this afternoon. I realize what you have done and the demonstration which this really symbolizes. And what it means is this: It means that no matter how many millions of dollars we get from Washington, no matter how much you are able to get from the State government or from your county government, no matter how much comes from the various volunteer organizations from all over America, that what really counts are the people.

Because, if the heart of the people and the spirit of the people and the strength of the people are not sound, then all of the money in the world will not help. As I

---

[1] See Item 341.

come to Mississippi today, I say that the heart and the spirit and the strength of the people of Mississippi has never been stronger. And that means you are going forward to a greater future than ever before.

Thank you.

Ladies and gentlemen, we won't have the time to meet and shake hands with everybody here because we have to fly on to Washington, but we would like to meet some of you and if we don't meet you all,

just remember, we wish that we could and maybe next time.

NOTE: The President spoke at 8:25 p.m. at the Gulfport Municipal Airport in Gulfport, Miss. Gov. John Bell Williams, Senators James O. Eastland and John Stennis, and Representative William M. Colmer, Chairman of the House Rules Committee were all from Mississippi.

White House releases announcing allocations of Federal disaster relief funds to Mississippi on August 18 and October 2, 1969, are printed in the Weekly Compilation of Presidential Documents (vol. 5, pp. 1165 and 1355).

359 Eulogy at Memorial Services for Senator Dirksen of Illinois. *September* 9, 1969

Mrs. Dirksen, Mr. Vice President, Mr. Chief Justice, Members of the Congress, Members of the Cabinet, Members of the Diplomatic Corps, Your Excellencies, and friends of Everett Dirksen throughout the Nation:

When Daniel Webster died more than a century ago, a man who differed strongly with him on many public issues rose in Congress to say this in eulogy: "Our great men are the common property of the country."

Everett Dirksen, of Illinois, was and is the "common property" of all the 50 States.

Senator Dirksen belonged to all of us because he always put his country first. He was an outspoken partisan, he was an individualist of the first rank, but he put his nation before himself and before his party.

He came to the Nation's Capital in 1932, and his public service spanned an era of enormous change in the life of our country. He played a vital part in that change. That is why it is so difficult to

think of the Washington scene, of this Capitol, without him.

Only his fellow legislators, the Senators and Representatives who have gathered here today and who mourn his loss across the Nation, know the full extent of his contribution to the process of governing this country.

They know the time and concern he put into their bills, their causes, their problems. They know another side to Everett Dirksen—the side in the committees and behind the scenes where so much of the hard work and the hard bargaining is done, where there is so little that makes headlines and so much that makes legislation.

Through four Presidencies, through the adult life of most Americans living today, Everett Dirksen has had a hand in shaping almost every important law that affects our lives.

Everett Dirksen was a politician in the finest sense of that much abused word. If he were here, I think he might put it this way:

A politician knows that more important than the bill that is proposed is the law that is passed.

A politician knows that his friends are not always his allies, and that his adversaries are not his enemies.

A politician knows how to make the process of democracy work, and loves the intricate workings of the democratic system.

A politician knows not only how to count votes, but how to make his vote count.

A politician knows that his words are his weapons, but that his word is his bond.

A politician knows that only if he leaves room for discussion and room for concession can he gain room for maneuver.

A politician knows that the best way to be a winner is to make the other side feel it does not have to be a loser.

And a politician—in the Dirksen tradition—knows both the name of the game and the rules of the game, and he seeks his ends through the time-honored democratic means.

By being that kind of politician, this "Man of the Minority" earned the respect and affection of the majority. And by the special way he gave leadership to legislation, he added grace and elegance and courtliness to the word "politician."

That is how he became the leader of a minority, and one of the leaders of our Nation. And that is why, when the Senate worked its way, Everett Dirksen so often worked his way.

That is why, while he never became President, his impact and influence on the Nation was greater than that of most Presidents in our history.

He was at once a tough-minded man

and a complete gentleman. He could take issue without taking offense. And if that is an example of the "old politics," let us hope that it always has a place in the politics of the future.

He is a man to be remembered, as we remember the other giants of the Senate—the Websters and Calhouns, the Vandenbergs and the Tafts.

Some will remember his voice—that unforgettable voice—that rolled as deep and majestically as the river that defines the western border of the State of Illinois he loved so well. Others will remember the unfailing—often self-deprecating—sense of humor which proved that a man of serious purpose need never take himself too seriously.

Others will remember the mastery of language, the gift of oratory that placed him in a class with Bryan and Churchill, showing, as only he would put it, that "The oil can is mightier than the sword."

But as we do honor to his memory, let us never forget the single quality that made him unique, the quality that made him powerful, made him beloved: the quality of character.

Everett Dirksen cultivated an appearance that made him seem old-fashioned, an incarnation of a bygone year. But that quality of character is as modern as a Saturn V.

As he could persuade, he could be persuaded. His respect for other points of view lent weight to his own point of view. He was not afraid to change his position if he were persuaded that he had been wrong. That tolerance and sympathy were elements of his character and that character gained him the affection and esteem of millions of his fellow Americans.

We shall always remember Everett

Dirksen in the terms he used to describe his beloved marigolds: hardy, vivid, exuberant, colorful—and uniquely American.

To his family, his staff, and his legion of friends who knew and loved Everett Dirksen, I would like to add a personal word.

There are memorable moments we will never know again—those eloquent speeches, the incomparable anecdotes, those wonderfully happy birthday parties.

But he, least of all, would want this to be a sad occasion. With his dramatic sense of history, I can hear him now speaking of the glory of this moment.

As a man of politics, he knew both victory and defeat.

As a student of philosophy, he knew the triumph of and the tragedy and the misery of life.

And as a student of history, he knew that some men achieve greatness, others are not recognized for their greatness until after their death. Only a privileged few live to hear the favorable verdict of history on their careers.

Two thousand years ago the poet Sophocles wrote: "One must wait until the evening to see how splendid the day has been."

We who were privileged to be his friends can take comfort in the fact that Everett Dirksen—in the rich evening of his life, his leadership unchallenged, his mind clear, his great voice still powerful across the land—could look back upon his life and say: The day has indeed been splendid.

NOTE: The President spoke at 12:14 p.m. at the Capitol Rotunda.

360   Memorandum on the Combined Federal Campaign for the National Capital Area.   *September* 11, 1969

Memorandum for Heads of Executive Departments and Agencies:

I am pleased to announce that the Honorable John A. Volpe, Secretary of Transportation, has agreed to serve as Chairman of this year's Combined Federal Campaign for the National Capital Area.

The Combined Federal Campaign covers in one single drive the campaigns of the United Givers Fund, the National Health Agencies, and the International Service Agencies. In this one drive Federal employees and military personnel in the Washington Metropolitan Area will have an opportunity to share in meeting the needs of over 160 local, national and international health, welfare and social service agencies.

This year, our support is needed more than ever. Citizens working together through the voluntary agencies can become partners with Government in the effort to build better communities, a healthier nation, and a more peaceful world. The voluntary organizations need the support of all Federal personnel in the National Capital Area to accomplish their important objectives. The extent to which they succeed will be a measure of our support.

I request that you serve personally as Chairman of the combined campaign in your organization and appoint a top assistant as your Vice Chairman. Please advise Secretary Volpe of the person you designate as your Vice Chairman.

RICHARD NIXON

NOTE: The United Givers Fund, in a September 30, 1969, press release, announced that the President and Mrs. Nixon had made the first contribution to the Fund's 1969 residential campaign.

361   Statement on United States Troops in Vietnam. *September* 16, 1969

AFTER careful consideration with my senior civilian and military advisers and in full consultation with the Government of Vietnam, I have decided to reduce the authorized troop ceiling in Vietnam to 484,000 by December 15. This compares with the ceiling of 549,500 which existed when this administration took office. Under the newly authorized troop ceiling, a minimum of 60,000 troops will have been withdrawn from Vietnam by December 15.*

Since coming into office, my administration has made major efforts to bring an end to the war:

—We have renounced an imposed military solution.

—We have proposed free elections organized by joint commissions under international supervision.

—We have offered the withdrawal of U.S. and allied forces over a 12-month period.

—We have declared that we would retain no military bases.

—We have offered to negotiate supervised cease-fires under international supervision to facilitate the process

of mutual withdrawal.

—We have made clear that we would settle for the *de facto* removal of North Vietnamese forces so long as there are guarantees against their return.

—We and the Government of South Vietnam have announced that we are prepared to accept any political outcome which is arrived at through free elections.

—We are prepared to discuss the 10-point program of the other side, together with plans put forward by the other parties.

—In short, the only item which is not negotiable is the right of the people of South Vietnam to determine their own future free of outside interference.

I reiterate all these proposals today.

The withdrawal of 60,000 troops is a significant step.

The time for meaningful negotiations has therefore arrived.

I realize that it is difficult to communicate across the gulf of 5 years of war. But the time has come to end this war. Let history record that at this critical moment, both sides turned their faces toward peace rather than toward conflict and war.

NOTE: The President also recorded portions of this statement for television and radio broadcast.

---

*Actually, the total reduction in authorized ceiling strength amounts to 65,500. But within the authorized ceiling, all units are shown at 100 percent strength. In actual practice, most units are slightly below full strength, so that actual strength normally is less than the authorized ceiling by 1 or 2 percent.

362   Toasts of the President and Prime Minister Keith J.
      Holyoake of New Zealand.   *September* 16, 1969

*Mr. Prime Minister, Mrs. Holyoake, and
our distinguished guests this evening:*

As the Prime Minister was surveying
this very elite group this evening, he reminisced about the fact that it was just 1
year ago that he was in this house and in
this room, and the host on that occasion
was President Johnson.

He noted one of the guests who is here
tonight who was also here 1 year ago.
He, of course, raised the question, and I
thought of it, too, as to whether or not
he was a Democrat or a Republican. I will
not reveal who that guest is, but I will
only say that in this room, Mr. Prime
Minister, are Democrats and Republicans.

There are people all the way from New
York to Hawaii to the State of Alaska,
and there are people from all walks of
life. And what unites them tonight is the
fact that they all are friends of New Zealand, and they are delighted to be here
to honor you and Mrs. Holyoake on this
occasion.

I want to speak quite personally in that
respect about my own debt to your country, and perhaps in speaking that way I
can bring to those of our guests who have
not been to New Zealand—and many of
you have not been there—some of the
feeling I have for this country which is
so far away geographically, but so close
to us in ways that are far more important.

Twenty-five years ago, in World War
II, I was stationed on a very barren island
at the tip of the Solomons—Green Island.
I don't know why they called it Green
Island; it had no water. All it had was

25,000 troops there, a Marine combat
air transport detachment—I was the
Naval Operations Officer with that detachment—and the 25,000 troops were a
New Zealand division.

I learned to know New Zealand
through New Zealanders and General
[Harold Eric] Barrowclough, who was the
commander of that division, who later became the Chief Justice of New Zealand.
And I, as did many Americans who served
with New Zealanders in World War I and
II and the later generations in Korea and
now in Vietnam—knowing New Zealanders you feel very much at home with them
and you realize that we have very much
in common.

Then in 1953, in this room, one of the
predecessors of the Prime Minister, Prime
Minister [Sir Sidney George] Holland, was
here as one of the very first state guests
of President Eisenhower. After the dinner,
Prime Minister Holland suggested to
President Eisenhower that the Vice President ought to take a trip. He said he ought
to go to New Zealand and Australia and
to the other countries of Asia.

President Eisenhower, who knew how
to take advice, particularly from a distinguished Prime Minister, did take that
advice and as a result of what the Prime
Minister of New Zealand in 1953 said to
the President of the United States, the
Vice President of the United States and
Mrs. Nixon took a 70-day trip to New
Zealand and other points in Asia.

It was then, in 1953, that we really
visited New Zealand for the first time. We
learned then to know the land as well as

the people, the greenest land I have ever seen—I can say that despite my half Irish background because I have never really seen all of Ireland—but this great, green land, with its spectacular beauty, but primarily with the great spirit in its people, a spirit that we know in America from its political leaders, a spirit that we know also from those like Edmund Hillary, who was the first man to climb Mount Everest, a spirit that again transcends differences in population, differences insofar as miles between our two countries are concerned.

What I would like really to say to this group tonight is this: The Prime Minister, in our meeting today in which we covered a number of very important issues, and in which we found we looked at the Pacific and Asia through basically the same principles, referred facetiously to the fact that New Zealand was a country of only 3 million, and the United States was one of 200 million, and New Zealand had 3 million people and 100 million sheep.

I can only say in response to that, that those 3 million people in New Zealand are a strong people, and I speak as one who knows them. They are a people who have stood with us and with the allies of freedom in two World Wars, and in Korea and in Vietnam.

The Prime Minister, a man that I have met briefly before and have learned to know on this trip, represents that country in the councils of the world, speaks for it with a voice that carries far beyond his land because he speaks to principles that transcend the size of a country and that, in effect, reach all the peoples of the world.

Because his country, as is ours, is deeply dedicated to the principles of independence, to the principles of self-determination, to the principles of freedom which allows us to survive, and his country to survive, and which must survive in other parts of the world if what we believe in is to remain for our children in the years to come.

Mr. Prime Minister, it has been a privilege for us to know you and we hope that our guests, after dinner—at least most of them—will have a chance to talk to you again.

I can only say in conclusion that next year, which will be the 200th anniversary of Captain Cook's discovery of New Zealand, will be a great year in the history of your country.

For those of us who will not be able to attend it, we salute you now. We salute New Zealand. We salute you for your leadership of a great people and in saluting you, we do so by raising our glasses in the traditional toast to Her Majesty the Queen.

NOTE: The President proposed the toast at 9:43 p.m. in the State Dining Room at the White House. Prime Minister Holyoake responded as follows:

Mr. President and Mrs. Nixon, Your Excellencies, especially Mr. and Mrs. Franzheim, who have come to New Zealand to represent your wonderful country, and ladies and gentlemen:

Can I say it is a tremendous pleasure and a tremendous honor, we think, Mrs. Holyoake and I, to be your guests in this great country, in this famous house, and to be your particular guests tonight, and with this distinguished company, as you say, all the way from Alaska—where is Alaska?—to Honolulu.

I want to take this opportunity publicly to offer my warmest congratulations to you, Mr. President, on my own personal behalf, but also on behalf of the people of New Zealand, in becoming the President of this, the greatest state that man has ever devised.

I know, because it is important for me to know, after studying what has happened in the last few months, that you come to this office with a sense of great dedication, with tremendous vigor, and, if I may say so without presumption, wisdom as well.

This means so much, not just to you and the people of the United States, but to all men who, as you said, love freedom, and to the men of those countries like ourselves, let us say humbly, that, when the chips are finally down, would rather die than lose their freedom. You, of course, have mentioned the occasions when we have joined together in such cases.

I often wonder what the casual observer would say and think when he observes Americans and New Zealanders together and realizes that they are friends—readily make friendships between each other.

Well, we do have some things in common, but there are a lot of things patently that we don't have. For instance, we are about on exactly the opposite ends in the matter of power in the world. You, whether you like it or not, you do and you must continue to regard everything from the global point of view. We haven't any such responsibility. We survey the world, but we have our particular interests in only two or three parts, here in the greater North America, Britain and Western Europe, and Southeast Asia.

But even these things, these differences too, I think, bring us sometimes together.

I observe, and over the years I am convinced, that we have much the same values; we place much the same values on most things in life. And I am amazed with the facility you American people understand our English. I think this is quite wonderful. So we have, we enjoy, the same rich language, the same culture, the same heritage. These things bring us so much together.

So, perhaps it is natural that we should form the ready habit of cooperation as we have and as has been mentioned by the President on a number of occasions, when we both felt that the pressures around the world demanded that we should go beyond our own shores.

The President has mentioned two World Wars, Korea, and now in Vietnam. I think, because I do study the American scene very closely, it is so important to us, and I think I know it reasonably well, and I think we come to these conclusions that we do have a duty and a proper place and a part to play, after

the same kind of self-searching and soul-searching and doubts; and we would not make the right decisions if we did not have all of those, including the doubts, before we finally came to our decisions.

I want to say that in our small and humble way down there in the South Pacific that it is for these same reasons that we have, in the wake of the British decision to leave our part of the world, east of Suez, in global terms, in 1971, that we, together with our Australian cousins, have decided to continue to make a military as well as other contributions in Singapore and Malaysia. This is something really new for us.

We have always gone in the shadow of a great power, perhaps in the reflected glow of a great power, but not on this occasion. And I guess, too, from studying your scene, from talking with Americans, reading, that you in your larger way and we in ours—but every man can only make up his mind for himself, and I claim with all the arrogance of a man from a small country that one New Zealander is just as important as one American or one Englander or one Asian; we are all individuals finally—and individually, and so collectively, too, we come to the same decision that we must get to know the people of Asia and particularly the people of the new and emerging Asia, the free countries, ringing the periphery of Asia and of the Pacific, our ocean, our lake, and one that you are interested in as much as we.

And we believe that the closer partnership that we have now with the people ringing the Pacific, this, we believe, is to our mutual advantage.

We talked today. I have had an opportunity of talking to your President and one or two of your ministers and others about our mutual interests and about trade. I am not going to talk much about it tonight, but it would be quite wrong for me not to mention it.

I wanted to make a quotation. The creation of a stronger and more balanced economy is one of our goals down in New Zealand—green as you say; farming is the base, but coming along is manufacturing—and to achieve our objective then we need, of course, to find wider fields for our products from the farm and from the factory. We need a world that I would like to describe, and this is a quotation from a quite famous man: We need a world more "open to the exchange of goods and people." I took those few words from your inaugural address, Mr. President. I was not quite sure whether you remembered them or whether you would not. So much has happened to you since then.

This, of course, is essential to our capacity to play our small part and to hoist our flag when we think it is time to hoist our flag beside that of our friends, large, medium, and small.

We ask for no favors. We are a donor country. We do ask for reasonable opportunities to trade fairly. We are, I think, the only country in the world that does not subsidize its farmers, either internally or on the export market.

So, we are free men, too. I know that you are as well. I am very, very heartened by what you have told me from time to time and I am very interested, too, when the Senate committee says: "Thou shalt not, and please don't send that stuff here, it's too good and it's too cheap."

Mr. President, and my friends, I must not speak to you at any greater length. I have probably spoken a little too long already. Looking at your faces reminds me of a story that I know my wife will tweak my ear for having told again.

A few years ago at a gathering something like this, and I was not sure whether we should have made speeches at all—it did not seem to me to be very appropriate—but quite late in the evening the master of ceremonies came along to me and very stuttering and stammering he said: "Mr. Holyoake, do you think you had better make your speech now or should we just let the people go on enjoying themselves?"

So, my speech is over. You can just go on enjoying yourselves, if first you will join me in a toast to the President of the United States of America.

363 Statement Announcing the Membership of the Advisory Council for Minority Enterprise. *September* 17, 1969

IT IS with great pleasure that I announce today the names of 63 distinguished leaders from a broad spectrum of American life who have volunteered to serve on the new Advisory Council for Minority Enterprise. I am grateful to these dedicated citizens who have recognized the importance of involving more members of minority groups in the American enterprise system.

Encouraging more successful enterprise by minority group members is a vital objective of this administration. We believe that every American should have the opportunity to share in the profits of our free enterprise system. With each new business that comes into being we enlarge the opportunities for more new careers. Thus the success that our minority people have in owning and managing their own businesses will provide a twofold value for

them and for the Nation.

Six months ago, I pointed out in creating the Office of Minority Business Enterprise that this effort is neither a panacea nor a substitute for other efforts to create more and better job opportunities for all Americans. We want to create new opportunity and foster the pride of accomplishment in both the management and the work force of the Nation.

We firmly intend that this long term effort shall succeed. As the appointment of this committee today indicates we are bringing together some of the best minds in America to eliminate roadblocks on the path of economic opportunity for every citizen of our country.

Both Secretary Stans and I look to this distinguished group for proposal of feasible methods to speed the flow of capital, ease credit facilities, obtain insurance and provide needed technical assistance, and thereby help eliminate many of the frustrations which have blocked so many minority Americans in their efforts to become a constructive part of our national economic life.

Through its collective experience, its wide knowledge of business and industry, and its understanding of the challenge confronting our minorities, this Council will broaden the base of opportunity by seeking out, recommending, and developing new types of business for minority involvement. It will provide the guidance which will help the Office of Minority Business Enterprise to execute those functions for which it was created.

Two outstanding Americans have agreed to serve as Chairman and Vice Chairman of the Council.

Sam E. Wyly of Dallas, Texas, will be the Chairman. As chairman of the board

of the Sam Wyly Foundation of Dallas, he has done much to aid the disadvantaged and contribute to minority economic development.

To work with him as Vice Chairman, I have named Berkeley G. Burrell, president of the National Business League, Washington, D.C. Mr. Burrell already has made a record as a successful pioneer in the promoting of businesses owned and operated by minority group members.

I am confident that the Council will assist this administration in making yesterday's dream today's specific effort and tomorrow's fact. There is no greater bridge to human dignity than the pride that comes with well-earned success in the free enterprise system.

NOTE: A list of the Council's members with brief biographies of each is printed in the Weekly Compilation of Presidential Documents (vol. 5, p. 1271).

364   Remarks on Signing the Older Americans Act Amendments of 1969.   *September* 17, 1969

BEFORE this bill-signing ceremony, I want to congratulate the Members of the House and Senate who have provided the leadership for the passage of this legislation.

These amendments to the Older Americans Act will further the objective that we are all very interested in, and that is of providing more useful and constructive lives for the 20 million Americans over 65 years of age.

I think, also, this is a very appropriate time to announce that next week I shall send to the Congress a message asking for an increase in social security benefits of 10 percent, effective April 1.

This is a matter of simple justice for those living on social security, because as we look at the record of rising costs over the past 5 years, those who have suffered most are our older citizens who are living on fixed incomes.

I know that all of those Members of the Senate and House who have worked with this legislation will provide the leadership for quick passage of the social security increase.

NOTE: The President spoke at 11:55 a.m. in the Roosevelt Room at the White House. As enacted, the Older Americans Act Amendments of 1969 is Public Law 91-69 (83 Stat. 108).

365 Address Before the 24th Session of the General Assembly of the United Nations. *September 18, 1969*

Madam President, Mr. Secretary General, distinguished Foreign Ministers, Prime Ministers, delegates—my fellow citizens of the world community:

I first wish to express my deep appreciation for the honor of addressing this organization for the first time and also to take this opportunity to welcome all of those from 126 countries who are here at the United Nations General Assembly session.

Particularly, on a personal note, I appreciate the opportunity to have been welcomed today by the Secretary General. It is hard to realize, as we were reminiscing, that just 16 years ago he welcomed me to Burma when he was Chief of Protocol and I was Vice President.

Since then, we have both come up in the world to a certain extent.

I think we would all agree that there is no nobler destiny, nor any greater gift that one age could make to the ages that follow, than to forge the key to a lasting peace.

In this great Assembly, the desirability of peace needs no affirmation. The methods of achieving it are what so greatly challenge our courage, our intelligence, our discernment.

Surely if one lesson above all rings resoundingly among the many shattered hopes in this world, it is that good words are not a substitute for hard deeds, and noble rhetoric is no guarantee of noble results.

We might describe peace as a process embodied in a structure.

For centuries, peace was the absence of war; stability was the absence of change. But in today's world, there can be no stability without change—so that peace becomes a continuing process of creative evolution. It is no longer enough to restrain war. Peace must also embrace progress—both in satisfying man's material needs and in fulfilling his spiritual needs.

The test of the structure of peace is that it ensure for the people of each nation the integrity of their borders, their right to develop in peace and safety, and their right to determine their own destiny without outside interference.

As long as we live with the threat of aggression, we need physical restraints to contain it.

But the truest peace is based on self-restraint—on the voluntary acceptance of those basic rules of behavior that are rooted in mutual respect and demonstrated in mutual forbearance.

The more closely the world community adheres to a single standard in judging international behavior, the less likely that standard is to be violated.

ROLE OF THE UNITED STATES

I am well aware that many nations have questions about the world role of the United States in the years ahead—about the nature and extent of our future contribution to the structure of peace.

Let me address those doubts and address them quite candidly before this organization.

In recent years, there has been mounting criticism here in the United States of the scope and the results of our international commitments.

This trend, however, has not been confined to the United States alone. In many countries we find a tendency to withdraw from responsibilities, to leave the world's often frustrating problems to the other fellow and just to hope for the best.

As for the United States, I can state here today without qualification: We have not turned away from the world.

We know that with power goes responsibility.

We are neither boastful of our power, nor apologetic about it. We recognize that it exists, and that, as well as conferring certain advantages, it also imposes upon us certain obligations.

As the world changes, the pattern of those obligations and responsibilities changes.

At the end of World War II, the United States for the first time in history assumed the major responsibility for world peace.

We were left in 1945 as the one nation with sufficient strength to contain the new threats of aggression, and with sufficient wealth to help the injured nations back to their feet.

For much of the world, those first difficult postwar years were a time of dependency.

The next step was toward independence, as new nations were born and old nations revived.

Now we are maturing together into a new pattern of interdependence.

It is against this background that we have been urging other nations to assume a greater share of responsibility for their own security, both individually and together with their neighbors. The great challenge now is to enlist the cooperation of many nations in preserving peace and in enriching life. This cannot be done by American edict, or by the edict of any

other nation. It must reflect the concepts and the wishes of the people of those nations themselves.

The history of the postwar period teaches that nationalism can be dangerously disruptive—or powerfully creative.

Our aim is to encourage the creative forms of nationalism; to join as partners where our partnership is appropriate, and where it is wanted, but not to let a U.S. presence substitute for independent national effort or infringe on national dignity and national pride.

It is not my belief that the way to peace is by giving up our friends or letting down our allies. On the contrary, our aim is to place America's international commitments on a sustainable, long term basis, to encourage local and regional initiatives, to foster national independence and self-sufficiency, and by so doing to strengthen the total fabric of peace.

It would be dishonest, particularly before this sophisticated audience, to pretend that the United States has no national interests of its own, or no special concern for its own interests.

However, our most fundamental national interest is in maintaining that structure of international stability on which peace depends, and which makes orderly progress possible.

TOWARD PEACE IN VIETNAM

Since I took office as President, no single question has occupied so much of my time and energy as the search for an end to the war in Vietnam—an end fair to the people of South Vietnam, fair to the people of North Vietnam, and fair to those others who would be affected by the outcome.

We in the United States want to end

this war, and we are ready to take every reasonable step to achieve that goal. But let there be no question on this one fundamental point: In good conscience we cannot—in the long term interests of peace we will not—accept a settlement that would arbitrarily dictate the political future of South Vietnam and deny to the people of South Vietnam the basic right to determine their own future free of any outside interference.

As I put it in my address to the American people last May: "What the United States wants for South Vietnam is not the important thing. What North Vietnam wants for South Vietnam is not the important thing. What is important is what the people of South Vietnam want for South Vietnam."

To secure this right—and to secure this principle—is our one limited but fundamental objective.

Both in public and at the Paris talks, we have offered a number of proposals which would bring peace and provide self-determination. And we are ready to consider any other proposals that have the same objective. The missing ingredient so far has been the willingness of the other side to talk on any terms other than those that would predetermine the result and deny the right of self-determination to the people of South Vietnam. Once that willingness exists, and once there is a genuine willingness by the other side to reach agreement, the practical solutions can readily be found.

This makes it urgent that the U.N. members, those in this room who have long taken an active interest in peace in Vietnam, now take an active hand in achieving it.

Many urged that if only we halted our bombing of the North, peace would follow. Nearly a year has passed since the bombing of the North was halted.

Three months have passed since we began the process of troop replacement, signaling both our own genuine desire for a settlement and the increased readiness of the South Vietnamese to manage their own defense.

As I announced on Tuesday, by December 15 our troop strength in Vietnam will have been reduced by a minimum of 60,000 men.

On September 2, 1969, North Vietnam's chief negotiator in Paris said that if the United States committed itself to the principle of totally withdrawing its forces from South Vietnam, and if it withdrew a significant number of troops, Hanoi would take this into account.

I repeat here today what I said in my speech of May 14: that we are prepared to withdraw all of our forces from South Vietnam.

And the replacement of 60,000 troops is a significant step.

The time has come for the other side to respond to these initiatives.

The time has come for peace.

And in the name of peace, I urge all of you here—representing 126 nations—to use your best diplomatic efforts to persuade Hanoi to move seriously into the negotiations which could end this war. The steps we have taken have been responsive to views expressed in this room. And we hope that views from this organization may also be influential in Hanoi. If these efforts are successful, this war can end.

The people of Vietnam, North and South alike, have demonstrated heroism enough to last a century. And I speak from personal observation. I have been to North Vietnam, to Hanoi, in 1953, and all over South Vietnam. I have seen the people of the North and the people of the South. The people of Vietnam, North and South, have endured an unspeakable weight of suffering for a generation. And they deserve a better future.

When the war ends, the United States will stand ready to help the people of Vietnam—all of them—in their tasks of renewal and reconstruction. And when peace comes at last to Vietnam, it can truly come with healing in its wings.

AN ERA OF NEGOTIATIONS

In relations between the United States and the various Communist powers, I have said that we move from an era of confrontation to an era of negotiation.

I believe our relations with the Soviet Union can be conducted in a spirit of mutual respect, recognizing our differences and also our right to differ, recognizing our divergent interests and also our common interests, recognizing the interests of our respective allies as well as our own.

Now, it would be idle to pretend that there are not major problems between us, and conflicting interests. The tensions of the past 30 years have not been caused by mere personal misunderstandings. This is why we have indicated the need for extended negotiations on a broad front of issues.

Already, as you know, we have had extensive consultations with the Soviet Union as well as with others about the Middle East, where events of the past few days point up anew the urgency of a stable peace.

The United States continues to believe that the U.N. cease-fire resolutions define the minimal conditions that must prevail on the ground if settlement is to be achieved in the Middle East. We believe the Security Council resolution of November 1967 charts the way to that settlement.

A peace, to be lasting, must leave no seeds of a future war. It must rest on a settlement which both sides have a vested interest in maintaining.

We seek a settlement based on respect for the sovereign right of each nation in the area to exist within secure and recognized boundaries. We are convinced that peace cannot be achieved on the basis of substantial alterations in the map of the Middle East. And we are equally convinced that peace cannot be achieved on the basis of anything less than a binding, irrevocable commitment by the parties to live together in peace.

Failing a settlement, an agreement on the limitation of the shipment of arms to the Middle East might help to stabilize the situation. We have indicated to the Soviet Union, without result, our willingness to enter such discussions.

In addition to our talks on the Middle East, we hope soon to begin talks with the Soviet Union on the limitation of strategic arms. There is no more important task before us.

The date we proposed for the opening of talks has passed for lack of response. We remain ready to enter negotiations.

Since the United States first proposed strategic arms talks 3 years ago, the task of devising an effective agreement has become more difficult.

The Soviet Union has been vigorously expanding its strategic forces; weapons systems themselves have become more sophisticated, more destructive. But as the difficulty of the talks increases, so, too, does their importance.

Though the issues are complex, we are

prepared to deal with them seriously, concretely, and purposefully—and to make a determined effort not only to limit the buildup of strategic arms, but to reverse it.

Meanwhile, I want to affirm our support for arms control proposals which we hope the Geneva conference will place before this Assembly, with regard to the seabed and chemical and bacteriological weapons. We hope also that the Nuclear Nonproliferation Treaty will soon enter into force.

We should be under no illusion, however, that arms control will in itself bring peace. Wars are fought by soldiers, but they are declared by politicians. Peace also requires progress on those stubbornly persistent political questions, questions that are considered in this room, questions that still divide the world—and it requires other exchanges, not only of words but of deeds, that can gradually weave a fabric of mutual trust among the nations and the peoples of the world.

We intend to conduct our negotiations with the Soviet Union soberly and seriously, neither encumbered by prejudice nor blinded by sentimentality, seeking to reach agreement, rather than to make propaganda.

Whenever the leaders of Communist China choose to abandon their self-imposed isolation, we are ready to talk with them in the same frank and serious spirit.

PEACE-KEEPING AND PEACE-BUILDING

For nearly a quarter of a century, the U.N. has struggled with the often thankless task of peace-keeping.

As we look to the future, however, keeping the peace is only part of our task. We also must concentrate on building the peace.

Let us be candid. There are many differences among the great powers, and among other powers, which as realists we know cannot be resolved quickly, cannot be resolved even by this organization. But we also know that there are at least five areas in particular of great concern to everyone here with regard to which there should be no national differences, in which our interests are common and on which there should be unanimity.

They are these:

—securing the safety of international air travel,

—encouraging international voluntary service,

—fostering economic development, population control,

—protecting our threatened environment,

—exploring the frontiers of space.

By any standards, aircraft hijackings are morally, politically, and legally indefensible. The Tokyo Convention [1] has now been brought into force, providing for prompt release of passengers, crew, and aircraft. Along with other nations, we also are working on a new convention for the punishment of hijackers. But neither of these conventions can be fully effective without cooperation; sky piracy cannot be ended as long as the pirates receive asylum.

Consequently, I urge the United Nations to give high priority to this matter. This is an issue which transcends politics;

------

[1] The Tokyo Convention on Offenses and Certain Other Acts Committed on Board Aircraft was favorably considered by the Senate on May 13, 1969. It was ratified by the President on June 30, 1969, and the instrument of ratification was deposited on September 5, 1969. The text is printed in United States Treaties and Other International Agreements (20 UST 2941).

there is no need for it to become the subject of polemics or a focus of political differences. It involves the interests of every nation, the safety of every air passenger, and the integrity of that structure of order on which a world community depends.

The creative, dynamic kind of peace I have spoken of, of course, requires more than such basic protections as the one I have just described.

To build this kind of peace, we must join together in building our societies—in raising a great cathedral of the spirit, which celebrates the infinite possibilities of man himself.

Such a peace requires a fuller enlistment, not only of government resources and of private enterprise resources, but also of the dedication and skill of those thousands of people all over the world who are ready to volunteer in the cause of human achievement. Our own Peace Corps has helped in many countries. And I especially welcome the consideration of the U.N. itself, which it is now giving to establishment of an International Volunteer Corps. We stand ready to give this exciting new venture our full and enthusiastic cooperation.

As the U.N. looks toward the beginning of its second development decade, it faces a time of enormous challenge, but enormous opportunity.

We can only guess at the new scientific discoveries that the seventies may bring. But we can see with chilling clarity the gap that already exists between the developed economies and the economies of the developing countries and the urgent need for international cooperation in spurring economic development.

If, in the course of that second development decade, we can make both significant gains in food production and signifi-

cant reductions in the rate of population growth, we shall have opened the way to a new era of splendid prosperity. If we do only one without the other, we shall be standing still, and if we fail in both, great areas of the world will face human disaster.

Increasingly, the task of protecting man's environments is a matter of international concern. Pollution of air and water, upsetting the balance of nature—these are not only local problems, and not only national problems, but matters that affect the basic relationships of man to his planet.

The United Nations already is planning a conference on the environment in 1972. I pledge the strongest support of the United States for that effort. I hope that even before then we can launch new national and international initiatives toward restoring the balance of nature, and maintaining our world as a healthy and hospitable place for man.

Of all of man's great enterprises, none lends itself more logically or more compellingly to international cooperation than the venture into space. Here, truly, mankind is one: as fellow creatures from the planet earth, exploring the heavens that all of us enjoy.

The journey of Apollo 11 to the moon and back was not an end, but the beginning.

There will be new journeys of discovery. Beyond this, we are just beginning to comprehend the benefits that space technology can yield here on earth. And the potential is enormous.

For example, we now are developing earth resource survey satellites, with the first experimental satellite to be launched sometime early in the decade of the seventies.

Present indications are that these satellites should be capable of yielding data which could assist in as widely varied tasks as these: the location of schools of fish in the oceans, the location of mineral deposits on land, the health of agricultural crops.

I feel it is only right that we should share both the adventures and the benefits of space. As an example of our plans, we have determined to take actions with regard to earth resource satellites, as this program proceeds and fulfills its promise.

The purpose of those actions is that this program will be dedicated to produce information not only for the United States, but also for the world community.

We shall be putting several proposals in this respect before the United Nations.

These are among the positive, concrete steps we intend to take toward internationalizing man's epic venture into space—an adventure that belongs not to one nation but to all mankind, and one that should be marked not by rivalry but by the same spirit of fraternal cooperation that so long has been the hallmark of the international community of science.

And now, Madam President, Mr. Secretary General, if I could speak a personal word to the representatives gathered in this room.

I recognize that those here are dedicating their lives to the cause of peace and that, in this room, what is done here will have an enormous effect on the future of peace.

I have had the great privilege over the past 23 years to travel to most of the countries represented in this room. I have met most of the leaders of the nations represented in this room. And I have seen literally thousands of people in most of the countries represented in this room.

There are differences between the nations and differences between the leaders and differences between the peoples in this world. But based on my own experience, of this one thing I am sure: The people of the world, wherever they are, want peace. And those of us who have the responsibilities for leadership in the world have an overwhelming world mandate from the people of the nations we represent to bring peace, to keep the peace, and to build the peace.

Now, I realize that a survey of history might discourage those who seek to establish peace.

But we have entered a new age, different not only in degree but in kind from any that has ever gone before.

For the first time ever, we have truly become a single world community.

For the first time ever, we have seen the staggering fury of the power of the universe unleashed, and we know that we hold that power in a very precarious balance.

For the first time ever, technological advance has brought within reach what once was only a poignant dream for hundreds of millions: freedom from hunger and freedom from want—want and hunger that I have personally seen in nation after nation all over this world.

For the first time ever, we have seen changes in a single lifetime—in our lifetime—that dwarf the achievements of centuries before, and those changes continue to accelerate.

For the first time ever, man has stepped beyond his planet—and revealed us to ourselves as "riders on the earth together," bound inseparably on this one bright, beautiful speck in the heavens, so tiny in the universe and so incomparably welcoming as a home for man.

In this new age of "firsts," even the goal of a just and lasting peace is a "first" we can dare to strive for. We must achieve it. And I believe we can achieve it.

In that spirit, then, let us press toward an open world—a world of open doors, open hearts, open minds; a world open to the exchange of ideas and of people, and open to the reach of the human spirit; a world open in the search for truth, and unconcerned with the fate of old dogmas and old isms; a world open at last to the light of justice, and the light of reason, and to the achievement of that true peace which the people of every land carry in their hearts and celebrate in their hopes.

NOTE: The President spoke at 11:23 a.m. at United Nations headquarters in New York. The President of the General Assembly was Miss Angie Brooks, Assistant Secretary of State of Liberia, and the Secretary General of the United Nations was U Thant of Burma.

366   Remarks Concerning Changes in Draft Calls and Pending Draft Legislation.   *September* 19, 1969

Ladies and gentlemen:

I have an announcement today, and the Secretary of Defense will answer questions on that announcement when it is concluded.

Acting on the recommendation of the Secretary of Defense, the programed draft calls for the months of November and December—32,000 for November and 18,000 for December—will be canceled.

The draft call previously announced for the month of October will be phased out over the final quarter of the year.

These actions have been made possible by the reduction in our forces of 60,000 in Vietnam which I announced on Tuesday,[1] and by other actions taken by the Department of Defense under the manpower program.

Further, with regard to the future of the draft program, as you know, we have been considering that in the National Security Council. The Secretary of Defense had a meeting yesterday with various congressional leaders on it. I have an announcement to make with regard to that program at this time.

On May 13, I submitted legislation to the Congress which would have removed from vulnerability to the draft all young men between the ages of 20 and 26, and which would provide for draft eligibility only those 19 years of age under a system of random selection.

The Congress has not yet acted on this legislation; and we have decided that if the Congress does not act on this legislation during this session of the Congress that then I shall take, by unilateral action, by Executive order, the recommendation of the Secretary of Defense which he will describe in detail, which will move toward that objective and which will remove uncertainties from the age group of 20 to 26, although it will not accomplish the objective as clearly and as fairly as would the legislation if it were passed.

The Secretary of Defense will be able to answer all your questions on the technical details of these two actions, and I

---

[1] See Item 361.

731

will now turn the press conference over to him.

NOTE: The President spoke at 11:36 a.m. in the Roosevelt Room at the White House.

The news briefing by Secretary of Defense Laird, following the President's remarks, is printed in the Weekly Compilation of Presidential Documents (vol. 5, p. 1283).

367   Remarks to Members of the Association of Student Governments. *September* 20, 1969

IN WELCOMING YOU to the White House this morning, or I should say this afternoon, I should point out that in this historic room over the past 8 months I have had the opportunity of welcoming many distinguished groups.

This is the room in which we receive heads of state, ambassadors, and all of the great of the world and of the United States.

And I have always tried to find the appropriate words with which to address each group. But I think the way that I can bring home to all of you here—and to those who may be witnessing this ceremony on television or hearing it on radio—the significance of this occasion is that for the first time in 8 months I can say "fellow presidents."

Now, this should call forth from me some profound remarks about the problems of education in the United States today, the problems of the generation gap, the problems of the world, or any of the others with which I know you are deeply concerned.

I am not going to provide that kind of information for you today. I don't think that is appropriate. I don't think that perhaps would be of the greatest interest to you. I do want to have the opportunity to meet each of you, the presidents of the student government associations, and the presidents of the universities and colleges

here, and to say a word to you as we go through the line.

But I would like to be permitted just a little personal reminiscence with regard to the position that you find yourselves in. And I speak now of those who are presidents of student government.

I have never been the president of a college or university. I don't think I could quite handle that problem.

I was once—and this gives me an opportunity, of course, to puff a bit—the president of student government at a small college in California and also president of my law school student body at Duke University.

I recall in those years—the years between 1930 and 1937—that we were concerned about the grave problems of the United States and the world. Perhaps as you compare the situation today with the situation then, it may seem that our problems were not too great.

We did not have nuclear weapons then. We have them now. But we did have a deep depression then. Our concern was, when we finished school, whether we could get a job and, if we got a job, whether we could be paid enough to make a living.

We also had on the horizon—and all of us could recognize it, particularly in the years between '35, '36, '37—the specter of World War II. Mussolini,

Hitler, the other potential dictators and warmakers were on the loose. And we were sensitive enough to international conditions to know the future—what it might hold for us.

Despite that, we—just as you—were not discouraged, although possibly we should have been discouraged. We tried to seek the answers. We perhaps did not seek those answers in as aggressive a way as the generation today does. That may be to our discredit and it may be to your credit that this generation is—in seeking the answers to the problems in both student relations with the university and the college and also with regard to the problems of America and the world—it seems to be more in tune with modern problems than we were at that time.

What I am really trying to say is this: that while there is a generation gap, a generation gap that my two daughters often remind me of—my daughter, Patricia, she even has a generation gap with those who are in college, because she is 2 years out of college. But while there is a generation gap, let me assure you that those of us in this administration, those in the House and the Senate, Democrats and Republicans alike, are concerned about the problems that you are concerned about.

We are concerned when we see on the campuses of this country the frustration boiling up into violence, and we want to find answers with you. That is why I was so delighted to hear of this conference and to note that what you were trying to do was to search together for the answers, to search together with the college and university presidents for the answers to these problems.

Of course, you know you are not going to find them. You may find a way to approach the problems. You will not find the answers in a conference of 2 or 3 days.

But this kind of dialogue, it seems to me, may be tremendously useful on the campuses from which you come, and I know could be very useful to you in your lives in the future.

And I would simply add perhaps a little bit more from my personal experience, again not with any thought that this is so profound as to make an impression on this group.

I have found in my travels around the world—and you may have recalled that when I spoke at the United Nations a couple of days ago—I have met most of the heads of government presently in the world and most of those who have been heads of government of the nations of the world over the past 22 years. I have had the opportunity, in meeting them, to learn from them.

And perhaps there are three lessons that I have learned over those years that are worth passing on:

First, I have found that I learned a great deal more in my travels by listening. I don't mean that I didn't have ideas that I tried to get across. But by listening—and, incidentally, listening to not just those who led the great nations, but those who led the small nations—I learned a great deal, because wisdom is not limited to those nations which happen to have power and wealth.

Some of the most exciting conversations I have had have been with prime ministers, presidents, foreign ministers, leaders in some of the smaller nations of Africa and Latin America and Asia.

And second, I have learned, too, over

those years that usually the man who talked the loudest had the least to say. I found that, and it is somewhat like a poker game—I am sure none of you play poker; at least you could afford it—but, nevertheless it is like a poker game. You can be sure that whoever is talking the loudest is pretty sure to be bluffing. And you watch out for that silent man who sits there and doesn't say too much. He has probably got the cards.

And I have found that those who talk quietly with firmness, firmness yes, but with some quietness, have an enormous effect compared with the others who bluster and shout and repeat without reasoning.

Then finally, this other lesson that I learned in these travels around the world and in the position that I now have the honor to hold. And it is: to have respect for the opinions of others. I find every day in this office, whether it is in foreign policy, in trying to find the answer to peace in the world, not only to bring peace in Vietnam, but to avoid other Vietnams, to have real peace in the world ahead; trying to find the answer to disarmament, trying to find the answer to the relations between the races in this country, to the answers to the problems of population in the world, which will eventually suffocate the world unless we do find a better answer, food production, the environment, all of these problems— I have found that I come in sometimes with a very well-briefed position and I am pretty sure that it is right.

Then, after listening for a couple of hours in a meeting to various groups of people express different points of view, it isn't that it means that you come away with an absolute certainty, but it does mean that you find a better answer, not

the one that is infallible, but a better answer than you would otherwise have found.

I just leave this final thought with you. Everybody has a hobby in this great house. Mine is not reading westerns or looking at television. We have removed some of the television sets, although they have the Colts and the Rams on tomorrow. I will look at that.

But, nevertheless, it is reading and particularly reading in the field of history, which was my major, and it carried over to both my daughters. In this field, I am always fascinated with that magnificent story—I think it is magnificent—of how the American Constitution came into being. Perhaps the American Constitution today seems rather obsolete.

But for its time, and considering how it has been able to be the framework upon which we were able to build the society in which we live, I think most observers outside the United States would say that some way or other in Philadelphia came together the genius of people in this very small and new land.

At the time the Constitution was being ratified, Benjamin Franklin, the oldest of the delegates—he was 82, which is very old even now and at that time it was very, very old—he was 82, 20 years older than any other of the delegates. He really had a generation gap.

He was too old to come to that meeting. And so one of the other delegates read his remarks.

His bit of advice is the advice that I take and the advice that from him I pass on to you. He said: "I know there are uncertainties among members of the delegations as they come now to ratify this Constitution. But I would urge each of you to have a doubt with regard to his own infallibility."

This, I think, is the lesson we all need to know, on the campuses, in government. We do not think we are infallible. And I know that you, as intelligent men and women, do not think you are.

If we start that way, with respect for the opinions that we disagree with, perhaps we will find some of the answers.

That is what I feel and that is why I am so delighted to welcome you here today and now to have the chance to greet each one of my fellow presidents.

Thank you.

NOTE: The President spoke at 12:45 p.m. in the East Room at the White House, where he greeted approximately 500 delegates to the conference. The delegates had convened in Washington to improve communications and understanding among student, academic, business, and Government leaders.

368   Statement on the Construction Industry Collective Bargaining Commission. *September 22, 1969*

IN MY September 4, 1969, statement on the construction industry I directed the Secretary of Labor to devise a way for union and employer groups to cooperate with each other and the Government in the solution of collective bargaining and related problems in the industry.

Secretary Shultz has recommended the establishment of a tripartite Construction Industry Collective Bargaining Commission. I am issuing an Executive order [11482] immediately to implement this recommendation.

Cooperative effort on the part of labor and management to work with government in times of stress is nothing new in the construction industry. Indeed, on numerous occasions in the past the Federal Government has requested the leaders of the industry to join together with the Government to solve its pressing problems.

Notable among these instances were the Board of Review and the Wage Adjustment Board of the World War II period, the Construction Industry Stabilization Commission of the Korean era, the Atomic Energy Labor Relations Panel established in 1948, and the President's Missile Sites Labor Commission, 1961–67.

The critical problems facing the industry today call again for special efforts both to meet the present challenge and to prepare the industry to cope with the unprecedented demands which will be placed on it in the decade of the seventies.

The Construction Industry Collective Bargaining Commission will be composed of four public representatives and an equal number from labor and from management. The Secretary of Labor, George P. Shultz, will serve as the Chairman and John T. Dunlop, Harvard University, as the Secretary of the Commission. George Romney, Secretary of the Department of Housing and Urban Development, and J. Curtis Counts, Director of the Federal Mediation and Conciliation Service, will serve as the other public representatives on the Commission.

The Commission will have two major roles. The first—vitally important in terms of the long-range growth and development of the construction industry—will be to bring together top management and labor representatives from all sectors and trades of the industry to discuss and seek solutions to a wide range of labor-management and manpower problems which directly affect the industry's ability to grow and adapt to changing needs. Among the problems to be considered are the training and development of construction manpower, instability and seasonality of employment opportunities, productivity and mobility of the construction labor force.

The second major role of the Commission is to develop voluntary tripartite procedures in settling disputes. The presence of a third party representing the public in matters so directly affecting the public interest is clearly desirable. The intent of these tripartite procedures is neither to provide for compulsory arbitration nor to abrogate rights to strike or lockout; the intent is to facilitate, through the collective bargaining process, industrial peace and stability in the construction industry.

The Commission is directed to work and coordinate its study activities with the recently established Cabinet Committee on Construction. In addition, I have asked all Federal agencies to cooperate with the Commission in discharging its activities. In this connection, I have directed the Bureau of the Budget to compile annually and furnish to both the Commission and the Cabinet Committee on Construction information regarding Federal or federally assisted construction in such forms as the Commission and Committee deem necessary in the discharge of their responsibilities.

This administration is deeply committed to the institution of free collective bargaining. As a fundamental premise, in order for the institution to survive and prosper, the parties must assume the full share of their responsibilities to the industry and to the Nation. Through the years the strains of our dynamic economy bring greater pressures upon one industry than on others. Today a combination of circumstances has produced serious stress within the construction industry. I call upon the leaders of this important industry, working through the Collective Bargaining Commission, to attack problems and to seek solutions which will meet the current and future challenges of the industry.

The Commission members are:

Public

George P. Shultz, Secretary of Labor, Washington, D.C., Chairman of the Commission; George W. Romney, Secretary, Department of Housing and Urban Development, Washington, D.C.; J. Curtis Counts, Director, Federal Mediation and Conciliation Service, Washington, D.C.; Dr. John T. Dunlop, Harvard University, Cambridge, Mass.

Unions

C. J. Haggerty, president, Building & Construction Trades Department, AFL–CIO, 815 16th Street, NW., Washington, D.C.; M. A. Hutcheson, president, United Brotherhood of Carpenters and Joiners of America, 101 Constitution Avenue, NW., Washington, D.C.; Peter T. Schoemann, president, United Association of Journeymen and Apprentices of the Plumbing and Pipe Fitting Industry of the United States and Canada, 901 Massachusetts Avenue, NW., Washington, D.C.; Hunter P. Wharton, president, International Union of Operating Engineers, 1125 17th Street, NW., Washington, D.C.

Employers

E. S. Torrence, executive director, Painting and Decorating Contractors Association, 1629 K Street, NW., Washington, D.C.; Robert Higgins, executive vice president, National Electrical Contractors Association, 1730 Rhode Island Avenue, NW., Washington, D.C.; Carl M. Halvorson, president, The Associated General Contractors of America, 1957 E Street, NW., Washington, D.C.; John A. Stastny, national vice president and treasurer, National Association of Home Builders, Chicago, Ill.

Alternate Commission members will be selected and announced shortly after consultation with the national labor organizations and contractor associations in the industry.

NOTE: Also released was the transcript of a news briefing by Vice President Spiro T. Agnew and Governor John A. Love of Colorado, chairman of the National Governors' Conference, on inflation and its impact on the construction industry, following a meeting with the President.

On September 30, 1969, the White House released the text of a news briefing by Secretary of Labor George P. Shultz following a meeting of the President with the Cabinet Committee on Construction.

369   Remarks Announcing Decision To Continue Development of the Supersonic Transport. *September 23, 1969*

Ladies and gentlemen:

The purpose of this briefing, which will be conducted by Secretary of Transportation Volpe, is to make a major announcement with regard to the future of American leadership in air transport.

I think all of us are aware that for 50 years the United States has led the world in air transport. The decision that we announce today means that we will continue to maintain leadership in this field.

The supersonic transport is going to be built. The question is whether in the years ahead the people of the world will be flying in American supersonic transports or in the transports of other nations. And the question is whether the United States, after starting and stopping this program, after stretching it out, finally decides to go ahead.

This has been a very difficult decision in terms of a very spirited debate within the administration and also within the Congress as to the proper priority for funds.

I have made the decision that we should go ahead.

I have made it first because I want the United States to continue to lead the world in air transport. And it is essential to build this plane if we are to maintain that leadership.

I have made the decision, also, because in another sense this means that through this plane we are going to be able to bring the world closer together in a true physical and time sense. This plane, which will fly at 1,700 miles an hour, will mean that in the year 1978, when it will fly commercially—the prototypes will fly in 1972—but in the year 1978 when it will fly commercially, that Tokyo will be as close to Washington, D.C., as far as hours are concerned, as London is today. And, in another sense, Argentina will be as close—the furthest tip of Latin America— to Washington, D.C., as London is today.

This is a massive stride forward in the field of transport and I think all of us want the United States to move forward in this area.

There are arguments that the Secretary will be able to answer with regard to the technical features of the plane. After listening to all of those arguments, I am convinced that the technical factors can be solved and that we should move forward.

And the decision is that now we do go forward and that the first prototype will be flown in 1972 and that the United States will continue to lead the world in air transport.

I want to congratulate at this time not only the Secretary of Transportation, who has felt very strongly within the administration that we should go forward with this decision, but to the leaders—particularly from the State of Washington where the planes will be built, I understand, in the first instance, although this art will spread around other parts of the country, and I am sure subcontracts will cover the whole country, as I understand—to Governor [Daniel] Evans, to Senator [Henry M.] Jackson, to Congresswoman [Catherine] May, to Congressman

[Thomas M.] Pelly, and also to the Representative from the Appropriations Committee of the House, Mr. Bill Minshall of Ohio—certainly he has an interest in aviation, being a pilot himself, and has long felt that we should go forward.

Thank you very much.

NOTE: The President spoke at 9:04 a.m. in the Roosevelt Room at the White House.

Also released on the same day was the text of a news briefing by Secretary of Transportation John A. Volpe which followed the President's remarks.

An announcement of February 27, 1969, on the establishment of an interdepartmental committee to review the supersonic transport program is printed in the Weekly Compilation of Presidential Documents (vol. 5, p. 329).

370   Statement on the Subway System for the District of Columbia.   *September* 24, 1969

I WANT to congratulate and thank all those who have made possible the beginning of construction of the new subway system for Washington. The people of the area, and indeed of the Nation, owe appreciation to many persons who have labored so many years to make this day possible, but of course special thanks are due to Members of the Congress, to the Mayor [Walter E. Washington] and Council of the city of Washington, and to the Washington Metropolitan Transit Authority.

More than a subway will begin in December. A city will begin to renew itself; a metropolitan area to pull itself together. That the Nation's Capital is involved makes this an event of national significance.

NOTE: The statement followed an announcement by Representative William H. Natcher, Chairman of the House Appropriations Subcommittee on the District of Columbia, that he would recommend that appropriations be made which would enable subway construction to begin.

371   Remarks of Welcome to Prime Minister Golda Meir of Israel at the White House.   *September* 25, 1969

Madam Prime Minister and our guests here at the White House today:

It is a very great privilege for me, speaking in behalf of the American people, to welcome you, Madam Prime Minister, in a very personal sense, because

you were raised in this country. You have been to this country many times, but we are particularly proud that for the first time we welcome you as the Prime Minister of Israel.

Speaking to you in that capacity, as

the head of government of a very courageous people, a people who are determined to maintain their independence, who also are determined to achieve a lasting peace in the area in which they live, I look forward to the talks we shall have individually, and also with other members of your party.

It would be less than candid for me not to say that the problems of the Mideast are terribly complex and not susceptible to solution in one meeting, or two or three, or even more, at the level at which we will be talking.

But it is also proper to say that the Mideast and peace in the Mideast is of interest not only to your nation and your neighbors but to the whole world, because of what could happen in the event that war were to break out there, the repercussions that that could have all over the world.

We know that you and your people want peace. We know that your neighbors want peace. Certainly the majority of the people in the whole area want peace. The question is how to achieve it. On this we shall have discussions that I hope will be helpful; the real peace, the peace that is not simply one of words but one in which both parties will have a vested interest in maintaining.

I would say finally, Madam Prime Minister, that a very famous British Prime Minister once said: "One should always talk as much as possible to women, because this is the best school."

I can assure you that I recognize the tremendous complexity of the problem we will be discussing. I recognize that it is necessary to get the very best answers that we can to find a solution to these problems, and I realize that in talking to you, not just because you are Prime Minister but because you are one of the outstanding women in political leadership in the world, that in talking to you, I will be truly going to the best school today and tomorrow.

NOTE: The President spoke at 10:37 a.m. on the South Lawn at the White House where Prime Minister Golda Meir was given a formal welcome with full military honors.

See also Items 373 and 376.

The Prime Minister responded as follows:

Mr. President, needless to say, I am deeply moved by the reception and by the words that you have spoken. Every official guest from abroad to the White House must surely sense the significance of the occasion. May I say this is particularly so for a representative of a people small in numbers and in resources.

May I say that in receiving me here in friendship and equality you are affirming that the attitude of the United States to other peoples is not determined by physical factors.

The history of Israel, reborn in the years preceding statehood and the more than two decades since its achievement, cannot be told without reference to the unwavering support and friendship shown by successive American governments and by the American people.

Within hours after the proclamation of our statehood, the United States Government recognized Israel, and Jewish remnants from the Nazi death camps, who had been largely liberated by American forces in Europe, came to our shores.

Mr. President, the ties between our two countries are rooted in the Biblical heritage and in the common dedication to human dignity, freedom, and to democracy.

We have done everything in our power to translate these ideals into the fabric of our national life. It is this sense of affinity that has encouraged us to ask for America's understanding and support in difficult times.

The story of modern Israel is essentially the story of the return to the ancestral homeland of exiles from persecution, insecurity, and fear in quest of freedom, human dignity, independence, and peace.

Today, no Jew need remain homeless because of oppression and insecurity. I am gratified to be able to say this here in this great land which has been a haven for the oppressed, including many of my own people.

I shall be able to tell you, Mr. President, of Israel's progress in many fields. Tragically, peace is still denied us. But that same faith that sustained us down the ages instills within us the confidence that the hour of peace will come.

I look forward to the day when an Israeli Prime Minister will be able to come here bearing to the President and the people of the United States the tidings that the Middle East has entered a new epoch of amity and regional cooperation.

Mr. President, the prayers and hopes of my people are with you in the heavy responsibility you carry, not only for your great country but for the freedom-loving mankind at large. We follow with deep sympathy your efforts for regional and world peace, the phenomenal scientific advance of America under your leadership, the results of which are open to all nations, and your interest in economic and social advancement for all peoples.

I am privileged, Mr. President, to convey to you the best wishes from the President, the Government, and the people of Israel, together with their deep appreciation for your invitation to me and for your interest in our welfare and progress.

From Jerusalem, the city of prophecy and universal inspiration, I bring you the traditional Hebrew greeting: *Shalom.*

372   Special Message to the Congress on Social Security. *September 25, 1969*

To the Congress of the United States:

This nation must not break faith with those Americans who have a right to expect that Social Security payments will protect them and their families.

The impact of an inflation now in its fourth year has undermined the value of every Social Security check and requires that we once again increase the benefits to help those among the most severely victimized by the rising cost of living.

I request that the Congress remedy the real losses to those who now receive Social Security benefits by increasing payments by 10 per cent.

Beyond that step to set right today's inequity, I propose that the Congress make certain once and for all that the retired, the disabled and the dependent never again bear the brunt of inflation. *The way to prevent future unfairness is to attach the benefit schedule to the cost of living.*

This will instill new security in Social Security. This will provide peace of mind to those concerned with their retirement years, and to their dependents.

By acting to raise benefits now to meet the rise in the cost of living, we keep faith with today's recipients. By acting to make future benefit raises automatic with rises in the cost of living, we remove questions about future years; we do much to remove this system from biennial politics; and we make fair treatment of beneficiaries a matter of certainty rather than a matter of hope.

In the 34 years since the Social Security program was first established, it has become a central part of life for a growing number of Americans. Today approximately 25 million people are receiving cash payments from this source. Three-quarters of these are older Americans; the Social Security check generally represents the greater part of total income. Millions of younger people receive benefits under the disability or survivor provisions of Social Security.

Almost all Americans have a stake in the soundness of the Social Security system. Some 92 million workers are contributing to Social Security this year. About 80 per cent of Americans of working age are protected by disability insurance and 95 per cent of children and mothers have survivorship insurance protection. Because the Social Security program is an essential part of life for so many Americans, we must continually reexamine the program and be prepared to make improvements.

Aiding in this Administration's review and evaluation is the Advisory Council on Social Security which the Secretary of Health, Education and Welfare appointed in May. For example, I will look to this Council for recommendations in regard to working women; changing work patterns and the increased contributions of working women to the system may make present law unfair to them. The recommendations of this Council and of other advisers, both within the Government and outside of it, will be important to our planning. As I indicated in my message to the Congress on April 14, improvement in the Social Security program is a major objective of this Administration.

There are certain changes in the Social Security program, however, for which the need is so clear that they should be made without awaiting the findings of the Advisory Council. The purpose of this message is to recommend such changes.

I propose an across-the-board increase of 10% in Social Security benefits, effective with checks mailed in April 1970, to make up for increases in the cost of living.

I propose that future benefits in the

Social Security system be automatically adjusted to account for increases in the cost of living.

I propose an increase from $1680 to $1800 in the amount beneficiaries can earn annually without reduction of their benefits, effective January 1, 1971.

I propose to eliminate the one-dollar-for-one-dollar reduction in benefits for income earned in excess of $2880 a year and replace it by a one dollar reduction in benefits for every two dollars earned, which now applies at earnings levels between $1680 and $2880, also effective January 1, 1971.

I propose to increase the contribution and benefit base from $7800 to $9000, beginning in 1972, to strengthen the system, to help keep future benefits to the individual related to the growth of his wages, and to meet part of the cost of the improved program. From then on, the base will automatically be adjusted to reflect wage increases.

I propose a series of additional reforms, to ensure more equitable treatment for widows, recipients above age 72, veterans, for persons disabled in childhood and for the dependent parents of disabled and retired workers.

I emphasize that the suggested changes are only first steps, and that further recommendations will come from our review process.

The Social Security system needs adjustment now so it will better serve people receiving benefits today, and those corrections are recommended in this message. The system is also in need of long-range reform, to make it better serve those who contribute now for benefits in future years, and that will be the subject of later recommendations.

THE BENEFIT INCREASE

With the increase of 10%, the average family benefit for an aged couple, both receiving benefits, would rise from $170 to $188 a month. Further indication of the impact of a 10 per cent increase on monthly benefits can be seen in the following table:

	Present Minimum	New Minimum	Present Maximum	New Maximum
Single Person:				
(A man retiring at age 65 in 1970)....	$55.00	$61.00	$165.00	$181.50
Married Couple:				
(Husband retiring at age 65 in 1970)..	82.50	91.50	247.50	272.30

The proposed benefit increases will raise the income of more than 25 million persons who will be on the Social Security rolls in April, 1970. Total budget outlays for the first full calendar year in which the increase is effective will be approximately $3 billion.

AUTOMATIC ADJUSTMENTS

Benefits will be adjusted automatically to reflect increases in the cost of living. The uncertainty of adjustment under present laws and the delay often encountered when the needs are already apparent is unnecessarily harsh to those who must depend on Social Security benefits to live.

Benefits that automatically increase with rising living costs can be funded without increasing Social Security tax rates so long as the amount of earnings subject to tax reflects the rising level of wages. Therefore, I propose that the wage base be automatically adjusted so that it corresponds to increases in earnings levels.

These automatic adjustments are interrelated and should be enacted as a package. Taken together they will depoliticize, to a certain extent, the Social Security system and give a greater stability to what has become a cornerstone of our society's social insurance system.

REFORMING THE SYSTEM

I propose a series of reforms in present Social Security law to achieve new standards of fairness. These would provide:

1. *An increase in benefits to a widow who begins receiving her benefit at age 65 or later.* The benefit would increase the current 82½% of her husband's benefit to a full 100%. This increased benefit to widows would fulfill a pledge I made a year ago. It would provide *an average increase of $17 a month to almost three million widows.*

2. *Non-contributory earnings credits of about $100 a month for military service* from January, 1957 to December, 1967. During that period, individuals in military service were covered under Social Security but credit was not then given for "wages in kind"—room and board, etc. A law passed in 1967 corrected this for the future, but the men who served from 1957 (when coverage began for servicemen) to 1967 should not be overlooked.

3. *Benefits for the aged parents of retired and disabled workers.* Under present law, benefits are payable only to the dependent parents of a worker who has died; we would extend this to parents of workers who are disabled or who retire.

4. *Child's insurance benefits for life* if

a child becomes permanently disabled before age 22. Under present law, a person must have become disabled before age 18 to qualify for these benefits. The proposal would be consistent with the payment of child's benefit to age 22 so long as the child is in school.

5. *Benefits in full paid to persons over 72,* regardless of the amount of his earnings in the year he attains that age. Under present law, he is bound by often confusing tests which may limit his exemption.

6. *A fairer means of determining benefits payable on a man's earnings record.* At present, men who retire at age 62 must compute their average earnings through three years of no earnings up to age 65, thus lowering the retirement benefit excessively. Under this proposal, only the years up to age 62 would be counted, just as is now done for women, and three higher-earning years could be substituted for low-earning years.

Changes in the Retirement Test

A feature of the present Social Security law that has drawn much criticism is the so-called "retirement test," a provision which limits the amount that a beneficiary can earn and still receive full benefits. I have been much concerned about this provision, particularly about its effects on incentives to work. The present retirement test actually penalizes Social Security beneficiaries for doing additional work or taking a job at higher pay. This is wrong.

In my view, many older people should be encouraged to work. Not only are they provided with added income, but the country retains the benefit of their skills and wisdom; they, in turn, have the feeling of usefulness and participation which employment can provide.

This is why I am recommending changes in the retirement test. Raising the amount of money a person can earn in a year without affecting his Social Security payments—from the present $1680 to $1800—is an important first step. But under the approach used in the present retirement test, people who earned more than the exempt amount of $1680, plus $1200, would continue to have $1 in Social Security benefits withheld for every $1 they received in earnings. A necessary second step is to eliminate from present law the requirement that when earnings reach $1200 above the exempt amount, Social Security benefits will be reduced by a full dollar for every dollar of added earnings until all his benefits are withheld; in effect, we impose a tax of more than 100% on these earnings.

To avoid this, I would eliminate this $1 reduction for each $1 earned and replace it with the same $1 reduction for each $2 earned above $3000. This change will reduce a disincentive to increased employment that arises under the retirement test in its present form.

The amount a retired person can earn and still receive his benefits should also increase automatically with the earnings level. It is sound policy to keep the exempt amount related to changes in the general level of earnings.

These alterations in the retirement test would result in added benefit payments of some $300 million in the first full calendar year. Approximately one million people would receive this money—some who are now receiving no benefits at all and some who now receive benefits but who would get more under this new arrangement. These suggestions are not by any means the solution to all the problems of the retirement test, however, and I am asking the Advisory Council on Social Security to give particular attention to this matter.

CONTRIBUTION AND BENEFIT BASE

The contribution and benefit base—the annual earnings on which Social Security contributions are paid and that can be counted toward Social Security benefits— has been increased several times since the Social Security program began. The further increase I am recommending— from its present level of $7800 to $9000 beginning January 1, 1972—will produce approximately the same relationship between the base and general earnings levels as that of the early 1950s. This is important since the goal of Social Security is the replacement, in part, of lost earnings; if the base on which contributions and benefits are figured does not rise with earnings increases, then the benefits deteriorate. The future benefit increases that will result from the higher base I am recommending today would help to prevent such deterioration. These increases would, of course, be in addition to those which result from the 10% across-the-board increase in benefits that is intended to bring them into line with the cost of living.

FINANCING

I recommend an acceleration of the tax rate scheduled for hospital insurance to bring the hospital insurance trust fund into actuarial balance. I also propose to decelerate the rate schedule of the old-age, survivors and disability insurance trust funds in current law. These funds taken together have a long-range surplus of income over outgo, which will meet much of the cost. The combined rate,

known as the "social security contribution," already scheduled by statute, will be decreased from 1971 through 1976. Thus, in 1971 the currently scheduled rate of 5.2% to be paid by employees would become 5.1%, and in 1973 the currently scheduled rate of 5.65% would become 5.5%. The actuarial integrity of the two funds will be maintained, and the ultimate tax rates will not be changed in the rate schedules which will be proposed.

The voluntary supplementary medical insurance (SMI) of title XVIII of the Social Security Act, often referred to as part B Medicare coverage, is not adequately financed with the current $4 premium. Our preliminary studies indicate that there will have to be a substantial increase in the premium. The Secretary of Health, Education and Welfare will set the premium rate in December for the fiscal year beginning July 1970, as he is required to do by statute.

To meet the rising costs of health care in the United States, this Administration will soon forward a Health Cost Control proposal to the Congress. Other administrative measures are already being taken to hold down spiraling medical expenses.

In the coming months, this Administration will give careful study to ways in which we can further improve the Social Security program. The program is an established and important American institution, a foundation on which millions are able to build a more comfortable life than would otherwise be possible—after their retirement or in the event of disability or death of the family earner.

The recommendations I propose today, which I urge the Congress to adopt, will move the cause of Social Security forward on a broad front.

We will bring benefit payments up to date.

We will make sure that benefit payments stay up to date, automatically tied to the cost of living.

We will begin making basic reforms in the system to remove inequities and bring a new standard of fairness in the treatment of all Americans in the system.

And we will lay the groundwork for further study and improvement of a system that has served the country well and must serve future generations more fairly and more responsively.

RICHARD NIXON

The White House
September 25, 1969

NOTE: The Social Security Amendments of 1969 were approved by the President on December 30, 1969, as title X of the Tax Reform Act of 1969 (Public Law 91–172, 83 Stat. 737).

373 Toasts of the President and Prime Minister Golda Meir of Israel. *September* 25, 1969

Madam Prime Minister and our very distinguished guests this evening:

As I look around this room, I see several Members of the Senate and the House who have been here before during this administration's dinners in this State Dining Room, and who have seen the heads of state and heads of government who have been here.

All of them were very distinguished leaders of their countries but, as you know, this is the first time that in this administration we have had the honor to receive the head of government of another state who also is a woman.

Now that, naturally, should give a great deal of opportunity for a President of the United States, in welcoming the Prime Minister, to remark about her unusual capabilities, not only in her official capacity but as a woman. And I can only say this, that I am reminded of the fact that David Ben-Gurion [Israel's first Prime Minister], in referring to our very distinguished guest this evening, referred to her as the best man in his Cabinet.

I also recall the old Jewish proverb to the effect that man was made out of the soft earth and woman was made out of a hard rib.

Now, I do not mean by these references to indicate that the Prime Minister whom we honor tonight, is one who does not have those very remarkable and unique qualities that we admire in the women of her country and the women of our own country, and the women of the world. But what I would like to say very simply is this: that throughout the history of her people, a history that we know very well in this country, a history that we heard even the Marine Band and our Strolling Strings attempt to represent by music very briefly a few moments ago, we know that very capable women and strong women have played a remarkable and important part in that history.

In Biblical terms, we remember Deborah, 3,000 years ago. The Bible tells us very little about Deborah, except that she loved her people and served them well. Then, if I may paraphrase, it concludes with this one thought: that there was peace in the land for 40 years.

Madam Prime Minister, as we welcome you here at this dinner, and as we meet

745

with you today and tomorrow on the occasion of this visit, what is really deepest in our hearts is the hope that history will record that after your service as Prime Minister there was peace in the land for 40 years and longer.

When we think back on your people, a war every 10 years; when we think back on your people going back through the century, how they have suffered, we know how much the word "peace" means.

We can say to you that while it is fashionable in the great councils of the world to talk rather casually about peace, and while it is, of course, expected that at events like this we use that term almost in an offhand way, that we feel it very deeply here. We feel it because the people of Israel deserve peace. They have earned peace, not the fragile peace that comes with the kind of a document that neither party has an interest in keeping, but the kind of peace that will last, one that will last for 40 years or even longer.

I say that for another reason, too. I have had the privilege and I know that many of our friends around this room have had the privilege of seeing what the people of this very small country have done in Israel, and it is a remarkable story.

With this immense military burden, with this tremendous budget that they have to bear in that respect, how they have made that land bloom, how they have made it productive. But also I have seen what the people of this country have done in other lands, in Africa, in Asia, in Latin America. People have gone from the State of Israel to these other lands in their own programs of assistance and advice and this kind of genius, this kind of ability, is very rare in the world. It is desperately needed in the world. It is desperately needed for the works of peace.

And for these and for so many other reasons, we simply want to say that we are very honored to have the Prime Minister, the Foreign Minister, and others in this distinguished party here in this room tonight. We are honored to pay tribute to a very brave and courageous people. We hope that as a result of our meeting that we will have taken a significant step forward toward that peace which can mean so much to the people of Israel, to the people of all the Mideast, and also to the people of the world.

Now I would like to ask you, in affirming that sentiment, to rise and raise your glasses with me to the Prime Minister.

NOTE: The President proposed the toast at 9:53 p.m. in the State Dining Room at the White House.

See also Items 371 and 376.

Prime Minister Meir responded as follows:

Mr. President, Mrs. Nixon, Mr. Vice President, friends:

There is no use my trying to hide the fact that this has been an exceptional day in my life. One reads sometimes that representatives of big powers get together, try to solve problems, make certain decisions. We know it is important.

Then one sentence reads that representatives of little countries, not very powerful, not very much, not very able to give each to the other, one has a feeling; well, they got together; they at least shared their troubles and problems; they at least feel sorry for each other. That helps sometimes.

But I think that this world would be entirely different if there was a possibility of meeting between the big and powerful and the small, in an atmosphere and a feeling not of one asking for something and one giving something, but in an atmosphere that in this world there must be a real partnership between large powers and small, rich and poor.

This world has become too small and too full of problems and troubles for any one of us to feel that he, by himself, can either separate himself from the world and be happy in his home, isolated because he is powerful, or that it doesn't matter.

There can be some that are secure and strong and resourceful and there are others that are small and poor and troubled, as though it did not affect all of us, what happens in any corner of the earth.

We have become too advanced in science. If any trouble is discovered in the moon, Mr. President, I am afraid it will affect us on earth. We are all a part of everything that is good and everything that is dangerous.

To me this has been a great day, not because I have come representing a people that has no worry in the world, that has no problems, that needs nothing. But this is a great day for me because I represent a small country, a small people. I represent a people that throughout its history for 2,000 years has known persecution, has known discrimination, has been driven from place to place. And for 2,000 years this people has refused to give up a dream, an ideal that some day it will come back to its home and rebuild it.

It is tragic that this happened when six million of our people were gone. Those six million in Eastern and central Europe—those were the centers of culture, of religion, of Zionism, of faith—withstood everything, all hardships, and did not give up their faith. They are gone.

Every one of us feels that he has to make up and he owes it to them, not only to those who are alive, those remnants that have remained, but owes it to them who are gone.

Those who went to the gas chambers went singing, "I believe the Messiah will come." They knew that they were going to their death, and we feel that they left us a legacy that we must implement and put into life, that which they believed in and that for which they died. It is not simple in this world, in the neighborhood in which we live.

When I say this was a great day for me, Mr. President, I shall remember it always, because you made it possible for me to speak to you, to bring before you all our problems, all our worries, all our hopes and aspirations; and if you will forgive me, I did not have a feeling for one single moment that I, representing little, tiny Israel, was speaking to the President of the great United States.

I felt I was speaking to a friend who not only

listens—in Hebrew we have two words, a word that means only listening, and a word that means that it really is absorbed—and I have a feeling that you were not merely kind to listen to me, but you shared what I was saying, what our worries are.

We discussed the problems of Israel as though they were our common problems. This means a lot. Israel has known in its short number of years too many hours when we felt we were all alone. And we made it.

In 1948, when we were attacked by six Arab armies and had nothing to fight with—but thank God we did not lose our sense of humor—we said, yes, but we have a secret weapon and our secret weapon is: no alternative, we must win because we have nowhere to run to except the sea. Therefore, we chose to fight and to fight it out and win. We had no alternative. We had known many hours that were dark, the hours before the 5th of June in 1967, none of us will ever forget them.

But we believe. We have not lost our confidence. We have faith, not only in the life and existence and development of Israel; we believe honestly and sincerely that the day will come when there will be peace in the area. The day will come when across the borders there will not be tanks and one will not listen only to the shelling, to the shells that will be sent from across the borders into villages, killing men and women and children. But I am convinced that the day will come when farmers from Israel, young men and women who have left their homes and left their towns and went to the desert and went to the hills at Galilee and brought life to the desert when nothing has bloomed for hundreds and hundreds and hundreds of years, and have brought forests to the hills and have absorbed human beings shattered in body and spirit after the Second World War, and made them alive again, and they straightened their backs, and the children who came to us with eyes full of fear are happy now and they sing.

These men and women and these scared children who have now become young men and women have made it possible for us to develop the desert, to do what we have done, and there is song on their lips and they teach and they study and they farm and they build.

No greater day can we envisage than when

these people merely step across the border and with a farmer of Jordan and with a farmer in the Nile Valley and with a farmer in Syria, not when we are on the Golan Heights—we see what was not done in the villages of the Golan Heights—and we will just step across the border and bring with us not only the fruits of our experience but the joy in being alive together, we and they, and making it possible for their children, too, to live as human beings and to hope for a life where one will bring joy to everyone around and where we can erase from the minds of young people, where we can erase the horror of mothers that they bring children into this world and, who knows, maybe when they are just beginning their life they will be sent into the battleground.

We believe in that, Mr. President, honestly and faithfully. We are a people who for 2,000 years believed in the impossible. And here we are, a sovereign state, accepted in the family of nations, with many problems, many troubles, but here we are.

And here we are speaking in the United States. Here I am as a guest of the President of the United States, having full understand-

ing of what this day means, and yet I will come home and I will tell my Cabinet and I will tell my people and I will tell our children and our young people: Don't become cynical, don't give up hope, don't believe that everything is just judged only by expediency.

There is idealism in this world. There is human brotherhood in this world. There is the great and powerful country, the United States, that feels that the existence of Israel is important to it because it is important that we all live and all exist, no matter how small and how troubled we are.

Mr. President, thank you, not only for your wonderful hospitality, not only for this great day and every moment that I had this day, but thank you for enabling me to go home and tell my people that we have a friend, a great friend and a dear friend. It will help. It will help us overcome many difficulties.

When the great day comes when this dream comes true, you will have had a great share in it.

Thank you very much.

To the President of the United States.

374 The President's News Conference of September 26, 1969

Questions

UNITED STATES PRESENCE IN VIETNAM

THE PRESIDENT. [1.] Mr. Cormier [Frank Cormier, Associated Press].

Q. How do you feel about the various proposals to propose an arbitrary cutoff time on our military presence in Vietnam?

THE PRESIDENT. I have considered a number of those proposals within the administration and, of course, have noted some of the references that have been made recently in the Senate in that regard. I know they are made with the best of intentions. However, it is my con-

clusion that if the administration were to impose an arbitrary cutoff time, say the end of 1970, or the middle of 1971, for the complete withdrawal of American forces in Vietnam, that inevitably leads to perpetuating and continuing the war until that time and destroys any chance to reach the objective that I am trying to achieve, of ending the war before the end of 1970 or before the middle of 1971.

I think this is a defeatist attitude, defeatist in terms of what it would accomplish. I do not think it is in the interest of the United States.

I also believe that even though these proposals, I know, are made with the best of intentions, they inevitably undercut and destroy the negotiating position that we have in Paris. We have not made significant progress in those negotiations. But any incentive for the enemy to negotiate is destroyed if he is told in advance that if he just waits for 18 months we will be out anyway. Therefore, I oppose that kind of arbitrary action.

JUDGE CLEMENT HAYNSWORTH'S NOMINATION

[2.] Q. Mr. President?

THE PRESIDENT. Mr. Hensley [M. Stewart Hensley, United Press International].

Q. At the time or shortly after your appointment of Mr. Burger [Chief Justice Warren Earl Burger] to the Supreme Court, it was said that you hoped, insofar as possible, to avoid appointments which would become controversial. The nomination of Judge Haynsworth [Clement F. Haynsworth, Jr.] has become controversial to a certain extent.

THE PRESIDENT. Yes, I understand.

Q. Has this become controversial enough to lead you to withdraw the nomination of Judge Haynsworth?

THE PRESIDENT. No, I do not intend to withdraw the nomination of Judge Haynsworth. I studied his record as it was submitted to me by the Attorney General before I sent the nomination to the Senate.

I have also noted the various items that have been brought up during the course of his hearings in the Senate. I still have confidence in Judge Haynsworth's qualifications, in his integrity. I believe that the Senate should approve him. I believe it will. I believe that he will be a great credit to the Supreme Court when he becomes a member of that Court, I hope in the fall term.

STUDENT ANTIWAR DEMONSTRATIONS

[3.] Q. Mr. President?

THE PRESIDENT. Mr. Horner [Garnett D. Horner, Washington Evening Star].

Q. What is your view, sir, concerning the student moratorium and other campus demonstrations being planned for this fall against the Vietnam war?

THE PRESIDENT. I have often said that there is really very little that we in Washington can do with regard to running the university and college campuses of this country. We have enough problems running the Nation, the national problems.

Now, I understand that there has been and continues to be opposition to the war in Vietnam on the campuses, and also in the Nation. As far as this kind of activity is concerned, we expect it. However, under no circumstances will I be affected whatever by it.

THE REPUBLICAN PARTY

[4.] Q. Mr. President, does the "heartland" theory, which is outlined in the book, "The Emerging Republican Majority," [1] by an assistant of John Mitchell coincide with your own approach toward strengthening the party?

THE PRESIDENT. I regret to say, and I hope this does not discourage sales of the book, which I understand are quite good, that I have not read the book. My own views with regard to the Republican Party have been often stated in backgrounders and also in public sessions.

I believe the Republican Party should be a national party. I don't believe in writ-

---

[1] By Kevin P. Phillips, published by Arlington House, New Rochelle, N.Y., 1969 (482 pp.).

ing off any section of the country. I have attempted to make our appeal nationally, to the South, to the North, the East, the West, and to all groups within the country.

To the extent that the book advocates theories that are inconsistent with that principle, of course, I would disagree with it.

SCHOOL DESEGREGATION

[5.] Q. Mr. President, sir, many civil rights groups are saying that your policy on school desegregation amounts to a retreat from the Supreme Court decision of 15 years ago.[2] Some even say that this amounts to an effort to build a party base for the Republicans in the South.

Where do you stand on school desegregation and how much more time do you think districts that haven't complied ought to have?

THE PRESIDENT. Well, on this very difficult problem, I would say first that we have had a lot of criticism from the South insofar as our integration and desegregation policies are concerned, as well as from the groups to which you refer.

It seems to me that there are two extreme groups. There are those who want instant integration and those who want segregation forever. I believe that we need to have a middle course between those two extremes. That is the course in which we are embarked. I think it is correct.

As I evaluate the situation this year, I found that there are twice as many schools that are desegregated at the opening of this term as was the case at the opening of the term a year ago. I think that is progress.

Now one other point that should be

made. I do not consider that it is a victory for integration when the Federal Government cuts off funds for a school and thereby, for both black and white students in that school, denies them the education they should have. That is not a victory for anybody. It is a defeat for education.

I believe, therefore, that that particular device should be used as we currently are using it: only when it is absolutely necessary for the purpose of achieving our objective of desegregated education. We are for it, but we are going to avoid both extremes.

OIL DEPLETION ALLOWANCE

[6.] Q. You told an audience in Houston last fall[3] that you opposed reduction of the oilmen's depletion allowance. Do you still oppose it?

THE PRESIDENT. As a matter of fact, I not only told the audience in Houston that, but that has been my position since I entered politics in California 22 years ago. It is still my position.

I believe that the depletion allowance is in the national interest because I believe it is essential to develop our resources when, as we look at the Mideast and other sections of the world, many of our oil supplies could be cut off in the event of a world conflict.

On the other hand, I am a political realist. I noted the action of the House of Representatives in reducing the depletion allowance. Also, my primary concern is to get tax reform—the tax reform which we submitted in April, which goes further than any tax reform in 25 years. We need that tax reform above everything else.

---

[2] *Brown* v. *Board of Education of Topeka, Kans.* (347 U.S. 483), May 17, 1954.

[3] At a campaign rally in Miller Memorial Amphitheater on September 6, 1968.

Some of the items that I recommended, the House did not follow my recommendations, and the same will be in the Senate. When the bill comes to my desk, I intend to sign that bill, even though it does not follow all of my recommendations—provided that it does not require a revenue shortfall. That is more than I believe the Nation can stand.

STRATEGIC ARMS LIMITATION TALKS

[7.] Q. Mr. President, can you tell us the reasons behind Russia's prolonged failure to respond to your proposal for prompt negotiations on strategic arms limitations?

THE PRESIDENT. We are trying to explore those reasons. Mr. Rogers [William P. Rogers, Secretary of State] met with Mr. Gromyko [Andrei A. Gromyko, Soviet Foreign Minister] on Monday. He will meet with him again on next Monday. He has no answer except a suggestion—and I don't think I am divulging any confidences in this respect—that we may expect an answer in the near future and that it is likely to be a positive answer.

Now, why the answer has been delayed is a question really that would have to be asked of those who have control of policy in the Kremlin.

GOVERNMENT PERSONNEL CHANGES

[8.] Q. Mr. President, would you please tell us when you are going to make some real, honest-to-goodness changes in personnel in these bureaucrats who have been in power through many generations, who are still wasting the taxpayers' money, and making errors on the war and policy and promoting their friends, who are unqualified, to high jobs? I refer particularly

to the office in the Pentagon of Assistant Secretary of Defense [for Installations and Logistics] Barry J. Shillito.

THE PRESIDENT. I don't know the gentleman, but after that question, I am going to find out who he is very soon.

SUPREME COURT NOMINATIONS

[9.] Q. Mr. President, could you give us some insight into your thinking, sir, as to the difference between the situation that required Supreme Court Justice [Abe] Fortas to resign and the recent disclosures concerning Judge Haynsworth?

THE PRESIDENT. Well, since the matter is still before the Senate committee, I am not going to comment on the specifics that are being considered by that committee.

I will simply stand on my statement that I was aware generally of Judge Haynsworth's background, of his financial status, before he was appointed. I had confidence then in his integrity. I think the Senate committee will overwhelmingly agree with that opinion.

SOCIAL SECURITY PROPOSAL

[10.] Mr. Healy [Paul F. Healy, New York Daily News].

Q. Mr. President, Congress has always taken a very dim view of the idea of automatically adjusting the social security benefits to the cost of living, as you proposed yesterday. As a political realist, do you think you can change their mind on this?

THE PRESIDENT. I am going to try. As far as that particular proposal is concerned, there are some who reach a different conclusion for a reason that all of us will understand. They believe that it

is an automatic escalator as far as inflation is concerned, and discourages those
fiscal policies that would control inflation
by assuming that we are going to have to
raise social security because we have to
accept the idea we are always going to
have inflation.

My view is different. I have found in
examining this situation that where the
Congress must always act to see to it
that those on social security keep up with
the rise in the cost of living, that the Congress tends to act either too late or with
perhaps even overreaction to the
situation.

I believe this is the sensible, sound way
to do it and I think that it will be de-
flationary rather than inflationary in the
long run.

VIETNAM PEACE EFFORTS

[11.] Mr. Kaplow [Herbert Kaplow,
NBC News].

Q. How are you doing, Mr. President,
in your efforts to end the Vietnam war?

THE PRESIDENT. Not as well as I would
hope. I will not be doing as well as I
would hope until the war is ended. I
would point, however, to some progress.

We point first to the fact that we have
announced that 60,000 Americans will be
returned from Vietnam.

We point, second, to the fact that as a
result of that and other actions, that
50,000 Americans who otherwise might
have been drafted before the end of the
year will not be drafted.

In addition to that, we find that infiltration, which tells us a lot about the enemy's
future capabilities, looking at the first
9 months of this year, is two-thirds less

than it was in the corresponding period
last year.

We find that American casualties are
down one-third from what they were over
the same 9-month period last year.

We find also that on the negotiating
front, that the United States has made a
far-reaching and comprehensive peace offer, a peace offer which offers not only
mutual withdrawal of forces, internationally guaranteed cease-fires, internationally
supervised elections in which we will accept the result of those elections and the
South Vietnamese will as well, even if it
is a Communist government, and by making that offer we have reversed the whole
tide of world public opinion.

I noted when I was at the U.N., I
found no significant criticism of the U.S.
policy. Now is the time for Hanoi to make
the next move. We certainly have made
it.

There is one thing, however, which I
should emphasize that is not negotiable.
We will talk about anything else. What
is not negotiable is the right of the people
of South Vietnam to choose their own
leaders without outside imposition, either
by us or by anybody else. We believe that
that limited goal must be one that we
must insist on. We believe it can be
achieved, and we believe that if we stay
on this course and if we can have some
more support in the Nation—we have a
lot of support, but even more support in
the Nation—for this steady course, the
enemy then will have the incentive to
negotiate, recognizing that it isn't going
to gain time; that it isn't going to wait us
out.

Once the enemy recognizes that it is not
going to win its objective by waiting us

out, then the enemy will negotiate and we will end this war before the end of 1970. That is the objective we have.

SENATOR GOODELL'S VIETNAM PROPOSALS

[12.] Mr. Theis [J. William Theis, Hearst Newspapers].

Q. Going back to Mr. Cormier's question about the Vietnam cutoff, Senator Goodell, who will be a candidate next year, is providing the vehicle for a new round of Senate hearings on this subject. Will this either embarrass you as a Republican President, or other Republican candidates next year?

THE PRESIDENT. Well, Mr. Theis, I, of course, can't control the course of Senate hearings, particularly in the Foreign Relations Committee. On the other hand, as far as those hearings are concerned, I believe that a discussion in the Senate of this matter, an open discussion, in which all the consequences of this very well-intentioned statement by Senator Goodell, all the consequences of it, the fact that it inevitably leads to the conclusion that the United States is going to be stuck in Vietnam until the end of 1970, that there is no hope of ending the war before then, that when that comes home, I think the Senate will overwhelmingly reject the Goodell proposition.[4]

THE SOUTH VIETNAMESE GOVERNMENT

[13.] Mr. Lisagor [Peter Lisagor, Chicago Daily News].

Q. Mr. President, does the insistence

---

[4] Senator Charles E. Goodell of New York on June 25, 1969, proposed legislation requiring withdrawal of all U.S troops from Vietnam by the end of 1970.

upon self-determination in Vietnam as an indispensable condition mean that you will support the present Thieu regime there until there is a negotiated settlement or until there are elections to change that regime?

THE PRESIDENT. It means, Mr. Lisagor, that the Thieu regime is there because of the result of an election, and until the people of South Vietnam have another opportunity to vote, I think that the United States should not reverse that election mandate. That is the answer that I think is only appropriate under the circumstances.

SCHOOL DESEGREGATION

[14.] Mr. Loory [Stuart Loory, Los Angeles Times].

Q. Going back to your response to the school desegregation question, it is now 15 years since the Supreme Court made its decision. How much longer do you think school segregation should be allowed to exist anywhere in the country?

THE PRESIDENT. Only as long as is absolutely necessary to achieve two goals— to achieve the goal of desegregated schools without, at the same time, irreparably damaging the goal of education now for the hundreds of thousands of black and white students who otherwise would be harmed if the move toward desegregation closes their schools.

Q. Mr. President, in connection with the school desegregation, one of the most controversial cases has been the action that the Government took in Mississippi in deciding to ask for a further postponement of some of the school integration there.

There have been published reports that

Senator John Stennis of Mississippi informed the administration that if the school integration went through there, he might not be able to handle the administration's defense bill, and that you, yourself, made the decision.

Would you tell us whether these reports are true, whether Senator Stennis did so inform the administration, and your connection, if any, with this Mississippi case?

THE PRESIDENT. Senator Stennis did speak to me, along with several other representatives from Mississippi, with regard to his concern on this problem. But anybody who knows Senator Stennis and anybody who knows me would know that he would be the last person to say: "Look, if you don't do what I want in Mississippi, I am not going to do what is best for this country."

He did not say that, and under no circumstances, of course, would I have acceded to it.

With regard to the action in Mississippi, that action was taken by this administration because it was felt that better than cutting off the funds with the disastrous effect on the black and white students affected by that, the better course was the one that we did take—the one which gave more time to achieve desegregation without impairing education.

THE UNITED STATES AND LAOS

[15.] Q. There has been growing concern, sir, about deepening U.S. involvement in the combat in Laos. If you could confirm that, would you also say whether this runs counter to your new Asian policy?

THE PRESIDENT. There are no Amer-

ican combat forces in Laos. At the present time, we are concerned by the North Vietnamese move into Laos. There are 50,000 North Vietnamese there at the present time, and more perhaps are coming.

As you know, the American participation in Laos is at the request of the neutralist government, which was set up in accordance with the 1962 Accords, which were agreed to, incidentally, by Hanoi, Peking, and the Soviet Union. That was during the administration of President Kennedy, negotiated by Mr. Harriman [Assistant Secretary of State for Far Eastern Affairs].

We have been providing logistical support and some training for the neutralist government in order to avoid Laos falling under Communist domination. As far as American manpower in Laos is concerned, there are none there at the present time on a combat basis.

Q. Mr. President?

THE PRESIDENT. Mr. Potter [Philip Potter, Baltimore Sun].

Q. You say there are no combat forces in Laos. How do you regard the airmen who bomb the Ho Chi Minh Trail from bases in Thailand and Vietnam? Would

Q. You say there are no combat forces

THE PRESIDENT. When we consider the situation in Laos, I think President Kennedy in his first major television speech, which we all remember, in 1961, put it very well. He pointed out that Laos was potentially the key to what would happen in Thailand as well as in Vietnam and the balance of Southeast Asia.

Now, Laos relates very much to Vietnam, because the Ho Chi Minh Trail runs through Laos. It is necessary, under those circumstances, that the United States take cognizance of that, and we do have aerial reconnaissance; we do have perhaps some other activities. I won't discuss those other activities at this time.

BLACK MEMBERSHIP IN CHICAGO CONSTRUCTION UNIONS

[16.] Q. Mr. President, yesterday in Chicago, your Assistant Secretary of Labor, Mr. Fletcher [Arthur A. Fletcher, Assistant Secretary of Labor for Wage and Labor Standards], tried to hold some hearings about getting more blacks into the construction unions, and he was prevented from doing so.

I wonder if you could tell us, first of all, your reaction to that specific situation in Chicago, and, secondly, your general feeling about getting more blacks into the trade unions?

THE PRESIDENT. Relating first to the second part of the question, it is essential that black Americans, all Americans, have an equal opportunity to get into the construction unions. There is a shortage in construction workers.

The interest of the Nation requires this, apart from the matters of simple justice which are involved.

Second, in this respect, we have, as you know, the Philadelphia Plan. We have had our problems in Pittsburgh which are presently being discussed through our mediation, at least discussed, although it is still a very volatile situation. And now, of course, we have the problem in Chicago.

We intend to continue through the Department of Labor to attempt to make progress in this field, because in the long-run, we cannot have construction unions which deny the right of all Americans to have those positions.

America needs more construction workers, and, of course, all Americans are entitled to an equal right to be a member of a union.

CONTROL OF INFLATION

[17.] Q. Mr. President, on the subject of inflation, a number of economists have said that they do not believe the administration can take the steam out of the economy without exerting pressure on specific price increases, such as the auto increase, the steel price increase, and the others.

Are you considering taking such steps, or do you feel that the corner has already been turned in the battle on inflation?

THE PRESIDENT. I would take those steps if history told me they would work. I would point out, however, that the previous administration tried, through jawboning, as it is called, to put the blame on business for price increases; the blame on labor for wage increases.

In 1966, the guidelines died. They died because when Government, which is the primary agent for increasing prices, fails to do its job, Government asking labor and management to do theirs simply won't work. It is hypocritical, it is dishonest, but most important, it is ineffective, because since 1966, as you will note, in 1966, 1967, 1968, despite all of the calling of the people to the White House, telling them to hold prices down, hold wages down, prices continued to escalate.

Now, we have attacked the source of the problem. We have cut the budget by $7 billion. We have monetary restraints. We have asked for an extension of the surtax rather than its complete elimination. And these basic policies, which go to the core of the problem, are beginning to work, as Mr. McCracken pointed out in his speech in Detroit on Monday.[5]

Now that the Government has set the example, I believe that labor and management would be well advised to follow the example. I am not jawboning and telling them to reform themselves, when we refuse to reform ourselves. But I do say this: that labor and management, labor that asks for exorbitant wage increases, management that raises prices too high, will be pricing themselves out of the market.

Anybody who bets on a continuing inflation will lose that bet, because our Government policies are beginning to work and we are going to stick to those policies until we cut the rise in the cost of living.

REDUCTION IN DRAFT CALLS

[18.] Q. Mr. President, my question concerns the draft, sir. The National Council to Repeal the Draft contends that your draft cut is a fraud, because the summer draft calls were inflated to allow for a preplanned cut.

Would you comment, please?

THE PRESIDENT. I don't consider that charge as one of merit. I know of no inflation in the summer draft calls. I would also point out the fact that when you look at the statistics with regard to the withdrawal of our forces from Vietnam, with regard to the reduction of our forces around the world, it is quite obvious that we don't need as many through the draft. That is why we did it, and not for the reason that is suggested here.

EFFECT OF THE CHANGE OF LEADERSHIP IN HANOI

[19.] Q. Mr. President, does the change of leadership in Hanoi, brought about by the death of Ho Chi Minh,[6] show any sign at all to you, sir, of any change of intent either in combat or in Paris, on the part of the enemy?

THE PRESIDENT. Not yet, and we would expect nothing yet. Each of our systems of government has a problem. The major problem in a Communist system of government is the problem of succession and the North Vietnamese are going through that.

Immediately after a change of leadership, there is a tendency for uncertainty and rigidity as the contest for power goes on. We think that is going on within North Vietnam at the present time. However, looking to the future, as new leaders emerge, as they look at the consequences of past policy and the prospects for future policy, and as long as the United States holds to its course, I think the prospects for a possible change are there.

I am not predicting it. I am not trying to raise false hopes. I am only suggesting that since there is new leadership, we can expect perhaps some reevaluation of policy.

GOVERNOR ROCKEFELLER'S REPORT ON LATIN AMERICA

[20.] Q. Mr. President, when do you plan to make Governor [Nelson A.] Rockefeller's report on Latin America public, and what is the main thrust of his recommendations to you?

---

[5] Chairman Paul W. McCracken of the Council of Economic Advisers spoke before the Economic Club of Detroit on September 22, 1969.

[6] President Ho Chi Minh of North Vietnam died in Hanoi on September 3, 1969.

THE PRESIDENT. During the time that I have been in Washington, and a few of you—not many—have been in Washington longer than I, in and out, I have found that we have had at least eight reports on Latin America.

And in talking to my Latin American friends in the diplomatic corps, they have begged me, "Please don't study us," because they have said, "All you do is study us and make headlines with the words and then have no actions."

Now, when I set up the Rockefeller task force, I made one commitment to him, to which he completely agreed: that he would make the report to me, and what we would try to do is to make our actions make the news rather than the words make the news.

I have already met with Governor Rockefeller. There are some very exciting recommendations in his report which we are going to adopt. I am going to meet with him for an extended visit tomorrow at Camp David, along with the Assistant Secretary of State for Latin America, Mr. [Charles A.] Meyer.

Then later in this month—I mean later in October—we will be making a major new pronouncement on Latin American policy, and a number of the Rockefeller recommendations will be in that announcement.

MEETING WITH VIETNAM ADVISERS

[21.] Q. Mr. President, 2 weeks ago today you had a major meeting with your top advisers and people directly involved in the Vietnam effort. I don't think we have had a report, as such, on that meeting. I wonder if there was a focus such as the death of Ho Chi Minh, or just what was it all about?

THE PRESIDENT. Well, naturally much of what was discussed in that meeting could not be appropriately discussed in a public forum like this. We looked over the military situation, the political situation in South Vietnam. And naturally we speculated privately, and I would never speculate publicly, as to what might happen with the change of leadership.

We did determine, however, that there were some good signs on the horizon: the failure of the enemy to be able to launch a summer offensive which everybody had predicted; the fact that the infiltration rate was down by two-thirds, which means that the possibility of an offensive this fall has receded, we took note of that; the fact that this Vietnamization program, despite some problems, was moving forward; and that political and economic stability in the South, despite some significant problems, was going forward.

All of these matters were taken into consideration. Generally, I would not like to leave the impression that this was an overly optimistic report, because I believe in looking at Vietnam and all of our problems in a very realistic, down-to-earth manner.

But I would say this: I think we are on the right course in Vietnam. We are on a course that is going to end this war. It will end much sooner if we can have to an extent, to the extent possible in this free country, a united front behind very reasonable proposals. If we have that united front, the enemy then will begin to talk, because the only missing ingredient to escalating the time when we will end the war is the refusal of the enemy in Paris to even discuss our proposals. The moment that they start discussing those proposals, then that means that we can bring the war to a conclusion sooner than if we just continue on our present course.

M. Stewart Hensley, United Press International: Thank you very much.

NOTE: President Nixon's seventh news conference was held in the East Room at the White House at 12 noon on Friday, September 26, 1969. It was broadcast on radio and television.

375 Remarks to Delegates to the 15th Biennial Convention of the National Federation of Republican Women. *September 26, 1969*

THAT IS the best introduction I have had in a long time.

I want to join Pat in welcoming all of you to this house, which belongs to the whole Nation, but which we presently are occupying, thanks to you. We realize that this is the first time in 8 years that the Republican Women's Federation could come here. We are glad you are here.

That does not mean you could not come always in any year, just as a tourist, but you are going to get a real, special tour today, believe me.

We are so delighted, too, that it was one of those days in the fall in Washington when the weather is good, when we could have, for the first time, these grounds fixed as they are. We hope you have enjoyed the punch and the cookies. I don't see much left.

But anyway, it is so colorful to see it and we are glad that your coming allowed us to set it up in this way and that no rain bothered us.

I would like to say, too, that having had this introduction, and since this is a group of the Women's Federation which has meant so much to us through the years, to the party, going back through campaigns, as far as we are concerned, to 1946—anybody here that old? Never admit it!—that on this occasion I would

like to say a word about the role of the women in this house, in this administration.

I know you always read about what the President does, and mostly about what he doesn't do. And some of it is true and some of it isn't. But you make up your own minds.

In any event, what the women do, I think, does not get the credit it really deserves. You are going to see this great house. And the First Ladies through the years have contributed to it. This First Lady, the First Lady in our house and in the White House, she has, of course, been engaged in a program, which is the responsibility of every First Lady, for redecoration. I hope you will like it. I hope you will like what she does. I certainly do. Of course, if I didn't, I wouldn't say so, but I like it.

She picked this tie, too, and I like it.

But that isn't all. I was just thinking, when Pat mentioned our two girls, the things that they do that you perhaps don't hear anything about. Let me brag a little on them.

For example, Tricia yesterday, a couple of days ago, was in Philadelphia—anybody here from Pennsylvania? Right— helping to open an exhibition of Romanian art there in Philadelphia. She represented us in a very unofficial but a very effective way at the investiture of the Prince of Wales in England a little earlier.

And Julie, while she is in school at the present time, still has found the time to go to Chicago. Anybody here from Illinois?

She has had time to go to Illinois with David for a meeting there, a Republican meeting, and then to New Mexico for a very historic meeting involving the Indians and job opportunities that are being provided in that area.

All that I want to say is this: We get a lot of invitations over there in that West Wing of the White House, but if you really want the stars of this outfit, you invite the girls or invite Pat, because they are the ones that can bring the message to you.

Now a word about the First Lady. Naturally, her first responsibility is to preside over a great dinner such as we had last night for Mrs. [Golda] Meir, the Prime Minister of Israel, and also this house with all of the responsibilities entailed in that.

But, as you know, she has been active in volunteer activities around the Nation, and there are more trips of that type that are planned. In addition, she has to travel with me. I say "has to" because, in a sense, she is such a great asset, as any wife can be to her husband when there are responsibilities that go far beyond what a husband is able to undertake.

I don't know whether any of you—I am sure some of you—had an opportunity to see Nancy Dickerson's [of NBC News] program on our trip around the world. I know that all of you heard the news commentators describing the hard schedule that I was going through, all the talks we were having, the hot weather and the rest. But I can tell you what I did was nothing compared to what she did.

As I look out over these grounds, I think halfway around the world to a wonderful reception that we had in Pakistan. On the occasion of that reception in Pakistan, in Lahore, out there on the parade grounds, we saw over 200 bagpipes in a great band, the best in the world, playing, that the Government of Pakistan arranged for us. There were awnings like this in the great style that the British through the years have had, and now those that are formerly British colonies have continued to perpetuate now that they have become independent.

We sat there in this particular place, and it was about 120° right under the awning. I was sitting there with the sweat pouring down my face. I didn't think, really, that the afternoon would be one that I could get through. I looked over at Pat, and she sat there just as cool as she could possibly be.

So I wondered about the mystery of that. You know, they talk about the weaker sex and the stronger sex. I found in studying a little prior to Mrs. Meir's visit here that there is an old Hebrew proverb to this effect: that man was made out of soft earth, and woman was made out of a hard rib.

Now, I only indicate that to say that in our family, certainly, I am very proud of the role the women have played, and in saying that I am very proud, in the Republican family, of the role the women have played. Without you, we couldn't win. With you, we will win.

Incidentally, if I could just make, for a minute, a couple of political comments. Anybody here from Virginia? All right, we want a Governor down there. How about it?

And how about New Jersey? Right. We

want a Governor in New Jersey, and we can get one.

And, of course, there are many other contests across the country.

I see you have a Holton [1] button right there.

There are many others across the country. We will not go into those now. I simply want to say that I know that with your help, the victories we have been working to achieve can be achieved in the years ahead.

Then just a word about some of the great issues in which you are interested. I know all of you are carrying not only your programs, but I see here the story on the issues and the rest.

You remember the campaign of 1968. You remember the things that all the candidates talked about. First and foremost was the issue of peace. The second issue was the issue of crime and reestablishing respect for law in this country. The third issue was the issue of inflation and high prices, and what we did about that. And the fourth, if we were to add a fourth, was the whole problem of the poor, welfare, and what we were going to do about that terrible mess, the way it had been handled.

I just want to give you a report very briefly on those four issues. I would like to say that we have solved them all, but the war still goes on. But I will say this: After 5 years of more and more men going to Vietnam, after 5 years of higher and higher draft calls, we have turned it around. We are bringing men home from Vietnam and we have reduced the draft calls.

---

[1] A. Linwood Holton was Republican candidate for Governor of Virginia in the 1969 elections.

I pledge to you we are on a path that we believe can bring an end to that war, bring the kind of an end to the war that will discourage that kind of aggression in the future—the real peace that we want, the peace that will be not only for this generation, but for the generations to come. I believe that we are on the right path, and I pledge the continued effort of this administration working toward that end.

On the issue of inflation, we have had to do some things that are rather unpopular, unpopular in this sense: You know, it would be very easy to sit back and blame business for raising prices, and then turn to the labor unions and say: "You are responsible. You are asking for too much wages." That is what the other administration did.

You know what happened. It didn't work. Prices went up 5 percent a year in 1966, 5 percent a year in 1967, 5 percent a year in 1968. So when we came in, we recognized that the problem, as far as high prices were concerned, was not either the demands of labor or business raising prices. But if you want to talk about the cause of the high cost of living, it is the high cost of Government, and we have done something about that.

We have cut the Federal budget by $7 billion. While that means that we are not able to give a lot of people the projects they want, and we would like to do it, while that means that we can't go as far as we would like to go on many of the programs that all of you are interested in at this time, it does mean this: As interested as anybody may be in this project or that one, or another one, in one part of the country, the overriding concern every person here has to have is in how we can reduce the cost of living for millions of people, and this affects every American— how we can enable people to balance the family budget.

We are trying to deal with that. If we have to make some unpopular decisions now, we are going to make it so that you are able to balance your family budgets all across America.

Now, on this whole field of law enforcement, I suppose that one would say: "Now, we have been in here 8 months. Why hasn't crime stopped?" The answer is: Crime will never stop. All we can do is slow it down. All we can do eventually, we hope, is to turn it around so that the statistics will be going down rather than up.

We have slowed the rate in the increase in crime. But I can tell you this: Not only in Washington, but all over this country, we have a new attitude with regard to law enforcement and respect for law, and we are going to continue that kind of an attitude in America.

I can also tell you: We have laid bills before the Congress, and if you really want action, ask the Congress to act on our bills, asking for stronger control of narcotics. Ask the Congress to act on our bills for control of obscenity. Ask the Congress to act on our bills for organized crime.

If Congress will give us the tools, we will control crime. That is what you want and that is what we are going to give you, so give us that chance.

And now, finally, in this field that everybody here is concerned about, the field of those who don't have that equal chance that I am sure all of you have had, or otherwise you wouldn't be here in Washington. I want to say that we have decided

that it was time for a new approach. It would have been easy to go on just the way we have been going, to just say: "Well, we have got a welfare program. We are just going to pile on more and more and more as the previous administration did."

But this is what we found, and this is what I concluded: After spending billions of dollars more, and finding that we had made no progress on the problems of the poor, that there were more people on welfare, and more frustration, we decided that was the wrong road; we better get off of it and get on another road. So we have taken a new road to deal with this problem.

That is why we have set forth the boldest, the most imaginative—yes, controversial, but it is the right way—a new program in which we are going to get people off of welfare rolls and onto payrolls in this country.

That is why, in addition to helping those and providing a minimum floor under our family assistance program for all of those who are poor and cannot find work, we are going to see to it that there are work incentives, and work requirements, and that the working poor are helped as well as those who do not work. We believe that is the kind of approach that Americans want.

I want to say finally that in this whole field we could go on, but this is no time for the laundry list of everything we have done and all of the hopes that we have. I simply want to say on the 20th of this month we concluded 8 months in office. I wish that we could have had solutions for all of these problems, but of this I am sure: We have turned this country around—we have turned this country around—we have turned this country around in terms of a new hope, not only for ending the war in Vietnam, but for avoiding other Vietnams. We have a new Asian policy, one in which we will help other countries, but help them in the event that they have a problem, help them fight the war rather than fight the war for them, and we think that Americans support that kind of a proposition.

We have a new approach and new hope that we are going to be able to get this great problem of crime under control, so that we can have a new attitude toward respect for law in this country.

We have turned the situation around with regard to inflation. The first statistics, and these are the first hopeful ones we have had, coming in August, indicate that the hope for the future is a good one, provided we just stay on course. We couldn't have done it unless we had had your support.

All that I can say is, we are grateful for the chance to live in this great house. I know that some who have been President have spoken of the awesome burdens and how lonely you are, and all of those things. Well, I am never lonely here, I can assure you.

Of course, I know others have said: "Well, why is it that a President goes away? Why does he go to California? Why does he go around the world? Why does he go to Key Biscayne? Why does he go to Camp David?"

I just want to say one thing in a very personal sense: A President can leave Washington; he never leaves the job. I can assure you that we will never leave the job.

I also want you to know that in terms of the future that we enjoy the privilege of living in this house. We welcome the challenge of meeting these great problems. We know how hard all of you worked to get us here and we are not going to let you down.

Thank you very much.

In saying goodby, you probably wonder, "Now, what is he going to do now?" I am going back over to that Oval Office which I hope many of you have an opportunity to see, at least sometime. And this afternoon, first I meet the Postmaster General. And incidentally, we need postal reform. We need better postal service. I will tell him you want it. That will really buck him up.

Then I will have a final meeting, a very important meeting, with the Prime Minister of Israel, one of the great leaders of the world, and one of the great women of the world as well.

And then I have a meeting of our national security group.

Let me see—what do I have after that?

Well, I am just suggesting that we do have some responsibilities, otherwise I would just love to stay here and greet every one of you personally.

Thank you.

NOTE: The President spoke at approximately 3:15 p.m. on the South Lawn at the White House to some 3,000 members of the Federation.

Preceding the President's remarks, Mrs. Nixon addressed the group. Her remarks are printed in the Weekly Compilation of Presidential Documents (vol. 5, p. 1332).

376 Remarks on the Departure of Prime Minister Golda Meir of Israel. *September* 26, 1969

Madam Prime Minister:

It seems that you have just arrived and, of course, your visit has been a short one. But in the brief hours you have been in Washington we have had very extended talks, private talks, on the relations between our two countries and, beyond that, I want the members of the press to know, on problems in the world generally.

This is the first opportunity I have had to talk to the Prime Minister, although I have known of her work in the field of diplomacy and in other areas over many, many years. She is, naturally, an expert and an advocate of the great principles that concern her own country, but she has a very deep understanding of those issues that divide the world.

And it has been very valuable for me to have the benefit of her counsel on those problems all over the world, including even the problems of youth, which we discussed at some length last night, although we found, I must admit, no solutions.

I would like to say, too, that in these talks we have discussed all of those matters that have been speculated about in the press. We will not announce any decisions at this time. There is no formal communiqué.

This was a meeting where we thought it was very important for us to have a direct discussion of, first, our past relations, where we are now, and what course of action should be followed in the future.

I think we have a very good understanding as to the positions that we both take, and I think growing from this meeting could come some progress toward a solution of the terribly difficult problems we confront in the Mideast. I say "could" because I want to be very realistic. Because I find that one thing the Prime Minister and I have in common is that we are "no nonsense" kind of people. We talk very directly, and we cover a lot of subjects in a very brief time.

The problems in the Mideast go back over centuries. They are not susceptible to easy solution. We do not expect them to be susceptible to instant diplomacy. On the other hand, we must try—and I was glad to find a willingness on the part of the Prime Minister and her colleagues— to try to find a way to peace.

We have no new initiatives to announce, but we do think that we have a better understanding of how we should move from here on out in attempting to meet this very difficult problem.

I can only wish you well on the balance of your trip. I know you will receive a wonderful welcome every place you go, and particularly in Milwaukee. Milwaukee lost the Braves, but they got you back.[1]

THE PRIME MINISTER. Thank you very much, Mr. President.

THE PRESIDENT. As a matter of fact, the Braves could use you as a pinch-hitter right now in order to win.

THE PRIME MINISTER. They lost that opportunity.

---

[1] Prime Minister Meir was born in Kiev, Russia, came to Milwaukee as a young girl, taught school, and married there before emigrating to Israel.

39–861—71——52

THE PRESIDENT. They are in Atlanta. You know that.[2]

THE PRIME MINISTER. I only want to express my extreme appreciation for the opportunity that I have had to spend so much time with the President. It was an exceptional opportunity for me personally.

The President says he knew about me.

You would be surprised, I suppose, if I said I knew about you, Mr. President.

Also, representing my country, speaking to the President of the United States, I am happy that I can go home and, without any announcement of news, say that I found in the President of the United States a friend of Israel, and found full understanding for our problems and difficulties; and that there is something that we share in common: and that is, that everything should be done that is possible to bring real peace in the area, knowing that the interest of peace is for the welfare of all in the area—not only

Israel but the tens of millions of Arabs and others in the various Arab countries.

It is good to know that in the search for peace, both of us, both of our countries, the populations in both of our countries, are deeply interested and dedicated to this quest, not something that is make-shift, but something that is real peace in the area of the Middle East and all over the world.

Mr. President, I don't know how to thank you for the time that you have taken, for the privilege that I have had to discuss many problems with you in an atmosphere of friendship and frankness, for the opportunity that you gave me to place upon your shoulders, that are carrying such a heavy burden for the entire world, also the burden of a little country somewhere put away in the Middle East, but that you have made me feel means something to you and to your people.

Thank you very much.

---

[2] As a result of franchise changes in the National Baseball League, the Milwaukee Braves became the Atlanta Braves in 1966.

NOTE: The President spoke at 5:12 p.m. in the Roosevelt Room at the White House.

See also Items 371 and 373.

377   Statement on Congressional Action on Electoral Reform. *September 30, 1969*

IN FEBRUARY of this year I committed this administration to support any reform of the electoral system that removed its most negative features. I said I would support any amendment approved by Congress that would make three specific reforms in the current system: one, eliminate the problem of the "faithless elector," two, make a 40 percent margin adequate for victory, and three, reform the system so that the electoral outcome more closely reflects the popular outcome.

It was my judgment then that the ap-

proach most likely to prevail in the country would be the proportional distribution method. I thought it had the best chance of being approved by the Congress and by three-fourths of the States.

Now there is an entirely new factor to be considered if we are to have electoral reform with all necessary speed. The House of Representatives has overwhelmingly supported the direct election approach. It is clear that unless the Senate follows the lead of the House, all opportunity for reform will be lost this year and possibly for years to come.

Accordingly, because the ultimate goal of electoral reform must prevail over differences as to how best to achieve that goal, I endorse the direct election approach and urge the Senate also to adopt it. While many Senators may prefer a different method, I believe that contrary views are now a luxury—that the need for electoral reform is urgent and should be

our controlling consideration. I hope, therefore, that two-thirds of the Senate will approve the House-passed amendment as promptly as possible so that all of us together can then urge the States also to give their approval.

NOTE: Also released was the transcript of a related news briefing held at the White House by Senate Minority Leader Hugh Scott of Pennsylvania and House Minority Leader Gerald R. Ford of Michigan.

378   Remarks on Presenting the Presidential Unit Citation to the First Marines (Reinforced). *September 30, 1969*

Ladies and gentlemen:

We are here today for a "first" activity—on the part of the administration and as far as I am concerned. That is the presentation of a Presidential Unit Citation.

The citation is for one of the most distinguished units in the whole history of the American Armed Forces, the First Marine Regiment of the First Marine Division.

The Secretary of the Navy will read the citation.

[Secretary of the Navy John H. Chafee read the citation, the text of which follows.]

The President of the United States takes pleasure in presenting the

PRESIDENTIAL UNIT CITATION

TO THE

FIRST MARINES (—) (REINFORCED)
FIRST MARINE DIVISION (REINFORCED)

for service as set forth in the following

CITATION:

For extraordinary heroism and outstanding performance of duty in action against enemy forces during Operation HUE CITY, conducted in Thua Thien Province, Republic of Vietnam, from 31 January to 2 March 1968. On 31 January 1968, Company A, 1st Bat-

talion, 1st Marines responded as a reaction force to relieve pressure on beleaguered free world forces in Hue City. As the reaction force moved by vehicle convoy toward the city, it was attacked by two battalions of the North Vietnamese Army and temporarily halted. Receiving reinforcements from Company G, 2d Battalion, 5th Marines and a provisional command group from 1st Battalion, 1st Marines, the reaction force fought its way into the city. Once within the city, it secured various objectives in order to rescue U.S. National and Republic of Vietnam government officials from the north side of the Perfume River. Engaging a numerically superior enemy force, the Marines performed superbly. The attack was a classical example of combat in a built-up area as the majority of the fierce fighting was performed at distances under 35 meters, on streets, in yards, from house to house, room to room, and in hand-to-hand combat. As time passed and the intensity of the fighting increased, the decision was made to declare the action a full-scale operation, and on 2 February control was passed to the 1st Marines. Reacting swiftly to reinforce the units in Hue, the 1st Marines (—) (Reinforced) proceeded from Phu Bai by vehicle convoy to exploit the contact already made. Engaging enemy troops as they drew near, the 1st Marines fought their way into and through the city to the MACV compound to find it under intense attack by a numerically superior force. Immediately deploying, they countered the attack and within 30 minutes placed the enemy on the defensive. The fighting continued and the Marines recaptured the provincial headquarters and hospital while driving the enemy from other critical areas. On 26 February, a portion of the Marines were withdrawn from the Citadel and, upon combining forces with Marines in another portion of the zone of responsibility, began conducting final clearing operations south of the Phu Cam River. Through the remaining four days, the Marines encountered stubborn resistance, but secured the city by 2 March with 1,889 enemy killed. By their effective teamwork, aggressive fighting spirit, and individual acts of heroism and daring, the men of the 1st Marines (—) (Reinforced) soundly defeated a numerically superior enemy force and achieved an illustrious record of courage and skill which was in keeping with the highest traditions of the Marine Corps and the United States Naval Service.

RICHARD NIXON

[At this point the President resumed speaking.]

We will present the citation to Colonel Hughes who will receive it for the regiment.

Colonel, in presenting it to you, I want to point out your very distinguished record. You joined the Marine Corps in 1940, served in World War II, served also in Korea, and now in Vietnam. These decorations indicate the distinction of that record, including the Navy Cross.

In congratulating the unit, we also congratulate you and thank you. We also thank Sergeant Manion and all of your colleagues for their splendid, superb service to the country.

If I could be permitted a personal word, when we speak of the Marine Corps it is very difficult to add to the words of that citation, but the Marine Corps has had somewhat of an effect on my own life.

During World War II, I happen to have been in the Navy, Mr. Secretary. In the Navy as an air operations officer, I was assigned to the First Marine Air Wing, a group called MAG-25, or better known as SCAT [South Pacific, Combat Air Transport Command]. SCAT flew up through the Solomons to Guadalcanal, Bougainville, Green Island, Vella Lavella, and all areas that are well known to Marines and perhaps to some who are here in this audience today.

I learned then to respect the Marines as individuals but particularly as a unit. That is why a unit citation to the Marine Corps is particularly appropriate.

Any Marine, whenever you speak to him, will say that it is the team that counts, the unit that counts, and the esprit de corps that Marines, some way, from the time of their foundation, have been able to maintain. This esprit de corps has certainly been exemplified by the record of this group.

Also, I am glad to see in this audience today General [Robert E.] Cushman, once the Commander of the Marines in Vietnam, and also my executive assistant when I was Vice President of the United States, and now the Deputy Director of the CIA.

Finally, this word: The record of this unit, I think, also speaks of the fighting men generally in Vietnam, the difficult task that they have. We know the problems that this war has caused in this country. We know some of the division in this country. We know also that day after day a half a million Americans in Vietnam are doing their job—doing their job because that is their duty.

Until the war is brought to a conclusion that will some way contribute to the cause of a lasting peace in that area and in the Pacific, these men will continue to do their duty.

It is very difficult to fight any kind of a war, difficult even when a nation is united as it was in World War II. It is much more difficult for men to fight day after day when the Nation appears to be divided.

I can only say that in hearing this citation read, I think of not only the officers, Colonel Hughes, Sergeant Manion, General Chapman, but I think of those men in Vietnam. I have seen them in the DMZ. I have seen them all over that country—the Marines, the Army, Navy, Air Corps—and they are splendid men doing their job day after day.

I trust that the political leadership that we have in this country will be able to match the sacrifice that they have made.

We think we can bring peace. We will bring peace. The peace that we will be able to achieve will be due to the fact that Americans, when it really counted, did not buckle, did not run away, but stood

fast so that the enemy knew that it had no choice except to negotiate—negotiate a fair peace, a peace which did not require from them anything more than anyone should ask for, and that is: the right of an equal chance to present their case to the people of South Vietnam and let the people decide.

We thank the Marines for what they have done and we are very proud to be here in your company again.

Thank you.

NOTE: The President spoke at 11:04 a.m. in the Rose Garden at the White House. Gen. Leonard F. Chapman, Jr., was Commandant of the Marine Corps, Col. Stanley S. Hughes was regimental commander, First Marines, at the time of the action, and Sgt. Maj. Harry C. Manion was regimental sergeant major.

The symbol (—) indicates the First Marine Regiment was operating without all of its assigned units.

379   Statement Issuing a Call for a White House Conference on Aging.   *October* 6, 1969

EVER SINCE Benjamin Franklin, at the age of 70, served on the committee which drafted the Declaration of Independence, older Americans have played a vitally important role in the life of this Nation.

Since Franklin's time the United States of America has grown in size and complexity. With that growth have come new challenges and new opportunities for the older citizens of this country. They have met these challenges and seized these opportunities with great determination and energy. At the same time, the entire Nation and its government have increasingly recognized their responsibility for helping older Americans to play active and constructive roles in our society.

This administration is fully committed to carrying out that responsibility. It was

in keeping with this commitment that I recently asked the Congress to raise social security benefits by 10 percent and to provide for automatic increases thereafter, so that payments will always keep pace with the cost of living. These measures, and other improvements which I have proposed for the social security system, will protect older Americans—so many of whom live on fixed incomes—against one of their worst enemies, the rising cost of living caused by inflation. My specific recommendations give maximum protection without further aggravating inflationary pressures. I earnestly hope that Congress will give these proposals its prompt consideration and approval.

Social security improvements are an important first step in our program for the older generation. But there are also other areas in which we must move forward. We must fully explore and carefully consider a variety of suggestions for helping the more than 19 million Americans who are now 65 and over—and the many millions more who will soon be in that category—to live healthier and more productive lives. We must find better ways for our society to tap their wisdom and talent and experience.

Much of the progress which has been made can be traced back to the last White House Conference on Aging which was called by President Eisenhower and held nearly a decade ago. Remembering that landmark conference and the valuable findings which it produced, the Congress last year authorized a new White House Conference on Aging. I enthusiastically supported such a conference in my campaign a year ago.

Today I am issuing a formal call for the second White House Conference on Aging to meet in Washington, D.C., in November in 1971. With careful advance

planning and with broad, representative participation, this Conference can help develop a more adequate national policy for older Americans. I hope that it will fully consider the many factors which have a special influence on the lives of the aging and that it will address precise recommendations, not only to the Federal Government, but also to government at other levels and to the private and voluntary sectors as well. The Conference will be directed by John B. Martin, Commissioner on Aging and Special Assistant to the President on Aging.

Members of the older generation have given much to their country. Through the White House Conference on Aging, a grateful nation can recognize these contributions. More than that, the Conference can move this Nation toward the goal of making old age a time of contribution and satisfaction.

NOTE: The White House Press Office released the text of a news briefing on the Conference held on October 6 by John B. Martin, Commissioner on Aging, Department of Health, Education, and Welfare.

380 Message to the Senate Transmitting the Consular Convention Between the United States and Belgium. *October* 8, 1969

To the Senate of the United States:

With a view to receiving the advice and consent of the Senate to ratification, I transmit herewith the consular convention between the United States of America and the Kingdom of Belgium, signed at Washington on September 2, 1969, and two exchanges of notes related thereto.

The convention deals with the conduct of consular relations between the two countries and the functions, privileges,

and immunities of their respective consular officers. Upon entry into force it will replace the consular convention of March 9, 1880 between the United States and Belgium. Like other recent consular conventions of the United States, the new convention with Belgium covers such important matters as the obligations of the two countries to assure free communication between a citizen and his consul, to inform consular officers of the arrest or detention of their countrymen, and to permit visits by consuls to any of their countrymen who are in prison. It covers consular functions and responsibilities in such fields as the issuance of visas and passports, and the performance of notarial services. It provides for the inviolability of consular communications, documents, and archives, and the obligations of the host country to protect consular premises against intrusion or damage.

I recommend that the Senate give early and favorable consideration to the convention and related exchanges of notes

and give its advice and consent to the ratification thereof.

I transmit also, for the information of the Senate, the report of the Secretary of State with respect to the convention and exchanges of notes.

RICHARD NIXON

The White House
October 8, 1969

NOTE: The convention was favorably considered by the Senate on November 10, 1969. The President signed the Instrument of Ratification on December 2, 1969. The text is printed in Senate Executive F (91st Cong., 1st sess.) which also includes the exchanges of notes and the report of the Secretary of State.

381   Remarks to Members of the American Revolution Bicentennial Commission.   *October* 8, 1969

Dr. Sterling, and members of the Bicentennial Commission:

As all of you know, we are gathered in this historic house for an opportunity that comes to a people once in a century, the celebration of the 200th anniversary of the United States, which will take place in 1976.

We are starting to plan now. We have representatives not only from the Federal Government, but from most of the States of the Nation here to plan that celebration.

I would like to speak to that subject very briefly, to speak to it in perhaps a way that most of you would not have thought of—would not have thought of because traditionally when we think of this kind of celebration, we think of the Nation's past and we glory in that past, as we should. We think of the Nation's present, and we consider the problems that we must deal with.

This celebration, I would hope, would

look to America's future, look to the year 1976, and set for ourselves goals for that year 1976 which we can achieve.

In the space of 7 years, we can achieve great goals, so that when 1976 comes we can look back over those 200 years with even greater pride than we did 100 years ago.

And I would only suggest that the pace of change and progress has escalated to the point in America today that we could accomplish as much in the next 7 years in achieving some of the goals that America wants to achieve—goals in the field of housing and transportation, and abolishing hunger and providing opportunity. We could achieve as much progress in achieving our ultimate goal as we did in all the history of the country up to this time.

This is possible. And we have to set for ourselves what not only is possible, but somewhat more than that and reach as high as we can.

Now with regard to what those goals should be, could I refer to the early days of this country, to the time that this Nation was founded and to the words that were spoken by those who, at the time of the Declaration of Independence, thought of the mission of America, what America could mean to the world? And one of them said that we act not just for ourselves, but for all mankind.

You know, we hear that today and we think that was perhaps a very appropriate statement to make because history has justified that kind of optimism.

But look at America 200 years ago—3 million people, 13 Colonies, and then States, a weak country, a poor country. And yet a founder spoke of acting for all mankind, which gives us the lesson, it seems to me, for the bicentennial.

Today we are the richest country in the world; we are the strongest country in the world. And, yet, in thinking of whether we are truly the hope of all mankind, we must recognize that that hope does not exist because of wealth or because of strength. It exists because of a spiritual quality that we have had from the time of our birth.

Somewhere along the line many of us perhaps have forgotten that spiritual quality. Many Americans need to be reminded of it. Perhaps we all have to discover it—why we are here; what we mean to the world.

In setting forth goals, I can tell you that this administration is thinking in terms that are tremendously exciting. In the field of hunger, it will be possible by the year 1976 to abolish hunger in the United States of America. It will be possible in the year 1976 to make enormous progress in the field of housing, in the field of transportation, in all of these areas that are

tremendously important to every American family and that are also admired and respected around the world.

Also, as we think of the year 1976 and what America means to the world, let us not discount ourselves too much. We do have enormous problems at home and problems abroad.

But I can tell you from having visited the major capitals of Europe, and from having also had the opportunity of visiting many of the capitals of Asia, that millions of people in the world today respect America, they admire America, and many of them love this country.

That is true even on the other side of the Iron Curtain, where I saw a million people in the streets of Bucharest who had not had an opportunity really to know about America for 35 years and, yet, some way, somehow, they sensed America meant something to them.

Our astronauts are finding it today, not just because they reached the moon, but because they stand for something more than the scientific achievement which enabled them to reach the moon.

What I am really trying to say is this: America in 1976 can be as it is today, the best fed, the best housed, the best clothed people in the world.

And we still will not have achieved our true goal of being the hope of the world in the ultimate sense, because going back to the beginning, when America was poor, when America was weak, when America was ill-housed and ill-clothed, let us never forget we had something then that caught the imagination of the world.

So, to those who come from the States and those here from the Federal Government, let us set for our goal in 1976 not just moving forward in all these material areas, but to move forward in the realm of the American spirit.

I know this sounds perhaps too illusory, too uncertain for us possibly to capture. But it is there. We must put our minds to it, we must put our hearts to it.

That brings me now to those from the States.

This celebration will not just be a national celebration, because Washington, great city that it is, is not America any more than New York is America or Los Angeles is America.

America is 50 States. America is big cities and small cities and small towns. It is all the homes and all the hopes of 200 million people.

That is why we want this celebration to be national. It must go directly to the people and derive its strength from the people.

And we want people all over this land to sense the greatness of this moment, to participate in it, to help us all to discover what that great spirit is.

So, I would charge this Commission, Dr. Sterling, to move forward, move forward, yes, in reaching the great material goals of which we know we are capable—that is the easiest part of the job—but

recognizing that the best fed, best clothed, best housed people in the world, that the strongest nation in the world, and the richest nation in the world still will not deserve to be the hope of the world unless it has that splendid spirit, the lift of a driving dream which meant so much to the world in 1776 and for 200 years since that time.

I would conclude simply by saying that by that year 1976, the world will be at peace. By that year 1976, America, we trust, will find the understanding that we perhaps do not have in many quarters today. But above everything else, I would trust in that year 1976 that more Americans can look back with pride and look to the future with hope, hope that the opportunity that everybody in this room has had is something that is a realizable dream that can be achieved for anyone who has the good fortune to be born in this country, for anyone who has the good fortune to come to this country.

Thank you.

NOTE: The President spoke at 12:15 p.m. in the Blue Room at the White House. Dr. John E. Wallace Sterling was Chairman of the Commission.

382 Remarks With Participants in the Bipartisan Congressional Leadership Meeting on Crime in the District of Columbia. *October 9, 1969*

LET ME OPEN the meeting by saying that, in speaking of crime in the District of Columbia, everybody around this table knows that we speak of an issue that is certainly not partisan. What we are talking about here is a problem that is national, and it is a problem in which the Congress traditionally has had a function

which is very special in relation to the District and also special in relation to what the District can be in its example to the Nation.

I have noted in reading the statements that all of us have made in campaigns, and on the subject generally in nonpolitical speeches about crime in this country, that we have pointed to the fact that the Nation's Capital, the first city in the world, should really be an example to the Nation and to the world of a safe city, a city in which not only the citizens of this city but the ambassadors and others who visit this city can feel safe, within reason, at least, having in mind the problem that any city, any place, is going to have some crime.

We all know that the situation with regard to crime in the District in the past, going back over several years, has not been one that we can be proud of. This is not said in any partisan sense. It has run through all administrations and today it has reached crisis proportions, as the presentation by the Chief will indicate.

Now, what we do about this is something we will discuss after the presentation has been made. But I will simply summarize my opening remarks by saying what is done is certainly related to the actions of three different groups.

First, the Congress has a responsibility. We are, in a sense, the legislative body of the city. It is true that home rule is now being established, but the Congress has the primary responsibility in terms of legislation in this field.

Second, the city government has some responsibility. It can take some action that will be indicated in this briefing.

Third, in the administration of justice, the Department of Justice has some responsibility, and we will have the Department of Justice here to make a presentation with respect to how they are going to meet their responsibilities.

All I am saying here, I emphasize, is simply to present in a preliminary way the situation as I see it. This is not a partisan question, it is a national question. It is a question which I think we want the facts

on. We want to know what to do and then it is time to get going and to do it because nobody feels comfortable about sitting on what I think is an explosive, and frankly, when we see these statistics, a disgraceful situation with regard to crime in the District of Columbia.

We cannot point our finger to the other cities or the national crime statistics unless we do something about crime here where we are and where we have the responsibility.

Chief, you tell us the facts.

CHIEF OF POLICE JERRY V. WILSON. *Mr. President, Members of Congress, members of the press:*

I have a few statistics here, but this is not a statistical presentation, because I think all of you are generally familiar with the statistics, but it is merely to set a stage for the problems we have.

This is the data of criminal index offenses, January through June of 1969. As you can see, the District of Columbia is second in actual number of offenses and second in offenses per thousand population.

In the more problem areas, for example, robbery, we were first, but there are other cities that are close to us. It is a national problem, as the President said. Baltimore is close and San Francisco is close behind. The San Francisco area has a higher rate than we have in the Washington area, but we do have an extreme problem with robbery in this city at this time, and with crime across the board.

We have also presented data which has been published in the press of comparisons of crime in the District, January through June of 1968 and 1969, showing a 22 percent increase in crime in D.C. and suburbs, compared to a national urban increase of 9 percent, an increase in our own metropolitan area of some 9.6 percent.

I would point particularly to the problem in robbery. We have, again, a real problem area in this city at this time of robberies. In this we have nearly a 50 percent increase in robberies during this period.

To put it in perspective with the past, I have presented data for 1958, 1962, 1966, and 1969. I want to say at the outset that our data for the past years has some question to it. I am not sure how much, precisely. When we say that 1958 was our low year for crime in the city, I am willing to say to you that we were fudging on our statistics some then.

I will give you a 10 or 15 percent edge, and say that our crime may have been 10 or 15 percent more than it is now, but even if you wanted to say that robberies were double in 1958—which was 348, and I don't believe it would double—we have had a tenfold increase in robberies. These are not pickpockets and purse snatching, these are FBI robberies which include force and violence and armed robberies.

We have had an increase in burglary from 1,700 to 10,000 offenses in 11 years, and in auto theft, some 900 offenses to some 4,600 offenses.

This is a projection of trends based on our data for 1966 through 1969, showing a projection indicating that we will rise, unless something is done, from 55,000 annually as of 1969, to some 80,000 offenses annually as of 1972. Note that in our total offenses and in our offenses against persons, we are already going ahead of the trend. That would indicate we may have even more.

These have been statistics, and again, I am not willing to make a statistical presentation. I want to talk a little bit about what crime is subjectively to people who live and come through the city. I want to talk about Safeway stores, and I don't mean to advertise them, but Safeway stores as a grocery chain, have a large number of innercity chain stores—42—and since July 1 they have had 53 holdups.

They have tried to combat this with armed guards. The consequence has been that they have had one armed guard killed and another shot. They have difficulties now hiring them. These holdups range from one individual who holds up a checkout clerk and the manager doesn't know she is held up until he is gone, to an incident 2 weeks ago in Northeast where five armed men go in and make 100 customers lie on the floor until they rob the store.

This does something to the stores. They can't get competent help to work in the store. It forces the residents of the downtown area to go to the suburbs to shop because they are afraid to go to the neighborhood store.

Safeway will have a quarter of a million dollars in holdups this year.

I will talk about High's stores, 156 holdups since July 1. It is a favorite of the holdup men. In this case, they tend to hire low-paid women who live in the neighborhood. These women often know who held them up, but they are afraid to tell the police because the man is often back on the street. So it is impossible to find out who held them up.

Liquor store holdups are generally down this year. The holdup man has learned that when he goes to the liquor store he is taking that man's money, and that man is going to shoot him. So they go to Safeway's, High's, or the deliverymen on the route.

THE PRESIDENT. What do you mean they know that the man is going to shoot them? Do you mean they are armed?

POLICE CHIEF WILSON. The liquor store people are armed. It is their money. In the High's store it is the clerk who is hired. The store has a good policy, I would suggest, of saying, give them the money, and the cleaning truck driver on the street is going to give it up, but when they go to the liquor store it is that man's money.

Let's talk about the downtown merchants. If you go downtown, you will see that the clerk is going to have a key on a chain around his neck, because the cash register is locked. They have groups of keys—10 or 15. They go into stores and take what they want and go.

Shoplifting is a problem, but it is not the old pilferage shoplifting, it is going in and grabbing and running. It is a real problem. We have worked hard with the downtown stores with this, because the city cannot afford to lose these stores to the suburbs, and this is what happens. The stores give up and move to the suburbs.

Talking about poor people, I had a call yesterday afternoon from a community leader of the Barry Farm Welfare Mothers. The woman was almost crying, saying that the mothers lose their money. The burglars go in and take furniture and appliances. She was telling me about the problem they have in public housing with the children on dope, the 12- and 13-year-olds.

This is the problem throughout our city. Two weeks ago a court of general sessions judge called me and said: "My God, I don't know what is going to happen. These holdup men stand in front of me and smirk because they know I have

to let them go."

I went to U Street 2 months ago, to one of the real estate offices. He had a sign: "All rent must be paid by check. No cash accepted." The door is locked and the clerk comes to see you before you go in.

I went to a Baptist church service. They had signs throughout the church: "All officers and employees are prohibited from leaving money on the premises." That is so the burglar will know there are no valuables on the premises.

Even prostitution is rampant in this city, and we arrest prostitutes who tell us they are brought to town with the promise that they are not going to get jail terms on the first or second arrest; they will get fines that they can pay.

Let's talk about the factors that have led to problems of crime. I will not beat the dead horse of the Mallory Rule.[1] That happened a long time ago. Our crime has come up. We had a ban on investigative arrests in 1962. We have had some crime increase since then.

There are other factors at work in crime. We have had crime throughout the city where these factors didn't come to work. It is very pointed though, that following enactment of the Bail Reform Act of 1966, crime has shot skyward, beginning in June or July of 1966, and again last fall, as I will discuss later, but largely when the many thousand cases from the April 1968 riots went to court.

These are the long term trends. I think there has been in effect just a general tendency to look towards hard law enforcement or firm law enforcement as being a bad policy.

Another factor that has come about has been an explosion of the narcotics prob-

---

[1] *Mallory* v. *United States,* 1957 (354 U.S. 449, 77 S. Ct. 1356, 1 L.Ed. 2d 1479).

lem, and this occurred in 1966. Part of the narcotics problem, of course, is the fact that we have no facilities in this city for treating narcotics. We have no facilities that realistically treat the narcotic addict.

There is a statute on the book which permits the involuntary hospitalization of the addict, but it has never been fully implemented. It was dropped almost entirely in 1966.

Again, I suggest we have poor sentencing policies. We have a policy in this city where all persons get concurrent sentences. The word is, when a man is arrested for a holdup, he knows he is free and he is going to get out on bail reform, and while he is out he might as well live high because he will get concurrent sentences for anything he does after that.

The growth of the juvenile problems has to be mentioned. That amounts to 45 percent of our robberies, 13 percent of the burglaries and 60 percent of the auto theft. All of these problems were accentuated by the 1968 riots, which clogged the total criminal justice system.

I am one who believes that the total criminal justice system is one that has to be treated. I do not believe that treating the police department is going to solve the problem. But the problem is, we don't have swift justice. Chief Justice Burger said that many people will be deterred from serious crime if they believe the justice is swift and sure. Nobody believes that now, and they are right.

With robbery, we had our long term trend of crime which literally exploded in our face last fall, especially in armed robberies. In November, December, and January our armed robberies went to unusual highs, from the level of about 300 a month to a level of almost 700 a month.

We had an abrupt drop in February, March, and April. What happened, of course, we think, is that the clogging of the courts from the riot cases probably made the holdup man know he was not going to get to trial.

The other thing was, of course, during Thanksgiving; in response to this, we beefed up police patrols, but in January before the drop came, Judge Hart[2] gave a 15-year-to-life sentence to an armed holdup man and said he would give it to any armed holdup man who came before him.

At the same time, a general sessions judge, with a petty larceny case, gave the man 2 years.

I think no doubt most important, the court of general sessions in February obviously began disregarding the Bail Reform Act of 1966. This change is clearly reflected by the fact that in April, just before our robberies jumped up again, the court of appeals footnoted their letters and opinions by saying they had more repeals under the act than they had during the entire preceding 8 months.

Mayor [Walter E.] Washington pointed out in August that something must be done. We need, as the President has said, movement on all fronts; legislative movement, appropriations movement. We need treating of the whole justice system.

I recommend, Mr. President, that the thing that we need most at this time is pretrial detention. I think the conclusion is inescapable that early action has to be taken on change of the Bail Reform Act of 1966. I think this action alone might abate our armed robberies.

We also need court reorganization, but

[2] Judge George L. Hart, Jr., of the United States District Court for the District of Columbia.

we know that that will take a year or two before it takes effect. We need stronger sentences. We need more than anything else, other than the Bail Reform, to institute the involuntary hospitalization for narcotic users. We need to take them off the street. Our estimates at this time are that as many as 35 to 50 percent of our holdup men are narcotic users. If we can get them off the street, it will be a lot harder for the pusher.

In police manpower, in August the mayor authorized us to spend a quarter of a million dollars in overtime for policemen; but frankly, we have not seen that much effect from it. I don't think this is really an economical way of achieving change. The total justice system has to be treated and I can't emphasize that too much. My greatest fear is that Congress may go home without this being done.

SENATOR JOSEPH D. TYDINGS.[3] Chief, I wonder if you would give the President an idea of how many—a conservative figure—narcotic addicts are released each month pending trial, without any facility whatever.

POLICE CHIEF WILSON. I have no count of the number.

SENATOR TYDINGS. Would 500 be a conservative figure?

POLICE CHIEF WILSON. There are at this point some 1,600 persons out on bail release at this time, and our data, which is not good data, indicates that about 50 percent of these serious offenders are probably narcotic addicts.

THE PRESIDENT. Fifty percent?

POLICE CHIEF WILSON. Of all serious offenders, probably 50 percent.

SENATOR TYDINGS. Would it be fair to say that in the last 8 to 12 months that

the narcotic addict has moved into the field of armed robbery, away from just burglary?

POLICE CHIEF WILSON. And no real sir. There is no question that the narcotic addict who formerly was involved strictly in crime against property has moved to armed robbery. There is no question.

SENATOR TYDINGS. As you pointed out, the average robber or holdup man is arrested; he figures he has about 1 year in which to commit as many more robberies as he wishes because of the concurrent sentencing and because he knows he will not be brought to trial for at least a year.

POLICE CHIEF WILSON. That is correct.

THE PRESIDENT. In concurrent sentencing, as all the lawyers around here understand, the point is that it doesn't make any difference if he is on that kind of a kick, or how many crimes he commits. He is just going to get the same sentence and that is why you get the double impact, as I understand, the moment you let him out. He has no incentive not to commit a crime.

POLICE CHIEF WILSON. And no real fear of getting caught, Mr. President. I am satisfied that this is why we have not had more policemen shot apprehending armed robbers, because their best bet is to give themselves up.

SENATOR TYDINGS. One more question, if you took 200 or 300 of these people out of circulation, what would happen to these statistics?

POLICE CHIEF WILSON. If we could get the right 300 people off the street, I think it would probably almost cure the problem. I think that it would do two things: It would get those committing most of the crimes, and the thing that I am afraid has happened is that we have created an atmosphere that not only per-

---

[3] Chairman of the Senate District of Columbia Committee.

petuates the hard criminal, but also draws into it the youngster who sees it.

THE PRESIDENT. Who are the right 300?

POLICE CHIEF WILSON. The narcotic addicts.

THE PRESIDENT. Not the young ones?

POLICE CHIEF WILSON. No.

THE PRESIDENT. These are the hard, tough ones who are completely hooked?

POLICE CHIEF WILSON. Yes, sir, but we also need to do something about the youngsters on narcotics, Mr. President.

THE PRESIDENT. I agree, but you are talking about the hard 200 or 300, and treat the others?

POLICE CHIEF WILSON. It is relatively few. There are probably less than 100 professional holdup men who repeatedly get out on bail bond, and we could probably lick the problem.

SENATOR MIKE MANSFIELD. Chief, to get away from this concurrent sentencing, some of us have introduced legislation which would make the sentencing mandatory if you used a gun in the perpetration of the crime, and it would not run on a concurrent basis with the crime itself, but you would be sentenced separately and positively.

The first offense would be 1 to 10 years, the second would be 25 years. The judge would have no discretion, and in that way the man would be punished, one, for carrying a gun, and secondly, for the crime he committed, but they would not run concurrently, which is the case in so many places today.

POLICE CHIEF WILSON. There is legislation now for additional penalties for a crime of violence while armed, and I have never heard of it being enforced, although it is on the books.

THE PRESIDENT. We can have more

questions later.

At this time Deputy Attorney General Kleindienst and Mr. Santarelli will make the presentation of Justice.

DEPUTY ATTORNEY GENERAL RICHARD G. KLEINDIENST. *Mr. President, Members of the Congress, and gentlemen of the press:*

I would like to divide this presentation into two parts: a brief thumbnail sketch of what the Justice Department has done, and then have Mr. Santarelli, the Associate Attorney General, who has been intimately involved in the details of the problem for the last several months, go more into depth.

In response to the President's message to the Congress on January 31 with respect to the District of Columbia and crime, the Attorney General brought about his first reorganization of the Justice Department to accommodate and meet this problem. That was done in the Office of Criminal Justice.

In the prior administrations, the Office of Criminal Justice had been a philosophical thing, with two or three people dealing conceptually with the whole problem of criminal justice in the United States.

On February 1, the administration converted this into an action team, addressing itself to the problem of crime in the District of Columbia. Instead of three persons thinking about the problem, we have a permanent staff of five persons, headed by Mr. Santarelli, together with a task force of ten lawyers who have been working continually on the problem, and together with the assistance of other persons and departments of the executive branch.

As a result of their efforts, working some 60 hours a week for some 5 months, within a 5-month period of time, they have put together nearly 500 pages of carefully thought-out legislation in response to the President's message on January 31 dealing in a comprehensive manner with the whole problem of crime in the District.

I would like to outline for you, just by name and description, the present status of this legislation which was presented to Congress on July 11, 1969.

The first bill was the bail reform bill to which the Chief alluded. It is in the Congress as Senate bill 2600 and in the House as House of Representatives bill 18036. So far as we know, no action is planned on it in the Senate. In the House, there is a hearing set on it on October 16. The second bill is the court reorganization bill and criminal law reform bill.

THE PRESIDENT. The hearing is in the District Committee?

MR. KLEINDIENST. It will be in the Judiciary Committee.

SENATOR TYDINGS. The Urban Subcommittee on Constitutional Rights.

THE PRESIDENT. I would like to have you tell us the committees.

MR. KLEINDIENST. That is the only bill that is not in the District Committee. It is in the Judiciary Committee. All the other bills I will be referring to are in the District Committee of both Houses.

The next bill is the court reorganization and criminal law reform bill. In the Senate that is divided by the Senate District Committee into two parts, the court reorganization part, which was passed on September 16, 1969, with slight modification, and the criminal law section of it remains in the Senate and is subject to scheduled hearings in the Senate.

SENATOR TYDINGS. The hearings are complete. It is subject to markup.

MR. KLEINDIENST. In the House, the bill has remained intact in both of its parts, and it is subject to hearings, and so far as we know, there are no immediate prospects or plans for hearings with respect to the entire bill in the House.

The public defender bill is pending in both Houses before the District Committees.

SENATOR TYDINGS. Hearings are completed in the Senate and we are pending markup on the public defender bill.

MR. KLEINDIENST. The fourth is the bail agency bill. The Senate passed a similar version of the administration's bill on July 8. The administration's bill was introduced on July 11, and both bills are scheduled for hearings in the House.

Then on September 26, a juvenile court and law reform bill was submitted to the Congress. The delay in the juvenile court bill was necessitated by virtue of its comprehensive nature and, although significant and important just in terms of priorities for congressional action dealing with the crime problem in the District, it was felt it would take less priority position so far as crime.

I would also like to make a comment with respect to a request by this administration for increased appropriations from the Congress. We have requested on behalf of the Department of Justice a loan of $1½ million additional to permit the Department of Justice to address itself to the specifics of crime in the District of Columbia, and the District government itself has requested an additional $8 million to deal specifically in terms of increases in crime in the District of Columbia. That $8 million would be part of a total package of $20.6 million.

The Department of Justice requests have passed the House and are before the

Senate and neither House has passed a request of the District of Columbia with respect to those increased appropriations.

At a later time, we might concern ourselves, Senator Tydings, with these requests for appropriations, particularly looking to the narcotics problem and the treatment of narcotic addicts in the District of Columbia.

That is a thumbnail sketch, Mr. President. I would like to have Mr. Santarelli briefly describe, in depth, the significance of each of these pieces of legislation.

ASSOCIATE DEPUTY ATTORNEY GENERAL FOR CRIMINAL JUSTICE DONALD E. SANTARELLI. *Mr. President and gentlemen:*

We will start with the bail reform proposal. By way of understanding the context of this, I think it is important to recognize that since 1789 we have assured the right of bail in capital cases. Over the years capital cases eroded, and now almost no serious offense is capital except murder.

Now under the reform of the bail law, there was enacted a statute which made it mandatory to release persons in noncapital cases, pending trial. The problem with this is that for 176 years, the courts devised a method by which to detain dangerous people. By doing that, the court detained persons prior to trial.

Since 1966 this is no longer possible. Now all persons who are no longer charged with capital offenses are released prior to trial, and since we now have a delay factor of up to 10 months to a year in the District of Columbia for serious felonies, this means that all persons are released.

We have proposed comprehensive legislation to revise the bail law that was passed in 1966. This bill, which Mr.

Kleindienst mentioned, does a number of things. It specifically allows the court to take into consideration dangerousness to the community by the defendant's release when it sets those conditions of release, or in the alternative, it can detain persons prior to trial in the event that the court finds them to be dangerous.

We have also provided in that bill for extensive due process procedures to assure that no person will be detained improperly. The court has to go through a series of findings before it can order detention, and then only for 60 days, and the trial shall be expedited in those 60 days, over and above other less dangerous persons.

We have provided in that bill additional conditions for bail jumping and we have provided that they are consecutive rather than concurrent in their application. That is in the Judiciary.

We have provided a comprehensive proposal for court reform. This applies to the District of Columbia. Presently, it is in the District Committee. The proposal would transfer all of the local, State-like felony crimes and civil jurisdiction from the present United States District Court to a newly created superior court of the District of Columbia.

The superior court would consist eventually, over a period of 3 years, of 50 judges. That is 23 more judges than presently sit on the court of general sessions.

The superior court would incorporate into it the court of general sessions, and we would have a very large court, hopefully able to keep very current with its calendar. We would also expand the present District of Columbia court of appeals and create a unified court system, trial court, appeal court, and the appeals going directly to the Supreme Court. We

779

would no longer have a double appeal in the local appeals court and the U.S. Court of Appeals which we presently have.

The jurisdiction would be transferred in stages over a period of 2 to 3 years. In the first stage, 15 or more felony crimes, and finally all civil jurisdiction over the 3-year period.

The new court would have some unique aspects to it. We would give life tenure to the judges of this superior court subject to mandatory retirement at age 70, and subject to good behavior removal. We would create a removal commission which would have the power to suspend, remove, or retire for cause judges who are convicted of crimes, who fail to perform their duty or conduct themselves in a manner prejudicial to the administration of justice and tend to bring disrepute to the office.

This panel would consist of seven members: one judge, three members of the bar, and three residents of the District of Columbia, two of which could be members of the bar.

Another aspect that it would have would be a chief executive for administration. This executive would have very broad powers to administer the court in the most technologically advanced and specific manner available.

We wrote into the bill that computers would be used to the greatest extent to calendar cases. We would have a comprehensive director of social services in charge of all the social programs in the court, both probation and in the family court structure. Part of this new court would consist of a family court division, a rather novel situation in which juveniles and their families could be treated together in one comprehensive civil type procedure with a civil remedy of sanction

and injunction rather than criminal penalties in a family situation.

A very significant part of the court reform bill is procedural change. We strongly believe that it was not enough to simply add more judges, but we have to have more efficient and fair procedures rather than to rock along with the obstacle-like procedures that we presently have.

We have changed the rules of evidence and changed the rules relating to mental health commitments. We have provided a local wiretap statute, a local conspiracy statute, which we do not have in the District of Columbia.

We have provided for recidivist statutes, including life status for three-time felons. We have rewritten the arrest power and made clear what the power of the police is to deal with crime. We have provided for citizen arrest provisions, a prohibition on resisting arrest, new notions on search and seizure, and new powers for the prosecution, including prosecution appeal.

Another aspect of our court reorganization and juvenile bill which was submitted on the 26th of September is a totally new treatment of the juvenile problem. We have made waiver of juvenile persons accused of crime to adult courts a much easier practice. We have lowered the age to 15, so those few hard-core 15-year-olds could be waived to adult prosecution.

We have provided that 16- and 17-year-olds charged with violent felony crimes shall be prosecuted as adults, and we have required the practice of requiring jury trials in juvenile cases.

We have elevated the standard of proof requiring new evidence, and we have safeguarded their rights, rights to lawyers, rights to medical examinations and recordkeeping confidentiality.

We have provided a bail agency bill. In this case we are very much concerned that persons who are released prior to trial on pretrial release, with or without a condition, have no effective sanctions against them for their conduct prior to trial. If they do not conform to the condition put on by the court, no one is to know the difference. If they commit crimes, no one is to know the difference.

Therefore, we propose to establish an agency for those people to insure that their conduct conforms to the order of the court.

SENATOR TYDINGS. That is the bill that passed the Senate in July.

MR. SANTARELLI. That is correct. We submitted our July letter somewhat different than yours, Senator.

We would also provide for a Public Defender's office in the District of Columbia, a comprehensive office, capable of representing 60 percent of the indigent persons accused of crime. We have a small agency now which represents 10 percent.

THE PRESIDENT. But no public defender. Is there any other city where there is not one?

SENATOR TYDINGS. Yes, Mr. President, but this is a good bill.

THE PRESIDENT. I was thinking of San Francisco and New York, for instance.

MR. KLEINDIENST. They are not adequate in any city, frankly.

THE PRESIDENT. This goes further?

MR. KLEINDIENST. Yes, sir.

THE PRESIDENT. It also goes back to the point we made earlier, and some of these are highly technical matters which lawyers can argue on the committee and on the floor, but what appeals to me about the program that has been presented is that it moves into areas in which you are looking around the country and picking the most advanced kinds of approaches. Things that have been tried before and didn't work, you have thrown out, and things that have been tried and worked, you have incorporated. Also there are some new approaches which brings us to this fundamental point that the District of Columbia could well be a city where we set an example for the rest of the major cities, and particularly because you have here, let's face it, on the Judiciary Committees of the House and Senate, and on the House District Committee, people from all over this country, people who should have the capability and also the responsibility to lead rather than to simply follow.

I think that is really the point. That is the spirit in which I think this has been prepared. I know when we talked about the matter earlier, I urged the Department of Justice in its recommendations to come up with a program not to just patch up some of the old laws we have, so that this city could be an example.

MR. KLEINDIENST. We think that is what this program is, Mr. President.

THE PRESIDENT. Incidentally, I want to say to Senator Tydings, we don't consider it to be the end result. I think your suggestion in terms of the treatment of the juveniles in the narcotics field is an area where we ought to be in the leadership, also. I think that is an area we ought to discuss.

MR. SANTARELLI. The bail agency bill would provide for new concepts in the representation by the Public Defender's office in all areas: parole, probation, juvenile representation which is not presently existing in the District of Columbia in all misdemeanors.

Turning to appropriations, I think it is

significant in view of the interest expressed here this morning to note that presently pending in the District of Columbia, in the government's request for a narcotics treatment program, is a request for $400,000 in addition for their narcotic treatment programs, and also a request for a reprograming of $200,000 previously requested into a narcotics treatment program.

With respect to correction, which everyone is interested in and does not lend itself to substantive specific legislation, but far more to appropriation legislation, the District Government has in its present budget $8 million in additional funds for an improved correctional system for almost 500 additional positions for persons in the system, for new administrative techniques, work-release programs, and a training academy for correctional officers.

In addition, the police budget for the District of Columbia has a $4 million request for 1,000 new police officers which the President called for back in his message.

THE PRESIDENT. I have one fundamental question. In this field of crime, as all of us who are lawyers are quite aware, it is imperative to have a balance between an approach which emphasizes stiff penalties and an approach which gets at what is perhaps the heart of the problem, the repeater.

In other words, it is the treatment of the first-offender and the treatment of those who commit a crime and then go out and commit another one.

Do you consider this program to have that proper balance?

MR. SANTARELLI. Yes, Mr. President.

MR. KLEINDIENST. I think we have also addressed ourselves to the essential interest in the care of the innocent at the same time.

THE PRESIDENT. Do you have a figure in the District of Columbia with regard to the percentage of crimes that are committed by people who have committed crimes before?

MR. KLEINDIENST. The recidivism rate in the District is one of the highest in the country.

SENATOR TYDINGS. I think it is something like 67 percent within 5 years and maybe a little less within 1 or 2 years.

THE PRESIDENT. That gets to the heart of the problem. The Chief mentioned a moment ago that if he could get the 300 most wanted that you could break the back, you think, of this crime wave in the District. I think, also, would you not agree, Chief, that in addition to getting those 300, that if we could have a new approach to the person who commits a crime and then who is going to continue to commit crimes, a new approach to attempt to reduce that tendency, that would also be helpful.

Do you agree with a need for that as well? I want this said while the press is here. Chief Wilson has impressed me with his presentation now and also because of his record, and also because he does not approach this simply in the routine way that sometimes very dedicated law enforcement officers do; saying, "more penalties will do it."

He recognizes the penalties and the modifications of the bail reform are needed. But you endorse this kind of an approach which gets at this, particularly these young people who commit a crime and then within a year commit another one?

POLICE CHIEF WILSON. Mr. President, I think one of the worst parts of our criminal justice system, not only in the District of Columbia, but in the Nation as a whole, because the recidivism rate is 73 percent within 5 years, is really that we don't rehabilitate criminals. Criminals really just grow too old to get out and commit crime.

What happens is that they come into the system at 16 or 17 or 18 and go in and out of the institutions until 26 or 27 and perhaps get married and settle down because they are too old to get out on the street at night.

This is what rehabilitates crime in the streets now and it is a sad commentary on our system.

I think at this point in time stricter penalties would help. I don't see that as a long term solution.

THE PRESIDENT. But you need the penalties now?

POLICE CHIEF WILSON. Yes, sir.

SENATOR TYDINGS. Between swifter penalties and stiffer penalties, which, in your opinion, would be the most effective?

POLICE CHIEF WILSON. If I could get a man 1 year, 3 weeks after the crime was committed, I would take the 1 year, if I could get it.

MR. KLEINDIENST. I think the Chief and the Senator have emphasized the due process as a preventive process to the arbitrary bail which is posed by judges on a very arbitrary basis. This gives us precise terms in which you can determine safety in a community with appropriate due process safeguards and I think it would be one of the most significant innovations with regard to this problem.

POLICE CHIEF WILSON. The 16-year-old sees the 18-year-old who held up a store and is arrested and he sees him on the street the next day. Two or three years later he has forgotten the fact when the holdup man goes to jail. If you could get them to jail sooner I think it would remove the idea that nobody goes to jail—and they are right.

THE PRESIDENT. To what extent has the question been raised about the increase in robberies, due to the fact that the narcotics enforcement has become more effective?

POLICE CHIEF WILSON. We don't see that as a large factor, Mr. President. This doesn't seem to have affected it.

THE PRESIDENT. I noted the speculation in the press to that effect. You don't see it?

POLICE CHIEF WILSON. Our observation was an immediate rise in narcotics prices which immediately dropped off and it was probably more in the area of profiteering than a real shortage in the market.

We have a feeling that some of the merchants were saying there was a shortage in order to jump the price, but this has dropped off and the price seems to be what it was before.

I think our real problem is almost obviously the problem with the court of appeals and the Leathers [4] decision and the subsequent decisions in June.

NOTE: The President opened the meeting at 8:47 a.m. in the Cabinet Room at the White House.

Also present were: Senators Winston L. Prouty of Vermont, Senate District of Columbia Committee; Roman L. Hruska of Nebraska, Senate Judiciary Committee; Representatives Gerald R. Ford of Michigan, House Minority Leader; Ancher Nelsen of Minnesota, House District of Columbia Committee; William M. McCulloch of Ohio, House Judiciary Committee; and Glenn R.

[4] *United States* v. *Leathers,* 1969 (412 F. 2d 169).

Davis of Wisconsin and William H. Natcher of Kentucky, both members of the House Committee on Appropriations Subcommittee on District of Columbia Appropriations.

Also on October 9, the White House Press Office released the text of a news briefing on the meeting by Representative Gerald R. Ford and Jerry V. Wilson, Chief of Police of the District of Columbia.

383   Remarks on Presenting the Medal of Honor to Four Members of the United States Army.   *October 9, 1969*

Ladies and gentlemen:

We are gathered here today at the White House for the purpose of presenting the Nation's highest decoration to four of the finest young men it has been my privilege to know. The Secretary of the Army, Mr. Resor, will read the citations and the presentations will now be made.

[Secretary of the Army Stanley R. Resor read the four citations, the texts of which follow.]

The President of the United States of America, authorized by Act of Congress, March 3, 1863, has awarded in the name of The Congress the Medal of Honor to

MAJOR PATRICK H. BRADY, MEDICAL SERVICE
CORPS, UNITED STATES ARMY

for conspicuous gallantry and intrepidity in action at the risk of his life above and beyond the call of duty:

Major Patrick H. Brady, Medical Service Corps, distinguished himself by conspicuous gallantry and intrepidity while serving with the 54th Medical Detachment, 67th Medical Group, 44th Medical Brigade in the Republic of Vietnam. On 6 January 1968 Major Brady, commanding a UH–1H ambulance helicopter in the vicinity of Chu Lai, volunteered to rescue wounded men from a site in enemy held territory which was reported to be heavily defended and to be blanketed by fog. To reach the site he descended through heavy fog and smoke and hovered slowly along a valley trail, turning his ship sideward to blow away the fog with the backwash from his rotor blades. Despite the unchallenged, close-range enemy fire, he found the dangerously small site, where he successfully landed and evacuated two badly wounded South Vietnamese soldiers. He was then called to another area completely covered by dense fog where American casualties lay only 50 meters from the enemy. Two aircraft had previously been shot down and others had made unsuccessful attempts to reach this site earlier in the day. With unmatched skill and extraordinary courage, Major Brady made four flights to this embattled landing zone and successfully rescued all the wounded. On his third mission of the day Major Brady once again landed at a site surrounded by the enemy. The friendly ground force, pinned down by enemy fire, had been unable to reach and secure the landing zone. Although his aircraft had been badly damaged and his controls partially shot away during his initial entry into this area, he returned minutes later and rescued the remaining injured. Shortly thereafter, obtaining a replacement aircraft, Major Brady was requested to land in an enemy minefield where a platoon of American soldiers was trapped. A mine detonated near his helicopter, wounding two crew members and damaging his ship. In spite of this, he managed to fly six severely injured patients to medical aid. Throughout that day Major Brady utilized three helicopters to evacuate a total of fifty-one seriously wounded men, many of whom would have perished without prompt medical treatment. Major Brady's conspicuous gallantry was in the highest traditions of the military service and reflects great credit upon himself and the United States Army.

RICHARD NIXON

The President of the United States of America, authorized by Act of Congress, March 3,

1863, has awarded in the name of The Congress the Medal of Honor to

CAPTAIN JACK H. JACOBS

UNITED STATES ARMY

for conspicuous gallantry and intrepidity in action at the risk of his life above and beyond the call of duty:

Captain Jack H. Jacobs (then First Lieutenant), Infantry, distinguished himself on 9 March 1968 while serving as Assistant Battalion Advisor, 2d Battalion, 16th Infantry, 9th Infantry Division, Army of the Republic of Vietnam, during an operation in Kien Phong Province, Republic of Vietnam. The 2d Battalion was advancing to contact when it came under intense heavy machine gun and mortar fire from a Viet Cong battalion positioned in well-fortified bunkers. As the 2d Battalion deployed into attack formation its advance was halted by devastating fire. Captain Jacobs, with the command element of the lead company, called for and directed air strikes on the enemy positions to facilitate a renewed attack. Due to the intensity of the enemy fire and heavy casualties to the command group, including the company commander, the attack stopped and the friendly troops became disorganized. Although wounded by mortar fragments, Captain Jacobs assumed command of the allied company, ordered a withdrawal from the exposed position and established a defensive perimeter. Despite profuse bleeding from head wounds which impaired his vision, Captain Jacobs, with complete disregard for his own safety, returned under intense fire to evacuate a seriously wounded advisor to the safety of a wooded area where he administered lifesaving first aid. He then returned through heavy automatic weapons fire to evacuate the wounded company commander. Captain Jacobs made repeated trips across the fire-swept open rice paddies evacuating wounded and their weapons. On three separate occasions, Captain Jacobs contacted and drove off Viet Cong squads who were searching for allied wounded and weapons, singlehandedly killing three and wounding several others. His gallant actions and extraordinary heroism saved the lives of one United States advisor and thirteen allied soldiers. Through his effort the allied company was restored to an effective fighting unit and

prevented defeat of the friendly forces by a strong and determined enemy. Captain Jacobs, by his conspicuous gallantry and intrepidity in action in the highest traditions of the military service, has reflected great credit upon himself, his unit and the United States Army.

RICHARD NIXON

The President of the United States of America, authorized by Act of Congress, March 3, 1863, has awarded in the name of The Congress the Medal of Honor to

CAPTAIN JAMES M. SPRAYBERRY

UNITED STATES ARMY

for conspicuous gallantry and intrepidity in action at the risk of his life above and beyond the call of duty:

Captain (then First Lieutenant) James M. Sprayberry, Armor, United States Army, distinguished himself by exceptional bravery on 25 April 1968 in the Republic of Vietnam while serving as Executive Officer of Company D, 5th Battalion, 7th Cavalry, 1st Cavalry Division (Airmobile). On this date his Company Commander and a great number of the men were wounded and separated from the main body of the company. A daylight attempt to rescue them was driven back by the well-entrenched enemy's heavy fire. Captain Sprayberry then organized and led a volunteer night patrol to eliminate the intervening enemy bunkers and to relieve the surrounded element. The patrol soon began receiving enemy machine gun fire. Captain Sprayberry quickly moved the men to protective cover and without regard for his own safety, crawled within close range of the bunker from which the fire was coming. He silenced the machine gun with a hand grenade. Identifying several one-man enemy positions nearby, Captain Sprayberry immediately attacked them with the rest of his grenades. He crawled back for more grenades and when two grenades were thrown at his men from a position to the front, Captain Sprayberry, without hesitation, again exposed himself and charged the enemy-held bunker killing its occupants with a grenade. Placing two men to cover his advance, he crawled forward and neutralized three more bunkers with grenades. Immediately thereafter, Captain Sprayberry was surprised by an enemy soldier who charged from a concealed position. He killed the soldier with his pistol and with continuing disregard for the danger, neutralized another enemy emplacement. Captain Sprayberry then established radio contact with the isolated men, directing them toward his position. When the two elements made contact he organized his men into litter parties to evacuate the wounded. As the evacuation was nearing completion, he observed an enemy machine gun position which he silenced with a grenade. Captain Sprayberry returned to the rescue party, established security, and moved to friendly lines with the wounded. This rescue operation, which lasted approximately seven and one-half hours, saved the lives of many of his fellow soldiers. Captain Sprayberry personally killed twelve enemy soldiers, eliminated two machine guns, and destroyed numerous enemy bunkers. Captain Sprayberry's indomitable spirit and gallant action at great personal risk to his life are in keeping with the highest traditions of the military service and reflect great credit upon himself, his unit, and the United States Army.

RICHARD NIXON

The President of the United States of America, authorized by Act of Congress, March 3, 1863, has awarded in the name of The Congress the Medal of Honor to

SERGEANT ROBERT M. PATTERSON
UNITED STATES ARMY

for conspicuous gallantry and intrepidity in action at the risk of his life above and beyond the call of duty:

Sergeant Robert M. Patterson, (then Specialist Four), distinguished himself on 6 May 1968 while serving as a fire team leader of the 3d Platoon, B Troop, 2d Squadron, 17th Cavalry during an assault against a North Vietnamese Army Battalion which was entrenched in a heavily fortified position near La Chu, Republic of Vietnam. When the leading squad of the 3d Platoon was pinned down by heavy interlocking automatic weapon and rocket propelled grenade fire from two enemy bunkers, Sergeant Patterson and the two other members of his assault team moved forward under a hail of enemy fire to destroy the bunkers with grenade and machine gun fire. Observing that his comrades were being fired on from a third enemy bunker covered by enemy gunners in one-man spider holes, Sergeant Patterson, with complete disregard for his own safety and ignoring the warning of his comrades that he was moving into a bunker complex, assaulted and destroyed the position. Although exposed to intensive small arm and grenade fire from the bunkers and their mutually supporting emplacements, Sergeant Patterson continued his assault upon the bunkers which were impeding the advance of his unit. Sergeant Patterson singlehandedly destroyed by rifle and grenade fire five enemy bunkers, killed eight enemy soldiers and captured seven weapons. His dauntless courage and heroism inspired his platoon to resume the attack and to penetrate the enemy defensive position. Sergeant Patterson by his conspicuous gallantry and intrepidity in action at the risk of his own life has reflected great credit upon himself, his unit and the United States Army.

RICHARD NIXON

[The President then resumed speaking.]

I am very proud to stand in the company of these men. I am proud to stand in their company because of what you have just heard in the citations that have been read.

I think all of us are proud to be Americans when we realize that America produces such fine young men. History will record that these men are heroes. They are heroes—heroes for what they have done, for the sacrifice that they were willing to make to save others, and for the sacrifice they were willing to endure for their country.

We wonder sometimes how we happen to have men like this, and I am reminded of the fact that often discussions take place as to whether heroes are made or whether they are born. The Carnegie Foundation made a study of this problem going over 30 years. They reached, it seems to me, a very interesting and profound conclusion.

Heroism, the Foundation reported, is not made. Like gold, it is uncovered. Danger does not make heroes; it finds them. Somewhere these men had in their character, character that they acquired from their families, from their homes, from their schools, from their churches, from the heart of America—they had this element of greatness and the danger brought it forth. So we know they are heroes.

It is for us a tragedy that this heroism which was there all the time had to be uncovered because of a war. But also, we are reminded of the fact that on such an occasion we dedicate ourselves anew to bringing the peace which we all want, so that men like this, who have this element of greatness within them, may become heroes, meeting the challenges of peace because heroism is the Nation's greatest asset, greater than gold. Like gold, heroism must be uncovered.

I am confident that the challenges of peace will uncover great heroism in America's younger people, just as the dangers of war have uncovered the heroism in these four splendid Americans we honor today.

NOTE: The President spoke at 10:24 a.m. on the South Lawn at the White House.

An announcement of the presentation ceremony dated October 8, 1969, is printed in the Weekly Compilation of Presidential Documents (vol. 5, p. 1380).

384   Statement About National Newspaperboy Day, 1969.
October 10, 1969

AS AMERICANS commemorate National Newspaperboy Day, we give deserving recognition to a youthful occupation that, perhaps more than any other, inspires the qualities of integrity, leadership and good citizenship in all walks of life.

There is no limit to the number of successful businessmen, doctors, lawyers, government officials, and countless other citizens who began their road to achievement on a newspaper delivery route.

Their experience taught them about people. It developed their sense of responsibility. And it showed them the satisfaction that derives from serving others.

As we applaud these young men, we salute America in the making—and we anticipate the future good that will come from the dedication of newspaperboys in their line of duty.

My personal admiration for them is second to none. And my best wishes are with them as they forge the tools for their chosen careers and build a promising future for themselves and for the nation that is so proud of them.

RICHARD NIXON

385 Statement Announcing the Appointment of Lieutenant General Lewis B. Hershey as Advisor to the President on Manpower Mobilization. *October 10, 1969*

FOR 33 YEARS, General Hershey has served with distinction in the Selective Service System. He has administered a program of paramount importance to the security of the United States, and few Americans have performed a more important service to their country through difficult and often turbulent days. The Nation owes General Hershey a hearty "well done."

I look forward to having the benefit of General Hershey's advice and counsel as we move ahead on a broad range of re-

forms designed to ensure that our manpower mobilization policies are equitable, efficient and geared to the requirements of the future. General Hershey brings to his new assignment vast experience and a perception into national manpower resources, perhaps unmatched in the country. The Nation is fortunate that it will continue to have his wise counsel.

NOTE: An announcement of the President's intention to nominate General Hershey is printed in the Weekly Compilation of Presidential Documents (vol. 5, p. 1394).

386 Special Message to the Congress on Legislative Reform. *October 13, 1969*

To the Congress of the United States:

In the nine months since Inauguration, a number of issues have arisen clearly calling for the Congress and the Administration to work together.

One such issue was the extension of the surtax, where our economic security was involved. Another was authority to build the Safeguard ballistic missile defense, where the national safety was the issue. On both occasions, when the time came to be counted, Congress subordinated partisan concerns and voted the country's interest.

The continuance of this working partnership between a Congress heavily Democratic and a Republican Administration, on occasions where great issues are involved, is imperative for the good of our country. I hope this partnership will survive the "spirit of party" that

grows more evident weekly in the national capital. Yet, in recent days, the call to partisan combat has grown more compelling.

I am aware that members of the Administration have criticized the Democratic-controlled Congress for "dragging its feet" in the enactment of legislation, for holding hearings thus far on only half the Administration proposals before it, for having enacted but a single appropriations bill for fiscal 1970, a full quarter of the way through the fiscal year. From Capitol Hill there have come similar charges—that the Administration has been laggard in proposing legislation, that the Executive Departments have been slow in giving the Congress the reports it has requested, that some of the most far-reaching Administration proposals have only lately been sent to the Congress, and so cannot be acted upon by the end of the year.

If a working partnership between men of differing philosophies and different parties is to continue, then candor on both sides is required. There may be merit in both charges; neither the Democratic Congress nor the Republican Administration is without fault for the delay of vital legislation.

But, in my view, the American people are not interested in political posturing between the Executive Branch and Capitol Hill. We are co-equal branches of government, elected not to maneuver for partisan advantage, but to work together to find hopeful answers to problems that confound the people all of us serve.

Both the President and Congress have been commissioned by the same American people, for a limited time, to achieve objectives upon which the great majority agree. For our part, we are willing to travel more than half-way to work with Congress to accomplish what needs to be done. The time for staking out political claims will come soon enough.

Let us resolve, therefore, to make the legislative issue of the 1970 campaign the question of who deserves greater credit for the Ninety-First Congress' record of accomplishment, not which of us should be held accountable because it did nothing. The country is not interested in what we say, but in what we do—let us roll up our sleeves and go to work. Before us are urgent legislative priorities.

The legislative program of this Administration differs fundamentally from that of previous administrations. We do not seek more and more of the same. We were not elected to pile new resources and manpower on the top of old programs. We were elected to initiate an era of change.

We intend to begin a decade of government reform such as this nation has not witnessed in half a century. Some months ago, a Washington columnist wrote in some pessimism that if ours is not to be an age of revolution then it must become an age of reform. That is the watchword of this Administration: *Reform.*

Reform of the draft. I have asked Congress to make the most extensive changes in the way we select young men for military service since the draft became an accepted feature of American life. We have the administrative power—and we will exercise it if Congress fails to act— to make far-reaching reforms in the selective service system, reducing the period of prime vulnerability for young Americans from seven years to 12 months. However, we need Congressional approval to shift from the inequitable requirement of choosing the "oldest first" to the more just method of random selection. I asked Congress five months ago for this power; I ask again today. Basic fairness to our young people is the prime reason for this recommendation. I see no reason why this vital piece of legislation cannot be enacted *now.*

Reform of the welfare system. Last summer I asked Congress to make the most sweeping changes in the American system of welfare since the beginning of the New Deal. Last week legislation went to Congress outlining the proposal I have made for a new family assistance system to replace the demeaning and bankrupt system that now exists.

Under the present system, sometimes a father must desert his wife and children to make them eligible for benefits. Under the present system, some mothers with three children must survive with only $39 a month for the entire family to live on.

The family assistance system is built on a different set of principles. It provides incentives for families to stay together. It provides economic rewards for men and women on welfare who enter training programs and search out jobs. It provides a floor under income that assures the minimum necessary for food and clothing and shelter.

The present system has led this country into a morass. It has laid a heavier and heavier burden on the American taxpayer. It has loaded the relief rolls with more and more families even in times of rising prosperity and low unemployment. I ask that Congress begin hearings on the new family assistance system at once. The welfare system should be abandoned as quickly as we can discard it and a new system established in its place.

Reform of the tax code. In April I recommended to Congress the most comprehensive set of tax reforms in many years. Subsequently the House of Representatives responded with an even more far-reaching proposal of its own. The national momentum behind tax reform—to make the code more fair and equitable, to shift part of the burden from those who have borne too much for too long to the shoulders of others who have not carried their fair share—must not be allowed to dribble away while a partisan wrangle goes on over who deserves the political credit. We will give Congress as much assistance and as many hours of labor as it requires to enact extensive and responsible reform in this calendar year.

I do ask, however, that Congress, in acting on this major reform, not compromise this Administration's effort to combat the most unjust tax of all, inflation. Specifically, I ask that Congress not convert this historic tax reform legislation into a sharp tax reduction that would unbalance the Federal budget and neutralize our campaign to halt the rising cost of living. I ask again that Congress repeal the seven per cent investment tax credit, and extend for another six months the income tax surcharge at one-half the present rate. To fail to take these steps would be an abdication by Congress of its vital role in controlling inflation.

Revenue reform. For the first time in the history of this government, we have recommended a national policy of permanent sharing of the Federal income tax revenues with the States and lesser political units in the country. For years, political students and leaders have contended that governments at the State, county and local levels have lost their creativity and lost the capacity to respond because they lack access to the great source of growing revenues available to the Federal government. I have recommended that Congress set aside a rising portion of Federal revenues each year and transmit them directly back to the States and communities to spend as they see fit and not as Washington sees fit. This concept has been debated by both parties and recommended by their majorities for years. The time has come to move it off the plane of discussion to make it a reality. I urge the Congress to move.

Postal reform. For more than a decade the American people have complained increasingly of the rising cost of postal service accompanied step by step with declining service. Today the United States postal system is inferior to that of many countries of Western Europe; it is grossly inadequate to the needs of our society. The nation has known this for years. I have acted in that knowledge—recommending that the existing postal system be scrapped, that a government-owned corporation replace the United States Post Office, that business principles replace partisanship in its management, and that merit and performance—rather than political affiliation—be the new criteria for appointment and advancement. Three years ago this month the Chicago postal system, a microcosm of the national system, collapsed under a flood of mail. The rapid delivery of mail is not a partisan issue. Distinguished leaders, of both parties, have endorsed the precise reform I have recommended. There is no reason why the Congress cannot enact the most complete reform of the United States Post Office in the nation's history—by the close of this session.

I am aware of the setback which postal reform sustained in a House Committee on October 8. That action must be reversed. I shall persist in behalf of both the taxpayers and the mail users in this country to press for this urgently needed reform. I still believe enactment should come by the end of this session of the Ninety-First Congress.

Here I must again urge responsible Congressional action, and promptly, on the proposed increase in postal rates for all three classes of mail. When this Administration entered office in January, it confronted a deficit in the postal budget for fiscal year 1970 of more than $1.2 billion. We are already three months into that fiscal year—and this deficit is being underwritten by the taxpayers, rather than the users of the postal service, who should rightly bear the cost. I recognize that such a measure is hardly a political delight. Yet it is required in the interest of equity and fiscal integrity. I request the Congress to face up to this task.

Manpower reform. The history of the

1960s chronicles an intense political debate that has resulted in the old centralism of the thirties losing converts to the new federalism of the seventies. More and more progressive men in both parties have become convinced from the failures of programs run from Washington that important areas of government decision-making must be returned to the regions and locales where the problems exist.

I have attempted to take that conclusion out of the forum of debate and into the arena of action—Congress. I have recommended that management of a Federal program—the multi-billion dollar manpower training program—be consolidated, and turned over in a three-stage operation to the States and communities to run in a way that fits the needs of the immediate areas involved. No reform of this magnitude has been attempted since centralism became the dominant national trend at the depths of the depression. This recommendation represents the beginning of a revitalized federalism, the gradual transfer of greater power and responsibility for the making of government decisions to governments closest to the people. I urge swift Congressional action.

Social security reform. I have requested an across-the-board increase of ten percent in Social Security benefits to compensate elderly Americans for the losses they are suffering because of an inflation they could do nothing either to prevent or avoid. In addition, I have proposed a new reform, an escalator in Social Security to insure that benefits will rise correspondingly whenever the cost of living goes up. When this reform is enacted, never again will those Americans least able to afford it be made to bear the brunt of inflation.

791

These necessary steps can and should be taken by Congress before the end of this year.

One word of caution. I know the political temptations here. Why not balloon the benefits now, far above 10 percent, for political rewards in 1970? I remind the Congress that it is long since time that we stopped the political over-reactions which fuel the inflation that robs the poor, the elderly, and those on fixed incomes. I urge Congress to hold to this 10 percent figure—and let the new escalator protect older Americans against the possibility of future inflation.

A second reform I have proposed is to alter the system of social security to encourage and reward the workers who want to go on working past age 65—rather than discourage them. I ask Congress to enact this measure without delay.

Reform of the grant-in-aid system. Among the first major pieces of legislation I asked of Congress was authority to make uniform the requirements for participation in many grant-in-aid programs that have proliferated in the last five years. If we are granted the power to draw these programs together, to group them by function—setting far more simple regulations—then States and communities will participate more and Congress' original purposes will be better served. We need that authority *now.* I know of no reason for delay.

Electoral reform. While I originally favored other methods of reforming the electoral college system, I have strongly endorsed the direct popular election plan approved by the House. I hope the Senate will concur so that final favorable action can be completed before the end of this session. This must be done if we are to have this needed reform amended to the Constitution in time for the presidential election of 1972.

D.C. Government reform. For years there has been broad support for granting the people of Washington, D.C., the same right to Congressional representation other Americans have always prized, and the right to conduct their public business themselves. The Federal city has been a federal colony far too long. Months ago I presented to Congress a program to bring about the orderly transfer of political power to the people of this community. I recommended a constitutional amendment giving the District of Columbia at least one representative in the House and such additional representatives as Congress may approve, and providing for the possibility of two United States Senators. I urged Congress further to grant the city one non-voting Congressional representative in the interim, and recommended creation of a commission to prepare and present to Congress and the President a program to improve the efficiency and competence of the District Government—looking to the day of complete self-government. Favorable action has been taken by the Senate. I ask that this work be completed before the end of the year.

OEO reform. I have provided the Office of Economic Opportunity with a new director, a new structure, and added responsibilities as the research and development arm of the nation's effort to deal with the problems of the poor. OEO is now strengthening its present operating programs, including the Community Action Agencies, VISTA, Legal Services, Neighborhood Health Centers, Family Planning, Emergency Food, Rural, Older Persons, Indian and Migrant Programs. In addition, there is new emphasis on research, the evaluation of existing Federal social programs, and developing and testing new approaches in community and economic development, manpower and education, to assist the poor to move into the economic life of the nation. I have asked for a two-year extension of the existing legislation, without crippling amendments. I believe that a reformed OEO has a major and continuing role to play in our national life. Here again, there is no need or justification for further delay.

In recent years the Federal Government has suffered a precipitous decline in public confidence. The reason can be found in the chronic gap that exists between the publicity and promise attendant to the launching of a new Federal program—and that program's eventual performance. If confidence in government is to be restored, the gap must be closed.

This is the purpose of the foregoing proposals and great goal of this Administration—not to establish some new arithmetical record for the number of programs proposed, but to do more than other Administrations have done—to devise new approaches, to make the worthy old programs work, and to make old institutions responsive. It is for this that we prize the mechanics and engineers of government who retool and improve its machinery as much as we do the planners and the idea men who develop new programs and new agencies. There is little publicity and less glamor in the labor of the mechanics and engineers of government but, with billions in tax dollars invested in scores and scores of on-going Federal programs, the need is certainly greater. Let us together make government's performance and responsiveness more commensurate with its size.

Reform of foreign aid. Our foreign aid program, sent to Congress in May, differs from earlier programs in three significant ways. First, it would place greater emphasis on technical assistance, especially in the areas of agriculture, education and family planning, where the return would be greatest when measured in terms of national and human development. Second, the new program would create an Overseas Private Investment Corporation to provide a greater thrust for the channeling of private investment to the low-income countries. Third, it would increase the share of our assistance contributed through multilateral institutions.

I know of the economic miracles which foreign aid has helped create in Western Europe and in parts of Asia. I know also that our program is far from perfect. With this in mind, I have recently appointed a Presidential Task Force on International Development, charged with proposing new approaches to aid for the 1970s.

One fundamental question must be faced as Congress prepares to vote on this issue: will we in the United States live out our lives in comparative affluence, while denying reasonable help to those who are our neighbors in the world community and who are struggling to help themselves achieve a better life? To enable us to answer this question positively, I have requested $2.7 billion—the smallest request in the history of the U.S. aid program but an amount vitally needed to maintain our relationship with the developing world.

In addition to the reforms already cited, I have made other recommendations that call for new commitments by the Federal government, and offer more hopeful avenues of progress than the paths of the past.

Specifically, I have asked Congress to:

—establish a national computer Job

Bank, which would enable the unemployed and the employer to come together through a computer matching system. The bank would have "branches" in every major labor market in the country. No longer would men have to go without work solely because they did not know where to find jobs.

—commit this country to the most extensive improvement of the nation's air facilities in history. Under this program, the annual Federal appropriation for improving air facilities will rise from $93 million a year— the average of the last decade—to $250 million annually over the next decade. I have proposed further aid for airport development of $2.5 billion dollars in Federal funds in the next ten years to be matched dollar-for-dollar by the States and local governments. This will mean an added $5 billion in funds for airport development. It will mean a running start on the national effort to build for the doubling of airline traffic expected by 1975 and its tripling by 1980.

—commit this country to the redevelopment of the nation's deteriorating public transportation system by providing an unprecedented measure of Federal support. In the six-year period ending with fiscal 1970, some $800 million will have been authorized by Congress to aid the nation's deteriorating public transit industry. I have proposed raising that commitment to $3.1 billion over the next five years and to a total of $10 billion over the next twelve.

—enact the most extensive improvements in the Federal-State unemployment system in a decade, with coverage extended to an additional 4.8 million workers, mostly low-income, with an automatic extension of benefits to workers during times of high unemployment.

—enact the strongest mine health and safety bill in history, one which empowers the Secretary of the Interior to upgrade health and safety standards for coal mines as the technology develops.

—establish a national occupational health and safety board, with power to set standards to protect workers.

—empower the Equal Employment Opportunity Commission to bring suit in a Federal District Court to enforce federal laws against discrimination.

—ban literacy tests as a prerequisite for voting throughout the United States.

New Initiatives

The hungry. For many years, in this richest of societies, we have heard rumors of malnourished children and hungry men and women. Now we know these rumors are true. This realization has prompted us to a commitment—that we eliminate every vestige of hunger and malnutrition from America. I have asked Congress to help us assure that every American family can have a nutritionally complete diet; I have asked that the poorest members of our national community be provided with food stamps free of cost.

The Senate has shown a willingness to join in this commitment and has acted with dispatch. I urge the House to move so as not to prolong any further the day when the ancient curse of malnutrition and hunger is eliminated in this most modern of nations.

Population. There is a widely-recognized correlation between population growth and poverty in the underdeveloped nations of the world. I have asked Congress to support our endorsement of those individuals and organizations seeking voluntary answers to this global question in other lands.

To approach this question as it applies at home, I have called on Congress to create a national commission to undertake now a study of how the nation is to provide for the 100 million new Americans expected before the turn of the century.

Beyond this, I have asked that a new philosophy become American government policy. We will interfere with no American's freedom of choice; we will infringe upon no one's religious convictions; but we shall not deny to any American woman the family planning assistance she may desire but cannot afford. That is the goal I ask Congress to support.

THE CONTROL OF CRIME

There is no greater need in this free society than the restoration of the individual American's freedom from violence in his home and on the streets of his city or town. Control and reduction of crime are among the first and constant concerns of this Administration. But we can do little more unless and until Congress provides more tools to do the job. No crisis is more urgent in our society. No subject has been the matter of more legislative requests from this Administration. Yet, not a single one of our major recommendations on crime has been acted upon favorably. I have not even received yet

the budget appropriation for the Department of Justice for this fiscal year which is three months old. In light of the rising crime statistics in the country—and in the nation's capital—I again call upon Congress to become a full-fledged ally in this national campaign.

Organized crime. To intensify the national effort against organized crime, I have asked for an arsenal of new legal weapons:

—a doubling of existing resources for the organized crime effort;

—authority for Justice Department agents to enter any community and shut down large-scale gambling operations;

—a modern general witness immunity statute under which witnesses in Federal criminal cases could be compelled to testify under threat of a prison sentence for contempt;

—finally, because organized crime would shrivel up without its enormous gambling resources, and because illegal gambling on a large scale cannot go on without cooperation of corrupt law enforcement, I have asked Congress to make corruption of local authorities who are tied in with such gambling operations a Federal crime. I must stress the great urgency of these measures. Let the Congress act—*now.*

D.C. crime. To deal with the increase in crime in the District of Columbia I have asked for an expansion and strengthening of the entire system of law enforcement and criminal justice, including a fundamental reorganization of the courts. I have stressed the urgent need for more police, more judges, more prosecutors, more courtroom space, a new public defender's office, better penal and rehabilitation facilities and reform in the procedures for dealing with juvenile offenders. Crime in the District of Columbia continues to rise to new records with each month. We cannot contain or control it with existing resources; we need more men and money; we need a speedier trial system and, as important as any other measure, the power to keep hard-core criminal repeaters in the District of Columbia off the streets, so they are not committing five and six crimes before they are ever brought to trial. The Congress should act—*now.*

Narcotics. In the Federal effort against the illicit narcotics trade, I have submitted a major revision of all Federal narcotics laws and requested more men and money to deal with a problem that long ago outstripped the capacity of government at every level. Existing manpower and resources are stretched to their elastic limits—they are demonstrably inadequate. We have to have the cooperation of Congress to attack this terrible problem. Let's get at it—*now.*

Pornography. To prevent the use of the nation's postal system for the mailing of unsolicited sex-oriented materials to families that do not want the material and to children to whom it might do psychological harm, I offered three legislative pro-

posals that will protect American citizens from the barrages of the filth peddlers, and will also be consistent with the decisions of the U.S. Supreme Court interpreting the First Amendment. These bills are still in Congress. I ask that they be promptly enacted.

———————

These are among my major legislative proposals in these first nine months in office. I believe they speak directly to the needs of a nation in distress. I can see no legitimate reason why—with good will and cooperation between us—we cannot make the great majority of these urgently needed programs law before the end of the year. We should have all of them—as well as the others now pending—on the statute books well before the Ninety-First Congress enters the history books.

To that end, I again pledge the cooperation of this Administration.

RICHARD NIXON

The White House
October 13, 1969

NOTE: On October 10, 1969, the White House Press Office released the text of a news briefing on the President's message on legislative reform by Bryce N. Harlow, Assistant to the President.

387   Remarks to Members of the Advisory Council for Minority Enterprise. *October 13, 1969*

Mr. Secretary, and gentlemen:

I wish to express my appreciation to this advisory committee for taking the time to come to Washington to give us the benefit of your views and also to gather from us our views that you can take them back to the country.

In a sense, you are ambassadors from the business community to Washington, and I trust ambassadors from Washington to the business community.

I read over the list of people that are attending this meeting. And, if you will look to the right of you and look to the left of you and look around this room, there is probably gathered here as much business power and examples of successes in private enterprise as you could find in any one room in America.

This is a powerful group, a very powerful group in terms of what individuals have done to build their own businesses and thereby to contribute to the building of America.

And what we want to do is to enlist this power, this creative power that all of you have, because I know the backgrounds of so many of you—how you started with very little and then built the business enterprises which have so much. We want that creative power enlisted in a very high risk enterprise.

Now I am going to be quite blunt. You all know that any business is a risk. You all know that a small business is a much bigger risk. And it is certainly no secret that a minority small business is the biggest risk of all. This is the truth. These are what the figures show.

But all of us know that the bigger the risk is, the bigger the potential gain is, whether it is in betting on a contest— the higher the odds, if you win, the greater the gain.

That is why in this whole field of minority business enterprise, much of which will begin small but can eventually grow until it is big, you have such a challenge— a challenge that we want to work with you on. Because, while the risk is great, the risk of minority enterprise, for reasons that are no fault of the minorities, while the risk is great, the risk of small business, because small business does not have the capital that big business has, it doesn't have the talent that big business has, nevertheless, it can be done. And it will be done provided we can add this ex-

tra ingredient of the talent and the ability that is represented in this room, not only by you, individually, but by all the people in your companies.

Now, one other word: I know from looking around this room that I have seen many of you over the years who have been to meetings in Washington, D.C. You have come here for this committee and that committee and the others, and you hear a lot of fine speeches. Sometimes you go home charged up and other times you go home and say, "Was this trip necessary?" or "Was this trip worthwhile?"

I am keenly aware of that. And, I suppose, too, that at a meeting like this, the real question is, "Was it necessary? Was the trip necessary? Was the meeting necessary?" And the question also is raised, "Can we really come forth from this meeting with something new that will change America—change it for the better?"

I believe we can. I spoke to this subject quite often long before I officially became a candidate for President and throughout the campaign. I spoke to the point that it was not enough simply to see that all people in this country had an equal opportunity to get a job—and that is an enterprise that many of you as businessmen have contributed to enormously—but that it was necessary for every individual in America to be able not only to get a job, but to have a chance to become an owner or a manager, to have a piece of the action in private enterprise in this country.

And, frankly, there are a lot of people that are skeptical about that. There are a lot of people who believe that this is so long away in the future, it is so much of a dream, that the concentration should be almost exclusively on the area of jobs.

I don't think that is enough. We don't want a minority that is a class apart simply as job holders. We want a group of people who not only can be employees, but who can honestly feel that they have an equal chance to go up, to go up from that job, that employee status, to become an owner and a manager—as a matter of fact, to become what the people in this room are, people who are eminently successful.

You know you wouldn't have had the chance, those of you who came from small beginnings to the big businesses that many of you represent—you wouldn't have had it unless you had a helping hand along the way.

What we are simply saying here today is, we need your help, the Government needs your help. A lot of people who won't have that chance need your help in order to get this program moving and to provide opportunity for literally hundreds of thousands at the beginning, and we hope millions in the end, of Americans to proudly stand up and have the dignity that comes from not simply being part of an organization, being an employee, but from being an owner and a manager just as those in this room, for the most part, are.

Finally, I want you to know that I feel very deeply that the trip that you have taken to Washington is worthwhile; that as a result of the impetus you give to this program that we are going to find that there will be a new hope, a new hope in the minds and the hearts of hundreds of thousands of young people in this country who otherwise wouldn't really think they had that chance—a chance that you have had, a chance that I have had.

Now this is America at its best. It is something I believe in. It is something you believe in. It is something that your successes prove. And for that reason, I appreciate your taking the responsibility as members of this committee. It has my complete support and I know it will have yours.

Together, working together, working with all elements in the Government and all elements in the business community, we can take this very high risk enterprise and we can get one of the greatest gains that America has ever had.

Thank you.

NOTE: The President spoke at 10:21 a.m. in the Indian Treaty Room at the Executive Office Building. In his opening words he referred to Secretary of Commerce Maurice H. Stans.

388   Letter to University Student Randy J. Dicks on the "Vietnam Moratorium."   *October 13, 1969*

Dear Mr. Dicks:

In reply to your comments about my press conference remark that "under no circumstances will I be affected whatever" by the demonstrations planned for October 15, I would suggest that there are several points you should bear in mind.

First, there is a clear distinction between public opinion and public demonstrations. To listen to public opinion is one thing; to be swayed by public demonstrations is another. A demonstration—in whatever cause—is an organized expression of one particular set of opinions, which may or may not be shared by the majority of the people. If a President—any President—

allowed his course to be set by those who demonstrate, he would betray the trust of all the rest. Whatever the issue, to allow government policy to be made in the streets would destroy the democratic process. It would give the decision, not to the majority, and not to those with the strongest arguments, but to those with the loudest voices. It would reduce statecraft to slogans. It would invite anarchy. It would allow every group to test its strength not at the ballot box but through confrontation in the streets.

The planned demonstrations will tell us that a great many Americans are deeply concerned about the war; that some of these consider U.S. participation immoral; that many want U.S. troops withdrawn immediately and unconditionally. But all of us in the Administration are already well aware of this sentiment. We are already well aware that it is widespread—indeed, that no matter how many people might participate, there would be many more who share their concern.

Therefore, there is nothing new we can learn from the demonstrations. The question is whether, in the absence of any new evidence or any new arguments, we should be turned aside from a carefully considered course. The policies we are now following reflect our own best judgment, based on exhaustive study of all the available evidence, of how to achieve that goal. To abandon that policy merely because of a public demonstration would therefore be an act of gross irresponsibility on my part.

One further point: I respect the right of each American to express his own opinion. I recognize that many feel a moral obligation to express their opinions in the most conspicuous way possible, and therefore consider such expression to be

their responsibility. I respect that. However, my responsibility is different. I must consider the consequences of each proposed course of action—short-term and long-term, domestic and world-wide, direct and indirect. Others can say of Vietnam, "Get out now;" when asked how, they can give the simple, flip answer: "By sea." They can ignore the consequences. But as I consider these consequences, in both human and international terms, I can only conclude that history would rightly condemn a President who took such a course.

One of the first acts of my Administration was to review, exhaustively and comprehensively, every aspect of the nation's policies in Vietnam. We have drastically altered the policies we inherited. We are on the road to peace. That road is not easy. It is not simple. But I am convinced it is the right one. There is no problem to which I have given more of my time and thought. For nine months, we have worked every day for a just end to a conflict which has been building for more than eight years.

On October 15th, I understand, many will simply be saying: "I am for peace." I ardently join with all Americans in working toward that goal.

Sincerely,

RICHARD NIXON

[Mr. Randy J. Dicks, Georgetown University, Washington, D.C. 20007]

NOTE: Randy J. Dicks' letter, dated September 28, 1969, and released by the White House Press Office along with the President's letter on October 13, 1969, read as follows:

Dear Mr. President:

I think that your statement at your recent press conference that "under no circumstances" will you be affected by the impending antiwar protests, in connection with the "Viet Nam Moratorium," is ill-considered to say the least.

It has been my impression that it is not unwise for the President of the United States to take note of the will of the people; after all, these people elected you, you are their President, and your office bears certain obligations. Might

I respectfully suggest that the President reconsider his pre-judgment.

Yours sincerely,

RANDY J. DICKS

[The President, the White House, Washington, D.C.]

389 Message to the Senate Transmitting the Estate Tax Convention Between the United States and the Netherlands. *October 13, 1969*

To the Senate of the United States:

With a view to receiving the advice and consent of the Senate to ratification, I transmit herewith the convention between the United States of America and the Kingdom of the Netherlands for the avoidance of double taxation and the prevention of fiscal evasion with respect to taxes on estates and inheritances, signed at Washington on July 15, 1969, and the related protocol signed on the same date.

I transmit also, for the information of the Senate, the report of the Secretary of State with respect to the convention and protocol.

The purposes of this convention are the same as those of the twelve other estate tax conventions now in force between the United States and other countries, namely, to minimize the burdens of double taxation at death and to prevent fiscal evasion with respect to taxes on estates and inheritances. In accomplishing these purposes, the convention departs from the pattern of our existing estate tax conventions in order (a) to take into account problems which employees of international businesses assigned to foreign countries have encountered under previous conventions, (b) to follow the direction indicated by the Foreign Investors Tax Act of 1966 in

assisting our balance of payments by minimizing deterrents to foreign investment in the United States, and (c) to conform to the extent practicable with the provisions of the Draft Double Taxation Convention on Estates and Inheritances published in 1966 by the Organization for Economic Cooperation and Development.

The convention contains four principal innovations:

1. The seven year domiciliary rule, whereby a decedent who is considered by each country as having been domiciled therein at death will generally be deemed to have been domiciled only in the country of which he was a citizen if he had been resident in the other country for less than seven years without the intent to remain there indefinitely.

2. As a corollary of the seven year domiciliary rule, the convention provides that if a citizen of one country was resident in the other country seven or more years, the country of citizenship grants a credit for the death taxes of the other country. In these cases, jurisdiction to tax real property and business assets will be retained by the country in which such property is situated, with the other country providing appropriate credits.

3. The convention exempts tangible and

intangible personal property (to the extent such property is not a business asset of a permanent establishment) from taxation by either country if the decedent is neither a domiciliary nor a citizen of such country. This exemption complements on a bilateral basis the liberalized treatment afforded foreign investors in the United States by the Foreign Investors Tax Act of 1966, aids our balance of payments by removing deterrents to investments in the United States, and reduces estate tax formalities for Dutch investors in the United States.

4. Under the convention, the Netherlands provides treatment analogous to the relatively liberal United States exemptions which the Federal estate tax law grants to estates of foreigners, by granting Americans who are not residents of the Netherlands (and who are taxable only on real estates and business assets situated in the Netherlands) an exemption for small estates and an exemption which cor-

responds to our marital deduction.

The related protocol, containing ten numbered paragraphs, sets forth understandings concerning certain matters of interpretation and application of the convention.

The convention and protocol have the approval of the Department of State and the Department of the Treasury. The Treasury will provide a detailed technical explanation of the convention at the time of the hearings before the Senate Foreign Relations Committee.

I recommend that the Senate give early and favorable consideration to the convention and protocol with the Netherlands.

RICHARD NIXON

The White House
    October 13, 1969

NOTE: The texts of the convention, protocol, and report of the Secretary of State are printed in Senate Executive G (91st Cong., 1st sess.).

390   Remarks at a Ceremony Commemorating the Establishment of the People-to-People Program. *October 14, 1969*

I WOULD LIKE to be permitted just a personal word as I stand here with Mrs. Eisenhower on this occasion of the General's birthday.

I think back to those days in this house when she, as the First Lady, presided with such dignity and such great credit to America and to the world. I think, too, of General Eisenhower and particularly of those last days. Last days can be sad days, but I think Mrs. Eisenhower would agree they were great days—great days because the General, to the very last, spoke of his family. He spoke of his country, and he

spoke of those causes that were very, very close to his heart.

I remember asking him shortly before he died, as he looked back over almost 60 years of public service, what he really rated the highest—and what a choice he had: commander of the armies that brought victory in World War II against aggression that would have otherwise swept Europe and possibly the world; President of the United States in which he brought peace to the Nation and kept the peace for 8 years; and then a distinguished career after he left the Presidency, in which he continued to give leadership on the highest ideological plane to the people of this Nation and to the people of the world.

It was interesting to note that the President often told me that among his activities that had not received as much publicity, of course, as the crusade in Europe and the Presidency and the end of the war in Korea, was the People-to-People program.

Six times after I left the Vice Presidency and before I came to this house in January of this year, I took trips around the world. Mrs. Eisenhower remembered that all six times I came to call on General Eisenhower, sometimes in California, and sometimes in Gettysburg, to get his advice about the affairs of the world and matters that I might discuss when I was abroad. He never failed to mention the fact that he had a tremendous interest in the People-to-People program, in the Eisenhower Fellows, another program that I might see abroad.

To show you the immense impact that one part of the whole People-to-People program can have, I recall one country I visited on one trip. There were six members of a cabinet in that country who had been Eisenhower Fellows. They started as young people in the People-to-People program and in a young country they moved up.

I think that if General Eisenhower were to look back on those great years of his service to the Nation he would put very high on the list People-to-People; and he would urge all of his friends to support it—support it because it is truly one of those paths to peace that we must explore and that we must expand—expand it not only among peoples who are allies and friends, but expand it between those areas

of the world that potentially might be enemies but that should be friends, whose peoples certainly should be friends.

That is why in this administration we strongly support not only the People-to-People program as it presently exists, but we hope that it can be expanded more and more to an exchange between the United States and the Soviet Union, between the United States and other Eastern European countries, and, eventually, we would hope, also between the United States and that great potential power of people that exists in mainland China.

All of these things are our goals, and all of these things will happen. They will happen in our time.

I would like to add just one other word with regard to the conversation with the General that I am sure Mrs. Eisenhower has often recalled because he has spoken to me as well as to others in these terms.

He had a very friendly smile. When General Eisenhower walked into a room, he just lit it up when he smiled. We all remember that.

But beneath that friendly smile all of us who knew him know that there was a very hard intelligence which knew the costs of war and also knew the costs of maintaining a peace.

Because he knew that balance, because he knew what war was and, knowing what it was, hated it so much, he was able to provide leadership that ended a war and kept the peace.

That, of course, is the responsibility we have today.

But this is what I particularly remember that he said. In his last days, particularly, he talked about history—the history of this Nation, the history of the world. And as he talked about history, he made what I thought was a very simple but a very profound comment about the United States of America in this century.

He said: "The debate in the United States of America in this century has never been about whether we should have war. The debate in the United States of America has always been about how we can achieve peace." Putting it more simply: "The debate," as he put it, "was never between people who wanted war and those who wanted peace, it was always between Americans deeply devoted to keeping the peace, maintaining the peace."

Yet, we have had four wars in this century.

And he responded to a question as to how he could justify the fact that that was an historical occurrence with his statement that "Americans were always debating about peace rather than war." He said: "In World War I, President Wilson said it was a war to end wars. We went to Europe for the cause of peace. In World War II, President Roosevelt said the American frontier is on the Rhine, and we went to Europe because we wanted peace and we knew that it was necessary to stop aggression if we were to have peace. In the Korean war, the question was not any desire on the part of the United States to wage war but to defend the cause of peace, the right to exist of a nation that was living in peace and whose identity and existence was threatened by those who were bent on war."

And so it is also in Vietnam. There is debate about this war. But let us understand that the debate is not about any desire of the American people for war. The debate is about peace—how to achieve it, how best to achieve it.

Honest men and honest women can disagree about those means, but let the world understand: The American people want peace. We believe in peace. We have fought our wars in this century because we wanted peace. And we want to bring the war in Vietnam to an end in a way that will promote not a temporary but a lasting peace.

I think I have spoken or paraphrased what General Eisenhower said to many visitors in those last days before he died.

Finally, may I say that with regard to the People-to-People program, sometimes I suppose those little things you do—receiving a foreign student, spending some time with some individual who may come in from a foreign country—seems rather inconsequential when you weigh it against the great decisions that have to be made in the Congress or in the State Department or in the White House.

But looking far down that road, down that road to the end of this century when, I am confident, we will have a world of peace, we must remember: Those young people you talk to today from foreign lands will be the leaders of those lands tomorrow. And the fact that they have been here, the fact that they know from visiting our homes and our offices that Americans are a people dedicated to peace—this fact will make them leaders in the cause of peace just as the American people, I know in the future, will always be dedicated to the cause of peace.

Thank you.

NOTE: The President, honorary chairman of the People-to-People program, spoke at 11:16 a.m. in the East Room at the White House. The ceremony was held on the 79th birthday of the late President Dwight David Eisenhower, who created and founded the program in 1956.

Prior to his remarks, the President presented Eisenhower People-to-People awards to Ambassador George V. Allen, chairman of the People-to-People Board of Trustees; Dr. Frank

H. Krusen, chairman of the People-to-People Committee for the Handicapped; and to Apollo 11 Commander Neil A. Armstrong. Commander Armstrong was on a good will tour with his fellow Apollo 11 astronauts. His award was accepted by Willis H. Shapley, Associate Deputy Administrator of the National Aeronautics and Space Administration.

The People-to-People program is a nonprofit, nongovernmental organization dedicated to promoting world peace through international educational and cultural exchange programs.

The Eisenhower Exchange Fellowship, awarded yearly to potential leaders from free nations and to Americans to go abroad, was established in 1953.

391 Letter to House Minority Leader Gerald R. Ford on a Proposed Federal Pay Raise. *October 14, 1969*

Dear Jerry:

I must frankly advise that our critically important national effort to contain inflation is bound to be seriously undercut if the federal employee pay bill now before the House were to become law.

In its present form H.R. 13000 would add approximately $4.3 billion a year to federal expenditures. It would balloon expenditures in the remainder of this fiscal year by $1.5 billion.

Spending increases of this magnitude cannot avoid nullifying many of the steps we have recently taken to stabilize the economy.

Less than three months ago, the Congress reflected the nation's determination to control inflation by imposing an expenditure ceiling for the current fiscal year. I gave a commitment at that time to restrict expenditures for this fiscal year to $192.9 billion. In keeping with this limitation I am cutting federal expenditures for this year by an additional $3.5 billion. But if H.R. 13000 should become law, additional deep cuts in federal services would have to be made.

The increase which the Post Office Department alone must absorb, for example, would require cut-backs in a variety of

services. They would include the elimination of Saturday deliveries and window service for rural, city and suburban areas alike.

Since our total expenditures must be limited, a new round of heavy pay increases for federal employees would be in effect a mandate to reduce, abruptly, the number of federal employees.

The national interest clearly requires reconsideration of H.R. 13000 because of its inflationary impact. Furthermore, it would grant disproportionate benefits to postal employees. These increases should be reexamined in light of another major legislative proposal now before Congress. Improvements in the condition of the postal worker are long overdue, but they ought to be secured through total reform of the present outmoded, inefficient and costly postal system.

The postal reform I have urged provides for the setting of wage levels for postal employees through collective bargaining. Any major increase in postal worker benefits should be secured through this process, or as part of legislation establishing a government-owned postal corporation which will have the means of operating, ultimately, on a self-sustaining basis.

I solicit your personal leadership in urging the House to recognize that, however appealing H.R. 13000 may appear politically at this moment, the consequences of its enactment would surely generate strong resentments throughout the public far outweighing presently anticipated political gains.

Sincerely,

RICHARD NIXON

[Honorable Gerald R. Ford, House of Representatives, Washington, D.C. 20515]

NOTE: The letter was dated October 13, 1969 and released October 14, 1969.

392 Statement About Cleaner Air Week. *October 14, 1969*

WITH the growth of our cities, the expansion of industry, and the increasing use of automobiles, the problem of air pollution becomes more critical each year. It is not only in our large urban areas that polluted air damages property and endangers health. Its impact is felt in many smaller agricultural and recreational areas where it damages farm crops, timber, and plants of all kinds.

To deal effectively with the threat of polluted air to our environment and lives, we must first apply the fullness of existing control technology to the sources of pollution. And second, we must seek new solutions to those technical difficulties which still stand in the way of adequate control.

In the Clean Air Act, we have a mechanism to translate our scientific and technical knowledge into responsible social and political action. Under this act, both government and business have an unprecedented opportunity to cooperate in the fight against air pollution for the benefit of all Americans.

However, no legislation can accomplish its expressed purpose without the fullest support of the people. Cleaner Air Week serves to remind individual citizens of the responsibilities they must meet if we are to decontaminate the air we breathe. I commend the Air Pollution Control Association on its sponsorship of this annual call for a stronger civic commitment to purifying our air and prolonging our lives.

NOTE: Cleaner Air Week was observed October 19–25, 1969.

393 Message to the Senate Transmitting an Agreement Between the United States and Canada on Flood Control Payments. *October 14, 1969*

To the Senate of the United States:

With a view to receiving the approval of the Senate, I transmit herewith the texts of two notes, signed at Washington and dated August 18 and 20, 1969, constituting an agreement between the Government of the United States of America and the Government of Canada concerning adjustments in the flood control payments by the United States Government to the Canadian Government as a result of early completion of projects (Arrow Dam and Duncan Dam) contemplated by Article II(2) (b) and (c) of the Columbia River Treaty.

It is provided in the agreement that it will enter into force upon notification by the United States Government to the Canadian Government that all internal measures necessary to give effect to the agreement for the United States have been completed.

Pursuant to the treaty relating to cooperative development of the water resources of the Columbia River basin signed at Washington on January 17, 1961, Canada constructed the Duncan Dam and the Arrow Dam in British Columbia. The treaty provides that the United States shall pay to Canada specified sums with respect to each of the dams for the flood control benefits. The sums specified were based on a period of 55 years of flood control benefits, and it was expected that the projects would be completed subsequent to the spring of 1969. The dams actually commenced operation well in advance of the expected dates, so that the United States has received additional benefits for two years in the case of Duncan Dam and one year in the case of Arrow Dam.

The treaty provides that the United States would pay less if full operation of the storage were not commenced within the time specified, but does not provide for additional payments if such operation were commenced prior to the time specified. By an exchange of notes dated January 22, 1964, prior to the entry into force of the treaty, the two Governments agreed to consult with a view to adjustments in the payments if there should be an early completion of the dams. The agreement transmitted herewith has resulted from such consultation. It provides for a payment to Canada of a total of $278,000 for the additional flood control benefits resulting from early completion of Duncan Dam and Arrow Dam.

The treaty of 1961 does not without modification provide a basis for authorizing the additional payments. It is desirable, therefore, that in effect the treaty provisions be modified so that there may be an adequate legal basis for an authorization for appropriations. The notes of August 18 and 20, 1969 have been exchanged for this purpose.

I also transmit for the information of the Senate a report by the Secretary of State relating to the agreement effected by that exchange of notes.

I urge that the Senate give early and favorable consideration to the agreement concerning adjustments in the flood control payments by the United States Government to the Canadian Government.

RICHARD NIXON

The White House
October 14, 1969

NOTE: The treaty was favorably considered by the Senate on November 10, 1969. The President signed the Instrument of Ratification on December 2, 1969. The treaty is printed in Senate Executive H (91st Cong., 1st sess.), which also includes the texts of the exchange of notes and the report of the Secretary of State.

394   Statement Announcing the Nomination of Dr. Arthur
        F. Burns as a Member of the Board of Governors,
        Federal Reserve System.   *October* 17, 1969

A PRESIDENT makes many important appointments during his term in office, but few are as important as the nomination I am announcing today. For the Chairman of the Board of Governors of the Federal Reserve System has an exceptionally significant influence upon the economic policies of the Government and the economic health of the Nation.

The term of the present Chairman, William McChesney Martin, Jr., will expire on January 31, 1970; the law stipulates that a member cannot be reappointed to the Board after serving the standard 14-year term. It is my judgment that the vacancy which will therefore occur on the Board at the end of next January should be filled by Dr. Arthur F. Burns. I will submit Dr. Burns' name to the Senate in the near future. When he is confirmed as a member of the Board, I will then designate him as Chairman—a designation which the President must make every 4 years.

Chairman Martin has headed the Federal Reserve Board with great distinction for more than 18 years, since April of 1951. During that time the Nation has had five Presidents, seven Secretaries of the Treasury, and seven Chairmen of the Council of Economic Advisers. It is difficult to think of any economic policymaker in this country, since the time of Alexander Hamilton, whose influence has been as considerable as Chairman Martin's over such an extended period of time.

As Chairman Martin's term of office comes to an end, a grateful Nation salutes him for the energy, the dedication, and the skill with which he has performed his important work. His tenure has coincided with an era of unsurpassed prosperity and economic growth.

The Nation is fortunate that a man of Dr. Burns' ability and experience stands ready to take on the Chairmanship of the Federal Reserve Board. One of the Nation's outstanding economic scholars, Dr. Burns has been a frequent adviser to the Federal Government on a broad range of economic and social questions. He performed distinguished service as Chairman of the Council of Economic Advisers during the Eisenhower administration and headed the National Bureau of Economic Research for many years. I have found him to be an invaluable adviser in his position as Counsellor to the President since last January.

Although Chairman Martin's term will extend for more than 3 additional months, I am announcing Dr. Burns' nomination at this time for two reasons. First, it will make possible a smooth and orderly transition as the responsibilities of the Chairmanship change hands for the first time in 18 years. Secondly, I believe that it will be helpful if the identity of the new Chairman is not a subject of widespread speculation during the intervening months.

Dr. Burns has been known for many years as a strong and effective leader in the fight against both inflation and recession. I know that under his leadership, the Federal Reserve Board will continue to work effectively for a stable and prosperous economy.

NOTE: Dr. Burns' nomination was confirmed by the Senate on December 18, 1969.

A release announcing the nomination of Dr. Burns and giving biographical information is printed in the Weekly Compilation of Presidential Documents (vol. 5, p. 1425).

395 Address to the Nation on the Rising Cost of Living. *October 17, 1969*

Good afternoon, my fellow Americans:

Today I would like to share my thoughts with you about a problem that worries millions of Americans—high prices that just keep getting higher.

All across this land, hard working men and women look at paychecks that say they have had a raise. But they wonder why those bigger checks just don't buy any more than their lower paychecks bought 4 years ago.

All across this land, men and women in their retirement, who depend on insurance and on social security and on their life savings, look at their monthly checks and wonder why they just can't seem to make ends meet anymore.

And all across this land, housewives wonder why they have to pay 66 cents a pound, and in some areas much more, for hamburger that cost 53 cents 4 years ago; people who are ill want to know why in those 4 years the cost of 1 day in a hospital has gone from $27 to $48; children who pay a nickel for a candy bar want to know why that bar is only half as big as it used to be.

When it comes to rising prices, it seems to most people that there is no end in sight. Many Americans are upset and many are even angry about this, and they have a right to be, because the ever-rising cost of food and clothing and rent robs them of their savings, cheats them of the vacations and those necessary extras that they thought they had been working for.

Now, why does everything cost so much? And what can we do to hold down the upward climb of prices?

For 5 long years, you have heard politicians and economists denouncing "the high cost of living." Back in 1966 and '67, when prices rose by 3 percent a year, everyone said how bad that was; and then in 1968, when prices speeded up by 4 percent, everyone agreed something ought to be done; and now, when momentum has carried the rise to nearly 6 percent, the same heads are shaking.

You might begin to wonder: If a rising cost of living has so many enemies, why has it been allowed to grow so fast? For years, in political speeches, the high cost of living has been as safe to denounce as the maneating shark; but after the speeches were over, nobody seemed to do anything about it.

Now, there was a very simple reason why your cost of living got out of hand: The blame for the spiral of wages and prices falls fundamentally on the past policies of your Government.

The Federal Government spent a lot more than it raised in taxes. Some of that spending was on the war in Vietnam, some of the spending was on new social programs, but the total spending was very heavy.

Now we are paying for all that red ink, not only in higher taxes, but in higher prices for everything you buy. To put it bluntly, the frequent failure to balance the Federal budget over the past 5 years has been the primary cause for unbalancing the family budgets of millions of Americans.

Today I want to tell you what we have been doing to make it easier for you to balance your family budget. I want you to know what results we are beginning to see, to understand the meaning of the news about the economy you will be reading in the coming months. And finally, I want to suggest what the American people—what you—can do together to hold down the cost of living.

When this administration took office 9 months ago, we decided that we were going to stop talking about higher prices and we were going to start doing something about them. We knew that some sophisticated investors could make out fairly well in a time of skyrocketing prices, but that the average family bore the brunt of the high cost of living, and the family on a fixed income was being driven right up the wall.

And so, to meet the real needs of most Americans, we began a steady effort to take the upward pressure off your cost of living.

Now, of course, there was a faster way available to bring prices down; many people suggested that we slam on the brakes hard and fast, and bring about a recession. But that kind of shock treatment is harsh and unnecessary; we want to level things off, not shake them up and down.

Step by step we took those measures

necessary to get our Nation's house in order.

Step one was to cut Federal spending, which more than anything else was pushing your prices up. We cut proposed Federal spending by more than $7 billion. We have taken it out of defense, we are cutting back on construction, we are squeezing it out of many other departmental budgets.

Now, we have been selective in these cuts, recognizing urgent national and social needs, but hardly anything has escaped some reduction. One area that was not cut, and I am sure you will agree with this decision, was the Department of Justice, which has fallen far behind in the war against crime—a war we are determined to win.

Next, working with the Congress, we proposed to phase out the tax surcharge over the course of a year. We could not afford to let the surtax lapse in the middle of 1969, because that would have driven up the prices you pay for everything.

And, also, we have supported our central banking system in its policy of keeping money hard to borrow. When too much money is borrowed, this money is simply used to bid prices up higher.

Now, let's face it: Holding down Government spending and holding up the tax rate and making it harder for people to get credit, is not the kind of policy that makes friends for people in politics. We have asked the American people to take some bitter medicine. We believe that the American people are mature enough to understand the need for it.

Well, here we are, 9 months later, and I can report to you that the medicine has begun to work. There will be no overnight cure, but we are on the road to recovery from the disease of runaway prices.

Now, let me be careful not to mislead anyone: Prices are still going up. They may continue to do so for a while; a 5 year momentum is not easy to stop. But now prices are no longer increasing faster and faster. The increases not only have slackened but the rates of increase are actually down. Without shock treatment, we are curing the causes of the rising cost of living.

For some time to come, you will be reading about how some business is not doing very well. Sales may be sluggish in department stores; new housing, which this Nation needs, has declined; the production of our industry has edged down for the first time in a year.

Now ordinarily, this is bad news. But today, these declines are evidence that our policy of curbing the rising cost of living is beginning to take hold.

We must be realistic. As we gently, but firmly, apply the brakes, we are going to experience some "slowing pains." Just like growing pains, these are a healthy development; but they are painful, nevertheless.

My point very simply is this: We have undertaken a policy that is slowing down the rise in prices. Unfortunately, some industries, some individuals will feel this necessary adjustment more directly than others. But difficult though it may be, and unpopular though it may become when the water gets a bit choppier, by curbing inflation, we do what is best for all the American people.

Just as we must be realistic, we must be compassionate; we must keep a close watch on the rate of unemployment. Now, there are some who say that a high rate of unemployment can't be avoided.

I don't agree. In our leveling-off process, we intend to do everything we can to resist increases in unemployment, to help train and place workers in new jobs, to cushion the effects of readjustment.

For example, we have overhauled and modernized our job training programs. We have proposed reforms extending unemployment insurance to millions not now covered, with higher benefits paid over longer periods to those in the system. We have proposed a computer job bank to match workers with hundreds of thousands of vacant jobs which exist all over this country.

The Nation must dedicate itself to the ideal of helping every man who is looking for a job to find a job. Today, about 96 percent of the work force is employed. We want it to be more. But we cannot effectively and fairly make it more by ignoring the widespread hardship that a runaway cost of living imposes on so many Americans.

Now that we have begun to detect the signs of success in slowing down, what can you expect your Government to do next?

Well first, let me tell you what we are not going to do. We are not going to change our game plan at the end of the first quarter of the game, particularly at a time that we feel that we are ahead. We are not going to turn away from treating basic causes to start treating symptoms alone.

In other words, we are not considering wage or price controls. My own first job in Government was with the old Office of Price Administration at the beginning of World War II. And from personal experience, let me just say this: Wage and price controls are bad for business, bad for the workingman, and bad for the consumer. Rationing, black markets, regimentation—that is the wrong road for America, and I will not take the Nation down that road.

Nor are we considering putting the Government into the business of telling the workingman how much he should charge for his services or how much the businessman should charge for his goods. Those are called "guidelines." They collapsed back in 1966 because they failed to get to the root of the problem.

What we are going to do is based on total realism.

This weekend, I am sending a letter to a cross section of leaders in labor and business across America calling their attention to the latest facts of economic life.

I am asking them to take a hard look at what Government has done in these 9 months—not just our words but our deeds. And I am asking them to make their own future plans on the basis of working and selling in a country that is not fooling about slowing down the rise in the cost of living.

Instead of relying on our jawbone, we have put some backbone in Government's determination to hold the line for the consumer. We are going to continue to exercise that backbone in the face of criticism by a lot of powerful special interests. You can rely on that. And, most important, you can make your plans on the basis that price rises are going to be slowed down.

As workingmen and businessmen get that message—as they see that Government is willing to live up to its responsibilities for doing what is needed to do to hold down prices—we can expect to see a new responsibility in the decisions of labor and management. By responding to the changed conditions, they will be following their self-interest and helping the national interest as well.

Today, I have laid out our strategy to take the pressure off the prices you pay. There is a good reason for spelling out the strategy right now, at the beginning of a turning point in the struggle. Because you see, there is a secret weapon that we intend to use in the battle against rising prices. That secret weapon is the confidence of the American people.

In recent years, that confidence in our ability to slow down the upward spiral has been missing. More and more, a paralyzing fatalism has crept into our view of prices. Too many of us have made the mistake of accepting ever-higher prices as inevitable, and, as a result, we have planned on higher and higher prices. And what we expected—we got.

Only our secret weapon of American confidence in ourselves will get us out of that vicious circle.

More than a generation ago, in the depths of the depression, an American President told you—over this medium of radio—that the only thing we had to fear was fear itself.

Today, in a prosperity endangered by a speedup of prices, the only thing we have to fear is fatalism, that destructive habit of shrugging our shoulders and resigning ourselves to a hopeless future on a wage-price treadmill.

I say to my fellow Americans today: The runaway cost of living is not a cross we are obliged to bear. It can be brought under control. It is being slowed by firm and steady action that deals with its root causes.

And as you plan for your own future on the assumption that the rise in prices will indeed slow down, you will be bringing our secret weapon into play. Your confidence in the strength of our economy, your confidence in the determination of America to win this battle, that is what will turn the tide.

On that note of confidence, let me issue this call:

I call upon the Congress to extend the surtax at half rate, 5 percent, from January 1 to June 30 of next year. Also I call upon the Congress, when it passes tax reform legislation, which I have recommended, which is greatly needed, that it do so in a way that we not have a net tax reduction of a size that will help push up prices that the consumer has to pay.

I call upon Americans to urge their Congressmen to pass those measures of manpower training and unemployment insurance that I have proposed, measures that would help make it easier for people to adjust to change.

And I call for your support in our policy of holding down Federal spending so that we are able to continue setting an example with a responsible budget for the next year, fiscal 1971.

I call upon the American people to urge their State and local governments to cooperate in postponing spending that can appropriately be delayed.

I call upon labor's leadership and labor's rank and file to base their wage demands on the new prospect of a return toward price stability.

I call upon businessmen to base their investment and price decisions on that new economic climate, keeping in mind it is in their private interest to be realistic in their planning and to help build a strong economy.

I call upon all Americans to bear the burden of restraint in their personal credit and purchasing decisions, so as to reduce the pressures that help drive prices out of sight.

I am convinced that Americans will answer this call.

I am convinced that a new confidence will be felt in this country when we match the strength of our resources with the strength of our resolution.

The dollar you earn should be worth a dollar. The dollar you save should stay worth a dollar. This is no impossible dream; this is something you are entitled to.

The cost of living affects the quality of life. Together we are going to improve the quality of life, and together, we are going to succeed in slowing down the rise in your cost of living.

NOTE: The President spoke at 4 p.m. in his office at the White House. His address was broadcast on radio.

On October 16, 1969, the White House Press Office released the text of a news briefing on inflation and the national economy by Dr. Paul W. McCracken, Chairman, Council of Economic Advisers, and Dr. Arthur F. Burns, Counsellor to the President.

An advance text of the President's address was also released by the White House on October 17, 1969.

396 Letter to Business and Labor Leaders on the Rising Cost of Living. *October 18, 1969*

IN VIEW of the growing concern about the rising cost of living, I would like to share with you at some length my thoughts about what is being done and what we must do to curb inflation.

The danger of inflation is real; the cure requires some unpleasant medicine, patience on the part of all and self-discipline by the government, business and labor.

This Administration is determined to control inflation without imposing controls upon the economy.

Four great forces make up the free market: government, business, labor and the consumer. A government that tolerated huge budget deficits could not fairly heap the blame for the ravages of inflation onto any of the other market forces. It was past government policy that caused our present inflation.

That is why I have refused to look for a scapegoat amid the genuine national concern about the rising cost of living.

That is why I have insisted government put its own economic house in order before enlisting other forces in the fight against inflation.

Hard decisions had to be made to extend the surtax; to slash Federal spending by more than seven billion dollars a year; to drastically curtail construction commitments by the Federal government; to place a strong budget surplus in tandem with a restrictive monetary policy. Economic policy needed backbone rather than jawbone, and backbone is exactly what our record shows.

We have taken the unpopular road to earn back government's credibility in fiscal affairs, and by our actions we have shown that we mean what we say about cooling inflation.

Because of this record, everyone should realize that government will continue to do whatever is necessary in the future to curb the rising cost of living.

Because government's house is now in order, we can turn to business and labor to remind them that inflation is everybody's problem and fighting inflation is everybody's business.

It is in the interest of private business to consider pricing policies in the light of government's determination to check inflation. The business that commits errors in pricing on the up side, expecting to be bailed out by inflation, is going to find itself in a poor competitive position. Betting on ever-higher prices is a sure way of losing.

It is in the interest of every union leader and workingman to avoid wage demands that will reduce the purchasing power of his dollar and reduce the number of job opportunities.

Government has set the example of restraint, and will continue to set that example. When we combine labor restraint and business restraint, we can build a foundation for an on-going prosperity.

In curbing inflation, we must continue to move deliberately, with a careful eye on the unemployment picture. The percentage of our work force unemployed is more than a statistic—it is a human condition that deserves the close attention of every American.

New laws and new restrictions are not required, if we treat with respect the law of supply and demand. Government's recent action in the construction industry, to increase the supply of skilled labor and materials so as to curb the excessive expansion of demand, is a case in point.

Because we add no artificial controls does not mean that there are no controls in operation. The free market has its own controls on those who flout responsibility: loss of profits to the businessman, loss of jobs to the workingman. These are losses that responsible action can avert.

A sense of responsibility must be part of every prudent judgment concerning prices and wages, now that government has repudiated the previous inflationary policies. Price and wage decisions that anticipate inflation's continuing at or near present levels would be shortsighted, imprudent, and unprofitable.

For your own planning, the policy of this Administration in the fight against inflation will be:

First, to continue stern restraints on Federal spending.

Second, to insist on a tax system that has the capacity to generate enough revenues to cover spending outlays. I shall not tolerate, for example, a tax bill that would result in an irresponsible budget.

Third, to rely strongly on the forces of reason and moderation within the private economy, so that governmental intervention will rarely be necessary.

The ultimate consequences of runaway inflation—the bust that follows, with the suffering that accompanies huge unemployment—must never again be inflicted upon the American people. Instead, we will take every measure necessary to build a sound prosperity, temporarily unpopular as some restraints may be.

I would be interested in your own views as to how the private sector and government can work together in holding down the cost of living. In this cause—hard to explain, hard to achieve, but fundamental to the economy of our nation and the progress of our people—I trust that I can count on your support.

Sincerely,

RICHARD NIXON

NOTE: This is the text of identical letters addressed to approximately 2,200 business and labor leaders throughout the Nation.

397 Remarks at an Informal Meeting With Members of the White House Press Corps on Judge Haynsworth's Nomination to the Supreme Court. *October* 20, 1969

RON ZIEGLER has suggested that it might be useful to members of the press if from time to time on a specific subject I brief the press myself and then take questions so you can follow through on that subject.

You may recall that I did this on the occasion of the Chief Justice Burger subject, and it seems to me that this type of procedure is one that we can follow.

I want also to say that as far as those who are here for television and radio, you, of course, can only comment on this because we do not have sound and do not have film. But we will have ready, I understand, on December 15th, the new press room in the West Wing. When that is available, we shall have this kind of a briefing session on a subject-by-subject basis in that room so that those who want to get sound or film can get it. We won't do it always that way. Sometimes we will do it this way, but I think that will be a very useful way to do it.

It will be a very nice room. I was there this morning and it is coming along very well.

This morning this will be on the record and a transcript will be made available to you when we finish.

This morning I have selected as a subject one you have been asking Ron about over the past several weeks, the Haynsworth matter.

In discussing that matter, I want to give you my own thinking with regard to the nomination of Judge Haynsworth, where it stands at the present time, and what my evaluation of the charges that have been made against him is.

You may recall that when I nominated Judge Haynsworth,[1] I said that he was the man, of all the circuit judges in the country—and a chief judge, with 12 years experience—that he was the man I considered to be, by age, experience, background, philosophy, the best qualified to serve on the Supreme Court at this time.

Three weeks ago at a press conference I not only had one question on this matter, as I recall, two. I reiterated that position, and today, after having had an opportunity to evaluate all the charges that have been made in the past 3 weeks I reaffirm my support of Judge Haynsworth, and in reaffirming it I reaffirm it with even greater conviction.

I say with greater conviction because when a man has been through the fire, when he has had his entire life and its entire record exposed to the glare of investigation, which, of course, any man who is submitted for confirmation to the Senate should expect to have; and in addition to that, when he has had to go through what I believe to be a vicious character assassination, if after all that he stands up and comes through as a man of integrity, a man of honesty, and a man of qualifications, then that even more indicates that he deserves the support of the President of the United States who nominated him in the first place and also the votes of the Senators who will be voting on his nomination.

I would like to touch upon perhaps three or four of the major points that have been raised. They are technical points, as many of you who have been studying the case will know.

I should say I have some experience in investigations myself, and I have studied this case completely in every respect.

I have read the income tax returns, the financial statements, all the charges that have been made by various Senators, and the answers that have been made on the Senate floor by Judge Marlow Cook,[2] by Senator Allott [of Colorado], and also the evaluation, of course, of the Department of Justice.

Based on that examination, I personally now have made and concluded, now that all the evidence is in, there are four or five points, perhaps, that are worth discussing, but more if you want to bring them up in your questions.

The charge is made that Judge Haynsworth should have disqualified himself in six cases involving litigants who were customers of a company in which he owned stock. I have examined those cases and that charge. I agree completely with the American Bar Association, with Judge Soboloff[3] who conducted an investigation of this matter in 1963 and 1964, and also with John [P.] Frank, the leading authority on conflict of interest, when he said that not only did Judge Haynsworth have no requirement to disqualify himself, he had a responsibility to sit in these cases because in not one of these instances or cases named did Judge Haynsworth use his influence in any way in behalf of the company in which he owned stock,

---

[1] The announcement of the nomination of Judge Clement F. Haynsworth, Jr., as Associate Justice of the Supreme Court on August 18, 1969, together with biographical information, is printed in the Weekly Compilation of Presidential Documents (vol. 5, p. 1164).

[2] Senator Marlow W. Cook of Kentucky.

[3] Simon E. Soboloff was the Chief Judge of the Fourth Circuit Court of Appeals at the time Clement F. Haynsworth, Jr., was a judge on the Court.

and in no instance was there any indication that he was influenced whatever in decisions by that stock ownership.

If you want to spread this out just a bit, if we were to apply that kind of a standard to all Federal court judges across this country, I would say that perhaps half of them would have to be impeached, and some in the Supreme Court, because carrying it to the ridiculous end result, if a judge owned stock in U.S. Steel, U.S. Steel has customers, a great number of them, and most of those customers or a great number of them get to the Supreme Court or the Circuit Court of Appeals.

So the judge should not disqualify himself because customers of a company he happens to own stock in are in the court. This charge has no substance.

The second major charge is that Judge Haynsworth had a substantial interest in litigation which he decided as a member of the Circuit Court of Appeals.

Let me be quite precise. The law refers not to a substantial interest in the company or the litigant, but a substantial interest in the case. Of course, that is the proper standard to apply.

In this case, I find that the Senator from Indiana [Birch Bayh] who made the charges cited six cases, and these six cases represent perhaps one of the most glaring examples of sloppy staff work that I have seen in the years of seeing what can happen in such cases. Two of the cases were mistakes, of course, and on the others the question of a substantial interest has been, again, reduced to an absurdity.

In the Brunswick case,[4] it is now found, as Judge Marlow Cook pointed out—and he was a judge before he became a Sena-

tor, as you know—Judge Haynsworth would have profited by $5.00, at the most—probably $4.92, the exact figure—if the litigant had recovered all the amount that was involved in the case.

In the Grace case,[5] which involved, incidentally, a parent-subsidiary relationship, Judge Haynsworth's stock would have been reduced in value by 48 cents as a result of the decision that he made.

As an indication of the staff work in this case, one of the other reasons was the Greenville Hotel case.[6]

It is true that Judge Haynsworth did have an interest in the Greenville Hotel. It appeared that years ago as an attorney he was a director for the hotel. Being a director of the hotel he was issued a share of stock in the hotel corporation.

Then after he became a judge, he received a stock dividend of 15 cents, a check which was mailed to him. The judge, of course, returned the check, thinking it was a joke. The company returned it to him. So Judge Haynsworth recorded 15 cents on his income tax return.

Then there is another group of cases that have been raised. That is that Judge Haynsworth should have disqualified himself in those cases involving former clients of his law firm. I should say his former law firm. The law is quite clear here. A judge does not have responsibility and should not disqualify himself in cases involving clients of his former law firm unless that relationship has been very close to the client and has continued close, and also, in point of time, unless the relationship has continued. In other words,

---

[4] *Brunswick Corp.* v. *Long,* 1967 (392 F2d 348).

[5] *Farrow* v. *Grace Lines, Inc.,* 1967 (381 F2d 380).

[6] *Darter* v. *Greenville Community Hotel Corp.,* 1962 (301 F2d 70).

the passage of time and the closeness of the relationship is a factor to be considered.

In all of the cases, the 12 which were raised in hearings involving the former clients, it appeared that Judge Haynsworth was beyond suspicion, and, as a matter of fact, not only should not have disqualified himself but had a duty to sit, in my opinion.

Now the Bobby Baker matter. This is guilt by association and character assassination of the very worst type.[7] Judge Haynsworth knew Bobby Baker. He saw him last 10 years ago. Many of you gentlemen of the press know I used to see him quite often when he was a clerk to the majority. He had three contacts with him. He had no influence on Bobby Baker, and Bobby Baker had no influence on him.

The so-called business deals in which they were partners have been completely laid before the Senate committee, and any suggestion of improper influence has been discounted by Senator Williams [of Delaware], who is kind of a bull on these matters.

I should say, incidentally, while we are talking, I knew Bobby Baker very well myself, too, as the Presiding Officer of the Senate. He was clerk to the majority.

One of the members of my staff, Rose Mary Woods [Personal Secretary to the President], pointed up something I had forgotten. As a matter of fact, Bobby Baker's wife served as a stenographer on

---

[7] Robert G. Baker resigned as Secretary for the Senate Majority on October 7, 1963. Findings of an investigation into charges against Mr. Baker are set forth in Senate Report 1175 of July 8, 1964 entitled "Financial or Business Interests of Officers or Employees of the Senate" by the Committee on Rules and Administration.

my staff for several months when I was a Senator from California.

The fact that I knew him does not make me guilty by association. The fact that Judge Haynsworth along with others knew him, Senator Hollings [of South Carolina] and others, does not make him guilty by association.

On this particular point, I stand very firmly against the use of that tactic.

Now I will go to something a little more fundamental because this involves the decision as to what Senators should consider as they determine whether they confirm a judge for the Supreme Court, or, for that matter, any court.

The question is raised, and one Senator, Senator Magnuson [of Washington], I thought, quite candidly and honestly faced up to this question. He said he did not raise any question with regard to Judge Haynsworth's impropriety charges, but that he simply disagreed with his philosophy on certain matters, civil rights and labor law.

That is a ground which a Senator can give for rejecting, perhaps, Judge Haynsworth. I do not believe it is a proper ground. I would agree with those Senators, many of whom are now opposing Judge Haynsworth, who, in the [Associate Justice Thurgood] Marshall confirmation, categorically said that a judge's philosophy was not a proper basis for rejecting him from the Supreme Court.

Looking back over the history of the cases, as I said when you were here before on the Burger matter, among my heroes of the Court is Louis Brandeis. If philosophy were a test for him, he would have been ruled out because he was too liberal.

Another was Charles Evans Hughes. If philosophy had been a test for him he would have been ruled out because he was too conservative in representing the business interests.

If you want to go back and read what really can happen in cases of this sort, I would suggest you read the debate over Louis Brandeis and also the confirmation of Charles Evans Hughes, in which they poured on him all the filth they could possibly amass because of his connection with insurance companies. Also like Judge Haynsworth, he had represented various other interests.

As far as philosophy is concerned, I would be inclined to agree with the writer for the St. Louis Post Dispatch [8] who said he thought Judge Haynsworth was a man with a razor sharp mind and a middle of the road record on the major issues.

But if Judge Haynsworth's philosophy leans to the conservative side, in my view that recommends him to me. I think the Court needs balance, and I think that the Court needs a man who is conservative—and I use the term not in terms of economics, but conservative, as I said of Judge Burger, conservative in respect to his attitude towards the Constitution.

It is the judge's responsibility and the Supreme Court's responsibility, to interpret the Constitution and interpret the law, and not to go beyond that in putting his own socio-economic philosophy into decisions in a way that goes beyond the law, beyond the Constitution.

Now the final point, and this one is one that troubles, I think, many people who are not prejudiced against Judge Haynsworth because he is a southerner or because of his civil rights record or because

---

[8] In an article on August 19, 1969, entitled "Judicial Restraint Shown in Rulings by Haynsworth."

of his labor record.

It is this: At this time in our history, it is very important to have a man that is beyond reproach.

An editorial in the Washington Post, I thought quite a thoughtful editorial, was quite candid in saying that the charges against him on the ethical side were not warranted, or at least were not with the foundation they should be, but because a doubt had been raised, that the name should be withdrawn.

I just want to say categorically here, I shall never accept that philosophy with regard to Judge Haynsworth.

The appearance of impropriety, some say, is enough to disqualify a man who served as judge or in some other capacity. That would mean that anybody who wants to make a charge can thereby create the appearance of impropriety, raise a doubt, and that then his name should be withdrawn.

That isn't our system. Under our system, a man is innocent until he is proven guilty.

Judge Haynsworth, when the charges were made, instead of withdrawing his name, as he could—and, incidentally, if he now asks for his name to be withdrawn, I would not do so—Judge Haynsworth, when the charges were made, openly came before the committee, answered all the questions, and submitted his case to the committee, and now to the full Senate.

I have examined the charges. I find that Judge Haynsworth is an honest man. I find that he has been, in my opinion as a lawyer, a lawyer's lawyer and a judge's judge. I think he will be a great credit to the Supreme Court, and I am going to stand by him until he is confirmed. I trust he will be.

Q. Mr. President, how much of this attack on Judge Haynsworth do you think is an attack, an end run attempt to get at you?

THE PRESIDENT. I have read some of the "spec stories" on that, but I am not going to be involved in that.

The Brandeis case was not a very proud moment in the history of the United States Senate. There was anti-Semitism in it and there was also a very strong partisan attitude towards Woodrow Wilson.

The Hughes debate was not a proud moment. There were a lot of partisan considerations that entered into it. This was a great man and a great Chief Justice, as was Judge Brandeis.

I don't think the Parker nomination [9] was a very happy moment either.

I don't hold any brief for any one of these men in terms of philosophy. I don't agree with them, but no lawyer agrees with every other lawyer on everything. But in Judge Parker's case, it was not proper to turn down a man because he was a southerner.

It is not proper to turn down a man because he is a southerner, because he is a Jew, because he is a Negro, or because of his philosophy.

The question is: What kind of a lawyer is he? What is his attitude toward the Constitution? Is he a man of integrity? Is he a man that will call the great cases that come before him as he sees them, and in this case will provide the balance that this great Court needs? I think Judge

[9] The nomination of Judge John J. Parker of North Carolina to the Supreme Court was rejected May 7, 1930.

Haynsworth does that.

Q. Mr. President, it has been suggested, and I wonder what you think of the idea, that every member of the Federal judiciary holding a lifetime appointment, to avoid this kind of trouble, place their investments perhaps in some kind of a blind trust or perhaps in some kind of fund.

THE PRESIDENT. Bill [*unidentified*], as you noticed, Judge Haynsworth said he would put his stocks into trust. I suppose the American Bar Association or, for that matter, the Senate, or the Congress, could lay down some sort of a rule about that to really meet the problem.

I don't happen to think that blind trusts, particularly in the public mind, are going to remove these questions. That is one of the reasons, as a matter of fact, before I came to office, I disposed of every stock I owned. I own nothing but real estate.

Q. What would you say, Mr. President, when people say you selected Haynsworth in large part because of political obligations?

THE PRESIDENT. I selected Judge Haynsworth for the reasons that I mentioned. I was looking for a man, first, who, like Judge Burger, had broad experience as an appeals judge, a Court of Appeals judge—that is the next highest court to the Supreme Court—who was the right age, and who also had a philosophy for the Constitution similar to my own because that is what a President is expected to do.

As far as a political obligation is concerned, I had no political obligation to select Judge Haynsworth or Judge Burger.

In fact, my acquaintance with Judge Haynsworth can only be casual. If he would walk into this room, I am afraid I wouldn't recognize him.

Q. Can you tell me on what you base your confidence in the confirmation, Mr. President?

THE PRESIDENT. The Senate is a body in which time and discussion work on the side of fairness and justice. That sounds like a cliché, I suppose.

As a former Member of the Senate it is perhaps a self-serving statement. But I am convinced that when Senators read the record, as I did, not just the editorials but the record, the evidence, and as they study every one of these cases—and believe me, I have studied every one of them—if I had found one case where there was a serious doubt, I would have had him removed because I want that Court to be above reproach.

If the Senators do that, I believe a majority of the Senators will vote for Judge Haynsworth's confirmation.

Let me say this too: It is not a partisan matter.

To answer your earlier question, sure, there is some partisanship, I suppose. That is perhaps part of the game, and perhaps with some Republicans. I am not questioning their motives.

All I ask is that every Senator should look very carefully into this record because he has to make the decision that I had to make.

Let me be quite candid. There were those, good friends of mine, who came to me a few weeks ago suggesting I withdraw Judge Haynsworth's nomination due to the fact that a doubt had been raised and that politically it was going to be very difficult to wield.

I had to consider then whether because charges had been made without proof, and whether there was a doubt, whether I would then take upon my hands the destruction of a man's whole life, to destroy his reputation, to drive him from the bench and public service.

I did not do so, and I think that as Senators consider what they will be doing as they vote on this matter, as they consider the evidence, they will realize that they are dealing here with an honest man, a man who has laid all the facts before them, a man who is qualified to serve on the Supreme Court, and I think they will conclude as I did that there is no dishonor in standing with an honest man.

Q. Senator Griffin [of Michigan] is one of the men you referred to, and he has studied this record, case by case. How do you account for Senator Griffin's point of view?

THE PRESIDENT. I hope he will study it further. I trust that after he studies it more, he will change his mind.

Q. One of the things that has happened in the Haynsworth case is that there has been a piecemeal revelation of details.

Is there a problem in our Government, a problem of confidence with Congress and with judges, that we do not have a more comprehensive disclosure law?

THE PRESIDENT. The matter of piecemeal disclosure is because the critics have chosen to make the charges this way.

Some Senators were worried about when the other shoe would drop. I saw the other shoe, and it wasn't even a slipper. We wondered why Senator Bayh wouldn't debate Senator Hollings. Senator Bayh is a very articulate man. But after reading the record I know why. He was well advised not to debate.

Reporter: Thank you, Mr. President.

NOTE: The President spoke at 11:18 a.m. in his office at the White House.

398   Remarks of Welcome at the White House to the Shah of Iran. *October* 21, 1969

Your Imperial Majesty and our guests here on the White House lawn this morning:

This is the ninth time over the past 20 years that Your Majesty has honored our country by a visit to the United States, and never in all that period will you be more welcome, both personally and officially, than you are today on this truly brilliant autumn day in Washington, D.C.

We welcome you because of the proud and ancient land that you represent. We welcome you because of the title which you bear with such distinction. But we welcome you also because of the personal qualities, which those of us who know you as I know you—those qualities you have exemplified in your leadership of your country.

Today on this parade ground we see the flag of the United States and your flag; and the colors of your flag are green and red and white—green standing for the rich spiritual heritage of your country, red standing for courage, and white standing for peace.

We know, Your Majesty, that you, in your life, stand for those great virtues. But we also know that you stand for more than that. In a period in which many new nations are being born, and in which old nations are being born again, and in which all nations are going through change, you have provided an example of leadership in your nation for all the world to see and for many to follow.

That example I have seen firsthand in my visits to your country. I recall that many years ago you gathered your ministers together; and speaking from the position of royalty which you held, you made a comment that has since been remembered around the world. You said to them: Make a revolution in this land.

And you have made a revolution in your land, a revolution in terms of literacy, the great progress that all of us have noted there; a revolution in terms of land reform in which you, yourself, set the example by giving much of your vast lands to the people; a revolution in terms of social and economic and political progress.

But the key to your success has been in the nature of that revolution. It has been a revolution designed not to destroy and to tear down, but a revolution to build—a peaceful revolution.

It is this example that the world sees in Iran. It is this example that is your legacy, not only to your country but to those who seek progress—peaceful progress in nations around the world.

Your Majesty, we welcome you here today—welcome you because of those qualities that I have mentioned and welcome you also because of the personal friendship that we have had the opportunity to enjoy, going back over so many years.

We know that all of the American people, during your brief stay here, will want to express, as I have tried to express in my words today, their admiration, their respect, their affection for you and for the people of Iran.

NOTE: The President spoke at 10:55 a.m. on the South Lawn at the White House where His Imperial Majesty Mohammad Reza Shah Pahlavi, Shahanshah of Iran, was given a formal welcome with full military honors.

See also Items 401 and 405.

His Imperial Majesty responded as follows:

Mr. President:

First of all I would like to thank you from deep in my heart for the words that you were kind enough to pronounce towards myself and my country.

It is true that I am not a newcomer to your wonderful land, but this time in particular it is a distinct pleasure and honor to be your guest; that is, the guest of the President of the United States of America, a President who has shown in all his life how well he understands the problems of our world, the problems of today and the problems of the future; in addition to this, to be welcomed by somebody who has been following with interest the development of our country in the last 20 years or so, in some days maybe the darkest days of our history, and today, I am happy to say, in a period of renaissance.

It is a comfort to know that you have, in this great country, a President who has those friendly sentiments and also that knowledge of your country.

You have mentioned that we have undertaken a revolution in our country which is really covering every aspect of our life. We believe that all of our countries are passing through periods of either evolution or revolution, but my prayers are that the result of all that will be for a better world, better understanding between the people, and the realization of the aspiration of mankind for the betterment of not only the living condition but also of the spiritual one.

I am very proud to say, on behalf of myself and the people of my country, that never in the long-established relationship between our two countries—although our relations have always been excellent—never have we enjoyed such a state of complete mutual trust, understanding, and respect.

I have to add that it is with deep gratitude of your attitude of the past, your unselfish and generous attitude toward my country—and, I could say, toward all the countries of the world—that we want to express this feeling of ours, and in return, wish for your people, your goodhearted people, ever increasing prosperity, and your great country ever increasing progress and order in the world of today.

Thank you, Mr. President.

399 Letter of Congratulations to Willy Brandt on His Election as Chancellor of the Federal Republic of Germany. *October* 21, 1969

Dear Mr. Chancellor:

It gives me great pleasure to congratulate you on your elevation to the high office of Chancellor of the Federal Republic of Germany. You have already done much for your people, as governing Mayor of Berlin and as Foreign Minister and Vice Chancellor. The admiration and respect you have won throughout the world in these earlier capacities promises much for the discharge of the even greater and more challenging duties you have now assumed. I think you are aware of the confidence you have won throughout the world in years.

In our complex and difficult world today, I particularly value such elements of stability as the close relationship that exists between the United States and the Federal Republic of Germany. I attribute the highest importance to the maintenance of this relationship, which I am convinced must be based on mutual understanding and confidence. Whenever occasion warrants, I would like to feel free to consult with you directly on matters of mutual interest. I will welcome it if you will do the same.

I look forward to the prospect of working with you in the interest of those objectives which join our two countries in responsibility as well as friendship.

With warm personal regards,
Sincerely,

RICHARD NIXON

400   Letter to Senator Ralph Yarborough on Proposed Increases in Veterans Educational Benefits. *October* 21, 1969

Dear Mr. Chairman:

In line with my talk last Friday [1] on the rising cost of living, I must tell you of my deep concern regarding certain provisions of H.R. 11959, now pending Senate consideration.

Title I of this measure, as amended by the Senate Committee on Labor and Public Welfare, would raise veteran's educational assistance allowances by an average of 46% over current rates. Such increases would be retroactive to September 1, and would mean added expenditures of more than 323 million dollars over present costs in the remainder of this fiscal year. Together with the costs of the bill's Title II provisions, total extra spending through June 30, 1970, would be nearly 393 million dollars.

The average additional outlay for each of the next four full fiscal years would be approximately 550 million dollars.

I am in sympathy with a justifiable increase in educational allowances for post-Korean and Vietnam Era veterans. Yet, I consider the magnitude of the increases contained in H.R. 11959 to require reconsideration for two reasons. The proposed rates are excessive and their effect would be inflationary.

In comparison to the actual rise in the cost of living since these allowances were

last increased, just two years ago, a 46% increase at this time is unrealistic and excessive. And, if we are to stay within the expenditure limit for fiscal 1970, the cost of H.R. 11959 as now drawn could not be borne without imposing severe cuts in other, also important programs.

It is not easy to criticize the pending bill for it promises some appealing benefits to a most deserving group. But our veterans have long known that they must be champions of responsible government. They know the basic truth that a veterans' program not good for the nation as a whole cannot ultimately be of benefit to veterans themselves.

This summer I appointed a Committee consisting of agency heads having responsibility for programs bearing on the welfare and readjustment of returning veterans. I have received an interim report from its Chairman, Mr. Donald E. Johnson, the Administrator of Veterans Affairs. A copy is attached, inasmuch as the Committee's main recommendation bears directly on the subject matter of this letter.

The Committee on the Vietnam Veteran addressed the issue as follows:

"Educational assistance allowances were last increased October 1, 1967. Since that date the cost of living has risen approximately 10%. Included in that increase is an even more dramatic rise in one

---

[1] Item 395.

of its components, the cost of education. Since the last increase in educational assistance allowances, colleges have increased their charges by roughly 15%. This means that today tuition and fees for an academic year are higher by an average of $94.

"Therefore, your Committee recommends an immediate increase in educational assistance allowance rates commensurate with the rise in education and living costs cited above."

I fully support this recommendation. For this reason and those expressed above, I seek your support in urging the Senate to recognize the inflationary impact that enactment of H.R. 11959 would have. The consequences flowing from its enactment would in the long run more than outweigh any temporary gain that may be realized. As President, I have no option but to view with extreme concern the possible enactment of this measure.

I have sent an identical letter to Senator Javits.

Sincerely,

RICHARD NIXON

[Honorable Ralph W. Yarborough, Chairman, Committee on Labor and Public Welfare, United States Senate, Washington, D.C.]

NOTE: Senator Jacob K. Javits was ranking Republican member of the Senate Labor and Public Welfare Committee.

The Interim Report of the President's Committee on the Vietnam Veteran and its letter of transmittal are printed in the Weekly Compilation of Presidential Documents (vol. 5, p. 1450).

On October 21, 1969, the White House Press Office also issued the text of a news briefing by Donald E. Johnson, Administrator of Veterans Affairs, concerning the Interim Report.

401 Toasts of the President and the Shah of Iran. *October 21, 1969*

Your Imperial Majesty and friends of Iran and the United States who are gathered here at the White House tonight:

We are honored again to receive His Imperial Majesty in this house and in this room. Before the dinner, I found that this, of course, is not the first time that His Majesty has been here; but you will be interested to note that he is one of the few leaders, heads of state in the world, who has been a guest in this house and in this room as the guest of President Truman and then of President Eisenhower and then President Kennedy and then President Johnson and now, tonight, as our guest.

I would say on that count he is far ahead of me. [*Laughter*] He is somewhat younger than I, although he will celebrate a birthday on Sunday.

I found in checking into his background that we had one thing in common—a love for sports. We both played football. There was a difference. I sat on the bench. He was captain of the team.

But in welcoming him here tonight, I could speak of those usual pleasantries and diplomatic clichés that grace such occasions; but I think because there are so many here who know his country and have for his country the affection and admiration that I have and Mrs. Nixon has; because there are so many here from his own country, that you would like it better if I shared with you a personal view of the leadership he has provided for his country and the cause of peace and freedom in the world.

In 1953, my wife and I had a very great privilege to travel around the world, and particularly through the countries of Asia. In that period, not too long after World War II, the great leaders of World War II were still living and still active and powerful on the world scene.

I remember them well, now. The names, most of them you will recall, some are still active: Yoshida in Japan, Syngman Rhee in Korea, Chiang Kai-shek in Taiwan, Menzies in Australia, Nehru in India, Ghulam Mohammed in Pakistan, and many others.

The last stop on that long trip of 70 days was Iran. On that stop we met for the first time our very honored guest tonight. He made a very deep impression on me and on my wife at that time, a deep impression because of his own personal character, and also with regard to the various other leaders that I had seen, each of whom had greatness in his own way, because in 1953 Iran had very difficult problems.

There was martial law in the land. The father of the now Secretary for Foreign Affairs was Prime Minister,[1] and His Majesty was the symbol, and not just the symbol but the actual leader of authority who kept the nation together, to whom all of those in government and the people of Iran turned in a moment of crisis.

There were those who thought that Iran in 1953 might not make it. When I left Iran, I knew it would make it. I knew

---

[1] Ardeshir Zahedi and his father Fazollah Zahedi.

it because of the men I had seen. I knew it not only because of the Government leaders to whom I have referred, but particularly because of the personality and the strength and the character of the man who is our honored guest tonight.

He was a young head of state then, just as he is really a young head of state today. I was a young Vice President. But what I recall was this: Despite the deep depression of spirit which seemed to infect many of those who observed Iran in that period of crisis, His Majesty saw the problems but also had a vision for the future.

Omar Khayyám has referred eloquently to the ability of a leader, a great leader, to heed the roll of distant drums. His Majesty had that ability. He saw his country in the future, and he proceeded to move his country into the future, and that story of progress is now one of the most exciting stories of all the development that has occurred in the world in the past 16 years.

I referred to it this morning: Progress in education, progress in economic development, progress in social development, until today Iran stands as one of the strongest, the proudest among all the nations of the world.

So today we honor a nation and a people with whom we are proud to stand as friends and allies. We honor also a man who has those elements of leadership which are too rare in the world.

In a moment you will rise with me and we will drink a toast. We will be drinking a toast, as has happened in this room for over 150 years, to His Majesty. But I can say that tonight I feel very deep in my heart, as everyone here who knows him and knows his country and his record, that when we say "His Majesty," we realize we are drinking to a man who has demonstrated majesty—majesty in his leadership, majesty in his reverence for the past, but in his vision for the future.

Our friends, will you please rise and raise your glasses to the Shahanshah.

NOTE: The President spoke at 10:10 p.m. in the State Dining Room at the White House.

See also Items 398 and 405.

His Imperial Majesty Mohammad Reza Shah Pahlavi, Shahanshah of Iran, responded as follows:

Mr. President, Mrs. Nixon, Your Excellencies, dear guests:

I was already once deeply moved by your kind words of greeting this morning; and tonight I am overwhelmed by the warmth of your sentiments which could only come from a true friend, someone who is sharing your problems and someone who is understanding your problems.

For our association, Mr. President—and the great honor and pleasure that I take and have by saying that our friendship started a long time ago—is this strong and this durable because I think it started in a period that for my country was a very vital one. That was the aftermath of the war, the period of the big drive forward of the policies that wanted to dominate the world.

We on our part tried to keep our independence and resist those pressures; and you on your part wanted to be the bearer of this flag that America has always waved with pride in the air, the flag of always standing for the people who are standing for righteousness and for freedom.

You were kind enough to say that our country in that meantime had succeeded. Much of our success is due to the deeply rooted sentiments of our country in being true to themselves, in being true to their history, in being true to what the human valor of the individual, the freedom of the individual, means, and also, I must admit, to the heartening effect of knowing that we had the friendship of a great nation like yours and great leaders like the late President and you, Mr. President, as his

very able Vice President at that time.

I can return back what you have said about me even more by saying that you have shown such human valor and dignity during your hours of triumph and success, and also during hours of trial. This is what makes a man great and reliable. This is what makes a man have the character of a leader.

Today more than ever we need the friendship of America as a friend and the leadership of America in the world and the leadership of the President of this great country to uphold all of what we are standing for: to implement the laws of equity, of justice; to encourage decency in relationships between states, countries, and people.

You might rest assured that nowhere you would find more than in our country—friendship, understanding, and sympathy in everything you do, in everything you enterprise, because we know in advance that it is being done in the path of justice and equity.

We can felicitate ourselves of the result of your friendship because, as it stands now, I hope and I believe that our country is trying to represent and to continue to do what our past history has tried to do, to give something to the world, something spiritual, something that could be of help to make life better, to render life more interesting.

We shall never stop in trying to do so because this is the history of our country, and no country could live without remaining true to its past while trying to still do better in the future.

We shall always remember your visit to our country and Mrs. Nixon's visit. I personally will always remember the long hours that we spent together in 1967, and above all, we shall be waiting with the greatest of anticipation to the future visit of the President of the United States, and especially of President Nixon, a person whom we respect, a person for whom we have such an admiration.

So I would like also to ask this distinguished audience to raise their glasses with me to the health of the President of the United States, a man to which I am sure we all are holding such very high sentiments of esteem and admiration.

402   Remarks at the Presidential Prayer Breakfast.
October 22, 1969

THIS MORNING we begin the National Day of Prayer. As I was determining what would be the most appropriate appearance for the President on this occasion— as you know, this is an annual occasion through the proclamation of the President of the United States—it occurred to me that it would give me an opportunity to participate again with many of my old friends and many who came to the Congress and the Senate years after I left it, from the House and Senate prayer groups. So, today we have the Wednesday group, the Thursday group, and the Friday group. And now and then I see some of you here on Sunday.

I simply want to say that I am most grateful for the fact that over these months that I have been here that you have invited me to come down to the prayer group. I was not, perhaps, as regular an attendant as I might have been, or should have been, when I was in the House and Senate.

I was a member of both groups, and I found it particularly helpful and particularly inspiring to meet with my colleagues and take that bit of time off on either a Wednesday, as it was in the House, or a Thursday, as it was in the Senate in those days, for the purpose of an inspirational meeting.

This morning we thought that all of you would like to have participation from both the House and the Senate.

We are going to have for our invocation, a Californian. That is only a coincidence. It just happens that he was selected by his colleagues as being one who could best participate—Del Clawson of California.

[Representative Clawson gave the invocation. The President then resumed speaking.]

For the Scripture reading we turn to the Senate side and to an old friend. I have served with him in the Senate, when I was presiding over the Senate and prior to that time—Wallace Bennett.

[Senator Wallace F. Bennett of Utah read selected Scripture verses. The President then resumed speaking.]

Before we turn to Billy Graham, who will be here to bring us our message this morning, the script calls for some remarks by the President of the United States, by your host.

I have been trying to think of what would be appropriate. Last night we had a great state dinner with the Shah of Iran, as is often the case in this room, and today we have a very different kind of a meeting, and yet it has very great meaning to all in this room.

This is truly an ecumenical meeting. There are Catholics and Protestants here; and among the Protestants, all the various groups or most of them are represented: the very large groups like the Baptists, the Presbyterians, the Methodists are in this room, some of the smaller ones like the Mormons, or medium-sized—the Mormons grow, I find.

I imagine I am the only Quaker in the room. No, there is one other. Well, the Quakers have a tradition of worshiping in silence. I suppose that is why so few of them ever got to the Senate.

39–861—71——56

But, nevertheless, it seemed to me that I could bring you two thoughts before Billy Graham speaks to you that would be very appropriate this morning.

Over that fireplace when Franklin Roosevelt was President, an inscription was carved into that marble. Those of you who are close enough can read it. I think it is a very memorable inscription, particularly because of the historical significance.

As you know, George Washington never lived in this house. The first President to live in it, and he lived in it even before it was completed, was John Adams. When John Adams, just prior to the completion of his term in office—his only term—returned to Washington, he was thinking of the future of this house and all who might live in it, and I am sure he, even with his great faith—as all had faith among those early founders—in the future of the Republic, would not have been able to predict what would have happened now to the strength of America and how strong we are, this great Nation.

But he wrote a prayer, a prayer about the Presidency, this house, and what it means. I think it is well that it is inscribed there and perhaps it might be well to read it now.

It says: "I pray Heaven to bestow the best of blessings on this house and on all that shall hereafter inhabit it. May none but honest and wise men ever rule under this roof."

Now, as we look over our Presidents through the past 190 years, I think most of us would agree they were honest men, and history will perhaps have a considerable debate as to whether all of them were wise men, or at least as to the extent of their wisdom.

But no matter how honest or how wise they were, I think all of us realize that at times of great challenge to our Nation, whether during the bitter War Between the States or whether during the other military challenges and economic challenges which this Nation has faced, particularly in this century, we know that during those periods there had to be something more than honesty and more than wisdom in the leadership of this country, whether it was in the President of the United States or in the Members of the House and the Senate.

There had to be, we believe—some call it destiny—I would prefer to say there had to be that spiritual quality which we can feel in this room this morning as we meet with this group of Senators and Congressmen who recognize the spiritual heritage of America, how important it is, that there are times that we need help beyond ourselves, beyond what any man can give us in order to make the right decision for the Nation.

Now among the Quakers—not all—but among the Quakers, at least as my mother and my grandmother on my mother's side knew them, there was a different tradition. The Quakers worshiped in silence. Well, the modern-day Quakers, most of them, have ministers just as do Methodists, the Baptists, and the rest, but even they always turn to silence now and then as the medium where each in his own way could think of his relationship to the problems around him and to the spiritual relationship he had with his Maker.

I am not going to suggest this morning that we worship in the manner of the Quakers, because those silent meetings, my mother used to tell me, would last for an hour, an hour when all would gather in the meetinghouse and would sit without a word being spoken during the whole period.

I do think this morning, though, that before Billy Graham speaks to us, that it would be appropriate if all of us, for a few moments, would sit in silence. I would not try to suggest what we would think about, except to say that at such a time we can think of our Nation and we can think of those who try to defend it abroad. We can think of its tragedies, and we can also think of what we can do to make life better for those who will follow us in this house and in the Halls of Congress.

But most of all, we can think of our own relationship to our colleagues, our own responsibilities, whether they not only have the ingredients of honesty and wisdom, but whether sometimes they have

that extra ingredient of a spiritual quality—a spiritual quality which history tells me every President who has ruled in this house has turned to or has exemplified when very difficult decisions were before him.

So if we could have that moment of silence in the manner of the Quakers now, and then Billy Graham will speak to us.

[A moment of silence was observed. The Rev. Billy Graham then addressed the group.]

NOTE: The annual prayer breakfast of a non-denominational group of laymen, marking the National Day of Prayer, was held in the State Dining Room at the White House. The President spoke at 8:41 a.m.

The invocation, selected Scripture verses, and the remarks of the Rev. Billy Graham are printed in the Weekly Compilation of Presidential Documents (vol. 5, p. 1453).

The National Day of Prayer for 1969 was designated in Proclamation 3940.

403　Statement About National Bible Week.
October 22, 1969

IT IS a great honor for me to join the American Bible Society, the Catholic Biblical Association, the Laymen's National Bible Committee, and all who participate in the special recognition of National Bible Week.

It is most fitting that this traditional observance is to be held during the week of Thanksgiving. For as each of us pauses to reflect on the meaning of the Bible in our lives, we surely have some special instance for which to express our thanks to God for strengthening our faith through Holy Writ.

I am especially reminded of Benjamin Franklin's immortal thought when he remarked that if no sparrow can fall to the ground without His notice, no nation can

rise from the ground without His help. Throughout our history, despairing men and women have found sustaining solace in the word of God as written in the Bible. Families have been guided by its enlightened precepts. Statesmen and leaders have drawn inspiration from its teachings, and courage from the enriching experience it records.

It is unique among books and treasured by men and nations. And the power of the universal truths it holds is appropriately refreshed within our hearts on this occasion. The past has truly proved that we have much to gain by our devotion to the Scriptures. And the future holds great promise if we heed past lessons well.

So in the spirit of this timely week,

let us draw upon the timeless wisdom of the Book of Books to guide us in our daily lives.

NOTE: In recognition of the President's service as honorary chairman of National Bible Week, W. Clement Stone, national chairman, pre-sented him with a miniature copy of a statue entitled "We Shall Beat Our Swords Into Plowshares" in a ceremony at the White House on October 22, 1969. The original statue stands in the garden of the United Nations Headquarters in New York.

404 Remarks at a Bipartisan Leadership Meeting on Narcotics and Dangerous Drugs. *October 23, 1969*

WE ARE sorry we are late. Mr. Ingersoll got caught in the traffic. I wonder about traffic around here.

If I could say a word with regard to the nature of this meeting in the beginning, and also an indication as to how we will proceed.

The subject this morning is one that we think is appropriate for a bipartisan meeting.

As I was telling Mike Mansfield last night, and I talked to the Speaker on this point, there are some subjects that are completely above partisan consideration, and this is one. The only question is the means. How do we deal with this problem of dangerous drugs in the United States, narcotics and so forth?

We thought, therefore, that the presentation should be made to a bipartisan group, Senators and Congressmen. We also thought that we would follow the practice on a matter of this sort, where one of the major needs is public information, to have the press in the room—the writing press—for the presentation.

Of course, during the presentation, any questions you might have you could ask, but we would like to move on. After the presentation is made, then the press will leave the room, and then we will have discussion among the members on the legislation situation. So that will be an executive session. We can have give-and-take as to where the bills are and what can be done and the like.

I don't know if there is any one of you who is more expert, but you will agree with me, I am sure, that with this particular issue there needs to be information as to what the problem really is so that we can deal with it as it is rather than deal with the headlines and all of our misconceptions as to what is dangerous and what isn't, what the penalties ought to be and why sometimes they have to be less for one or more for another, and so on.

We are going to go into some of those subjects here this morning in some depth. Having heard some of this in advance, I can tell you that it was extremely educational to me. I had the idea that I knew something about it, but I find that this is a subject that we all, frankly, in this country, have too little information on. There is just too much ignorance in the country.

I hope this morning, while this will be old to some of you, it will be very helpful to all of you, and I hope the press will be able to record it, too.

We are going to begin with an expert, Mr. Ingersoll, who will, as Director of the Bureau of Narcotics and Dangerous Drugs, have the primary responsibility within the administration in this field.

He will begin the briefing and he will be followed by Secretary Finch on other aspects of the problem. After that, Art Linkletter [1] will make a presentation in terms of the public problem, which he discussed with me last night, and which I think you will find extremely interesting.

As I said, feel free to ask any questions during the presentation that you would like to, but remember that we will discuss the legislative situation at the conclusion of this.

Mr. Ingersoll.

MR. JOHN E. INGERSOLL. Thank you very much, Mr. President.

Distinguished Members of Congress and members of the news media:

I can't really say it is a pleasure to discuss this topic. However, I am very grateful for the opportunity to discuss this most serious problem with you and to urge your support for the swift passage of the administration's controlled dangerous substances act.

As many of you know, the Bureau of Narcotics and Dangerous Drugs is the Federal agency charged with the principal responsibility for eliminating the illicit traffic of narcotics and dangerous drugs in the United States and for destroying the major illicit drug conspiracies that exist in the United States to peddle their wares.

In order to meet these law enforcement responsibilities and objectives more efficiently, the administration has proposed legislation that, first of all, would bring together the many divergent Federal laws in this area. The legislation would also unify the jurisdictional base for law enforcement and give the Bureau of Nar-

cotics and Dangerous Drugs the law enforcement and regulatory tools that are necessary to meet the challenge, not only for today but for the 1970's as well.

Today, the Bureau, along with the other Federal law enforcement agencies, is focusing its major law enforcement efforts on halting the supply of drugs that are coming into the United States, hopefully before they reach the shores, and particularly in respect to narcotics, drugs, and marihuana.

Operation Intercept [2] was a first step in the administration's plan towards finding ways to effectively spur multilateral cooperation among the family of nations in slowing down international illicit drug traffic.

Operation Intercept was very, very successful. While it was in effect, and even to this day, the flow of narcotics and marihuana from Mexico into this country was substantially curtailed. Marihuana is still in short supply in the United States, and in most places where it is available, at least the Mexican form, the prices have doubled and in some cases tripled.

Presently, a less economically severe plan called Operation Cooperation has replaced Operation Intercept. While this is also an intensive surveillance effort involving the cooperation of numerous Federal agencies and the Government of Mexico, it is less burdensome economically to those persons who are engaged in lawful commerce between the United States and Mexico.

At the President's direction, we are now working out detailed procedures for inter-

---

[1] Radio and television personality

[2] Operation Intercept, initiated September 21, 1969, was replaced with Operation Cooperation on October 10, 1969.

dicting the flow of heroin into the United States from its two principal sources, Turkey and France.

The chart here is a schematic representation of the worldwide flow of heroin, particularly from the Middle East and the various routes of illicit traffic through Europe to the United States, and in some cases using Canada and Mexico as transshipment points.

Additionally, we are currently engaged in discussions with the Government of Mexico in order to stop the flow of heroin as well as other drugs, including marihuana, from that country.

If our efforts are in any way successful in halting the flow of heroin from the primary sources, we will have come a long way toward eliminating the principal supplies of this drug.

While we look to other countries for their support in helping us to solve what is a major American problem, the international community also looks to the United States for assistance in preventing drug abuse on a worldwide basis. There is presently great pressure from the international community to revise penal and regulatory laws in order to more effectively stop the narcotic and dangerous drug traffic within and without our borders.

For example, the 38th General Assembly of the International Organization of Criminal Police, which is known to most non-law-enforcement people as INTERPOL, agreed last Friday to recommend the prohibition of all cultivation of the opium poppy that is a source of heroin, and cantharis which is a source of marihuana in those countries which belong to INTERPOL.

Additionally, it was recommended that member countries exercise greater national control over the hallucinogenic, the depressant, and stimulant drugs.

Specific steps called for include these:
—first, the making of these substances available on prescriptions only;
—secondly, governmental supervision of all transactions from production to retail distribution;
—third, licensing of all producers;
—fourth, limiting trade to authorized persons;
—and, finally, prohibition of non-authorized possession for distribution.

This international body also recommended that member nations clearly designate between mere users of narcotics and dangerous drugs and those persons who are involved in the illicit traffic in these substances. The latter group, under the INTERPOL recommendation, is to be given heavy prison sentences, while mere users should be allowed the benefit of maximum flexibility in sentencing.

This recommendation was made last Friday.

The proposed controlled dangerous substances act specifically provides for a marihuana eradication program within the United States of the type recommended by the INTERPOL conference.

Additionally, this legislation imposes much tougher regulatory controls over the legitimate manufacturers, distributors, and dispensers of hallucinogens, depressants, and stimulants in order to prevent the widespread illicit diversion of these drugs that presently exist.

Tighter controls would also be placed over the importation and exportation of all narcotics and dangerous drugs to protect against both domestic and international diversion of these substances.

The controlled dangerous substances act not only evidences the good faith of the United States in meeting international obligations with respect to control of narcotics and dangerous drugs, but also provides a law enforcement framework within which our very own domestic drug problem can be resolved.

This bill is tough. But it is also fair. It metes out harsh penalties for persons identified as professional traffickers or professional criminals. But it also permits flexible penalties for the lesser trafficker and a great deal of flexibility for those persons who are drug users but do not traffic in the drugs.

There is a tendency in some quarters to label the alternative penalties recommended by the administration as being soft in dealing with the drug problem. I, as the head of the law enforcement agency responsible for this problem, consider that charge a misnomer, unfair, and false of fact.

A sentencing structure, in order to be effective, must be acceptable to the courts, to those who prosecute criminal cases, and, of course, to the public. Today's penalties, in some instances, do not meet these tests; that is, penalties, to be effective, must be tough for the more severe trafficking offenses and offenders while having sufficient flexibility for dealing with persons possessing for their own use.

As to narcotic drugs offenses, there is agreement among the courts and the United States attorneys that the nonaddict who traffics in large amounts of narcotics for his own gain ought to be punished severely. And under our proposal, he will be.

There is also agreement that those persons who sell small amounts for personal gain and not just to support a habit should also be punished, but the courts should have some flexibility in meting out the sentence, especially for the first offender.

So what we have done is to build more flexibility into the sentencing structure and allow the courts to exercise their judicial prerogatives more fully.

This does not mean that the criminal is to go free. The outer penalty limits are more than sufficient for the protection of society, which is all of our first concern.

What it does mean is that we have recognized that heroin and marihuana, for example, are not co-equal in danger and we affix the penalties accordingly.

We believe that we now have a structure which distinguishes more carefully between the different offenders in a realistic way. We feel this approach will increase respect for the law and overcome public apathy to some of the inequities in the present penalty structure.

We also anticipate less reluctance to prosecute and less reluctance to sentence, as the penalties would now more closely fit the offenses committed and the individuals who commit them.

In short, we feel that we will see more and better enforcement of the law under the new approach than at the present.

Specific provisions of the bill would also expand the arrest authority of special agents of the Bureau of Narcotics and Dangerous Drugs and give the Attorney General some greater flexibility in employing them where needed. In addition, existing search warrant provisions have been retained with regard to nighttime search warrants, except that they have been expanded to include offenses involving all controlled dangerous substances.

Presently, such warrants that are able to be served at night are not available for investigations involving stimulants, depressants, and the other non-narcotic dangerous drugs.

In addition, a "no-knock" provision has been included to permit agents to obtain court warrants which designate that they need not announce their authority before they enter the place where the warrant is to be executed, where they can demonstrate to the court that if they had to knock and announce their authority, the result would either be dangerous to the special agent or it would inevitably involve the rapid destruction of evidence.

Many States already have this "no-knock" authority. It has been tested in the Supreme Court and has been found to be constitutionally sufficient. We feel that this most useful law enforcement tool is vitally necessary also at the Federal level in order to enable us to reach those persons who are trafficking in drugs before they are able to dispose of the evidence.

In addition to these search warrant provisions, the bill would permit administrative or inspection warrants. There is a need for this type of warrant, as has been dictated by recent Supreme Court decisions, which have held that administrative searches are no less subject to the protection of the fourth amendment than are inspections in pursuance of criminal investigations.

This provision is of vital importance to the Bureau, since we are also involved in the regulation of the legitimate drug industry and must have the ability to inspect their records, books, and facilities in the event that we were denied access to them under voluntary circumstances. It is the legitimate end of the drug industry which is the major source of the supply of depressant and stimulant drugs which find their way into the illicit drug channels.

Because recent Supreme Court decisions have attacked the validity of certain sections of the existing narcotic and marihuana laws, the Federal Government is no longer able to make possession cases involving marihuana or cocaine.

In addition, the legality of the very basis of the existing narcotic laws dealing with the sale of heroin is currently pending before the Supreme Court.

As you know, narcotics and marihuana are jurisdictionally based on the taxing power of the Constitution. Should these laws ultimately be found to be constitutionally deficient, the Federal Government, for all practical purposes, would be out of the narcotic and marihuana enforcement business.

It is obvious, therefore, that the need for swift enactment of the pending legislation is imperative.

Registration provisions under the existing Drug Abuse Control Amendments, which deal with the regulation of depressants, stimulants, and hallucinogens, are inadequate for effective regulation of the legitimate industry. There are just too many people dealing with these drugs that are not presently required to register. At the same time, many of the drugs under the Drug Abuse Control Amendments no longer require an inventory so that we can keep track of them or keep account of their supply and their distribution, as the original 3-year inventory in the basic law has expired.

The changes found in the controlled dangerous substances act will remedy this situation and permit better supervision over the principal sources of these dangerous drugs. Prompt action is needed if we are to effectively meet the challenge which faces us today.

The Senate hearings have been concluded on the bill and swift action is urged to report this bill out of the Senate

Judiciary Committee and to achieve passage in the Senate. The House of Representatives has yet to start hearings. A bifurcated form of the bill is presently divided between the House Ways and Means Committee and the Interstate and Foreign Commerce Committee.

The regulatory tools, the new penalty structures, and the law enforcement tools found in the controlled dangerous substances act will give us the equipment that we have to have in order to effectively combat the traffic in narcotics and dangerous drugs. I would urge you to act swiftly and favorably on this legislation.

REPRESENTATIVE CARL ALBERT. Mr. President, may I ask one question?

In recommending more flexible sentences, you are not recommending that the maximum be taken off, but that the minimums be lowered at the discretion of the enforcement and judicial authorities, is that correct?

MR. INGERSOLL. That is correct.

SENATOR JACOB K. JAVITS. Is the presentation this morning to be confined solely to this question? Will we in any way talk about treatment or how to deal with the offender or the user in the United States?

MR. INGERSOLL. The present law, Senator Javits, the law under consideration, is primarily a law enforcement package, as you well know. There are recognitions placed in the law, and also in the President's message of July 14, of the need for better rehabilitation techniques, and at the present time we are reviewing the Narcotic Addict Rehabilitation Act with the view in mind of perhaps recommending in the near future some amendments.

THE PRESIDENT. Secretary Finch is going to cover some of this, Jack [Javits], in his presentation. This is a very important phase of it.

SENATOR MANSFIELD. Mr. Ingersoll, do you have new agents?

MR. INGERSOLL. We are making requests for additional personnel, Senator.

SENATOR MANSFIELD. Enough?

MR. INGERSOLL. I think that we had to go rather slowly during the 1960's. The predecessor bureaus of the Bureau of Narcotics and Dangerous Drugs were simply small organizations. In the last year and a half since the Bureau of Narcotics and Dangerous Drugs has been formed, we have practically doubled our strength, and by the fiscal year 1971, our resources, if our pending budget requests are effected, will have increased about $2\frac{1}{2}$ or $2\frac{3}{4}$ times.

I don't think we are going to have enough right away, but I also feel that we have to build systematically and slowly. We have to train our people adequately. I don't want to have a large organization that is inadequately trained.

THE PRESIDENT. Isn't it true that you found the situation—well, there had to be considerable housecleaning?

MR. INGERSOLL. That is correct.

THE PRESIDENT. Why don't you talk about that a little bit. This is the problem, again, that has to do with the nature of what we are dealing with in this area particularly. You have to be extremely careful to be sure that you don't simply offer an opportunity for those who have the habit or are trying to traffic, of becoming, frankly, agents of the Government.

Isn't that the problem you run into?

MR. INGERSOLL. Yes. During the first year that I was Director of the Bureau, I had the unhappy job of separating over 50 people, indicting about 14 or 15 agents and former agents for Federal criminal offenses, some of which involved trafficking in narcotics, some of which involved other forms of corruption, and at least three or four cases which involved perjury.

THE PRESIDENT. Do some of these become users? Is that the problem?

MR. INGERSOLL. We have had some instances of that, Mr. President. That is not too extensive, but there have been a few.

Q. But now you are going on a training program, highly selective, to upgrade the whole Bureau?

MR. INGERSOLL. Yes. The standards for employment were relatively low and lax. We have tightened these up considerably. The last 100 men or so who have been employed have been of very high caliber. They have a wide variety of educational backgrounds, almost all of which—I think 100 percent—have at least a 4-year college degree.

They have language capabilities, for example, to illustrate the diversity, ranging from Thai to Spanish. Some of them have previous investigative backgrounds, law enforcement backgrounds, and others do not.

We are trying to obtain the very best people that we can. This kind of work offers the most fantastic temptations that I have found in some 18 or 19 years of law enforcement work.

THE PRESIDENT. Because of the profit in it?

MR. INGERSOLL. The money is terrific. I have seen traffickers who can make $150,000 to $200,000 a year. These are not the bigtime fellows. These are the middle level.

In one of our integrity cases, it was estimated that $1 million exchanged hands between our man, our former agent who was involved in this, and the trafficker he was working with. So we have to be extremely careful.

THE PRESIDENT. Would you talk a moment about the tie-in of the organized crime with the whole drug problem? Is that part of the problem? Is that where so much money comes in?

I think it would be of interest to have some discussion of that.

MR. INGERSOLL. This is a very substantial part of the problem. The Mafia, for many, many years, traditionally has offered heroin as one of its vice commodities. It has controlled the trafficking of heroin, at least on the eastern seaboard of the United States, for the last 20 or 30 years. It has direct links with organized criminal elements in France and in the other parts of Europe, principally the Corsicans of France. It controls the importation and the initial distribution of heroin in the eastern part of the United States and then it filters down through a lot of other channels.

But many of the big names, the leaders of the Mafia, never touch the drug. They never see it. Many of them, as in any large corporate enterprise, are probably not aware of daily transactions that their organization is involved in, in specific detail.

This is, in further response to your question, Senator Mansfield, one of the things that we badly need in the Bureau. In addition to manpower, we need to be able to have more money available for investigative funds, because in order to reach these very high levels of the criminal syndicate, we have to, in all frankness, be able to buy our way in. In order to do this, we have to have large resources and investigative funds available to us.

THE PRESIDENT. Is it not true, as I understand it, the organized crime, syndicates and the rest, are funded to a great extent by, and the very heart of their operation is, the drug traffic?

MR. INGERSOLL. This is true in the case of a few Mafia families. Some of the families have gotten out of the narcotics business over the years. I suppose that narcotics is not the major source of organized crime finances at this time, but it does represent a substantial source of income for a few prominent figures in the Mafia.

SENATOR JAVITS. Mr. President, about the Mafia, we have the testimony of Valachi [3] before the Government Operations Committee. Valachi testified that they were getting out of the heroin business, that it was not liked by the Mafia families and there was a new crime structure being established in the United States by non-Mafia operators, strictly for the drug traffic.

The reason I mentioned this is only because we don't want to get diverted by advertising. The Mafia is blamed for everything. It is guilty of plenty, but at the same time this could be a very false impression.

THE PRESIDENT. The point I was trying to bring out is that it is not the Mafia, but it was organized crime—those operators are the ones, from the investigations that I have read.

Senator Hruska, you have been in some of this, I have heard. The whole body of organized crime, they are the ones that have the network that can distribute this stuff and bring it in from abroad and the rest, apart from the Mafia.

SENATOR ROMAN L. HRUSKA. They

have the organization and they have the discipline to go with that organization that makes it a highly efficient proposition. It is very difficult to deal with, too.

MR. INGERSOLL. May I add something to that?

I agree with you Senator, that the Mafia was not the only one. I was not referring exclusively to it. The traffic in LSD, for example, was, in one instance, very highly organized. As a matter of fact, we have a case pending in court at this time where it involves a national syndicate, manufacturing, distributing, and finally street sales of LSD, which stretched from San Francisco to Washington, D.C.

There are smaller organizations involved in the trafficking of marihuana, which are not connected with the Mafia. At the present time, our Bureau is identifying all of these structures. This is one thing, again, that has not been done in the past.

At the beginning of next year we intend to attack the drug problem on the basis of the structures of the criminal conspiracies that are operating throughout the United States and linking them with their international overseers.

SPEAKER McCORMACK. Where does the Customs Service come in?

MR. INGERSOLL. The Customs Service is responsible for guarding the ports of entry. The Bureau of Customs intercepts and interdicts a substantial amount of drugs that are coming into the United States through those ports.

I point out that some of the drugs are manufactured within the United States, and that it is also necessary to cooperate with the foreign law enforcement agencies which represent the source of these substances so that we can prevent them from reaching the ports at all.

---

[3] Joseph Valachi testified before the Committee in September and October 1963.

SENATOR RALPH W. YARBOROUGH. May I say a word about the Customs Service?

My State alone, bordered with Mexico, is the one that had the greater experience with Operation Intercept than any other. The aims and ideals of that had widespread acceptance in my State, but the border cities were greatly in opposition to it because of the 5 or 6 hour delay.

I talked to many people along the border there. They say they think it is a good thing if there were enough customs agents, so that instead of waiting you have enough to keep examining the cars rapidly. They do examine them rapidly.

So, as Chairman of the Appropriations Subcommittee that has jurisdiction over the appropriations of the Customs Bureau, I would expedite any request of the administration for more customs agents. I believe we added 500 customs agents in the recent appropriations bill, but most of those were to go to the big airports because of this great increase in air traffic from overseas. I think only 100 went to the Canadian and Mexican borders.

But that was the big complaint over Intercept. I think the overwhelming majority of the people of my State approved of it, except for the delay in the commerce between the cities.

REPRESENTATIVE ALBERT. Doesn't it come down to this, that the major operators in this field are so well organized, financed, and disciplined that we have got to step up in order to compete with them as a Government enforcing operation?

MR. INGERSOLL. I think that is true to a large extent.

THE PRESIDENT. You can't fight organized crime with the weapons of the 1800's.

REPRESENTATIVE WILLIAM H. NAT-CHER. Mr. Ingersoll, a week ago last Friday, the Speaker of the House of the Mexican Government [4] called me on the telephone—he also happens to be a good friend of Mike Mansfield—with reference to this Intercept. I said: "What is your problem?" He said: "This is all bringing us ill will. Are you working out the problem? There is a problem here between the two countries."

I talked with him one other time on the telephone and I don't get any definitive answer to this.

But are you, at the present time, getting the cooperation of the Mexican Government in this thing?

MR. INGERSOLL. We will be down in Mexico for talks next week. When we go there, we will bring with us a set of requests and also offer assistance.

I think I would be able to answer your question better following those meetings.

THE PRESIDENT. The problem, Bill [Natcher], I think, on this point, as all of you know—you don't have to be in foreign affairs or foreign relations to know it—is a very difficult one. We need cooperation. Operation Intercept was shock treatment and it was believed necessary and it did accomplish a great deal.

Now, however, the Mexican Government and the President [Gustavo Diaz Ordaz], when I talked to him, gave every assurance of the desire to be cooperative. The Mexican Government has indicated a desire to work out a cooperative venture with the United States.

I should also point out that we have the same problem, a very delicate and sensitive problem, with regard to the Turkish and French problem. It would not be

---

[4] President of the Permanent Commission of the Congress of Mexico, Luis M. Farias.

well to discuss that problem here. I can only say that every effort is being made cooperatively with those Governments to work out this problem.

Is that a fair statement?

MR. INGERSOLL. Yes, sir, very much.

THE PRESIDENT. You can be assured we will leave no stone unturned, but we do have to have in mind the fact that we are dealing with sovereign governments in these instances, and the foreign policy consequences can be very significant, as it turns out to be in Operation Intercept.

But that is turning around now, and the Mexican Government, I think, is working with us in a cooperative manner. Would that be correct?

MR. INGERSOLL. Yes, sir. My latest report came in yesterday and indicated that very definitely there is evidence that the Government of Mexico has stepped up its eradication program and is destroying substantial amounts of marihuana and opium poppies.

THE PRESIDENT. Senator Dodd?

SENATOR THOMAS J. DODD. That pretty well answered what I was going to ask about. I was in Turkey a few weeks ago. I was working with Mr. Ingersoll's people in the area. I said it seems to me we are running into a lot of opposition in the operations abroad. We ought to make provision for this.

THE PRESIDENT. Let me ask one question before we go on to Secretary Finch. As I understand from your presentation, the passage of the dangerous substances act, the passage also of the organized crime proposals that have been submitted to the Congress, that these two would give you, your colleagues, and others in this field, very necessary weapons that are needed to wage a more effective fight on this whole drug problem, the dangerous drug problem.

MR. INGERSOLL. Yes, sir.

THE PRESIDENT. At the present time you feel you are inhibited in that you don't have the adequate weapons to deal with this whole infrastructure which has grown up over the years, which is making the drug available to people by the hundreds of thousands in the country. Is that the problem?

MR. INGERSOLL. Yes.

THE PRESIDENT. How many years have you been with this problem?

MR. INGERSOLL. I have been in charge of this Bureau for only a little over a year. However, I have been in law enforcement, as you know, 18 or 19 years. I have had direct contact with these problems over that period of time.

THE PRESIDENT. Let me be a little more blunt. Too often—as a former Member of the House and Senate, I know this is true—too often people say when there is a problem, "Pass a law." Then they think the law is passed and the problem is solved, when really the problem is not the passage of the law. The problem is the administration of the law. The problem is the personnel.

From what you have indicated here, there has been a very serious problem of personnel, putting it more bluntly, the Bureau of Narcotics has been a disgrace, a disgrace in terms of the way that it was allowed to be operated. I am not referring to the top leadership. I am referring to the fact that you referred to just a moment ago.

At the present time, you are not contending that your administration is perfect, right? You have got to step that up. Even with the existing law you can do a better job.

MR. INGERSOLL. Yes.

THE PRESIDENT. But what you are saying is that if you are in it with near perfection, you still need weapons that can come only from the Congress.

MR. INGERSOLL. That is correct.

THE PRESIDENT. Change, for example, with regard to the penalties which will be discussed later; also the organized crime, which is not in your field, but attacked from another direction. All of these changes you think are essential for you to do the job, even if you have all the personnel and best that you can get. Because that is the fundamental problem.

MR. INGERSOLL. I think you have to have both, Mr. President. You have to have both adequate personnel, competent, adequate in numbers and quality. You also have to have the tools to do the job. You can't build a house with a rock. You have got to have modern tools.

One of these tools is modern legislative tools, the modern law. We are dealing with laws which were passed. Today we are trying to administer laws which were passed in a completely other era, as long ago as 1914.

THE PRESIDENT. When you didn't have this great network of organized crime and this enormous profit that was being made, when it was basically an individual problem rather than an organized problem. That is really the difference, is it not?

MR. INGERSOLL. Yes.

THE PRESIDENT. Senator Hughes.

SENATOR HAROLD E. HUGHES. I don't know, Mr. Ingersoll, whether this is in the field you are concerned about, yourself, or maybe part of it is Secretary Finch's or someone else's.

But I would like to ask, we seem to have an increasing amount of information coming to the hearing that even though a man is processed through the courts and

imprisoned, that he has already accessible narcotics in almost every prison in the country also, including Federal, State, and jails in the country, and the fact that the backlog of the courts themselves, you know, have left these people on the streets, even though your men may have processed—I am not talking about the Federal, it is probably local and State more than Federal.

This doesn't deal with the particular law, I believe, but are the prisons under your jurisdiction or are they under the Bureau of Prisons?

MR. INGERSOLL. The Bureau of Prisons is in the Department of Justice, Senator. They are not under our jurisdiction. We do work with the Director of the Bureau of Prisons at the Federal level on this problem. He is aware of the existence of drug trafficking in some of his institutions and has taken appropriate steps or has taken steps to not only counter or react to the problem as he finds it, but also to prevent the problem from continuing.

THE PRESIDENT. And the problem, as you know, Senator, your former experience as Governor, is that most of the prison problems are in the State and local communities. I think what we need here is to get cooperation of State and local communities. But there isn't any question but the Senator's point is well taken. It is not just talk. They go to prison, and they find it right there.

MR. INGERSOLL. We found it right out here at Lorton [5] just a few months ago, as you may recall, quite a substantial traffic in and out of Lorton.

SENATOR HUGHES. The next question deals again with some of our own prob-

---

[5] District of Columbia Corrections Department, Correctional Complex at Lorton, Va.

lems internally. Again, I just question, but there seems to be some evidence coming through that there is a limited amount of traffic, at least within the Armed Forces of our country. I don't know what we are doing. If this is the place to ask that question, I would like to ask it.

THE PRESIDENT. It is.

SENATOR HUGHES. What we are doing and what we can do.

MR. INGERSOLL. I think the principal problem lies in Vietnam. We have had an agent stationed there since last April, a very high ranking and very experienced man, who is working closely with the military and serves as a bridge between our military and the Government of Vietnam, together with our AID [Agency for International Development] public safety people, who are in that area.

One of the most significant things that this man, our agent, has done is, he has undertaken a location and eradication program. He surveys areas from low-flying helicopters and when he discovers cultivation of cantharis, for example, of marihuana, then they call in troops to destroy it. Through this operation, I think already in the first 4 or 5 months of his time there, something in the neighborhood of four or five times as much as was found in all of last year.

In addition to that, he is working extensively in a prevention program using the Armed Forces broadcast media throughout Vietnam in bringing educational materials to the attention of the troops together with the military.

In addition, he is working with military investigators in Vietnam, assisting them in their individual investigations and is also providing training assistance to the military from his own expertise.

In Europe, our agents, who are sta-tioned there, work closely with the military upon request. As an example of this kind of cooperation, sometime in the next few months the military has asked us to transport an entire training instructors team to Germany for the purpose of providing training to military investigators who are stationed in Germany. We intend to respond to this.

In the United States, domestic posts, again, we receive information and exchange information with the military on a daily, weekly, monthly basis and I think that we work very closely with them.

One of my men is a member of the Department of Defense Drug Control Coordinating Committee, I believe it is called, and I am virtually in daily contact with people of the Department of Defense.

I might add that they are part of an interagency committee that is under the White House chair at the present time. They were also represented on the Operation Intercept Task Force.

SENATOR HUGHES. Mr. President, could I ask just a couple more questions?

THE PRESIDENT. Surely.

SENATOR HUGHES. I would like to ask you, if you know, are there any sort of chemical analysis tests being used in the Armed Forces, for example, analysis for heroin users of detection on the systematic use?

MR. INGERSOLL. I am not aware of it.

SENATOR HUGHES. I was going to wait until Secretary Finch was here to talk about education but you touched on education.

Undoubtedly, as I listened to you before, you have a part of the educational field yourself, do you not?

MR. INGERSOLL. Yes, we feel that we can supplement the program which is primarily the Department of Health, Education, and Welfare's.

As I have mentioned to you in my testimony some time ago, we have a great demand placed upon us for educational materials. In addition to that, I think we have a particular perspective of the problem and a particular expertise which has to be made a part of the total educational process that we are involved in.

SENATOR HRUSKA. Could you touch on the development on the State level with reference to the model plan for penalties? I think that would be of special interest since we are getting into it on a national basis.

What are there, some 14 States now that have adopted those same approaches which you are now advocating?

MR. INGERSOLL. I believe it is 11. I think one of the very important things about this Federal legislation, in addition to the improved law enforcement tools that it will provide, is that it also will provide Federal leadership to the States.

The State laws in many, many cases are in as much a jumble, if not more so, than the Federal laws.

I think already that we are seeing signs, because of the hearings of your committee, that the States and localities are beginning to think and beginning to think along the lines that the Federal Government seems to be moving. We are preparing a proposed model State act which is being sent out at this time for review and comment.

Some 26 States have recently asked us for assistance in preparing and modifying their legislation. We are responding to these requests.

SENATOR MANSFIELD. Mr. President, appropos to what Senator Hruska said and the answer made by Mr. Ingersoll that 11 States have indicated an interest

in legislation on the basis of the Federal model, first let me say that I think the sooner we get this legislation out of the committee and onto the floor the better.

Secondly, Mr. President, I would like to make a suggestion because of the emphasis placed on State-Federal relations on this particular subject. It is all-embracing as far as the Nation is concerned.

I would like to suggest that you consider the possibility of having a Governors' conference.

SENATOR DODD. I think our subcommittee [6] will report the bill out within a week.

SENATOR MANSFIELD. If you get it out, we will get it up in the next day or two.

MR. INGERSOLL. We also have a very active State-Federal relations program within the Bureau which provides assistance.

THE PRESIDENT. You may have that, but I think what the Senator is suggesting is something else; that we have had a Narcotics Bureau for the last 50 years with the tools of 1914 dealing with the nuclear weapons in that field, if I may use an analogy, that are used by organized crime of the 1960's. We have been ridiculously outgunned. That is part of the problem.

So we tend to just blame it all on the kids and the others that are drawn into this field. It has been made available to them. The sale has been made. The Government hasn't done its job.

I think a lot of responsibility rests right with the Government, Federal, State, and local. We can cooperate with the States when they ask. But, as Governor Hughes knows, it does help to get the States to-

---

[6] Juvenile Delinquency Subcommittee of the Senate Judiciary Committee.

gether and it jogs them into action. Isn't that true, Governor?

SENATOR HUGHES. It helps a great deal if you do have a conference and you place the emphasis on it.

THE PRESIDENT. Exchange ideas and then they go back and have a concerted approach rather than just doing it, "If the State asks, we will be glad to cooperate."

If the Governor gets behind it, it is one thing; if it is the fellow down the line, it is something else.

MR. INGERSOLL. You mentioned this in your message of July 14. We have already begun to work on that.

THE PRESIDENT. We will put Secretary Finch on now, if you will stay for questions later.

SECRETARY ROBERT H. FINCH. *Mr. President and gentlemen:*

I can be very brief and pretty well spell this out.

We were in the preparation of legislation and we support it fully.

As the law is now, there are no controls at all. This legislation is on the basis of flexibility, the tailoring of regulatory and penal controls. We are satisfied that we have sufficient input in the decisions of the Attorney General to exercise the functions designating these dangerous substances as well as securing persons who will be permitted to engage in research in the drugs themselves.

We don't anticipate any problem in the administration of this area. We think we have a really rational means of bringing these drugs under control.

That is simply not true under the legislation where administrative procedures and legal requirements are different for marihuana and narcotics than they are for the depressants, stimulants, and other kinds of drugs. We think that for the first time this is met in this bill.

This is enforcement law, enforcement thrust. It certainly does not pretend to cover, and we are not covering now, the educational aspects and the research aspects and the rehabilitation aspects. I don't think we should kid ourselves that we are.

Our studies now cover a great aspect of this whole problem, such as the addicts potential of new drugs, basic biochemical and neuro-physiological aspects, the nature and extent of the drugs in the United States, the biological and sociological consequences of drug abuse.

We have over 150 grants out now. We are satisfied that we still don't know what these various drugs do in terms of the nervous system, genetic influence, and consequences. And in many other areas, we are finding out that there is a lot we don't know which we should know.

THE PRESIDENT. You have a limited budget. Is it too limited? Do you have enough to do what you are doing?

SECRETARY FINCH. Certainly not in the field of education, Mr. President, and certainly not in the field of rehabilitation.

THE PRESIDENT. Will you ask for more?

SECRETARY FINCH. We will in the next budget.

THE PRESIDENT. Do you have people expert enough that you could use them effectively?

SECRETARY FINCH. I am not sure we have people. We are trying through the regional programs to educate the educators so that we get more into the public school system.

THE PRESIDENT. I am not going to raise this point, but I think Senator Javits raised it earlier. From at least a cursory knowledge of this thing, this educational and rehabilitation thing could be even more important than this whole law enforcement side. It is the repeater.

REPRESENTATIVE ALBERT. It destroys their market.

THE PRESIDENT. Is this what you find?

SECRETARY FINCH. Yes, sir.

Last year we finally isolated the active constituents of marihuana. This means that for the first time the scientific community has a standardized substance that they can use in controlled studies of marihuana. Because, otherwise, the quality of marihuana, the natural product, varies so much from area to area that we can't make any definite conclusions.

THE PRESIDENT. On the education side, I was talking to Art Linkletter about this last night. I said: "Don't they start in high school?" He said: "No, in junior high school."

This, apparently, is the problem.

SECRETARY FINCH. We had 28 workshops regionally. That is hard to cover. But these are in the active areas, the Northeast, the Far West, and one in Chicago.

THE PRESIDENT. You have a number? What is the percentage of people or would you like to even propose it? I know I have seen a number of polls and studies and so forth. Are you prepared to say approximately how many in the schools are involved?

SECRETARY FINCH. We have some very spotty data, and it is frightening, given by high school superintendents and districts. But it is another weakness. Another proposal that you have before your desk is a mechanism which will enable us to get data of this kind.

But any guess I would make right now would be purely speculative. I can tell you

that from very high income districts, for example in Virginia, affluent districts, we have superintendents come in and say it is better than half their students they think who are using marihuana or other drugs.

THE PRESIDENT. In other words, it gives a lie to the idea that this is something that simply happens to the poor. It is moving to the upper middle class and so forth.

SECRETARY FINCH. This brings us to what I would like to support, the penalty provisions, because I have been both a prosecutor and in the district attorney's office and so forth. Here, again, I believe very firmly that the flexibility that goes into this law is sound. Because here are a few kids and they get hold of some marihuana and under some States laws that is a felony. You might as well write him off right at that point because he is branded a felon from then on.

The courts have an understanding of the situation, and the school system, in some cases, cannot take him back into the school. So that I would like to argue very strongly for the flexibility that is built into this law in terms of sentencing and in terms of the probation aspect.

I think the rest of the prepared statement I would like to submit and respond to questions.

SENATOR JAVITS. Mr. President, the one thing I hope you realize is that a two-pronged attack is absolutely essential. You can't hope to get anywhere, this is my judgment, unless at the same time you attack the sources as well as the customers.

What Bob [Finch] is saying is entirely right. The kids question us sociologically and even politically on this issue of "pot." I hope very much that you will get the very best counsel and guidance so that we won't have 1914 ideas of "pot." They think it is no worse than taking a drink or having a martini. We had better take account of that.

You know as a lawyer, it isn't what the facts are, it is what the judge thinks that counts. That is what we think. It gets down to almost the upper public school level.

THE PRESIDENT. Mr. Poff?

REPRESENTATIVE RICHARD H. POFF. Mr. President, not by way of rebuttal, but while it is true that the administration's proposal does not deal with techniques of rehabilitation, the penalty package in the administration's proposal does have two very useful mechanisms to promote new rehabilitation techniques.

The first of those is the flexibility to which you referred, which makes it possible for the court to expunge the record and spare the first offender of the possibility of bearing a stigma which will follow him all of his life.

And the second, equally important, I think, is that with respect to all penalties imposed, it is possible for the court to consider the degradations of the crime as to the gravity of the offense and fit the punishment to suit the crime. Under the present penalty structure, that is simply impossible.

SECRETARY FINCH. Or they will tell them to cop out, take the lesser plea.

REPRESENTATIVE POFF. Exactly.

The second important mechanism to which I refer is that which is called, for the lack of a better phrase, the mandatory parole component. Built into each felony sentence will be a segment which is mandatory in its impact and requires that the convicted felon be subjected to a period of supervised rehabilitation following customarily the conclusion of his serv-

ice in the institution.

SENATOR YARBOROUGH. Mr. President, the Labor and [Public] Welfare Committee in the Senate, of which our distinguished neighbor is the ranking minority member [Senator Javits], and we work closely on such matters. I have concern over the traditional division of duties between the Justice Department and HEW. HEW has charge of education, medical treatment, doctors, drugs, some of the things the Secretary mentioned, rehabilitation, and research.

I have had the staff analysis of these different bills pending. We have some bills before our committee. The Justice Department bill is before the Judiciary Committee.

We have some concern of the part of the functions of HEW being put over to the Justice Department which is not a department of medical doctors and medical education.

Part of the bill provides for educational research programs. Another provision of it is authority for any educational research program necessary for the enforcement.

We have in the bills pending before our committee specific authorizations of appropriations going up through fiscal '74 for building facilities under the jurisdiction of the Secretary of HEW. He is the administrator.

The House bill, I believe Chairman Staggers [7] in the House, is very similar with the bill in the Senate.

So we have two sets of bills, one to deal with the treatment, research, the things that the Secretary talked about.

---

[7] Representative Harley O. Staggers of West Virginia, Chairman of both the House Interstate and Foreign Commerce Committee, and the Special Subcommittee on Investigation of Interstate and Foreign Commerce.

I would like to raise a question as to the wisdom of creating, as part of the bill before the Judiciary Committee, the necessity, it seems to me, of putting up educational and medical treatment under the Justice Department.

SECRETARY FINCH. To get at the very thing we are talking about, where we have a penal institutions study, people who have been addicts, and when they are brought back in it is necessary for us to have that kind of educational language in there.

It is also my understanding that just as with the classification of the so-called hard drugs, we will require the concurrence of the Secretary of HEW in writing for these programs. That is my understanding.

SENATOR YARBOROUGH. You are satisfied that none of your research——

SECRETARY FINCH. We have worked with the Attorney General, our technical people have worked right from the beginning. This has been a matter of months since the day we came into office.

I can tell you no one is more cognizant or jealous of their prerogatives than doctors and psychiatrists or researchers.

THE PRESIDENT. If I may suggest, and I think the Senator has put his finger on a very important jurisdictional point, but I personally think it would be very harmful for the cause we are working for here to have too much isolation.

The difficulty is that too many of our educators and doctors have too little information or too little interest in the necessity for the use of the law and the penal weapons that are necessary. And, also, it isn't a very healthy situation to have people in law enforcement who have very little understanding or interest in education.

We want law enforcement people who understand the educational problems, who have compassion, and, by the same token, we don't want educators that are sitting out here on the side saying: "The problem is solely educational. You don't need to have these penalties and the rest."

I would hope that whatever we work out that you have some cross-fertilization there. I think it is impressive to have the Bureau of Narcotics, being a man who is a law enforcement official but, as you noted, putting great emphasis on the rehabilitation and the necessity for flexible penalties and the rest. It is that kind of attitude that I think is sophisticated and subtle, but perhaps not as spectacular as saying: "Go out and toss them all in jail." But, nevertheless, it will get to the problem.

I think what we really need is a new breed here. We need people who can understand both and who will not emphasize one to the exclusion of the other. That is what I think you are trying to do.

SECRETARY FINCH. Particularly, Mr. President, at the board of education level, high school and even elementary, they have got to face up to this.

I know Senator Hughes feels very strongly about this. We have encountered such resistance because they don't want to face the thing. It is so unpleasant. In terms of shaking up curricula and everything else——

THE PRESIDENT. You mean the educators?

SECRETARY FINCH. Yes, local boards and principals. They don't want to admit it is going on.

SENATOR HUGHES. Mr. President, I don't want to make a speech about this, but I talked to the Secretary about it. It is a very tragic situation in this country.

There is absolutely, in my opinion, in the way of educational materials and experience and qualifications and technical know-how, almost a total void throughout the United States of any ability to reach the young people of this country in relation to this problem.

Also, in the material we are putting out and the information we are putting out is absolutely baloney as far as the kids are concerned in this country in the way they are getting it.

I talked to the Secretary about it again and asked him if he minded that. I very emphatically stated that we are totally infracted at the national level in approaching this.

In Senator Yarborough's committee, we have had medical library bills up, Indian education bills up, and so forth. And in every one of those you have to distinctly and from a fractured approach get in something in the field of narcotics, drug abuse, and alcoholism. There is no unification of purpose of what we are doing.

As a result of that, we are not even instructing in our medical schools. We are not instructing in our professional disciplines. We have got to begin at the top and the bottom because they have no exposure. In fact, most of the testimony has indicated they receive prejudice in those schools against alcoholics, narcotic users, and drug abusers. As a result, they want nothing to do with them.

Our social workers, in very small part, have a specialized interest. We have not given this type of work any prestige or any dignity or any continuity of funding, so as the researchers will not dedicate their life to it, they will not spend their total talents with it.

In my opinion, in a city of the size of Washington, D.C., in every high school in this city, there ought to be an expert on narcotics and drugs. The drug scene is changing so rapidly, as Mr. Ingersoll and Mr. Finch will tell you, that what is the problem this year may well fade into history next year and we have a totally new one. There is nothing in the library that is current. It is all antiquated. They can't get the information. A school counselor cannot talk to a kid with a drug problem. It has been absolutely, almost universally, my total experience.

They need specialty in the field, completely, which means the development of a completely new line of people in the field of education, treatment in health. Then if you get to rehabilitation, you have got the other side of it.

I found, also, in the community mental health centers, which is another approach we have tried to take on this thing, a total prejudice against it, an unwillingness to even cope with the problem in the process of suffering.

We talk about what we are doing in our prisons. We are running post-graduate schools to train criminals and to train those people to find out where they can get heroin in Chicago, Los Angeles, New Orleans.

Senator Dodd could communicate more eloquently than I on this. He has been examining it very thoroughly.

But we are actually giving those people freedom to move all over the country because they have then made the contacts where they can get it anywhere. They can pick up a fix within 30 minutes after they are out of the prison.

I want to thank the Secretary, and you, sir, for allowing me to let out a little pent-up emotion on this, I guess. This is a very critical stage in this country. It is in the elementary schools. It is in the junior high schools. It is in the great, broad, white middle class as well as the black ghetto. It is a unique problem of the American Indian. It has just absolutely invaded every home in America. And every parent in America is scared to death to talk to them. They are literally scared to death of what is happening. I am, too.

THE PRESIDENT. Senator Griffin?

SENATOR ROBERT P. GRIFFIN. To state the obvious, a big part of the education on this subject, regardless of what you do in the school—and we should do a great deal—is the education that our young people get from the media. I think that they can be very helpful, particularly the television and the newspapers. Whatever we can do to get their cooperation would obviously be very important.

SECRETARY FINCH. We have current films now.

THE PRESIDENT. Leaving out what your doctors and researchers and so forth are trying to find out about the diet drugs and so forth, but speaking specifically to the subject the Senator has referred to of education, in the education material for high schools and students, how much do you have?

SECRETARY FINCH. I think we have raised it from about $1½ million to $3 million.

THE PRESIDENT. What are you asking? It seems to me that that is a pitifully inadequate amount. How can you possibly do the job with that?

You will reexamine this. I think it is important to reexamine this, and to the extent that you can find qualified personnel, it seems to me, is just as important to reduce the market.

We have got to get at the demand. It seems to me the job is totally inadequate.

Do you need a supplemental now? Mr.

Mayo [Director, Bureau of the Budget] isn't here to speak for himself.

SECRETARY FINCH. We will make sure we have it.

THE PRESIDENT. Get the people.

SENATOR HUGHES. Mr. President, we also have a great problem in the adult education which I didn't touch on. Senator Griffin reminded me of it. I find most parents in America don't mind discussing the war in Vietnam or the nuclear bomb, but they absolutely forbid you to bring up the subject of marihuana in front of their children. The children know more about marihuana than they do by far, and whatever the street language is, they know that, too.

I think we need a tremendous adult education program in this country, too, to try and educate the parents to the fact that they are not in communication with the youngsters. They don't understand the problems the youngsters are facing and the culture that these youngsters are living in now with narcotics and drugs.

SENATOR MANSFIELD. I think the Congress could stand a good deal more in the way of education, too.

SENATOR YARBOROUGH. Mr. President, I am hopeful that in our supporting of the desire of the Chief Executive for speedy action on the law, I am hopeful in our speed, we are careful about this language on education and research; that it doesn't impinge on the traditional jurisdiction of the Secretary of HEW, because he has the framework. We have bills here that would give the money to authorize the grants, give the monies for administration and also construction. It seems to me that education basically should remain there in HEW.

SECRETARY FINCH. We will examine that, Senator, but both my Education people and Health people who work with the Department of Justice are not at all apprehensive at this point.

SENATOR YARBOROUGH. You feel you will still have jurisdiction?

SECRETARY FINCH. Yes.

THE PRESIDENT. I would like to see consideration given, Senator, to the strike force. I think we need cross-fertilization between the law enforcement and education group.

The trouble is too many of us live in a vacuum on this thing. We think of only one isolated part of it. I think it is well for the educators to talk to the law enforcement people and not to say: "This is my jurisdiction and this is yours."

To the extent you can work it out that way, it would be very helpful.

Bob, if you will stay there, we will turn to Art Linkletter, who will present this situation from the public standpoint. This is an unusual presentation.

REPRESENTATIVE ANCHER NELSEN. One thing I think we can immediately get at right here in the District of Columbia— Chief Wilson pointed out the other day [8] that about 300 to 400 criminals are engaged in armed robbery particularly for the purpose of feeding their habit, and we have no detention or treatment center right here in the Nation's Capital.

He called attention to the fact that if about 300 were taken off the streets, a great percentage of our armed robbery problems would be solved here.

We are aware of it on the District Committee. But I think the Congress will be helpful if we move in this direction and do something about it.

THE PRESIDENT. As you know, in a bipartisan meeting, it seems to me that in

the District we could use this as a model, and get the District crime package as well as some of the other items underway. We could perhaps make an enormous contribution here, and also that can be educational to the whole Nation and to the Congress.

SENATOR DODD. Mr. President, I would like to say to Senator Mansfield and to you, sir, last year we asked for $12 million for that Addict Rehabilitation Act and only got $5 million. Even that got out to the States late. I think this is where we certainly need more money. If there had been more money available, I think we could have made a great difference.

THE PRESIDENT. Senator, as you know, this year and despite our budget cutting which was essential for the reasons we are all aware of, the one area that we didn't cut, in fact we increased, was in the field of law enforcement.

I think, however, we are getting into here a broader subject. Let's not put law enforcement over here in one area, more police, more judges, more penalties, and the rest and say: "We are shortchanged in the same field."

That, I think, is the fundamental point you are getting at, Senator Hughes.

SENATOR DODD. I feel very strongly that that is the right way.

SENATOR MANSFIELD. Secretary Finch says he has approximately $3 million to spend on educational aspects of this program. That is the cost of just one hour of the war in Vietnam. It is abominable.

SENATOR HUGHES. I would like to just state, if I might, sir, going back to Mr. Ingersoll and agents, that though I am primarily interested in the health and education end of it, that we have had this subject slip into the hearings held.

In New York, for example, they said

in their area alone they needed 100 additional agents. This is a lot of manpower. If you divided that in half and talked to Mr. Ingersoll about it, I am sure it would be reduced greatly. But the need for agents I want to emphasize also. Because though my interest is on the other side of it primarily in committee work, I do agree that all of it is essential.

THE PRESIDENT. This is, as I was indicating earlier, an unusual procedure; but from time to time, we are trying to bring to meetings of this type people from outside of government who have an understanding of the problem, particularly when the problem involves massively one of education.

In this field, Art Linkletter, who is an old personal friend and, of course, known to everyone around this table, can speak, I think, with great knowledge and great eloquence.

Art, if you want to talk and you will be glad to answer questions I understand, too, but if you would tell us what you think of what you have heard here, or anything you want.

MR. LINKLETTER. Let me begin on purely a personal note of course. Two weeks ago, my beautiful 20-year-old daughter leaped to her death from her apartment while she was in a depressed, suicidal frame of mind and of panic believing that she was losing her mind from recurring bad trips from an LSD experiment some 6 months before.

That this was a shock to the family and to the Nation goes without saying. I made the decision that this tragic death would not be hushed up, it would not be covered over as is the case with so many prominent children and people, but that I would seek out to shock the Nation into the realization that this is not happening to other people's children in some part of the town, but that it can happen to a well-educated, intelligent girl from a family that has traditionally been a Christian family and has been straight.

I must say that Hollywood is pretty generally tarred with a brush of excesses of all kinds. Our family has been an outstanding example, I think you would agree, in the opposite. So, that my daughter would have this happen to her has certainly been a salutary experience to the Nation.

The result of it is that in the last 10 days I have had over 25,000 letters, hundreds and hundreds of telegrams, as well as phone calls which I couldn't accept, asking me to appear at a variety of aroused citizens' meetings, ranging from Honolulu to Boston, from Governors to sheriffs to PTA's; but also an alarming number of letters from parents saying that they know that this is happening in their own family and what should they do.

I was horrified, gentlemen, to find out on the examination of my own experience and my own mind that I don't know what to tell them. I had been aware that my daughter, along with all the kids of her age, had done a little experimenting.

But she had—I want to make it very clear—told me this months ago. She had said that it was ridiculous, that the bum trips and the bad experiences of her colleagues had frightened her, and that she certainly was never going to do it again.

My son [Robert Linkletter], who was very close to Diane, my 24-year-old boy, told me that she had not taken any more and not experimented any more, but that for months these trips kept recurring against her own wishes, no way for her to stop it, which led her to believe that she might be losing her mind.

It was a terrible, lonesome experience. She couldn't tell anybody about it. It was a shock to me that she couldn't tell us about it, because we are a very close family.

But instead of that, she went the other way and talked against it, and told us how her friends were such fools and she was trying to talk herself into believing that she was leaving it and it was all right.

The reason I bring this up is because it is not a theory, it is not a supposition of what can happen. It is a vital personal experience in our own family.

Diane was not a hippie. She was not a drug addict. She was not a nutty girl. She had everything to live for. She had no deep depressions. She had no problems in her life that were not the normal growing up problems of all children, of being frustrated and disappointed and anxious about life which we all go through.

The point is that the kids of America today are reacting to the drug society in which they have grown up, where from the time they are born, on the television tube everybody popping things into their mouths, whether they want to get thin, fat, or happy or go to sleep or wake up or erase tension or take away headaches or whatever. So, they are used to putting chemicals and seeing everybody putting chemicals into their body.

Then when you add to that the normal teenage and the upper teenage desire to do something risqué and daring—in our case, some of our older folks remember stealing an apple or taking a joy ride in the car, something a little bit against the law or against rules. The kids now have available to them every kind of amphetamine, barbiturate; they take "downers," "uppers," and the language has become a completely different cul-

ture. They talk about "bummers" and "smack"; and while most of the kids in my opinion in this country are afraid of heroin, and are becoming frightened of LSD and are becoming frightened of methionine, they still want the kicks that come from chemicals.

In certain regions, they are so crazy and insane as to inject into their bloodstream peanut butter, because somebody said that peanut butter gives you a high, and they die from that. Mayonnaise they are inserting into their bodies.

So what we have is the syndrome of the growing-up child with anxieties, frustrations, turning to drugs of any kind.

So I am using this platform of my personal tragedy, number one, to alert every parent in America that it not only can happen to their child, but it probably will happen to their child; that he will be exposed to some kind of an offer to take some kind of a stimulant. Where we used to think that it might happen, now we know it is going to happen.

What can we do about it? I believe in education first, and I believe in education starting in the fourth grade, long before the children get to the level where they are playing "chicken" with their teenage contemporaries to show how reckless and bold they are.

I am talking about teaching children at the fourth and fifth and sixth grades that you no more put anything into your mouth or bloodstream than you walk out in front of a car on the highway, set fire to your dress, or drink iodine out of the medicine chest. It is just a plain, simple statement of fact, rather than a "no-no" or a moralism.

Number two, I think parents have got to learn that they must keep open every avenue of communication; and they must know all the telltale signs; and they must be understanding and not treat their children like juvenile delinquents when they try something, but merely like experimentalists who are doing something dangerous like walking on a pipe across a culvert or anything else that kids do.

I am in favor of the new law, projected law, on treatment of marihuana cases, because I have grown up in southern California. In San Diego, the story of marihuana is an old story. We have been down there next to Tijuana for all of my life. Marihuana has been a curse; and I have been arguing against it for many years, not that it is a dangerous drug, which it isn't, but when they say it is no worse than alcohol, I say to the kids: "In other words, tuberculosis is no worse than hepatitis. They are both bad. That is no argument for taking it."

Alcohol has probably done more harm than any drug in the history of the United States. So it is not to be equated that while it is used, it is harmless.

I think too often mothers and fathers who know their children are smoking marihuana have not reported it because it is a felony. They have been unable to get treatment for fear the child will have a mark against him for the rest of his life.

I know personally of families whose children have tried marihuana, have been arrested and have had felony charges processed against them; and in one case, the daughter of a very prominent Hollywood woman, her son is today somewhere in India, Nepal—God knows under what influence—because he has a felony charge against him and he left the country rather than go to prison. His life is ruined; whereas, if he had been treated, as the proposed law indicates, he would have been saved.

I speak at 15 colleges a year, and have for 5 years, all across the country. I talk to the kids at lunch and breakfast and also in my main speech. If you think the kids of today think that marihuana is the same as heroin, you have got another think coming. They have the same attitude toward marihuana and the legal prosecution of marihuana smokers as we did in 1929 against alcohol and the prohibition law.

They think it is unfair, so they are laughing at it. When the judges don't follow the law, they said: "See, they don't believe it either. So the whole thing is wrong."

I think that having marihuana be a felony is as bad as marihuana being legal. I think both are extremes. I think we can't legalize it. I think by over-punishing it, we overemphasize and over stress it.

As with amphetamines and all of these things, I have a very single attitude about it. The kids reflect to me the fact that our own American manufacturers have many, many different ways of selling and flooding the market with these available drugs. We know they come across from Mexico. They know they are bought in large multimillion quantities from American manufacturers.

That is why I noticed in this bill the wonderful provision that from the manufacturer through the distribution, these kinds of drugs should be supervised by Federal law and by Federal supervision of some kind, because it does no good to be "holier than thou" and have millions of these things going right out and coming right back in where the kids can get them.

Most of the kids are too smart, as I say, to take heroin. But it leads to it when they can't get some of these other things. I feel very, very keenly about this. I intend to make public appearances. I am not an expert. I do not profess to be an authority on drugs, but I know something about human beings; and I have spent my life talking to kids. My special field is going to be the parents and the young children.

I think we should make the next generation understand what they are putting into their blood is not an answer to life's problems. It only exaggerates and accentuates them.

I am delighted that the President and his wife feel as keenly as I know they do about it, because from the top of this country down, we need to be aware of the problem, and fight it.

Thank you.

SENATOR JAVITS. Art, would you say a word about why you think that we should not legalize it in the light of prohibition? I am arguing the kids' case.

You talk the same language I do. If medical research shows that it is no more harmful than alcohol, what is the case against not having the prohibition? As we found, prohibition law made criminals of everybody. So we might just as well forget it and deal with other means of control, regulation, et cetera.

MR. LINKLETTER. As a practical politician, you probably realize that the country would probably not accept that kind of a lengthy step.

You know we are in danger even talking about this liberalization of the law of causing vast numbers of people to rise up and say: "You are being soft."

Marihuana has been painted for so long as a terrible drug, equating it with drug addiction of the worst type. We know now that it is not physically addictive; and it is not a narcotic in the sense it is not a painkiller, but certainly it is psychologically, in some cases, addictive. It certainly does hurt anybody by the virtue of the

fact that it takes away motivation; it makes things seem what they are not.

I don't think it would be possible to take that far a step. Some day it might happen. But I just think you have got to do the best you can with alleviating the worst of a situation.

SECRETARY FINCH. If I may respond to that point.

The research we are doing now for the first time tells us that, in the case of one out of 20, you get a very marked differential depending on body chemistry and a lot of other factors.

MR. LINKLETTER. Then, Bob, you have marihuana of two kinds. Then you get into hashish. They say: "If you can smoke marihuana, why can't you smoke hashish?" Except it is six times as strong.

SENATOR JAVITS. Let's take Bob's position; we still don't know. And if we don't know, we must say no.

We are not making any moral judgments. We don't know. Therefore, we say no.

THE PRESIDENT. In our view that can be made, Jack and you have probably discussed it, too. When you look at some of the societies of Asia, committees and others—marihuana of course is all-related in the family—you see what has happened to them when they accept this and move in that direction. You don't want it to happen here.

I think Art has made a very sophisticated political judgment there. We were just checking some recent polls on this. A very substantial majority of the people disagree with the assumption that marihuana is not dangerous because they don't know what it is, and they think it is dangerous.

So, I think you are exactly right. Moving in that direction, apart from that, on the merits, I don't think we are certainly in a position to say now, and I think it would be very bad to come out of this meeting with the idea that marihuana is perhaps not something to be too concerned about.

It is just the fact that we have an antiquated law and people who are too unsophisticated to understand it; because there are real dangers, as Art has already indicated, apart from the physical addiction, that psychological breakthrough that occurs may then take the individual on into the other drugs.

MR. LINKLETTER. Yes, habituation more than addiction. But it is still just as serious.

I think my own judgment on it is that it is worse than alcohol because it has worse effects on some people. God knows, alcohol has been bad enough. We could go back and do it all over again and probably make a different set of laws for that, too.

SENATOR JAVITS. The main point in marihuana is you can't take one drink. Once you have it, you have had it.

SENATOR MANSFIELD. Isn't it true, Mr. President, that within the past several weeks there has been a high-level governmental commission created for the purpose of determining the points which Senator Javits has brought out and which Mr. Linkletter and Senator Hughes and others have emphasized just to find out what marihuana is, if it is really addictive in other than a physical sense and if it is dangerous?

SENATOR DODD. That is in the bill before us.

SENATOR HUGHES. Mr. President, I would like to ask Mr. Linkletter another question. He has very emphatically pointed to alcohol two or three times. All of you know I am a recovered alcoholic. You know that I came through this route.

I would like to inquire, wouldn't it be also helpful in the field of marihuana usage—and I want everyone to know I thoroughly agree we don't need alcohol, marihuana, or anything else; we are an intoxicated society, depending on where we begin, with a cup of coffee and a cigarette and on down that route all during the day—if a real, honest look at alcohol, without any intentions of trying to go back to prohibition, but at least telling the truth about alcohol in this country, wouldn't help in alleviating a lot of the pressure on marihuana?

It is not a beautiful drug as everyone has been led to think it is.

MR. LINKLETTER. At least it would answer the charges of all the kids who were hypercritical, a great cry of all the young college kids today that we are hypocritical. We say it is okay to drink alcohol but not the other. This would at least equate that and say we do recognize they are all troublesome.

I was amazed, when speaking up at Yale University a few months ago, to find a high level of intelligent, top students arguing very seriously for the legalization of marihuana.

But I had to argue with them that they were just asking for the impossible and that it was not a good idea to spread further a thing which we already agree is not good.

Of course, the kids are pretty clever. Up there they had a rule, for instance, no girl could be in a room with a boy unless there is a book between the door and jam. So they put in a book of matches. These kids know within thousandths of an inch how far to go. They will go all the way.

I want to say one word, too, about the

media, since I am identified with the media.

You gentlemen may not realize it but almost every time a "top 40" record is played on the radio, it is an ad for "acid," marihuana, and trips. The lyrics of the popular songs and the jackets on the albums of the popular songs are all a complete, total campaign for the fun and thrills of trips. If you don't believe it, you ought to take a good, long look at some of the lyrics and some of the albums with the hidden symbols, with the language that the kids know that you don't even realize they are talking about.

They have words for trips and marihuana and "speed" that you have never even heard of. When those lyrics are sung, the kids are all rapping, as they call it, talking, rapping with each other, on this subject.

I personally am going to do what I can out in Hollywood to see if we can't get creative rock and roll people to do songs in the same idiom, the same vernacular and in the same acceptable language of the kids that is away from that.

But every major record company and every rock and roll radio station is sending out, 18 hours a day, messages to the kids that are right over the heads of our generation.

THE PRESIDENT. Art, let me ask you one question about the media in another field. Among the most popular programs, of course, on television, apart from soap operas and all the other things and sports, are programs like the FBI story, in other words, investigative programs; people like mystery.

Has television done, is it doing, an adequate job, from the standpoint of public service? We all understand that the public service aspects of television are somewhat exaggerated despite what they may claim because they have to be in it for the money, for the ads and so forth.

MR. LINKLETTER. It is an advertising medium.

THE PRESIDENT. I am speaking now in terms of sometimes making a virtue out of necessity here. Would it not be possible for television not to put on a dull educational program about the evils of marihuana, heroin, "speed," LSD, and so forth? It would seem to me that some exciting programs on this could have an enormous educational impact on the country.

Is it adequately being done and is anything being planned?

MR. LINKLETTER. I don't think it is adequately being done. But I think it is being planned.

I know of several programs, one of which I am intimately connected with, which has that as one of its principal goals. The only reason that I would not care to go any further with the details of it is that there are 4,000 of my colleagues waiting to steal it if I mention it. I prefer to get it on and then tell you about it.

But I couldn't agree more.

THE PRESIDENT. You think there are possibilities?

MR. LINKLETTER. Yes, especially since the networks have in recent months been very painfully and sensitively aware of violence, and so they are going to have to get into the more intriguing aspects of crime.

One of them certainly is this field rather than the shoot-'em-up cops and robbers which we all know is just a dramatic smoke and flame, and the real crime occurs in many other areas where it is deep and insinuated into our fabric of our civilization.

855

But I think there will be more of that done.

SENATOR YARBOROUGH. Mr. President, in support of what Mr. Linkletter said, in the days of hearings that I have held this year on the problem, we learned that the average narcotic addict today is under 21 years of age, where 20 years ago he was over 30.

Furthermore, these young people who become heroin addicts, generally, most of them started with marihuana or some of these goofballs or pep pills and went to LSD and from LSD into the heroin.

I agree with everything you have said about how dangerous marihuana is. I was district judge in Austin, Texas, and in the cases before that court I saw what people did under the influence of marihuana.

Senator Javits said it isn't taking one drink. They smoke these and they do incredible things, try to fight six armed policemen. A 16-year-old boy, with his bare fists, says, "I can whip all of you." They wrestle them to the ground to keep from beating them up. He is not as brutal as a lot of these people.

THE PRESIDENT. We would like to go on with this, but Senator Mansfield and the Speaker reminded me that we do want a little time left for discussion.

SENATOR MANSFIELD. May I say, Mr. President, that I leave with deep regret. I want to thank Mr. Ingersoll and Secretary Finch for their effectual summation of a difficult problem; and Mr. Linkletter for, in effect, opening up a new world to me, as far as some of these problems connected with drugs which we have been discussing today.

I would like to say, I am an hour late now, which is the best compliment I can give to all of you.

But I do want to promise, Mr. Presi-dent, that if the committee gets out this legislation—I hope they do shortly—that we will handle it expeditiously on the floor and we will get it passed.

Thank you very much.

SPEAKER MCCORMACK. We will do the same thing.

REPRESENTATIVE STAGGERS. If I might say this, Mr. President, in speaking for the Interstate and Foreign Commerce Committee, we will do all we can. I want to assure you of our concern to bring this to a successful ending; and I have just yesterday made a release on drug abuse, the evils of it in the country.

Here is an article I wrote some time ago for one of our magazines in the country on drug abuse.

I want to also compliment Secretary Finch. I think he did an excellent job.

I especially want to thank Mr. Ingersoll because I think you have two men who understand sort of the problem, and we can work together in a bipartisan way. As you say, it is certainly something that has to be approached by everyone. I think the whole country will be appreciative of the fact that you are attacking this, and they are tackling it and we can all work on it together.

THE PRESIDENT. I want to thank all the Members of the Congress who have been here.

As they say, this is one subject let's decide right today, and I think the Speaker and Mike Mansfield will agree, and all of you, one subject we are going to keep completely above the partisan level.

It is just as important as the defense of the country abroad. I think we all feel that way. I know these jurisdictional problems.

Wilbur, would you like to say anything? Ways and Means always acts expeditiously.

REPRESENTATIVE WILBUR D. MILLS. We try to.

No, thank you, Mr. President.

THE PRESIDENT. On these jurisdictional problems, we want to work with the Congress. We do need the action. If we can have that kind of spirit, I think we will move in this field, and then the administration will have the responsibility for executing with the proper personnel.

SENATOR YARBOROUGH. It is my pleasure, as chairman of my committee, to be entirely nonpartisan.

REPRESENTATIVE STAGGERS. Again, I would like not to forget Mr. Art Linkletter, because he has been the idol of most

of the people of this country. The fact that he has come here to give his contribution, I think, is terrific.

SPEAKER McCORMACK. I think we should all convey to Mr. Linkletter and his loved ones our deep sympathy.

NOTE: The President began the meeting at 8:45 a.m. in the Cabinet Room at the White House. Also present for the bipartisan meeting were: Representatives John Jarman of Oklahoma, Gerald R. Ford of Michigan, William M. McCulloch of Ohio, and William L. Springer of Illinois.

The text of a news briefing on narcotics and dangerous drugs by Director Ingersoll, Bureau of Narcotics and Dangerous Drugs, Senator Roman L. Hruska, Art Linkletter, and Ronald L. Ziegler, White House Press Secretary, was released the same day and is printed in the Weekly Compilation of Presidential Documents (vol. 5, p. 1474).

405   Remarks on the Departure of the Shah of Iran. *October 23, 1969*

Your Imperial Majesty:

As you leave this Capital, after your visit here, I can echo what the Secretary of State just said in reflecting on your visit. He said: "The weather today is like our relations."

And, certainly on this beautiful day as we complete our talks, I believe that the relations between Iran and the United States have never been better. That is due to your leadership. It is due also to the fact that we feel a special relationship not only to your country, but to you, a relationship which, in my case, goes back many years.

We have had bilateral talks which have been most constructive.

But I, too, want to thank you for giving the Secretary, myself, and our colleagues the benefit of your analysis of the problems in the Mideast which are tremen-

dously explosive at the present time and also the problems in the world, because Iran, in a sense, is a bridge between the East and the West, between Asia and Europe, and, for that matter, Africa.

And at that vantage point you are able to see those problems perhaps better than almost any leader in the world.

We thank you for coming to us.

And I can say, in conclusion, that I look forward to visiting Iran again. I have not yet set a date. But you have very cordially invited me to come. I accept the invitation, and we will set a date at a later time.

Thank you.

NOTE: The President spoke at 11:20 a.m. in the Rose Garden at the White House.

See also Items 398 and 401.

His Imperial Majesty Mohammad Reza Shah Pahlavi, Shahanshah of Iran, responded as follows:

Thank you very much, Mr. President.

I must say once more how honored I was by your hospitality and friendship that you have shown to me once more, and how deeply appreciative I am of the frankness and the friendliness in which we have had our talks with you, Mr. President, and your associates.

As you very well mentioned, our relations have never been as good as they are now, because they are based on an absolute trust and mutual interests.

We are defending the same principles, upholding the same moral values that we understand and for which we are living and, if necessary, dying; the interest of your country that the world should be a good place to live in, a free place to live in; that everybody should be given the opportunity of progressing, of living better without fear and in health and happiness.

For these ideals that we respect, we wish you an evergrowing strength.

We wish you success in all your enterprises and, in addition to this, we hope that you will always feel—maybe sometimes it is a burden—but feel the responsibility that you have towards the human race, because you can provide it. When you can provide it, if I could be bold enough to say, you must provide it.

We shall continue on our part to play whatever constructive role that we can in our part of the world, upholding the same principles, trying to be of any assistance and cooperation for the maintenance of peace, stability, and assistance to all those who would ask for it without any second thought and as liberally as possible.

The state of relationships between our two countries, I hope, will continue in this manner for the better of our two countries, of our region, and I hope maybe even for the world.

As you mentioned, Mr. President, my country is a crossroad between various civilizations and various interests. It will be our duty to be able to honor this task faithfully, with dignity and, I hope, also in a constructive way.

We will be more able to do it always when we have the moral support, assistance, of our friends, the greatest of them being this great country of yours, and your personal friendship, Mr. President, which I personally, and I am sure my people, value to the greatest possible extent.

Thank you very much.

———————

THE PRESIDENT. On behalf of all of the American people, we wish you a very happy birthday Sunday.

HIS IMPERIAL MAJESTY. Thank you very much.

406   Special Message to the Congress on a New Program for the United States Merchant Marine.   *October 23, 1969*

To the Congress of the United States:

The United States Merchant Marine—the fleet of commercial ships on which we rely for our economic strength in time of peace and our defense mobility in time of war—is in trouble.

While only one-fourth of the world's merchant ships are more than twenty years old, approximately three-fourths of American trading vessels are at least that antiquated. In the next four years, much of our merchant fleet will be scrapped. Yet we are now producing only a few new ships a year for use in our foreign trade.

Building costs for American vessels are about twice those in foreign shipyards and production delays are excessive. Operating expenses also are high by world standards, and labor-management conflicts have been costly and disruptive.

Both government and industry share responsibility for the recent decline in American shipping and shipbuilding. Both government and industry must now make a substantial effort to reverse that record. We must begin immediately to rebuild our merchant fleet and make it more competitive. Accordingly, I am announcing today a new maritime program for this nation, one which will replace the drift and neglect of recent years and restore this country to a proud position in the shipping lanes of the world.

Our program is one of challenge and opportunity. We will challenge the American shipbuilding industry to show that it can rebuild our Merchant Marine at reasonable expense. We will challenge American ship operators and seamen to move toward less dependence on government subsidy. And, through a substantially revised and better administered government program, we will create the opportunity to meet that challenge.

The need for this new program is great since the old ways have not worked. However, as I have frequently pointed out, our budget constraints at this time are also significant. Our program, therefore, will be phased in such a way that it will not increase subsidy expenditures during the rest of fiscal year 1970 and will require only a modest increase for fiscal year 1971. We can thus begin to rebuild our fleet and at the same time meet our fiscal responsibilities.

THE SHIPBUILDING INDUSTRY

Our shipbuilding program is designed to meet both of the problems which lie behind the recent decline in this field: low production rates and high production costs. Our proposals would make it possible for shipbuilders to build more ships and would encourage them to hold down the cost of each vessel. We believe that these two aspirations are closely related. For only as we plan a major long-range building program can we encourage builders to standardize ship design and introduce mass production techniques which

have kept other American products competitive in world markets. On the other hand, only if our builders are able to improve their efficiency and cut their costs can we afford to replace our obsolescent merchant fleet with American-built vessels. These cost reductions are essential if our ship operators are to make capital investments of several billion dollars over the next ten years to build new, high-technology ships.

Our new program will provide a substantially improved system of construction differential subsidies, payments which reimburse American shipbuilders for that part of their total cost which exceeds the cost of building in foreign shipyards. Such subsidies allow our shipbuilders—despite their higher costs—to sell their ships at world market prices for use in our foreign trade. The important features of our new subsidy system are as follows:

1. We should make it possible for industry to build more ships over the next ten years, moving from the present subsidy level of about ten ships a year to a new level of thirty ships a year.

2. We should reduce the percentage of total costs which are subsidized. The government presently subsidizes up to 55 percent of a builder's total expenses for a given vessel. Leaders of the shipbuilding industry have frequently said that subsidy requirements can be reduced considerably if they are assured a long-term market. I am therefore asking that construction differential subsidies be limited to 45 percent of total costs in fiscal year 1971. That percentage should be reduced by 2 percent in each subsequent year until the maximum subsidy payment is down to 35 percent of total building expenses.

We are confident that the shipbuilding industry can meet this challenge. If

859

the challenge is not met, however, then the Administration's commitment to this part of our program will not be continued.

3. Construction differential subsidies should be paid directly to shipbuilders rather than being channeled through shipowners as is the case under the present system. A direct payment system is necessary if our program is to encourage builders to improve designs, reduce delays, and minimize costs. It will also help us to streamline subsidy administration.

4. The multi-year procurement system which is now used for other government programs should be extended to shipbuilding. Under this system, the government makes a firm commitment to build a given number of ships over a specified and longer period of time, a practice which allows the industry to realize important economies of scale and to receive lower subsidies.

5. The increased level of ship construction will require a corresponding increase in the level of federally insured mortgages. Accordingly, we should increase the ceiling on our present mortgage insurance programs from $1 billion to $3 billion.

6. We should extend construction differential subsidies to bulk carriers, ships which usually carry ore, grain, or oil and which are not covered by our present subsidy program.

7. A Commission should be established to review the status of the American shipbuilding industry, its problems, and its progress toward meeting the challenge we have set forth. The Commission should report on its findings within three years and recommend any changes in government policy which it believes are desirable.

THE SHIP OPERATING INDUSTRY

My comments to this point have related to the building of merchant vessels. The other arm of our maritime policy is that which deals with the operation of these ships. Here, too, our new program offers several substantial improvements over the present system.

1. Operating differential subsidies should be continued only for the higher wage and insurance costs which American shipping lines experience. Subsidies for maintenance and repair and for subsistence should be eliminated. Instead of paying the difference between the wages of foreign seamen and actual wages on American ships, however, the government should compare foreign wages with prevailing wage levels in several comparable sectors of the American economy. A policy which ties subsidies to this wage index will reduce subsidy costs and provide an incentive for further efficiencies. Under this system, the operator would no longer lose in subsidies what he saves in costs. Nor would he continue to be reimbursed through subsidies when his wage costs rise to higher levels.

2. At the same time that we are reducing operating subsidies, it is appropriate that we eliminate the "recapture" provisions of the Merchant Marine Act of 1936. These provisions require subsidized lines to pay back to the government a portion of profits. If the recapture provisions are removed, the purpose for which they were designed will be largely accomplished by corporate taxes, which were at much lower rates when these provisions were instituted. We will also save the cost of administering recapture provisions.

3. Many bulk carriers presently receive indirect operating subsidies from the government because of the statutory requirement that certain government cargos must be shipped in United States vessels at premium rates. When the Department of Agriculture ships grain abroad, for example, it pays higher rates out of its budget than if it were allowed to ship at world market rates. We will propose a new, direct subsidy system for such carriers, thus allowing us to phase out these premium freight rates and reduce the costs of several nonmaritime government programs.

4. Ship operators now receiving operating differential subsidies are permitted to defer Federal tax payments on reserve funds set aside for construction purposes. This provision should be extended to include all qualified ship operators in the foreign trade, but only for well-defined ship replacement programs.

5. Past government policies and industry attitudes have not been conducive to cooperation between labor and management. Our program will help to improve this situation by ending the uncertainty that has characterized our past maritime policy. Labor and management must now use this opportunity to find ways of resolving their differences without halting operations. If the desired expansion of merchant shipping is to be achieved, the disruptive work stoppages of the past must not be repeated.

6. The larger capital investment necessary to construct a modern and efficient merchant fleet requires corresponding port development. I am therefore directing the Secretary of Commerce and the Secretary of Transportation to work with related industries and local governments in improving our port operations. We must take full advantage of technological advances in this area and we should do all we can to encourage greater use of intermodal transportation systems, of which these high-technology ships are only a part.

EQUAL EMPLOYMENT OPPORTUNITIES

The expansion of American merchant shipbuilding which this program makes possible will provide many new employment opportunities. All of our citizens must have equal access to these new jobs. I am therefore directing the Secretary of Commerce and the Secretary of Labor to work with industry and labor organizations to develop programs that will insure all minority groups their rightful place in this expansion.

RESEARCH AND DEVELOPMENT

We will also enlarge and redirect the maritime research and development activities of the Federal government. Greater emphasis will be placed on practical applications of technological advances and on the coordination of Federal programs with those of industry.

The history of American commercial shipping is closely intertwined with the history of our country. From the time of the Colonial fishing sloops, down through the great days of the majestic clipper ships, and into the new era when steam replaced the sail, the venturesome spirit of maritime enterprise has contributed significantly to the strength of the nation.

Our shipping industry has come a long way over the last three centuries. Yet, as one of the great historians of American seafaring, Samuel Eliot Morison, has written: "all her modern docks and terminals and dredged channels will avail nothing, if the spirit perish that led her founders to 'trye all ports.'" It is that spirit to which our program of challenge and opportunity appeals.

It is my hope and expectation that this program will introduce a new era in the maritime history of America, an era in which our shipbuilding and ship operating industries take their place once again among the vigorous, competitive industries of this nation.

RICHARD NIXON

The White House
October 23, 1969

NOTE: Also released were a White House announcement and the transcript of a news briefing on the merchant marine program by Under Secretary of Commerce Rocco C. Siciliano and Federal Maritime Administrator Andrew E. Gibson.

407   Statement on a Safety Policy for the Federal Government. *October* 24, 1969

THE HUMAN suffering and economic waste caused by accidents are principal concerns of this administration. Federal, civil, and military personnel and the public must be protected; governmental programs must be efficiently run. These two goals can best be realized by a unified, dedicated, and on-going program of accident elimination in government.

We are making progress in this area. In 1965 when Mission SAFETY–70 was begun, the disabling injury frequency rate was 7.7. The rate for 1968 was 6.9, a three percent improvement over the previous year and an overall 10.4 percent improvement. Through this effort an estimated $12,210,000 was saved, and 16,200 disabling injuries were prevented.

There is still great progress to be made. Department or agency heads play a major role in the elimination of accidents. If a department or agency has an effective program in this area, it should be continued; if it does not have an adequate program, one should be developed; if the program needs the necessary resources to make it effective, resources should be provided. Everyone in a department or agency should know that a safety program is effective only to the degree that it is supported and participated in by employees.

In a united effort, the Federal Government will work with labor unions representing government employees, with State and local governments, and with appropriate safety organizations in developing and applying sound accident prevention principles and practices.

The Secretary of Labor is directed to advise me annually, and at such other times as he deems appropriate, of the actions taken and the progress made by each agency.

408   Statement Announcing the White House Conference on Children and Youth.   *October* 26, 1969

ADDRESSING the Conference on the Care of Dependent Children in 1909, President Theodore Roosevelt said: "There can be no more important subject from the standpoint of the Nation than that with which you are to deal; because, when you take care of the children you are taking care of the Nation of tomorrow. . . ."

Sixty years have passed since Theodore Roosevelt spoke those words. The world has moved from the beginning of the Age of Flight to the beginning of the Age of Space. Yet, despite the numerous changes in practically every major field of human endeavor, one thing has remained constant: the importance of children in the life of our Nation. We must make certain that every child born in the United States of America has the opportunity to fulfill his potential.

Ever since that first conference, there has been a White House Conference on Children and Youth held upon the personal call of the President in each decade of this century. Each Conference has had the support and participation of State, Federal, and voluntary organizations.

The seventh decennial White House Conference on Children and Youth will meet in Washington, D.C., December 13–18, 1970. In the near future I shall appoint a National Chairman and a National Committee to direct the Conference.

This Conference will have a three-part emphasis and will focus upon:

1. Infants and young children from birth to age 5.
2. Children from approximately 6 to 14.
3. Youth aged 14 to 21.

On April 14 of this year, in a message to Congress, I made clear that an area of deep concern to this administration is the most dependent constituency of all: the child under 5. A commitment to the first 5 years of life is one of the basic pledges of this administration.

Thus, while I am convinced that attention must be given to every age group of childhood and youth, I am particularly gratified to know that the early childhood years, of such vital intellectual and emotional importance to children, will be studied and discussed.

In keeping with the historic emphasis placed upon voluntary contributions to the success of the White House Conference on Children and Youth, and in keeping with this administration's conviction of the importance of voluntarism in our national life, I call upon all relevant private voluntary organizations to lend their support and provide leadership in this undertaking.

It is my hope that the States, voluntary organizations, professional groups, Federal departments and agencies, and the general public, including young people, will, working together, make this Conference as successful in its results as it is significant in its meaning.

America is a nation young at heart, and the needs of its youth are at the center of its concern. Nothing can be more important than making the coming generation the great generation.

409 Letter to the Governors of the States and Territories and the Mayor of the District of Columbia on the White House Conference on Children and Youth. *October 26, 1969*

THE SEVENTH DECENNIAL White House Conference on Children and Youth will be convened in Washington, D.C. on December 13–18, 1970.

In the near future I shall appoint a National Chairman and a National Committee to direct the Conference.

This Conference will have a three-part emphasis and will focus upon:

1. Infants and young children from birth to age five.
2. Children from approximately six to fourteen.
3. Youth aged fourteen to twenty-one.

At this time I am asking that you take all necessary steps at your earliest convenience to fully mobilize your State in complete cooperation with the national preparation which is now under way.

It is my hope that the States, voluntary organizations, professional groups, Federal departments and agencies, and the general public, including young people, will, working together, make this Conference as successful in its results as it is significant in its meaning.

In keeping with the historic emphasis placed upon voluntary contributions to the success of the White House Conference on Children and Youth, and in keeping with this Administration's conviction of the importance of voluntarism in our national life, I urge you to call upon all relevant private voluntary organizations to lend their support and provide leadership in this undertaking.

America is a nation young at heart, and the needs of its youth are at the center of its concern. Nothing can be more important than making the coming generation the great generation.

Sincerely,

RICHARD NIXON

NOTE: The texts of identical letters were dated October 24, 1969, and released October 26, 1969.

410 Message to the Congress Transmitting the National Science Foundation Report on Weather Modification. *October 27, 1969*

To the Congress of the United States:

In recent months many American communities were ravaged by storms that were among the most violent and destructive in our history. Although our civilization has been able to perform the incredible feat of placing a man upon the moon and returning him to earth, we have only a very incomplete understanding of the forces which shape our weather and almost no power to control or change them. That is why this Tenth Annual Report on Weather Modification, as submitted by the National Science Foundation for Fiscal Year 1968, is of special interest.

This report tells of the important progress that is taking place in the field of weather modification—on projects ranging from augmenting precipitation and dissipating fog to simulating the life cycle of hurricanes. Such advances may someday permit us to manipulate our weather in ways which protect us from natural disasters and substantially improve the quality of our environment.

I congratulate those Americans who, in cooperation with scientists of other nations, are doing so much to achieve these goals.

RICHARD NIXON

The White House
    October 27, 1969

NOTE: The report is entitled "Weather Modification, Tenth Annual Report, 1968: National Science Foundation" (Government Printing Office, 141 pp.).

---

411   Letter to Congressional Leaders on Appropriations for Fiscal Year 1970. *October 28, 1969*

Dear Mr. President:

My great respect and regard for the leadership of the Congress and of the Senate and House Appropriations Committees make me extremely reluctant to send this letter.

I must, however, call attention to an impending crisis in the handling of the Nation's financial affairs. We are already almost four months into the new fiscal year. Only the second appropriation bill has come to me for signature. Authorizing legislation still lags. For the country the situation is fast becoming intolerable.

The Executive Branch has already begun the preparation of the 1971 budget. Under the law, this budget must be submitted in January. It must be completed, therefore, in December. But unless the Congressional pace is sharply accelerated, it is clear that many appropriation bills will not pass in time for Federal agencies to assemble the voluminous details necessary to meet the budget deadlines.

To array and print the vast amount of technical detail required by the Congress in time to meet this schedule, Congressional action on appropriation bills must be substantially completed within the next few weeks. *If this is not done, it may be impossible for me to transmit the 1971 budget in January.*

The Nation clearly has a right to question a Government which cannot conduct its financial affairs in an efficient manner. I urgently request your cooperation, therefore, in securing swift action by the Congress on the pending 1970 appropriation bills. Otherwise we will be frustrated in our efforts to move ahead efficiently on the 1971 budget.

I write in this vein neither to criticize the Congress for delay nor to exonerate the Executive Branch for delay. At this critical point in the appropriations and budgetary process I am less interested in why we are where we are than I am in where we now seem to be headed. I am confident that you share these concerns.

This same letter is being sent to the Speaker of the House, the Majority and Minority Leaders of both Houses, and the Chairmen and senior Minority Members of the Senate and House Appropriations Committees.

Sincerely,

RICHARD NIXON

[The Honorable Spiro T. Agnew, President of the Senate, Washington, D.C.]

412 Message to the Congress Transmitting Reports on Incentive Awards to Military Personnel. *October 28, 1969*

To the Congress of the United States:

Forwarded herewith in accordance with the provisions of 10 U.S.C. 1124 are reports of the Secretary of Defense and the Secretary of Transportation on awards made during the first six months of 1969 to members of the Armed Forces for suggestions, inventions, and scientific achievements.

The last previous report on the military awards program covered the calendar year 1968. Following the present six-month report, future annual reports will be submitted on a fiscal year basis. This will increase efficiency by facilitating the compilation of the report in conjunction with the Incentive Awards Program report which departments and agencies submit annually to the Civil Service Commission.

Participation by military personnel in the cash awards program was authorized by the Congress in September 1965. The success of the program in motivating military personnel to seek and suggest ways of reducing costs and improving efficiency is shown by the steadily increasing participation and the notable growth in measurable first-year benefits from adopted suggestions.

Tangible benefits from suggestions submitted by Department of Defense and Coast Guard military personnel that were adopted during the period from January 1 through June 30, 1969 totalled over $57,000,000. This figure, if projected for the entire year, would substantially exceed the total for calendar year 1968. Tangible first-year benefits derived from the suggestions of military personnel in the relatively short period since the program went into effect have now reached a total of more than $272,000,000.

130,861 suggestions were submitted by military personnel during the reporting period, and 20,757 were adopted. Cash awards totalling $924,742 were paid for these adopted suggestions, based not only on the tangible benefits cited above but also on many additional benefits and improvements of an intangible nature.

A substantial majority of the cash awards paid went to enlisted personnel at Grade E–6 and below. The size of the cash awards varied from the minimum of $15 to several awards in excess of $1,000.

Brief descriptions of some of the more noteworthy contributions made by military personnel through the suggestion program during the first six months of 1969 are contained in the attached reports of the Secretary of Defense and the Secretary of Transportation.

RICHARD NIXON

The White House

October 28, 1969

413 Statement on the Virginia Gubernatorial Campaign.
        October 28, 1969

LINWOOD HOLTON has my unqualified and enthusiastic support in his campaign to become Governor of the Commonwealth of Virginia. He has the character and the capability to be one of the truly great Governors in the history of this State which has produced many of America's greatest political leaders.

I know this to be true because I have worked beside Lin Holton in many causes in recent years. He is not a man discouraged by temporary reversals; he has the perseverance, dedication, intelligence, and drive that are among the prime ingredients of great executive leadership.

When the times were most difficult in my own career, it was to men like Lin Holton that I turned, and on whom I counted.

The victory of Lin Holton and his team of State Senator Buz [H. Dunlop] Dawbarn and Dick [Richard D.] Obenshain will give Virginia exactly the kind of administration it needs in the years ahead. They have the new ideas, and they offer the fresh and aggressive leadership that are indispensable to the future of strong and sound government at the State level in this country.

NOTE: The statement was released at Roanoke, Va.

414 Remarks at Roanoke, Virginia.
        October 28, 1969

I WOULD just like to take a moment of your time to thank you all for giving me such a wonderful welcome on my return to Virginia and to Roanoke.

I well recall that my first speech in Virginia in a campaign was in 1952. It was in Roanoke. Some of you here are old enough to remember that, I am sure.

I recall out there in the football field that day that Dick Poff [Representative Richard H. Poff of Virginia] said it was the biggest crowd you have ever had in Roanoke or in Virginia; isn't that right?

REPRESENTATIVE POFF. It was the largest crowd before or since assembled for a political gathering, Mr. President.

THE PRESIDENT. I was going to say that I understood that the rally was going to be downtown. I don't know how anybody could be there when you are all out here.

But I do want you to know that coming back to this State and to this city and to this part of this State is a very heartwarming thing for me. I only wish that my wife could be here with me. She was with me on all the previous occasions, but for the last 2 days she has been down in bed with the flu bug. But she sends her very best and knows that the "Ladies for Lin" are going to come through for Holton.

Finally, as I will say a little later at the rally downtown, generally a President does not find it possible to go into all of the contests and all of the campaigns that he would like to. This is the first time that I have made an appearance since becoming President of the United States in behalf of a candidate. And I am proud that it is in behalf of Lin Holton, proud be-

cause he is my friend, proud because, of course, he happens to be a member of my party, but proud also because he is one of those new, young leaders of this country who will make all Virginians proud of him. I look forward to working with him when he is Governor of this State. Thank you very much for sending him there.

NOTE: The President spoke at 7:48 p.m. at Woodrum Airport, Roanoke, Va.

415   Remarks at Salem, Virginia. *October 28, 1969*

Ladies and gentlemen:

All I can say is that that is quite a welcome for an outside agitator.

On this visit to the Roanoke Valley— and I know I am in Salem, incidentally, and not in Roanoke—I can assure you that it is a great honor to be here, to have this wonderful welcome, to remember the time that I was here in 1960 with one of the largest—according to Dick Poff, the largest—political crowd that had ever been gathered in this part of the State, either before or since.

Tonight as I stand before you, I realize that you are here because not only would you like to hear from the President of the United States, but because you are vitally concerned in the election of your next Governor and his campaign team.

Just so I can lay to rest—I know of very friendly comments of some of the opposition with regard to outsiders. I want you to know something: I don't think the President of the United States is an outsider in any country or any State in this Nation.

I can particularly say that in the State of Virginia, because when I happened to have the privilege to be on the ticket

in 1952 and 1956, that ticket carried Virginia, and in 1960 and 1968 we carried Virginia.

Also, for those of you who would like a little historical reference, you might be interested to know that except for my native State of California, and for Washington, D.C., I have lived in the State of Virginia longer than any other State of the Union, because my wife and I were very proud and happy to live in Arlington, Virginia, in the year 1942 before I went into the Navy, and then for 5 years during the years I was a Congressman, and for 1 year when I was a Senator we also lived in Arlington.

So I speak to you as a former Virginian speaking for the next Governor of the State of Virginia.

I also want you to know that it has been a very great privilege for me to come here in the company of my colleagues—I call them my colleagues, because having started in the House of Representatives all Congressmen are really, I feel, my colleagues—who are here from the House. They came down on the plane with me. They are going back with me to continue the Nation's business in the Halls of

Congress.

They have been introduced already. Most of them are from districts other than this one, of course: Bill Whitehurst, Bill Scott, Bill Wampler—Joel Broyhill would be here except that he is making a speech in another part of the State. I could speak about all of them. They are a fine team.

But I do want to say in his home county and in his own area, that among the leaders of the Congress on the Republican and Democrat side, there is not a man who has a higher standing and higher respect from his colleagues than your own Congressman, Dick Poff, of the State of Virginia, and particularly in that great field of law enforcement which is such an important objective for this administration, a field in which all we need from this Congress are the laws to be passed, laws that deal with narcotics, laws that deal with obscenity, laws that deal with organized crime, particularly in this field he is one of the real experts.

If the Congress follows his leadership, the Congress will give your new administration the laws that it needs to deal with those problems, and I am sure that is what all Virginians and all Americans want at this time in our history.

I am proud also to be here because not only do I speak for Lin Holton, but for the whole ticket, for Buz Dawbarn,[1] for Dick Obenshain.[2] I have spoken with them before. This is a fine team, and later on when I finish, I want them all to come up here so you can show that you are for the whole team, from the top to the bottom, just as I am.

I am happy also to speak here because

I like the distaff side of the Holton team. I think that Jinks [Mrs. A. Linwood] Holton is one of the best campaigners that I have ever seen on the campaign trail. She will make a great first lady of the State of Virginia.

Also I am happy to be here because of some personal matters that have already been referred to in the press, and that I would like to speak to you just briefly about this evening.

This is the first time since becoming President that I have gone into any State or into any district speaking specifically for a candidate. I think you wonder why I came to Virginia.

Well, first I was invited; second I have a great respect for the man who is running for Governor. I have respect for him first as a man. He ran once before in 1965. It was a hard race. There was very little chance for him to win. He knew it, but he ran. He ran well, and he came back to run again, and I know what it means to lose and then to win, and he is going to win, too. It is that kind of comeback spirit that the people of Virginia like in their political leaders, and that kind of spirit he has.

Also, I remember that when I became a candidate for the Presidency, then for the nomination, he was one of the first to support me, and of course I appreciated that. And I suppose that that is enough reason to come into a State for a man, the fact that he has been your friend, the fact that you do happen to admire him.

But my support for him goes to much more important issues than those, important as those are. It goes to something else that he has referred to. It goes to the philosophy of the man. I like the way he talks. I like what he stands for. I like the fact that Lin Holton is not a man of the

---

[1] H. Dunlop "Buz" Dawbarn, Republican candidate for Lieutenant Governor.

[2] Richard Obenshain, Republican candidate for Attorney General.

past, but a man for the future of Virginia, and that is what the people of Virginia want. Because, my friends, there is a new era beginning in national politics.

We are going to provide the leadership in Washington, D.C., for that new era, for a new relationship between the States and the Federal Government, for a relationship which this State and the people of this State have always believed in and which they deeply want, I am sure, now.

It is called the New Federalism. Lin Holton has referred to it; Dick Poff has referred to it. Let me put it to you quite directly. During the campaign some of you may have heard me say right in this State that after 40 years of power going from the people and from the States to Washington, D.C., it was time to have it turn around and have the power come from Washington back to the States and back to the people of the United States of America.

Now, the fact that I said that was not an unusual thing, because I want to tell you something—for 50 years politicians in both parties have been talking that way, saying that we had to decentralize government, saying that power should go back to the States, but for 50 years nobody has really done anything about it until this administration came to power, and we are doing something about it.

We have offered the most revolutionary legislation in the history of the Republic in this respect. Too much power is in Washington. Governors today, in order to get what they need for their States have to go hat in hand to the Halls of Congress or to the West Wing of the White House. This should stop. That is why we say that a portion of the Federal revenues, because the Federal Government has the greatest tax base, should now be shared with the States without strings, so that the people of the States and the Governors of the States can do and spend the money the way the States want it rather than the way the people in Washington, D.C., want it.

Also, that is why in this program for the first time since power began to flow to Washington we have through our manpower training program—we have asked the Congress to provide the means whereby a billion dollar program for the training of manpower, training people for jobs, a billion dollars which is now spent by the Federal Government will be distributed to the States so that they can make those decisions and do that training because, believe me, the States know better how to train manpower than does the Federal Government in Washington, D.C.

I could give other examples. Whether it is in the field of water pollution, whether it is in the field of the environment, and all of the others you have been hearing about, a new relationship is developing.

This administration is for it in Washington and what we need in the States are men, men with new ideas, men with progressive ideas, men who will recognize as Dick Poff said a moment ago, not only States rights, but States responsibilities, men who will look to the future and who, as they get the funds that will be made available to them over the next years, will use those funds wisely and effectively for the people of those States.

That is the way this country began. That was certainly the dream of the Founding Fathers, and it is that dream now that is necessary if this country is going to be able to govern itself effectively in the future because government in Washington is too big, I know. Government in Washington is too inefficient and there is only one way to cure it, through redistributing that power by sending from Washington to the States the funds and those powers which can better be handled by the States.

Let me say in that connection, in Lin Holton you have a man who believes in this program. I believe in it at the Federal level. You have a man who will know what to do with it as we work together in years ahead, and you have a man who in my opinion will lead this State among the first ranks of all the States of the Union with the new programs, as the State of Virginia should be an example with its great political tradition, an example to all the other States.

Now, my friends, could I also leave one other thought with you? I noted the reference tonight to the two-party system. I noted the reference tonight to the fact that all the people of Virginia should have a chance to participate in politics. I recognize the tradition in this State that goes back for many years of one-party government. I recognize, too, that under that tradition this State has produced some fine political leaders. But I know this: Whether it is in business, or whether it is in the athletic field or whether it is in politics, it is better to have competition because the better the competition, the better the man who wins and that is what you are going to have with Lin Holton and the two-party government.

For Virginia, which has provided for this whole Nation this great heritage of democracy, for it to set the example for the whole Southland, for it to set the example of a real two-party system and two-party responsibility, this will serve Virginia well, but it will also serve the Nation well.

Finally, one other thought that impresses me as I speak to this great crowd here—and speaking of a great crowd, when we stopped in at the airport, I thought that was where the rally was, there were as many there as there are here. After we got in the car Lin Holton took me down a bit. He said they were just there to see Air Force One, to see whether it would make it or not. But in any event we made it. I don't know whether it will get off or not, but we got in.

I was going to say that one of the things that impressed me at that airport, one of the things that impresses me about this crowd tonight, is the great number of young people who are here. That is one of the reasons that I think Lin Holton will win, and deserves to win.

His wife told me that the campaign headquarters is primarily staffed by volunteers from 20 to 30 years of age. This means that a vote for Holton is a vote for the future.

It reminds me of one of my favorite stories about the two-party system and how it developed in the neighboring State of Tennessee where they have always had, as you have in Virginia now, some Republicans, but where it has not been particularly an asset to have that party label.

Howard Baker, the fine young Republican Senator, said that after a very stirring speech to an audience in one of his campaigns a very old man came up to him and said: "Son, for all my life up to this time I have voted the straight Democratic ticket because that is the way my grandfather would have wanted me to vote. But," he said, "this year I am voting Republican because that is the way my grandson wants me to vote."

My friends, I say to you tonight, I do not put the case for Lin Holton on the basis of my personal friendship or on the basis of my partisan affiliation and his. I put it it on the basis of the man. He is the best man for the job.

Democrats or Republicans will vote for the best man for the job. I am convinced that measuring the man, measuring the times and the need of the times, the people of Virginia will be convinced that here is the man who will provide the new look, the new leadership, the new strength that Virginia should have. That is what you want. That is why his campaign is rolling and that is why it will roll on, in my opinion, to victory on next Tuesday.

I say to you finally on a personal note that I am most grateful for your very warm welcome this evening, for this great demonstration of support for a fine candidate and for also the personal welcome you have given to me.

I only regret that my wife could not have been with me. She unfortunately is a victim of the flu bug. She went to New York on Sunday to dedicate the final wing of the Juilliard School of Music at the Lincoln Center—I am not blaming the flu bug on New York, incidentally—but nevertheless she has been in bed since. She sends her best to all of you.

My daughter Tricia will be in Friday to campaign in northern Virginia.

I just leave this final thought. I am convinced as I stand here that we are at a watershed period in the history of this Nation, in the Federal-State relationship and at a watershed time in the history of Virginia. Something is happening in this State. I can feel it in this room. I sensed it at that airport. I can feel it in the enthusiasm of these candidates. Something is happening, and you are going to help make it happen.

I say to you: Go out and work for these men. Vote for them because as you work and vote for them you can be proud of your vote. You can be proud of Virginia and believe me, I will be proud to work as President of the United States with Lin Holton, the next Governor of the State of Virginia.

NOTE: The President spoke at 8:35 p.m. at the Salem-Roanoke Valley Civic Center, Salem, Va.

416 Statement on the New Jersey Gubernatorial Campaign. *October 29, 1969*

WILLIAM CAHILL is a Congressman whose integrity, whose knowledge of the problems of urban America, whose abilities as a leader, and whose experience in Congress uniquely qualify him to become a great Governor of the State of New Jersey.

Among the problems confronting the people of this great industrial State are the quality of education, the modernization of transportation, and the security of the citizen against crime and violence. Eleven years of distinguished service in the Congress and on the Judiciary Committee have given Bill Cahill the background to deal successfully with all of them.

His contribution to the omnibus crime bill was a major and a vital one; it gave the State governments a stronger hand in dealing with crime. In the areas of transportation and education, his record is among the most progressive and responsible on Capitol Hill. He offers New Jersey new leadership, new ideas, and a fresh point of view—he has the kind of vision the States of this Union need to become strong and vital partners of the National Government in a new kind of federalism for America. I endorse his candidacy without reservation, and with great enthusiasm.

NOTE: The statement was released at Morristown, N.J.

417   Remarks on Arrival at Morristown, New Jersey. *October* 29, 1969

Congressman Cahill, Mrs. Cahill, Congressman Frelinghuysen, Senator Case—I am being very formal with all of my colleagues and former colleagues—Mr. Mayor:

I do want you to know that this is a wonderfully heartwarming welcome.

And I think I got a little bit of bad advance dope about this meeting, Peter [H. B. Frelinghuysen]. I thought the rally was downtown. I didn't know it was out here.

And I think also you will be interested to note that my background information told me some interesting background with regard to this county and the visits of Presidents. This is a county which has been very good to Republican candidates. It was very good to me in 1960 and in 1968.

But I think you will be interested to know this is the first time in history that a President of the United States has ever visited Morris County. I am glad to be here.

I have had the privilege of visiting this county as a candidate on other occasions. And I have always had a wonderful welcome. But, believe me, this tops them all. And we are most grateful.

I simply want to leave with you, if I can, one thought: I am here not in my own behalf, but in behalf of a man for whom I have very great respect. I like Bill Cahill as a person. I like him because of his experience in the Congress of the United States.

He is a man who is trained for the job that he is seeking. I like him because I believe that he is the man for the future of this State. He is a man who has no commitments to those mistakes of the past, and he is a man that can lead New Jersey in the seventies. And that kind of a man, I think, New Jersey wants.

Let me put it this way: I just happen to think that Bill Cahill, because of his integrity, because of his experience, because of his program, because of his idealism—I think he is ready to lead New Jersey and, from what I see here, New Jersey is ready for Cahill.

I wish we had more time. I do know that there are many, many problems that you would like to hear discussed.

On Monday night, I urge you, incidentally, to listen to Bill Cahill's final wrap-up.

I also will tell you that I will be speaking to the Nation Monday on a subject—the subject of Vietnam—and I would invite you all to listen to that particular matter.

But let me say, finally, that apart from these political remarks that I have made, you can't really understand or estimate how heartwarming it is for a man who serves as President of the United States to come to a State, which has been very

873

good for him and to him on election day, and gets such a wonderfully warm welcome.

And I particularly say that because I know how hard it is to get to an airport.

I know how far you had to walk to get here.

Thank you very much.

NOTE: The President spoke at 7:30 p.m. at Morristown Airport, Morristown, N.J. The mayor of Morristown was Victor L. Woodhull.

418 Remarks at Morristown, New Jersey. *October* 29, 1969

I WANT to express my appreciation to all of you for giving me such a warm welcome on a return to Morris County, and, also, as I speak to you here this evening briefly—because, as you know, we are going on to Hackensack, and I also understand we are going to even talk to the area of Monmouth County by telephone tonight, so we will make three meetings before I get back to Washington—I want you to know that it is a great privilege to be here on this platform with the whole New Jersey delegation, Republican delegation from Washington, D.C.

I could mention them all—Cliff Case, the Senator from New Jersey, who has spoken so eloquently for the candidacy of our candidate, Bill Cahill.

I could speak, too, of all the Congressmen, but this is after all, Peter Frelinghuysen's district, and I am so glad to be here in this district again.

I want to say, too, that he has given me all the background about the district. He told me we would get a good welcome. We certainly did. I thought the rally was at the airport. All the way along there were huge crowds.

And I mention to you something that I did learn from him on the way up. This is the first time in history that a President of the United States has ever spoken in Morris County. I am glad to be the first

President to do that. Because even during the time that Woodrow Wilson was President—as you know, he went to the Presidency from the Governorship of this State—he never spoke here while he was the President. So I would like to be first in that respect.

And I have something to say to you today. I can say it very briefly. I can say it very much from the heart. I want to tell you why.

In 1960, when I was a candidate for President the first time, I had a very busy year. There were very few times that I could go out and make speeches for others. I was too busy speaking for myself. But in that year, I remember that a young Congressman came to me from Camden, New Jersey. He had been in only one term. He had had a close race.

And he said, "Will you come over to Camden for a fundraising dinner?" Some way or other, he appealed to me, the way he talked, the cut of his jib, that good Irish smile. And I said, "Yeah, I will do it."

Well, I went over to Camden. And I remember it was such an exciting, really joyful meeting. There was a spirit there that I sense here tonight, and that I sensed in those crowds—people like Bill Cahill, because he is a fine man and that is one of the reasons he is going to be elected

Governor of the State of New Jersey.

It is hard to realize now that I am speaking in behalf of an 11-year veteran of the House of Representatives, one of the most respected men in the whole Congress, a man that is respected by the Republicans, of course, his own party, but respected by the Democrats as well; a man that is respected because he has integrity, he is an honest man, a fine man, and a hardworking man; a man who is respected because of that wonderful family—and that tells you something about the man, too—but a man also who is respected because of his record in the Congress of the United States.

Now, naturally, you would expect me to say nice things about him tonight. And I am not going to disappoint you in that expectation.

But I want you to know, my friends, that when I look at that record, when I see 11 years on the Judiciary Committee of the House of Representatives where he has the first-hand experience in the field of law enforcement and crime, when I see that he preceded that with experience in the FBI, when I know that one of the issues in this State, perhaps not in this county, but in this State, is the issue of law enforcement, is the issue of control of crime, just as it is the issue across the Nation, I say there isn't a better man in the Congress or in this country better qualified to deal with crime than Bill Cahill. And I look forward to working with him.

But there are other great problems and I speak of them only briefly—the problem of education to which he referred. We know the proud tradition of this State in the field of education, higher education, the great universities that it has and the great colleges.

We know also that this State, in recent years, has had problems with regard to maintaining educational quality, particularly at the secondary and primary level.

Here is a man who understands that problem. Here is a man who has a program for the future for it. Here is a man who doesn't have to defend what didn't happen in the last 16 years and tell you what is going to happen for the next 8 years. And that is the kind of a man you want in the field.

So it is with the other subjects that I could mention, transportation. He has gotten out there. He has been in the traffic. He knows what it is. He knows what the problems are. He knows the needs of this State, and he will meet those needs.

He also is a man who knows of the new issues. The young people will know now what I am talking about: the whole area of the environment, the problem of pollution, the problem of the quality of life, the problem of our consumers, all of these, those that people are talking about, those that people want new action about. He knows about that and I am for him for those reasons.

But I want to add one other word: I believe Bill Cahill is the man for the times, the man for the job, because, you see, whether you ever mention any of these problems—the problems of education, the problems of the environment, the problems of transportation, all of the rest—what we conclude is that the old ways won't do; what we conclude is that the old leadership won't do. It has failed.

We need reform—reform of State government, reform of Federal Government. And I am proud of the fact that in this administration we have sent to the Congress the most significant series of reform requests ever submitted by a Chief Executive over the past 25 years.

I am proud of the fact that after 40 years of leaders talking about revenue sharing with the States, we have submitted a program for revenue sharing with the States so that it will reduce your tax burden, which is one of the highest in the whole Nation.

After 40 years of everybody talking about turning from the Federal Government, turning some of the functions now being handled at that level back to the States, we have come forth with the program in job training where a $1 billion program is going to be turned back to the States.

I am proud of the fact that in the field of pollution, in the field of transportation, in the field of highways, that a new relationship is being developed by our administration. It will be developed with the help of the Congress, with its cooperation, in which the States and the people get control of their government once again, in which Governors do not have to go to Washington hat-in-hand and pace the floors of Congress or the corridors, as the case might be, or come to the White House, but where they will have the opportunity to develop the strong leadership here in these programs.

Now let me conclude with this thought: You see, if revenues are going to be shared by the Federal Government with the States, if the Federal Government is going to turn back to the States, as it should, the functions that the States can handle better, if we are going to have progress in all these fields, we need a new, strong State leadership. We need a man who is a man of the seventies, a man who shares the convictions that I have just now expressed and that he has expressed before me, a man who will look at the problems

of education and the problems of environment and the problems of transportation and the problems of law enforcement and who will brush aside all the failures of the past and say, "Here is a new way. Here is a better way." That is Bill Cahill.

And, my friends, I want to say one other thing. I know this is Morris County. I know that in this county being a Republican is a great asset. I know that I carried the county by 33,000 votes, and that helped us carry the State by 60,000 votes.

I know, too, as I speak in Morris County, when all you would really have to do is say, "He is a Republican; vote for him for he is a Republican." I want to say that isn't enough of a reason, and it isn't the only reason that I think he deserves your support.

Whether you are a Republican, or a Democrat, or an Independent, he is the man for the job. That is the way the people of New Jersey are thinking, that is the way they vote, and that is why he is going to win.

I look back over the history of this State, and you know I think you would be interested to know that in my office I had a choice of the desk I could have of the former Presidents. I chose Woodrow Wilson's. I chose his desk not because he was a Democrat, as he was, but because he was one of my favorite Presidents. And I have that desk now.

Before I came up here, as I was sitting there making some notes, I thought of the great Governors of the State of New Jersey. He was one of the greatest Governors of this State. He was a reform Governor when New Jersey needed reform.

At that period in its history, New Jersey needed a Democratic Governor because the Republicans had not provided the

876

leadership they should.

And then time went by, and in another 40 years another Governor came on. This time it was a Republican. It was Al Driscoll.[1] He gave the State reform.

My friends, now 16 years have passed

---

[1] Alfred Driscoll, Governor of New Jersey 1947–1953.

since those years. Now this State needs reform again. And in the tradition of Woodrow Wilson, in the tradition of Al Driscoll, you have got the man, Bill Cahill.

What I say to you is that Bill Cahill is ready to lead New Jersey and the people of New Jersey are ready for Bill Cahill.

NOTE: The President spoke at 8:10 p.m. at the Gouverneur Morris Inn in Morristown, N.J.

419 Remarks at Hackensack, New Jersey. *October 29, 1969*

I WANTED to get all of the group that you have just seen up here so that you could see the people who came up from Washington with me on Air Force One tonight.

And I simply want to say, by way of introduction, that I am very proud to serve in Washington with those who represent the State of New Jersey in the Congress and particularly with those that are here tonight.

You saw that team here. It is a great team. We would like to keep them all there, but, believe me, we need a Governor in New Jersey and Bill Cahill we are going to spare for that job.

I realize that we are running a little late this evening. I think you will be glad to know the reason why. We had enormous crowds at the airport and on the way in to the meeting at Morristown and, consequently, we are delayed.

Then there was another reason we were delayed slightly and I would like to be permitted a personal note. I have Mrs. Cahill's permission to share it with you.

When we were in the holding room a moment ago, we made a call. You see, the Cahills and the Nixons have a number of things in common. I served in the House

and they served in the House. And I have two daughters. They have more than that.

But, nevertheless, one of my daughters' name, the older one, is Tricia. They have a Tricia, too. You all know that she had an accident and she is in the hospital. She is a brave, fine girl.

So we called the hospital tonight. They got her on the phone. I said, "Tricia, your daddy is going to win." And let's make him win.

And I do want you to know that some of the girls up here in front asked where Mrs. Nixon was. As you probably read, she, after speaking in New York or going to New York to help dedicate one of the new units of the Lincoln Center—she got the flu and was unable to go with me to Virginia yesterday or to New Jersey tonight.

But, believe me, she is here in spirit and she joins me in wishing the Cahills the best and everybody the best.

And, too, may I say that coming to Bergen County means something to me. I want to tell you what I know about Bergen County.

I have campaigned it a lot. It is a tremendously important county from the standpoint of this State, because what you

877

do in Bergen determines whether you carry this State. It is a big county. For a Republican, he has got to bring it in real big.

I remember in 1952 I came up to a rally in Bergen County after the election in '53. It was one of the biggest rallies I have ever heard or seen. I remember Bergen County was proud that year, Nelson Gross [State Republican Committee chairman], to point to the fact that it gave the biggest majority to the Eisenhower-Nixon ticket of any county in the Nation.

Now, in the year 1968, we knew New Jersey was a key State. We knew that it was a must State. It was one of those we really had to win. We campaigned it hard.

You know what happened? We carried the State of New Jersey by 60,000. We carried Bergen County by 60,000. This county did it. You put us over the top.

So I thank you in a personal note for that support in that campaign of 1968.

Now, tonight, I am here in behalf of another man. I want to speak to you quite directly, as I did to the people in Morris County a few moments ago. I want to tell you why I am for him.

I am for him because I like him personally, and I like his wonderful family, as you do.

I am for him, too, because I think that Bill Cahill has the experience to qualify him to be the Governor of this State.

I like him because he is a Republican, a member of my party. But I know that in this county, while it is a great Republican county, I know that here, as throughout this State, there are Independents, there are Democrats as well as Republicans that are going to make up their minds not on the basis of a party label, but on the basis of who is the best man for that job.

And that is why I am for Bill Cahill.

He is the best man for that job.

So for a moment, and I ask all of you tonight, whatever you are, Republicans, Democrats, or Independents, forget your party label or affiliation. And those of you who are going to go out and work these last critical 6 days, remember what I say now because this is what counts. Think of the race in New Jersey in terms of the man, not the party; think in terms of what New Jersey needs; think of what the other party offers; think of what this party, the Republican Party offers; but above everything else, think of the man, his experience, and his background, and then determine what New Jersey needs.

It seems to me the choice is clear. I am not going to try to give a judgment as to what the people of New Jersey should do about their own business, except to say this: that when you consider the background of the man, the people of New Jersey have never had a man who, from the standpoint of experience at the national level, was better qualified to be the Governor of this State than Bill Cahill.

Look at him. Eleven years in the House of Representatives, 11 years on the key Judiciary Committee of the House.

What does that mean? It means that here is a man who, instead of just talking about law enforcement, talking about controlling crime, will do something about it.

We are going to help him do something about it with your help.

And Bill Widnall, your Congressman and the man who comes from this town, and who has been a great friend of mine, has for many years told me when you look at Bill Cahill's record in all fields, whether it is in the field of education or the field of transportation or the field of the environment, all of these matters in which you are so vitally concerned in this great county, Bill Cahill has the kind of progressive action record that recommends itself to people who are looking at the man and not just at his party label.

That brings me, really, to the key point. As some of you are probably aware, as President of the United States I have had the responsibility and also the great privilege to travel abroad twice during the Presidency—once to Europe and then around the world visiting several Asian countries.

This was a very great experience for me as a man and also as one representing a great people. It was very exciting to see the marvelous crowds and to see the exciting events that were planned on that trip.

But after traveling abroad, no matter where you go, and when you return to the United States you always come home realizing what truly a great country this is.

I just want you to know that we have problems in this country. We have problems that all of you are aware of. You have problems in this State—the problems of transportation, the problems of law enforcement, the problems of education, the others to which I have referred and to which Bill Cahill has referred in his campaign. But the difference between America and most of the other nations of the world is that we have what it takes to solve the problems.

We are by far the richest country in the world. We have certainly the greatest well of intelligence and trained people, from the standpoint of our education, in the world.

What we need to do in order to solve our problems is to get the leadership and we also need new programs, new methods, new approaches to those problems.

And that brings me to the key reason why I think the independent voter, be he a Republican or Democrat or unregistered, either one, why he is going to be for Cahill rather than his opponent.

Usually, the choice is simply on the basis of one party or the other. This year, the choice is: Is New Jersey satisfied with the leadership that it has had for the last 16 years? Does it want 4 more years or 8 more years of that?

Or are the people of New Jersey, with a great tradition over the past of some great Governors, going to turn to a vigorous man, a man well qualified by experience and background, a man with the program for the '70s rather than talking about what he did in the '50s or the '60s, a man who says to the people of New Jersey, "Give me the chance" and he is going to do something about crime in this State.

He is going to do something about education in this State. He is going to do something about transport problems in this State. He is going to make New Jersey first again in the quality of its State government. That is what he is going to do.

At the national level, my friends, I want you to know that we have made a beginning in that direction, and with the cooperation of the Congress, we will present to the American people a record of accomplishment in terms of a new approach to the problems of the State of the Nation, a new approach such as we have not had over the past 25 years.

After 25 to 40 years, as a matter of fact, with the power flowing from the States and the people to Washington, D.C., we finally turned it around. We have a program in which we have asked the Congress to enact legislation in which the Federal Government will do what it should have done, what people have

879

talked about doing for many, many years, and that is share the Federal revenues with the States so you can handle your problems here and reduce your own tax burden.

We have a new program in the field of welfare, a program in which we provide that minimum assistance, which is needed by any family that is in need in America, but which we also provide that if an individual is able to work, and if a job is found for him, and we should try to find jobs, then he should be given that opportunity to work—in other words, job incentives, getting people off the welfare rolls and onto payrolls. We think that is a good line for the United States to follow.

We have, too, a program in which the Federal Government is going to turn over to the States, first in the field of job training, a billion dollar program, where the States can better administer than the Federal Government.

What I am really saying to you is this: We are looking at an entirely new situation for State government of the decade of the 70's. We are having in Washington, D.C., a new attitude, in which Washington, instead of grabbing the power from the people in the States and taking it to Washington, we are bringing it back to the people. We are bringing government to the people.

We are giving the people of New Jersey a chance to decide their own problems.

But, my friends, you see, that is the challenge. If that is going to work, you have to have a man who is thinking new, who is thinking about action for the future, who will assume those responsibilities, and who will develop the new programs rather than to think of the way that it used to be done, and Bill Cahill is that kind of a man.

I know it. You know it. And that is the reason that I believe that he deserves your vote, not just because you happen to be Republicans, if you are, but because he is the best man for the job this year.

Now my friends, I would close on one personal note. In my office in Washington, D.C., like all Presidents who have the great privilege and the high responsibility of assuming that Office, I had the chance to choose the desk I was to have. And there was the Eisenhower desk, and the desk of others who had been in that Office, and, of course, they all have a history.

I chose the Wilson desk, because it had been my desk when I was Vice President. It had been Woodrow Wilson's desk when he was President. I chose it because I was always an admirer of Woodrow Wilson.

He, of course, was a Democrat. He also was the Governor of this State. Incidentally, right after he had run for Governor, he became a candidate for President. I am just saying to Bill Cahill, wait 4 years at least before you do that.

And my friends, as I sit at that desk, I sometimes think of that man and some of the things that he said. He was one of our most eloquent Presidents and among the most eloquent of all the inaugurals was Wilson's first inaugural.

Go back and read it, those of you in school here, and you will find it had the great prose which he developed probably to the highest point in terms of eloquence of any President in our history.

He spoke of the challenge that he faced in an era of reform for America in the time he became President, in the year 1913. He was elected in 1912.

But in reading the history of that inaugural, I found something very interesting. While there were many great phrases in it, there is one that is not in the text of the speech that is more remembered than any other. This is the way it came about.

The Secret Service in that year 1912, 1913, March 1913, at the Inauguration, protecting the President, as they always have the responsibility to do, had put the fences way out beyond the Capitol steps. And when Wilson got up to speak, he saw the people far away from him.

And very softly, before he started to speak, he said, "Let the people come forward." And the people came forward.

And that came to be, really, the watchword of Wilson's first term as President of the United States.

I think of Bill Cahill today, Bill Cahill, a Republican rather than a Democrat—

but when great ideas are involved, they transcend all partisan politics—is as he indicated in his own brief remarks trying to bring government to the people. He is listening to the people.

He, like Woodrow Wilson, is saying, "Let the people come forward." My friends, that is what kind of government the people of New Jersey want. You want to participate. You want to make your own decisions. You want a chance to go into the future with a man of the future.

Bill Cahill is ready to serve the people of New Jersey, and, I think, too, that New Jersey is ready for Bill Cahill.

NOTE: The President spoke at 9:22 p.m. in the gymnasium at Hackensack High School.

420   Remarks to Participants in the Heritage Groups Nationalities Conference of the Republican National Committee. *October 30, 1969*

Mr. Vice President, ladies and gentlemen:

In accepting this resolution and in accepting it for the Vice President and myself, I do want you to know how grateful we are for your support in the 1968 campaign, and also how grateful we are for your presence here today in the White House.

Your very eloquent remarks give me an opportunity to respond briefly as to the significance of this group, a significance that goes far beyond your partisan affiliations. We are glad you are supporting the Republican Party and the Republican candidates. I realize, however, that those in your groups cover Democrats and Independents, all of those who are interested in what our party and our administration stand for.

What we stand for is something that

America needs. It is something that those who love freedom in the world want. It is this that I think brings you together here in support of us during this administration.

You mentioned the fact that there were 29 different nationalities here. I am delighted that there are that many. Of course, there could be more, because when we think of the United States of America and what makes it a great country, one of the primary factors is that we have drawn upon all of the peoples and all of the races and all the nationalities of the world, and that has made us richer—richer in the diversity of our people, richer in our customs and richer in many other ways, one in particular that I am going to mention.

When I speak to you, I speak as one of

you, too. I should point out that the Vice President, from time to time, feels that he is very much in touch with the Heritage Groups, or as it is sometimes called, as an ethnic group, because of his Greek background.

Now, I don't happen to have a Greek background, but I am very proud to have the Vice President with his Greek background in our administration, and he has done a great job for this administration.

I think you should also know that my great, great grandparents did not come over on the Mayflower. I remember when I was in grammar school, I was a student of history, and there was a very fine teacher who was on one occasion telling us about the background of the United States, and of those magnificent people who came over on the Mayflower, the early Americans.

I went home that day—I think I was in the fifth grade—and talked to my father a bit about it because he also had a great interest in politics and that sort of thing.

I said, "I note this background of the United States and I also note that many people could point to the fact that they were sons and daughters of the American Revolution." I said to my father, "What about us? What are we?"

He thought a moment, and he said, "We are Heinz—57 varieties."

Of course, he was right. My mother was an Irish Quaker. My father had an English, German, and Irish background. My wife's mother was born in Germany and her father was Irish. So you see, I am one of you, too, and most Americans are.

What I want to say is, the name you have selected for this group is very appropriate. I don't like the term "ethnic group." That separates some Americans from others. The word "heritage" is something else again, because the heritage of America is very rich and it is rich for the reasons that I mentioned; it is rich because it draws from the peoples of the world.

In this room we see so much wealth—wealth in the diversity, wealth in what you have contributed to America, contributed in terms of your backgrounds, the arts, and in so many other areas, and also, as I mentioned earlier, in one respect above all others.

In these days when people look at the United States of America and wonder about whether or not there is that degree of patriotism, patriotism in the best sense, love of country that we ought to have, I more than often find that those who love America the most are those who adopted it, those who love America the most are those who come from backgrounds from other nations, because they know from having either been in another country or having been only one generation from another country, much as they loved the other country or their mother's or their father's country, they know that anyone who lives in America, lives in America even with all its problems, is the most fortunate person in the world. This is the place.

It is that message that I hope we can get across through the Heritage Groups. This administration wants to work with all Americans. We want to work particularly with those in this group who have been so kind to come to the White House this morning. We are proud to have your support. We only hope that in this administration we can follow those policies that will make everyone who came to America proud that he chose this country, that can make everyone who has a background from a different country thankful that

America is his country.

This is what I believe. It is what you believe. It is the great factor that will bring us on to greater victories in the future.

Just so that the Irish and the Germans and the English backgrounds do not rule out the other American heritage, I think we ought to hear from one with a Greek background.

The Vice President.

NOTE: The President spoke at 10:25 a.m. in the State Dining Room at the White House. Introductory remarks by Laszlo C. Pasztor, Director of the Heritage Groups Nationalities Division, and concluding remarks by Vice President Spiro T. Agnew are printed in the Weekly Compilation of Presidential Documents (vol. 5, p. 1514).

421 Special Message to the Congress on Consumer Protection. *October* 30, 1969

To the Congress of the United States:

Consumerism—Upton Sinclair and Rachel Carson would be glad to know— is a healthy development that is here to stay.

That does not mean that *caveat emptor*—"let the buyer beware"—has been replaced by an equally harsh *caveat venditor*—"let the seller beware". Nor does it mean that government should guide or dominate individual purchasing decisions.

Consumerism in the America of the 70s means that we have adopted the concept of "buyer's rights."

I believe that the buyer in America today has the right to make an intelligent choice among products and services.

The buyer has the right to accurate information on which to make his free choice.

The buyer has the right to expect that his health and safety is taken into account by those who seek his patronage.

The buyer has the right to register his dissatisfaction, and have his complaint heard and weighed, when his interests are badly served.

This "Buyer's Bill of Rights" will help provide greater personal freedom for individuals as well as better business for everyone engaged in trade.

The program I am outlining today represents the most significant set of Presidential recommendations concerning consumer interests in our history. Specifically, I propose:

—A new Office of Consumer Affairs in the Executive Office of the President with new legislative standing, an expanded budget, and greater responsibilities. This will give every American consumer a permanent voice in the White House.

—A new Division of Consumer Protection in the Department of Justice, to act as a consumer advocate before Federal regulatory agencies in judicial proceedings and in government councils.

—A new consumer protection law which would be enforced by the Department of Justice and United States Attorneys across the land. Such a law would also better enable consumers either as individuals or as a class to go into court to obtain redress for the damages they suffer.

—Expanded powers for a revitalized Federal Trade Commission, to en-

883

able it to protect consumers promptly and effectively.

—A newly activated National Commission on Consumer Finance to investigate and report on the state of consumer credit.

—Expanded consumer education activities, including government review of product-testing processes, a new *Consumer Bulletin,* and the release of certain government information regarding consumer products.

—Stronger efforts in the field of food and drug safety, including a thorough re-examination of the Food and Drug Administration and a review of the products on the "generally regarded as safe" list.

—Other reforms, including an expansion of consumer activities in the Office of Economic Opportunity and greater efforts to encourage the strengthening of state and local programs.

To their credit, producers and sellers have generally become far more responsible with the passing years, but even the limited abuses which occur now have greater impact. Products themselves are more complicated; there is more about them that can go wrong and less about them that can be readily understood by laymen. Mass production and mass distribution systems mean that a small error can have a wide effect; the carelessness of one producer can bring harm or disappointment to many. Moreover, the responsibility for a particular problem is far more difficult to trace than was once the case, and even when responsibility for an error can be assigned, it is often difficult to lodge an effective complaint against it.

All too often, the real advantages of mass production are accompanied by customer alienation; many an average buyer is intimidated by seemingly monolithic organizations, and frequently comes to feel alone and helpless in what he regards as a cruelly impersonal marketplace. In addition, many of the government's efforts to help the consumer are still geared to the problems of past decades; when it is able to act at all, government too often acts too slowly.

Fortunately, most businessmen in recent years have recognized that the confidence of the public over a long period of time is an important ingredient for their own success and have themselves made important voluntary progress in consumer protection. At the same time, buyers are making their voices heard more often, as individuals and through consumer organizations. These trends are to be encouraged and our governmental programs must emphasize their value. Government consumer programs, in fact, are a complement to these voluntary efforts. They are designed to help honest and conscientious businessmen by discouraging their dishonest or careless competitors.

NEW OFFICE OF CONSUMER AFFAIRS

One of the central roles in present government efforts in the consumer rights field is performed by the President's Special Assistant for Consumer Affairs and those who work with her. This position has been created by Presidential order rather than by statute, however, and it is neither as visible nor as effective as it should be. It is important that both the prestige and the responsibility of this office be strengthened.

I am therefore asking the Congress to establish within the Executive Office of the President a new Office of Consumer

Affairs to play a leading role in the crusade for consumer justice. This Office and its director would have central responsibility for coordinating all Federal activities in the consumer protection field, helping to establish priorities, to resolve conflicts, to initiate research, and to recommend improvements in a wide range of Government programs. The Office would advise the President on consumer matters and would alert other government officials to the potential impact of their decisions on the consumers' interests. It would receive complaints from individual consumers and refer them to appropriate agencies or to the businesses concerned.

The new Office of Consumer Affairs would not work solely within the Executive Branch of the Government, however; it would continue to carry out other assignments which the Special Assistant to the President for Consumer Affairs now performs. For example, when called upon, it would assist in the legislative process, testifying at Congressional hearings, and consulting with individual Congressmen. It would aid schools and media in educating the public in consumer skills. The new Office will continue the constructive interchange of information which the Special Assistant has established with businesses and industries, and carry forward its assistance to state and local consumer protection programs.

As I will explain in greater detail later in this message, I am also asking the Special Assistant for Consumer Affairs to undertake specific surveillance responsibilities in the area of product safety, to review the government's policy concerning the release of its own information on consumer products, and to publish a new *Consumer Bulletin* on a regular basis. When the new Office of Consumer Affairs

is established, it would take over these and related duties.

A new Office of Consumer Affairs would be a focal point for a wide variety of government efforts to aid people who buy. I urge the Congress to grant it the legislative standing and the added resources necessary to do this work effectively.

A DIVISION OF CONSUMER PROTECTION
  AND A NEW CONSUMER PROTECTION
  LAW

A second important structural reform which I am recommending is the establishment by statute of a new Consumer Protection Division in the Department of Justice. This Division would be headed by an Assistant Attorney General and would be staffed by lawyers and economists. It would be adequately financed and given appropriate investigative power so that it could effectively ascertain consumer needs and advance consumer causes. The head of the new Division would act, in effect, as the consumers' lawyer representing the consumer interest before Federal agencies, in judicial proceedings and in government councils.

I also propose that Congress arm this new Consumer Protection Division with a new law—one which would prohibit a broad, but clearly defined, range of frauds and deceptions. The legislation I will propose will be of sufficient scope to provide substantial protection to consumers and of sufficient specificity to give the necessary advance notice to businessmen of the activities to be considered illegal.

The role of the new Assistant Attorney General for Consumer Protection would be similar to that of the Assistant Attorney General who heads the Antitrust Division in the Department of Justice. Just as the Antitrust Division enforces the antitrust laws and intervenes in various governmental proceedings to preserve competition, so the Consumer Protection Division would enforce consumer rights and intervene in agency proceedings to protect the consumer. In enforcing these rights, the Assistant Attorney General for Consumer Protection would also have the assistance of United States Attorneys throughout the country. Their power to take quick and effective action under the new statute would be particularly important for protecting low-income families who are frequently victimized by fraudulent and deceptive practices.

Effective representation of the consumer does not require the creation of a new Federal department or independent agency, but it does require that an appropriate arm of the Government be given the tools to do an effective job. In the past a lone Justice Department lawyer— the Consumer Counsel—has attempted to carry out a portion of this task. Our proposal asks that the new Division of Consumer Protection be adequately staffed and independently funded, as is the Antitrust Division, so that it can vigorously represent the interests of the consumer and enforce the newly proposed legislation.

The new Assistant Attorney General and his Division would, of course, work closely with the Office of Consumer Affairs, the Federal Trade Commission, and state and local law enforcement agencies.

Consumers in the Federal Courts— Individual and Class Suits

Present Federal law gives private citizens no standing to sue for fraudulent or deceptive practices and State laws are often not adequate to their problems. Even if private citizens could sue, the damage suffered by any one consumer would not ordinarily be great enough to warrant costly, individual litigation. One would probably not go through a lengthy court proceeding, for example, merely to recover the cost of a household appliance.

To correct this situation, I will recommend legislation to give private citizens the right to bring action in a Federal court to recover damages, upon the successful termination of a government suit under the new consumer protection law.

This measure will, for the first time, give consumers access to the federal courts for violation of a federal law concerning fraudulent and deceptive practices, without regard to the amount in controversy. Under Federal court rules, consumers would have the right to sue as a class and not only as individuals. In other words, a group of people could come into court together if they could show that the act in question affected all of them. This is a significant consideration, for it would allow a number of citizens to divide among themselves the high costs of bringing a law suit. Although each person's individual damage might be small, the cumulative effect of a class complaint could be significant and in some circumstances could provide a significant deterrent to expensive fraud or deception. At the same time, the fact that private action must follow in the wake of a successful government action will prevent harassment of legitimate businessmen by unlimited nuisance lawsuits.

The Federal Trade Commission

The problems of the American consumer first became a central matter of

Federal concern in the late years of the nineteenth century and the early years of the twentieth. One of the important elements in the Government's response at that time was the establishment in 1914 of the Federal Trade Commission, an independent body which was designed to play a leading role in the fight against unfair and deceptive trade practices. While new legislation has given the FTC additional and more specific duties, there has been increasing public concern over the Commission's ability to meet all of its many responsibilities. I believe the time has now come for the reactivation and revitalization of the FTC.

The chairman-designate of the FTC has assured me that he intends to initiate a new era of vigorous action as soon as he is confirmed by the Senate and takes office. A report prepared at my request by a commission of the American Bar Association should help considerably in this effort, for it presents a valuable description of the problems which face the FTC and the ways in which they can be remedied. I urge the FTC to give serious consideration to these recommendations. I have also asked the Bureau of the Budget to help with the revitalization process by supervising an even more detailed management study of this commission.

I am particularly hopeful that a number of specific improvements in the FTC can be quickly accomplished. For example, the Commission should immediately begin to process its business more rapidly so that it can reduce its unacceptably large backlog of cases. I also believe that it should seek out new information on consumer problems through more energetic field investigations, rather than waiting for complaints to come in through its mailrooms or from other government agencies. This initiative could begin with pilot field projects in a limited number of cities, as the ABA task force has suggested. Whatever the strategy, I would hope that it could be accomplished through a more efficient use of existing personnel and finances; if that proves impossible, added funds should later be appropriated for this purpose.

Administrative reforms will provide only part of the answer, however. I believe the Commission should also consider the extent to which Section 5 of the Federal Trade Commission Act, broadly interpreted, may be used more effectively to cope with contemporary consumer problems. This is the section which gives the Commission its legislative mandate to move against unfair or deceptive practices. The language of this section might well provide an appropriate instrument for policing more effectively some of the more prevalent abuses described by the ABA task force study.

Even if the Commission does apply Section 5 more broadly, however, there remains a question about its jurisdiction which the Congress should promptly resolve. Past FTC enforcement activities have been inhibited by a Supreme Court decision of some twenty-five years ago, holding that activities "affecting" interstate commerce were not subject to FTC jurisdiction since the language of the law was limited to activities "in" interstate commerce. This means that there is a doubt at present concerning the FTC's ability to consider many unfair and deceptive practices which have a nationwide impact but are local in terms of their actual operation.

I am therefore recommending that the Congress amend Section 5 so as to permit the FTC to take action concerning consumer abuses which "affect" interstate commerce, as well as those which are technically "in" interstate commerce. This amendment would make it clear that the FTC has a jurisdiction consistent with that of several other Federal agencies and commissions. The purpose of the amendment is to clarify FTC jurisdiction over cases which have true national significance; it should not be interpreted in a way which burdens the Commission with a large number of cases which are of only local importance.

One of the most important obstacles to the present effectiveness of the FTC is its inability to seek an injunction against an unfair or deceptive business practice. The result of this inability is an unacceptable delay between the time a harmful practice is discovered and the time it is ended. Often two years will pass between the time the FTC agrees to hear a complaint and the time it issues its final order and another two years may pass while the order is reviewed by the courts.

I recommend that the Congress remedy this situation by giving to the Federal Trade Commission the power to seek and obtain from the Federal courts a preliminary injunction against consumer practices which are unfair or deceptive. The judicial process includes safeguards which will assure that this authority is fairly used. Courts will retain their usual discretion to grant or deny an injunction in the light of all the consequences for both the accused and the plaintiff. Parties will, of course, retain their right to a fair hearing before any injunction is issued.

NATIONAL COMMISSION ON CONSUMER FINANCE

The buying public and businessmen alike have been concerned in recent years about the growth of consumer credit. Twenty-five years ago the total consumer credit outstanding was only 5.7 billion dollars; today it is 110 billion dollars. The arrangements by which that credit is provided are subject to government supervision and regulations, an assignment which has recently become increasingly complex and difficult. For this reason a National Commission on Consumer Finance was established by law in 1968. It was instructed to review the adequacy and the cost of consumer credit and to consider the effectiveness with which the public is protected against unfair credit practices.

The National Commission on Consumer Finance should begin its important work immediately. I will therefore announce shortly the names of three new members of the Commission, including a new chairman, and I will ask the Congress for a supplemental appropriation to finance the Commission's investigations during the current fiscal year. I look forward to receiving the report of the National Commission on Consumer Finance in January of 1971.

CONSUMER EDUCATION—INFORMATION ON PRODUCT TESTING

No matter how alert and resourceful a purchaser may be, he is relatively helpless unless he has adequate, trustworthy information about the product he is considering and *knows what to make of that information.* The fullest product description is useless if a consumer lacks the understanding or the will to utilize it.

This Administration believes that consumer education programs should be expanded. Our study of existing consumer education efforts in both the public schools and in adult education programs has been funded by the Office of Education and will report its results in the near future.

The Special Assistant to the President for Consumer Affairs is focusing many of the resources of her office on educational projects. One new project which I am asking that office to undertake is the preparation and publication, on a regular basis, of a new *Consumer Bulletin.* This publication will contain a selection of items which are of concern to consumers and which now appear in the daily government journal, *The Federal Register.* The material it presents, which will include notices of hearings, proposed and final rules and orders, and other useful information, will be translated from its technical form into language which is readily understandable by the layman.

The government can help citizens do a better job of product evaluation in other ways as well. First, I recommend that Congress authorize the Federal Government to review the standards for evaluation which are used by private testing laboratories and to publish its findings as to their adequacy, working through appropriate scientific agencies such as the National Bureau of Standards. Laboratories presently issue quality endorsements, of one kind or another, for a wide variety of products. Some of these endorsements have meaning, but others do not. It would be most helpful, I believe, if the testing procedures on which these endorsements were based were evaluated by government experts. Manufacturers whose products had been tested under government-evaluated testing standards would be allowed to advertise the fact. If no testing standard existed or if the standard in use was found to be inadequate, then the appropriate agency would be authorized to develop a new one.

Secondly, I propose that we help the consumer by sharing with him some of the knowledge which the government has accumulated in the process of purchasing consumer items for its own use. Government agencies, such as the General Services Administration and the Department of Defense, have developed their own extensive procedures for evaluating the products they buy—products which range from light bulbs and detergents to tires and electric drills. As a result of this process, they have developed considerable purchasing expertise; in short, they know what to look for when they are buying a given product. They know, for example, what general types of paint are appropriate for certain surfaces; they know what "check-points" to examine when a piece of machinery is being purchased. The release of such information could help all of our people become more skillful consumers. I am therefore asking my Special Assistant for Consumer Affairs to develop a program for disseminating general information of this sort and to carry on further studies as to how the skill and knowledge of government purchasers can be shared with the public in a fair and useful manner.

FOOD AND DRUGS

The surveillance responsibilities of the Food and Drug Administration extend not only to food and drugs themselves, but also to cosmetics, therapeutic devices, and other products. Both the structure and the procedures of the FDA must be fully adequate to this sizeable and sensitive assignment, which is why this Administration has made the FDA the subject of intensive study.

I have asked the Secretary of Health, Education, and Welfare to undertake a thorough re-examination of the FDA, and I expect that this review will soon produce a number of important reforms in the agency's operations. This study is taking up several central questions: What further financial and personnel resources does the FDA require? Are laboratory findings communicated as promptly and fully as is desirable to high Administration officials and to the public? What should be the relationship of the FDA to other scientific arms of the government? What methods can bring the greatest possible talent to bear on the critical questions the FDA considers?

There are a number of actions relating to FDA concerns which should be taken promptly, even while our study of that institution continues. For example, I have already asked the Secretary of Health, Education, and Welfare to initiate a full review of food additives. This investigation should move as fast as our resources permit, re-examining the safety of substances which are now described by the phrase, "generally recognized as safe" (GRAS). Recent findings concerning the effects of cyclamate sweeteners on rats underscore the importance of continued vigilance in this field. The major suppliers and users of cyclamates have shown a sense of public responsibility during the recent difficulties and I am confident that such cooperation from industry will continue to facilitate this investigation.

I also recommend that the Congress take action which would make possible, for the first time, the rapid identification of drugs and drug containers in a time of personal emergency. When overdosage or accidental ingestion of a drug presently occurs, a physician is often unable to identify that drug without elaborate laboratory analysis. Many manufacturers are already working to remedy this problem on a voluntary basis by imprinting an identification number on every drug capsule and container they produce. As many in the industry have urged, this simple process should now be required of all drug producers, provided they are given suitable time to adjust their production machinery.

Another important medical safety problem concerns medical devices—equipment ranging from contact lenses and hearing aids to artificial valves which are implanted in the body. Certain minimum standards should be established for such devices; the government should be given additional authority to require premarketing clearance in certain cases. The scope and nature of any legislation in this area must be carefully considered, and the Department of Health, Education, and Welfare is undertaking a thorough study of medical device regulation. I will receive the results of that study early in 1970.

OTHER PROPOSALS

THE OFFICE OF ECONOMIC OPPORTUNITY

The problems which all American consumers encounter are experienced with particular intensity by the poor. With little purchasing experience to rely upon and no money to waste, poorer citizens are the most frequent and most tragic victims of commercial malpractices. The Office of Economic Opportunity is therefore establishing its own Division of Consumer Affairs to help focus and improve its already extensive consumer activities for poorer Americans. The nationwide network of Community Action Agencies can be one instrument for extending consumer education into this area.

HELPING THE STATES AND LOCALITIES

An important segment of consumer abuses can be handled most effectively at the state and local level, we believe, provided that each state has a strong consumer protection statute and an effective mechanism for enforcing it. Several States set examples for the Federal government in this field; every State should be encouraged to explore the need for an adequately financed Division of Consumer Protection as a part of its State Attorney General's office. Both the Special Assistant for Consumer Affairs and the Federal Trade Commission can do much to help States and localities to improve their consumer protection activities. The codification of state consumer protection laws which the Special Assistant is now conducting promises to be a useful part of the States in this effort.

GUARANTEES AND WARRANTIES

Consumers are properly concerned about the adequacy of guarantees and warranties on the goods they buy. On January 8, 1969, a task force recommended that the household appliance industry disclose more fully the terms of the warranties it provides. It recommended that, if at the end of one year, voluntary progress had not occurred, then legislative action should be considered.

In order to evaluate the industry's recent progress, I am today reactivating that task force. It will be chaired by my Special Assistant for Consumer Affairs and will include representatives from the Department of Commerce, the Department of Labor, the Federal Trade Commission, the Department of Justice, and the Council of Economic Advisors. I am asking the task force to make its report by the end of this year and to comment on the need for guarantee and warranty legislation in the household appliance industries and in other fields.

PRODUCT SAFETY

The product safety area is one which requires further investigation and further legislation, as the hearings of the National Commission on Product Safety have already demonstrated. I am asking my Special Assistant for Consumer Affairs to provide continued surveillance in the area of product safety, particularly after June 30, 1970, when the National Commission on Product Safety is scheduled to complete its work. And I am also instructing the appropriate agencies of the government to consult with the Commission and to prepare appropriate safety legislation for submission to Congress.

Finally, I am asking the Congress to require that any government agency, in any written decision substantially affecting the consumers' interest, give due consideration to that interest and express in its opinion the manner in which that interest was taken into account. I would also note that the major review which will be conducted this December by the White House Conference on Food, Nutrition, and Health will provide further welcome advances in the protection and education of the American consumer.

Interest in consumer protection has been an important part of American life for many decades. It was in the mid-1920's, in fact, that two of the leading consumer advocates of the day, Stuart Chase and F. J. Schlink, reached the following conclusion: "The time has gone—possibly forever—," they wrote, "when it is possible for each of us to become informed on all the things we have to buy. Even the most expert today can have knowledge of only a negligible section of the field. What sense then in a specialized industrial society if each individual must learn by trial and error again and forever again?" It was clear at that time and it is clear today, that the consumer needs expert help. The consumer has received some of that needed help through the years, from a variety of sources, private and public.

Our program is a part of that tradition. Its goal is to turn the "Buyer's Bill of Rights" into a reality, to make life in a complex society more fair, more convenient and more productive for all our citizens. Our program is fair to businessmen and good for business, since it encourages everyone who does business to do an even better job of providing quality goods and services. Our action is intended to foster a just marketplace—a marketplace which is fair both to those who sell and those who buy.

RICHARD NIXON

The White House
October 30, 1969

NOTE: Also released was the transcript of a White House news briefing on the message by Virginia H. Knauer, Special Assistant to the President for Consumer Affairs, Patricia Reilly Hitt, Assistant Secretary of HEW for Community and Field Service, Richard W. McLaren, Assistant Attorney General, Antitrust Division, and Dr. Jesse L. Steinfeld, Deputy Assistant Secretary of HEW for Health and Scientific Affairs.

422   Statement About the Supreme Court Decision on Timing of School Desegregation.   *October 30, 1969*

THE SUPREME COURT has spoken decisively on the timing of school desegregation. There are, of course, practical and human problems involved. With all of us working together in full respect for the law, I am confident we can overcome these problems.

I intend to use the leadership resources of the executive branch of Government to assist in every possible way in doing so. I call upon all citizens, and particularly those in leadership positions, to work together in seeking solutions for these problems in accordance with the mandate of the Court.

NOTE: The statement was read by Press Secretary Ronald L. Ziegler at his news briefing at 12:15 p.m. on Thursday, October 30, 1969.

The decision handed down on October 29, 1969, was in *Alexander* v. *Holmes County Board of Education* (396 U.S. 19).

423   Statement About the Decision of the Democratic Leadership To Defer Consideration of Draft Reform. *October 30, 1969*

I DEEPLY REGRET the announced decision of the Democratic leadership to deny the United States Senate an opportunity to consider draft reform until next year. It is clear that the vast majority of Americans share the sense of urgency which I feel concerning reform of the Selective Service System. The House of Representatives by an overwhelming vote has today indicated that it holds the same opinion. Yet the action of the Senate Democratic leaders means that the Members of that body—even including, apparently, the members of the duly constituted committees—will not even have a chance to vote on my recommendation.

The American people, and particularly our young people, have questioned from time to time whether our political institutions can still be responsive to clearly felt needs. The proposed Selective Service reforms present the Senate of the United States with an opportunity to confirm those doubts—or to dissipate them. I am still hopeful that the Senate will approve—during this session—this high priority legislation.

Pointing to the further reforms which might be made is no excuse to make no reforms at all. Clearly, this is not a matter which should be casually dismissed or made a political football. I respectfully, but urgently, suggest that the decision of the Democratic Senate leadership to block action be reconsidered.

NOTE: On November 8, 1969, the White House Press Office released the text of a news briefing by Secretary of Defense Laird on pending draft legislation.

424   Remarks at the Annual Meeting of the Inter American Press Association.   *October 31, 1969*

President Copley, President Edwards, Mr. Secretary of State, Governor Rockefeller, all of the distinguished guests here, Your Excellencies, the Ambassadors from the American States, and members and guests of the Inter American Press Association:

As we stand here on this 25th anniversary meeting of the Inter American Press Association, I should like to be permitted some personal comments before I then deliver my prepared remarks to you.

I have learned that this is the first occasion in which the remarks of the President of any one of the American nations has been carried and is being carried live by Telstar to all the nations in the hemisphere. And we are proud that it is before the Inter American Press Association.

I am sure that those of you, and I know that most of you here are members and

893

publishers of the newspaper profession, will not be jealous if this is on television tonight.

Also, I am very privileged to appear before this organization again. I was reminded it was 15 years ago that I, as Vice President, addressed the organization in New Orleans. It is good to be with you tonight, and particularly as the outgoing president is an old friend, Mr. [Agustín] Edwards from Santiago. The new president is also an old friend, Mr. [James] Copley from San Diego—sister cities, one in the Northern Hemisphere of the Americas and the other in the Southern Hemisphere.

There is one other remark that Mrs. Edwards brought eloquently to my attention as we heard that magnificent rendition by the Army Chorus of "America the Beautiful." She said, "That is for all of us. We are all Americans in this room."

And it is in that spirit that I want to address my remarks tonight to our partnership in the Americas. In doing so, I wish to place before you some suggestions for reshaping and reinvigorating that partnership.

Often we in the United States have been charged with an overweening confidence in the rightness of our own prescriptions, and occasionally we have been guilty of the charge. I intend to correct that. Therefore, my words tonight are meant as an invitation by one partner for further interchange, for increased communication, and, above all, for new imagination in meeting our shared responsibilities.

For years, we in the United States have pursued the illusion that we alone could remake continents. Conscious of our wealth and technology, seized by the force of good intentions, driven by our habitual impatience, remembering the dramatic success of the Marshall Plan of postwar Europe, we have sometimes imagined that we knew what was best for everyone else and that we could and should make it happen. Well, experience has taught us better.

It has taught us that economic and social development is not an achievement of one nation's foreign policy but something deeply rooted in each nation's own traditions.

It has taught us that aid that infringes pride is no favor to any nation.

It has taught us that each nation, and each region, must be true to its own character.

What I hope we can achieve, therefore, is a more mature partnership in which all voices are heard and none is predominant—a partnership guided by a healthy awareness that give-and-take is better than take-it-or-leave-it.

My suggestions this evening for new directions toward a more balanced relationship come from many sources.

First, they are rooted in my personal convictions. I have seen the problems of this hemisphere. As those in this room know, I have visited every nation in this hemisphere. I have seen them at first hand. I have felt the surging spirit of those nations—determined to break the grip of outmoded structures, yet equally determined to avoid social disintegration. Freedom, justice, a chance for each of our people to live a better and more abundant life—these are goals to which I am unshakably committed because progress in our hemisphere is not only a practical necessity, it is a moral imperative.

Second, these new approaches have been substantially shaped by the report of Governor Rockefeller, who, at my request and at your invitation, listened perceptively to the voices of our neighbors and incorporated their thoughts into a set of farsighted proposals.

Third, they are consistent with thoughts expressed in the Consensus of Vina del Mar,[1] which we have studied with great care.

Fourth, they have benefited from the counsel of many persons in government and out, in this country and throughout the hemisphere.

And, finally, basically they reflect the concern of the people of the United States for the development and progress of a hemisphere which is new in spirit, and which, through our efforts together, we can make new in accomplishment.

Tonight I offer no grandiose promises and no panaceas.

I do offer action.

The actions I propose represent a new approach. They are based on five principles:

—First, a firm commitment to the inter-American system, to the compacts which bind us in that system—as exemplified by the Organization of American States and by the principles so nobly set forth in its charter.

—Second, respect for national identity and national dignity, in a partnership in which rights and responsibilities are shared by a community of independent states.

—Third, a firm commitment to continued United States assistance for hemispheric development.

—Fourth, a belief that the principal future pattern of this assistance must

be U.S. support for Latin American initiatives, and that this can best be achieved on a multilateral basis within the inter-American system.

—Finally, a dedication to improving the quality of life in this new world of ours, to making people the center of our concerns, and to helping meet their economic, social, and human needs.

We have heard many voices from the Americas in these first months of our new administration—voices of hope, voices of concern, and some voices of frustration.

We have listened.

These voices have told us they wanted fewer promises and more action. They have told us that United States aid programs seemed to have helped the United States more than Latin America. They have told us that our trade policies were insensitive to the needs of other American nations. They have told us that if our partnership is to thrive or even to survive, we must recognize that the nations of the Americas must go forward in their own way, under their own leadership.

Now it is not my purpose here tonight to discuss the extent to which we consider the various charges that I have just listed right or wrong. But I recognize the concerns. I share many of them. What I propose tonight is, I believe, responsive to those concerns.

The most pressing concerns center on economic development and especially on the policies by which aid is administered and by which trade is regulated.

In proposing specific changes tonight, I mean these as examples of the actions I believe are possible in a new kind of partnership in the Americas.

Our partnership should be one in which the United States lectures less and listens

---

[1] A list of 46 specific proposals for United States trade and aid policy changes drawn up at Vina del Mar, Chile, by ministers from 21 Latin American nations in May 1969.

more. It should be one in which clear, consistent procedures are established to insure that the shaping of the future of the nations in the Americas reflects the will of those nations.

I believe this requires a number of changes.

To begin with, it requires a fundamental change in the way in which we manage development assistance in the hemisphere.

That is why I propose that a multilateral inter-American agency be given an increasing share of responsibility for development assistance decisions. CIAP— the Inter-American Committee on the Alliance for Progress—could be given this new function, or an entirely new agency could be created within the system.

Whatever the form, the objective would be to evolve an effective multilateral framework for bilateral assistance, to provide the agency with an expert international staff and, over time, to give it major operational and decisionmaking responsibilities.

The other American nations themselves would thus jointly assume a primary role in setting priorities within the hemisphere, in developing realistic programs, in keeping their own performance under critical review.

One of the areas most urgently in need of new policies is the area of trade. In my various trips to the Latin American countries and the other American countries, I have found that this has been uppermost on the minds of the leaders for many, many years. In order to finance their import needs and to achieve self-sustaining growth, the other American nations must expand their exports.

Most Latin American exports now are raw materials and foodstuffs. We are attempting to help the other countries of the hemisphere to stabilize their earnings from these exports, to increase them as time goes on.

Increasingly, however, those countries will have to turn more toward manufactured and semimanufactured products for balanced development and major export growth. Thus they need to be assured of access to the expanding markets of the industrialized world. In order to help achieve this, I have determined to take the following major steps:

—First, to lead a vigorous effort to reduce the nontariff barriers to trade maintained by nearly all industrialized countries against products of particular interest to Latin America and other developing countries.

—Second, to support increased technical and financial assistance to promote Latin American trade expansion.

—Third, to support the establishment, within the inter-American system, of regular procedures for advance consultation on trade matters. United States trade policies often have a very heavy impact on our neighbors. It seems only fair that in the more balanced relationship we seek, there should be full consultation within the hemisphere family before decisions affecting its members are taken, and not after.

—And finally, most important, in world trade forums, I believe it is time to press for a liberal system of generalized trade preferences for all developing countries, including Latin America. We will seek adoption by all of the industrialized nations of a scheme with broad product coverage and with no ceilings on preferential imports. We will seek equal access to industrial markets for all developing countries, so as to eliminate the discrimination against Latin America that now exists in many countries. We will also urge that such a system eliminates the inequitable "reverse preferences" that now discriminate against Western Hemisphere countries.

There are three other important economic issues that directly involve the new partnership concept and which a number of our partners have raised. They raised them with me, they raised them with Governor Rockefeller, with the Secretary of State, and others in our administration.

These are "tied" loans, debt service, and regional economic integration.

For several years now, virtually all loans made under United States aid programs have been "tied," that is, as you know, they have been encumbered with restrictions designed to maintain United States exports, including a requirement that the money be spent on purchases in the United States.

These restrictions have been burdensome for the borrowers. They have impaired the effectiveness of the aid. In June, I ordered the most cumbersome restrictions removed, three additionality requirements.

In addition, I announce tonight that I am now ordering that effective November 1, loan dollars sent to Latin America under AID be freed to allow purchases not only here, but anywhere in Latin America.

As a third step, I am also ordering that all other onerous conditions and restrictions on U.S. assistance loans be reviewed, with the objective of modifying or eliminating them.

Now, if I might add a personal word, this decision on freeing AID loans is one of those things that people kept saying ought to be done but could not be done. In light of our own balance of payments problems, there were compelling arguments against it. I can assure you that within the administration we had a very vigorous discussion on this subject. But I felt, and the rest of my colleagues within the administration felt, that the needs of the hemisphere had to come first, so I simply ordered it done, showing our commitment in actions rather than only in words. This will be our guiding principle in the future.

And with the presence of many Members of the House and the Senate here tonight, I am sure they realize that there are not too many occasions when the President can accomplish something by just ordering it to be done.

The growing burden of external debt service has increasingly become a major problem of future development. Some countries find themselves making heavy payments in debt service which reduce the positive effects of development aid. Therefore, tonight I suggest that CIAP might appropriately urge the international financial organizations to recommend possible remedies.

We have seen a number of moves in the Americas toward regional economic integration, such as the establishment of the Central American Common Market, the Latin American and Caribbean free trade areas, and the Andean Group. The decisions on how far and how fast this process of integration goes, of course, are not ours to make. But I do want to stress this: We in the United States stand ready to help in this effort if our help is requested and is needed.

On all of these matters, we look forward to consulting further with our hemisphere neighbors and partners. In a major related move, I am also directing our representatives to invite CIAP, as a regular procedure, to conduct a periodic review of U.S. economic policies as they affect the other nations of the hemisphere, and to consult with us about them.

Similar reviews are now made of the other hemisphere countries' policies, as you are aware, but the United States has not previously opened its policies to such consultation. I believe that true partnership requires that we should and, henceforth, if our partners so desire, as I gather from your applause you do, we shall.

I would like to turn now to a vital subject in connection with economic development in the hemisphere, namely, the role of private investment. Now, clearly, each government in the Americas must make its own decision about the place of private investment, domestic and foreign, in its development process. Each must decide for itself whether it wishes to accept or forgo the benefits that private investment can bring.

For a developing country, constructive foreign private investment has the special advantage of being a prime vehicle for the transfer of technology. And certainly, from no other source is so much investment capital available, because capital, from government to government on that basis, is not expansible. In fact, it tends now to be more restricted, whereas, private capital can be greatly expanded.

As we have seen, however, just as a capital-exporting nation cannot expect another country to accept investors against its will, so must a capital-importing country expect a serious impairment of its ability to attract investment funds when it acts against existing investments in a way which runs counter to commonly accepted norms of international law and behavior. Unfortunately, and perhaps unfairly, such acts by one nation in the Americas affect investor confidence in the entire region.

We will not encourage U.S. private investment where it is not wanted or where local political conditions face it with unwarranted risks. But I must state my own strong belief, and it is this: I think that properly motivated private enterprise has a vital role to play in social as well as economic development in all of the American nations. We have seen it work in our own country. We have seen it work in other countries—whether they are developing or developed—other countries that lately have been recording the world's most spectacular rates of economic growth.

Referring to a completely other area of the world, the exciting stories of the greatest growth rates are those that have turned toward more private investment, rather than less. Japan we all know about, but the story is repeated in Korea, in Taiwan, in Malaysia, in Singapore, and in Thailand.

In line with this belief, we are examining ways to modify our direct investment controls in order to help meet the investment requirements of developing nations in the Americas and elsewhere. I have further directed that our aid programs place increasing emphasis on assistance to locally-owned private enterprise. I am also directing that we expand our technical assistance for establishing national and regional capital markets.

As we all have seen, in this age of

rapidly advancing science, the challenge of development is only partly economic. Science and technology increasingly hold the key to our national futures. If the promise of this final third of the 20th century is to be realized, the wonders of science must be turned to the service of man.

In the Consensus of Vina del Mar, we were asked for an unprecedented effort to share our scientific and technical capabilities.

To that request we shall respond in a true spirit of partnership.

This I pledge to you tonight: The nation that went to the moon in peace for all mankind is ready, ready to share its technology in peace with its nearest neighbors.

Tonight, I have discussed with you a new concept of partnership. I have made a commitment to act. I have been trying to give some examples of actions we are prepared to take.

But as anyone familiar with government knows, commitment alone is not enough. There has to be the machinery to assure an effective followthrough.

Therefore, I am also directing a major reorganization and upgrading of the United States Government structure for dealing with Western Hemisphere affairs.

As a key element of this—and this is one of those areas where the President cannot do it, he needs the approval of the Congress—but as a key element of this, I have ordered preparation of a legislative request, which I will submit to the Congress, raising the rank of the Assistant Secretary of State for Inter-American Affairs to Under Secretary—thus giving the hemisphere special representation.

I know that many in this room, 15 years ago urged that upon me, and I see Mr. Pedro Beltrán [2] here particularly applauding. He urged it upon me just a few years ago, too.

I trust that we will be able, through the new Under Secretary of State, to do a more effective job with regard to the problems of the hemisphere, and the new Under Secretary will be given authority to coordinate all United States Government activities in the hemisphere, so that there will be one window for all those activities.

And now, my friends in the American family, I turn to a sensitive subject. Debates have long raged, they've raged both in the United States and elsewhere, over what our attitude should be toward the various forms of government within the inter-American system.

Let me sum up my own views very candidly.

First, my own country lives by a democratic system which has preserved its form for nearly two centuries. It has its problems. But we are proud of our system. We are jealous of our liberties. And we hope that eventually most, perhaps even all, of the world's people will share what we consider to be the blessings of genuine democracy.

We are aware that most people today in most countries of the world do not share those blessings.

I would be less than honest if I did not express my concern over examples of liberty compromised, of justice denied, or rights infringed.

Nevertheless, we recognize that enor-

---

[2] Prime Minister and Minister of Finance of Peru 1959–1961, and presently owner and publisher of the daily newspaper La Prensa in Lima.

mous, sometimes explosive, forces for change are operating in Latin America. These create instabilities; they bring changes in governments. On the diplomatic level, we must deal realistically with governments in the inter-American system as they are. We have, of course—we in this country—a preference for democratic procedures, and we hope that each government will help its own people to move forward to a better, a fuller, and a freer life.

In this connection, however, I would stress one other point. We cannot have a peaceful community of nations if one nation sponsors armed subversion in another's territory. The ninth meeting of American Foreign Ministers clearly enunciated this principle. The "export" of revolution is an intervention which our system cannot condone, and a nation like Cuba which seeks to practice it can hardly expect to share in the benefits of this community.

And now, finally, a word about what all this can mean—not just for the Americas but for the world.

Today, the world's most fervent hope is for a lasting peace in which life is secure, progress is possible, and freedom can flourish. In each part of the world we can have lasting peace and progress only if the nations directly concerned take the lead themselves in achieving it, and in no part of the world can there be a true partnership if one partner dictates its direction.

I can think of no assembly of nations better suited than ours to point the way to developing such a partnership. A successfully progressing Western Hemisphere, here in this new world, demonstrating in action mutual help and mutual respect, will be an example for the world. Once

again, by this example, we will stand for something larger than ourselves.

For three quarters of a century, many of us have been linked together in the Organization of American States and its predecessors in a joint quest for a better future. Eleven years ago, Operation Pan America was launched as a Brazilian initiative. More recently, we have joined in a noble Alliance for Progress, whose principles still guide us. And now I suggest that our goal for the seventies should be a decade of "action for progress" for the Americas.

As we seek to forge a new partnership, we must recognize that we are a community of widely diverse peoples. Our cultures are different. Our perceptions are often different. Our emotional reactions are often different. May it always be that way. What a dull world it would be if we were all alike. Partnership—mutuality—these do not flow naturally. We have to work at them.

Understandably, perhaps, a feeling has arisen in many Latin American countries that the United States really "no longer cares."

Well, my answer to that tonight is very simple.

We do care. I care. I have visited most of your countries, as I said before. I have met most of your leaders. I have talked with your people. I have seen your great needs as well as your great achievements.

And I know this, in my heart as well as in my mind: If peace and freedom are to endure in this world, there is no task more urgent than lifting up the hungry and the helpless, and putting flesh on the dreams of those who yearn for a better life.

Today, we in this American community share an historic opportunity.

As we look together down the closing decades of this century, we see tasks that summon the very best that is in us. But those tasks are difficult precisely because they do mean the difference between despair and fulfillment for most of the 600 million people who will live in Latin America in the year 2000. Those lives are our challenge. Those lives are our hope. And we could ask no prouder reward than to have our efforts crowned by peace, prosperity, and dignity in the lives of those 600 million human beings—

in Latin America and in the United States—each so precious, each so unique—our children and our legacy.

NOTE: The President spoke at 9:35 p.m. at the Washington Hilton Hotel.

Copies of the advance text of the President's remarks were sent to Presidents Emilio Garrastazu Medici of Brazil, Carlos Lleras Restrepo of Colombia, José Joaquín Trejos Fernandez of Costa Rica, and Gustavo Diaz Ordaz of Mexico. Letters of appreciation from the Latin American Presidents are printed in the Weekly Compilation of Presidential Documents (vol. 5, pp. 1565–1566 and 1627).

425   Address to the Nation on the War in Vietnam. *November 3, 1969*

Good evening, my fellow Americans:

Tonight I want to talk to you on a subject of deep concern to all Americans and to many people in all parts of the world—the war in Vietnam.

I believe that one of the reasons for the deep division about Vietnam is that many Americans have lost confidence in what their Government has told them about our policy. The American people cannot and should not be asked to support a policy which involves the overriding issues of war and peace unless they know the truth about that policy.

Tonight, therefore, I would like to answer some of the questions that I know are on the minds of many of you listening to me.

How and why did America get involved in Vietnam in the first place?

How has this administration changed the policy of the previous administration?

What has really happened in the negotiations in Paris and on the battle-front in Vietnam?

What choices do we have if we are to

end the war?

What are the prospects for peace?

Now, let me begin by describing the situation I found when I was inaugurated on January 20.

—The war had been going on for 4 years.

—31,000 Americans had been killed in action.

—The training program for the South Vietnamese was behind schedule.

—540,000 Americans were in Vietnam with no plans to reduce the number.

—No progress had been made at the negotiations in Paris and the United States had not put forth a comprehensive peace proposal.

—The war was causing deep division at home and criticism from many of our friends as well as our enemies abroad.

In view of these circumstances there were some who urged that I end the war at once by ordering the immediate withdrawal of all American forces.

From a political standpoint this would

have been a popular and easy course to follow. After all, we became involved in the war while my predecessor was in office. I could blame the defeat which would be the result of my action on him and come out as the peacemaker. Some put it to me quite bluntly: This was the only way to avoid allowing Johnson's war to become Nixon's war.

But I had a greater obligation than to think only of the years of my administration and of the next election. I had to think of the effect of my decision on the next generation and on the future of peace and freedom in America and in the world.

Let us all understand that the question before us is not whether some Americans are for peace and some Americans are against peace. The question at issue is not whether Johnson's war becomes Nixon's war.

The great question is: How can we win America's peace?

Well, let us turn now to the fundamental issue. Why and how did the United States become involved in Vietnam in the first place?

Fifteen years ago North Vietnam, with the logistical support of Communist China and the Soviet Union, launched a campaign to impose a Communist government on South Vietnam by instigating and supporting a revolution.

In response to the request of the Government of South Vietnam, President Eisenhower sent economic aid and military equipment to assist the people of South Vietnam in their efforts to prevent a Communist takeover. Seven years ago, President Kennedy sent 16,000 military personnel to Vietnam as combat advisers. Four years ago, President Johnson sent American combat forces to South Vietnam.

Now, many believe that President Johnson's decision to send American combat forces to South Vietnam was wrong. And many others—I among them—have been strongly critical of the way the war has been conducted.

But the question facing us today is: Now that we are in the war, what is the best way to end it?

In January I could only conclude that the precipitate withdrawal of American forces from Vietnam would be a disaster not only for South Vietnam but for the United States and for the cause of peace.

For the South Vietnamese, our precipitate withdrawal would inevitably allow the Communists to repeat the massacres which followed their takeover in the North 15 years before.

—They then murdered more than 50,000 people and hundreds of thousands more died in slave labor camps.

—We saw a prelude of what would happen in South Vietnam when the Communists entered the city of Hue last year. During their brief rule there, there was a bloody reign of terror in which 3,000 civilians were clubbed, shot to death, and buried in mass graves.

—With the sudden collapse of our support, these atrocities of Hue would become the nightmare of the entire nation—and particularly for the million and a half Catholic refugees who fled to South Vietnam when the Communists took over in the North.

For the United States, this first defeat in our Nation's history would result in a collapse of confidence in American leadership, not only in Asia but throughout the world.

Three American Presidents have recognized the great stakes involved in Vietnam and understood what had to be done.

In 1963, President Kennedy, with his characteristic eloquence and clarity, said: ". . . we want to see a stable government there, carrying on a struggle to maintain its national independence.

"We believe strongly in that. We are not going to withdraw from that effort. In my opinion, for us to withdraw from that effort would mean a collapse not only of South Viet-Nam, but Southeast Asia. So we are going to stay there."

President Eisenhower and President Johnson expressed the same conclusion during their terms of office.

For the future of peace, precipitate withdrawal would thus be a disaster of immense magnitude.

—A nation cannot remain great if it betrays its allies and lets down its friends.

—Our defeat and humiliation in South Vietnam without question would promote recklessness in the councils of those great powers who have not yet abandoned their goals of world conquest.

—This would spark violence wherever our commitments help maintain the peace—in the Middle East, in Berlin, eventually even in the Western Hemisphere.

Ultimately, this would cost more lives.

It would not bring peace; it would bring more war.

For these reasons, I rejected the recommendation that I should end the war by immediately withdrawing all of our forces. I chose instead to change American policy on both the negotiating front and battlefront.

In order to end a war fought on many fronts, I initiated a pursuit for peace on many fronts.

In a television speech on May 14, in a speech before the United Nations, and on a number of other occasions I set forth our peace proposals in great detail.

—We have offered the complete withdrawal of all outside forces within 1 year.

—We have proposed a cease-fire under international supervision.

—We have offered free elections under international supervision with the Communists participating in the organization and conduct of the elections as an organized political force. And the Saigon Government has pledged to accept the result of the elections.

We have not put forth our proposals on a take-it-or-leave-it basis. We have indicated that we are willing to discuss the proposals that have been put forth by the other side. We have declared that anything is negotiable except the right of the people of South Vietnam to determine their own future. At the Paris peace conference, Ambassador Lodge has demonstrated our flexibility and good faith in 40 public meetings.

Hanoi has refused even to discuss our proposals. They demand our unconditional acceptance of their terms, which are that we withdraw all American forces immediately and unconditionally and that we overthrow the Government of South Vietnam as we leave.

We have not limited our peace initiatives to public forums and public statements. I recognized, in January, that a long and bitter war like this usually cannot be settled in a public forum. That is why in addition to the public statements and negotiations I have explored every possible private avenue that might lead to a settlement.

Tonight I am taking the unprecedented step of disclosing to you some of our other initiatives for peace—initiatives we undertook privately and secretly because we thought we thereby might open a door which publicly would be closed.

I did not wait for my inauguration to begin my quest for peace.

—Soon after my election, through an individual who is directly in contact on a personal basis with the leaders of North Vietnam, I made two private offers for a rapid, comprehensive settlement. Hanoi's replies called in effect for our surrender before negotiations.

—Since the Soviet Union furnishes most of the military equipment for North Vietnam, Secretary of State Rogers, my Assistant for National Security Affairs, Dr. Kissinger, Ambassador Lodge, and I, personally, have met on a number of occasions with representatives of the Soviet Government to enlist their assistance in getting meaningful negotiations started. In addition, we have had extended discussions directed toward that same end with representatives of other governments which have diplomatic relations with North Vietnam. None of these initiatives have to date produced results.

—In mid-July, I became convinced that it was necessary to make a major move to break the deadlock in the Paris talks. I spoke directly in this office, where I am now sitting, with an individual who had known Ho Chi Minh [President, Democratic Republic of Vietnam] on a personal basis for 25 years. Through him I sent a letter to Ho Chi Minh.

I did this outside of the usual diplomatic channels with the hope that with the necessity of making statements for propaganda removed, there might be constructive progress toward bringing the war to an end. Let me read from that letter to you now.

"Dear Mr. President:

"I realize that it is difficult to communicate meaningfully across the gulf of four years of war. But precisely because of this gulf, I wanted to take this opportunity to reaffirm in all solemnity my desire to work for a just peace. I deeply believe that the war in Vietnam has gone on too long and delay in bringing it to an end can benefit no one—least of all the people of Vietnam. . . .

"The time has come to move forward at the conference table toward an early resolution of this tragic war. You will find us forthcoming and open-minded in a common effort to bring the blessings of peace to the brave people of Vietnam. Let history record that at this critical juncture, both sides turned their face toward peace rather than toward conflict and war."

I received Ho Chi Minh's reply on August 30, 3 days before his death. It simply reiterated the public position North Vietnam had taken at Paris and flatly rejected my initiative.

The full text of both letters is being released to the press.

—In addition to the public meetings that I have referred to, Ambassador Lodge has met with Vietnam's chief negotiator in Paris in 11 private sessions.

—We have taken other significant initiatives which must remain secret to keep open some channels of communication which may still prove to be productive.

But the effect of all the public, private, and secret negotiations which have been undertaken since the bombing halt a year ago and since this administration came into office on January 20, can be summed up in one sentence: No progress whatever has been made except agreement on the shape of the bargaining table.

Well now, who is at fault?

It has become clear that the obstacle in negotiating an end to the war is not the President of the United States. It is not the South Vietnamese Government.

The obstacle is the other side's absolute refusal to show the least willingness to join us in seeking a just peace. And it will not do so while it is convinced that all it has to do is to wait for our next concession, and our next concession after that one, until it gets everything it wants.

There can now be no longer any question that progress in negotiation depends only on Hanoi's deciding to negotiate, to negotiate seriously.

I realize that this report on our efforts on the diplomatic front is discouraging to the American people, but the American people are entitled to know the truth— the bad news as well as the good news— where the lives of our young men are involved.

Now let me turn, however, to a more encouraging report on another front.

At the time we launched our search for peace I recognized we might not succeed in bringing an end to the war through negotiation. I, therefore, put into effect another plan to bring peace—a plan which will bring the war to an end regardless of what happens on the negotiating front.

It is in line with a major shift in U.S. foreign policy which I described in my press conference at Guam on July 25. Let me briefly explain what has been described as the Nixon Doctrine—a policy which not only will help end the war in Vietnam, but which is an essential element of our program to prevent future Vietnams.

We Americans are a do-it-yourself people. We are an impatient people. Instead of teaching someone else to do a job, we like to do it ourselves. And this trait has been carried over into our foreign policy.

In Korea and again in Vietnam, the United States furnished most of the money, most of the arms, and most of the men to help the people of those countries defend their freedom against Communist aggression.

Before any American troops were committed to Vietnam, a leader of another Asian country expressed this opinion to me when I was traveling in Asia as a private citizen. He said: "When you are trying to assist another nation defend its freedom, U.S. policy should be to help them fight the war but not to fight the war for them."

Well, in accordance with this wise counsel, I laid down in Guam three principles as guidelines for future American policy toward Asia:

—First, the United States will keep all of its treaty commitments.

—Second, we shall provide a shield if a nuclear power threatens the freedom of a nation allied with us or of a nation whose survival we consider vital to our security.

—Third, in cases involving other types of aggression, we shall furnish military and economic assistance when requested in accordance with our treaty commitments. But we shall look to the nation directly threatened to assume the primary responsibility of providing the manpower for its defense.

After I announced this policy, I found that the leaders of the Philippines, Thailand, Vietnam, South Korea, and other nations which might be threatened by Communist aggression, welcomed this new direction in American foreign policy.

The defense of freedom is everybody's business—not just America's business. And it is particularly the responsibility of the people whose freedom is threatened. In the previous administration, we Americanized the war in Vietnam. In this administration, we are Vietnamizing the search for peace.

The policy of the previous administration not only resulted in our assuming the primary responsibility for fighting the war, but even more significantly did not adequately stress the goal of strengthening the South Vietnamese so that they could defend themselves when we left.

The Vietnamization plan was launched following Secretary Laird's visit to Vietnam in March. Under the plan, I ordered first a substantial increase in the training and equipment of South Vietnamese forces.

In July, on my visit to Vietnam, I changed General Abrams' orders so that they were consistent with the objectives of our new policies. Under the new orders, the primary mission of our troops is to enable the South Vietnamese forces to assume the full responsibility for the security of South Vietnam.

Our air operations have been reduced by over 20 percent.

And now we have begun to see the results of this long overdue change in American policy in Vietnam.

—After 5 years of Americans going into Vietnam, we are finally bringing American men home. By December 15, over 60,000 men will have been withdrawn from South Vietnam—including 20 percent of all of our combat forces.

—The South Vietnamese have continued to gain in strength. As a result they have been able to take over combat responsibilities from our American troops.

Two other significant developments have occurred since this administration took office.

—Enemy infiltration, infiltration which is essential if they are to launch a major attack, over the last 3 months is less than 20 percent of what it was over the same period last year.

—Most important—United States casualties have declined during the last 2 months to the lowest point in 3 years.

Let me now turn to our program for the future.

We have adopted a plan which we have worked out in cooperation with the South Vietnamese for the complete withdrawal of all U.S. combat ground forces, and their replacement by South Vietnamese forces on an orderly scheduled timetable. This withdrawal will be made from strength and not from weakness. As South Vietnamese forces become stronger, the rate of American withdrawal can become greater.

I have not and do not intend to announce the timetable for our program. And there are obvious reasons for this decision which I am sure you will understand. As I have indicated on several occasions, the rate of withdrawal will depend on developments on three fronts.

906

One of these is the progress which can be or might be made in the Paris talks. An announcement of a fixed timetable for our withdrawal would completely remove any incentive for the enemy to negotiate an agreement. They would simply wait until our forces had withdrawn and then move in.

The other two factors on which we will base our withdrawal decisions are the level of enemy activity and the progress of the training programs of the South Vietnamese forces. And I am glad to be able to report tonight progress on both of these fronts has been greater than we anticipated when we started the program in June for withdrawal. As a result, our timetable for withdrawal is more optimistic now than when we made our first estimates in June. Now, this clearly demonstrates why it is not wise to be frozen in on a fixed timetable.

We must retain the flexibility to base each withdrawal decision on the situation as it is at that time rather than on estimates that are no longer valid.

Along with this optimistic estimate, I must—in all candor—leave one note of caution.

If the level of enemy activity significantly increases we might have to adjust our timetable accordingly.

However, I want the record to be completely clear on one point.

At the time of the bombing halt just a year ago, there was some confusion as to whether there was an understanding on the part of the enemy that if we stopped the bombing of North Vietnam they would stop the shelling of cities in South Vietnam. I want to be sure that there is no misunderstanding on the part of the enemy with regard to our withdrawal program.

We have noted the reduced level of infiltration, the reduction of our casualties, and are basing our withdrawal decisions partially on those factors.

If the level of infiltration or our casualties increase while we are trying to scale down the fighting, it will be the result of a conscious decision by the enemy.

Hanoi could make no greater mistake than to assume that an increase in violence will be to its advantage. If I conclude that increased enemy action jeopardizes our remaining forces in Vietnam, I shall not hesitate to take strong and effective measures to deal with that situation.

This is not a threat. This is a statement of policy, which as Commander in Chief of our Armed Forces, I am making in meeting my responsibility for the protection of American fighting men wherever they may be.

My fellow Americans, I am sure you can recognize from what I have said that we really only have two choices open to us if we want to end this war.

—I can order an immediate, precipitate withdrawal of all Americans from Vietnam without regard to the effects of that action.

—Or we can persist in our search for a just peace through a negotiated settlement if possible, or through continued implementation of our plan for Vietnamization if necessary—a plan in which we will withdraw all of our forces from Vietnam on a schedule in accordance with our program, as the South Vietnamese become strong enough to defend their own freedom.

I have chosen this second course.

It is not the easy way.

It is the right way.

It is a plan which will end the war and

serve the cause of peace—not just in Vietnam but in the Pacific and in the world.

In speaking of the consequences of a precipitate withdrawal, I mentioned that our allies would lose confidence in America.

Far more dangerous, we would lose confidence in ourselves. Oh, the immediate reaction would be a sense of relief that our men were coming home. But as we saw the consequences of what we had done, inevitable remorse and divisive recrimination would scar our spirit as a people.

We have faced other crises in our history and have become stronger by rejecting the easy way out and taking the right way in meeting our challenges. Our greatness as a nation has been our capacity to do what had to be done when we knew our course was right.

I recognize that some of my fellow citizens disagree with the plan for peace I have chosen. Honest and patriotic Americans have reached different conclusions as to how peace should be achieved.

In San Francisco a few weeks ago, I saw demonstrators carrying signs reading: "Lose in Vietnam, bring the boys home."

Well, one of the strengths of our free society is that any American has a right to reach that conclusion and to advocate that point of view. But as President of the United States, I would be untrue to my oath of office if I allowed the policy of this Nation to be dictated by the minority who hold that point of view and who try to impose it on the Nation by mounting demonstrations in the street.

For almost 200 years, the policy of this Nation has been made under our Constitution by those leaders in the Congress and the White House elected by all of the people. If a vocal minority, however fervent its cause, prevails over reason and the will of the majority, this Nation has no future as a free society.

And now I would like to address a word, if I may, to the young people of this Nation who are particularly concerned, and I understand why they are concerned, about this war.

I respect your idealism.

I share your concern for peace.

I want peace as much as you do.

There are powerful personal reasons I want to end this war. This week I will have to sign 83 letters to mothers, fathers, wives, and loved ones of men who have given their lives for America in Vietnam. It is very little satisfaction to me that this is only one-third as many letters as I signed the first week in office. There is nothing I want more than to see the day come when I do not have to write any of those letters.

—I want to end the war to save the lives of those brave young men in Vietnam.

—But I want to end it in a way which will increase the chance that their younger brothers and their sons will not have to fight in some future Vietnam someplace in the world.

—And I want to end the war for another reason. I want to end it so that the energy and dedication of you, our young people, now too often directed into bitter hatred against those responsible for the war, can be turned to the great challenges of peace, a better life for all Americans, a better life for all people on this earth.

I have chosen a plan for peace. I believe it will succeed.

If it does succeed, what the critics say now won't matter. If it does not succeed, anything I say then won't matter.

I know it may not be fashionable to speak of patriotism or national destiny these days. But I feel it is appropriate to do so on this occasion.

Two hundred years ago this Nation was weak and poor. But even then, America was the hope of millions in the world. Today we have become the strongest and richest nation in the world. And the wheel of destiny has turned so that any hope the world has for the survival of peace and freedom will be determined by whether the American people have the moral stamina and the courage to meet the challenge of free world leadership.

Let historians not record that when America was the most powerful nation in the world we passed on the other side of the road and allowed the last hopes for peace and freedom of millions of people to be suffocated by the forces of totalitarianism.

And so tonight—to you, the great silent majority of my fellow Americans—I ask for your support.

I pledged in my campaign for the Presidency to end the war in a way that we could win the peace. I have initiated a plan of action which will enable me to keep that pledge.

The more support I can have from the American people, the sooner that pledge can be redeemed; for the more divided we are at home, the less likely the enemy is to negotiate at Paris.

Let us be united for peace. Let us also be united against defeat. Because let us understand: North Vietnam cannot defeat or humiliate the United States. Only Americans can do that.

Fifty years ago, in this room and at this very desk,[1] President Woodrow Wilson spoke words which caught the imagination of a war-weary world. He said: "This is the war to end war." His dream for peace after World War I was shattered on the hard realities of great power politics and Woodrow Wilson died a broken man.

Tonight I do not tell you that the war in Vietnam is the war to end wars. But I do say this: I have initiated a plan which will end this war in a way that will bring us closer to that great goal to which Woodrow Wilson and every American President in our history has been dedicated—the goal of a just and lasting peace.

As President I hold the responsibility for choosing the best path to that goal and then leading the Nation along it.

I pledge to you tonight that I shall meet this responsibility with all of the strength and wisdom I can command in accordance with your hopes, mindful of your concerns, sustained by your prayers.

Thank you and goodnight.

NOTE: The President spoke at 9:32 p.m. in his office at the White House. The address was broadcast on radio and television.

On November 3, 1969, the White House Press Office released an advance text of the address.

---

[1] Later research indicated that the desk had not been President Woodrow Wilson's as had long been assumed but was used by Vice President Henry Wilson during President Grant's administration.

426   Letters of the President and President Ho Chi Minh of the Democratic Republic of Vietnam. *November 3, 1969*

Dear Mr. President:

I realize that it is difficult to communicate meaningfully across the gulf of four years of war. But precisely because of this gulf, I wanted to take this opportunity to reaffirm in all solemnity my desire to work for a just peace. I deeply believe that the war in Vietnam has gone on too long and delay in bringing it to an end can benefit no one—least of all the people of Vietnam. My speech on May 14 laid out a proposal which I believe is fair to all parties. Other proposals have been made which attempt to give the people of South Vietnam an opportunity to choose their own future. These proposals take into account the reasonable conditions of all sides. But we stand ready to discuss other programs as well, specifically the 10-point program of the NLF.

As I have said repeatedly, there is nothing to be gained by waiting. Delay can only increase the dangers and multiply the suffering.

The time has come to move forward at the conference table toward an early resolution of this tragic war. You will find us forthcoming and open-minded in a common effort to bring the blessings of peace to the brave people of Vietnam. Let history record that at this critical juncture, both sides turned their face toward peace rather than toward conflict and war.

Sincerely,

RICHARD NIXON

[His Excellency Ho Chi Minh, President, Democratic Republic of Vietnam, Hanoi]

NOTE: The President's letter was dated July 15, 1969, and released November 3, 1969.

President Ho Chi Minh's reply dated August 25, 1969, was released by the White House Press Office along with the President's letter. It read as follows:

To His Excellency Richard Milhous Nixon
President of the United States
Washington

Mr. President:

I have the honor to acknowledge receipt of your letter.

The war of aggression of the United States against our people, violating our fundamental national rights, still continues in South Vietnam. The United States continues to intensify military operations, the B-52 bombings and the use of toxic chemical products multiply the crimes against the Vietnamese people. The longer the war goes on, the more it accumulates the mourning and burdens of the American people. I am extremely indignant at the losses and destructions caused by the American troops to our people and our country. I am also deeply touched at the rising toll of death of young Americans who have fallen in Vietnam by reason of the policy of American governing circles.

Our Vietnamese people are deeply devoted to peace, a real peace with independence and real freedom. They are determined to fight to the end, without fearing the sacrifices and difficulties in order to defend their country and their sacred national rights. The overall solution in 10 points of the National Liberation Front of South Vietnam and of the Provisional Revolutionary Government of the Republic of South Vietnam is a logical and reasonable basis for the settlement of the Vietnamese problem. It has earned the sympathy and support of the peoples of the world.

In your letter you have expressed the desire to act for a just peace. For this the United States must cease the war of aggression and withdraw their troops from South Vietnam, respect the right of the population of the South and of the Vietnamese nation to dispose of themselves, without foreign influence. This is the correct manner of solving the Vietnamese problem in conformity with the national rights of the Vietnamese people, the interests of the United States and the hopes for peace of the peoples of the world. This is the path that will allow the United States to get out of the war with honor.

With good will on both sides we might arrive at common efforts in view of finding a correct solution of the Vietnamese problem.

Sincerely,

Ho Chi Minh

427 Statement About the National Program for Voluntary Action. *November 4*, 1969

FROM the beginning of our country, Americans have worked together voluntarily to help master common needs and problems. A major goal of this administration is to recognize and enlist the energies and resources of the people themselves, as well as government, in a renewal of this historic American approach. To further that goal, I announced last March the initial steps in building a National Program for Voluntary Action.

For the past 6 months, my Special Consultant on Voluntary Action, Max M. Fisher of Detroit, and Secretary Romney of the Department of Housing and Urban Development, Chairman of the Cabinet Committee on Voluntary Action, have been developing the National Program. It is based on three assumptions:

1. Many Americans would like to start working as volunteers on community problems. A recent survey reported that two-thirds of us were willing to volunteer regularly if shown something worthwhile to do.

2. The role of the government is to help these Americans become effective volunteers—not to direct them, or to impose priorities upon them, or to organize them in any kind of master plan.

The government should respond to the desires of the people, not the other way around.

3. For volunteer Americans to be most effective, they need to be able to draw

upon professional skills and organized experience. Therefore, it is also important to work with existing organizations as well as to encourage new activities.

Mr. Fisher and Secretary Romney have met with hundreds of voluntary action leaders—both from established organizations and emergent groups, representing the broadest cross section of American life. They have sought advice on how best to realize our goal of a "creative partnership" between governmental and private effort to carry out the National Program for Voluntary Action.

As a result of these consultations, private voluntary action leaders now are ready, with our encouragement, to formalize the private part of this national partnership. I am therefore announcing these actions today:

1. Creation of a nonprofit, nonpartisan National Center for Voluntary Action, which will encourage and assist effective voluntary action throughout the private sector. It will be established by distinguished private citizens working with government officials and using private funds.

2. Appointment of Mr. Fisher as Chairman of the National Center for Voluntary Action.

3. Appointment of W. Clement Stone of Chicago, an insurance executive and leader in voluntary action, to serve as Finance Committee Chairman of the

National Center.

4. Appointment of the following leaders of the private voluntary sector to serve as members of a nominating committee, which will propose 80 to 90 private citizens for membership on the National Center's Board of Directors:

Arthur Ashe, Jr., First Service Insurance Agency, Inc., Richmond, Va.; Philip Bernstein, executive vice president, Council of Jewish Federations & Welfare Funds, New York, N.Y.; Arch N. Booth, executive vice president, U.S. Chamber of Commerce, Washington, D.C.; Victor Carter, president, retired chairman, Republic Pictures, Los Angeles, Calif.; Martin Castillo, Inter-Agency Committee on Mexican American Affairs, Washington, D.C.; Jack Conway, president, Center for Community Change, Washington, D.C.; Bayard Ewing, Graham, Reid, Ewing and Stapleton, Providence, R.I. (president-elect of United Funds & Councils of America, Inc.); John W. Gardner, chairman, The Urban Coalition, Washington, D.C.; Miss Dorothy Height, president, National Council of Negro Women, Washington, D.C.; Mrs. Elsie Hillman, Standard Life Building, Pittsburgh, Pa.; Mrs. Laura Leonard, Westminister Community Center, Bell Gardens, Calif.; George Lindsay, attorney, Debevoise, Plimpton, Lyons and Gates, New York, N.Y.; Mrs. Alfred Anita Martinez, Dallas, Tex.; Aloysius A. Mazewski, president, Polish National Alliance of the US of NA, Northbrook, Ill.; Irwin Miller, president, Cummins Engine Co., Columbus, Ind.; Frank Pace, Jr., president, International Executive Service Corps, New York, N.Y.; Dr. W. Robert Parks, president, Iowa State University, Ames, Iowa; Leo Perlis, director, AFL–CIO Department of Community Services,

Washington, D.C.; Joseph Rhodes, Jr., Harvard University, Cambridge, Mass.; H. I. Romnes, chairman of the board, American Telephone and Telegraph Co., New York, N.Y.; Paul Sonnabend, executive vice president, Hotel Corporation of America, Boston, Mass.; William Toomey, Santa Barbara City College, Santa Barbara, Calif.

5. The call for a conference involving several hundred leaders, representing every facet of American life, to meet in Washington this winter, where they will have an open opportunity to discuss, determine and support the organization and future direction of the Center, the overall mission of the National Program for Voluntary Action, and their participation in it.

The Cabinet Committee with Chairman Romney and the Office of Voluntary Action will continue to represent the governmental side of this national effort and will work in closest harmony with the National Center and representatives of the private sector.

The total National Program for Voluntary Action, on both the private and governmental sides, will aim to:

1. Help motivate vast numbers of citizens to get involved in local voluntary efforts.

2. Help requesting communities mobilize for greater and more effective voluntary action.

3. Collect and transmit successful experience and expertise for strengthening voluntary action at all levels.

4. Stimulate all governmental levels to cooperate fully in voluntary efforts.

5. Achieve greater recognition of the role of voluntary action and those individuals, organizations, and communities which excel in their contributions.

I am confident that the National Program for Voluntary Action will be a significant and helpful instrument for enabling many more individual Americans to make their needed contributions toward solving the pressing problems of their neighborhoods, their communities, their States, and their Nation.

NOTE: The text of a news briefing on the National Program for Voluntary Action by Secretary of Housing and Urban Development George W. Romney and Special Consultant on Voluntary Action Max M. Fisher was released by the White House Press Office on November 4, 1969.

An announcement on December 22, 1969, designating Charles B. (Bud) Wilkinson as the President of the National Center for Voluntary Action is printed in the Weekly Compilation of Presidential Documents (vol. 5, p. 1778). The text of a news conference by Mr. Wilkinson was also released.

428   Remarks During a Television Interview Prior to a Congressional Breakfast. *November 5, 1969*

MISS BARBARA WALTERS. Good morning, Mr. President. We are very pleased to see you.

THE PRESIDENT. Good morning. Good morning, Herb. How are you? You were here last night.

MR. HERBERT KAPLOW. Yes, I hardly left.

THE PRESIDENT [*turning to Miss Walters*]. You were not here because it was stag.[1]

MISS WALTERS. I wish I could say that I had been here, Mr. President.

MR. KAPLOW. Mr. President, this time last year, let's see, we were all setting off from California back to New York to wait for the election returns.

THE PRESIDENT. Yes.

MR. KAPLOW. So it has been a year and you give the impression of a man who likes his job, even though there have been some pretty tough problems you have had to cope with.

THE PRESIDENT. Well, I am in pretty good shape. This morning I am rather happy, not because of the anniversary, but because we won a couple of good victories yesterday.

MR. KAPLOW. Tell me about the main problems you, yourself, have outlined in terms of priorities—Vietnam, inflation, cities, crime. Are you on schedule in getting somewhere in solving them?

THE PRESIDENT. We can never be on schedule until we solve the problems, but I suppose the problems, to a certain extent, will be with us in some of those fields. But we have made significant progress, I believe in all areas.

As far as the future is concerned, I think that our record here will be one that we can be very proud of. I think we have moved in all areas. We have moved in our pursuit for peace in Vietnam in an effective way. We have a plan now that will end the war, and end it in a way that we think will contribute to the cause of a just and lasting peace.

On the inflation front, we have had to take the hard medicine of cutting back on Government spending so that millions of people are going to be able to spend a little more and have more, have their dol-

---

[1] A stag dinner hosted by the President in honor of His Royal Highness Prince Philip, Duke of Edinburgh, was held in the State Dining Room at the White House at 8 p.m. on November 4, 1969.

lars mean more; and we think on the crime area, really, the problem is the Congress. The Congress has not given us the tools, but we are going to keep their feet to the fire until we get them.

MISS WALTERS. Mr. President, you mentioned a moment ago, of course, about the elections. You personally campaigned in New Jersey and in Virginia, and both of these men won their gubernatorial elections in great part because of the support of the people for you.

I understand also that this morning it was released that 77 percent of the country, according to a Gallup poll, is behind your Vietnam program. Do you think this kind of very large response will have an effect on your critics in Congress?

THE PRESIDENT. It could. Of course, let me say that there are very honest people who are going to be critical of a program, and they are not going to be affected by polls or by the fact that we won a couple of elections. I understand that.

There, of course, are others who probably just wonder which is the best way to go in this area. I believe that the public reaction has had considerable reaction in Washington. Washington does react to the country.

Incidentally, speaking of those two victories in New Jersey and Virginia, though, while I was in the States—and incidentally, Julie and David campaigned in New Jersey and Tricia in Virginia—the man wins it. I mean, Holton in Virginia and Cahill in New Jersey were great candidates and when we have a good candidate we will win in those States. So I don't take the credit.

I am rather happy we won because their opponents both made me the issue. Of course, in New Jersey Mr. [Robert]

Meyner made the war in Vietnam a straight up and down issue, and that 60 percent vote that Mr. Cahill got, I thought that was very reassuring in this bellwether State.

MISS WALTERS. Mr. President, here with your congressional supporters, I wonder if you can comment on how you feel you have fared in general with Congress, what your greatest success is and, perhaps, what your biggest disappointment has been with them.

THE PRESIDENT. Well, I think that generally you cannot put the Congress in a sort of bag and say the Congress is bad or good, and you cannot put, say, the Democratic leadership in a bag and say it is bad or good.

I have been very pleased and heartened by the way that the top Democratic leadership on great issues, issues involving war and peace, has supported the Presidency, just as when we, as Republicans in the 80th Congress, supported Mr. Truman in the Marshall Plan and the Greek-Turkish loan. That is the way it should be in this country.

Now when you get to the domestic issues, the crime package that Herb referred to, and the inflation package, and the tax bill, and the rest, it is a little harder, but that is the way the game is played. But I am going to fight just as hard as I can here, because this Nation wants this Congress to get to work and give us the tools to deal with narcotics, and deal with crime, to deal with all of these problems. We cannot do it until we get this legislation passed.

Also, the country wants this administration to have the tools to cut back on the cost of living. We cannot do it until the Congress passes a responsible tax bill and also passes the appropriations bill at the present level.

Now I have made a little bit of a political comment, but I just want to say, don't lump that Congress together and say Republicans are good, Democrats are bad. When you really look at it, I would say there are the responsible men in Congress and there are those that I don't think are quite as responsible. I am not going to name names. I am just glad that there have been enough responsible ones for us to win the close votes, but we need to win some more for the good of the country.

MR. KAPLOW. Mr. President, I think we will let you get to breakfast with the men you obviously feel are responsible.[2]

THE PRESIDENT. I should say. This is a very interesting group.

Barbara, you are sort of covering it from the standpoint of the social affairs. We were talking about this yesterday. Last night in this room—this is the State Dining Room, of course—it was set up with a great E-shaped table and Herb was here as one of our guests, and Prince Philip was a guest. He was really scintillating, didn't you think, Herb?

MR. KAPLOW. He certainly was.

MISS WALTERS. Oh, you are rubbing it in, Mr. President.

THE PRESIDENT. [Former Secretary of State] Dean Acheson and [former Secretary of State] Dean Rusk and Secretary [of State] Rogers and Vice President Agnew all spoke, so it was really quite an interesting evening. I did not have to speak long. I told the people in the audience I had made my speech the night before.

But I thought you would be interested to know that when I was talking to Prince Philip, we happened to talk about television. I just mentioned, incidentally, that the "Today Show," if he could work it into his schedule, would be a very good thing for him to do. I don't know whether he is going to do it, but if he doesn't do it this year, he will do it next year.

MISS WALTERS. Mr. President, you are the best agent the "Today Show" has ever had. We received a telephone call at 1:00 in the morning that Prince Philip will indeed be able to do the interview.

THE PRESIDENT. Tomorrow in New York, isn't that right?

MISS WALTERS. Yes, I am flying to New York to do it. I know it is your doing.

THE PRESIDENT. This morning, the reason he could not do it is because he is having breakfast with the Vice President. You know he has to do all these protocol things. But now you remember, ask him the right questions.

MISS WALTERS. Would you write them for me?

THE PRESIDENT. I don't need to. He is really quick.

MR. KAPLOW. Feel free, Mr. President, to come forth with any other suggestions.

THE PRESIDENT. I made one point, Barbara, that you should mention in this story. A recent poll in Britain showed that Prince Philip, if they elected a President, would run first. So you can see that he has what it takes, all that political charisma—I guess that is the popular word these days. You are going to see that tomorrow on television and your audience, I think, is going to enjoy it.

MISS WALTERS. That will be my opening question.

THE PRESIDENT. Thank you.

MISS WALTERS. Thank you, Mr. Presi-

---

[2] After his TV appearance, Mr. Nixon presided at a White House breakfast for Members of Congress who were his early supporters in the 1968 campaign.

dent, for inviting us here today. It is so kind of you.

THE PRESIDENT. It is nice to be on the morning show after so many mornings.

MISS WALTERS. Thank you, Mr. President. Enjoy your breakfast.

THE PRESIDENT. Thank you. Herb, it was good to see you.

NOTE: The interview with NBC reporters Barbara Walters and Herbert Kaplow began at 8:34 a.m. It was broadcast live on the "Today Show."

429 Remarks With the Governors-Elect of New Jersey and Virginia. *November 5, 1969*

I WANT to take this opportunity to welcome the two new Governors-elect from New Jersey and Virginia.

It is rather interesting to note that, while they are both Republicans and both outstanding winners in these States, this is the first time they have met. So, we have brought you together right here at the White House.

In speaking of them, I want to say that many will try to attribute their victories to what others did. They had a lot of support, a lot of support from outside the State and within the State, friends across the country. But having been a candidate many times, I know that the one who wins it is the man. These are two superb candidates. I could say that the only ones who really deserve any other credit are their wives.

Each of the Governors, as candidates, pledged that they were going to work with the Federal administration on the programs for their States. We thought we ought to start that working together today, the day after the election. That is why they are here. We are going to have lunch in the White House. We are going to discuss some of these problems and get going.

Would you like to say a word first, Bill? You are back in Washington where you have been awhile.

GOVERNOR-ELECT WILLIAM T. CAHILL. Mr. President, Governor Holton, first I certainly want to express on behalf of Mrs. Cahill and myself and our entire family and the family of Republicans in the State of New Jersey our appreciation to you for your tremendous assistance in the campaign and for your always generous efforts on our behalf.

We in New Jersey look to the White House, of course, for the leadership, not only of the country, but as far as our State is concerned. We look forward in this new administration to a truly cooperative effort to implement the "New Federalism" announced by you, and hopefully one that will bring to our State the necessary assistance to cope with the many problems of our State.

I really believe, Mr. President, that the victory at the polls yesterday was an expression of all of the people of the State of New Jersey, Republicans, Democrats, and Independents alike, expressing their desire for a change, expressing the hope that we can really bring new solutions to these old problems.

I look forward with great anticipation and great pleasure to future work with you and your associates here in Washington.

Thank you very much, Mr. President.

THE PRESIDENT. And now to Governor-elect Holton, the first Republican to be elected in the State of Virginia as Governor for 87 years.

I should say, incidentally, Governor-elect Cahill is the first Republican to be elected in the State of New Jersey in 16 years, since 1953.

Would you like to say a word about your new responsibilities, Governor Holton?

GOVERNOR-ELECT A. LINWOOD HOLTON. Thank you, Mr. President. I must say, it is going to take a little while to get used to that title.

We are, of course, tremendously pleased, too, and I think that the things Governor-elect Cahill has said about cooperation with you and the administration and the better allocation of power and responsibility back to the States is something that you have very forcefully presented and is really good news in Virginia.

I think that certainly there is a great deal of that element involved in our election.

We appreciate, Jinks[1] and I, what you said about our efforts, but we do want you to know, and I can bring this to you from all Virginians, that we appreciated your assistance and your help. You came at the right time. Your appearance with us was a magnificent assist.

I am not going into anything else, except just to say "many thanks," Mr. President. It is great to be with you here today in this victory seat. It feels pretty good.

THE PRESIDENT. Well, I do want to say to both of these successful candidates that as I saw them come up today and how well they looked and how healthy, that there is nothing like winning to make you look very good and very healthy.

I know how it can feel the other way, too.

NOTE: The President spoke at 1:05 p.m. on the North Lawn at the White House, where he and Mrs. Nixon and Vice President and Mrs. Agnew greeted Governors-elect Cahill and Holton and their wives.

---

[1] Virginia R. (Jinks) Holton, wife of Governor-elect Holton.

430   Remarks Welcoming the Apollo 11 Astronauts Following Their Goodwill Tour.   *November 5, 1969*

IT IS my privilege to speak for all of the American people in expressing the heartfelt thanks of this Nation to the Armstrongs, the Aldrins, and the Collinses for what I think is the most successful goodwill trip in the history of the United States of America.

We have noted from the press the magnificent receptions they have received all over the world, in Asia, in Africa, in Latin America, and in Europe. We know that the crowd gathered here on the White House lawn is not as large as some

you have seen, but the hearts of the American people are here, and through us, we are trying to indicate to you our appreciation, not only for what you did in your travel to the moon, but also what you did for the cause of peace and better understanding through your travel on this earth.

Certainly the first men ever to land on the moon have demonstrated that they are the best possible ambassadors America could have on this earth.

Finally, I do know that over these past

few weeks you had long hours, many speeches, lots of entertainment, and lots of protocol. I think those listening here and on television and radio would be interested to know what the plans are for the rest of the day.

We have invited our astronauts and their wives to come to the White House, spend the afternoon and the evening, a quiet dinner, and spend the night. We think that after all they have done publicly, it is time that they had an evening by themselves and why not in "everybody's house," the White House of the United States of America.

I think all of us would like to have Neil Armstrong say a word on behalf of his colleagues and their wives.

So if you would like to say a word, we would like to hear from you.

NOTE: The President spoke at 3:27 p.m. on the South Lawn at the White House, where he welcomed Apollo 11 astronauts Neil A. Armstrong, Col. Edwin E. Aldrin, Jr., and Col. Michael Collins and their wives following their 38-day goodwill tour of 22 countries.

The remarks of Neil A. Armstrong are printed in the Weekly Compilation of Presidential Documents (vol. 5, p. 1563).

431 Statement Announcing Establishment of the Council for Rural Affairs. *November 6, 1969*

SHORTLY after I became President, I established a new Cabinet-level Urban Affairs Council to help me develop an overall strategy for meeting the problems of the cities and to coordinate the wide variety of government efforts in this area. It is a fact of our national life that the concerns of rural America also deserve more careful consideration and more effective coordination at the highest levels of government.

We are a nation of cities, to be sure, but we are also a nation of small towns and villages, farms and forests, mines and ranches, mountains and rivers and lakes. The people who live in rural America have urgent problems which deserve our attention. More importantly, they represent a great resource upon which all of us can draw.

It is for these reasons that I am announcing today the establishment of a new Rural Affairs Council at the Cabinet level. The Council will meet next week for the first time. The following officials will join me as members of the Council: The Vice President, the Secretary of Agriculture, the Secretary of the Interior, the Secretary of Commerce, the Secretary of Housing and Urban Development, the Director of the Office of Economic Opportunity, the Secretary of Health, Education, and Welfare, the Secretary of Labor, the Director of the Bureau of the Budget, and the Chairman of the Council of Economic Advisers.

It is to this Council that the Task Force on Rural Development will submit its report and recommendations.

As I announce the formation of the Rural Affairs Council, I would note several facts which underscore the importance of its work. It is shocking, for example, to discover that at least one-third of the housing in rural America is presently substandard. It is disturbing to realize that more than 3 million rural Americans have not completed 5 years of school. It is disheartening to see that one-third of our rural communities with a population over

1,000 have no public sewage facilities.

It is also important to note that the population of our country is likely to grow by 50 percent in the next 30 years. Where these next hundred million persons locate is a tremendously important question for our society. After an era in which people have moved steadily from the countryside to large and crowded cities, we must now do what we can to encourage a more even distribution of our population throughout our country. The Rural Affairs Council can help our Nation to meet this challenge by helping rural America, once again, become an area of opportunity.

NOTE: Executive Order 11493 of November 13, 1969 establishes the Council for Rural Affairs.

The White House Press Office released the text of a news briefing on the establishment of the Council for Rural Affairs by Secretary of Agriculture Clifford M. Hardin.

An announcement of the appointment of John R. Price, Jr., as Executive Secretary of the Council for Urban Affairs and the Council for Rural Affairs is printed in the Weekly Compilation of Presidential Documents (vol. 5, p. 1700).

432   Letter to Congressional Leaders Recommending Additional Air Traffic Controller Positions. *November 7, 1969*

AIR TRANSPORTATION is a rapidly growing and vital part of the national economy. It is essential that we keep our air transportation system safe, economic and efficient. I have stressed many times my determination to take the steps necessary to maintain the safety and improve the effectiveness of the nation's air traffic control system.

The airport and airway development bill now moving through Congress will provide the revenues and the means for assuring that the facilities which support air transportation will keep pace with its growth. I strongly urge that the Congress approve this legislation promptly. As soon as it is enacted, including the new user charges, I will propose the additional appropriations for new and expanded programs for airways facilities and airports so that we can begin to meet air transportation needs of the 1970s.

Meanwhile, I am now proposing that we take a step toward meeting and anticipating the needs for additional air traffic controllers. These men and women carry much of the responsibility for facilitating the efficient and rapid flow of air traffic, and for preventing mid-air collisions of aircraft. The system requires many controllers, and it takes up to two years to train a beginner until he reaches journeyman status.

Accordingly, at the recommendation of the Secretary of Transportation, Mr. Volpe, I ask that the Congress approve the addition of 1,000 more controller positions in the current fiscal year. These are in addition to the 2,800 positions already included in the Department of Transportation's budget estimates now being considered by the Appropriations Committees. Supporting documentation for this proposal will be supplied to the Committees by the Department.

Since the continuing resolution has

held the operations of the Department of Transportation so far in this fiscal year to the fiscal year 1969 level, no additional appropriations beyond the pending 1970 budget request will be required to support these additional 1,000 traffic controller positions.

I urgently request that the Congress approve this proposal.

Sincerely,

RICHARD NIXON

NOTE: This is the text of identical letters addressed to Vice President Spiro T. Agnew, President of the Senate, and to Senator Richard B. Russell, Chairman, Committee on Appropriations, United States Senate. The letter was dated November 6, 1969 and released November 7, 1969.

The Department of Transportation and Related Agencies Appropriation Act, 1970, which was passed on December 26, 1969 (Public Law 91–168, 83 Stat. 454), included the President's request for 1,000 additional traffic controller positions but did not provide appropriations for the positions.

The text of the letter was released at Key Biscayne, Fla.

433   Statement Announcing Inauguration of the "Very Important Patients" Program.   *November* 8, 1969

NOVEMBER 11th, Veterans Day, will mark the inauguration of a significant national program called VIP—Very Important Patients.

The VIP program will involve nearly 500 outstanding Americans volunteering their time to visit Veterans Administration hospitals throughout the country. These volunteers include famous names from the fields of entertainment, professional football, baseball, and basketball, as well as Olympic stars, noted cartoonists, and prominent individuals from government, industry, the arts, literature, and religion.

As President of the United States, I am serving as patron of the VIP program. I am pleased to announce that Presidents Johnson and Truman are joining me in that role. As men who have served in our Armed Forces, and as Commander in Chief, all three of us are aware of the need to give special attention to the some 800,000 patients treated annually in 166 VA hospitals.

These patients include men who fought in the Spanish-American War, as well as veterans of World War I, World War II, Korea, and Vietnam. Many of them have been hospitalized a long time. Many are a long distance from home. Others have no homes at all. Almost all are lonely.

While the Veterans Administration can and does attend to the physical needs of these men, the VIP program will let them know that the Nation has not forgotten their service and sacrifices. I want to thank the public spirited citizens who are joining me in supporting the VIP program. Those of us who participate will surely receive more in gratitude and self-satisfaction than any of us can possibly give.

NOTE: The President and Mrs. Nixon visited with patients and staff at the Washington, D.C., Veterans Administration Hospital on November 11, 1969, as part of the VIP program.

The statement was released at Key Biscayne, Fla.

434   Statement on Governor Rockefeller's Report on Latin America.   *November* 10, 1969

THERE ARE two points I want to stress in connection with Governor Rockefeller's report which is being released today:

First, as I said in my October 31 speech, this report constituted a major contribution to the formulation of our policy for this hemisphere. Both our general conceptual approach and the specific lines of action we intend to follow have been substantially shaped by that report.

Secondly, this report is still very much under active consideration. Many of its recommendations which are far-reaching and complex are still being staffed and examined with a view to their implementation. Therefore, a good many of the things we will be doing in the weeks and months ahead will have had their genesis in this report.

Let me give you an example: In his report, Governor Rockefeller recommends a unique and imaginative technique that might be used in cases where this type of action is indicated in the debt service area. He recommended the possibility of maintaining equivalent local currency payments in instances where the dollar repayments are suspended or stretched out. The local currency would be paid into a fund which could in turn be used for development purposes in that country. Now there are a number of technical points to be clarified, but the concept is an imaginative one, and I believe it is something that can be useful. Accordingly, I have directed the Secretary of the Treasury to undertake an immediate study of this proposal with a view to adopting it as a technique in those cases where it is ap-

propriate. Mr. George [D.] Woods, who was a senior adviser to the Governor on his mission and is former President of the World Bank, will be a consultant to the Secretary of the Treasury for this purpose.

Now let me make a more general point. My speech on October 31 was intended as a philosophical foundation for what I envisage as a continuous process of policy formation over the months ahead. It outlined our view of the nature of our relationship with the other states in the hemisphere; the principles which should underlie that relationship; the policies which should implement it; and the directions those policies should take, together with some concrete examples.

I did not want to promise things which would have been unattainable, such as greatly increased aid levels. On the other hand, I want to do the maximum of what is possible and "doable." This is what I meant by an action program, and we intend now to take such concrete measures in conjunction with the other American nations. We intend to propose over the next several months further concrete actions. We will be discussing and exchanging views with our sister nations on key issues and problems, and jointly we will be developing programs and policies to meet our problems. One of the things I want to explore very carefully when budget considerations make it possible is a program to finish the highway net down the center of the South American Continent. This is a program which I think would have an immense effect economically and be a great boost to integration of the region.

Next week the Inter-American Economic and Social Council will convene here in Washington at the technical level. The United States will be making some specific proposals in a number of fields; we will want to have the views of the other nations, and we will then be developing proposals and lines of action accordingly over the next several months.

Let me give you a concrete example: All of the American nations want to see the early establishment of a liberal worldwide system of generalized trade preferences for all developing countries. I stated in my speech that the United States intended to press vigorously with the developed countries for the adoption of such a system. This week U.S. representatives at OECD [Organization for Economic Cooperation and Development] meetings in Paris took that position. The United States will work actively now for such a system. I want to say, however, that if for any reason we find it not possible to establish a satisfactory system of generalized preferences within a reasonable time, then the United States will be prepared to consider other alternative actions it can take to assure that the American nations will have preferential access to the U.S. market.

As another example, we are also going to propose to the other American nations

at the IA–ECOSOC [Inter-American Economic and Social Council] meetings joint initiatives whose costs we are prepared to share:

—expansion of regional science programs, emphasizing research and training;

—promotion of an intensified hemispheric effort in basic and applied food research;

—establishment of an inter-American science information exchange program.

I am, in short, most serious about undertaking an action program and implementing a mature partnership with the countries of this hemisphere. Our fundamental objective, as Governor Rockefeller so eloquently expressed it, is to help improve the quality of life of the people of this hemisphere.

The Governor knows how personally grateful I am for all of the time and energy he spent on this mission, and how deeply appreciative I am for his insights and imaginative ideas. Let me once more take this opportunity publicly to express my appreciation.

NOTE: The report of Gov. Nelson A. Rockefeller of New York is entitled "Quality of Life in the Americas" (137 pp., processed). The complete text of the report, except for charts, graphs, and index, is printed in the Department of State Bulletin (vol. 61, p. 495).

435   Remarks at Governor Rockefeller's News Briefing on His Report on Latin America. *November* 10, 1969

Ladies and gentlemen:

You have already had distributed to you the copies of the Rockefeller report.

And Governor Rockefeller is here to answer questions on that report or any

other questions on our Latin American policy which you would like to ask him.

Before he answers those questions, I would like to say a word about that report and the part that it has played in developing our Latin American policy.

There have been numbers of reports on Latin America that have been made by various missions, going back over the 20 years that I recall studying Latin American policy. This is by far the most comprehensive, with 83 specific recommendations for action. Also, I believe that this report will see more of its recommendations implemented by action than any report on Latin America ever made.

Several of the recommendations in the report were implemented in my speech of the 31st.

There are others, which are under active consideration within the administration at the present time, which Governor Rockefeller will be glad to discuss in answer to your questions. Two particularly I would like to mention.

One is with regard to debt service. I had only one brief paragraph in my speech on debt service because we have not yet completed our studies on this matter. But I think the very imaginative recommendations that were made by the Rockefeller committee, and particularly by George Woods,[1] deserve not only the most active consideration, but deserve implementation within the administration, and Governor Rockefeller will be discussing the recommendations that are made.

I do not mean implementation exactly as recommended, because this involves a number of financial details with which I am not familiar. But I think this is the direction toward which this very basic problem of debt service, which plagues virtually every country in Latin Amer-

ica—this is the direction in which we should move.

The other is with regard to trade preferences. You will have noted in my speech I referred to the necessity for having special trade preferences for all the developing countries. I pointed out that there were countries outside of the Western Hemisphere that had special relationships with other countries, and particularly their former colonial countries, and that our first step would be to attempt to work out a general system of trade preferences which would apply equally and fairly to all of the developing countries, including those of Latin America.

We are beginning to implement that recommendation as contained in my speech. However, the Rockefeller report indicates that, if it is not possible to work out a satisfactory arrangement in the direction of implementing a recommendation for trade preferences for all the developing countries because of the ties that many of those countries will have with former colonial nations, then the goal that we have is to have special trade preferences for Latin America.

This incidentally is not a new goal as far as I am concerned. The Governor will remember I recommended this in 1958 when I returned. He has been recommending it long before that.

But our goal is overall trade preferences for all the developing countries, but specifically and particularly for Latin America, if it is not possible to work it out for all.

These two points I wanted to emphasize before presenting the Governor.

Now, Governor, you are welcome to answer any questions, and if you will

---

[1] George D. Woods, senior adviser on Governor Rockefeller's mission to Latin America.

expand on the debt service thing particularly.

NOTE: The President spoke at 11:27 a.m. in the Roosevelt Room at the White House.

The text of Governor Rockefeller's news briefing concerning his report was also released by the White House Press Office on November 10, 1969.

436   Thanksgiving Day Message to the Armed Forces. *November 10, 1969*

THE PILGRIMS at Plymouth had good reason to express their gratitude to God on that first Thanksgiving Day nearly three and a half centuries ago. Those who enjoyed the abundance of that first harvest had survived in a wilderness where suffering and want were their constant companions. Their faith in God's mercy was strengthened and sustained in spite of hardship.

Throughout our history, Americans have celebrated this day in both a spiritual and festive fashion, rejoicing in the blessings bestowed upon them by our Creator. Among these, for which we are indeed grateful, is our precious heritage

of freedom which you today protect and defend wherever you may serve. Your admirable contribution to our national security insures that this heritage will be preserved.

This Thanksgiving Day provides an ideal occasion for all Americans to acknowledge and give thanks for the courage, devotion to duty, and the loyalty you have demonstrated in service to our nation.

RICHARD NIXON

NOTE: The message was dated November 7, 1969 and released November 10, 1969.

On November 12, 1969, the President signed Proclamation 3944 "Thanksgiving Day, 1969."

437   Statement Outlining a 13-Point Program for Reform of the Federal Corrections System. *November 13, 1969*

NINETEEN out of every twenty persons who are sent to prison eventually return to society. What happens to them while they are in confinement is a tremendously important question for our country.

Are they effectively rehabilitated? In some instances, the answer is yes. But in an appalling number of cases, our correctional institutions are failing.

According to recent studies, some 40 percent of those who are released from confinement later return to prison. Or, to put it another way, a sizable proportion of serious crimes are committed by per-

sons who have already served a jail sentence. Eight out of every ten offenders sampled in a recent FBI study had at least one prior arrest and seven out of ten had a prior conviction. Of those charged with burglary, auto theft, or armed robbery, between 60 and 70 percent had been arrested two or more times in the preceding 7 years.

For youthful offenders, the picture is even darker. The repeater rates are greater among persons under 20 than over and there is evidence that our institutions actually compound crime problems by bringing young delinquents into contact with experienced criminals.

A nation as resourceful as ours should not tolerate a record of such futility in its correctional institutions. Clearly, our rehabilitative programs require immediate and dramatic reform. As a first step in that reform, I have today issued a broad directive to the Attorney General, asking him to take action to improve our correctional efforts in 13 specific ways. He will report to me on his progress after 6 months and will at that time make such further recommendations as he believes are necessary.

The primary purpose of my directive is to improve the Federal corrections system. If this goal can be speedily accomplished, then the Federal system can serve as a model for State and local reforms. The Federal Government will make every effort to help the States and localities make needed improvements, providing them with information, technical aid, and funds. We will also encourage greater cooperation and coordination between government and the private sector and among all the various units of government. I have specifically asked that our rehabilitative programs give greater attention to the special problems of distinct categories of offenders, such as juveniles, women, narcotics and alcoholic addicts, the mentally ill, and hard-core criminals. Closely supervised parole, work-release, and probationary projects should be accelerated, as should our basic research into rehabilitative methods.

THIRTEEN-POINT PROGRAM

The 13 specific concerns of my directive are as follows:

1. To end the crisis-oriented, stopgap nature of most reform efforts, I have asked the Attorney General to develop a 10-year plan for reforming our correctional activities.

2. I have directed that explorations begin on the feasibility of pooling the limited resources of several governmental units in order to set up specialized treatment facilities. Several counties within a State or several States can often accomplish together what none of them could accomplish alone. Regional cooperation could be especially helpful in dealing with women offenders who are so few in number that their treatment in local institutions is often inefficient and inadequate, with hard-core criminals who require close supervision and particularly secure quarters, and with the mentally ill and narcotics and alcoholic addicts who need extensive medical treatment.

3. It is a tragic fact that juveniles comprise nearly a third of all offenders who are presently receiving correctional treatment and that persons under the age of 25 comprise half of that total. Yet our treatment facilities are least adequate for these same age groups. This is the reason that so many young offenders are thrown in with older criminals. I have asked the Attorney General to give special emphasis to programs for juvenile offenders—including group homes, modern diagnostic and treatment centers, and new probation mechanisms. This effort should be closely coordinated with the Department of Health, Education, and Welfare.

4. We must expedite the design and construction of the long-planned Federal psychiatric study and treatment facility for mentally disturbed and violent offenders. Since the late 1950's, this project has been delayed by a series of administrative problems. It should be delayed no

925

longer, for our understanding of mentally disturbed offenders is distressingly inadequate.

5. Federal law, like many State laws, has never been adequately concerned with the problem of the mental incompetent who is accused of a crime, sentenced for a crime, or found innocent because of his mental condition. I do not believe, for example, that present law adequately protects the civil rights of the accused mental incompetent. Nor does the disposition of such cases always give adequate protection to society. We need a comprehensive study of this matter, one which takes up both the constitutional and the medical problems involved. A new law should be drafted which could not only serve the Federal jurisdiction but which might aid State authorities who have similar problems.

6. A great number of existing city and county jails are antiquated and overcrowded. Correctional experts believe that the local jail concept should be replaced with a comprehensive, community-oriented facility which would bring together a variety of detention efforts, adult and juvenile court diagnostic services, treatment programs both for those who are incarcerated and for those on supervisory release, and the half-way house concept. Pilot projects along these lines have already been designed for New York City and Chicago. They should be given the highest priority and available funds should, wherever possible, be used to encourage other centers of this sort.

7. Ninety percent of convicted criminals and accused persons held in custody are housed in State or local institutions. The Federal Government should do all it can to help the States and localities carry this burden through programs of technical and financial aid. This Federal assistance should be especially directed toward the development of parole and probation programs and other alternatives to incarceration.

8. The lack of adequate public money for Federal and State prisons suggests that we should look to the private sector for supplementary assistance. Private industry can help rehabilitate criminals in many ways, such as retraining and hiring those who have served time. Voluntary agencies and professional organizations can also help those who are released from jail, tutoring them in new skills, helping them locate jobs, advising them as they readjust to civilian society, and cooperating with the courts in their probationary programs. A number of industries and volunteer organizations have already started successful programs of this sort; their example should be used to stimulate broader private efforts.

9. An adequate corrections system is only as effective as those who run it. Unfortunately too many rehabilitative programs are staffed with untrained personnel. I am therefore asking the Department of Justice to significantly expand its existing training programs for those who work in correctional institutions, both newcomers and experienced employees. The Justice Department's informal efforts to disseminate information should also be expanded.

10. I have asked the Attorney General to establish a task force which will make recommendations concerning a unified Federal corrections system. The various stages of rehabilitation are often poorly coordinated at present. The offender cannot proceed in an orderly manner from

confinement to work-release to release under supervision and finally to an unsupervised release. The unification of the various programs involved could bring to this process the coordination and sense of progression it badly needs.

11. Our experience with so-called "half-way houses," institutions which offer a mediating experience between prison and complete return to society, has been most successful to this point. The per capita cost of operating half-way houses is not significantly higher than that of maintaining a man in prison, and the rate of recidivism among those who leave half-way houses is lower than among those who return directly to society after confinement. I am asking the Attorney General to prepare legislation which would expand the half-way house program to include a greater number of convicted offenders, specifically, those on parole and probation who cannot participate in the program at present. The Department of Justice will also assist States and localities in establishing and expanding half-way house projects.

12. Many correctional programs are based more on tradition and assumption than on theories which have been scientifically tested. Few of our programs have been closely studied to see just what results they bring. Clearly the poor record of our rehabilitative efforts indicates that we are doing something wrong and that we need extended research both on existing programs and on suggested new methods. I have asked the Attorney General to marshal the combined resources of the Department of Justice in a major new research effort.

13. Correctional programs have proliferated in recent years with little or no effort at consolidation or coordination. Among the Federal agencies presently involved in correctional activities are the Bureau of Prisons, the Board of Parole, the Office of the Pardon Attorney, and the Law Enforcement Assistance Administration—all at the Department of Justice. Also involved are the Social and Rehabilitation Service, the Office of Education, and the Public Health Service of the Department of Health, Education, and Welfare. The Manpower Administration of the Department of Labor and the Office of Economic Opportunity also play major roles.

If all of these efforts are to be effectively coordinated then some one authority must do the coordinating. I have asked the Attorney General to take on that assignment.

A WORD TO THE CONCERNED CITIZEN

Many millions of words have been written about the crime crisis in our country. Surely it is among the most severe domestic crises of our times. Its successful solution will require the best efforts of the government at every level and the full cooperation of our citizens in every community.

One of the areas where citizen cooperation is most needed is in the rehabilitation of the convicted criminal. Men and women who are released from prison must be given a fair opportunity to prove themselves as they return to society. We will not insure our domestic tranquility by keeping them at arm's length. If we turn our back on the ex-convict, then we should not be surprised if he again turns his back on us.

None of our vocational education programs, our work-release efforts, our halfway houses, or our probation and parole systems will succeed if the community to which an offender returns is unwilling to extend a new opportunity. Unions, civic groups, service clubs, labor organizations, churches, and employers in all fields can do a great deal to fight crime by extending a fair chance to those who want to leave their criminal records behind them and become full and productive members of society.

NOTE: The White House Press Office also released the text of a news briefing on the President's program by Richard W. Velde, Associate Administrator, Law Enforcement Assistance Administration, and Myrl E. Alexander, Director, U.S. Bureau of Prisons.

438 Memorandum to Attorney General Mitchell on Reform of the Federal Corrections System. *November 13, 1969*

Memorandum for Honorable John N. Mitchell, the Attorney General:

The American system for correcting and rehabilitating criminals presents a convincing case of failure. No realistic program to substantially reduce crime can ignore the appalling deficiencies of our prisons and rehabilitation efforts.

Today, at least 40 percent of all offenders released from custody eventually return to prison. The FBI Uniform Crime Reports for 1968 [1] show that 82 percent of a sample of offenders arrested in 1967–1968 had been arrested previously. 70 percent had a prior conviction and 46 percent had been imprisoned on a prior sentence.

The FBI report also shows that 67 percent of persons charged with burglary, 71 percent charged with auto theft and 60 percent charged with armed robbery, had been arrested at least twice in the preceding seven years. For those under 20 years of age the repeater rates are even higher.

We must remember that crime control does not end with conviction and imprisonment: 19 out of every 20 men who enter prison one day return to society.

The purpose of this directive is to make the Federal correction system a prototype for the much needed overhaul of our generally archaic State and local corrections institutions. The Federal government should make every possible resource available to help States and local systems in similar reform efforts.

There has been some improvement in certain correctional programs in recent years, but it has not been enough. The problems of crime continue to outpace the solutions.

We must immediately begin to make greater progress in dealing with these problems. The processes for returning both criminal and juvenile offenders to a useful life in our society must be rapidly improved. It is most important that we improve not only the Federal system, however, but also the State and local systems which handle the majority of offenders.

Unsuccessful correctional programs must be abandoned. Those which have proved successful must be accelerated and expanded. And new, bold and imaginative programs must be developed and im-

---

[1] "Crime in the United States, Issued by J. Edgar Hoover, Uniform Crime Report—1968" (Government Printing Office, 187 pp.).

plemented if we are to succeed where past efforts have failed.

I am therefore requesting you to take the following actions:

1. Prepare a ten-year program for complete modernization of the physical plants and correctional programs in the Federal prison system, with emphasis on developing model facilities and programs which State and local systems can follow.

2. Initiate discussions with State and local officials to explore the advisability and feasibility of constructing *regional* institutions to house State, local and Federal female offenders.

3. Give particular priority in the Federal corrections effort to the special problems presented by special categories of offenders, such as juveniles, women, and the mentally disturbed, with special emphasis on the use of alternatives to traditional institutionalization. These efforts should be consistent with the objectives of the Juvenile Delinquency Prevention and Control Act of 1968.

4. Expedite the planning and construction of a new Federal psychiatric study and treatment facility for mentally disturbed and violent offenders, and assist in the development of appropriate regional and State facilities for this largely neglected class of offender.

5. Develop recommendations for revising the Federal laws relating to the handling of the mentally incompetent charged with a Federal crime, serving a sentence for a Federal crime, or found not guilty solely because of a mental condition.

6. Expedite the planning and construction of Federal demonstration centers for urban areas. Consideration should be given to community-oriented facilities which combine detention efforts, adult and juvenile court diagnostic services, treatment programs for those incarcerated and for those on supervisory release and the half-way house concept.

7. Expand the Federal program of technical assistance to State and local governments that need help in improving correctional facilities and the quality of parole, probation and other alternatives to imprisonment.

8. Work to provide new vocational, educational and employment opportunities for persons on probation, in prison, and on parole, seeking out the cooperation and resources of private industry, and developing a government-wide system of coordination of this effort.

9. Expand training programs for correctional personnel at the Federal, State and local level.

10. Conduct a study to determine if the Federal corrections system can be made more effective by consolidating existing programs in a Unified Corrections Service.

11. Expand the use of "Half-Way House" Community Treatment Centers to include offenders on probation and parole as well as inmates preparing to return to society. Assist in the development of similar programs at the State and local level.

12. Institute a program of research, experimentation and evaluation of correctional methods and practices so that successful techniques may be identified quickly and applied broadly in all correctional systems.

13. In cooperation with other Departments and agencies, coordinate all Federal corrections programs, particularly those programs which assist State and

local corrections activities.

I am asking that you report to me on your progress in six months and that you make any recommendations you may have for further action at that time.

RICHARD NIXON

439 Executive Order 11494, Establishing the Presidential Citizens Medal. *November 13, 1969*

BY VIRTUE of the authority vested in me as President of the United States, it is ordered as follows:

SECTION 1. *Medal established*. The Presidential Citizens Medal (hereinafter referred to as the Medal), together with accompanying ribbons and appurtenances, is hereby established for the purpose of recognizing citizens of the United States of America who have performed exemplary deeds of service for their country or their fellow citizens.

SEC. 2. *Award of the Medal*. (a) The Medal may be bestowed by the President upon any citizen of the United States at the sole discretion of the President.

(b) The announcement of the granting of the Medal and the presentation ceremonies may take place at any time during the year.

(c) Subject to the provisions of this order, the Medal may be conferred posthumously.

SEC. 3. *Design of the Medal*. The Army Institute of Heraldry shall prepare for the approval of the President a design of the Medal, citation, and ribbon.

SEC. 4. *Prior orders*. The establishment of the Medal shall not operate to terminate any other medal and this order shall not be deemed to supersede the whole or any part of any other Executive order.

RICHARD NIXON

The White House,
November 13, 1969

440 Remarks in the Chamber of the United States House of Representatives. *November 13, 1969*

Mr. Speaker, my colleagues in the House of Representatives:

I do feel very much at home in this House. My heart is truly in this House, because, as the Speaker has so very generously indicated, my first service in Government was here 22 years ago.

I have come here today for an unusual purpose, perhaps an unprecedented purpose. If it is, and can be expressed quite briefly, I want to express appreciation to the Members of this House, the Members on both sides of this aisle, for their support of a just peace in Vietnam.

Yesterday I was informed by a bipartisan group from the House of Representatives that over 300 Members of the House had joined in sponsoring a resolution [1] for a just peace in Vietnam

---

[1] The House Resolution, which was approved by the House Foreign Affairs Committee by a vote of 21 to 8, is printed in the Weekly Compilation of Presidential Documents (vol. 5, p. 1592).

along the lines of the proposals that I made in a speech on November 3.

As I saw that resolution, I realized its great significance, its great significance from an historical standpoint and its great significance in terms of the effect it might—and I believe could—have in hastening the day that that just peace may come.

First, from an historical standpoint, if I could be permitted to reminisce for a moment, 22 years ago in this House, the breakdown on the Democratic and the Republican sides was approximately the opposite of what it is today. In the 80th Congress, it was 3 to 2 Republican, and today in this Congress it is 3 to 2 Democratic.

I remember in that period immediately after World War II, there were those who thought that with the President being a Democrat—Harry Truman—and the Congress being Republican, that this would mean that the United States in the critical areas of foreign policy, when it was vitally important to have a consistent foreign policy, would not speak with one voice to the world. And even one critic, a Member of the other body, suggested that President Truman should resign so that there could be a Republican President working with a Republican Congress.

Those predictions of division on the great issues of national security and foreign policy proved to be wrong. They proved to be wrong, and those of you who were in the House then will remember that on those great initiatives which were recommended to the country and to this House and to the other body by President Truman—the Greek-Turkish aid program, the Marshall Plan, NATO—received the support not only of the major-ity of Democrats, but of the majority of Republicans.

As a result, America adopted policies then that, in my opinion, have been the primary factor in stopping the aggression that could have taken place, particularly through Europe in that period, and in avoiding a world war over these past 22 years.

And now today, we face a different situation, a situation of a Republican President and a Democratic House and a Democratic Senate. And the question arose at the beginning of this adminis-tration as to whether or not this could be the kind of Government, the kind of leadership, that the Nation needed in a period of very great problems abroad as well as at home.

I want to be quite candid with regard to the relationship of the President with the House of Representatives and with the Senate when it is under the control of the other party. As one who has been a Member of both bodies, I understand and I respect differences of opinion in both foreign and domestic policy.

As one who has been a Member of both bodies, I understand and respect the fact that particularly in domestic policy, there will be occasions when the administration will not be able to get perhaps the sup-port for its programs that it might get if it controlled the majority of its own party on this side of the aisle.

But I also know this—and this goes back to that experience 22 years ago—I do know that when the security of Amer-ica is involved, when peace for America and for the world is involved, when the lives of our young men are involved, we are not Democrats, we are not Repub-licans, we are Americans.

I do not suggest by that remark that there should be no criticism and no division with regard to foreign policy, because we need the constant discussion which produces superior ideas that come from debate and from constructive suggestions.

But I do know that when the great issues are involved, that in this House, that what happened yesterday with that announcement on the part of Members on both sides of the aisle of well over a majority supporting the policy of the President of the United States, I realize that that was in the great tradition of this country.

Mr. Speaker, if I could be permitted just one closing and personal note, one in reminiscence and one with regard to the present. I look over this House and I see some older Members, a few who were here then; I see many younger Members. I can imagine that some of the younger Members perhaps are frustrated by their committee assignments and are wondering when they are going to get into positions of leadership.

To give you some encouragement, I recall that when I came to the House I was assigned to the Committee on Education and Labor, and there were a number of new Members on both the Republican and the Democratic side assigned in that 80th Congress to the Committee on Education and Labor.

The new Members drew straws to see what position we would have in the seniority. On the Republican side I drew the last straw. I was the 15th member of the Committee. On the Democratic side, a young Congressman, a war veteran from World War II from Massachusetts, drew the last straw, John F. Kennedy.

I can only suggest to those who think

sometimes that the luck of the draw is not with them, that we both did rather well politically since that time.

But more important, the record will show that John F. Kennedy and Richard Nixon—on those great issues in that 80th Congress and in the 81st Congress, involving security of the Nation, involving foreign policy—voted together.

Now, a personal word with regard to the present. I realize that Members of this House receive great numbers of letters on the great issues of the day. Some of them are quite partisan and some of them are stimulated and some of them come from the hearts of the people who write them. There are two, very briefly, that I would read to you that express the sentiments I was trying to express on November 3d, and I think express the sentiments of most of the Members of this House.

One is from Pittsburgh, Pennsylvania: "Dear Mr. President:

"A brave man, a splendid son, a devoted husband and father, Warrant Officer Robert Satterfield, was killed in Vietnam, April 16, 1969. His parents strongly support your plan to Vietnamize the war. One of Bob's taped messages to his family from Vietnam said:

" 'We are not here to quarrel as to whether or not we should have entered the war, as only history may disclose the validity. We do have a purpose of keeping a nation of people free from aggression and we work with the trust that our children will remain free.'

"Monday evening you echoed Bob's wishes and we urge you to maintain your commitment and be as flexible as need be, that our son's life and that of others was not in vain."

The other letter comes from Colorado. It reads:

"Dear President Nixon:

"As a registered Democrat who did not vote for you in 1968, and a father with a son in Vietnam, I want you to know that I am in back of you 100 percent in your stand on this crisis. I feel like you are acting like an American and you can count on me telling other people that I feel this way."

So to my colleagues in the House I say: History will look back on this period in the House of Representatives and it will judge us and judge those of us in the executive as to our leadership. In a way, the problem that you confront was more difficult than that we confronted in that 80th Congress 22 years ago, because then the lines were more clearly drawn.

Today we have a war that is difficult, that is controversial. But in the pursuit for peace we can act, and I believe we should and will continue to act, with a majority of Americans supporting a just peace. I can say as I stand here today, I believe that we will achieve a just peace in Vietnam. I

cannot tell you the time or the date, but I do know this: that when that peace comes, that it will come because of the support that we have received, not just from Republicans, but from Democrats, from Americans in this House and in the other body and throughout this Nation.

And history will record that the United States of America, in a period of crisis, in a period of controversy, met the challenge of greatness, and that the Representatives of the people thought of themselves as Americans, put their country first rather than their party first in the great tradition of this House.

Thank you.

NOTE: The President spoke at 12:53 p.m. in the House Chamber at the Capitol.

The text of a news briefing on November 12, 1969, concerning congressional support of the President's program for peace in Vietnam by Senator Gordon Allott of Colorado, Representatives James C. Wright, Jr., of Texas, Wayne L. Hays of Ohio, E. Ross Adair of Indiana, and Leslie C. Arends of Illinois is printed in the Weekly Compilation of Presidential Documents (vol. 5, p. 1589).

441 Remarks in the Chamber of the United States Senate. *November 13, 1969*

Mr. President, and my colleagues in the Senate:

I can use that term because I shared the opportunity of serving in this body, and I always feel that I belong here whenever I have the chance to return.

I do want to say on this occasion that this is only the second opportunity I have had to speak in this Chamber since I presided over this body; as you know, the presiding officer has very little chance to speak. He makes a few rulings but not often does he speak.

In speaking to you, I shall do so only

briefly, but I do feel that at this time, with the calendar year nearing an end, it would be well to refer to the relations between the executive and the legislative branches of our Government.

When this administration came into office on January 20, we had a problem with regard to those relationships, which had not existed for nearly a hundred years, after an election—the President a member of one party, and both Houses controlled by members of the other party.

Of course, the usual dire predictions

were made that, under the situation, progress would grind to a halt, and that whether it was domestic or foreign policy, we would not be able to give the Nation the kind of government that the Nation should be entitled to under our system.

I think the predictions have proved to be wrong. I do not mean to suggest, as I indicated in, I thought, a temperate message to Congress a few weeks ago, that there are not some areas where the executive would appreciate more action on the part of the legislative branch of the Government. But I do say this: I look back over these months with great appreciation for the fact that on some of the great national issues and on the great international issues involving the security of the Nation, we not only have had consultation, but we have had support.

I also want to recognize a fact of life— a fact of life that I learned when I was in the Senate and when I presided over it: Senators, more so than Members of the House of Representatives, are individuals. Senators have a great pride, and rightly so, in their right to make up their own minds with regard to the propositions that are sent to them by the executive branch of the Government. This is true whether they are members of the President's party or not members of the President's party.

I find, looking back over this period of time, that this administration has been subjected to some sharp criticism by some Members of this body, both from the Democratic side and from the Republican side. I want the Members of this body to know that I understand it. I recognize this as being one of the strengths of our system, rather than one of its weaknesses;

and I know that, in the end, out of this kind of criticism and debate will come better policies and stronger policies than would have been the case had we simply had an abject Senate—or House of Representatives, for that matter—simply approving whatever ideas came from the executive branch of the Government.

This does not mean that we do not feel very strongly about our proposals when we send them here. It does mean that I, as a former Member of this body, one who served in it and who presided over it for 8 years, recognize this great tradition of independence, and recognize it as one of the great strengths of our Republic.

I would address a very brief remark to a subject that I had an opportunity to discuss with the majority leader this morning at breakfast, and then with members of the leadership at lunch today.

In the next few months, a number of matters will be undertaken on the world scene, some of which will require not only Senate consultations, but also, if there is agreement among world powers, including ourselves, Senate advice and consent.

This administration wants to develop a relationship in which we will have that consultation, and in which we will have the advice, not just the consent. This is not always easy, because when such negotiations take place—negotiations involving, as is the case in the strategic arms limitation talks which will begin next week, the very future, not only of this Nation, but of all of the nations in the world who depend on America's power for their own security—we must recognize that it is vitally important that the position of our negotiators not be weakened or compromised by discussions that might publicly take place here, discussions that could weaken or compromise us with those representing the other side.

On the other hand, recognizing the role of the Senate, recognizing the importance of getting the best ideas and the best thinking of the Members of this body on both sides of the aisle on these great matters, we are attempting to set up a process—a process in which we can consult, in which we can get your advice, and, at the same time, not weaken the position of our negotiators as they attempt to meet the goals of this Nation—the goal of limiting arms and the goal of a just and lasting peace.

Finally, on one other point: I am very grateful for the fact that a number of Members of the Senate—more than 60— have indicated by a letter to Ambassador Lodge [1] their support of a just peace in Vietnam and their support of some of the proposals I made in my speech of November 3 on that subject.

I am grateful for that support; and at the same time, while being grateful for the support of more than half the Members of this body, I also have respect for those who may have disagreed with the program for peace that I outlined.

I know that this war is the most difficult and most controversial of any war in the Nation's history. But I know that while we have our differences about what is the best way to peace, there are no differences with respect to our goal. I think Americans want a just peace; they want a

lasting peace. It is to that goal that this administration is dedicated and that I am dedicated.

I may say this in conclusion: that in the next few months we hope that progress— we know that progress—will be made toward that goal. I am sure, as I stand here, that we are going to reach the goal of a just and lasting peace in Vietnam, one that will, I trust, promote rather than discourage the cause of peace not only in Vietnam but in the Pacific and in the whole world.

As that happens, I want everyone in this great Chamber to know that when it happens it will not be simply because of what a President of the United States may have been able to do in terms of leadership; it will happen, and it will only have happened because the Members of this body and the Members of the House of Representatives, in the great tradition of the Nation, when the security of America is involved, when the security of our young men is involved, and when peace is involved, have acted and have spoken not as Democrats or Republicans but as Americans.

It is in that spirit that I address you today. It is in that spirit that I ask, not for your 100 percent support, which would not be a healthy thing for me personally, for this country, and certainly not for this body, but I ask for your understanding and support when you think we are right and for your constructive criticism when you think we are wrong.

I thank you very much.

---

[1] The text of the letter is printed in the Weekly Compilation of Presidential Documents (vol. 5, p. 1590).

NOTE: The President spoke at 2:37 p.m. in the Senate Chamber at the Capitol.

442   Remarks to NASA Personnel at the Kennedy Space Center.   *November 14, 1969*

Dr. Paine and all of you here at Cape Kennedy for this occasion:

I do want to say that it has been a very great privilege to be here. And speaking for Mrs. Nixon and my daughter, who are here with me, we think this trip—our trip from Washington to here—was definitely worthwhile.

When I announced earlier in the week that I was trying to arrange my schedule to come down, there were those who said, "Well, why can't you see it all on television?" It is true that I have seen some previous launches on television but I thought I would share with you the experience of one who has never seen a launch live before and what the difference is.

Perhaps if I may use the analogy of sports—I really believe while I like to go to a football game live and feel the crowd and the rest, I really believe that when you sit at home and see a football game on television, you can probably see it as well or even better than you can see it by being there, because the camera will watch that T formation or the quarterback and will be sure you're watching the ball rather than the fake.

But while that is true in the field of sports, football and baseball, it simply is not true in the case of what we have just seen a few moments ago. Here it is a sense of not just the sight and the picture but of feeling it—feeling the great experience of all that is happening.

I would add to that by saying that coming here and coming to this room brings an extra dimension to this great space launch that we saw a moment ago.

Dr. Paine, Frank Borman, Colonel [Thomas P.] Stafford, a lot of my friends in this activity, have often told me: Remember that the three who are up there couldn't be there except for tens of thousands on the ground, tens of thousands of people who sometimes may seem to be—and you may feel you are faceless—just numbers, just like these computers that we see in front of you.

I do want you to know that I realize that except for what you are doing here, they could not be there and they could not make this mission successful.

I think that you can be proud of the fact—and we are proud of the fact—that every one of our astronauts, when they have come to the White House—and I have had the privilege of entertaining several of them—every one of them makes the point that those on the ground, the engineers, and the technicians, and the scientists, and all of those who work in the program, that they are really the heart of this great, successful experience for the American people and for all the people of the world.

Finally, I simply want to say that I know there has been a lot of discussion as to what the future of the space program is. As you know, we have been discussing that in the Cabinet and within the administration.

I do think you can be assured that in Dr. Paine and his colleagues you have men who are dedicated to this program, who are making the case for it, making the case for it as against other national priorities and making it very effectively.

I leaned in the direction of the program before. After hearing what they have had to say with regard to our future plans, I must say that I lean even more in that direction.

Announcements will be made in the future as they have been made in the past as to the commitment of this Nation to the program. I realize that within those in the program, between scientists, engineers, and others, there are different attitudes as to what the emphasis should be, whether we should emphasize more exploration or more in taking the knowledge we have already acquired and making practical applications of it.

All of these matters have been brought to my attention. I can assure you every side is getting a hearing. We want to have a balanced program, but most important, we are going forward. America, the United States, is first in space. We are proud to be first in space. We don't say that in a jingoistic way. We say it because as Americans we want to give the people of this country, and particularly our young people, the feeling that here is an area we can concentrate on for a positive goal, concentrate and be proud of being Americans, be proud of what we have accomplished, not only for ourselves but for future generations and for the whole world.

In that vein, I simply want to say I am proud of those three men up there. I talked to them on the phone before they left and I am just as proud of everybody in this room and the thousands across this country who made it possible. You are part of a great organization. The whole Nation owes you a debt of gratitude and, as President of the United States, I express that debt and acknowledge it today.

Here is Mrs. Nixon. I think you would like to know that she is the woman I am with today and every day. The girl in lilac is Tricia, our daughter.

Also, while, of course, he needs no introduction because he has been to several of these launches as Chairman of the Space Council, we are very happy to have today the Vice President of the United States and Mrs. Agnew.

We have a few other celebrities here you should know. I don't think I can see them all, but we have Senator Margaret Chase Smith of the State of Maine, a real space enthusiast. And Senator [Edward J.] Gurney of Florida who told me the weather would be perfect today if I would just come.

We have several Congressmen here: Congressman [Louis, Jr.] Frey, your own Congressman from this area; Congressman [James G.] Fulton from Pennsylvania, also on the Space Committee. Cheer for them real hard because they get your appropriations for you. Congressman [J. Herbert] Burke from that little pocket of poverty, Fort Lauderdale; and Congressman [William C.] Bill Cramer, is he here? He must be campaigning.

And then I think, too, you would like to see the Science Adviser from sunny California, Lee DuBridge, over here—the President's Science Adviser.

Well, after being an emcee here, I think I will ask for Johnny Carson's [1] job next week.

Thank you very much.

NOTE: The President spoke at 11:57 a.m. at the Kennedy Space Center, Fla., after watching the launch of spacecraft Apollo 12. Dr. Thomas O. Paine was Administrator of the National Aeronautics and Space Administration.

---

[1] A television emcee.

443   Memorandum on Expenditures by Government Departments and Agencies.   *November 14, 1969*

Memorandum for the Heads of Executive Departments and Agencies:

I have approved H.J. Res. 966, which provides temporary appropriations to finance governmental programs for which 1970 appropriations have not been enacted as of October 31, 1969.

This legislation is required for continued operation of our government. But I must express my deep concern with the particular terms which would permit some agencies, such as the Department of Health, Education, and Welfare, to commit the government to make expenditures at a rate inconsistent with our efforts to keep the budget under strict control and thereby restrain inflation.

I am fully aware of our needs in health, education, training, and other social areas, and have reflected those in my budget proposals as best I can. At the same time, I feel strongly that the soundness and stability of our economy demand stringent fiscal measures on all fronts, and that such stringency will better serve the long-run interests of all the American people.

I take this occasion, therefore, to reconfirm my statement of August 12, 1969, on the action by the House of Representatives that added $1.1 billion to the appropriations for the Department of Health, Education, and Welfare when I stated "my intention not to spend in this fiscal year any funds appropriated in excess of my budgetary estimates of April this year. No commitments will be made to spend these additional appropriations until the Congress has completed action on all appropriation bills and revenue measures."

Any increases in appropriations that permit spending beyond that level must be offset by equivalent reductions, either by the Congress or by the executive branch. Therefore, I direct you to make no commitments at this time which will lead to spending in excess of the 1970 outlay ceiling which the Director of the Bureau of the Budget communicated to you at my direction.

I expect your full cooperation in demonstrating our fiscal responsibility. It is imperative that this Administration do everything in its power to fight the inflationary pressures which are eroding the purchasing power of the American people.

RICHARD NIXON

NOTE: As enacted, H.J. Res. 966, is Public Law 91–117 (83 Stat. 191).

444   Message to Ambassador Gerard C. Smith at the Opening of the Strategic Arms Limitation Talks in Helsinki.   *November 17, 1969*

YOU ARE embarking upon one of the most momentous negotiations ever entrusted to an American delegation.

I do not mean to belittle the past. The

Antarctic Treaty, the Limited Test Ban Treaty, the Outer Space Treaty, and most recently the Non-Proliferation Treaty, which we hope will soon enter into force, were all important steps along the road to international security. Other tasks remain on the agenda of the United Nations and the Conference of the Committee on Disarmament. Today, however, you will begin what all of your fellow citizens in the United States and, I believe, all people throughout the world, profoundly hope will be a sustained effort not only to limit the build-up of strategic forces but to reverse it.

I do not underestimate the difficulty of your task; the nature of modern weapons makes their control an exceedingly complex endeavor. But this very fact increases the importance of your effort.

Nor do I underestimate the suspicion and distrust that must be dispelled if you are to succeed in your assignment.

I am also conscious of the historical fact that wars and crises between nations can arise not simply from the existence of arms but from clashing interests or the ambitious pursuit of unilateral interests. That is why we seek progress toward the solution of the dangerous political issues of our day.

I am nevertheless hopeful that your negotiations with representatives from the Soviet Union will serve to increase mutual security. Such a result is possible if we approach these negotiations recognizing the legitimate security interests on each side.

I have stated that for our part we will be guided by the concept of maintaining "sufficiency" in the forces required to pro-

tect ourselves and our allies. I recognize that the leaders of the Soviet Union bear similar defense responsibilities. I believe it is possible, however, that we can carry out our respective responsibilities under a mutually acceptable limitation and eventual reduction of our strategic arsenals.

We are prepared to discuss limitations on all offensive and defensive systems, and to reach agreements in which both sides can have confidence. As I stated in my address to the United Nations, we are prepared to deal with the issues seriously, carefully, and purposefully. We seek no unilateral advantage. Nor do we seek arrangements which could be prejudicial to the interests of third parties. We are prepared to engage in bona fide negotiations on concrete issues, avoiding polemics and extraneous matters.

No one can foresee what the outcome of your work will be. I believe your approach to these talks will demonstrate the seriousness of the United States in pursuing a path of equitable accommodation. I am convinced that the limitation of strategic arms is in the mutual interest of our country and the Soviet Union.

NOTE: An announcement on July 5, 1969, of the senior membership of the United States delegation to the strategic arms limitation talks (SALT) is printed in the Weekly Compilation of Presidential Documents (vol. 5, p. 948).

An announcement on October 25, 1969, of the opening of SALT with the Soviet Union in Helsinki on November 17, 1969, is printed in the Weekly Compilation of Presidential Documents (vol. 5, p. 1485).

The text of a news briefing by Ambassadors Gerard C. Smith and Llewellyn E. Thompson concerning SALT was released by the White House Press Office on December 29, 1969.

445   Special Message to the Congress on United States Trade Policy.   *November 18, 1969*

To the Congress of the United States:

For the past 35 years, the United States has steadfastly pursued a policy of freer world trade. As a nation, we have recognized that competition cannot stop at the ocean's edge. We have determined that American trade policies must advance the national interest—which means they must respond to the whole of our interests, and not be a device to favor the narrow interest.

This Administration has reviewed that policy and we find that its continuation is in our national interest. At the same time, however, it is clear that the trade problems of the 1970s will differ significantly from those of the past. New developments in the rapidly evolving world economy will require new responses and new initiatives.

As we look at the changing patterns of world trade, three factors stand out that require us to continue modernizing our own trade policies:

First, world economic interdependence has become a fact. Reductions in tariffs and in transportation costs have internationalized the world economy just as satellites and global television have internationalized the world communications network. The growth of multi-national corporations provides a dramatic example of this development.

Second, we must recognize that a number of foreign countries now compete fully with the United States in world markets.

We have always welcomed such competition. It promotes the economic development of the entire world to the mutual benefit of all, including our own consumers. It provides an additional stimulus to our own industry, agriculture and labor force. At the same time, however, it requires us to insist on fair competition among all countries.

Third, the traditional surplus in the U.S. balance of trade has disappeared. This is largely due to our own internal inflation and is one more reason why we must bring that inflation under control.

The disappearance of the surplus has suggested to some that we should abandon our traditional approach toward freer trade. I reject this argument not only because I believe in the principle of freer trade, but also for a very simple and pragmatic reason: any reduction in our imports produced by U.S. restrictions not accepted by our trading partners would invite foreign reaction against our own exports—all quite legally. Reduced imports would thus be offset by reduced exports, and both sides would lose. In the longer term, such a policy of trade restriction would add to domestic inflation and jeopardize our competitiveness in world markets at the very time when tougher competition throughout the world requires us to improve our competitive capabilities in every way possible.

In fact, the need to restore our trade surplus heightens the need for further movement toward freer trade. It requires us to persuade other nations to lower barriers which deny us fair access to their markets. An environment of freer trade will permit the widest possible scope for the genius of American industry and agriculture to respond to the competitive challenge of the 1970s.

Fourth, the less developed countries need improved access to the markets of the industrialized countries if their economic development is to proceed satisfactorily. Public aid will never be sufficient to meet their needs, nor should it be. I recently announced that, as one step toward improving their market access, the United States would press in world trade forums for a liberal system of tariff preferences for all developing countries. International discussions are now in progress on the matter and I will not deal with it in the trade bill I am submitting today. At the appropriate time, I will submit legislation to the Congress to seek authorization for the United States to extend preferences and to take any other steps toward improving the market access of the less developed countries which might appear desirable and which would require legislation.

The Trade Act of 1969

The trade bill which I am submitting today addresses these new problems of the 1970s. It is modest in scope, but significant in its impact. It continues the general drive toward freer world trade. It also explicitly recognizes that, while seeking to advance world interests, U.S. trade policies must also respect legitimate U.S. interests, and that to be fair to our trading partners does not require us to be unfair to our own people. Specifically:

—It restores the authority needed by the President to make limited tariff reductions.

—It takes concrete steps toward the increasingly urgent goal of lowering non-tariff barriers to trade.

—It recognizes the very real plight of particular industries, companies and workers faced with import competition, and provides for readier relief in these special cases.

—It strengthens GATT—the General Agreement on Tariffs and Trade— by regularizing the funding of United States participation.

While asking enactment of these proposals now, the trade program I will outline in this message also includes setting preparations underway for the more ambitious initiatives that will later be needed for the long-term future.

TARIFF REDUCTION

I recommend that the President be given authority to make modest reductions in U.S. tariffs.

The President has been without such authority for over two years. This authority is not designed to be used for major tariff negotiations, but rather to make possible minor adjustments that individual circumstances from time to time require—as, for example, when it becomes necessary to raise the duty on an article as the result of an "escape clause" action or when a statutory change is made in tariff classification. Our trading partners are then entitled to reasonable compensation, just as we would be entitled to receive it from them in reverse circumstances. Lack of this authority exposes our exports to foreign retaliation. Therefore, the Bill would provide to the President, through June 30, 1973, the authority to reduce tariffs by limited amounts.

NON-TARIFF BARRIERS

The time has come for a serious and sustained effort to reduce non-tariff barriers to trade. These non-tariff barriers have become increasingly important with the decline in tariff protection and the growing interdependence of the world economy. Their elimination is vital to our efforts to increase U.S. exports.

As a first step in this direction, I propose today that the United States eliminate the American Selling Price system of customs valuation.

Although this system applies only to a very few American products—mainly benzenoid chemicals—it is viewed by our principal trading partners as a major symbol of American protectionism. Its removal will bring reciprocal reductions in foreign tariffs on U.S. chemical exports, and a reduction in important foreign non-tariff barriers—including European road taxes, which discriminate against our larger automobiles, and the preferential treatment on tobacco extended by the United Kingdom to the countries of the Commonwealth. Beyond this, its removal will unlock the door to new negotiations on the entire range of non-tariff barriers. Because of the symbolic importance our trading partners attach to it, the American Selling Price system has itself become a major barrier to the removal of other barriers.

Essentially, the American Selling Price system is a device by which the value of imports for tariff purposes is set by the price of competitive American products instead of the actual price of the foreign product, which is the basis of tariff valuation for all other imports. The extraordinary protection it provides to these few products has outlived its original purposes. The special advantage it gives particular producers can no longer justify its heavy cost in terms of the obstacles it places in the way of opening foreign markets to American exports.

Reducing or eliminating other non-tariff barriers to world trade will require a great deal of detailed negotiating and hard bargaining.

Unlike tariffs, approaches to the reduction of non-tariff barriers are often difficult to embody in prior delegation of authority. Many—both here and abroad—have their roots in purely domestic concerns that are only indirectly related to foreign trade, and many arise from domestic laws.

Many would require specific legislative actions to accomplish their removal—but the nature of this action would not finally be clear until negotiation had shown what was possible.

This presents a special opportunity for Congress to be helpful in achieving international agreements in this vital area.

I would welcome a clear statement of Congressional intent with regard to non-tariff barriers to assist in our efforts to obtain reciprocal lowering of such barriers.

It is not my intention to use such a declaration as a "blank check." On the contrary, I pledge to maintain close consultation with the Congress during the course of any such negotiations, to keep the Congress fully informed on problems and progress, and to submit for Congressional consideration any agreements which would require new legislation. The purpose of seeking such an advance declaration is not to bypass Congress, but to strengthen our negotiating position.

In fact, it is precisely because ours is a system in which the Executive cannot commit the Legislative Branch that a general declaration of legislative intent would be important to those with whom we must negotiate.

At the same time, I urge private interests to work closely with the govern-

ment in seeking the removal of these bar-riers. Close cooperation by the private sector is essential, because many non-tariff barriers are subtle, complex and difficult to appraise.

AID FOR AFFECTED INDUSTRIES

Freer trade brings benefits to the entire community, but it can also cause hardship for parts of the community. The price of a trade policy from which we all receive benefits must not fall unfairly on the few—whether on particular industries, on individual firms or on groups of workers. As we have long recognized, there should be prompt and effective means of helping those faced with adversity because of increased imports.

The Trade Act of 1969 provides significant improvements in the means by which U.S. industry, firms, and workers can receive assistance from their government to meet injury truly caused by imports.

This relief falls into two broad categories: 1) the escape clause, which is industry-wide; and 2) adjustment assistance, which provides specific aid to particular firms or groups of workers.

These improvements are needed because the assistance programs provided in the Trade Expansion Act of 1962 have simply not worked.

Escape Clause

The escape clause provisions of the 1962 Act have proved so stringent, so rigid, and so technical that in not a single case has the Tariff Commission been able to justify a recommendation for relief. This must be remedied. We must be able to provide, on a case-by-case basis, care-ful and expedited consideration of petitions for relief, and such relief must be available on a fair and reasonable basis.

I recommend a liberalization of the escape clause to provide, for industries adversely affected by import competition, a test that will be simple and clear: relief should be available whenever increased imports are the primary cause of actual or potential serious injury. The increase in imports should not—as it now is—have to be related to a prior tariff reduction.

While making these escape clause adjustments more readily obtainable, however, we must ensure that they remain what they are intended to be: temporary relief measures, not permanent features of the tariff landscape. An industry provided with temporary escape-clause relief must assume responsibility for improving its competitive position. The bill provides for regular reports on these efforts, to be taken into account in determining whether relief should be continued.

Adjustment Assistance

With regard to adjustment assistance for individual firms and groups of workers, the provisions of the Trade Expansion Act of 1962 again have not worked adequately.

The Act provides for loans, technical assistance and tax relief for firms, and readjustment allowances, relocation and training for workers. This direct aid to those individually injured should be more readily available than tariff relief for entire industries. It can be more closely targeted; it matches the relief to the damage; and it has no harmful side effects on overall trade policy.

I recommend that firms and workers be considered eligible for adjustment assist-

ance when increased imports are found to be a substantial cause of actual or potential serious injury.

Again, the increase in imports would not have to be related to a prior tariff reduction. The "substantial cause" criterion for adjustment assistance would be less stringent than the "primary cause" criterion for tariff relief.

I also recommend two further changes in existing adjustment provisions:

—That the Tariff Commission continue to gather and supply the needed factual information, but that determinations of eligibility to apply for assistance be made by the President.

—That adjustment assistance be made available to separate units of multi-plant companies and to groups of workers in them, when the injury is substantial to the unit but not to the entire parent firm.

With these modifications, plus improved administrative procedures, our program of assistance to import-injured firms and workers can and will be made to work. Taken together, they will remedy what has too long been a serious shortcoming in our trade programs.

These changes in our escape clause and adjustment assistance programs will provide an adequate basis for government help in cases where such help is justified in the overall national interest. They will thus help us move away from protectionist proposals, which would reverse the trend toward interdependence, and toward a constructive attack on the existing trade barriers of others.

The textile import problem, of course, is a special circumstance that requires special measures. We are now trying to persuade other countries to limit their textile shipments to the United States. In doing

so, however, we are trying to work out with our trading partners a reasonable solution which will allow both domestic and foreign producers to share equitably in the development of the U.S. market.

Such measures should not be misconstrued, nor should they be allowed to turn us away from the basic direction of our progress toward freer exchange.

FAIR TREATMENT OF U.S. EXPORTS

By nature and by definition, trade is a two-way street. We must make every effort to ensure that American products are allowed to compete in world markets on equitable terms. These efforts will be more successful if we have the means to take effective action when confronted with illegal or unjust restrictions on American exports.

Section 252 of the Trade Expansion Act of 1962 authorizes the President to impose duties or other import restrictions on the products of any nation that places unjustifiable restrictions on U.S. agricultural products. *I recommend that this authority be expanded in two ways:*

—By extending the existing authority to cover unfair actions against all U.S. products, rather than only against U.S. agricultural products.

—By providing new authority to take appropriate action against nations that practice what amounts to subsidized competition in third-country markets, when that subsidized competition unfairly affects U.S. exports.

Any weapon is most effective if its presence makes its use unnecessary. With these new weapons in our negotiating arsenal, we should be better able to negotiate relief from the unfair restrictions to which American exports still are subject.

944

Ever since its beginning in 1947, U.S. participation in GATT—the General Agreement on Tariffs and Trade—has been financed through general contingency funds rather than through a specific appropriation.

GATT has proved its worth. It is the international organization we depend on for the enforcement of our trading rights, and toward which we look as a forum for the important new negotiations on nontariff barriers which must now be undertaken.

I recommend specific authorization for the funding of our participation in GATT, thus both demonstrating our support and regularizing our procedures.

FOR THE LONG-TERM FUTURE

The trade bill I have submitted today is a necessary beginning. It corrects deficiencies in present policies; it enables us to begin the 1970s with a program geared to the start of that decade.

As we look further into the Seventies, it is clear that we must reexamine the entire range of our policies and objectives.

We must take into account the far-reaching changes which have occurred in investment abroad and in patterns of world trade. I have already outlined some of the problems which we will face in the 1970s. Many more will develop—and also new opportunities will emerge.

Intense international competition, new and growing markets, changes in cost levels, technological developments in both agriculture and industry, and large-scale exports of capital are having profound and continuing effects on international production and trade patterns. We can no longer afford to think of our trade policies in the old, simple terms of liberalism vs. protectionism. Rather, we must learn to treat investment, production, employment and trade as interrelated and interdependent.

We need a deeper understanding of the ways in which the major sectors of our economy are actually affected by international trade.

We have arrived at a point at which a careful review should also be made of our tariff structure itself—including such traditional aspects as its reliance upon specific duties, the relationships among tariff rates on various products, and adapting our system to conform more closely with that of the rest of the world.

To help prepare for these many future needs, I will appoint a Commission on World Trade to examine the entire range of our trade and related policies, to analyze the problems we are likely to face in the 1970s, and to prepare recommendations on what we should do about them. It will be empowered to call upon the Tariff Commission and the agencies of the Executive Branch for advice, support and assistance, but its recommendations will be its own.

By expanding world markets, our trade policies have speeded the pace of our own economic progress and aided the development of others. As we look to the future, we must seek a continued expansion of world trade, even as we also seek the dismantling of those other barriers—political, social and ideological—that have stood in the way of a freer exchange of people and ideas, as well as of goods and technology.

Our goal is an open world. Trade is one of the doors to that open world. Its continued expansion requires that others move with us, and that we achieve reciprocity in fact as well as in spirit.

Armed with the recommendations and analyses of the new Commission on World Trade, we will work toward broad new policies for the 1970s that will encour-

age that reciprocity, and that will lead us, in growing and shared prosperity, toward a world both open and just.

RICHARD NIXON

The White House
    November 18, 1969

446   Statement on the Death of Joseph P. Kennedy. *November 18, 1969*

JOSEPH P. KENNEDY leaves a long and distinguished record of service to his country—a genuinely unique record that involved his entire family in the making of American history. He inspired his family to share his own strong sense of dedication to his Nation. He enjoyed with grace the triumphs of his life, and he endured its tragedies with great dignity. And surely he also felt great satisfaction in his own

and in his family's service and accomplishments. Mrs. Nixon and I know that we are joined by countless Americans and by people all over the world as we express our deepest sympathy to the Kennedy family.

NOTE: Joseph P. Kennedy, financier, former U.S. Ambassador to Great Britain, and father of the late President John F. Kennedy, died at the age of 81 at his home at Hyannis Port, Mass., after a long illness.

447   Remarks of Welcome at the White House to Prime Minister Eisaku Sato of Japan. *November 19, 1969*

Mr. Prime Minister, ladies and gentlemen gathered here on the South Lawn of the White House:

It is a very great honor for me, not only in my official capacity representing the American people, but also personally, to welcome you, Mr. Prime Minister, to the United States again.

This is your third visit to the United States but this is indeed an historic day. As we meet here this ceremony is being carried live by television to millions of people in Japan as well as people in the United States.

And at this same moment millions of people all over the world can see two

Americans from earth walking on the face of the moon.

The magnificent welcome which was given to our astronauts when they visited Tokyo just a few weeks ago is an indication of the ties that bind our two peoples together. Today, as we look to the future of the Pacific, we recognize that whether peace survives in the last third of the century will depend more on what happens in the Pacific than in any other area of the world. And whether we have peace and prosperity and progress in the Pacific will depend more than anything else upon the cooperation of the United States and Japan, the two strongest and the two most prosperous nations in the Pacific area.

In this period, Japan, which has the fastest growing economy of any major country in the world, will play a key role. That is why our talks are so important, because we must discuss those areas of cooperation where our two peoples and our two Governments can work together for our common goal of peace and prosperity for the whole Pacific area.

Mr. Prime Minister, I believe that these talks will very probably be the most successful talks that have been held between representatives of our two Governments going back over many years. I say this not only because the talks have been well prepared by both sides but also because we have the good fortune not only of being official friends but personal friends.

Just a few yards to the south of us at the Tidal Basin, we can see the cherry trees that were presented by the people of Tokyo to the people of Washington many years ago. There is a Japanese proverb that "There are no strangers under the cherry blossoms." This is not cherry blossom time, but I can assure you that as we meet today we meet as friends— official friends, personal friends—working together for the peace, the friendship, and the prosperity that both of our countries want.

NOTE: The President spoke at 10:13 a.m. on the South Lawn at the White House where Prime Minister Eisaku Sato was given a formal welcome with full military honors.

See also Items 449, 452, and 453.

The Prime Minister responded in Japanese. A translation follows:

Mr. President, Mrs. Nixon, distinguished guests, ladies and gentlemen:

I am deeply touched by your kind words, Mr. President. Having visited Japan six times,

you understand our country as she really is better than any previous American President, and I am heartily delighted to have this opportunity to call on you at the White House.

The timing is perfect for me. I am grateful for my good fortune to be able to stand on this platform right after the successful landing on the moon of Apollo 12, which has so closely followed the historic feat of Apollo 11, and express my profound respect and heartfelt congratulations to you and to the American people.

The relations between Japan and the United States are becoming increasingly closer in recent years, and it is my earnest desire to strengthen further the relationship of mutual trust and friendship between our two countries through my talks with you.

The purpose of my present visit here is, as you already know, to solve the Okinawa problem, the biggest issue pending between Japan and the United States, and thereby lay a foundation for the new Japanese-American relations of the 1970's. I am convinced that the ties of mutual trust and friendship binding the peoples of our two countries are strong enough to make it possible for us to reach a mutually satisfactory solution to this problem.

Cooperative relations between Japan and the United States are assuming ever greater importance for the maintenance of world peace and stability in the fluid international situation. Especially in Asia, where there are a number of developing countries, our two countries are expected to play a role of their own in concert with each other for the economic independence and stabilization of people's livelihood of these countries. I would like to take this opportunity to have an unreserved exchange of views on various matters of common interest to our two countries with you, Mr. President, and with other leaders of your administration.

I am confident that the talks between our two countries, with a similar social system and a common conception of values, at this time when we are about to greet the 1970's, will bring about a substantial effect upon the peace and progress of the world.

Thank you.

448 Statement on Signing the National Science Foundation Authorization Act, 1970. *November 19, 1969*

I HAVE APPROVED S. 1857, the bill which authorizes appropriations for the activities of the National Science Foundation for fiscal year 1970.

Section 6 of the bill warrants a few words of comment. It would require the Director of the National Science Foundation to keep the appropriate committees of the Congress fully and currently informed with respect to the activities of the Foundation.

In my memorandum of March 24, 1969, to heads of executive departments and agencies, I said: "The policy of this Administration is to comply to the fullest extent possible with Congressional requests for information. While the Executive branch has the responsibility of withholding certain information the disclosure of which would be incompatible with the public interest, this Administration will invoke this authority only in the most compelling circumstances and after a rigorous inquiry into the actual need for its exercise." I reaffirm that policy here.

At the same time, there must be some limits on what information can be reported. Voluminous reporting of detailed day-to-day activities of an agency can be unduly burdensome without providing any significant assistance to the Congress in discharging its legislative responsibilities. More importantly, premature disclosure of information can seriously impair the ability of executive branch agencies to carry out effectively their responsibilities, e.g., in law enforcement or in executive branch communications leading to the development of legislative and budgetary proposals for possible presentation to the Congress.

I think that the Congress and the executive branch agencies appreciate the importance of striking a working balance between the needs of Congress for information and those of the agencies for candid and free communication in carrying out their responsibilities. I interpret statutory provisions to keep the Congress fully and currently informed with respect to all of the activities of executive branch agencies and the intent of the Congress in enacting such legislation to be consistent with the proper division of powers between the Congress and the executive branch.

NOTE: As enacted, the bill (S. 1857) is Public Law 91–120 (83 Stat. 203), approved November 18, 1969.

The memorandum of March 24, 1969, from which the President quoted, was not released by the White House Press Office.

449 Toasts of the President and Prime Minister Sato of Japan. *November 19, 1969*

Mr. Prime Minister, Madame Sato, and our guests from Japan and from the United States:

It is a very great honor for me to welcome the Prime Minister and Mrs. Sato and the members of their party to our country and to this house, and in welcoming them, to do so both officially and personally.

I cherish memories of my visits to Japan

when the Prime Minister has been my host. We are very honored to have him here in his capacity as Prime Minister of a great and friendly country in the Pacific and in Asia.

I have been trying to think of something that would be appropriate to say to this company made up of so many people from the United States and Japan who are so deeply interested in Japanese-American friendship.

I think first of our honored guest, the Prime Minister. I think of his leadership of his country which goes back over many years. He has been Prime Minister now for 5 years. And I think that perhaps the success of his leadership is best indicated by what I understand is the literal translation of his first name, Eisaku Sato. Eisaku, as I understand, means to "create prosperity," and Japan has created prosperity under Prime Minister Sato.

We who have visited Japan and we who have read about it know that Japan is the modern miracle of economic progress. We know that its economic growth at 10 percent a year is the highest of all the advanced countries, if not the highest in the world.

We know, too, that looking down to the end of the century, that there are those who predict that if the present rate of growth continues, that Japan may well have the highest per capita income of all the people in the world 25 years from now.

I could dwell on those subjects which are usually the subjects emphasized when our friends from Japan are present, because in economic growth and economic statistics, Japan leads the world.

But I think for our guests tonight it would be well to point out a very different aspect of this great country, this friendly

country in the Pacific, something that I know from knowing the country and from knowing its people.

We should not think of Japan as simply a nation of statistics, of economic growth, an economic giant, but we should think of it as it really is. It is a great country though a very small country.

I think it could well be said that never in the world's history have so many people done so much with so little in the way of resources.

I think, too, that it can be said by those who have visited Japan that it is a country that captures the imagination, captures it because of the magnificent landscapes, landscapes that I think Mr. Andrew Wyeth, the great American painter who honors us with his presence tonight, would agree cannot be captured except in a Japanese painting.

We know Japan, those of us who have visited it, because of the incomparable hospitality and the friendship of the people that we have met there, and we know Japan, and I emphasize this particularly tonight, for another reason: because of the character of its people.

I saw Japan with my wife in 1953. I saw a people who were recovering from the devastation of war. And I knew then what the future would be for Japan, although it exceeded even my own predictions and those of my colleagues as to what would happen. I knew it because of the people that I met, people who did work hard, yes, but people who had the will and also the character of greatness. And it is that character of greatness that is represented by our honored guest tonight.

I said when the Prime Minister arrived, that looking to the future, in the last third of this century, whether peace and freedom survive would depend more on what happened in Asia than in any other section of the world.

I think we could put it another way. As we look at the Pacific, the Pacific and Asia is the area of the greatest promise and also the greatest peril. Whether Asia and the Pacific becomes an area of peace, as the Pacific literally translated means, or an area of devastation for Asia and the world, will depend upon what happens between the United States and Japan more than between any other peoples in the world. That is because we are the nations with the greatest wealth; we are the nations with potentially the greatest power.

This is not the time to discourse at length on the great problems that are involved in that future as we look down to the end of the century, but this I know: As I think of the people of Japan, as I think of the character that has brought Japan now to the pinnacle of economic power and wealth which it now has, I look upon this great country not in terms of its richness economically but in terms of a wealth that money cannot buy, of the character and strength and courage of a great people.

That is why, Mr. Prime Minister, we in the United States, the American people, are proud that we stand with the people of Japan, working toward the progress and harmony for all mankind which is the slogan of Expo '70, the Osaka World's Fair of 1970.

I know that all of us will want to raise our glasses, not only to those thoughts and to our honored guest, but particularly to His Imperial Majesty, the Emperor of Japan.

To the Emperor.

NOTE: The President proposed the toast at 10:05 p.m. at a dinner in the State Dining Room at the White House.

See also Items 447, 452, and 453.

Prime Minister Sato responded in Japanese. His remarks, as translated by an interpreter, follow:

Mr. President, Mrs. Nixon, Mr. Vice President, Mrs. Agnew, distinguished guests, ladies and gentlemen:

I wish to express my deep appreciation to you, Mr. President, for this warm and cordial reception extended to us this evening.

First, I should like to take this opportunity to offer you my heartiest congratulations on the successful landing on the moon of the Apollo 12 spacecraft. As you may have already heard, the Japanese people were greatly excited by the lunar landing of the Apollo 11 spacecraft. Almost all of the 100 million Japanese people, young and old, men and women, were glued to their television sets the whole time, as long as they could, watching the astronauts' activities on the moon with breathless suspense. They shared a feeling of great joy when they saw you, Mr. President, smiling a welcome to the three astronauts upon their return from the Pacific.

They were fascinated by the revelation to human sight of the mysterious lunar world, and wholeheartedly applauded the United States success. This event gave the Japanese people the opportunity to witness the advent of the space age as a personal experience and to be able to imagine in all its vividness the future development of human society.

It can be said that the United States has created a sense of solidarity among mankind by appealing directly to the hearts of the peoples of various countries in the world through this project. In my opinion, this is not only the victory of the superb power of organization of the United States, but also the victory of the imagination and courage of the American people.

Only a short time ago, when they visited Japan, I had the opportunity of hearing in person from the three astronauts the story of their experiences. It therefore gives me special pleasure to be informed of the successful landing on the moon of Apollo 12 during my stay in Washington.

Mr. President, at this time, when United States-Japan relations are about to make a new development, we have found it extremely heartening to have you as the highest leader of the United States, especially since you have visited Japan as many as six times after the war and have such a deep understanding of the actual state of our country.

Your reference to my name is but another demonstration of your great knowledge of our culture of which I am deeply appreciative.

I had the pleasure of first meeting you, Mr. President, when you came to Japan in your capacity as Vice President under the administration of the late President Eisenhower. Please allow me to confess here frankly that since then, I have always had a sense of special closeness to you, by drawing an analogy between your relations with the late President and my own relations with the late Prime Minister Shigeru Yoshida.

In recent years, Japan's national strength has been greatly enhanced through steady economic growth and technological innovation. Our development up to the present time represents the fruits of the Japanese people's many years of diligent effort, but, at the same time, it owes a great deal to the close cooperation between our two countries which many of our predecessors have done so much to promote.

On the other hand, the difficulties confronting the present world are numerous and deep-rooted. I feel, Mr. President, that the amount of painstaking effort you expend in carrying out your responsibilities as the President of the United States cannot be measured. No per-

son can help respecting you for your faith, your indomitable stateman's spirit, so to speak, in overcoming the many difficulties you have faced, by exercising your firm will, and in finally reaching your present exalted position. We have also heard that behind your successes there has always been the warm presence of Mrs. Nixon.

Unshakable faith and untiring aspiration: These are the two qualities of which the present world is in the utmost need. I am convinced that your excellent leadership combined with the wisdom and power of action of the American people as symbolized in the Apollo project, will not fail to contribute to the reduction of international tensions and to the enhancement of the progress of mankind.

We are also firmly determined to establish a relationship of mutual trust between the United States and Japan on this foundation, to carry out such international responsibilities and roles as would be commensurate with our national strength.

It is my sincere hope that, under the leadership of President Nixon, the United States will continue to achieve even higher development as the vanguard of world civilization.

Ladies and gentlemen, I wish now to ask you all to join me in a toast to the good health and further success of the President and Mrs. Nixon, as well as to the everlasting friendship and mutual trust between the United States and Japan.

450 Letter to Ambassador Henry Cabot Lodge Accepting His Resignation as Head of the U.S. Delegation to the Paris Meetings on Vietnam. *November 20, 1969*

Dear Cabot:

It is with great regret that I accept your resignation as head of the U.S. Delegation at the Paris Meetings on Vietnam. I could have asked for no better representative, and will miss your counsel and efforts as we seek to negotiate a just peace in Vietnam.

You have the satisfaction of knowing

that you have done all that imagination and dedication to peace could accomplish.

Please accept my warmest thanks for your service to the Nation in this demanding job.

It is reassuring that you have agreed to serve as an advisor so that I will continue to have the benefit of your experience and wisdom on Vietnam.

With best personal regards,
Sincerely,

RICHARD NIXON

[The Honorable Henry Cabot Lodge, Head of U.S. Delegation to the Paris Meetings on Vietnam, American Embassy, Paris, France]

NOTE: Ambassador Lodge served as head of the delegation from January 21 to December 8, 1969. His letter of resignation, dated November 18, 1969, is printed in the Weekly Compilation of Presidential Documents (vol. 5, p. 1630).

451   Letter to Lawrence E. Walsh Accepting His Resignation as Deputy Head of the U.S. Delegation to the Paris Meetings on Vietnam. *November 21, 1969*

Dear Ed:

It is with special regret that I accept your resignation as Deputy Head of our Delegation to the Paris Meetings on Vietnam. This was a difficult assignment and I understand your disappointment with the progress achieved thus far.

Your fellow countrymen owe you a debt of gratitude for your efforts in behalf of peace—your contribution has been a great one. I want you to know how much I appreciate your outstanding work as well as the generous sacrifice of your personal interests which this assignment

required. It was particularly heartening to learn that we can count on your help in the future.

With warm personal regards,
Sincerely,

RICHARD NIXON

[The Honorable Lawrence E. Walsh, Judge, 1 Chase Manhattan Plaza, New York, New York]

NOTE: Mr. Walsh served as deputy head of the delegation from January 17, 1969, to January 16, 1970. His letter of resignation, dated November 20, 1969, is printed in the Weekly Compilation of Presidential Documents (vol. 5, p. 1631).

452   Remarks on the Departure of Prime Minister Sato of Japan From the White House. *November 21, 1969*

Mr. Prime Minister and Your Excellencies who are present here today:

There have been many meetings between the heads of government of Japan and the United States over the past 25 years. I am confident that history will record that this is the most significant meeting that has occurred since the end of World War II.

It is customary on such occasions to say that a new era begins in the relations be-

tween the two countries involved. I believe today, however, that there is no question that this is a statement of the fact that a new era begins between the United States and Japan, in our relations not only bilaterally in the Pacific but in the world.

As the joint communique which will be issued at 11:30 indicates, we have resolved the last major issue which came out of World War II, the Okinawa problem. And further, we have made significant progress in the resolution of other bilateral issues in the economic field, as well as in the field of investment and trade, not only between our two countries, but in the Asian area.

Mr. Prime Minister, I believe that as we stand here today that in the years ahead, our two Governments and our two peoples will work together toward that great goal which is contained in the slogan of the Expo 1970 in Osaka, "Harmony and Progress for all Mankind."

NOTE: The President spoke at 11:10 a.m. in the Rose Garden at the White House.

See also Items 447, 449, and 453.

Prime Minister Eisaku Sato responded in Japanese through an interpreter, as follows:

I am leaving Washington this afternoon after having successfully completed 3 days of talks with President Nixon and other leaders of the United States Government.

It gave me the greatest pleasure to have been able to strengthen the ties of mutual trust and friendship between the United States and Japan in such an openhearted atmosphere as prevailed throughout our meetings.

Although we still face a number of difficult problems in the present international society, I firmly believe that the paths we have to tread will open up by themselves if we both continue our efforts with hope in the future and in the spirit of mutual understanding and cooperation.

In particular, it is an event of historic significance that an agreement has been reached on the reversion of Okinawa through our talks.

On my return to Japan, I am determined to make every possible effort to set up new relations between the United States and Japan, based on the accomplishments of this visit, which would also contribute toward the establishment of world peace.

As I take my leave, may I express to President and Mrs. Nixon, as well as to the Government and the people of the United States, my heartfelt gratitude for your warm solicitude and my best wishes for the good health and continued prosperity of you all.

453   Joint Statement Following Discussions With Prime Minister Sato of Japan.   *November* 21, 1969

1. PRESIDENT NIXON and Prime Minister Sato met in Washington on November 19, 20 and 21, 1969, to exchange views on the present international situation and on other matters of mutual interest to the United States and Japan.

2. The President and the Prime Minister recognized that both the United States and Japan have greatly benefited from their close association in a variety of fields, and they declared that guided by their common principles of democracy and liberty, the two countries would maintain and strengthen their fruitful cooperation in the continuing search for world peace and prosperity and in particular for the relaxation of international tensions. The President expressed his and his government's deep interest in Asia and stated his belief that the United States and Japan should cooperate in contributing to the peace and prosperity of the region. The Prime Minister stated that Japan would make further active contributions to the peace and prosperity of Asia.

3. The President and the Prime Minister exchanged frank views on the current international situation, with particular attention to developments in the Far East. The President, while emphasizing that the countries in the area were expected to make their own efforts for the stability of the area, gave assurance that the United States would continue to con-

tribute to the maintenance of international peace and security in the Far East by honoring its defense treaty obligations in the area. The Prime Minister, appreciating the determination of the United States, stressed that it was important for the peace and security of the Far East that the United States should be in a position to carry out fully its obligations referred to by the President. He further expressed his recognition that, in the light of the present situation, the presence of United States forces in the Far East constituted a mainstay for the stability of the area.

4. The President and the Prime Minister specifically noted the continuing tension over the Korean peninsula. The Prime Minister deeply appreciated the peacekeeping efforts of the United Nations in the area and stated that the security of the Republic of Korea was essential to Japan's own security. The President and the Prime Minister shared the hope that Communist China would adopt a more cooperative and constructive attitude in its external relations. The President referred to the treaty obligations of his country to the Republic of China which the United States would uphold. The Prime Minister said that the maintenance of peace and security in the Taiwan area was also a most important factor for the security of Japan. The President described the earnest efforts made by the United States for a peaceful and just settlement of the Viet-Nam problem. The President and the Prime Minister expressed the strong hope that the war in Viet-Nam would be concluded before return of the administrative rights over Okinawa to Japan. In this connection, they agreed that, should peace in Viet-Nam not have been realized by the

time reversion of Okinawa is scheduled to take place, the two governments would fully consult with each other in the light of the situation at that time so that reversion would be accomplished without affecting the United States efforts to assure the South Vietnamese people the opportunity to determine their own political future without outside interference. The Prime Minister stated that Japan was exploring what role she could play in bringing about stability in the Indochina area.

5. In light of the current situation and the prospects in the Far East, the President and the Prime Minister agreed that they highly valued the role played by the Treaty of Mutual Cooperation and Security in maintaining the peace and security of the Far East including Japan, and they affirmed the intention of the two governments firmly to maintain the Treaty on the basis of mutual trust and common evaluation of the international situation. They further agreed that the two governments should maintain close contact with each other on matters affecting the peace and security of the Far East including Japan, and on the implementation of the Treaty of Mutual Cooperation and Security.

6. The Prime Minister emphasized his view that the time had come to respond to the strong desire of the people of Japan, of both the mainland and Okinawa, to have the administrative rights over Okinawa returned to Japan on the basis of the friendly relations between the United States and Japan and thereby to restore Okinawa to its normal status. The President expressed appreciation of the Prime Minister's view. The President and the Prime Minister also recognized the vital role played by United States forces

in Okinawa in the present situation in the Far East. As a result of their discussion it was agreed that the mutual security interests of the United States and Japan could be accommodated within arrangements for the return of the administrative rights over Okinawa to Japan. They therefore agreed that the two governments would immediately enter into consultations regarding specific arrangements for accomplishing the early reversion of Okinawa without detriment to the security of the Far East including Japan. They further agreed to expedite the consultations with a view to accomplishing the reversion during 1972 subject to the conclusion of these specific arrangements with the necessary legislative support. In this connection, the Prime Minister made clear the intention of his government, following reversion, to assume gradually the responsibility for the immediate defense of Okinawa as part of Japan's defense efforts for her own territories. The President and the Prime Minister agreed also that the United States would retain under the terms of the Treaty of Mutual Cooperation and Security such military facilities and areas in Okinawa as required in the mutual security of both countries.

7. The President and the Prime Minister agreed that, upon return of the administrative rights, the Treaty of Mutual Cooperation and Security and its related arrangements would apply to Okinawa without modification thereof. In this connection, the Prime Minister affirmed the recognition of his government that the security of Japan could not be adequately maintained without international peace and security in the Far East and, therefore, the security of countries in the Far East was a matter of serious concern for Japan. The Prime Minister was of the view that, in the light of such recognition on the part of the Japanese Government, the return of the administrative rights over Okinawa in the manner agreed above should not hinder the effective discharge of the international obligations assumed by the United States for the defense of countries in the Far East including Japan. The President replied that he shared the Prime Minister's view.

8. The Prime Minister described in detail the particular sentiment of the Japanese people against nuclear weapons and the policy of the Japanese Government reflecting such sentiment. The President expressed his deep understanding and assured the Prime Minister that, without prejudice to the position of the United States Government with respect to the prior consultation system under the Treaty of Mutual Cooperation and Security, the reversion of Okinawa would be carried out in a manner consistent with the policy of the Japanese Government as described by the Prime Minister.

9. The President and the Prime Minister took note of the fact that there would be a number of financial and economic problems, including those concerning United States business interests in Okinawa, to be solved between the two countries in connection with the transfer of the administrative rights over Okinawa to Japan and agreed that detailed discussions relative to their solution would be initiated promptly.

10. The President and the Prime Minister, recognizing the complexity of the problems involved in the reversion of Okinawa, agreed that the two governments should consult closely and cooperate on the measures necessary to assure a smooth transfer of administrative rights to the Japanese Government in

accordance with reversion arrangements to be agreed to by both governments. They agreed that the United States-Japan Consultative Committee in Tokyo should undertake overall responsibility for this preparatory work. The President and the Prime Minister decided to establish in Okinawa a Preparatory Commission in place of the existing Advisory Committee to the High Commissioner of the Ryukyu Islands for the purpose of consulting and coordinating locally on measures relating to preparation for the transfer of administrative rights, including necessary assistance to the Government of the Ryukyu Islands. The Preparatory Commission will be composed of a representative of the Japanese Government with ambassadorial rank and the High Commissioner of the Ryukyu Islands with the Chief Executive of the Government of the Ryukyu Islands acting as adviser to the Commission. The Commission will report and make recommendations to the two governments through the United States-Japan Consultative Committee.

11. The President and the Prime Minister expressed their conviction that a mutually satisfactory solution of the question of the return of the administrative rights over Okinawa to Japan, which is the last of the major issues between the two countries arising from the Second World War, would further strengthen United States-Japan relations which are based on friendship and mutual trust and would make a major contribution to the peace and security of the Far East.

12. In their discussion of economic matters, the President and the Prime Minister noted the marked growth in economic relations between the two countries. They also acknowledged that the leading positions which their countries occupy in the world economy impose important responsibilities on each for the maintenance and strengthening of the international trade and monetary system, especially in the light of the current large imbalances in trade and payments. In this regard, the President stressed his determination to bring inflation in the United States under control. He also reaffirmed the commitment of the United States to the principle of promoting freer trade. The Prime Minister indicated the intention of the Japanese Government to accelerate rapidly the reduction of Japan's trade and capital restrictions. Specifically, he stated the intention of the Japanese Government to remove Japan's residual import quota restrictions over a broad range of products by the end of 1971 and to make maximum efforts to accelerate the liberalization of the remaining items. He added that the Japanese Government intends to make periodic reviews of its liberalization program with a view to implementing trade liberalization at a more accelerated pace than hitherto. The President and the Prime Minister agreed that their respective actions would further solidify the foundation of overall U.S.-Japan relations.

13. The President and the Prime Minister agreed that attention to the economic needs of the developing countries was essential to the development of international peace and stability. The Prime Minister stated the intention of the Japanese Government to expand and improve its aid programs in Asia commensurate with the economic growth of Japan. The President welcomed this statement and confirmed that the United States would continue to contribute to

the economic development of Asia. The President and Prime Minister recognized that there would be major requirements for the post-war rehabilitation of Viet-Nam and elsewhere in Southeast Asia. The Prime Minister stated the intention of the Japanese Government to make a substantial contribution to this end.

14. The Prime Minister congratulated the President on the successful moon landing of Apollo XII, and expressed the hope for a safe journey back to earth for the astronauts. The President and the Prime Minister agreed that the exploration of space offers great opportunities for expanding cooperation in peaceful scientific projects among all nations. In this connection, the Prime Minister noted with pleasure that the United States and Japan last summer had concluded an agreement on space cooperation. The President and the Prime Minister agreed that implementation of this unique program is of importance to both countries.

15. The President and the Prime Minister discussed prospects for the promotion of arms control and the slowing down of the arms race. The President outlined his Government's efforts to initiate the strategic arms limitations talks with the Soviet Union that have recently started in Helsinki. The Prime Minister expressed his Government's strong hopes for the success of these talks. The Prime Minister pointed out his country's strong and traditional interest in effective disarmament measures with a view to achievement of general and complete disarmament under strict and effective international control.

454   Statement Following the Senate Vote on the Nomination of Judge Clement F. Haynsworth, Jr., as Associate Justice of the Supreme Court. *November 21, 1969*

AN OUTSTANDING jurist, who would have brought great credit to the Supreme Court of the United States, has been rejected by the United States Senate.

I deeply regret this action. I believe a majority of people in the Nation regret it.

Especially I deplore the nature of the attacks that have been made upon this distinguished man. His integrity is unimpeachable, his ability unquestioned. The Supreme Court needs men of his legal philosophy to restore the proper balance to that great institution.

The Nation is fortunate that Clement Haynsworth's ability and judgment will remain available to the judiciary through his continuance as Chief Judge of one of the largest and busiest Appellate Courts in the Nation.

When the Congress returns for its second session in January I will nominate another Associate Justice. The criteria I shall apply for this selection, as was the case with my nomination of Judge Haynsworth, will be consistent with my commitments to the American people before my election as President a year ago.

NOTE: The President's intention to nominate Judge Haynsworth was announced on August 18, 1969 (5 Weekly Comp. Pres. Docs., p. 1164).

455 Remarks at the "Briefing for Businessmen" Meeting. *November* 21, 1969

Secretary Stans, Secretary Kennedy, all of the distinguished guests here in the Sheraton Park today:

I am very honored to be here in this company and, also, I want to express my appreciation to those who have come from all over the Nation to this meeting of business leaders.

I am delighted that you have had the opportunity to hear from the top members of our Cabinet and of our White House team in the economic field. I hope you have agreed with them. If they are wrong, I am wrong, and I want to be sure that they are right.

I can assure you, too, that in working with them over these past 10 months I have learned to respect them—I respected them before—but to respect them even more for their devotion, their dedication, and their ability to analyze difficult problems and to come up with what I hope are the right answers.

Now, I am not going to take your time today in any detail in covering the ground that they have already covered in the field of trade, in the field of tax reform, in the area of budget, and all the others that may have been discussed prior to my getting here.

I would simply like to underline some of the administration's basic economic decisions so that there will be no doubt in your minds or in the minds of the Nation as to where we stand and where we are going.

On January 20th we had to make a basic decision. We had had inflation in this country for a period of 4 years in excess of the amount that we thought was

tolerable. We felt it was necessary to make some decisions to deal with that problem. There were two ways to move. One was an easy way. One was to do what had been done in the past and that is to call businessmen in and labor leaders in, blame business for raising prices when prices were raised, blame labor for asking for more wages when wages went up.

Now, while rises in prices and rises in wages of course are contributory factors to the whole problem of inflation, we realized that it was essential for us to deal with our own house and to put it in order. We moved on those points. I can assure you it was not the easiest way, to cut a budget by $7 billion, to ask for an extension of a tax rather than to get rid of a tax which we do want to get rid of—sooner than will be the case—and finally to follow at this time a policy of monetary restraint. These certainly were not the easy courses to follow.

We instituted these courses of action. We now see the first signs that those courses of action are working. We believe that they will work in cooling the inflation. We intend to continue on this course of action until we are sure that they will work.

We simply want to say to the businessmen here gathered—and I believe this—that those who bet on inflation are going to lose their bets in making their business plans, and those who bet on cooling the inflation will win their bets because we are committed and we believe that that is the first step which is essential to deal with this problem.

I realize that in talking about the cutting of budgets and the extension of taxes and monetary restraints that this is not particularly pleasant for any audience to hear, including an audience of businessmen.

I simply want you to know that this is the short-range policy, but because of these short-range, sound steps, we believe that we can look to the future with some optimism.

I understand that Paul McCracken [Chairman, Council of Economic Advisers] indicated that for the year 1980 we could expect an economy of a trillion and a half dollars. I believe that that estimate is one, based on what I have seen, that is reasonable, one that might prove even to be conservative. But whatever the case might be, I don't want to leave the impression that I am pessimistic with regard to the long-range future of this country or even with regard to the immediate future, once we get these inflationary factors under control.

In that connection, I think I can bring my thoughts to you in a rather direct way by sharing with you some correspondence that I have had recently on a very interesting subject with a major publication in this country. I am not going to criticize the publication, as a matter of fact.

The letter is dated November 13th. It is from Miss Ann Bayer, Assistant Editor of Life Magazine. It seems that Life is doing a photographic essay on teddy bears. The letter says:

"Dear Mr. President:

"We thought perhaps you might belong to that select fraternity who still cling to the same teddy bear they had as a child. If you do, please write and tell us no later than Monday, December 1, such specifics as your teddy bear's name, age, and physical condition and something of

the life you and he have shared together. Feel free to express whatever personal feelings you have about your bear."

Well, I thought there could not be a better forum in which to answer that letter. Miss Bayer will also receive her answer in due time by mail—I think it takes 5 days. Is the Postmaster General here? We are also asking for your support of postal reform, incidentally, among other things.

But I am going to answer it this way, so she can see it on television, if it is carried on television, or in the newspapers, or in Life. I shall read the answer to you.

"Dear Miss Bayer:

"I regret that I never belonged to the select fraternity you described. To the extent of not having a teddy bear, my early childhood might be described as disadvantaged.

"However, on January 20th of this year the Dow-Jones averages were 930. Today they are around 830. That means to me that the age and condition of my bear is ten months and about 100 points.

"As to my personal feelings, I am looking forward to the day when this bear turns into a bull."

So, to this group of American businessmen today from all over this Nation, we are optimistic about the future. We are optimistic about the future because we are doing the responsible things about the present. And we ask your cooperation in dealing responsibly with your decisions so that that future may indeed be a bright one for business and for all of the American people.

I would like in my remarks today to go beyond the subjects that have been discussed, go beyond them and perhaps put them in a larger perspective.

It has been said that the business of

959

America is everybody's business. I have just concluded a series of meetings with the Prime Minister of Japan. As I talked to him, the leader of that tremendously productive nation, the third most productive nation in the world and second to the United States in the free world, I realized the truth of that statement. I have realized it as I have talked to the leaders of every major European nation and to the leaders of Asian nations on a trip around the world earlier in the summer.

What we face is this simple fact: Because of the power and the size of the American economy, because of the strength that that economy allows us to have on the military side, what happens in the United States affects the whole world.

This we know. And this is brought home to us every time we talk to a visiting leader, whether he is in the field of government or whether he is in the field of business or labor or education.

As we think of that awesome responsibility that we have, that the decisions we make, whether they are at the highest level in government or in business or in your communities, that those decisions may affect not only our Nation but the world, it gives us certainly a sense of not only national destiny, but also it gives us a sense of perspective as to what our future may be and also it requires us at times to look to our past to see where we have been.

It was, of course, not always this way. Two hundred years ago the United States was a very weak country militarily; it was a very poor country economically. But even then the United States of America, to millions of people who were never

to see it, was the hope of the world.

F. Scott Fitzgerald, in an unfinished novel, unfinished at his death, wrote this: "France is a land; England is a people; America has about it the quality of an idea and is more difficult to describe."

It was that idea that 200 years ago caught the imagination of the world. It was that idea that over these 200 years has continued to mean something in the world far beyond how wealthy we were and how strong we were.

Today America is the strongest nation in the world militarily. We are the richest nation in the world economically. The question is: Do we still have the quality of an idea, an idea that goes far beyond military strength and economic wealth?

Alastair Buchan, the distinguished British Director of the Institute for Strategic Studies in London, wrote recently: "If the United States proves ungovernable in the face of new pressures, then there is no hope for a world order. If the problems of racial integration prove intractable in the United States, then the prospects elsewhere are in doubt. If the problems of developing an effective and orderly system of higher education have been misjudged in the United States, then they have been misjudged elsewhere."

There is the confused feeling in the world today that the United States has ceased to be the last best hope of man, and has become the cockpit of violence, adolescent malaise, racial tension, a network of decaying cities in which the virtues of the American past have been obliterated.

That was not his judgment. He was simply indicating what many people in the world were now concluding about the United States.

So I would like to leave with this audience a challenge that goes far beyond the vitally important responsibility you have in terms of the business decisions that you will make.

I know that reference has been made to the importance of the employment of hard-core unemployed. I know that reference has been made, too, to the community action responsibilities that businessmen increasingly, in this Nation, have undertaken—undertaken with a high sense of purpose.

I would add to that, that whether we are talking about the generation gap, whether we are talking about giving to our young people a sense of participation—participation in business, if they go into business—that sometimes they do not presently have, that in all of these areas we are, in a sense, working at this problem—this problem that goes beyond mere wealth and goes beyond mere military strength, the quality of an idea that once caught the imagination of the world and that is still here, that we can still be very proud of.

We can look at America today and look down to the end of this century and we can see that we will then be the best clothed, and the best housed, and the best fed people in the world, as we are today, but the critical question will be: What has happened to the American idea? Have we become all of those things and are we torn apart by division? Are we torn apart by strife? Do we have gaps between the generations, between the races, between the regions of this country which could pull apart even a nation as strong as this?

I pose these only as rhetorical questions. I do not believe that is the case. I think there has been a tendency in this country in talking about our faults to overlook our virtues.

I believe in America, and I think we have to speak up more for America and the strength of America and what it means to us and what it means to the world.

We talk about hunger in America, and we have some. We are having a conference on nutrition and hunger in which we are going to deal with some of those problems. But as we consider the problem of hunger in America, let us not overlook the fact that American agriculture produces enough to make Americans the best fed people in the world and enough to give billions of dollars of food away to other nations in the world. That is the strength of America.

We can talk about our problems in other fields. We can talk, for example, about that fact that there are inequities in this country. There are some who are rich and there are some who are poor. But as we look at the overall situation among the 200 million Americans, and over the history of mankind, from the beginning, never in the history of the world has more wealth been more fully shared by more people than in the United States of America, and we should not be defensive or apologetic about that.

I know the concern about dissent in America. We have had some evidences of it in this city, and you have seen it in your own cities. But let us not overlook the fact, and this is the important fact, that the right of peaceful dissent has been and is recognized and is protected in America. That is the point that should be emphasized.

If there is any doubt on that score, even the Vice President has the right to dissent in the United States of America.

I do not intend to try to speak to this group in what is usually described in the "Chamber of Commerce" fashion, about a Pollyanna-ish view of the United States and its problems. Our problems are serious at home and our burdens are very great abroad.

But I leave with all of you this thought: When we consider where we would like to be, where we would like to live, and we look at America and we look at the other nations in the world, as I have often said, this is the time and this is the place in which I would like to live.

Yes, we do have problems abroad. We have responsibilities that Americans did not ask for. We are the only nation in the history of the world that acquired a position of world leadership as a result of a policy which was not designed to reach that position.

Nevertheless, however, as we look at that position of world leadership, would we have it another way? We do not say this, and I do not express it in any arrogant or jingoistic way, but I do say that the United States of America, at this time in its history, having no designs of conquest or of domination over any other nation of the world, can and will furnish the leadership that the world needs.

The fact that, in four wars in this century—in World War I, in World War II, in Korea, and in Vietnam—we have given our men, we have spent our money. We have done so generously and we have done so without regard to what we might gain in the way of territory or domina-tion over other nations; the fact that the United States does honestly stand for the right of every other people in this world to choose their own way without any domination from us or anybody else— this is, in itself, a great idea. We should be proud of it. We should not be defensive about it and we should stand up for it.

To you, the members of the American business community, I simply conclude with these words: I have no question about the future of America from the standpoint of its economic growth. It is in good hands and our prosperity is assured by what you will do, the decisions you will make.

But we need more than that from you. The men who can create the tremendous business establishment that we see in this Nation have leadership capabilities that are needed. They are needed in your communities, they are needed in your States, and they are needed in this Nation.

We have appreciated that leadership that you have offered so voluntarily to this administration and to previous administrations.

One of the reasons I am confident about the future is that in addition to the business leadership you will provide, that the brains and the ability and the dedication in this room also are going to be available to this Nation to see to it that America at this critical time in the world's history will meet its responsibility—meet its responsibility not only to make America rich and strong, but meet its responsibility to make America as it was in the beginning, the hope of the whole world.

NOTE: The President spoke at 4:20 p.m. in the Sheraton Park Hotel in Washington to some 1,600 businessmen attending briefings by Government officials.

456   Remarks on Presenting the Medal of Honor to Three Members of the United States Army. *November 24, 1969*

Ladies and gentlemen:

We welcome you all to the White House today. We are gathered here for a very special ceremony, one that will mean a great deal to all of us personally, particularly to the families of those who are being honored and also a great deal to this Nation.

At the present time, coming back from the moon are three very brave men. They will splash down in the Pacific later today. The whole Nation, the whole world, will honor their exploits—our three astronauts, the second team to go to the moon and to land on the moon and to return safely.

Today in this room, we honor three other very brave men. They did not go to the moon. They went to Vietnam. And along with hundreds of thousands of other young Americans they have helped there to defend the principles of this Nation, and they have served with uncommon courage and uncommon valor.

Oliver Wendell Holmes once spoke about the "contagion of courage," that courage some way, when we see it in others, helps to build it up in all of us, and in a whole nation.

Those men who have gone to the moon have raised the spirit of the Nation.

These men, too, by their courage helped raise the spirit of the whole Nation.

At this time, it is a very great honor for all of us to join here in this room to confer upon these three men the highest distinction that this Nation has, the Medal of Honor.

The Secretary of the Army will read the citations.

[At this point, Secretary of the Army Stanley R. Resor read the citations, the texts of which follow:]

The President of the United States of America, authorized by Act of Congress, March 3, 1863, has awarded in the name of The Congress the Medal of Honor to

SERGEANT FIRST CLASS WEBSTER
ANDERSON
UNITED STATES ARMY

for conspicuous gallantry and intrepidity in action at the risk of his life above and beyond the call of duty:

Sergeant First Class Webster Anderson, (then Staff Sergeant), distinguished himself by conspicuous gallantry and intrepidity in action while serving as Chief of Section in Battery A, 2d Battalion, 320th Artillery, 101st Airborne Infantry Division (Airmobile) against a hostile force near Tam Ky, Republic of Vietnam. During the early morning hours on 15 October 1967, Battery A's defensive position was attacked by a determined North Vietnamese Army Infantry unit supported by heavy mortar, recoilless rifle, rocket propelled grenade and automatic weapon fire. The initial enemy onslaught breached the battery defensive perimeter. Sergeant Anderson with complete disregard for his personal safety mounted the exposed parapet of his howitzer position and became the mainstay of the defense of the battery position. Sergeant Anderson directed devastating direct howitzer fire on the assaulting enemy while providing rifle and grenade defensive fire against enemy soldiers attempting to overrun his gun section position. While protecting his crew and directing their fire against the enemy from his exposed position, two enemy grenades exploded at his feet knocking him down and severely wounding him in the legs. Despite the excruciating pain and though not able to stand, Sergeant Anderson valorously propped himself on the parapet and continued to direct howitzer fire upon the closing enemy and to encourage his men to fight on. Seeing an enemy grenade land within the gun pit near a wounded member of his gun crew, Sergeant Anderson, heedless of his own safety, seized the grenade and attempted to throw it over the parapet to save his men. As the grenade was thrown from the position it exploded and Sergeant Anderson was again greviously wounded. Although only partially conscious and severely wounded, Sergeant Anderson refused medical evacuation and continued to encourage his men in the defense of the position. Sergeant Anderson by his inspirational leadership, professionalism, devotion to duty and complete disregard for his own welfare was able to maintain the defense of his section position and to defeat a determined enemy attack. Sergeant Anderson's conspicuous gallantry and extraordinary heroism at the risk of his own life above and beyond the call of duty are in the highest traditions of the military service and reflect great credit upon himself, his unit and the United States Army.

RICHARD NIXON

The President of the United States of America, authorized by Act of Congress, March 3, 1863, has awarded in the name of The Congress the Medal of Honor to

STAFF SERGEANT NICKY D. BACON
UNITED STATES ARMY

for conspicuous gallantry and intrepidity in action at the risk of his life above and beyond the call of duty:

Staff Sergeant Nicky D. Bacon distinguished himself by conspicuous gallantry and intrepidity while serving as a squad leader with the 1st Platoon, Company B, 4th Battalion, 21st Infantry, Americal Division during an operation west of Tam Ky, Republic of Vietnam, on 26 August 1968. When Company B came under fire from an enemy bunker line to the front, Sergeant Bacon quickly organized his men and led them forward in an assault. He advanced on a hostile bunker and destroyed it with grenades.

As he did so, several fellow soldiers, including the 1st Platoon leader, were struck by machine gun fire and fell wounded in an exposed position forward of the rest of the platoon. Sergeant Bacon immediately assumed command of the platoon and assaulted the hostile gun position, finally killing the enemy gun crew in a single-handed effort. When the 3rd Platoon moved to Sergeant Bacon's location, its leader was also wounded. Without hesitation Sergeant Bacon took charge of the additional platoon and continued the fight. In the ensuing action he personally killed four more enemy soldiers and silenced an antitank weapon. Under his leadership and example, the members of both platoons accepted his authority without question. Continuing to ignore the intense hostile fire, he climbed up on the exposed deck of a tank and directed fire into the enemy position while several wounded men were evacuated. As a result of Sergeant Bacon's extraordinary efforts, his company was able to move forward, eliminate the enemy positions, and rescue the men trapped to the front. Sergeant Bacon's conspicuous gallantry at the risk of his own life was in the highest traditions of the military service and reflects great credit upon himself, his unit and the United States Army.

RICHARD NIXON

The President of the United States of America, authorized by Act of Congress, March 3, 1863, has awarded in the name of The Congress the Medal of Honor to

STAFF SERGEANT PAUL R. LAMBERS
UNITED STATES ARMY

for conspicuous gallantry and intrepidity in action at the risk of his life above and beyond the call of duty:

Staff Sergeant (then Sergeant) Paul R. Lambers distinguished himself by conspicuous gallantry and intrepidity in action on 20 August 1968 while serving with the Third Platoon, Company A, 2d Battalion, 27th Infantry, 25th Infantry Division, in Tay Ninh Province, Republic of Vietnam. The unit had established a night defensive position astride a suspected enemy infiltration route, when it was attacked by an estimated Viet Cong battalion. During the initial enemy onslaught, the platoon leader fell seriously wounded and Sergeant Lambers assumed command of the platoon. Disregarding the intense enemy fire, Sergeant Lambers left his covered position, secured the platoon radio and moved to the command post to direct the defense. When his radio became inoperative due to enemy action, Sergeant Lambers crossed the fire swept position to secure the 90mm recoilless rifle crew's radio in order to re-establish communications. Upon discovering that the 90mm recoilless rifle was not functioning, Sergeant Lambers assisted in the repair of the weapon and directed cannister fire at point blank range against the attacking enemy who had breached the defensive wire of the position. When the weapon was knocked out by enemy fire, he single-handedly repulsed a penetration of the position by detonating claymore mines and throwing grenades into the midst of the attackers, killing five of the enemy. He then attacked a number of the enemy who were moving on the northwest sector of the perimeter, killing four more of the Viet Cong with well aimed hand grenades. Sergeant Lambers maintained command of the platoon elements by moving from position to position under the hail of enemy fire, providing assistance where the assault was the heaviest and by his outstanding example inspiring his men to the utmost efforts of courage. He displayed great skill and valor throughout the five hour battle by personally directing artillery and heli-copter fires, placing them at times within five meters of the defensive position. He repeatedly exposed himself to hostile fire at great risk to his own life in order to redistribute ammunition and to care for seriously wounded comrades and to move them to sheltered positions. Sergeant Lambers' superb leadership, professional skill and magnificent courage saved the lives of his comrades, resulted in the virtual annihilation of a vastly superior enemy force and were largely instrumental in thwarting an enemy offensive against Tay Ninh City. His conspicuous gallantry at the risk of his own life is in keeping with the highest traditions of the military service and reflects great credit upon himself, his unit and the United States Army.

RICHARD NIXON

[The President resumed speaking.]

We thank you very much for coming to this ceremony. I think you would like to know that at the conclusion of these ceremonies we always provide a very special tour of the White House for, of course, the winners of the Medal of Honor and their families.

We are going to give you that tour now. We hope you enjoy it.

Thank you very much.

NOTE: The President spoke at 10:35 a.m. in the East Room at the White House.

457 Remarks on Signing the Instrument of Ratification of the Treaty on the Non-Proliferation of Nuclear Weapons. *November 24, 1969*

Ladies and gentlemen:

We have invited you here today to witness the signing of the Instrument of Ratification of the Treaty on the Non-Proliferation of Nuclear Weapons to which the Senate gave its advice and consent on March 13th of this year.

This act of ratification completes a process which has spanned the adminis-trations of three Presidents in which this treaty was negotiated and it is now being ratified.

It is our hope that after the ratification on the part of the United States that the necessary additional number of nations will ratify the treaty so that it will go into effect.

In speaking of this treaty, we believe

that this action today underlines the commitment of this Nation, not only for a policy of limiting armaments generally, but also to reduce those areas of conflict that potentially would result in a threat to the peace and security of the world.

And finally, I believe that this act of ratification clearly demonstrates that this Nation, through the administrations of all our Presidents in this century, is dedicated to the cause of peace, and we will continue to pursue that cause in every possible, effective way.

The Secretary of State, I think, will explain to you the final action with regard to the treaty and the ceremony which will be scheduled at that time. We have not set the date for it yet, but if you would explain it, Mr. Secretary.

NOTE: The President spoke at 11:09 a.m. in his office at the White House. The remarks of Secretary of State Rogers are printed in the Weekly Compilation of Presidential Documents (vol. 5, p. 1658).

458   Statement on Signing the Instrument of Ratification of the Treaty on the Non-Proliferation of Nuclear Weapons.   *November 24, 1969*

I HAVE today signed the Instrument of Ratification of the Treaty on the Non-Proliferation of Nuclear Weapons to which the Senate gave its advice and consent on March 13, 1969.

This Government is thus completing the process of ratifying a major international agreement designed to make our world a safer home for all mankind.

The negotiation and ratification of this treaty spans the administrations of three Presidents and reflects our country's dedication to the cause of peace.

It is my earnest hope that ratification of the treaty by the necessary number of additional states will soon occur so that it may enter into force at an early time.

This administration seeks equitable and meaningful agreements to limit armaments and to resolve the dangerous conflicts that threaten peace and security. In this act of ratification today, this commitment is demonstrated anew.

459   Statement on the Successful Completion of the Apollo 12 Mission.   *November 24, 1969*

ANOTHER CHAPTER in the history of American exploration has ended successfully. I extend the congratulations of all Americans to the crew of Apollo 12 and to the thousands who made its success possible. This mission has shown conclusively that the system we have developed has enormous scientific potential, and we can now look forward to utilizing that capability.

We have all been impressed over the last several days with both the technical proficiency and the high spirits of Commander Conrad, Commander Gordon, and Commander Bean.

The triumph of Apollo 12 is not only

an American triumph. This second voyage to the surface of the moon represents another great victory of the human mind and spirit, one which will lift the sights and raise the spirits of men everywhere.

460   Telephone Conversation With the Crew of Apollo 12 Following Splashdown and Recovery. *November 24, 1969*

THE PRESIDENT. Hello, Commander? Are you all three on?

COMMANDER RICHARD F. GORDON, JR. Yes, sir, we are all on the phone.

THE PRESIDENT. I am delighted to have this opportunity to welcome you back. I only wish that I could be out there for the splashdown.

We all went with you on television. I can't say that I followed every bit of it. But I can assure you that millions here in the United States and around the world were watching.

I am just tremendously proud, personally, and speaking also representing the American people, of what you have done.

As you know, before you took off, we talked on the phone that night and I invited you and your wives to come to the White House for dinner. I just want to be sure you can make that date.

COMMANDER GORDON. Yes, sir, we will be there.

THE PRESIDENT. Fine. We will expect to see you after you get out of quarantine.

And now there is one other thing that I think I should tell you. I have noticed that you have been responsible for several firsts. You weren't the first on the moon. But I think, Commander Conrad, you were the first to sing from the moon, right?

COMMANDER CHARLES CONRAD, JR. I guess so, sir.

THE PRESIDENT. That is right.

Also, we have had the first moonquake as a result of your flight and the first press conference from outer space.

Now, after all of those firsts, I think that the Nation wants some recognition. And I have been trying to think of what would be the best way to recognize you.

Over these past 10 days I have noticed that Walter Cronkite and the other commentators are always referring to you as "Commander Conrad," and "Commander Gordon," and "Commander [Alan L.] Bean."

And I, exercising my prerogative as Commander in Chief of the Armed Forces, have decided that you should be promoted and that from this day forth, you shall be "Captain Conrad," and "Captain Gordon," and "Captain Bean."

Congratulations.

CAPTAIN GORDON. Thank you, Mr. President.

CAPTAIN BEAN. Thank you very much.

CAPTAIN CONRAD. Thank you, sir.

THE PRESIDENT. We look forward to seeing you.

CAPTAIN GORDON. Yes, sir. We look forward to being there.

Thank you very much, sir.

NOTE: The President spoke at 5:45 p.m. in his office at the White House to the astronauts on board the aircraft carrier U.S.S. *Hornet.*

461   Statement on Chemical and Biological Defense Policies and Programs.   *November 25, 1969*

SOON AFTER taking office I directed a comprehensive study of our chemical and biological defense policies and programs. There had been no such review in over 15 years. As a result, objectives and policies in this field were unclear and programs lacked definition and direction.

Under the auspices of the National Security Council, the Departments of State and Defense, the Arms Control and Disarmament Agency, the Office of Science and Technology, the intelligence community, and other agencies worked closely together on this study for over 6 months. These Government efforts were aided by contributions from the scientific community through the President's Science Advisory Committee.

This study has now been completed and its findings carefully considered by the National Security Council. I am now reporting the decisions taken on the basis of this review.

CHEMICAL WARFARE PROGRAM

As to our chemical warfare program, the United States:

—Reaffirms its oft-repeated renunciation of the first use of lethal chemical weapons.

—Extends this renunciation to the first use of incapacitating chemicals.

Consonant with these decisions, the administration will submit to the Senate, for its advice and consent to ratification, the Geneva Protocol of 1925 [1] which prohibits the first use in war of

"asphyxiating, poisonous or other Gases and of Bacteriological Methods of Warfare." The United States has long supported the principles and objectives of this Protocol. We take this step toward formal ratification to reinforce our continuing advocacy of international constraints on the use of these weapons.

BIOLOGICAL RESEARCH PROGRAM

Biological weapons have massive, unpredictable and potentially uncontrollable consequences. They may produce global epidemics and impair the health of future generations. I have therefore decided that:

—The United States shall renounce the use of lethal biological agents and weapons, and all other methods of biological warfare.

—The United States will confine its biological research to defensive measures such as immunization and safety measures.

—The Department of Defense has been asked to make recommendations as to the disposal of existing stocks of bacteriological weapons.

In the spirit of these decisions, the United States associates itself with the principles and objectives of the United Kingdom Draft Convention which would ban the use of biological methods of warfare. [2] We will seek, however, to clarify specific provisions of the draft to assure that necessary safeguards are included.

---

[1] League of Nations Treaty Series (vol. 94, p. 65).

[2] Annex to United Nations General Assembly Document of November 3, 1969 (A/7741 DC/232).

Neither our association with the Convention nor the limiting of our program to research will leave us vulnerable to surprise by an enemy who does not observe these rational restraints. Our intelligence community will continue to watch carefully the nature and extent of the biological programs of others.

These important decisions, which have been announced today, have been taken as an initiative toward peace. Mankind already carries in its own hands too many of the seeds of its own destruction. By the examples we set today, we hope to contribute to an atmosphere of peace and understanding between nations and among men.

462   Remarks Announcing Decisions on Chemical and Biological Defense Policies and Programs. *November 25, 1969*

Ladies and gentlemen:

I have just completed a meeting with the legislative leaders of the House and the Senate, the Foreign Relations and the Armed Services Committees.

In that meeting, we discussed some major initiatives in the disarmament field, initiatives that are the result of decisions that have been made after a Security Council meeting that was held last week.

I would like to summarize the decisions that have been made as a result of the Security Council meeting and the meetings with the legislative leaders, and also to indicate the actions that we hope will be taken by the Senate to affirm the decisions that the administration has made.

The United States is taking two steps today toward advancing the cause of peace and reducing the terror of war. Since this administration took office, the National Security Council has been reviewing our policy regarding chemical warfare and biological warfare. This has been the first thorough review ever undertaken of this subject at the Presidential level.

I recall during the 8 years that I sat on the National Security Council in the Eisenhower administration that these subjects, insofar as an appraisal of what the United States had, what our capability was, what other nations had, were really considered taboo.

And it was felt when we came into the administration that we should examine all of our defense policies and defense capabilities, because it has always been my conviction that what we don't know usually causes more fear than what we do know.

What we have tried to do in this examination by the Security Council, an unprecedented examination, is to find the facts and to develop the policies based on the facts as they are, rather than on our fears as to what the facts might be.

On the basis of this review, I made a number of decisions which I believe will sharply reduce the chance that these weapons, either chemical or bacteriological, will ever be used by any nation.

First, in the field of chemical warfare, I hereby reaffirm that the United States will never be the first country to use chemical weapons to kill. And I have also extended this renunciation to chemical weapons which incapacitate.

I am asking the United States Senate for its advice and consent in the ratification of the Geneva Protocol of 1925, which prohibits the first use in war of chemical warfare weapons.

Since 1925, this proposal has been affirmed by the United States as a matter of policy, but never approved by the United States Senate.

And I have asked the leaders this morning to expedite action in this field.

These steps should go a long way toward outlawing weapons whose use has been repugnant to the conscience of mankind.

Second, biological warfare, which is commonly called germ warfare—this has massive, unpredictable, and potentially uncontrollable consequences. It may produce global epidemics and profoundly affect the health of future generations.

Therefore, I have decided that the United States of America will renounce the use of any form of deadly biological weapons that either kill or incapacitate.

Our bacteriological programs in the future will be confined to research in biological defense, on techniques of immunization, and on measures of controlling and preventing the spread of disease.

I have ordered the Defense Department to make recommendations about the disposal of existing stocks of bacteriological weapons.

This program of research and development, incidentally, can have a very important byproduct for the United States and for the world, because we thereby, we think, can break new ground with regard to immunization for any kind of diseases that might spread either nationally or internationally.

The United States positively shall associate itself with the principles of the Draft Convention prohibiting the use of biological weapons of warfare presented by the United Kingdom and the U.N. Eighteen-Nation Disarmament Conference on August 26, 1969.

Up to this time, only Canada has indicated support of this United Kingdom initiative.

The United States, as of today, now indicates its support of this initiative and we hope that other nations will follow suit.

Mankind already carries in its own hands too many of the seeds of its own destruction. By the examples that we set today, we hope to contribute to an atmosphere of peace and understanding between all nations.

Thank you.

NOTE: The President spoke at 10:31 a.m. in the Roosevelt Room at the White House.

463   Remarks on Signing the Draft Reform Bill. *November 26, 1969*

Mr. Secretary, Members of the Senate and House, and members of the Youth Advisory Committee who are present here today:

I am here for the purpose of signing the draft reform bill, which has been passed by the House and the Senate.

In signing this bill, I think it might be well to refer to a statement that was made over 100 years ago by General Grant with regard to the draft that was then in effect.

He said that the agony of suspense is worse than the effect of the law itself.

As far as this draft reform bill is concerned, it does not remove all of the inequity of the draft, because there will be inequity as long as any of our young men have to serve when others do not have to serve. But the agony of suspense and uncertainty which has hung over our younger generation for 7 years can now be reduced to 1 year, and other very needed reforms in the draft can be made by Executive order.

In signing the bill, I want to impress upon everybody here that while the administration took the initiative through the Secretary of Defense's recommendation in sending this bill to the Congress, it could not be here for signature by the President had it not had strong bipartisan support by members of the Democratic Party in the House and the Senate, as well as members of the Republican Party. This is truly a bipartisan measure and the credit should be taken by both parties

as the bill signing occurs.

Finally, I would say that looking to the future, while this measure will remove a great number of the inequities and particularly remove the uncertainty to which I refer, we shall not be satisfied until we finally can have the system which I advocated during the campaign of a completely volunteer armed force. We cannot move to that now because of the requirements for armed services. That is, however, our ultimate goal.

Now I will sign the measure.

NOTE: The President spoke at 10:11 a.m. in the Roosevelt Room at the White House. As enacted, the bill is Public Law 91–124 (83 Stat. 220).

On November 26, 1969, the White House Press Office released a news briefing on the bill by Secretary of Defense Melvin R. Laird and Assistant to the President Peter M. Flanigan. A fact sheet on the new draft selection system is printed in the Weekly Compilation of Presidential Documents (vol. 5, p. 1662).

Proclamation 3945 and Executive Orders 11497 and 11498 implement the draft reform legislation.

464   Remarks at a Thanksgiving Day Dinner for Senior Citizens at the White House.   *November 27, 1969*

Ladies and gentlemen:

We are just delighted to welcome you here on this Thanksgiving Day. We apologize for the delay but apparently some of the buses were a little bit late and we wanted to be sure everybody could be seated before the Thanksgiving dinner began.

This is really a very historic occasion for this house—this very great house which belongs to all the people of America. This is the biggest dinner that has been held in the White House since this administration came to Washington, and

one of the biggest ever.

This room is full. We have never, in this administration, had dinner in this room, the famous East Room. And the dining room is full, too. We think there is a very good reason for it to be at this dinner, because of the people we are honoring.

We were trying to think on this Thanksgiving Day what group we could invite to be with us. In our family we always had Thanksgiving as a family day. We have in the past, and we do now.

Our parents cannot be here now, but

we wanted people who have been with this Nation for so many years, who have lived good lives, to be here as our guests today. We feel that you are part of our family and we invite you here and we hope you enjoy this house as part of our family—the White House family, the American family.

I also would like to say that in this room you are going to have, as your very special hostess today, a very great lady, who for 8 years presided over this house as the First Lady of America, Mrs. Dwight Eisenhower. She is accompanied by her uncle,[1] who came all the way from Iowa here.

Now I am not going to tell you his age, but I do understand that among our guests here, everyone is young in heart, but I understand there is at least one who might be 98. Is that one person in this room or is he in the other room?

Hold up your hand. Nobody is going to admit it anyway. [*Laughter*]

Oh, here we are. Let's be sure that everybody sees him. How about a hand for the oldest person in the room—98 years old.[2]

Incidentally, right now I invite you back to the White House on your 100th birthday, right here. You are going to be here.

Now I just close with this final thought. You have seen the menu. It is the usual kind of menu that we have, of course, the turkey, with all of the things that go with it, and pumpkin pie for dessert. And when I noticed that we were having turkey, I was reminded of the fact that

when this country began, that Benjamin Franklin, when there was a great debate as to what the national symbol of the country should be, argued that it should be the turkey rather than the eagle.

Now I think he was a very wise man, but I think the decision to have it the eagle was a little better. I think when Neil Armstrong landed on the moon, it would have sounded rather funny to say, "Turkey has landed," and today I think you will all agree you would not want to eat eagle.

So we do have turkey today. We hope you will enjoy being here as much as we enjoy having you.

I want you to meet your other hosts in this room, my daughter, Tricia, and Susie Eisenhower,[3] the granddaughter of Mrs. Eisenhower.

Now if you will excuse us, we will go into the other room to welcome the guests there.

And Mrs. Eisenhower, you take over. You have lots of experience.

[The above remarks were addressed to a group of senior citizens dining in the East Room. The President then went to the State Dining Room to address other members of the group there.]

We want to welcome you here to the White House today and to tell you how honored we are to have you in this room. Our dinner has been a bit delayed because, as some of you who may have been on the last bus know, the last bus didn't get here until about 10 minutes ago, and we wanted to be sure that everybody was in the room before we had a chance to come in to welcome you, very

---

[1] Joel Carlson, 89, of Boone, Iowa.

[2] Michael Dunnigan, from the Little Sisters of the Poor home.

[3] Susan Eisenhower, daughter of U.S. Ambassador to Belgium John Eisenhower, the late President's son.

briefly, before you have what we think will be a very good White House Thanksgiving dinner.

You, in this room, are in what is called the State Dining Room. This is the room normally which is set up to seat approximately 100 people. I thought you would be interested to know how usually it is fixed. Usually the table is set in a "U" shape or "E" shape, with the heads of state or government sitting at that end of the room and then coming down this way.

But for occasions like this, we find we can get a few more in if we use the round tables. So in order to get all the people in as guests today—and I think there are 120 in this room today—we have the round tables.

But it gives you a chance to talk a little more around the round tables rather than that big, long table. And we knew you would enjoy doing that, meeting perhaps some of your friends and also others who may be living in this neighborhood.

Also, I would like you to know that in this room over the years many great events have occurred, going back to all of our Presidents except for General Washington, who, of course, did not use the White House because it was not built until John Adams became President.

But in this room many great people have been honored. There have been kings, emperors, prime ministers, presidents, and other distinguished people. I have been here for dinners honoring Winston Churchill, Prime Minister Nehru, and, just recently, the Shah of Iran and Prince Philip of England—all of these people whom you have heard about and who have been here.

But I want you to know that for Mrs. Nixon and for me and for our family, we don't think that on this Thanksgiving Day anyone deserves being honored more in the White House than our guests today, those who are here. Because for us, Thanksgiving is always a special family day and we like to have our family with us.

We think you are family. You feel that way to us and you are part of the great American family. Today, in honoring you, we honor all of you across the country who have lived good lives, long lives in America, and who are here today with us.

I would just conclude with this thought. On Thanksgiving we do tend to try to think of those things we should be thankful for, and we also try not to put emphasis on some of the things that perhaps bother us so much. This is good, because if we were always thinking of our troubles, it would be a pretty sad world in which to live.

I think in terms of you who are here, of the lives you have led and what has happened, if you were to look at the dark side of it, it has been a rather bad time to be alive. You can point to the fact that we have had four wars. You can point to the fact that we have had a depression during your lifetime, most of you who have lived here. And this, of course, is the bad side.

Then, on the other side, of course, you can think of what has happened to America in this period—some of the good things—and what has happened to the world. I was thinking that 66 years ago— it is only that long ago—the Wright brothers first flew. Just think what has happened since then. The astronauts twice have landed on the moon, and who would have thought that would happen. And we are lucky enough to have seen it all happen in our lifetime.

We have seen other things happen. We have seen the United States grow to be the strongest nation, the richest nation in the world. And we also know that as we look around the world, despite our difficulties—difficulties that we constantly attempt to resolve—that when you go to other countries of the world, as I have traveled to most of them, along with Mrs. Nixon, as we have traveled, we see many great things, we see many fine people; but when we return I can say we realize that we are very fortunate to be in the United States of America, to live in this country.

This is a great country and a good country and if you have any doubt about it, just go other places and then come back again.

I think you should know that in the other room, the East Room, that Mrs. Dwight Eisenhower stayed there as the special hostess for that room. As you know, she presided over this house with such great distinction and also with such great charm for 8 years.

In this room we have Mrs. Nixon, my wife, and then you get an Eisenhower, too—you get two of them—David and Julie Eisenhower. They will be in this room.

I would like to tell you, incidentally, that Mrs. Nixon baked the turkey. She did not. But I want you to know this: that up until about 4 or 5 years ago, she always did. She can bake a real good turkey, and I hope it is as good today as she can bake, I can assure you.

Now I hope all of you have a wonderful Thanksgiving dinner. We are honored to have you with us.

Incidentally, I understand that there might be one other person in this room who is 98 years of age. There is one in the other room.

Ninety-three over here? Is there anybody else over 90 in this room?

Ninety-three? Well, let's give a hand to the oldest guest.[5] We are very happy to have you here.

From Missouri? We are glad to have somebody from what we call the very heart of the country here. I know President Truman will be glad we had a Missourian right here today. Independence?

Just let me say this: After hearing you talk at 93 years of age, those people in Missouri must be real strong. We wish you many happy returns, and many good birthdays in the future. Thank you very much, and we hope you have a wonderful Thanksgiving dinner.

Did you hear that? He has never had a sick day. I am going to have the Secretary of Health, Education, and Welfare come over to talk to you and get your formula so we can pass it around the country. I want to get your formula, too.

NOTE: The President spoke at 1:36 p.m. in the East Room and at 1:42 p.m. in the State Dining Room at the White House to some 220 senior citizens from the Washington area.

Following the President's remarks, his daughter, Julie Eisenhower, offered a short grace before the meal. Her prayer is printed in the Weekly Compilation of Presidential Documents (vol. 5, p. 1667).

---

[5] The 93-year-old Missourian was John W. Graves of Neosho, a resident of the National Lutheran Home for the Aged in Washington, D.C.

465 Statement on the Occasion of the 100 Millionth Smallpox Vaccination Under the AID Program in Africa. *November 30, 1969*

OF THE MANY humanitarian programs conducted by the United States through the Agency for International Development, none is more important—or more expressive of our national concern with peaceful progress in the developing world—than the work to eliminate the scourge of disease.

The challenge is measured in cruel statistics. Smallpox epidemics in Africa have killed one in four stricken by the disease. Measles kills about 10 percent of the African children it infects. Gastrointestinal diseases have taken a fearful toll. Even for those who survive, these diseases often leave behind continuing misery in disfigurement, crippling arthritis, blindness, and increased susceptibility to other illnesses. There is also the tragedy visited upon the families of the victims.

Beyond the suffering of the individual, there is a loss to the larger community. For disease ravages the energy of body and mind which is the engine of national development.

But the progress you mark today in Niger is dramatic proof that man can be free of these age-old bonds.

This one hundred millionth vaccination against smallpox is not only an impressive measure of technical assistance. It is one hundred million opportunities to be productive citizens of the new Africa.

And like most great strides in development, it was made possible by people working together—20 nations of West and Central Africa, the World Health Organization, regional groups, and AID—all doing their share in a common cause.

My warmest congratulations to all those who have helped reach this milestone.

NOTE: The statement was read at a ceremony in Niamey, the Republic of Niger, by Dr. John A. Hannah, Administrator, Agency for International Development. The text was released at Key Biscayne, Fla.

466 Remarks at a Dinner for the Board of Directors of the Boys' Clubs of America. *December 1, 1969*

Chairman Al, President John, and all of my fellow members of the Board of the Boys' Clubs of America:

I am most grateful to all of you for presenting me my first Christmas present. I don't think they will all come from Tiffany's. I am glad to have one.

This obviously got by the Secret Service. It is empty.

But, nevertheless, I do want you to know that I am very proud to be the host tonight.

And I think that all of you are aware of the fact that this is an evening that is a first. You might be interested to know this is the first evening dinner that has been held in this room since I have been President of the United States. I am honored that it is for the Boys' Clubs Board.

This is the first time, at least in this administration, that the board of a national organization like the Boys' Clubs has met in the White House for dinner. And I am honored it is this board.

There is, of course, a reason for this. And I am sure that, as you sit in this room, you will realize the historical moment in which we are participating. I do not believe there is any other organization in the United States which has had as its chairmen two men who have served as President of the United States.

President Hoover, of course, became chairman of the Boys' Clubs in 1936 after having served as President of the United States.

I did it the other way around. I became chairman first of the Boys' Clubs before becoming President.

And that allows me to answer a question that is often asked. I was talking to John Burns a few moments ago. He was asking me how it was, after I had suffered a couple of political defeats, that I had the nerve or whatever it is, or the rashness to go into the political arena again and to run for office again.

I will tell you how it came about. When I moved to New York, I became the chairman of the Boys' Clubs on the recommendation of Mr. Hoover. And at the first meeting as chairman of the Boys' Clubs of America, I found that I was the first chairman of the Boys' Clubs of America that had never served as president of the Boys' Clubs before. As a matter of fact, I was the first chairman of the Boys' Clubs of America that had never been president of anything before.

And so, I decided that I would have to correct that deficiency. And I looked first at the Boys' Clubs. I couldn't run for president of the Boys' Clubs because Al Cole was president of the Boys' Clubs.

So, consequently, I picked what was most natural—I ran for the President of the United States. That is why I am here.

It is indeed, therefore, a very great honor to remind all of us on this occasion that two Presidents of the Nation now have been associated with this great organization and are proud to have been associated with it.

I am going to speak to you very briefly tonight, as the evening is late. But before I speak, I think you should have the opportunity to hear very briefly from two others, who are here at the head table, who I know will, perhaps, appear before meetings of this board or at national conferences in the future, and at least one has appeared in the past.

But I know you would not want to come to Washington without hearing briefly from each of them.

First—and it is very appropriate that he is the youngest member of the Cabinet, and it is also very appropriate that he is the head of the largest domestic Cabinet office, the office of Health, Education, and Welfare—Robert Finch from California.

[Following Secretary Finch's remarks (5 Weekly Comp. Pres. Docs., p. 1683), the President resumed speaking.]

And now a man who has received the highest award of the Boys' Clubs of America, one who had the deep affection and respect of President Hoover and one who is respected by everyone in this room and by millions of Americans, one who is known for his effectiveness in dealing with the problems of juvenile delinquency, but one who is also highly known in another field of knowing the importance of and emphasizing juvenile decency as representative of the Boys' Clubs of America, J. Edgar Hoover.

[Following remarks by J. Edgar Hoover, Director of the Federal Bureau of Investigation (5 Weekly Comp. Pres. Docs., p. 1683), the President resumed speaking.]

My fellow board members:

The last official state visitor that we had in the White House was the Prime Minister of Japan, Mr. Sato. And before we made our toasts for the evening, he was telling me at the table about a Japanese proverb, which is very brief, but I think very pertinent at this hour in the evening.

It said, "Many words, little sense." I am going to take that hint tonight. My words will be brief: And I hope they make some sense.

I want to say that in terms of the Boys' Clubs and its contributions, that I look around this room and see people from all over the United States, from California and Florida, and from the Northeast, the Midwest, the Southwest, the South, and I realize that virtually everybody in this room is very busy in either his business or professional career.

And I know how much time you contribute, not only to this organization but to other organizations that depend upon volunteer activity.

I know, too, that when you come to Washington, and you think of a country with what is approaching a $200 billion budget, you must wonder whether the efforts of the Boys' Clubs of America, with a very substantial budget—I noted these three $1 million contributions that Al Cole referred to; we could use him in helping to balance our budget, I can assure you— but when you think of that effort, it must seem very small compared with the budget that we have in the Federal Government,

even if you compare it with Bob Finch's budget of around $40 billion. I haven't cut it yet. But, nevertheless, we are just working that out at the present time. [*Laughter*]

But I want to return to a favorite theme of mine in speaking not only to the Boys' Clubs but to similar organizations across this country. You are doing something that government cannot do.

Since almost a year ago, those of us in this administration have been working toward what we believe are some very important government goals. We have offered a very bold program in the field of family assistance, one which we hope, when adopted by the Congress, will mean that every family in America will have a minimum income, either through work or, if they are unable to work, through government assistance.

We have advocated a revenue-sharing program in which revenues now collected by the Federal Government will be shared with the States so that our cities and States will have a better opportunity to meet their responsibilities.

And then we have programs which you may have heard about in a number of other fields, which will be coming along, programs for cleaning up the air, cleaning the water, programs in the field of what is generally called the environment. We could go on.

Whether we are talking, however, about revenue-sharing or family assistance, or clean air or clean water, we finally come to a conclusion, and that is that government efforts can only contribute so much to the solution of a problem.

There is another ingredient that is needed, an ingredient which comes from an organization like this, either from an organization like this or from the home, from the church, or from some similar organization outside of government.

Let me put it another way quite graphically. J. Edgar Hoover has referred to the problems of juvenile delinquency with some statistics from 1960 to 1968.

On Wednesday of this week, in this very room, we will be meeting with the Governors of the 50 States, in which we will hear a report with regard to narcotics, particularly among young people in the United States.

It will be significant to note that that report on narcotics and the crime that develops from narcotics, among that group of young people in the United States, primarily covers not the deprived, not those from the poor families, but those from the middle income or, more often, the upper middle income families of the United States.

Now the purpose of my making this point is a very simple one. A few moments ago we saw the Bunker Hillbillies, and we saw a young boy from Tampa, Florida.[1] They come from relatively poor families.

They are, we hope, well fed. They were well clothed. They certainly seemed to be well trained in the field of music, which they exhibited so very well before this audience.

But what is even more important is this: Those boys had character. Where did that character come from? It may have come from the home. It may have come from the church. But I think as members of the Boys' Clubs Board, we can say that it very likely got a big assist from their association with the Boys' Clubs of America.

---

[1] The Bunker Hillbillies, a musical group formed by the Boys' Club of Boston, Mass., and Gregory Torres, an accordionist from the Boys' Club of Tampa, Fla., entertained at the dinner.

Yes, government can do a lot of things. We can provide food stamps for those who do not have an adequate diet. We can provide family assistance for those who are unable to earn a living. We can provide programs that will clean up the air and clean up the water and clean up our cities and make them more livable places in which to live.

But, then there comes that critical break point when the future of the society is really involved. And that is: What will be the character of the people of this country? And here it is that we need the efforts of organizations like the Boys' Clubs across this Nation, organizations which will refer, as your president and your chairman tonight have referred to them, refer to such things as patriotism and character without being ashamed of it, being proud of the fact that in this country we can produce fine young men, and that this Nation does have a mission—a mission which sometimes we do not fulfill as well as we would like—but a mission which can only be fulfilled, not simply by seeing that we are the best-fed, best-housed, best-clothed people in the world, with the best transportation system in the world, but it will only be fulfilled if our young people at some time at a very early age have instilled in them the character that we saw in those young Boys' Clubs members tonight.

That is the message I would like to leave with you. Yes, this trip to Washington was worthwhile. It was worthwhile to me, to Edgar Hoover, to Bob Finch, to see so many men who will devote their time and their energy to this cause, time and energy to a cause and to a purpose that government, with all of its immense resources, simply cannot meet.

We commend you for what you are doing and we hope that you will spend just as much of your time, your efforts, and your money in meeting this responsibility in the years ahead.

Thank you.

NOTE: The President spoke at 10:55 p.m. in the East Room at the White House. Albert L. Cole was chairman, and John L. Burns, president of the Boys' Clubs of America. Mr. Cole had presented the President with a gold and silver apple on behalf of the Boys' Clubs of America.

467   Remarks at the White House Conference on Food, Nutrition, and Health.   *December 2, 1969*

Members of the Cabinet, Mr. Mayor, all of the distinguished guests on the platform, and all the distinguished representatives to this Conference:

I very much appreciate the opportunity to be here, and before speaking myself, I want to express my appreciation to those who are arranging the Conference, to Dr. [Jean] Mayer and others, for the introductions that have been arranged.

I understand that Ezra Ellis,[1] who came from my hometown of Whittier, California, gave the invocation, and I am most grateful for that, and I am most grateful, too, that the Mayor of my city, Washington, D.C., Mayor Washington, is here today. I think he is doing a fine job as Mayor of this city.

I am not going to talk about the problems of the District, except indirectly at this point, but as I speak about the legislative imperatives, three of which I will mention in my address, I want you to know that at the very top of the list of other imperatives are the programs for the District of Columbia.

We have offered a number of programs that are new in this field and some that are old, but we have talked about the Dis-

trict for years. It is time to act about the District of Columbia, and under the Mayor's leadership we do plan to act, and with your help we will do so.

As all of you are aware, this is an historic Conference. It is particularly an historic Conference for me because it is the first White House Conference that I have had the opportunity to address as President of the United States. I have addressed others as Vice President. And it is the first that we have had in this administration.

This meeting marks an historic milestone. What it does is to set the seal of urgency on our national commitment to put an end to hunger and malnutrition due to poverty in America.

At the same time, it marks the beginning of a new, more determined, and more concerted drive than ever before, to reduce the malnutrition that derives from ignorance or inadvertence.

I recognize that many of you who are here and who have participated in the panels have been under enormous pressure, because you have had a relatively short time for the vast amount of work that it took to put this Conference together and to prepare for it.

However, that pressure reflects the priority of the subject we are here to discuss. It reflects the sense of urgency that

---

[1] Rev. Ezra Ellis, formerly of the First Friends Church of Whittier, who studied with the President at Whittier College.

we all feel.

Until this moment in our history as a nation, the central question has been whether we as a nation would accept the problem of malnourishment as a national responsibility.

That moment is past. On May 6 I asserted to the Congress that "the moment is at hand to put an end to hunger in America itself. For all time."

Speaking for this administration, I not only accept the responsibility—I claim the responsibility.

Malnourishment is a national concern because we are a nation that cares about its people, how they feel, how they live. We care whether they are well and whether they are happy.

First of all there is a moral imperative: Our national conscience requires it. We must because we can. We are the world's richest nation. We are its best educated nation. We have an agricultural abundance that ranks as a miracle of the modern world. This Nation cannot long continue to live with its conscience if millions of its own people are unable to get an adequate diet.

Even in purely practical terms there are compelling considerations requiring this challenge to be met.

A child ill-fed is dulled in curiosity, lower in stamina, distracted from learning. A worker ill-fed is less productive, more often absent from work. The mounting cost of medical care for diet-related illnesses; remedial education required to overcome diet-related slowness in school; institutionalization and loss of full productive potential; all of these place a heavy economic burden on a society as a whole.

And for many of us, and for me, as I know for many of you, this subject also evokes vivid personal memories. I grew up in the Great Depression. I shall never forget the hopelessness that I saw so starkly etched on so many faces—the silent gratitude of others lucky enough to enjoy three square meals a day, or sometimes even one.

I recall in my native State of California in the '30's, families that I knew, that I went to school with, subsisting on bread and gravy, bread and milk, beans. And later on in the '30's, in North Carolina, families who knew nothing much more than black-eyed peas, turnip greens.

We have come a long way since then, but we still have a long way to go.

The question now is: What will we do about it?

We begin with the troublesome complex of definitions and causes.

Now experts can argue—and they do and you will—about the magnitude of the problem: how many are hungry, how many malnourished, how severely they are malnourished. Precise statistical data remain elusive and often contradictory. However, Dr. Arnold Schaefer, the man in charge of the National Nutrition Survey, recently made this cautious but very forceful observation. He said:

"We have been alerted by recent studies that our population who are 'malnutrition risks' is beyond anticipated findings, and also that in some of our vulnerable population groups—pre-school children, the aged, teenagers and the poor—malnutrition is indeed a serious medical problem."

We don't know just how many Americans are actually hungry and we don't know how many Americans suffer from malnutrition, who eat enough but do not eat the right things. But we do know there are too many Americans in both categories.

We can argue the extent, but hunger exists.

We can argue the severity, but malnutrition exists.

The plain fact is that a great many Americans are not eating well enough to sustain health.

We see, then, that the problem of hunger and malnutrition is, really, two separate problems. One is to insure that everyone is able to obtain an adequate diet. The second is to insure that people actually are properly fed, where they have the ability to obtain the adequate diet.

On the one hand, we are dealing with problems of income distribution. On the other hand, with problems of education, habit, taste, behavior, personal preferences—the whole complex of things that lead people to act the way they do, to make the choices they do.

The answers to many of these questions are difficult to come by. The very fact that the same question evokes so many different, conflicting answers is itself testimony as to how fragile is the basis of our knowledge.

Assuming we can agree on definitions, and the causes of malnourishment, how do we eradicate it?

Now some will answer that the magic ingredient is money, and money certainly is one ingredient, and a very important one. The more than $5 billion that I have proposed for new or expanded programs for food and family assistance next year would go a long way toward bringing the problem under control.

And in this connection, I would urge each of you in this great Conference to enlist yourself in an effort to win passage of three landmark pieces of legislation I have already recommended to Congress.

One of these is what many observers consider to be the most important piece of domestic legislation proposed in the past 50 years, the establishment of a floor under the income of every American family.

For the first time—Mr. Moynihan [Counsellor to the President] please notice—for the first time, this new family assistance plan would give every American family a basic income, wherever in America that family may live. For the first time, it would put cash into the hands of families because they are poor, rather than because they fit certain categories. When enacted, this measure alone will either supplement the incomes or provide the basis for the incomes of 25 million American men, women, and children.

Our basic policies for improvement of the living conditions of the poor are based on this proposition: that the best judge of each family's priorities is that family itself, that the best way to ameliorate the hardships of poverty is to provide the family with additional income—to be spent as that family sees fit.

Now, some will argue with this proposition. Some argue that the poor cannot be trusted to make their own decisions, and therefore, the Government should dole out food and clothing and medicine, according to a schedule of what the Government thinks is needed.

Well, I disagree. I believe there are no experts present in this great gathering who know more about the realities of hunger and malnutrition than those among you who are here because you have suffered from it, or than those among you who are here who do suffer from it, from great cities, from wornout farms, from barren reservations, from frozen tundra, from tiny islands half a world away.

The task of government is not to make

decisions for you or for anyone. The task of government is to enable you to make decisions for yourselves. Not to see the truth of that statement is fundamentally to mistake the genius of democracy. We have made too many mistakes of this type—but no more. Our job is to get resources to people in need and then to let them run their own lives.

And now I would stress that all of you who have been so strong and effective in achieving a breakthrough on national awareness on hunger, will become an equally strong citizen lobby for welfare reform. The needs of the poor range far beyond food, though that is often the most visible and heart-rending aspect of poverty. More basically, the poor need money with which they can meet the full range of their needs, from basic shelter to medicine, to clothes for school, to transportation. And they need these resources in a program framework that builds incentives for self-support and for family stability.

Let the reform of the bankrupt welfare system in this country be the next great cause of those who come together here today.

Now the second measure that I would especially urge your support for is one that you will be considering in your deliberations. It is the reform and expansion of the food stamp program. I requested this in my May 8 message on hunger. This has been designed to complement the welfare program. While the welfare proposals may be subject to long debate, I hope and I expect that Congress will act quickly on the expanded food stamp plan.

The Nation's food programs have been shot through with inequities, as you will find, notably, the fact that many counties have not participated, and the fact that because food stamps had to be bought with cash many of the neediest were unable to participate.

We are pressing hard to bring every county into one or other of the food distribution programs, and the new food stamp bill would provide stamps free to those most in need—while expanding the program to a level that would reach $2.5 billion a year when fully implemented.

In a related matter, we already are greatly expanding our school lunch programs, with the target of reaching every needy schoolchild with a free or reduced-cost lunch by the end of the current fiscal year.

Now, there is a third measure, a third measure which at first will seem unrelated, but which is directly related to this conference. I ask your support for the Commission on Population Growth and the American Future which I have proposed to Congress and which has been most favorably received, not only in the Congress, but by church and civic organizations throughout the Nation.

America, I believe, has come to see how necessary it is to be responsibly concerned with this subject. In proposing the Commission, I also declared that it would be the goal of this administration to provide "adequate family planning services within the next 5 years to all those who want them but cannot afford them." And there are some 5 million women in low-income families who are in exactly that situation. I can report that the steps to meet that goal—a goal 5 years away—have already been taken within the administration. The program is underway.

Now taken together, these three measures would virtually eliminate the problem of poverty as a cause of malnutrition.

Their dollar cost is high, but their practical benefits to the Nation are immense.

I know that your panels have advanced proposals for massive efforts on many fronts. They demonstrate that the goal cannot be won by government alone.

It is for each to ask how he, individually, can respond to the questions being asked here. For example:

—can foods be better labeled, can they be made more nutritious, be fortified with available additives?

—can industry, the schools, government, and citizens individually join effectively in a program of public education?

—can school lunch programs feasibly be improved?

—can voluntary programs by citizens and community organizations teach people what to eat, to close the knowledge gap?

The fact that so many groups are represented here today is itself evidence of a new sense of community responsibility, of industry responsibility, of individual responsibility. The fact that so many women are represented here, especially, is evidence of an enormous resource, particularly in the volunteer field, a resource that can do so much to insure our success.

I, of course, in my official capacity, have already indicated legislative programs that I shall be supporting. But speaking now as one who from time to time can act in a volunteer capacity, I know the power of simply dropping a word as to what a President or a potential President does in certain fields.

I recall in your field, about 18 months ago I was being interviewed on a talk show. I was asked how I kept my weight down—that was my problem rather than the other way around. I answered—I thought rather low-key—that the doctor had told me to eat cottage cheese. The difficulty is I don't like cottage cheese. And so I said I took his advice, but I put catsup on it.

You can't imagine how many letters I got. The dairy industry wrote and told me that I should like cottage cheese. The catsup industry wrote and told me to try it on my cereal. And others wrote and said that catsup with cottage cheese had to be unhealthy. I pointed to the fact that my grandmother lived to be 93 and she ate it all her life, so that was the answer.

I use this facetious example to only indicate that the power of example—not just from a President, but from those in this room in this whole field—of not just how much, but how and what we eat with regard to diet can be tremendous.

Now, I want to turn to—with Dr. Mayer's suggestion and his approval—to a very important procedural point, one that I discussed with him when he took the position which he is filling and one that I want to speak very directly to you about.

We have not attempted to program those in this room. We have not attempted to program you as to the questions you may ask or the answers and recommendations that you will make.

I expect to read that you had a lively difference of opinion during this Conference. As a matter of fact, I have already read about a lively difference of opinion that you have had during this Conference and that is as it should be. From an airing of views of all sides, answers and ideas will appear. Answers and ideas are what we seek in this process. Obviously, if we knew all the answers we would not have convened the Conference in the first place.

That is why you are here.

I will say this: I want to speak quite directly. I can imagine that in this room are many people who have attended White House conferences before. For 22 years I have been watching White House conferences. I have attended them and I have seen the effort that went into them, an enormous volunteer dedicated effort. I have seen it too often wither away in futility as the reports gathered dust on Government shelves.

Well, beginning with this Conference, that is going to change. It will be the policy of this administration to follow up each White House conference, beginning with this Conference, with a second meeting one year later, bringing together the key participants of the original conference to reexamine its findings, to measure what has been done about implementing them. We believe that is the only proper procedure.

I know that you take your work seriously and we are going to take your report seriously. I expect the results of this Conference to be not just words, but action.

This Conference marks a coalescing of the national conscience; it marks a triumph of the American system.

Now, I realize that there is a ready disposition, whenever we confront an ill that is still uncorrected in America, to cry that "the system" is corrupt, or "the system" has failed.

Our so-called "system" has been under heavy and sustained assault, not from one quarter but from many quarters.

But let us not forget, that system is what brought us here together today in this Conference. It is a system that embraces compassion and practicality; it has given us the abundance that allows us to consider ending hunger and malnutrition.

Ours is the most productive and most generous country the world has ever seem. Less than 5 percent of our population—according to Secretary Hardin, Secretary of Agriculture—produces enough food to feed all the American people and to supply the needs of millions in other countries as well. In the years since World War II the United States has provided more than $30 billion in food, in the form of aid, to needy nations and peoples abroad.

I have traveled to most of the nations of the world, in Asia, in Africa, and Latin America. Do you realize that in most of the world today a conference like this would be meaningless because those nations would lack the resources to produce the food to meet the objectives that this Conference may decide should be met or lack the resources to purchase the food which they themselves would not be able to produce?

It is precisely because our system has succeeded so well that we are now able to address the goals of this Conference and the fact that we are gathered here is an example of one of the greatest strengths of that same system. It has a capacity for self-correction, for self-regeneration; its constant reaching out to identify new or additional needs and to meet those needs, the readiness of its citizens to join in that effort, volunteering their time and their talents, as you are volunteering your time and your talents today.

This Nation has the capacity to provide an adequate diet for every American. The calling of this Conference demonstrates that we have the will to achieve this goal. What we need is to find the most effective means for doing so consistent with maintaining the vitality of the system that makes it all possible.

And so I will review your recommendations with great care.

And I will ask you to go about drawing up those recommendations with equally great care.

My fellow Americans, as you begin this Conference I commit to your concern the lives of millions of Americans, too young, too old, or too hurt by life to do without your help. I commit to your concern the not less serious task of helping to bring the rest of America to understand what we seek and to join us in adding this new dimension to the concept of American democracy. For at this very moment we are gathered at one of those great historical moments when it

becomes possible for all of us to act a little better than we are, and in so doing, to leave this great and good Nation a little better because we were there.

NOTE: The President spoke at 10:28 a.m. in the Sheraton Hall at the Sheraton Park Hotel in Washington. The mayor of the District of Columbia was Walter E. Washington.

The Conference report was transmitted to the President by Dr. Jean Mayer with a covering letter dated December 24, 1969. It is entitled "White House Conference on Food Nutrition, and Health: Final Report" (Government Printing Office, 341 pp.).

Also released on December 24 was a news briefing on the Conference report by Dr. Jean Mayer, Edward J. Heckman, Administrator of the Food and Nutrition Service, and John R. Price, Jr., Executive Secretary of the Urban Affairs Council.

468   Letter to Senate Leaders Mike Mansfield and Hugh Scott on the Tax Reform Bill.   *December 2, 1969*

THE SENATE is to be commended for the deliberate speed with which it is considering H.R. 13270, the Tax Reform Act of 1969. I hope that meaningful and acceptable legislation can be passed by Congress before the end of this year. But to be acceptable, such legislation must be equitable and it must meet the test of fiscal responsibility.

Certain amendments scheduled to be considered by the Senate this week fail these tests. I refer to the proposals to raise the personal exemption from $600 to either $800 or $1,000, and to establish a $1,000 uniform standard deduction. Those proposals would be substituted for the major tax-relief provisions of H.R. 13270 as voted by the Senate Finance Committee.

The Finance Committee bill would result in a net revenue gain for fiscal years

1970 and 1971, and a minor loss in 1972. It is consistent with our determined efforts to control inflation.

This bill fights inflation by extending the income tax surcharge at 5 percent until mid-1970; postponing scheduled reductions in certain excises; and repealing the 7-percent investment credit. It is simply not in the national interest then to add new inflationary pressures through reductions in personal income taxes which are too early and too generous.

The proposed amendments would substitute imbalanced, inequitable relief for the Committee's evenhanded tax rate reductions in all income brackets.

The proposal to raise the personal exemption to $1,000 would fall some $6 billion short of the Committee bill during the next 2½ years. The $800 exemption would result in a $4.8 billion short-fall.

The Administration's economical Low Income Allowance, which would take some 5 million citizens off the tax rolls and lower taxes on 7 million others, goes far enough this time.

The spirit of this legislation is tax reform which attempts to make taxation fairer to all Americans not tax reduction. It would be unfortunate indeed if Congress violated this spirit of reform and thereby jeopardized both the source of revenue for vital national goals and the fight against inflation.

This Administration is strongly committed to tax reform. I have stated that I will sign a good tax reform bill. I still intend to do so, but it must be equitably constructed and it must be fiscally responsible.

I urge the Senate to accept the tax relief provisions so carefully constructed by the Senate Finance Committee.

Sincerely,

RICHARD NIXON

469   Statement on Signing Bills for the Preservation of Presidential Birthplaces and Homes. *December 2, 1969*

WE HAVE DEVELOPED a tradition of preserving the birthplaces and homes of our Presidents to commemorate their dedication and service to the Nation and to serve as a tangible symbol and inspiration for present and future generations of Americans. Today we have an unprecedented opportunity to do honor simultaneously to three American Presidents—William Howard Taft, Dwight David Eisenhower, and Lyndon Baines Johnson.

The legislation I am approving carries this tradition forward in three steps. H.R. 7066 and S. 2000 will preserve and establish as national historic sites the birthplaces and boyhood homes of President Taft in Cincinnati, Ohio, and President Johnson in Johnson City, Texas. S.J. Res. 26 will authorize the necessary funds to preserve and develop President Eisenhower's home and farm at Gettysburg, Pennsylvania, already established as a national historic site.

The approval of these three measures will now make these American homes as much a part of the Nation's history as are the achievements of the men who occupied them. I am sure everyone will understand my very special personal feeling at being able to pay such a tribute to President Eisenhower, with whom I was privileged to work closely for many years and for whom I will always have the deepest affection and admiration.

NOTE: As enacted, the bills (H.R. 7066, S. 2000, and S.J. Res. 26) are Public Laws 91–132, 91–134, and 91–133, respectively (83 Stat. 273–274).

470   Remarks at the Opening Session of the Governors' Conference at the Department of State. *December 3, 1969*

Ladies and gentlemen:

It is my pleasure to welcome all of you, also, and to make one other presentation.

We presented the First Lady and Mrs. Agnew, and I think the first lady of the Governors' Conference, Mrs. [John A.]

Love, also ought to stand and be heard later. She will represent all the first ladies from the various States who are here.

This Conference is an unusual one, as you have heard, because not only are the Governors in attendance but their wives and their families.

I would like to tell you how this Conference came about. We had a presentation in the Cabinet, which, I think those present agreed, was one of the most impressive and certainly one that had greater effect on our thinking than any that we have had.

We had the same presentation for Members of Congress. I happened to sit by Speaker McCormack that day on the one side, and Mike Mansfield, the Democratic leader, on the other side. Each individually told me that in all of the years they have attended bipartisan conferences at the White House, that presentation on narcotics and dangerous drugs was the most effective that they had ever heard.

For this reason, the fact that this presentation had been so effective before the Cabinet and before the legislative leaders, we thought it also should be made to the Governors. It should be made to you also, because if we are to do what needs to be done, we not only have to do it at the Federal level, we need of course, State cooperation, city cooperation, county cooperation, government volunteer activities at all levels.

Now the presentation itself will cover in more specific terms the general points I would like to make.

First, with regard to the magnitude of the problem—and I am going to use statistics that are deliberately cautious but which certainly can be sustained by any reasonable objective observer: The number of people in the United States who use marihuana is 8 million; the number of people who use heroin—and when they use it, that means they will not be able to get off its use—is 180,000.

But now putting it in another dimension, the number of people of college age who use marihuana or have used it, is one-third of all the college students of the Nation. The number of students of high school age who have used marihuana is 16 percent.

Now let's look at where those various groups break down. There has been sort of a general thought that so far as drugs were concerned, we find them in the ghettos, among the deprived, those who are depressed and turn to drugs as a last resort. That may have once been the case. It is not the case today.

The primary use, as far as drugs are concerned, has moved to the upper middle class, those families who have better opportunities than others who have less of this world's goods. Consequently, we see that the problem is not limited to any region of the country, it isn't limited to any segment of the society. It hits the young as well as the old and is indeed a national problem.

Now, what is its effect? Here we get some arguments. There are those who say marihuana has perhaps as little effect as alcohol has, and, of course, that all depends on the quantity in either case. There are others who point out that when we start with marihuana, then the inevitable result is to move on to LSD or whatever provides the bigger thrill, until eventually the individual moves to heroin or the so-called hard narcotics from which there is virtually no recovery. But we do know effects in terms of hard statistics.

987

I notice that Mayor [Walter E.] Washington is here from Washington, D.C., who has major responsibilities—we were talking about this problem the other day, the problem of robberies in the city, and it is interesting to note that over half of the robberies in the city of Washington are committed by people who are addicted to drugs, which indicates either cause or effect, or both. Whether one leads to the other or vice versa is not really material to the point. There is a direct relationship in one way or the other.

We can also go further in terms of that effect. In the city of New York alone, I was looking at some statistics that were presented by Mr. Moynihan, and in 1 week 100 people died in the city of New York alone because of overdoses of drugs—heroin, or some other types. This is an indication of what drugs can do.

But let's put it in other, certainly broader, more important dimensions. When we look to the history of civilizations we find that those civilizations that have turned on a broad, general basis to drugs, and particularly when that affliction reaches the leader classes of those civilizations, those civilizations inevitably lose their spirit. They go down. They are destroyed. This is what happens.

The question is, is it going to happen to America? We have many problems in this country—material problems, problems we will deal with in this Conference when we meet again in February, and which we will deal with in Washington, and you will deal with in your State capital, problems of the environment and other problems that can be dealt with in a material way. But when the spirit of the people is destroyed, it is almost impossible to restore that spirit.

There is not any question but that when drug addiction becomes a national malady, affecting all segments of the population, that there is the danger that the spirit of a nation may certainly be impaired.

These are some of the factors we have to have in mind.

There is one final point which will indicate a personal commitment. You will hear later from Art Linkletter, who will put this in very personal terms, as he put it to us when he spoke to the Cabinet and the legislative leaders.

Shortly after my nomination last year, I received a number of letters as you might imagine. I received one that was unsigned, by a girl in San Diego, who said she was 19 years of age. She told me her story. She came from a good family. She went to Sunday school and church as a little girl. She started on marihuana and then went to LSD, and she was now hooked on heroin and she was in some hospital for whatever therapy could be provided in order to restore her to some degree of health.

It was a letter which moved me emotionally, as it would have moved anyone here. The concluding paragraph of that letter was this. She said: "Mr. Nixon, I think you are going to be elected. If you are, as President, will you try to do something to see that what happened to me does not happen to other young people across this country?"

I am going to keep my promise to that young girl, and I want all of you to help me keep that promise, not because I personally have a stake in it, in the sense of politics, just as you personally would not think in those terms, but because we have a national responsibility—a national responsibility to all of the young people of this Nation to see to it that they have a chance to grow up, to grow up without having their spirit destroyed and their health destroyed by turning to drugs.

Then I would add this final point. I have learned a lot in these presentations. I must say that when they first started, I thought the answer was more penalties. I thought that the answer was simply enforce the law and that will stop people from the use of drugs. But it is not that.

When you are talking about 13-year-olds and 14-year-olds and 15-year-olds, the answed is not more penalties. The answer is information. The answer is understanding.

It is very important to be quite precise, to distinguish between marihuana and LSD and heroin so that we can all know what the effect of each is and so that we will be able to make the case against each, if the case is to be made against each on the facts as they are, rather than on the facts as we thought they were before we received the knowledge which we are going to receive in this briefing today.

We are glad that all of you are here, the Governors, their wives, and particularly their children, so that we can get the facts, and so that all of us can go back to our communities and be able to wage a campaign—a campaign of information and education that will reach all of the people in the States of this Nation, because that campaign of education and in-

formation, in my opinion, is probably more important than the criminal penalties that we will be talking about later in this session today.

That is part of the process. But when you get to the point that you have to apply criminal penalties to the users and dispensers of drugs, then the damage has already been done. What we are trying to do is get at it before they reach that point. We ask your assistance in that.

Now the presentation will go on, and you can judge for yourself whether you agree with the Congressmen and the Cabinet and the Senators about the importance of this Conference, and whether you think, in your judgment, this trip to Washington by the Governors and their families was worthwhile.

Thank you.

NOTE: The President spoke at 9:10 a.m. in the West Auditorium of the Department of State following an introduction by Vice President Spiro T. Agnew (5 Weekly Comp. Pres. Docs., p. 1693). The remarks of Secretary Finch, Art Linkletter, television and radio personality, and Dr. Daniel P. Moynihan, Counsellor to the President, together with introductory remarks by John D. Ehrlichman, Assistant to the President for Domestic Affairs, were also released by the White House Press Office.

An announcement of a presentation to the Governors of mementos from the Apollo 11 moon landing is printed in the Weekly Compilation of Presidential Documents (vol. 5, p. 1696).

471 Toasts of the President and Governor John A. Love of Colorado at a Dinner Honoring Governors Attending the Governors' Conference. *December 3, 1969*

Mr. Vice President, members of the Cabinet, Governor Love, members of the Governors' Conference:

We want to welcome you here tonight

in this house, which is your house, and to say that it is a very great privilege for us to have you here at this time.

This is the first occasion at which we

have hosted the Governors and their wives. We are delighted you are all here. We also, in welcoming you, want you to know that it has made it a special day for us, because in an unprecedented invitation, I understand, we not only have the honor of having you here but having your children here. We just wish they could be in this room with us.

Now, I am not going to impose on your time long, because they are having dinner in another part of the house or on the grounds, and we are all going to join in a few moments in what I understand is some very exciting entertainment. I thought it was the Temptations, but I understand it is the Fifth Dimension [singing group], and Al Hirt [jazz musician]. I know him, but I don't know the Fifth Dimension. But I will know them before we finish. In any event, they are waiting for that, and we are, too.

But I did not want this occasion to pass in this room, in this historic house and in this meeting, without saying a word about our program today and about our children—all of our children.

I had the sense this morning, which I am sure you also felt, that perhaps we have a greater responsibility than we have realized, to provide for our children a challenge and excitement that they are seeking in other directions.

I noted that over and over again in the theme that ran through the drug abuse briefings, that those who turned toward drugs were turning to escape or turning for challenge or turning for excitement.

And now I am going to say something that will be unfashionable, unfashionable perhaps not in this room but certainly it will be unfashionable in most of the academic community, if I may use that term, Dr. Kissinger. I know that we say these

days that the problem with American youth, where they have problems, is that life is so hard. I don't agree. I think the problem with American youth is that life is so easy. Perhaps what American youth needs is a challenge.

As they turn to these drugs and to all of the other things other than drugs, to give that lift, it is because of boredom, the boredom of a life in which, perhaps, they do not have the necessities, the necessities that some of us may have had to work to achieve in order to meet the challenges of life.

What I am really trying to say is this: We sit here in a room tonight that is full of history, and all of the memories of the men who were here. Every man who has been President of the United States has been in this house except George Washington. John Adams was the first one who was here. And then through the years you can think of them in this room. Andrew Jackson was here—Abraham Lincoln, Grover Cleveland, Theodore Roosevelt, Woodrow Wilson, Herbert Hoover, Franklin Roosevelt, Harry Truman, Dwight Eisenhower, John Kennedy.

We think of all of those men. We think of the history that has passed through these rooms. The heads of state and heads of government and all the rest have been here.

And we think of this country, what it means to us, what it meant to them. We think of this country at the beginning, what it was then, not very populous, 3 million people, certainly not very strong. Militarily it was a weakling among the nations of the world, even though they won the Revolutionary War.

It was a poverty stricken nation among the nations of the world, even though it had great physical resources. And yet when America was only 3 million and 13 States, and weak and poor, America even then had something—let's call it a fifth dimension. It meant something to the world. It was the hope of the world. It was a challenging, exciting place in which to live.

I should say something else. The air was clean then and the water was clean then and America had all of its frontiers in front of it.

So now we move through 190 years and we look at America today, the strongest nation in the world, the richest nation in the world. Sure we have some problems, problems that I will refer to very briefly before I close.

But as we look at our strength and our wealth, we find, too, this enormous frustration that seems to infect so many of our people—and I refer not to those who are poor. They have their problems but they are different. But I refer to those who are really our children and the children of our friends and our neighbors, others whom we have known.

And the problem, it seems to me, is summarized in the fact that sometimes we have lost sight of the fact that great wealth and great military strength is not enough, that a nation and a people must have something more. It must have a great ideal and it is the idealism of America that has made this country great. That is what we had in the beginning. That is what we really have now, if we only knew it. And if you have any doubt about it, go abroad. Go to all the countries of the world, and I have seen all of them. Go to Bucharest, Romania, and see 1 million people on the streets shouting and cheering, not for a President—they don't know me from anybody else—but for an idea. America stood for them and meant for

them something that was far more important than military strength, something far more important than economic might.

This is what I would remind us of on this occasion.

Now I come to the concluding point. How can we give a challenge, a challenge to young America? As your conference in February—and I would just like to lift the curtain a bit on what I am going to talk about then. I think it is time to move forward on the whole subject of the quality of life in America, the environment, how we can clean up our rivers and our water, how we can clean up our air, how we can clean up our streets and our cities, how we can move forward on all fronts so that life in this country in addition to being very rich and very strong, can also have that extra dimension, the extra dimension of idealism that somehow caught the imagination of the world, that still has a great deal of that imagination, but that has been lost upon a great part of the younger generation, a great part of it—not all, not a majority—but a part of that generation who may be the leaders of the future.

This is our challenge. You as Governors, all of us in leadership positions, we have a responsibility, a responsibility to deal with the hard facts, the problems of crime and the problems of delinquency and the problems of environment and all the others, and budget and so forth that we wrestle with day by day. But our greatest challenge is to provide some sense of idealism and some sense of challenge to the younger generation so that they can be proud of this country as they should be proud of it.

They are lucky to be born in the United States of America. Anyone who has a choice in the world today would not choose any other country but the United

States. Never let them forget it. Never let us forget it.

Having said all these things, let me say, I enjoyed meeting your children. They are wonderful children. It is difficult, as Art Linkletter said, for a child to grow up any time and it is particularly difficult for a child to grow up as the child of any celebrity, and particularly a politician.

There is one thing Harry Truman and I share in common. When he wrote the letter to that music critic,[1] I was with him all the way.

And I can tell you, they can say and write anything about me they want, and they will, but if they say anything about Tricia or Julie, believe me, I am going to be after them.

And so, I, in the last conference, proposed a toast to the first ladies of the 50 States. At this conference, will you all rise and join in a toast to our children?

NOTE: The President proposed the toast at 10:03 p.m. in the State Dining Room at the White House.

Governor John A. Love of Colorado, Chairman of the Conference, responded as follows:

---

[1] In a strongly worded letter in 1950, President Truman took issue with music critic Paul Hume over Mr. Hume's unfavorable review of a singing performance by the President's daughter Margaret.

Mr. President, Mrs. Nixon, Mr. Vice President, Mrs. Agnew:

I thought of so many great things that I wanted to say, but to follow and respond to those wonderful words leaves me in a position where I can't say all that I would like to say.

I know I speak for all the Governors and their wives and their children here in voicing our gratitude for this wonderful day. I am sure that the various participants on the great problem of drugs, the briefing on foreign affairs, the opportunity to be with, and ask and exchange ideas with the various Cabinet members and, of course, to be here this evening in this, as you say, historic house, and perhaps most important of all, to be here with our families and in a minor way, but the first time I have ever come in the front door [*laughter*]—which is wonderful.

I couldn't agree more with your definition of the problem that confronts us all. It has been said in many ways today, by you more eloquently than anybody else. But perhaps for the first time in the history of mankind a substantial portion of the population of this Nation has a choice. Now this has not been true forever, or ever before this.

And choice is an uncomfortable thing and it presents, perhaps, even a greater challenge than our forefathers were faced with.

We were most appreciative of the opportunity to be here. We are appreciative of this increment and additional commitment to your belief in the viability, the necessity of the Federal system.

I would simply like to, with a great deal of affection and gratitude and respect, propose a toast to the President of the United States.

472   Remarks on the Decision of Judge Clement F. Haynsworth, Jr., To Continue as Chief Judge of the United States Court of Appeals for the 4th Circuit. *December 4, 1969*

Ladies and gentlemen:

Immediately after the Senate action in a very close vote in not confirming Judge Haynsworth for the Supreme Court I called the Judge on the phone. I asked him

if he would continue to serve as Chief Judge of the 4th Circuit.

The Judge at that time said he wanted to think about it. He felt that the primary consideration was whether the confirmation hearings and the refusal of the Senate to confirm him had impaired his ability to serve on that Court in an effective way, in the way that was justified.

I have discussed the matter with the Judge. We have had an exchange of correspondence and I have talked to him today.

I must say that after the brutally vicious and, in my opinion, unfair attack on his integrity, I would well understand why the Judge would retire to private life. A weak man would; a fearful man would. The Judge is not a weak man. He is a strong man.

I told him of my philosophy which is that a great philosophy is one that is never without defeat, but it is always without fear. The Judge has suffered a defeat, but he is without fear.

A man of his courage, his integrity, is needed on one of the highest courts of this land and I am very delighted to announce today that the Judge will continue to serve as Chief Judge of the 4th Circuit.

NOTE: The President spoke at 11:10 a.m. in the Roosevelt Room at the White House.

Judge Haynsworth's response is printed in the Weekly Compilation of Presidential Documents (vol. 5, p. 1698).

473 Statement Announcing the Appointment of Stephen Hess as National Chairman of the White House Conference on Children and Youth. *December* 5, 1969

ONCE EACH DECADE, since the days of Theodore Roosevelt, the President of the United States calls together a large and representative body of his fellow citizens to assess the present circumstances and future prospects of the Nation's children and youth. Out of these efforts have come valuable stocktaking, heightened awareness, and much useful legislation and action on all levels of government.

This oldest of all White House Conferences, the White House Conference on Children and Youth, will take place in Washington on December 13–18, 1970. Through individuals, State committees, voluntary and professional organizations, and Federal agencies, 6 million Americans ultimately will become involved in its planning and deliberations.

Today I am pleased to announce the appointment of Stephen Hess as National Chairman of the White House Conference on Children and Youth.

I will serve as Honorary Chairman, but it will be the responsibility of Mr. Hess, acting on my behalf, to organize and direct this considerable undertaking.

Never has this White House Conference come at a time of greater national questioning. Long held attitudes on such subjects as family planning, pornography, health services, school curricula, sex education, family structure, drug abuse, moral standards, governance of higher education, responsiveness of government—all are now openly debated and challenged.

The White House Conference can and will define problems, seek new knowledge, evaluate past successes and failures, and outline alternative courses of action.

Earlier this year I made a national commitment to providing all American children an opportunity for healthful and stimulating development during the first 5 years of life. We now know that the process of learning begins in the earliest months of life and that much of a child's intelligence is set long before he enters his first classroom. It is thus incumbent upon us to invent new social institutions and techniques to respond to this knowledge. I will look to the work of the White House Conference to advance this commitment.

Also earlier this year work was begun in the Urban Affairs Council, under the direction of Dr. Moynihan and Mr. Hess, to assist me in formulating a National Youth Policy. It is clear that the many Federal programs that affect youth are often contradictory in effect. Some may indeed lengthen that period between childhood and adulthood which we call youth, thereby increasing the sense of frustration and alienation felt by so many young people. This effort to find ways to decrease this period of dependency and bring our youth more rapidly into full participation in society will now be joined by Mr. Hess and his colleagues.

At a time when government often seems far away and immovable—when many of our youth are rightly asking, "Who's listening? Who cares?"—I hope that this White House Conference, especially through the active involvement of a great many young people, will provide a positive answer. In this regard, I have asked Mr. Hess to listen well to the voices of young America—in the universities, on the farms, the assembly lines, the street corners. I have known Steve Hess a long time, and I know him to be a good listener.

As he begins this challenging new assignment, I pledge him the full cooperation of the Federal Government.

NOTE: Also released by the White House Press Office was biographical data about Mr. Hess, and a news briefing on a meeting of the Urban Affairs Council by Dr. Daniel P. Moynihan, Counsellor to the President, Robert H. Finch, Secretary of Health, Education, and Welfare, Mr. Hess, and John R. Price, Jr., whose appointment as a Special Assistant to the President and Executive Secretary of the Urban and Rural Affairs Councils was announced at the briefing by Ronald L. Ziegler, Press Secretary to the President.

474   Memorandum Requesting Support for the Minority Business Enterprise Program.   *December 5, 1969*

Memorandum to Heads of Departments and Agencies:

SUBJECT: Federal Procurement and Minority Business Enterprise

Minority business enterprise is a major concern of this Administration. For that reason, on March 5, 1969, I established by Executive Order the Office of Minority Business Enterprise in the Department of Commerce to coordinate the efforts and resources of Federal departments and agencies and private enterprise in this field.

One of the most important ways to promote this effort is to develop a program which will increase the involvement of minority group contractors in the multibillion dollar Federal procurement program. The Office of Minority Business Enterprise, the Small Business Administration, and a Federal Task Force on Procurement—under the leadership of Robert L. Kunzig, Administrator of General Services—are working closely with members of my staff to develop such a program.

Leonard Garment, my Special Consultant, and Robert J. Brown, my Special Assistant, will assist in the development of that program, keep me informed of progress, and make such recommendations as they feel are necessary.

I request that during the period of program development, all departments and agencies provide to the Office of Minority Business Enterprise and the Small Business Administration full support in the following ways:

—Provide procurement opportunities.

—Supply management and technical experts.

—Help to set goals to measure progress of the efforts being made.

—Name a representative of your department or agency to pursue these efforts.

This program has high priority on this Administration's agenda. I trust that all of you will give it your best attention and effort.

RICHARD NIXON

475   Statement on Signing the Wildlife Bill. *December 5, 1969*

IN APPROVING H.R. 11363 today, I am signing into law the most significant action this Nation has ever taken in an international effort to preserve the world's wildlife.

This act protecting wild creatures serves three purposes: It will help the States to conserve such species as our endangered alligators and other reptiles and lesser life as well; it will help other nations preserve species threatened with extinction by prohibiting importation of such animals into the United States; and it will provide additional authority and funds for this country to acquire land for the protection of native wildlife which is endangered. In addition, this legislation calls for an international meeting to develop binding conventions for worldwide conservation of animals.

This bill represents the culmination of many years of activity by many people in and out of government. It is effective and just legislation, and I take great pleasure in signing it into law.

NOTE: As enacted, the bill (H.R. 11363) is Public Law 91–135 (83 Stat. 275).

476   Remarks on Arrival at Fort Smith, Arkansas, To Attend the Arkansas-Texas Football Game.   *December 6, 1969*

GOVERNOR [Winthrop] Rockefeller and all of the people who are here at the airport at Fort Smith, I want you to know how much I appreciate this very warm welcome. It is warm, at least as far as the welcome is concerned.

I want you to know, too, that, as I come here to this great football game at Fayetteville, that I have to be in somewhat of a nonpartisan position, because on the airplane we brought down some members of the delegation from the State of Arkansas—Senator [John L.] McClellan, Senator [J. William] Fulbright, John Paul Hammerschmidt, your own Congressman—but I also brought along some members of the delegation from Texas. So I have to be in between the two.

All that I know is that we are going to see today, in this 100th anniversary of football, one of the great football games of all time, and both of them I wish could be Number 1. But at the end, whichever is Number 1 will deserve it, and the Number 2 team will still go to a bowl and be a great team.

We want to also say, clearly apart from football, that as we flew over the airport and I saw the cars parked for, well, actually not just feet nor yards, but miles down the road, and then as I went down this line and shook hands with people and I felt how cold your hands were, and your noses a little red, and the rest, I realized some of you have been here a long time.

I just want you to know how much we appreciate it. To come from Washington, to get this kind of a welcome, in the heart of the country, right here in Arkansas, means a great deal to us.

We are going to take back memories of that welcome.

I want you to know, too, that I did not have the opportunity of visiting Arkansas during the 1968 campaign. This is the first time I have had a chance to visit Arkansas, since becoming President. After this warm welcome, it isn't going to be the last. I want to come back here.

Now, if I could just close my remarks with one other thought, I realize that this is the beginning of a holiday season. It isn't going to be much of a holiday season for the Congress. I think we are going to have to stay and work during most of that Christmas season, although I haven't worked that out yet with the Congressmen and Senators. But I do want you to know, for everybody here, that Mrs. Nixon and I and our two daughters extend our very best wishes for a very Merry Christmas and a Happy New Year to all of you.

Thank you.

NOTE: The President spoke at 11:20 a.m. at Fort Smith Municipal Airport, Fort Smith, Ark.

477 Remarks During a Television Interview in Fayetteville, Arkansas. *December 6, 1969*

MR. SCHENKEL.[1] Mr. President, Bud and I are so pleased that you came up into our office to pay us a visit at half time.

THE PRESIDENT. Well, Chris, it is a little warmer up here than it is down in the stands. I must say I have never seen a football game where there is more excitement in the air than there is today. This whole State is just alive. I can feel it.

We stopped at an airport about an hour away by car and everybody there—

that is all they are talking about, this game.

MR. SCHENKEL. And of course, with their nickname, the Razorbacks, and the calling of the hogs, it is a most unusual setting for this game.

THE PRESIDENT. I have never heard a yell like that before.

I am sitting, incidentally, in a very interesting spot. I have four Texas Congressmen sitting in back of me and two Senators from Arkansas and a Congressman. Believe me, there is a lot of rivalry here in the stands.

MR. SCHENKEL. You talk about the

---

[1] The President was interviewed by Chris Schenkel, ABC sportscaster, along with Charles B. (Bud) Wilkinson, widely known sports figure who was a Special Consultant to the President.

pep rallies, Mr. President. In Austin, the night before the team flew here, at the stadium, their pep rally for the Longhorns drew 28,000 fans, most of them students, and that is most heartwarming.

THE PRESIDENT. Well, looking at this game, it is for the ranking of Number 1. Incidentally, I say it is for that, having in mind the fact that Penn State has been giving me a lot of flak this week for coming down here.

MR. SCHENKEL. Did you get many wires?

THE PRESIDENT. Yes. Penn State is the team that will have the longest undefeated streak for the year. You have covered them, and I know they are a great team. Maybe we ought to have a super college bowl after this.

But whatever the case might be, looking at these two teams today, either one is going to be Number 1 by vote of the writers. What is more important is the tremendous spirit that they generate.

It is good for people to be for somebody, to be for a team. You can learn a lot from losing as well as winning. I have had a little experience in that.

MR. SCHENKEL. Well, Mr. President, with the favorite team, Texas, down seven to nothing here at half time, that is true. The first half of your career you were down but, boy, you came back a winner.

THE PRESIDENT. I was down more than seven to nothing, I would say. It was sort of a fourth quarter finish, you know, and a pass perhaps in the last 30 seconds to win. But that is what counts.

MR. SCHENKEL. I am one of the many millions who are glad you won.

You watched football for years, and I know you watch it from an analytical standpoint, whether it be on television or in person. Could you just predict, maybe,

what might transpire in this second half?

THE PRESIDENT. Let me say, first, the reason I watch it is that I sat on the bench when I was in college, and you learn a lot from the coach when you sit on the bench.

As I looked at this game in the first half, I think that Texas has enormous power that is really not unleashed yet, and that in the second half they are likely to be much better offensively.

However, they are not going to run over Arkansas. They can't do it by just going that 3 yards and a cloud of dust, the old Woody Hayes [head football coach at Ohio State University] formula—not the Woody Hayes formula this year.

I think they are going to have to throw more. They have an excellent passer and they will have to throw to open up the Arkansas defense. I think under those circumstances they are likely to score once or twice.

Also, I would suggest that Arkansas looks better offensively than I had realized. They could score in this second half. They have a fine passer. I don't think I have seen a cooler passer than [Quarterback Bill] Montgomery. He is really cool under very great pressure.

Texas has got a great pass rush. But Montgomery is cool. He gets out there and goes off.

I would rather say I expect both teams to score in the second half. The question is whether Texas' superior manpower, and I mean probably a stronger bench, may win in the last quarter. That is the way I see it.

MR. SCHENKEL. Mr. President, if Bud Wilkinson, our analyst, ever falters, we at ABC may call on you to do our commentary. Excellent.

THE PRESIDENT. I am not thinking,

Chris, of what I am going to do when I finish my present job, but there is nothing I would like better than to have Bud's job right with you. I like football and this is the first game I have seen this year in college football, and I am glad it is the greatest of the year.

MR. SCHENKEL. You have paid all of us a great deal of honor by coming to this, the number one game of the year, in the centennial year. Enjoy the second half.

THE PRESIDENT. Thank you.

MR. SCHENKEL. Thank you, Mr. President.

NOTE: The interview began at 1:40 p.m. at Razorback Stadium, University of Arkansas, Fayetteville, Ark.

478 Remarks With Texas Coach Darrell Royal. *December 6, 1969*

THE PRESIDENT. This was one of the great games of all time, without a question. I was up in the booth, the ABC booth, at halftime, and, incidentally, I have got to brag a little. They asked what was going to happen in the second half. I said both teams were going to score, but I thought that what would really determine the second half would be whether Texas had the ability in the fourth quarter to come through. And you did. How do you feel?

MR. ROYAL. I have got to be the happiest guy in America tonight.

THE PRESIDENT. I just want to say this in presenting the plaque: In presenting this plaque, I want to say first that the AP [Associated Press] and the UPI [United Press International] will name Texas Number 1, as we know, after this game. This is a great honor in the 100th year of football.

I also want to say that, having seen this game, what convinced me that Texas deserves that is the fact that you won a tough one. For a team to be behind 14 to 0 and then not to lose its cool and to go on to win, that proves that you deserve to be Number 1, and that is what you are.

MR. ROYAL. Mr. President, it is a great thrill for us to win the football game, but the big thrill, I know I speak for all of our squad, is for the President of the United States to take time to endorse college football and to honor us with your presence in our locker room. This is a big moment in all of our lives. I am speaking for the coaching staff and all the players.

THE PRESIDENT. I want all of you to know that we didn't make up the plaque in advance. It doesn't say what team. I am taking it back to Washington and putting in Texas.

If I could add one thing, Darrell, while we are talking here, I do want to say that Penn State, of course, felt that I was a little premature in suggesting this, so we are going to present a plaque to Penn State as the team in the 100th year with the longest undefeated, untied record. Is that fair enough?

MR. ROYAL. That is fair enough.

NOTE: The President visited the Texas locker room at 3:05 p.m. at Razorback Stadium, University of Arkansas, Fayetteville, Ark.

479   Remarks With Arkansas Coach Frank Broyles. *December 6, 1969*

THE PRESIDENT. It is an honor to be here with a great team.

MR. BROYLES. Thank you, sir. We are proud and we feel that way, too.

THE PRESIDENT. I would like to say something to the team, because I know how you feel.

In my field of politics, I have lost some close ones and I have won some close ones. But I want you to know that in the 100th year of football, in the game to prove which was to be Number 1, we couldn't have had a greater game. Arkansas was magnificient throughout the game, and Texas, in order to win, had to beat a great team.

On any Saturday, if we were to make a bet, I would say we wouldn't know which team to choose, whether it would be Arkansas or Texas.

I also want you to know this: I think you can be awfully proud of the way your fans are with you. I have never seen stands so full of life. The whole State was behind you. There was a spirit there about it, Coach, and that means that your team has done something that is really great for this State.

MR. BROYLES. Thank you, sir. We are very proud of our fans. They have had a big part in the success that we have had.

But we are doubly proud that you are a big sports fan and believe in our program across the State. This will mean a lot to football for years to come.

THE PRESIDENT. I know how the fellows feel, being right down there on that 8-yard line, ready to go over, and then losing the game after what they have done. But I do know this, that in that Sugar Bowl, watch out.

BILL FLEMMING [ABC Sports]. Mr. President, this has been, of course, the climax of the centennial year of college football, and we, indeed, are very indebted to you, sir, for not only taking your television set to your dentist so you could watch a college game, but also being here at this final game.

THE PRESIDENT. Well, I wouldn't have missed it. I am only sorry that both teams couldn't have won.

Thank you, fellows.

NOTE: The President visited the Arkansas locker room at 3:15 p.m. at Razorback Stadium, University of Arkansas, Fayetteville, Ark.

480   Remarks at the 50th Anniversary Meeting of the American Farm Bureau Federation. *December 8, 1969*

President Shuman, Secretary Hardin, all of the distinguished guests who are here on the platform, and all of the distinguished delegates and guests here in the audience:

It is a very great honor for me to appear before this 50th anniversary meeting of the American Farm Bureau Federation. I have just come from rural America. I have been to Camp David and just got back a few minutes ago.

I am delighted to have the opportunity to drop by on this occasion. I say drop by, because I have not prepared a formal speech. I thought that the Secretary of Agriculture could take care of that phase of my activities.

But I did not want this occasion to pass without coming before this organization and, through you, to speak to rural America, to the farmers of this Nation and those in related agricultural activities.

I would begin with rather a blunt statement. I think there is a tendency these days to make agriculture the whipping boy for many of our problems. We hear a lot of talk about farm subsidies and parity and all the rest. We hear very little talk about how it came about, that the reason that farmers have the present problems they have is because they made their investments at the request of government and as a result of the initiative of government, in order to increase agriculture production at a certain time.

Also, as we look at those problems, we overlook another very important, it seems to me, conclusion; one that was emphasized by a convention which preceded yours, incidentally, in this city just a few days ago. It was the first convention of its type in the history of this country, the first White House conference in the history of America on hunger in the United States.

Four thousand people came from all over the United States, and that conference made recommendations—recommendations for action by the President, action by the Department of Agriculture and other departments of Government, and action by the Congress of the United States.

There were differences of opinion

within the conference as to what that action should be but only as to degree. Some thought that the guarantee that the Government should provide as a floor under the income of all Americans and particularly as a floor under their income as far as the ability to purchase necessary food was concerned, should be higher than others thought. But there was no difference at all about, first, the need for some action in that field and, second and even more important, the fact that we had the capacity to do the job.

Let's look at America today. Let's compare the situation in America with other nations in the world. This is one of the few nations in the world where the United States can make a decision that we are going to provide an adequate diet for everyone in this country and be able to do it, and we could not do it if it were not for the American farmer, so let's give credit where credit is due.

And so we look at the great agricultural community of this country and what do we find? Only 5 percent are actually engaged in agriculture, and, of course, you know and you have heard that because you are only 5 percent that your political influence is not as great as it maybe once was.

Well, let's look at it another way. As I look at that 5 percent of America, I find that it produces enough food to feed all of the American people and feed them well, and enough in addition to provide the means whereby the United States can aid other countries around the world.

Look at what we have done since World War II alone: $30 billion in food distributed to other countries around the world—some gifts, some loans—but nevertheless provided, provided out of our surplus. This is a magnificent achievement, an achievement again which is due to the productivity, the efficiency, the dynamism of the American farm community.

And so I say to you today that I am very proud as the President of the United States to recognize American agriculture for what it has achieved, for what it means to America. No nation can long be great without a sound, strong, agricultural base. This is true of virtually all the great nations of the world. It is even true of a nation like Japan, which has very little, certainly, land which is arable, and yet has a strong agriculture. But it, of course, is doubly true of the United States of America.

Agriculture has been at the foundation of our economic strength from the time of our beginning and all of our plans for the future will depend upon having a strong, healthy agriculture. This administration is going to see to it that we have that kind of agriculture throughout this Nation's history.

We can have differences of opinion, of course, as to how that can be achieved. But we will welcome, as the Secretary of Agriculture has indicated in his remarks, your recommendations, the recommendations of others, but the goal is the same, the commitment is sure and the commitment is firm.

I would like to go a step further, however. I have talked about agriculture and the American farm in terms of the production of food. I would like to talk about agriculture and American farmers in terms that are much broader than that.

I have learned from appearing before this organization and other farm organizations on several occasions that you are interested not only in the production of farm commodities, efficiency and the like,

and the Government programs that may relate to that production, but you are interested in all the problems of America. You want a program that will bring peace and keep peace for America. You want a program that will provide for the young people of America the idealism, the challenge that is needed if this Nation is to survive as a great nation.

So, at a time when you are 50 years of age and looking back, there is naturally a tendency, a welcome tendency for you, at this very important time in your history, which has never happened before and never will happen again, for you to look forward, to look forward not just to the next crop season, not just to the next 2 years or 4 years, but down to the end of the century.

What kind of a country is this going to be, and what kind of a country it will be is a decision that you will help to make. You have noted that early in this administration we set up an Urban Affairs Council because of the fact that we have many problems in our cities.

Just recently, during the last month, we have set up a Rural Affairs Council. I will tell you why we did so: first, because while great numbers of people, approximately 150 million people, by definition, live in what is called urban America, at least 50 million, maybe as many as 75 million—depending upon your definition of what a large and a small city is—live in rural America.

So, this is a very important segment of our country, and it is important, therefore, that a national administration have a program to deal with the problems of rural America as well as urban America.

We are doing some very exciting thinking in this direction. We want your views, your views as to how we can contribute and you can contribute to a better life, to raising the quality of life all over America and particularly in rural America.

Look ahead to the end of this century. There are 200 million Americans now. By the end of the century there will be 300 million. Where are those 100 million going to be? You can't pour them into New York, into Los Angeles, into Chicago and the rest and choke those cities to death with smog and crime and all of the rest that comes with over population. It is going to be necessary for America to grow toward its heartland, toward the center. It is going to be necessary for Americans to find again the excitement and the challenge of what is basically rural America.

I don't mean by that that this Nation becomes completely industrial and that farmers have no place in the future of our Nation. I have already covered that point. But I am saying that there is a need for a balanced approach to the development of America: new cities, new towns, out across this great heartland of our country.

I do not have the answers now. I do know, however, that for the first time in the history of this country we are thinking about these problems and we are very fortunate to have a Secretary of Agriculture who is able to look beyond the next crop year, but looks down to the end of this century, just as you will. That is the kind of a man we need. It is the kind of thinking we want for America at this particular time in our history.

There is another reason that we emphasize rural America, because the spirit of America will be the better for it. There is no substitute for a nation's spirit. It comes from the people. It comes from the family.

It comes from the schools. It comes from the churches of this Nation. And as we look toward rural America we find much of the strength and much of the character of America is there. We want to keep it. We want to recognize it. We want to strengthen it. We want to nurture it.

I mention all these things because if I were a farmer in America today I would be proud of it, proud because of what you are producing and what you are achieving, and proud because of what you add to America in terms of character and strength.

Finally, one personal point: I mentioned that I had appeared before this organization before. Mr. Shuman will recall that I have appeared several times as Vice President of the United States. And I have appreciated all of those invitations. But most of all, I appreciated an invitation to appear before you the last time that I met you at a convention at Las Vegas.[1] Incidentally, I went there for the convention and for no other purpose.

In this football season perhaps I can illustrate why I appreciated that invitation with a little story. I have a good friend in the football coach at Ohio State, Woody Hayes. After Ohio State beat Purdue, Mr. Secretary, I wrote him a letter of congratulations and talked to him on the phone.

Then after he lost to Michigan and they were therefore eliminated as Number 1—and then I thought Texas was Number 1 until I heard from Penn State, now I am not sure—I wrote Woody Hayes another letter. I will try to remember it as I said it and then you will see why all this talk about Woody Hayes and football and

---

[1] On December 6, 1966.

Ohio State and Michigan and Purdue relates to that invitation to Las Vegas.

I said, "Dear Woody: From experience, I know that when you win you hear from everybody. I know that when you lose you only hear from your friends, and as your friend, I write you today when you lose to Michigan."

I want you to know that I appreciated the fact that when I had lost I was invited to appear before the American Farm Bureau Convention. Therefore, I believe that those in this great organization, despite your partisan affiliations, you are my friends. And I want you to know that, win or lose, you can be sure that at least during the balance of this term that you will have a friend in the White House and a friend in the Department of Agriculture.

Thank you very much.

NOTE: The President spoke at 3:11 p.m. at the Washington Hilton Hotel.

481   The President's News Conference of *December 8, 1969*

QUESTIONS

THE PRESIDENT. [1.] Won't you be seated.

THE OUTLOOK IN VIETNAM

Mr. Smith [Merriman Smith, United Press International].

Q. Mr. President, do you see any signs of the Vietnam war cooling off?

THE PRESIDENT. Well, looking over the long period, yes—as far as recent weeks are concerned, since my speech of November 3, no significant change. When we compare the situation with regard to infiltration and casualties this year with last year, there is a great difference.

Looking to the future, if that situation continues, I believe that we can see that the Vietnam war will come to a conclusion regardless of what happens at the bargaining table. It will come to a conclusion as a result of the plan that we have instituted on which we are embarked for replacing American troops with Vietnamese forces.

MYLAI

[2.] Mr. Cornell [Douglas B. Cornell, Associated Press].

Q. In your opinion, was what happened at Mylai [1] a massacre, an alleged massacre, or what was it? And what do you think can be done to prevent things like this?

If it was a massacre, do you think it was justifiable on military or other grounds?

THE PRESIDENT. Well, trying to answer all of those questions and sorting it out, I would start first with this statement: What appears was certainly a massacre, and under no circumstances was it justified.

One of the goals we are fighting for in Vietnam is to keep the people from South Vietnam from having imposed upon them a government which has atrocity against civilians as one of its policies.

We cannot ever condone or use atroci-

---

[1] Allegations against a U.S. infantry unit concerning an incident which occurred on March 16, 1968, first appeared in the press on November 17, 1969.

ties against civilians in order to accomplish that goal.

Now when you use the word "alleged" that is only proper in terms of the individuals involved. Under our system a man is not guilty until proved to be so. There are several individuals involved here who will be tried by military courts. Consequently, we should say "alleged" as far as they are concerned until they are proved guilty.

As far as this kind of activity is concerned, I believe that it is an isolated incident. Certainly within this administration we are doing everything possible to find out whether it was isolated and so far our investigation indicates that it was.

As far as the future is concerned, I would only add this one point: Looking at the other side of the coin, we have 1,200,000 Americans who have been in Vietnam. Forty thousand of them have given their lives. Virtually all of them have helped the people of Vietnam in one way or another. They built roads and schools. They built churches and pagodas. The Marines alone this year have built over 250,000 [2] churches, pagodas, and temples for the people of Vietnam.

Our soldiers in Vietnam and sailors and airmen this year alone contributed three-quarters of a million dollars to help the people of South Vietnam.

Now this record of generosity, of decency, must not be allowed to be smeared and slurred because of this kind of an incident. That is why I am going to do everything I possibly can to see that all

of the facts in this incident are brought to light and that those who are charged, if they are found guilty, are punished. Because if it is isolated, it is against our policy and we shall see to it that what these men did, if they did it, does not smear the decent men that have gone to Vietnam in a very, in my opinion, important cause.

VICE PRESIDENT AGNEW'S SPEECHES ON THE NEWS MEDIA

[3.] Q. Vice President Agnew, in recent weeks, has made two speeches in which he has criticized the news media, broadcasting in particular——

THE PRESIDENT. Yes, I know.

Q. What, if anything, in those speeches is there with which you disagree?

THE PRESIDENT. Before this audience?

The Vice President does not clear his speeches with me, just as I did not clear my speeches with President Eisenhower. However, I believe that the Vice President rendered a public service in talking in a very dignified and courageous way about a problem that many Americans are concerned about, that is, the coverage by news media, and particularly television news media, of public figures.

Now, let me be quite precise. He did not advocate censorship. On the contrary, he advocated that there should be free expression. He did not oppose bias. On the contrary, he recognized, as I do, that there should be opinion.

Let me say on that score that I don't want a bunch of intellectual eunuchs, either writing the news or talking about the news. I like excitement in the news, whether it is on television or whether it is in the columns.

---

[2] The White House Press Office later explained that the President had inadvertently used an incorrect figure. The Marines had built 251 schools and 117 churches, pagodas, and temples.

He did say, and perhaps this point should be well taken, that television stations might well follow the practice of newspapers, of separating news from opinion. When opinion is expressed, label it so, but don't mix the opinion in with the reporting of the news.

It seems to me these were useful suggestions. Perhaps the networks disagreed with the criticisms. But I would suggest that they should be just as dignified and just as reasonable in answering the criticisms as he was in making them.

THE TAX REFORM BILL

[4.] Mr. Bailey [Charles W. Bailey 2d, Minneapolis Star and Tribune].

Q. Sir, if the final version of the tax reform bill now pending in Congress includes the Senate-adopted $800 exemption provision and the 15 percent social security increase, can you sign it?

THE PRESIDENT. No.

A CIVILIAN COMMISSION ON MYLAI

[5.] Mr. Theis [J. William Theis, Hearst Newspapers].

Q. May I go back to Mr. Cornell's question to ask, in the light of the Mylai incident, would you prefer a civilian commission, something other than a military inquiry in this case?

THE PRESIDENT. Mr. Theis, I do not believe that a civilian commission at this time would be useful. I believe that the matter now is in the judicial process, and that a civilian commission might be, and very properly could be, used by the defendants' attorneys as having prejudiced their rights.

Now, if it should happen that the judi-

cial process, as set up by the military under the new law passed by Congress,[3] does not prove to be adequate in bringing this incident completely before the public, as it should be brought before the public, then I would consider a commission, but not at this time.

TROOP CUTBACKS IN VIETNAM

[6.] Q. Mr. President, today Secretary of Defense Laird is reported to have said that you would be expected to announce a further troop cutback from Vietnam later this month, probably 40,000 men. Also, today, Senator George Aiken is reported as having said that you have already withdrawn or ordered withrawn another 9,000 that were not announced.

Could you give us your thinking on the prospects and the substance of both of those reports?

THE PRESIDENT. As I indicated in my speech on television on November 3, the reports from Vietnam with regard to infiltration, with regard to casualties, and with regard to the training of the South Vietnamese, indicate more progress on all fronts than we had anticipated when we started our troop scheduled withdrawal in June.

There will be a troop cut with a replacement by South Vietnamese later this month, I would say within the next 2 to

---

[3] The Military Justice Act of 1968 (Public Law 90–632, 82 Stat. 1335) which took effect August 1, 1969, provided for increased participation of military judges and counsel on courts-martial.

On June 19, 1969, the President issued Executive Order 11476, effective August 1, 1969, prescribing the use of a revised edition of the Manual for Courts-Martial, United States Army.

3 weeks. As far as the number is concerned, the number is still under consideration. It will depend upon the events and our analysis of the events between now and the time I make the announcement.

PENTAGON PERSONNEL

[7.] Q. Sir, there are two flagrant instances of intimidation and harassment and threats against Pentagon personnel who may have divulged information to Congress and to the public about cost overruns and mismanagements and irregular industrial alliances.

These two instances are related because some of the same people are involved. I refer, one, to the Gestapo-like interrogation of Pentagon personnel to see who leaked information to Sarah McClendon [representing several newspapers and news services] for news stories. This involves Barry J. Shillito and Edward [J.] Sheridan.[4]

I also refer to the firing of A. Ernest Fitzgerald,[5] whose divulgement of cost overruns saved the American people $2 billion. His greatest critics were Dr. Robert [C.] Moot[6] and Barry J. Shillito.

Will you do something about this, please, sir?

THE PRESIDENT. Miss McClendon, perhaps I'd better, after the way you put that question.

---

[4] Assistant Secretary Installations and Logistics (and Deputy Assistant Secretary Installations and Housing), Department of Defense.

[5] Deputy Assistant Secretary for Management Systems, Department of the Air Force.

[6] Assistant Secretary of Defense (Comptroller).

WHITE HOUSE CONFERENCE ON FOOD, NUTRITION, AND HEALTH

[8.] Q. Mr. President, last week the White House conference on food and nutrition strongly recommended approval of a bill which has passed the Senate to reform the food stamp program that is blocked in the House and another bill which would reform the school lunch program which has passed the House, but is blocked in the Senate.

Your administration is reported to be lobbying against both bills. Will you follow the recommendations of your White House Conference, and what course of action will you take?

THE PRESIDENT. I favor the approach that our administration has put before the Congress as being the more responsible approach on both scores. I will, of course, consider the recommendations of the White House Conference, which will be made to me at my request within approximately 30 days.

There is another recommendation by the White House Conference which I, unfortunately, cannot give really sympathetic consideration to, and that is the one recommending a $5,400 minimum for a family of four in America. That would cost approximately $70 billion to $80 billion in taxes, or $70 billion to $80 billion in increased prices. Now, I do not say that to discredit the Conference.

I simply say that all of us in this country want to end hunger in the United States. All of us want the poor to have a minimum floor, and that minimum to be as high as possible.

All of us, for example, want social security to be higher. But when I consider all of these matters, I have to think also of this fact: the fact that I, as President, am the one who has the primary responsibility for the cost of living in this country.

Referring a moment ago to the tax question, it would be very easy for me to sign a bill which reduces taxes. But if I sign the kind of a bill which the Senate is about to pass, I would be reducing taxes for some of the American people and raising the prices for all the American people.

I will not do that.

NEWS MEDIA REPORTING ON THE ADMINISTRATION

[9.] Mr. Kaplow [Herbert Kaplow, NBC News].

Q. How fair do you think the news media has been in reporting on you and on Vice President Agnew and on your administration generally?

THE PRESIDENT. Generally, I think the news media has been fair. I have no complaints about, certainly, the extent of the coverage that I have received.

I also will have no complaints just so long as the news media allows, as it does tonight, an opportunity for me to be heard directly by the people and then the television commentators to follow me. I will take my chances.

STATEMENTS BY THE WIFE OF THE ATTORNEY GENERAL

[10.] Miss Thomas [Helen Thomas, United Press International].

Q. Do you think that the wife [Mrs. Martha Mitchell] of the Attorney Gen-

eral, like the Vice President, has rendered a public service by her statements on the protest movement and on her political activities?

THE PRESIDENT. Well, now, Miss Thomas, I decided when this administration came to Washington that I would take the responsibility for answering for my own personal family and for my Cabinet family, but that each Cabinet member would answer for his family. So I will leave that question to the Attorney General.

PUBLIC OPINION AND PRESIDENTIAL POLICIES

[11.] Mr. Semple [Robert B. Semple, Jr., New York Times].

Q. To broaden that a little bit, on November 3 you called for support for your policies in Vietnam. You since received a response that some of your aides feel is gratifying.

My question is, however, have you not, with the help of Vice President Agnew, and I am referring to some of his recent speeches, purchased this support at the cost of alienating a sizable segment of the American public and risking polarization of the country?

THE PRESIDENT. Well, Mr. Semple, one of the problems of leadership is to take a position. I like to be liked. I don't like to say things that everybody doesn't agree with.

When peace marchers come to Washington it would be very easy to say that I agree with them and I will do what they want. But a President has to do what he considers to be right, right for the people, right, for example, in pursuing a just peace—not just peace for our time, for a little time.

I believe that I pursued that path. I do not believe that that is a disservice to the public interest, because I believe that sometimes it is necessary to draw the line clearly, not to have enmity against those who disagree, but to make it clear that there can be no compromise where such great issues as self-determination and freedom and a just peace are involved.

SPECIAL SESSION OF CONGRESS

[12.] Q. Will you assess for us how you see now the prospects of a special session of Congress during the Christmas holidays?

THE PRESIDENT. Well, I have had some conversations with some of the Members of the House and Senate since I indicated to the Republican leaders that I might call that session.

I would say the jury is still out. The House is moving much more speedily; the Senate has begun to move more speedily. If the present progress continues at this rate, it may be that we can all have some vacation after Christmas. But if they do not pass the appropriations bills as I indicated, I will have to call a special session as much as I would not want to do so.

STRATEGIC ARMS LIMITATION TALKS

[13.] Q. The United States today asked for a postponement in the SALT talks, the strategic arms [limitation] talks. Can you tell us why and assess the talks for us, please?

THE PRESIDENT. Well, the postponement does not have any long-range signif-

icance. It is only for the purpose of developing positions in a proper way. As far as the progress is concerned, I would say it is encouraging. I say that somewhat cautiously, because I would not want to leave out the hope that we would have an agreement within a matter of weeks or even months.

But it is encouraging because both sides are presenting positions in a very serious way and are not trying to make propaganda out of their positions. Both sides, I believe, therefore, want a limitation on strategic arms. As long as this is the case, there is a chance for an agreement.

Now, it is going to take some time, because what is involved here, as distinguished from the test ban, as distinguished from the nonproliferation treaty, both of which were important, but which were basically peripheral issues, here you have the basic security of the United States of America and the Soviet Union involved. Therefore, both must bargain hard. But I believe that the progress to date has been good. The prospects are better than I anticipated they would be when the talks began.

TROOP WITHDRAWALS

[14.] Q. Mr. President, as the Vietnamization process moves along, are there any circumstances, such as, perhaps, a series of defeats by the South Vietnamese Army, that might lead you to want to reverse the process of troop withdrawals and increase our troops in Vietnam?

THE PRESIDENT. I do not anticipate that at this time. I want to make it, of course, clear, that we do not anticipate that there will not be troubles. The enemy still has the capability of launching some offensive actions. Not, certainly, the capability that it had a year ago. It is much less because their infiltration has been less. But the present prognosis that I think I can make is this: that we can go forward with our troop withdrawal program and that any action that the enemy takes, either against us or the South Vietnamese, can be contained within that program.

THAI COOPERATION IN VIETNAM

[15.] Mr. Horner [Garnett D. Horner, Washington Evening Star].

Q. Mr. President, is there any truth in the reports that have been rather persistent for the last couple of weeks that we paid Thailand something like a billion dollars for their cooperation in Vietnam?

In that connection, where do our allies, like Thailand, South Korea, and their troops fit into our withdrawal program?

THE PRESIDENT. Well, first, with regard to the second part of the question, both Thailand and South Korea have no intention, at least none that has been indicated to us, of withdrawing forces at the time that we are withdrawing ours, because we have a much greater commitment there than they have.

Second, with regard to the billion dollars that allegedly has been paid to Thailand, the amount is, of course, far less than that. But quite candidly, yes, the United States is subsidizing the Thai troops. We also are subsidizing the South Korean troops. We are doing exactly what we did in Western Europe immediately after World War II when we subsidized virtually all of Western Europe due to the fact that they could not maintain forces themselves for their own defense.

These are newly developing countries.

They are unable to maintain their forces for their own defense. Therefore, we think that subsidy is correct. I can only say this, it seems to me it makes a great deal of sense. The Thais are in Vietnam as volunteers, and if they are willing to go there as volunteers, I would much rather pay out some money to have them there than to have American men fighting there in their place.

PARIS PEACE TALKS

[16.]   Q. Since Ambassador Lodge resigned, you have not named a successor as chief negotiator. Is this in effect downgrading the Paris talks, because they have been nonproductive?

THE PRESIDENT. No. Mr. [Philip C.] Habib is a very competent career diplomat, and he will be able to discuss anything that is brought up seriously by the other side. We are simply waiting for a serious proposal.

Q. Considering how things have gone in Paris, how do you now rate the chances of a negotiated settlement of the war?

THE PRESIDENT. Not good. Quite candidly, I would like to say that they were good, but looking at the present situation, the enemy's line continues to be hard, their proposals quite frivolous, as the ones by the VC today, and I do not anticipate any progress on the negotiating front at this time.

But I put in this one condition: As our program for Vietnamization continues to work, and as it becomes apparent, as I believe it increasingly will, that it will succeed, I think the pressures for the enemy then to negotiate a settlement will greatly increase, because once we are out and the South Vietnamese are there, they will have a much harder individual to negotiate with than they had when we were there.

SCHOOL INTEGRATION

[17.] Q. Before the Supreme Court ordered immediate school integration,[7] you said you preferred a middle road policy, that is between segregation forever and instant integration.

What is your policy now?

THE PRESIDENT. To carry out what the Supreme Court has laid down. I believe in carrying out the law even though I may have disagreed as I did in this instance with the decree that the Supreme Court eventually came down with. But we will carry out the law.

TAX PHILOSOPHY

[18.] Q. A question on your broad philosophy on the tax problem that we are all struggling with. You have often pointed out that this is a very rich country and there are some people who argue that the American people can tax themselves whenever they want to and when they are prepared to make the sacrifice in order to provide the very substantial sums that are necessary for the very big problems at home, the cities, getting their housing program rolling and so forth, and that we might very well do it now and get on with the job because the end of the Vietnam war apparently is not going to release very substantial amounts of fresh funds.

Could you comment on this rather hairshirted approach to the tax problem?

THE PRESIDENT. Well, it is, of course,

a very complicated but a very fundamental question. I would put it briefly and answer in this way: Approximately 35 to 37 percent of the total income in the United States goes to taxes, that is in Federal, State, and local taxes. I believe that amount is high enough.

I believe that when a nation takes a substantially larger portion of the national income than that for taxes, that then that nation loses its character as a free, private enterprise economy and turns over and becomes primarily a state-controlled and oriented economy.

Therefore, while I believe that the United States can afford what it needs to do in many fields, including the environment and others that I will be touching upon in the State of the Union, I do not want to see a substantial increase in the tax burden as a percentage of our gross national income.

CONGRESS AND THE ADMINISTRATION

[19.] Mr. Lisagor [Peter Lisagor, Chicago Daily News].

Q. Mr. President, getting back to the Congress for a moment, House Democratic Leader Carl Albert today said that administration spokesmen have issued misleading statements about the Congress in an effort to undermine public confidence in it. He went on to say, and I quote him as saying it is the fault of the administration for delays, obfuscations, and confusion and lack of leadership on the part of the administration.

Would you care to comment?

THE PRESIDENT. Well, that sounds like a pretty good political statement by Mr. Albert. I can understand why he is the majority leader and might find it necessary to make that statement. However, I

---

[7] *Alexander* v. *Holmes County Board of Education* (396 U.S. 19).

think he knows, as all of you know, that for 6 months we have had a major crime control package before the Congress with no action. For months we have had other programs in a number of fields there without action.

This Congress has the worst record in terms of appropriations bills of any Congress in history.

Now let me say I am a defender of the Congress and, having said all of this, I am also a defender of Carl Albert. I like him and I want to continue to work with him. I don't want to answer that question any further at this point.

All right.

PRESIDENTIAL NEWS CONFERENCES

[20.] Q. I have two related questions, sir. Why have you only had three full-dress news conferences in 6 months? And what is your reaction to the general philosophy among some of us in the press that the press is not doing its job, if it doesn't hold an administration, any administration, to account without, shall we say, coziness?

THE PRESIDENT. Well, I don't think I have had any problem with regard to the press holding me to account in my political lifetime. I think, if I could paraphrase Winston Churchill's statement made in 1914, I have always derived a great deal of benefit from criticism and I have never known when I was short of it.

Now as far as the press conferences are concerned, I try to have press conferences when I think there is a public interest—not just a press interest or my interest, but the public interest in having them—and also to use various devices. As you know, I have had conferences in my office. I had a conference in Guam. I have also made three major television addresses in

prime time.

If I considered that the press and the public needs more information than I am giving through press conferences, I will have more. I welcome the opportunity to have them. I am not afraid of them—just as the press is not afraid of me.

VIETNAM INVOLVEMENT

[21.] Q. Mr. President, will our Vietnam involvement be reduced in your administration to the point where it will command no more public attention than, say, Korea does now?

THE PRESIDENT. Well, that is certainly our goal and I think we are well on the way to achievement of that goal. We have a plan for the reduction of American forces in Vietnam, for removing all combat forces from Vietnam, regardless of what happens in the negotiations.

That plan is going forward. As I will report to the Nation, when I announce the troop withdrawal 2 or 3 weeks from now, I believe that developments since my November 3 speech have been on schedule.

THE UNITED STATES AND LAOS

[22.] Q. Mr. President, what limits do you put on what the people of the United States ought to know about the war that is going on in Laos, and the American involvement in it?

THE PRESIDENT. The public interest. As far as I am concerned, the people of the United States are entitled to know everything that they possibly can with regard to any involvement of the United States abroad.

As you know, in answer to a question I think Mr. Potter [Philip Potter, Balti-

more Sun] asked at the last press conference, I pointed out what were the
facts. There are no American combat
troops in Laos. Our involvement in Laos
is solely due to the request of Souvanna
Phouma, the neutralist Prime Minister,
who was set up there in Laos as a result
of the Laos negotiation and accords that
were arranged by Governor Harriman
during the Kennedy administration.[8]

We are attempting to uphold those accords and we are doing that despite the
fact that North Vietnam has 50,000
troops in Laos. We are also, as I have
publicly indicated and as you know, in-
terdicting the Ho Chi Minh Trail as it
runs through Laos. Beyond that, I don't
think the public interest would be served
by any further discussion.

All right.

BUDGET ESTIMATES AND THE SURTAX

[23.] Q. Mr. President, Budget Director [Robert P.] Mayo said recently that
uncontrolled Federal spending is likely to
push the fiscal '71 budget beyond the $200
billion mark and that the eventual elimination of the surtax could produce a
deficit that year. I have two questions:
Do you foresee the possibility of a deficit
in '71, and, if that is the prospect, will
you recommend continuing the surtax
beyond June 30?

THE PRESIDENT. The answer to the
second question is that I do not intend
to recommend the continuation of the
surtax beyond June 30.

With regard to the first part of the
question, only by use of the Presidential

veto and by impounding funds are we
going to be able to avoid the kind of a
situation that Director Mayo has described. But I can assure you that I
intend to use all the powers of the Presidency to stop the rise in the cost of
living, including the veto.

ENEMY INFILTRATION IN VIETNAM

[24.] Q. Mr. President, the enemy's infiltration has been up recently in Vietnam.
Could you give us your assessment of
this, specifically whether you think he is
replacing losses, or building up for an offensive, and what significance could this
fact have in terms of your own plans for
troop reduction?

THE PRESIDENT. It has great significance because, as I have pointed out,
enemy infiltration, the fact that it was
down, is one of the reasons that we have
been able to go forward with our own
troop withdrawal programs.

However, I have been analyzing these
reports week by week. The figures that
we got 2 weeks ago seem to have been
inflated. The infiltration rate is not as
great as we thought then. It is higher than
it was a few months ago. It is still lower
than it was a year ago.

We do not consider the infiltration significant enough to change our troop withdrawal plans. Now, something may occur
in the next 2 to 3 weeks that may give me
a different view on that, but at this time
that would be my observation.

THE ANTIPOVERTY PROGRAM

[25.] Q. Mr. President, a move is underway in the House, and it is supported
by the Republican leadership, to change
the structure of the antipoverty program,

---

[8] W. Averell Harriman, former Governor
of New York, who served as Ambassador-at-
Large and Assistant Secretary of State for Far
Eastern Affairs 1961–1963.

to give the Governors a veto over programs in their States. What is your position on that?

THE PRESIDENT. I support the Director of OEO [Donald Rumsfeld]. He has asked for a 2-year extension. He has pledged to reform the OEO, and I think he should be given the chance to reform it.

I hope he is able to work out with the leadership in the House, most of whom are Republicans in this instance, who want the changes, and some Democrats—will be able to work out some kind of accommodation with them. But, of course, I support my Director that I have appointed.

YOUNG PEOPLE AND THE ADMINISTRATION

[26.] Mrs. Dickerson [Nancy H. Dickerson, NBC News].

Q. Getting back to the polarization question, Mr. President, your administration has been charged with the failure to reach the young people, both those who protest and march and those who don't.

Have you any specific plans for reaching the young people of this country?

THE PRESIDENT. I think you reach the young people more by talking to them as adults than talking to them as young people. I like to treat them as adults. I like to talk to them.

I was rather encouraged by the number of letters and calls I received with regard to my Vietnam speech from young people. They didn't all agree. But at least they had listened, they had paid attention. I know a way not to reach them, and that is to try to pick number one as far as the football teams are concerned.

Merriman Smith, United Press International: Thank you, Mr. President.

NOTE: The President's eighth news conference was held in the East Room at the White House at 9 p.m. on Monday, December 8, 1969. It was broadcast on radio and television.

482   Remarks at the National Football Foundation and Hall of Fame Dinner in New York City.   *December* 9, 1969

Mr. Chairman and Mr. Toastmaster, Your Eminence Cardinal Cooke, all of the distinguished guests at the head tables and all of the distinguished award winners and all of those who are here on this very momentous occasion:

It would be momentous because of this organization meeting to honor the men that you have honored—and I speak of others, of course, than myself—but it would be momentous, too, because it is the 100th year of a very great game.

I was trying to think of something that would appropriately describe how I feel in accepting this award. I would have to be less than candid if I were not to say that because of the offices I have held I have received many awards.

But I think Archibald MacLeish, in that perfectly eloquent tribute to football, quoting Secretary of State Dean Acheson [1949–1953], put it very well. He said, "The honors you don't deserve are the ones you are most grateful to receive."

I simply want to set the record straight with regard to my football qualifications. This is a candid, open administration. We believe in telling the truth about football and everything.

I can only say that as far as this award is concerned, that it is certainly a small step for the National Football Foundation and a small step for football, but it is a giant leap for a man who never even made the team at Whittier.

I have looked around that wall. Whittier is not up there, I can assure you. I didn't hear the Whittier song, either, a moment ago. In fact, only the coach from Loyola [Loyola University of Los Angeles] knows where Whittier is. We used to play Loyola.

I got into a game once when we were so far behind it didn't matter. I even got into one against Southern Cal once when we were so far behind it didn't matter.

Now just to tell you a little about Whittier because I want the record to be straight: It is a school with very high academic standing. We had a very remarkable coach.

Today as we pay tribute to the players, I am glad that one of those who made the Hall of Fame is a coach, Bud Wilkinson.[1]

I pointed out in my acceptance address in Miami that one of the men who influenced me most in my life was my coach and I think that could be true of many public men.

My coach was an American Indian, Chief Newman. He was a perfectly remarkable man and a great leader. I learned more from him about life really than I did about football, but a little about football.

One of the reasons, I guess, he didn't put me in was because I didn't know the plays. Now there was a good reason for that. It wasn't because I wasn't smart enough. I knew the enemy's plays. I

---

[1] Head coach of the University of Oklahoma 1947–1964.

played them all week long. Believe me, nobody in the Southern California Conference knew Occidental's or Pomona's or Redlands' or Cal Tech's or Loyola's plays better than I did, because I was on that side.

I learned a lot sitting by the coach on the bench—learned about football and learned about life.

Incidentally, since this is a night for confession, I want to tell you one thing about Chief Newman. He went to Southern California. He played on Southern California's first Rose Bowl team and that first Rose Bowl team beat Penn State in the only game Penn State ever played in the Rose Bowl.

Now, because Governor [of Pennsylvania Raymond P.] Shafer is here, and because I had an uncle who taught at Penn State and had a very distinguished record, and because somebody suggested that some day I might want to visit the campus—after I have left the Presidency—of Penn State, I can only say that they have a great football team.

As a matter of fact, I was going to suggest that we have a super college bowl after the November or the January 1 games and then I thought I was in deep enough already because look what could happen: Southern Cal could beat Michigan and they would claim they were Number 1; Notre Dame might beat Texas and they would claim they were Number 1; and of course, you never know what would happen with Penn State and Missouri. I understand they are pretty good.

So all that I can say now is this: I understand that Penn State certainly is among those that should be considered for Number 1 in the United States of America.

Now, could I share with you for a moment, in a somewhat serious vein, what football means to me? I think that is what the man who receives this award, particularly one who really doesn't deserve it because of his football prowess, that is something he is expected to do.

First, without talking about those factors that are tremendously important that Archibald MacLeish touched on, the character, all of the great spirit that comes into individuals who either are in the game, participate in it, or watch it, I look back on football and have many pleasant memories. I just enjoyed playing it, watching it, reading about it over the years.

Among all of the people who have been honored tonight, let me just say a good word about sports writers. After all, I must say that this is not an unselfish statement, most sports writers become political writers in the end—"Scotty" Reston, Bob Considine, Bill Henry. So I am just planning for the future.

But, in any event, thinking of sports writers for the moment, they have made football live before the days of television and even now for many who never got to the games.

My first recollection of big-time college football was Ernie Nevers against Notre Dame in 1925—I see Ernie Nevers here. And I sat in the stands with Father Hesburgh [2] when Southern Cal played and lost to Notre Dame, and I know the great spirit between those two schools. But I remember that game. I remember the score. I think it was 25 to 10, or four touchdowns to a touchdown and a field goal, and I remember that the sports writers, Bill Henry of the Los Angeles

Times, and others were writing about the game, wrote about one play where Nevers went through the line close to the goal and there was a dispute as to whether he went over and was pushed back.

I wondered whether or not, with the replays we have on television, the game might have turned out differently if we had had television in 1925. I am not saying it would, Father Hesburgh. I have got enough trouble with Penn State. I don't want any with Notre Dame.

Then my memory goes on, just to share them with you, and interestingly enough I remember performances by men who lost as well as those who won. That is rather natural, I am sure you can understand.

The first Rose Bowl game I saw was between one of the great Howard Jones' teams of the early thirties and Jock Sutherland's Pitt team. Pitt was overmanned. They had a fine quarterback in Warren Heller, a good passer. And Howard Jones had a team that beat them 35 to 0.

But my memories of that team were not of the awesome power of Howard Jones' team moving down with the unbalanced single wing going down, down, down the field and scoring again and again with that tremendous blocking, but of two very gallant Pittsburgh ends, Stedani and Dailey.

For the first half, I remember they plowed into that awesome USC interference and knocked it down time and time again and held the score down. The game was lost, but I remember right to the last they were in there fighting and that spirit stayed with me as a memory; and the years go on.

I think of another game, Southern Cal and Duke, 1938. I had attended Duke University for law school, and I remember that Duke came there undefeated, un-

[2] Father Theodore Hesburgh, president of the University of Notre Dame.

tied, unscored upon. The score was 3 to 0 going into the last few minutes of the game. So out came a fourth-string quarterback, not a third-string, Doyle Nave, and he threw passes as they throw them today, one after another, to Al Kreuger, an end from Antelope Valley, California. And finally Southern California scored. It was 7 to 3.

I must say that I was terribly disappointed, of course, but the woman who was to be my future wife went to Southern Cal and that is how it all worked out. We met at that game.

The years go on and I am not going to bore you with more of my own recollections, except to give you a feel of what football has meant to me as a spectator, and college football particularly.

I remember some Ohio State games. I recall going to Ohio State to a football game, and until you have been in Columbus to see an Ohio State game—in fact, until I went to Fayetteville, Arkansas, I thought the Columbus crowds were the most exciting. But in any event, that year, I think it was about 1958, I went there with Senator John Bricker [Senator from Ohio 1947–1959]. Iowa had a great team. They were a favorite over Ohio State.

They led going into the last quarter. Woody Hayes—in those days, it was just 3 yards and a cloud of dust—he didn't have the passers. But he had a great big fullback by the name of White and he ran him, starting at the 35-yard line of Ohio State, ten different times over the same hole in the Iowa line, going off the left side, until they scored, and they won the game 17 to 14.

If you think enthusiastic crowds developed in other places, you ought to see an Ohio State crowd when they beat anybody.

But in any event, on through the years, I come to more recent years, years that these younger men here will remember and recall with the same zest and enthusiasm, I am sure, that I do.

This year, 1969—certainly of all the hundred years of football none could be more exciting. There were never so many great teams, never so many Saturdays when the favorite could not be sure that he was going to come through, never so many times when a team that was behind came on to win or tie in the last quarter.

I am referring, of course, to Southern Cal, what they did to UCLA [University of California at Los Angeles].

If you talk to somebody from UCLA they say it should not have happened. So, watch out, Michigan, for Southern Cal; it could happen. I am not predicting now. I have had enough trouble with Penn State. I don't want any with Michigan. Before I get through I will only have friends in Texas and I didn't carry Texas. So let's not talk any further about that.

But now, one serious moment. Archibald MacLeish did say what I wish I could have written about what football means to this country, what it means to me as an individual, what it means to me as one who is serving as President of the United States. I can only tell you that in the Cabinet Room there are the pictures of three men whom I consider to be great Presidents: President Eisenhower, President Woodrow Wilson, President Theodore Roosevelt. There were other great ones, but these three in this century, I consider to be among the great Presidents.

All of them had one thing in common. They were very different men: Eisenhower, the great general; Theodore Roosevelt, the tremendous extrovert, explorer, writer, one of the most talented men of our time in so many fields; Woodrow Wilson, probably the greatest scholar who has ever occupied the Presidency, a man with the biggest vocabulary of any President in our history, in case you want to put it down in your memory book.

But each of them had a passion for football. Woodrow Wilson, when he taught at Wesleyan [Wesleyan University, Middletown, Conn.] used to talk about the spirit of football, and later on when he was president of Princeton, he insisted on scholarship, but he recognized and tried to encourage football.

T. R. was dictating a speech one day, a very important one. He got a call telling of two of his sons participating in a prep school game which they had won. He dropped the speech and ran shouting for joy to his wife and said, "They won, they won!"

I remember President Eisenhower talking to me after his heart attack. He said one of the things he hated to give up was that the doctor said he should not listen to those football games because he got too excited and became too involved.

What does this mean, this common interest in football of Presidents, of leaders, of people generally? It means a competitive spirit. It means, also, to me, the ability and the determination to be able to lose and then come back and try again, to sit on the bench and then come back. It means basically the character, the drive, the pride, the teamwork, the feeling of being in a cause bigger than yourself.

All of these great factors are essential if a nation is to maintain character and greatness for that nation. So, in the 100th year of football, as we approach the 200th year of the United States, remember that our great assets are not our military strength or our economic wealth, but the character of our young people, and I am glad that America's young people produce the kind of men that we have in American football today.

I close on a note that will tell you why I think Texas deserved to be Number 1. It was not because they scored the second touchdown, but it was because after the first touchdown when they were ahead [behind] 14 to 0, the coach sent in a play. They executed the play and they went for two. When they went for two and the score was 18 [8] to 14, they moved the momentum in their direction. They were not sure to win because Arkansas still had a lot of fight left and I remember that great Arkansas drive in those last few minutes. But Texas, by that very act, demonstrated the qualities of a champion, the qualities to come back when they were behind and then when they could have played it safe just to tie, they played to win.

This allows me to tell a favorite anecdote of mine in the world of sports. In another field, one of the great tennis players of all time, of course—the first really big tennis player in terms of the big serve and the rest, in our time—was Bill Tilden.

When he was coaching, after he completed his playing years, a young player had won a match in a minor tournament and won it rather well. He came off the court and expected Tilden to say something to him in words of congratulation, and Tilden didn't.

The player said to him, "What is the matter, I won, didn't I?" Tilden said, "Yes, you won, but playing that way you will never be a champion, because you played not to lose. You didn't play to win."

That is what America needs today. What we need in the spirit of this country and the spirit of our young people is not playing it safe always, not being afraid of defeat—being ready to get into the battle and playing to win, not with the idea of destroying or defeating or hurting anybody else, but with the idea of achieving excellence.

Because Texas demonstrated that day that they were playing to win, they set an example worthy of being Number 1 in the 100th year of college football.

Thank you.

NOTE: The President spoke at 10:15 p.m. in the Ballroom at the Waldorf-Astoria Hotel in New York City. Roger Blough, cochairman of the General MacArthur Advisory Board of the National Football Foundation and Vincent Draddy, chairman of the dinner, were both seated at the head table with the President. The toastmaster was Chris Schenkel, ABC television sportscaster and His Eminence Terence Cardinal Cooke, Archbishop of New York gave the invocation.

Mr. Blough presented the Foundation's Gold Medal for 1969 to the President. Archibald MacLeish, noted poet and dramatist, received the Foundation's Distinguished American Award.

Also honored were 9 newly elected members to the National Football Hall of Fame, 11 university scholar-athletes receiving graduate fellowships, and the University of Texas football team, awarded the MacArthur Bowl for being the outstanding football team of the 1969 season.

483 Special Message to the Congress About Funding and Authorization of the National Foundation on the Arts and the Humanities. *December* 10, 1969

To the Congress of the United States:

Americans have long given their first concerns to the protection and enhancement of Life and Liberty; we have reached the point in our history when we should give equal concern to "the Pursuit of Happiness."

This phrase of Jefferson's, enshrined in our Declaration of Independence, is defined today as "the quality of life." It encompasses a fresh dedication to protect and improve our environment, to give added meaning to our leisure and to make it possible for each individual to express himself freely and fully.

The attention and support we give the arts and the humanities—especially as they affect our young people—represent a vital part of our commitment to enhancing the quality of life for all Americans. The full richness of this nation's cultural life need not be the province of relatively few citizens centered in a few cities; on the contrary, the trend toward a wider appreciation of the arts and a greater interest in the humanities should be strongly encouraged, and the diverse culture of every region and community should be explored.

America's cultural life has been developed by private persons of genius and talent and supported by private funds from audiences, generous individuals, corporations and foundations. The Federal government cannot and should not seek to substitute public money for these essential sources of continuing support.

However, there is a growing need for Federal stimulus and assistance—growing because of the acute financial crisis in which many of our privately-supported cultural institutions now find themselves, and growing also because of the expanding opportunity that derives from higher educational levels, increased leisure and greater awareness of the cultural life. We are able now to use the nation's cultural resources in new ways—ways that can enrich the lives of more people in more communities than has ever before been possible.

Need and opportunity combine, therefore, to present the Federal government with an obligation to help broaden the base of our cultural legacy—not to make it fit some common denominator of official sanction, but rather to make its diversity and insight more readily accessible to millions of people everywhere.

Therefore, *I ask the Congress to extend the legislation creating the National Foundation on the Arts and the Humanities beyond its termination date of June 30, 1970, for an additional three years.*

Further, *I propose that the Congress approve $40,000,000 in new funds for the National Foundation in fiscal 1971 to be available from public and private sources. This will virtually double the current year's level.*

Through the National Foundation's two agencies—the National Endowment for the Arts and the National Endowment for the Humanities—the increased appropriation would make possible a variety of activities:

—We would be able to bring more productions in music, theatre, literature readings and dance to millions of citizens eager to have the opportunity for such experiences.

—We would be able to bring many more young writers and poets into our school system, to help teachers motivate youngsters to master the mechanics of self-expression.

—We would be able to provide some measure of support to hard-pressed cultural institutions, such as museums and symphony orchestras, to meet the demands of new and expanding audiences.

—We would begin to redress the imbalance between the sciences and the humanities in colleges and universities, to provide more opportunity for students to become discerning as well as knowledgeable.

—We would be able to broaden and deepen humanistic research into the basic causes of the divisions between races and generations, learning ways to improve communication within American society and bringing the lessons of our history to bear on the problems of our future.

In the past five years, as museums increasingly have transformed themselves from warehouses of objects into exciting centers of educational experience, attendance has almost doubled; in these five years, the investment in professional performing arts has risen from 60 million dollars to 207 million dollars and attendance has tripled. State Arts agencies are now active in 55 States and territories; the total of State appropriations made to these agencies has grown from $3.6 million in 1967 to $7.6 million this year. These State agencies, which share in Federal-State partnership grants, represent one of the best means for the National Endowment to protect our cultural diversity and to encourage local participation in the arts.

In this way, Federal funds are used properly to generate other funds from State, local and private sources. In the past history of the Arts Endowment, every dollar of Federal money has generated three dollars from other sources.

THE FEDERAL ROLE

At a time of severe budget stringency, a doubling of the appropriation for the arts and humanities might seem extravagant. However, I believe that the need for a new impetus to the understanding and expression of the American idea has a compelling claim on our resources. The dollar amounts involved are comparatively small. The Federal role would remain supportive, rather than primary. And two considerations mark this as a time for such action:

—Studies in the humanities will expand the range of our current knowledge about the social conditions underlying the most difficult and far-reaching of the nation's domestic problems. We need these tools of insight and understanding to target our larger resources more effectively on the solution of the larger problems.

—The arts have attained a prominence in our life as a nation and in our consciousness as individuals, that renders their health and growth vital to our national well-being. America has moved to the forefront as a place of creative expression. The excellence of the American product in the arts has won worldwide recognition. The arts have the rare capacity to help heal divisions among our own people

and to vault some of the barriers that divide the world.

Our scholars in the humanities help us explore our society, revealing insights in our history and in other disciplines that will be of positive long-range benefit.

Our creative and performing artists give free and full expression to the American spirit as they illuminate, criticize and celebrate our civilization. Like our teachers, they are an invaluable national resource.

Too many Americans have been too long denied the inspiration and the uplift of our cultural heritage. Now is the time to enrich the life of the mind and to evoke the splendid qualities of the American spirit.

Therefore, I urge the Congress to extend the authorization and increase substantially the funds available to the National Foundation for the Arts and the Humanities. Few investments we could make would give us so great a return in terms of human understanding, human satisfaction and the intangible but essential qualities of grace, beauty and spiritual fulfillment.

RICHARD NIXON

The White House
  December 10, 1969

NOTE: The National Foundation on the Arts and the Humanities was established by Public Law 89–209 of September 29, 1965 (79 Stat. 485), assuming the functions of the National Council on the Arts.

Also released was the transcript of a news briefing held by Miss Nancy Hanks, Chairman of the National Endowment for the Arts, following a meeting with the President.

484 Remarks Following a Meeting With Wives and Mothers of Prisoners of War and Servicemen Missing in Action in Vietnam. *December* 12, 1969

Ladies and gentlemen:

I have the very great honor to present in this room today five of the most courageous women I have had the privilege to meet in my life.

Mrs. Nixon and I have met with 26 women, of which these were a part, representing approximately 1,500 women, mothers and wives of American servicemen who are missing in Vietnam and who are or may be prisoners of war. Some of these men have been prisoners or missing for as long as 5 years, most of them 2 to 3 years.

Insofar as the treatment of prisoners is concerned, it would probably not be inaccurate to say that the record in this war is one of the most unconscionable in the history of warfare. And there have been, of course, some very bad examples in past wars, as we know.

What I have assured these very courageous women is that, first, in reaching a settlement of the war, that an integral part of any settlement that is agreed to must be a settlement which is satisfactory on the prisoner issue and, second, that clearly apart from reaching an overall settlement of the war that this Government will do everything that it possibly can to separate out the prisoner issue and have it handled as it should be, as a separate issue on a humane basis.

Finally, I would simply add that while we all know that there is disagreement in this country about the war in Vietnam and while there is dissent about it on several points, that on this issue, the treatment of prisoners of war, that there can be and there should be no disagreement.

The American people, I am sure, are unanimous in expressing their sympathy to these women, to their children, and also in supporting their Government's attempt to get the Government of North Vietnam and the VC to respond to the many initiatives which we have undertaken to get this issue separated out and progress made on it prior to the time that we reach a complete settlement of the war.

Thank you very much, and I understand they will be here to answer other questions if you have them.

NOTE: The President spoke at 10:50 a.m. in the Roosevelt Room at the White House. The five women to whom he referred in his opening remarks were Mrs. Sybil Stockdale of Coronado, Calif., wife of Capt. James Bond Stockdale, USN; Mrs. Mary A. Mearns of Los Angeles, Calif., wife of Lt. Col. Arthur S. Mearns, USA; Mrs. Andrea Rander of Baltimore, Md., wife of S. Sgt. Donald Rander, USA; Mrs. Carole L. Hanson of El Toro, Calif., wife of Capt. Stephen P. Hanson, USMC; and Mrs. Louise Mulligan of Virginia Beach, Va., wife of Comdr. James A. Mulligan, USN.

The transcript of a news conference held by the five women about their meeting with the President was also released.

485   Remarks at a White House Dinner and Dress Rehearsal of the Bob Hope Christmas Show for Overseas Troops. *December 14, 1969*

EXCHANGE OF TOASTS

THE PRESIDENT. We want to welcome all of you rather officially in this famous State Dining Room of the White House. Of course I have been sitting here thinking of something appropriate to say this evening.

Perhaps one of the things I can do is to describe to you this room—not physically, because, of course, you can see it—but what it has meant to this country and what it means to us tonight to have this very special group here.

The only President who did not live in this house was George Washington. His picture, of course, was in the great East Room where you will be performing in a few moments. John Adams was the first President—ever since then the Presidents have lived here.

Of course, this house has had its problems. The British burned it once, but it was restored pretty much as it was originally planned. Then during the period of President Truman's Presidency, he lived in Blair House for awhile, while the White House was being redone.

But when you think back to all of the people who have lived here and of the great events that have been held here, you get a sense of the history of the room and what it means to the Nation—the Presidents that have been here, Lincoln, Theodore Roosevelt, Franklin Roosevelt, Eisenhower. And then, some of the people who have been honored here. I have been here for dinners with Chancellor Adenauer, De Gasperi of Italy, Winston Churchill, the King of England, the Emperor of Ethiopia, Yoshida of Japan, and of course for other people, prime ministers, presidents, kings, emperors, and one duke—Duke Ellington.

Now this is a special occasion tonight. Usually we honor men, or sometimes a woman. For example, Golda Meir, the Prime Minister of Israel, was here just a couple of months ago.

Tonight we honor a whole group. This is the first time that, rather than having the guests for dinner and the entertainment after, we are having the entertainers for dinner.

We are having you here for a special reason. We know that you are embarking on a long journey. We know what this journey means to our men abroad and all of those that will be there. We know, also, what it means to you, the fact that you have to be away from home during this Christmas and holiday season. And we are very grateful for that.

Also, another reason that I thought it was appropriate to have you here was the present one. It shows you what kind of a man Bob Hope is. Now I know he is going to follow me at some time, so I am not going to try to be funny; he says I don't have to try.

But, nevertheless, just so he doesn't beat me with this gag, it isn't true that my favorite song is: I have been dreaming of a White Christmas in the White House.

Whatever the case may be, this is our first Christmas in the White House and this is the first occasion that we have had an entertainment at night in the White

House, and we thought that having Bob Hope and his great group would be the proper way to kick it off.

I could say that for a number of reasons, because I remember him from the days of radio, Radio City with all the various ways—on the stage, on the screen, on television, and other places. I remember him—not very fondly—on the golf course. Some day I am going to be his partner and I will win.

But we also remember particularly the great things he has done, which we are all aware of. Things like this: I recall he went to Mississippi a few weeks ago and they called it the "We Care Fund." He went there and contributed his time and raised a lot of money for people who had been made homeless by the hurricane. The last time I was on the phone with him— it just seems like a week ago—he was raising money for the Eisenhower Medical Center in Palm Springs.

And all over the country he is doing something of that sort. To show you the real greatness of the man, when I suggested that on this occasion when he said he would stop by and open this Christmas season, that we would like to give a dinner in his honor, he said: "I would like to have the whole troupe here. I would like to have everybody here."

That is why you are here. And we are very honored to have you here. It shows you what kind of a man he is. It shows you also what he thinks of you. A man who is a real star in his own right recognizes that it takes a great team, a team around him of other stars to make him. That is a sign of his greatness and that is one of the reasons we appreciate him.

I just want to say that from all this you would gather I have known him for a long time. I have. I have known him since before most of you were born, at least most of those I met in the line. I have known Bob 22 years. And if you think that is a long time, I have known Les Brown [1] for 34 years.

Enough of that. I know that Dolores is over in Berlin waiting for you, but I thought that there would be no greater pleasure during the time I will be proposing toasts in this great room to the great of the world than to ask you to join me in proposing a toast tonight to Bob and Dolores Hope.

To Bob and Dolores.

MR. HOPE. Thank you very much, Mr. President. I feel that I must catch up.

Mr. President, we do have our show coming on, and you are going to see the final rehearsal of our show. I think Mrs. Nixon—we talked it over—and I think she understands most of it. She may go to bed.

I am not going to try to tell a lot of jokes here because I am trying to think of what I am going to say to your guests out there.

I must say we appreciate this, and I can't think of a greater way to launch this trip. We have had the pleasure of being in Thailand and being invited to the palace every year by the King [Bhumibol Adulyadej] and Queen [Sirikit]. But everybody got a very special glow when they walked in here and they said, "How about this!" I said, "Yes, we are playing our palace."

So I just want our troupe to stand up and just toast our President and our First Lady. Thank you very much.

---

[1] Leader of the "Band of Renown," which played later in the evening.

THE PRESIDENT'S REMARKS INTRODUC-
ING THE PERFORMANCE

*Mr. Vice President, Members of the
Cabinet, Members of the Congress, Members of the Joint Chiefs of Staff, all of the
distinguished guests:*

This is a very special occasion and a
first for the White House—the first time
that we have had an evening at the White
House, an evening of entertainment only.

We thought it was appropriate that we
should begin what we think will now be
a good precedent to follow, to begin in
this Christmas season.

As we were trying to think of someone
who could best kick off this series, the man
who came to mind was, of course, Bob
Hope.

I would like to say just a word before
the show begins and then I will get off
and leave it to him and to others.

But it has been said that probably no
man in contemporary America has done
more to make American men happy
around the world than Bob Hope each
Christmas season.

I asked him how long, and he said for
25 years. Year after year he has spent
Christmas away from home, along with
his wonderful troupe, some of whom have
been with him almost that long and others
who were born after he started his first
show, something he will not admit.

He has gone almost all around the
world, but this is the first time that he
will be traveling clear around the world.
He will be in Europe tomorrow, and then
to various stations, until he finally reaches
Vietnam, and then will return to the
United States.

Those of you who will want to see what
happens abroad can see the television
show which will be carried, I understand,
in the middle of January, an hour and a
half special. But tonight we have something very special.

This is the first time in White House
history that we have what is in effect an
opportunity to see a dress rehearsal. This
show has not been rehearsed before. It
comes on completely unrehearsed and
anything can happen—and it will.

And now finally, I would simply like
to say this one thing about Bob Hope.
We know him from television. We know
him, too, from radio. And we know him,
of course, as one who has given so much
of his time and so much of his energy
for good causes. This is a contribution
that he makes with his appearance at the
White House tonight and his trip around
the world.

Somebody asked me whether or not we
were paying for this performance and the
answer is, we don't have room in the
budget for it, and the other answer is if
we put it in the budget, he couldn't afford to pay the taxes he would have to
pay.

But in any event, in presenting the beginning of the show, it is my privilege, not
to present Bob Hope, because he doesn't
come on at the beginning, but an old
friend. Thirty-five years ago at Duke
University, when I was a student of law,
working my way through, a man in the
undergraduate school was working his
way through with an orchestra—Les
Brown.

Here he is—the master of ceremonies.

REMARKS AT THE CONCLUSION
OF THE PERFORMANCE

I know that I am expressing, Bob, the
thoughts of everyone in this room of appreciation to you and the wonderful mem-

bers of the Bob Hope troupe as you start this journey around the world.

I just consulted with the Secretary of Defense; he thinks the boys will get the message.

I think for you, Bob, I would like to say that we have a number of very special guests tonight, the members of the Cabinet, of course, the Vice President, and the members of the Joint Chiefs, and others. But on this night, too, I think all of the people here in the room would be very happy to know that we have one of our men who served with very great distinction in Vietnam, made a splendid record there, and who is now stationed in the Washington area. He also has another distinction; he was married in this house. And we are very happy to have Major Robb and Lynda Bird Johnson Robb here tonight.[2]

Can you come up for a minute?

MR. HOPE. Lynda Robb volunteered to go with our unit a couple of years ago,

and one of these days we are going to take her. How are you, darling?

He said when he was in Vietnam last year he couldn't see us from where he was standing.

THE PRESIDENT. I just want to say, Bob, as this evening comes to a conclusion, that James Thurber once wrote that the oldest and most precious national asset of this country is humor, and that we must do everything we possibly can to preserve it. Certainly no man in our generation has done more to preserve that asset than you have.

We wish you well as you take it around the world and bring a very Merry Christmas and Happy New Year to all of our men abroad.

Thank you very much.

NOTE: The exchange of toasts began at 8:21 p.m. in the State Dining Room at the White House. Following the dinner the President introduced the performance in the East Room at 9:15 p.m. and spoke again at its conclusion at 10:43 p.m.

The show was a final dress rehearsal before the cast left on a 15-day round-the-world tour to entertain servicemen abroad. It was Bob Hope's 21st Christmas tour and his 6th to Vietnam.

---

[2] Maj. Charles S. Robb, USMC, and President Johnson's daughter, Lynda Bird Johnson, were married in the East Room of the White House on December 9, 1967.

486   Address to the Nation on Progress Toward Peace in Vietnam.   *December* 15, 1969

Good evening, my fellow Americans:

I have asked for this television time tonight to give you a progress report on our plan to bring a just peace in Vietnam, which I described in my television address on November 3.

As you will recall, I said then that we were proceeding in our pursuit for peace on two fronts: a peace settlement through negotiation, or if that fails, ending the war

through Vietnamization, a plan we have developed with the South Vietnamese for the complete withdrawal, first, of all U.S. combat troops, and eventually of other forces and their replacement by South Vietnamese forces on an orderly scheduled timetable.

I must report to you tonight with regret that there has been no progress whatever on the negotiating front since November 3. The enemy still insists on a unilateral, precipitate withdrawal of American forces and on a political settlement which would mean the imposition of a Communist government on the people of South Vietnam against their will, and defeat and humiliation for the United States.

This we cannot and will not accept.

Typical of their attitude is their absolute refusal to talk about the fate of the American prisoners they hold and their refusal even to supply their names so as to ease the anguish of their loved ones in the United States. This cruel, indefensible action is a shocking demonstration of the inflexible attitude they have taken on all issues at the negotiating table in Paris.

But despite their attitude, we shall continue to participate in the Paris talks and to seek a negotiated peace—one which is fair, fair to North Vietnam, fair to the United States, but most important, fair to the people of South Vietnam. Because as I have indicated, anything is negotiable except the right of the people of South Vietnam to determine their own fate.

As you know, Ambassador Lodge has had to leave his assignment in Paris because of personal reasons. I have designated Philip Habib, one of our most experienced Foreign Service officers who has been participating in the negotiations for over 18 months, as the acting head of our delegation with the personal rank of Ambassador. He has been given full authority to discuss any proposal that will contribute to a just peace.

Let me turn now to the progress of our plan for Vietnamization and our troop withdrawal program.

When I announced this program in June, I said that the rate of withdrawal would depend on three criteria: progress in the Paris negotiations, progress in the training of South Vietnamese forces, and the level of enemy activity.

Now, while there has been no progress on the negotiating front, I have a much more favorable report to give to you tonight with regard to the training of South Vietnamese forces.

First, let me share with you how I reached this conclusion. In making decisions, I believe a President should listen not only to those who tell him what he wants to hear, but to those who tell him what he needs to hear. It is most important to get independent judgments from individuals who are expert on the factors to be considered, but who are not directly involved in the operations themselves. This is particularly essential when the lives of American men are involved.

Several months ago I read a book by Sir Robert Thompson,[1] a British expert who was one of the major architects of the victory over the Communist guerrillas who attempted to take over Malaya in the 1950's. In his book, which was published just as this administration took office, he was very pessimistic about the conduct of the war in Vietnam. He particularly noted the failure to prepare the South Vietnamese to take over the responsibilities for their own defense.

On October 7, I met with Mr. Thompson and asked him to go to Vietnam and to give me a firsthand, candid, and completely independent report on the situation there. After 5 weeks of intensive in-

---

[1] "No Exit from Vietnam" was published in 1969 by David McKay Company, Inc. (224 pp.).

vestigation he gave me his report on December 3.

His full report, which makes several very constructive recommendations, must remain confidential since it bears on the security of our men. But let me read to you from his summary of his findings.

"I was very impressed by the improvement in the military and political situation in Vietnam as compared with all previous visits and especially in the security situation, both in Saigon and the rural areas.

"A winning position in the sense of obtaining a just peace (whether negotiated or not) and of maintaining an independent, non-Communist South Vietnam has been achieved but we are not yet through. We are in a psychological period where the greatest need is confidence. A steady application of the 'do it yourself' concept with continuing U.S. support in the background will increase the confidence already shown by many South Vietnam leaders."

Mr. Thompson's report, which I would describe as cautiously optimistic, is in line with my own attitude and with reports I have received from other observers and from our civilian and military leaders in Vietnam.

Now, there is one disturbing new development, however, with regard to enemy activity. Enemy infiltration has increased substantially. It has not yet reached the point where our military leaders believe the enemy has developed the capability to mount a major offensive, but we are watching the situation closely to see whether it could develop to that extent.

Now for the decision. Taking all these developments into consideration, I am announcing tonight a reduction in our

troop ceiling of 50,000 more U.S. troops by April 15 next year. This means that the ceiling which existed when I took office on January 20 has now been reduced by 115,500 men. This reduction has been made with the approval of the Government of South Vietnam, and in consultation with the other nations which have combat forces in Vietnam.

Now there are some who believe that to continue our withdrawals at a time when enemy infiltration is increasing is a risk we should not take. However, I have consistently said we must take risks for peace.

And in that connection, let me remind the leaders in Hanoi that if their infiltration and the level of enemy activity increases while we are reducing our forces they also will be running a risk. I repeat the statement I made in my speech on November 3:

"Hanoi could make no greater mistake than to assume that an increase in violence will be to its advantage. If I conclude that increased enemy action jeopardizes our remaining forces in Vietnam, I shall not hesitate to take strong and effective measures to deal with that situation."

This reduction in our forces is another orderly step in our plan for peace in Vietnam.

It marks further progress toward turning over the defense of South Vietnam to the South Vietnamese.

And it is another clear sign of our readiness to bring an end to the war and to achieve a just peace.

Before concluding this report, I wish to express my appreciation to the great number of people from all over this Nation who have indicated their support for our program for a just peace since my speech on November 3.

This support was particularly underlined by the action of the House of Representatives and the Congress in which a majority of both Democrats and Republicans voted overwhelmingly 334 to 55 for a resolution supporting the plan for peace which I announced on November 3.

The leaders in Hanoi have declared on a number of occasions that division in the United States would eventually bring them the victory they cannot win over our fighting men in Vietnam. This demonstration of support by the American people for our plan to bring a just peace has dashed those hopes.

Hanoi should abandon its dreams of military victory.

It is time for them to join us in serious negotiations.

There is nothing to be gained by delay.

If Hanoi is willing to talk seriously they will find us flexible and forthcoming.

I am glad that I was able to report tonight some progress in reaching our goal of a just peace in Vietnam. After 5 years of increasing the number of Americans in Vietnam, we are bringing American men home.

Our casualties continue to be at the lowest rate in 3 years.

But I want you to know that despite this progress, I shall not be satisfied until we achieve the goal we all want: an end to the war on a just and lasting basis.

This is the fifth Christmas when Americans will be fighting in a war far away from home.

I know that there is nothing the American people want more, and there is nothing I want more, than to see the day come when the Christmas message of "peace on earth, good will to men" will be not just an eloquent ideal but a reality for Americans and for all others who cherish peace and freedom throughout the world.

Your continued support of our plan for peace will greatly strengthen our hopes that we can achieve that great goal.

Thank you and goodnight.

NOTE: The President spoke at 6:02 p.m. in his office at the White House. His remarks were broadcast on radio and television.

On the same day the White House released an advance text of the address.

487   Remarks Following a Meeting With Representative Rogers C. B. Morton, Chairman, Republican National Committee. *December 16, 1969*

Ladies and gentlemen:

There has been considerable speculation about the future of Rogers Morton, the national chairman of the Republican Party.

As you know, he is a Congressman from Maryland and he has been one who has been mentioned as possibly the strongest candidate to run for the Senate in Maryland in 1970.

It is time now to end that speculation, and I am going to end it and then see if the Congressman will corroborate what I say.

I believe that he would make an outstanding Senator. He has had 6 years in the House. I believe he, if he ran, would win, and we need him in the Senate.

However, I believe that he has been one of the most outstanding national chairmen that either party has had in many years. He has not only been loyal to the administration, but, more importantly, he is presenting a positive picture of the Republican Party across this Nation and has unified the party as no chairman in my memory has been able to do it in recent years.

Under the circumstances, after considering all the factors, I have made a decision—and it was a very close one when he asked me for my advice, not that my advice would have been absolutely, shall we say, decisive—that he can better serve not only his party and the Nation and the administration, but also, I think, serve his own interests by remaining as national chairman.

I requested that he remain as national chairman and he has agreed to do so. I am delighted with his decision from the standpoint of the party and the administration.

I regret that he cannot run for the Senate, but he assures me that he will find another very strong candidate for the Senate in Maryland.

Mr. Chairman, we will keep you right where you are.

NOTE: The President spoke at 10:35 a.m. in the Roosevelt Room at the White House.

The text of a news conference by Representative Morton on his decision to continue as chairman of the Republican National Committee was also released by the White House Press Office on December 16, 1969.

488   Remarks on Signing a Proclamation Honoring Reserve Components of the Armed Forces. *December* 16, 1969

I APPRECIATE the opportunity to join in this ceremony; and it is one that I wish I could participate in more often, where a proclamation expresses appreciation for service rendered, and where those involved have completed that service and have returned to civilian life, where that is their choice.

I should point out, of course, that you are still in the Reserve. That means that you can still be called, something which I know you understand and something I know which will always be the great tradition in this country.

I think it is worth saying, however, something about the Reserve components that were called up as a result of this proclamation of 1968,[1] to which [Deputy] Secretary [of Defense David] Packard has referred.

Thirty-six thousand men have been called up under that proclamation. Twenty-two thousand of those 36,000 served overseas. Those 22,000 received over 4,000 citations, including over 250 Purple Hearts.

This is, it seems to me, eloquent demonstration of the service that is rendered to the United States, not only by our regular forces, and those who are brought into the service through the Selective

---

[1] Executive Orders 11392 of January 25, 1968, and 11406 of April 10, 1968, together called up 36,000 men.

Service, but also those who are in the Reserves, as are the people who are here.

The Nation is grateful to you, grateful to you for the service you have rendered. The Nation is also grateful to you for the fact that you are in the Reserves, that you are ready, ready to serve the Nation again, as you have in the past.

And in this Christmas season, we can only say that this is the appropriate time to sign the proclamation, a proclamation which recognizes the service, recognizes what you have done. And it also gives me the opportunity in this East Room, which is appropriately decorated, to wish all of you the very best for Christmas and the New Year.

I should point out, incidentally, to the Secretary, as I see all of this rank in the front row, that I am reminded of the fact that I, too, am in the Reserves, although it is now inactive—I understand inactive, at least.

But, while, because of the position I hold—I hold the rank of Commander in Chief of our Armed Forces—I realize that except for that election that I would be a lieutenant commander in the U.S. Naval Reserve, showing proper respect to my superiors here in the front row.

We hope you all have a chance to look at the Christmas decorations and take anything that isn't nailed down.

NOTE: The President spoke at 10:50 a.m. in the East Room at the White House on signing Proclamation 3949. More than 130 people were present for the ceremony which honored the National Guard and the Reserves.

489   Message to the Congress Transmitting Annual Report on the Trade Agreements Program for 1968.   *December 16, 1969*

To the Congress of the United States:

With this message I am transmitting the Thirteenth Annual Report on the Trade Agreements Program, as required by the Trade Expansion Act of 1962. The report covers the year 1968.

In 1968, free world trade increased by 11.6 percent; U.S. exports increased by 9.6 percent; and U.S. imports rose by 23.7 percent, largely due to the inflationary forces in our economy which stimulated imports and also hampered the competitiveness of our exports.

The Trade Bill of 1969, which I recently submitted to the Congress, will equip us to build on the past gains of the Trade Agreements Program and to move forward toward a new trade program for the 1970s. It will give us the capability to continue to move toward freer world trade, defend our own trade interests, and provide constructive adjustment to changes in world trade patterns. The Commission on World Trade, which I am appointing, will examine the complex trade issues that will confront us in the 1970s, and will make recommendations for the U.S. policies needed to deal with them.

This Administration is committed to a freer exchange of goods among nations. We must continue to strive for further growth in mutually advantageous world trade and, in part through such trade, for the eventual dismantling of the barriers that have stood in the way of the freer interchange of people and ideas.

RICHARD NIXON

The White House
December 16, 1969

NOTE: The report is entitled "Thirteenth Annual Report of the President of the United States on the Trade Agreements Program—1968" (processed, 60 pp.).

490   Remarks at the Lighting of the Nation's Christmas Tree.   *December* 16, 1969

Mr. Secretary, Mr. Congressman, Mr. Mayor, members of the Diplomatic Corps, and my fellow Americans:

I wish to express appreciation for the very generous statements that have been made and the citation read just a few moments ago and also for the flowers that have been presented to Mrs. Nixon, and also to the choir from Chattanooga, Tennessee, which has entertained us in such, it seems to me, a moving way in this Christmas season.

As we look at this great tree, we are reminded of the fact that all over America during these next 2 weeks there will be trees in American homes. Forty-five million American homes will have Christmas trees that they will be lighting each in their own way.

This tree has a special meaning. It belongs to all the Nation. And that is why, as we look at this tree we think of America; we think of its role in the world; we think of the past, and we think of the future and, particularly, I think we understand that this is a very significant year in the history of our country, because it is the last Christmas of the sixties.

Next year, we enter the year of the seventies; and in the period of the seventies, the United States has a great challenge, a great challenge for the role of leadership which is ours, one that we accept, one that we did not ask for, but one in which we will meet that challenge and meet it effectively.

As we enter the years of the seventies, I think it might be well for us to get a historical perspective—to think a moment of this tree, a tree, incidentally, that grew up in the home county of my father in Ohio.[1] That tree, incidentally, is 70 years of age, and I was thinking and you probably now may think with me of what America was just 70 years ago.

There were only 75 million people in America then. There were no automobiles. There was no television. There were no radios. There were no airplanes.

America was not the major power of the world. It was a strong nation, but not as strong as many others in the world. And now in just 70 years, we look at America today as we enter the decade of the seventies. We have 200 million people, and by the end of the century, just 35 years more, 30 years more, we will be

[1] The President's reference to Ohio was intended to be related to the 57 small trees which were a part of the setting, rather than the large tree which came from the State of New York.

300 million people.

And if we want to get the statistics on the other points that I mentioned, there are 85 million television sets, there are 80 million automobiles, there are 300 million radios in America, and 150,000 airplanes.

And we can point to the fact, too, that in this country of ours today, as distinguished from just 70 years ago when that tree was just a sapling out in Ohio—today America is the richest nation in the world; we are the strongest nation in the world. All of these things of course we look to; we point to them with a certain sense of pride. We also recognize that there is another difference, a difference which we should recognize and a difference that we want to correct. Seventy years ago, America was at peace. Today, America is not at peace.

And what we want for this Nation is not only peace now but peace in the years to come, peace for all people in the years to come.

What we must realize, too, that while America did not seek this role of world leadership, that except for the United States of America and the power that we have, that no other nation in the free world today could be free and could expect to have peace unless it were for the strength of the United States.

They could not have peace, except the kind of peace that suffocates freedom. This, as I said, is a role America did not seek. We are the first power to be the major power in the world that did not ask for it; but America, nevertheless, recognizes its role, and we are trying in our own way, sometimes imperfectly, but always, I trust, with high idealism, to meet that responsibility.

So, today I say to you that as we enter the decade of the seventies, America will continue to be rich; America will continue to have more of this world's goods; there will be more television sets and more radios and more automobiles; and, Mr. Secretary, we hope during the decade of the seventies that we will be able to have clean air, clean water, and make progress in all the great problems, including an end to hunger in this country, something we are capable of doing today that we couldn't have done 70 years ago.

But above everything else in this Christmas season, as we open this Pageant of Peace and as we light this Nation's Christmas tree, our wish, our prayer, is for peace, the kind of peace that we can live with, the kind of peace that we can be proud of, the kind of peace that exists not just for now but that gives a chance for our children also to live in peace.

That is what we believe in. That is what Americans stand for and that, believe me, is what we shall have.

And my friends, I also say to you that as we look at this great tree, there is an old saying about Christmas trees. It goes something like this: May a Christmas tree be as sturdy as faith, as high as hope, as wide as love. And I could add, may a Christmas tree, our Christmas tree, be as beautiful as peace.

I think it is. I think it will be. And may this moment be one that history will record was one in which America looked forward to a decade of the seventies in which we could celebrate our Christmases at peace with all the world.

And now with this electronic device, which also did not exist 70 years ago, we light the tree.

NOTE: The President spoke at 5:50 p.m. at the 16th annual Pageant of Peace ceremonies on the Ellipse near the White House. The National Community Christmas Tree was a 65-foot Norway spruce from Crandall Park in Glens Falls, N.Y.

In his opening words he referred to Secretary of the Interior Walter J. Hickel, Representative Carleton J. King of New York, and

Mayor of the District of Columbia Walter E. Washington.

The President's remarks were broadcast on radio and television.

491 Letter to the House and Senate Leadership on Federal Spending and Revenues. *December 17, 1969*

WHEN GOVERNMENT spending gets out of hand, consumer prices go out of sight. To combat rising prices, I proposed last April to hold down Federal spending to $192.9 billion, cutting $4 billion from the programs proposed by the prior administration.

The integrity of the $192.9 billion budget total was seriously threatened in the summer by Congressional actions and by increases in uncontrollable payments such as interest on the public debt. To hold the line, I directed a further cut of $3½ billion in controllable budget outlays. Six out of seven dollars of this reduction was in Defense, a cut which was last week concurred in by the House of Representatives.

The Congress, in midsummer, also expressed its concern for overall fiscal responsibility, fixing a ceiling of $191.9 billion on total budget spending. This is one billion dollars less than my own target.

The Congressional limit, however, was a rubber ceiling. It provided—quite appropriately—an allowance for further increases in those uncontrollable payments, but it also—quite wrongly—removed the incentive for the Congress to exercise continued restraint by providing that increased spending later enacted by the Congress would be added to the ceiling and decreases taken away. The *only* significant decrease the Congress has considered thus far is the defense cut we had already made last summer. Every other major change has been up—more spending, which would have the effect of driving prices upward.

Furthermore, the legal allowance for uncontrollables was limited to $2 billion. But committed government payments in 1970 are likely to exhaust that $2 billion allowance and go an additional $2 billion beyond. Interest cost on the public debt has mounted by another $½ billion. In addition, quite apart from newly proposed Social Security benefit increases, existing Social Security, Medicare and similar benefit payments fixed by law will add another billion dollars to the April estimate. Still another $½ billion overrun is imminent, reflecting increased spending because of the loss of offsetting offshore oil receipts, and a potential shortfall in the sale of government financial assets, due to the persistence of high interest rates. In all, about six billion dollars in fixed, built-in increases have swelled government spending since we took office in January.

Therefore, both the Congressional ceiling and my own fiscal target are in jeopardy. The responsible path toward protecting the buying power of the consumer's dollar is clear. But the Congress has not appeared to be willing to take that path.

Congressional actions that have already passed at least one House could add about $4 billion to Federal spending this fiscal year. Such spending includes:

—Increased educational aid provided by the Labor-HEW appropriations bill.

—A premature civilian and military pay raise, following on the heels of substantial raises just this past summer.

—A 15 per cent increase in Social Security benefits in place of my 10 per cent recommendation, and effective months earlier.

—New legislation, worthy though it may be, to benefit veterans, children and others.

In addition, a billion dollars this year has been lost through Congressional inaction on Administration requests to make the postal system self-supporting and to permit sales of certain financial assets of the Farmers Home Administration and the Veterans Administration—actions which do not affect at all the benefits of these programs.

Taken together, this combination of action and inaction would load an additional five billion dollars onto an already overheated economy.

In spite of these actions that increase *expenditures,* recent Senate tax actions to increase personal income tax exemptions and retain part of the investment credit would, if approved, actually take $1.6 billion away from *revenues.*

The Congress appears to be well on its way to substituting tax reduction for tax reform. This will harm rather than help the average taxpayer. Sugar-coating a bitter pill is understandable, but all sugar coating and no pill will not help the patient. A tax cut for some citizens would

mean a rise in prices for every citizen.

In a situation without parallel in our history, we came into the month of December, almost halfway through the fiscal year, with most of the regular appropriation bills yet to be passed. If the Administration is to achieve its goal of slowing down the rise in prices, it will have to reserve funds on many popular spending programs. The other course—of appealing to sundry interests—would run directly counter to the public interest.

A dollar of spending does not add just one dollar to the spending stream: It is spent, and in turn provides income to someone else to spend again, multiplying its effects. Every dollar released through reduced taxes or increased expenditures will produce several dollars of additional price pressures in the economy as those who receive the initial benefit in turn spend the money. A billion dollars of Federal spending or tax relief can add many times that amount to the escalation of our rising price levels. And inflation—the hole in everybody's pocket—is the most unfair tax of all.

If the American people do not believe that their government will maintain its commitment to a responsible fiscal policy, inflationary expectations will raise prices and interest rates further.

In a year that is already half gone, the Administration's ability to make expenditure cuts in the few areas where we have discretion is quite limited. Significant cuts would adversely affect the proper execution of ongoing government programs.

With the full loss of the surtax by July 1, revenues for the year beginning that day must be calculated from a base $8½ billion lower than the present base. At the same time, increases in uncontrollable Federal payments will raise next year's budget expenditures substantially—probably above $200 billion—quite apart from further Congressional spending actions or Administration initiatives to meet critical national challenges.

The achievement of a sound prosperity with steady economic growth demands restraint now. New Federal programs and increased benefit payments would be dissipated by ever-rising prices.

The Congress, along with the Executive Branch, carries the responsibility for the economic health of the nation.

This budget whipsaw—and the proposed increase in spending and reduction of revenues does whipsaw the consumer—comes at a particularly ironic time in the course of economic events. While restoring order in an economy racked by inflation for over five years requires the patience of Job, the fact is that some results have already been showing up:

— Retail sales have been relatively flat since midsummer.

— Business inventories have been piling up more rapidly, and this may require some further easing of production schedules.

— The consumer price index was rising at the rate of 6.4% per year in the first half of 1969, but the rate has dropped to 5.3% per year since June.

This is tangible evidence that we are beginning to make some progress in relieving those excessive pressures on the economy that have been driving up the cost of living.

We are now, therefore, at a critical moment. If we persevere in strong, responsible fiscal policies, we can expect to see confidence building steadily in the year ahead—confidence that government really does intend to manage economic policies responsibly. The way we handle the Fed-

eral budget will determine whether millions of consumers can balance their family budget.

Unfortunately, reluctance by the Congress to come to grips with the need to hold down prices is recreating doubts about the will of government to persevere. An increase in personal exemptions or further large increases in Federal expenditures, let me repeat, do not make people better off in an economy already under pressure. They simply guarantee that price tags in the grocery stores, and the cost of living generally, will be higher.

These actions go a long way toward explaining why our financial markets find it hard to believe that Washington is capable of responsible budget policy.

Recently high quality bond issues could be marketed only at interest rates in excess of 9 per cent. It is difficult to develop a flourishing mortgage market when high grade corporate bond yields are at these levels. Why are bond rates so high? Contrary to what some believe, the primary reason is not Federal Reserve policy. Interest rates are high because savers and managers of money are insisting that nominal rates be high enough to give them a worthwhile rate of return after the inflation which they are assuming will continue.

We stand at the crossroads of credibility. If we can regain a fiscal grip on ourselves and carry through with a strong budget and fiscal policy, we can build on the growing evidence that policies of 1969 are beginning to exert a stabilizing effect. But if we miss this opportunity, it will be a long time before the public will ever believe that government can manage its finances in any way other than to produce sustained and serious inflation.

For this reason, I urge the Congress to

join with the Executive Branch in a continuing display of determination to hold down spending and maintain revenue so as to contain the cost of living, no matter what the cost in political popularity. At stake is nothing less than the future of the American economy.

Sincerely,

RICHARD NIXON

NOTE: This is the text of identical letters sent to Senator Mike Mansfield of Montana, Senate Majority Leader; Senator Richard B. Russell of Georgia, President pro tempore of the Senate; Senator Hugh Scott of Pennsylvania, Minority Leader of the Senate; Representative Carl Albert of Oklahoma, House Majority Leader; Representative Gerald R. Ford of Michigan, House Minority Leader; and Representative John W. McCormack of Massachusetts, Speaker of the House.

492 Letter to the House and Senate Leadership on HEW-Labor-OEO Appropriations. *December 19, 1969*

I FEEL obliged to inform the Congress, before adjournment, that the development of the HEW-Labor-OEO appropriations has been such as to compel me to veto these appropriations when they arrive on my desk.

I send this advance notice in order to afford the Congress, if it wishes, an opportunity to enact a continuing resolution for these agencies and thereby permit them to operate without the necessity of recalling the Congress in special session.

The HEW appropriations in large part involve mandatory Federal spending. Even the level of appropriations passed by the House of Representatives is more than $1 billion above my budget request. The Senate increased the appropriations further by another $.6 billion. As much as I sympathize with the objectives of some of the programs for which the Congress has voted increased appropriations, I cannot, at this critical point in the battle against inflation, approve so heavy an increase in Federal spending.

The Congress, it appears to me, may meet this situation in one of three ways: first, by sending the Appropriations Act to me for veto, but then to return in special session immediately after Christmas;

second, pass a continuing resolution for these three agencies, send the appropriations to me for veto, and then consider the veto after January 19; or, third, defer further action on these appropriations until after January 19, and provide authority to continue the current level of funding for these agencies in the interim.

The choice among these alternatives rests, of course, with Congress. In the interest of affording a respite for Congress, I suggest either of the continuing resolutions approaches. But, of course, should the special session route be preferred, I will cooperate.

Sincerely,

RICHARD NIXON

NOTE: This is the text of identical letters, dated December 18, 1969, and addressed to Senator Mike Mansfield of Montana, Senate Majority Leader; Senator Hugh Scott of Pennsylvania, Senate Minority Leader; Representative Gerald R. Ford of Michigan, House Minority Leader; and Representative John W. McCormack of Massachusetts, Speaker of the House.

On December 19, 1969, the Senate passed a continuing resolution by a vote of 65 to 10 allowing the Departments of Health, Education, and Welfare, Labor, and the Office of Economic Opportunity to continue spending at their present levels through January 30, 1970.

493   Message to the Senate Transmitting Convention on the Privileges and Immunities of the United Nations.   *December 19, 1969*

To the Senate of the United States:

I transmit herewith the Convention on the Privileges and Immunities of the United Nations with a view to receiving the advice and consent of the Senate to accession.

The United Nations General Assembly unanimously approved the Convention on February 13, 1946, to give precision to the obligations of members under Articles 104 and 105 of the United Nations Charter. Of the 126 United Nations Members, 100 have already become parties to the Convention.

As host to United Nations headquarters the United States bears special responsibility for the status of the United Nations, its officials, and representatives of its members. We should have acceded to the Convention long ago. Over the years, our failure to do so has become a source of embarrassment to the United States as well as increasingly troublesome to the U.N. Secretariat and to a growing number of U.N. Member states.

The Convention was submitted to the first session of the 80th Congress for approval by Joint Resolution together with the Headquarters Agreement Between the United States and the United Nations. The Headquarters Agreement was approved by both Houses of Congress and entered into force on November 21, 1947. The Convention was approved by the Senate and the House Committee on Foreign Affairs, but the House as a whole took no action. It was resubmitted to the 81st Congress, but once again no action was taken. It has not subsequently been resubmitted up to this time although I understand the Chairman of the Foreign Relations Committee inquired during the last Congress as to its status.

In accordance with the more usual practice concerning conventions dealing with diplomatic and consular matters, I have decided now to submit the Convention to the Senate for action under the treaty power of the Constitution. The enclosed report of the Secretary of State explains the Convention and its relation to existing law. Many of the privileges and immunities provided by the Convention are already accorded by the Headquarters Agreement or by the 1945 International Organizations Immunities Act. But under existing law full diplomatic status is not accorded to the Secretary-General to Under Secretaries-General or to non-resident representatives from other countries to United Nations meetings. Accession to this Convention would close these and other anomalous and unintended gaps.

It is my hope that the Senate of the United States will consider this long overdue matter and consent to United States accession at an early date.

RICHARD NIXON

The White House
December 19, 1969

494 Statement Urging Senate and House Conferees To Permit Continued Implementation of the Philadelphia Plan. *December* 19, 1969

THE civil rights policy to which this administration is committed is one of demonstrable deeds—focused where they count. One of the things that counts most is earning power. Nothing is more unfair than that the same Americans who pay taxes should by any pattern of discriminatory practices be deprived of an equal opportunity to work on Federal construction contracts.

The Philadelphia Plan does not set quotas; it points to goals. It does not presume automatic violation of law if the goals are not met; it does require affirmative action if a review of the totality of a contractor's employment practices shows that he is not affording equal employment opportunity.

The Attorney General has assured the Secretary of Labor that the Philadelphia Plan is not in conflict with Title VII of the Civil Rights Act of 1964. I, of course, respect the right and duty of the Comptroller General to render his honest and candid views to the Congress. If in effect we have here a disagreement in legal interpretation between the Attorney General and the Comptroller General the place for the resolution of this issue is in the courts.

However, the rider adopted by the Senate last night, would not only prevent the Federal departments from implementing the Philadelphia Plan, it could even bar a judicial determination of the issue.

Therefore, I urge the conferees to permit the continued implementation of the Philadelphia Plan while the courts resolve this difference between congressional and executive legal opinions.

NOTE: The rider to which the President referred was section 904 of H.R. 15209, a supplemental appropriations bill for fiscal year 1970. A statement on the rider, dated December 20, 1969, by Secretary of Labor Shultz is printed in the Weekly Compilation of Presidential Documents (vol. 5, p. 1762).

Texts of news briefings on the Philadelphia Plan on December 18 and 20 by Secretary Shultz and Assistant Secretary of Labor for Wage and Labor Standards Arthur A. Fletcher were also released by the White House Press Office.

495 Statement on a House of Representatives Amendment to the Philadelphia Plan. *December* 22, 1969

THE House of Representatives now faces an historic and critical civil rights vote.

Tucked into the supplemental appropriations conference report is a provision vesting the Comptroller General with a new quasi-judicial role. The first effect of this proposal will be to kill the "Philadelphia Plan" effort of this administration to open up the building trades to nonwhite citizens. It is argued that the administration seeks to restrict the role of the General Accounting Office and the Comptroller General. This is a false issue.

I wish to assure the Congress and the public of this Nation that I consider the independence of the Comptroller General of the United States of the utmost importance in the separation of powers in our Federal system. The amendment now under discussion by the Congress will not and should not be permitted to bring this principle into any doubt.

Of course, in the conduct of his independent review of all executive actions, the Comptroller General may raise, and has often raised, questions about the legality of Federal contracts and whether funds, according to the law, should be spent under such contracts. The executive has always, will always, give the fullest attention to his recommendations and his rulings.

When rulings differ, however, when the chief legal officer of the executive branch and the chief watchdog of the Congress end up with opposing views on the same matter of law, the place for resolution of such differences is the courts— just as it is for the resolution of differences between private citizens.

The amendment as presently written makes a court review extremely difficult,

even questionable. For example, 14 contracts have been let under the Philadelphia Plan. If the amendment passes, these contracts will have to be canceled. If the contractors should not elect to sue, the executive branch of the Federal Government could not—and the matter would not reach the courts unless a member of my Cabinet were intentionally to violate the law.

The position I am taking is, therefore, that the amendment need not be stricken but that it should be modified to permit prompt court review of any difference between legal opinions of the Comptroller General and those of the executive, and to permit the Comptroller General to have his own counsel (rather than the Attorney General) to represent him in such cases.

To be quite candid, I share the Attorney General's serious doubts as to the constitutionality of this amendment and may have to withhold my signature from any legislation containing it.

---

496   Statement Urging the Establishment of the Position of Under Secretary of State for Western Hemisphere Affairs. *December* 22, 1969

THE UNITED STATES has long had a special concern for its relations with the other nations of the Western Hemisphere. Our relationship has been forged by ties of geography, history, and common interests and aspirations. It is embodied in the web of treaties and commitments that constitute the inter-American system. Above all, the nations of the hemisphere share a common commitment to improve the quality of life for all the peoples of this hemisphere.

To meet the pressing needs of the decade ahead, I have proposed that the nations of the inter-American system develop—in a more mature partnership—a program of action for progress in the 1970's. We have made a start, and are continuing a process of consultation with our hemisphere neighbors, in the crucial areas of expanding trade and accelerating development.

To fulfill more effectively our commitment in this new partnership program will require a significant reorganization and upgrading of our governmental structure dealing with Western Hemisphere affairs. The proposal which the Secretary of State submitted to the Congress on December 20 to establish an Under Secretary of State for Western Hemisphere Affairs is a key element of that effort. It is an important first step designed to:

—produce more effective and efficient implementation of new policy approaches in the Western Hemisphere. The new Under Secretary will be given authority to coordinate all U.S. Government activities in the Western Hemisphere.

—create one place in the U.S. Government where other hemisphere nations can come to discuss their problems. The new Under Secretary will

have the personal authority and responsibility to speed decisions and be responsive to the concerns of our hemisphere partners.

—signify to the nations of the hemisphere the special importance we attach to our relations with them. The new Under Secretary will have the stature and authority to symbolize our commitment to the special Western Hemisphere relationship.

The proposal to establish an Under Secretary for Western Hemisphere Affairs has received wide approval in the hemisphere. It is a step which is long overdue. Early passage of the proposed amendment by the Congress will help to demonstrate our good faith and serious intentions in the quest for a better life for the peoples of the hemisphere.

497 Statement About Congressional Action on the Philadelphia Plan. *December 23, 1969*

I AM deeply gratified that the Congress has acted responsibly to allow continuation of the Philadelphia Plan and our program of positive steps to assure equal job opportunity. The Members of the Congress who contributed to this wise action have my thanks and congratulations.

There is no civil right more central to the American system than the right of equal opportunity. Every American should have equal opportunity for new jobs created by the taxes paid by all Americans. I have worked for implementation of this principle since 1953 when President Eisenhower appointed me Chairman of the President's Committee

on Government Contracts. This administration is determined to see that this right—so long denied or given lip service—becomes national policy.

The Philadelphia Plan has been opening new jobs for minority workers in the construction industry, an industry with a severe labor shortage in skilled crafts. With this action by the Congress, this program of economic opportunity can go forward as planned.

NOTE: By a vote of 208 to 156 the House of Representatives agreed to delete from the conference report on H.R. 15209 the Senate amendment which in effect rejected the Philadelphia Plan. Later the Senate voted 39 to 29 to accept the action of the House of Representatives.

498 Statement on Signing a Bill Affecting Interest, Credit, and Lending. *December 24, 1969*

AS ENACTED by the Congress, S. 2577 contains a number of provisions that the administration did not request and does not desire. However, despite my serious reservations and objections about these provisions, one provision of the bill is of such overwhelming urgency that I must reluctantly give the total legislation my approval. That provision preserves the authority of Federal supervisory agencies to regulate rates of interest paid on accounts at banks and savings and loan associations. That authority is essential to avoid the risk of destructive competition among these institutions.

The Congress could have acted responsibly on this problem merely by extending the authority to regulate these interest rates. However, the Congress chose to do otherwise and included provisions that are both unnecessary and undesirable.

Three provisions either require or increase the likelihood of additional budget outlays at a time when responsible fiscal policy and control of inflation demand restraint:

1. Authority for the Secretary of the Treasury to lend an additional $3 billion to the Federal home loan banks.

2. A reduction in the insurance premiums for Federal savings and loan insurance, which has the effect of increasing budget outlays by $63 million in fiscal year 1970 and $102 million in 1971.

3. An increase of $70 million in the level of lending by the Small Business Administration to small business investment companies in fiscal year 1970.

Two provisions of the bill would authorize voluntary and mandatory credit controls, which, if invoked, would take the Nation a long step toward a directly controlled economy and would weaken the will for needed fiscal and financial discipline.

These aspects of the bill made the decision to sign it a very difficult one, but the need to prevent chaos in our interest rate situation has made my approval imperative.

NOTE: As enacted, the bill (S. 2577), which was signed on December 23, 1969, is Public Law 91-151 (83 Stat. 371).

499 Remarks at a News Briefing on Vice President Agnew's Forthcoming Trip to Asia. *December 24, 1969*

Ladies and gentlemen:

This meeting with the press brings back some reminiscences for me, because I recall when I was in my first year as Vice President, when President Eisenhower sent me on a trip to Asia, a trip which took me clear around the world and which was really my first opportunity to see that part of the world except for service in World War II.

The Vice President is now going to leave on a trip to Asia, which will take him to a number of countries, 37,000 miles, which is more than around the world, although he will be coming back from Asia to the United States directly rather than going on around.

We have the map here just to give you an indication of the scope of the trip. And I should say that in selecting the countries that the Vice President is visiting, the Philippines was selected first, because he is going there as the representative of the President to the inauguration of President [Ferdinand E.] Marcos. The other countries in Asia are for the most part nations that I was unable to visit on my recent Asian trip and in fact, he will be visiting one country, Nepal, that I have never visited. That is quite unusual.

In terms of where he would be going, the map of course is self-explanatory.

He will be swinging out across the Pacific, stopping at Guam, going first to the Philippines, then to the Republic of China, to Thailand, Nepal, Afghanistan, Malaysia, Singapore, Indonesia, Australia, New Zealand, and then back to the United States.

The Vice President will be taking messages to each of the heads of state and heads of government from me to them. He will be prepared to discuss bilat-

eral matters between the United States and the various governments involved, and he also will be prepared to talk to the leaders there with regard to the Nixon Doctrine, which I announced on my trip to Asia at Guam.

In addition to that, I have asked him particularly to emphasize in his talks with Asian leaders the desire of the United States to develop programs, economic programs and other programs, for Asian development after Vietnam.

The Vice President will be prepared to have such discussions with each of the Asian leaders wherever they may be interested in those subjects.

It is a 3-week trip. He will be returning in time for the beginning of the next session, and I wish him very well. And I only wish that I could go along with him, because I have some very pleasant memories of those countries that I visited.

So, we wish you a good trip and a safe return. We might need that one vote margin in the Senate.

NOTE: The President spoke at 12:41 p.m. in the Roosevelt Room at the White House. Following his remarks, Vice President Spiro T. Agnew made a statement and answered questions on his itinerary and plans. A text of the session was released by the White House on December 24, 1969.

The Vice President left on his 25-day Asian trip on December 26, 1969, from Andrews Air Force Base.

---

500 Statement on Signing the Departments of State, Justice, and Commerce, the Judiciary, and Related Agencies Appropriation Act, 1970. *December 29, 1969*

I HAVE SIGNED H.R. 12964, the Departments of State, Justice, and Commerce, the Judiciary, and Related Agen-

cies Appropriation Act, 1970.

While taking this action, I want to point out that I disagree with one of the bill's provisions. Section 706 provides that no funds appropriated under the act may be used to assist any person who has engaged in certain forms of coercive conduct at an institution of higher education. The institution would have an opportunity to initiate or complete appropriate proceedings in order to determine whether the provisions of this limitation applied. Institutions concerned would be required to certify their compliance with this provision to the Secretary of Health, Education, and Welfare at quarterly or semester intervals.

In connection with this provision, I wish to reaffirm a point I have often made: I do not approve of interference by the Federal Government in the internal affairs of our colleges and universities.

I am gravely concerned, of course, about the problem of student unrest. At the same time, I have recognized that the enforcement of discipline and the maintenance of order in our schools is primarily the responsibility of the schools themselves. The Federal Government is ill-fitted to play the role of policeman on our college and university campuses.

The Congress has already enacted into law an appropriate mechanism for cutting off Federal funds to those who participate in serious campus disruptions. In passing Section 504 of the Higher Education Amendments of 1968, the Congress carefully protected the value of academic freedom, the principle of self-policing, and the rights of the individuals concerned. Congress reaffirmed these values when it recently included similar provisions in the authorization acts for the National Aeronautics and Space Administration and the National Science Foundation.

But this approach is not the one which is followed in Section 706 of the bill I am signing. Both the standards for cutting off funds under the current bill and its vague procedural stipulations are different from those in earlier legislation. These inconsistencies could create considerable confusion for institutions which are affected by both the old and the new legislation. Moreover, I know that students and faculty members are giving considerable attention to the fairness of campus disciplinary proceedings, and I am concerned about the possibility that Section 706 might engender further confusion in this area.

In order to minimize confusion and alleviate unwarranted fears, I emphasize that I do not interpret Section 706, including its requirements that institutions periodically certify their compliance with its provisions, as placing the Government in the role of a campus policeman. Under this legislation, as I interpret it, the Federal Government will not take on the role of an enforcer or overseer of college rules and regulations. I appreciate and share fully the concern of the Congress that the taxpayers' money should not go to those who bring disorder to our institutions of higher learning. But I believe that it would be more appropriate if the Congress implemented this concern by extending the coverage of Section 504 of the Higher Education Amendments of 1968.

NOTE: As enacted, the bill (H.R. 12964), approved on December 24, 1969, is Public Law 91–153 (83 Stat. 403).

The National Aeronautics and Space Administration Act, 1970 is Public Law 91–119 (83 Stat. 196) and the National Science Foundation Authorization Act, 1970 is Public Law 91–120 (83 Stat. 203).

501   Statement on Signing the Tax Reform Act of 1969.   *December 30, 1969*

EIGHT MONTHS AGO, I submitted a sweeping set of proposals to the Congress for the first major tax reform in 15 years, one which would make our tax system more fair.

My proposals were carefully balanced to avoid increasing the pressure on prices that were already rising too fast.

Congress has passed an unbalanced bill that is both good and bad. The tax reforms, on the whole, are good; the effect on the budget and on the cost of living is bad.

When the Congress reduces revenues, and at the same time increases appropriations, it causes budget deficits that lead to higher prices.

In terms of long-overdue tax reform, most of my major reform proposals were adopted. Other proposals were worked out between the Congress and the administration; still others were the handiwork of the Congress alone.

—More than 9 million low-income people who pay taxes will be dropped from the tax rolls. This results primarily from the special low income allowance that I proposed last April as a means of making sure that people at or below the poverty level do not have to pay Federal income taxes.

—A large number of high-income persons who have paid little or no Federal income taxes will now bear a fairer share of the tax burden through enactment of a minimum income tax comparable to the proposal that I submitted to the Congress, which closes the loopholes that permitted much of this tax avoidance. However, the highest rates on wages and other earned income, not otherwise tax-sheltered, will be reduced from 70 percent to 50 percent in 1972.

—The Congress accepted my recommendations to reduce sharply the discrimination against single persons in the tax laws.

—Over 19 million additional people who pay taxes will find their annual task easier because they will find it advantageous to use the simple standard deduction, which is being significantly increased, rather than listing each deduction separately.

—Measures are also included that will guard against over-withholding of income taxes. For example, students who work in the summer and who in the past have had taxes withheld and retained by the Government until refund checks were mailed out the following spring, will no longer be subject to such withholding.

—The application of our low income allowance will permit a student in 1970 to earn $1,725—$825 more than at the present time—without paying Federal taxes or being subject to withholding.

—The 255-page bill represents a sweeping revision of the Internal Revenue Code. Section after section is tightened to prevent the avoidance of taxes that has permitted far too many of our citizens to avoid the taxes that others have had to pay.

—Our continuing efforts to meet the Nation's housing needs will be aided. The tax bill encourages rehabilitation of old housing and investment in residential construction.

—Tax-free foundations were brought under much closer Federal scrutiny although Congress wisely rejected provisions that would have hampered legitimate activities of the voluntary sector. At the same time, we must recognize that congressional consideration of this matter reflected a deep and wholly legitimate concern about the role of foundations in our national life.

Congress also accepted this administration's recommendation to increase social security payments, enabling our older citizens to maintain their standard of living in the face of rising prices. Earlier I proposed that this be accomplished through a "catch-up" increase in payments coupled with automatic increases in the years ahead to meet any future rises in living costs. Congress provided instead for a higher one-time increase with no automatic increases in the years ahead. I believe my position was more responsive to the long-range needs of the elderly, but the overriding consideration is that 25 million recipients of social security benefits have fallen behind financially, which makes my approval of this short-range revision necessary.

Despite the achievement of these worthy goals, the decision to sign the bill was not an easy one.

The bill unduly favors spending at the expense of saving at a time when demands on our savings are heavy. This will restrict the flow of savings to help build housing, to provide credit for small business firms and farmers, and to finance needed State and local government projects. It will make our fight against the rising cost of living more difficult.

The critical moment for this legislation came after the Senate had passed a totally irresponsible bill that would have led to a sharp increase in the cost of living for every family in America. In a letter to the leaders of the Congress, I left no doubt that such a bill would be vetoed.

As a result, when Members of the Congress met to work out the differences between the House and Senate bills, the bill that came out of that conference was over $6 billion less inflationary for the next fiscal year than the bill that had passed the Senate. It still falls almost $3 billion short of my original proposals, but this response to my appeal to budgetary sanity makes it possible for me to sign the bill into law.

I am, however, deeply concerned about the reluctance of the Congress to face up to the adverse impact of its tax and spending decisions. If taxes are to be reduced, there must be corresponding reductions on the expenditure side. This has not been forthcoming from the Congress. On the contrary: In the very session when the Congress reduced revenues by $3 billion, it increased spending by $3 billion more than I recommended.

A deficit in the budget at this time would be irresponsible and intolerable. We cannot reduce taxes and increase spending at a time and in a way that raises prices. That would be robbing Peter to pay Paul. That is why I shall take the action I consider necessary to present a balanced budget for the next fiscal year.

I am also concerned about the constraint this act imposes on Government revenues in future years, limiting our ability to meet tomorrow's pressing needs.

Seldom is any piece of major legislation fully satisfactory to a President. This bill is surely no exception. But I sign it because I believe that, on balance, it is a necessary beginning in the process of making our tax system fair to the taxpayer.

NOTE: As enacted, the bill (H.R. 13270) is Public Law 91–172 (83 Stat. 487).

The White House also released a text of

portions of the statement as read by the President for later television and radio broadcast and the text of a news briefing on the act by Secretary of the Treasury David M. Kennedy and Assistant Secretary of the Treasury Edwin S. Cohen.

502   Statement on Signing the Federal Coal Mine Health and Safety Act of 1969. *December 30, 1969*

THE HEALTH and safety of American workers is a primary concern of this administration. With this concern in mind, one of my very early legislative recommendations was in the area of coal mine health and safety. This has culminated today in my signing of the Federal Coal Mine Health and Safety Act of 1969. The health and safety provisions of this act represent an historic advance in industrial practices.

However, I do have reservations about certain serious issues raised by the act. In signing it I wish to bring to the attention of the Congress and the Nation three points I consider to be of major importance:

First, workmen's compensation has been and should be a State responsibility. Title IV of this act gives the Federal Government responsibility in this area. I want to emphasize very strongly that Title IV is temporary, limited, and unique and in no way should it be considered a precedent for future Federal administration of work-

men's compensation programs. With the exception of continuing benefit payments to claimants establishing eligibility during the period prior to December 31, 1972, all Federal responsibility in this area will expire within 7 years.

Next, this act creates confusion about the consistency of standards in federally administered disability programs. I have therefore instructed the Secretary of Health, Education, and Welfare in administering this program to apply wherever possible standards consistent with those under the existing Social Security Act disability program.

Finally, the act may present problems of administration that require legislative changes. If such problems arise, I will propose corrective legislation.

While I have these concerns about the problems presented by the act, I have great pride in this historic legislation. It represents a crucially needed step forward in the protection of America's coal miners.

NOTE: As enacted, the bill (S. 2917) is Public Law 91–173 (83 Stat. 742).

503   Remarks on Arrival at El Toro Marine Corps Air Station, California. *December 30, 1969*

WE WOULD LIKE to express our appreciation to all of you who have come out to the airport and have given us such

a wonderful welcome as we return home to California.

I noted that a few of you wore coats. I

can't understand it. We just came from Washington and we have a wonderful white Christmas there. It feels very warm to me here in California, not only because of the weather but because of the warmth of your welcome.

And too, I want you to know that on this trip we are going to participate in only one public event. It is one we have been looking forward to, and it is something which I think you, because most of you are residents of Orange County and of California, will be interested in. While we are here on this trip, the three of us are going to register as voters in California, our home State. So I wanted to be sure that my Congressman, Jimmy [James B.] Utt, was aware of the fact that he better

be nice to me and answer my mail from now on, all the letters that I send to him.

And here he is—Jimmy.

So we simply want to say that after 4 months it is very good to be back here. We know that returning to California has always meant a great deal to us but particularly now in the middle of this holiday season.

We want to take this opportunity to wish every one of you a very Happy New Year, and we hope we can make it a peaceful new year, too.

Thank you.

NOTE: The President spoke at 4:35 p.m. after he arrived with his wife and daughter Tricia for a 12-day vacation at their home in San Clemente, Calif.

504   Statement on Signing the Foreign Assistance Act of 1969.   *December* 31, 1969

THE Foreign Assistance Act which I have signed today represents evidence of the continuing commitment of the United States to provide assistance to the less developed nations of the world. It is my personal conviction that such assistance remains vitally necessary if we are to effectively cooperate with less wealthy countries struggling to improve the lives of their citizens.

It is also my personal conviction, as I stated in submitting this year's foreign assistance legislation, that substantial improvements in our aid program are necessary. Several such improvements are already underway: This act authorizes an Overseas Private Investment Corporation, to give new direction to U.S. private investment abroad; we have increased our emphasis on technical assistance; we will channel a greater percentage of our assist-

ance through multilateral institutions; and we will expand our assistance to food production and family planning programs.

I recognize that many Members of Congress and many Americans believe that a more extensive renovation of our foreign assistance program is necessary. I share that belief. For that reason I look forward to the forthcoming report of my Task Force on International Development, of which Rudolph Peterson is Chairman, and expect its recommendations to form the basis of an innovative and more effective foreign assistance program which will justify even greater support from the Congress and the American people. The 2-year authorization provided in the Foreign Assistance Act of 1969 will facilitate careful consideration of that report.

While our new program is being formulated, however, it is essential that we maintain an adequate level of foreign assistance. I submitted the lowest aid request in history and regret that this act reduced that request substantially. Further large cuts in the appropriations bill would have serious consequences for U.S. foreign policy.

The task of overcoming poverty and human misery at home and abroad is a formidable one. It is the most ambitious and most crucial challenge in human history. It is one to which this country has made a great contribution, of which we should be proud. It is also one which will call upon us and other wealthy nations for greater efforts in the future.

NOTE: As enacted, the bill (H.R. 14580), approved on December 30, 1969, is Public Law 91–175 (83 Stat. 805).

The text of the announcement of the appointment of Rudolph A. Peterson as Chairman of the Presidential Task Force on International Development is printed in the Weekly Compilation of Presidential Documents (vol. 5, p. 1221).

The statement was released at San Clemente, Calif.

505   Statement on Signing the Bill Establishing the Cabinet Committee on Opportunities for Spanish-Speaking People.   *December 31, 1969*

IN THE 1970 census we will learn, for the first time, exactly what portion of the American public is made up of Spanish-speaking and Spanish-surname Americans. It is estimated that between 8 and 10 million of our people draw upon a Mexican, Puerto Rican, or Cuban heritage.

Many members of this significant minority group have been too long denied genuine, equal opportunity. For example, many have been denied the dignity that comes from useful job training, good jobs, and a real share in American business enterprise.

The bill before me transforms the Inter-Agency Committee on Mexican American Affairs into a statutory Cabinet Committee on Opportunities for Spanish-Speaking People, and authorizes funding for this important activity. This was made necessary when legislation passed in 1968 prohibited financing of interagency committees through contributions from member agencies.

In signing this bill, I reaffirm the concern of this Government for providing equal opportunity to all Spanish-speaking Americans—to open doors to better jobs and the ownership and management of business.

The Cabinet Committee will foster a new awareness within Government of the specific needs of this significant group and will insure that existing and future Government programs in fact reach the Spanish-speaking people.

It will, for example, immediately address itself to enlisting support of the private sector in a national housing corporation to provide technical assistance to Spanish-speaking people preparing proposals to the Department of Housing and Urban Development. It will also work closely with the Department of Commerce's Office of Minority Business Enterprise in assisting Spanish-speaking people to launch their own businesses and generate new job opportunities. It will point up the need for a bilingual dimension in education.

This Committee will depend for its success upon four elements: the dedication of its membership, the support of government, the receptivity of private enterprise, and the proven drive and talent of the Spanish-speaking peoples.

Working together, we can swing wide the door to dignity and self-help to millions of our fellow citizens. This administration is determined to speed the day when every member of this group has his fair share of opportunity, and the American system fully benefits from the resourcefulness and traditions of the Spanish-speaking heritage. Those traditions include an admirable respect for law, strong family and religious ties, and a proud individualism.

Accordingly, I sign this bill *con gusto*— with the enthusiasm and determination to make equal opportunity a reality in these United States.

NOTE: As enacted, the bill (S. 740), approved December 30, 1969, is Public Law 91–181 (83 Stat. 838).

The statement was released at San Clemente, Calif.

Appendix A—Additional White House Releases

NOTE: This appendix lists those releases which are neither printed as items in this volume nor listed in subsequent appendices.

January

22 Announcement of nomination of Phillip S. Hughes as Deputy Director of the Bureau of the Budget

22 Secretary Kennedy's remarks to the press on introducing the nominees for Treasury Under Secretaries

22 Announcement of nomination of Dr. Charls E. Walker as Under Secretary and Paul A. Volker as Under Secretary for Monetary Affairs, Department of the Treasury

23 Announcement by the Assistant to the President for Urban Affairs, Dr. Daniel P. Moynihan, of appointment of six members to his staff

23 Announcement of signing of Executive Order 11452 establishing the Council for Urban Affairs

23 Biographical data on Alexander P. Butterfield, appointed Deputy Assistant to the President

24 Announcement of nomination of David A. Hamil as Administrator, Rural Electrification Administration

24 Announcement of nomination of William Eugene Galbraith as Deputy Administrator for State and County Operations, Department of Agriculture

24 List of 67 Air Force officers to be nominated for promotion to the temporary grade of Brigadier General

25 Announcement of nominees for five key positions in the Department of Housing and Urban Development

January

25 Biographical data on Richard C. Van Dusen, nominated to be Under Secretary, Department of Housing and Urban Development

25 Biographical data on Floyd H. Hyde, nominated to be Assistant Secretary for Model Cities and Government Relations, Department of Housing and Urban Development

25 Biographical data on Samuel C. Jackson, nominated to be Assistant Secretary for Metropolitan Development, Department of Housing and Urban Development

25 Biographical data on Samuel J. Simmons, nominated to be Assistant Secretary for Equal Opportunity, Department of Housing and Urban Development

25 Biographical data on Sherman Unger, nominated to be General Counsel, Department of Housing and Urban Development

26 Telegram to Mrs. Charlie Everett following the death of her son, Representative Robert A. Everett

26 Announcement of flood disaster assistance following heavy rains in California.

28 News briefing by Senator Dirksen and Representative Ford following the President's meeting with Republican congressional leadership

28 Announcement of nomination of George B. Hansen as Deputy Under Secretary for Congressional Relations, Department of Agriculture

1051

39–861—71——70

January

28 Announcement of nomination of Fred J. Russell to be Deputy Director, Office of Emergency Preparedness

28 Biographical data on Fred J. Russell, nominated to be Deputy Director, Office of Emergency Preparedness

28 Announcement of nomination of Russell E. Train to be Under Secretary of the Department of the Interior

28 Biographical data on Russell E. Train, nominated to be Under Secretary of the Department of the Interior

28 Background release on the President's Irish setter, King Timahoe

29 Biographical data on Gerard C. Smith, nominated to be Director, United States Arms Control and Disarmament Agency

29 Announcement of nomination of Allen L. Donielson and Richard A. Dier to be United States Attorneys

29 Announcement of nomination of Rear Adm. Jackson D. Arnold for promotion to the grade of vice admiral

29 Announcement of approval of selection board recommendations on promotion of three United States Marine Corps Reserve officers

30 Biographical data on Elizabeth Duncan Koontz, nominated to be the representative of the United States on the Commission on the Status of Women of the Economic and Social Council of the United Nations

30 Announcement of the first group in a series of directives to the heads of Federal agencies

30 Announcement of nominees for five key positions in the Post Office Department

30 Biographical data on Elmer Theodore Klassen, nominated to be Deputy Postmaster General, Post Office Department

January

30 Biographical data on James W. Hargrove, nominated to be Assistant Postmaster General, Bureau of Finance and Administration, Post Office Department

30 Biographical data on Kenneth A. Housman, nominated to be Assistant Postmaster General, Bureau of Personnel, Post Office Department

30 Biographical data on John L. O'Marra, nominated to be Assistant Postmaster General, Bureau of Facilities, Post Office Department

30 Biographical data on David A. Nelson, nominated to be General Counsel, Post Office Department

31 Announcement of nomination of J. Curtis Counts to be Director, Federal Mediation and Conciliation Service

31 News conference of Secretary of Labor George P. Shultz and J. Curtis Counts announcing Mr. Counts' nomination as Director, Federal Mediation and Conciliation Service

31 Biographical data on Donald Eugene Santarelli nominated as Associate Deputy Attorney General for the Administration of Criminal Justice, Department of Justice

February

1 Announcement of itinerary of Astronaut Frank Borman's goodwill tour of Western Europe

1 Biographical data on Albert W. Sherer, Jr., nominated as Ambassador Extraordinary and Plenipotentiary of the United States of America to the Republic of Equatorial Guinea

1 Biographical data on Maj. Gen. Frederick J. Clarke, appointed Chief of Engineers, United States Army

1 Biographical data on Maj. John V. Brennan, United States Marine Corps, appointed Assistant Military Aide at the White House

February

1 Biographical data on Lt. Comdr. Charles R. Larson, United States Navy, appointed Assistant Military Aide at the White House

1 Biographical data on Lt. Col. Vernon C. Coffey, Jr., United States Army, appointed Assistant Military Aide at the White House

3 Announcement of additional directives to the heads of Federal agencies

3 Biographical data on James E. Allen, Jr., nominated as Assistant Secretary for Education and United States Commissioner of Education, Department of Health, Education, and Welfare

3 Announcement of recommendations that planning for post-Vietnam economic adjustment be assigned to the Cabinet Committee on Economic Policy

3 Biographical data on Rita E. Hauser appointed as United States Representative on the Human Rights Commission of the Economic and Social Council of the United Nations

4 Announcement of 13 new metropolitan chairmen for the National Alliance of Businessmen

4 Biographical data on Dr. Paul W. McCracken, Chairman of the Council of Economic Advisers

4 Biographical data on Herbert Stein, a member of the Council of Economic Advisers

4 Biographical data on Hendrik S. Houthakker, a member of the Council of Economic Advisers

4 Biographical data on Dr. Arthur F. Burns, appointed Counsellor to the President

4 Biographical data on George A. Lincoln, Director of the Office of Emergency Preparedness

4 Biographical data on Martin J. Hillenbrand, nominated to be Assistant Secretary for European Affairs, State Department

February

4 Biographical data on Joseph J. Sisco, nominated to be Assistant Secretary for Near Eastern and South Asian Affairs, State Department

4 Biographical data on Samuel DePalma, nominated to be Assistant Secretary for International Organization Affairs, State Department

4 Biographical data on Lt. Col. Ralph D. Albertazzie, appointed Commander of the President's aircraft

4 Biographical data on Col. Walter R. Tkach, appointed Physician to the President

5 News briefing by Senator Dirksen and Representative Ford following the President's meeting with Republican congressional leadership

5 Statement by Postmaster General Winton M. Blount on appointment of postmasters and rural carriers

5 News briefing of Postmaster General Winton M. Blount on appointment of postmasters and rural carriers

5 News briefing of Dr. Lee A DuBridge, Director, Office of Science and Technology, on the expenditure ceiling for the National Science Foundation

6 Tentative schedule of the President's trip to Western Europe

6 News conference of Dr. John A. Hannah, nominated as Administrator, Agency for International Development

6 Biographical data on Dr. John A. Hannah, nominated as Administrator of the Agency for International Development

7 Announcement on the structure, role, and staff of the National Security Council

7 Biographical data on newly appointed members of the National Security Council.

February

7 Biographical data on John G. Veneman, nominated as Under Secretary of the Department of Health, Education, and Welfare

7 Announcement of Executive Order 11454 granting authority to the Senate Committee on Government Operations to inspect certain tax returns

7 Announcement of intention to nominate four persons to positions in the Department of Transportation

7 Biographical data on James M. Beggs, nominated as Under Secretary, Department of Transportation

7 Biographical data on Dr. Paul Cherington, nominated as Assistant Secretary of Transportation for Policy and International Affairs, Department of Transportation

7 Biographical data on James D'Orma Braman, nominated as Assistant Secretary for Urban Systems and Environment, Department of Transportation

7 Biographical data on Charles D. Baker, nominated as Deputy Under Secretary, Department of Transportation

7 News briefing of John A. Volpe, Secretary, Department of Transportation on various transportation programs

7 Announcement of resignations of Ralph M. Paiewonsky as Governor of the Virgin Islands and Ridgway B. Knight as U.S. Ambassador to Belgium

8 Announcement of directive on prompt release of statistics by Federal agencies

8 Announcement of additional directives to the heads of Federal agencies

8 News briefing by the Vice President following a meeting of the Council for Urban Affairs on the poverty program and the Manpower Administration

9 Announcement of investigation by Presidential Assistant Robert J. Brown of tornadoes and gas explosion in Mississippi

February

10 Announcement of additional directives to the heads of Federal agencies

10 Memorandum from Robert Ellsworth, Assistant to the President, on the transpacific route investigation

11 Announcement of nomination of James D. O'Connell to be Assistant Director, Office of Emergency Preparedness

11 Announcement of nomination of Jerome M. Rosow to be Assistant Secretary for Policy Development and Research, Department of Labor

11 Announcement of the visit to Washington on March 31, 1969, of Prime Minister John G. Gorton of Australia

11 Biographical data on Prime Minister John G. Gorton of Australia

11 Announcement of appointment of 19 members to the 1969 Assay Commission

11 Biographical data on 19 members appointed to the 1969 Assay Commission

11 Announcement of assignment of Lt. Gen. Frederick C. Weyand, United States Army, as Military Adviser to the Chairman of the United States Delegation, United States Embassy, Paris

11 Biographical data on Lt. Gen. Frederick C. Weyand, United States Army

11 Biographical data on John L. Campbell, appointed Staff Assistant to the President's Special Consultant Charles B. Wilkinson

11 Biographical data on William B. Mullins, appointed Staff Assistant to the President's Special Consultant Charles B. Wilkinson

11 News conference of Attorney General John N. Mitchell and Arthur J. Sills, President, Executive Committee of the National Association of Attorneys General, on efforts to control crime

February

11 List of members of the Executive Committee of the National Association of Attorneys General

11 List of members of 1968 U.S. Davis Cup tennis team who lunched with the President

11 Biographical data on Miss Willie Mae Rogers, appointed Consultant to the President for Consumer Affairs

12 Announcement of appointment of Richard T. Burress as Deputy Counsel to the President

12 Announcement of appointment of Tom Cole as Deputy Special Assistant to the President

12 News conference of Robert H. Finch, Secretary; James Farmer, Assistant Secretary for Administration-designate; and Creed C. Black, Assistant Secretary for Legislation-designate, Department of Health, Education, and Welfare, on the nominations of Mr. Farmer and Mr. Black

12 Biographical data on James Farmer, nominated as Assistant Secretary for Administration, Department of Health, Education, and Welfare

12 Biographical data on Creed C. Black, nominated as Assistant Secretary for Legislation, Department of Health, Education, and Welfare

12 Biographical data on Bruce Rabb, appointed as a Staff Assistant to the Special Assistant to the President Robert J. Brown

12 News briefing by Governor Nelson A. Rockefeller of New York and Dr. Daniel P. Moynihan, Assistant to the President for Urban Affairs, on Federal-State relations

12 News conference by Miss Willie Mae Rogers on the position of Consultant to the President for Consumer Affairs

13 Biographical data on Gilbert Hahn, Jr., nominated to be Chairman of the District of Columbia Council for the term expiring February 1, 1972

February

13 Biographical data on Sterling Tucker, nominated to be Vice Chairman of the District of Columbia Council for the term expiring February 1, 1972

13 Biographical data on Jerry A. Moore, nominated to be a member of the District of Columbia Council for the term expiring February 1, 1972

13 Announcement of report of Emergency Board No. 174 on a railway labor dispute

13 Announcement of appointment of a 14-member panel to consider oil spillage problems

13 List of members of the National Science Board of the National Science Foundation

13 List of winners of the Arthur S. Flemming Award

14 List of officials attending the ceremony for the signing of Executive Order 11455, establishing the Office of Intergovernmental Relations

14 Biographical data on Nils A. Boe, appointed as Director of the Office of Intergovernmental Relations

14 News briefing by the Vice President on the Office of Intergovernmental Relations

14 Announcement of intention to nominate Rear Adm. Robert L. Townsend, United States Navy, for appointment to the grade of vice admiral and assignment as Commander, Naval Air Force, U.S. Atlantic Fleet

14 Biographical data on Rear Adm. Robert L. Townsend

14 Announcement of intention to nominate Rear Adm. Vincent P. de Poix, United States Navy, for appointment to the grade of vice admiral and assignment as Deputy Director for Administration, Evaluation and Management, Office of Director of Defense Research and Engineering, Defense Department

14 Biographical data on Gen. Robert L. Schulz, appointed as Special Assistant to the President for Liaison with Former Presidents

14 Biographical data on Gen. Frank Schaffer Besson, Jr., assigned as Chairman, Joint Logistic Review Board

15 Announcement of decision of Miss Willie Mae Rogers not to serve as Consultant to the President for Consumer Affairs

15 Announcement of the renaming of two Presidential cabin cruisers in honor of the President's daughters

17 List of officers of the Urban Coalition attending a meeting of the Council for Urban Affairs

17 News conference by John Gardner, Chairman, Urban Coalition, and Dr. Daniel P. Moynihan, Assistant to the President for Urban Affairs following a meeting of the Urban Affairs Council

17 Announcement of nomination of Vice Adm. Andrew McB. Jackson, Jr., United States Navy, for appointment to the grade of vice admiral on the retired list; Vice Adm. John M. Lee, United States Navy, for appointment as a senior member of the Military Staff Committee of the United Nations; and of assignment of Maj. Gen. Charles A. Corcoran, United States Army, as Commanding General, I Field Force, United States Army, Vietnam, and appointment to the grade of lieutenant general

18 News briefing by Senator Dirksen and Representative Ford following the President's meeting with Republican congressional leadership

18 Announcement of presentation of awards of the American Heart Association

18 Announcement of transmittal to the Congress of annual report of the National Science Board

18 Announcement of a study of the operation of the Bureau of Indian Affairs

19 Biographical data on Donald L. Jackson, nominated to be a member of the Interstate Commerce Commission

20 Announcement of intention to nominate seven key officials to positions in the Department of Commerce

20 Biographical data on Kenneth N. Davis, Jr., nominated to be Assistant Secretary of Commerce for Domestic and International Business, Department of Commerce

20 Biographical data on Robert A. Podesta, nominated to be Assistant Secretary of Commerce for Economic Development

20 Biographical data on James T. Lynn, nominated to be General Counsel for the Department of Commerce

20 Biographical data on Andrew E. Gibson, nominated to be Maritime Administrator

20 Biographical data on C. Langhorne Washburn, nominated as Director of the United States Travel Service

20 Biographical data on G. Fred Steele, nominated as Federal Cochairman of the Coastal Plains Regional Commission

20 Biographical data on W. D. Brewer, nominated as Federal Cochairman of the Four Corners Regional Commission

20 Announcement of request for supplemental appropriation for the Commodity Credit Corporation

20 Announcement of approval of foreign air carrier permit

20 Announcement of nomination of Rear Adm. Edwin B. Hooper, United States Navy, for promotion to the grade of vice admiral and assignment as Navy member, Joint Logistic Review Board

February

20 Announcement of nominations of Lt. Gen. Ferdinand J. Chesarek for promotion to the grade of general and for assignment as Commanding General, United States Army Materiel Command; of Maj. Gen. William E. DePuy for promotion to the grade of lieutenant general and assignment as the Assistant Vice Chief of Staff, United States Army; and of Lt. Gen. Harry J. Lemley, Jr., for assignment as Senior United States Army Member, Military Staff Committee, United Nations

20 News conference by Maurice H. Stans, Secretary of Commerce, on appointments to the Department

20 Biographical data on Hilary J. Sandoval, Jr., nominated to be Administrator of the Small Business Administration

20 Biographical data on James F. Battin, nominated to be United States District Judge for the District of Montana

20 Biographical data on Mrs. Jean Picker, appointed as Representative of the United States on the Social Commission of the Economic and Social Council of the United Nations

21 Statement on the appointment of Donald M. Kendall as Chairman of the National Alliance of Businessmen

21 Biographical data on Donald M. Kendall

21 Announcement of intention to nominate Albert L. Cole as a member of the Board of Directors, Corporation for Public Broadcasting

22 Announcement of flood disaster relief funds for California

22 Biographical data on Clarence Clyde Ferguson, Jr., appointed as Special Coordinator on relief to civilian victims of the Nigerian civil war

22 List of members of the President's party and of the news media accompanying the President on his trip to Europe

February

22 Background information on previous Presidential visits abroad

22 Biographical data on Hamer H. Budge, nominated as Chairman of the Securities and Exchange Commission

26 List of German citizens who met with the President

26 List of resignations of Government officials accepted by the President

27 Announcement of establishment of an interdepartmental committee to review the supersonic transport program

27 Biographical data and nomination of Robert L. Kunzig to be Administrator of the General Services Administration

March

1 Announcement of discussions in Paris between Secretary Rogers and Sigismund von Braun, Ambassador to France from the Federal Republic of Germany

1 List of French citizens meeting with the President

1 Announcement concerning threat of floods from accumulated snow

1 White House statement on the President's 94 directives to Federal agencies

4 Announcement of Executive Order 11457 on inspection of certain tax returns by the House Committee on Government Operations

5 Biographical data on Thomas O. Paine, nominated to be Administrator of the National Aeronautics and Space Administration

5 Background information on the Apollo 8 flight and Astronauts Borman, Lovell, and Anders

5 Background information on the Robert H. Goddard Memorial Trophy

1057

March

5 News conference of Secretary of Commerce Stans and Robert J. Brown, Special Assistant to the President on minority business enterprise

5 List of individuals attending the signing of Executive Order 11458 on minority business enterprise

5 Announcement of assignment of Maj. Gen. Oren E. Hurlbut as Army member, Joint Logistic Review Board, and of his promotion to the grade of lieutenant general

6 List of winners of the Federal Woman's Award

6 Announcement of intention to nominate Lt. Gen. Robert E. Cushman, Jr., as Deputy Director, Central Intelligence Agency

6 Biographical data on Nathaniel Samuels, nominated to be a Deputy Under Secretary of State for Economic Affairs

6 News conference of Secretary of State Rogers and Nathaniel Samuels, Deputy Under Secretary of State for Economic Affairs-designate on his nomination

7 Announcement of intention to nominate Peter A. Bove to be Governor of the Virgin Islands

7 Announcement of intention to nominate Henry Kearns to be President of the Export-Import Bank of the United States

7 Announcement of report on a railway labor dispute by Emergency Board No. 175

11 News briefing on Presidential legislation submitted to Congress by Senator Dirksen, Representative Ford, and Press Secretary Ziegler following the President's meeting with Republican congressional leadership

11 Background information on the Easter Seal ceremony

11 Statement on the appointment of John N. Irwin II as special emissary to Peru

March

11 Announcement of intention to nominate William B. Buffum, Christopher H. Phillips, and Glenn A. Olds as United States Representatives to the United Nations

11 Biographical data on William B. Buffum, nominated to be the Deputy Representative of the United States to the United Nations

11 Biographical data on Christopher H. Phillips, nominated to be Deputy Representative of the United States in the Security Council of the United Nations

11 Biographical data on Glenn A. Olds, nominated to be the Representative of the United States on the Economic and Social Council of the United Nations

12 Announcement of nomination of Preston Martin to be a member and Chairman of the Federal Home Loan Bank Board

12 Announcement of forthcoming retirement of Gen. Lyman Lemnitzer, to be succeeded by Gen. Andrew J. Goodpaster as Supreme Allied Commander, Europe

12 Announcement of intention to nominate Henry Loomis to be Deputy Director, United States Information Agency

12 Announcement of intention to nominate Lawrence H. Silberman to be Solicitor, Department of Labor

13 Announcement of appointment of Lynn Townsend as Vice Chairman and Paul W. Kayser as Executive Vice Chairman, National Alliance of Businessmen

13 Announcement of intention to nominate William H. Brown III to be a member, Equal Employment Opportunity Commission

13 News briefing by Secretary of Labor Shultz, Assistant Secretary for Manpower Weber, and Press Secretary Ziegler on reorganization of the Manpower Administration of the Labor Department

March

14 Announcement of intention to nominate Marshall Green to be Assistant Secretary of State for East Asian and Pacific Affairs, Department of State

14 Announcement of intention to nominate Art Fletcher as Assistant Secretary of Labor for Wage and Labor Standards, Department of Labor

14 List of people attending the White House dinner of March 14, 1969

17 Announcement of intention to nominate John D. J. Moore as United States Ambassador to Ireland

17 Statement by the Vice President on the National Summer Youth Program

17 Fact sheet on the National Summer Youth Program

17 Biographical data on Capt. James A. Lovell, Jr., United States Navy, appointed as the President's Consultant on Physical Fitness and Sports

17 News briefing by the Vice President, Capt. James A. Lovell, United States Navy, Consultant to the President on Physical Fitness and Sports, and Ronald L. Ziegler, Press Secretary, on the summer youth program

17 Letter from the President's Science Adviser on the proposed antiballistic missile system

17 List of members attending the meeting of the President's Science Advisory Committee

18 News briefing by Senator Dirksen and Representative Ford following the President's meeting with Republican congressional leadership

18 Announcement of intention to nominate Randolph W. Thrower as Commissioner, Internal Revenue Service

18 Announcement of intention to nominate Walter C. Sauer for reappointment as First Vice President, Export-Import Bank of the United States

18 Announcement of intention to nominate Joseph H. Blatchford as Director, Peace Corps

March

18 Biographical data on Maj. Gen. Carl C. Turner, United States Army, retired, head of the United States Marshals

18 Biographical data on James Elliott Williams, nominated to be United States Marshal for the District of South Carolina

19 Announcement of actions on task force recommendations concerning lumber and plywood prices

19 Announcement of intention to nominate Otto F. Otepka as a member, Subversive Activities Control Board

19 Announcement of intention to nominate Maj. Gen. Louis B. Robertshaw for promotion to the rank of lieutenant general, United States Marine Corps

19 Announcement of the presentation of the Boy of the Year award

20 Announcement of report on increased job opportunities for minorities

20 Announcement of intention to nominate John B. Waters, Jr., as Federal Cochairman, Appalachian Regional Commission

20 Announcement of Executive Order 11460 reconstituting the President's Foreign Intelligence Advisory Board

24 Announcement of assignment of Lt. Gen. William B. Rosson, United States Army, as Deputy Commander, United States Military Assistance Command, Vietnam, and Maj. Gen. Julian J. Ewell, United States Army, as Commanding General, II Field Force, Vietnam

24 Announcement of appointment of Col. S. H. Bear, United States Air Force, as Assistant Physician to the President

25 News briefing of Senator Dirksen and Representative Ford following the President's meeting with Republican congressional leadership

25 Background information on the Walt Disney Commemorative Medal

Appendix A

Appendix A

April

19 Announcement of flood relief funds for Nevada

21 Announcement of intention to nominate Donald Rumsfeld as Director of the Office of Economic Opportunity

21 Statement by Representative Donald Rumsfeld

21 News conference by Representative Rumsfeld on his appointment

21 Announcement of report on a railway labor dispute by Emergency Board No. 173

22 News briefing by Senator Dirksen and Representative Ford following the President's meeting with Republican congressional leadership

22 Announcement of intention to nominate Guilford Dudley, Jr., to be United States Ambassador to Denmark

23 Announcement of intention to nominate Dr. Theos J. Thompson as a member, Atomic Energy Commission

23 Announcement of intention to nominate Robert H. McBride of the District of Columbia to be United States Ambassador to Mexico

24 Announcement of intention to nominate Edward E. Johnston as High Commissioner, Trust Territory of the Pacific Islands

24 Announcement of intention to nominate Francis J. Galbraith to be United States Ambassador to Indonesia

24 Announcement of appointment of five new members of the President's Science Advisory Committee

24 Biographical data on the five new members of the President's Science Advisory Committee

24 News briefing by Vice President Agnew, Dr. Daniel P. Moynihan, Mayor Carl B. Stokes of Cleveland, and Mayor Kevin White of Boston following the President's meeting with mayors

April

25 Announcement of intention to nominate Francis E. Meloy, Jr., to be United States Ambassador to the Dominican Republic

25 Announcement of intention to nominate Sheldon B. Vance to be United States Ambassador to the Democratic Republic of the Congo (Kinshasa)

25 Announcement of flood and storm disaster assistance for Iowa and Arkansas

28 Announcement of intention to nominate Armin H. Meyer to be United States Ambassador to Japan

28 Announcement of appointment of a 10-man Commission on Presidential Scholars

28 Announcement of appointment of five new members to the White House Staff

29 Announcement of intention to nominate Matthew J. Looram, Jr., to be United States Ambassador to Dahomey

29 Announcement of intention to nominate Oliver L. Troxel, Jr., to be United States Ambassador to Zambia

29 News briefing of Senator Dirksen and Representative Ford following the President's meeting with Republican congressional leadership

29 Announcement of selection of Presidential Australian Science Scholars

29 News briefing by Roy Ash, Chairman of the President's Advisory Council on Executive Organization on organization of Government agencies

30 News briefing by Secretary of Housing and Urban Development George W. Romney, Special Consultant on Voluntary Action Max M. Fisher, and Press Secretary Ronald L. Ziegler on voluntary action

30 Announcement of intention to nominate Daniel Z. Henkin as Assistant Secretary for Public Affairs, Department of Defense

30 Announcement of appointment of Sterling Cole as Representative of the United States to the Southern Interstate Nuclear Board

April

30 Announcement of intention to nominate John Davis Lodge to be United States Ambassador to Argentina

30 Announcement of intention to nominate Spencer M. King to be United States Ambassador to Guyana

May

1 Announcement of intention to nominate Jack Hood Vaughn to be United States Ambassador to Colombia

1 Announcement of Federal disaster assistance for Wisconsin following floods

1 List of guests accompanying the President to the Kentucky Derby

2 Announcement of new program for Federal executive interns

2 News briefing by Charles B. Wilkinson, Special Assistant and Jeffrey Donfeld, Staff Assistant to Mr. Wilkinson on the executive intern program

2 Announcement of intention to nominate Bert M. Tollefson, Jr., to be Assistant Administrator for Legislative and Public Affairs, Agency for International Development

2 Announcement of appointment of J. William Henderson, Jr., as a member of the Golden Spike Centennial Celebration Commission

2 Announcement of intention to nominate Frank Q. Nebeker to be an Associate Judge, District of Columbia Court of Appeals

2 News briefing by John W. Dean III, Associate Deputy Attorney General, and David A. Nelson, General Counsel, Post Office Department, on obscene and pornographic materials

2 Announcement of intention to nominate James F. Leonard, Jr., as Assistant Director for International Relations, United States Arms Control and Disarmament Agency

2 Announcement of appointment of Charles F. Butler as Representative of the United States, Council of the International Civil Aviation Organization

May

2 Announcement of intention to nominate Murray Weidenbaum to be Assistant Secretary for Economic Policy, Department of the Treasury

5 News conference of Joseph H. Blatchford, Director, Peace Corps, following swearing-in ceremony

5 Announcement of intention to nominate Nicholas G. Theodore to be Superintendent of the Mint of the United States at Philadelphia

5 Announcement of intention to nominate R. Alex McCullough to the Board of Directors, Export-Import Bank of the United States

5 Announcement of intention to nominate Dr. Carlos Camacho to be Governor of Guam

5 Announcement of intention to nominate Kingdon Gould, Jr., to be United States Ambassador to Luxembourg

5 Announcement of intention to nominate David H. Popper to be United States Ambassador to Cyprus

5 Announcement of signing of bill relating to the rank of Assistant Commandant, Marine Corps

5 Announcement of intention to nominate James A. Washington, Jr., to be General Counsel, Department of Transportation

5 List of members of the AFL–CIO Executive Council at a meeting with the President

6 News briefing by Senator Everett M. Dirksen and Representative Gerald R. Ford following the President's meeting with Republican congressional leadership

6 Announcement of intention to nominate Philip H. Trezise to be Assistant Secretary for Economic Affairs, Department of State

6 Announcement of appointment of John H. Reed as Chairman, National Transportation Safety Board

May

6 News conference by William H. Brown III, following his appointment as Chairman, Equal Employment Opportunity Commission

6 Announcement of promotion of Lt. Gen. John L. Throckmorton, United States Army, to the grade of general and assignment of Maj. Gen. Melvin Zais, United States Army, as Commanding General, XXIV Corps, Vietnam, and promotion to the grade of lieutenant general

7 Announcement of signing of bill concerning the Winston Churchill Memorial and Library, Westminster College, Fulton, Missouri

7 Announcement of intention to nominate David W. Williams of Los Angeles, Calif., to be United States District Judge for the Central District of California

8 Announcement of intention to nominate G. McMurtrie Godley to be United States Ambassador to the Kingdom of Laos

8 Announcement of intention to nominate Carl O. Kamp, Jr., to the Federal Home Loan Bank Board

8 List of advisers accompanying Governor Nelson A. Rockefeller to Latin America

9 Announcement of intention to nominate J. William Middendorf II to be United States Ambassador to the Kingdom of the Netherlands

9 Announcement of intention to nominate Richard Funkhouser to be United States Ambassador to the Gabon Republic

9 Announcement of graduation exercises at the White House for the 83d class of the FBI National Academy

9 Announcement of appointment of Vice Adm. Ralph W. Cousins as Deputy Chief of Naval Operations (Fleet Operations and Readiness), and appointment of Rear Adm. Maurice F. Weisner as Commander, Attack Carrier Striking Force, Seventh Fleet, and Commander, Carrier Division Five, and promotion to the grade of vice admiral

May

10 Announcement of promotion of Lt. Gen. Lewis W. Walt, Assistant Commandant of the Marine Corps, to the grade of general

10 Announcement of hurricane disaster assistance for Florida

12 Announcement of appointment of six members of the Board of Governors of the American Red Cross

12 Announcement of establishment of the Richard Nixon Foundation and designation of trustees

12 Announcement of the President's report on his personal finances

12 Announcement of intention to nominate Judge George Harrold Carswell to be United States Circuit Judge for the Fifth Circuit and Judge John F. Kilkenny to be United States Circuit Judge for the Ninth Circuit

13 News briefing by Representative Gerald R. Ford following the President's meeting with Republican congressional leadership

13 Letter accepting the resignation of Lee C. White as Chairman, Federal Power Commission

13 Announcement of supplemental appropriations request

13 News briefing by Dr. Daniel P. Moynihan following a meeting of the Urban Affairs Council

13 Announcement of intention to nominate Donald E. Lane as an associate judge, United States Court of Customs and Patent Appeals

15 News briefing by Secretary of the Treasury David M. Kennedy, Robert P. Keim, president of the Advertising Council, Dr. M. L. Frankel, Joint Council on Economic Education, and Archie Davis, chairman, Board of Wachovia Bank and Trust Co., Winston-Salem, N.C., following a meeting with the President on the control of inflation

May

16 Announcement of the resignation of William H. Stewart as Surgeon General, Public Health Service

16 Announcement of intention to nominate John C. Clark as a member of the Board of Directors, Export-Import Bank of the United States

16 Announcement of a ceremony for the presentation of the Medal of Honor

19 Announcement of flood disaster assistance for Colorado

19 Announcement of intention to nominate Aubrey J. Wagner to be a member of the Board of Directors, Tennessee Valley Authority

19 Announcement of signing of bill concerning the 100th anniversary of the American Fisheries Society

19 Announcement of appointment of Huntington Hartford to be a member of the National Council on the Arts

19 Announcement of intention to nominate William E. Amos to be a member of the Board of Parole, Department of Justice

19 Announcement of intention to nominate John N. Nassikas as a member and Chairman, Federal Power Commission

19 Information on World Trade "E" Awards presented by the President

20 News briefing by Representative Gerald R. Ford and Press Secretary Ronald L. Ziegler following the President's meeting with Republican congressional leadership

20 Announcement of nomination of Lane Dwinell as Assistant Administrator for Administration, Agency for International Development

21 Announcement of appointment of Robert J. Brown and Charles B. Wilkinson as members and of the Secretary of Transportation as a permanent member of the President's Council on Youth Opportunity

May

21 Announcement of intention to nominate Haakon Lindjord as an Assistant Director, Office of Emergency Preparedness

21 Announcement of appointment of Charles A. Meyer as Chairman of the United States Section and of Antonio F. Rodriguez as Commissioner and Director, United States-Mexico Commission for Border Development and Friendship

21 Announcement of appointment of Isabella J. Jones as United States Representative on the Executive Board, United Nations Children's Fund

21 Announcement of intention to nominate Maj. Gen. Andrew P. Rollins, Jr., United States Army, as a member and President of the Mississippi River Commission

21 Biographical data on Judge Warren Earl Burger of the United States Court of Appeals for the District of Columbia Circuit, nominated as Chief Justice of the United States

22 Announcement of intention to nominate John Richardson, Jr., to be Assistant Secretary of State for Educational and Cultural Affairs, Department of State

22 Announcement of intention to nominate Thomas J. Houser to be Deputy Director, Peace Corps

22 News briefing by Dr. Daniel P. Moynihan, Assistant to the President for Urban Affairs following a meeting on national urban policy

23 Announcement of intention to nominate J. Ronald Fox as Assistant Secretary for Installations and Logistics, Department of the Army

23 Citations of posthumous awards of the Medal of Honor to M. Sgt. Charles E. Hosking, Jr., and Sp4c. Don L. Michael, United States Army

26 Announcement of selection of 121 students as Presidential Scholars of 1969

May

26 Announcement of intention to nominate Joseph John Jova as Representative of the United States on the Council of the Organization of American States

26 Announcement of intention to nominate David D. Newsom to be Assistant Secretary for African Affairs, Department of State

26 Announcement of flood disaster assistance for North Dakota

26 News briefing by Dr. Daniel P. Moynihan, Assistant to the President for Urban Affairs and Mayor John V. Lindsay of New York following a meeting of the Urban Affairs Council

26 News briefing by Dr. Daniel P. Moynihan, Assistant to the President for Urban Affairs and Gerald Christensen, Executive Director, President's Council on Youth Opportunity, on the summer youth program

27 News briefing by Postmaster General Winton M. Blount on the postal reform message

27 Announcement of names of Executive Interns for 1969

27 News briefing by Governor Nelson A. Rockefeller on his Latin American trip

27 Announcement of intention to nominate Charles A. Bane to be United States Circuit Judge for the Seventh Circuit

27 Announcement of nomination of Maj. Gen. Frederick E. Leek, United States Marine Corps, as Commanding General, Fleet Marine Force, Atlantic, and promotion to grade of lieutenant general

27 Announcement of nomination of Brig. Gen. Hal B. Jennings, Jr., United States Army, to the position of Surgeon General, United States Army, and promotion to the grade of lieutenant general

28 Announcement of intention to nominate William F. Buckley, Jr., as a member, United States Advisory Commission on Information

May

28 Announcement of intention to nominate Hamer H. Budge for reappointment as member and Chairman, Securities and Exchange Commission

28 Announcement of intention to nominate James J. Needham to be a member, Securities and Exchange Commission

28 Announcement of flood disaster assistance for California

28 Announcement of appointment of Martin G. Castillo as member and Chairman, Inter-Agency Committee on Mexican American Affairs

28 News briefing by Dr. John A. Hannah, Administrator and Rutherford Poats, Deputy Administrator of Agency for International Development, on the foreign aid message

28 List of names of graduates of the 83d session of the FBI National Academy

28 Attorney General Mitchell's remarks at the graduation exercises of the FBI National Academy

28 Report by Robert J. Brown, Special Assistant to the President, on a meeting with members of the National Newspaper Publishers Association

29 Announcement of appointment of Arthur F. Sampson and Hugh C. Cannon as members, Committee on Purchases of Blind-Made Products

29 Announcement of intention to nominate William Henry Harrison and William School Whitehead as members, Renegotiation Board

29 Announcement of intention to nominate Stephen Horn as a member and Vice Chairman, Commission on Civil Rights

29 News briefing by Dr. Lee DuBridge, Science Adviser to the President, and Dr. John L. Buckley, staff member of the Science Advisory Committee, following a meeting on environmental quality control

June

2 Announcement of appointment of Walter N. Thayer as Special Consultant to the President and member of the President's Advisory Council on Executive Organization

2 Announcement of intention to appoint Clarence A. Arata as a member, National Visitor Facilities Advisory Commission

5 Announcement of intention to nominate Donald E. Johnson as Administrator of Veterans Affairs

5 News briefing of Donald E. Johnson on his nomination as Administrator of Veterans Affairs

5 Announcement of intention to nominate John R. Stevenson as Legal Adviser, Department of State

5 Announcement of appointment of 15 members of the General Advisory Committee, United States Arms Control and Disarmament Agency

6 Announcement of intention to nominate John C. Pritzlaff, Jr., to be United States Ambassador to Malta

6 Announcement of intention to nominate Hubert B. Heffner as Deputy Director, Office of Science and Technology

6 Announcement of establishment of Nationwide Youth Advisory Committees to the Selective Service System

6 News briefing by members of five experimental Youth Advisory Committees to the Selective Service System

6 Announcement of flood disaster assistance to Illinois

11 Announcement of intention to nominate John R. Petty for reappointment as Assistant Secretary for International Affairs, Department of the Treasury

11 Announcement of intention to nominate Spurgeon M. Keeny, Jr., as Assistant Director for Science and Technology, United States Arms Control and Disarmament Agency

June

11 Announcement of designation of Jerome K. Kuykendall as Chairman, Indian Claims Commission

11 Announcement of appointment of Dr. Jean Mayer as Special Consultant to the President to plan the White House Conference on Food, Nutrition, and Health

11 News conference by Dr. Moynihan and Dr. Jean Mayer on Dr. Mayer's appointment as Special Consultant to the President

11 Announcement of appointment of Leonard Garment as Special Consultant to the President

12 Announcement of intention to nominate Terence A. Todman of the Virgin Islands to be United States Ambassador to the Republic of Chad

12 Announcement of intention to nominate Joseph Palmer II to be United States Ambassador to the Kingdom of Libya

12 Announcement of intention to nominate John G. Hurd to be United States Ambassador to the Republic of Venezuela

12 Announcement of intention to nominate Harold F. Faught to be Assistant Postmaster General, Bureau of Research and Engineering, Post Office Department

12 Announcement of intention to nominate Gen. John D. Ryan to be Chief of Staff, United States Air Force

12 News briefing of Governor Nelson A. Rockefeller of New York on his recent trips to Latin America

12 Announcement of intention to nominate Gerald S. Levin to be a United States District Judge for the Northern District of California

13 News briefing held by Donald Kendall, chairman of the National Alliance of Businessmen, and Roger Lewis, chairman of Plans for Progress, on the merger of the two organizations

June

13 Announcement of intention to nominate Ridgway B. Knight to be United States Ambassador to Portugal

13 Announcement of intention to nominate Adolph W. Schmidt to be United States Ambassador to Canada

13 Announcement of intention to nominate Dr. Melvin H. Evans to be Governor of the Virgin Islands

16 Announcement of intention to nominate Kenneth Rush to be United States Ambassador to the Federal Republic of Germany

16 Announcement of intention to nominate Luther I. Replogle to be United States Ambassador to the Republic of Iceland

16 Announcement of intention to nominate John A. Calhoun to be United States Ambassador to the Republic of Tunisia

16 Announcement of intention to nominate Howard A. Glickstein to be Staff Director, Commission on Civil Rights

16 Announcement of appointment of White House Fellows for 1969–1970

16 Announcement of appointment of Michael Rapuano as a member, Temporary Commission on Pennsylvania Avenue

16 Announcement of intention to nominate Samuel Z. Westerfield, Jr., to be United States Ambassador to the Republic of Liberia

17 News briefing by Senator Everett M. Dirksen and Representative Gerald R. Ford following the President's meeting with Republican congressional leadership

17 Announcement of appointment of four new members and reappointment of two members to the Advisory Commission on Intergovernmental Relations

18 Announcement of approval of bill providing for the appointment of Thomas J. Watson, Jr., as a Citizen Regent on the Board of Regents, Smithsonian Institution

June

18 Announcement of intention to nominate J. Fife Symington, Jr., to be United States Ambassador to Trinidad and Tobago

19 Announcement of intention to nominate Dr. William D. McElroy to be Director, National Science Foundation

19 Announcement of Executive Order 11476 prescribing a new edition of the Manual for Courts-Martial

20 Citations of posthumous awards of the Medal of Honor to three members of the Marine Corps

20 Announcement of intention to nominate Eileen Roberta Donovan to be United States Ambassador to Barbados

23 Announcement of intention to nominate Albert B. Brooke for reappointment as a member, Federal Power Commission

23 Announcement of intention to nominate Kenneth Franzheim to be United States Ambassador to New Zealand

23 Announcement of intention to nominate Orville H. Lerch to be Alternate Federal Cochairman, Appalachian Regional Commission

23 Announcement of intention to nominate Eugene A. Wright to be a United States Circuit Judge for the Ninth Circuit

23 Telegram to the widow of Representative William H. Bates of Massachusetts

24 News briefing by Senator Everett M. Dirksen and Representative Gerald R. Ford following the President's meeting with Republican congressional leadership

24 Announcement of intention to appoint John B. Martin, Jr., to be Special Assistant to the President for the Aging

24 News briefing by Secretary of Transportation John A. Volpe on transportation in the District of Columbia

25 Announcement of intention to nominate John Raymond Ylitalo to be United States Ambassador to Paraguay

June

25 Announcement of intention to nominate Joseph Adolph Greenwald to be United States Representative to the Organization for Economic Cooperation and Development

25 Announcement of flood disaster relief for North Dakota

25 Announcement of sale of communications systems in Alaska

25 Announcement of intention to nominate Ozell M. Trask to be a United States Circuit Judge for the Ninth Circuit

26 Announcement of intention to nominate David W. Oberlin as Administrator, Saint Lawrence Seaway Development Corporation

26 Announcement of intention to nominate Brig. Gen. Willard Roper, United States Army, to be a member, Mississippi River Commission

26 Announcement of intention to appoint John Dolibois as a member, Board of Foreign Scholarships

26 Announcement of intention to nominate five members to the Advisory Board, Saint Lawrence Seaway Development Corporation

26 Announcement of intention to nominate Roderic L. O'Connor as Assistant Administrator for East Asia, Agency for International Development

28 Announcement of the President's trip to Asia and to Romania

28 Announcement of intention to nominate Dr. Roger O. Egeberg as Assistant Secretary for Health and Scientific Affairs, Department of Health, Education, and Welfare

30 Announcement of intention to nominate Clarence E. Larson as a member, Atomic Energy Commission

June

30 Announcement of intention to appoint Carter L. Burgess to be an Incorporator, National Corporation for Housing Partnerships

July

1 News briefing by Senator Everett M. Dirksen and Representative Gerald R. Ford following the President's meeting with Republican congressional leadership

3 Announcement of appointment of Henry Arthur Hendrickson to be Chairman of the Souris-Red-Rainy River Basins Commission

3 Announcement of intention to nominate Henry A. Byroade to be United States Ambassador to the Republic of the Philippines

3 Announcement of membership of the American Revolution Bicentennial Commission

5 Announcement of the senior membership of the United States delegation for proposed strategic arms limitation talks with the Soviet Union

5 White House statement on the assassination of Minister Tom Mboya of Kenya

5 Announcement of intention to nominate Leonard Carpenter Meeker to be United States Ambassador to the Socialist Republic of Romania

7 Announcement of appointment of John E. Nidecker as Deputy Special Assistant to the President

7 Announcement of appointments to the Board of Governors and to the Corporation of the United Service Organizations, Inc.

8 News briefing by Representative Gerald R. Ford following the President's meeting with Republican congressional leadership

8 News briefing by Secretary of Labor George P. Shultz on the unemployment insurance message

8 News briefing on revenue sharing by Dr. Arthur F. Burns, Governor Daniel Evans, Mayor Jack Maltester of San Leandro, Calif., and Edwin Michaelian, County Executive of Westchester County, in New York

July

9 Announcement of order on the reduction of United States personnel overseas

9 Announcement of appointment of Roger A. Freeman as Special Assistant to the President

10 Text of citations for the Medal of Honor awarded posthumously to three members of the United States Army

10 Announcement of intention to nominate Walter L. Rice to be United States Ambassador to the Commonwealth of Australia

10 Announcement of intention to nominate Taylor G. Belcher to be United States Ambassador to the Republic of Peru

11 Announcement of intention to nominate Jack W. Lydman to be United States Ambassador to Malaysia

12 News briefing on the National Goals Research Staff by Dr. Daniel P. Moynihan

15 News briefing by Senator Everett M. Dirksen and Representative Gerald R. Ford following the President's meeting with Republican congressional leadership

15 Announcement of tornado and flood disaster assistance for Kansas

15 Announcement of tornado and flood disaster assistance for Ohio

16 Announcement of appointment of Eugene S. Cowen as Special Assistant to the President

17 News briefing by Governor Raymond P. Shafer on his trade mission to Latin America, following his meeting with the President

17 Announcement of the appointment of Lt. Gen. John H. Michaelis, USA, for assignment as Commanding General, Eighth United States Army, Korea, and Commander in Chief, United Nations Command/Commander, United States Forces, Korea

21 News conference by Press Secretary Ronald L. Ziegler and Col. Frank Borman following the President's conversation with the Apollo astronauts

July

22 Announcement of intention to nominate George M. Moore as a member of the United States Tariff Commission

22 Announcement of intention to nominate Thomas Hal Clarke as a member of the Federal Home Loan Bank Board

22 News briefing on the reorganization plan for the Interstate Commerce Commission by Press Secretary Ronald L. Ziegler and Assistant to the President Peter M. Flanigan

22 News briefing on the President's statement concerning the 1970 budget by Robert Mayo, Director of the Bureau of the Budget

30 Statement by President Thieu at the conclusion of discussions with President Nixon

30 News briefing by Vice President Agnew, Secretary of the Treasury Kennedy, and Budget Director Mayo on the surtax

August

5 Announcement of intention to nominate Charles T. Cross to be United States Ambassador to the Republic of Singapore

5 Announcement of intention to nominate Robert Strausz-Hupé to be United States Ambassador to the Kingdom of Morocco

6 News briefing by James D. Hodgson, Under Secretary of Labor, Lawrence H. Silberman, Solicitor of the United States on the President's message on occupational safety and health

7 News briefing by Dr. Daniel P. Moynihan, Assistant to the President for Urban Affairs, James M. Beggs, Under Secretary of Transportation, and Carlos Villarreal, Administrator, Urban Mass Transportation Administration, on the President's message on public transportation

8 Memorandum for the President from the Chairman, Civil Service Commission, on equal employment opportunity in the Federal Government

August

9 Announcement of intention to nominate Mrs. Helen D. Bentley as member of the Federal Maritime Commission

9 Announcement of intention to nominate Robert M. Sayre to be United States Ambassador to the Republic of Panama

9 Announcement of intention to nominate William E. Schaufele, Jr., to be United States Ambassador to Upper Volta

9 Announcement of intention to nominate Charles W. Adair, Jr., to be United States Ambassador to Uruguay

11 Announcement of intention to nominate William H. Quealy to be a judge on the United States Tax Court

11 Statement by Ambassador to the Philippines Henry A. Byroade following a meeting with the President

11 Description of the President's San Clemente residence

11 Information on administrative and support buildings for the western White House located on the Coast Guard Loran Station at San Clemente, Calif.

11 News briefing by Secretary of State William P. Rogers following a meeting with the President on the Secretary's Asian trip

12 News briefing by Secretary of Labor George P. Shultz on the President's manpower message

12 Announcement of a dinner honoring the Apollo 11 astronauts

12 Partial list of guests attending the dinner honoring the Apollo 11 astronauts

13 News briefing by Dr. Arthur F. Burns on the President's message on revenue sharing

13 Announcement of the President's letter authorizing the Director of the Bureau of the Budget to establish new Federal Executive Boards

13 Guest list for the dinner at the Century Plaza Hotel honoring Apollo 11 astronauts

August

15 Announcement of appointment of Chairman and 19 members of the Citizens' Advisory Council on the Status of Women

15 Announcement of designation of Governor Ronald Reagan of California to represent the President at ceremonies opening the Cultural Center of the Philippines in Manila

15 Announcement of flood disaster assistance for California

18 Announcement by the Press Secretary of the nomination of Judge Clement F. Haynsworth, Jr., as Associate Justice of the Supreme Court

18 Announcement of hurricane disaster assistance for Mississippi

19 Announcement of flood disaster assistance for Louisiana

20 Announcement of intention to nominate Vincent de Roulet to be United States Ambassador to Jamaica

20 Announcement of intention to nominate Robinson McIlvaine to be United States Ambassador to the Republic of Kenya

20 Announcement of intention to nominate John Patrick Walsh to be United States Ambassador to the State of Kuwait

20 Announcement of intention to nominate Graham A. Martin to be United States Ambassador to the Italian Republic

20 Announcement of intention to nominate Douglas MacArthur II to be United States Ambassador to Iran

25 Announcement of intention to nominate Joel Bernstein to be Assistant Administrator for Technical Assistance, Agency for International Development

25 Announcement of intention to nominate William C. Trueheart to be United States Ambassador to the Republic of Nigeria

25 News briefing by Dr. Daniel P. Moynihan, Assistant to the President for Urban Affairs following a meeting of the Urban Affairs Council

August

26 Announcement of flood disaster assistance for New York

26 Announcement of intention to nominate Robert F. Keller to be Assistant Comptroller of the United States, General Accounting Office

26 Announcement of intention to nominate Ernest Stern as an Assistant Administrator, Agency for International Development

26 News briefing by Dr. Lee A. DuBridge following a meeting of the Environmental Quality Council

27 Background information on Redwood National Park

27 Text of plaque dedicating the Lady Bird Johnson Grove, Redwood National Park

28 Announcement of intention to nominate Joseph S. Farland to be United States Ambassador to the Islamic Republic of Pakistan

28 Announcement of intention to nominate Henry J. Tasca to be United States Ambassador to the Kingdom of Greece

28 Announcement of intention to nominate Dr. Thomas K. Cowden to be a member of the Board of Directors of the Commodity Credit Corporation

28 Announcement of appointment of four new members and reappointment of one member to the Advisory Board of the Commodity Credit Corporation

28 Announcement of study of economic effects of certain tariff items

28 Announcement of designation of Dr. Daniel P. Moynihan as coordinator of U.S. effort and head of U.S. delegation to a preparatory committee meeting on a NATO study of the challenges of modern society

29 Announcement of intention to nominate U.S. delegation to the 24th regular session of the United Nations General Assembly

30 Announcement of flood disaster assistance for Illinois

August

30 Announcement of flood disaster assistance for Ohio

30 Announcement of flood disaster assistance for Vermont

September

2 News briefing on postal reform by Postmaster General Winton M. Blount, Lawrence F. O'Brien, and Senator Thruston Morton

2 Announcement of appointment of two members of the National Selective Service Appeal Board

2 Announcement of appointment of Rudolph A. Peterson as Chairman of the Presidential Task Force on International Development

2 Announcement of intention to nominate A. Sydney Herlong as a member of the Securities and Exchange Commission

3 Announcement of hurricane disaster assistance for West Virginia

3 Announcement of appointment of Charles L. Clapp as Special Assistant to the President

3 Announcement of intention to nominate Nancy Hanks to be Chairman of the National Council on the Arts

3 News conference by Nancy Hanks following announcement of her nomination as Chairman of the National Council on the Arts

4 News briefing by Dr. Arthur F. Burns, Counsellor to the President on the President's statement on the construction industry

4 Announcement of appointment of William E. Casselman II as Deputy Special Assistant to the President

4 Announcement of appointment of Richard K. Cook as Special Assistant to the President

Appendix A

September

19 Announcement of intention to nominate Thomas Patrick Melady to be United States Ambassador to Burundi

19 Announcement of intention to nominate Scott Heuer, Jr., as Inspector General of Foreign Assistance, Department of State

19 Announcement of intention to nominate Anthony Faunce as Deputy Inspector General of Foreign Assistance, Department of State

19 Announcement of appointment of Jack McDonald as a member of the Citizens Advisory Board on Youth Opportunity

19 Itinerary for the world tour of the Apollo 11 astronauts

22 News briefing by Dr. Arthur F. Burns on the Presidential task forces to assist the administration with ideas and recommendations

22 News briefing by Vice President Agnew and Governor John A. Love of Colorado following a meeting on inflation with regard to the construction industry

22 Announcement of intention to nominate Harold C. Passer as Assistant Secretary for Economic Affairs, Department of Commerce

22 Announcement of report of the Board of Visitors to the United States Naval Academy

23 News briefing by John A. Volpe, Secretary of Transportation, on the supersonic transport

23 Announcement of intention to nominate John Frick Root to be United States Ambassador to the Republic of Ivory Coast

23 Announcement of flood disaster assistance for California

23 Announcement of flood disaster assistance for Iowa

23 Announcement of intention to nominate Dr. Henry S. Robinson, Jr., as a member of the District of Columbia Council

September

23 Announcement of intention to nominate Frank Charles Carlucci III as Assistant Director for Operations of the Office of Economic Opportunity

23 Announcement of Executive Order 11483 granting authority to the House Select Committee on Crime to inspect certain tax returns

24 Announcement of intention to nominate Paul J. O'Neill as a member of the Subversive Activities Control Board

24 Announcement of appointment of the membership of the Presidential Task Force on International Development

24 Announcement of flood disaster assistance for Minnesota

24 Announcement of flood disaster assistance for West Virginia

24 Announcement concerning applications for the 6th annual program of White House Fellows

25 Announcement of intention to nominate Robert Coleman Gresham to be Commissioner of the Interstate Commerce Commission

25 Announcement of intention to nominate Robert Louis Johnson to be Assistant Secretary of the Army for Research and Development

25 Announcement of intention to nominate Jack Malcolm Layton as a member of the Board of Regents of the National Library of Medicine

25 Announcement of intention to nominate Dr. Carl Walske for reappointment as Chairman of the Military Liaison Committee to the Atomic Energy Commission

25 News briefing by Dr. Arthur F. Burns and officials of the Department of Health, Education, and Welfare on the President's message on social security

September

29 Announcement of intention to nominate William B. Dale for reappointment as United States Executive Director of the International Monetary Fund

30 Announcement on reduction of United States Forces in Thailand

30 News briefing by Senator Hugh Scott and Representative Gerald R. Ford following the President's meeting with Republican congressional leadership

30 Announcement of intention to nominate Robert E. Wieczorowski as United States Executive Director of the International Bank for Reconstruction and Development

30 Announcement of appointment of Chairman and 15 members of the President's Commission on Personnel Interchange

30 News briefing by George P. Shultz, Secretary of Labor, on a meeting of the President and the Cabinet Committee on Construction

October

1 Announcement of intention to nominate Lewis Hoffacker to be United States Ambassador to the Federal Republic of Cameroon

1 Announcement of National Security Council memorandum recommending draft postponements for graduate students

2 Announcement of intention to nominate Caspar W. Weinberger to be a member of the Federal Trade Commission

2 News conference by Caspar W. Weinberger, Chairman-designate of the Federal Trade Commission

2 Announcement of intention to nominate Samuel C. Adams, Jr., as Assistant Administrator for Africa, Agency for International Development

2 Announcement of flood disaster assistance for California

2 Announcement of hurricane disaster assistance for Louisiana

October

2 Announcement of hurricane disaster assistance for Mississippi

4 Announcement of intention to nominate Dr. S. Paul Ehrlich, Jr., and Dr. Benjamin D. Blood as United States representative and alternate representative on the Executive Board of the World Health Organization

6 News briefing on the White House Conference on Aging by John B. Martin, Jr., Commissioner on Aging, Department of Health, Education, and Welfare

7 Announcement of appointment of James A. Skidmore, Jr., as a member of the Citizens Advisory Board on Youth Opportunity

7 Announcement of appointment of Jeb S. Magruder as Special Assistant to the President

7 Announcement of intention to nominate John H. Schneider as Assistant Commissioner of Patents, Department of Commerce

7 News briefing by Senator Hugh Scott and Representative Gerald R. Ford following the President's meeting with Republican congressional leadership

7 Announcement of intention to nominate Charles Clark, of Jackson, Miss., to be United States Circuit Judge for the Fifth Circuit

8 Announcement of intention to nominate Manuel Ruiz, Jr., as a member of the Commission on Civil Rights

8 Announcement of ceremony for the presentation of the Medal of Honor to four members of the United States Army

8 Announcement of intention to appoint William B. Taylor III as a United States Commissioner on the South Pacific Commission

9 News briefing by Representative Gerald R. Ford and Jerry V. Wilson, Chief of Police of the District of Columbia, on crime in the District of Columbia

October

9 Announcement of intention to nominate Clarence M. Coster as an Associate Administrator of the Law Enforcement Assistance Administration, Department of Justice

10 Announcement of intention to appoint Lt. Gen. Lewis B. Hershey to be Advisor to the President on Manpower Mobilization

10 News briefing by Bryce N. Harlow, Assistant to the President on the President's special message to the Congress on legislative reform

10 News conference by former Vice President Hubert H. Humphrey following a meeting with the President (2 releases)

14 News briefing by Senator Hugh Scott and Representative Gerald R. Ford following the President's meeting with Republican congressional leadership

14 Announcement of appointment of members of the President's Committee on Mental Retardation

14 News briefing by Vice President Agnew on a letter to the American people from Premier Pham Van Dong of North Vietnam

16 Announcement of intention to nominate Wesley L. Hjornevik as Deputy Director of the Office of Economic Opportunity

16 News briefing by Dr. Paul W. McCracken, Chairman, Council of Economic Advisers, and Dr. Arthur F. Burns, Counsellor to the President, on inflation and the national economy

17 Announcement of intention to nominate Dr. Arthur F. Burns as member of the Board of Governors, Federal Reserve System

17 Announcement of intention to nominate Lewis Hoffacker as United States Ambassador to Equatorial Guinea

October

20 Announcement of intention to nominate David R. Derge, Jewel LaFontant, and William C. Turner as members of the United States Advisory Commission on International Educational and Cultural Affairs

21 Letter to the President on the interim report of the President's Committee on the Vietnam Veteran

21 News briefing by Donald E. Johnson, Administrator of Veterans Affairs, on the interim report of the President's Committee on the Vietnam Veteran

22 Announcement of appointment of Paul M. VanWegen as alternate U.S. Representative to the Delaware River Basin Commission

22 Announcement of appointment of Ellis L. Armstrong to be Commissioner of Reclamation, Department of the Interior

22 News briefing by Roy L. Ash, Chairman, President's Advisory Council on Executive Organization, following a Council meeting

23 News briefing by John E. Ingersoll, Director, Bureau of Narcotics and Dangerous Drugs, Senator Roman L. Hruska, Art Linkletter, and Ronald L. Ziegler, Press Secretary, following the bipartisan leadership meeting on narcotics and dangerous drugs

23 Announcement of the President's new program for the United States Merchant Marine

23 News briefing by Rocco C. Siciliano, Under Secretary of Commerce, and Andrew E. Gibson, Federal Maritime Administrator, on the President's Merchant Marine message

23 Announcement of additional membership of the Task Force on Rural Development

23 Announcement of membership of the Task Force on Model Cities

October

25 Announcement of opening of strategic arms limitation talks with the Soviet Union

27 Announcement concerning the "President's Listening Post" in Philadelphia

28 News briefing by Senator Hugh Scott and Representative Gerald R. Ford following the President's meeting with Republican congressional leadership

29 Announcement on the signing of Executive Order 11491 on labor-management relations in the Federal service

29 News briefing by Secretary of Labor George P. Shultz and Assistant Secretary W. J. Usery, Jr., on the Executive order concerning labor-management relations in the Federal service

30 News briefing by Virginia H. Knauer, Special Assistant to the President for Consumer Affairs, Patricia Hitt, Assistant Secretary of Health, Education, and Welfare for Community and Field Services, Richard McLaren, Assistant Attorney General, Antitrust Division, Department of Justice, and Deputy Assistant Secretary of Health, Education, and Welfare for Health and Scientific Affairs on the President's consumer protection message

30 Announcement of appointment of new members and designation of Robert E. Merriam as Chairman of the Advisory Commission on Intergovernmental Relations

30 Announcement of intention to appoint Richard L. Herman as United States Commissioner on the International Boundary Commission, United States and Canada

31 Announcement of annual report of the Board of Visitors to the United States Military Academy

31 Announcement of intention to appoint Andy Leroy Borg as Chairman of the United States Section of the Permanent Joint Board on Defense—United States and Canada

November

3 Announcement of report of Presidential Emergency Board No. 176 investigating a railway labor dispute

4 Announcement of appointments of Bryce N. Harlow and Dr. Daniel P. Moynihan as Counsellors to the President and of John D. Ehrlichman as Assistant to the President for Domestic Affairs, and assignments in the Domestic Affairs Council staff

4 News briefing by Dr. Daniel P. Moynihan, Bryce N. Harlow, John D. Ehrlichman, and H. R. Haldeman on White House Staff assignments

4 News briefing by Secretary of Housing and Urban Development George W. Romney and Special Consultant on Voluntary Action Max M. Fisher on the National Program for Voluntary Action

5 Announcement of a report on university programs on environmental problems to the Environmental Quality Council

5 News briefing by Dr. Lee A. DuBridge and John S. Steinhart, Office of Science and Technology, on the report to the President's Environmental Quality Council

6 News briefing by Edmund Gullion, Charles Tyroler II, and Mrs. Oswald B. Lord, members of the Citizens Committee for Peace with Freedom in Vietnam on their meeting with the President

6 News briefing by Secretary of Agriculture Clifford M. Hardin on establishment of the Rural Affairs Council

6 Announcement of appointment of Charles W. Colson as Special Assistant to the President

6 Announcement of designation of Dr. Daniel P. Moynihan to represent the United States at the NATO Committee's first meeting in Brussels on challenges of modern society

7 Text of letter from President Emilio Garrastazu Medici of Brazil to President Nixon on his address to the Inter American Press Association

November

7 Text of letter from President Carlos Lleras Restrepo of Colombia to President Nixon on his address to the Inter American Press Association

7 Text of letter from President José Joaquín Trejos Fernandez of the Republic of Costa Rica to President Nixon on his address to the Inter American Press Association

7 Announcement of designation of Chairman and appointment of members of the National Commission on Consumer Finance

7 Announcement of appointment of Gen. William H. Draper as United States Representative to the United Nations Population Commission

8 News briefing by Secretary of Defense Melvin R. Laird on pending draft legislation

10 News briefing by Governor Nelson A. Rockefeller on his report to the President on Latin America

10 Announcement concerning the status of the uranium enrichment facilities within the Atomic Energy Commission

11 News briefing by Jacqueline Goyette Gutwillig, Chairman, Citizens' Advisory Council on the Status of Women, on a meeting with the President

12 Announcement of intention to nominate Graham W. Watt as Assistant to the Commissioner (Deputy Mayor) of the District of Columbia

12 News conference by Mayor Walter E. Washington of the District of Columbia, Thomas Fletcher, former Deputy Mayor, and Graham W. Watt on Mr. Watt's nomination as Deputy Mayor

12 Announcement of appointment of Ralph E. Carpenter, Jr., as a member of the Committee for the Preservation of the White House

12 Announcement of the appointment of George H. Hildebrand as United States Representative on the governing body of the International Labor Office

November

12 News briefing by Secretary of Health, Education, and Welfare Robert H. Finch, Dr. Daniel P. Moynihan, Counsellor to the President, and Ben Heinemann, Chairman of the President's Commission on Income Maintenance Programs, following a meeting with the President on the report of the Commission

12 News briefing by Senator Gordon Allott and Representatives James C. Wright, Jr., Wayne L. Hays, E. Ross Adair, and Leslie C. Arends on congressional support of the President's program for peace in Vietnam

13 News briefing by Richard W. Velde, Associate Administrator, Law Enforcement Assistance Administration, and Myrl E. Alexander, Director, U.S. Bureau of Prisons, on the President's program for reform of the Federal corrections system

13 Announcement of intention to nominate George M. Low as Deputy Administrator of the National Aeronautics and Space Administration

17 Announcement of intention to nominate Anthony D. Marshall as United States Ambassador to the Malagasy Republic

18 News briefing by Postmaster General Winton M. Blount following his return from a trip to the Far East

18 News briefing by Senator George Murphy and Representatives Wayne N. Aspinall and Don H. Clausen following a meeting with the President on the Point Reyes National Seashore area

19 Letter to the President on his remarks at the annual meeting of the Inter American Press Association from President Gustavo Diaz Ordaz of Mexico

19 News briefing by Senator George D. Aiken on his meeting with the President

20 Announcement of review by the Environmental Quality Council of a report by the Commission on Pesticides

Appendix A

December

17 Announcement of intention to nominate Gardiner L. Tucker as Assistant Secretary of Defense for Systems Analysis, Department of Defense

18 Announcement of report of the Board of Visitors to the United States Air Force Academy

18 News briefing by Secretary of Labor George P. Shultz and Assistant Secretary Arthur A. Fletcher on the Philadelphia Plan

19 Remarks of Vice President Spiro T. Agnew at the end-of-the-year Cabinet meeting

20 Statement by Secretary of Labor George P. Shultz on the Philadelphia Plan

20 News briefing by Secretary of Labor George P. Shultz and Assistant Secretary Arthur A. Fletcher on the Philadelphia Plan

22 News briefing by Senator Hugh Scott and Representative Gerald R. Ford following the President's meeting with Republican congressional leadership

22 Announcement of designation of Charles B. Wilkinson as President of the National Center for Voluntary Action

22 News conference by Charles B. Wilkinson on his designation as President of the National Center for Voluntary Action

22 Announcement of intention to nominate Robert Strausz-Hupé as United States Ambassador to Ceylon and the Maldive Republic

22 Announcement of intention to nominate Lyle S. Garlock as member of the Foreign Claims Settlement Commission of the United States

22 Announcement of Executive Order 11501, administration of foreign military sales

23 Announcement of appointment of Martin Anderson as Special Consultant to the President for Systems Analysis

December

23 Announcement of reassignment of Tom Cole as Special Assistant to the President

23 Announcement of appointment of Dr. Edwin L. Harper as Special Assistant to the President

24 Announcement of Proclamation 3950, duties on chemicals

24 News briefing by Dr. Jean Mayer, Special Consultant to the President, Edward J. Hekman, Administrator, Food and Nutrition Service, John Price, Executive Secretary, Urban Affairs Council, and Ronald L. Ziegler, Press Secretary, on the report of the White House Conference on Food, Nutrition, and Health

24 News briefing by Vice President Spiro T. Agnew on his forthcoming trip to Asia

29 Announcement of signing of Proclamation 3951 on imports of sheet glass

29 Letter accepting the resignation of William W. Scranton as United States Representative to the INTELSAT Conference

29 Announcement of intention to appoint Abbott M. Washburn as United States Representative to the INTELSAT Conference

29 Announcement of flood disaster assistance for California

29 Announcement of intention to appoint Robert L. Hess as a member of the National Highway Safety Advisory Committee

29 News briefing by Ambassadors Gerard C. Smith and Llewellyn E. Thompson on the strategic arms limitation talks with the Soviet Union

30 News briefing by Secretary of the Treasury David M. Kennedy and Assistant Secretary Edwin S. Cohen on the Tax Reform Act of 1969

31 Announcement of the 1969 recipients of the National Medal of Science

*Appendix B—*Presidential Documents Published in the Federal Register

[The texts of these documents are also printed in title 3 of the Code of Federal Regulations and in Volume 5 of the Weekly Compilation of Presidential Documents.]

PROCLAMATIONS

Appendix B

Appendix B

EXECUTIVE ORDERS

Appendix B

Appendix B

PRESIDENTIAL DOCUMENTS OTHER THAN PROCLAMATIONS AND EXECUTIVE ORDERS

Appendix C—Presidential Directives and Task Forces

PRESIDENTIAL DIRECTIVES

Presidential request	*Addressee*	*Date 1969*

A. ELECTION REFORM

1. Recommendations on reforming the electoral college. — The Attorney General. — Jan. 29

2. A recommendation as to whether or not the administration should support a constitutional amendment that would lower the voting age to 18. — The Attorney General. — Feb. 9

3. A suggested program for clean elections legislation. — The Attorney General. — Feb. 4

4. A report on congressional redistricting legislation. — The Attorney General. — Feb. 21

5. A review of the Voting Rights Act of 1965, an evaluation of what it has accomplished and recommendations concerning its proposed renewal. — The Attorney General. — Feb. 18

B. GOVERNMENT REORGANIZATION

6. Suggestions concerning the direction and operation of the Office of Executive Management. — The Director of the Bureau of the Budget. — Feb. 4

7. Methods for upgrading the Arms Control and Disarmament Agency. — The Secretary of State. — Jan. 29

8. A comprehensive program for improving the postal service. — The Postmaster General. — Jan. 29

9. Recommendations concerning the reorganization of the Federal Government's educational activities and the possible appointment of a special commission to study the matter. — The Secretary of Health, Education, and Welfare. — Jan. 30

10. An assessment of the proposal that a separate Department of Health be established and that a Council of Health Advisers be created within the Executive Office of the President. — The Secretary of Health, Education, and Welfare. — Feb. 11

11. A review of proposed reforms in the Internal Revenue Service. — The Secretary of the Treasury. — Feb. 4

12. A report on the advisability of establishing a Labor Court to help deal with labor-management problems. — The Secretary of Labor. — Feb. 11

C. FEDERAL EXPENDITURES

13. Suggestions for revising the budget for fiscal year 1969. — The Director of the Bureau of the Budget. — Jan. 29

Appendix C

Presidential request	*Addressee*	*Date 1969*

C. FEDERAL EXPENDITURES—continued

14. Recommendations concerning a contingency reserve fund for fiscal year 1969. — The Director of the Bureau of the Budget. — Jan. 29

15. Suggestions for revising the budget for fiscal year 1970. — The Director of the Bureau of the Budget. — Jan. 29

16. An assessment of the proposal that the Federal Government share a portion of its income tax revenues with the States and localities. — The Secretary of the Treasury. — Feb. 9

17. Recommendations for modifying the present grant-in-aid program so that States and localities will have greater freedom in making use of grant funds. — The Director of the Bureau of the Budget and the President's Assistant for Urban Affairs. — Feb. 11

D. FEDERAL TAX POLICY

18. Recommendations concerning tax reform and the possible establishment of a Commission on Federal Tax Policy. — The Secretary of the Treasury. — Feb. 9

19. A judgment on specific suggestions for changing business income tax policy. — The Secretary of the Treasury. — Feb. 13

20. A judgment on specific suggestions for altering the personal income tax laws. — The Secretary of the Treasury. — Feb. 13

21. Recommendations concerning the present rates of excise taxes. — The Secretary of the Treasury. — Feb. 13

E. THE FEDERAL DEBT

22. A report on the advisability of raising the ceiling on the Federal debt. — The Secretary of the Treasury. — Feb. 4

23. A review of the present interest rate ceilings on Treasury issues. — The Secretary of the Treasury. — Feb. 19

F. FEDERAL CREDIT PROGRAMS

24. Establishment of a committee to investigate existing Federal direct loan and loan guarantee programs. — The Director of the Bureau of the Budget. — Feb. 4

25. Implementation of recommendations concerning the utility of loan insurance vis-a-vis enlarged Federal loan programs. — The Director of the Bureau of the Budget. — Feb. 4

26. Recommendations concerning the establishment of an office within the Department of the Treasury to coordinate new debt issues of Federal credit agencies with direct U.S. Treasury financing operations. — The Secretary of the Treasury. — Feb. 6

1088

Appendix C

Presidential request	*Addressee*	*Date* 1969

G. RESOURCES AND ENVIRONMENT

27. A recommendation concerning the problems of population growth and family planning. — The President's Assistant for Urban Affairs. — Feb. 9

28. Evaluation of the report of the Commission on Marine Science, Engineering, and Resources. — The Secretary of the Interior. — Feb. 1

29. Proposals concerning American agriculture; recommendations for changes in present Department of Agriculture policies. — The Secretary of Agriculture. — Feb. 1

30. A review of the operation of the Economic Development Assistance Act, its general concept, the way it has been implemented, and suggested reforms. — The Secretary of Commerce. — Feb. 9

31. A review of the Appalachian regional development program, together with a judgment as to whether regional programs are more desirable than the generalized EDA approach. — The Secretary of Commerce. — Feb. 9

32. A report on the present Water Pollution Control Act and on the soundness of proposals to amend it. — The Secretary of the Interior. — Feb. 4

H. SCIENCE AND TECHNOLOGY

33. An assessment of various proposals for reorganizing the science activities of the Federal Government. — The Science Adviser to the President. — Feb. 18

34. A specific recommendation on raising the expenditure ceiling for the National Science Foundation for fiscal year 1969. — The Director of the Bureau of the Budget. — Jan. 29

35. Recommendation concerning the building of prototypes in the development of new weapons systems. — The Secretary of Defense. — Feb. 9

36. Establishment of a committee to review the supersonic transport program. — The Secretary of Transportation. — Jan. 29

37. Recommendations concerning Federal funding of the National Accelerator Laboratory Project. — The Science Adviser to the President. — Feb. 9

38. An assessment of the proposal to appoint an interagency committee to advise the President on the post-Apollo space program. — The Science Adviser to the President. — Feb: 4

39. A report on the possibility of significant cost reductions in the launching and boosting operations of the space program, together with a judgment on how best to assess future developments in this area. — The Science Adviser to the President. — Feb: 4

I. TRANSPORTATION

40. Recommendations on airport development and air traffic control. — The Secretary of Transportation: — Jan. 29

Appendix C

Presidential request	*Addressee*	*Date* *1969*

K. EDUCATION

56. The establishment of an interdepartmental study group to make an overall review of the Federal role in education. — The Secretary of Health, Education, and Welfare. — Jan. 30

57. Comments concerning the proposed consolidation of categorical grants under the Elementary and Secondary Education Act. — The Secretary of Health, Education, and Welfare. — Feb. 18

58. A special study of the deficiencies of education in large cities and ways in which they can be remedied. — The Secretary of Health, Education, and Welfare. — Jan. 30

59. A program for establishing a National Student-Teacher Corps. — The Secretary of Health, Education, and Welfare. — Jan. 30

60. An evaluation of the proposed National Institute for the Educational Future, along with a draft plan for such an institute. — The Secretary of Health, Education, and Welfare. — Feb. 11

L. URBAN PROBLEMS

61. Recommendations concerning the various programs of the Office of Economic Opportunity and particularly the Job Corps. — The Secretary of Labor and the Secretary of Health, Education, and Welfare. — Feb. 1

62. Recommendations concerning voluntary programs that will involve businessmen more intensively in meeting social and economic problems, together with a recommendation concerning the proposed White House conference of business leaders. — The Secretary of Commerce and the Secretary of Housing and Urban Development. — Jan. 29

63. A study of proposals to improve economic and social conditions in poverty areas through a variety of tax incentives for private efforts. — The Secretary of the Treasury. — Jan. 30

64. Recommendations concerning the proposed Human Investment Act to expand employment and improve job skills by offering tax credits to private industry. — The Secretary of the Treasury. — Jan. 30

65. An evaluation of the Community Self-Determination Act. — The Secretary of the Treasury, the Secretary of Commerce, and the Secretary of Housing and Urban Development. — Jan. 30

66. An appraisal of the present supply of skilled construction workers and the membership practices of construction unions, together with recommendations concerning this problem. — The Secretary of Labor and the Secretary of Housing and Urban Development. — Feb. 18

67. An evaluation and recommendations concerning the role which the Davis-Bacon Act may have played in increased construction costs. — The Secretary of Labor. — Feb. 13

Presidential request	*Addressee*	*Date 1969*

L. URBAN PROBLEMS—continued

68. A report concerning the adequacy of the inforcement authority of the Equal Employment Opportunity Commission. — The Attorney General. — Feb. 13

M. OLDER AMERICANS AND VETERANS

69. An evaluation of the proposal that an automatic cost-of-living increase be applied to social security benefits, and suggestions for other reforms in social security. — The Secretary of Health, Education, and Welfare. — Feb. 11

70. A recommendation concerning the appointment of a White House Staff member with special responsibility for the problems of older Americans. — The Assistant to the President (Mr. Haldeman). — Feb. 4

71. Recommendations concerning the employment of veterans, particularly Negroes, when the war in Vietnam ends. — The Secretary of Labor and the Secretary of Defense. — Feb. 13

N. HEALTH CARE

72. A review and recommendations concerning the rising costs of the Medicaid program. — The Secretary of Health, Education, and Welfare. — Jan. 30

73. An analysis and suggestions with respect to the Medicare program; its effectiveness and its rising costs. — The Secretary of Health, Education, and Welfare. — Jan. 30

74. A reevaluation of the Hill-Burton Act and a new set of recommendations concerning Federal aid for the construction of community hospitals and other health facilities. — The Secretary of Health, Education, and Welfare. — Feb. 11

O. WELFARE PROGRAMS

75. A thoroughgoing, critical review of welfare programs in America. — The President's Assistant for Urban Affairs. — Feb. 1

76. Suggestions as to how Federal food distribution programs can be more effectively coordinated. — The Director of the Bureau of the Budget. — Feb. 9

77. Recommendations concerning the mandatory use of declaratory applications for establishing eligibility for public assistance. — The Secretary of Health, Education, and Welfare. — Jan. 30

P. BUSINESS REGULATION

78. Recommendations concerning one-bank holding companies. — The Secretary of the Treasury. — Feb. 4

79. Recommendations concerning the interest rate ceilings on bank deposits. — The Secretary of the Treasury. — Jan. 29

80. Recommendations concerning new occupational safety legislation. — The Secretary of Labor. — Feb. 11

81. Recommendations concerning possible amendments to the Pension and Welfare Disclosure Act. — The Secretary of Labor and the Secretary of Commerce. — Feb. 18

Appendix C

| *Presidential request* | *Addressee* | *Date 1969* |

82. Suggestions concerning the establishment of a National Law Enforcement Council.
The Attorney General.
Jan. 30

83. An assessment of various recommendations for meeting the narcotics problem, along with plans for their implementation.
The Attorney General.
Feb. 9

84. Suggestions as to how the problem of obscene materials in the U.S. mails can be dealt with more effectively under present law, together with recommendations for such further legislation as is believed necessary.
The Attorney General and the Postmaster General.
Feb. 4

85. Suggestions concerning a task force to study the correction and rehabilitation problem and to review proposals for a consolidated Federal Correction Service.
The Attorney General.
Feb. 4

86. Recommendations toward a Presidential message on organized crime.
The Attorney General.
Jan. 29

R. INTERNATIONAL ECONOMIC PROBLEMS

87. A report on ways in which the Government can move away from controls over foreign lending and investing.
The Secretary of the Treasury.
Jan. 29

88. An analysis of the report of the International Private Investment Advisory Council, proposing the creation of a federally chartered corporation for the purpose of promoting private capital investment in the developing nations.
The Secretary of State.
Feb. 13

89. Recommendations for legislative or administrative action concerning trade and tariff policies.
The Secretary of State and the Secretary of Commerce.
Feb. 21

90. A review of new proposals concerning the Foreign Investors Tax Act of 1966.
The Secretary of the Treasury.
Feb. 4

91. An assessment of past recommendations concerning telecommunications, along with such new proposals as are deemed necessary.
The Science Adviser to the President.
Feb. 1

92. Recommendations concerning the international conference to establish arrangements for a Global Commercial Communications Satellite System.
The Secretary of State.
Feb. 11

93. A review of various recommendations concerning international space cooperation.
The Secretary of State.
Feb. 21

94. Instructions concerning the prompt and regular release of statistical information by Federal agencies.
The Director of the Bureau of the Budget.
Jan. 31

Appendix C

PRESIDENTIAL TASK FORCES

[The text of this group of releases is not printed in this volume but appears in Volume 5 of the Weekly Compilation of Presidential Documents as cited below.]

Appendix D—Presidential Unit Citations

[The text of this group of releases is not printed in this volume but appears in Volume 5 of the Weekly Compilation of Presidential Documents as cited below.]

Appendix D

Appendix E—Presidential Reports to the 91st Congress, First Session

Subject	Published	Sent to the Congress	Date of White House release
National Science Board (1st annual)		Feb. 18	Feb. 18
Government Employees Training Act of 1958 (fiscal year 1968)		Feb. 19	. . . .
Head Start Report	H. Doc. 75	Feb. 19	Feb. 19
Cash Awards to Members of the Armed Forces and the Coast Guard:			
For calendar year 1968		Mar. 4	Mar. 4
For the period January 1–June 30, 1969		Oct. 28	Oct. 28
Commodity Credit Corporation (fiscal year 1968)	H. Doc. 88	Mar. 11 (S) Mar. 12 (H)	. . . .
U.S. Arms Control and Disarmament Agency (8th annual)		Mar. 11 (S) Mar. 12 (H)	. . . .
World Weather Program (1st annual)		Mar. 13	Mar. 13
Federal Disaster Act (1968)	H. Doc. 89	Mar. 24	. . . .
International Educational and Cultural Exchange Program (fiscal year 1968)		Mar. 25	. . . .
National Capital Housing Authority (1968)		Apr. 21	Apr. 21
Food for Peace Program under P.L. 480, 83d Congress (1968) .	H. Doc. 104	Apr. 22	Apr. 22
Highway Safety Act of 1966 (2d annual)	H. Doc. 109	Apr. 28 (S) Apr. 29 (H)	. . . .
National Traffic and Motor Vehicle Safety Act of 1966 (2d annual).	H. Doc. 110	Apr. 28 (S) Apr. 29 (H)	. . . .
Board of Actuaries for the Retired Serviceman's Family Protection Plan (14th annual).		May 19	May 19
Natural Gas Pipeline Safety Act of 1968 (1st annual)		May 20	. . . .
Railroad Retirement Board (fiscal year 1968)	H. Doc. 27	May 28	. . . .
Office of Economic Opportunity (4th annual)	H. Doc. 128	May 28	. . . .
Administration of Radiation Control for Health and Safety Act (1st annual).	H. Doc. 126	June 3	. . . .

Appendix E

Subject	Published	Sent to the Congress	Date of White House release
National Advisory Council on Economic Opportunity (2d annual).	H. Doc. 129	June 11	. . . .
Federal Statutory Salary Systems	H. Doc. 131	June 17	June 17
Special International Exhibitions (6th annual)		June 17	. . . .
Automotive Products Trade Act of 1965 (3d annual)		July 7	. . . .
International Coffee Agreement (1968)		Aug. 5	Aug. 5
Atlantic-Pacific Interoceanic Canal Study Commission (5th annual).	H. Doc. 143	Aug. 6	Aug. 6
Antidumping		Aug. 13	. . . .
Special Project Grants for Health of School and Preschool Children.		Sept. 12	. . . .
National Advisory Council on Extension and Continuing Education (3d annual).	H. Doc. 161	Sept. 23	. . . .
St. Lawrence Seaway Development Corporation (1968)	H. Doc. 162	Sept. 24	. . . .
National Advisory Committee on Adult Basic Education (2d annual).	H. Doc. 176	Oct. 9	. . . .
Acid Mine Drainage in Appalachia	H. Doc. 180	Oct. 15	. . . .
United Nations (23d annual)	H. Doc. 118	Oct. 27	Oct. 27
Weather Modification (10th annual and final)	H. Doc. 186	Oct. 27 (H) Oct. 28 (S)	Oct. 27
Alien Property (fiscal year 1968)		Oct. 29	. . . .
Department of Transportation (2d annual)	H. Doc. 189	Oct. 31 (H) Nov. 3 (S)	. . . .
National Aeronautics and Space Administration (20th semi-annual).	H. Doc. 153	Nov. 13	. . . .
Surgeon General (13th annual)	H. Doc. 193	Nov. 17	. . . .
Trade Agreements Program (13th annual).	H. Doc. 204	Dec. 16	Dec. 16

Appendix F—Rules Governing This Publication

[Reprinted from the Federal Register, vol. 34, p. 19118, dated December 2, 1969]

TITLE 1—GENERAL PROVISIONS

Chapter I—Administrative Committee of the Federal Register

PART 32—PRESIDENTIAL PAPERS

Subpart A—Annual Volumes

Publication and Format

AUTHORITY: The provisions of this Part 32 issued under 44 U.S.C. 1506. Sec. 6, E.O. 10530, 19 F.R. 2709; 3 CFR 1954–58 Comp.

Subpart A—Annual Volumes

Publication and Format

§ 32.1 *Publication required.* There shall be published forthwith at the end of each calendar year, a special edition of the FEDERAL REGISTER designated "Public Papers of the Presidents of the United States." Ordinarily each volume shall cover one calendar year and shall be identified further by the name of the President and the period covered.

NOTE: This program started with the year 1957.

§ 32.2 *Coverage of prior years.* After conferring with the National Historical Publications Commission with respect to the need therefor, the Administrative Committee may from time to time authorize the publication of similar volumes covering specified calendar years prior to 1957.

NOTE: The Committee has approved the publication of volumes starting with the year 1929.

§ 32.3 *Format, indexes, ancillaries.* Each annual volume, divided into books whenever appropriate, shall be separately published in the binding and style deemed by the Administrative Committee to be suitable to the dignity of the office of President of the United States. Each volume shall be appropriately indexed and shall contain appropriate ancillary information respecting significant Presidential documents not published in full text.

Scope

§ 32.10 *Basic criteria.* The basic text of the volumes shall consist of oral utterances by the President or of writings subscribed by him.

§ 32.11 *Sources.* (a) The basic text of the volumes shall be selected from: (1) Communications to the Congress, (2) public addresses, (3) transcripts of press conferences, (4) public letters, (5) messages to heads of state, (6) statements released on miscellaneous subjects, and (7) formal executive documents promulgated in accordance with law.

(b) In general, ancillary text, notes, and tables shall be derived from official sources.

OFFICIAL DISTRIBUTION

§ 32.15   *The Congress.* Each Member of the Congress, during his term of office, shall be entitled to one copy of each annual volume published during such term. Authorization for furnishing such copies shall be submitted in writing to the Director and signed by the authorizing Member.

§ 32.16   *The Supreme Court.* The Supreme Court of the United States shall be entitled to 12 copies of the annual volumes.

§ 32.17   *Executive agencies.* The head of each department and the head of each independent agency in the executive branch of the Government shall be entitled to one copy of each annual volume upon application therefor in writing to the Director.

§ 32.18   *Governmental requisitions.* Legislative, judicial, and executive agencies of the Federal Government may obtain, at cost, copies of the annual volumes for official use upon the timely submission to the Government Printing Office of a printing and binding requisition (Standard Form 1).

§ 32.19   *Extra copies.* All requests for extra copies of the annual volumes must be addressed to the Superintendent of Documents, Government Printing Office, Washington, D.C. 20402. Extra copies must be paid for by the agency or official requesting them.

PUBLIC SALE

§ 32.22   *Sale of annual volumes.* The annual volumes shall be placed on sale to the public by the Superintendent of Documents, Government Printing Office, Washington, D.C.

20402, at prices determined by him under the general direction of the Administrative Committee.

Subpart B—Weekly Compilation

§ 32.30   *Publication required.* There shall be published promptly, once each week, a special edition of the FEDERAL REGISTER designated "Weekly Compilation of Presidential Documents."

§ 32.31   *Format and indexes.* The Weekly Compilation shall be published in the style and binding deemed by the Administrative Committee to be most suitable for public and official use. The Director of the Federal Register shall provide indexes and such other finding aids as may be appropriate to effective use.

§ 32.40   *Official distribution.* The Weekly Compilation shall be furnished regularly to members of Congress and to officials of the legislative, judicial and executive branches of the Government in such numbers as are needed for official use. Authorization to make such distribution shall be made in writing to the Director and signed by the authorizing officer. Special needs for selected issues in substantial quantity shall be filled by the timely submission to the Government Printing Office of a printing and binding requisition (Standard Form 1).

§ 32.50   *Public sale.* The Weekly Compilation shall be placed on sale to the public by the Superintendent of Documents, Government Printing Office, Washington, D.C. 20402, at a price to be determined by him under the general direction of the Administrative Committee.

INDEX

[Main references are to item numbers except as otherwise indicated]

Index

[Main references are to item numbers except as otherwise indicated]

Index

[Main references are to item numbers except as otherwise indicated]

[Main references are to item numbers except as otherwise indicated]

Index

Index

Index

[Main references are to item numbers except as otherwise indicated]

Index

Index

Index

Index

Index

Index

[Main references are to item numbers except as otherwise indicated]

Index

Index

[Main references are to item numbers except as otherwise indicated]

Index

[Main references are to item numbers except as otherwise indicated]

Index

[Main references are to item numbers except as otherwise indicated]

Index

Index

[Main references are to item numbers except as otherwise indicated]

Index

[Main references are to item numbers except as otherwise indicated]

Index

Index

Index

Index

Index

[Main references are to item numbers except as otherwise indicated]

Index

Index

[Main references are to item numbers except as otherwise indicated]

[Main references are to item numbers except as otherwise indicated]

Index

[Main references are to item numbers except as otherwise indicated]

Index

[Main references are to item numbers except as otherwise indicated]

Index

[Main references are to item numbers except as otherwise indicated]

Index

[Main references are to item numbers except as otherwise indicated]

[Main references are to item numbers except as otherwise indicated]

Index

[Main references are to item numbers except as otherwise indicated]

Index

Index

[Main references are to item numbers except as otherwise indicated]

Index

[Main references are to item numbers except as otherwise indicated]

39–861—71——76

Index

[Main references are to item numbers except as otherwise indicated]

Index

[Main references are to item numbers except as otherwise indicated]

Index

[Main references are to item numbers except as otherwise indicated]

Index

[Main references are to item numbers except as otherwise indicated]

Index

[Main references are to item numbers except as otherwise indicated]

[Main references are to item numbers except as otherwise indicated]

Index

Index

Index

[Main references are to item numbers except as otherwise indicated]

Index

Index

Index

Index

[Main references are to item numbers except as otherwise indicated]

Index

[Main references are to item numbers except as otherwise indicated]

Index

39–861—71——77

Index

Index

Index

[Main references are to item numbers except as otherwise indicated]

Index

[Main references are to item numbers except as otherwise indicated]

Index

Index

Index

Index

Index

[Main references are to item numbers except as otherwise indicated]